McCORMICK ON EVIDENCE

Eighth Edition

by

Robert P. Mosteller

General Editor
J. Dickson Phillips Distinguished Professor of Law Emeritus
University of North Carolina

Contributing Authors

Kenneth S. Broun

Henry Brandis Professor of Law Emeritus, University of North Carolina

George E. Dix

George R. Killam, Jr. Chair Emeritus of Criminal Law, The University of Texas

Edward J. Imwinkelried

Edward L. Barrett, Jr. Professor of Law Emeritus, University of California, Davis

David H. Kaye

Distinguished Professor of Law Emeritus, The Pennsylvania State University and Regents' Professor Emeritus, Arizona State University

Eleanor Swift

Professor of Law Emerita, University of California at Berkeley School of Law

This book is an abridgement of "McCormick on Evidence, Eighth Edition, Volumes 1 & 2. Practitioner Treatise Series".

HORNBOOK SERIES®

Preface

This edition of *McCormick on Evidence* attempts to do what the prior editions accomplished: to set out the law of Evidence in as complete and understandable a manner as possible in a work of moderate length. The authors have tried to be faithful to the pragmatic approach to analyzing evidence issues taken by the original author of this book, Dean Charles McCormick.

Although the Federal Rules of Evidence and their state counterparts make up much of the basis for the law, many aspects depend heavily on case analysis. The book attempts to meld rules and case law in a way that is useful for practitioners, scholars, the courts, and students. As in prior editions, important cases containing helpful discussions of precedent and policy are noted in the extensive footnotes found in the practitioner's edition.

As with the recent editions, there will be two versions of this edition, a two-volume practitioner's edition, which is published by Thomson Reuters, and this one-volume student edition. The only significant difference between the two editions is the absence of extensive footnoting in the student edition.

With this edition, Professor Ernest Roberts, who covered judicial notice, has retired, and we will greatly miss his contributions. All the other authors of the Seventh Edition have continued. Their responsibility for chapters is as follows: Professor Edward Imwinkelried, Chapters 1–7, covering preparing and presenting evidence, examination of witnesses, procedure for admitting and excluding evidence, and competency; Professor Kenneth Broun, Chapters 8–11, dealing with common law and statutory privileges and Chapter 36, the burdens of proof and presumptions; Professor George Dix, Chapters 13–15, covering certain constitutional rights and privileges; Professor David Kaye, Chapters 16–20, dealing with relevancy considerations (including scientific evidence covered in Chapter 20); Professor Eleanor Swift, Chapters 21–23, dealing with real and demonstrative evidence and authentication and contents of writings; and myself, Chapter 12, privileges for governmental secrets, Chapters 24–34, dealing with the hearsay rule and its exceptions and confrontation, and Chapter 35, examining judicial notice.

This edition contains updates to all the subjects covered in the treatise. Chapter 3, which deals, inter alia, with the introduction of expert testimony, has been substantially reorganized. Special note should be taken of the continuing developments in the forensic science community that affect how forensic science findings can and should be presented in court (Chapter 20); the increased use of electronic evidence and its impact on evidentiary rules (Chapters 21 and 22); and the resolution of some issues in the evolution of the Confrontation Clause jurisprudence arising from the *Crawford* case (Chapter 24).

On behalf of all the authors, I hope that we have both continued the traditional excellence of this treatise and taken steps to bring it fully up to date in terms of both the law and the age of technology in which we now live.

ROBERT P. MOSTELLER

May 2020

iii

Summary of Contents

TITLE 11. JUDICIAL NOTICE

TITLE 12. BURDEN OF PROOF AND PRESUMPTIONS

Table of Contents

CHAPTER 9. THE PRIVILEGE FOR MARITAL COMMUNICATIONS 209

CHAPTER 10. THE CLIENT'S PRIVILEGE: COMMUNICATIONS BETWEEN CLIENT & LAWYER 219

TITLE 7. RELEVANCE

TITLE 8. REAL EVIDENCE, OTHER NONTESTIMONIAL EVIDENCE, AND DEMONSTRATIVE AIDS

CHAPTER 21. REAL EVIDENCE, OTHER NONTESTIMONIAL EVIDENCE, AND DEMONSTRATIVE AIDS

TITLE 9. WRITINGS

TITLE 10. THE HEARSAY RULE AND ITS EXCEPTIONS

TITLE 11. JUDICIAL NOTICE

TITLE 12. BURDEN OF PROOF AND PRESUMPTIONS

McCORMICK ON EVIDENCE

Eighth Edition

Title 1

INTRODUCTION

Chapter 1

PREPARING AND PRESENTING THE EVIDENCE

Table of Sections

§ 1   Planning and Preparation of Proof as Important as the Rules of Evidence

The rules of evidence are arguably the most important doctrinal area in the law. Evidentiary doctrines are critical to maintaining the legitimacy of any legal system because they help to ensure that the system's announced rules are applied properly. Actors in the market place cannot have confidence in the safety of their investments if their legal system's evidentiary rules do not assure the accurate determination of facts in commercial disputes. Likewise, citizens cannot have confidence that their most precious civil liberties are secure if the evidentiary rules do not provide a solid basis for believing that the facts relevant to the existence and exercise of those liberties will be adjudicated accurately. An inadequate set of evidentiary rules can render the citizenry's substantive rights hollow. The legal rights may exist on paper, but they will not be consistently enforced in court.

The law of evidence is the system of rules and standards regulating the admission of testimony and exhibits at the trial of a lawsuit. The last section in this chapter, § 4, is an overview of the procedural regulations governing the sequence of evidentiary presentations at trial. However, the trial stage, when evidentiary rules govern, is a relatively late phase in a long litigation process. Thus, in every case dealing with a trial dispute over the application of a rule of evidence, the lawyers have already completed many other tasks in the planning and production of testimony and exhibits. The lawyers must perform these pretrial tasks in anticipation of problems of proof under the law of evidence—weeks, months, or years before any evidentiary question is submitted to a trial judge. Some of these earlier stages in the litigation process are mentioned in this chapter. In particular, the next to last section in this chapter, § 3, discusses the use of formal discovery devices to prepare to gather evidence for trial while § 2 reviews the informal methods of readying for trial.

§ 2   Preparation for Trial on the Facts Without Resort to the Court's Aid

In many cases, especially cases with relatively small monetary stakes, the lawyers collect evidence for trial without resorting to formal discovery devices. The lawyer can either personally perform the collection task or delegate the task to an assistant such as a clerk or private investigator. Informal discovery techniques tend to be faster and less expensive than formal discovery. Moreover, the use of informal discovery methods can preserve the element of surprise. There is no element of surprise at trial when the lawyer deposes a witness to an accident; the opponent can attend the deposition and is entitled to a transcript of the deposition hearing. In contrast, the opponent may gain little or no advance notice if the lawyer is content to informally interview the witness. Although these investigative steps are informal, the attorney taking these steps must keep formal evidence law in mind.

As a starting point in informal discovery, the lawyer must interview the client to learn his version of the facts. At some point, these interviews ought to include a tactful but searching mock cross-examination to overcome the client's natural tendency to mention only the facts favorable to his side in the litigation. The lawyer conducting these interviews should endeavor to ensure that the attorney-client evidentiary privilege applies to these interviews.[1] More specifically, at the time of the communication there ought to be physical privacy—ideally without the presence of any third parties. Moreover, the attorney should instruct the client to maintain the secrecy of their communications and not disclose their content to any third party outside the circle of confidence.

The lawyer ought to contact not only the client but also other witnesses with personal knowledge of the relevant facts. The witnesses who have firsthand knowledge of the transaction in controversy must be interviewed; and where possible, their written statements ought to be taken. The statement might become evidence at trial, or the lawyer could need to resort to the statement to refresh the witness's memory at trial if the witness has difficulty recalling the pertinent facts. In the case of statements by non-party witnesses, the lawyer should do her best to make certain that the evidentiary protection for work product attaches to the witnesses' statements. For example, the lawyer could attach the label "Attorney Work Product" to documents that she thinks are protected.

Apart from the ordinary lay eyewitnesses, it is increasingly necessary to arrange for experts such as molecular biologists and psychiatrists in criminal cases, epidemiologists in toxic tort actions, physicians in personal injury cases, chemists and physicists in patent litigation, engineers and architects in controversies over construction contracts, and questioned document examiners in will contests. Some have suggested that in the United States, trial by jury is becoming trial by expert. That suggestion is obviously hyperbole, but there is a large measure of truth in the suggestion. In one Rand Corporation study of California courts, 86% of the trials reviewed involved expert testimony.[2] Once again, the lawyer must keep evidence law in mind. In some jurisdictions, in certain circumstances the attorney-client privilege extends to reports obtained from the lawyer's own experts; and in an even larger number of jurisdictions, there is conditional work product protection for such reports. Moreover, in many jurisdictions the courts have construed the state medical privilege statutes as forbidding a civil defense lawyer from making ex parte contact with the plaintiff's treating physician.

---

[1]   See infra § 3 concerning the right to interview witnesses.

[2]   Gross, Expert Evidence, 1991 Wis. L. Rev. 1113, 1119.

In addition to contacting potential expert and lay witnesses, it is often necessary to assemble exhibits. Exhibits can take the form of documentary evidence such as contracts, letters, receipts, certified copies of deeds, judgments, and decrees. In the computer age, it can also be vital to collect electronic files, e-mail messages, and social media postings, which can be voluminous. The compilation of electronic files can be such a massive, complicated undertaking that attorneys frequently hire digital forensics experts to oversee the collection process. Other physical evidence, such as the assailant's revolver or a sample of the goods in an action for breach of warranty, should be located and preserved for use at the trial. At trial the lawyer needs to be in a position to authenticate these items by, for example, proving a chain of custody to establish the identity of each item. Chain of custody testimony can demonstrate that the exhibit tendered at trial is the same revolver found at the crime scene.

The lawyer is not restricted to objects which have an original, historical connection to the case such as the very revolver found at the homicide scene. The lawyer can be creative in planning demonstrative aids to appeal to the senses such as still photographs, videotapes, motion picture films, X-rays, plats, diagrams, and models. Visual aids not only help the lawyer arrest the jurors' short-term attention; more importantly, they significantly increase the jurors' long-term memory of the data depicted by the aid. The use of visual aids is especially important when the lawyer contemplates offering scientific evidence. Jurors sometimes find scientific testimony confusingly complex and abstract. A visual aid such as a computer-generated animation (CGA) can powerfully simplify the testimony for the jury's benefit. If the lawyer hires a consultant to generate a CGA, the lawyer must ensure that consultant follows procedures that will enable the lawyer to lay an evidentiary foundation to justify the introduction of the item at trial.

Where practicable, counsel should endeavor to lighten the task of proof at trial by securing the opponent's pretrial written stipulations to facts not in controversy such as the validity of the software used to generate a CGA, the authorship of documents, or the ownership of a vehicle involved in the suit. Even if the opposition is unwilling to enter into a stipulation of fact, they may be agreeable to a stipulation of expected testimony: If a certain person appeared as a witness, she would be willing to testify to specified facts. A stipulation can substitute for evidence and eliminate the need for counsel to present evidence at trial. In addition, if counsel will have to offer a copy to prove the terms of a document in the adversary's possession, counsel must give the opposing counsel written notice to produce the original at trial in order to satisfy the best evidence rule discussed in Chapter 23.

All these steps should be carefully planned with evidence law in mind. A tentative plan may emerge early in the litigation process. As the trial approaches, the lawyer evolves a theory of the case; and the lawyer ought to formulate a final plan to ensure that the attorney can prove up the theory at trial. Each essential factual element of the claim or defense ought to be listed, specifying the witnesses and documents by which it will be proved. The plan can be supplemented with (1) a list of the witnesses in the order in which they will be called, including the subjects on which they will be testify, and (2) a master exhibit list, identifying the witnesses to authenticate each exhibit. Finally, on the eve of trial before the witnesses take the stand, the counsel calling a witness may need to reinterview the witness to confirm what he is prepared to swear to, to refresh his memory if necessary, and to ready him for the probable cross-examination. Again, the counsel must keep evidence law in mind as she takes these preparatory steps. In particular, the counsel must be aware that if the witness resorts to his pretrial statement during the interview to revive his memory, that may waive any evidentiary privilege that would otherwise attach to the statement at trial. Every task must be performed with a view to the ultimate objective of ensuring that there will be ample, admissible, persuasive evidence at trial.

Informal discovery has taken on added importance since 2007. In that year, the United States Supreme Court handed down its decision in *Bell Atlantic Corp. v. Twombly*,[3] an antitrust case. Prior to *Bell,* most American jurisdictions had endorsed the liberal philosophy of notice pleading. Thus, in 1957, in *Conley v. Gibson*, the Supreme Court had observed that "a complaint should not be dismissed for failure to state a claim unless it appears beyond doubt that the plaintiff can prove no set of facts in support of his claim which would entitle him to relief."[4] However, in *Bell Atlantic* the Court declared that "this famous observation has earned its retirement." In essence, the *Bell Atlantic* Court announced that in order to satisfy Federal Rule of Civil Procedure 8, the plaintiff must allege enough facts to demonstrate that she could plausibly win at trial. In 2009 in *Ashcroft v. Iqbal,*[5] the Court ruled that the new standard applies across the board to all types of civil cases. After *Bell* and *Ashcroft,* the plaintiff may have to conduct additional informal discovery before filing in order to be in a position to draft a sufficient complaint. It is true that in rare cases, a litigant may conduct formal discovery before a complaint has been filed. However, in the typical case the litigant will have to rely on the informal discovery methods discussed in this section to satisfy the enhanced pleading requirements.

§ 3 Invoking the Court's Aid in Preparing for Trial: Right to Interview Witnesses; Discovery and Depositions; Requests for Admission; Pretrial Conferences

The Right to an Opportunity to Interview Witnesses

As the preceding section pointed out, one of the essential steps in informal trial preparation is interviewing the potential witnesses with firsthand knowledge of the relevant facts. From time to time the question arises whether counsel has a legal right to a pretrial opportunity to interview a witness. The question usually arises when opposing counsel has instructed a witness not to "talk" at all or only on certain conditions. Counsel may have to resort to the court to settle the matter. Several courts have ruled that a criminal defendant has such a right to interview, enforceable against the prosecution in a limited sense; that is, prosecutors may not pressure a potential witness to refuse to cooperate with the defense. Generally, under the Sixth Amendment, a criminal defendant has the right to an opportunity to interview witnesses privately. There is respectable authority that the prosecution in a criminal case has a similar right. Certain types of defense interference with prosecution access to witnesses and potential evidence could constitute obstruction of justice. There is also an emerging parallel right for both parties in civil cases. A civil litigant's interference with the opposition's access to witnesses and evidence might amount to sanctionable spoliation of evidence.

Nevertheless, there are situations in which a court will refuse to interfere even when counsel have suggested to witnesses that they limit or refuse interviews. Absent a subpoena, on her own motion, the witness is generally free to refuse to submit to an

---

[3] Bell Atlantic Corp. v. Twombly, 550 U.S. 544 (2007).

[4] Conley v. Gibson, 355 U.S. 41 (1957).

[5] Ashcroft v. Iqbal, 556 U.S. 662 (2009).

informal interview. As § 2 explained, despite the existence of formal discovery devices, the opportunity to informally interview witnesses is important in trial preparation. When the witness refuses to submit to an interview, the lawyer may need to resort to court to secure an opportunity to question the witness. At this juncture, the formal discovery devices come into play.

Formal Discovery Devices—Civil Cases

Adequate trial preparation often requires the use of the official fact-gathering procedures available after the lawsuit commences. The formal discovery procedures in the various jurisdictions[6] are treated at length in treatises and one-volume works concerning civil and criminal procedure. Consequently, this section includes only a very short, summary review of these procedures. Especially if the jurisdiction does not follow *Twombly* and *Iqbal,* the pleadings in civil cases may be fairly general and need not specify the facts in any great detail. Notice pleadings give the defense little insight into the evidence that the plaintiff will adduce at trial. To furnish the necessary detail, the civil rules provide for fairly thorough post-pleading discovery processes by which each party can learn the possible evidence in the case and identify the specific fact issues that will be genuinely disputed at trial.

In many states and federal judicial districts, the official procedures include a statute or court rule requiring mandatory pre-discovery disclosures. For example, under a 1993 amendment to Federal Rule of Civil Procedure 26(a), even absent a request by the opposing attorney, the litigant must reveal specified information about potential witnesses, relevant documents, and experts. The amendment forced plaintiffs to frontload their expenditures for expert services. If the mandatory disclosures do not satisfy the opposing attorney, the attorney can turn to formal discovery devices. The federal mandatory pre-discovery disclosure requirements were so controversial that when they were originally promulgated in 1993, the amendment provided that individual judicial districts could opt out of the requirements. However, in 2000, the rule was amended again to eliminate the opt-out provision. Especially after the amendment, the rule has had a major impact on the admissibility of expert testimony at trial. The rule requires most testifying experts to file a relatively complete report describing their anticipated testimony. If the expert does not file any report, the trial judge may altogether bar the expert's testimony as a discovery sanction. If the expert files an incomplete pretrial report but at trial the expert attempts to give testimony that was not revealed in the report, the judge may exclude that part of the expert's testimony.

One of the most important devices in civil cases is the "discovery" deposition procedure enabling each party to orally examine the other party under oath and likewise question other persons who have knowledge of the subject matter of the lawsuit. Over half the states have substantially copied the federal rules on deposition procedure. Although a judicial order for a commission authorizing an officer to preside at an oral examination is still necessary in some states, the more popular, simplified procedure for taking oral depositions ordinarily requires only a notice to the person to be examined, a subpoena ordering her to appear at a certain time and place for the examination before a court reporter/notary public, and a notice of the examination for the opposing party if she is not the deponent. In many jurisdictions, following the lead of the federal civil discovery process, at an oral deposition the examiner may seek any information

---

[6] Fed. R. Civ. P. 26–37.

reasonably calculated to lead to the discovery of admissible evidence even if the information will not be admissible at the trial. Thus, at a deposition a lawyer can demand that the deponent disclose hearsay statements that would be inadmissible at trial. However, the lawyer cannot entirely ignore evidentiary doctrine during a deposition. To begin with, if the lawyer neglects to assert an evidentiary privilege during the deposition, the privilege may be waived for trial. Moreover, while most substantive evidentiary doctrines such as hearsay are inapplicable at a deposition, the opponent must make form objections such as the objection that the question is argumentative or misleading.

Effective use of depositions will enable a party to discover the evidence both for and against his position. Furthermore, the deposition of an opposing witness allows the attorney to evaluate the witness's demeanor: Will the deponent probably be an effective witness at trial? The witnesses' performance during their depositions can have a major impact on the settlement value of the case. That impact is especially likely if the deposition is videotaped. In 1993, Federal Rule of Civil Procedure 30(b)(2) was amended to give the moving party the presumptive right to specify "the method of recording." A videotaped deposition can capture "that moment of shocked silence when the witness is confronted with an awful truth or incredible surprise" or "the look of perplexed consternation or shocked embarrassment."[7] That demeanor may do irreparable damage to the witness's credibility.

Of course, depositions are not the only formal discovery devices. In many states in civil cases, written interrogatories may also be directed to the opponent; and with few exceptions the opponent must answer them. Interrogatories can be employed hand in hand with oral depositions. For instance, if the opponent is a corporation, the lawyer might use interrogatories about the corporation's organizational structure to identify potential deponents.

Further, a party often demands production, that is, that the adversary permit him to examine papers and things—even real property—relating to the subject matter of the suit. At one time depositions were the central events during pretrial discovery. However, with the advent of electronically stored information (ESI), production has eclipsed the importance of depositions in major commercial lawsuits. In particular, the production context generates more published opinions dealing with the waiver of evidentiary privileges than any other setting. In many cases, the question presented is whether the opponent's inadvertent production of privileged documents waives the privilege. The issue arose so frequently and pretrial privilege reviews to preclude waiver became so costly that in 2008, Congress took the extraordinary step of intervening to pass legislation governing the waiver of the attorney-client privilege in this setting.

Next, in over half the states in personal injury actions and sometimes other suits in which a party's physical or mental condition is in issue, the judge may issue an order for the physical or mental examination of a party. The findings at the examination can serve as the bases for expert opinions at trial.

Lastly, although not strictly speaking a discovery device, in many states a party can send requests for admissions to her opponent who must either admit or deny the specified fact. For instance, a lawyer might ask that the opponent admit the facts necessary to lay the evidentiary foundation for introducing an exhibit at trial.

---

[7]   Neubauer, Videotaping Depositions, 19 Litig., 60, 60 (Sum. 1993).

In many jurisdictions, after the close of discovery a pretrial hearing or conference is authorized for civil cases, although it is rarely used in some states. When the time for trial approaches—usually two or three weeks before the date set for trial—the judge summons counsel for both sides and sometimes the parties as well. At the conference, the judge seeks to narrow the scope of the dispute and secure stipulations as to the facts not genuinely at issue. The text of the original federal rule[8] authorizing conferences mentions, *inter alia,* the following objectives of the hearing:

(1)　The simplification of the issues;

(3)　The possibility of obtaining admissions of fact and of documents which will avoid unnecessary proof;

(4)　The limitation of the number of expert witnesses; [and]

(5)　The advisability of a preliminary reference of issues to a master for findings to be used as evidence when the trial is to be by jury.

The pretrial conference can serve as a vehicle for reaching agreement on various factual issues, although the conference does not always yield that result. By process of elimination, the conference helps the parties identify the remaining disputed issues which the trial evidence will focus on.

One other procedure should be mentioned before concluding this summary: the procurement of the issuance and service of writs of subpoena for the witnesses who are to be called at trial. If a third party has custody of a relevant document or other physical evidence, the party who desires its production at trial may secure a subpoena duces tecum (SDT) addressed to the third party. The SDT commands her to attend the trial and to bring with her the document or other object. Once again evidence law comes into play. Like a party resisting a production request, a witness opposing a subpoena may occasionally assert an evidentiary privilege to quash the subpoena.

The use of some of these discovery devices can result in creating testimony and exhibits which can be introduced at trial. One of the risks of resorting to formal discovery is that the lawyer might inadvertently preserve unfavorable evidence for trial. (That risk explains why experienced litigators routinely conduct informal discovery before using formal discovery devices; a deposition is less risky if beforehand the lawyer gains at least a general sense of what the deponent is likely to testify to.) In certain circumstances, deposition testimony may be introduced at trial. Under the federal rules, an opposing party's deposition may be admitted virtually without any restrictions or conditions. The opposing party's statements at the deposition routinely fall within the hearsay exemption for statements by opposing parties (formerly called admissions of a party-opponent). The most common conditions for introducing the deposition testimony of non-party witnesses are the requirements set out in the Federal Rules of Civil Procedure. The Federal Rules of Evidence also contain provisions regulating the admissibility of depositions under the former testimony hearsay exception. By way of example, in most jurisdictions, a non-party deponent's deposition is admissible only if the deponent is unavailable to testify in person at trial.

---

[8]　Fed. R. Civ. P. 16.

Formal Discovery Devices—Criminal Cases

Discovery procedures are also available to criminal defendants. However, extensive criminal discovery is a relatively recent development. Only in the past few decades have rules or statutes been enacted to accord criminal defendants extensive discovery rights, and even these procedures are limited. The 1970 Crime Control Act authorizes the defense to conduct witness depositions primarily for the preservation of the evidence (for future use as evidence), rather than merely for the purpose of discovery. To obtain judicial authorization for such a "preservation" deposition or conditional examination, the defendant must make a preliminary showing that the prospective deponent will probably be unavailable at trial. Today some jurisdictions also authorize the prosecution to conduct such depositions. Federal Rule of Criminal Procedure 16 is a broad discovery provision concerning defense discovery of reports, scientific tests, grand jury testimony, books, documents, tangible objects, and places. There is a more limited provision for reciprocal discovery of similar matters by the government. Rule 16 has been amended several times. The 1993 amendment is particularly noteworthy, since it expands the discovery of expert testimony which either the government or the defense contemplates offering at trial. Unlike civil parties, however, criminal litigants do not have any duty to make mandatory pre-discovery disclosure; one side must take the initiative to seek discovery from the other side.

Whether the case is criminal or civil and whether the lawyer relies primarily on formal or informal discovery techniques to prepare for trial, the objective is the same: gathering a large quantity of believable, admissible evidence for trial. If the lawyer achieves that pretrial objective, the lawyer's client should gain either an advantageous settlement or a favorable trial verdict. In the vast majority of instances, the case settles without going to trial; in 2002 only 1.8% of the civil cases filed in federal court were disposed of by trial, and the percentage was even lower in many states.[9] In most cases, pretrial is *the* trial of the attorney's case. Pretrial discovery has become the center of gravity in modern litigation. The settlement is largely driven by the quantity and quality of the admissible evidence unearthed during formal and informal pretrial discovery.

§ 4 The Order of Presenting Evidence at the Trial

If the case does not settle, the litigants proceed to trial. Evidence law figures even more prominently at this stage than it does during the pretrial phase.

If the hearing will be a jury trial, the jury must be selected before the lawyers present their evidence. Depending on the jurisdiction, during the voir dire examination of the panelists the judge might permit the attorney to question them about potential items of evidence in the case. A panelist could conceivably have such an adverse reaction to an item of evidence that he would be challengeable for cause, or the attorney might want to employ a peremptory strike to remove him from the jury. Even if the panelist's attitude is not unfavorable enough to necessitate striking him, the attorney might engage in factual indoctrination and attempt to obtain the panelist's promise that the panelist will not vote against the attorney's client "solely" or "merely" because of that item of evidence.

After the jury selection, the attorneys present opening statements. During the statements, the attorneys preview their evidence for the jury. The attorney will typically

---

[9]   Refo, The Vanishing Trial, 30 Litig. 1, 2 (Wint. 2004).

discuss both the anticipated evidence in the case and the ultimate burden of proof that the jury will eventually have to apply to evaluate the sufficiency of the evidence. According to American Bar Association Model Rule of Professional Conduct 3.4(e), in opening a lawyer may not "allude to any matter that the lawyer does not reasonably believe . . . will . . . be supported by admissible evidence . . ." at trial. By far, the most common objection during opening statement is that a particular statement is argumentative. In this context, "argumentative" means that the statement is a conclusion which would be inadmissible under the evidence rules governing lay and expert opinion testimony. As a rule of thumb, an attorney may not make a statement during opening unless, under the governing opinion rules, it would be permissible for one of the attorney's scheduled witnesses to make the statement on the stand. The attorney might be uncertain whether he or his opponent may refer to a particular item of potential evidence in opening. If so, even before opening statement the lawyer can file a pretrial in limine motion seeking an advance ruling on the admissibility of the evidence.[10] It is especially advisable to raise the issue before trial when the lawyer intends to rely on a novel type of expert testimony or an unconventional noncharacter or nonhearsay theory of admissibility.

After the opening statements, testimony begins. Under the usual order of proceeding at the trial, including a trial under the Federal Rules of Evidence, the party with the ultimate burden of establishing her claim, the plaintiff or prosecutor, first introduces the evidence to prove the facts necessary to enable her to recover or obtain a conviction. This initial phase is called the plaintiff's or prosecutor's main case or case-in-chief. For instance, in a contract lawsuit, the plaintiff would introduce evidence relating to the formation of the contract, his fulfillment of the conditions to the defendant's duty, the defendant's breach of duty, and the amount of damages caused by the breach. At this stage the plaintiff calls all the witnesses on whom he relies to establish these facts, together with the pertinent exhibits. The exhibits are formally offered into evidence when they have been authenticated by a sponsoring witness's testimony. During this stage, each witness is initially questioned by the plaintiff's counsel on direct examination and then cross-examined by opposing counsel. These examinations can be followed by redirect and re-cross examinations. When all the plaintiff's or prosecutor's witnesses in her main case have been subjected to this process of questioning and cross-questioning, the plaintiff or prosecutor signals the completion of her case-in-chief by announcing that she rests.

In most jurisdictions, the judge presiding at trial has a discretionary power to permit testimony to be presented out of normal order. Thus, if it is impossible for a key defense witness to appear later in the hearing, the judge could allow the witness to testify early even before the plaintiff's or prosecutor's case-in-chief has concluded. Suppose, for example, that a civil defendant contemplates calling a doctor as a witness but that the physician is scheduled to conduct a life-or-death surgery on a day that will probably fall within the defense case-in-chief. The defense could seek the judge's leave to present the physician's testimony "out of order." In these circumstances, the trial judge might grant the defense permission to interrupt the plaintiff's case in order to present the surgeon's testimony.

Assume, though, that in the normal order, the plaintiff or prosecutor has rested. If the defense counsel believes that at this point the plaintiff or prosecutor has not

---

[10]   See infra § 52.

presented a legally sufficient case, the counsel moves for a nonsuit, directed verdict, or judgment of acquittal as a matter of law. The counsel asserts the weakness of the plaintiff's or prosecutor's body of evidence and claims that the plaintiff or prosecutor has not met the initial burden of production or going forward, discussed in Chapter 36.[11] For purposes of this motion, the judge assumes that all the evidence introduced by the plaintiff or prosecutor is admissible. The motion poses this question: If the trier of fact decides to believe all of the plaintiff's or prosecutor's testimony, does the testimony have sufficient cumulative probative value to rationally sustain a plaintiff's verdict or conviction? If the testimony lacks adequate probative worth, the judge makes a peremptory ruling against the plaintiff or prosecutor. Otherwise, the trial continues.

If the trial continues, the next major phase is the defense case-in-chief or case in defense. The defendant now presents the witnesses and the tangible evidence supporting her case. At this stage the defendant produces evidence disputing the plaintiff's or prosecutor's claim. Thus, the defendant could present testimony that the alleged contract was never agreed on. Similarly, in a negligence case the defense might offer testimony that some bodily injury was not permanent as the plaintiff alleged. The defense can also support any properly pleaded affirmative defenses, such as fraud in the inducement of a contract sued on or the execution of a release of a personal injury claim. Here again each witness's story on direct examination is subject to being tested by cross-examination and supplemented on re-direct. When the defendant has completed the presentation of her proof of affirmative defenses, if any, and her evidence rebutting the plaintiff's or prosecutor's claims, the defendant announces that she rests.

At the conclusion of the defense case-in-chief, the defense could renew the motion for a directed verdict or nonsuit. At this point, the defense can argue alternatively that it has so weakened the plaintiff's or prosecutor's case that no rational juror could convict or find for the plaintiff or that the evidence of an affirmative defense is so strong that no rational juror could reject the defense.

The plaintiff or prosecutor now has another turn at bat; she may present a case in rebuttal. At this stage, the plaintiff or prosecutor is not entitled as of right to present witnesses who merely support or corroborate the allegations of the complaint or accusatory pleading. Rather, the plaintiff or prosecutor is confined to testimony refuting the defense evidence, unless the trial judge in his discretion permits her to exceed the regular scope of rebuttal. The plaintiff's or prosecutor's rebuttal witnesses may be new ones, but she can also recall witnesses who testified for her during the case-in-chief to answer some point first raised by the defendant's witnesses. In this, as in the other stages, the witness may not only be examined on direct, but also cross-examined, redirected, and re-cross-examined. When the plaintiff's or prosecutor's case in rebuttal is finished, she closes her case.

If the rebuttal case raises new points for the first time, the defendant may meet them by evidence in rejoinder or surrebuttal. Otherwise, she closes his case. In a rare case, after a party has closed, the judge may permit the party to reopen the case to present additional evidence.

When witnesses are called during the various phases of the case, the attorneys may not be the only ones to question the witnesses. To begin with, the judge may question the witnesses. Indeed, on her own motion or at a party's request a judge may call a

---

[11]   See infra §§ 336, 338.

witness. The judge is not a mere umpire at trial. The judge has discretion to exercise the power to interrogate witnesses in order to clarify the witness's testimony and fill in key gaps in the record. However, the judge must avoid giving the jury the impression that she has reached a conclusion as to the merits of the case or the witness's credibility. In addition, in many jurisdictions, either the jurors have the right to pose questions or the trial judge has discretion to allow them to do so. The judge typically screens juror questions and rules on their propriety before the question is put to the witness in open court.

When both parties have announced that they have closed, the evidentiary hearing comes to a halt, and the trial proceeds with the closing arguments of counsel and the court's instructions to the jury. The instructions frequently include jury charges about the evidence in the case. For example, if the judge earlier ruled inadmissible certain proffered testimony the jury was exposed to, the judge might give the jury a *curative* instruction to disregard the testimony. Even if the judge ruled certain evidence admissible, the judge might give the jury a *limiting* instruction that they may use the item of evidence only for a particular purpose or only against a particular party. Or the judge could read the jurors a *cautionary* instruction informing them that they should be especially wary in evaluating a certain type of evidence such as eyewitness or accomplice testimony. Or if an issue such as the authenticity of a document falls under Federal Rule of Evidence 104(b), the judge would tell the jury that they must decide the issue and disregard the evidence during the balance of their deliberations if they decide that the document is not genuine.[12] In addition, the judge instructs the jury on the allocation and measure of the ultimate burden of proof on each essential element of the causes of action, crimes, and affirmative defenses at issue.

To sum up, the major stages of the trial are:

(1)   the plaintiff's or prosecutor's main case or case-in-chief;

(2)   the defendant's case-in-chief or case in defense;

(3)   the plaintiff's or prosecutor's rebuttal; and

(4)   the defendant's rejoinder or surrebuttal.

In each stage, each witness's examination may pass through these steps:

(1)   the direct examination conducted by the party who calls the witness;

(2)   the cross-examination by the adversary;

(3)   redirect;

(4)   re-cross; and

(5)   questions by the judge or jurors.

The Federal Rules of Evidence do not prescribe an order for the presentation of evidence at trial. However, under Rule 611(a), the trial judge customarily follows the common law order. According to Rule 611(a), the court "shall exercise reasonable control over the . . . order of examining witnesses and presenting evidence so as to (1) make those procedures effective for determining the truth, (2) avoid wasting time, and (3) protect witnesses from harassment or undue embarrassment." As a practical matter, judges rarely find a sufficient reason to depart from the normal sequence of the major

---

[12]   See infra § 53.

stages of the hearing described above. The primary focus of the explicit provisions of Rule 611 is the control of the steps in examining individual witnesses. The upshot is that trials conducted under the Federal Rules ordinarily follow the traditional common law norms for the major stages of the case.

In the common law order, the witnesses testify one after another. Exercising their discretion, though, some American courts are now experimenting with concurrent expert testimony at bench trials. In this procedure, in order to identify and narrow the real points of disagreement between opposing experts, the experts take the stand at the same time, are subject to questioning by the judge, and can respond to testimony by the opposing expert. This procedure is increasingly being used in bench trials and administrative hearings in the United States.

Title 2

EXAMINATION OF WITNESSES

Chapter 2

THE FORM OF QUESTIONS ON DIRECT; THE JUDGE'S WITNESSES; REFRESHING MEMORY

Table of Sections

§ 5   The Form of Questions: (a) Questions Calling for a Free Narrative Versus Specific Questions

Any experienced litigator knows that at trial, the vast majority of objections relate to the issue of the form of the question rather than substantive evidence doctrines such as hearsay.[1] Form objections can arise on either direct or cross-examination. Cross-examination can be more dramatic than direct examination. Furthermore, skill in cross-examination may be more difficult to develop than the essential skill of direct examination, constructing a coherent, compelling narrative from the mouths of your own witnesses. However, skill in conducting direct is far more important.

One of the key tactical decisions on direct is whether it would be more effective to elicit a particular witness's testimony by several questions about particular facts rather than by a more open-ended question. In the latter case, the lawyer directs the witness's attention to the relevant incident by asking her whether she was on the scene at the time and then inviting her to generally recount what she saw and heard. This method, narrative testimony, is often more persuasive. From the jurors' perspective the account does not seem to come from the counsel, as it might when the counsel poses very specific questions to the witness. If the witness has a good memory, a pleasant personality, and an effective speaking style, her spontaneous narration of her own story may be more interesting and impressive. Narrative testimony allows the witness to put her honesty and intelligence on better display for the jury. Furthermore, empirical research indicates that spontaneous narrative is more accurate (because it is less influenced by suggestion).

The Downsides of Narrative Testimony

However, the same studies show that fully interrogated testimony tends to be more complete. Moreover, specific interrogation can be preferable because it can make it easier to present complicated testimony in proper order, help a nervous witness, or prevent boring testimony by a dull witness. In addition, there are risks to relying on questions calling for narrative responses. When a witness is examined by the narrative method,

---

[1]   Capra & Greenberg, The Form of the Question: Text, Materials and Exercises on the Evidentiary Rules of Form (2014).

the proponent must be ready to interrupt with specific questions to supplement the narrative to bring out omitted facts or if the testimony becomes confusing. For example, if an expert uses a potentially confusing technical term of art, counsel should step in and invite the expert to define the term for the jury. A further problem is that the opponent has to be especially attentive; at any point in the narrative, the witness might inject a reference to inadmissible material.

Given these conflicting considerations, it is no surprise that trial judges vary in their attitude toward questions calling for a narrative. Some trial judges enforce a general prohibition of questions calling for a narrative. These judges fear that that the witness will narrate in a jumbled, confusing fashion. Under the prevailing view, though, there is no general rule of law requiring or even preferring either form of questioning. For example, there is no provision in the Federal Rules of Evidence forbidding narrative questions. Indeed, in rare situations in some states, the rules of legal ethics require the direct examiner to attempt to elicit the witness's testimony in narrative fashion. Admittedly, a number of courts have placed special stress on the possibility that when asked to narrate his story, the witness will mention hearsay or other inadmissible testimony. However, together with counsel's careful phrasing of the question, a proper caution by the judge, on the adversary's request, can usually prevent the risk from materializing.

The Judge's Discretion

It is true that if the witness blurts out an improper statement, the only remedy is striking that part of the evidence and giving the jury a curative instruction to disregard the stricken testimony; and sometimes it is very difficult to unring the bell. Moreover, there is the further problem that the opposing counsel may waive an objection if he does not interrupt promptly and move to strike. Opposing counsel must listen very intently to identify the objectionable parts of a narrative answer. Nevertheless, the legitimate interest in eliciting the witness's knowledge in the most accurate way trumps these dangers. The trial judge ought to have discretion, reviewable only for abuse, to control the form of examination, to the end that the testimony is accurately presented. Hence, the judge may permit either method discussed. On balance, whenever circumstances make narrative testimony feasible, its use is usually in the interest of both the examining party and the system; narrative testimony is not only more persuasive, but it also can yield a more accurate account of the truth.

Enlightened judges rarely curb the use of questions calling for short narrative responses, except in criminal trials when they pose the risk of exposing the jury to constitutionally inadmissible testimony. As a practical matter, at the outset of a direct examination in a civil case many judges entertain a presumption that the lawyer may elicit the witness's testimony in narrative form. The presumption is rebutted—and the judge will insist on more specific questions—only if the witness's narrative becomes confused or the witness makes repeated references to inadmissible matter. So long as the witness avoids those two pitfalls during her testimony, the judge will permit the examiner to elicit the witness's testimony by questions calling for answers the length of a short paragraph. To ensure that the presumption remains unrebutted throughout the direct examination, the attorney must properly prepare the witness before trial. The witness has to learn the chronology well, and the witness must know what not to mention—for example, inadmissible hearsay—unless the questioner asks point blank about that information.

These principles are consistent with restyled Federal Rule of Evidence 611(a), which provides:

> The court shall exercise reasonable control over the mode and order of examining witnesses and presenting evidence so as to:
>
> (1)   make those procedures effective for determining the truth;
>
> (2)   avoid wasting time; and
>
> (3)   protect witnesses from harassment or undue embarrassment.

Rule 611(a) does not purport to announce any categorical "rules" governing the form of the question. The accompanying Advisory Committee's Note contains the sensible observation that "[s]pelling out detailed rules to govern the mode . . . of interrogating witnesses and presenting evidence is neither desirable nor feasible. The ultimate responsibility for the effective working of the adversary system rests with the judge."

§ 6 The Form of Questions: (b) Leading Questions

The preceding section compared the technique of presenting the witness's free narrative on direct examination with that of eliciting testimony by specific questions. One danger of the latter method is that the witness may acquiesce in a false suggestion in the question. The same danger gives rise to another major form problem on direct examination, namely, leading or suggestive phrasing. The suggestion can plant a belief in its truth in the witness's mind. Some empirical studies confirm many judges' belief that this danger is greater than the average layperson supposes. A friendly or pliant witness may follow suggestions on direct examination. Yet, a case can be made that there is little reason to bar suggestive questions. To be frank, before trial the witness is exposed to numerous, far more powerful suggestive influences. In that light, by the time of trial the "leading" objection seems comparatively trivial.

The Definition of "Leading"

Nevertheless, subject to the limitations discussed in the remainder of this section, objections to leading questions are still permissible under the modern common law and Rule 611(c) of the Federal and Revised Uniform Rules of Evidence. The first sentence of Rule 611(c) announces a general norm that "[l]eading questions should not be used on direct examination . . . ." The Advisory Committee's Note underscores the choice of the verb "should" rather than "must" or "shall"; the Note emphasizes that the sentence is purposely "phrased in words of suggestion rather than command."

Although the norm against leading on direct is not an inflexible rule, it is still important to develop a working definition of "leading," since again there is a general prohibition of leading on direct. A leading question is one that suggests to the witness the answer desired by the examiner. Of course, the starting point in analysis should be the precise wording of the question. A question may be leading because of its form, but sometimes the mere form of a question does not dictate whether it is leading. Some types of phrasing such as "Did he not?" are obviously leading,[2] but almost any other type of

---

[2]   There are degrees of leading:

Some questions such as "Did he stop?" are mildly leading. The phrasing refers to an event and carries the suggestion that the event occurred. Especially in bench trials, many judges routinely permit leading questions on direct examination.

wording can be leading, depending on its content and context. It is sometimes categorically asserted both that any question which can be answered yes or no is ipso facto leading and that the neophyte attorney can always take refuge in neutral, alternative wording ("State whether or not . . .") or " 'fig leaf' words" such as "if any" to escape the charge of leading. However, sometimes the former kind of question is not leading, and often the latter type of wording is.

The wording of the question itself is only the starting point in analysis. The context of the previous questioning may signal that the questioner desires a specific answer. Or the questioner's nonverbal conduct can make an otherwise properly worded question objectionably leading. It would obviously be leading for the prosecutor to ask a witness whether the perpetrator is in the room while the prosecutor simultaneously points at the defendant. Yet, the most important consideration can be the substantive content of the question, especially its particularity. When the question describes an incident in detail and asks if the incident happened, the natural inference is that the questioner expects an affirmative answer that the incident occurred. Similarly, if one alternative branch of a question is concrete and detailed but the other vague ("Was the sound like the loud scream of a woman in fear or soft?"), the wording sends the message that the first alternative is preferred. In contrast, when the phrasing of a question is neutral ("At what time did this occur?") or balanced ("Was the water hot or cold?"), it is not leading. All these factors—the context of the prior questioning, the question's wording and content, and the questioner's demeanor—are pertinent considerations. However, the bottom line is this: The judge should adopt the witness's perspective and inquire whether, in these circumstances, the witness would likely form the impression that the questioner desired a particular answer. So long as the circumstances create that impression, the question is leading. To avoid leading question objections, experienced direct examiners consistently begin their questions with natural interrogatory words such as who, what, which, when, where, why, and how. When laypersons are conversing and one wants to obtain information from the other, they frequently begin their questions with such words.

The Propriety of Leading Questions

After we have defined the expression, "leading question," the next issue that arises is when it is permissible to employ leading phrasing. The courts have developed different norms for direct and cross-examination. As Chapter 1 noted, before trial diligent lawyers normally informally interview all the witnesses whom they expect to call for direct examination. This practice is perfectly ethical in the United States. However, the practice creates a probability that by the time of trial, the lawyer and the witness will have reached a friendly *entente* making the witness susceptible to the lawyer's suggestions. In contrast, when a lawyer cross-examines a witness called by the adversary, the lawyer may have had little or no prior contact with the witness; and there is less likelihood of an understanding between them about the facts. Hence, a common

---

The more negative phrasing, "Did he not?," carries a stronger suggestion. Fairly leading questions of this nature often prompt an objection, and especially in jury trials many judges sustain the objection.

Then there are brutally leading questions. A question can be made brutally leading in one of three ways. First, the examiner might use prefatory language such as "Isn't it true . . .?:" Second, the examiner could add a tag after a declarative sentence: "He came to a full stop. Right?" Finally, if the cross-examiner and a compliant witness get into a rhythm, the questioner utters a declarative sentence, omits the tag, and signifies that the statement is a question by raising her voice at the end of the sentence. The last style is sometimes referred to as "conversational" cross-examination.

sense rule of thumb evolved: On objection, the judge ordinarily forbids leading questions on direct examination but usually permits them on cross-examination. Yet, in the final analysis, the permissibility of leading questions is discretionary, and the judge's deviation from the usual practice will not be reversed unless it contributed to an unfair trial.

When the normal assumption about the relation between the witness and the counsel conducting the direct examination does not hold true, the usual practice is reversed. Thus, if on direct the witness is legally identified with the opponent, appears hostile to the examiner, or is reluctant or uncooperative, the danger of suggestion disappears. In these circumstances, the judge will permit leading questions on direct. Conversely, when on cross-examination the witness appears biased in the cross-examining attorney's favor, the judge may prohibit counsel from leading. By way of example, in civil cases, the plaintiff can call the defendant as an adverse witness. After the plaintiff's direct examination of the defendant, the defendant's own counsel has the opportunity to cross-examine. However, the defendant's relationship with her own counsel is hardly hostile.

In many situations, especially at bench trials, judges routinely permit mildly leading phrasing during direct examination. For instance, leading questions may be used to bring out preliminary matters such as the witness's name and occupation, or to elicit matters that are not seriously disputed. Leading phrasing may also be employed to suggest a subject or topic, as distinguished from an answer. Other relaxations are justified on the ground of necessity. Thus, when the need appears, the judge ordinarily allows leading questioning of children or adult witnesses who are so ignorant, hesitant, timid, weak-minded, or deficient in the English language that they cannot otherwise convey the information they possess. Admittedly, in these cases, especially as to children, there is a risk of false suggestion. However, on balance, it is better to run that risk than to abandon altogether the effort to elicit the witness's knowledge. Similarly, when a lawyer has directed a witness to the subject by non-leading questions without securing a complete account of the witness's knowledge, the witness's memory is said to be "exhausted." In that event, the judge may permit the examiner to ask more specific questions whose particularity can revive the witness's memory (but which simultaneously to some degree might suggest the desired answer). Likewise, many courts liberally allow specific, leading questions during the direct examination of experts. These courts reason that if the expert were allowed free rein, her testimony could easily become "complicated" and confuse the jury.

In some jurisdictions, longstanding practice permits putting leading questions to a second witness who, for impeachment purposes, is called to testify about a previous witness's statement that is inconsistent with the previous witness's testimony. Here too necessity is the stated justification. It might otherwise be difficult to quickly get to the point and direct the second witness's attention to the subject of the testimony. It has been argued that the practice should be discontinued. But most courts have rejected the argument and upheld the common practice.

§ 7 The Form of Questions: (c) Argumentative, Misleading, and Indefinite Questions

Sections 5 and 6 discussed form problems that arise mainly during direct examination. We turn now to form problems of primary importance on cross-examination.

Argumentative Questions

The first problem is that of the argumentative question. This problem can conceivably arise during direct examination, particularly when the direct examiner calls an adverse party or hostile witness to the stand. However, the objection is lodged far more frequently on cross-examination.

The examiner may not ask a question that merely pressures the witness to assent to the questioner's inferences from or interpretations of the testimony already admitted. Rather than attempting to elicit new substantive information, the cross-examiner is challenging or arguing with the witness about an inference from the testimony already in the record. For instance, evincing disbelief in her demeanor, the cross-examiner might ask, "Do you really expect the jury to believe that?" or "How can you reconcile those statements?" This kind of question is objectionable as "argumentative" or "badgering the witness." The trial judge has a wide range of discretion in enforcing the rule, particularly on cross-examination where such questions are more common. It is certainly fair for judges to enforce the rule during cross-examination. When the cross-examiner becomes argumentative, she is in effect previewing her summation; and she will later have an ample opportunity to argue the inferences during her summation to the jury.

Misleading Questions Assuming Facts Not in Evidence

Another common form problem occurs when the examiner words the question so that it assumes as true matters which no witness has yet testified to, and which are disputed between the parties. The danger is two-fold. First, when the examiner puts the question to a friendly witness, the recitation of the assumed fact may be leading, suggesting the desired answer. Second, whether the witness is friendly or hostile, the answer can be misleading. The witness deserves a fair opportunity to affirm or deny the fact. If the witness is inattentive and answers the question without identifying the assumption, it may impossible for the trier of fact to later determine whether the witness affirmed or simply ignored the assumption. When the question suffers from this vice, the opposing counsel usually objects that the question "is misleading" or "assumes facts not in evidence."

Indefinite or Vague Questions

Occasionally questions are considered objectionable because they are too broad or indefinite. Sometimes this objection is in reality an objection of lack of relevancy. The objection can arise on direct or cross. However, indefinite or ambiguous cross-examination questions about a witness's personal background can be especially dangerous. Suppose, for instance, that the cross-examiner asks a witness whether he has had any "troubles," "contacts," "brushes," "encounters," "problems," "difficulties," or "run-ins with the law." In response to that question, the witness might mention convictions admissible for impeachment as well as other misconduct that is both prejudicial and inadmissible. The witness's answer could violate the restrictions on credibility or character evidence. Likewise, indefinite wording is dangerous when the wording includes a legalism. The meaning of the legalistic term may differ from the general, popular meaning of the expression.

The principles mentioned in this section are not expressly codified in the Federal or Revised Uniform Rules (1974), but they may be enforced in the trial judge's discretion under Rules 403 and 611(a).[3]

§ 8 The Judge May Call Witnesses; the Judge and Jurors May Question Witnesses

Judges

Sections 5 to 7 deal with some of the form issues that arise when attorneys call and question witnesses. Problems can also materialize when judges call or question witnesses. Under the Anglo-American adversary trial system, the parties' counsel have the primary responsibility for finding, selecting, and presenting the evidence. However, our system of party-investigation and party-presentation has limitations. The system is a means to the end of discovering the truth and administering justice. In order to achieve that end, the judge may exercise various powers to intervene to supplement the parties' evidence.

More specifically, the judge has the powers to call and question witnesses. Under the case law and Federal Rule of Evidence 614(b), the judge has discretion to examine any witness to clarify testimony or to bring out needed facts omitted by the parties. The trial judge is not a mere umpire or passive moderator. Some appellate courts have even gone to the length of stating that the trial judge may have a "duty" to question witnesses. If there were such a duty, an appellant could conceivably predicate error on the judge's failure to ask questions that would have yielded answers favorable to the appellant. However, the judicial references to "duty" seem to be rhetorical dicta; the supposed duty does not appear to have been enforced by any appellate decision.

In the great majority of states, the judge has lost the traditional common law power to comment on the weight of the evidence. In those jurisdictions, the judge's questioning in jury cases must be cautiously guarded to avoid implied comment. If the judge uses highly leading questions suggesting the desired answer, the questions may strongly imply that the judge views the desired answer as the truth and thus amount to forbidden comment. To be sure, courts have occasionally held that the policy against leading questions by counsel, namely, avoiding false testimony prompted by partisan suggestion,[4] does not apply to judges. After all, the judge's office is supposed to be impartial. However, this reasoning is unrealistic. Especially since the judge is an authority figure, there is a grave risk that the witness will adopt any suggestion implicit in the judge's question. Some witnesses are more likely to adopt the suggestion in a judge's question than in a question posed by counsel. Leading judicial questions clearly aimed at discrediting or impeaching the witness, though allowable for counsel, can intimate the judge's belief that the witness has lied, and hence constitute a verboten implied comment.

In the federal courts and the few states retaining the common law power to comment, these restrictions on judicial questions are relaxed. In all jurisdictions, the restrictions are enforced more laxly in judge-tried cases. Nevertheless, even then the

---

3   As to Rule 403, see infra § 185.

4   See supra § 6.

judge must avoid extreme exercises of the power to question. In a judge-tried case, the judge's questions can amount to error if they betray an actual, premature judgment. In a jury trial, functionally the judge must not assume the role of an advocate or a prosecutor—in actuality or appearance. If her questions are too partisan and extensive, the judge runs the risk that the appellate court will find that she crossed the line between judging and advocacy. However, the mere number of judicial questions is not dispositive. The nature of the questions and the identity of the witness are the two most important considerations.

Not only may the judge examine witnesses called by the parties. In her discretion, again to bringing out needed facts, the judge may call witnesses whom the parties have chosen not to call at all. Judges most frequently exercise the power to call witnesses when a necessary witness will probably be hostile to the government and the prosecutor desires to escape the necessity of calling him and being handicapped by the traditional rule against impeaching one's own witness. Concededly, under the Federal Rules of Evidence, the prosecutor has another option; the rules allow a party to impeach the party's own witness. Yet, as a practical matter the prosecutor may not wish to call the witness and thereby be identified with the witness in the jurors' minds. If the witness has a long unsavory criminal record, his "affiliation" with the government might taint the prosecution case in the jurors' eyes. In these circumstances, the prosecutor could invoke the judge's discretion under Rule 614(a) to call the witness. If the judge calls the witness, both parties may cross-examine and impeach the witness.

As we have seen, Rule 614(a) generally empowers the judge to call witnesses. Rule 706 deals specifically with court appointed expert witnesses. At common law another use of the judicial power to call witnesses, codified in some state statutes, is to mediate the battle of partisan expert witnesses employed by the parties. In effect, the practice resurrects the judge's ancient power to call an expert of her own choosing to give impartial testimony to aid her or the jury in resolving a scientific issue. In its celebrated 1993 *Daubert* decision, the Supreme Court decided that in order to determine the admissibility of purportedly scientific testimony, federal trial judges must evaluate the extent and quality of the empirical validation of the underlying theory or technique.[5] In his concurring opinion in the 1997 *Joiner* case elaborating on *Daubert*, Justice Breyer encouraged trial judges to exercise their power under Rule 706.[6] Those decisions have prompted trial judges to appoint experts with greater frequency under Rule 706. However, as we have seen, under Rule 614(a) the scope of the judge's power of calling witnesses in aid of justice is broader and is not limited to expert testimony cases. The key difference between Rules 614 and 706 is that while a normal witness must obey a summons or subpoena issued by a judge, an expert may decline to accept a Rule 706 appointment.

Jurors

The preceding section points out that judges may question witnesses called by the parties. Should jurors be allowed to do so?

There are conflicting policy considerations. On the one hand, there are obvious dangers to permitting jury questions. One fear is that if jurors actively participate in the trial before they have heard all the evidence, they may develop biases inconsistent with

---

[5]   Daubert v. Merrell Dow Pharms., Inc., 509 U.S. 579 (1993).

[6]   General Elec. Co. v. Joiner, 522 U.S. 136, 147, 149–50 (1997).

"their . . . role as neutral factfinders." Moreover, there is the risk that the jurors will attach inordinate weight to the witnesses' answers to the jurors' questions and slight the testimony elicited by the parties. On the hand, there is a strong case for allowing the jurors to pose questions. The argument runs that if the jurors realize that they can pose questions, they will be motivated to be more engaged and attentive to the witnesses' testimony. Furthermore, there are perils to the factfinding process if, even at the close of evidence, the jurors have nagging questions that are unanswered. It is a distinct possibility that the jurors will speculate as to the answer and base a verdict on conjecture. Unanswered questions relating to expert testimony are especially problematic. The jurors can often draw on common experience to correctly close gaps in a lay witness's account, but they are much more likely to err if they attempt to fill in a missing blank in an expert's analysis. Another possibility is that the litigant might suffer a wrongful loss; even if the litigant could easily have supplied the missing evidence, the jurors may hold the gap in the evidence against the litigant and for that reason decide the case adversely to the litigant.

It is understandable that given these conflicting policies, there is a wide split of authority over the propriety of juror questions.

- At one extreme, in a few jurisdictions such as Kentucky petit jurors have the right to ask questions.

- The polar extreme view is that juror questions are absolutely forbidden, at least in criminal cases.

- However, both the majority view and the growing trend is to accord the trial judge discretion to allow juror questioning. Some courts restrict this discretion to complex cases. While acknowledging that the complexity of a case makes it more appropriate for the judge to permit juror questioning, other courts do not strictly limit the discretion to complicated cases. The latter position is the most sensible view. However, even in the jurisdictions following the majority view, the appellate courts often caution the trial bench that juror questioning is risky and should be carefully monitored by the trial judge.

When the judge exercises discretion to permit juror questioning, the judge can monitor and minimize the risks by observing certain safeguards. The rules of evidence apply to juror questions; and there would obviously be a substantial danger if, without prior screening, jurors could simply orally pose questions. Thus, the judge ought to instruct the jurors that when they want to ask a question, they should raise their hand. When a juror does so, the judge directs the juror to reduce the question to writing. The juror hands the slip of paper to the court reporter or bailiff, who in turn delivers the slip to the judge. At that point at sidebar the judge and attorneys can discuss the propriety of the question. The judge ought to give the jury an additional instruction, cautioning them against reaching conclusions or prematurely taking positions before all the evidence has been presented to them. In addition, if a juror question is permitted, the attorneys should be allowed to follow-up and examine the witness on the topic of the juror's question.

§ 9 Refreshing Recollection

Whether the questioner is a counsel, the judge, or a juror, an anxious witness may forget a relevant fact. Testifying is a novel, frightening experience for many witnesses.

It is clear from everyday experience that the latent memory of an experience can sometimes be revived by a familiar image or statement. In the words of one court, the inspiration for the revival "may be a line from Kipling or the dolorous strain of 'The Tennessee Waltz'; a whiff of hickory smoke; the running of the fingers across a swatch of corduroy; the sweet carbonation of a chocolate soda; [or] the sight of a faded snapshot in a long-neglected album."[7] This is an illustration of the phenomenon that the classical psychologists called association. A person's retrieval of any part of a past experience can help the person recall other parts in the same field of awareness, and a new experience can stimulate the recall of prior similar events. The effect is a reminder. The reminder prompts our memory to retrieve associated experiences.[8]

As Chapter 1 noted, the interviewing of witnesses by counsel who will examine them in court is a necessary step in preparing for trial.[9] Before trial, the counsel can best refresh the witness's memory about the facts of the case by giving her the opportunity to read her own previous written statements, letters, maps, or other documents. However, again testifying at trial can be an intimidating experience. On occasion, even if the attorney properly prepared the witness before trial, the witness becomes anxious and forgets on the stand. In that event, the attorney must attempt to refresh or revive the witness's memory in order to elicit the witness's testimony about the forgotten fact. The use of the statement or map to refresh the witness's memory is more likely to be successful if the witness has physically handled and discussed the document during the pretrial interview.

Suppose that at trial, when asked about a particular fact or event, the witness answers that she cannot remember. At least when the witness admits forgetfulness on the record, it has long been the practice that counsel may hand her a memorandum to inspect for the purpose of "refreshing her recollection." When she speaks from a memory thus revived, her testimony is the evidence, not the writing. This is the process of *refreshing recollection at trial* in the original, strict sense.

Confusion with the Past Recollection

Recorded Hearsay Exception

However, after the courts accepted that simple, uncontroversial practice, it was natural for counsel to seek to carry it a step further. Suppose that even after inspecting the writing, the witness states that her memory is not revived and that she cannot testify from a refreshed recollection. But she vouches that she recognizes the writing as a memorandum she made when the facts were fresh in her mind. She adds that although she has no present memory of the facts, she remembers correctly recording the facts in the memorandum. Here the writing itself becomes the evidence. This latter situation is quite different than the process of *refreshing recollection*. In refreshing recollection, after reviewing the memory aid the witness testifies orally on the basis of her present refreshed memory. In contrast, when her memory is not jogged, the counsel relies on the witness's voucher as a basis for introducing the writing. The writing is the real evidence.

In both cases, the questioner tenders a memorandum to the witness, but the underlying justification in the second situation is fundamentally different. Here the justification rests on the reliability of a writing which the witness swears is an accurate

---

[7]   Baker v. State, 371 A.2d 699 (Md. Ct. Spec. App. 1977).

[8]   See infra § 279.

[9]   See supra § 2.

record of her past recollection. The writing itself is formally introduced into evidence. The courts formulated special foundational rules and restrictions for this kind of memorandum. Hence, the common law rules generally require that the memo must have been written by the witness or examined and found correct by her. There is a further restriction that the memo must have been prepared so promptly after the events recorded that the events were still fresh in the witness's mind when the record was made, or examined and verified by her. Memoranda satisfying these restrictions fall within the past recollection recorded exception to the hearsay rule.

Apparently, the earlier English cases on genuine refreshment of recollection placed no comparable restrictions on the use of memoranda at the trial to revive a witness's memory. Those memoranda were not required to have been written by the witness or under her direction, or to have been made near in time to the event. The memorandum need not be accurate or independently admissible. Theoretically, the questioner could use anything to fresh the witness's memory. However, in the case of the practice of introducing records of *past recollection,* the additional restrictions were prescribed with good reason. Unfortunately, since the old name of "refreshing recollection" was often applied indiscriminately to both practices, the two practices became confused. Predictably, the restrictions developed for one kind of memorandum (past recollection recorded) spilled over to the other (present recollection refreshed).

The Case for Distinguishing Between the Two Practices

Which is the wiser practice: (1) the older rule, championed by Wigmore and most modern courts, that any memorandum, without restriction of authorship, time, or correctness, may be used to revive memory, or (2) the doctrine requiring that a memorandum used to refresh meet the same restrictions as a record of past recollection? Even if the latter doctrine is an historical blunder, by serendipity it could be a desirable practice enhancing the search for truth.

Any kind of stimulus, "a song, a face, or a newspaper item," can produce the "flash" of recognition, the subjective feeling that "it all comes back to me now." But the sincerity of the feeling is no guarantee of the objective correctness of the information purportedly recalled. There is a danger that the mind will "remember" something that never happened. That danger is at least as great here as in the case of leading questions. "Imagination and suggestion are twin artists ever ready to retouch the fading daguerrotype of memory."[10] Thus, there is a plausible policy argument for extending to refreshing memory the safeguards developed for memoranda of past recollection recorded, namely, the requirements that the witness must have created the writing or recognized it as correct, and that the creation or recognition must have occurred while the event was still fresh in the witness's memory.

Nevertheless, today most courts adhere to the "classical" view that any memorandum or object may be used as a stimulus to present memory without regard as to authorship, admissibility, guarantee of correctness, or time of making. On balance, this liberal view is sounder. There are other, sufficient safeguards against abuse. The first safeguard is the trial judge's power under Federal Rule of Evidence 104(a). It is a preliminary question for her decision under Rule 104(a) whether the memorandum actually does refresh. When there is no seeming connection between the contents of the memorandum and the witness's testimony, the judge may find that it does not; she need

---

[10]   Gardner, The Perception and Memory of Witnesses, 18 Cornell L.Q. 390, 401 (1933).

not accept at face value the witness's claim that reviewing the memo revived the witness's memory. The judge has additional control under Rules 403 and 611(a). In the exercise of her discretion to control the manner of the witness's examination, the judge may decline to permit the use of the memory aid when, under 403 and 611, she regards the danger of undue suggestion as substantially outweighing the probative value.

When the witness seeks to resort to the memorandum, another safeguard is the rule entitling the adverse party to inspect the memorandum so that she may (1) object to its use if a ground appears, and (2) use the memorandum to cross-examine the witness. With the memorandum in hand, the cross-examiner has a good opportunity to test the credibility of the witness's claim that her memory has been revived, and to search out any discrepancies between the writing and the testimony. For instance, if there is no evident nexus between the contents of the writing and the fact purportedly remembered, the cross-examiner can attack the plausibility of the witness's testimony that viewing the writing helped the witness remember that fact. In the past, this inspection right was usually limited to writings used by the witness on the stand. However, the policy reasons for inspection seem equally applicable to writings used by the witness to refresh her memory before she testifies. The subject of inspection and use of writings to which the witness referred before testifying at trial is discussed at the end of this section.

Not only may the adversary inspect the memoranda used to refresh memory during the witness's examination, but she may also submit them to the jury for their examination. If there is no evident connection between the content of the memorandum and the fact the witness purported to remember, the jurors may disbelieve the witness's testimony that reviewing the memorandum revived the witness's memory of the fact. In contrast, the party calling the witness may not introduce the memorandum unless it is independently admissible under the hearsay rule. The consensus is that unless they qualify as nonhearsay or fall within an exemption from or exception to the hearsay rule, memoranda used to refresh are not substantive evidence that can be relied on to support a finding of fact. They are merely memory joggers or aids. Consequently, the best evidence rule is inapplicable; and a copy may be used to refresh memory without accounting for the original.

The line between using the writing merely as a memory jogger and treating it as a record of past memory can be shadowy. Must the proponent show that the witness has no present recollection whatsoever of the matters embodied in the memorandum before she can resort to it as a memory aid? Even in opinions issued under the Federal Rules of Evidence, it is sometimes asserted that that showing is required, but that assertion is unsound. Rule 803(5) permits the proponent to rely on the past recollection recorded hearsay exception when, after viewing the writing, the witness "cannot recall well enough to testify fully and accurately." The courts should apply a similarly realistic standard under Rule 612. The witness may believe that she remembers completely; but, after reading the memorandum, she might well recall additional facts. As the ancient proverb has it, "The palest ink is clearer than the best memory." There is an undeniable danger that a suggestible witness may mistakenly think that she remembers a specific fact merely because she reads it. However, that danger is not so acute that it justifies a categorical rule prohibiting the use of present recollection refreshed in these situations. The judge should enjoy discretion in the matter. Even if a witness recognizes from present memory the correctness of a set of facts recorded in a memorandum, the witness may be unable to detail the individual facts such as numbers from memory without consulting the writing. Accordingly, it is too inflexible to hold that, once refreshed, a witness must testify independently without viewing the writing. Again, the matter ought to be entrusted to the trial judge's discretion. The judge may permit the witness to consult the memorandum as she speaks, especially when it is so lengthy and detailed that even a witness with a fresh memory would realistically be unable to recite unaided all the items.

As previously stated, many older cases refused to enforce a demand for production at trial of matter reviewed by a witness to refresh memory before testifying. However, even prior to the enactment of the Federal Rules of Evidence, a growing number of cases reached the contrary conclusion. Nevertheless, the most important factor in accelerating this trend has been the adoption of Federal Rule of Evidence 612. Rule 612(a)(2) explicitly announces that when a witness uses a writing to refresh her memory even before testifying, an adverse party is entitled to have the writing produced at the hearing, to inspect it, to cross-examine the witness about the writing, and to introduce into evidence the portions relating to the witness's testimony, if the court in its discretion determines production is necessary in the interests of justice.

Consider the significance of the sweeping wording of Rule 612. A writing consulted to refresh memory could be a privileged one, such as a letter written by the client-witness to her attorney about the case. In that event, there is a possible conflict between Rule 612's disclosure requirement and the privilege for confidential communications between attorney and client. Should the pretrial act of consulting the writing effect a waiver of the privilege? Finding a waiver when the writing is consulted by the witness while testifying is obviously warranted; it would be patently unfair for a witness to consult the writing while testifying in open court but refuse to allow the opposing counsel to see the writing. The proper result is more debatable when a privileged writing is consulted before trial. Ordinarily the privilege involved will be either the absolute attorney-client privilege[11] or the qualified protection for "work product."[12] Section 93 of this treatise discusses the problem of waiver of those privileges. The Advisory Committee's Note to Rule 612 states that "access" should be granted "only to those writings which may fairly be said in fact to have an impact upon the testimony of the witness." In the early federal cases a clear trend emerged to hold that Rule 612 overrides all privileges claims, at least when the witness consulted the passage in the writing pretrial for the precise purpose of reviving his memory in order to testify. Some of the more recent decisions override the privilege only when the record establishes that consulting the writing actually refreshed the witness's memory and affected the witness's trial testimony. The position taken in those decisions is the most consistent with the wording of the Advisory Committee's Note—again, "in fact . . . have an impact upon the testimony of the witness."

A further matter connected to Federal Rule of Evidence 612 is the relationship between that rule and Federal Rule of Criminal Procedure 26.2. Rule 26.2 is the successor to the so-called Jencks Act, 18 U.S.C.A. § 3500. That relationship is explored in a later section.[13]

Lastly, hypnosis is sometimes employed as a technique to refresh a witness's recollection.[14] That subject is analyzed in the chapter on scientific evidence.

---

[11]   See generally infra Ch. 10.

[12]   See infra § 96.

[13]   See infra § 97.

[14]   See infra § 206.4.

Chapter 3

THE REQUIREMENT OF FIRSTHAND KNOWLEDGE: THE OPINION RULE & EXPERT TESTIMONY

Table of Sections

§ 10   The Requirement of Firsthand Knowledge from Observation

The common law system of evidence embodies a strong preference for admitting the most reliable sources of information. This preference is reflected in the hearsay rule, the documentary original doctrine, and the opinion rule. These doctrines are not absolute exclusionary rules; rather, as just stated, each doctrine reflects a preference for a more reliable types of evidence. For example, by virtue of the opinion rule, the law prefers that a witness testify to facts, based on personal knowledge, rather than opinions inferred from such facts. The common law model assumes that the lay witness can articulate the relevant primary sensory data and that the lay jurors are then competent to decide what inferences to draw from the data.

One of the most pervasive manifestations of the common law preference[1] is the rule that a witness testifying about a fact which can be perceived by the senses must: (1) have had an opportunity to observe, (2) have actually observed the fact, and (3) presently recall the observed fact. More broadly, the requirement is that the witness have gained knowledge of the fact through her sensory experience. Thus, a lay witness may testify not only about events she observed but also about sensations such as pain she experienced. The same general requirement applies to declarations admitted under most exceptions to the hearsay rule; as a general proposition, the out-of-court declarant must have had an opportunity to observe the fact declared.

---

[1]   Daubert v. Merrell Dow Pharms., Inc., 509 U.S. 579, 592 (1993).

31

This requirement can easily be confused with the rule barring the in-court repetition of out-of-court statements considered hearsay.[2] Technically, if on its face the witness's testimony purports to describe observed facts but the testimony rests on statements of others, the objection is that the witness lacks firsthand knowledge. In contrast, when on its face the testimony indicates the witness is repeating out-of-court statements, a hearsay objection is appropriate. Courts often blur this distinction.

The party offering the testimony has the burden of laying a foundation showing that the witness had an adequate opportunity to observe, actually observed, and presently recalls the observation. Suppose that on direct examination, the witness initially purports to testify from personal knowledge. If it later appears for the first time that the witness lacked opportunity or did not actually observe the fact, on motion his testimony will be stricken; and on request the jury will be given a curative instruction to disregard the stricken testimony. Although the requirement for showing the witness's personal knowledge exists, the proponent's burden is a minimal one. The judge applies the Rule 104(b) conditional relevancy procedure in deciding whether the proponent has made an adequate showing of personal knowledge. As § 53 explains, the Rule 104(b) standard is relaxed. When reasonable persons could differ as to whether the witness had an adequate opportunity to observe, the witness's testimony is admissible; and the jury will later make its own appraisal of his opportunity to know in evaluating the weight of the testimony during deliberations.

In laying the foundation, the examiner may elicit from the witness the particular circumstances that led her to notice, observe, or remember the fact. What called the witness's attention to the fact or event? How clear a view did the witness have? Why was the fact so memorable for the witness? If the witness had a special reason to be attentive, the jury is likely to attach more weight to the witness's purported recollection.

While the law demands firsthand observation, the law does not unrealistically insist on either precise perception or certainty in recalling the facts. Accordingly, even when a witness uses qualifying language such as "I think," "My impression is," "In my opinion," or "To the best of my recollection," the testimony is admissible if he is merely acknowledging an inattentive observation or an unsure memory. However, an objection will be sustained if the judge concludes that the witness means that he is speaking from conjecture or hearsay. When the state of the record is unclear, the judge may exercise her power under Rule 614 to question the witness to clarify the testimony before making a final ruling on the objection.

Of course, a person who has no knowledge of a fact except what another has told her does not satisfy the requirement of knowledge from observation for that fact. However, when the witness bases her testimony partly on firsthand knowledge and partly on the accounts of others, the situation calls for a practical compromise. As a case in point, when a witness speaks about her own age or her kinship with a relative, the courts routinely allow the testimony. Strictly speaking, it is impossible for the witness to have personal knowledge of those facts. No matter how precocious a child might be, she will not recall her own birth. Hence, there is an element of necessity in this situation. Moreover, the witness's knowledge of this type of fact is likely to have a trustworthy basis, namely, reports from close relatives who possess firsthand knowledge. In short, when the witness testifies to facts that she knows partly firsthand and partly from

---

[2]   See infra § 247.

hearsay reports, the judge should admit or exclude according to the judge's assessment of the overall reliability of the evidence. Thus, a witness's industry experience is a sufficient predicate for the witness's testimony about practices within the industry. Similarly, lay employees of a business are often held to have enough "personalized knowledge" of the business' operation to testify about such topics as the amount of its profits.

§ 11 The Evolution of the Rule Against Opinions: Opinions of Laypersons; Applicability of Restrictions to Out-of-Court Statements

The restrictions on lay opinions go beyond the requirement that laypersons base their testimony on personal knowledge. Even when a layperson possesses personal knowledge, the restrictions limit the form of her testimony.

The Original English View

The opinion rule was enforced more widely and far more inflexibly here than in England. The original rule against "opinions" had a different, limited meaning for the English judge. In English usage of the 1700s and earlier, the primary meaning of "opinion" was an unsupported "notion" or "persuasion of the mind without proof or certain knowledge."[3] Thus, the original expression implied a lack of grounding in personal knowledge, which is quite different than the contemporary meaning of the term "opinion" in this country. In the United States today the word denotes an inference, belief, or conclusion without necessarily suggesting that the inference is completely unfounded.

The requirement that witnesses have personal knowledge, discussed in the preceding section, has roots in medieval law. The early courts demanded that witnesses testify about only "what they see and hear." Coke's classic 1622 dictum, that "It is no satisfaction for a witness to say that he 'thinketh' or 'persuadeth himself' "[4] and Mansfield's 1766 statement, "It is mere opinion, which is not evidence"[5] ought to be understood as condemning only testimony not based on personal knowledge. Statements founded purely on hearsay or conjecture fall under this ban. But as Wigmore interprets the historical evidence, until the 1800s there was no judicial support for a broader, more restrictive "opinion" rule excluding even inferences by witnesses possessing personal knowledge.

The Evolution of the American Law—The Early Exclusionary Rule

By the middle of the 1800s the disparagement of "mere opinion" in the limited sense of conjecture not based on observation evolved into a broader, much more questionable canon of exclusion. This canon was the doctrine that witnesses generally must restrict their testimony to recitations of the "facts" and avoid "inferences, conclusions, or opinions," even ones drawn from their own personal knowledge of the facts.

That canon is based on the simplistic assumption that "fact" and "opinion" differ in kind and are readily distinguishable. But this basic assumption is largely an illusion. As the Supreme Court has remarked, "the distinction between statements of fact and

---

[3]   Samuel Johnson's Dictionary (1st ed. 1755).

[4]   Adams v. Canon, Dyer 53b, quoted in 7 Wigmore, Evidence § 1917, at 2 (Chadbourn rev. 1979).

[5]   Carter v. Boehm, 3 Burr. 1905, 1918 (1766), quoted in 7 Wigmore, Evidence § 1917, at 7 (Chadbourn rev. 1979).

opinion is, at best, one of degree."[6] The witness's words cannot "give" or "recreate" the facts, that is, the objective situations or events about which the witness is testifying. Drawings, maps, photographs, and even motion pictures are only remote, partial portrayals of those "facts." Word pictures—oral or written descriptions—of events are even more distant approximations of reality. Even the seemingly most specific, detailed, and "factual" statements are in some measure the product of inference as well as observation and memory. Consider the statement, "He was driving on the left-hand side of the road" (which would be categorized as "fact" under the rule) and the statement "He was driving carelessly" (which would be called "opinion"). To be sure, it is an overstatement to entirely dismiss the contrast and characterize it as nothing more than a difference between a more concrete form of descriptive statement and a less specific form. The latter statement is more ambiguous and might be excluded on that ground. However, the distinction between the so-called "fact" and "opinion" is not a bright-line difference between opposites or contrasting absolutes, but instead a difference in degree on a spectrum without sharp boundaries.

If trial judges must distinguish on the spur of the moment between "fact" and "opinion," no two judges, acting independently, will always reach the same result in every case. Of course, many questions have recurred and have customarily been classified as calling for either "fact" or "opinion." But in a changing world there will be a myriad of new statements to which the judge must apply the distinction. Thus, good sense demands that the law accord the trial judge considerable discretion at least in classifying evidence as "fact" or "opinion," and probably also in admitting evidence classified as opinion. Several courts have expressed this viewpoint. Federal Rule of Evidence and Uniform Rule of Evidence 701 should be construed as conferring that latitude on the trial judge.

———

The Gradual Relaxation of the Admissibility Standard

The recognition of the impossibility of administering the opinion standard as a mandatory rule came slowly. The relaxation began at common law and accelerated under the Federal Rules.

At common law, the relaxation of the strictness of the standard was initially limited to cases of strict necessity. A norm excluding opinion except in instances of strict necessity survives today as the "orthodox" view in a few states. However, even in states which have not adopted the Federal Rules of Evidence or a similar statutory reform, the practice is becoming far more liberal than the older formulas. The practice is more accurately reflected in a formula used by some courts sanctioning the admission of opinions on grounds of "helpfulness," "expediency," or "convenience" rather than absolute "necessity."

Of course, before deciding whether a particular lay opinion is helpful, the judge must decide whether laypersons are capable of reliably drawing that type of conclusion or inference. That issue is rarely litigated. When it does arise, the judge tends to implicitly fall back on her own personal experience. Driving to and from work, the judge is constantly forming opinions about the speed of the car in front of her car and the distance between that car's rear bumper and her car. The judge acts on those opinions;

---

[6]   Beech Aircraft Corp. v. Rainey, 488 U.S. 153, 168 (1988).

for example, she decelerates to avoid colliding with the car in front of her. The opinions turn out to be reliable enough to be helpful; she arrives at work without incident. As laypersons, on a daily basis judges form and successfully act on opinions on topics such as distance, speed, and the handwriting style of acquaintances. Judges then justifiably project that other laypersons can form trustworthy, helpful opinions on such topics.

The so-called "collective fact" or "short-hand rendition" rule illustrates the helpfulness/convenience notion. That case law doctrine, permitting opinions on such topics as a person's age, a car's speed, the height of a fixture, or a person's intoxication, rests on this liberal notion. The same notion underlies the acceptance of "skilled lay observer" opinions on such subjects as the identification of a person or of a person's handwriting style. In the words of Federal Rule 701(a), these opinions must be "rationally based on the witness's perception." It is not enough that the opinion has some basis in the witness's personal knowledge. The inclusion of the adverb "rationally" signals that the judge must decide whether, as a matter of logic, the extent of the witness's knowledge is sufficient to support the proffered opinion. In the case of collective fact opinions, the proponent has to lay a foundation establishing an adequate opportunity for observation such as a sufficiently long period to observe the allegedly speeding car. If a witness hears a passing car without seeing it, some courts allow the witness to opine whether the car sounded as if it was going "fast" or "slow" but forbid the witness from estimating the car's speed in miles per hour. In the case of skilled lay observer opinions, the proponent lays a foundation demonstrating a sufficiently large number of prior opportunities for observation such as previous occasions when the witness saw exemplars of the person's cursive writing.

Federal Rule of Evidence 701 strengthened the common law trend toward admitting such opinions. Rule 701 codifies helpfulness/convenience as the standard. Rather than restricting lay opinion to cases of strict necessity, Rule 701 authorizes the receipt of any lay opinion "helpful" to the trier of fact. As a general proposition, Rule 701 liberalizes the common law standard.

The standard actually applied by many contemporary trial judges at common law and under Rule 701 reflects Wigmore's position. His position was that lay opinions should be rejected only when they are superfluous in the sense that they will be of no value to the jury. The helpfulness or value of opinions to the jury is the principal test under Federal Rule of Evidence and Uniform Rule of Evidence 701. In light of Rule 701, the prevailing practice in respect to the admission of lay opinions should be described not as a rigid rule excluding opinions, but rather as a preference. The more concrete description is preferred to the more abstract. To the extent reasonably feasible, the witness ought to attempt to convey the concrete primary facts to the trier of fact. However, when it is impractical for the witness to verbalize all the data supporting an inference—when the "poor, poor power of speech" fails—the preference yields; and the witness's inferential testimony is admissible. The principal impact of the rule is on the form of examination. The questions, while they cannot suggest the particular details desired, should call for the most specific account that the witness can give. For example, the witness should not be asked, "Did they reach an agreement?" but rather "What did they say?" The opinion rule ought to be conceived as a matter of the form of the examination rather than the substance of the testimony—again, a difference of degree. So conceived, like the form regulations of leading questions and questions calling for a free narrative, the opinion rule falls in the realm of discretion. The habit of Anglo-American lawyers to examine about specific details to develop a vivid, interesting story is a valuable tradition. Many veteran litigators have an instinctive sense that jurors find more concrete testimony more persuasive. The challenge is to preserve this habit while curbing time-wasting quibbles over trivial "opinion" objections. Unfortunately, those objections can still be voiced in jurisdictions wedded to a literal application of the older formulas.

A simple, clean solution would be to remove the matter of lay opinion from the category of matters governed by "rules." Supporters of that solution find sufficient substitutes in lawyers' natural desire to present a detailed, convincing case and the cross-examiner's ability to expose the non-existence or inconsistency of details not developed on direct. Federal Rule of Evidence 701 does not go quite that far, but it embraces a viable alternative short of altogether jettisoning the opinion doctrine. Under Rule 701 and Rule 602, the witness must have personal knowledge of the matter forming the basis of testimony of opinion; the testimony must be based rationally on the witness's perception; and the opinion must be helpful to the jury (the principal test). Given these liberal statutory standards, many courts have become more receptive to lay opinions about the state of mind of third parties. Modernly, the courts tend to accept such opinions so long as the witness makes it clear to the jury that she is expressing an inference about the third party's apparent state of mind based on factors such as the third party's demeanor and behavior. Contrary to some early decisions, if the proponent adequately establishes the witness's personal knowledge, the witness need not recite all the observed matters that are the bases of opinion, although the judge has discretion to require preliminary testimony about those matters. Of course, as parts of the same legislative scheme, Rules 701 and 403 must be harmonized. Thus, even if a lay inference passes muster under Rule 701, Rule 403 permits exclusion of an inference that is prejudicial, confusing, misleading, or time-wasting.

The Distinction Between Lay and Expert Opinions

The preceding paragraphs discuss the various requirements for admitting an inference as proper lay opinion. However, a proffered lay opinion can not only be excluded due to failure to satisfy those requirements; the opinion could also be barred on the ground that the topic of the testimony necessitates expert testimony. Effective December 1, 2000, Federal Rule of Evidence 701 was amended to provide that an admissible lay opinion may "not [be] based on scientific, technical, or other specialized knowledge within the scope of Rule 702." As the accompanying Advisory Committee's Note explains, there were two reasons for the amendment. One was "to eliminate the risk that the reliability requirements of Rule 702 will be evaded through the simple expedient of proffering an expert in lay witness clothing." The other reason was to prevent litigants from evading the mandatory discovery requirements for expert testimony, set out in Federal Rule of Civil Procedure 26 and Criminal Rule 16.

Of course, the difficulty in administering the 2000 amendment is drawing the line between lay and expert testimony. Since 2000, the courts have frequently been called on to draw that line when prosecutors have offered "lay" opinions by experienced police officers. Testimony by physicians in civil cases can pose the same line-drawing problems. The line is critical because in many cases, lay and expert witnesses can testify on the same topic.

In general terms, the judge can draw the line by focusing on the fundamental question of why the opinion is being admitted: Is it being accepted because it is impractical to verbalize the primary data such as the witness's personal experience (the rationale for lay opinion) or because the witness has a methodology (a technique or theory) for drawing a more reliable inference from the primary data (the rationale for expert opinion)? The Note accompanying the 2000 amendment suggests that the trial judge follow that approach. The Note states that the amendment is not intended to affect the "prototypical example[s]" of proper lay opinions such as inferences on the topics of "the appearance of persons or things, identity, the manner of conduct, competency of a person, degree of light or darkness, sound, size, weight, distance, or an endless number of things that cannot be described factually in words apart from inferences"—all examples of either "collective fact" or "skilled lay observer" opinion. In these cases, the lay witness simply cannot verbalize all the underlying data to put the trier of fact in as good a position to decide whether to draw the inference.

More specifically, though, the Note expressly endorses the reasoning in a 1992 Tennessee decision, *State v. Brown*.[7] The *Brown* court explained that lay opinion "results from a process of reasoning familiar in everyday life" while expert opinion "results from a process of reasoning which can be mastered only by specialists in the field." *Brown* ruled that although a layperson could testify that a substance appeared to be blood, only an expert could opine that bruising around the eyes was indicative of skull trauma. The issue is not what topic the witness's opinion relates to; rather, the question is how the witness reaches the opinion on that topic.

At first blush, the difference in reasoning processes between lay and expert opinion may seem indistinct. However, the key insight is that any witness—lay or expert—who forms and opinion about the significance of the facts in the case is making a comparative judgment:

- One term of the comparison is a generalization such as one about the normal appearance of a particular person's handwriting style or the symptomatology of a disease. Lay and expert witnesses differ in how they derive their generalization. For lay opinion, the witness must develop the generalization exclusively or primarily through firsthand experience such as personal observation of other examples of the author's handwriting. In contrast, for expert opinion, the witness can rely on earlier lectures, treatises, and empirical studies. To paraphrase Sir Isaac Newton, modern experts stand on the shoulders of the giants who preceded them. A contemporary physicist need not duplicate the research conducted by Fermi or Feynman before utilizing a generalization derived from or reported in their research.

- The second term of the comparison is a case-specific fact such as questioned document or a set of case-specific facts such as a patient's case history. Lay and expert witnesses also differ in how they acquire their information about the case-specific fact. In the case of lay opinion about the speed of an automobile, the witness must have personally observed the auto in question. In contrast, as § 14 explains, in the case of expert opinion, the expert can gain the information from a variety of sources: personal knowledge, the contents of a hypothetical question, admissible hearsay, and even inadmissible secondhand, out-of-court reports if it is the

---

[7] 836 S.W.2d 530, 549 (Tenn. 1992).

customary, reasonable practice of experts in the witness's field to consider reports from such sources.

In short, in order to justify the admission of a layperson's opinion, the proponent must demonstrate that: (1) the witness is relying on a generalization developed through personal experience, and (2) the witness has personal knowledge of the case-specific fact. If either element is missing, the conclusion may not be admitted as a lay opinion. When either element is missing, if the opinion is to be admitted at all, it must satisfy the requirements for expert testimony. The remaining sections of this chapter discuss those requirements.

The Applicability of the Limitations to Out-of-Court Statements

However, before turning to the requirements for expert testimony, there is one remaining issue with respect to lay opinions. To date, we have discussed the limitations on the admissibility of lay opinions by testifying witnesses. Again, before admitting a lay witness's inference, the judge must not only be convinced that the witness possesses firsthand knowledge about the topic of the opinion; the judge must also conclude that it is impractical for the witness to verbalize the underlying facts to the extent that the lay jurors themselves would just as readily decide whether to draw the inference. However, do these limitations apply to out-of-court statements offered in court under some exemption from or exception to the hearsay rule? More specifically, suppose that the judge believes that laypersons can reach reliable conclusions on the topic in question but that if the layperson appeared as a witness, the judge would have to exclude the opinion on the ground that the witness could ordinarily articulate the underlying facts and enable the jurors to decide whether to draw the inference. As we have seen, the early view was that the opinion doctrine is a categorical canon of exclusion. Positing that view, the courts naturally assumed that if this kind of evidence is inadmissible when elicited from a witness on the stand, it should be rejected when offered in hearsay form. Consequently, many older decisions analyze the admissibility of lay opinions contained in hearsay declarations as if they were proffered by a witness on the stand, apply the normal limitations, and reject or admit them accordingly.

However, the emerging view is that the opinion doctrine should not be viewed as an absolute rule of exclusion. Rather, as we have seen, the doctrine is best conceived as a relative norm for the examination of witnesses, preferring when it is feasible the more concrete testimony to the more general and inferential. Given that conception, the opinion rule has little or no sensible application to out-of-court statements, especially when the declarant is unavailable as a witness. At trial, an objection to counsel's question as calling for an "opinion" is usually not a serious matter; in most cases, counsel can easily rephrase the question on the spot to elicit the more concrete statement. But to automatically reject the same statement by an out-of-court declarant in a dying declaration mistakes the function of the opinion rule and may altogether foreclose a valuable source of proof. When the source is an unavailable declarant, the stark choice facing the court may be between admitting the opinionated hearsay statement or denying the jury any information from that source. The legislatures and courts should choose the first option. Many cases and Wigmore take this enlightened view as to an opposing party's statements (formerly called admissions of a party-opponent).[8]

---

[8]   See the treatment of the various exemptions from and exceptions to the hearsay rule in infra Chs. 25–33.

Fortunately, that view is spreading to the other classes of out-of-court statements admitted under exceptions to the hearsay rule.[9]

Distinguish the superficially similar question of the declarant's lack of personal knowledge. If the out-of-court declarant had not observed firsthand the fact declared, that deficiency goes not to form but to substance; and it is often fatal to admissibility when the statement is offered as substantive evidence to prove the fact.[10] As previously stated, the personal knowledge requirement generally applies to hearsay declarants as well as trial witnesses.

§ 12 Expert Witnesses: Overview—Necessity; Proper Subjects for Expert Testimony; Reliability; Qualifications

While Sections 10 to 11 deal with lay testimony, including lay opinion evidence, this section shifts to expert testimony. In a Rand study of California Superior Court trials, experts appeared in 86% of the trials; and on average, there were 3.3 experts per trial.[11] A more recent study found that the average had risen to 4.31 experts per trial.[12] Some commentators claim that the American judicial hearing is becoming trial by expert. That claim is hyperbole, but there is a large measure of truth in the claim.

Commentators often refer to the widespread "use" of expert witnesses—in the singular. The implicit assumption is that there is only one way to use a witness who happens to be an expert. In truth, there are four different ways to employ such a witness:

- First, the witness could testify to observed facts under Rule 602. For instance, suppose that a toxicologist, driving to work, witnesses a car run through a red light and strike another car. Any layperson could testify to that fact, and the witness's expert credentials do not disqualify her from doing so.

- Second, the witness could testify to a lay opinion under Rule 701. After witnessing the accident, the toxicologist walks up to the car that ran the red light. When the driver exits his car, the toxicologist notices that his speech is slurred, his eyes are red, and there is a strong odor of alcohol on his breath. In Section 11, we saw that laypersons may express opinions on the subject of intoxication. The toxicologist can do so as well.

- Third, the witness could give the jury a lecture or exposition about an expert methodology (a technique or theory) without attempting to apply the technique or theory to the facts. Federal Rule of Evidence 702 states that a qualified expert may testify in the form of "an opinion or otherwise." The Advisory Committee's Note explains that the drafters included "or otherwise" in the text of Rule 702 to signal that "an expert on the stand may give a dissertation or exposition of scientific or other principles relevant to the case, leaving the trier of fact" or another expert "to apply them to the facts" of the case. Suppose that the toxicologist was called as a witness in a lawsuit arising from the accident. The prosecutor or plaintiff

---

[9]   As to dying declarations, see infra § 313. As to the entry of items in business records, see infra § 290.

[10]   See infra §§ 280 & 313. But the state of the law is to the contrary with respect to an opposing party's statements (formerly termed admissions), see infra § 255.

[11]   Gross, Expert Evidence, 1991 Wis. L. Rev. 1113, 1118–19.

[12]   Allen, Kuhns & Swift, Evidence: Text, Problems and Cases 649 (5th ed. 2011).

has already called the police officer who administered an intoxilyzer test to the driver to measure his breath alcohol concentration. The plaintiff or prosecutor could ask the toxicologist to testify about the reliability of intoxilyzers. Soft science testimony often fits this format. For example, as Section 13 will explain, although courts often permit psychologists to give general background testimony about the factors that increase the risk of mistaken eyewitness identification, most courts forbid the psychologist from opining that a particular eyewitness is mistaken.

- Fourth, the witness could not only describe an expert methodology (a technique or theory) but also derive an opinion by applying the methodology to a case-specific fact or facts. In the overwhelming majority of cases, this is the underlying model of expert trial testimony. Essentially, after qualifying as an expert, the witness: (1) describes a technique or theory; (2) specifies the case-specific fact or facts the witness contemplates evaluating; (3) applies the technique or theory to those facts; and (4) thereby draws a conclusion about the significance of those facts or facts in the case.

As Section 10 explained, the common law model assumes that a witness can verbalize all the necessary sensory data for the jury and that the lay jurors are competent to decide what inferences to draw from that data. We permit lay opinion when the first assumption breaks down: A lay observer has relevant firsthand knowledge, but it is impractical for her to articulate all the relevant data for the trier of fact. We permit expert opinion when the second assumption breaks down. In other words, the expert has something different to contribute. That something is the ability—the knowledge or skill—to draw inferences from the facts which a jury could not draw at all or as reliably.

The Necessity Factor: Proper Subjects for Expert Inference

The common law preferential rules such as hearsay, best evidence, and opinion typically yield when two factors concur: some element of necessity for resorting to the non-preferred type of evidence and a showing of the reliability of the proffered evidence. In the context of the opinion rule, the threshold necessity question relates to the subject matter of the expert's opinion. On some subjects such as the standard of care in medical malpractice cases, expert testimony is required. However, in the published opinions, more commonly the question is whether expert testimony is permissible on a certain subject. In the distant past, the courts commonly announced the rule that the subject of the inference must be so distinctively related to a science, profession, business, or occupation as to be completely "beyond the ken" of lay persons. Although that expression still appears in an occasional modern case, today that expression is nowhere near as commonplace as it formerly was. Moreover, even some of the early cases held that the judge has discretion in administering this rule.

Section 11 noted that although the early cases admitted lay opinion testimony only in the case of strict necessity, under Rule 701 the modern standard is relative helpfulness. The evolution of the law of expert testimony followed a similar, parallel path. In the middle of the 20th century, cases began moving toward a more liberal standard, admitting expert opinion concerning matters about which the jurors may have general knowledge if the expert opinion would refine their understanding of the issue. The latter standard is codified in Federal Rule of Evidence and Revised Uniform Rule of Evidence 702. Rule 702 seems to permit expert opinion even when the matter is barely within the jurors' competence if specialized knowledge will be "help[ful]." Under this liberal reading of Rule 702, although the courts permit lay opinions on the speed of a passing car, they also accept speed estimates based on the application of physics principles by accident reconstruction experts. Similarly, a psychologist may testify about the supposed unreliability of eyewitness testimony; and human factors engineers may opine about the behavior of an average person in some settings. In the words of a respected state judge,

> [Rule 702's] helpfulness gate does not mean that an expert can only testify about something that the jury knows nothing about. While the expert might possess some additional [insight] beyond that possessed by the average person, the gap need not necessarily be monumental. An expert may aid the jury in understanding even familiar matters if the expert's experience or training provide a more thorough understanding than ordinary experience provides. Evidence is helpful when it provides a further depth or precision of understanding about subjects that lie well within common experience.[13]

The Reliability Factor: The Witness's Qualification as an Expert

In addition to establishing the helpfulness or necessity for resorting to expert opinion, the proponent must show its reliability. The initial step in doing so is proving the witness's status as an expert. Even if the inference relates to a proper subject, the witness must be competent to draw the inference. Hence, it is a traditional requirement is that on objection the witness's proponent show that the witness has sufficient skill or knowledge related to the pertinent field or calling that her inference will probably aid the trier in the search for truth. The knowledge may be derived from reading alone in some fields (education), from practice alone in other fields (experience), or as is more commonly the case from a combination of both. Of course, a statute may prescribe to the contrary and mandate both educational and experiential requirements as a condition to testifying as an expert on certain subjects. However, such provisions are rare outside the medical malpractice context. Although a certain subject of inquiry may require calling a member of a particular profession such as a doctor, engineer, or chemist, a specialist in a particular branch of a discipline or profession is usually not required. The question is not whether this witness is more qualified than other experts in the field; that is not the standard of comparison. Rather, the issue is whether the witness is more competent to draw the inference than the lay jurors and judge.

However, there is a trend to toughen standards, especially in jurisdictions that have adopted the *Daubert*[14] standard for the admissibility of scientific testimony. In *Daubert* and its progeny, the Supreme Court emphasized that the witness must be competent to perform the specific "task at hand." As a practical matter, that emphasis pressures the proponent to call a specialist to the stand. Many courts now take a closer look at the connection between the expert's credentials and the specific subject of the question posed to the expert. Yet, even after *Daubert,* for the most part the substantive qualification standards have not crystallized into hard-and-fast rules. Instead, the appellate courts have entrusted the question to the trial judge's discretion reviewable only for abuse. Reversals for abuse are rare.

---

[13]   Brown & Davis, *Eight Gates for Expert Witnesses: Fifteen Years Later,* 52 Houst. L. Rev. 1, 35 (2014).

[14]   Daubert v. Merrell Dow Pharms., Inc., 509 U.S. 579 (1993).

§ 13 Reliability: The Validity of the Expert's Methodology

After establishing her status as an expert, the witness ordinarily describes and testifies about the reliability of the methodology she used to assess the significance of certain case-specific facts. The methodology can be technical or theoretical. For example, the methodology might be the technique for using gas chromatography/mass spectrometry (GC/MS) to identify unknown drugs. Or the methodology could be the diagnostic criteria set out in the American Psychiatric Association's *Diagnostic and Statistical Manual* for determining whether a patient suffers from a particular mental disorder. The witness's testimony about her methodology raises several issues: What test should the judge use to determine whether the expert may rely on this methodology as the basis for an opinion? What is the scope of the test? And how can the expert's proponent satisfy the test?

The Tests for Determining Which Methodologies the Expert May Rely on

As Section 203 notes, prior to 1993 under the *Frye*[15] test most jurisdictions held that purportedly scientific testimony has to be based on a generally accepted methodology.

However, in its 1993 *Daubert* decision, the Supreme Court enunciated a new test.[16] The Court announced that when the proponent proffers the witness as a scientific expert, the proponent must establish that the witness's methodology (the underlying theory or technique) qualifies as reliable "scientific . . . knowledge" within the meaning of that expression in Federal Rule 702. The Court stated that to constitute "knowledge," the expert's methodology must rest on "more than subjective belief or unsupported speculation." The Court explained that to be reliable in a "scientific" sense, the expert's methodology must be empirically validated. The Court stated that in evaluating the validation of the expert's methodology, trial judges should consider the following factors, *inter alia*: whether the validity of the methodology is testable and has been tested; whether the methodology has been subjected to peer review and publication; whether the methodology has a known error rate; whether there are accepted standards for using the methodology; and whether the methodology is generally accepted. As we shall see in Section 203, the clear majority of states now apply some version of the *Daubert* validation standard. Indeed, in recent years some of the states which had been the staunchest advocates of the *Frye* standard have incorporated the validation/reliability standard into their jurisprudence.

The Scope of the Daubert Test

When the general acceptance test was dominant, at least if the witness's expertise was nonscientific character, most courts did not subject the expert's reasoning to scrutiny other than requiring that the opinion relate to a proper subject (the necessity factor) and that the witness qualify as an expert—the two traditional requirements discussed in Section 12.

The courts adopted an essentially laissez-faire attitude toward the methodologies that non-scientific expert testimony rested on. Any doubts about the reliability of the expert's methodology went "largely unregarded." As Section 203 explains, in the mind of the courts in most *Frye* jurisdictions, the primary rationale for that test was the risk that uninitiated lay jurors would ascribe undue weight to purportedly scientific testimony.

---

[15]   293 F. 1013 (D.C. Cir. 1923).

[16]   *Daubert*, 509 U.S. at 590.

However, they believed that non-scientific expert testimony—for example, the testimony of musicians and dog handlers—did not present that risk to the same acute degree. In the same vein, some *Frye* courts even refused to extend the general acceptance requirement to "soft" science such as psychology for the stated reason that a psychologist's testimony was much less likely to overawe the jury than the testimony of a nuclear physicist.

However, post *Daubert* most courts examine non-scientific expert methodology more carefully. In footnote 8 in *Daubert,* the Court noted that that case involved only scientific testimony. After the rendition of the *Daubert* decision, the question then arose as to whether *Daubert*'s reliability test for "scientific . . . knowledge" applies to other types of expert testimony. On its face, Rule 702 refers in the alternative to "scientific, technical, or other specialized knowledge." Thus, the wording of the statute suggests that there can be nonscientific "technical" and nonscientific, nontechnical "specialized" experts in addition to scientific experts. Do *Daubert*'s reliability test and list of factors apply to nonscientific experts?

In an automobile collision case, the plaintiff might call an automotive mechanic to testify about the proper technique or manner for maintaining the anti-lock braking system on a truck. Concededly, the mechanic will not testify about the physics principles underlying the design of automobiles in general or braking systems in particular. However, based on her experience, conversations with other mechanics, and the study of various automotive manuals, the mechanic can testify about the maintenance techniques—how the brakes should be maintained. The mechanic is testifying on the basis of experience accumulated in her field. Rather than pointing to published empirical studies of the effectiveness of the various maintenance techniques, the mechanic is relying on maintenance manuals, the aggregate experience in the field, and a feedback loop from customers (who will voice their complaints if their brakes are not successfully repaired). The mechanic is arguably testifying about "technical . . . knowledge."

Likewise, a prosecutor might call an experienced police officer to testify about the typical modus operandi for a crime such as drug trafficking. The officer's testimony can amount to "specialized knowledge" gleaned from sharing experiences with other drug investigators and the study of D.E.A. manuals. However, the officer will not be opining on the basis of systematic, controlled scientific research. Should the court subject the reliability of the underlying assumptions of the auto mechanic and officer to scrutiny under *Daubert*? Are those types of expertise exempt from the new empirical validation test, as they had been under the general acceptance test in many, if not most, *Frye* jurisdictions?

Prior to 1999, the courts divided into three camps. For their part, some courts ruled that "technical" and "specialized" expertise were exempt from the *Daubert* test. Again, in footnote, the *Daubert* Court disclaimed any intention to pass on the question of admissibility standards for nonscientific expert testimony. At the polar extreme, other courts took the position that the entirety of the *Daubert* opinion extends to other types of expert testimony. Some not only applied the general *Daubert* reliability test but also attempted to evaluate the validity of nonscientific expert methodologies in terms of the specific factors enumerated in *Daubert*. The second camp, insisting that nonscientific testimony satisfy the *Daubert* factors, was obviously wrong-minded. As we shall see, these cases strained to fit round non-scientific pegs into square scientific holes.

A third position is the most sensible: While the proponent of nonscientific testimony must demonstrate the reliability of the expert's underlying assumptions, the trial judge need not necessarily use the *Daubert* factors to gauge reliability. Those factors are derived from a classic scientific model. Rather, the judge ought to engage in a more flexible analysis; the judge should pose such questions as whether in the real world members of the public routinely turn to this profession for services other than testimony and whether there is a feedback loop, alerting a member of the profession when she has erred. An auto mechanic may lack the formal education to qualify as a scientific expert, but her customers are likely to provide her with feedback as to whether her repair work on their car was successful. As we shall soon see, in its 1999 *Kumho* decision, the Supreme Court declared that the basic reliability test prescribed by *Daubert* extends to all types of expert testimony. Even before *Kumho,* the Judicial Conference had proposed an amendment to Rule 702 which extended a foundational reliability requirement to methodologies used by all types of experts, nonscientific as well as scientific. The amendment was eventually adopted in 2000.

However, even before the amendment took effect, the issue reached the Supreme Court in 1999 in *Kumho Tire Co. v. Carmichael.*[17] In the majority opinion authored by Justice Breyer, the Court cited the proposed amendment to Rule 702 and essentially endorsed the third position. On the one hand, the Court stated that the basic *Daubert* test—"a *Daubert*-style [reliability] scrutiny"—is appropriate for all types of expert testimony. As a matter of statutory construction, the Court concluded that all kinds of expert testimony must amount to reliable "knowledge" to qualify for admission under Rule 702. In effect, the Court mandated that trial judges test the validation and epistemological basis of any proffered expert testimony. The expert is making a knowledge claim, and the judge must inquire whether there is a sufficient warrant for the expert's claim. The Court added that "the evidentiary rationale" underlying *Daubert* is a concern about reliability, and in the Court's judgment that rationale is equally applicable to non-scientific expertise. Furthermore, the Court asserted that "it would prove difficult, if not impossible, for judges to administer evidentiary rules under which a gatekeeping obligation depended upon a distinction between 'scientific' knowledge and 'technical' or 'other specialized' knowledge."

On the other hand, the *Kumho* majority made it clear that, as with even strictly scientific testimony, non-scientific testimony need not satisfy each of the *Daubert* factors in order to qualify for admission. The trial judge should consider the *Daubert* factors, but in a given case some or most of those factors might be inapposite. The Court commented that "we can neither rule out, nor rule in, for all cases . . . the applicability of the factors mentioned in *Daubert.* . . ." In 1997 in *General Electric Co. v. Joiner,*[18] the Court had ruled that abuse of discretion is the appropriate standard for appellate review of trial judge rulings under *Daubert. Joiner* ruled that the trial judge enjoys discretion in applying the factors listed in *Daubert* to purportedly scientific testimony. In *Kumho,* the Court analogized to *Joiner.* The *Kumho* Court declared that "[t]he trial court must have the same kind of latitude in deciding how to test a [non-scientific] expert's reliability. . . ." The Court stressed that "whether *Daubert's* specific factors are, or are not, reasonable measures of reliability in a particular case is a matter that the law grants the trial judge broad latitude to determine." For that matter, the judge may enjoy even greater latitude

---

[17]   Kumho Tire Co., Ltd. v. Carmichael, 526 U.S. 137 (1999).
[18]   General Elec. Co. v. Joiner, 522 U.S. 136 (1997).

in a bench trial. In any event, *Kumho* goes beyond *Joiner*; in the case of non-scientific expertise, at a more fundamental level the judge has discretion to choose the factors to apply. In 2000, the proposed amendment to Rule 702 took effect, largely codifying *Kumho*'s prescriptions. However, *Kumho* and the amendment are such relatively recent developments and the conceivable varieties of expertise are so numerous that, understandably, the admissibility standards are in flux.

Determining Whether the Daubert Test Has Been Satisfied

Nevertheless, a basic approach is emerging. Under the approach, the judge should address three basic questions.

—First, What Is the Particular Methodology (the Technique or Theory) That the Expert Will Rely on?

It is certainly unacceptable for the expert to rely on a methodology that is literally ineffable. An ineffable notion borders on mysticism. It is not enough for the witness to assert in conclusory fashion that she is relying on her general "expertise," "knowledge," "skill," "education," or "training." Those credentials can qualify the witness as an expert, but they do not speak to the separate issue of the validity of the expert's methodology. To provide a useful expert insight, the witness must identify a particular methodology (a technique or theory); the witness must articulate that technique or theory. Otherwise, the witness is only intuiting and venturing nothing more than a guess. In both *Joiner* and *Kumho,* the Court explicitly stated that the expert must present more than *ipse dixit* reasoning. When the witness asks the court to admit her opinion merely because the witness possesses relevant education or experience, the opinion is *ipse dixit.*

In gauging the admissibility of the proffered opinion, the trial judge must focus on the particular methodology the expert relies on rather than the "global" reliability of the expert's discipline. Admittedly, *Kumho* contains language carrying a contrary suggestion. In his lead opinion, citing the examples of astrology and necromancy, Justice Breyer commented that sometimes "the discipline itself lacks reliability."[19] However, most of the language in the *Daubert-Joiner-Kumho* trilogy indicates that the judge's focus should be narrow. In the summary at the end of his opinion in *Daubert,* Justice Blackmun stated that the proponent's foundation must convince the trial judge that the expert's theory or technique is sufficiently reliable "to perform the task at hand."

Joiner lends itself to the same interpretation. There Chief Justice Rehnquist analyzed the question of whether the animal studies cited by the plaintiff were an adequate basis for the expert's opinion as to the cause of Joiner's small-cell cancer. The Chief Justice initially listed the criticisms of the animal studies. He then wrote:

> Respondent (plaintiff) failed to reply to this criticism. Rather than explaining how and why the experts could have extrapolated their opinions from these seemingly far-removed animal studies, respondent chose "to proceed as if the only issue [was] whether animal studies could ever be a proper foundation for an expert opinion." Of course, whether animal studies could ever be a proper foundation for an expert's opinion was not the issue. The issue was whether *these* experts' opinions were sufficiently supported by the animal studies on which they purported to rely.[20]

---

[19]   *Kumho Tire Co., Ltd.,* 526 U.S. at 151.
[20]   *Joiner,* 522 U.S. at 144.

Kumho fits the same mold as *Daubert* and *Joiner*. In reviewing the foundation laid by the plaintiffs for the expert Carlson's opinion, Justice Breyer engaged in a highly particularized analysis:

> [T]he specific issue before the [trial] court was not the reasonableness in general of a tire expert's use of a visual and tactile inspection to determine whether overdeflection had caused the tire's tread to separate from its steel-belted carcass. Rather, it was the reasonableness of using such an approach, along with [the expert's] particular method of analyzing the data thereby obtained, to draw a conclusion regarding the particular matter to which the expert testimony was directly relevant.[21]

The Justice acknowledged that "as a general matter, tire abuse can be identified . . . through visual or tactile inspection of the tire." However, Carlson claimed to have developed a more "particular" methodology, namely, the theory that there are four characteristic signs of tire abuse and that the absence of at least two of the signs indicates that the accident was caused by a manufacturing defect in the tire; and Carlson had not tested the theory. Later in the opinion, the Justice stressed that Carlson had not rested his opinion "simply [on] the general theory that, in the absence of evidence of abuse, a defect will normally have caused a tire's separation. Rather, the expert employed a more specific theory to establish the existence (or absence) of such abuse." "[T]he question before the trial court was specific, not general."

United States v. Fujii[22] is a perfect example of the narrow analytic focus demanded by the *Daubert* trilogy. There the issue was whether a questioned document examiner could identify the author of Japanese handprinting. The rub was that students of Japanese handprinting are taught to suppress individuality in printing style and instead strictly follow a prescribed style. The court stated that it was not passing on the general trustworthiness of the discipline of forensic document examination. Rather, the issue before the court was whether the record established the examiner's ability to perform the specific task at hand. The court found the record lacking and excluded the testimony. The *Fujii* approach is the soundest. At any given time in a scientific discipline, the theories and techniques circulating in the discipline will vary in the extent of their empirical validation. Some may rest on extensive validation, others might have barely enough supporting data to pass muster under *Daubert,* and still others will fall far short. Rather than generalizing about the validity of the whole discipline, it makes much more sense to focus on the particular methodology upon which the expert is relying.

—Second, Which Type of Inference Is the Expert Attempting to Draw?

How does the expert propose using the methodology? In other words, what type of inference is the expert using the methodology to draw? At the first step, the mistake to be avoided is framing the inquiry too broadly and treating the global validity of the discipline as dispositive. Here the mistake to be avoided is the converse—framing the inquiry too narrowly. The focus must be on the type or kind of inference the expert contemplates drawing, not the particular inference that the expert will testify to. Deciding whether the particular inference is correct is the province of the trier of fact, not that of the judge passing on the admissibility of the opinion. In the words of the 2000 Advisory Committee Note to Rule 702, "[P]roponents 'do not have to demonstrate to the

---

[21]   *Kumho Tire Co., Ltd.,* 526 U.S. at 153–54.

[22]   152 F.Supp.2d 939 (N.D. Ill. 2000).

judge by a preponderance of the evidence that the assessments of their experts are correct . . . The evidentiary requirement of reliability is lower than the merits standard of correctness.' "

There are several possible categories of inferences, including a normative use. However, most of the published opinions involve one of three categories of use: a descriptive inference, a credibility inference, or an inference related to the historical merits.

One category is a descriptive or summational inference. The expert essentially describes or summarizes experience in her field. The expert's only conclusion is an immediate inference from the experience that a practice, custom, or condition exists. Suppose, for instance, that in a contract lawsuit, there is a dispute as to the meaning of a term in the written agreement. To support his interpretation of the term, the plaintiff calls an experienced member of the industry as an expert. According to the witness, in the industry there is a trade custom or usage, that is, a linguistic convention as to the meaning of that term. The expert's specific theory is that the usage exists within the industry. The witness is prepared to testify that she has been a member of the industry for a considerable period of time and that her inference rests on her personal experience as well as conversations with other industry members.[23] She will testify that she and her colleagues have encountered that usage of the term by industry members on numerous occasions and have never or rarely encountered a different usage. Her testimony, summarizing her experience and that of her colleagues, points to the existence of the usage.

The same rationale explains the approving mention of police testimony about drug argot in both Justice Breyer's *Kumho* opinion and the Advisory Committee's Note to the 2000 amendment to Federal Rule 702. Drug trafficking is a business. Just as a term can acquire a specialized meaning for members of a lawful commercial trade, a term can take on a peculiar significance for criminal drug traffickers. Hence, just as a veteran member of the meat scrap industry could explain the meaning of "50% protein" in a lawful contract between two industry members, an experienced undercover narcotics officer may testify as to the meaning of "lid" in an unlawful agreement for the purchase of a contraband drug. As the 2000 Advisory Committee Note states, in this situation "experience alone . . . may . . . provide a sufficient foundation for expert testimony."[24]

However, in other cases—the second and third categories—the proponent of the expert testimony wants the expert to do more than merely summarize experience and infer fact *A,* the existence of a practice, custom, or condition. It is not enough to establish the existence of fact *A.* Instead, the proponent contemplates inviting the expert to draw another inference from the experience. The expert evaluates the experience and draws a further inference as to fact *B.*

In the second category, the further inference relates to the credibility of a witness. Suppose that on cross-examination in a rape case, the defense attempts to impeach the complainant by showing that she delayed reporting the alleged assault to the police. To rehabilitate the complainant's credibility, the prosecution might call a psychologist

---

[23]   If the expert relied solely or primarily on personal experience, her testimony could be admitted as lay opinion under Rule 701. See supra § 11.

[24]   Again, if the officer were relying exclusively or primarily on personal experience, the proponent might be able to introduce the testimony as lay opinion under Rule 701. See supra § 11. However, if the officer is relying on conversations with other officers and the contents of training manuals, Federal Rule 702 governs.

familiar with the rape trauma syndrome (RTS) theory. The psychologist will testify that in many cases, even victims who honestly believe that they have been raped delay reporting the offense. The psychologist will not only testify that like the alleged victim in the instant case, a high percentage of other alleged victims delay reporting the alleged offense; the psychologist will venture the further opinion that such conduct is consistent with an honest belief that there has been a rape. Or a defense polygrapher might attempt to testify that the accused was being truthful during the test when he denied committing the rape. The polygrapher will not only testify that the accused produced certain markings on the polygraph chart; the polygrapher will offer the additional opinion interpreting the markings as an indication that the accused did not lie during the test. The two experts' opinions differ—one takes the form of a generalization about alleged rape victims while the second relates to a specific accused—but both conclusions relate to credibility.

In the third category, as in the second, again the expert contemplates drawing a further inference. However, in this category, that inference relates to the historical merits of the case: A disputed historical event occurred or that a disputed fact is true. By way of example, a drug dog handler may be prepared to go beyond describing the dog's behavior and add that the dog's behavior constituted an "alert" indicating the presence of contraband drugs in the defendant's luggage. Likewise, a fingerprint examiner might be ready to go beyond describing the latent impressions found at a crime scene and a set of known prints from the defendant and opine that a comparison of the two sets of impressions indicates that the defendant is the source of the latent crime scene prints at the scene.

—Third, Has the Proponent Validated the Claim That the Expert's Use of the Methodology Will Enable the Expert to Accurately Draw That Type of Inference?

Finally, having identified the expert's particular methodology and categorized the expert's claim about the type of inference that the methodology supports, in the words of *Daubert* the judge must determine whether the proponent has established "appropriate validation." The answers to the first two questions specify the hypothesis or claim that must be validated: The expert asserts that by using a particular methodology, that is, a specific theory or technique, she can accurately draw a certain type of inference. The bottom line is the validation of that claim. The sufficiency of the validation is a question of logic, not technical legal rules. The required validation varies with two factors: the type of inference or claim the expert is making and the specificity of the claim.

Factor 1: The type of inference. One factor is the category or type of inference that the expert claims to be able to draw. When the expert is making a summational claim, the trial judge should demand a foundation establishing that on a significant number of occasions, the witness or other members of her specialty have had experiences similar to the incident in question. How many times has an industry member encountered a meat scraps transaction in which the expression, "50% protein," was used? In what proportion of those transactions was the buyer willing to accept a delivery with 49.5% protein? Or how often has the undercover agent or fellow officers been involved in a contraband drug transaction in which the word, "lid," was employed or heard about such a transaction from other agents? In what proportion of those transactions did a participant produce a certain quantity of drugs? It is not enough for the witness to testify that she has been an industry member or an undercover agent for several years. The experience must be sufficiently particularized to prove to the judge that the expert is competent to perform the specific task at hand, namely, to draw an inference about the existence of a linguistic convention as to "50% protein" or "lid."

It is true that summational claims do not usually describe data compiled in controlled laboratory experiments or by systematic field observation. However, the Advisory Committee's Note to the 2000 amendment to Rule 702 explicitly rejected the contention that "experience alone . . . may not provide a sufficient foundation for expert testimony." Quite to the contrary, the Note states that "extensive experience" can furnish adequate validation. Although the *Daubert* Court referred to "validation," that term should be interpreted in the broad Rationalist tradition, not the narrower scientific tradition. There is a longstanding, strong Rationalist tradition in Anglo-American Evidence law.[25] That tradition is founded on the empiricism of the 17th century English philosopher John Locke and his belief that human knowledge derives from experience. That experience need not be amassed by formal scientific studies.

In contrast, if the expert is making an inferential claim, a foundation merely showing the expert's experience—no matter how extensive—is inadequate. If the prosecution rape trauma syndrome expert proposes making a claim in the second category about the credibility of the typical complainant, it is not enough that there have been tens or even hundreds of complaints by alleged victims who delayed reporting. The expert cannot accept the self-reports at face value. Instead, to validate the credibility inference, the expert must submit additional testimony. For instance, the expert might at least present foundational testimony that the complainants received follow-up treatment for post-traumatic stress disorder (PTSD) and that in the vast majority of cases, therapists perceived an improvement in the complainant's condition. Of course, it is possible that some of the complainants were feigning, but a large number of successful clinical interventions provides common sense support for the credibility inference. The proponent could supplement that testimony with evidence that many of the complainants had taken and successfully passed polygraph tests about their reports of rape.[26]

In the third and final category related to the historical merits, the judge should insist on a foundation demonstrating that the expert's technique or technique "works"; that is, the methodology enables the expert to accurately make the determination as to which she proposes to testify. The foundation must include a showing of the results when the technique was used on prior occasions. Do the outcomes demonstrate a connection between facts *A* and *B*? Neither the expert's personal voucher nor general acceptance in the field nor even long-term, repeated use of the theory suffices. Subdivision (b)(9) of Federal Evidence Rule 901 furnishes a helpful parallel. When the question is the authentication of "a process or system," the statute explicitly requires a "showing that the process or system produces an accurate result." In *Kumho*, Justice Breyer asserted that in evaluating the reliability of an expert's methodology, the judge ought to consider "how often an . . . expert's methodology has produced erroneous results . . . ."[27] The 2000 Advisory Committee Note to amended Rule 702 likewise states that a pertinent consideration is the "results" reached when the theory or technique is utilized. That

---

[25]   Twining, Rethinking Evidence: Exploratory Essays (2d ed. 2006).

[26]   It is true that numerous courts have held that polygraph testimony is inadmissible. See infra §§ 206.1–206.3. However, here the proponent is offering the testimony to a judge under Federal Rule 104(a) to establish the admissibility of the psychologists' testimony. By virtue of Rule 104(a), other than privilege, the technical exclusionary rules are inapplicable to foundational testimony.

[27]   Kumho Tire Co., Ltd. v. Carmichael, 526 U.S. 137, 151 (1999).

consideration is a key when, for instance, a forensic chemist uses gas chromatography/ mass spectrometry (GC/MS) to infer the identity of the drug found in the defendant's automobile. Is there empirical research demonstrating that the use of GC/MS enables an analyst to correctly determine the elemental composition of the unknown sample? In the case of GC/MS, the answer to that question is Yes.

Under this standard, if the expert is employing a classic scientific instrumental technique to support an inference, the judge should consider: the size of the data set the expert is relying on (Does it constitute a mere handful of anecdotes?), the composition of the data set (Is it representative of the population of persons or objects involved in the case?), the test conditions (Do they approximate the real world conditions in the instant case?), and the findings (the false positive and false negative percentages indicating the accuracy of the methodology). If the proffered expert is a drug or explosive dog handler, there should be a showing of the dog's training and track record. Were the conditions in the training tests comparable to those in the real world? What were the dog's false positive and false negative rates during the training? In the past when the dog has alerted in the field, what percentage of the alerts led to the seizure of contraband drugs? In the case of fingerprint examiners, on validation tests in what percentage of the cases have the examiners correctly identified the source of the impressions? Again, the bottom line is whether this particular methodology leads to accurate inferences of the type in question. So long as the accuracy rate exceeds 50%, the evidence can be helpful to the trier of fact.[28]

Factor 2: The specificity of the claim. The nature and extent of the required validation vary not only with the type of claim but also with its specificity. The more specific the inference, ordinarily the more extensive the foundation must be. Consider the following, illustrative opinions:

- Opinion A. Suppose that the proposed testimony is the generalization that a certain phenomenon exists. For instance, the expert might be prepared to opine that mistaken eyewitness identifications are more common than most laypersons realize. To validate that relatively general opinion, it would probably suffice if the foundation described empirical data from two types of studies. One type of study involved witnesses to simulated or staged crimes. These studies estimated the incidence of mistaken eyewitness identifications. The second type of study would be a follow-up to the first; in this research, the witnesses testified at mock trials; and mock jurors were asked to decide whether to accept the witnesses' identifications. Assume that both studies were well designed, the first indicated that the incidence of mistaken identifications was 25%, but the second found that the jury concluded that only ten percent of the identifications were erroneous. That foundation would arguably suffice to validate the expert's theory.

- Opinion B. Now the expert proposes taking the next step and testifying to the more specific theory that certain factors can cause or prevent mistaken identifications. By way of example, the expert might be prepared to testify that a racial difference between the alleged perpetrator and the witness

---

[28] Faigman, Kaye, Saks & Sanders, Science in the Law: Standards, Statistics, and Research Issues § 1– 3.4.2, at 35 (2002). Of course, if the accuracy rate of the methodology barely exceeds random chance, the testimony might be vulnerable to an objection under Federal Rule 403.

can cause a mistaken identification. As a matter of logic, the foundation for opinion A is inadequate to validate this hypothesis. Indeed, it is simply irrelevant to the conclusion being offered. The expert would have to testify to a very different type of research project. Assume, though, that: The expert conducted a study involving two groups of subjects; with one exception, the two groups were similar—the same age and visual acuity and identical observation conditions; the exception was that while the first group was asked to identify a perpetrator of the same race, the second group was required to attempt to make a cross-racial identification; and the error rate for the second group was significantly higher than the rate for the first group. Now the foundation might be adequate. Other experiments could demonstrate that conversely, improved lighting conditions reduce the probability that the phenomenon will occur.

- <u>Opinion C</u>. The particular facts of the instant case are a manifestation of the general phenomenon—this particular witness is mistaken. This opinion demands a more sophisticated understanding of the interplay and relationship among the various casual factors. The research supporting opinion B might indicate that the cross-racial factor can cause a mistaken identification but that excellent lighting conditions reduce the risk of error. To give opinion C, though, the expert must have further research exploring the relationship between the factors. What is likely to occur when the identification is cross-racial but the lighting is excellent? The research answering that question is lacking because such experiments are difficult to design and conduct. This is sometimes termed the G2i problem[29]—the challenge of justifying an inference from the general to the individual. In the past, especially when the witness was a doctor or mental health expert, the courts often overlooked the G2i problem and routinely allowed witnesses to employ subjective diagnostic criteria to draw inferences such as opinion C. However, gradually, the courts are coming to appreciate that whether the expert's inference is of type A, B, or C, the expert's knowledge claim requires validation. The courts' treatment of psychological testimony about the supposed unreliability of eyewitness identification is a case in point. The virtually universal view is that the currently available research does not justify a G2i inference and that consequently, the expert may not opine as to whether a particular eyewitness is mistaken.

Although the courts have made progress in clarifying the meaning and reach of *Kumho*, there is still a remaining tension in the area. Suppose that the proponent's showing satisfies the bottom line test, but it would be possible to subject the expert's methodology to formal scientific testing to determine its accuracy. The pivotal question is this: If a controlled scientific experiment could feasibly be devised to validate a non-scientific expert claim and the practitioners of the expertise have neglected to conduct the experimentation, how strongly, if at all, should that neglect cut against admissibility? By way of example, should the courts bar the introduction of fingerprint evidence even as non-scientific expertise if scientists have failed to conduct the rigorous

---

[29]   Faigman, Monahan & Slobogin, Group to Individual (G2i) Inference in Scientific Expert Testimony, 81 U. Chi. L. Rev. 417, 419, 430, 432, 451—52 (2014).

scientific experiments that could verify their underlying premises? In *Kumho*, Justice Breyer commented that the Court wanted to "make certain that an expert . . . employs in the courtroom the same level of intellectual rigor that characterizes the practice of an expert in the relevant field."[30] If a certain type of testing is customary in the real world practice of the expert's discipline, the lack of testing could be fatal to admissibility. More broadly, some respected commentators on expert evidence have argued that expert evidence law ought to be structured to create incentives for litigants to present "the best possible information" or at least "better evidence." A number of courts have found this argument persuasive. It strikes these courts as "exactly backwards"[31] to approve the expert's validation reasoning when the expert has failed to resort to a superior, available validation methodology. Significantly, the 2000 Advisory Committee Note to amended Rule 702 evidences sympathy with the argument. The Note asserts that "[a]n opinion from an expert who is not a scientist should receive the same degree of scrutiny for reliability as an opinion from an expert who purports to be a scientist."

The weakness in the argument is that at least prior to the 2000 amendment to Rule 702, it was difficult to discern such a principle in the text or legislative history of the Federal Rules of Evidence. At trial, the opponent may certainly point to the factor of the expert's (or an entire discipline's) failure to use a superior, scientific methodology to validate a technique or theory as a basis for attacking the weight of the expert's testimony. However, it is a very different question whether that failure should also factor into admissibility analysis. The question is not whether the proponent has presented the best possible validation, but rather enough validation to establish the reliability of the theory or technique. A scientific experiment can conceivably be devised to test virtually any proposition. The North Carolina Court of Appeals has declared that "there is . . . no requirement that a party offering [expert] testimony must produce evidence that the testimony . . . has been proven through scientific study."[32] In addition, several courts have expressly rejected the argument that the expert must base her opinion on the best available methodology. As previously stated, the bottom line should be the question of whether, as a matter of logic, the expert has presented sufficient empirical data and reasoning to validate the hypothesis that by applying the specific theory or technique he or she proposes relying on, the expert can accurately draw the particular inference he or she contemplates testifying to.

It remains to be seen how the courts will ultimately resolve this tension. In Justice Blackmun's original opinion in *Daubert,* he referred to the "liberal thrust" of the Federal Rules and their "permissive" approach. It is undeniable, though, that the federal courts are generally taking a harder line on expert testimony, including non-scientific evidence. In 2000, reflecting on the *Daubert* line of precedent, the Supreme Court itself remarked that that line of authority prescribes "exacting" standards of reliability.[33] In the same year, the Federal Judicial Center released a study of federal judges' receptivity to expert testimony.[34] In 1991, the Center had asked federal trial judges whether they had admitted all the expert testimony proffered to them in their last trial. In that year 75% of the respondents answered in the affirmative. In 1998 after the Supreme Court had

---

[30] *Kumho Tire Co, Ltd.*, 526 U.S. at 152.

[31] Watkins v. Telsmith, Inc., 121 F.3d 984, 991 (5th Cir. 1997).

[32] Taylor v. Abernethy, 560 S.E.2d 233 (N.C. Ct. App. 2002).

[33] Weisgram v. Marley Co., 528 U.S. 440 (2000).

[34] Kaye, Bernstein & Mnookin, The New Wigmore: Expert Evidence § 7.4.1, at 331–32 (2d ed. 2010).

handed down *Daubert,* that figure fell to 58%. Again, in 1991 the Center asked trial judges whether they had ever excluded expert testimony. In that year only 25% answered in the affirmative. In 1998 post *Daubert* that number rose to 41%. If the courts construe the 2000 amendment to Rule 702 as manifesting an intention to tighten the standards for the admissibility of non-scientific expertise, the proponents of expert testimony will find it more difficult to introduce such testimony over objection. As we shall see in Chapter 20, that trend is most evident in civil cases involving novel causation theories, but even in criminal cases involving traditional forensic science techniques such as fingerprint examination and microscopic hair analysis, a growing number of courts are more carefully policing the wording of the expert's opinion to ensure that the expert does not overstate her opinion by testifying to inferences that are unsupported by the available empirical data.

§ 14   Reliability: The Case-Specific Facts Analyzed; Personal Knowledge; Hypothetical Questions; Secondhand Reports

Section 12 pointed out that in most cases the proponent wants the expert to derive an opinion by applying a methodology (some technique or theory) to the case-specific facts. Section 13 dealt with the topic of the validity of the methodology. This section answers the question of how the expert obtains information about the case-specific fact or facts to be evaluated. Expert opinion need not be admitted if the judge believes that the truth of a particular fact is an essential premise of the expert's opinion but it is unreasonable to assume the truth of the fact. If the expert proposes opining about the significance of specific facts in the pending case, there must be a proper basis for the assumptions about those facts. There are three basic methods by which an expert can acquire such information: directly perceiving the facts, hypothetically assuming them to be true, or relying on an out-of-court, secondhand report.

Personal Knowledge

It is ideal if the expert on the stand has personal, firsthand knowledge of the case-specific facts. For example, a treating physician who personally examined the patient may testify to the observations that serve as the basis for her opinion. An expert witness who has firsthand knowledge may describe the observations and testify to inferences from them under traditional views as well as the Federal Rules of Evidence. Initially, the common law insisted on personal knowledge. At that time, personally known facts were the only permissible bases for expert opinions.

Hypothetically Assumed Facts

The next step in the evolution of the common law was to allow an expert to rest an opinion on facts shown by evidence already in the record. The expert could learn the facts by sitting in court and listening to the trial testimony (if the expert was not excluded from the courtroom by a sequestration order). Alternatively and more commonly, after other witnesses have testified to the facts, the facts are furnished to the expert by including them in a hypothetical question. A hypothetical question asks the expert to assume that certain facts are true and then requests an opinion based on them:

Q   Doctor, please assume facts *A, B,* and *C.* Assuming those facts, can you form an opinion about my client's diagnosis to a reasonable degree of medical probability?

Q   What is that opinion?

The hypothetical question technique enabled the courts to capitalize on the expertise of witnesses when, due to the expert's location or schedule, it was impractical or impossible for the expert to gain firsthand knowledge of the case-specific facts. At common law the use of hypothetical questions became the orthodox method of taking advantage of the witness's knowledge and skill. In the judge's discretion, the use of hypothetical questions is still permissible under the federal and other liberal rules.

Although American litigators have posed hypothetical questions to experts for decades, the hypothetical question technique has been sharply criticized. In response to the criticisms, this method has been reformed in a growing number of jurisdictions, including those adopting the Federal and Revised Uniform Rules of Evidence. There have been two major changes. First, by virtue of Federal Rule 705, on direct examination an expert may state an opinion and the theoretical "reasons" for the opinion without prior disclosure of the underlying data or facts. This change eliminates the need for a lengthy statement of the underlying case-specific facts on direct examination. Rule 705 gives the cross-examiner the choice whether to expose the underlying data. Second, under Rule 703 the expert need not base her opinion on either firsthand knowledge or an hypothesis; in certain circumstances, otherwise inadmissible out-of-court reports are now considered proper bases for the expert's opinion. This change brings the legal practice more in line with the practice of experts outside the courtroom, since in their own practice they often rely on trustworthy out-of-court reports. At the same time, in these more liberal jurisdictions a trial attorney may still employ the traditional methods of eliciting expert opinion, including the hypothetical question. The use of the hypothetical question is not only permissible at contemporary common law; it is still popular and in widespread use. Since the proponent can specify the content of the hypothesis, the hypothetical question gives the proponent maximum control; and if the proponent keeps the hypothesis short and sweet, the jury will clearly understand the factual basis of the expert's opinion.

When the questioner specifies the assumed facts, the expert is to rely on, it is often said that the questioner is using the "long form" hypothetical. In most jurisdictions committed to the more traditional views, the judge has discretion to allow an expert witness to remain in court during testimony by other witnesses. Later when the expert is called as a witness, the counsel can simplify a hypothetical question by merely instructing the witness to assume the truth of the previous testimony the witness has heard, or some specified part of it—the so-called "short form" of a hypothetical question. This practice is also permissible under the Federal Rules of Evidence and other contemporary state rules. The practice has some advantages but several limitations. The assumed testimony must be clear to the jury and not conflicting; otherwise, the witness's answer may confuse the jurors rather than assist them. A question asking the witness to assume the truth of a single previous witness's testimony usually meets these requirements. However, as the range of assumption widens to cover the testimony of several witnesses or all the testimony for one side, the risk of confusing the jury increases. When a hypothetical question covers all the testimony in the case, the question can be approved only if the testimony relating to the question is consistent and simple enough for the jury to recall its basic outlines.

—The Mechanics of Using the Hypothetical Question

At common law, whether the proponent employs the long or short form, before posing a hypothetical question, the proponent must ordinarily present admissible, independent evidence of every fact included in the hypothesis. The traditional requirement rests on the notion that if the opinion is premised on a fact which the jury, for lack of evidence, cannot find to be true, the jurors may not use the opinion as the basis for a finding. There must be admissible evidence supporting each assumed fact. Direct testimony as to the fact is not required. It suffices if the fact is fairly inferable from the circumstances proved. Moreover, at common law in most jurisdictions there is no invariable requirement that the supporting evidence be admitted before the interrogating counsel poses the hypothetical question to the expert. As an officer of the court, counsel can assure the judge that the evidence will be forthcoming because the trial judge has discretion to vary the order of proof.

Further, it is no objection that the evidence supporting the case-specific facts is controverted. The proponent is entitled to present her side of the case to the witness as the basis for the witness's opinion. However, there is a danger that by omitting some critical facts, the proponent will present an unfair, slanted version of the facts to the expert and that the jury may give undue weight to the opinion without considering its faulty basis. For instance, the proponent might elicit an unreliable estimate of a car's speed from an accident reconstruction expert if the proponent's hypothesis omitted any mention of critical, undisputed evidence about the length of the skidmarks left by the car. Are there any safeguards against this danger? Some decisions require that all facts material to the question be mentioned in the hypothesis. However, such an inflexible requirement is undesirable; it multiplies disputes over the sufficiency of the hypothesis and can cause counsel, out of an excess of caution, to propound lengthy questions that are tedious and confusing to the jury. The sounder, prevailing view is that the hypothesis need not include all material facts. However, even under the prevailing view, there are safeguards. One safeguard is the cross-examiner's rights; on cross-examination the adversary may supply omitted facts and ask the expert if those additional facts would modify his opinion or at least be relevant. A further safeguard is the judge's authority; if she deems the question unfair, the trial judge may require that the questioner reword the hypothesis to supply an adequate basis.

Section 16 of this chapter deals with the ultimate issue prohibition. That section notes that while the original version of Rule 704 purported to abolish the prohibition, to a degree the prohibition was resurrected when Congress amended the statute to add Rule 704(b). The question arises whether a direct examiner can in effect circumvent Rule 704(b) by using a hypothetical question. Suppose, for example, that the direct examiner crafts an hypothesis that closely mirrors the facts in the case. After instructing the witness to assume the truth of the hypothesis, may the direct examiner elicit an ultimate opinion otherwise barred by Rule 704(b)? Admittedly, it is sometimes difficult to determine whether the opinion solicited by the question is one barred by Rule 704(b). However, assuming that the judge decides that the opinion coincides with such a question, the trial judge should not permit the examiner to avoid Rule 704(b) by the simple expedient of resorting to a hypothetical question. In that situation, a mirroring hypothetical is an all too transparent device for evading Rule 704(b).

—The Wisdom of Retaining the Hypothetical Question

The preceding discussion of the strengths and weaknesses of the hypothetical question technique naturally leads to this question: Should the technique be retained? In theory, the hypothetical question is an ingenious device for enabling the jury to benefit from the expert's scientific knowledge even if the expert lacks personal knowledge of the facts. If properly used, the device permits the judicial system to capitalize on the witness's expertise even when the expert has not had the time to acquire firsthand knowledge of the facts. Nevertheless in practice, it suffers from significant flaws and can be abused to obstruct the search for truth. If we require that the hypothesis recite all the relevant facts, it becomes intolerably wordy. If we allow, as most courts do, the interrogating counsel to select whatever facts he sees fit, we tempt him to shape a one-sided hypothesis. Many commentators view this opportunity for partisan slanting of the hypothesis as a major weakness of the practice. The commentators who have studied the problem generally condemn the current common law practice.

What is the optimal solution? It hardly seems practical to require the trial judge to undertake the thorough study of the case necessary to enable her to personally select the facts to include in the hypothesis. It might be feasible for the questions to be framed by both counsel in conference with the judge, either at a pretrial hearing or during the trial in the jury's absence. But that conferral process could be unproductive or at the very least time-consuming. The only remaining expedient is the one generally advocated, namely, on direct examination dispensing with the requirement that the question be accompanied by a recital of a hypothesis, unless the trial judge requires it. This is the procedure authorized by Federal and Uniform Rule of Evidence 705 and analogous statutes and rules.

Under Rule 705, the cross-examiner has an election whether to bring out the factual basis for the expert's opinion. This approach does not lessen the partisanship of the question or the answer on direct examination. However, it simplifies the examination and removes the occasion for reversing the trial judgment by appellate rulings on technical deficiencies in the form of hypothetical questions. Rule 705 does, however, give the judge discretion to require prior disclosure of basic facts on direct. Judges tend to do so when there has not been adequate pretrial opportunity to discover the facts, especially in criminal cases.

Secondhand, Out-of-Court Reports

As we have seen, at common law an expert could base an opinion either on personally known facts or facts stated in an hypothesis. However, today those two bases do not exhaust the possibilities. The expert may also rest an opinion on third party out-of-court statements, sometimes referred to as secondhand reports.[35] The former majority view was that a question is improper if it calls for the witness's opinion on the basis of out-of-court reports that are inadmissible in evidence under the hearsay rule. The rationale for this view was that as a matter of logic, the jury could not accept the opinion based on the facts if the only evidence of the facts is inadmissible. This view applied even when the witness was asked to give an opinion, not merely on the basis of reports of this kind, but on those matters supplemented by the witness's own observation. However, there has been a strong case law trend toward a contrary view. (There is also a related, incipient trend in the cases toward the somewhat more conservative view that opinions based on out-of-court reports are less objectionable when they concern subjects that have an indirect relation to the fact issues in the case, rather than the central facts in issue.)

The case law trend culminated in the broader modern view codified in Federal Rule of Evidence 703, adopted in many states. Under Rules 703 and 705, on direct examination an expert may give an opinion based on facts and data, including

---

[35]   See infra § 324.3.

technically inadmissible reports, if "experts in the particular field would reasonably rely on those kinds of facts or data in forming an opinion on the subject." These secondhand reports are supposedly put to a nonhearsay use. Rather than receiving the reports as substantive evidence, the judge admits the testimony about the reports for the limited purpose of showing the basis of the expert's opinion. Irrespective of the truth of the reports, a consideration of the reports can assist the trier to assess the caliber of the expert's reasoning. The focus is on the effect of the report on the expert's state of mind; the fact that the expert has received the report indicates that her opinion is better grounded. The jury may consider the reports in the process of evaluating the quality of the expert's reasoning: Are the stated bases adequate to support the opinion? Did the expert commit any obvious logical fallacies in reasoning about the bases? According to the Advisory Committee's Note accompanying Rule 703, the primary rationale for permitting the expert to rely on such reports is that in the real world experts follow this practice: "The physician makes life-and-death decisions in reliance upon" such reports. In the Note's words, Rule 703 "bring[s] the judicial practice into line with the practice of the experts themselves when not in court." If this type of data can be an acceptable basis for critical decisions in the operating room, it seems silly to preclude experts from relying on such reports in the courtroom.

—The Substantive Question Under Rule 703

The principal substantive problem presented by Rule 703 is the interpretation of the language, "reasonably rely on." The courts are divided over the proper interpretation of that expression.

- The liberal approach is that the judge must accept the expert community's view in deciding whether the rule is met at least in matters in which the judge is not equipped to "second guess" the expert. The courts subscribing to this approach equate "reasonably" with "customarily."[36] According to this approach, the judge's only task is to make a factual finding under Rule 104(a) as to whether it is the customary practice of the expert's specialty to consider a certain type of report. If there is such a custom, the judge's hands are tied; the judge must allow the expert to rely on that type of report.

- There is a competing, restrictive approach to Rule 703 that even when it is the field's customary practice to consider a type of report, the trial judge has a residual discretion to decide that such reports are insufficiently reliable to serve as the basis for an expert opinion.

- Indeed, there are two versions of the restrictive approach. As previously stated, one is that although the proof of the specialty's custom is relevant, the only finding that the judge must make is that the practice of relying on that type of information is reasonable. The second variation sets an even higher standard: The judge must find that the practice is both customary and reasonable.

None of these approaches is flawless. The difficulty with the liberal approach is that a party can employ an expert witness to place untrustworthy facts, data, or opinions before

---

[36]   In re Japanese Electronic Products Antitrust Litig., 723 F.2d 238, 277 (3d Cir. 1983). The Third Circuit later shifted to the restrictive approach. In re Paoli R.R. Yard PCB Litig., 35 F.3d 717, 748 (3d Cir. 1994).

the jury—a sort of "backdoor" hearsay exception. The criticism of the restrictive approach is that it seems presumptuous for a non-expert judge to tell a qualified expert the types of information that she may rely on to formulate an opinion.

On the whole, the restrictive approach is preferable as a matter of both policy and statutory construction. To be sure, the judge should typically defer to the specialty's customary practice. However, in an extreme case, the judge ought to have a residual power to second guess the customary practice and rule that a particular type of hearsay source is too untrustworthy. When the analogous Tort question arises as to whether an industrial practice is negligent, the courts consider evidence of the industry's customary practice; but the custom is not dispositive. At most the existence of the custom should give rise to a presumption, but the presumption ought to be rebuttable. The restrictive approach is also sounder as a matter of statutory interpretation. When the drafters wanted to make the application of an evidentiary rule turn on the existence of a custom or routine practice, as they did in Rules 406 and 803(17), they found apt words to manifest their intention. In Rule 703, they opted to use the adverb "reasonably" rather than "customarily." "Reasonably" connotes an objective standard to be applied by the trial judge.

The judge and the attorneys may litigate this matter at a hearing under Rule 104. At such a Rule 703 hearing in a criminal case, one of the potential questions is whether, before trial, the defendant should or must have the opportunity to cross-examine the persons who originated the data on which a prosecution expert relies. Even absent a prior opportunity to question the declarant, the judge should ordinarily apply Rule 703 unless a government expert is in effect being used as a conduit to bring before the jury otherwise inadmissible matter (particularly hearsay implicating the Confrontation Clause). The courts have taken a similar approach where the criminal defendant's mental health expert relies on the defendant's statements as support for an opinion about sanity. It was hoped that the Supreme Court's decision in *Williams v. Illinois*[37] would shed some light on this issue; but, as we shall see at the end of this section, the Court decided *Williams* on another basis and, in the process, raised significant questions about the future of Rule 703.

—The Procedure for Administering Rule 703

In addition to the substantive question of the meaning of "reasonably" in Rule 703, the rule presents a procedural issue. Assuming that it is substantively permissible for an expert to rely on a secondhand out-of-court report as part of the basis of her opinion, how far may the expert go in describing the content of the report? The expert should certainly be allowed to indicate the general type of report she is relying on. Thus, the expert could state that in forming her opinion, she considered reports from investigating police officers or findings from a toxicology laboratory. However, when the report is oral, may she quote the report in detail? If the report is in writing, may the proponent formally introduce the report, have the expert quote it, and even submit it to the jurors for their inspection? As § 324.3 points out, the courts have divided over this question. It has been argued that as a matter of logic, the jurors cannot thoroughly evaluate the expert's reasoning unless they have an in-depth understanding of all the bases of the opinion. Further, a case can be made that the wording of Rule 705 indicates that the drafters contemplated that the expert should be permitted to give the jurors a detailed

---

[37]   567 U.S. 50 (2012).

description of the content of the report. That rule states that the expert "may" state the opinion and the reasons for the opinion "without first testifying to the underlying facts or data"—suggesting that the expert's proponent may choose to elicit the testimony about the underlying facts or data during the expert's direct examination.

However, the operative assumption here is that the report is not independently admissible; that is, it is not reliable enough to qualify for admission under any hearsay exemption or exception. With some support in the empirical studies, several commentators caution that allowing the expert to detail the report's content creates a grave risk that the jurors will misuse the content as substantive evidence. A number of jurisdictions have amended their version of Rule 703 to preclude the expert from elaborating on the content of the report, and a 2000 amendment to Federal Rule 703 is to the same effect.

Of course, in a broad sense almost all expert opinion about scientific propositions embodies hearsay indirectly. Whenever an expert testifies, she implicitly draws on such material as lectures she heard and textbooks she read during her education. It would be ridiculous to apply the hearsay rule to that material. However, that problem is distinguishable from the issue analyzed in this section. Newton's and Fermi's writings relate to the expert's methodology discussed in § 13, that is, the research underpinning the expert's technique or theory. In this section, the question is quite different; the focus here is on the content of the expert's other premise, namely, the trustworthiness of the case-specific information about how the traffic accident occurred or the accused's behavior just before he shot the decedent. There is less justification for lifting the bar of the hearsay rule when the expert rests her opinion on out-of-court reports about that kind of information. There is also greater probative danger because the case-specific data are more likely to overlap with the disputed facts on the historical merits in the case.

———

The Impact of Williams v. Illinois *on the Future of Rule 703*

As previously stated, the conventional wisdom is that secondhand reports admitted under Rule 703 are used for a legitimate, nonhearsay purpose. However, in 2012, five Supreme Court justices challenged the orthodoxy. In *Williams v. Illinois*,[38] a DNA expert opined that there was a match between the defendant's DNA profile and a profile extracted from a rape victim's vaginal swab. In her direct testimony, the expert referred to the profile that Cellmark had extracted from the vaginal swab. In particular, the expert referred to "the male DNA profile found in semen from vaginal swabs" of the victim. The question was whether that reference violated the defendant's Sixth Amendment rights.

Ultimately, the Court affirmed the defendant's conviction. The Court did so because five justices—the plurality led by Justice Alito and Justice Thomas in concurrence—held that Cellmark's report was not testimonial. The plurality reasoned that the report was not testimonial because it did not target a specific defendant. In Justice Alito's words, the primary purpose of the report "was to catch a dangerous rapist who was still at large, not to obtain evidence for use against petitioner, who was neither in custody nor under suspicion at that time." Although Justice Thomas agreed that the report was not testimonial, he rejected the plurality's reasoning; instead, he contended that the report

---

[38]   567 U.S. 50 (2012).

was not formal or solemn enough to trigger the Confrontation Clause. In any event, there were five votes to affirm the defendant's conviction on the ground that the report was non-testimonial. Nevertheless, lower courts are beginning to take note that five justices—"the 703 majority" (Justice Thomas and the four dissenters)—forcefully stated in dictum that any secondhand report relied on under Rule 703 must be used for the truth of the assertion. The disagreement between those justices and the plurality raises significant questions about the future of Rule 703. Assuming that the proponent has otherwise satisfied Rule 703, does the proponent's failure to present independent, admissible evidence of 703 facts render the expert's opinion irrelevant and inadmissible or merely give the opponent an argument for attacking the weight of the opinion?

Initially, posit the 703 majority's view that the utilization of a report under Rule 703 necessarily entails the use of the report as substantive evidence. If the 703 majority is right, there may be an admissibility problem; there is a strong argument that the jury ought to be permitted to consider the resulting opinion only when there is admissible, independent evidence of the 703 case-specific facts. If such evidence is lacking, the judge should bar the opinion. As in the case of a hypothetical question, when the proponent attempts to introduce the opinion, the opponent should have a parallel right to object on the ground that there is no extrinsic, admissible evidence of the 703 facts. Even when the judge exercises discretion to allow the proponent to submit the admissible evidence later—again as in the case of a hypothetical question—on the opponent's motion the judge should strike the opinion if the proponent rests without submitting the admissible evidence. At first blush, the view of the 703 majority seems to lead to the conclusion that the lack of independent evidence of the 703 facts creates an admissibility problem; and the judge ought to exclude the opinion.

Alternatively, posit the conventional wisdom, endorsed by the plurality, that the utilization of a secondhand report under Rule 703 is a legitimate, nonhearsay use of the report. On that assumption, the proponent's failure to present independent, admissible evidence of the 703 facts creates a weight problem rather than an admissibility issue. The Advisory Committee's Note to Rule 703 lends support to the plurality's view. The first paragraph of the Note discusses the hypothetical question. That discussion appears to contemplate that trial judges will continue to enforce the traditional, common law requirement that the proponent present independent, admissible evidence of the hypothesized facts. For instance, the Note mentions the situation in which an expert exempted from a sequestration order "hear[s] the testimony establishing the [hypothesized] facts." Later the same paragraph turns to the expert's reliance on out-of-court reports. The Note expressly states that when an expert relies on this type of basis for the opinion, the proponent can dispense "with the expenditure of substantial time in producing and examining various authenticating witnesses." As previously stated, the Note observes that experts such as "physician[s] make[ ] life-and-death decisions in reliance" on such reports and that the expert's reliance on customary sources of information should "suffice" to warrant admitting the opinion.

However, even the plurality conceded that the proponent's failure to present independent, admissible evidence of a 703 secondhand report can sometimes render the opinion itself irrelevant. The plurality approvingly quoted a judicial instruction generally informing the jury that in assessing the weight of the expert's opinion, they may consider whether the 703 facts "are sustained by the [other] proof." More specifically, the plurality endorsed an instruction that if an essential assumption was "not supported by the proof," the expert's opinion deserves "no weight." Perhaps the best analogy is to the conditional relevance procedure codified in Federal Rule 104(b).[39] In the case of preliminary facts such as a lay witness's personal knowledge and an exhibit's authenticity, the jury ordinarily makes the ultimate relevance decision. The judge plays a limited, screening role and answers only this question: If the jury decides to accept the testimony at face value, does the foundational testimony possess sufficient probative value to support a rational jury finding that the fact exists? If the jury decides that the witness did not see the accident or that the writing is a forgery, common sense will lead the jury to disregard the evidence during the remainder of their deliberations. A case can be made that even lay jurors without legal training can understand that the falsity of an essential premise renders the opinion irrelevant and that they should ignore an irrelevant opinion. If so, the sort of jury instructions discussed in Justice Alito's plurality opinion may be a satisfactory solution. The judge would have to intervene to exclude the opinion only when there is no or clearly insufficient independent, admissible evidence of an essential premise of the opinion.

The dicta by the 703 majority in *Williams* will muddy the 703 jurisprudence in the near future. On its face, *Williams* is a constitutional criminal procedure decision of interest only to criminal practitioners. However, civil practitioners must also pay attention to the language in *Williams* about the evidentiary status of secondhand reports relied on under Rule 703. The logic of the 703 majority extends to civil cases.

§ 15 Reliability: The Manner in Which the Expert Applied the Methodology to the Case-Specific Facts

As previously stated, the starting point for the expert's reasoning is usually the premise that her methodology—the particular technique or theory she is relying on—is valid. The 2016 President's Council of Advisors on Science and Technology (PCAST) report refers to this question as "foundational validity."[40] Section 13 discusses that topic. Next, the expert describes the case-specific facts that she is evaluating. Section 14 analyzes the question of the manners in which the expert can gain her information about those facts. To derive her final opinion, the expert applies the methodology to those facts. The application step introduces another possibility of error in the expert's reasoning. A misapplication of the methodology can result in a flawed conclusion. In the words of the PCAST report, the "validity as applied" issue arises at this step. At common law, there was a split of authority whether the foundation for an expert opinion must include a showing that the expert followed proper test procedure or protocol. One court broadly asserted that "[c]areless testing affects the weight of the evidence and not its admissibility."[41] However, there is a plausible policy argument supporting the contention that such a showing should be essential. Of course, it is dangerous to read too much into the results of proficiency studies; their difficulty can vary, and the analysts sometimes know beforehand that their work is being evaluated. However, in some instances in which a proficiency test identified analyst errors, the follow-up investigation revealed that the root cause of the error was faulty test procedure. The expert may be employing a valid methodology and applying it to trustworthy information about the

---

[39]   See infra § 53.

[40]   Report to the President: Forensic Science in Criminal Courts: Ensuring Scientific Validity of Feature-Comparison Methods (2016).

[41]   People v. Farmer, 765 P.2d 940, 956 (Cal. 1990).

case-specific facts, but sloppy test procedure can result in a misapplication of the technique or theory and, hence, an erroneous final conclusion.

After the Supreme Court's 1993 decision in *Daubert v. Merrell Dow Pharmaceuticals, Inc.,*[42] it was argued that any common law foundational requirement for a showing of proper test procedure had not survived the enactment of the Federal Rules of Evidence. Section 203 points out that in *Daubert,* the Court held that the enactment of the Rules had impliedly overturned the *Frye* general acceptance test for the admissibility of scientific testimony. The Court premised that holding on Rule 402. Rule 402 generally provides that relevant evidence is admissible unless it is excludable under some other provisions of law such as the Constitution, a federal statute, the Rules of Evidence, or a provision of a set of rules that the Supreme Court has adopted pursuant to statutory authority such as the Federal Rules of Civil and Criminal Procedure. Rule 402 makes no mention of case, common, or decisional law. The remainder of the Evidence Rules—in particular, Rule 702—did not codify any general acceptance test; and consequently, the adoption of the Federal Rules dispensed with the common law *Frye* test. Just as the original provisions of Article VII were silent on a general acceptance test, they said nothing about a requirement for a showing of proper test procedure. The argument ran that just as Rule 702 overturned *Frye,* it impliedly superseded any common law requirement for a showing of proper test procedure.

It is true today as it was at the time of the *Daubert* decision that it would be overstated to claim that the clearly prevailing view among state courts is that there is such a foundational requirement. Some state cases have recognized the requirement, but most state supreme courts have yet to reach the issue. However, there is greater clarity in federal practice. Effective December 1, 2000, Rule 702 was amended to prescribe a requirement that the proponent show that "the [expert] witness has applied the principles and methods reliably to the facts of the case." The accompanying Advisory Committee's Note states that under the amendment, "the trial court must scrutinize not only the principles and methods used by the expert, but also whether those principles and methods have been properly applied to the facts of the case." The Note approvingly cites a Third Circuit decision declaring that "any step [in the expert's reasoning] that renders the analysis unreliable . . . renders the expert's testimony inadmissible" and that the judge should exclude the testimony when the judge concludes that the expert has "misapplie[d] th[e] methodology." The restyled Rules incorporate that requirement in Rule 702(d).

As a practical matter, where does one go to learn how a particular methodology should be applied? If the expert used a commercially available instrument such as a particular model gas chromatograph/mass spectrometer (GC/MS), the best starting place is usually the manufacturer. The manufacturer usually prepares an operations and maintenance manual. In addition, the American Academy of Forensic Sciences (AAFS) has a Standards Board. For its part, the International Standardization Organization (ISO) and the American Society for Testing and Materials International (ASTM) develop consensus standards for both industrial and forensic techniques. ASTM committee E-30 is specifically tasked to develop standards for the forensic sciences. An ASTM standard might apply. After the *Daubert* decision, the FBI established technical working groups (TWGs), which were eventually replaced by scientific working groups (SWGs). In turn, they have been supplanted by the Organization of Scientific Area Committees (OSAC).

---

[42]   509 U.S. 579 (1993).

The Scientific Area Committees (SAC) and Subcommittees are now operating under the aegis of the National Institute of Standards and Technology (NIST). Their mission is to generate guidelines and standards for the application of forensic techniques. The parties can cite to these standards when they litigate the Rule 702(d) issue. Another possibility is locating a standard in a learned treatise falling within the hearsay exception codified in Federal Rule 803(18).[43]

§ 16 Reliability: The Expert's Conclusion; the Limitations on the Phrasing of the Expert's Opinion

Section 13 discussed the validity of the expert's methodology. Section 14 turned to the case-specific information that the expert applies the methodology to evaluate. The end result of the application of the methodology to the case-specific facts is the expert's conclusion. There are several limitations on the wording of the conclusion. This section reviews the three most important traditional limitations: the requirement that the opinion be couched as a reasonable scientific certainty and the prohibitions of opinions on ultimate questions of fact and questions of law.

The Requirement That Factual Inferences Be Stated as a Reasonable Scientific Certainty

At one time, many common law courts required that an expert couch her opinion as a certainty or at least as being true to a reasonable degree of scientific certainty. Two factors contributed to the emergence of this requirement. The first was that at the time, the popular view was that science was capable of attaining absolute certainty. The assumption was that the universe was governed by invariable, physical laws that were discoverable by the classic scientific methodology of formulating hypotheses, testing the hypotheses, and evaluating the results of the testing. Given that assumption, there was a widespread belief—shared by many, if not most, judges—that an expert should be able to vouch for her opinion as a certainty. The second factor, which reinforced the requirement, came into play later after questions had arisen about the orderliness of the physical world. As § 203 explains, for most of the 20th century, the dominant standard for the admissibility of scientific evidence in the United States was the *Frye* general acceptance test. The leading rationale for that test was the belief that lay jurors naively view almost any expert opinion as dispositive. If lay jurors will probably treat expert opinions in that fashion, it makes sense to admit only opinions that measure up to the jurors' high expectations.

However, the traditional requirement has come under attack. There were several bases for the attack:

- There is a growing realization that the old, simplistic assumption about science's ability to attain true certainty is flawed:

  Around the turn of the twentieth century, . . . advances in physiology and psychology and the advent of the quantum and relativity theories in physics destroyed simple, mechanistic certainty. Quantum theory tells us that certainty is a physical impossibility, relativity that time is not

---

[43] See infra § 321.

absolute, and psychology that preconceptions color supposedly objective accounts of the natural world.[44]

Indeed, one of the most important foundations of modern physics is Heisenberg's 1927 discovery of the uncertainty principle relating to the unpredictable behavior of electrons. Investigational science relies on inductive and abductive reasoning rather than pure deduction. Investigators formulate their hypotheses and then subject them to empirical testing. If a number of tests appear to verify the hypothesis, there can be growing confidence in the hypothesis—sometimes enough confidence to treat the hypothesis as a basis for making very important decisions such as whether to convict an accused. However, another empirical test is always conceivable; and so long as that is the case, there is a possibility of subsequent falsification of the hypothesis. Thus, in principle an investigator can never regard an hypothesis as certainly or conclusively validated. In *Daubert,* drawing on several amicus briefs filed by individual scientists and scientific organizations, Justice Blackmun declared that "arguably there are no certainties in science."

- As the former National Commission on Forensic Science noted, courts increasingly came to understand that "reasonable degree of scientific certainty" has no settled scientific meaning. Scientists do not use that expression in communicating with each other or publishing their research. From a lay perspective, the expression is nonsensical. For a layperson, the choice is binary: Either a proposition is certain or it is not. There is no such thing as a "reasonable degree" of certainty.

- Furthermore, jury research began to undermine the elitist assumption that lay jurors routinely ascribe undue weight to expert testimony. In 1998 during the *Kumho* litigation, a group of some of the leading legal psychologists in the United States filed an amicus brief reviewing the empirical investigations of laypersons' assessment of expert testimony.[45] Their review of the studies led them to conclude that "[t]he heavy preponderance of the data from more than a quarter century of empirical jury research points to just the opposite view of jury behavior."

- Finally, advocates mounted a statutory construction attack on the traditional requirement. As § 203 explains, in *Daubert* the Court held that the enactment of the Federal Rules of Evidence in 1975 had impliedly superseded the *Frye* standard. Frye was a common law rule, and Article VII of the Federal Rules did not include any language that could reasonably bear the interpretation that it codified a general acceptance test. By the same token, Article VII did not contain language lending itself to the construction that the Rules impose a rigid requirement that all expert opinions be stated as certainties or propositions that are true to a reasonable degree of certainty.

Admittedly, some jurisdictions still insist that experts couch their opinions in those terms. However, judicial support for the traditional view is quickly eroding. The trend is

---

[44]   Black, A Unified Theory of Scientific Evidence, 56 Fordham L. Rev. 595, 616 (1988).

[45]   Brief Amici Curiae of Neil Vidmar et al. in Support of Respondents, Kumho Tire Co., Ltd. v. Carmichael, No. 97–1709, at 25 (Oct. 1998).

definitely toward the view that an expert opinion may be admissible even if it is stated only as a probability or possibility. (For that matter, as a matter of logic, if science cannot attain certainty, expert witnesses should be neither required nor permitted to describe their opinions as certainties.) When the wording of the expert's opinion explicitly acknowledges its uncertainty, the wording may: make the opinion more vulnerable to discretionary exclusion under Federal Rule 403, render the opinion legally insufficient to satisfy the proponent's initial burden of production, and reduce the weight of the opinion in the jurors' eyes. However, that wording does not render the opinion automatically inadmissible, as was formerly true in some jurisdictions.

Although there is growing consensus that expert need not use the language of certainty in stating her opinions, there is controversy over how experts may affirmatively state their opinions. That is the new "hot button" battleground relating to the phrasing of expert opinions. In 2015, the United States Army's Defense Forensic Science Center took the position that its fingerprint experts could use the language, "The likelihood of observing this amount of correspondence when two impressions are made by different sources is considered extremely low." The Department of Justice's Uniform Language for Testimony and Reports permits its examiners to state that they "would not expect to see that arrangement of features repeated in an impression that came from a different source." For that matter, may the expert assert a probability that a particular fingerprint or item of trace evidence is attributable to a particular source? These disputes are discussed in Chapter 20 devoted to scientific evidence.

The Limitation on Opinions on Ultimate Questions of Fact

—The Traditional View

The early cases sometimes purported to enunciate a general view that an expert could not opine on the ultimate issue in the case. As Section 11 pointed out, for the most part the terms "fact" and "opinion" denote merely a difference of degree in concreteness of description or a distinction in nearness or remoteness of inference.[46] The opinion rule prefers the more specific description to the less concrete, and the direct form of statement to the inferential. But there is still another variable in the equation: the purpose of the testimony has an impact on the required degree of concreteness. In the outer circle of collateral fact near the limit of relevancy, the courts receive evidence with relative freedom. However, as the testimony moves closer to the central issue, the courts are understandably more insistent on details instead of inferences. Trial judges tend to be more liberal in exercising discretion to admit opinions about collateral matters and less indulgent when testimony relates to more crucial matters. But is it advisable to go farther and to tie the judge's hands by a categorical rule forbidding opinion evidence as to "ultimate" matters?

Some highly opinionated statements by the witness amount to nothing more than an expression of her general belief as to how the case should be decided or the amount of damages which ought to be awarded as just compensation. All courts exclude such extreme, conclusory expressions. There is no necessity for this kind of evidence; its receipt would suggest that the judge and jury may shift responsibility for the decision to the witnesses. In any event, the opinion is worthless to the trier of fact.

---

[46]   Beech Aircraft Corp. v. Rainey, 488 U.S. 153, 168 (1988).

But until about a half century ago, a large number of courts went far beyond this common sense reluctance to listen to the witness's views as to how the judge and jury should perform their functions; these courts went to the length of announcing a general doctrine that witnesses may never give their opinions or conclusions on an ultimate fact in issue. The stated justification was sometimes that such opinions "usurp the function" or "invade the province" of the jury. These expressions were not meant to be taken literally. Rather, they were intended to convey the fear that the jury might forego independent analysis of the facts and bow too readily to the opinion of an expert witness.

—*The Modern View*

Although many states followed that doctrine prior to 1942, a trend later emerged to abandon it. In most state courts today, an expert may express her opinion on an ultimate fact, provided that all the other requirements for the admission of expert opinion are met. The trend culminated in the adoption of Federal Rule of Evidence 704, now subdivision 704(a). As Rule 704(a) reads: "In General—Not Automatically Objectionable. An opinion is not objectionable just because it embraces an ultimate issue."

On its face, Rule 704(a) is not limited to expert opinions and thus seemingly authorizes the receipt of lay opinions on ultimate questions. Some courts had already adopted the view that laypersons' opinions on ultimate facts are permissible. After all, the courts routinely admit skilled lay observer opinions about identity, and identity is often an ultimate question in a lawsuit. However, such opinions may run afoul of other restrictions in particular instances, e.g., opinions as to how the case should be decided and what amount of money damages would be "just" or "appropriate." Neither a lay witness nor an expert may simply in effect tell the jury what decision it should reach. Even in the most liberal jurisdictions, those opinions are excludable under either Rule 702 on the ground that the inference is unhelpful or exceeds the limits of the witness's expertise or Rule 403 on the ground that the probative value of the inference is outweighed by "a danger of one or more of the following: unfair prejudice, confusing the issues, misleading the jury, undue delay, wasting time, or needlessly presenting cumulative evidence." However, there is no categorical ban on opinions, either lay or expert, addressing ultimate facts. The only meaningful question is whether the opinion satisfies the requirements prescribed by Rules 701–703 and 705.

This change in viewpoint concerning "ultimate fact" opinion resulted from the realization that the rule excluding opinion on ultimate facts is unduly restrictive, and can pose many close, technical questions of application. The rule can unfairly obstruct the presentation of a party's case. In jurisdictions where the traditional prohibition survives, there can be time-consuming, wasteful arguments over whether an opinion concerns an ultimate fact.

Although the statutory provision that is now Rule 704(a) appears to abolish any ultimate issue prohibition, to a degree subdivision (b) resurrects the prohibition. 704(b) was enacted in part as a backlash against the acquittal of John Hinckley on the ground of insanity after his attempted assassination of President Reagan. Unlike Rule 704(a), by its terms Rule 704(b) applies only to expert testimony. Rule 704(b) provides that when an accused's state of mind or mental condition is in issue (such as lack of predisposition in entrapment or the true affirmative defense of insanity), an expert witness may not testify that the defendant did nor did not have the mental state or condition constituting an element of the crime charged or of the defense.

Rule 704(b) sought to eliminate the confusing spectacle of competing psychiatric and psychological experts testifying to directly contradictory conclusions on the ultimate issue to be resolved by the trier of fact. Yet, even under Rule 704(b), presumably a mental health expert may answer the questions, "Was the accused suffering from [a specific mental disease]?", "Explain the characteristics of that mental disease," and "Was his act the type of conduct that can be a product of that disease or defect?" These conclusions fall squarely within the domain of the witness's expertise. However, if Rule 704(b) is to have any teeth, the expert may not take the final step and directly answer the question, "Was the accused able to appreciate the nature and quality of his acts" or "Did the accused appreciate the wrongfulness of his acts?" To some extent, Rule 704(b) has had the intended effect of moderating courtroom battles of mental health experts, but it has not made a dramatic difference. Rule 704(b) forbids dueling experts from expressing conflicting opinions on the ultimate topics, but many courts still permit them to express diametrically opposed opinions on penultimate questions before the jury. Thus, most trial judges would allow the expert to testify about the defendant's mental illness, the classic symptoms of the illness, and the likely impact of the illness on the defendant's cognitive and volitional capabilities. The expert can go to the very brink of Rule 704(b)'s prohibition but must refrain from testifying to the opinion explicitly forbidden by the rule.

The Limitation on Opinions on Questions of Law

Regardless of the jurisdiction's rule concerning opinions on ultimate facts, at common law courts do not allow opinion on a question of law, unless the issue concerns foreign law.[47] Nor do the Federal Rules of Evidence explicitly authorize opinions on law except questions of foreign law. One federal court voiced the typical judicial attitude when it wrote that "in a trial there is only one legal expert—the judge."[48]

Even a court which does not blanketly ban opinions on the ultimate issue may condemn a question phrased in terms of a legal criterion that is not adequately defined by the questioner. Absent an adequate definition, the lay jurors may misunderstand the witness's answer. However, some jurisdictions still adhere to a broader, general rule that a witness may never opine on a pure question of law (e.g., whether the defendant had a duty of care to the plaintiff pedestrian) or a mixed question of law and fact (e.g., whether, on the facts of the instant case, the defendant violated the duty of care she owed the plaintiff pedestrian).

But it is often convenient or desirable to use questions partially phrased in terms of a legal standard. The crux of the problem is the jurors' interpretation of the reference to the standard in the question. How do we ensure that the jury properly interprets the part of the question alluding to the legal standard? An expert opinion is not automatically inadmissible because it refers to the law. Thus, if the expert's opinion tracks the language of the legal rule and the technical meaning of the legal term happens to coincide with the term's colloquial meaning, there is little danger that the opinion will mislead the jury. Alternatively, suppose that the meanings differ. Even then the danger is minimal if the expert enables the jury to exercise independent judgment by clearly specifying the criteria on which the opinion is based so long as the criteria themselves are expert in nature.

---

[47]   See infra § 335.

[48]   Pivot Point Intern., Inc. v. Charlene Products, Inc., 932 F. Supp. 220, 225 (N.D. Ill. 1996).

The problem frequently arises in relation to testimony on the issue of capacity to make a will. Thus, a court allowing opinions on an ultimate issue would approve a question, "Did X have mental capacity sufficient to understand the nature and effect of her will?" That phrasing expressly incorporates the substantive legal standard for testamentary capacity. However, even such a court would disapprove of the conclusory wording, "Did X have sufficient mental capacity to make a will?" That question can easily be misunderstood by the witness and the jury if they do not know the law's definition of "capacity to make a will." But a court completely prohibiting opinions on the ultimate issue might condemn both forms of questions—and perhaps even one where the questioner breaks down "testamentary capacity" into its legally defined constituent elements. This issue is by no means confined to estate litigation; similar problems might arise in respect to such issues as undue influence, total and permanent disability, and negligence.

On the whole, opinions on mixed questions of law and fact tend to have minimal probative value. But the danger posed by these questions is also slight, since attorneys seldom ask such questions except when the popular meaning is roughly the same as the legal meaning. In a jurisdiction where there is no general rule against opinions on the ultimate issue, a request by the adversary that the questioner define her terms should be the only recourse. If the questioner makes the definition of the legal term clear to the jury, many jurisdictions accept opinions couched as conclusions on mixed questions of law and fact.

§ 17 The Cross-Examination of Experts

There are not only special rules for an expert's direct examination; peculiar problems can also arise during cross. How deeply can the cross-examiner probe the facts underlying the expert's opinion? How far may the cross-examiner go in using texts and articles to challenge the expert's technique or theory? And to what extent may the cross-examiner question the expert about sources of potential bias?

On cross-examination, opposing counsel may require the expert to reveal facts and data underlying the expert's opinion that were not disclosed on direct. With respect to the facts and data forming the basis of the expert's opinion, the cross-examiner may explore whether, and if so how, the change or invalidation of any fact or the existence of a contrary fact, would or might affect the opinion. Counsel is permitted to test the expert's reasoning process by inquiring as to what changes of conditions would alter her opinion or at least be relevant. For example, the cross-examiner is free to add facts to, subtract facts from, or modify facts in any hypothetical that the expert relied on during direct. In conducting this inquiry, the cross-examiner is not limited to facts supported by the record.

The Use of Treatises for Impeachment

However, there are limitations on the cross-examiner's ability to use passages in published treatises and articles to attack the theory or technique underlying the expert's opinion. An expert witness may, of course, be confronted with a learned treatise, admissible as substantive evidence under the hearsay exception set out in Fed. R. Evid. 803(18). As Section 321 notes, at common law only a few jurisdictions recognized a learned treatise hearsay exception; but by virtue of the widespread adoption of state provisions patterned after Rule 803(18), the recognition of the exception is now the majority view. Many jurisdictions, though, go farther and allow the cross-examiner to use texts and articles for impeachment even when the publication does not fall within the scope of the hearsay exception. Some jurisdictions do so by statute. Others allow the practice by case law. Depending on the jurisdiction, the cross-examiner may confront the expert with a contrary passage in a publication: the expert relied on, the expert consulted, the expert recognizes as authoritative, or is judicially noticeable as a standard authority in the field or which the cross-examiner has shown to be authoritative. When the publication is used for the limited purpose of impeachment, it is admitted only to attack the quality of the expert's reasoning, not as substantive evidence. On request, under Rule 105 the trial judge should give the jury a limiting instruction to that effect. In the instruction, the judge should identify the theory on which the passage in the publication is logically relevant to impeach the expert's reasoning process, not as substantive evidence. For instance, if the witness concedes that he is unfamiliar with an authoritative text in his field, the concession calls into question the degree of the witness's claimed expertise. Or when the witness admits that the text is authoritative but concedes that he did not bother to consult the text, the concession raises a doubt about how painstakingly the witness has analyzed the case-specific facts.

Bias Impeachment

Cross-examination of an expert directed at establishing bias through financial interest is also quite common. The cross-examiner may seek to establish: (1) financial interest in the instant case by reason of compensation for services, including services performed which enabled him to testify, (2) continued employment by a party, or (3) the fact of prior testimony for the same party or the same attorney. The common law authorities disagree over the propriety of cross-examination about such subjects as the amount of previous compensation from the same party, the percentage of the witness's total income generated by testifying on behalf of a party or a category of party, and the mere fact of prior testimony on behalf of other similarly situated litigants. However, financial interest can have a powerful biasing effect on an expert's testimony. Most contemporary judges realize that many professional experts earn huge fees by spending more time in court than in the laboratory or hospital. Consequently, the better view is that in the judge's discretion, such inquiries are permissible.

The cross-examiner can also point to the expert's doctrinal bias. Suppose, for example, that a psychiatrist testifies that the defendant had an irresistible impulse to commit the actus reus. It is certainly relevant to point out that the psychiatrist is a thoroughgoing determinist who believes that everyone has an irresistible impulse to do everything they do. During the cross-examination of a defense psychiatrist in the trial of Sirhan for the assassination of Senator Robert Kennedy, the prosecutor forced the witness to concede that the witness "considered the concept of free will . . . a delusion."

A growing body of cognitive research has shown that bias can also arise from an expert's exposure to prejudicial information that is "domain-irrelevant," that is, unnecessary to the performance of the expert's task.[49] For example, before a fingerprint examiner compares a suspect's known print to a latent crime scene print, a police officer might tell the examiner about other evidence incriminating the suspect. The examiner does not need that information to perform her comparison, and at a subconscious level the exposure to that information could bias the examiner when she conducts the more subjective aspects of her task. Laboratories are now implementing case or context

---

[49]   Dror & Charlton, Why Experts Make Errors, 56 J. Forensic Sci. 600 (2006).

management procedures to reduce that risk. For example, the laboratory can structure the flow of information within the laboratory to "blind" the expert to prejudicial information that she has no need for. Alternatively, if at some later point in the analysis the examiner needs the information, there can be "sequential unmasking," disclosing the information to the expert only subsequently at the step in the analysis when she requires the information. This problem can be a profitable area for cross-examination, especially if the expert has ignored context management safeguards in place in her laboratory.

The precise scope of cross-examination of expert witnesses rests in the trial judge's discretion. However, the judge should give the cross-examiner latitude, especially when the expert testifies to opinions about matters far beyond the common knowledge and experience of laypersons. According to the California Supreme Court, experts may be cross-examined more extensively and searchingly than lay witnesses; experts may be forced to respond to inquiries that ordinarily would have no place in the cross-examination of a lay witness.[50] When the witness is an expert, there is a risk that the jurors will overvalue the direct testimony. In *Daubert*, Justice Blackmun approvingly cited an article by Judge Weinstein, recognizing that danger.[51] Probing cross-examination can help reduce that risk.

§ 18   Proposals for Improving the Practices Relating to Expert Testimony

The Primary Weaknesses

Common law countries employ the adversary or contentious system of trial, in which the opposing parties, not the judge as in other systems, have the primary responsibility and initiative in selecting and presenting proof. Advantageous as this system is in many respects, its application to the procurement and presentation of expert testimony is widely considered a sore spot in judicial administration.

The critics point to two chief weaknesses in the system. The first is that before trial the experts are chosen by the parties, who are naturally interested in finding not the best scientist, but the "best witness." As an English judge observed:

> [T]he mode in which expert evidence is obtained is such as not to give the fair result of scientific opinion to the Court. A man may go, and does sometimes, to half-a-dozen experts . . . . He takes their honest opinions, he finds three in his favor and three against him; he says to the three in his favor, "will you be kind enough to give evidence?" and he pays the three against him their fees and leaves them alone; the other side does the same . . . [T]he result is that the Court does not get that assistance from the experts which, if they were unbiased and fairly chosen, it would have a right to expect.[52]

The second weakness is that the adversary method of eliciting scientific testimony at trial, frequently by hypothetical questions based on a partisan choice of only favorable facts, is ill-suited to a balanced presentation. Section 14 pointed out that by virtue of Rule 703, the attorney need not present the case-specific facts to the experts in the form

---

[50]   People v. Henriquez, 406 P.3d 748 (Cal. 2017).

[51]   Daubert v. Merrell Dow Pharms., Inc., 509 U.S. 579, 595 (1993).

[52]   Jessel, M.R., in Thorn v. Worthington Skating Rink Co., L.R. 6 Ch. D 415, 416 (1876).

of a hypothetical question; Rule 703 permits the attorney to invite the expert to rely on a secondhand, out-of-court report.

Nevertheless, the hypothetical question remains popular because it gives the attorney maximum control over the expert and a clearly worded hypothesis can give the jury a better understanding of the factual basis of the opinion. However, the hypothesis may include only the facts favoring the proponent's position.

The cumulative effect of these two weaknesses is that in many cases at trial, the expert testimony overstates the extent of the disagreement between the experts and makes it more difficult for the jury to decide the case.

Potential Remedies for the Primary Weaknesses

There are several proposals for either remedying these weaknesses or reducing their impact. Some proposals relate to pretrial procedure while others relate to the handling of expert opinion testimony at trial.

The Court Appointment of Experts to Testify on the Ultimate Issues in the Case

A potential remedy for the first weakness lies in the use of trial judges' common law power to call experts. As early as the 14th century—before witnesses were heard by juries—there are recorded cases of judges summoning experts to aid them in determining scientific issues. The existence of the judge's power to call witnesses generally and expert witnesses in particular is well settled in this country.[53] The power is recognized by rules and statutes in a substantial number of states. Some provisions apply to scientific issues in any case, civil or criminal, others are limited to criminal cases, and still others refer narrowly to sanity issues in criminal cases. The general principle is implemented in the Model Expert Testimony Act approved by the Commissioners on Uniform State Laws, and embodied in Uniform Rule of Evidence and Federal Rule of Evidence 706. Unfortunately, in the past judges have rarely exercised their power under Rule 706. That reluctance is understandable. Before their appointment to the bench, most judges are schooled as litigators in the adversary tradition. That tradition is so ingrained that some commentators believe that to overcome the judicial reluctance to appoint court experts, court appointment must be made mandatory in certain types of cases.

Limited Court Appointments of Experts to Provide the Judge and Jury with a Primer on the Relevant Expertise

It has been proposed that by adapting existing procedures, American courts could shift from a dialectic (adversary) model to a more didactic (educational) model for presenting expert testimony. One of the weaknesses in the current model is that at the typical trial, all the expert testimony is presented by witnesses hired by the litigants. When all the expert testimony comes from potentially biased sources, it is difficult for the trier of fact to separate the wheat from the chaff. Unlike many prior recommendations, this proposal does not contemplate that the judge will appoint an expert who would duplicate the work of the partisan experts and opine on the ultimate

------

[53]   See supra § 8.

disputed issues. Rather, the limited extent of the proposal is to modify existing procedures to give the trier of fact a primer on the basics in the relevant discipline. Armed with a primer, the trier would be in a better position to perform the task described by the *Joiner* Court, namely, deciding which partisan expert is making the more reasonable extrapolation and which is making "too great an analytical" leap.[54] Under this proposal, pursuant to Rule 201 the judge would judicially notice the well settled propositions in the discipline and instruct the jury about them. Then, pursuant to a very limited Rule 706 appointment, an independent expert would respond to the jury's questions about those propositions. In effect, the judge is the master teacher, the court-appointed expert is the teaching assistant, and the jurors are the students. After the judge's instructions and the jury's opportunity to question the court-appointed expert, the jury would hear the testimony by the partisan experts. All of these procedures— judicial notice, court appointment, and juror questioning—are permissible under the current law in most jurisdictions.

These procedures would better enable the trier of fact to choose intelligently between the conflicting opinions advanced by the competing partisan experts. Moreover, the use of limited appointments might make courtroom appearance more attractive to some experts. Outstanding scientists often express the sentiment that they dislike serving as expert witnesses because they find adversary litigation too combative. Although Rule 706 authorizes the judge to appoint experts, they have the right to decline the appointment; and some of the most eminent scrupulous experts are unwilling to accept such appointments. That sentiment is understandable because, in the typical case, they are asked to opine on an ultimate issue in the case and directly oppose one or more partisan experts who have formed a contrary opinion on the very same issue. In that scenario, the parties' attorneys have the maximum incentive to aggressively attack the court-appointed expert. If these potential experts were offered the opportunity to play a more limited role and merely teach the judge and jury about the general theories and techniques in their field, these scientists might be more willing to participate in litigation.

The Establishment of Panels of Impartial Experts

Another possible antidote for the first weakness is establishing panels of impartial experts designated by groups in the appropriate specialty fields. The judge could then select an expert from the panel. An American Bar Association committee approved in principle this procedure for impartial medical expert witnesses. However, little headway has been made in implementing this procedure.

Pretrial Conferences to Narrow the Disagreements Between the Opposing Expert

The second weakness in the status quo may also be remediable. In the current system, lay jurors are often called on to arbitrate a "battle of experts." In some kinds of controversies, a well-devised plan of scientific investigation and report could greatly reduce the need for contested trials. The Uniform Act provides that the court may require

------

[54] General Electric Co. v. Joiner, 522 U.S. 136, 146 (1997).

a conference of the experts, whether chosen by the court or the parties. The conference gives the experts an opportunity to resolve or reduce their disagreements in interpreting the data. The conference might lead to a complete agreement which practically settles the issue. If not, the conference may at least narrow the controversy. The Act provides that two or more experts may join in a single report. At the trial, the individual expert's report or a joint report can be read to the court and jury as a part of the expert's testimony, and he may be cross-examined about the report. The Act dispenses with the requirement to use hypothetical questions. There was a striking, if bizarre, example of the utility of joint reports in a famous New York DNA case, *People v. Castro*.[55] In that case,

> [i]n an unusual move, four of the expert witnesses—representing both the prosecution and the defense—met to review the scientific evidence after they had already testified. The result of this meeting was a two-page consensus statement that addressed the inadequacy of the scientific evidence and the legal procedures for assessing [the] evidence. Although the statement itself was not accepted as evidence in the pretrial hearing, the substance of the consensus document was introduced by the defense's recall of two prosecution expert witnesses to testify on its substance.[56]

Although these pretrial proposals addressing the two system's two major weaknesses have merit, the proposals themselves have been targets of criticism. For example, the expanded use of court appointed experts has its critics. The critics argue that there is no such thing as a truly impartial expert and that, even assuming such experts exist, courts lack the ability to identify and locate them. To address this problem, the American Association for the Advancement of Science established the Court Appointed Scientific Experts (CASE) project. At this stage, CASE is a pilot project to better enable federal judges to find suitably qualified, independent experts. In addition, critics contend that at trial identifying the witness as an appointed expert could result in excessive emphasis by the trier of fact on that expert's opinion. Once the jury learns that one expert is the "court's" witness, the jurors might leap to the conclusion that they should accept her opinion and ignore the opinions of the parties' experts.

———

Concurrent Testimony by Experts

The focus of the next proposal is on the trial rather than the pretrial stage. Some other common law jurisdictions, notably Australia and Canada, have developed a practice of concurrent expert testimony—sometimes referred to as "hot-tubbing."[57] In this practice, the opposing experts are required to meet before trial. At trial, the opposing witnesses take the stand at the same time. After preliminary statements, the witnesses are questioned by the judge and can respond to statements by each other. In one survey of Australian judges, 94.9% responded that they were satisfied with the procedure and thought that the practice had improved the presentation of expert testimony in that jurisdiction. There are several advantages to the procedure. One is that the procedure

---

[55]   545 N.Y.S.2d 985 (Sup. Ct. 1989).

[56]   Office of Technology Assessment, U.S. Cong., Genetic Witness: Forensic Uses of DNA Tests 103 (1990).

[57]   Sonenshein & Fitzpatrick, The Problem of Partisan Experts and the Potential for Reform Through Concurrent Evidence, 62 Defense L.J. 60 (Nov. 2013).

helps the trier of fact identify the real points of agreement and disagreement between the experts. Narrowing the scope of the controversy is especially helpful. Another advantage is that the procedure creates a disincentive to overstated testimony; the expert realizes that the opposing expert is immediately available to point out any exaggeration and explain why the overstatement is fallacious. Some American administrative agencies have used the procedure at their hearings, and a few American trial judges have employed the procedure during bench trials. It may prove difficult to adapt the procedure to jury trials. A free-flowing exchange between the opposing experts could expose the jury to inadmissible evidence. Further, it might be awkward to employ the procedure at a trial during which all the jurors are permitted to pose questions. Yet, it certainly seems worthwhile to explore the use of this innovative practice at American bench trials.

The two primary weaknesses mentioned earlier are not the only features of common law procedures which hamper the effectiveness of expert testimony. Other problem areas include: the asserted unsuitability of the lay jury as a tribunal for resolving highly technical assessing scientific; the rules of privilege, especially the attorney-client privilege, the physician-patient privilege, and the privilege against self-incrimination which can impede a full inquiry into the bases of the expert's opinion; and the use of legal standards of civil liability and criminal responsibility, that do not accord with the scientific standards which the experts are accustomed to, as in the case of the "understanding of right and wrong" test for legal sanity.

More broadly, the courts' need for better employment of the technical resources goes beyond the use of expert witnesses. One judge has observed:

> The methods of courts might well be supplemented by the use of well tested examples of administrative tribunals, of expert investigators acting for the court—engineers, scientists, physicians, economic and social investigators, as needed—in addition to, not in substitute for, similar experts acting for the parties . . . Why should not judge and jury in cases involving multitudinous scientific exhibits, or scientific questions, have the benefit of the assistance of those competent to organize such data and analyze such questions? Why should not courts have adequate fact finding facilities for all kinds of cases? Boards of directors do. Administrative tribunals do. The parties, and in a large sense the public, have an interest in the decision of cases on whole truth, not on partial understanding. The machinery and expert staffs developed by the interstate commerce commission, state public service commissions, and workmen's compensation boards have values for fact finding which may profitably be studied in reference to judicial reorganization . . . .[58]

Even if in the long term we are unwilling to fundamentally reorganize the legal system to better integrate expertise, there are more modest steps that can be taken in the short term. The American legal tradition has devised a number of procedures which might conceivably be adapted to better utilize experts' services. For instance, special pretrial conferences could be tailored to deal exclusively with matters involving expert opinion. In addition, judges possess authority, often conferred by statute or rule but in any event an "inherent" judicial power, to refer a question to a master, referee, auditor or similar officer, standing or special. The reference may go beyond a mere investigation

---

[58]   Stephens, *What Courts Can Learn From Commissions*, 21 A.B.A.J. 141, 142 (1933).

and report and authorize an adversary hearing followed by a report or a preliminary decision. Even if the courts are reluctant to extend these procedures to expert testimony problems, the legislatures could intervene and mandate the procedures by statute. It has also been suggested that the courts make wider use of the executive branch's technical resources, specifically those of the administrative agencies and commissions. To be more specific, their staffs could serve as a source for neutral expert witnesses.

There are small signs of progress. As previously stated, until recently most judges have been reluctant to resort to techniques such as court appointment under Rule 706. However, in its 1993 *Daubert* decision, the Supreme Court announced the new, reliability test for the admissibility of purportedly scientific testimony. That test requires trial judges to directly assess the validity of scientific hypotheses; the judges may no longer rely on "proxies" or "surrogates" for validity such as the popularity or general acceptance of the hypothesis. The shift to the new validation test should encourage trial judges to appoint experts under 706. Indeed, in the course of its opinion, the *Daubert* Court mentioned the possibility that in applying the new test, judges would find it useful to appoint experts under the rule. In his concurrence in *Joiner*, Justice Breyer encouraged trial judges to exercise their appointment power. There is some evidence that the incidence of court appointment is increasing. However, it has been over a quarter century since the *Daubert* decision; and, to be frank, the progress on this front is barely perceptible.

During the same period, though, there has undeniably been a dramatic increase in the number of continuing legal and judicial education programs devoted to scientific evidence. In addition, judges and attorneys now have far greater access to specialized scientific evidence tools such as the *Reference Manual on Scientific Evidence* released by the Federal Judicial Center. These programs and tools have not only raised the trial bar's and bench's awareness of expert testimony issues; to some extent, they have also increased the scientific literacy of the bar and bench. Unlike her counterpart 30 years ago, today the typical civil attorney trying a toxic tort case knows something about the rudiments of epidemiology. Unlike his counterpart 30 years ago, the average contemporary criminal practitioner who defends drug cases possesses at least an elementary understanding of gas chromatography/mass spectrometry (GC/MS). Admittedly, the progress has been gradual—some would say painfully slow. However, that growing awareness and literacy are probably the two most hopeful developments.

Chapter 4

CROSS-EXAMINATION AND SUBSEQUENT EXAMINATIONS

Table of Sections

---

§ 19 The Right of Cross-Examination: Effect of Denial of Opportunity to Cross-Examine

For two centuries, common law judges and lawyers have regarded the opportunity for cross-examination as an essential safeguard of the accuracy and completeness of testimony. They have insisted that the opportunity is a right, not a mere privilege. This right is available at the taking of depositions as well as during the examination of witnesses at trial. The premise that the opportunity of cross-examination is an essential safeguard has become the principal justification for the general exclusion of hearsay statements.[1] The same premise underpins the recognition of a hearsay exception for former testimony taken at a prior hearing where the present adversary was afforded the opportunity to cross-examine.[2] State constitutional provisions guaranteeing the accused's right of confrontation have been interpreted as codifying this right of cross-examination, and the Sixth Amendment confrontation clause of the federal constitution has likewise been construed as guaranteeing the accused's right to cross-examination in criminal proceedings. Indeed, although other rights are subsumed under the

---

[1]   See infra § 245.

[2]   See infra § 302.

confrontation clause, in the Supreme Court's 2004 decision in *Crawford v. Washington*[3] a majority of the justices appeared to embrace the notion that the right to cross-examination is the primary interest secured by the confrontation clause. Under the rubric of procedural due process, the courts have even granted a measure of constitutional protection to the right in civil cases.

The Consequences of a Denial of the Opportunity for Cross-Examination

A denial of an opportunity for cross can be caused by a party, a witness, or the judge.

Denials Caused by a Party or Witness

When a party alleges that the conduct of an opposing party or a witness denied them an opportunity for cross-examination, several questions arise: Did the conduct amount to a denial of the opportunity to cross? What are the legal consequences of a denial? And do the usual consequences vary if the denial is temporary rather than permanent or partial rather than complete?

Of course, the threshold question is whether the party's or witness's responses amount to a refusal to testify. If the witness suffers a genuine memory loss, many courts refuse to characterize the witness's response as a refusal necessitating the striking of the testimony. However, it can be argued that if the witness untruthfully claims a memory loss, the witness is impliedly refusing to testify. Yet, there is authority that even if the witness is feigning memory loss, the witness is still deemed available for cross-examination; " '[t]he witness . . . is in fact subject to cross-examination, providing a jury with the opportunity to see the demeanor and assess the credibility of the witness . . . .' "[4] After all, in summation the cross-examiner can treat the witness's claimed forgetfulness as the basis for an effective attack on the quality of the witness's memory and therefore for discounting the rest of the witness's testimony. The jury is especially likely to accept that attack if there is a hint that the witness is faking the memory loss.

Assuming that there has been a denial, what are the legal consequences? The consequences depend on the cause of the denial. There are four common, recurring situations.

First, a party testifying on his own behalf might unjustifiably refuse to answer questions necessary to a complete cross-examination. In this fact situation, the consensus is that the adversary is entitled to have the direct testimony stricken—a result that seems fair. The party suffers the loss of the direct testimony, but the party himself is responsible for the denial of cross-examination.

Second, a non-party witness might similarly refuse to be cross-examined or to answer proper cross-examination questions. Assume that the witness expressly refuses to answer questions. The loss of the non-party witness's testimony can be a severe hardship to the party calling the witness, and the party may not be responsible in any way for the witness's refusal. Nevertheless, many courts and writers approve of the same drastic remedy of excluding the direct. This remedy minimizes the party's temptation to procure the witness's refusal—a collusion which is often hard to prove; the remedy forcefully protects the right of cross-examination.

---

[3]   Crawford v. Washington, 541 U.S. 36 (2004).

[4]   People v. Noriega, 188 Cal. Rptr. 3d 527, 535–36 (Cal. Ct. App. 2015).

However, there is a split of authority in the second situation. There is case law rejecting the drastic remedy of exclusion and holding that the matter should be left to the judge's discretion. In particular, there is precedent that if the witness invokes the privilege against self-incrimination to refuse to answer cross-examination questions which are merely collateral, that is, logically relevant only to the witness's credibility, the judge should not automatically strike the direct testimony. Here many cases accord the judge a measure of discretion in ruling on the cross-examiner's motion to strike.

Third, the witness may become, or purport to become, sick or otherwise physically or mentally incapacitated, before cross-examination is begun or completed. The facts in many of these cases raise a suspicion of simulation, particularly when the witness is a party. Consequently, the courts often strike the party's direct examination. In the case of the non-party witness, the same result usually obtains. However, at least in civil actions, a case can be constructed that the judge should not exclude the direct if she is clearly convinced that the incapacity is genuine. In that event she ought to let the direct testimony stand. She can then give the jury a cautionary instruction to explain the weakness of uncross-examined evidence. (Temporary incapacity may change this result, as indicated below.)

In the fourth situation, the witness dies before the conclusion of the cross-examination. Here again it is usually held that the party denied cross-examination is entitled to have the direct testimony stricken, unless, presumably, the death occurred during a postponement of the cross-examination consented to or procured by that party. Indeed, exclusion may be constitutionally compelled if the person was a state's witness in a criminal case. Yet, at least in case of death, it has been suggested that striking the direct ought to be discretionary. That suggestion has merit. No matter how valuable cross-examination may be, common sense tells us that the half-loaf of direct testimony is better than no bread at all. It seems excessive to deny the jury all the testimony from a potential source of valuable information. It was the accepted practice in equity to let the direct testimony stand. It is submitted that except for the testimony of prosecution witnesses, the judge should let the direct testimony stand but on request instruct the jury to consider the lack of opportunity to cross-examine in weighing the direct testimony.

The above paragraphs describe the usual legal consequences of a denial. But what if the denial is merely temporary rather than permanent? There is authority that where the incapacity is temporary, the cross-examiner may not insist on immediate exclusion of the direct testimony. Rather, she must be content with the offer of a later opportunity to cross-examine even when doing so makes it necessary for her to submit to a mistrial. The temporary disability of a crucial witness can be sufficient necessity for a mistrial declaration, permitting a later retrial. If the initial trial proceeded to decision without the benefit of the witness's testimony, the outcome might be a wrongful verdict. A second trial could avoid a miscarriage of substantive justice.

Or what if the denial is partial rather than complete? The preceding paragraphs assumed for simplicity's sake that although the witness answered some cross-questions, a failure to secure a complete cross-examination would be treated as if cross-examination had been wholly denied. That assumption is an oversimplification. Even when the cross-examination is cut off before it is finished, under the circumstances the questioning could be substantially complete enough on a topic to satisfy the requirement for an opportunity to cross-examine on that subject. At the very least, in a given case, cross-examination as to part of the direct testimony may be extensive enough to allow at least that part to stand though the rest must be stricken. If the cross-examination on a particular topic has been in depth, the trial judge should refuse to strike the direct testimony on that topic.

Denials Caused by the Judge

Although the preceding paragraphs deal with the conduct of parties and witnesses, the infringement of the right of cross-examination may result from the judge's action. The judge has wide discretionary control over the *extent* of cross-examination on particular topics. Yet, the complete denial of cross-examination or its arbitrary curtailment on a proper, important subject of cross-examination is ground for reversal. In particular, in decisions such as *Davis v. Alaska*,[5] the Supreme Court has emphasized that evidence of a witness's bias can have significant probative value on the question of a witness's credibility. When a trial judge completely forecloses or severely limits cross-examination about a prosecution witness's bias, the trial judge is flirting with reversal on appeal.

A related issue is whether the trial judge may impose a time limit on the duration of the cross-examination. Again, it is well-settled that the judge has discretion to reasonably limit the, extent of the cross-examination. However, an unduly severe time limitation might preclude the questioner from exploring an important topic during the cross-examination. Consequently, before announcing a firm time limit, the judge should engage in a particularized assessment to ensure that the allotted time is adequate.

§ 20 Form of Interrogation

Assuming that a litigant has the right to cross-examine, questions can arise as to the scope and form of the cross. In contrast to direct examination, cross-examination may usually be conducted by questions that are leading in form. When the cross-examiner uses leading, narrowly-phrased questions, under the guise of asking questions the cross-examiner can make factual assertions on the record and force the witness to assent. The cross-examiner can virtually testify for the witness. The cross-examiner's purpose is often to weaken the effect of the direct testimony, and the witness is commonly assumed to be more or less uncooperative. Consequently, there is little risk that the witness will acquiesce in the cross-examiner's suggestions.

The courts permit leading on cross-examination on the assumption that there is usually a hostile relationship between the witness and the cross-examiner. Given the nature of their relationship, the witness is unlikely to blindly accept the suggestions implicit in the questions' leading phrasing. However, in many jurisdictions when it appears that the witness is biased in the cross-examiner's favor and likely to yield to the suggestions of leading questions, the judge may forbid the cross-examiner from leading. If a civil plaintiff calls the defendant as a witness, on cross-examination there will obviously be a friendly relationship between the defendant and her own counsel. There are, however, a number of somewhat illogical decisions permitting leading questions on cross-examination even when the witness is biased in the cross-examiner's favor.

---

[5]   Davis v. Alaska, 415 U.S. 308 (1974).

The Cross-Examiner's "Adoption" of the Witness

In jurisdictions limiting the scope of cross-examination, if the examiner goes beyond the proper scope of cross-examination she may be required to refrain from leading the witness as to the new subject. The cross-examiner "adopts" the witness with respect to the new topic. Although the questioning is formally cross-examination, it is functionally a direct examination; and the general prohibition against leading consequently comes into play.

§ 21 Scope of Cross-Examination: Restriction to Matters Opened up on Direct: The Various Rules

The judicial sentiment varies widely among the different jurisdictions over the question of whether the cross-examiner is confined to the subjects on the historical merits testified about in the direct examination and, if so, to what extent. However, the differences of opinion should not be overstated. Although this section reviews those varying practices, there is a good deal of consensus over the proper scope of cross-examination. As § 22 notes, all the courts agree that the proper scope includes matters relevant to the witness's credibility. In addition, as we shall see again in § 24, most jurisdictions accord the trial judge a measure of discretion over the scope of cross-examination on the merits. The point of sharpest disagreement is the normal scope of cross-examination on the historical merits of the case. There are three major schools of judicial thought on that topic: the wide-open view, the restrictive view, and the half-open door view.

The Traditional Rule of Wide-Open Cross-Examination

England and a few states follow the simplest and freest practice. In these jurisdictions, the cross-examiner is not limited to the topics which the direct examiner has chosen to open. The cross-examiner is free to question about any subject relevant to any issue on the merits of the entire case, including facts relating solely to the cross-examiner's own case or affirmative defense.

The "Restrictive" Rule, in Various Forms, Limiting
Cross-Examination to the Scope of the Direct

In the United States, the majority of the states agree that the cross-examination is limited to the aspects of the merits that were testified to on the direct examination. The Federal Rules of Evidence adopt this approach. While all these jurisdictions purport to embrace the restrictive rule, they differ markedly in the rigor with which they enforce the rule:

- One version of the doctrine strictly confines the cross-questions to those relating only to the same, specific facts or historical events mentioned on direct, and, perhaps, those occurring at the same time and place. This version of the doctrine is sometimes called the factual or historical test. Under this narrow view, the cross-examination is limited to "the same points" brought out on direct, the "matters testified to," or the "subjects mentioned."

- There is a slightly more expansive version of the restrictive rule. That version extends the scope to "facts and circumstances connected with" the matters stated on direct. However, even this phrasing still suggests a requirement of basic identity of transaction and proximity in time and space.

- Another variation gives cross-examination a somewhat wider scope. Under this variation, the cross-examination may touch on the matters opened in direct and facts tending to explain, contradict, or discredit the direct testimony.

- The broadest formula includes facts tending to "rebut" any inference or implication from the matters testified on direct. As we shall see in the next paragraph, under the "legal test" version of this formula, many judges permit cross-examination about any matter related to any essential element of a cause of action, crime, or defense, which was touched on during direct.

There is little consistency in the phrasing and use of these formulas, even in the same jurisdiction. All these express criteria are too vague to be employed with precision. Even assuming that cross-examination is limited to the subject matter of the direct examination, the subject matter of questions on direct examination can always be defined with greater or lesser generality regardless of the express formula.

As previously stated, the Federal Rules codify a version of the restrictive approach. Federal Rule of Evidence 611(b) refers to "the subject matter of the direct examination." The courts should interpret that statutory language as endorsing the broader, more liberal views described above. That interpretation is consistent with the provision in Rule 611(b) that the court may permit inquiry into additional matters as if on direct. As a practical matter, many federal trial judges apply the so-called legal test. This test equates "the subject matter of the direct" with the essential elements of the cause of action, crime, or defense mentioned on direct. At the end of the trial, the judge gives the jury substantive law instructions on the pertinent causes of action, crimes, and defenses. These instructions list the essential legal elements which the burdened party must prove to prevail on that theory. One of the essential elements of a true crime is a *mens rea* element. Suppose that on direct examination, a defense witness testified about the accused's mens rea at the time of the *actus reus*. Under the legal test, on cross-examination the prosecutor could inquire about distinct acts by the accused so long as the other acts were logically relevant to the element of *mens rea*; the prosecution would not be limited to the historical events mentioned during the witness's direct examination.

All these limiting formulas share an escape valve, namely, the common law notion that where part of a transaction, contract, conversation, or event has been mentioned on direct, the remainder may be brought out on cross-examination.[6] This particular aspect of the rule of completeness is still in effect in modern federal practice. In substance, this notion merely states the converse of the limiting rule itself. However, that does not detract from the notion's practical utility as an alternative argument to persuade a judge to expand the scope of cross-examination.

In civil cases, the trial judge sometimes exercises discretion to enforce a "one-appearance" rule. In the interest of judicial economy and the witness's convenience, the witness is called only once. After one side's direct examination of the witness, the other

---

[6]   See infra § 56.

side is permitted to cross-examine the witness without being limited to the matter covered on direct examination. The judge is most likely to adopt this practice when the witness is of only marginal importance to the case and the practice will not substantially lengthen the cross-examination.

The Half-Open Door: Cross-Examination Extends to Any Matters Except Cross-Examiner's Affirmative Case

A third view as to the scope of cross-examination represents a middle course between the two extremes. Under this view—now mostly obsolete—the cross-examiner may question the witness about any matters relevant to any issue in the action *except* facts relating only to the cross-examiner's own affirmative case such as defendant's affirmative defenses or cross-claims or, in case of a plaintiff, her new matter in reply. In some states, this compromise standard served as a temporary half-way house for courts which later embraced the "wide-open" practice. Compared with the restrictive practice, the third view has the practical advantage of reducing the number of disputes by widening the scope of examination. Its chief drawback is that, particularly under modern liberal pleading rules, it is often difficult to determine whether the matter inquired about relates solely to the cross-examiner's "distinct grounds of defense or avoidance."

The Questioner's Ability to Introduce Exhibits During Cross

Suppose that the cross-examiner would like to introduce an exhibit relevant to a fact that is within the scope of cross-examination under whatever view the jurisdiction takes. The question is whether the trial judge may enforce a rule that a questioner may not introduce exhibits during cross-examination. The better view is that if the cross-examiner can lay the foundation for an exhibit, the cross-examiner may proffer the exhibit at that time. Nevertheless, in their courtroom some trial judges do not permit cross-examiners to introduce exhibits. Appellate courts have generally upheld the practice for the stated reason that the practice affects only the timing of the introduction of the exhibit.

§ 22 Cross-Examination to Impeach Not Limited to the Scope of the Direct

One of the main functions of cross-examination is to afford an opportunity to elicit answers impeaching the witness's veracity, capacity to observe and remember, impartiality, and consistency. Even in jurisdictions adopting the most restrictive practice on the historical merits, impeaching cross-examination is not limited to matters brought out in the direct examination. As we shall see in §§ 33 and 47, on direct examination, a witness's proponent ordinarily may not bolster the witness's credibility; during direct—before there has been any attack on the witness's credibility—the proponent generally may not elicit testimony which is logically relevant only to enhancing the witness's believability. Until cross-examination, we often do not know whether the opponent will attack the witness's credibility; and if the opponent does not do so, it was a waste of time to receive testimony enhancing the witness's credibility. However, by the simple act of testifying, the witness places her credibility in issue. For that reason, the witness's credibility is fair game on cross-examination. Federal Rule of Evidence 611(b) adopts this view.

§ 23   Formal and Practical Consequences of the Restrictive Rules: Effect on Order of Proof: Side-Effects

It is sometimes asserted that the only "essential" formal difference between the "wide-open" and the restrictive views of scope of cross-examination is the time or stage at which the witness may be called on to testify to the facts inquired about. The primary difference among the views is supposedly their effect on the order of proof. Under the "wide-open" rule the witness may be immediately questioned about the new matter during cross-examination. In contrast, under the restrictive rules the cross-examiner postpones the questions until her own next stage[7] of putting on proof and then calls the witness to prove the same facts.

This assertion, though, overlooks the real world impact of the restrictive practice. At a given trial, timing can be critical; and even a "mere" postponement can be important. For dramatic effect, the questioner wants to strike while the iron is hot. As a practical matter in many instances a postponement of the questions will not be the only result of a ruling excluding a cross-question as outside the scope of the direct. Unless the question is vital and she is fairly confident of a favorable answer, the cross-examiner might be unwilling to run the risk of calling the adversary's witness at a later stage as her own witness. A cautious cross-examiner might well decide to abandon the inquiry. Getting concessions from the opponent's witness hot on the heels of the direct while his story is fresh is worth trying for. It is a much chancier and less attractive option to have to call an unfriendly witness later when his initial testimony is stale. Admittedly, to a degree the restrictive rules promote the orderly presentation of proof.[8] However, in some cases the application of those rules does not foster that policy. For example, suppose a direct examiner injects an issue by witness #1 but not by witness #2 who cannot be cross-examined on the issue under the restrictive view although witness #2 has knowledge highly relevant to that issue. In that situation, from the jury's perspective it might be more orderly and sensible to have both witnesses testify about the fact in the same phase of the case. However, the scope rules will force the opponent to recall witness #2 later.

Moreover, postponing questions exceeding scope of direct is not even the only formal consequence of the restrictive rule. There are many incidental effects. By way of example, the courts adopting the restrictive practice frequently say that if the cross-examiner, perhaps without objection, questions the witness about new matter, he makes the witness his own. Although the questioning is formally cross-examination, the questioning about the new topic is functionally direct examination. The cross-examiner "adopts" the witness with respect to the new matter. Federal Rule of Evidence 611(b) embraces this adoption notion. The cross-examiner normally may not ask leading questions about the new matter; and under the traditional rule against impeaching one's own witness, he may be precluded from impeaching the witness as to those facts. However, since one may impeach one's own witness under Federal Rule of Evidence 607, the cross-examiner would not be precluded from impeaching the witness concerning the new matter brought out pursuant to Rule 611(b).

Furthermore, the invocation of the restrictive rule to exclude unfavorable testimony from the plaintiff's witness which might otherwise be elicited on cross-examination,

---

[7]   As to the order of proof, by stages, of the respective parties, see supra § 4.

[8]   The Supreme Court itself has acknowledged the litigant's felt need to tell a coherent, compelling story at trial. Old Chief v. United States, 519 U.S. 172 (1997).

could have another critical formal effect: It might save the plaintiff from a directed verdict at the close of her case-in-chief. Otherwise, during the plaintiff's case-in-chief, the defense could introduce new matter that arguably dictated a defense verdict. In that light, the application of the restrictive rule can be a significant advantage for the plaintiff. The plaintiff both survives the directed verdict motion and, during the later defense case, gains an opportunity to strengthen her case by eliciting favorable facts from his opponent's witnesses.

Finally, in one situation, the restrictive doctrine operates as a rule of complete exclusion, not a mere postponement. In this situation, the witness has a privilege not to be called as a witness by the cross-examiner. Thus, the privileges of the accused and the accused's spouse not to be called by the state may prevent the prosecutor from eliciting the new facts at a later stage, if the prosecutor cannot adduce them on cross-examination.

§ 24 The Scope of the Judge's Discretion Under the Wide-Open and Restrictive Rules

In the early 19th century Gibson, C.J.[9] and Story, J.[10] modified the orthodox "wide-open" cross-examination by suggesting that questioning about new matter was improper at the stage of cross-examination. When they did so, they conceived of their modification as relating solely to the order of proof. Traditionally the order of proof and the conduct and extent of cross-examination were subject to the trial judge's discretionary control. In keeping with that tradition, Federal Rule 611(a) empowers the judge to "exercise reasonable control over the . . . order of examining witnesses and presenting evidence. . . ." For its part, Rule 611(b) allows the judge to a degree to "exercise . . . discretion" over the scope of cross.

The earlier decisions and many contemporary cases adopting the restrictive rule emphasize the trial judge's discretionary power to allow deviations. Indeed, it has been said that both the courts following the wide-open view and those adopting the restrictive practice "recognize the discretionary power of the trial court to allow variations from the customary order and decline ordinarily to consider as an error any variation sanctioned by the trial court."[11] If this statement were completely accurate, the hazards of injustice at trial or appellate reversal would be relatively minor. But the statement paints too bright a picture.

In the states adopting the restrictive "scope of the direct" test, many trial judges often find it easier to administer the test as a mechanistic rule rather than as a flexible discretionary standard. In the past, appellate courts reversed many cases for error in applying the test. Fortunately, the modern trend is to accord wider latitude to the trial judge.

In states following the traditional wide-open view, there also has been little tendency to apply the notion that the order of proof is discretionary. Their tradition has not been shaped in terms of order of proof, but rather in the language of a right to cross-examine on the whole case. The situation putting the greatest strain on the wide-open rule is the one in which a party, usually the plaintiff, finds herself compelled at the outset

---

9   Ellmaker v. Buckley, 16 Serg. & Rawle 72, 1827 WL 2669 (Pa. 1827).

10   Philadelphia & Trenton R. Co. v. Stimpson, 39 U.S. 448 (1840).

11   St. Louis, I.M. & S. Ry. Co. v. Raines, 119 S.W. 665, 668 (Ark. 1909).

to call either the opposing party himself or an ally of the opponent to prove a formal fact not substantially in dispute. Should the opponent then be allowed to disrupt the proponent's case at this stage by cross-examining the willing witness about defensive matters unrelated to the direct examination? This is an appealing situation for the exercise of discretion to deviate from the wide-open practice; to the prevent the disruption of the proponent's case, the trial judge could require the cross-examiner to recall the witness for these new matters when the cross-examiner later puts on his own case. Yet, as the decisions indicate, even in this extreme fact situation, in "wide-open" jurisdictions trial judges rarely exercise their discretion to force a recall.[12]

§ 25 Application of Wide-Open and Restrictive Rules to the Cross-Examination of Parties: (a) Civil Parties

In the cross-examination of party witnesses, two situations must be distinguished: (1) the hostile cross-examination by the adversary of a party who calls himself as witness in his own behalf, and (2) the friendly cross-examination by the counsel of a party who has been called as an adverse witness by his opponent.

In the first situation, in jurisdictions following the restrictive rules courts sometimes hold that while the judge should normally apply the general limitation to the "scope of the direct," the trial judge's range of discretion to relax the restrictive practice is wider when the witness is the opposing party. However, Federal Rule of Evidence 611(b) does not appear to authorize a relaxation of the restrictive practice *only* for parties; on its face, 611(b) does not differentiate between the cross-examination of parties and non-parties. Yet, without much discussion, a few cases have announced that the limitation to the scope of the direct is inapplicable during the hostile cross-examination of a party. In the "wide-open" states, the courts routinely accord the cross-examiner the usual freedom from the restriction to the scope of direct.

Contrast the second situation: A statute or rule often provides that when a party calls the adverse party as a hostile witness, the party may question the witness "as upon cross-examination." Hence, the party may ask leading questions; and she is not "bound" by the adverse witness's answers—meaning chiefly that she may impeach the testimony by showing inconsistent statements. When this direct examination, savoring of cross, ends, some jurisdictions give the witness no right to be examined immediately by his own counsel; rather, the judge has discretion whether to permit immediate questioning or to instead require that his examination be deferred until the next stage of the witness-party's own case. Most jurisdictions, though, allow the witness's immediate examination by his own counsel. However, even if the witness's own counsel is permitted to conduct an immediate examination, on request the trial judge should forbid leading questions. In restrictive jurisdictions, during this "cross-examination" of a friendly witness, there is no discernible judicial tendency to relax the usual limitation confining the questions to the scope of the direct.

§ 26 Application of Wide-Open and Restrictive Rules to the Cross-Examination of Parties: (b) The Accused in a Criminal Case

As a means of implementing the prescribed order of producing evidence, the restrictive rules limiting cross-examination to the scope of the witness's direct or to the proponent's case are burdensome, but understandable. The cross-examiner is

---

[12] See infra § 25.

temporarily blocked, but she has a theoretical remedy: She may later recall the witness for questioning when she puts on her own next stage of evidence. However, when the restrictive practice is applied to the criminal accused, as it is in most jurisdictions following that practice, the accused can permanently preclude the prosecution from questioning the accused about facts outside the scope of the accused's direct. There is authority that if the prosecution cannot question the accused during the defense case-in-chief about a certain issue on cross-examination, the prosecution may not later recall the accused during its rebuttal to query the accused about that fact. The accused may carefully narrow his direct examination to a single aspect of the case such as age, sanity, or alibi and then invoke the jurisdiction's rule normally restricting the cross-examination to that topic. At the very beginning of the direct examination, the defense counsel might expressly announce that she intends to question the accused "only" about a specified topic; counsel does so to put herself in a better position to later urge scope objections. This application of the restrictive practice to the cross-examination of the accused has been criticized. However, that criticism has not persuaded the courts to exempt prosecution cross-examination of the accused from the restriction. (Of course, the accused will not escape a searching inquiry on the whole case in a jurisdiction where the scope of cross-examination is "wide-open.")

Regardless of whether the result under the restrictive rule is desirable as a matter of policy, the scope of the accused's cross-examination might not be controlled solely by evidence case law, statutes, or rules.[13] Federal Rule 611(b) does not purport to define the extent to which a testifying accused waives the constitutional privilege against self-incrimination.[14] Eventually, constitutional doctrine may dictate the outer limits of cross-examination concerning the degree to which the accused waives his privilege of self-incrimination by taking the stand and testifying. Some judicial language suggests that under the Fifth Amendment of the United States Constitution, the accused's waiver extends only to questions concerning matters mentioned on direct examination. If this position ultimately prevails, state practice will be partially controlled by federal constitutional limits on waiver. Those limits could render unconstitutional "wide-open" cross-examination of criminal defendants, and perhaps even liberal variations of the restrictive rules.

§ 27 A Comparison of the Systems of Wide-Open and Restricted Cross-Examination

The principal virtue of the restrictive rules is that they pressure the parties to present their facts in logical order: first the facts on which the plaintiff has the burden, then those which the defendant must prove, and so on. The restrictive rules minimize the danger that one party's plan of presenting his facts will be interrupted by cross-examination interjecting new and damaging matters constituting his adversary's case. If permitted, such interjection can lessen the impact and persuasiveness of the proponent's case. The proponent planned to lay out an orderly case fact by fact. However, during its very presentation, the carefully crafted case is disrupted by contrary facts drawn out in cross-examination of the proponent's own witnesses. The proponent's "case," conceived as a single melody, is converted to counterpoint. The contemporary litigator views herself as a storyteller—telling the jury a coherent, compelling narrative

---

13   See generally infra § 132.
14   The scope of the waiver by a testifying accused is discussed in infra § 129.

of the disputed events. The litigator understandably resents it when the opposition attempts to disrupt the continuity and flow of the story. For that reason, most practitioners probably prefer the restrictive views of the scope of cross.

Like virtually all conventions as to order, the common law order of proof by "cases" or stages is to some extent arbitrary. Since two witnesses cannot speak at once, some rules must be worked out as to who shall call the witnesses and in what order. However, it seems artificial to impose a further restriction that a witness who knows many facts about the case may tell only certain facts at his first appearance, and must be recalled later to testify as to other facts. There is a sort of natural order to the freer, wide-open practice; on direct examination the general order of proof of the respective parties' "cases" is maintained, but the adversary is free to draw out damaging facts on cross-examination. An alternative procedure would allow each witness successively to tell everything she knows about the case. That is the system which laypersons tend to follow in any informal investigation untrammeled by legal rules. Jeremy Bentham, the great critic of "artificial" procedural rules, favored a "natural" system of evidence. By that expression, he meant the practices which a lay family might use to investigate a factual question. That system better serves the witnesses' convenience and may strike the jury as a more natural way of developing the facts. Of course, it could be objected that a detour into new paths on cross-examination lessens the persuasiveness of the direct examiner's presentation of her story. However, it is hardly self-evident that the direct examiner has a right to the psychological advantage of presenting her facts in an oversimplified, one-sided way. Is she entitled to make a favorable first impression on the jurors which, although answered later, can be hard to dislodge?

Another policy consideration is economy of time and energy. The wide-open rule leaves little or no opportunity for wrangling over its application at either the trial or appellate level. In contrast, the restrictive practice can produce petty courtroom bickering over the choice among the numerous variations of the "scope of the direct" criterion, and the application of the chosen standard to particular cross-questions. These technical controversies often resurface on appeal, and there is the possibility of reversal for error. Compliance with these ambiguous restrictions is a matter of constant concern to the cross-examiner. If these disputes and delays were necessary to safeguard fundamental substantive rights, they might be worth the cost. But as the price of enforcing a debatable regulation of the order of evidence, the sacrifice is misguided. The American Bar Association's Committee for the Improvement of the Law of Evidence observed:

> The rule limiting cross-examination to the precise subject of the direct examination is probably the most frequent rule (except the Opinion rule) leading in trial practice today to refined and technical quibbles which obstruct the progress of the trial, confuse the jury, and give rise to appeal on technical grounds only. Some of the instances in which Supreme Courts have ordered new trials for the mere transgression of this rule about the order of evidence have been astounding. We recommend that the rule allowing questions upon any part of the issue known to the witness . . . be adopted . . . .[15]

In short, there is a strong case for the "wide-open" rule.

---

[15]   See 6 Wigmore, Evidence § 1888, at 711 (Chadbourn rev. 1976), setting out the relevant part of the committee's report.

The upshot is that while most practitioners favor the restrictive approach, the "wide-open" rule enjoys the support of many reformers, academics, and jurists.

§ 28 Cross-Examination About Witness's Inconsistent Past Writings: Must Examiner Show the Writing to the Witness Before Questioning About Its Contents?

A fatal weakness of many liars is letter writing.[16] Betraying letters are often inspired by the liar's boastfulness or stupidity. Properly used, letters have exposed many a witness intent on perjury. An eminent trial lawyer, Louis Nizer, remarked:

> ... There is an art in introducing the letter contradicting the witness' testimony. The novice will rush in. He will obtain the false statement and then quickly hurl the letter in the face of the witness. The witness, faced with it, very likely will seek to retrace his steps, and sometimes do it skillfully, and the effect is lost.
>
> The mature trial counsel will utilize the letter for all it is worth. Having obtained the denial which he wishes, he will, perhaps, pretend that he is disappointed. He will ask that same question a few moments later, and again and again get a denial. And he will then phrase—and this requires preparation—he will then phrase a whole series of questions not directed at that particular point, but in which is incorporated the very fact which he is ready to contradict—each time getting closer and closer to the language in the written document which he possesses, until he has induced the witness to assert not once, but many times, the very fact from which ordinarily he might withdraw by saying it was a slip of the tongue. Each time he draws closer to the precise language which will contradict the witness, without making the witness aware of it, until finally, when the letter is sprung, the effect as compared with the other method is that, let us say, of atomic energy against a firecracker.[17]

The Rule in Queen Caroline's Case

However, some courts erected a major obstacle to effectively using this impeachment technique. The obstacle is the rule in *Queen Caroline's Case,* pronounced by English judges in an 1820 advisory opinion.[18] The opinion announced that the cross-examiner cannot ask the witness about any written statements by the witness, or ask whether the witness has ever written a letter of a given tenor, without *first* both producing the writing *and* exhibiting it to the witness. The cross-examiner must permit the witness to read the writing or the part of it that the cross-examiner seeks to ask him about. In effect, the examiner must telegraph her punch. Thus, the potential trap is laid before the eyes of the intended prey. While reading the letter, the witness will be forewarned not to deny it. Worse still, a clever witness may be able to quickly weave a new web of deception to explain away the inconsistency.

---

[16]   Of course, today the inconsistent statement could take the form of an email, a text message, or a social media post.

[17]   Nizer, The Art of Jury Trial, 32 Cornell L.Q. 59, 68 (1946). An instructive analysis of the technique of "exposure by document" is found in Love, Documentary Evidence, 38 Ill. Bar J. 426, 429–30 (1950). *See also* 4 Belli, Modern Trials § 63.30 (2d ed. 1982).

[18]   2 B. & B. 284, 286–90, 129 Eng. Rep. 976, 11 Eng. Rul. C. 182 (1820).

As previously stated, *Queen Caroline's Case* announced that the writing must first be shown to the witness before he can be questioned about it. The judges conceived of the rule as an application of the best evidence doctrine requiring the production of the original document *when its contents are sought to be proved*. This rule was a misconception in at least two respects. First, *at this stage* the cross-examiner is not seeking to prove the contents of the writing. Quite to the contrary, her hope is that the witness will deny the existence of the letter. Second, the original document rule requires the production of the document as proof of its contents to the judge and jury, not to the witness. The Victorian barristers found the rule in the *Queen's Case* so obstructive that they lobbied vigorously and secured its abrogation by Parliament in 1854.[19]

However, this practice requiring exhibition to the witness was unquestioningly accepted by many American courts and occasionally by American legislatures. The actual invocation of the rule at trial is relatively infrequent in most states in which the rule is still in effect. Even today some judges and practitioners in these jurisdictions are unaware of this pitfall in the cross-examiner's path.

The preceding paragraphs discussed the operation of the rule in situations in which the thrust of the attempted impeachment is the exposure of attempted perjury. In this situation, the rule seems to blunt one of counsel's most potent weapons. However, worse still, in the more typical case in the real world the weapon may be misdirected. Honest witnesses frequently write letters, forget their contents, and years later testify mistakenly—but innocently—to facts inconsistent with assertions in the letters. On the one hand, the cross-examiner undeniably has a right to reveal the witnesses' forgetfulness and discredit their present testimony to that extent. On the other hand, the cross-examiner arguably should not be allowed to encourage an honest witness by subtle questioning to widen the gap between their present testimony and their past writings. In this situation, the judge ought to have discretion whether to permit the questioning about the writing without requiring its exhibition to the witness. When it seems clear to the judge that at most the witness is guilty of innocent misrecollection, the judge should have discretion to require the cross-examiner to show the writing to the witness.

In recognition of the disadvantages of the rule of *Queen Caroline's Case,* the Federal Rules of Evidence abolish the rule by permitting cross-examination without a prior showing of the writing to the witness. Rule 613 substitutes a requirement that the writing be shown or disclosed to opposing counsel on request as an assurance of the cross-examiner's good faith. However, there is federal authority that the trial judge retains discretion to require the exhibition of the writing to the witness. As previously stated, it could be appropriate for the judge to exercise that discretion in a case in which it is apparent that the thrust of the impeachment is innocent misrecollection rather than outright perjury.

§ 29 The Standard of Relevancy as Applied on Cross-Examination: Trial Judge's Discretion

There are three main functions of cross-examination: (1) to attack the credibility of the direct testimony of this witness and other opposing witnesses, (2) to elicit additional facts on the historical merits related to those mentioned on direct,[20] and (3) in states

---

[19] St. 17 & 18 Vict. C. 125, § 24.

[20] See supra § 21.

following the "wide-open" rule, to bring out additional facts relevant to any issue in the case. The normal standard of relevancy governing testimony offered on direct examination applies to the subject-matter of cross-examination questions intended to serve the second and third functions.

However, when she is performing the first function of attacking the credibility of the direct testimony, the cross-examiner's purpose is radically different than in pursuit of the other two functions. In the first function, the cross-examiner is not directly targeting the historical merits of the case. Here the common law test of relevancy is not whether the answer sought will shed light on any issue on the merits, but rather whether it aids the trier of fact in appraising the witness's credibility and assessing the probative value of the witness's direct testimony. In general the common law principles stated in this section also obtain under Federal Rule of Evidence and Revised Uniform Rule of Evidence 611(b). The Federal Rule explicitly authorizes cross-examination about "matters affecting the witness's credibility."

At common law and in modern federal practice there are many recognized lines of questioning for this purpose, none of which has any direct relevance to the historical merits. For instance, one familiar type of credibility inquiry is the preliminary series of cross questions asking about residence and occupation, designed to place the witness in his setting. Either the witness's residence or occupation might give rise to an inference of bias. Another common question is, "Have you talked to anyone about this case?" Like a witness's residence or occupation, a witness's pretrial contacts could have a biasing influence. Still another popular type of credibility inquiry is the testing, exploratory question. In this kind of question, the cross-examiner (who may not have had the advantage of previously interviewing the witness) poses questions somewhat remote from the main inquiry. The questions are designed to experimentally test the witness's ability to remember detailed facts similar to those recited on direct, his capacity accurately to perceive facts, or his willingness to tell the truth without distortion or exaggeration. This kind of inquiry is part of the tradition and art of cross-examination, and some of the most famous instances of successful cross-examinations are of this variety. A final example of credibility cross-examination is the attack by questions seeking to show such matters as inconsistent statements or conviction of crime. Again, these facts have no necessary relevance to the historical merits. The courts recognize that a rule strictly limiting cross questions to those relevant to the issues on the historical merits would cripple these kinds of examination.

With respect to all the lines of inquiry mentioned in the preceding paragraph, the criteria of relevancy are vague, since the cross-examiner's purpose is frequently exploratory. Too tight a rein on the cross-examiner may rob the examination of its utility. However, the dangers of undue prejudice to the party or the witness and of potential waste of time are apparent. Consequently, the trial judge has a discretionary power to control the extent of examination. Appellate courts overturn this exercise of discretion only for abuse resulting in substantial harm to the complaining party. A survey of a large number of these cases reveals that in practice, the appellate courts more often find abuse when complaint is that the trial judge unduly limited the examination than when undue expansion is alleged. In a criminal case, the court is especially likely to find an abuse of discretion when the trial judge restricts cross-examination probing a prosecution witness's bias.

§ 30 The Cross-Examiner's Art

Section 5 of this treatise noted that although at the typical trial the direct examinations are more determinative of the outcome than the cross-examinations, many attorneys find it more difficult to master the art of cross-examination. An overview of the art of cross-examination, gleaned from the prolific literature on the subject, may help the beginning advocate appreciate some of the wisdom that lawyers have learned from hard experience. It may also aid in considering the topic of the next section, namely, evaluating the broader policy significance of cross-examination. The following are some of the most important generalizations.

Pretrial preparation is the key. Some lawyers seem to have a natural, intuitive talent for cross-examination. A great Victorian advocate, Montagu Williams, voiced this view when he said, "I am by trade a reader of faces and minds."[21] Today, however, the stress is on painstaking preparation, not divine inspiration. Improvisation is often necessary, but its results are usually small compared to those achieved by planned questions based on facts methodically discovered before trial. The planning steps are explained in several classic works on cross-examination. Not all steps have to be taken for all adverse witnesses; the testimony of some adverse witnesses is simply not damaging enough to warrant the time and expense of thorough preparation. If the witness's testimony is only mildly damaging, a lengthy cross-examination might have the unintended effect of magnifying the witness's importance in the jurors' minds. Nevertheless, preparation before trial is the soil from which, in the average case, successful cross-examination grows.

At trial, listen intently to the direct testimony. If you properly prepare before trial, during an opposing witness's direct examination you should have nothing to do other than concentrate on exactly what is being said. Some lawyers recommend that at trial, any notes in preparation for later questions be made by an associate or the client, rather than the cross-examiner. Likewise, distracting oral suggestions to the cross-examiner at the counsel table should be kept to the bare minimum. During the direct examination, the cross-examiner cannot afford to spend a good deal of time preparing notes or conversing; the task at hand for the cross-examiner is to listen intently to every word coming out of the mouth of the direct examiner and witness.

Do not cross-examine unless you believe that you can probably achieve a specific strategic or tactical objective. In the movies, desperate fishing expeditions on cross-examination routinely yield startling revelations. In the real world, they are usually ineffective and often counter-productive. The cross-examiner typically succeeds only in having the witness repeat the damaging testimony, and during cross hostile witnesses frequently add damning facts which were deliberately omitted on direct to set a trap for the cross-examiner.

As a general proposition, the attorney should not cross at all unless, in her best professional judgment, she is convinced that she can probably achieve one of the useful purposes of cross. As we have seen, these purposes are: first, to elicit new facts on the historical merits, qualifying the direct or in some states bearing on any issue in the case; second, to test the witness's story by exploring its details and implications, in the hope of disclosing inconsistencies or implausibilities; and third, to elicit impeaching facts such as prior inconsistent statements, bias, and criminal convictions to attack the credibility

---

[21] Quoted in Elliott, The Work of the Advocate 231 (2d ed. 1912).

of either this witness or another opposing witness. If you prepared thoroughly before trial, you are in position to predict whether you can probably achieve one or more of these objectives. The cross-examiner should rarely pose a question about a pivotal fact to an adverse witness unless the cross-examiner is reasonably confident the answer will be favorable. In deciding whether to pursue any of these objectives, but particularly the last two, the cross-examiner must be conscious that the odds are stacked against her. An unfavorable answer is more damaging when elicited on cross-examination. It is hard for an attorney to win her case on cross-examination, but it is easy for her to lose it. Hence, if the witness's direct testimony has done little or no harm, a cross-examination for the second or third purpose is often ill-advised. In many cases, when the direct examiner tenders the witness to the cross-examiner, the cross-examiner should say only, "No questions, Your Honor. This witness may be excused."

But what if the witness's direct testimony has been damaging or even threatens to destroy the cross-examiner's case if the jury believes it? Suppose that although the testimony has been damaging, the cross-examiner has little ammunition against the witness. Should the attorney launch an exploratory cross-examination? The cross-examiner must make a situational, on-the-spot judgment: Was the direct testimony so devastating that the jurors will probably regard a waiver of cross as an admission of the truth of the testimony, and, on that basis, find against the cross-examiner's client? In that situation cross-examination is usually necessary even if the chances of success are remote. To be blunt, if the direct testimony was devastating and the cross-examiner has no real ammunition against the witness, the cross-examiner must contemplate either launching a fishing expedition or seeking a recess to renew settlement discussions.

If out of desperation you decide to conduct a fishing expedition, it is inadvisable to follow the sequence of topics in the witness's direct testimony. One commentator suggests: "If the witness is falsifying, jump quickly with rapid-fire questions from one point of the narrative to the other, without time or opportunity for a connected narrative: backward, forward, forward, backward from the middle to the beginning, etc."[22] Of course, there are common sense limits to this suggestion. If the cross-examiner jumps around too quickly and abruptly, the cross-examination will confuse the jurors rather than impressing them.

Know when to conclude the cross-examination and try to end on a high note. If the cross-examiner succeeds in eliciting a favorable fact, it is frequently better to wait and stress the inconsistency in closing argument rather than to continue to press the witness to embellish. Immediately after conceding the favorable fact, the witness might realize how damaging the concession was. If the cross-examiner presses with a follow-up question, the additional question may give the witness an opportunity to recover and explain away the concession. When the cross-examiner has gained an important admission, she ordinarily should not risk the witness's recantation by continuing the questioning to obtain additional details or to demand a repetition of the admission. Instead, she ought to move to another important point if she has one, and conclude the examination after her last big point. End on a high note: "When you have struck oil, stop boring."[23] The impact of a cross-examination depends on the overall impression left at

---

[22] Ramage, A Few Rules for the Cross-Examination of Witnesses, 9 Cent. L.J. 354 (1920).

[23] Credited to Josh Billings in Steeves, The Dangers of Cross-Examination, 86 Cent. L.J. 206, 207 (1918).

the end of the cross rather the number of technical debating points which the cross-examiner scores against the witness during the cross.

Cross-examine for the jury, not for your client. As just stated, be conscious of the overall impression left by your cross-examination. It is often tempting for the cross-examiner to display his wit and skill for his client, or to satisfy the client's hostility toward an opposing witnesses by humiliating them. This temptation frequently presents itself in bitter family law disputes. Small victories on collateral matters are often easy to secure. However, the odds between the experienced advocate and the witness, nervous in new surroundings, are not even. The jury is keenly aware of this disparity, and most jurors are prone to imagine themselves in the witness's shoes. The jurors tend to sympathize—and side—with the witness. Impress the jury with your civility.

The cross-examiner must be ultra-polite in questioning sympathetic witnesses such as children, crime victims, and bereaved relatives. The cross-examiner usually obtains better results with the witness and makes a better impression on the jury, by tactful sensitivity rather than sarcastic bullying. However, in the rare case when the cross-examiner is convinced that a crucial witness has committed perjury and that she can expose it, the cross-examiner should press aggressively. Once it is clear to the jury that the cross-examiner has "the goods" on the witness, it is safe for the cross-examiner to adopt a more overtly aggressive attitude toward the witness.

Project sincerity. While these generalities are worthwhile guidelines, the cross-examiner must adapt her techniques to the specific situation she faces. Different seasoned litigators might use widely varying techniques in cross-examining the same witness. As on direct, during cross-examination the litigator needs to adopt a questioning style suited to her personality. Whatever else the litigator does during trial, she must project sincerity to the jury. If the cross-examiner attempts to mimic another attorney's style and persona, her presentation may strike the jury as insincere. The jurors suspect that the lawyer knows the truth; after all, she has had the benefit of privileged conversations with the client. If the jurors view the attorney as insincere, they may infer that the attorney realizes that the client's case lacks merit.

§ 31 Cross-Examination Revalued

Early Victorian writers on advocacy waxed poetic about cross-examination and exaggerated its importance. One wrote, "There is never a cause contested, the result of which is not mainly dependent upon the skill with which the advocate conducts his cross-examination."[24] This romanticism contrasts with the realism of Scarlett, a great "leader" of a later day. Scarlett remarked, "I learned by much experience that the most useful duty of an advocate is the examination of witnesses, and that much more mischief than benefit generally results from cross-examination. I therefore rarely allowed that duty to be performed by my colleagues. I cross-examined in general very little, and more with a view to enforce the facts I meant to rely upon than to affect the witness's credit—for the most part a vain attempt."[25] Reed, one of the most sensible early 20th century writers on trial tactics, observed, "Sometimes a great speech bears down the adversary, and sometimes a searching cross-examination turns a witness inside out and shows him up to be a perjured villain. But ordinarily cases are not won by either speaking or cross-

---

[24]   Quoted from Cox, The Advocate 434, in Reed, Conduct of Lawsuits 277 (2d ed. 1912).

[25]   Memoir of Lord Abinger, quoted in Reed, Conduct of Lawsuits 278 (2d ed. 1912).

examining."[26] Yet, even today many lawyers who write about the art of cross-examination believe that failure to use this tool effectively can lose a case. That belief often holds true for criminal defense counsel.

Most contemporary commentators have a less romantic and more realistic view of the importance of cross-examination. To the modern advocate, cross-examination is more valuable as a means of gleaning additional facts on the merits corroborating the cross-examiner's own theory of the case; in the real world—as opposed to movies and television—the cross-examiner rarely destroys the credibility of an opposing witness. It is true that cross-examination of experts is critical in many cases. Federal Rule of Evidence 705 makes the opportunity to cross-examine particularly important when, as the rule permits, on direct examination an expert states only her opinion and the theoretical reasons for the opinion. In that situation, Rule 705 places the burden on the cross-examiner to explore the facts or data about the specific case on which the opinion is based. However, even in this context, the focus is ordinarily on the validity of the expert's reasoning process rather than the expert witness's personal credibility. In summary, while cross-examination can be an important tool at some trials, in most cases it does not loom as large a determinant of victory as direct examination.

We should not only consider this assessment in critiquing the norms and procedures for cross-examination. More broadly, a reappraisal of cross-examination as an engine for discovering truth should factor into any discussion of the reform of American evidence law, notably hearsay doctrine. The traditional assumption has been that if there is no opportunity for cross-examination, the statement of an out-of-court declarant is so lacking in reliability that it is not even worth hearing at trial. The traditional mindset is that the opportunity for cross-examination is essential.

To be sure, cross-examination is a useful device to ensure greater accuracy and completeness in the witness's testimony. In the hands of a skillful advocate, it will sometimes expose fraud or honest error. But it can also produce errors. The litigator can use cross-examination to expose perjury; but it is sometimes the honest, timid witness who goes down under the fire of cross-examination. As a matter of fairness, every important witness in judicial proceedings should be made available for cross-examination when it is feasible to do so. However, where cross-examination is impossible, as in the case of an out-of-court statement of a witness who dies before cross-examination, it is dubious to insist that the statement normally be excluded for that reason alone. Cross-examination ought to be considered useful, but not indispensable, as a means of discovering truth. The lack of an opportunity to cross-examine should be only one relevant factor in deciding whether to admit a statement. A sensible, reformist approach to the hearsay doctrine would be that when the opportunity to cross-examine a witness is permanently cut off without either party's fault, the hearsay testimony should be admissible. Hearsay statements arguably ought to be admitted if: (1) the declarant based the statement on personal knowledge, and the declarant is now dead or unavailable for cross-examination, or (2) the declarant is alive and still available for

---

[26]   Reed, Conduct of Lawsuits 276 (2d ed. 1912). *See also* Kilner & McGovern, Successful Litigation Techniques § 14.10, at 14-1 (1981) ("The right to thoroughly cross-examine all witnesses makes our adversary system work, because it is through that examination that the accuracy, truthfulness and trustworthiness of the testimony is tested. Some jurors, unfortunately, expect the cross examining attorney to pull a Perry Mason on every witness and eventually to have him completely repudiate everything he said on direct examination. The trial practitioner, however, must recognize that things like that happen in television shows but seldom do they occur in a real courtroom.").

cross-examination. Perhaps written statements should be admitted wherever production for cross-examination can fairly be dispensed with.

Although this reformist approach is generally defensible, there are special constitutional concerns in criminal cases. The source of those concerns, of course, is the accused's right of cross-examination under the Sixth and Fourteenth Amendments. Those constitutional guarantees constrain the liberalization of cross-examination practice and the hearsay rule. To a degree, asymmetry between the hearsay rules in prosecutions and those in civil actions may be inevitable.

§ 32 Redirect and Subsequent Examinations

Redirect Examination

The courts have developed what might be termed a "rule of first opportunity" to define the scope of redirect and recross-examination. As a general proposition, an attorney who calls a witness is normally required to elicit on the witness's first direct examination all the testimony that the attorney wishes to prove by the witness. This norm of proving everything feasible at the first opportunity is in the interest of fairness and efficiency. As previously stated, there is a split of authority over the question of whether the cross-examiner should be limited to answering the direct, with the vast majority of states favoring the restrictive approach.[27] However, when the question is the scope of redirect and the subsequent examinations, there is no such division; the consensus is that the party's examination is typically limited to answering any new matter drawn out in the adversary's immediately preceding examination. It is true that under her general discretionary power to vary the normal order of proof, the judge may permit the redirect examiner to bring out relevant matter which through oversight he failed to elicit on direct. Under Federal Rule of Evidence 611(a), the judge has discretion over the scope of redirect. However, even in Federal Rules jurisdictions, the courts view replying to new matter adduced on cross-examination as the customary, limited function of redirect. Examination for this purpose is often deemed a matter of right, but even then its extent is subject to the judge's discretionary control.

A skillful re-examiner can frequently remove the sting of an apparently devastating cross-examination. The most intelligent use of redirect is usually to give the witness an opportunity to deny or explain a seemingly impeaching fact mentioned during cross-examination. The reply on redirect can take the form of explanation, avoidance, or qualification of the new substantive facts or impeachment matters elicited by the cross-examiner. Suppose, for example, that on cross-examination, the witness conceded that she made an apparently inconsistent statement. On redirect, the examiner might invite the witness to explain away the apparent inconsistency by telling the jury that she used a key term in the statement in a peculiar sense. The straightforward approach, such as "What did you mean by" or "What was your reason for" a witness's statement on cross-examination, is frequently effective. However, a mere reiteration of assertions made on the direct or cross-examination is usually prohibited, although the judge has discretion in this matter.

The re-examiner often invokes the common law rule of completeness, permitting proof of the remainder of a transaction, conversation, or writing when a part has been proven by the adversary if the remainder relates to the same subject-matter. In *Beech*

---

[27] See supra § 21.

Aircraft Corp. v. Rainey,[28] the Supreme Court announced that that aspect of the common law is still in effect in federal practice. Moreover, the redirect examiner can sometimes resort to the principle of curative admissibility, permitting her to respond to irrelevant or inadmissible evidence elicited during cross-examination.

Re-Cross Examination

Like redirect, recross-examination follows the norm of first opportunity. Consequently, the scope of recross as of right is normally confined to questions directed to explaining or avoiding new matter brought out on redirect. As a practical matter, if the previous examinations of the witness have been lengthy, by this point the jury's patience may be exhausted. Even if the opposing counsel would be legally entitled to conduct recross, it may be foolish to exercise that right.

---

[28]   488 U.S. 153 (1988).

Chapter 5

IMPEACHMENT AND SUPPORT

Table of Sections

§ 33 Introduction: Bolstering, Impeachment, and Rehabilitation

Assume that a witness on the stand gives some testimony or that a counsel introduces an out-of-court declarant's hearsay statement as substantive evidence. As soon as the testimony or hearsay statement is admitted, the credibility of the witness or declarant becomes a fact of consequence within the range of dispute at trial under Federal Rule 401.

There are three groups of credibility rules. The first relates to the attempts by a witness's proponent to bolster the witness's credibility even before the opponent attempts to impeach the witness. The second concerns the various techniques which the opponent may employ to attack or impeach the witness's credibility. Finally, a third set of rules addresses the methods which the witness's proponent may use to rehabilitate the witness's credibility after attempted impeachment, in effect to undo the damage done by impeachment.

Both at common law and under the Federal Rules, the general norm is that the witness's proponent may not bolster the witness's credibility before any attempted impeachment. For example, on direct examination it would be improper for the witness's proponent to elicit the witness's own testimony that the witness "always tells the truth."

Federal Rule of Evidence 608(a)(2) partially codifies the ban on bolstering; the rule provides that the "evidence of [a witness's] truthful character is admissible only after the character . . . has been attacked . . . ." There are some exceptional situations discussed in § 47—fresh complaints and prior identifications—in which the witness's proponent is permitted to bring out bolstering evidence on direct examination. However, as a general proposition, bolstering evidence is inadmissible. As of the time of the direct examination, it is uncertain whether the cross-examiner will attack the witness's credibility; the counsel might later waive cross-examination or cross-examine solely for the purpose of eliciting new facts on the historical merits which support that counsel's theory of the case. If the opposing counsel does so, all the time devoted to the bolstering evidence on direct examination will have been wasted. For that reason, the witness's proponent must ordinarily hold information favorable to the witness's credibility in reserve for rehabilitation on redirect or the next stage of the case.

Although the common law was hostile to bolstering evidence, the common law and the Federal Rules liberally admit impeaching evidence. There are five main modes of attack on a witness's credibility. The first, and probably most frequently employed, is proof of a prior inconsistent statement or "self contradiction," as it is sometimes imprecisely described. That technique consists of proof that the witness previously made statements inconsistent with his present testimony. The second is an attack showing that the witness is biased on account of emotional influences such as kinship for one party or hostility to another, or motives of pecuniary interest, whether legitimate or corrupt. The third is an *ad hominem* attack on the witness's character, but lack of religious belief is not available as a basis for this type of attack on credibility. The fourth is an attack showing a deficiency in the witness's capacity to observe, remember, or recount the matters testified about. The fifth is specific contradiction, that is, proof by other witnesses that material facts are not as testified to by the witness being impeached. Some of these attacks such as bias are not specifically or completely treated by the Federal or Revised Uniform Rules of Evidence. Nevertheless, they are authorized in federal practice. Article VI of the Federal Rules contains several provisions expressly regulating impeachment techniques[1] such as proof of prior inconsistent statements. Thus, Article VI implicitly recognizes that a witness's credibility is a fact of consequence under Rule 401. Absent an express Article VI provision, the admissibility of facts such as bias that are logically relevant to witness credibility is governed by the general analytic framework set out in Federal Rules 401 to 403.

The process of impeachment can proceed in two different stages. First, the facts discrediting the witness or his testimony may be elicited from the witness herself on cross-examination. Of course, the cross-examiner must have a good faith basis in fact. Some modes of attack are limited to this stage; the shorthand expression is, "You must take his answer." When the mode of attack is limited in this manner, the cross-examiner is sometimes said to be restricted to "intrinsic" impeachment. Second, in other situations, the facts discrediting the witness may be proved by extrinsic evidence. For example, the plaintiff's witness to be impeached has already left the stand; and the impeaching defense attorney waits until her own case-in-chief and then proves the facts discrediting the testimony of the plaintiff's witness by a second witness or documentary evidence.[2]

---

[1]   See infra § 49.

[2]   See infra §§ 45 & 49.

There is a cardinal rule of impeachment. Never launch an attack implying that the witness has lied deliberately, unless the attack is provable and essential to your case. An unsuccessful attack often produces in the jury's mind an indignant sympathy for the witness. Unless you can convince the jury that you have "the goods" on the witness, an aggressive attack on the witness can easily backfire. The attack will be worse than ineffective; it will be counterproductive.

In general, today there is less emphasis on impeachment of witnesses than formerly. The courts now apply the elaborate, common law system of rules regulating impeachment less strictly. The system has been simplified by relying less on rules and more on judicial discretion.

§ 34   Prior Inconsistent Statement Impeachment: Degree of Inconsistency Required

As § 33 observed, the most widely used impeachment technique is proof that the witness made a pretrial statement inconsistent with her trial testimony. This observation is certainly true in civil actions where pretrial depositions are commonplace. In many jurisdictions, when the cross-examiner employs this impeachment technique, just before asking the witness about the statement the cross-examiner customarily says "Calling court's and counsel's attention to page _ line _ in (witness's name) deposition . . . ."[3] Sections 34 and 35 address the threshold question of whether there is sufficient inconsistency between the witness's trial testimony and a pretrial statement to allow the opponent to resort to this impeachment technique. Section 36 discusses the question of when the proof of the inconsistent statement is restricted to intrinsic impeachment, that is, cross-examination. Finally, assuming that the opponent is not confined to cross-examination, § 37 addresses the other conditions that the opponent must satisfy before presenting extrinsic evidence of the inconsistent statement.

Before turning to this impeachment technique, though, we must distinguish the technique from the related issue of the substantive use of prior inconsistent statements.[4] When a witness testifies to facts material in a case, the opponent may have available proof that the witness previously made statements inconsistent with his present testimony. Under a modern view of the hearsay rule, some or all such previous statements are exempt from the rule and consequently admissible as substantive evidence of the facts stated. After all, the primary purpose of the hearsay rule is to safeguard the opportunity for cross-examination; if the witness is on the stand, she can be cross-examined about her prior out-of-court statement as well as her courtroom testimony. This view is discussed in detail in the chapter concerning hearsay. However, under the more traditional views these previous statements are often inadmissible as evidence of what they assert because they constitute hearsay not within any exemption from or exception to the hearsay rule.[5] Even though the statements are inadmissible hearsay as evidence of the facts asserted, they are admissible for the limited purpose of impeaching the witness.[6] They may be admitted for that purpose with a limiting instruction under Federal Rule 105. The trial judge informs the jury that although they

---

[3]   Bodiford, Cross-Examination in a Nutshell 424 (2018).

[4]   See infra § 251.

[5]   See infra Ch. 24.

[6]   The use of unconstitutionally obtained evidence for purposes of impeachment is discussed in infra § 183.

may consider the statement for whatever light it sheds on the witness's credibility, they may not treat the statement as substantive evidence of the facts asserted in the statement. Subject to the exception that some prior inconsistent statements are exempt from the hearsay rule if they were made under oath subject to the penalty of perjury at a trial, hearing, or deposition, the Federal and Revised Uniform Rules of Evidence preserve this traditional view.

The treatment of inconsistent statements in this chapter is confined to the situation in which the statements are introduced for impeachment purposes but may not be used as substantive evidence (over the opponent's proper objection).[7] For this purpose, the previous statements may be drawn out in cross-examination of the witness himself; and at common law if on cross-examination the witness denied making the statement or failed to remember it,[8] the statement may later be proved by extrinsic evidence such as another witness's testimony. In contrast, under the Federal and Revised Uniform Rules of Evidence in limited circumstances the making of the statement may also be brought out by the second witness without prior inquiry during the cross-examination of the witness who made the statement.[9]

This form of impeachment is sometimes imprecisely called "self-contradiction." It must be distinguished from "specific contradiction" impeachment, the production of other evidence as to material facts conflicting with the testimony of the assailed witness. The production of other evidence conflicting with a witness's testimony is discussed in § 45. The characterization of the prior inconsistent statement as "self" contradiction is accurate only in the sense that the inconsistent statement must be attributable to the witness to be impeached. As we shall see, to be admissible, the prior statement need not flatly contradict the witness's trial testimony. The statement need be merely inconsistent with the testimony.

The attack by prior inconsistent statement is not based on the theory that the present testimony is false and the former statement true. Rather, the theory is that talking one way on the stand and another way previously is blowing hot and cold, raising a doubt as to both statements. Suppose that although at trial the witness testified that a car was going 70 miles an hour, pretrial she told the police that the car was going 50 miles an hour. The pretrial statement is relevant to the witness's credibility even if both that statement and the trial testimony are wrong. The fact *of* the inconsistent statement is relevant to the witness's credibility even when the fact asserted *in* the statement—the car's speed—is false. Even if in truth the car was going 60 miles an hour, the fact of the inconsistency gives the jury an insight into the witness's state of mind; the inconsistency shows that the witness is either uncertain or untruthful. In either event, the inconsistency calls into question the witness's believability. Assuming the statement is inadmissible as substantive evidence under the hearsay rule, the prior statement may be used in this context only as an aid in judging the credibility of the trial testimony inconsistent with the previous statement.[10] On request, under Federal Rule 105 the trial judge will give the jury a limiting instruction about the evidentiary status of the statement.

---

[7]   The use of prior inconsistent statements as substantive evidence is discussed in infra § 251.

[8]   See infra § 37.

[9]   See infra § 37. This discussion assumes that the matter is noncollateral, infra §§ 36 & 49.

[10]   See the discussion in infra Ch. 24.

The Required Degree of "Inconsistency"

On an appropriate objection, the judge must make a preliminary determination whether the pretrial statement is inconsistent with the witness's trial testimony. What degree of inconsistency between the witness's testimony and his previous statement is required to create a doubt about the witness's credibility? The language of some cases, suggesting that there must be a flat contradiction, is too restrictive. Under the better, more widely accepted view, any material variance between the testimony and the previous statement suffices. The pretrial statement need "only bend in a different direction" than the trial testimony. For instance, if the prior statement omits a material fact presently testified to and it would have been natural to mention that fact in the prior statement, the statement is sufficiently inconsistent. In the same vein, the impeachment can take the form of a witness's earlier statement disavowing knowledge of facts that he now testifies to. For that matter, some argue that there is sufficient inconsistency when the pretrial statement refers to a fact but at trial the witness claims to be unable to remember the fact. The test ought to be: Could the jury reasonably find that a witness who believed the truth of the facts testified to at trial would be unlikely to make a prior statement of this tenor?

The Federal and Uniform Rules of Evidence do not expressly prescribe a test for inconsistency. Under these statutory schemes, most courts apply the more liberal standards. Thus, if the previous statement is ambiguous and according to one meaning inconsistent with the testimony, it ought to be admitted. The jury can later decide which sense of the term the witness had in mind at the time of the statement. Reasonable judges can differ in applying the criterion of material inconsistency, and a fair range of discretion must be accorded the trial judge. Instead of restricting the use of prior statements by a mechanical test of inconsistency, in case of doubt the courts should lean toward receiving such statements to aid in evaluating the trial testimony. After all, the pretrial statements were made when memory was fresher and when there was less time for the play of bias. Thus, they are often more trustworthy than the testimony. A logical extension of this reasoning justifies the admission of prior testimony about an independent, unrelated event so strikingly similar to the present testimony as to raise a suspicion of fabrication. At the very least, the trier of fact may find such an extraordinary coincidence curious and consider the coincidence negatively in assessing the witness's credibility.

§ 35 Prior Inconsistent Statements: Opinion in Form

The question addressed in this section is a variation of the issue analyzed in § 34: What type of pretrial statement may be considered "inconsistent" with a witness's trial testimony? If a witness, such as an expert, testifies in terms of opinion, all courts permit impeachment by showing the witness's previous expression of an inconsistent opinion. However, courts have struggled with the question which arises when the witness testifies to specific facts but then is sought to be impeached by prior inconsistent expressions of opinion. For example, in a collision case the plaintiff's witness testifies to particular facts pointing to the conclusion that the bus driver involved in the accident was at fault. The defense proposes to show that just after seeing the collision, the witness said, "The bus was not to blame." The witness's pretrial, opinionated statement is inconsistent with the effect or impression created by the witness's trial testimony. Is that enough?

However, even before reaching the issue under Rule 613, we must confront the logically antecedent question: Should the opinion rule be invoked to exclude such an impeaching statement? The early, strict rule against opinions has been substantially relaxed in recent years.[11] Most courts appreciate that what was once supposed to be a fundamental difference in kind between fact and opinion is a mere difference in degree.[12] Wigmore contended that the opinion rule ought to go no farther than excluding an opinion as superfluous when the proponent can conveniently resort to more concrete statements.[13] Thus, at trial the principal value of the opinion rule is as a regulation requiring the examining counsel to bring out her facts by more specific questions if practicable, before introducing more general ones. It is often a mistake to apply the rule to out-of-court statements, since the out-of-court declarant might be unavailable and the proponent may not have the option to elicit the testimony in a more concrete form.[14] Moreover, when the out-of-court statement is not offered as evidence of the fact asserted but only to show the asserter's inconsistency, the essential purpose of the opinion rule, to improve the objectivity and hence reliability of testimonial assertions, is inapposite. Thus, the inconsistent opinion should be admitted for purposes of impeachment even if the proponent does not lay the normal opinion foundation discussed in Chapter 3. Concededly, many earlier American decisions, influenced perhaps by a passage in Greenleaf,[15] a casual English *nisi prius* holding[16], and some later opinions, routinely excluded impeaching statements in opinion form. However, the trend and the majority view are in accord with the common sense notion that if there is a substantial inconsistency, the form of the impeaching statement is immaterial. Federal and Revised Uniform Evidence Rule 701 lends support to that view by codifying a broad version of the opinion rule.

§ 36 Prior Inconsistent Statements: Extrinsic Evidence and Previous Statements as Substantive Evidence of the Facts Stated

Inadmissibility of Extrinsic Evidence of a Prior Inconsistent
Statement Related to a "Collateral" Matter

Assume that there is sufficient inconsistency between the witness's pretrial statement and trial testimony to permit the opposing attorney to resort to this impeachment technique. The next question that arises is whether the attorney will be restricted to cross-examination or "intrinsic" impeachment. The courts relax the strict rules of relevancy on cross-examination.[17] Generally in her discretion the trial judge may permit the cross-examiner to inquire about any previous statements inconsistent with assertions that the witness has testified to on direct or cross. At the cross-examination stage, there is no categorical rule that the previous impeaching statements must not deal with "collateral" matters; even if the matter has no relevance to the historical merits of the case, it can bear on the witness's credibility, and credibility is in issue on cross. But as the next paragraph notes, at common law when the cross-examiner inquires about inconsistent statements on "collateral" matters, the cross-examiner must "take the

---

[11]   See supra Ch. 3.

[12]   See supra §§ 11, 12.

[13]   7 Wigmore, Evidence § 1918 (Chadbourn rev. 1978).

[14]   See supra § 11.

[15]   Greenleaf, Evidence § 449 (3d ed. 1846).

[16]   Elton v. Larkins, 5 Car. & P. 385, 172 Eng. Rep. 1020 (1832).

[17]   See supra § 29.

answer"—she cannot later call other witnesses to prove the making of the alleged statement. This restriction, the collateral fact rule, evolved as a creature of case law, but some courts continue to enforce it under the Federal and Revised Uniform Rules of Evidence.

Extrinsic evidence of inconsistent statements, that is, the production of other witnesses' testimony about the statements, is restricted for obvious reasons of economy of time. The bromide, "You cannot contradict as to collateral matters," applies. Here the bromide means that to escape from the reach of the collateral fact rule, the subject of the statement must relate to the issues on the historical merits in the case. Although the Federal and Revised Uniform Rules of Evidence do not codify a categorical prohibition on the use of extrinsic evidence to impeach about collateral matters, the judge may factor the same policy considerations (for example, balancing probative worth against time consumption) into her analysis under Rule 403.

Distinguish the collateral fact rule from a distinct but somewhat cognate notion. According to that notion, if a party questions a witness about a fact which would be favorable to the examiner if true but receives a reply which has only a negative effect on examiner's case, the examiner may not introduce extrinsic evidence to prove that the witness earlier stated that the fact was true. An affirmative answer would be material and subject to impeachment by an inconsistent statement. However, a negative answer is not affirmatively damaging to the examiner; a negative answer is merely disappointing. According to this notion, a disappointing answer may not be impeached by extrinsic evidence; when the witness's only response is a negative answer, the opponent is limited to intrinsic impeachment on cross. In this situation the policy consideration is not saving time and preventing confusion, but rather the protection of the other party against the risk that the jury will misuse the statement as substantive proof in violation of the hearsay rule. With respect to the Federal and Revised Uniform Rules of Evidence view, see § 38. As a general proposition, modern courts do not recognize this technical distinction between damaging and disappointing answers. Rather, under Rule 403 the judge makes a pragmatic judgment as to the importance of the inconsistent statement impeachment.

As previously stated,[18] a witness's inconsistent statements are analyzed in this chapter primarily on the assumption that they are inadmissible as substantive evidence under the traditional hearsay rule still administered in numerous states and under the limited exemption in the Federal and Revised Uniform Rules of Evidence (1974) 801(d)(1). Of course, under that exemption or special hearsay exceptions in various jurisdictions, some inconsistent prior statements of a witness are admissible as substantive evidence as well as for impeachment purposes. More broadly, under another view adopted in a few jurisdictions, despite the hearsay rule all prior inconsistent statements of trial witnesses may be considered substantive evidence and consequently are not restricted to their use as impeachment. Section 251 discusses the latter view.

---

[18]　See supra § 34.

§ 37   Prior Inconsistent Statements: Requirement of Preliminary Questions on Cross-Examination as "Foundation" for Proof by Extrinsic Evidence

The Historical Origins of the Common Law Practice

Assume both that there is sufficient inconsistency between the witness's pretrial statement and trial testimony and that the collateral fact rule does not confine the counsel to intrinsic impeachment on cross-examination. Even on those assumptions, there may be further conditions that the counsel must satisfy before the judge will permit the introduction of extrinsic evidence of the inconsistent statement. To be specific, before presenting the extrinsic evidence, the counsel might have to: (1) lay a foundation during the witness's cross-examination; and (2) elicit the witness's denial of making the inconsistent statement. At common law, the genesis for these conditions was *Queen Caroline's Case.*

In 1820, in their answers in *Queen Caroline's Case,* the judges announced: "If it be intended to bring the credit of a witness into question by proof of anything he may have said or declared touching the cause, the witness is first asked, upon cross-examination, whether or not he has said or declared that which is intended to be proved."[19] The announcement crystallized a practice which had previously been occasional and discretionary. Later the practice was almost universally accepted in this country. The rule came to be applied to both written and oral inconsistent statements.[20] The purposes of this traditional requirement are: to avoid unfair surprise to the adversary; to save time, since an admission by the witness may make extrinsic proof unnecessary; and to give the witness a fair chance to explain the discrepancy.

To satisfy condition (1) of a foundational question, the cross-examiner asks the witness whether the witness made the alleged statement, giving its substance and naming the time, the place, and the person to whom made. The purpose of specifying these details is to refresh the witness's memory of the supposed statement by reminding the witness of the surrounding circumstances. According to condition (2), the witness's answer to the foundational question must necessitate the cross-examiner's resort to extrinsic evidence. If the witness denies making the statement or fails to admit it, for example by saying "I don't know" or "I don't remember," the element of necessity is satisfied. At the next stage of giving evidence, the cross-examiner may then prove the making of the alleged statement. When, however, the witness fully and unequivocally admits making the statement on cross, may the cross-examiner still choose to prove it again by another witness? Surprisingly, with some support, Wigmore suggests that the cross-examiner may. However, for the most part permitting cross-examination in these circumstances is a waste of time. Consequently, the prevailing view is to the contrary of Wigmore's suggestion, and in the usual situation this view is the wiser practice.

The Impact of Federal Rule of Evidence 613 on the Common Law

Under Federal and Revised Uniform Rule 613, the only express requirements for introducing a witness's prior inconsistent written or oral statements are that: (1) when the cross-examiner questions the witness concerning written statements or the substance of the statements, the statement must be shown or disclosed to the opposing

---

[19]   2 Brod. & Bing, 284, 313, 129 Eng. Rep. 976 (1820).

[20]   See supra § 28.

counsel on request; and (2) at some point in time—even after the introduction of the extrinsic evidence—the witness is afforded a chance to deny or explain the statement, and the opposing counsel has the opportunity to question the witness about the statement. Moreover, in her discretion the judge may dispense with the witness's opportunity to explain or deny later and the opposing counsel's opportunity to question later in the interests of "justice." For instance, suppose that despite the exercise of reasonable diligence the counsel did not discover the witness's inconsistent statement until after the witness was permanently excused from further testimony. In that situation, on balance it serves the interest of justice to permit counsel to introduce extrinsic evidence of the statement.

On their face, the Federal and Revised Uniform Rules of Evidence adopt a liberal view, abolishing the rigid notion that on cross-examination the witness must be shown an inconsistent statement or be advised of its contents before being questioned about its substance. Rule 613 goes even farther and abandons the traditional requirement that the foundational questions be put to the witness on cross-examination before extrinsic evidence of the statement is introduced, i.e., before other witnesses testify to it or before an inconsistent writing is introduced. As the Advisory Committee's Note to Federal Rule 613 indicates, "[t]he traditional insistence that the attention of the witness be directed to the statement on cross-examination is relaxed in favor of simply providing the witness an opportunity to explain and the opposite party an opportunity to examine on the statement, with no specification of any particular time or sequence." The Note approvingly cites California Evidence Code § 770. That statute expressly allows the counsel attacking the witness's credibility to offer extrinsic evidence of an inconsistent statement so long as the witness is excused subject to recall; excusing the witness in that manner obviates the need for any foundation during the witness's cross-examination. The opposing party can then later recall the witness to give the witness an opportunity to deny or explain away the statement.

The Advisory Committee's Note suggests that Rule 613 facilitates the questioning of collusive witnesses by permitting several such witnesses to be examined before disclosure of a joint prior inconsistent statement. Such joint inconsistent statements are rare. That rather infrequent benefit hardly justifies Rule 613's general dispensation with the requirement for a foundation on cross-examination. According to the Note, the rationale for Rule 613's general dispensation derives from two factors: (1) Rule 801(d)(1), as proposed by the Advisory Committee and the Supreme Court, gave substantive effect to all prior inconsistent statements, and (2) widespread attorney incompetence.

The Case for Granting the Trial Judge Discretion to Require a Foundation

To understand the policy rationale for the common law limitations on extrinsic evidence of inconsistent statements, one must keep in mind that if prior inconsistent statements are admissible only for purposes of impeachment, the traditional foundation requirement serves the useful function of helping confine the use of such statements to credibility and discouraging the trier of fact from misusing them as substantive evidence. The foundation requirement placed a prior pretrial statement in relatively immediate juxtaposition to the trial testimony of the witness sought to be impeached; in the same line of questioning, the cross-examiner mentions both the witness's statement on direct examination and the inconsistent pretrial statement. The juxtaposition makes it easier for the jurors to understand that they are to simply contrast the testimony and the statement for whatever insight that gives them into the witness's credibility. In addition, by giving the witness the opportunity to admit a prior statement, the foundation requirement reduces the likelihood that extrinsic evidence of the prior inconsistent statement will have to be introduced at all. Without a foundation on cross, it may be harder for the jury to avoid treating the extrinsic testimony as substantive evidence; when the extrinsic evidence is introduced later during the trial, there may be no mention of the direct testimony that the extrinsic evidence is theoretically being admitted to impeach. Furthermore, if the witness fully admits the prior statement during cross-examination, at least in her discretion the judge could bar the extrinsic evidence.

It is critical to remember that, under the proposed evidence rules as originally drafted by the Advisory Committee, all prior inconsistent statements were admissible as substantive evidence pursuant to Rule 801(d)(1). The proposed substantive admissibility of all prior statements would have rendered the function served by the foundation requirement obsolete. A more practical consideration then became paramount. Again according to the original Note, the practicality was that trial lawyers often forget to lay or never learned how to lay a proper foundation for the extrinsic evidence. The Advisory Committee politely referred to such forgetfulness or incompetence as "oversight." Positing wholesale substantive admissibility, though, these "oversight[s]" are less problematic. Even when the opponent does not lay a foundation on cross, the draft rule authorized the introduction of the inconsistent statement so long as the witness was eventually given an opportunity to deny or explain.

However, as finally enacted by Congress, Rule 801(d)(1) does not sanction the substantive admission of all prior inconsistent statements. Congress balked at embracing the Advisory Committee's radical position. Under the final versions of Rules 613 and 801, as at common law, some inconsistent statements are admissible only for the limited purpose of impeachment. Thus, the traditional foundation requirement can still serve the useful function of encouraging the jury to consider a prior inconsistent statement solely as to credibility and not as substantive evidence. Since all prior inconsistent statements are not substantively admissible, counsel should not have the unfettered right to introduce extrinsic evidence of the statement before the witness has an opportunity to admit, deny, or explain the declaration. When the extrinsic evidence of the prior statement is admitted without explicitly relating it to the witness's trial testimony and there is a significant time lapse between the witness's testimony and the later introduction of the extrinsic evidence about the inconsistent statement, the circumstances virtually invite the jury to treat the prior statement as substantive evidence.[21] Accordingly, a strong case can be constructed that under Rules 403 and 611, federal courts and state courts with an identical scheme should require the traditional foundation be laid on cross-examination before the introduction of extrinsic evidence of prior statements admissible solely to impeach unless the interests of justice require otherwise. Admittedly, as a matter of statutory interpretation, it is difficult to find in the text an invariable requirement that there be a foundation on cross-examination. However, several courts have held that under the statutes, they possess the discretion to mandate in light of the specific facts in a given case that the cross-examiner follow the traditional practice. It is especially justifiable to require a foundation if the judge anticipates a major time gap between the witness's cross-examination and the subsequent presentation of the extrinsic testimony; the more time that is likely to elapse,

---

[21]   Graham, Prior Inconsistent Statement Impeachment, Fed. R. Evid. 613(b): Current Practice and Proposed Changed Foundation Requirement, 54 Crim. L. Bull. 676 (2018).

the greater is the risk that the jurors will misuse the later testimony as substantive evidence. Some authorities assert that "most (though not all) of the [federal] circuits" which have passed on the question still adhere to "the traditional common law requirement" for a foundation on cross. Furthermore, most states still enforce the traditional requirement.

Miscellaneous Issues

Suppose that the person attacked is not on the stand but instead the testimony introduced was given at a deposition, prior trial, or some other hearing, and the person made an inconsistent statement before the hearing. At common law, most prior decisions applying the traditional requirements exclude the inconsistent statement unless the foundation question was asked at the prior hearing. In contrast, under the Federal and Revised Uniform Rule 613 the trial judge arguably has discretion to dispense with compliance with any general requirement that the opposing counsel have given the witness a previous opportunity for denial or explanation. Even when otherwise applicable, the traditional requirements ought to be abandoned in the case of depositions based on written interrogatories (which must be prepared in advance) and inconsistent statements made after the prior testimony was taken.

If a party takes the stand as a witness and the adversary desires to use the party's prior inconsistent statement, the statement is receivable on two theories—first as an opposing party's statement (formerly termed the admission of a party-opponent)[22] and second as an inconsistent statement to impeach the witness. On the first theory, the statement is relevant to the factual issues on the historical merits of the case; on the second theory, it is not. Yet, even in jurisdictions requiring traditional foundational questions for impeachment, the prevailing view is that the requirement for a foundation is inapplicable here. There is less danger of surprising a party than a witness. Furthermore, the party has an ample opportunity to deny or explain after the inconsistent statement is proved; as a litigant, the party can simply call himself as a witness later. In these jurisdictions, on occasion the courts inadvertently assume that the foundational requirement applies to the party-witness. Sometimes courts have imposed the requirement if the proponent offers the statement only for impeachment, and one appellate court held the trial judge has discretion to impose the requirement for a foundational question as prerequisite to introducing an opposing party's admission. These petty qualifications are hardly worthwhile. In jurisdictions which otherwise require the foundation question, the more sensible practice is entirely dispensing with the "foundation" for parties' admissions.

The bottom line is that Federal Rule of Evidence 613 and the Revised Uniform Rule 613 evidence of statements or admissions of the party-opponent, even if the admissions also have some incidental impact on the party's credibility as a witness. Nor do the rules have any impact on the introduction of a statement pursuant to a hearsay exception in Federal and Revised Uniform Rules 803 when the out-of-court declarant testifies. However, Federal and Revised Uniform Rule 613 applies when a prior inconsistent statement is admitted as substantive evidence solely by virtue of Federal and Revised Uniform Rule 801(d)(1)(A); the terms of Rule 801(d)(1)(A) render 613 applicable because they expressly refer to statements admitted as being "inconsistent with the declarant's [trial] testimony. . . ."

---

[22]　See infra Ch. 25.

Again in jurisdictions in which a foundational question is required but the cross-examiner overlooks it, the judge should have discretion to admit extrinsic evidence of the inconsistent statement based on such factors as the cross-examiner's ignorance of the inconsistent statement at the time when the witness was cross-examined, the importance of the testimony under attack, and the impracticability of recalling the witness. After weighing these factors, the judge can permit the impeachment without the foundation or allow a departure from the traditional time sequence if it seems fairer to do so.

§ 38 Prior Inconsistent Statements: Rule Against Impeaching One's Own Witness

The Common Law Voucher Rule

The case law voucher rule forbidding a party to impeach her own witness has an obscure origin. It is probably a late manifestation of the evolution of the common law trial procedure from an inquisitorial to an adversary or contentious system. The prohibition generally applied to all forms of impeachment. It applied not only to an attack by inconsistent statements but also to an attack on character or a showing of bias, interest, or corruption. However, the voucher rule never forbade the party from introducing other evidence specifically contradicting the facts testified to by her witness.

Several reasons (or rationalizations) have been advanced for the voucher rule: first, by calling the witness the party vouches for the witness's trustworthiness; and second, the power to impeach is the power to coerce the witness to testify as desired, under the implied threat of assassinating the witness's character. Both rationales are flawed. The answer to the first is that, except in a few instances such as character witnesses and experts, the party usually has little or no choice of witnesses. The party may have to call the persons who happen to have observed the particular events in controversy. For the most part, you take your percipient witnesses as you find them. The answers to the second reason are that: (a) it applies only to two kinds of impeachment, the attack on character and the showing of corruption; and (b) to forbid the attack by the calling party leaves that party at the mercy of the witness and the adversary. When the truth lies on the side of the calling party but the witness's character is bad, the adversary can attack the witness if the witness tells the truth. However, if the witness lies, the adversary will not attack; and, under the voucher rule, the calling party cannot impeach. The voucher rule should certainly not be carried to an absurd extreme; if the witness has been bribed to change his story, the calling party ought to be allowed to expose the bribe.

As previously stated,[23] the most frequently used kind of impeachment is by inconsistent statements. Most voucher cases involve this type of impeachment. It is difficult to see any justification for prohibiting proof of a prior inconsistent statement by a witness who has testified contrary to a previous statement. Perhaps there is a fear that the jurors will misuse the previous statement as substantive evidence of the facts asserted if, as in some jurisdictions, the use of the statement for that purpose would be inadmissible hearsay. However, at common law the voucher rule is not limited to prior inconsistent statement impeachment. Except in those jurisdictions which have altogether abandoned it, the common law rule against impeaching one's own witness also persists largely intact with respect to proof of bias and attacks upon character.

---

[23] See supra § 33.

The Early Reforms

By decision and statute, a number of jurisdictions relaxed the rule insofar as it prohibits impeachment by inconsistent statements. A provision in the draft of the 1849 Field Code of Civil Procedure bore fruit in the 1854 English Common Law Procedure Act (St. 17 & 18 Vict. c. 125, § 22), reading: "[1] A party producing a witness shall not be allowed to impeach his credit by general evidence of bad character; [2] but he may, in case the witness shall in the opinion of the judge prove adverse, [3] contradict him by other evidence, [4] or by leave of the judge prove that he has made at other times a statement inconsistent with his present testimony." A few states copied this statute. Other state legislatures, following the example of Massachusetts, adopted the English statute but omitted the statutory condition that the witness must have proved "adverse." Still other courts reached a similar result by decision.

These statutes and decisions open the door to the most important type of impeachment of one's own witness, namely, prior inconsistent statements. However, whether the reform was effected by statute or decision, at this point in the evolution of the voucher rule some courts imposed two troublesome limitations. One is that the party seeking to impeach must show that she is surprised at the witness's testimony. The second is that she cannot impeach unless the witness's testimony is positively harmful or adverse to her cause. The witness's testimony must be worse than a mere failure ("I do not remember" or "I do not know") to give expected favorable testimony. A simple, negative failure is merely disappointing, not damaging to her case in the sense that the testimony would positively aid the adversary.[24] These limitations are explicable only as attempts to safeguard the hearsay policy preventing the party from proving the witness's prior statement in situations where its only realistic value to the proponent is as substantive evidence of the facts asserted. The rule against substantive use of the prior inconsistent statements, and the debatable soundness of its rationale, are the subject of a subsequent section.[25]

Federal Rule of Evidence 607

More and more states have gone farther and altogether abandoned the voucher rule prohibiting the impeachment of one's own witness. Likewise, Federal Rule of Evidence 607 and Uniform Rule of Evidence 607 repeal the rule. Rule 607 permits resort to the standard methods of impeachment. Under Rule 607, there is no requirement that the proponent show that the witness's testimony was either surprising or positively harmful.

Yet, in some situations, several courts have refused to give Rule 607 a literal construction. In particular, there is some dispute whether and under what circumstances impeachment of one's own witness is impermissible because of prejudice to the opposing party, particularly in criminal cases. For instance, there is a sizeable body of precedent that a prosecutor may not employ a prior inconsistent statement to impeach a witness as a "mere subterfuge" or for the "*primary* purpose" of placing before the jury substantive evidence which is otherwise inadmissible. The application of the "mere subterfuge" or "*primary* purpose" doctrine focuses on the content of the witness's testimony as a whole. If the witness's testimony is useful to establish any fact of consequence significant in the litigation, the party may call the witness, elicit the witness's testimony to that fact, and impeach the witness on the other fact that the inconsistent statement relates to. In the

---

[24]   See supra § 36.

[25]   See infra § 251.

words of one commentator, the pivotal question is whether the "party [is] calling a witness with the reasonable expectation that the witness will testify something helpful to the party's case *aside from* the prior inconsistent statement."[26] Subject to that limitation, a rule excluding prior inconsistent statements of one's own witness can sometimes be a serious obstruction to the ascertainment of truth, even in criminal cases. In a given case with the right facts, a criminal defendant could plausibly contend that the application of the rule to prevent him from mounting a critical attack on a key defense witness is unconstitutional.[27]

§ 39 Bias and Partiality

Case law recognizes the powerful distorting effect on human testimony of the witness's emotions or feelings toward the parties or the witness's self-interest in the outcome of the case. Thus, the courts have long acknowledged that bias, or any acts, relationships, or motives reasonably likely to produce it, may be proved to impeach credibility. Indeed, the right to cross-examine to expose a prosecution witness's bias has a constitutional dimension. While Article VI of the Federal Rules of Evidence does not explicitly refer to attacking the witness by showing bias, interest, corruption, or coercion, the rules impliedly authorize the use of that ground of impeachment. The inclusion of Article VI in the Federal Rules reflects the drafters' realization that a witness's credibility is a fact of consequence under Rule 401; and Rule 402 states that evidence logically relevant to a fact of consequence is admissible unless there is a statutory basis for exclusion. In short, Rule 402 is the only statutory authorization needed for the continued use of the bias impeachment technique in federal practice. In any event, though, the cross-examiner must have a good faith basis in fact for the inquiry about the fact or event.[28]

The kinds and sources of partiality are too varied to list exhaustively, but a few of the common instances will be mentioned. *Favor* or friendly feeling *toward* a party may be evidenced by family or business relationship, employment by a party or the party's insurer, intimate or sexual relations, membership in the same organization, or the witness's conduct or expressions evincing such feeling. In auto collision cases, it is commonly held that when a witness appears for defendant, the fact that he earlier made a claim against the defendant and has already been paid a sum in settlement tends to show bias in defendant's favor.[29] Similarly, *hostility against* a party may be shown by the fact that the witness has had a fight or quarrel with him, has a lawsuit pending against him, has contributed to the defense, employed special counsel to aid in prosecuting the party, or has a racial bias against (or in favor of) members of the party's ethnic group. In criminal cases, the witness's attitude toward the victim sheds light on his feeling about the charge. A defense witness's bias may arise from the fact that the same district attorney's office recently prosecuted one of the witness's relatives. The witness's *self-interest* is evident when he is himself a party or a surety on the debt sued on. Similarly, it is relevant that he is being paid by a party to give evidence, even when, as in the case of an expert witness, a payment exceeding the regular witness fee is completely lawful. *Self-interest* may also be shown in a criminal case when the witness testifies for the state and an indictment is pending against him, the witness could be but

---

[26]   Saltzburg, Using Prior Statements, 24 Crim. Just., Spr. 2009, at 45, 48.

[27]   Chambers v. Mississippi, 410 U.S. 284 (1973).

[28]   See infra § 49.

[29]   See infra § 266.

has not yet been charged with a crime, has been promised leniency, has been granted immunity, is awaiting sentence, is in protective custody, or is an accomplice or co-indictee in the crime on trial. Self-interest in an extreme form may be manifest in the witness's *corrupt* activity such as seeking to bribe another witness, taking or offering to take a bribe to testify falsely, or making similar baseless charges on other occasions. As this wide array of cases suggests, the courts generally tend to permit the impeachment whenever the underlying facts "support a reasonable inference of bias that relates to a witness's credibility . . . ."[30] For example, cognitive research indicates that a forensic scientist conducting a test involving subjective judgment, such as fingerprint examination, can be biased by her exposure to prejudicial domain-irrelevant information, for example, a police officer's statement to the examiner that an eyewitness has already identified the source of one of the known prints. However, the trial judge has a great deal of discretion in deciding whether particular evidence indicates bias. The large majority of published appellate decisions approve the trial judge's discretionary ruling on this score.

Foundational Question on Cross-Examination

At common law, most courts impose the requirement of a foundational question on cross-examination as in the case of impeachment by prior inconsistent statements. Before the witness can be impeached by calling other witnesses to prove acts or declarations showing bias, the witness under attack must be asked about these facts during cross-examination. There is pre-Rules federal case authority to this effect. Fairness to the witness is most often cited as the reason for the requirement, but saving time by making extrinsic evidence unnecessary seems even more important. Analogizing to inconsistent statements, some courts distinguish between declarations and conduct evidencing partiality and require the preliminary question for the former but not for the latter. However, as a leading English case observed, words and conduct are usually intermingled in proof of partiality; and in applying this rule, the courts should avoid "nice and subtle distinctions." It is better to require a "foundation" as to both or neither. However, even jurisdictions imposing the general requirement ought to accord the judge discretion to dispense with a foundation in several fact situations: when matters of indisputable relationship, such as kinship, are concerned; where the foundation was overlooked and it is infeasible to recall the witness; or where other exceptional circumstances make it unfair to insist on the foundation.

At common law a minority of holdings do not require any foundational question on cross-examination of the principal witness as a condition precedent to the introduction of extrinsic evidence of partiality. The Federal and Uniform Rules are silent on the subject. The discretion granted the judge in Rule 611(a) is adequate authority to follow the same practice for partiality as that employed for prior inconsistent statements under Rule 613(b).[31] However, given Rule 402, the judge could not announce the practice as a categorical, invariable requirement. Rather, the judge should have the discretion to require a foundation if the specific facts of the instant case warrant. The case for imposing a foundational requirement here is weaker than in the case of prior inconsistent statement impeachment. In the latter setting, the requirement serves two purposes: saving time if the witness admits the inconsistent statement as well as reducing the risk that the jury will misuse the impeaching statement as substantive

---

[30]   United States v. Sigillito, 959 F.2d 913, 938 (8th Cir. 2014).

[31]   See supra § 37.

evidence. Here the foundational requirement serves only the first purpose. But the weaker the inference of bias from the fact and the more time-consuming the presentation of the extrinsic evidence is likely to be, the more sense it makes for the judge to exercise discretion to require a foundation on cross.

Assume that the judge exercises her discretion to require a foundation. On that assumption, following the traditional method for impeachment by a prior inconsistent statement, on cross-examination the witness under attack would first be asked about the acts or statements supposedly showing bias.

The Extent of the Inquiry on Cross-Examination and by Extrinsic Evidence

As we have seen, at common law in many states the impeacher must inquire about the facts of partiality on cross-examination as the first step in impeachment. If the witness fully admits the facts, the impeacher should not be allowed to prolong the attack by calling other witnesses to the admitted facts. At the very least, when the main circumstances from which the partiality proceeds have been proven, the trial judge has a discretion to determine how far the details may be probed, whether on cross-examination or by other witnesses. After all, impeachment is not relevant to the historical merits of the case. Although the trial judge may not deny a reasonable opportunity at either stage to prove the witness's bias, she has a discretion to control the extent of the proof. She has the responsibility to see that the sideshow does not take over the circus. Numerous cases decided under the Federal Rules of Evidence confirm the existence of this discretion. The discretion follows from the trial judge's power to "exercise reasonable control" under the terms of Rule 611(a).

At common law, if the witness on cross-examination denies or does not fully admit the facts claimed to show bias, the attacker has a legitimate need to prove those facts by extrinsic evidence. In courtroom parlance, facts showing bias are considered so highly probative of credibility that they are never deemed "collateral"; the cross-examiner is not required to "take the answer"[32] of the witness but may call other witnesses to prove them. There are similar holdings under the Federal Rules of Evidence.

§ 40 Character: In General

The witness's character for truthfulness or mendacity is relevant circumstantial evidence on the question of the truthfulness of the witness's testimony. The fact that the witness previously engaged in deception is some evidence that the witness has a character trait for untruthfulness, and in turn the existence of that character trait at least slightly increases the probability that the witness lied during his testimony. The topic of character impeachment raises several questions, notably: In any particular situation, when does the danger of unfair prejudice against the witness and the party calling her from this type of impeachment outweigh the probative value of the light shed on credibility? Should character-impeachment be limited to an attack on the particular trait of truthfulness, or should it extend to "general" character for its undoubted, albeit more remote, bearing on credibility?[33]

The growing tendency is to use this form of attack more sparingly. The empirical studies of untruthfulness indicate that a person's general character trait for truthfulness

---

[32]   See references to "taking the answer" in supra § 36 supra and infra §§ 45 & 49.

[33]   See the general discussion of relevancy and its counterweights in infra Ch. 16, and of the relevancy of character evidence in various other situations in infra Ch. 17.

is a poor predictor of whether she is untruthful on a specific occasion. It was part of the melodrama of the pioneer trial to find "the villain of the piece." In all of Perry Mason's trials, he established his client's innocence by unmasking the real culprit. That attack does not fit as well in the more realistic, businesslike atmosphere of the modern trial. Moreover, as a matter of advocacy, the danger to the attacker is great if the attack misses its mark or is pressed too far. The jurors naturally sympathize with the witness, and the attacker should not level this accusation unless she has "the goods" on the witness. In this situation, the attack can easily backfire, and the jurors may resent the attacker. Finally, the legal ethics rules reinforce the trial advocacy lesson; lawyers must be conscious of their duty not to ask a question that the lawyer realizes serves only to degrade a witness. For that matter, Federal Rule 611(a)(3) directs the trial judge to protect the witness from "undue embarrassment."

The following sections discuss three different types of character evidence: specific acts that have not resulted in a conviction (§ 41), convictions (§ 42), and reputation and opinion (§ 43).

§ 41 Character: Misconduct, for Which There Has Been No Criminal Conviction

The methods of proving a witness's character trait for untruthfulness include prior convictions and proof of untruthful acts which have not resulted in a conviction, the subject of this section. As we shall see, evidence of prior convictions is more liberally admissible than the latter type of proof of bad character for truthfulness. The differential treatment of the two types of evidence is justifiable. To begin with, when the witness has already been convicted of the act, there is strong evidence that the witness in fact committed the act calling his credibility into issue. Moreover, the availability of the written judgment of conviction reduces the risk that there will be a time-consuming, potentially distracting dispute over the question of whether the witness committed the act. In short, in terms of the policy considerations recognized in Federal Rule of Evidence 403, there is a much stronger case for permitting conviction impeachment.

The Split of Authority over the Propriety of This Impeachment Technique

Yet, the English common law tradition of "cross-examination as to credit" permits counsel to broadly inquire about the witness's associations and personal history including any misconduct tending to discredit his character, even though it has not been the subject of a conviction. In the common law tradition, the English courts trusted the bar's disciplined discretion to avoid abuse.

In this country, there is a confusing variety of decisions, occasionally even in the same jurisdiction. At present, however, the majority of courts limit the cross-examination attack on character to acts which have a significant relation to the witness's credibility. By its terms, Federal Rule 608(b) permits the cross-examiner to inquire only about acts which are relevant to the witness's "character [trait] for . . . untruthfulness. . . ." However, a minority of American courts allow a broader attack on character by wide-ranging cross-examination about acts of misconduct which show bad moral character and have only an attenuated relation to credibility. Finally, at the other extreme, a few jurisdictions altogether prohibit cross-examination as to acts of misconduct for impeachment purposes; the cross-examiner must have a conviction. This latter view has considerable merit given the dangers of prejudice (especially if the witness is a party), of distraction and confusion, of abuse by asking unfounded questions, and the difficulties, as demonstrated in the appellate cases, of determining whether particular acts relate to character for untruthfulness.

The dangers of victimizing witnesses and of undue prejudice to the parties have led most American courts permitting this character-impeachment technique to recognize that the trial judge has discretionary control over cross-examination concerning acts of misconduct. To emphasize the existence of that control, the former version of Rule 608(b) expressly used the phrase, "in the discretion of the court." Some of the factors that inform the exercise of the discretion are: (1) whether the witness's testimony is crucial or unimportant, (2) the relevancy of the act of misconduct to untruthfulness, (3) the nearness or remoteness of the misconduct to the time of trial, (4) whether the matter inquired into is likely to lead to time-consuming, distracting explanations on cross-examination or re-examination, and (5) whether there will be unfair humiliation of the witness and undue prejudice to the party who called the witness.

Safeguards Against Abuse

Assume that the jurisdiction in question recognizes this impeachment technique. Nevertheless, there are important safeguards intended to prevent the abuse of the technique.

To begin with, the cross-examiner may not pose the question unless she has a good faith basis in fact for the inquiry.[34] There is no invariable requirement that the cross-examiner demonstrate the good faith basis at sidebar before posing the question. However, if the direct examiner objects, the judge can require that the cross-examiner establish the basis before asking the question. The information furnishing the good faith basis need not be independently admissible evidence; but if the cross-examiner has no basis or a flimsy basis, the judge may bar the question.

Secondly, even if the cross-examiner has the right to ask the question, the witness may have a non-constitutional right to refuse to answer. In the formative period of evidence law, some courts recognized, as a sort of corollary of the privilege against self-incrimination, a witness's privilege not to answer questions calling for answers which would degrade or disgrace him when the questions were irrelevant to the historical merits in the case. Though sporadically recognized during the 1800s, today that privilege has been generally abandoned, except as it is preserved by the codes of a few states. Assume *arguendo* that the forum state still recognizes the privilege. Even in such a jurisdiction, although the privilege affords the witness some protection, the protection is not as effective as that afforded by a rule altogether prohibiting such cross-examination; the privilege must be claimed by the witness, and a claim in open court is almost as degrading as an affirmative answer. Taking an intermediate position, Federal and Uniform Rule of Evidence 611(a) gives the court discretion to prevent harassment or embarrassment of witnesses when they are cross-examined about acts of misconduct.

Another important safeguard against abuse is the constitutional privilege against self-incrimination.[35] The privilege may entitle the witness to refuse to answer the question. A witness who without objecting partially discloses incriminating matter cannot later invoke the privilege when she is asked to complete the disclosure. However, the mere act of testifying does not waive the privilege as to criminal activities relevant solely to attacking the witness's credibility. While an accused, unlike an ordinary

---

[34] See infra § 49.

[35] For more detailed information, see infra §§ 133–35.

witness, has an option whether to testify at all, exacting a waiver as the price of taking the stand is somewhat inconsistent with the right to testify in one's own behalf. Therefore, Federal Rule of Evidence and Revised Uniform Rule of Evidence 608(b) provides that the giving of testimony by any witness, including an accused, does not waive the privilege as to matters relating only to credibility.

The final safeguard is the accepted rule limiting the proof to intrinsic impeachment, that is, cross-examination. Thus, if the witness stands his ground and denies the alleged misconduct, the examiner must ordinarily "take his answer." That expression does not mean that the cross-examiner may not press further to extract an admission, for instance, by reminding the witness of the penalties for perjury. Rather, it means that the cross-examiner may not later call other witnesses to prove the discrediting acts. This limitation is incorporated in Federal Rule of Evidence 608(b). On cross-examination, the questioner should ask the witness directly and bluntly whether he committed the untruthful act. It is improper to inquire whether the witness was "fired," "disciplined," or "demoted" for the alleged act—those terms smuggle into the record implied hearsay statements by third parties who may lack personal knowledge.

However, there has been slippage from a broad, absolute prohibition of extrinsic evidence. For example, if the witness himself authored a writing mentioning the act, by the better view it is permissible for the cross-examiner to confront the witness with the writing. The principal rationale for the collateral fact rule is that the presentation of extrinsic evidence on collateral matters entails an undue consumption of trial time. However, when the witness is competent to authenticate the writing in question during cross, there is little expenditure of additional time. Thus, it does not serve the purpose of the rule to apply it in this situation. In these circumstances, some courts refuse to construe Rule 608(b) as forbidding the use of extrinsic documents during the witness's cross-examination.

Some jurisdictions have gone farther and allow extrinsic evidence of judicial and jury findings that the witness has given untruthful testimony. These courts believe that those types of findings are so reliable that extrinsic evidence of the findings should be admissible despite the seemingly absolute prohibition codified in Rule 608(b).

§ 42   Character: Conviction of Crime

At common law a person's conviction of treason, any felony, or a misdemeanor involving dishonesty or false statement (crimen falsi) or the obstruction of justice, rendered the convict completely incompetent as a witness. These were said to be "infamous" crimes. Thanks to statutes or rules virtually universal in the common law world, this primitive absolutism has been abandoned. The disqualification for conviction of crime has been repealed, and by specific provision or decision it has been reduced to a mere ground for impeaching credibility. Unfortunately, just as the common law definition of disqualifying crimes was not very precise, many of the repealing statutes and rules suffer from indefiniteness. In particular, the list of crimes for which a conviction is a ground of impeachment varies widely among the states that have not adopted Federal Rule of Evidence 609.

This section initially discusses the types of convictions which may be used for purposes of impeachment and the related question of the judge's discretion to bar the use of an otherwise admissible conviction. The section then takes up the topic of the mechanics of this impeachment technique, including the use of written copies of convictions and the extent to which the cross-examiner may elicit the details of the underlying criminal act.

The Types of Convictions Usable for Impeachment

A rule strictly limiting impeachment to conviction of crimes involving deceit or false statement would have the virtue that those crimes have an obvious connection to truthfulness. It would have the further virtue that it is fairly definite and simple for administrative purposes.

However, the federal statutory scheme is more complex. The Federal Rule governing impeachment by proof of conviction of crime is the product of compromise. Under Rule 609(a)(2), regardless of the imposable punishment, crimes of "dishonesty or false statement" may be used against any witness, including an accused. In contrast, Rule 609(a)(1) authorizes the use of felony-grade convictions for impeachment. The upshot is that misdemeanor-grade crimes (punishable by less than imprisonment in excess of one year) that do not involve dishonesty or false statement are never usable. Under Rule 609(a)(1), against an accused who takes the stand, felony-grade crimes (punishable by death or imprisonment in excess of one year) may be used, if the court determines that the probative value of the conviction outweighs its prejudicial effect to the accused. In civil cases or against all criminal witnesses other than the accused, 609(a)(1) convictions are usable unless under the normal Rule 403 standard the court determines that the probative value of the conviction is substantially outweighed by its prejudicial effect.

The Meaning of "Dishonesty or False Statement" in Rule 609(a)(2)

It is understandable that there has been a good deal of litigation over the interpretation of "dishonesty or false statement" in Rule 609(a)(2). Crimes involving "dishonesty or false statement" are sometimes said to be automatically admissible. That statement is true in the sense that crimes involving "dishonesty or false statement" are not subject to the normal Rule 403 balancing of probative value against prejudice under 609(a)(2). However, they can still arguably be excluded as remote in time under Rule 609(b).

Even if such convictions are not always admissible, it is still critical to determine the meaning of "dishonesty or false statement" in 609(a)(2). As a practical matter, if a conviction falls within that category, it is highly likely that the judge will admit it. The meaning of that expression has been much debated. The original Report of the Conference Committee stated:

> By the phrase "dishonesty and false statement" the Conference means crimes such as perjury or subornation of perjury, false statement, criminal fraud, embezzlement, or false pretense, or any other offense in the nature of *crimen falsi*, the commission of which involves some element of deceit, untruthfulness, or falsification bearing on the accused's propensity to testify truthfully.

Given the explicit language in the Conference Committee Report limiting the phrase "dishonesty or false statement" to offenses involving *crimen falsi*, even immediately after the enactment of the Federal Rules the courts should have ascribed little meaning to the term "dishonesty" with the possible exception of embezzlement. Yet, a controversy initially surfaced in reported decisions trying to determine whether the expression "dishonesty or false statement" applied to convictions involving petty larceny, robbery, shoplifting and narcotics. Despite the initial controversy, it quickly became the prevailing view that negatively crimes involving solely the use of force such as assault and battery, and crimes such as drunkenness and prostitution do not involve "dishonesty or false statement," while affirmatively the crime of fraud does. In 1990, when Rule 609 was amended, the Advisory Committee issued a new Note to the rule. The Note expressed disapproval of the minority of cases which read Rule 609(a)(2) broadly as including theft offenses.

Especially after the 1990 amendment, the published opinions display a willingness to follow the Conference Committee Report. Hence, the trend is to restrict "dishonesty or false statement" to a crime "which involves some element of deceit, untruthfulness, or falsification bearing on the accused's propensity to testify truthfully." A few other crimes have now been held to categorically meet this definition. However, federal courts and most state courts are unwilling to classify offenses such as petty larceny, receipt of stolen property, shoplifting, robbery, possession of a weapon, and narcotic violations as per se crimes of "dishonesty or false statement." Moreover, standing alone a post-offense attempt to evade detection or arrest does not convert the prior offense into a crime involving dishonesty or false statement.

Suppose, though, that by going beyond the face of the judgment, the party proffering a conviction not considered per se a crime of "dishonesty or false statement" can show that by going behind the face of the judgment, the particular offense was perpetrated by deceit, untruthfulness or falsification, i.e., involved some element of active misrepresentation. On that supposition, the prior conviction perhaps is logically relevant to impeach credibility. However, until recently many, if not most, jurisdictions did not permit the party to go beyond the judgment. As previously stated, the courts are receptive to this impeachment technique in part because the use of the written judgment reduces the risk of undue time consumption. If the parties were routinely allowed to go behind the judgment, the amount of time entailed by this technique could increase dramatically. To address this issue, the Evidence Rules Advisory Committee proposed amending Federal Rule 609(a)(2) to read: "evidence that any witness has been convicted of a crime shall be admitted, regardless of the punishment, if it readily can be determined that establishing the elements of the crime required proof or admission of an act of dishonesty or false statement by the witness." The Committee acknowledged that probing beyond the face of the judgment might consume some additional time, but the Committee believed that the amendment was circumscribed enough to prevent "a 'mini-trial.'" The amendment took effect in 2006. Restyled Rule 609(a)(2) incorporates the amendment. In its Note to the amendment, the Committee stated that it is appropriate to invoke the amendment when certain specific types of evidence enable the proponent to "readily" make the required showing without consuming an undue amount of trial time. More specifically, the Note explains that the amendment applies in situations in which "the proponent . . . offer[s] information such as an indictment, a statement of admitted facts, or jury instructions to show that the factfinder had to find, or the defendant had to admit, an act of dishonesty or false statement for the witness to have been convicted."

Assuming that the offense qualifies under 609(a), final convictions in any state or federal court are usable to impeach. The question sometimes arises, though, whether the testimony establishes a "final conviction." To begin with, what does "finality" denote? The trend is to hold that a conviction is sufficiently final as soon as the guilty verdict is entered even if sentence has not been imposed yet. The fact of the conviction establishes the witness's commission of the underlying act; and for that purpose, the verdict suffices even if the formal judgment on the verdict has not yet been entered. However, there is a split of authority over the admissibility of a guilty plea prior to the entry of judgment; there is an argument that the conviction is not yet final, since at that point there is still a possibility that the judge will permit the withdrawal of the plea. By the predominant view, including the Federal Rules of Evidence, the pendency of an appeal does not preclude the use of the conviction. The pending appeal does not deprive the trial court judgment of the requisite finality.

Of course, even before reaching the finality issue, the court must be persuaded that the evidence establishes a "conviction." Although a civil judgment against a lawyer of suspension or disbarment for criminal misconduct is not technically a conviction, there is authority that either is provable to impeach. Statutes relating to juvenile court proceedings frequently provide that a finding of delinquency shall not be used in evidence against the child in any other court and is not deemed a "conviction." These statutes are usually construed as precluding treating the juvenile court finding as an adult conviction for impeachment purposes. In various jurisdictions, as under the Federal Rules of Evidence, this matter is expressly dealt with by evidence rule or statute. Under such provisions, juvenile adjudications are admissible only in limited, defined circumstances.

Other Issues Relating to Whether a Conviction Qualifies Under Rule 609

There are several miscellaneous issues related to conviction impeachment. To begin with, the conviction must not only be final; it must also be constitutionally valid. A conviction cannot be used if it was obtained in violation of the defendant's right to counsel. In contrast, by case law, a pardon does not prevent the use of the conviction to impeach. The Federal Rules of Evidence adopt the same rule with limited exceptions under stated conditions. The primary condition is that under Rule 609(c)(2), a pardon bars the use of the conviction only if the pardon "or other equivalent procedure" was "based on a finding that the person has been rehabilitated" or "a finding of innocence."

Most courts hold that lapse of time may prevent use of a conviction too remote in time from trial when the judge in his discretion finds that under the circumstances it lacks sufficient probative value. The Federal Rule of Evidence is more specific; under Rule 609(b), convictions are presumptively remote and inadmissible when more than 10 years have elapsed. As previously stated, the wording of Rule 609(b) is broad enough to apply even to convictions involving dishonesty or false statement under Rule 609(a)(2).

Case authority is divided over the use of a judgment based on a plea of *nolo contendere*. The Federal Rule of Evidence should be interpreted as permitting the use of such a judgment. Other Federal Rules such as Rules 410 and 803(22) expressly refer to *nolo* pleas. Those references suggest that the drafters purposely omitted any reference to such pleas in Rule 609 and decided against excluding convictions resting on such pleas from the scope of Rule 609.

The Mechanics of Using a Conviction for Impeachment

Assume that the conviction in question is usable for impeachment purposes. What mechanical steps should the attorney follow to employ the conviction for that purpose? Of course, the attorney must establish that the witness is the person who suffered the proffered conviction. Federal Rule 104(b) governs that preliminary fact. The identity between the witness's name and the name stated on the judgment can support a permissive inference that the witness is the convict.

At common law, the general rule in other situations is that if feasible, proof of an official record must be made by a certified or examined copy rather than oral testimony about its contents. The English courts applied that rule to proof of records of conviction and precluded the cross-examiner from asking about convictions. This practice still persists in a few states. However, the inconvenience of the requirement, and the obvious reliability of the witness's answer acknowledging his own conviction, have led most jurisdictions to abandon that practice; by statute, rule, or decision, the vast majority of jurisdictions permit the proof by either production of the record or a copy, or the oral acknowledgment by the convicted witness himself. Hence, the cross-examiner need not "lay a foundation" by copy or record. Nor is she bound to "take the answer"; if the witness denies the conviction, she may prove it by introducing the record.

Sometimes the direct examiner elicits the testimony about the witness's conviction. It is a common tactic for the party who calls a witness with a provable criminal record to bring out the prior conviction on direct examination.[36] This practice is not genuine impeachment of a party's own witness. Rather, it is an anticipatory, preemptive disclosure designed to reduce the prejudicial effect of a revelation of the evidence for the first time on cross-examination. It is "a time-honored trial tactic" to attempt to beat the opposing attorney to the punch. When the witness's proponent discloses the impeaching fact on direct, the jury may have a higher regard for the proponent's candor; and the disclosure might take some of the sting out of the later cross-examination. Anticipatory disclosure is particularly common when the criminal defendant testifies on her own behalf. Section 55 of this treatise discusses the question of whether the direct examiner's mention of the evidence waives any objection that the direct examiner's client would otherwise have to the opponent's introduction of the conviction.

However, more often than not the initial mention of the conviction occurs on cross-examination. How far may the cross-examiner go in inquiring about convictions? There is consensus that at the very least, she may ask about the name of the crime committed, i.e. murder or embezzlement. The name is stated on the face of the copy of the judgment of conviction. Where the crime was aggravated, it would certainly add moral force to the impeachment if she could also ask about any lurid circumstances, for example, whether the murder victim was both a baby and the witness's own niece. A few courts have suggested that since proof by the trial record is allowable, cross-examination should be permitted to disclose all the facts mentioned in the record of trial. On balance, however, the more reasonable position restricts the cross-examiner to the basic facts reflected on the face of the judgment: the name of the crime, the time and place of conviction, and sometimes the punishment. That position minimizes the risks of prejudice and distraction from the central issues in the case. Further details such as the victim's name and the aggravating circumstances may not be inquired into unless the specific circumstance in question is independently admissible under another theory of logical relevance such as Rule 404(b) or 608(b).

It could be argued that if the impeacher is foreclosed from showing aggravating details, even-handedness dictates that the witness be precluded from explaining or extenuating the conviction or denying his guilt. It is unquestionably impractical and forbidden to retry the case on which the conviction was based. Many decisions completely prohibit any explanation, extenuation, or denial of guilt even by the witness himself on redirect. This prohibition is supposedly a logical consequence of the premise of finality

---

[36]   As to impeaching one's own witness, see infra § 38.

or conclusiveness of the judgment. However, that prohibition does not satisfy our feeling that the witness ought to have some opportunity for self-defense, if it can be done without too much distraction from the business at hand. Accordingly, while not opening the door to retry the conviction, numerous courts accord the witness the right to make a brief, general statement in explanation, mitigation, or denial of guilt, or grant the trial judge a discretion to permit it. Wigmore aptly terms it a "harmless charity to allow the witness to make such protestations on his own behalf as he may feel able to make with a due regard to the penalties of perjury."[37]

The most prejudicial impact of conviction impeachment (as is true also of cross-examination as to misconduct, see § 42, above) affects one particular type of witness, namely, the criminal accused who elects to take the stand. Suppose that the accused is forced to admit that he has a "record" of past convictions, particularly convictions for crimes similar to the one on trial. In this situation, despite any limiting instructions, there is an obvious danger of misuse of the evidence. The jurors might give more weight to the past convictions as evidence that the accused is the kind of person who would commit the crime charged or even that he ought to be imprisoned without much concern for present guilt, than to the convictions' legitimate bearing on credibility. The accused who has both a "record" and a meritorious defense to the present charge, thus faces a harsh dilemma. One horn of the dilemma is the realistic fear that if he stays off the stand, despite contrary judicial instructions his silence alone might prompt the jury to believe him guilty. The other horn is that if he elects to testify, his "record" becomes provable to impeach him, and this again could doom his defense.

Where does the proper balance lie? Most prosecutors argue forcefully that it is misleading to permit the accused to implicitly portray himself as having led a blameless life, and this argument has prevailed widely. One intermediate position, between routinely admitting all the convictions and excluding them all, is that the admissible convictions should be restricted to those bearing directly on character for truthfulness. Another intermediate view—but with the disadvantage of uncertainty—permits the introduction of the defendant's prior convictions in the judge's discretion. In each instance, the judge would have to balance the possible prejudice against the probative value of the conviction as to credibility. As already noted, Federal Rule 609 is a compromise. Rule 609 essentially embraces the latter intermediate view. However, even these intermediate views do not exhaust the possibilities. In Pennsylvania, under certain circumstances, the accused who takes the stand is shielded from cross-examination as to misconduct or conviction of crime offered to impeach but not from subsequent proof by the record of conviction. Finally, the former Uniform Rule provided that if the accused does not offer evidence supporting his own credibility, the prosecution may not, on cross-examination or otherwise, use his conviction for impeachment purposes. The very variety of proposed solutions indicates the vexing difficulty of the problem.

In view of that difficulty, the suggestion has been made that the "mere fact" method be employed for convictions punishable by death or imprisonment in excess of one year. The method is described as follows:

> [T]he proper procedural approach is simply to ask the witness the straightforward question as to whether he had ever been convicted of a crime. The inquiry must end at this point unless the witness denies that he has been

---

[37] 4 Wigmore, Evidence § 1117, at 251 (Chadbourn rev. 1972).

convicted. In the event of such denial the adverse party may then in the presentation of his side of the case produce and file in evidence the record of any such conviction. If the witness admits prior conviction of a crime, the inquiry by his adversary may not be pursued to the point of naming the crime for which he was convicted. If the witness so desires he may of his own volition state the nature of the crime and offer any relevant testimony that would eliminate any adverse implications; for example, the fact that he had in the meantime been fully pardoned or that the crime was a minor one and occurred many years before.[38]

The "mere fact" method of proving the accused's prior conviction is intended to reduce the prejudice to an accused who wants to testify at trial. Some commentators have gone farther and argued that this impeachment is so highly prejudicial that conviction impeachment of an accused should be forbidden. The suggestion has even been made that impeachment of the accused by showing prior convictions is unconstitutional. Under the Sixth Amendment the accused has a constitutional right to testify, and the admissibility of convictions for impeachment purposes pressures the accused to forego exercising that right. However, to date, no federal or state court has embraced the suggestion.

§ 43 Character: Impeachment by Proof of Opinion or Bad Reputation

This section deals with the last type of bad character evidence related to credibility.

The Form of the Testimony: Reputation or Opinion

In most jurisdictions the impeacher may attack a prior witness's character by posing the following formulaic questions to a second witness:

Q.   "Do you know William Witness's current general reputation for truth and veracity in the community in which he lives?"

A.   "Yes."

Q.   "What is that reputation?"

A.   "It is bad."

Q.   "Given that reputation, would you believe William Witness under oath?"

A.   "No."

This formula is the product of traditions which became established in a majority of American courts. The common law tradition is the result of several choices between alternative solutions. As we shall see, some of the traditional choices were wise, but others were misguided.

One misguided choice was the threshold view that this attack on character for truth must be limited to the abstract, debilitated form of proof of reputation. By what is apparently a misreading of legal history, at common law the American courts generally prohibited proof of character by having a witness describe his opinion of the prior witness's character even when the opinion is based on extensive personal experience with the witness under attack and observation of his conduct. The courts defended the limitation to reputation on the ground that admitting an opinion would provoke

---

[38]   McArthur v. Cook, 99 So.2d 565, 567 (Fla. 1957).

distracting side disputes about the impeached witness's specific conduct, since the impeaching witness could be cross-examined about the basis of his opinion. That danger undoubtedly exists, and the judge would need to confine the disputes to reasonable limits. However, the choice of reputation (instead of opinion based on observation) eliminated much of the objectivity from the attempt to appraise character, and it encouraged the parties to select character witnesses who, under the guise of reputation, voiced opinions based on prejudice and ill-will. As Dean McCormick wrote, the hand is that of Esau, but the voice is Jacob's. In addition, reputation in modern, impersonal urban centers is often evanescent or non-existent.

The Federal Rules of Evidence and the Revised Uniform Rules of Evidence break with tradition and permit attack by opinion, while at the same time continuing to authorize the traditional reputation attack. (At this point, note the interpretive argument that the Federal Rules seem to authorize the admission of expert opinion on the topic. Although Article VII of the Federal Rules expressly distinguishes between lay and expert opinion, Rule 608(a) refers generally to "opinion." The argument runs that if the drafters had wanted to limit Rule 609(a) opinions to lay testimony, the drafters would have said so. However, at the end of this section we shall see that many judges reject this argument.)

The Scope of the Testimony

—General Character or a Specific Character Trait

At common law, the courts faced a further choice. The choice related to the question of whether the inquiry should extend to "general character" and other specific bad traits such as sexual immorality, or whether it ought to be directed solely to the trait of veracity. In the realm of "character," it is best to insist on a high degree of relevancy. Fortunately, the great majority of courts strictly limit the inquiry to "reputation for truth and veracity." Under Federal and Revised Uniform Rule of Evidence 608(a) , both opinion and reputation are similarly restricted; the rule mentions solely "character for truthfulness or untruthfulness." Only a few jurisdictions open the door to reputation for "general character" or "general moral character." Fewer still permit proof of reputation for specific traits other than veracity.

—The Temporal Focus: The Time of Trial

As we shall see in Chapter 17, the common law and the Federal Rules allow an accused to introduce character evidence on the historical merits of the case; when the accused does so, the evidence must relate to the accused's character at the time of the alleged *actus reus*. However, in impeachment analysis the temporal focus is different. The crucial time when the witness's character influences her truth-telling is the time she testifies. But obviously reputation takes time to form and is the result of the witness's earlier conduct. Hence, the reputation does not reflect character precisely and only at the trial date. The practical solution is to do what most courts do, that is, (1) to permit the reputation-witness to testify about the impeachee's "present" reputation as of the time of the trial, and (2) to accept testimony about reputation as of any pretrial time period which the judge in her discretion finds is not too remote. Most courts follow this practice under Federal Rule of Evidence 608(a). Likewise, a witness's opinion permitted by the rule must have a similar temporal relation to the trial.

—The Basis for the Reputation (Community Membership)
or Opinion (Personal Acquaintance)

As to the place of reputation, the traditional inquiry is about general reputation for veracity "in the community where he (the witness to be impeached) lives." The purpose of this geographic limitation was to restrict evidence to reputation among the people who know the witness best. The residential limitation was appropriate for the living conditions in England (and to a degree in America) before the Industrial Revolution, when most people resided in small towns or rural villages. But as an exclusive limitation, it is inappropriate today. A person may be virtually anonymous in the suburb or city neighborhood where she lives, but well known in another locality where she works or several localities where she regularly does business. Thus, the courts now generally agree that proof may be made of the witness's reputation not only where she lives, but also in any substantial group of people among whom she is well known, such as the persons with whom she works, does business, or goes to school. Even a large jail population can qualify as a community. To give reputation testimony, the witness must be a member of such a "community," not a mere acquaintance of the witness being impeached. These standards apply under Federal Rule of Evidence 608(a). The rule gives the trial judge a measure of discretion to determine whether the group in question meets these standards and whether the witness has a sufficient nexus to the group. Was the witness a member of the group long enough to have gained a reliable sense of the person's reputation within the group?

Other problems arise when the attack on character is by opinion, as authorized by Federal Rule of Evidence 608(a). To begin with, the opinion must relate to the prior witness's character trait for untruthfulness, not the question of whether the witness's specific trial testimony was truthful. Moreover, a lay person's opinion should rest on some firsthand knowledge pursuant to Rule 602; the opinion ought to be based on rational perception and aid the jury, as required by Rule 701. The lay witness must be sufficiently familiar with the person to make it worthwhile to present the witness's opinion to the jury. However, specific untruthful acts cannot be elicited during the witness's direct examination even for the limited purpose of showing the basis of the opinion. An adequate preliminary showing to meet the requirements of Rule 701 consists of evidence of sufficient acquaintance with the witness to be impeached.

As previously stated, on its face, Rule 608(a) refers generically to "opinion" without distinguishing between lay and expert opinion. The generic reference suggests that expert opinion may also be admissible under Rule 608(a). However, many judges are unconvinced that there is such a thing as genuine psychiatric or psychological expertise on the topic of "truthfulness." "Truthfulness" is a lay notion, not an expert concept such as schizophrenia or bipolar disorder. These judges distinguish between opinion on that topic and expert testimony about specific mental and emotional conditions that are likely to affect a witness's testimonial qualities. Impeachment by expert opinion on the latter subject is considered in the next section.

§ 44 Defects of Capacity: Sensory or Mental

Assume that the witness has a sensory deficiency but not one which is so extreme that it renders the person incompetent as a witness under the standards discussed in Chapter 7. Any deficiency of the senses, such as deafness or color blindness, which would substantially lessen the ability to perceive the facts which the witness purports to have observed, ought to be provable to attack the witness's credibility.

As to the mental qualities of intelligence and memory, there is a distinction between attacks on competency[39] and attacks on credibility, the subject of this section. Sanity in a general sense is no longer a test of competency, and a so-called "insane" person is generally permitted to testify if she can report correctly the matters to which she testifies and understand the duty to speak the truth. Federal Rule of Evidence 601, applicable at least in federal question cases in federal court, precludes the trial judge from treating insane persons as automatically incompetent to testify. However, as we shall see in § 62, at common law a prospective witness could conceivably be treated as incompetent if in an extreme case she did not have the capacity to acquire personal knowledge, recall, or understand the duty to tell the truth. Much more commonly, though, in the judge's discretion both at common law and under the Federal Rules, the fact of mental "abnormality" at the time of either observing the facts or testifying can serve as a basis for impeachment on cross or by extrinsic evidence. (The use of expert opinion as extrinsic evidence in this situation is discussed in the last part of this section.)

What about mental deficits within the range of normality, such as a slower than average mind or a poorer than usual memory? A skilled questioner can sometimes expose these deficiencies in a testing cross-examination. May they be proved by other witnesses? The decisions are divided. It is eminently a question for the judge's discretion. The trial judge determines whether the relative importance of the testimony attacked and the insight gained into the witness's credibility outweigh the time consumption and potential distraction involved in opening this side-dispute. The development of standardized tests for intelligence and their widespread use in business, government and the armed forces, suggest that they may eventually serve as useful aids in evaluating courtroom testimony. However, that day has not yet arrived.

Alcohol and Substance Abuse

Abnormality is a horse of a different color. It is a standard ground of impeachment. One form of abnormality comes into play when a person is under the influence of drugs or alcohol. If the witness was under the influence at the time of the events which he testifies to or at the time he testifies, the witness's condition is provable to impeach on cross or by extrinsic evidence. The courts, though, treat habitual addiction differently. Standing alone, the mere fact of chronic alcoholism is ordinarily not provable on credibility. Apart from the minimal probative value of evidence of alcoholism, its admission arguably violates the general prohibition against using character as circumstantial proof of conduct; in the final analysis, the attorney is arguing that since the witness was intoxicated on previous occasions, it is more likely that the witness was intoxicated when he observed the relevant events—a variation of the simplistic argument, "He did it once, therefore he did it again."

Yet, when the abnormality is a drug addiction carrying even more social odium, some decisions routinely allow it to be shown, even without expert testimony that addiction to the particular drug has a long-term effect on some aspect of credibility such as perception or memory. However, more contemporary courts exclude it, absent a showing of a specific effect on the witness's veracity. Most federal cases concur with the majority view. The majority courts have the better of the argument. There is insufficient

---

[39] See infra § 62.

scientific consensus to warrant judicial notice that addiction in and of itself usually affects credibility. Worse still, the evidence is pregnant with prejudice.

Psychiatric Testimony

In recent decades with the progress of psychiatry, expert testimony about issues of sanity in cases of wills and crimes has become commonplace. The use of expert psychiatric testimony about mental disorders and defects is also a potential aid in determining a witness's credibility in any kind of litigation. In one specific type of litigation, namely sex offense prosecutions, Wigmore and several other commentators characterized this kind of testimony as indispensable; and in the distant past the courts routinely approved its admission.[40] Wigmore even generalized that women who testify they have been sexually attacked *often* report such matters falsely and that a judge should *always* be sure that the female victim's mental history is closely scrutinized by a mental health expert. Today we know that those generalizations are both chauvinist and inaccurate. Most courts now hold that the admission of psychiatric testimony is in the judge's discretion. More often than not judges exercise the discretion to exclude evidence of the witness's past psychiatric problems. Further, many appellate courts hold that a trial judge should exercise the power to order an examination to generate such testimony only for compelling reasons in exceptional circumstances. The criteria for identifying such circumstances are unclear; if compelled examinations are to be permitted at all, the courts ought to specify strict limiting conditions. Indeed, there is respectable state authority that judges have no inherent power to order a psychiatric examination with a view to possibly admitting testimony about the findings in rape trials.

Although the use of psychiatric testimony in sex offense cases has garnered the most attention, psychiatric testimony has been offered in other types of cases. A number of courts have taken the position that the use of expert psychiatric testimony to impeach a principal witness is not confined to sexual assault cases. However, as a general proposition the federal courts are disinclined to exercise their discretion to broadly permit attacks by experts on mental capacity. In the final analysis, though, when there is a solid ground for believing that a principal witness suffers from a severe mental abnormality affecting credibility, there may be a legitimate need to employ the resources of psychiatry. Many contemporary courts accept the principle that psychiatric evidence should be received, at least in the judge's discretion, whenever its probative value outweighs the cost in time, distraction, and expense.

The value of such evidence depends, *inter alia*, on the importance of the witness's testimony and the adequacy of the expert's opportunity to form a reliable opinion. This first factor, the importance of the testimony, is relevant to the justifiability of subjecting witnesses (even party-witnesses) to the ordeal of psychiatric attack. The second factor is the adequacy of the expert's opportunity to form a trustworthy opinion. An opinion based solely on a hypothetical question is virtually worthless. Only slightly more reliable is an opinion resting on the expert's observation of the subject's courtroom demeanor and testimony. The courtroom is not only a foreign environment for most witnesses; worse still, the prospect of testifying can create anxiety which distorts the witness's normal demeanor. Most psychiatrists agree that a reliable opinion can be formed only after the witness has been subjected to a thorough clinical examination. A few decisions have held that the trial judge has a discretionary power to order an examination of a prosecuting

---

[40]   *See* 3A Wigmore, Evidence §§ 924a, 924b & 934(a) (Chadbourn rev. 1970).

witness, but the conditions for exercising that discretion are unclear. Many of those decisions involve sexual assault prosecutions, but the decisions at least implicitly recognize a broader principle. If it exists at all, the discretionary power ought to extend to any type of case. The exercise of the discretion should be informed by such factors as whether undue expense or time consumption will result, whether the person is a key witness, and whether there are solid indications that the witness is suffering from mental abnormality at the time of trial or the relevant event. An expert opinion based on courtroom observation and reading the trial record ought to be admitted only as a last resort if the judge lacks the power to order an examination. Even then, permitting opinion based on such flimsy bases is dubious—so dubious that in a given case, the opinion might be vulnerable to an objection under Federal Rule 403.

The types of expert opinion relevant to credibility discussed in this section must be distinguished from the topic discussed in § 43, that is, opinion about the witness's character trait of "truthfulness." Rule 608(a) is not direct authority for the admission of the type of opinion testimony discussed in this section. As in the case of bias impeachment, Article VI does not contain any provision expressly regulating this type of testimony. As the preceding paragraphs demonstrate, in determining the admissibility of such testimony, rather than looking to Rule 608(a), the courts should rely on the general framework set out in Federal Rules 401–03.

§ 45 Impeachment by "Specific Contradiction"[41]

"Specific contradiction" may be explained as follows. In the course of testifying about an accident or crime, Witness One mentions that at the time she witnessed the event, the day was snowy and she was wearing a green sweater. Suppose that the statements about the snow and the sweater can be "disproved." Disproof can happen in several ways. Witness One on direct or cross-examination may later acknowledge that she was in error. Or, based on an official United States Weather Service report, the judge might take judicial notice that at the time and place—Tucson in July—it was not snowing. But often disproof or "contradiction" involves calling Witness Two to testify to the contrary that the day was sunny and warm. This is the sense in which the term "contradiction" is meant in this section.

What impeaching value does the contradiction have in the above situation? If Witness One is wrong and Witness Two right, it tends to show that Witness One has erred about or falsified certain facts, and therefore is capable of error or lying. That showing can be considered negatively in weighing other testimony by Witness One. But that insight has negligible probative value. After all, all human beings are fallible; and all testimony ought to be discounted to some extent for this weakness. It is true that the trial judge in her discretion may permit the cross-examiner to test the power of Witness One to observe, remember, and recount facts unrelated to the case to "explore" these capacities. However, to permit a prolonged dispute about such extraneous, "collateral" facts as the weather and the witness's clothing by allowing the attacker to call other witnesses to disprove them, is impractical. There are evident dangers of surprise, jury confusion, and waste of time.

To combat these dangers, at common law many courts enforced the restriction that a witness may not be impeached by producing extrinsic evidence of "collateral" facts

---

[41]   The extent to which evidence obtained in violation of a constitutional right may be used to impeach is treated in infra § 183. The use of treatises to impeach experts is dealt with in supra § 17 & infra § 321.

"contradicting" the first witness's assertions about those facts. Section 49 discusses the collateral fact rule in detail. A matter is deemed "collateral" if the matter itself is irrelevant to establish any fact of consequence in the litigation, i.e., irrelevant for a purpose other than mere contradiction of the prior witness's in-court testimony. When the collateral fact sought to be contradicted is elicited on cross-examination, this restriction is often expressed by saying that the answer is conclusive or that the cross-examiner must "take the answer." By the better view, if the "collateral" fact happens to have been drawn out on direct, the rule against extrinsic contradiction still applies. The danger of surprise is lessened, but the policy considerations of waste of time and confusion of issues are still present.

Article VI of the Federal Rules does not expressly mention specific contradiction as a permissible method of impeachment. However, the federal courts continue to permit resort to this technique. They are correct in doing so. As previously stated, the drafters' decision to include Article VI in the Federal Rules reflects their recognition that a witness's credibility is a fact of consequence under Rule 401. The Supreme Court's reasoning in *United States v. Abel*[42] is apposite. As in the case of specific contradiction, Article VI is silent on the bias impeachment technique. However, the *Abel* Court noted that bias is logically relevant to a witness's credibility; and consequently, Rule 402 is sufficient statutory authorization for the continuation of the practice of bias impeachment. Like bias, specific contradiction is relevant to impeach a prior witness's credibility and, by parity of reasoning, permissible in federal practice. Although the Rules do not expressly limit specific contradiction on collateral matters, some federal courts continue to apply the common law restriction. To be sure, the judge may exercise her discretion under Rule 403 to limit specific contradiction impeachment; but when it is logically relevant, specific contradiction evidence is presumptively admissible under Rule 402. For that matter, the amended version of Rule 408 refers to "impeach[ment] by . . . contradiction."

§ 46 Beliefs Concerning Religion

As § 63 indicates, the early common law competency rules required that the prospective witness believe in a God who would punish untruth as a qualification for taking the witness's oath. This requirement arose in a religious climate which has weakened with the passage of time. Most common law jurisdictions have abandoned the requirement. Many jurisdictions have general provisions such as that in the Illinois constitution to the effect that "no person shall be denied any civil or political rights, privilege or capacity on account of his religious opinions." The courts have construed these provisions as abrogating the rule of incompetency to take the oath. Nor is belief in God required by the Federal Rules of Evidence.

As indicated in §§ 43 and 65, the overall trend has been to convert the old grounds of testimonial incompetency, such as interest and infamy, into bases for impeaching credibility. This general principle of conversion has sometimes been expressly enacted in constitutional provisions and statutes. But should the same principle be applied to permit a witness's credibility to be attacked by showing that she is an atheist or agnostic and does not believe in divine punishment for perjury? Most courts that have addressed the question have concluded no; they reached that conclusion by interpreting either general provisions such as that in the Illinois constitution, or more specific

---

[42]   469 U.S. 45 (1984).

constitutional, statutory, or rule language. Thus, many states recognize a witness's privilege not to be examined about her own religious faith or beliefs, except so far as the judge finds that the relevance of the inquiry to some fact of consequence in the case outweighs the interest of privacy and the danger of prejudice. A few old cases, either reasoning from the conversion of grounds of incompetency into bases for impeachment or following the peculiar language of a specific statutory provision, seemingly allowed this ground of impeachment. However, those cases are badly dated and have little modern precedential value. Even under the old cases, courts would not permit inquiry about particular creeds, faiths, or affiliations except as they shed light on the witness's belief in a God who will punish untruthfulness.

There is a strong argument that, in addition to recognizing a witness's privilege not to answer questions about her own religious beliefs, the legislatures and courts should forbid the party to impeach by bringing other witnesses to attack the first witness's faith. Today, there is an insufficient basis for believing that the lack of faith in God's avenging wrath is an indication of greater than average untruthfulness. Without that basis, the evidence of atheism is irrelevant to the question of credibility.

Federal Rule of Evidence 610 provides: "Evidence of a witness's religious beliefs or opinions is not admissible to attack or support the witness's credibility." A juror might wrongfully discount the credibility of the member of an unconventional or unusual religion. Rule 610 guards against that type of prejudice. However, the prohibition is not complete. In some cases, evidence of the witness's religion will be admissible on an alternative theory of logical relevance. For example, the Advisory Committee's Note to Rule 610 adds that "disclosure of affiliation with a church which is a party to the litigation would be allowable under the rule," since it could bear on the witness's bias.

§ 47 Supporting the Witness

As § 33 noted, there are three stages in credibility analysis: bolstering before attempted impeachment, impeachment, and rehabilitation after attempted impeachment. Impeachment is not a dispassionate study of the witness's capacities and character, but rather an *attack* on his credibility. Under our adversary trial system, the witness's proponent must be given an opportunity to meet this attack by presenting evidence rehabilitating the witness. As we have seen, one general principle, recognized under both case law and the Federal Rules of Evidence, is that absent an attack on the witness's credibility, no bolstering evidence is allowed. Conversely, after the witness's opponent has introduced evidence of impeaching facts, the witness's proponent may present contradictory evidence disproving the allegedly impeaching facts. Such disproof is relevant and generally allowable.

The General Ban on Bolstering

As just stated, absent the introduction of impeaching facts, the witness's proponent ordinarily may not bolster the witness's credibility. The rationale is that we do not want to devote court time to the witness's credibility and run the risk of distracting the jury from the historical merits unless and until the opposing attorney attacks the witness's credibility.

Admittedly, there are exceptions to this general norm. For instance, the fact of a complaint or outcry of rape and in some instances certain details of the complaint have been held admissible. If a person has been raped, the person will normally make a complaint about the incident. Both the fact of complaint and, where allowed, the details of the complaint may be admissible on the theory of bolstering the complaining witness. However, since this evidence may sometimes come in as substantive evidence under some theories, the matter is dealt with at length later. Likewise, prior consistent statements of identification can be admissible substantively or to bolster. If the declarant later appears as a witness and during direct examination identifies a person, it is permissible to elicit the witness's testimony that she previously identified the same person—even before cross-examination and any opportunity for impeachment. However, precisely because prior identifications may be introduced as substantive evidence and trigger constitutional requirements, that subject is also discussed elsewhere. With the exception of fresh complaints and prior identifications, the witness's proponent may proffer evidence of the witness's truthfulness as rehabilitation only after attempted impeachment.

Corroboration

Suppose that the witness completes her testimony about fact *A* and that the opposing attorney does not attempt any impeachment. Absent attempted impeachment, the witness's proponent cannot offer later testimony for the purpose of rehabilitating the witness's credibility. Thus, the proponent could not call witness #2 to testify that witness #1 has a reputation as a truthful person. However, the proponent may call witness #2 to give additional testimony about fact *A*. On its face, that testimony is relevant to the historical merits rather than witness #1's credibility. This type of testimony is classified as corroborating rather than rehabilitating. Under Federal Rule of Evidence 403, the trial judge has discretion to limit the amount of corroborating testimony about fact *A*, but such testimony is not subject to the special limitations on either bolstering or rehabilitation. At trial, many elements of a litigant's theory of the case are likely to be formally or virtually undisputed. On those elements, the litigant can be content to present enough evidence to barely satisfy the initial burden of going forward. However, on the key elements that are sharply controverted, the litigant must present ample corroboration.

Rehabilitation

While corroborating testimony is relevant to the historical merits, rehabilitating testimony relates to the credibility of a witness who has been impeached. A discussion of rehabilitation is best organized around the techniques employed. The two most common rehabilitative methods are: (1) introduction of supportive evidence of good character of the witness attacked, and (2) proof of the witness's consistent statements. The basic question is whether these two types of rehabilitation evidence represent a proper response to the specific methods of impeachment that have been used. The general test of admissibility is whether evidence of the witness's good character or consistent statements is logically relevant to explain the impeaching fact. The rehabilitating facts must meet the impeachment with relative directness. The wall, attacked at one point, may not be fortified at another, distinct point. Credibility is a side issue, and judges should draw the circle of relevancy tightly in this context. When we reach the stage of rehabilitation after impeachment, we are rather far afield from the historical merits of the case; and the courts justifiably insist on a stronger showing of relevance to minimize the risk that the jury will lose sight of the merits. As a rule of thumb, the courts demand that the rehabilitation be a response in kind to the impeachment. Precisely how responsive is a question of degree as to which reasonable courts differ.

———

Proof of the Witness's Character Trait for Truthfulness

When may the party supporting the impeached witness offer evidence of the witness's good character for truthfulness? Certainly attacks by evidence of bad reputation, bad opinion of character for truthfulness, conviction of crime, or misconduct which has not resulted in conviction, all open the door to character support. In the words of the Advisory Committee's Note to Rule 608,

> Opinion or reputation that the witness is untruthful specifically qualifies as an attack, and evidence of misconduct, including conviction of crime, and of corruption also fall within this category. Evidence of bias or interest does not. Whether evidence in the form of contradiction is an attack upon the character of the witness must depend upon the circumstances.

The evidence of good character for truth is a logically relevant, direct response in kind to all these modes of impeachment. Moreover, a slashing cross-examination can carry strong accusations of misconduct and bad character, which even the witness's forceful denial will not remove from the jury's mind. If the judge considers that fairness requires it, she may admit evidence of good character as a palliative for the insinuation of an accusatory cross-examination.

Proof of a witness's corrupt conduct showing bias should also be regarded as an attack on veracity-character and thus warrant character support. However, impeachment for bias or interest by facts not involving corruption, such as proof of family relationship, does not open the door to proof of good character for truthfulness.

The courts divide over the propriety of supporting the witness by showing his good character for truthfulness when the witness has been impeached only by evidence of an inconsistent statement or evidence specifically contradicting the facts to which the witness testified. If the witness has been impeached by an inconsistent statement, in the past perhaps the numerical majority of courts routinely permitted a showing of his good character for truthfulness. However, if the adversary has merely introduced evidence contradicting the facts to which the witness testified, most cases forbade a showing of the witness's good character for truthfulness. Convenient as hard-and-fast answers to these questions may be, it is unsound to resolve those questions in a mechanical fashion. A more sensible view is that in each case the judge should consider whether a particular impeachment for inconsistency or a conflict in testimony amounts in effect to an attack on the witness's character trait for truthfulness. In many fact situations, it is more realistic to view the impeachment as a limited attack on the veracity of the specific testimony the witness has given in the instant case, rather than a broader assault on the witness's truthfulness. One relevant consideration is whether the inconsistency or contradiction relates to a matter on which the witness could be innocently mistaken. Is the inconsistency or contradiction so flat that the irresistible common sense inference is a lie rather than an innocent mistake? Even a witness with a stellar character for truthfulness can commit a mistake. Another pertinent consideration is the number of inconsistencies mentioned by the cross-examiner. The larger the number, the stronger is the inference that by character the witness is a liar, not simply a witness who has told an isolated lie. Under the Federal Rules of Evidence, the trial judge may arguably consider the factor of the number of inconsistencies in deciding whether to permit the rehabilitation.

Proof of the Witness's Prior Consistent Statements

Turning to attempts to rehabilitate an attacked witness by introducing a prior statement consistent present testimony, a similar threshold question arises: What kinds of attack on the witness open the door to evidence of the witness's prior statements consistent with his present testimony? When the attack takes the form of character impeachment by showing misconduct, convictions, or bad reputation, there is no justification for rehabilitating by consistent statements. The rehabilitation does not meet the attack and fails the response-in-kind rule of thumb. As we shall now see, there are additional restrictions on the introduction of prior consistent statements for rehabilitative purposes.

Prior consistent statements satisfying the temporal priority doctrine. At common law under the prevailing temporal priority doctrine, if the attacker has charged bias, interest, corrupt influence, contrivance to falsify, or want of capacity to observe or remember, the prior consistent statement is deemed irrelevant to refute the charge unless the consistent statement was made *before* the source of the bias, interest, influence or incapacity originated. If the statement was made later, proof of the statement does not assist the jury to evaluate the witness's testimony because the reliability of the consistent statement is subject to the same doubt as the trial testimony. After the enactment of the Federal Rules many courts continued to enforce the temporal priority doctrine under the Federal Rules; but there was a large body of contra authority. In 1995 in *Tome v. United States*,[43] the Supreme Court held that Rule 801(d)(1)(B), governing the admission of consistent statements as substantive evidence, incorporates the temporal priority doctrine. *Tome* thus construed the original version of the rule as codifying a temporal priority requirement. Although the Court disclaimed ruling on the question of whether the doctrine applies when the consistent statement under "any other evidentiary principle" such as rehabilitation, some commentators read *Tome* as a signal that the Court would eventually extend the same limitation to consistent statements proffered for the limited purpose of rehabilitation.

Other prior consistent statements. Post *Tome* a prior consistent statement could be admitted as credibility evidence if there was a charge such as bias and the statement antedated the source of the bias or other improper influence; if the statement passed muster as substantive evidence under *Tome,* it could certainly be used for the more limited purpose of impeachment. After *Tome,* the real question was whether a prior consistent statement could be admitted as rehabilitation only if the statement satisfied the temporal priority doctrine. In 2014 Rule 801(d)(1)(B) was amended to add a new provision. That provision, (ii), permits the admission of consistent statements as substantive evidence if the statements are relevant "to rehabilitate the declarant's credibility when attacked on another ground." The Advisory Committee's Note accompanying the amendment states that "[t]he intent of the amendment is to extend substantive effect to consistent statements that rebut other attacks on a witness—such as the charges of inconsistency or faulty memory." Since (ii) is distinct from the provision

---

[43]   513 U.S. 150 (1995).

incorporating *Tome*'s temporal priority restriction, the courts should not apply that restriction to later consistent statements that are otherwise relevant for rehabilitative purposes.

The pivotal, remaining question is whether a particular prior consistent statement that does not satisfy the temporal priority rule nevertheless possesses legitimate probative worth on a rehabilitation theory. There is a division of opinion over the question whether impeachment by inconsistent statements opens the door to rehabilitation by proving consistent statements. A few courts usually rule that this type of support is permissible. This holding has the merit of easy application. At the polar extreme, some courts generally hold that impeachment by prior inconsistent statement does not permit rehabilitation by prior consistent statement. The rationale for this holding is that despite the consistent statement, the inconsistency remains; now the inconsistent statement is simply at odds with the consistent statement as well as the trial testimony. That general holding seems preferable, but certain qualifications should be recognized. The most important qualification is that when the attacked witness denies making the inconsistent statement, evidence of consistent statements very near the time of the alleged inconsistent one is relevant to corroborate his denial. Again, the Advisory Committee's Note accompanying the 2014 amendment to Rule 801(d)(1)(B) expressly refers to the use of prior consistent statements for rehabilitation after a "charge[ ] of inconsistency . . . ."

Moreover, on the particular facts of the specific case, an attack by inconsistent statement might be accompanied by or interpretable as a charge of a recent plan or contrivance to give false testimony. If so, given the right timing, the consistent statement would be admissible as rehabilitation under the temporal priority doctrine. Proof of a consistent statement antedating the plan or contrivance tends to disprove that the testimony was the result of contrivance; the testimony could not be the product of the alleged contrivance because the witness said the same thing before the supposed contrivance. Here all courts concur. It is up to the judge to decide whether the impeachment at least implies a charge of contrivance. Most courts agree that there has been an express charge if the cross-examiner asks the witness to admit that he "didn't come up with this story" until the witness spoke with an attorney or party. However, if there is no such charge, the attack often amounts to nothing more than an imputation of inaccurate memory. If so, as the prior paragraph noted, only consistent statements made when the event was recent and the witness's memory fresh should be admitted for rehabilitation. Recognition of these qualifications still allows the courts to exclude many statements procured after the inconsistent statement, and thus to discourage attorneys from harassing witnesses and pressuring them to furnish counter-statements.

These principles can be recognized consistently with the text of the Federal Rules of Evidence. As the Advisory Committee's Note to the 2014 amendment to Rule 801(d)(1)(B) reflects, the common law temporal priority doctrine does not apply to all consistent statements offered for the limited purpose of rehabilitation in federal practice. The judge has discretion under the framework codified in Rules 401 and 403 to determine whether the particular circumstances justify admission of consistent statements to rehabilitate the witness. Suppose, for instance, that the cross-examiner forced the witness to concede that the witness had made a seemingly inconsistent statement. To rehabilitate the witness, it would be logically relevant to elicit the witness's description of other out-of-statements in which she used a key term in a peculiar sense which eliminated the seeming inconsistency. The other statements could conceivably be relevant on that theory even if they were made after the apparently inconsistent statement. By virtue of the 2014 amendment to Rule 801(d)(1)(B), if the other statements are admissible as rehabilitation, they may also be used as substantive evidence.

However, the caveat is that the pre-2014 version of Rule 801 is still in effect in many states. In those jurisdictions, the statements might be admissible only for the limited purpose of rehabilitation and not as substantive evidence under Rule 801. When the proponent offers the evidence in this manner, on request under Rule 105 the trial judge would give the jury a limiting instruction about the proper use of the evidence.

Even when part of a witness's prior statement is logically relevant to the witness's rehabilitation, only that part of the witness's earlier overall narrative is admissible for that purpose. The witness's proponent does not have carte blanche to introduce the entire narrative simply because one passage has legitimate evidentiary value as rehabilitation.

§ 48　Attacking the Supporting Character Witness

As § 41 explained, Rule 608(b)(1) permits the cross-examiner to impeach a witness by forcing the witness to admit that she had committed an untruthful act, even if the act has not resulted in a conviction. Rule 608(b)(2) also deals with impeachment, but now the target of the impeachment is different.

Under Fed. R. Evid. 608(b)(2) and Uniform Rule 608(b)(ii)[44] and at common law, a character witness who has testified to her favorable opinion or the good reputation of another witness ("principal witness") for truthfulness and veracity can be cross-examined about the principal witness's specific prior acts that are probative of untruthfulness. The courts usually deem specific instances of conduct involving dishonesty or false statement sufficiently probative of untruthfulness;[45] such specific acts are fair game on cross-examination even if they have not resulted in a conviction.[46] However, extrinsic evidence of the specific instances of the principal witness's conduct not resulting in a conviction is inadmissible; the cross-examiner must take the character witness's answer.[47] The Advisory Committee's Note accompanying the 2003 amendment to Rule 608 states that "the absolute prohibition on extrinsic evidence applies . . . when the sole reason for proffering that evidence is to attack the witness' character for truthfulness." In this line of inquiry, the only legitimate relevance of the answers is to impeach the character witness's credibility.

To be sure, whether the character witness gives reputation or opinion testimony, the opponent may probe the basis of the witness's testimony. Thus, a character witness testifying about the principal witness's reputation for truthfulness may be cross-

---

[44]　Former Fed. R. Evid. 608(b) provided:

Specific instances of the conduct of a witness, for the purpose of attacking or supporting the witness' credibility, other than conviction of crime as provided in rule 609, may not be proved by extrinsic evidence. They may, however, in the discretion of the court, if probative of truthfulness or untruthfulness, be inquired into on cross-examination of the witness (1) concerning the witness' character for truthfulness or untruthfulness or (2) concerning the character for truthfulness or untruthfulness of another witness as to which the character the witness being cross-examined has testified.

Uniform Rule of Evidence 608(b) is identical in content.

[45]　See supra § 42 with respect to the admissibility of prior convictions to impeach.

[46]　See supra § 41.

[47]　See also infra § 49.

examined concerning with whom, where, and when the witness has discussed the principal witness's reputation. Opinion testimony must be based on the character witness's personal knowledge of the principal witness; and consequently, the extent of her relationship with the principal witness is a proper subject of inquiry on cross-examination. Moreover, as the next paragraph explains, the cross-examiner may go farther and ask about specific inconsistent acts by the principal witness.

When a character witness testifies on direct as to the principal witness's reputation for truthfulness, at the common law the traditional phasing of the cross-examination question about specific instances of the principal witness's untruthful conduct is "Have you heard?" In contrast, where the direct testimony of the character witness takes the form of an opinion, according to the common law the proper form of the question is either "Do you know?" or "Are you aware?" While correct in theory, the distinction is of such slight practical importance that it could easily be eliminated at common law. For their part, the Federal Rules do precisely that and abandon the distinction.[48] The character witness may be asked directly not only about the principal witness's specific acts probative of untruthfulness, but also about her familiarity with the principal witness's convictions, arrests, and indictments. All these matters have a natural bearing on the principal witness's reputation and the character witness's opinion of the principal witness. They are disreputable acts, inconsistent with the good reputation for truthfulness which the character witness has vouched for. Lack of familiarity with such matters is relevant to an assessment of the basis for the character witness's testimony. If the witness answers that she is unfamiliar with these matters, the witness's answer impeaches the extent of the witness's knowledge of the principal witness's character. Alternatively, familiarity with the matters impeaches the character witness's standard of "truthfulness" or "untruthfulness" or suggests the witness's bias; if the witness answers that she is familiar with the unfavorable fact and yet vouches for the principal witness's good character, the character witness is either lying or using a rather strange standard for evaluating good character.

Whatever the form of the question, the cross-examiner must have a good faith basis in fact supporting the inquiry. If the opposing attorney objects and at sidebar the cross-examiner cannot demonstrate a good basis, the judge should bar the inquiry.

The judge may also preclude inquiry on cross-examination of the character witness about the principal witness's acts probative of untruthfulness not resulting in a conviction if the judge determines that the probative value of such cross-examination is substantially outweighed by the danger of unfair prejudice. The tenuous relevance of character testimony to veracity, coupled with the risk of unfair prejudice when the principal witness is also a party, will often militate in favor of the court exercising discretion under Rule 403 to prohibit inquiry into specific acts. In principle, a strong case can be made for a blanket prohibition of cross-examination about specific acts allegedly committed by the principal witness. However, to date there is neither judicial holding nor even dictum approving such a sweeping prohibition.

§ 49 Collateral and Non-Collateral Matters

On cross-examination, one of the purposes of every permissible type of impeachment is to test the witness's credibility. The use of extrinsic evidence to contradict is more restricted due to considerations of confusion of the issues, misleading the jury, and

---

[48]   See infra § 191.

undue consumption of time. If a matter is considered collateral, the counsel may be limited to intrinsic impeachment. In other words, the witness's testimony on direct or cross-examination stands—the cross-examiner must take the witness's answer; and contradictory extrinsic testimony, evidence offered other than through the witness himself, is barred. In contrast, when the matter is not collateral, extrinsic evidence may be introduced to dispute the witness's testimony on direct examination or cross.

The topic of the collateral fact rule can be confusing. It is helpful to approach the topic in the following sequence. First, we shall explore the limited procedural significance of a determination that the rule bars extrinsic evidence to impeach a witness. Second, we will identify the impeachment techniques exempt from the rule and, by process of elimination, the techniques subject to the rule. Finally, we shall explore how the courts determine whether a particular matter is "collateral" for purposes of the rule.

The Procedural Significance of a Determination That the Rule Bars Extrinsic Evidence

The rule does not limit cross-examination. During cross-examination, the questioner may attempt to challenge virtually any aspect of the witness's direct testimony. An error in any facet of the direct examination can reflect adversely on the witness's perceptual ability, memory, narrative ability, or sincerity; and all those factors are relevant to the jury's assessment of the witness's credibility. Subject to the trial judge's discretionary control under Rule 403, the cross-examiner can question about these factors to her heart's content. Moreover, even if the witness initially gives the cross-examiner an unfavorable answer, the questioner may apply pressure during cross by, for example, reminding the witness of the penalties for perjury. The courts sometimes say that when the collateral fact rule applies, the cross-examiner must "take the witness's answer," but that expression does not mean that the cross-examiner is obliged to accept the initial answer out of the witness's mouth. Lastly, although there is a split of judicial sentiment on the issue, there is modern authority that to apply further pressure for a truthful answer, the cross-examiner may confront the witness with any contrary writing which the witness would be competent to authenticate. The witness might have made the relevant statement in a letter that she personally authored. Again, one of the principal justifications for the rule is the courts' desire to minimize the amount of court time devoted to matters relevant only to a witness's credibility. There might be a considerable time expenditure if, after the witness leaves the stand, the attorney calls a second witness to impeach the prior witness. However, little additional time will be consumed if the cross-examiner presents the witness with a writing he can authenticate.

What then is the procedural significance of the rule? The core prohibition applies when the witness to be impeached has already left the stand and the former cross-examiner later calls a second witness or proffers an exhibit to impeach the earlier witness's credibility. At common law if the collateral fact rule applies at this juncture, the second witness's testimony or the exhibit is automatically inadmissible.

Which Impeachment Techniques Are Exempt from, and Which Subject to, the Collateral Fact Rule?

Most impeachment techniques are exempt from the collateral fact rule. In some cases, the exemption arises from the very nature of the impeachment technique. Suppose, for instance, that the question arises in one of the few jurisdictions which admits polygraph evidence. As a matter of policy, the jurisdiction has decided to permit impeachment by polygraphists or the testimony of other persons about a prior witness's character trait for untruthfulness. Those impeachment techniques necessarily involve extrinsic evidence: After the witness to be impeached leaves the stand, the former cross-examiner calls the polygraphist or the bad character witness. If the policy decision has been made to countenance these impeachment techniques, the techniques must necessarily be exempted from the collateral fact rule.

Moreover, other techniques are exempted because the impeaching facts are deemed so highly probative of credibility. For example, proof of (1) bias, interest, corruption, or coercion, (2) alcohol or drug use, (3) deficient mental capacity, (4) want of physical capacity or lack of exercise of the capacity to acquire personal knowledge and (5) a prior conviction[49] are exempt. These matters can possess such great probative worth on the issue of the witness's credibility that the courts tolerate the expenditure of the additional time entailed in the subsequent presentation of extrinsic evidence.

Which techniques are then subject to the collateral fact rule? By process of elimination, we conclude that there are only three: proof the witness has committed untruthful act which has not resulted in a conviction, proof that the witness made an inconsistent pretrial statement, and specific contradiction.

When Is a Particular Topic Deemed Collateral?

Assume both that the former cross-examiner is proffering extrinsic evidence to impeach the prior witness and that the counsel is using one of the impeachment techniques subject to the collateral fact rule. When is the specific impeaching evidence deemed collateral and inadmissible?

In the case of proof of the witness's untruthful acts which have not resulted in a conviction, the answer is relatively simple. With one exception, extrinsic evidence of such acts is always deemed collateral. On the one hand, even under the general rule if the witness initially denies perpetrating the act, the cross-examiner may pressure the witness for an honest answer by reminding the witness of the penalties of perjury and perhaps by confronting the witness with his own writing mentioning the act. On the other hand, when the witness sticks to his guns and adamantly refuses to concede the act, the cross-examiner must "take the answer" even though it would be relatively easy for the cross-examiner to expose the perjury. Even if a person with personal knowledge of the witness's act were sitting in the courtroom, the cross-examiner could not later call that person to the stand to prove the prior witness's commission of the deceitful act.

The solitary exception to the general rule for untruthful acts comes into play when the witness's testimony triggers the curative admissibility or "door opening" doctrine. Extrinsic evidence concerning a collateral matter may be admitted under the doctrine of "door opening." The courts tend to admit evidence under this doctrine where the government seeks to introduce evidence on rebuttal to contradict specific factual assertions raised during an accused's direct examination.[50] Suppose, for example, that on direct examination, an accused witness made a sweeping, superlative assertion that he had "never" committed a deceitful act. That assertion is such a serious violation of the rules limiting character evidence that on a curative admissibility theory many courts allow the opposing counsel to both cross-examine about the assertion and later introduce

---

[49]   See supra § 42.
[50]   See infra § 57.

extrinsic evidence rebutting the assertion. In effect, the accused has forfeited the protection of the general rule. However, with this single exception, at common law impeaching evidence of a witness's other untruthful acts which have not resulted in a conviction is always subject to the collateral fact rule.

Putting that exception aside, the determination of whether the extrinsic impeachment evidence relates to a collateral matter is more complex when the former cross-examiner resorts to extrinsic evidence to prove a prior inconsistent statement or specifically contradict the earlier witness's testimony. Although extrinsic evidence of untruthful acts is almost always considered collateral, extrinsic evidence offered for these purposes is sometimes collateral but sometimes non-collateral.

In these situations, there are two ways in which the extrinsic impeaching evidence can qualify as non-collateral.

First, the matter is non-collateral and extrinsic evidence consequently admissible if the matter itself is relevant to a fact of consequence on the historical merits of the case.[51] When the fact is logically relevant to the merits of the case as well as the witness's credibility, it is worth the additional court time entailed in hearing extrinsic evidence.

Secondly, the extrinsic evidence is non-collateral and again admissible when it relates to a so-called "linchpin" fact. Under this prong of the test, for purposes of impeachment a part of the witness's story may be attacked where as a matter of human experience, she could not be mistaken about that fact if the thrust of her testimony on the historical merits was true.

Consider the following illustration. An accident occurred on Apple Street at the intersection at its intersection with Maple Street. Bob is called to testify that the color of the traffic light facing Apple Street was red at the time of an automobile accident he witnessed at the corner of Apple and Maple. Fault and liability for the accident turn on the color of the light. On direct examination, Bob testifies that he distinctly recalls that when he witnessed the accident, he was driving "west on Apple, the street Piagano's Pizza Restaurant is situated on," and was heading toward the restaurant. He adds that Piagano's is located on the corner of Apple and Peach. On cross-examination counsel asks, "Isn't it true that Piagano's Pizza Restaurant is located on Apple three blocks east of Peach at *Maple?*" This cross-examination question is permissible as potentially affecting the jury's assessment of Bob's powers of perception and recollection. However, if Bob continues to maintain that the cross street for the restaurant is Peach Street, extrinsic evidence proffered on a specific contradiction theory may not be admitted during the cross-examiner's case-in-chief as to the cross street. The matter is collateral because the cross street at which the restaurant is located is not relevant in the litigation other than to contradict Bob's testimony. Likewise, even if Bob denied on cross-examination making a prior statement in which he allegedly said that the restaurant was on Apple and Maple, extrinsic evidence of the prior statement would be inadmissible because the matter is collateral. Although Bob may be mistaken about the cross street, his testimony on the historical merits about the accident on Apple Street could still be completely accurate.

However, the color of the traffic light facing Apple is non-collateral in the first way; the color of the traffic light is relevant to the merits of the case. Thus, specific

---

[51]   With respect to prior inconsistent statements, see also supra § 36.

contradiction evidence that the light facing Apple Street was green is admissible. By the same token, if Bob denies on cross-examination having previously stated that the traffic light was green, extrinsic evidence of Bob's prior inconsistent statement is admissible.

Finally, vary the initial illustration. Again, on direct Bob testified that when he witnessed an accident, he was driving "Keywest on Apple, the street on which Piagano's is located." Now the specific contradiction evidence is extrinsic testimony that Piagano's Pizza Restaurant is situated on Front Street that runs parallel to Apple. Or the opponent offers extrinsic evidence of an inconsistent statement by Bob that Piagano's is on Front. If Bob was on Front, not Apple, the extrinsic would be admissible; the fact is non-collateral in the second way. In this variation of the illustration, an error as to the location of the restaurant brings into question the trustworthiness of Bob's testimony on the historical merits of the case. The mistake no longer relates only to the minor detail of the cross street. If Bob was driving on Front Street, he might have seen another accident; but it would have been physically impossible for him to witness the accident that occurred on Apple. The location of the restaurant on Apple would be considered a "linchpin" fact, and extrinsic evidence would therefore be admissible to impeach Bob. A fact negating the fundamental assumption that the witness was in the right place at the right time to observe what she testified to is a classic example of a "linchpin" fact.

What is the status of the common law collateral fact rule under the Federal Rules? The continued application of the standard theory of collateral contradiction in federal practice has been criticized on the ground that it is a mechanistic doctrine which ignores pertinent policy considerations. It has been urged that the courts should substitute the discretionary approach of Rule 403. That approach is the better construction of the federal statutes. Although Rule 608(b) expressly prohibits extrinsic evidence of a witness's untruthful acts, the Federal Rules do not expressly codify a categorical collateral fact restriction. For example, there is no mention of that restriction in Rule 613 governing prior inconsistent statement impeachment. Given Rule 402, there is a powerful argument that the enactment of the Federal Rules impliedly overturned the technical collateral fact rule. Under this reading of the Federal Rules, there is no rigid prohibition of introducing extrinsic evidence to impeach a witness on a collateral matter; rather, under Rule 403, the judge would make a practical judgment as to whether the importance of the witness's testimony and the impeachment warrants the expenditure of the additional trial time. However, the collateral fact rule was so ingrained at common law that many federal opinions continue to mention "collateral" evidence.

The abolition of the collateral fact doctrine by the Federal Rules is a two-edged sword. The preceding paragraph noted that under Rule 403, the witness's testimony and the impeaching evidence could conceivably have such importance that the judge might permit extrinsic evidence which would have been barred at common law. The judge must make a pragmatic judgment call. However, it is equally true that the judge could bar evidence which would technically have been considered non-collateral and admissible at common law. Thus, standing alone, compliance with the common law rule does not guarantee the admissibility of extrinsic evidence under the federal statutes. Even if the evidence is otherwise admissible, it could be vulnerable to a Rule 403 objection.

§ 50 Exclusion and Separation of Witnesses

The immediately preceding sections in this chapter discuss the evidentiary techniques which counsel may use to either attack or support a witness's credibility.

However, there are also procedural steps which the judge can take to help ensure credible testimony. Judicial exclusion and separation orders are illustrative. There is no constitutional right to the exclusion of witnesses from the courtroom. However, exclusion orders are available in virtually every jurisdiction. If a witness hears the testimony of others before she takes the stand, it is much easier for the witness to deliberately tailor her own story to that of other witnesses. Witnesses may also be influenced subconsciously. In either event, the cross-examiner will find it more difficult to expose fabrication, collusion, inconsistencies, or inaccuracies in the testimony of a witness who has already heard other witnesses testify. Separation prevents improper influence during the trial by prohibiting witness-to-witness communication both inside and outside the courtroom.

At common law the court in its discretion may exclude witnesses. The court is empowered to order exclusion on its own motion; but in many, if not most, cases the judge enters the order at the request of a party. Rather than adopting a discretionary approach, Federal and Uniform Rule of Evidence 615 treats the exclusion of witnesses as a matter of right. Federal Rule 615 states: "At a party's request, the court must order witnesses excluded . . . ." A request to exclude witnesses is often referred to as "invoking the rule on witnesses." Rule 615 does not specify a deadline for making the request. The appellate courts have applied several standards in determining whether a trial judge's failure to order a witness's exclusion constitutes reversible error.

Exemptions from a Sequestration Order

Even if a litigant makes a proper, timely Rule 615 motion, not all witnesses may be excluded and separated. Neither case law nor Rule 615 authorizes exclusion of: (1) a party who is a natural person, (2) a person who is an officer or employee of a party which is not a natural person and who has been designated as its representative by its attorney which includes a government's investigative agent, (3) a person whose presence is shown by the party to be essential to the presentation of the party's case, or (4) as of 1997, the victim of the offense that an accused is charged with when the prosecution contemplates calling the victim as a witness during a subsequent sentencing hearing.

In criminal cases, judges routinely invoke (2) to permit the attendance of the investigating case agent at trial. Sometimes the courts classify an expert as a witness whose presence is essential under (3). It can be vital to give counsel the benefit of an expert's assistance while an opposing expert is testifying. In particular, assistance may be necessary in connection with technical matters as to which counsel lacks sufficient familiarity to try the case effectively on her own. When the counsel lacks that familiarity, she may need an expert "at her elbow" during the opposing expert witnesses' testimony; without the expert's assistance, the counsel would be handicapped in preparing on the spot to conduct an immediate cross-examination. A strong argument can also be made for permitting the presence of an expert witness who intends to give an opinion based in part on evidence presented at trial. Congress added exception (4) to Rule 615 in the 1997 Victim Rights Clarification Act. In addition to these four exceptions, there is a further limitation on the scope of Rule 615; some courts have held that the rule does not apply to rebuttal witnesses or witnesses called to impeach credibility.

On its face, Rule 615 authorizes only the exclusion of the prospective witness from the courtroom. While Rule 615 does not explicitly provide for the separation of witnesses outside court, the prevailing view is that courts have inherent procedural authority to take further steps designed to prevent communication between witnesses such as ordering them to remain physically apart, not to discuss the case with one another, and not to read a transcript of another witness's trial testimony.

Sanctions for Violating a Sequestration Order

If a witness violates an order of exclusion or sequestration, the trial judge has discretion to select the appropriate remedy. The court may refuse to permit a witness to testify, declare a mistrial, or give the jury a cautionary instruction to weigh the witness's credibility in light of the witness's presence in court or discussions with another witness. The instruction could authorize the jury to treat the witness's violation of the judge's order as evidence of the witness's bias. The court can also hold the witness in contempt. The courts are markedly reluctant to resort to the drastic remedy of disqualifying the witness. The strongest case for altogether barring the witness's testimony is a fact situation in which the witness heard testimony which could influence his own testimony and the party or counsel calling the witness colluded in the witness's violation of the sequestration order. Unfortunately, once it is decided to permit the witness to testify, the alternatives of comment or contempt have their drawbacks. The best approach is to avoid the problem beforehand. Before trial, the judge should emphatically impress on both the witnesses and counsel the importance of obeying the court's ruling excluding and separating the witness. If the witness is absent at the hearing at which the judge issues the order, the judge ought to direct the attorney to inform the witness of the order.

Title 3

ADMISSION AND EXCLUSION

Chapter 6

THE PROCEDURE OF ADMITTING AND EXCLUDING EVIDENCE

Table of Sections

---

§ 51   The Proponent: Presentation of Evidence: Offer of Proof

To gain a working knowledge of evidence law, you must appreciate the procedural framework within which evidence doctrine operates. The procedural rules impact every participant in the trial process, and a matter of procedural fairness the rules must be sufficiently clear to all the participants: The proponent needs to know when and how to introduce evidence, the opponent must understand when and how to object, and the judge has to appreciate when and how to rule. The rules of practice concerning presentation of evidence, offers of proof, and objections are designed to secure this result.

The presentation of exhibits such as writings, photographs, knives, guns, and other tangible objects often proves troublesome to neophytes. There are variations in local procedures, but the general process can be briefly described here. The attorney essentially walks the legs of a triangle—from the court reporter to the opposing attorney, then to the witness, and finally back to the judge. The party wishing to introduce evidence of this type should first have the object marked "for identification" as an exhibit. After the proponent has the thing marked by the court reporter or clerk for identification as an exhibit, the proponent submits the proposed exhibit to the opposing attorney for his inspection, at least on his request. After showing the exhibit to the opponent, the proponent approaches the witness. At this point, the proponent "lays the foundation" for its introduction as an exhibit by having it appropriately authenticated or identified by the witness's testimony. Although the courts often speak of laying "the foundation" in the singular, in truth the proponent may have to lay multiple foundations. Thus, a single exhibit such as a letter might require authentication, best evidence, and hearsay foundations.

The procedures for handling exhibits vary to a degree not only from jurisdiction to jurisdiction but also even among judges sitting in the same jurisdiction. However, the following generalizations hold true in most courtrooms in most jurisdictions. After laying

145

all the required foundations or predicates, the proponent tenders the exhibit to the judge by stating, "Plaintiff offers this (document or object, describing it), marked 'Plaintiff's Exhibit No. 2' for identification, into evidence as Plaintiff's Exhibit No. 2." At this juncture, the opponent can object to its receipt in evidence, and the judge will rule on the objection. Assuming the judge rules the exhibit admissible, if the item of evidence is a writing, with the judge's permission it may be read to the jury by the counsel offering it or by the witness. Again, with the judge's permission, the writing could also be passed to the jury or displayed on a screen. Likewise, when the exhibit is a gun or knife, in the judge's discretion or in accordance with local rule or custom, it may be shown or handed to the jurors for their physical inspection. (Some judges do not permit the proponent to submit his exhibits to the jury until the conclusion of the proponent's case-in-chief.)

When the courtroom is fully equipped with computer technology, the mechanics are even simpler. The court staff may include a technologist to operate the computer equipment. There will be monitor screens in front of the judge, at the counsel tables, on the witness stand, and in the jury box. Even before the trial session begins, the attorney can present an electronic version of the exhibit to the technologist. During trial, the attorney need not walk the legs of the triangle; instead, the attorney can stand in one position and simply make various requests of the technologist. Initially, the attorney asks that the technologist "display," "release," or "show" the exhibit to the judge. Next, the attorney requests that it be shown to opposing counsel. Then the attorney asks the technologist to show the exhibit to the witness. At this point the attorney elicits the witness's foundational testimony for the exhibit. The attorney then tenders the exhibit to the judge. If the judge rules that the foundation is complete, the attorney lastly requests that the exhibit be displayed on the monitor screens in the jury box.

Of course, the usual way of presenting oral testimony is to call the witness to the stand and ask her questions. Normally (but not always), the opponent must challenge the admissibility of the testimony by voicing objections to the questions before the witness answers the question.[1] Ordinarily, the admissibility of testimony is decided by the judge's sustaining or overruling objections to questions. If the court sustains an objection to a question, the witness is prevented from answering the question and from testifying to that extent.

Offers of Proof

When the judge sustains an objection, the proponent of the question should usually make "an offer of proof" or avowal. The usual practice is for the proponent to explain to the judge what the witness would say if the witness were permitted to answer the question and what the expected answer is logically relevant to prove. There are two reasons for this practice. One is that it permits the trial judge to reconsider the proponent's claim for admissibility. Before the offer of proof, the judge might not have realized the logical relevance of the line of inquiry. However, the second, formal reason is to preserve the issue for appeal by including the expected answer in the official record of trial. In the event of an appeal from the judge's ruling, the appellate court can better understand the scope and effect of the question and proposed answer. That understanding enables the appellate court in a better position to decide: whether the judge's ruling sustaining an objection was error, whether the error was prejudicial, and what final disposition to make on appeal. The trial judge usually requires the offer of

---

[1]   See infra § 52.

proof to be made outside the jury's hearing. The judge has already ruled the evidence inadmissible; and if the offer were made in the jury's hearing, the jurors would be exposed to inadmissible testimony which could improperly influence their deliberation.

The offer of proof is not only a traditional common law practice. Federal Rules of Evidence 103(a) and (b) also impose the requirement for an offer of proof. Significantly, on cross-examination, the requirement is often relaxed; some jurisdictions entirely eliminate the need for an offer of proof on cross-examination while most courts accept less specific offers on cross than they demand on direct. The courts realize that it is often more difficult to predict the answers on cross-examination than on direct, since cross-examination is sometimes exploratory. It would therefore be unfair to demand the same degree of specificity in offers of proof during cross-examination.

Occasionally, in the context of the record, the question itself can so clearly indicate the tenor of the expected answer that the appellate court will consider the propriety of the ruling on the question without an offer of proof. However, when an offer of proof is required before the appellate court will consider a ruling sustaining an objection to a question, the statement constituting the offer of proof must be reasonably specific; the offer should factually describe the witness's probable answer and identify the purpose of the proffered testimony. Thus, the proponent must tell the judge what the tenor of the evidence would be and why the evidence is logically relevant. Where the sustained objection challenges the relevancy of the testimony, the offer of proof should indicate the facts on which relevancy depends. When the objection is on a ground other than relevancy, the offer must also explain why the objection is unsound. These general guidelines apply under Federal Rule of Evidence 103 as well as at common law.

Effective December 1, 2000, Rule 103 was amended. By virtue of the amendment to Rule 103(a), if before trial the proponent makes a proper offer of proof and the trial makes a purportedly final ruling excluding the evidence, the proponent need not renew the offer at trial to preserve the issue for appeal. The Advisory Committee's Note accompanying the 2000 amendment points out that even before the amendment, some courts had distinguished offers of proof from pretrial objections (in limine motions) and not required a proponent to renew an offer at trial.

Under these guidelines, the proponent has significant burdens. If the proponent counsel specifies a purpose for which the proposed evidence is inadmissible and the judge excludes, counsel cannot complain of the ruling on appeal although the evidence could have been admitted for another purpose. Likewise, if part of the evidence offered such as a deposition transcript, letter, or conversation is admissible but another part is not, it is incumbent on the proponent, not the judge, to separate out the admissible part. When counsel offers both the admissible and inadmissible matter together and the judge rejects the entire offer, the proponent may not complain on appeal.

The offer of proof procedure described above assumes that a single witness is being questioned on the stand. Suppose that there are several other available witnesses, but not yet on the witness stand, to prove a fact. Assume further that the judge's rulings already indicate that he will probably exclude this entire line of testimony, or the judge rules in advance that the line of testimony is inadmissible. Given the normal requirement for an offer, must the party produce each witness, question him, and on exclusion, describe each expected answer? A few decisions mandate this procedure. Obviously that procedure wastes time and risks annoying the jury. The better view is that it is not invariably required to call the other witnesses. Under this view, an adequate offer of proof can be made without producing all the witnesses if the offer is sufficiently specific and there is nothing in the record to indicate the proponent's bad faith or inability to produce the proof.

§ 52 The Opponent: Objecting

If the administration of the exclusionary rules of evidence is to be fair and workable, the judge must be informed promptly of any contention that evidence should be excluded, and the reasons supporting the contention. This burden is placed on the party opponent, not the judge. Accordingly, the general approach is that a failure to make a specific objection at the time the evidence is proffered, is a waiver for appeal of any ground of complaint against its admission. However, this general approach is modified by the doctrine of plain error, discussed at the end of this section.

Time of Making: Motions to Strike

The opponent may not gamble on the possibility of a favorable answer. Rather, the opponent must object to the admission of evidence as soon as the ground for objection becomes apparent. Usually, during a witness's testimony, an objection is apparent as soon as the question is asked, since the wording of the question is likely to indicate that it calls for inadmissible evidence. If there is an opportunity at that time, counsel must then state her objection before the witness answers. But sometimes an objection before an answer is infeasible. An eager witness may answer so quickly that counsel does not have enough time and a fair chance to object. In that event, the counsel may move to strike the answer for the purpose of interposing an objection to the question; if the judge thinks that the witness prematurely "jumped the gun" and grants the motion, the counsel then states her objection to the question. Or a question which is unobjectionable may be followed by a partially or completely nonresponsive answer. In this situation, the questioner has the right to have the nonresponsive material stricken. Or after the evidence is received, a ground of objection to the evidence may later surface for the first time. For example, although on direct examination the witness purported to testify from personal knowledge, it might become evident for the first time on cross that in reality, the witness is relying on inadmissible hearsay. In all these cases, an "after-objection" may be stated as soon as the ground appears. The proper technique is to move to strike the objectionable evidence and request a curative instruction to the jury to disregard the evidence. Ideally, counsel should use the term of art "motion to strike," but any phraseology directing the judge's attention to the grounds as soon as they appear suffices.

Suppose that the evidence is a transcript of an earlier pretrial deposition. The time when objections must be made to deposition questions varies, depending on the type of objection. Usually objections going to the "manner and form" of the questions or answers, such as challenges to leading questions or nonresponsive answers must be made during the deposition hearing. Some jurisdictions treat opinion and best evidence issues in the same manner. The rationale is that in these cases, if the opponent had objected on the spot, the proponent could have cured the problem. For instance, the proponent might have rephrased the question or established an excuse for the non-production of the original writing. In contrast, objections going to the "substance," such as relevancy and hearsay, may ordinarily be urged for the first time when the deposition is later offered at trial.

Assume that there was a prior trial rather than a prior deposition hearing. Suppose further that evidence was introduced at the earlier trial of the case, and an available objection was not made then. In those circumstances, may the opponent object for the first time when the same evidence is tendered at a second trial? The trial and deposition settings differ markedly. As previously stated, the opponent can forego most types of objections at a deposition hearing while, at a trial, the opponent must generally urge the objections. Thus, if the opponent neglects to object at an earlier trial in the case, the opponent may be precluded from raising the objection at the retrial. Section 259 addresses this issue.

Pretrial Motions In Limine

Although the Federal Rules of Evidence do not expressly authorize in limine motions, federal courts have inherent procedural authority to entertain such motions. A motion for an advance ruling on the admissibility of evidence is a relatively modern device for obtaining rulings on evidence even before the evidence is proffered at trial. The proponent of evidence can file an offensive in limine motion to obtain an advance ruling that an item of evidence is admissible. It is especially advisable to make such a motion when the proponent contemplates relying on a novel type of expert testimony or a creative nonhearsay or noncharacter theory. The advance motion gives the judge more time to think through the proponent's argument for admissibility.

However, in the vast majority of cases, the opponent files the motion defensively to obtain an advance ruling that a particular item of evidence is inadmissible. The purpose of such motions may be to shield the jury from exposure to prejudicial inadmissible evidence or to afford a basis for strategic decisions. For instance, an advance ruling might help the counsel decide whether to mention an item of evidence during opening statement or advise her client whether to take the stand. Advance rulings on objections can be sought before or during trial prior to the presentation of the evidence. Although there is some old authority forbidding advance rulings, today the prevailing rule is that the judge has considerable discretion to make or refuse to make advance rulings, Unless the resolution of the motion requires a prediction of the state of the evidence at the later trial, and as long as the matter is left primarily within the trial judge's discretion, appellate courts should encourage pretrial rulings on in limine motions. In the pretrial setting, the judge has more time to carefully think through the evidentiary issue; there are no jurors impatiently waiting for the sidebar conference to end. In addition, an in limine motion may prevent the jurors' exposure to prejudicial information and thereby avoid a mistrial.

When a party files an in limine motion, the judge can make three different types of rulings:

- First, the judge can refuse to entertain the motion and defer the issue until trial. In most but not all cases, the judge has discretion whether to rule on the issue before trial.

- Secondly, the judge can make a preliminary or tentative ruling on the motion. By way of example, suppose that the opponent moves to exclude an item of evidence as unduly prejudicial under Rule 403. Although the judge agrees that the evidence might prejudice the jury, the judge can conceive of a state of the record in which the proponent's need for the evidence would be so great that the need would trump the risk of prejudice.

If so, the judge might tentatively exclude the evidence. However, the judge would also inform the proponent that the ruling is not final; if at any point during trial, the proponent thought that the state of the record had sufficiently sharpened the need for the evidence, the proponent could approach sidebar and request permission to introduce the evidence.

- Thirdly, the judge could make a definitive or final ruling on the merits of the motion. (However, even when the judge makes a purportedly definitive pretrial ruling, the judge has the power to reconsider and change the ruling at trial.)

Suppose that a party moves in limine to exclude certain evidence, but the judge denies the motion. To preserve the issue for appeal, must the party repeat the objection at trial when the opposing party offers the evidence? There is a split of authority over this question. At common law the traditional, prevailing view was that if she loses a pretrial in limine motion, the opponent has to renew the objection at trial in order to preserve the issue for appeal. Of course, that view robs the in limine motion of much of its utility. One of the foremost advantages of an in limine motion is that the opponent makes the motion outside the jury's hearing, and there is no risk that the jury will form the impression that the opponent is objecting to hide the truth. If the opponent must renew the motion in the jury's presence, that risk rears its ugly head again.

However, even at common law some appellate courts dispensed with a requirement for renewal when the trial judge's ruling is explicit and purportedly definitive. In 2000, Federal Rule of Evidence 103 was amended to codify that approach, and restyled Federal Rule of Evidence 103(a)(2) provides that "(o)nce the court rules definitively on the record—either before or at trial—a party need not renew an objection or offer of proof to preserve a claim of error for appeal." The caveat is that the Advisory Committee Note accompanying the 2000 amendment adds that the opponent has an "obligation . . . to clarify whether an in limine or other evidentiary ruling is definitive when there is doubt on that point."

An in limine motion is distinguishable from a motion to suppress.[2] Suppression motions typically rest on constitutional grounds such as the Fourth Amendment exclusionary rule rather than statutory and common law evidence rules. Moreover, in most jurisdictions, the party must make suppression motions before trial under pain of waiver. Further, if the suppression motion is timely, the judge ordinarily must dispose of it before trial. As previously stated, in the case of in limine motions, the judge usually has discretion whether to rule on the merits of the motion before trial.

General and Specific Objections

To help the judge make an intelligent ruling on the merits, the opponent should make a specific objection. Specificity has three aspects: specificity as to grounds, part, and party.

---

[2]   See infra Ch. 15.

Specificity as to Grounds

Objections have to be accompanied by a definite statement of the grounds; in other words, objections must reasonably indicate the appropriate rules of evidence relied on as reasons for the objections. These objections are labeled "specific" objections in contrast to so-called general objections. The specificity requirement serves two important purposes at the trial level. First, the requirement helps to ensure that the trial judge understands the objection raised and that the adversary has a fair opportunity to remedy the defect, if possible. However, the requirement for a specific objection does not *per se* ban the use of general trial objections (objections which state no distinct grounds). When the evidence is objectionable on some ground, the judge has discretion to entertain and sustain a general objection. However, as we shall soon see, the specificity requirement is enforced to a certain extent on appeal. The second purpose of the requirement is to make a proper record for the reviewing court in the event of an appeal.

If the judge *overrules* a general objection, on appeal the objecting party ordinarily may not attack the ruling by urging a ground not mentioned when the objection was made at trial. Yet, there are three exceptional situations in which the appellate court will disregard this requirement and consider a meritorious objection that was not voiced to the trial judge. First, if the ground for exclusion should have been obvious to judge and the proponent, the lack of specification of the ground is immaterial for the purpose of appealing the judge's action overruling the general objection. This exception is simple good sense. Second, some courts hold that if the evidence is inadmissible for any purpose, a general objection suffices to secure appellate review of the judge's overruling the objection. This exception makes little sense if the ground is not apparent; when the ground is not evident, there is still a need for specification. If the opponent had put the proponent on notice of the dispute over the admissibility of the evidence, the proponent might have substituted alternative proof to establish the fact. Third, it has been suggested that if the omitted ground could not have been obviated, a general objection permits appellate consideration of an unstated, specific objection. The case for this exception overlooks an important consideration. Assume *arguendo* that the objection to the particular evidence could not have been obviated. Nevertheless, if the objection had been stated and the proponent realized the validity of the objection, again the proponent might have withdrawn the inadmissible evidence and substituted other admissible evidence to fill the gap. Fortunately, Federal Rule of Evidence 103(a)(1) does not codify the third exception.

The cumulative impact of the above rules is that the appellate court typically upholds a trial judge's action in *overruling* a general objection. If the trial judge *sustains* a general objection, the appellate court is again charitable to the trial judge's ruling. "When evidence is *excluded* upon a mere general objection, the ruling will be upheld, if any ground in fact existed for the exclusion. It will be assumed, in the absence of any request by the opposing party or the court to make the objection more definite, that the objection was understood, and that the ruling was placed upon the right ground."[3]

Examples of general objections are "I object;" objections on the ground that the evidence is "inadmissible," "illegal," "incompetent," "foundation," is not "proper" testimony, or an objection "on all the grounds ever known or heard of." One of the most overworked objections is the formula that the evidence is "incompetent, irrelevant and

---

[3]   Tooley v. Bacon, 70 N.Y. 34, 37 (1877).

immaterial." Its rhythm and alliteration seduce some lawyers to employ it as a routine ritual. Courts frequently treat this formula as merely equivalent to the general objection, "I object." As applied to evidence, the word "incompetent" means no more than inadmissible and thus does not state a ground of objection. However, although somewhat general in wording, the expression "irrelevant and immaterial" states a distinct, substantive ground for exclusion under Federal Rule 401. A requirement that the objector state specifically the reason why the evidence is irrelevant or immaterial, as some courts demand, can be unduly burdensome; it requires the opponent to prove a negative. It is more practical to consider the irrelevancy objection in this form as a specific objection with one qualification. The qualification is that if the judge has any doubt as to relevancy, before ruling she may ask the proponent to explain the purpose of the proof.

To make a sufficiently specific objection, the opponent should name the generic evidentiary rule being violated: "calls for information protected by the attorney-client privilege," "lack of authentication," "not the best evidence," or "hearsay"—the level of specificity found in the phrasing of the titles of the various articles in the Federal Rules of Evidence. Under the prevailing view, it is unnecessary to be any more specific. From a tactical perspective, it is usually undesirable to be more specific. If the opponent names the specific deficiency in the foundation, the opponent has in effect educated the proponent, and the proponent now knows exactly how to cure the defect in the foundation. However, a minority view requires the opponent to specify the missing foundational element. This view has the advantage of forcing the opponent to get right to the point and thereby saving trial time. In the pretrial setting when the judge is ruling on an in limine motion, the judge is more likely to follow the minority view. At trial, an objection can surface unexpectedly; and it is often impractical to insist that the opponent specify the precise deficiency in the proffered testimony. In contrast, when the context is pretrial, the opponent typically has more time to formulate a specific objection. Understandably, the judge demands greater precision in objections in the pretrial context.

While an "irrelevancy" objection has occasionally been held sufficient to preserve a claim of prejudice in the sense of arousing personal animus against the party, that holding is questionable; that phrasing does not explicitly raise any of the policy concerns listed in Federal Rule 403. Those concerns can easily be raised specifically, and a reference to one of those concerns does not require the opponent to establish a negative. The judge should demand that the opponent cite Rule 403 or at least identify a probative danger mentioned in Rule 403.

In the above cases, the judge pressures the objecting party to be more specific. In other cases, though, the objector faces exactly the opposite problem: the judge might make it difficult for the attorney to verbalize a sufficiently specific objection to make the record for appeal. As we shall see, the trial judge has a right to preclude "speaking" objections, in which under the guise of objecting the objector endeavors to make a speech to the jury. However, in an effort to prevent a speaking objection, the trial judge sometimes cuts off the attorney too early and unduly interferes with the attorney's ability to articulate a complete objection satisfactory to the appellate court. When the record shows that the trial judge's interference is responsible for the generality of the objection stated in the court below, the appellate courts are more liberal in deciding whether the objection was sufficiently specific with respect to ground.

A variation of the problem of specificity as to ground arises when an evidentiary rule limits the purposes for which an item of evidence may be admitted. Assume that evidence offered is properly admissible on a particular issue but not upon some other issue, or is admissible against one party but not against another. Here, although she assigns grounds, an objector who asks only that this evidence be excluded cannot complain on appeal if her objection is overruled. Instead, under Federal Rule of Evidence 105, she should request that the admission of the evidence be limited to the particular purpose or party.

Ordinarily, to obtain a reversal on appeal, the litigant must not only have made a specific objection in the trial court; the litigant must also rely on the same ground on appeal. A "hearsay" objection does not preserve the contention that the admission of the statement violates the Sixth Amendment Confrontation Clause. Likewise, a general "relevance" objection does not raise the objection that the admission of the evidence would violate Rule 403 or the character rules. If the litigant attempts to shift to another ground on appeal, the court will apply the plain error doctrine codified in Federal Rule 103(e). As we shall see, appellate courts rarely find plain error.

————

Specificity as to Part

Objections ought to be specific not only with regard to the ground, but also with respect to the particular part of an offer. Suppose that evidence sought to be introduced consists of several statements or items tendered as a unit in a deposition, letter, conversation, or trial transcript. Assume that the opponent objects to the whole of the evidence when some parts are subject to the objection made but other parts are not. In this situation, the judge does not err by overruling the objection. It is not the judge's responsibility to sever the bad parts if some are good. That is the opponent's burden. Obviously this rule should not be administered rigidly by the appellate courts; rather, the courts ought to apply the rule realistically with a sensitivity to the realities of the particular trial situation.

————

Specificity as to Party

When the counsel represents only one party at trial and objects, she is obviously claiming that the evidence is inadmissible against her client. However, when counsel appears on behalf of multiple clients at the same trial, the evidence might be admissible as against one but inadmissible as against the other. In this situation, counsel runs the risk of waiving the objection if she does not identify the client whom the evidence is inadmissible against. There is a division of authority over "vicarious" objections; while some appellate courts allow one co-party to rely on a co-party's trial objection on appeal, other courts are contra.

Assume that the opponent makes an objection that lacks specificity with respect to ground, part, or party. On appeal, the court will uphold the *overruling* of an untenable specific objection even if there was a tenable ground for exclusion which was not urged in the trial court. In an adversary system of litigation, it is the opponent's responsibility to specifically articulate a justifiable basis for excluding the proponent's evidence.

When an untenable specific objection is *sustained,* there is authority that the appellate court will uphold the ruling if there is any other ground for doing so, even though the ground was not cited below. There is no point in ordering a retrial if the evidence would have to be excluded on the proper ground. However, some qualifications are necessary. When the correct objection, had it been made, could have been obviated, or admissible evidence could have been substituted, a retrial is appropriate. But consider the perspective of a trial judge presiding at a hearing on a new trial motion. Assume that a ruling on the proper objection at the second trial would involve the judge's discretion but, reflecting on the state of the record, the judge concludes that she would exercise discretion in favor of exclusion. In that situation, it would be a waste of time to grant the new trial motion. A similar result should follow where a ruling on the proper objection at a second trial would require certain factual findings but the judge concludes that given the state of the record, she would make findings adverse to the opponent seeking a new trial. Once again, it would make no sense to grant the motion and order a second trial.

Repetition of Objections

A offers one witness's testimony which his adversary, B, thinks is inadmissible. B objects, and the objection is *sustained.* In that event, when A offers similar testimony by the same or another witness, B must repeat her objection if she is to complain about the later evidence. Suppose, however, the first objection is *overruled.* Must B repeat her objection when other similarly objectionable evidence is offered? A few decisions intimate that she must—a requirement which wastes time and casts B in the unenviable role of an obstructionist in the jurors' eyes. Most courts sensibly hold that B is entitled to assume that the judge will continue to make the same ruling and she need not repeat the objection. The logical consequences of this view are that the first objection is not waived by the objector's subsequent conduct and that in addition, the reach of the initial objection extends to all subsequent, similar evidence vulnerable to the same objection. In any jurisdiction where the law on this point is at all unsettled, it is a wise precaution for objecting counsel to ask the judge to have the record reflect a "running" or "continuing" objection, going to all other like evidence.

"The Exception"

Closely associated with the objection but distinct from it was the classic common law exception; if the objector disagreed with the judge's overruling of the objection, the objector had to "except" to the ruling on the record to preserve the issue for purpose of appeal. The federal rules and the practice in most states dispense with exceptions. Rules such as Federal Rule of Criminal Procedure 51(b) provide that for all purposes, "it is sufficient to 'inform[ ] the court—when the court ruling or order is made or sought—of the action the party wishes the court to take, or the party's objection to the court's action and the grounds for that objection."[4] Nevertheless, for motivations such as a desire to impress a jury, some attorneys persist in announcing that they "except" to rulings at jury trials even in jurisdictions where exceptions are unnecessary. These attorneys do so at the risk of irritating the trial judge—and having the judge embarrass them by admonishing them in the jury's hearing.

---

[4]   Fed. R. Civ. P. 46; Fed. R. Crim. P. 51.

The Tactics of Objecting

Jurors want to know the facts. They may resent objections as attempts to hide the facts, and view sustained objections as the successful suppression of the truth. If this description of the jury's attitude is accurate, certain conclusions as to desirable tactics follow.

Even when a question is technically objectionable, the opponent should not object unless making the objection will do more good than harm. Conduct a cost/benefit analysis. In some situations, an objection can be counterproductive. On net, objections to leading questions or opinion evidence frequently result in strengthening the examiner's case by requiring her to elicit the testimony in more concrete, convincing form. In a given case, an authentication, best evidence, or hearsay objection can have the same result and backfire. Further, if an objection has little chance of being sustained at trial or on appeal, it usually should not be made. An unsuccessful objection may succeed only in magnifying the importance of unfavorable evidence; the jurors might think that the opponent must have thought that the evidence was damning because she went to the length of trying to exclude it. Objections ought to be few in number, and they should target only evidence which will do substantial harm to the objector's theory of the case.

Finally, when objections are made in the jury's presence, the objector's demeanor and the phrasing of the objection are important. An objection ought to be phrased to prevent the objection from sounding as if it rests exclusively on some technical rule. Thus, an objection to a copy under the best evidence rule should not be stated solely in terms of "secondary evidence" but should also mention the unreliability of an incomplete or blurry copy. Likewise, the objection "hearsay" ought to be expanded to mention the need to produce the declarant so that the jury can see him and evaluate his credibility. The art of making effective objections at a jury trial consists in adding a short adjective, adverb, or phrase which signals the jury that the ground of the objection relates to substantive justice. However, most judges do not tolerate lengthy "speaking" objections. If a counsel is foolish enough to attempt such an objection, the judge might admonish counsel in the jury's hearing.

Withdrawal of Evidence

The Federal and Uniform Rules of Evidence do not deal explicitly with the subject of withdrawal of evidence. However, reasonably construed, Rule 611(a) permits withdrawal as an aspect of the court's discretionary control over the presentation of evidence. The discretion could be exercised in accordance with the principles historically recognized in the case law:

- The cases sometimes imply that if a party has introduced evidence which is not objected to and which turns out to be favorable to the adversary, the offering party may withdraw the evidence as of right. The accepted rule, however, is that withdrawal is not of right. Rather, the adversary is entitled to have the benefit of the testimony, unless exceptional facts make it fair for the judge in her discretion to allow withdrawal.

- However, if the evidence is admitted over the adversary's objection, and the proponent later decides to yield to the objection and asks to withdraw the evidence, the court may revoke its ruling and permit the withdrawal.

Plain Error Rule

Many of the criteria for so-called "plain error" and "harmful error" (as opposed to harmless error) are similar. Yet, the two concepts should be distinguished. Like Uniform Rule of Evidence 103(a), restyled Federal Rule Evidence 103(a) codifies the "harmless error" concept with the statement, "A party may claim error only if the error affects a substantial right of the party . . . ." Thus, only harmful errors warrant relief. Plain error is defined in restyled Rule 103(e): "A court may take notice of a plain error even if the claim of error was not properly preserved." In contrast to harmful error, harmless error denotes a ruling which is incorrect but which is not cause for reversal. Plain error denotes a harmful error that is sufficiently serious to justify considering it on appeal despite the opponent's failure to observe the usual procedures for preserving error for review.

There are several key distinctions between plain and harmful error. To begin with, there is a difference in degree between harmful and plain error. For error to be harmful, the error must be prejudicial to the appellant; but for plain error, the error must have *very* prejudicial effects. To qualify as plain error, the error must be a "blockbuster." Harmful error is the genus, and plain error is the species. Plain error fact situations represent a small subset of the larger class of harmful error cases; in the plain error cases, the damage has to be extreme. Moreover, to trigger the plain error doctrine, the error must create a risk of a miscarriage of substantive justice. Some exclusionary rules of evidence bar the admission of relevant, reliable evidence in order to promote an extrinsic social policy. While those rules are certainly legitimate, it may be difficult to persuade an appellate court that a ruling admitting relevant, trustworthy evidence was likely to cause justice to miscarry. Despite the fundamental theoretical distinctions between the two concepts, surprisingly little difference can be found in the way the harmful and plain error concepts are applied in the published opinions.

The published opinions clearly demonstrate the appellate courts' hesitancy to overturn the trial judge's evidentiary decisions. There are many reasons for that hesitancy. The appellate courts are loathe to second guess the trial judge who usually has a better feel for the case.[5] Moreover, appellants frequently fail to marshal facts demonstrating that the alleged error was prejudicial. On appeal, it is often easy to demonstrate error but quite difficult to demonstrate prejudice; establishing prejudice can be the more important half of the battle. This judicial reluctance to reverse is evident even in criminal cases. However, a holding of plain error is far more likely in cases involving the constitutional rights of criminal defendants. Reversals on the basis of plain error are much less common in civil suits than in criminal cases, in part because liberty and life are not at stake in a civil action.

The application of the plain error doctrine depends upon a fact intensive, case specific analysis. Findings of plain error are not only rarities; they also have very limited precedential value.

§ 53 The Trial Judge: Deciding Preliminary Questions of Fact Arising on Objections

Most evidentiary rules operate to exclude relevant evidence. Examples are the hearsay doctrine, the best evidence rule preferring original writings, and the privileges

---

[5]   See supra § 55.

for confidential communications. All these exclusionary rules are "technical" in the sense that they were developed by a special professional group, judges and lawyers, and in the further sense that for long-term ends they sometimes obstruct the ascertainment of truth in the particular case. Most of these technical exclusionary rules and their exceptions are conditioned on the existence of certain facts. These are not the facts on the historical merits of the case under Federal Rule of Evidence 401. Rather, these are foundational, preliminary, or predicate facts falling under Rule 104. For example, a copy of a writing will not be received unless the original is lost, destroyed, or otherwise unavailable.[6] Suppose a copy is offered and there is conflicting evidence as to whether the original is destroyed or intact. It is, of course, the judge who decides the legal question of whether there is a rule of evidence law establishing the criterion of admission or exclusion. However, who decides the question of fact whether the original is lost, destroyed or unavailable—the preliminary question on which the *application* of the rule of evidence law hinges?

Procedural law usually assigns "issues of fact" to the jury, but there are strong reasons for not doing so here. If the special question of fact were submitted to the jury when objection was made, cumbersome problems about unanimity would arise. More importantly, if the judge submitted the evidence (such as the copy in the hypothetical) to the jury and directed them to disregard it unless they found that the disputed fact existed, the aim of the exclusionary rule might be frustrated for two reasons. First, the jury would often be unable to erase the evidence from their minds even after, at a conscious level, they found that the conditioning fact did not exist. For instance, even if the jury found that an accused's statement to his attorney was technically privileged and inadmissible, common sense suggests that they would have a difficult time forgetting that they had learned that the accused admitted committing the charged offense. Second, to be frank, some jurors might be unwilling to perform the mental gymnastic of "disregarding" the evidence. They are primarily intent on reaching a verdict in accord with what they believe to be true, rather than in promoting the long-term policies of evidence law. The law-trained judge appreciates that the policy of protecting privacy interests justifies enforcing privileges, but the lay jurors might view a privilege unfavorably as an impediment to their tasks to find the truth and do justice in the case before them. Just as in fact jurors can nullify substantive rules of law, they could nullify exclusionary rules of evidence.

Foundational Facts Conditioning the Application of Technical Exclusionary Rules

Accordingly, under the traditional and still generally accepted view, the trial judge finally decides the preliminary questions of fact conditioning the admissibility of evidence objected to under exclusionary rules such as the hearsay doctrine.[7] This principle is incorporated in Federal and Uniform Rule of Evidence 104(a) . The same practice extends to the determination of preliminary facts conditioning the application of the rules as to witnesses' competency and privileges. On all these preliminary questions, both sides have a right to present testimony on the foundational issue before the judge rules. For example, on request the judge may hold a hearing—perhaps even at sidebar—at which each side can produce evidence. When the opponent objects, she can request the opportunity to conduct voir dire in support of the objection. In effect, the voir

---

6   See infra §§ 231, 237.

7   See infra § 163 for rules concerning the admission of a criminal accused's confession.

dire is a mini cross-examination. During the voir dire, the opponent questions the witness solely about the foundational fact which the proponent attempted to establish, not the historical merits. Between the proponent's foundation and the opponent's voir dire, the judge hears all the testimony both pro and con on the foundational issue. With the exception of the privilege rules, the technical exclusionary rules do not apply to foundational testimony; and the judge may thus consider any unprivileged testimony, even hearsay. The judge acts as a factfinder in determining the existence of the foundational fact and ordinarily applies the preponderance of the evidence standard of proof. The judge may consider the credibility of the foundational testimony. Hence, the judge can decide to disbelieve the proponent's testimony even if it is facially sufficient.

Foundational Facts Conditioning the Fundamental Logical Relevance of the Evidence

The preceding discussion involves situations where the evidence is sought to be excluded under a "technical" exclusionary rule. Those situations must be distinguished from another type of situation, namely one in which the logical relevancy—the fundamental probative value—of the evidence depends on the existence of a preliminary fact. As the Advisory Committee's Note to Federal Rule of Evidence 104(b) observes:

> Thus when a spoken statement is relied upon to prove notice to X, it is without probative value unless X heard it. Or if a letter purporting to be from Y is relied upon to establish an admission by him, it has no probative value unless Y wrote ... it. Relevance in this sense has been labelled "conditional relevancy." Morgan, Basic Problems of Evidence 45–56 (1962).[8]

These factual questions of conditional relevancy under Rule 104(b) not only differ from questions falling under Rule 104(a). They also differ from questions whether particular evidence is relevant as a matter of law under Rule 401, such as the issue of whether evidence that on the day before a murder the accused purchased a weapon of the type used in the killing is relevant. Questions of the latter nature are, of course, for the judge. Distinguish that Rule 401 question of law from the Rule 104(b) question of fact whether the gun marked as prosecution exhibit #3 for identification is the very gun the accused purchased.

Conditional relevancy questions under 104(b) are well within the jurors' competency; they involve the kind of questions which jurors are accustomed to decide. Did A actually make a particular oral statement? Did B sign the letter offered in evidence? The jury's role and power on the merits would be greatly curtailed if judges made the final decisions on these questions. The judge is not, however, entirely eliminated from the picture; rather, the judge divides responsibility with the jury in the following manner. The judge requires the proponent to bring forward evidence from which a rational jury could find the existence of the preliminary fact. At this point, the judge plays a limited, screening role. The judge cannot pass on the credibility of the foundational testimony. Rather, the test is a hypothetical jury finding. The judge must accept the testimony at face value and ask only this question: If the jury decides to believe the testimony, is there a rational, permissive inference of the existence of the preliminary fact? When the judge determines that the jury could not find the existence

---

[8]   Fed. R. Evid. 104(b) advisory committee's note. *See also* Morgan, Functions of Judge and Jury in Preliminary Questions of Fact, 43 Harv. L. Rev. 164, 164–75 (1929). See the general treatment of authentication as an aspect of conditional relevancy, infra Ch. 22.

of the preliminary fact, she excludes the evidence. Otherwise, the question is for the jury to decide during deliberations. The jury makes the real factual determination whether the witness has personal knowledge or whether the letter is authentic. Although in fact some trial judges permit the opponent to conduct voir dire on conditional relevance issues, strictly speaking the opponent has no right to voir dire on this type of issue. When the opponent has contrary evidence, the opponent submits it to the jury rather than the judge. On request, in the final instructions the judge directs the jury to determine the existence of the foundational fact and to disregard the evidence if they find that the foundational fact has not been proven. Unlike the judge at the first step, the jury considers the credibility of the testimony.

At first blush, the Rule 104(b) scheme can seem complex, but it is reducible to a simple, two-step procedure:

- The judge screens the foundational testimony for the jury. The judge accepts the proponent's foundational testimony at face value and inquires only: If the jury chooses to believe this testimony, does it have sufficient probative value to support a permissive inference of the existence of the preliminary fact? If the answer is no, the judge sustains the objection, excluding the foundational testimony and the proffered item of evidence.

- If the answer is yes, the judge overrules the objection, admitting the foundational testimony and the proffered item of evidence. The jury makes the real factual determination.

This procedure is followed at modern common law and prescribed by Federal Rule of Evidence 104(b) and Uniform Rule of Evidence 104(c) and Federal Rule 104(b). Restyled Federal Rule 104(b), reads:

> When the relevance of evidence depends on whether a fact exists, proof must be introduced sufficient to support a finding that the fact does exist. The court may admit the proposed evidence on the condition that the proof be introduced later.[9]

Federal Rule 602 expressly applies this procedure to the preliminary issue of a lay witness's personal knowledge, and Rule 901(a) extends the procedure to the foundational issue of the authenticity of exhibits. The drafters reasoned that the jurors could be trusted to decide these preliminary issues. If the jurors find that a lay witness did not see the accident he testified about or that a letter allegedly written by the accused is a forgery, common sense should naturally lead them to disregard the witness's testimony or the letter during their deliberations. These preliminary facts condition the logical relevance of the evidence in a fundamental sense that is obvious even to lay jurors who lack legal training but have common sense. The jury has determined that the witness "doesn't know what he is talking about" or the exhibit "is not worth the paper it's written on." Once the jurors have made that determination, their common sense will prompt the jurors to disregard the evidence during the balance of their deliberations. In short, it is safe to allow the jurors to make these determinations.

---

[9]   In *Huddleston v. United States*, 485 U.S. 681 (1988), the Court held that Federal Rule 104(b) governs the foundational question of whether the accused committed an act of uncharged misconduct proffered under Rule 404(b), for example, another murder allegedly committed with the same distinctive modus operandi. A number of states have refused to follow *Huddleston* and required a stronger showing.

Three Troublesome Types of Issues

Some situations have not readily lent themselves to classification as falling in either of the two categories of facts and accordingly require further discussion.

First, confessions are subject to their own special rules, which are treated elsewhere in this treatise.[10]

Second, in cases involving dying declarations some jurisdictions assign the jury a role in deciding the preliminary question whether declarant had the settled, hopeless expectation of death required for that hearsay exception.[11] This practice is not followed under Federal and Uniform Rule of Evidence 104.

In a third, troublesome group of cases, the preliminary fact question coincides with one of the ultimate disputed fact-issues that the jury normally decides. There are several examples. (1) In a bigamy prosecution, the first marriage is disputed, the second wife is called as a state's witness, and the defendant objects under a statute disqualifying the wife to testify against her husband. (2) Plaintiff sues on a lost writing, and defendant raises a best evidence objection and contends that it was not lost because it never existed. (3) In a prosecution, the state offers an alleged co-conspirator's declaration made during the course of and in furtherance of the conspiracy. Defendants deny that the conspiracy ever existed. The published common law opinions on these three issues are split.

In Example (1) the preliminary question involves the witness's competency. Competency would be a question for the judge at common law or under Rule 104(a) if it were not for the overlap with the jury issue on the merits of whether she was validly married to the accused. However, allowing the judge to initially decide her competency does not interfere with the jury's function in any way; her decision need not be disclosed to the jury, and additional relevant evidence may be made available to the jury. Accordingly, the cases tend to leave the competency decision to the judge. For example, in a bigamy prosecution, even if the judge decides that the second marriage was invalid, overrules the competency objection, and permits the spouse's testimony, the accused can later litigate the question of the validity of the second marriage to the jury during the trial on the merits.

In Example (2) the preliminary question whether a writing was lost is ordinarily for the judge at common law or under Rule 104(a), but the writing obviously cannot have been lost if it never existed. Aside from the question of loss, the execution of the document would be a jury question; the preliminary question of authentication under Rule 901 is allocated to the jury at common law and under Rule 104(b). The basic issue is whether the original writing ever existed; the question whether it has been lost is subsidiary. Sound judgment dictates assigning the decision of the basic question to the jury, rather than subsuming it under the judge's authority to determine the application of the best evidence rule. This is the result both in the case law and under Rule 1008(a). If the judge decided that the writing never existed and excluded the secondary evidence, the case would end without ever going to the jury on the central issue.

In Example (3), the common law cases divide over whether the judge should make the preliminary determination whether a conspiracy existed and defendant and declarant were members of it, or whether the judge ought to admit the evidence upon a

---

[10]   See infra § 163.

[11]   The nature of the requirement is discussed in infra § 310.

prima facie showing and instruct the jury to disregard it if they find these matters not proved. Supporting the first position is the argument that the judge is dealing with the applicability of a hearsay doctrine, the exemption for co-conspirator declarations. Moreover, even when the prosecution's foundation is inadequate, the foundation often shows that the declarant had both personal knowledge and a close relationship with the defendant. In those circumstances, it is unrealistic to think that the jurors can readily put the foundational testimony and the hearsay statement out of mind even if the jurors decide that the foundation is technically insufficient. Those factors cut in favor of applying Rule 104(a) under the Federal and Revised Uniform Rules. In contrast, under one view of the hearsay definition, virtually all co-conspirator declarations qualify as "verbal acts"[12] and hence nonhearsay in the first place. This reasoning lends some support to empowering the jury to make the determination, after screening by the judge, as a question of conditional relevancy under Rule 104(b). Whatever the relative merits of these conflicting positions, in *Bourjaily v. United States*[13] the Supreme Court declared authoritatively that determining the admissibility of a co-conspirator's statement is solely a matter for the judge under Rule 104(a) and that the judge must apply the more probably true than not (preponderance) standard of proof. This result reflects two considerations: the awkward procedural consequences of submitting the preliminary question to the jury, and the courts' understandable wish to limit the use of conspiracy charges by prosecutors.

A closely related question is whether Rule 104(a) or 104(b) governs the foundational facts conditioning the hearsay exemption for authorized admissions in civil cases. One would think that the same procedure should govern the foundations for both hearsay exemptions; after all, a conspiracy is a criminal agency. However, even after the Supreme Court rendered its decision in *Bourjaily*, there was a strong statutory construction argument that Rule 104(b) controlled the foundational facts for the civil exemption. As previously stated, the original Advisory Committee's Note to Rule 104 approvingly quotes Professor Morgan as indicating that it is a conditional relevance question whether a principal "authorized" an admission made by an alleged agent. Some jurisdictions remain firmly committed to the view that these are conditional relevance questions. However, a 1997 amendment to Federal Rule 801 makes it clear that the federal courts are to apply the same procedure to both sets of foundational facts. Since *Bourjaily* squarely holds that Rule 104(a) governs the facts conditioning the coconspirator exemption, a fortiori 104(a) also controls the preliminary facts for authorized admissions. *Bourjaily* comes to the right conclusion. Even if at a conscious level the jurors decide that the technical elements of the foundation are missing, the record may show that the declarant had both personal knowledge and a special relationship to the party opponent. In these circumstances, there is a grave risk that at a subconscious level the jurors will be tempted to misuse the testimony as evidence against the party opponent.

§ 54 Availability as Proof of Evidence Admitted Without Objection

As § 52 indicated, a failure to make a sufficient objection to incompetent evidence waives any ground of complaint as to the admission of the evidence. But it has another equally important effect. If the testimony is received without objection, the testimony

---

[12]   See infra § 259.
[13]   483 U.S. 171 (1987).

becomes part of the evidence in the case and is usable as proof to the extent of its rational persuasive power. The fact that it was inadmissible does not prevent its use as proof so far as it has probative value. The inadmissible evidence, unobjected to, may be relied on in argument; and alone or in part it can support a verdict or finding. At the trial court level, a party may rely on the evidence to defeat a directed verdict motion; and on appeal, the party may use the evidence to uphold the legal sufficiency of the evidence to support a judgment. This principle is almost universally accepted. The Federal and Revised Uniform Rules of Evidence are silent on this subject but raise no doubt as to the continued viability of the common law rule. The principle applies to any ground of incompetency under the exclusionary rules. It is most often invoked with respect to hearsay, but it has also been applied to secondary evidence of writings, opinions, evidence elicited from incompetent witnesses, privileged information, and evidence objectionable due to the lack of authentication of a writing, firsthand knowledge, or expert qualification.

However, relevancy and probative worth stand on a different footing. If the evidence has no probative force or insufficient probative value to sustain the proposition for which it is offered, the lack of objection adds nothing to its worth; and the evidence will not support a finding. It is still irrelevant or insufficient. However, in some cases in some jurisdictions, the failure to object to evidence related to the controversy but not covered by the pleadings, can informally frame new issues and impliedly amend the pleadings. The evidence may be relevant to such a new issue. When this occurs, the failure to object on the ground that the evidence is irrelevant to any issue raised by the original pleadings is waived; and the evidence can support the proponent's position on the new informal issue.

§ 55 Waiver of Objection

As a general proposition, the party's failure to object promptly and specifically effects a waiver.[14] What other conduct constitutes a waiver?

A Failure to Testify After the Loss of a Motion In Limine

When a party has unsuccessfully moved in limine motion to exclude credibility evidence, some authorities, including the Supreme Court, require the witness to testify to preserve the issue for appeal. When the testimony is logically relevant only to credibility, the party can preclude the admission of the testimony by foregoing the witness's testimony. If the witness in question is the party, the party can simply elect not to testify; and if the witness is a non-party, the party can decide against calling them to the stand. Thus, the cost of a ruling admitting the evidence can be the loss of the witness's testimony. The argument runs that the appellate court cannot intelligently gauge that cost unless the court has the benefit of the testimony; the appellate courts reason that without the benefit of the witness's actual testimony, they cannot properly evaluate the trial judge's ruling denying the in limine motion.

However, the holdings in those authorities are limited in scope. Many of these authorities relate to evidence logically relevant only on a credibility theory. Moreover, in some jurisdictions a detailed offer of proof or a voir dire of the witness outside the jury's presence obviates the need for the witness to testify at trial to preserve the issue for

---

[14]   See supra § 52.

purposes of appeal. Finally, some jurisdictions flatly reject the view that the party must call the witness in order to preserve the issue.

Demand for Inspection of a Writing

Federal Rule of Civil Procedure 34 authorizes a litigant to demand that the opponent produce writings and objects for pretrial inspection. Suppose that one party, D, gives notice to his opponent, O, to produce a document, and O produces it. Then D asks to inspect it and is allowed to do so. Assume that under some evidentiary doctrine, the document, if offered by O, would be inadmissible except for the facts of notice, production, and inspection. Do these facts preclude D from objecting when O offers the document into evidence? Old precedents in England, Massachusetts, and a few other states said yes: D may not object. This result was originally rationalized on the notion that it would be somehow unfair to permit the demanding party to examine the producing party's private papers without incurring some corresponding risk. A later case, however, attempted to justify the result on another theory; according to that case, at least when the demand is made in open court, the jury may suspect the party who is called on to produce the writing of evasion or concealment unless he can introduce the writing. That argument has limited validity, though; that risk is present only when, under local procedure, the demand must be made in the jury's hearing. Modernly, the demand is ordinarily made out of court before trial.

The modern cases recognize that the traditional policy against compelled disclosure of relevant writings in a party's possession is outmoded. The contemporary policy is just the opposite, namely, pressuring full disclosure except for privileged matter.[15] Accordingly, today the overwhelming majority of states reject the old rule and permit D to assert any pertinent objection if O later offers the writing. This rule is consistent with Federal and Uniform Rule of Evidence 103(a)(1) . The older view is at odds with the liberal pretrial discovery policy of the federal civil rules, which have been adopted widely in the states. In this fact situation, it is silly to infer that the party requesting production has waived all evidentiary objections to the introduction of the writing; the party cannot forecast the potential objections until she has had an opportunity to review the contents of the writing.

Failure to Object to Earlier Similar Evidence

A party has introduced evidence of particular facts without objection. Later he offers additional evidence, perhaps by other witnesses or writings, of the same facts. May the adversary now object, or has he waived his right by his earlier quiescence? Some opinions summarily state that he may not object.

However, in the more carefully reasoned opinions, courts usually conclude that standing alone, the earlier failure to object to other like evidence is not a waiver of objection to the new inadmissible evidence. This conclusion should be reached under the Federal and Revised Uniform Rules of Evidence. (Of course, overruling the new objection will sometimes be harmless error, since the earlier evidence could render the error harmless; but that is a different question.) As § 52 points out, even when evidence is technically objectionable, experienced trial attorneys do not object unless the evidence is clearly damaging. Their practice is in the interest of judicial economy and encouraged by the nonwaiver rule. The conventional wisdom is that an attorney should not assert

---

[15]　Fed. R. Civ. P. 26.

every technically available objection; to avoid alienating the jury, the attorney ought to object only when the objection is both legally meritorious and tactically sound—such as when the evidence in question would do major damage to the attorney's theory of the case. It might have been tactically inadvisable to object to the earlier evidence; although the testimony was technically objectionable under evidence law, its contents might have been innocuous or positively helpful. Hence, it would be wrong-minded to infer a waiver from the earlier failure to object.

However, when the evidence of the fact, admitted without objection, is extensive, and the evidence though inadmissible has some probative value, the trial judge should have discretion to find that the objector's conduct amounted to a waiver. Again, this approach can be followed under the Federal and Revised Uniform Rules of Evidence.

The Offering of Similar Evidence by the Objector

If a party who has objected to evidence of a certain fact herself later produces affirmative evidence of the same fact from her own witness, she has waived his earlier objection. This result should obtain under the Federal and Revised Uniform Rules of Evidence. However, when her objection is made and overruled, she is entitled to treat this ruling as the "law of the trial" and to negatively rebut or explain, if she can, the evidence admitted over her protest. Consequently, as a general rule there is no waiver if she cross-examines the adversary's witness about the matter. There is also no waiver even though the cross-examiner repeats the fact or even meets the testimony with other evidence which, under the theory of her objection, would be inadmissible. Here too the courts can reach the same result under the Federal and Revised Uniform Rules of Evidence.

However, some courts have carved out an exception to the above general rule. Suppose that the defense counsel believes that the prosecutor will attempt to use an inadmissible conviction to impeach the defendant but unsuccessfully moves in limine to bar the use of the conviction. Assume further that to blunt the impact of the expected impeachment, during the defendant's direct examination the defense counsel has the defendant acknowledge the conviction. In 2000 in *Ohler v. United States,* the Court held that by mentioning her conviction on direct, the defendant waived any error in the in limine ruling. The Court's syllabus states:

> A defendant who preemptively introduces evidence of a prior conviction on direct examination may not challenge the admission of such evidence on appeal. Ohler attempts to avoid the well-established commonsense principle that a party introducing evidence cannot complain on appeal that the evidence was erroneously admitted by invoking the Federal Rules of Evidence 103 and 609. However, neither Rule addresses the question at issue here. She also argues that applying such a waiver rule in this situation would compel a defendant to forgo the tactical advantage of preemptively introducing the conviction in order to appeal the in limine ruling. But both the Government and the defendant in a criminal trial must make choices as the trial progresses.[16]

The Court's holding has been sharply criticized. The essence of the criticism is that it is an accepted, reasonable trial tactic to blunt anticipated damaging evidence and that

---

[16]   529 U.S. 753 (2000).

the cost of resorting to such a legitimate tactic should not include forfeiting the right to challenge an erroneous trial court ruling. Since the decision is non-constitutional in character, the states are free to adopt a contrary view. Several have done so.

Exclusion by Judge on Her Own Motion Absent an Objection

A party's failure to object usually waives the objection and forecloses that party from complaining if the evidence is admitted. But the party's failure does not preclude the trial judge from excluding the evidence on her own motion if the prospective witness is incompetent or the evidence is inadmissible, and the judge believes the interests of justice require the exclusion of the testimony. The judge is especially likely to intervene in criminal cases to bar inadmissible evidence that might severely prejudice the defendant. The judge can step in both to protect the accused's rights and to decrease the risk that any conviction will later be vulnerable to collateral attack on the ground of ineffective representation of counsel. The Federal and Revised Uniform Rules of Evidence grant the judge sufficiently broad power to intervene *sua sponte* in such circumstances.

However, many types of technically inadmissible evidence such as reliable affidavits or copies of writings can be probative and trustworthy. When the evidence falls into this category, absent an objection, the trial judge would be unjustified in excluding the evidence. The judge should exercise her discretionary power to intervene only when the evidence is irrelevant, unreliable, misleading, or prejudicial as well as technically inadmissible.

However, privileged evidence, such as confidential communications between husband and wife, ought to be treated differently. The privileges protect the holder's outside private interests, not the parties' interest in securing justice in the present litigation. Accordingly, when a question calls for privileged matter and the holder is present, if necessary the judge may explain the privilege to the holder; but the judge should not assert it on her own motion if the holder decides against claiming the privilege. In contrast, when the holder is absent, the judge in some jurisdictions has a discretionary power to assert it on the holder's behalf.

§ 56 The Effect of the Introduction of Part of a Writing or Conversation

The preceding sections discuss the procedures applicable when the opposing attorney negatively attempts to exclude the evidence proffered by the proponent. In some cases, though, the opponent endeavors to turn the proponent's proffer to affirmative advantage; the opponent argues that the proponent's proffer allows the opponent to introduce evidence that might otherwise be inadmissible. Sections 56 and 57 discuss these cases. Like § 32, this section addresses the rule of completeness while § 57 describes the curative admissibility doctrine.

Two competing considerations come into play when a party offers in evidence only a portion of a writing, oral statement, or conversation. One consideration is the danger of admitting only a portion of the expression, wresting that part out of its context. "The fool hath said in his heart, there is no God,"[17] where only the last phrase is quoted, is Wigmore's classic example of the possibilities of distortion. You can indeed quote the Bible as saying "there is no God;" but to do so would be a misleading half-truth because

---

[17] For the oft-quoted classic illustration, see 7 Wigmore, Evidence § 2094 (Chadbourn rev. 1978).

it rips the quotation from its context. Moreover, this danger may not be completely averted by a later, separate reading of the omitted parts. The distorted impression can sometimes linger and work its influence at the subconscious level. The second consideration is the countervailing danger of requiring that the whole be offered, possibly wasting time and cluttering the trial record with passages which have no bearing on the present controversy.

The Common Law

What is the proper balance between these two considerations? In the light of the dangers, is a party who seeks to introduce part of a writing or statement required to offer it in its entirety, or at least all the passages relevant to the facts sought to be proved? The common law version of the rule of completeness permits the proponent to prove whatever part she desires. At common law, the opponent cannot force the proponent to broaden the scope of her questioning of the witness. However, when the proponent turns the witness over to the opponent for questioning, the opponent can then elicit the other parts relevant to the same topic. Although the Federal Rules of Evidence do not expressly codify this facet of the rule of completeness, under the Supreme Court's 1988 decision in *Beech Aircraft v. Rainey*[18] the opponent can still invoke this doctrine in modern federal practice.

Federal Rule of Evidence 106

However, there is a strong policy argument that to guard against the danger of an ineradicable, false first impression, the adversary should have an additional right—the adversary ought to be permitted to require the proponent to introduce both the part which the proponent wants to introduce and other passages which are an essential part of its context. Federal and Uniform Rule of Evidence 106 go beyond the common law completeness rule and grant the opponent the further right to demand that the proponent expand the scope of his questioning of the witness to avoid creating a misleading initial impression. The statutes prescribe this rule for writings or recorded statements. The party invoking Rule 106 must specify the omitted portion of the writing or tape which supposedly serves as essential, integral context for the part the opposing party wants to introduce.

It is sometimes stated that the additional material may be introduced only if it is otherwise admissible. However, as a categorical rule, that statement is unsound. In particular, the statement is sometimes inaccurate as applied to hearsay law. At least when the other passage of the writing or statement is so closely connected to the part the proponent contemplates introducing that it furnishes essential context for that part, the passage becomes admissible on a nonhearsay theory. For that matter, the contextual nonhearsay theory does not exhaust the proponent's arguments. As we shall see, the complex of pertinent admissibility doctrines includes the concept of waiver of objection through "door opening."[19] In some cases, under that doctrine the proponent can successfully argue that the adversary's prior conduct has "opened the door" and rendered an otherwise inadmissible part admissible. In the final analysis, the question of whether an otherwise inadmissible part offered to explain, modify, or qualify the part already received is admitted should turn on whether its probative value for that purpose is

---

[18]   In Beech Aircraft Corp. v. Rainey, 488 U.S. 153 (1988), the Court stated that Rule 106 "partially codified" the completeness doctrine.

[19]   See infra § 57.

substantially outweighed by dangers of unfair prejudice, confusion of the issues, misleading the jury, or waste of time.

Of course, the adversary has another alternative, namely, later invoking the more limited, common law completeness rule. The state of the law governing this alternative is clearer and more consistent. The adversary may wait until her own next opportunity to present evidence. Then merely by virtue of the fact that the first party has earlier introduced a part, she has the right to introduce other parts of the writing, recording, statement, correspondence, former testimony, or conversation relating to the same subject matter. The more drastic doctrine, Rule 106, does not come into play unless the other passage is so closely related to the part the proponent offers that presenting only that part to the jury would be a half-truth which might mislead the jury. In contrast, the common law right applies so long as the other passage is logically relevant to the same topic as the part the proponent offers. This right is subject to the previously mentioned qualification which comes into play when there is an independent evidentiary objection to the remainder.

§ 57 Fighting Fire with Fire: Inadmissible Evidence as Opening the Door

One party successfully offers inadmissible evidence. There are various potential explanations for the introduction of the inadmissible evidence: The evidence might come in because the adversary neglects to object, he has no opportunity to object, or the judge erroneously overrules an objection. Is the adversary entitled to answer this evidence, with testimony by way of denial or explanation?

The question has prompted a sharp split of authority. In some jurisdictions the adversary is not entitled to meet the evidence, in others she may do so, and in still others she may do so if he would be prejudiced by denying her an opportunity to meet the evidence. However, it may be significant that the end result in many, if not most, decisions is the affirmance of the trial judge's action. The majority of courts appear to subscribe to the general proposition that "one who induces a trial court to let down the bars to a field of inquiry that is not competent or relevant to the issues cannot complain if his adversary is also allowed to avail himself of the opening."[20] Federal cases occasionally apply the same general notion.

Unfortunately, the published appellate opinions afford little guidance on the question as to how the trial judge should deal with the problem. Because of the many variable factors affecting the solution in a particular case, the diverse situations do not lend themselves easily to neat generalizations. However, the published decisions identify two key factors, the prejudicial nature of the evidence and whether the opponent made a timely objection to block the admission of the evidence. Given those two factors, it is possible to synthesize the case law. The following generalizations, having some support in the decisions, are reasonable:

(1) If the inadmissible evidence sought to be answered is irrelevant and not prejudice-arousing, to save time and to avoid distraction from the issues the judge should refuse to hear answering evidence. However, under the prevailing view, if the judge does admit it, the party opening the door has no standing to complain. Consider, for example, a case in which one party

---

[20] Warren Live Stock Co. v. Farr, 142 F. 116, 117 (8th Cir. 1905).

improperly injects evidence of the good character of one of his distant relatives who played a minor role in the litigated event. That type of evidence is unlikely to change the outcome of the trial. It would hardly be an abuse of discretion for the judge to exclude the opponent's evidence attacking the relative's character.

(2)   Suppose alternatively that, although inadmissible, the evidence is relevant to the issues and hence presumably damaging to the adversary's case, or though irrelevant is materially prejudicial and the adversary seasonably objected or moved to strike. Here the adversary should be entitled to present answering evidence as of right. By objecting, he did his best to save the court from committing error. His remedy of assigning appellate error to the ruling is inadequate. He needs a fair opportunity to win his case at the trial level by refuting the damaging evidence. In many cases, the adversary simply cannot afford the expense of a second trial after an appeal. Assume that the opponent succeeds in introducing inadmissible evidence of his own good character. That type of evidence is much more likely to affect the verdict than testimony about a distant relative's character. (This situation should be distinguished from the question, considered in § 55, whether the prior objection is waived if the answering evidence is permitted.)

(3)   Suppose that the first inadmissible evidence is relevant or that albeit irrelevant, the evidence is prejudicial and the adversary failed to object or to move to strike out where an objection might have avoided the harm. Here in principle the admission of answering evidence should rest in the judge's discretion. The judge ought to weigh the probable impact of the first evidence, the time and distraction incident to answering it, and the likely effectiveness of a curative instruction to the jury to disregard it. However, here several courts have indicated that introduction of the answering evidence is a matter of right and not allowed merely in the judge's discretion.

(4)   In any event, if the inadmissible evidence or even the inquiry eliciting it is so prejudice-arousing that an objection or motion to strike would not have erased the harm, the adversary should be entitled to answer it as of right.

This section is devoted to the question of rebutting inadmissible evidence. That question differs from the issue of whether a party's introduction of evidence inadmissible under some exclusionary rule (such as hearsay) gives the adversary license to introduce other evidence which (1) is inadmissible under the same exclusionary rule but (2) bears on a different issue or is irrelevant to the original inadmissible evidence. The "opening the door" doctrine has not been extended that far; the door does not swing open that widely.

§ 58   Admissibility of Evidence Dependent on Proof of Other Facts: "Connecting up"

The relevancy or admissibility of evidence of a particular fact frequently hinges on the proof of other facts. Thus, proof that a speeding automobile passed a particular spot at a certain time, or that there was a conversation between the witness and an unidentified stranger at a given time and place, will become relevant only when the automobile is identified as the defendant's or the stranger is shown to be the plaintiff. In the same manner, evidence of certain acts and declarations might not become material until they are shown to be those of the defendant's agent. Likewise, a copy of a writing does not become admissible until the original is proven to be lost or destroyed. In terms of logic, some of these missing facts may be thought of as preliminary to the fact offered, and others as coordinate with it. In either event, often only one fact can be proven at a time by a witness. In a given case, the most convenient sequence of calling witnesses might not coincide with the order of strict logic. Logic might dictate that a doctor testify first, but logic might have to yield to an emergency surgery.

Who decides the order of facts? In the first instance, the proponent does so by making the offer. However, in her general discretionary supervision over the order of proof to avoid confusion, the judge may require that the missing fact be proved first. But the trial judge seldom does so. At common law, when the adversary objects to the relevancy or the competency of the offered fact, the everyday method of handling the situation is to admit it conditionally; that is, the judge accepts the evidence on the proponent's express or implied assurance as an officer of the court that she will "connect up" the tendered evidence by proving the missing facts later. Federal Rule of Evidence 104(b), Uniform Rule 104(c), and Rule 611(a) in both codes grant the trial judge this same authority.

However, in a long trial with many witnesses and complex facts, it is easy for the offering counsel to later forget the need to present the required "connecting" proof, and for the judge and the adversary to overlook this gap in the evidence. Who has the burden of invoking the failure of the condition subsequent? The burden is on the objecting party to renew the objection and invoke the condition. According to the majority view, the opponent must move to strike the evidence conditionally received, when the failure of condition becomes apparent. The failure should become apparent to the objecting party when the offering party completes the particular stage of the case in which the evidence was offered. When the proponent "rests" without introducing the missing proof, the adversary should then "move to strike"; if the opponent fails to do so at that juncture, she cannot later as of right invoke the condition either during the trial or on appeal. Although some courts have considered the difference in form dispositive, a motion to strike, a motion to withdraw the fact from the jury, and a request for a curative instruction to disregard the evidence all should be regarded as a sufficient invocation of the condition. This analysis is compatible with Federal and Revised Uniform Rules of Evidence 104(b) and 611(a).

However, the proponent assumed some responsibility by promising to furnish the connecting proof. That responsibility can best be enforced by according the trial judge a discretion to allow the adversary to invoke the condition at any time before the case is submitted to the jury or before final judgment in a bench case, so long as the continued availability of the missing proof makes it fair to litigate the issue later. It is especially appropriate for the judge to exercise discretion in the adversary's favor when the offering party's case-in-chief was a lengthy one. The longer the case-in-chief is, the greater the probability that the adversary will innocently forget about the issue; and hence, the adversary's failure is relatively excusable.

Distinguish between the practice of "conditional" receipt pending further proof and the "provisional" admission of evidence where the opponent has objected and the judge admits the evidence while taking the objection under advisement. If the judge admits evidence provisionally, the final ruling on the objection is subject to a later decision when the judge has had more time to think through the issue. Unlike conditional admission situations, when the judge takes the matter under advisement there is nothing further for either side to submit. When the judge's ruling is provisional, to preserve the objection the objecting counsel must renew the objection and request a final ruling before the case concludes. The practice seems appropriate enough in a judge-tried case. However, in a jury trial there is a risk that letting the evidence in, even provisionally, might make an impression on the jury that a later instruction cannot erase. It is ordinarily unnecessary to run that risk. Understandably, the use of this practice in jury trials has been criticized. Although the published opinions sometimes indicate that the trial judge has discretion to employ this procedure, in many, if not most, instances resort to this practice is unnecessary and should be avoided. Rather than taking the issue under advisement and delaying a ruling, the judge should simply rule.

§ 59 Evidence Admissible for One Purpose, Inadmissible for Another: "Limited Admissibility"

A Limitation as to Purpose

An item of evidence may be logically relevant in several aspects, leading to distinct inferences or bearing upon different issues. For one of these purposes it may be admissible but for another inadmissible. In this common situation, subject to the limitations outlined below, the normal practice in case law and under Federal and Uniform Rule of Evidence 105 is to admit the evidence. The opponent's legitimate interest is protected, not by an objection to its admission, but rather by a request at the time of the offer for a limiting instruction that the jury consider the evidence only for the allowable purpose. Realistically, the instruction may not always be effective, but admission of the evidence with the limiting instruction is normally the best reconciliation of the competing interests.

However, there are exceptional situations where the danger of the jury's misuse of the evidence for the inadmissible purpose is acute, and the value of the evidence for the legitimate purpose is slight or the point for which it is admissible can readily be proved by other evidence. In such situations, both the cases and the Federal and Revised Uniform Rules of Evidence 403 recognize the judge's power to exclude the evidence altogether. Some hearsay problems cry out for the invocation of Rule 403. Assume that the proponent offers an out-of-court statement for a nonhearsay purpose but on its face the declaration asserts facts directly relevant to a critical issue in the case and the declarant would presumably have personal knowledge of the facts. Here common sense suggests that there is a grave risk that the jurors will misuse the testimony as substantive evidence.

A Limitation as to Party

Similarly, subject to the restrictions stated in the above and following paragraphs, evidence is frequently admissible as against one party, but not as against another. In that event, the accepted practice is to admit the evidence with an instruction, if requested, that the jurors are to consider the evidence only as to the party against whom it is properly admissible.

Yet, even limiting instructions are insufficient to insure against jury misuse of the confessions or admissions of a codefendant who does not take the stand when the confession implicates the defendant. In this situation, the confession is admissible against the non-testifying codefendant as an opposing party's statement (formerly termed a personal admission). But it may be inadmissible against the defendant. For instance, the confession might not qualify as a vicarious, co-conspirator admission against the defendant because a codefendant made the statement after he had been arrested and ceased being an active member of the conspiracy with the defendant. In similar situations, at a joint trial the traditional solution was to admit the evidence with a limiting instruction barring its use against the defendant. However, when the other evidence in the record indicates that there is a close relationship between the two and that the codefendant had personal knowledge of the facts asserted in his confession, there is an intolerable risk that the jury will disregard any limiting instruction and misuse the confession as proof of the defendant's guilt. There would be a violation of the Sixth Amendment right to confront witnesses. If the jurors treat the non-testifying codefendant's confession as evidence against the defendant, functionally the codefendant has become an accuser of the defendant; but since the codefendant will not testify, the defendant will be denied the right to cross-examine the accuser. Since the due process clause of the Fourteenth Amendment incorporates the Sixth Amendment confrontation guarantee, this rule is directly enforceable in state courts. However if, apart from the codefendant's confession, the case against the defendant was so overwhelming that its admission was harmless beyond a reasonable doubt, the appellate court will not reverse.

It would be a mistake, though, to generalize that if one purpose of two or more uses of evidence against a criminal defendant violates the defendant's constitutional rights, the evidence is completely inadmissible.[21] For example, in several cases, the Supreme Court has ruled that although a constitutional exclusionary rule precluded the use of an item of evidence as substantive proof, the evidence was admissible for impeachment purposes subject to a limiting instruction.

§ 60 Admission and Exclusion of Evidence in Bench Trials Without a Jury

The evidentiary rules at common law and under the Federal and Uniform Rules of Evidence apply in bench trials without a jury. Nevertheless as Thayer famously described the conventional wisdom, the law of evidence is to a great extent a "product of the jury system . . . where ordinary untrained citizens are acting as judges of fact." The Advisory Committee's Note to Federal Rule of Evidence 104 reiterates the received orthodoxy that the common law courts developed the exclusionary rules in large part due to their doubts about the capacity of lay jurors. For their part, judges possess professional experience in valuing evidence, greatly lessening the need for exclusionary rules. At common law, there was a sense that it was inexpedient to apply these restrictions to judges. That sense caused appellate courts to conclude that the same strictness need not be observed in applying the rules of evidence in bench trials as in jury trials. An appellate court should arguably reach the same result under the Federal and Uniform Rule of Evidence.

The most important influence encouraging trial judges to take a relaxed attitude toward evidence rules in nonjury cases is a doctrine recognized by most appellate courts. According to this doctrine, on an appeal from a bench trial, the receipt of inadmissible evidence over objection is ordinarily not ground for reversal if there was other, admissible evidence sufficient to support the findings. The judge is presumed to have disregarded the inadmissible evidence and relied on the admissible evidence. However, when the judge errs in the opposite direction by excluding evidence which ought to have

---

[21]   *See, e.g.,* United States v. Havens, 446 U.S. 620 (1980); Harris v. New York, 401 U.S. 222 (1971).

been received, the judge's ruling is subject to reversal if it is substantially harmful to the losing party. But some appellate decisions decline to apply the presumption when the evidence was objected to and the objection overruled. According to these decisions, the judge's action in overruling the objection suggests that the trial judge wanted to consider the evidence in question. Moreover, the presumption may be rebutted by a contrary showing. The rebuttal showing could take the form of the judge's statements from the bench during trial, or references to improperly admitted evidence in specific findings of fact prepared either separately or as part of an opinion or memorandum of decision.

In practice, considerations of waste of time, predictability and consistency lead most trial judges to apply the rules of evidence in a nonjury trial to exclude evidence that "is *clearly* inadmissible, privileged, or too time consuming in order to guard against reversal." However, where the admissibility of evidence proffered at a bench trial is debatable, many experienced, cautious judges follow a practice calculated to minimize the risk of reversal. That practice is to provisionally admit all arguably admissible evidence, even if objected to, with the announcement that all admissibility questions are reserved until all the evidence is in. In considering any objections renewed by motion to strike at the end of the case, the judge leans toward admission rather than exclusion but seeks to find clearly admissible testimony on which to base her findings of fact. To minimize the risk of appellate reversal, a prudent trial judge makes it a practice to explicitly identify on the record the admissible evidence that she is basing her factual findings on. The practice lessens the time spent in arguing objections and helps ensure that appellate courts have in the record the evidence that was rejected as well as that which was admitted. A more complete trial record sometimes enables the appellate court to dispose of the case by entering a final judgment rather than merely remanding to the trial court for further proceedings.[22]

---

[22]   See also the discussion of offers of proof, supra § 51.

Title 4

COMPETENCY

Chapter 7

THE COMPETENCY OF WITNESSES

Table of Sections

§ 61   Competency of Witnesses, in General

Most evidentiary rules regulate the content of proposed testimony. However, competency rules address the threshold question of whether a prospective witness is qualified to give any testimony at all in the case. For the most part, the competency standards relate to the prospective witness's status and personal capacities rather than the content of the testimony the witness is prepared to give. The early common law rules of incompetency were harsh, but they have been undergoing a process of piecemeal statutory liberalization for well over a century. During that period, most of the former grounds for altogether barring a witness have been converted into mere bases for impeaching her credibility.

Since the disqualification of witnesses for incompetency is thus dwindling in importance, and since the statutory reforms of the common law competency rules vary from state to state, this treatise does not present a detailed review of the law in the different jurisdictions. Instead, the following sections summarize the common law grounds of incompetency and describe the general directions of reform.

§ 62   Mental Incapacity and Immaturity: Oath or Affirmation

The Common Law

At modern common law, there is no rule automatically precluding an insane person as such from testifying. Moreover, although some states base a youth's competency or presumed competency on the child's chronological age, most jurisdictions do not preclude a child of any specified age from testifying. In each case, the test is whether the witness has enough intelligence to make it worthwhile to hear her at all and whether she recognizes a duty to tell the truth. Does she possess enough capacity to perceive, record, recollect, and narrate to probably add valuable knowledge of the facts to the record? At common law, following the procedure for foundational facts conditioning the competency of evidence,[1] the trial judge determines as a matter of fact whether the prospective witness possesses the requisite testimonial qualities, that is, the capacities to perceive, remember, narrate, and understand the duty to tell the truth under oath. Children as young as three years old have been ruled competent as witnesses. Similarly, persons with disabilities such as deafness and muteness may be competent witnesses. Likewise, persons suffering from mental disorders often satisfy the competency standards. Without more, neither past drug use nor even drug addiction is automatically disqualifying. By way of example, a crack cocaine user with the intelligence of a seven-year-old has been held to be a competent witness. The upshot is that a person is deemed incompetent only in extreme cases such as when he experiences insane delusions directly relevant to the subject-matter of his testimony or suffers from a psychosis very likely to grossly distort his testimony.

The major reason for the severe, early common law disqualification standards was the judges' distrust of a lay jury's ability to critically assess the words of a small child or a deranged person. Conceding *arguendo* the jury's deficiencies, the remedy of excluding such a witness—who may be the only person possessing knowledge of the facts—is primitive and Draconian. Even if the trier of fact lacks legal training and the testimony is difficult to evaluate, on balance it is still better to let the evidence come in for what it is worth with cautionary instructions.

The Federal Rules of Evidence

Although the more contemporary common law rules are relatively lax, the statutory reforms go even farther. Many states have enacted statutes specifically providing that the alleged victim is per se a competent witness in a child abuse prosecution. Furthermore, most modern evidence codes contain general provisions radically liberalizing the competency standards. Federal Rules 601–03 and 403 are pertinent.

———

Rules 601–603—the Plain Meaning Interpretation

Revised Uniform Rule of Evidence 601 and the first sentence of Federal Rule of Evidence 601 typify such codes. Rule 601 announces that "every person is competent to be a witness unless these rules provide otherwise." The only general competency requirements expressly "otherwise provided" by the Federal and Revised Uniform Rules of Evidence are contained in Rule 603 (prescribing that every witness declare by oath or affirmation that she will testify truthfully) and Rule 602 (mandating that the witness possess personal knowledge). A plain meaning interpretation of Rule 601 is that there are no remaining competency standards and that all the prospective witness need do is to take the oath. The most relevant legislative history, the very first sentence of the Advisory Committee's Note to Rule 601, confirms that plain meaning interpretation. The Note states that "[n]o mental or moral qualifications for testifying as a witness are specified." The Note dictates the conclusion that the drafters meant what Rule 601 unambiguously says. As a matter of statutory interpretation, this construction is the preferable view.

———

---

[1]   See supra § 53.

The Conservative Position

However, that sweeping interpretation of Rule 601 has evidently struck some courts as too revolutionary. Rather than construing Rule 601 literally, they take the more conservative position that the rule has a more limited impact, merely creating a presumption of competency. If that is the only impact of Rule 601, the substantive common law competency requirements survive; and procedurally, the judge must still find as a matter of fact that the prospective witness possesses the traditionally required capacities. However, the conservative position is highly questionable, since at common law in many jurisdictions the opposing party already had the burden of proof on the question of the witness's competency. In such a jurisdiction, the enactment of Rule 601 would be virtually meaningless because it would effect little change. It is true that many jurisdictions still follow the interpretive maxim that statutes in derogation of the common law are to be strictly construed, but here the drafters could not have made their intent more explicit. Short of saying "and we really mean it" in the text of Rule 601, the drafters could not have manifested their intent more clearly.

Some have suggested that the judge has implicit authority to bar a potential witness's testimony under Rule 603. That rule requires that the witness take an oath or make an affirmation that he will testify truthfully. The argument runs that to ensure that the oath is meaningful rather than a empty ritual, the trial judge should be empowered to determine in common law fashion whether the prospective witness is qualified to take the oath or make the affirmation. That argument, though, reads too much into the wording of Rule 603. The text of the rule refers only to the prospective witness's willingness to take an oath; neither the rule nor the accompanying Note even suggests that the judge is empowered to pass on the witness's qualification to take an oath.

———

The Intermediate Position

As we have seen, the conservative argument does violence to the statutory language of Rules 601 and 602. However, short of disregarding the language of the rules and Notes, a court might be willing to strain the language of Rule 601. Even then, at the very most, the Federal Rules can be construed as adopting an intermediate position, imposing four substantive requirements: (1) the witness have the capacity to accurately perceive, record, and recollect impressions of fact (physical and mental capacities); (2) the witness perceived, recorded, and recollects impressions tending to establish a fact of consequence in the litigation (the exercise of the capacities); (3) the witness declare that he will tell the truth, understands the duty to tell the truth (oath or affirmation), and appreciates the difference between the truth and a lie or fantasy; and (4) the witness possess the capacity to comprehend questions and express himself intelligibly, if necessary with an interpreter's aid (narration).

The intermediate position rests on a very broad reading of Rules 601 to 603. Its proponents argue that on an appropriate objection, the witness's proponent must make this four-fold showing to satisfy both the letter and spirit of the rules. Rule 602 expressly requires the proponent to show that the witness acquired firsthand knowledge. The proponents of the intermediate position argue that as a matter of logic, the witness could not have gained that knowledge unless she possessed the substantive capacities listed in this foundation. After all, how can you perceive anything unless you have the capacity to perceive? Given the wording of Rules 601 and 602, it is untenable to require anything more than this minimal foundation. It is certainly indefensible to announce any hard-and-fast rules concerning the incompetency of children of a specified age or adults suffering from a particular mental disorder. Moreover, especially since Rule 602 indicates that the judge must use the Rule 104(b) conditional relevance procedure for determining whether the proponent's showing of personal knowledge is satisfactory, the judge should apply the same lax procedure to all four substantive requirements.

Even the intermediate interpretation of the Federal Rules, though, leads to a substantial relaxation of the common law competency standards. As previously stated, at common law the trial judge decided as a question of fact whether the prospective witness possessed all the requisite capacities—the preliminary factfinding procedure now employed under Federal Rule 104(a). However, if the common law requirements have survived to an extent, as a matter of statutory interpretation they must largely be implied from the statutory scheme including Rule 602. Again, Rule 602 expressly indicates that the judge is to apply the conditional relevance procedure set out in Rule 104(b). To qualify a person as a witness, the witness's proponent need introduce only evidence sufficient to support a permissive inference of personal knowledge, i.e., that the witness had the capacity to and actually did observe, record, and can now recollect and narrate impressions obtained through any sense. That minimalist intermediate approach is consistent with the Advisory Committee's Note to Rule 601. The Note asserts that the common law standards of mental capacity proved elusive, few witnesses were actually disqualified, and a witness wholly without mental capacity is difficult to imagine.

Rule 403. Whatever construction of Rule 601 that the court adopts, the testimony of a witness whose mental capacity has been seriously impaired could still conceivably be excluded under Rule 403 on the ground that no reasonable juror could possibly believe that the witness possesses personal knowledge, or understands the difference between the truth and a lie or fantasy. With the exception of convictions qualifying under Federal Rule 609(a)(2), all evidence is subject to discretionary exclusion under Rule 403. The opponent's evidence of the prospective witness's deficiencies might be so strong that the trial judge could justifiably bar the witness under Rule 403. Admittedly, in assessing the probative value of an item of evidence for purposes of Rule 403, the trial judge ordinarily may not consider the credibility of the source of the evidence. However, especially if the contents of the prospective witness's testimony are garbled and virtually incoherent, her testimony would have minimal probative value and pose a significant danger of jury confusion.

In sum, even positing the intermediate interpretation of Rule 601, a witness's competency to testify at most requires only a minimal ability to observe, recollect, and recount as well as an understanding of the duty to tell the truth. Where a witness's capacity is brought into question, the ultimate issue is whether a reasonable juror must believe that the person's powers of perception, recollection, or narration are so deficient that it is not worth the time listening to her testimony. This test of competency requires only minimum credibility. The marked trend is to resolve doubts about the witness's credibility in favor of permitting the jury to hear the testimony and evaluate the witness's credibility for itself. Thus, proof of mental deficiency ordinarily has the limited effect of reducing the weight to be given to testimony rather than keeping the witness off the stand. Nevertheless, as previously stated, in an extreme case under Rule 403 the judge might exclude the testimony of a witness passing the test of minimum credibility on the basis of perceived probative dangers such as misleading or confusing the jury.

§ 63 Religious Belief

At early common law, as a prerequisite to taking the oath the witness had to believe in a divine being who, in this life or hereafter, will punish false swearing. Members of many major religions met the test, but followers of other religions, as well as atheists and agnostics, could not satisfy the test. That early approach is obviously inconsistent with the democratic principle of freedom of conscience. The state courts have invoked various theories for overturning this ground of incapacity. To reach that result, the courts have: relied on explicit state constitutional or statutory provisions, expansively interpreted state provisions forbidding deprivation of rights for religious beliefs, adopted Federal Rules of Evidence or Revised Uniform Rules of Evidence 601 and 603, or modified the common law "in the light of reason and experience" because such a requirement is inconsistent with the tolerant spirit of contemporary legal thought. In any event, the enforcement of this early common law rule of incapacity appears prohibited in any state or federal court by the First and Fourteenth Amendments of the national constitution.

The witness herself can object to an oath that directly or inferentially requires her to avow a belief in God. If the witness has a scruple against oaths, the witness may "affirm" under penalty of perjury rather than "swear." No particular form of oath or affirmation is necessary. However, it has been held that routinely swearing witnesses to tell the truth by using the phrase, "so help me God," does not warrant reversal when the witness herself did not object; requiring the use of that phrase might violate the witness's freedom of conscience, but in the typical case the losing litigant probably lacks standing to object on appeal. However, in some circumstances, as when it is evident to the jury that the losing party shared the beliefs which prevented the witness from swearing, the party could make a plausible argument that he was prejudiced. Inquiry into the witness's religious opinions for impeachment purposes is discussed in another section.[2]

§ 64 Conviction of Crime

The common law disqualified altogether a prospective witness who had been convicted of certain offenses, namely, treason, felony, or a crime involving fraud or deceit. In England and most states during the last hundred years, legislation has swept away this disqualification. In 1917, the United States Supreme Court determined that "the dead hand of the common law rule" of disqualification no longer applies in federal criminal cases.[3] The disqualification is not recognized in Federal Rule of Evidence and Uniform Rule of Evidence 601. However, a few states retain the disqualification for conviction of perjury and subornation. Even these statutes are now of debatable validity under the Supreme Court's decision in *Washington v. Texas*.[4] There the Court invalidated Texas legislation that barred persons charged or convicted as co-participants

---

[2]   See supra § 46.

[3]   Rosen v. United States, 245 U.S. 467 (1917).

[4]   388 U.S. 14 (1967). However, the opinion can be read more narrowly. In that case, the Court invalidated the Texas statutes primarily because they irrationally differentiated between the witness's appearance for the prosecution and the defense. That concern is inapplicable if the statute bars the convict from appearing as a witness for either side. However, the majority did reject Justice Harlan's suggestion in his concurrence that the Court remedy the infirmity by allowing Texas to deny the evidence to both sides.

in the same crime from testifying for each other. The Court found that it was irrational to permit such persons to testify for the prosecution while categorically barring their testimony for the defense.

§ 65 Parties and Persons Interested: The Dead Man Statutes

By far the most drastic common law incompetency rule was the doctrine excluding testimony by parties to the lawsuit and all persons with a direct pecuniary or proprietary interest in the outcome. In effect, this rule both imposed a disability on the party to testify in his own behalf and granted him a privilege not to be called as a witness against himself by the adversary. The disability had the specious justification of preventing self-interested perjury. The privilege lacked even that dubious rationale. It is almost unbelievable that the rule continued in force in England until the middle of the 19th century—and in this country for a few decades longer. In England, the reform was sweeping, and no shred of disqualification remains in civil cases.

In this country, however, the reformers were forced to accept a political compromise. An objection was raised with respect to controversies over consensual transactions, such as contracts, and other events such as traffic accidents where one party died but the other survived. The thrust of the objection was that fraud might result if the surviving parties or interested persons were permitted to testify about the transaction or the event. The survivor could still testify although death had sealed the adverse party's lips. This is a seductive argument. It was accepted in nearly all the states at a time when the real policy dispute was whether the general disqualification should be abolished or retained. At that time, the recognition of the exception for survivors' cases undoubtedly struck the reformers as a minor concession. Minor or not, the concession survives in many states.

State Survivors' Evidence Statutes

Accordingly, statutes in numerous states still provide that the common law disqualification of parties and interested persons is abolished with a single exception. The exception was that they remain disqualified to testify concerning a transaction or communication with a person since deceased in a suit prosecuted or defended by the decedent's executor or administrator. However, the statutes largely operate as a one-way street; there is often a proviso by statute or case law that the surviving party or interested person may testify if called by the adversary, that is, the decedent's executor or administrator. Thus, the proviso abrogates the privilege feature of the common law rule. The practical consequence of these statutes comes into play when a survivor has rendered services, furnished goods, or lent money to a person whom she trusted without an independent, corroborating witness or admissible written evidence. The survivor is helpless if the other dies and the representative of his estate declines to pay. The statute may also close the survivor's mouth in an action arising from a fatal automobile collision, or a suit on a note or account bill which the survivor paid in cash without obtaining a receipt.

Today, these restrictions are purely creatures of statute. Consequently, when a case raises a dead man's issue, the primary task is statutory construction. As Felix Frankfurter famously remarked, "Read the statute." To dissect the statute, keep the following questions in mind:

- What types of proceedings does the statute apply to? Must the decedent's personal representative be formally joined as a party? Does the statute apply only to causes of action directly derived from the decedent such as suits for the decedent's pain and suffering prior to death, or does it also extend to causes of action for wrongful death which are conferred by statute directly on the heirs? In a few states, the statute applies not only to proceedings involving a decedent's representative but also to actions involving the representative of a litigant who has been declared mentally incompetent.

- Who is disqualified? All statutes disqualify the surviving party. Some statutes also bar the surviving party's spouse. Many similarly exclude testimony by "interested persons." The courts tend to limit the scope of the latter expression to persons such as a surviving party's business partner who would benefit by the direct legal operation of the judgment in the case.

- What is the nature of the incompetence? Is the statute's bar limited to "communications" with the decedent? Or does the statute use broader language, typically "transactions"? How expansively should the term "transaction" be interpreted? Since the decedent's death has deprived the estate of the decedent's testimony based on personal knowledge, there is a strong argument that the "transaction" should purposively be construed broadly to include any fact or event which the decedent had firsthand knowledge of.

- Are there any special exceptions to the scope of the prohibition? Many statutes lift the bar of the statute when the survivor and the decedent stood in the relationship of employer and employee or partners. If the statute applied to such relationships, it would be difficult to enforce routine agreements between such parties. Those are important relationships in the business world, and the law should not impede them.

- What acts constitute a waiver of the statute? The estate certainly loses the protection of the statute when it calls an otherwise disqualified person as a witness at trial. Is there also a waiver if the estate merely deposes the person before trial? In some states, there is deep-seated judicial hostility to the continued existence of the statutes; and that hostility translates into the courts' willingness to strain to find a waiver.

More fundamentally, most commentators agree that the expedient of refusing to listen to the survivor is, in Bentham's words, "blind and brainless." In seeking to avoid injustice to one side, the statutory drafters ignored the equal possibility of creating injustice to the other. The survivor's temptation to fabricate a claim or defense is evident enough—so obvious that any juror should realize that her story must be evaluated cautiously. In case of fraud, a searching cross-examination will often reveal discrepancies in the "tangled web" of deception. In any event, the survivor's disqualification is more likely to disadvantage the honest than the dishonest survivor. A litigant who would resort to perjury will hardly hesitate at suborning a third person, who is not disqualified, to swear to the same false story.

Legislators and courts are gradually coming to realize the stupidity of the traditional survivors' evidence acts, and adopting liberalizing changes. A few states provide that the survivor may testify but that her testimony is legally insufficient to support a judgment unless the testimony is corroborated by other evidence. Others authorize the trial judge to permit the survivor to testify when it appears that her testimony is necessary to prevent injustice. Both of these solutions have evident drawbacks which are avoided by a third type of statute. The third kind of statutory scheme sweeps away the disqualification entirely and allows the survivor to testify without restriction. However, the scheme even-handedly minimizes the danger of injustice to the decedent's estate by admitting any relevant writings or oral statements by the decedent, both of which would ordinarily be excluded as hearsay.

Federal Law

Except in diversity cases, Federal Rule of Evidence and Uniform Rule of Evidence 601 completely abandon the instant disqualification. However, not all states that have generally copied the Federal Rules have followed suit. The disqualification not only survives in some states; the disqualification can also come into play in federal court. The second sentence of Federal Rule 601 reads: "But in a civil case, state law governs the witness's competency regarding a claim or defense for which state law supplies the rule of decision."

In short, interest as a disqualification in civil cases has been discarded, except for the relic of the survivors' evidence statutes. The common law disqualification which prevented the criminal accused from being called as a witness by either side has been abrogated in England and this country to the extent it disabled the defendant from testifying in her own behalf. However, it survives in that the prosecution cannot call the defendant. In this form, it is a privilege and constitutes one aspect of the broader Fifth Amendment privilege against self-incrimination, discussed in §§ 116 and 131.

While the disqualification of parties and persons interested in the result of the lawsuit has been almost entirely repealed, evidence law still acknowledges the obvious relevance of the fact of a witness's interest. Interest or bias may still be proved to impeach credibility.[5] Indeed, under the Sixth Amendment Confrontation Clause a criminal defendant has a constitutional right to cross-examine a prosecution witness to expose the witness's bias. In most jurisdictions the trial judge instructs the jury that a party's testimony should be weighed in the light of his self-interest and stake in the outcome of the trial.

§ 66 Husbands and Wives of Parties

Closely related to the parties' disqualification—and even more arbitrary and misguided—was the early common law disqualification of the party's husband or wife. This disqualification prevented the party's husband or wife from testifying either for or against the party in any case, civil or criminal. The disability of the husband or wife as a witness to testify *for* the party-spouse was a disqualification, based on the supposed infirmity of interest. In contrast, the rule enabling the party-spouse to prevent the husband or wife from testifying *against* the party functioned as a privilege.

Of course, the common law rule has been modified. After the Supreme Court's 2015 decision recognizing a constitutional right to same-sex marriage,[6] in all probability the rule's protection will be extended to same-sex couples. However, even before that landmark decision, the rule underwent major change. In the majority of jurisdictions today, statutes make the husband or wife fully competent to testify for or against the party-spouse in civil cases. In criminal cases, the disqualification of the husband or wife

---

[5]   See supra § 39.

[6]   Obergefell v. Hodges, 135 S. Ct. 2584 (2015).

to testify for the accused spouse has been removed everywhere; but in many states the prosecution may not call the spouse, without the accused spouse's consent, thus preserving the accused's privilege to keep the spouse off the stand altogether. To distinguish this competency doctrine from the more limited spousal communications privilege, this doctrine is often referred to as the anti-marital fact or spousal testimonial privilege. In some jurisdictions either spouse may assert the testimonial privilege. However, in its 1980 *Trammel* decision, the Supreme Court announced that in federal criminal cases, only the witness spouse (the spouse who is to be called by the prosecution as a witness) may claim the privilege.[7] The identification of the holder of the privilege is critical because it also determines who is competent to waive the privilege.

The privilege has occasionally been defended on the ground that it protects family harmony. However, family harmony is usually past saving when the witness spouse is willing to aid the prosecution. There are not only serious questions about the soundness of the policy rationale for the doctrine; at least at first blush, it is also difficult to defend the recognition of the doctrine as a matter of statutory construction. In recognizing the existence of the witness spouse's testimonial privilege, the Supreme Court looked to Rule 501 rather than Rule 601. Initially, one might think that Rule 601 on competency would govern. If Rule 601 governed and the Court gave 601 a literal interpretation, 601 would preclude the recognition of any privilege. After all, as the Advisory Committee's Note to Rule 601 states, "[n]o . . . qualifications" are "specified" in the text of the rule. However, in *Trammel* the Court correctly noted that its original draft of Article V of the Federal Rules touched on this privilege and that Congress had not objected to the treatment of the issue as an Article V problem. If Rule 501 controls, the Court had the power to recognize the privilege. Some states, though, have gone beyond *Trammel* and taken the step of abolishing the privilege in criminal cases; in those jurisdictions, spouses may be called to the stand to testify in criminal cases just as any other witness.

The Injured-Spouse Limitation on the Scope of the Privilege

Even when this privilege would otherwise apply, the prosecution may be able to defeat the privilege claim by invoking the so-called injured spouse exception. Even at common law the instant privilege was denied to an accused spouse in prosecutions for wrongs directed against the other spouse's person. In these cases, the spouse is the victim named in the indictment or information. The application of the privilege in these prosecutions would frustrate the enforcement of the criminal statutes in question, since the victim spouse is typically an important or even essential source of prosecution evidence. The public interest in the effective enforcement of criminal law overrides the spouses' private interest in the protection of their relationship. Most statutes retaining the instant privilege broaden the scope of the exception to encompass prosecution of any "crime committed by one against the other" and various other offenses, including crimes against children or the marital relation itself such as adultery.

Most jurisdictions limit the privilege in another respect, namely, its duration. There is some disagreement over the duration of the privilege. However, most courts regard the initial time at which it comes into existence as the date of the creation of the marriage and the terminus as the date of termination of marriage, as by divorce. As we shall see in Chapter 9, in contrast the spousal communications privilege survives the termination of the marriage by divorce and, in some jurisdictions, even death.

---

[7]   Trammel v. United States, 445 U.S. 40 (1980).

There are several related procedural questions. Of course, the holder of the privilege must be identified. As previously stated, there is a division of authority over the identity of the holder. There is a further disagreement whether it is error for the prosecution to call the spouse to the stand, thereby forcing the accused spouse or the witness spouse to object in the jury's presence. Most courts reinforce the privilege by precluding comment on its exercise. In some but not all jurisdictions, the trial judge must inform the spouse witness of the availability of the privilege.

The privilege is sometimes extended to the spouse's extra-judicial statements. However, in *Trammel* the Supreme Court indicated that the federal version of the privilege is limited to in-court testimony.

Limiting the scope of the privilege in these various respects is a step in the right direction. The privilege is an archaic survival of an almost mystical dogma. The privilege reflects an outmoded social attitude toward marriage. The Supreme Court's draft of Federal Rule of Evidence 504 would have abolished the privilege; and on balance, the abolition of the privilege would probably be desirable.

Both the instant privilege and the ancient disqualification must be distinguished from another, narrower privilege—the privilege against disclosure of confidential communications between husband and wife. The spousal communications privilege is discussed in Chapter 9. The disqualification and the instant testimonial privilege can have the effect of keeping the spouse completely off the witness stand. In contrast, the spousal communications privilege has a far more limited procedural effect; while the spouse is on the stand, the communications privilege merely bars the spouse from disclosing certain communications passing between the spouses. In that respect, the communications privilege is more defensible than either the ancient disqualification or the modern version of the instant testimonial privilege.

§ 67   Incompetency of Husband and Wife to Give Testimony on Non-Access

In 1777, in an ejectment case involving the issue of the claimant's legitimacy, Lord Mansfield delivered a pronouncement which apparently was new-minted doctrine. He declared "that the declarations of a father or mother cannot be admitted to bastardize the issue born after marriage . . . [I]t is a rule founded in decency, morality and policy, that they shall not be permitted to say after marriage that they have had no connection and therefore that the offspring is spurious . . . ."[8] Wigmore criticized Mansfield's invention as obstructive.[9] Yet, the doctrine was followed by later English decisions until overruled by statute, and has been accepted by some American courts. A few courts have wisely rejected the doctrine by construing the general statutes abolishing the incompetency of parties and of spouses as overturning this eccentric incompetency, but other courts have rejected that statutory construction argument.

Even the jurisdictions which recognize the exclusionary rule differ over the scope of the rule. The points of controversy about the rule's scope are: (a) whether it is limited strictly to evidence of non-access, or whether it reaches other types of evidence showing that someone other than the husband is the father; (b) whether the rule applies only in proceedings where legitimacy is in issue or extends to divorce suits where the question

---

[8]   Goodnight v. Moss, 2 Cowp. 291, 98 Eng. Rep. 1257 (1777).

[9]   7 Wigmore, Evidence § 2064 (Chadbourn rev. 1978).

is adultery rather than the child's legitimacy; and (c) whether it prohibits only the testimony of husband and wife on the stand, or also excludes evidence of the spouse's previous out-of-court declarations. In view of the fundamental unsoundness of the rule, in each instance the courts should adopt the narrower view of the scope of the doctrine.

§ 68 Judges, Jurors and Lawyers

Judges

A judicial officer called to the stand in a case in which she is not sitting as a judge is not disqualified by her office from testifying. For example, if an assault occurred during trial, the judge at that trial could appear as a witness in a subsequent assault prosecution presided over by another judge. But when a judge is called as a witness in a trial then before her, her appearance as witness is obviously inconsistent with her impartial role in the adversary system of trial. Nevertheless, under the older common law view she was generally regarded as a competent witness, although she had a discretion to decline to testify. Shockingly, this view still seems to be in effect under a few state statutes. The view is obviously subject to criticism.

The criticism led to a decided shift toward a second view that the judge is disqualified from testifying about material, disputed facts but may testify as to matters that are merely formal or undisputed. Although the second view is a step in the right direction, it can be hard to distinguish between material and formal matters. Moreover, there seems little need for the judge's testimony on these topics, since formal matters nearly always can be proved by other witnesses.

Accordingly, there is growing support for a third view that a judge is incompetent to testify in a case which she is trying. The view is as sensible as it is simple. This view is codified in Federal Rule of Evidence 605 and Revised Uniform Rule of Evidence 605. The rule provides for an "automatic" objection.

It is ordinarily easy to recognize this issue. The problem is obvious when the judge attempts to slide from the bench onto the witness stand. However, it can be more difficult to recognize the issue in another setting. Suppose that during trial, the judge injects her personal knowledge of facts that are not judicially noticeable. In effect, the judge has become a witness; and in principle the judge's conduct is objectionable under Rule 605.

Jurors

Three distinct doctrines relate to the question of when a juror can be a source of evidence: an incompetency, an exclusionary rule, and a privilege.

The Incompetency

On occasion, persons who formerly served as jurors testify to events that occurred at the previous hearing. Like a judge at a prior trial, a person who had served as a juror at that trial could appear as a witness in a subsequent prosecution to testify about an assault that occurred during the earlier trial. However, a threat to the tribunal's impartiality arises when a juror then sitting in the case is called as a witness. Nevertheless, some early common law authorities allowed such testimony. To eliminate that danger, Federal and Revised Uniform Rule of Evidence 606(a) overturned the common law by providing that the juror is incompetent as a witness. Many jurisdictions have adopted statutes and court rules patterned after Rule 606(a). Consequently, substantial inroads have been made on the traditional common law and the early statutes that had been construed as allowing juror testimony. Modernly these problems rarely arise, since in the vast majority of cases panelists with pre-knowledge of the facts of the case are identified and stricken during jury selection.

————

The Exclusionary Rule

While Rule 606(a) deals with the question of whether a sitting juror can give any testimony in the case, there is a separate traditional doctrine that a juror may not furnish an affidavit or testify to impeach the juror's verdict. By virtue of this doctrine, the juror is barred from testifying about matters that "inhere" in the deliberation process. Although occasionally criticized, this doctrine is now firmly entrenched. The traditional version of the doctrine, often termed the Mansfield rule, broadly prohibits jurors from testifying about both their subjective mental processes and objective events that transpire during deliberations. Barring juror impeachment of the verdict promotes the finality of verdicts and encourages frank jury deliberation, while discouraging later harassment of jurors by losing parties.

At common law a few courts have abandoned the Mansfield rule, and permit jurors to testify to misconduct and irregularities which are grounds for new trial. Under this so-called Iowa view, jurors may testify about "objective" facts and events occurring during deliberation—occurrences which are objective in the sense that other jurors could observe them and independently corroborate the juror's testimony about the fact or event. To protect the finality of deliberations, these courts rely on a narrower doctrine excluding evidence of the jurors' arguments during deliberations and evidence as to their own subjective motives, beliefs, mistakes, and mental operations. Even in jurisdictions subscribing to the Iowa view, the juror cannot even testify about the subjective impact of objective events on the juror's own state of mind; rather, the judge inquires whether the event was likely to affect a hypothetical reasonable juror. Federal and Uniform Rule of Evidence 606(b) is generally accord with prior federal case law following the traditional, Mansfield doctrine.

It is important to appreciate the limits to the scope of statutory provisions such as Rule 606(b). First, these rules do not specify the substantive grounds for a new trial. These rules merely govern the jurors' competency to testify or supply an affidavit or declaration to establish such grounds. Second, in addition to barring evidence of jurors' subjective thought processes, discussions, motives, beliefs, and mistakes, the rules exclude testimony about most irregular juror conduct in the jury room. Again, Rule 606(b) is a version of the Mansfield approach. Thus, the federal courts have held that the rule bars testimony about the jurors' consumption of alcohol at lunch and (prior to 2017) racist remarks during deliberations. Third, in one respect, Federal Rule 606 appears to broaden the scope of the common law rule. While that rule barred juror testimony and affidavit only when it was offered to impeach a verdict, the wording of 606(b)(1) is so expansive that it seemingly applies whether the evidence is offered to impeach or support the verdict. Fourth, the rules do not exclude juror testimony about outside influences or extraneous prejudicial information. Thus, a criminal juror could testify that he had received a threatening phone call; and in a civil case involving accident reconstruction testimony, one juror could supply an affidavit indicating that another juror had brought a text on accident reconstruction into the deliberation room and read aloud passages to the other jurors. Fifth, the rules appear to apply only post-indictment or post-verdict. On their face, the rules do not apply directly to a hearing to determine whether to discharge a juror during deliberations for misconduct. Sixth, some jurisdictions interpret even the original, unamended version of Rule 606(b) as permitting the jurors to correct an improperly transmitted or announced verdict. Amended Rule 606(b)(2)(C) permits the use of juror testimony and affidavits to prove that "a mistake was made in entering the verdict on the verdict form." Finally, the rules do not preclude testimony by other persons who know of jury misconduct. The bar applies only to jurors. Hence, if the door to the jury deliberation room was ajar and a passing bailiff heard one juror threaten another, the bailiff would be competent to testify about the threat.

In its 2014 decision, *Warger v. Shauers,*[10] a lawsuit arising from a motor vehicle accident, the Supreme Court dealt with another limitation on the scope of the doctrine, recognized in some jurisdictions. As Justice Sotomayor noted in her opinion, "[a]lthough some common-law courts . . . permit[ ] evidence of jury deliberations to be introduced to demonstrate juror dishonesty during voir dire, the majority do not . . . ." The courts allowing such evidence reason that the exclusionary rule bars the use of the evidence to demonstrate jury misconduct during deliberations, but not during voir dire. However, the Court adopted the majority view that the language of Rule 606(b) is sweeping enough to preclude the use of the evidence to prove a panelist's lie during jury selection. In dictum in footnote three, though, the justice stated that in rare cases, the evidence might demonstrate a "juror bias so extreme that . . . the [constitutional] jury trial right has been abridged. If and when such a case arises, the Court can consider whether the usual safeguards are . . . sufficient to protect the integrity of the process." In *Warger,* the evidence did not tend to establish an invidious, intense bias such as racism. Rather, the evidence showed only that the jury foreperson's daughter had been at fault in a motor vehicle accident and that the lawsuit based on that accident had adversely affected the daughter's life. In the Court's view, that evidence was insufficient to invalidate the judgment on constitutional grounds.

In 2017, the Supreme Court revisited the topic in *Pena-Rodriguez v. Colorado*[11]. The Court found an extreme situation in which the Constitution overrode Rule 606(b). The majority characterized the fact situation as a case in which a "juror made clear and explicit statements indicating racial animus was a significant motivating factor in [their] vote to convict." Writing for the majority, Justice Kennedy argued that in several respects, evidence of racial animus differs from the types of juror misconduct that the Court had previously ruled subject to the no-impeachment rule. To begin with, racial bias is "a familiar and recurring evil" in the American justice system. In contrast, Justice Kennedy found no evidence that "the jury system is rife" with the sort of irregularity present in *Warger.* Moreover, since panelists are especially reluctant to either admit racial bigotry or call another panelist a racist, the traditional trial safeguards "may be less effective in rooting out" racial bias. Before concluding his opinion, Justice Kennedy attempted to define the standard for admitting the evidence: Again, the statement must exhibit "overt racial bias," and the proponent of the evidence must show that "racial animus was a significant motivating factor in the juror's vote to convict." The Court accorded trial judges "substantial discretion" in weighing such factors as "the content

---

[10]   574 U.S. 40 (2014).
[11]   137 S. Ct. 855 (2017).

and timing of the alleged statements and the reliability of the proffered evidence" in deciding whether the moving party has met the standard.

The Privilege

Distinguish these rules of incompetency and exclusion, codified in Rules 606(a)–(b), from a third doctrine supported by Wigmore[12] and a few judicial opinions According to this doctrine, each juror has a personal privilege against disclosing in court her communications to the other jurors during their deliberations. There is little judicial support for this doctrine.

Lawyers

Although in some instances an attorney's testimony can violate the rules of legal ethics, those rules do not govern the admissibility of the testimony under evidence law. At common law and under Federal and Revised Uniform Rule of Evidence 601, a lawyer for a party is not per se incompetent to testify. Nevertheless, the court has wide discretion to bar testimony by a lawyer presently in the case, especially when the lawyer endeavors to testify in her client's favor. Judges routinely exercise this discretion to prevent such testimony where other sources of evidence about the fact of consequence are available or where the necessity for the lawyer's testimony could easily have been foreseen and avoided. Even where no other witness is available and the lawyer is willing to withdraw, judges usually exercise their discretion to preclude the lawyer from testifying. Permitting the lawyer to withdraw and substituting new counsel will delay, if not disrupt, the proceeding. The judicial discretion is ordinarily exercised in that manner whether the lawyer is being called by her client's side or the opposition. If the lawyer both testified and continued to try the case, there is a risk that the jury might confuse the lawyer's testimony as a witness with the lawyer's arguments as an advocate—a risk that brings Federal Rule of Evidence 403 into play. Rule 403 authorizes the trial judge to exclude logically relevant evidence when its probative value is substantially outweighed by probative dangers such as "confusing the issues."

ABA Model Rule of Professional Conduct, 3.7, Lawyer as Witness, originally promulgated in 1983, reads:

> (a)   A lawyer shall not act as advocate at a trial in which the lawyer is likely to be a necessary witness unless:
>
>> (1)   the testimony relates to an uncontested issue
>>
>> (2)   the testimony relates to the nature and value of legal services rendered in the case; or
>>
>> (3)   disqualification of the lawyer would work substantial hardship on the client.
>
> (b)   A lawyer may act as advocate in a trial in which another lawyer in the lawyer's firm is likely to be called as a witness unless precluded from doing so by [conflict of interest] Rule 1.7 or Rule 1.9.

Subdivision (a) generally bars the attorney's testimony when the attorney is personally involved in the trial of the case. However, subdivision (b) rejects vicarious

---

[12]   8 Wigmore, Evidence § 2346 (McNaughton rev. 1961).

disqualification; the attorney may testify at a trial being conducted by another member of the attorney's firm.

California has gone even farther in liberalizing the advocate-witness prohibition. As revised effective November 1, 2018, California Rule of Professional Conduct 4.7(a)(3) lifts even the personal disqualification by providing that a lawyer-advocate may testify before a jury if the lawyer "has the informed, written consent of the client." As previously stated, the courts which routinely bar such testimony reason that there is a danger that the jury will confuse the lawyer's testimony and lawyer's arguments. However, the proponents of the California rule counter that the courts often permit the same witness to testify in a dual role about facts as well as opinions. By way of example, many cases allow an experienced police officer to both describe an accused's conduct and voice an opinion that the conduct fits the modus operandi for a particular type of crime. If anything, such testimony presents the risk to a greater degree than a lawyer-advocate's testimony. When a police officer testifies in that manner, during the same direct examination the officer states both opinions and facts. In contrast, if the lawyer's testimony is restricted to facts, at least there is a substantial time gap between the factual testimony and the opinionated summation. That gap should reduce the risk of confusion.

In most cases, it is easy to recognize this issue: There is a red flag when a party calls a trial attorney in the case to the witness stand. However, it is more difficult to identify some variations of the problem. Suppose that before trial, the trial attorney interviewed the witness who is now on the stand. The trial attorney believes that the witness has testified inconsistently with his pretrial statements to the attorney. In principle, the same restrictions come into play if in open court the attorney then inquires whether the witness's testimony is at odds with what "you told us" or "said to us" before trial. Even though the attorney has not attempted to take the witness stand, the opponent should object that the attorney has in effect become a rebuttal witness.

§ 69 Firsthand Knowledge and Expertness

Two other rules, previously mentioned, relate to the general subject of witnesses' competency. These rules are the requirement that a witness testifying to objective facts must have had the means of learning them from observation,[13] and the doctrine that one testifying to an inference or opinion in matters requiring special knowledge or skill must qualify as an expert in the field.[14] Unlike most other competency doctrines going to the capacity to testify at all, these two rules are directed at the person's capacity as a witness to testify to a particular matter, not the person's fundamental competency to be a witness.

§ 70 The Procedure of Disqualification

Under the common law practice, the witness is not sworn until she is placed on the stand to begin her testimony. At early common law, before the oath was administered,

---

[13]   See supra § 10. The requirement of firsthand knowledge on the part of lay witnesses is not a question of competency in the traditional sense. Thus, Federal Rule 104(a), stating that a person's qualification to be a witness is a question for the court, is inapplicable to issues of firsthand knowledge. Rather, as the Advisory Committee Note to Rule 602 explains, these are questions of conditional relevancy, with the judge playing a limited, screening role and the jury making the final determination. *See* Joy Mfg. Co. v. Sola Basic Industries, Inc., 697 F.2d 104 (3d Cir. 1982); supra § 53 as to conditional relevancy generally.

[14]   See supra § 12.

the adversary had an opportunity to object to the prospective witness's competency. The judge or counsel would then examine the witness about her qualifications, before she was sworn as a witness. This was known as a voir dire examination. Traditionally when the witness was first called to the stand to testify, the opponent had to immediately challenge her competency if the opponent was then aware of grounds of challenge. If the opponent did not voice a competency objection before the witness took the oath, the objection was waived.

As we have seen, Federal and Uniform Rules of Evidence 601 significantly liberalize the substantive standards for witness competency. That substantive liberalization has a procedural impact. Except possibly for federal diversity cases, the procedure followed under either Federal Rule of Evidence 601 or Revised Uniform Rule of Evidence 601 differs sharply from the common law procedure described in the preceding paragraph. Under those rules, the common law incompetency standards have largely been supplanted by specific provisions such as Rules 602 and 603. Rule 602 requires that a witness possess firsthand knowledge. An objection premised on 602 must be urged after the witness takes the oath but before he answers a question relating to a fact which he lacks personal knowledge of. Rule 603 mandates that the prospective witness take an oath, but again the opponent could not object before the person took the oath; quite to the contrary, an objection would usually be appropriate only after the person refused to take the oath. The procedure for challenging judges and jurors as witnesses is prescribed by Rules 605 and 606.[15] Hence, under the new statutes, there appears to be only one case in which the opponent must routinely follow the common law procedure; in federal criminal cases, objections based on the spouse witness's privilege not to be called by the prosecution must still arguably be asserted before the spouse witness takes the oath. With that exception, in jurisdictions giving Rule 601 a literal, plain meaning interpretation, there are no competency objections to be raised independently of Rules 602 and 603; and there would consequently be no potential challenge to interpose before the witness begins to testify.[16] Even in federal diversity cases, the judge need not comply with the procedures followed in any particular state for disposing of competency objections. It is one thing to require the federal judge to apply the state's substantive competency standard, as Rule 601 sometimes mandates. It is quite another matter to import state procedure into a federal courtroom.

Under both case law and the Federal and Uniform Rules of Evidence, before eliciting an expert opinion from a witness, the offering party must show the witness's knowledge or skill. The proponent usually establishes the witness's expert status by eliciting the witness's own testimony about her qualifications.[17] However, those requirements come into play after the witness has begun to testify. Although the opponent could raise the issue in advance of the witness's testimony by filing an in limine motion, the opponent is not required to do so. Thus, here again the opponent would not waive the objection by neglecting to raise the issue before the witness takes her oath.

In the competency context, when a foundational question of fact is disputed or doubtful on the evidence, the trial judge sitting with a jury ordinarily does not submit this question of fact to the jury. The solitary exception is the question of whether under

---

[15]   See supra § 68.

[16]   See supra § 62.

[17]   See supra §§ 10, 12.

Rule 602 the witness possesses firsthand knowledge.[18] Hence, if a spousal disqualification objection raises the preliminary question of whether under Rule 501 the party and witness spouse are validly married, the judge follows the procedure prescribed by Rule 104(a). In contrast, the judge would apply Rule 104(b)'s conditional relevance procedure to the preliminary question of whether the witness had personal knowledge. In federal court the procedure for determining the competency of a child witness is governed by statute, 18 U.S.C.A. § 3509(c).

§ 71 Probable Future of the Rules of Competency

The rules disqualifying witnesses with knowledge of relevant facts and mental capacity to convey that knowledge are serious obstructions to the ascertainment of truth. In the first edition of this treatise, Dean McCormick famously remarked, "The manifest destiny of evidence law is a progressive lowering of the barriers to truth."[19] For over a century, the steady course of legal reform has been in the direction of sweeping away these obstructions. To that end all states should adopt Federal Rules of Evidence 601 to 606 or the similar provisions of the Revised Uniform Rules of Evidence. For its part, Congress ought to exercise the power to mandate these rules without qualification for diversity cases.

---

[18]   See supra § 69.
[19]   McCormick, Handbook of the Law of Evidence § 81 (1954).

Title 5

PRIVILEGE: COMMON LAW AND STATUTORY

Chapter 8

THE SCOPE AND EFFECT OF THE EVIDENTIARY PRIVILEGES

Table of Sections

---

§ 72 The Purposes of Rules of Privilege: (a) Other Rules of Evidence Distinguished

The overwhelming majority of all rules of evidence have as their ultimate justification some tendency to promote the objectives set forward by the conventional witness's oath, the presentation of "the truth, the whole truth, and nothing but the truth." Thus such prominent exclusionary rules as the hearsay rule, the opinion rule, the rule excluding bad character as evidence of crime, and the original documents (or "Best Evidence") rule, have as their common purpose the elucidation of the truth, a purpose that these rules seek to effect by operating to exclude evidence which is unreliable or which is calculated to prejudice or mislead.

By contrast the rules of privilege, of which the most familiar are the rule protecting against self-incrimination and those shielding the confidentiality of communications between husband and wife, attorney and client, and physician and patient, are not designed or intended to facilitate the fact-finding process or to safeguard its integrity. Their effect instead is clearly inhibitive; rather than facilitating the illumination of truth, they shut out the light.

Rules that serve to render accurate ascertainment of the truth more difficult, or in some instances impossible, may seem anomalous in a rational system of fact-finding.

195

Nevertheless, rules of privilege are not without a rationale. Their warrant is the protection of interests and relationships which, rightly or wrongly, are regarded as of sufficient social importance to justify some sacrifice of availability of evidence relevant to the administration of justice.

The interests allegedly served by privileges, as might be expected, are varied. The great constitutional protections that have evolved around self-incrimination, confessions, and unlawfully obtained evidence are considered elsewhere.[1] They are commonly classed as privileges.

Of the rules treated here, a substantial number operate to protect communications made within the context of various professional relationships, e.g., attorney and client, physician and patient, clergyman and penitent. The rationale traditionally advanced for these privileges is that public policy requires the encouragement of the communications without which these relationships cannot be effective. This rationale, today sometimes referred to as the utilitarian justification for privilege, found perhaps its strongest supporter in Dean Wigmore who seems to have viewed it as the chief, if not the exclusive, basis for privilege. Wigmore's views have been widely accepted by the courts, and have largely conditioned the development of thinking about privilege.

More recently other, and analytically distinct, rationales for privilege have been advanced. According to one theory, certain privacy interests in society are deserving of protection by privilege irrespective of whether the existence of such privileges actually operates substantially to affect conduct within the protected relationships. Thus, while it has been suggested that communications between husband and wife and physician and patient are not primarily induced by the privileges accorded them, some form of these privileges is nevertheless seen as justified on the alternative basis that they serve to protect the essential privacy of certain significant human relationships. Similarly, but not identically, other writers have formulated humanistic theories of privilege that emphasize autonomy, creating privacy enclaves with particular types of consultants to enable the citizen to make more intelligent, independent life preference choices. Given their comparatively recent origin, these latter rationales probably have not operated as a conscious basis for either the judicial or legislative creation of existing privileges. Today's judicial tendency to pour new wine into old bottles, however, may serve to make nonutilitarian theories factors in the subsequent development of thinking about privilege.

It is open to doubt whether all of the interests and relationships that have sometimes been urged as sufficiently important to justify the creation of privileges really merit this sort of protection bought at such a price. Moreover, even if the importance of given interests and relationships be conceded, there remain questions as to whether evidentiary privileges are appropriate, much less sufficient, mechanisms for accomplishing the desired objectives. In any event, it is clear that in drawing their justifications from considerations unrelated to the integrity of the adjudication process, rules of privilege are of a different order than the great bulk of evidentiary rules.

---

[1]   See infra Chs. 13, 14 & 15.

§ 72.1 The Purposes of Rules of Privilege: (b) Certain Rules Distinguished

As developed in a subsequent section,[2] true rules of privilege may be enforced to prevent the introduction of evidence even though the privilege is that of a person who is not a party to the proceeding in which the privilege is involved. This characteristic serves to distinguish certain other rules that, like privileges, are intended to encourage or discourage certain kinds of conduct. Among these latter rules may be included those excluding offers of compromise[3] and subsequent remedial measures following an injury.[4]

Functionally, the policies toward which these latter rules are directed may be fully realized by implementing the rules only in litigation to which the person sought to be actuated by the rule is a party. For example, the rule excluding evidence of offers of compromise is designed to encourage compromise; admitting the evidence in a case to which the offeror is not a party will in no wise operate to discourage compromises. Accordingly, such rules may be asserted only by a party. This consideration, in addition to the fact that these rules are also justified in part by considerations relating to relevancy, makes classification as rules of privilege analytically imprecise.

Again, true rules of privilege operate generally to prevent revelation of confidential matter within the context of a judicial proceeding. Thus, rules of privilege do not speak directly to the question of unauthorized revelations of confidential matter outside the judicial setting, and redress for such breaches of confidence must be sought in the law of torts or professional responsibility.

§ 73 Procedural Recognition of Rules of Privilege

In one important procedural respect, rules of privilege are similar to other evidentiary rules. The fact that most exclusionary rules are intended to protect the integrity of the fact-finding process while rules of privilege look toward the preservation of confidences might lead the casual reflector to conclude that the former will operate inexorably to exclude untrustworthy evidence while the latter will only be enforced at the option of the holder of the privilege. Such, we know, is not the case. Neither set of rules is self-executing: rules of exclusion, no less than rules of privilege, must be asserted to be effective, and if not asserted promptly will ordinarily be waived. Instead, the distinction in purpose between the two types of rules is reflected by a difference in the persons who may claim their benefit and, perhaps today, in what forum.

§ 73.1 Procedural Recognition of Rules of Privilege: (a) Who May Assert?

This difference in foundation between the two groups of rules manifests itself in another line of cleavage. The rule of exclusion or preference, being designed to make the trial more efficient as a vehicle of fact disclosure, may be invoked as of right only by the person whose interest in having the verdict follow the facts is at stake in the trial. Thus, when evidence condemned by one of these rules is offered, only the adverse party may object, unless the judge elects to interpose. But by contrast, if the evidence is privileged, the right to object does not attach to the opposing party as such, but to the person vested

---

[2]   Infra § 73.

[3]   See infra § 266.

[4]   See infra § 267.

with the outside interest or relationship fostered by the particular privilege. True, other persons present at the trial, including the adverse party, may call to the court's attention the existence of the privilege, or the judge may choose to intervene of his own accord to protect it, but this is regarded as having been done on behalf of the owner of the privilege.

The right to complain on appeal is a more crucial test. If the court erroneously recognizes an asserted privilege and excludes proffered testimony on this ground, clearly the tendering party has been injured in his capacity as litigant and may complain on appeal. But if a claim of privilege is wrongly denied, and the privileged testimony erroneously let in, the distinction that we have suggested between privilege and a rule of exclusion would seem to be material. If the adverse party to the suit is likewise the owner of the privilege, then, while it may be argued that the party's interest as a litigant has not been infringed, most courts decline to draw so sharp a line, and permit him to complain of the error.

Where, however, the owner of the privilege is not a party to the suit, it is somewhat difficult to see why this invasion of a third person's interest should be ground of complaint for the objecting party, whose only grievance can be that the overriding of the outsider's rights has resulted in a fuller fact-disclosure than the party desires. It has not been thought necessary to afford this extreme sanction in order to prevent a breakdown in the protection of privilege. In at least two classes of privileges, the privileges against self-incrimination[5] and against the use of evidence secured by unlawful search or seizure,[6] this distinction has been clearly perceived and the party is quite consistently denied any ground for reversal, despite the constitutional bases of the two privileges. The results in cases of erroneous denials of other privileges are more checkered; a considerable number of the older cases seem to allow the party to take advantage of the error on appeal.

The California Code of Evidence, one of the few modern codifications to address the question, is clear-cut. It provides: "A party may predicate error on a ruling disallowing a claim of privilege only if he is the holder of the privilege, except that a party may predicate error on a ruling disallowing a claim of privilege by his spouse . . . ."[7]

§ 73.2 Procedural Recognition of Rules of Privilege: (b) Where May Privilege Be Asserted? Rules of Privilege in Conflict of Laws[8]

Under traditional choice of law doctrine all rules of evidence, including those of privilege, were viewed as procedural and thus appropriately supplied by the law of the forum. This approach naturally tended to suppress any consideration of the differences in purpose clearly existing between rules of exclusion and preference on the one hand, and rules of privilege on the other.

Modern conflict of laws analysis, by contrast, inclines toward resolution of choice of law questions through evaluation of the policy interests of the respective jurisdictions that have some connection with the transaction in litigation. Under this approach, the forum will almost invariably possess a strong interest in a correct determination of the facts in dispute before its courts, and therefore a strong interest in the application of its

---

[5]   See infra § 119.

[6]   See infra § 175.

[7]   Cal. Evid. Code § 918.

[8]   Choice of law questions arising in federal courts are further treated in infra § 76.1.

rules of exclusion and preference. By contrast, the forum may have virtually no interest in applying its rules of privilege in a case where the relationship or interest sought to be promoted or protected by the privilege had its contacts exclusively with another jurisdiction.

Thus, for example, if a given professional relationship is carried out exclusively in State X which itself does not extend a privilege to protect that relationship, there would seem to be no compelling reason for the forum, State Y, to apply its own rules of privilege, thus denying its court the benefit of helpful evidence. No interest either of the forum or of State X argues for recognition of the forum's privilege in such a case.

On the other hand, if the relationship is carried out exclusively in State X, which does extend a privilege to the communication in question, circumstances may exist in which in which the forum, State Y, may want to recognize that privilege even though there would be no comparable privilege under its law.

§ 74 Limitations on the Effectiveness of Privileges: (a) Risk of Eavesdropping and Interception of Letters

Since privileges operate to deny litigants access to every person's evidence, the courts have generally construed them no more broadly than necessary to accomplish their basic purposes. One manifestation of this tendency is to be seen in the general rule that a privilege operates only to preclude testimony by parties to the confidential relationship. Accordingly, a number of older decisions held that an eavesdropper may testify to confidential communications, and that a letter, otherwise confidential and privileged, is not protected if it is stolen or otherwise intercepted by a third person. This principle, however, has only infrequently been carried to the extent of allowing a privilege to be breached if the interception is made possible by the connivance of a party to the confidential relationship.

Though the same general rule is still sometimes applied, most modern decisions do no more than hold that a privilege will not protect communications made under circumstances in which interception was reasonably to be anticipated. Certainly, a qualification of the traditional rule in terms of the reasonable expectations of the privileged communicator may provide a desirable common law readjustment to cope with the alarming potential of the modern eavesdropper. While in earlier times the confidentiality of privileged communications could generally be preserved by a modest attention to security, homespun measures will hardly suffice against the modern panoply of electronic paraphernalia.

The vastly enhanced technology of eavesdropping has drawn a variety of legislative reactions more directly responsive to the problem. These have included state statutes prohibiting wiretapping and electronic surveillance and denying admissibility to evidence obtained in violation. Such provisions are of course in addition to the protection that may rest on constitutional grounds. Moreover, statutes and rules defining the privileges have begun to include provisions entitling the holder to prevent anyone from disclosing a privileged communication.

§ 74.1 Limitations on the Effectiveness of Privileges: (b) Adverse Arguments and Inferences from Claims of Privilege

The underlying conflict comes most clearly in view in the decisions relating to the allowability of an adverse inference from the assertion of privilege. Plainly, the inference may not ordinarily be made against a party when a witness for that party claims a privilege personal to the witness, for this is not a matter under the party's control.[9] But where the party himself suppresses evidence by invoking a privilege given to him by the law, should an adverse inference be sanctioned? The question may arise in various forms, for example, whether an inquiry of the witness, or of the party, calling for information obviously privileged, may be pressed for the pointed purpose of forcing the party to make an explicit claim of the privilege in the jury's hearing, or again, whether the inference may be drawn in argument, and finally, whether the judge in the instructions may mention the inference as a permissible one.

Under familiar principles an unfavorable inference may be drawn against a party not only for destroying evidence, but for the mere failure to produce witnesses or documents within his control.[10] No showing of wrong or fraud seems to be required as a foundation for the inference that the evidence if produced would have been unfavorable. Why should not this same conclusion be drawn from the party's active interposing of a privilege to keep out the evidence? A leading case for the affirmative is *Phillips v. Chase*,[11] where the court said:

> It is a rule of law that the objection of a party to evidence as incompetent and immaterial, and insistence upon his right to have his case tried according to the rules of law, cannot be made a subject of comment in argument. . . . On the other hand, if evidence is material and competent except for a personal privilege of one of the parties to have it excluded under the law, his claim of the privilege may be referred to in argument and considered by the jury, as indicating his opinion that the evidence, if received, would be prejudicial to him.

An oft-quoted statement by Lord Chelmsford gives the contrary view:

> The exclusion of such evidence is for the general interest of the community, and therefore to say that when a party refuses to permit professional confidence to be broken, everything must be taken most strongly against him, what is it but to deny him the protection which, for public purposes, the law affords him, and utterly to take away a privilege which can thus only be asserted to his prejudice?[12]

The first of these arguments is based upon an unfounded distinction between incompetent and privileged evidence, namely, a supposition that the privilege can be waived and the incompetency cannot.[13] As we have seen, both may be waived with equal facility. As to the second, it may be an overstatement to say that permitting the inference "utterly takes away" the privilege. A privilege has its most substantial practical benefit when it enables a party to exclude from the record a witness, document, or line of proof that is essential to the adversary's case, lacking which he cannot get to the jury at all on a vital issue. The inference does not supply the lack of proof.[14] In other situations, the benefit accruing from a successful claim of privilege will depend upon circumstances. It

---

9   See supra § 73.1 and more particularly as to self-incrimination infra § 119.

10   See infra § 264.

11   87 N.E. 755, 758 (Mass. 1909).

12   Wentworth v. Lloyd, 10 H.L. Cas. 589, 591 (1864).

13   See supra § 73.

14   See infra § 264.

is evident, however, that in a case that survives a motion for a directed verdict or its equivalent, allowing comment upon the exercise of a privilege or requiring it to be claimed in the presence of the jury tends greatly to diminish its value. In *Griffin v. California*[15] the Supreme Court held that allowing comment upon the failure of an accused to take the stand violated his privilege against self-incrimination "by making its assertion costly." Whether one is prepared to extend this protection to all privileges probably depends upon her attitude towards privileges in general and towards the particular privilege involved. The cases, rather naturally, are in dispute. It is submitted that the best solution is to recognize only privileges that are soundly based in policy and to accord those privileges the fullest protection. Thus comment, whether by judge or by counsel, or its equivalent of requiring the claim to be made in the presence of the jury, and the drawing of inferences from the claim, all would be foreclosed.

§ 74.2 Limitations on the Effectiveness of Privileges: (c) Constitutional Limitations on Privilege

A previously unrecognized source of limitations on privilege in criminal cases emerged in the late 1960s and early 1970s as a result of decisions of the Supreme Court dealing with the Compulsory Process and Confrontation Clauses of the Constitution of the United States.

The three cases that have figured in this development are *Washington v. Texas*,[16] *Davis v. Alaska*,[17] and *United States v. Nixon*.[18] In *Washington v. Texas*, the Court held the provisions of the Compulsory Process Clause binding upon states as a component of due process, and struck down a Texas statute that rendered persons charged or convicted as co-participants in the same crime incompetent to testify for one another. The Court's decision stressed the "absurdity" of the statute and specifically held only that the constitutional provision is violated by "arbitrary rules that prevent whole categories of defense witnesses from testifying . . . ."[19] The Court expressly disclaimed any implied disapproval of testimonial privileges that it noted are based upon quite different considerations.

In *Davis v. Alaska*, the Court held that the Confrontation Clause was violated by application of a state statute privileging juvenile records where the result was to deny the defendant the opportunity to elicit on cross-examination the probationary status of a critical witness against him. Recognizing the strength of the state policy in favor of preserving the confidentiality of juveniles' records, the Court nevertheless held that this policy must yield to the superior interest of the defendant in effective confrontation. Significantly, the Court's decision did not compel disclosure of the juvenile record, but only remanded the case for further proceedings not inconsistent with the Court's opinion.

Finally, in *United States v. Nixon*, the Court held that a claim of absolute privilege of confidentiality for general presidential communications in the performance of the office would not prevail "over the fundamental demands of due process of law in the fair

---

[15]   380 U.S. 609 (1965).
[16]   388 U.S. 14 (1967).
[17]   415 U.S. 308 (1974).
[18]   418 U.S. 683 (1974).
[19]   Washington v. Texas, 388 U.S. 14, 22 (1967).

administration of criminal justice. The generalized assertion of privilege must yield to the demonstrated, specific need for evidence in a pending criminal trial."[20]

Taken together, and despite the somewhat distinctive fact situations involved, these cases fairly raise the question as to the viability of a claim of privilege when a criminal defendant asserts: (1) a need to introduce the privileged matter as exculpatory, or (2) a need to use the privileged matter to impeach testimony introduced by the state. The question is of course not altogether a novel one. Privileges running in favor of the government, such as the informer's privilege, have long been qualified to accommodate the defendant's rights of confrontation. Similarly, the state has frequently been precluded from relying upon the testimony of a witness whose claim of privilege on self-incrimination grounds prevents effective cross-examination.[21]

A number of state decisions, purporting to give effect to the constitutional holdings of *Davis* and *Nixon*, have resolved conflicts between the rights of a defendant on the one hand and claims of private privilege on the other by overriding the latter and forcing (or attempting to force) the testimony of the privilege holder.

Despite such decisions, the extent to which protection of the interests of a criminal defendant constitutionally requires invasion of private privilege was never clear, and has been placed even further in doubt in the decision of the Supreme Court in *Pennsylvania v. Ritchie*.[22] In *Ritchie*, the defendant, charged with rape and other related crimes, sought pretrial access to files of a state child protective agency. The defendant's chief interest in the files, which were protected by a qualified privilege under state statute, was to discover material of possible use in the cross-examination of his daughter, the complaining witness. The state supreme court, relying on *Davis*, held that the defendant had the right to inspect the files in question by virtue of the Confrontation and Compulsory Process clauses. The Supreme Court reversed this portion of the state judgment, a majority of the court concurring that the defendant was entitled only to have the file inspected in camera by the trial court. Only four justices, however, joined in the plurality opinion which based this result on due process grounds and stated that the Pennsylvania court's reliance on *Davis* was "misplaced" and that the Confrontation Clause creates only a "trial" right.

Not surprisingly, the *Ritchie* decision has been accorded a variety of interpretations. One approach adopted by several courts is to require that the defendant make a showing that there is reasonable ground to believe that failure to produce material which has been found privileged will be likely to impair defendant's right of confrontation. Once such a showing is made, the state must then obtain the privilege holder's waiver for purposes of an in camera inspection and, if the matter is found relevant, for trial presentation; otherwise the privilege-holder's testimony will be inadmissible. However, many decisions have failed to find that the defendant's constitutional rights require even so limited an intrusion on private privilege.

Even more dubious today is any right of the criminal defendant to obtain and present matter protected by private privilege that is relevant to the issues of the case but has no direct bearing upon the credibility of a witness for the prosecution.

---

[20]   418 U.S. 683, 713 (1974).

[21]   See supra § 19.

[22]   480 U.S. 39 (1987).

§ 75 The Sources of Privilege

The earliest recognized privileges were judicially created, the origin of both the husband-wife and attorney-client privileges being traceable to the received common law.[23] The development of judge-made privileges, however, virtually halted over a century ago. Though it is impossible definitely to ascribe a reason for this cessation, a contributing factor was undoubtedly a judicial tendency to view privileges from the standpoint of their hindrance to litigation. Certainly the vantage point of the legal profession in general, and of the judiciary in particular, is such as to force into prominence the more deleterious aspects of privilege as impediments to the fact-finding process. By contrast, many of the beneficial consequences claimed for privilege can be expected to be observable only outside the courtroom, and even then are often difficult to demonstrate empirically.

Perhaps as a consequence, during the 19th century the source of newly created privileges shifted decisively from the courts to the legislatures. New York enacted the first physician-patient privilege in 1828, and the vast majority of new privileges created since that time have been of legislative origin. The trend extended to codification even of the preexisting common law privileges, and today the husband-wife and attorney-client privileges are statutorily controlled in most states.

It may be argued that legitimate claims to confidentiality are more equitably received by a branch of government not preeminently concerned with the factual results obtained in litigation, and that the legislatures provide an appropriate forum for the balancing of the competing social values necessary to sound decisions concerning privilege. At the same time, while there is no doubt that some of the statutorily created privileges are soundly based, legislatures have on occasion been unduly influenced by powerful groups seeking the prestige and convenience of a professionally based privilege. One result of the process has been that the various states differ substantially in the numbers and varieties of privilege that they recognize.

Until very recently, the heavy consensus among commentators has favored narrowing the field of privilege, and attempts have been made, largely without success, to incorporate this view into the several 20th century efforts to codify the law of evidence. The draftsmen of both the Model Code of Evidence and the 1953 Uniform Rules of Evidence favored limitations on the number and scope of privileges. The final versions of both of these codifications, however, contained the generally recognized common law and statutory privileges substantially unimpaired.

The Federal Rules of Evidence as proposed by the Advisory Committee and approved by the Supreme Court contained provisions recognizing and defining nine non-constitutional privileges: required reports, attorney-client, psychotherapist-patient, husband-wife, clergyman-communicant, political vote, trade secrets, secrets of state and other official information, and identity of informer. In addition, proposed Rule 501 specifically limited the privileges to be recognized in the federal courts to those provided for by the Rules or enacted by the Congress.[24] When the Rules were submitted to the

---

[23] See infra §§ 78 & 87.

[24] Deleted Federal Rule 501, 56 F.R.D. 230, reads:

Except as otherwise required by the Constitution of the United States or provided by Act of Congress, and except as provided in these rules or in other rules adopted by the Supreme Court, no person has a privilege to:

Congress the privilege provisions excited particular controversy, with the result that all of the specific rules of privilege were excised from the finally enacted version of the Rules.[25] Indeed, Congress went a step further than simply rejecting the proposed rules. It enacted a statute that requires that any "rule creating, abolishing, or modifying an evidentiary privilege" must be approved by an Act of Congress' rather than through the usual Court initiated rulemaking process.[26]

The Congressional action reflects the policy considerations discussed earlier in this section. Although some evidentiary privileges arose out of the common law, most have been the result of legislative action involving the balancing of competing social values. The federal courts are free to deal with privileges on a case by case basis in the context of the facts before them, but the development of broader rules has been left to the legislative process.

The failure of Congress to enact specific rules of privilege left the Federal Rules of Evidence with a large gap when viewed as a potential model code for possible adoption by the states. Therefore, in promulgating the Revised Uniform Rules of Evidence (1974), based almost entirely on the Federal Rules, the National Conference of Commissioners on Uniform State Laws included specific rules of privilege. These rules were substantially rules submitted to Congress, but contained some notable changes. Some states adopting rules or codes based upon the Federal Rules have adopted the proposed Federal Rules concerning privilege, others have adopted the 1974 Uniform Rules on this subject, and some have retained their antecedent rules of privilege.

§ 76 The Current Pattern of Privilege

The failure of Congress to enact specific rules of privilege for the federal courts effectively precluded any immediate prospect of substantial national uniformity in this area. It is arguable that, in light of the strength and contrariety of views which the subject generates, hope for such a consensus was never realistic. In any event, the present form of Federal Rule of Evidence 501 perpetuates a fluid situation in the federal law of privilege and affords the states little inducement to adopt identical or similar schemes of privilege. The variegated pattern of privilege in both federal and state courts, described below, thus seems likely to remain the case for the foreseeable future.

§ 76.1 The Current Pattern of Privilege: (a) Privilege in Federal Courts; What Law Applies?

The Proposed Federal Rules of Evidence recognized only privileges emanating from federal sources and their enactment would have created a unitary scheme of privilege applicable to all cases regardless of jurisdictional ground. The congressionally enacted rules, however, establish a bifurcated system of privilege rules. Federal Rule of Evidence 501 provides:

---

(1)   Refuse to be a witness; or

(2)   Refuse to disclose any matter; or

(3)   Refuse to produce any object or writing; or

(4)   Prevent another from being a witness or disclosing any matter or producing any object or writing.

[25]   For the text of present Fed. R. Evid. 501, see infra § 76.1.

[26]   28 U.S.C.A. § 2074(b).

The common law—as interpreted by United States courts in the light of reason and experience—governs a claim of privilege unless any of the following provides otherwise:

- the United States Constitution;

- a federal statute; or

- rules prescribed by the Supreme Court.

But in a civil case, state law governs privilege regarding a claim or defense for which state law supplies the rule of decision.

Under Rule 501, then, common law, "as interpreted . . . in the light of reason and experience," will determine the privileges applicable in federal question and criminal cases, while privileges in diversity actions will derive from state law. In the former types of cases, it seems likely that the rules promulgated by the Supreme Court will prove influential as indicators of "reason and experience." But it is also apparent that the intent of Rule 501 is not to limit the number and type of privileges recognized to those included in the proposed rules. A significant question exists whether this freedom should be used to recognize and apply state privileges in cases where Rule 501 does not require such to be done.

The situation with respect to cases in which state law provides the rule of decision, primarily diversity cases, is somewhat clearer. Presumably a federal court today would not, as was sometimes done prior to the enactment of Rule 501, enforce a privilege in a diversity case that is not recognized by applicable state law. A major question remains, however, as to the process by which the existence or absence of an "applicable" state privilege will be determined in conflict of law situations.

It has been argued that, given the status of Rule 501 as an Act of Congress, the federal courts, in determining the applicable state law of privilege, are not constrained to accept state conflict of laws principles. Though this position has been supported by a number of commentators, a majority of the cases decided since enactment of the Federal Rules have continued to follow the doctrine of *Klaxon Co. v. Stentor Electric Manufacturing Co.*[27] and thus to look to state choice of law rules in determining what state's privilege should be applied.

Issues of the application of state or federal privilege law also arise in cases in which there are both federal and state claims. In such instances, the better practice would seem to be to consider the predominant nature of the claims and the issues to which the arguably privileged information would be relevant. Most federal courts facing that question have applied the federal law of privileges, although the problem has most commonly arisen in situations where the predominant claims are federal. A few courts have considered the predominant nature of the claims and the issues to which the arguably privileged information would be relevant.

---

[27]　313 U.S. 487 (1941).

§ 76.2 The Current Pattern of Privilege: (b) State Patterns of Privilege; Recognizing New Privileges

State patterns in the recognition of privileges vary greatly. As developed in succeeding chapters, all states possess some form of husband-wife,[28] and attorney-client privilege.[29] All afford some protection to certain government information.[30] Most, though not all, allow at least a limited privilege to communications between physician and patient.[31] In addition several other privileges are worthy of specific mention.

Though probably not recognized at common law, a privilege protecting confidential communications between clergymen and penitents has now been adopted in all 50 states. Wigmore's seemingly grudging acceptance of the privilege perhaps reflects the difficulty of justifying its existence on exclusively utilitarian grounds, since at least where penitential communications are required or encouraged by religious tenets, they are likely to continue to be made irrespective of the presence or absence of evidentiary privilege. A firmer ground appears available in the inherent offensiveness of the secular power attempting to coerce an act violative of religious conscience. Implementing a decent regard for religious convictions while at the same time avoiding making individual conscience the ultimate measure of testimonial obligation has proved to be attended by some difficulties. Early statutory forms of the privilege undertook to privilege only penitential communications "in the course of discipline enjoined by the church" to which the communicant belongs. This limitation, however, has been urged to be unduly, perhaps unconstitutionally, preferential to the Roman Catholic and a few other churches. The statutes have, accordingly, generally been broadened. Uniform Rule of Evidence 505, as promulgated in 1974, is typical in extending the privilege generally to "confidential communication[s] by a person to a clergyman in his professional character as spiritual advisor."

The states are split on the question of who can waive the clergyman-penitent privilege. Some provide that the privilege belongs only to the communicant, others provide that it belongs to the clergy member and still others hold that it belongs to both.

One of the most persistently advocated privileges for many years, but particularly during the past decade, has been one shielding journalists from being required in court to divulge the identities of news sources. The rationale asserted for this privilege is analogous to that underlying the long-standing governmental informers privilege and is exclusively utilitarian in character. Thus, it is contended that the news sources essential to supply the public's need for information will be "dried up" if their identities are subject to compelled disclosure. Numerous attempts to have the privilege enacted by federal statute have failed, and it is not one of those privileges that was incorporated into the Revised Uniform Rules of Evidence (1974). Moreover, the argument that a journalist's privilege is constitutionally to be implied from the First Amendment guarantee of a free press was seemingly rejected by the Supreme Court in *Branzburg v. Hayes*.[32] However, taking note that this rejection did not command an absolute majority of the Court, a substantial number of lower federal courts have undertaken to recognize a qualified

---

[28] See infra Ch. 9.

[29] See infra Ch. 10.

[30] See infra Ch. 12.

[31] See infra Ch. 11.

[32] 408 U.S. 665 (1972).

journalist's privilege that may be penetrated by appropriate showings on the part of the party desiring the privileged information. Several federal Courts of Appeal have recognized a limited privilege in civil cases while denying the privilege in criminal cases. Though occasionally referred to as a common law creation, despite *Branzburg*, the privilege has generally been said to derive from the First Amendment. Some form of privilege for journalists has been created by statute, nor in a few cases by judicial decision, in a substantial number of states. A few state courts have also found the privilege to be implied by state constitutional provision. Unlike other professional privileges, it is generally conceived as belonging to the journalist, to be claimed or waived irrespective of the wishes of the news source.

Communications to accountants are privileged in perhaps a third of the states. This privilege is most closely analogous to that for attorney-client, though the social objective to be furthered is arguably a distinguishable and lesser one.

In recent years much attention has been bestowed upon the plight of the rape victim, and some sort of sexual assault victim-counselor privilege has been created by statute or court decision in a substantial number of states. Such a privilege can claim a substantial basis in public policy, but inevitably comes into conflict with the constitutional rights of the criminal defendant.[33]

Even broader acceptance has been achieved by the principle that protection by evidentiary privilege is necessary for the deliberations of medical review committees.

There is occasional recognition of privilege for communications to confidential clerks, stenographers and other "employees" generally, school teachers, school counselors, participants in group psychotherapy, nurses, marriage counselors, private detectives, and social workers. A privilege for parent-minor child communications has been recommended but has received little judicial approval. Privileges for scientific researcher-subject and self-critical analysis have fared only somewhat better.

An attempt to obtain recognition of a federal privilege protecting against disclosure of confidential peer review materials of academic institutions has been rejected by the Supreme Court.[34]

§ 77 The Future of Privilege

Despite the rejection by the Congress of the Proposed Federal Rules of Evidence relating to privilege and the resultant failure to effect substantive changes in this area, several concurrent developments may portend certain new directions in the development of the law of privilege.

The vehemence of the attacks leveled at certain of the proposed Federal Rules on privilege suggests that the basic concept of evidentiary privilege, despite its deleterious consequences for the administration of justice, will not be abandoned in the foreseeable future. Many of these attacks, predictably, came from groups specifically interested in the preservation or creation of particular privileges. Much more significantly, the cause of privilege was also espoused by an unprecedentedly large segment of the academic community. The latter response was in large part precipitated by a generalized concern over the increasing intrusiveness of modern society into human privacy, a concern

---

[33] See supra § 74.2.
[34] University of Pennsylvania v. E.E.O.C., 493 U.S. 182 (1990).

reflected in several Supreme Court decisions conferring constitutional status upon certain aspects of privacy.

While the ultimate strategic significance of evidentiary privilege as a bastion for defending privacy values may be doubted, the focus on privacy or on similar humanistic justifications as an operative basis for the recognition of many privileges is believed to be a healthy and overdue development. At the optimum, such a focus may offer a theoretical basis for a more satisfactory accommodation than has heretofore been achieved between the legitimate demands for freedom against unwarranted intrusion on the one hand and the basic requirements of the judicial system on the other.

The traditionally felt need, stemming largely from Wigmore's dictum, to justify all privileges in terms of their utilitarian value leads not only to the assertion of highly questionable sociological premises but also affords little prospect for meaningful reconciliation of values in this area. Traditional evidentiary privilege necessarily paints with a broad brush since the achievement of utilitarian objectives requires privileges that are essentially absolute in character. But if it is recognized that not all privileges are based on identical considerations or will have identical effects if allowed in litigation, it will be seen that not all privileges need make such large demands. If the object aimed at is not the inducement of conduct in certain relationships but the protection of individual privacy from unnecessary or trivial intrusions, the implementation of the privilege is amenable to the finer touch of the specific solution. Thus, a decision in the particular case that sufficiently grave considerations demand disclosure will, to be sure, impact adversely on the privilege holder, but no more extended societal interest will be impaired.

Another factor may also contribute to a greater use of qualified or conditional privileges that are subject to suspension on ad hoc determination of particular need for evidence in a given case. It is already clear that the law of privilege must to some extent accommodate to the developing rights of criminal defendants under the Confrontation and Compulsory Process Clauses.[35] At the same time it is desirable, whenever possible, to avoid a choice between the automatic and total override of privilege whenever a criminal defendant asserts a need for privileged matter, and the dismissal of the charges if the privilege is to be sustained. At least in those instances where accomplishment of the privilege objective does not necessitate absolute protection, an in camera weighing of the potential significance of the matter sought as against the considerations of privacy underlying the privilege may represent a desirable compromise.

Though necessarily entailing a certain amount of procedural inconvenience and a considerable amount of judicial discretion, this solution has recommended itself to a number of commentators and courts. It is perhaps reasonable to predict that an increased involvement of judges in the general area of privacy and confidentiality may be in the making.

---

[35]   See supra § 74.2.

Chapter 9

THE PRIVILEGE FOR MARITAL COMMUNICATIONS

Table of Sections

§ 78   History and Background, and Kindred Rules

We are dealing here with a late offshoot of an ancient tree. The older branches are discussed in another chapter.[1] Those earlier rules, to be sharply distinguished from the present doctrine, are first, the rule that the spouse of a party or person interested is disqualified from testifying in favor of the other spouse, and second, the privilege of a party against having the party's husband or wife called as an adverse witness. These two earlier rules forbid the calling of the spouse as a witness at all, for or against the party, regardless of the actual testimony to be elicited, whereas the privilege presently discussed is limited to a certain class of testimony, namely communications between the spouses or more broadly in some states, information gained on account of the marital relation.

The movement for procedural reform in England in the first half of the 1800s found expression in the evidence field in agitation for the break up of the system of disqualification of parties and spouses. One of the auxiliary reasons that had been given to justify the disqualification of spouses was that of preserving marital confidences. As to the disqualification of spouses the reform was largely accomplished by the Evidence Amendment Act, 1853. On the eve of this legislation, Greenleaf, writing in this country in 1842, clearly announced the existence of a distinct privilege for marital communications, and this pronouncement was echoed in England by Best in 1849, though seemingly there was little or no support for such a view in the English decisions. Moreover, the Second Report of 1853 of the Commissioners on Common Law Procedure, after rejecting the arguments for the outmoded rules of disqualification, calls attention to the special danger of "alarm and unhappiness occasioned to society by . . . compelling

---

[1]   See supra § 66.

the public disclosure of confidential communications between husband and wife . . .” and declares that “[a]ll communications between them should be held to be privileged.”

However, though the policy supporting a privilege for marital communications had thus been distinctly pointed out, there had been little occasion for its judicial recognition, since the wider disqualifications of the spouses of parties left small possibility for the question of the existence of such a privilege to arise.

Nevertheless, the English Act of 1853, mentioned above, after it abolished the disqualification of husbands and wives of the parties, enacted that “no husband shall be compellable to disclose any communication made to him by his wife during the marriage, and no wife shall be compellable to disclose any communication made to her by her husband during the marriage.”[2] Moreover, nearly all the states in this country, while making spouses competent to testify, have included provisions disabling them from testifying to communications between them.

In the light of this history the Court of Appeal in England has denied that there was any common law privilege for marital communications. In this country, however, the courts have frequently said that the statutes protecting marital communications from disclosure are declaratory of the common law. Moreover, some courts have even held the “common law” rule to be in effect without benefit of statute, at least until legislatively abrogated.

In addition to the vitality that it has displayed in the courts, the rule discussed here has been viewed by some legal commentators as the most defensible of the various forms of marital privilege. However, Federal Rule of Evidence 505 as approved by the Supreme Court but deleted by the Congress, recognized no privilege for confidential communications between spouses, limiting the privilege to that of an accused in a criminal proceeding[3] to prevent his spouse from testifying against him. The marital privilege under the Revised Uniform Rules, limited under the 1974 version of those rules to a privilege of the accused to prevent disclosure of confidential communications, was subsequently broadened by amendment of Uniform Rule of Evidence 504. The revised rule recognizes a privilege on the part of a spouse to refuse to testify against an accused spouse in a criminal proceeding as well as one for confidential communications in criminal and civil cases. Under Federal Rule of Evidence 501, as adopted by Congress, the federal courts have continued to recognize a marital communications privilege as effective by common law.

§ 79 What Is Privileged: Communications Only, or Acts and Facts?

Greenleaf, arguing in 1842 for a privilege distinct from marital incompetency, and furnishing the inspiration for the later statutes by which the privilege was formally enacted, spoke only of “communications” and “conversations.”[4] Those later statutes themselves (except one or two) sanctioned the privilege for “communications” and for nothing beyond. Accordingly it would seem that the privilege should be limited to expressions intended by one spouse to convey a meaning or message to the other. These expressions may be by words, oral, written or in sign-language, or by expressive acts, as where the husband opens a trunk before his wife and points out objects in the trunk to

---

[2]   St. 16 & 17 Vict. c. 83, § 3.

[3]   The cognate privilege for adverse spousal testimony is treated in supra § 66.

[4]   See supra § 78.

her. Moreover, the protection of the privilege will shield against indirect disclosure of the communication, as where a husband is asked for his wife's whereabouts which he learned only from her secret communication. It seems, nevertheless, that logic and policy should cause the courts to halt with communications as the furthest boundary of the privilege, and a substantial number have held steadfast at this line.

A significant number of courts, however, have construed their statutes that say "communications" to extend the privilege to acts, facts, conditions, and transactions not amounting to communications at all. One group seems to announce the principle that acts done privately in the wife's presence amount to "communications." Another would go even further and say that any information secured by the wife as a result of the marital relation and which would not have been known in the absence of such relation is protected. Some at least of this latter group would hold that information secured by one spouse through observation during the marriage as to the health, or intoxication, habitual or at a particular time, or the mental condition of the other spouse, would be protected by the privilege.

All extensions beyond communications seem unjustified under either the instrumental or humanistic justifications for this privilege. The attitude of the courts in these cases seems to reflect a confusion with the quite distinguishable purpose of preserving family harmony by disqualifying one spouse from giving any testimony whatsoever against the other.[5] It is unrealistic to think that it would occur to anyone other than an attorney would consider the existence of the privilege before taking action in the presence of a spouse or, even more certainly, that a spouse would not even have entered into a marital relation but for the existence of the broader privilege—a premise one would have to believe in order to justify the exclusion of all information received as a result of the marital relation. Furthermore, it seems equally difficult to justify a private enclave between spouses that extends beyond confidential communications and information obtained through marital confidence.

A specific instance of development in a direction consistent with the underlying policies behind the privilege has recently been evident in statutes and cases that exclude from the protection of the privilege communications in furtherance of crime or fraud. This exception, long recognized to restrict the cognate privilege for attorney-client communications, seems amply justified in the present context as well.

§ 80 The Communication Must Be Confidential

Most statutes expressly limit the privilege to "confidential communications." However, even where the words used are "any communication" or simply "communications," the notion that the privilege is born of the "common law" and the fact that the pre-statutory descriptions of the privilege had clearly based it upon the policy of protecting confidences,[6] have caused most courts to read into such statutes the requirement of confidentiality. Communications in private between husband and wife are assumed to be confidential, though of course this assumption will be strengthened if confidentiality is expressly affirmed, or if the subject is such that the communicating spouse would probably desire that the matter be kept secret, either because its disclosure would be embarrassing or for some other reason. However, a variety of factors, including the nature of the message or the circumstances under which it was delivered, may serve

---

[5]   See supra § 66.
[6]   See supra § 78.

to rebut a claim that confidentiality was intended. In particular, if a third person is present to the knowledge of the communicating spouse, this stretches the web of confidence beyond the marital pair, and the communication is unprivileged. Even the presence of children of the family will deprive the conversation of protection unless the children are too young to understand what is said. The fact that the communication relates to business transactions may show that it was not intended as confidential. Examples are statements about business agreements between the spouses, or about business matters transacted by one spouse as agent for the other, or about property or conveyances. Usually such statements relate to facts that are intended later to become publicly known. To cloak them with privilege when the transactions come into litigation would be productive of special inconvenience and injustice.

§ 81   The Time of Making the Communication: Marital Status

The privilege is created to encourage marital confidences and is limited to them. Consequently, communications between the husband and wife before they were married, or after their divorce, are not privileged. And attempts to assert the privilege by participants in living arrangements argued to be the functional equivalents of marriage have to date uniformly been rejected by the courts. The requirement of a valid marriage may be satisfied by a valid common law marriage, if it can be proved, but a bigamous marriage will not suffice. Although this latter holding should probably, by analogy to other privileges, be relaxed where the party seeking the benefit of the privilege was ignorant of the status of the other purported spouse, the courts have not consistently done so.

What of a husband and wife living apart? It has been urged that communication in this context is far more likely to be related to preservation of the marriage than are the vast bulk of admittedly privileged communications. This fact, coupled with the pragmatic difficulty involved in determining when hostility between the spouses has become implacable, argues for the more easily administered approach of terminating the privilege only upon a decree of divorce. Some courts have adopted such a view. However, other courts, especially the federal circuits, have refused to apply the privilege where the parties are separated at the time of the communication.

§ 82   Hazards of Disclosure to Third Persons Against the Will of the Communicating Spouse

The weight of decision seems to support the view that the privilege does not protect against the testimony of third persons who have overheard (either accidentally or by eavesdropping) an oral communication between husband and wife, or who have secured possession or learned the contents of a letter from one spouse to another by interception, or through loss or misdelivery by the custodian.

In addition, several courts, especially more recently, have held that particular statutes provide only that a spouse may not be examined about confidential statements. Under such statutes, the privilege does not prevent another person from testifying to the statements or the introduction of documents containing references to such communications.

Such rulings are perhaps best sustained on the view that, since the privilege has as its only effect the suppression of relevant evidence, its scope should be confined as narrowly as is consistent with reasonable protection of marital communications. In this view, it seems, since the communicating spouse can ordinarily take effective precautions against overhearing, he should bear the risk of a failure to use such precautions. Moreover, if he sends a messenger with a letter, he should ordinarily assume the risk that the chosen emissary may lose or misdeliver the message. The rationale that the spouses may ordinarily take effective measures to communicate confidentially tends to break down where one or both are incarcerated. However, communications in the jailhouse are frequently held not privileged, often on the theory that no confidentiality was or could have been expected.

As has been observed elsewhere, the development of sophisticated eavesdropping techniques has led to curbs upon their use and upon the admissibility of evidence obtained thereby.[7] It has also led to inclusion in rules governing privileged communications provisions against disclosure by third persons.

Except in those jurisdictions where the privilege is held only to prevent the spouse from testifying and not the introduction of other testimony or documents, most of the cases have held that the privilege will not be lost if the eavesdropping, or the delivery or disclosure of the letter is due to the betrayal or connivance of the spouse to whom the message is directed. Just as that spouse would not be permitted, against the will of the communicating spouse, to betray the confidence by testifying in court to the message, so he or she may not effectively destroy the privilege by out-of-court betrayal.

If the spouse to whom a letter is addressed dies and it is found among the effects of the deceased, may the personal representative be required or permitted to produce it in court? Here there is no connivance or betrayal by the deceased spouse, and on the other hand this is not a disclosure against which the sender could effectively guard. If the privilege is to be held, as most courts do,[8] to survive the death of one of the spouses, it seems that only a court that strictly limits the effect of the statute to restraining the spouses themselves from testifying, could justify a denial of the privilege in this situation.

§ 83 Who Is the Holder of the Privilege? Enforcement and Waiver

Greenleaf in 1842, in foreshadowing the protection of marital communications, wrote of the projected rule as a "privilege" based on "public policy." Many legislatures, however, when they came to write the privilege into law phrased the rule simply as a survival in this special case of the ancient incompetency of the spouses, which the same statutes undertook to abolish or restrict. So it is often provided that the spouses are "incompetent" to testify to marital communications. Consequently, the courts frequently overlook this "common law" background[9] of privilege and permit any party to the action to claim the benefit of the rule by objection. Doubtless counsel often fail to point out that privilege, not incompetency, is the proper classification, and that the distinctive feature of privilege is that it can only be claimed by the holder or beneficiary of the privilege, not by a party as such.[10] The latter principle is clearly correct.

Who is the holder? Wigmore's argued that the policy of encouraging freedom of communication points to the communicating spouse as the holder. Under this view, in

---

[7]   See supra § 74 and infra §§ 169, 176.

[8]   See supra § 85.

[9]   See supra § 78.

[10]   See supra § 73.1.

the case of statement of a husband to his wife, only the husband could assert the privilege, where the sole purpose is to show the expressions and attitude of the husband. However, even under this limited view, if the object were to show the wife's adoption of the husband's statement by her silence, the husband's statement and her conduct both become her communication and she can claim the privilege. Similarly, if a conversation or an exchange of correspondence between them is offered to show the collective expressions of them both, either could claim privilege as to the entire exchange.

Despite Wigmore's argument, most jurisdictions now provide that both spouses hold the privilege. More than half of the states reach this result by statute or rule. Most federal circuit decisions have reached the same conclusion. The rationale articulated by one court in its decision to disregard earlier precedent placing the privilege only in the communicating spouse was that a failure to permit the non-communicating spouse to assert the privilege would eviscerate the privilege by inviting attempts to prove the statements of the other spouse circumstantially. Despite the view expressed in earlier editions of this text, the rationale expressed is convincing.

A failure by the holder to assert the privilege by objection, or a voluntary revelation by the holder of the communication, or of a material part, is a waiver. The judge, however, may in some jurisdictions in his discretion protect the privilege if the holder is not present to assert it, and objection by a party not the holder may serve the purpose of invoking this discretion, though the party may not complain if the judge fails to protect this privilege belonging to the absent spouse.

§ 84 Controversies in Which the Privilege Is Inapplicable

The common law privilege against adverse testimony of a spouse was subject to an exception in cases of prosecution of the husband for offenses against the wife, at least those of violence.[11] When nineteenth century statutes in this country limited and regulated this privilege and the incompetency of spouses as witnesses and defined the new statutory privilege for confidential communications, the common law exception above mentioned was usually incorporated and extended, and frequently other exceptions were added. Under these statutes it is not always clear whether the exceptions are intended to apply only to the provisions limiting the competency of the spouses as witnesses, or whether they apply also to the privilege for confidential communications. Frequently, however, in the absence of a contrary decision, it is at least arguable that the exception does have this latter application, and in some instances this intent is clearly expressed. Any other result would, in principle, indeed be difficult to justify.

The types of controversies in which the marital communication privilege is made inapplicable vary, of course, from state to state. They may be derived from express provision, from statutory implication, or from decisions based upon common law doctrine. They may be grouped as follows:

- Prosecutions for crimes committed by one spouse against the other or against the children of either. Besides statutes in general terms, particular crimes, most frequently family desertion and pandering, are often specified, and as to these latter the withdrawal of the privilege for communications is usually explicit.

---

[11] See supra § 66.

- Actions by one of the spouses against an outsider for an intentional injury to the marital relation. Thus far this exception has been applied, sometimes under statutes, sometimes as a continuation of common law tradition, chiefly in actions for alienation of affection or for criminal conversation. It is usually applied to admit declarations expressive of the state of affection of the alienated spouse.

- Actions by one spouse against the other. Some of the statutes are in this broader form. Some apply only to particular kinds of actions between them, of which divorce suits are most often specified. This exception for controversies between the spouses, which should extend to controversies between the representatives of the spouses, seems worthy of universal acceptance. In the analogous case of clients who jointly consult an attorney, the clients are held to have no privilege for such consultation in controversies between themselves.[12] So here it seems that husband and wife, while they would desire that their confidences be shielded from the outside world, would ordinarily anticipate that if a controversy between themselves should arise in which their mutual conversations would shed light on the merits, the interests of both would be served by full disclosure.

- A criminal prosecution against one of the spouses in which a declaration of the other spouse made confidentially to the accused would tend to justify or reduce the grade of the offense.

§ 85 If the Communication Was Made During the Marriage, Does Death or Divorce End the Privilege?

The incompetency of husband or wife to testify for the other, and the privilege of each spouse against adverse testimony are terminated when the marriage ends by death or divorce.[13] The privilege for confidential communications of the spouses, however, was based, in the mind of its chief sponsor, Greenleaf, upon the policy of encouraging confidences, who thought that encouragement required not merely temporary but permanent secrecy. The courts in this country have accepted this need for permanent protection and about one-half of the statutes codifying the privilege explicitly provide that it continues after death or divorce. In fact, this characteristic accounts for a large proportion of the attempted invocations of the communications privilege, since if the marriage has not been terminated one of the other, more embracive marital privileges will frequently apply.

In earlier editions of this text, the opinion was given that, "where the marital tie has been severed that the supposed policy of the privilege has the most remote and tenuous relevance, and the possibilities of injustice in its application are most apparent." The text quoted Wigmore, who stated, "there must arise occasional instances of hardship where ample flexibility should be allowed in the relaxation of the rule." The English case of *Shenton v. Tyler*,[14] was cited as an example of an instance of hardship. There, the plaintiff sued a widow and alleged that her deceased husband had made an oral secret trust, known to the widow, for the benefit of plaintiff, and sought to interrogate the widow. The widow relied on section 3 of the Evidence Amendment Act, 1853, as follows:

---

[12]   See infra § 91.1.
[13]   See supra § 66.
[14]   L.R. [1939] Ch. Div. 620 (C.A.).

"no wife shall be compellable to disclose any communication made to her during the marriage." The court rejected the Greenleaf theory of a common law privilege for communications surviving the end of the marriage, and was "unable to find any warrant for extending the words of the section by construction so as to include widowers and widows and divorced persons." The earlier versions of this text then stated: "However debatable may be the court's position that there was no common law privilege for marital communications,[15] it seems clear that the actual holding that the privilege for communications ends when the marriage ends is preferable in policy to the contrary result reached under American statutes and decisions."

The present authors take a somewhat different position with regard to the survival of the privilege after death or divorce. Rather than concluding that a holding that the privilege ends when the marriage ends is preferable in policy, we would argue that a humanitarian, rather than utilitarian, justification for the privilege may call for a qualified privilege generally. Such a privilege would survive death or dissolution of the marriage but might give way in circumstances such as *Shenton v. Tyler*. The possibility of a qualified privilege is discussed in the next section.

§ 86   Policy and Future of the Marital Communications Privilege

The argument traditionally advanced in support of the marital communications privilege is that the privilege is needed to encourage marital confidences, which confidences in turn promote harmony between husband and wife. This argument, now reiterated for almost a century and a half, obviously rests upon certain assumptions concerning the knowledge and psychology of married persons. Thus it must be assumed that spouses will know of the privilege and take its protection into account in determining to make marital confidences, or at least, which is not the same thing, that they would come to know of the absence of the privilege if it were withdrawn and be, as a result, less confiding than at present.

In the absence of any empirical validation, these propositions have appeared highly suspect to many, though not all, commentators. The most convincing answer to the argument of policy appears to be that the contingency of courtroom disclosure would almost never (even if the privilege did not exist) be in the minds of the parties in considering how far they should go in their secret conversations. What encourages them to fullest frankness is not the assurance of courtroom privilege, but the trust they place in the loyalty and discretion of each other. If the secrets are not told outside the courtroom there will be little danger of their being elicited in court. In the lives of most people appearance in court as a party or a witness is an exceedingly rare and unusual event, and the anticipation of it is not one of those factors which materially influence in daily life the degree of fullness of marital disclosures. Thus, while the danger of injustice from suppression of relevant proof is clear and certain, the probable benefits of the rule of privilege in encouraging marital confidences and wedded harmony are marginal.

But probably the policy of encouraging confidences is not the prime influence in creating and maintaining the privilege. It is really a much more natural and less devious matter. It is a matter of emotion and sentiment. All of us have a feeling of indelicacy and want of decorum in prying into the secrets of husband and wife.

---

[15]   See supra § 78.

As pointed out in an earlier section,[16] such humanistic considerations in support of the marital communications and other privileges have been widely advanced in recent years. Increasing recognition of the true operative basis for affording privilege to the marital partners may argue for the treatment of the privilege as qualified rather than absolute. The humanistic need for the creation of a private enclave within a marital relationship may not stand in the balance where there is a need for otherwise unobtainable evidence critical to the ascertainment of significant legal rights.

However, neither the courts nor the legislatures have made moves to convert the marital communications privilege from absolute to qualified. Indeed, the most recent pronouncements of the United States Supreme Court with regard to other privileges suggest a rejection of any notion that the more commonly accepted privileged be anything other than absolute. And the trend with regard to the marital communications privilege seems to be going in the direction of continuing recognition of the privilege in a fairly broad and certainly absolute form.

---

[16]   See supra § 72.

Chapter 10

THE CLIENT'S PRIVILEGE: COMMUNICATIONS BETWEEN CLIENT & LAWYER

Table of Sections

§ 87 Background and Policy of the Privilege: (a) Theoretical Considerations

The notion that the loyalty owed by the lawyer to his client disables him from being a witness in his client's case is deep-rooted in Roman law. This Roman tradition may or may not have been influential in shaping the early English doctrine of which we find the first traces in Elizabeth's time, that the oath and honor of the barrister and the attorney protect them from being required to disclose, upon examination in court, the secrets of the client. But by the eighteenth century in England the emphasis upon the code of honor had lessened and the need of the ascertainment of truth for the ends of justice loomed larger than the pledge of secrecy. So a new justification for the lawyer's exemption from disclosing his client's secrets was found. This theory, which continues as the principal rationale of the privilege today, rests upon three propositions. First the law is complex and in order for members of the society to comply with it in the management of their affairs and the settlement of their disputes they require the assistance of expert lawyers. Second, lawyers are unable to discharge this function without the fullest possible knowledge of the facts of the client's situation. And last, the client cannot be expected to place the lawyer in full possession of the facts without the assurance that the lawyer cannot be compelled, over the client's objection, to reveal the confidences in court. The consequent loss to justice of the power to bring all pertinent facts before the court is, according to the theory, outweighed by the benefits to justice (not to the individual client) of a franker disclosure in the lawyer's office.

This clearly utilitarian justification, premised on the power of the privilege to elicit certain behavior on the part of clients, has a compelling common-sense appeal. The tendency of the client in giving his story to his counsel to omit all that he suspects will work against him is a matter of every day professional observation. It makes it necessary for the prudent lawyer to cross-examine his client searchingly about possible unfavorable facts. In criminal cases the difficulty of obtaining full disclosure from the accused is well known, and would certainly become an absolute impossibility if the defendant knew that the lawyer could be compelled to repeat what he had been told.

These justifications, however, have never been convincing to all. Jeremy Bentham, perhaps the most famous of the privilege's critics to date, argued that the privilege is not needed by the innocent party with a righteous cause or defense, and that the guilty should not be given its aid in concerting a false one. Bentham's apocalyptic division of the client world into righteous and guilty seems somewhat naive in a time when even the best-intended may doubt their compliance with an ever more overwhelming body of law. Nevertheless, none can deny the privilege's unfortunate tendency to suppress the truth, and it has commonly been urged that it is only the greater benefit of increased candor that justifies the continuation of the privilege. Wigmore, the great champion and architect of the privilege, subscribed to this view, though he acknowledged that "Its benefits are all indirect and speculative; its obstruction is plain and concrete."[1]

The trend of recent years toward attempted empirical verification of the intuitive judgments of the past has lent a special cogency to Wigmore's assessment. For the degree of efficacy of the privilege in achieving its avowed aims, speculated to be quite low by critics, is ironically likely to prove indemonstrable by reason of the privilege itself. Despite these difficulties, it is of course possible to proceed from the Cartesian postulate that the privilege effects some unknown and unknowable marginal alteration in client behavior. But such minimal claims, even when combined with efforts to structure the privilege so as to confine its operation to contexts in which it will most probably have an effect, seem to fall short of an adequate justification.

As a possible ancillary justification, it is today suggested with increasing frequency that considerations of privacy should play a role in supporting and ultimately defining the privilege. To date, this rationale has achieved only very little recognition in the courts as a supporting, much less a sufficient, justification for the attorney-client privilege. It is probable that the ultimate fate of this theory will depend upon the success of its advocates in suggesting what implications for the parameters for the privilege are implied by such a rationale.

At the present time it seems most realistic to portray the attorney-client privilege as supported in part by its traditional utilitarian justification, and in part by the integral role it is perceived to play in the adversary system itself. Our system of litigation casts the lawyer in the role of fighter for the party whom he represents. A strong tradition of loyalty attaches to the relationship of attorney and client, and this tradition would be outraged by routine examination of the lawyer as to the client's confidential disclosures

---

[1]   8 Wigmore, Evidence § 2291, at 554 (McNaughton rev. 1961).

regarding professional business. To the extent that the evidentiary privilege, then, is integrally related to an entire code of professional conduct, it is futile to envision drastic curtailment of the privilege without substantial modification of the underlying ethical system to which the privilege is merely ancillary.

The foregoing state of affairs is clearly less than optimum from the standpoint that predictability in the application of the privilege, logically indispensable for any utilitarian effect, is largely lacking in many areas. Advocates of the supposedly inviolate privilege of yesteryear perceive even greater uncertainties interjected by the increasing uses of in camera inspection to determine the legitimacy of claims of privilege, and even in some jurisdictions the use of a balancing test to determine whether the privilege will be honored. While a balancing approach to the privilege is not consistent with the privilege's current rationales, one could argue that increased use of these expedients may ultimately result in a more rational administration of the privilege than could be achieved through the traditional methodology of controlling its scope through the liberal extension of exceptions and application of waiver doctrine.

A clear statement of the scope of the privilege as now generally accepted is embodied in the Uniform Evidence Rules as amended in 1999.

§ 87.1 Background and Policy of the Privilege: (b) Applications in Corporate, Governmental and Other Entity Settings

The application of the privilege for the benefit of a corporate client, as distinguished from a natural person, was never questioned until a federal district court in 1962 held that a corporation is not entitled to claim the privilege.[2] The decision attracted wide attention and much comment, most of which was adverse, until reversed on appeal.[3] There seems to be little reason to believe that the issue will arise soon again.

The scope of the privilege in the corporate context, however, has presented an exceptionally troublesome question that is even yet not fully resolved. The difficulty is basically one of extrapolating the essential operating conditions of the privilege from the paradigm case of the traditional individual client who both supplies information to, and receives counsel from, the attorney. Are both of these aspects of the relationship to be protected in the corporate setting, in which the corporate agents in a position to furnish the pertinent facts are not necessarily those empowered to take action responsive to legal advice based upon those facts? Early decisions focused upon the first half of this dichotomy, and extended the privilege expansively to communications from any "officer or employee" of the client corporation. This emphasis was dramatically reversed by the case of *City of Philadelphia v. Westinghouse Electric Corp.*[4], which propounded a "control group" test under which the privilege was restricted to communications made by those corporate functionaries "in a position to control or even to take a substantial part in a decision about any action which the corporation may take upon the advice of the attorney."

The "control group" theory was widely, though not universally, followed by the courts until the 1981 decision of the Supreme Court in *Upjohn Co. v. United States.*[5]

---

[2]   Radiant Burners, Inc. v. American Gas Ass'n, 207 F. Supp. 771 (N.D. Ill. 1962).

[3]   Radiant Burners, Inc. v. American Gas Ass'n, 320 F.2d 314 (7th Cir. 1963).

[4]   210 F. Supp. 483 (E.D. Pa. 1962).

[5]   449 U.S. 383 (1981).

While the Court specifically declined in Upjohn to attempt the formulation of a definitive rule, it did specifically reject the control group principle as one which "cannot . . . govern the development of the law in this area." The principal deficiency that the Court noted as inherent in the control group test is its failure to recognize the function of the privilege as protecting the flow of information to the advising attorney. The opinion does suggest limitations however, in that such information will be privileged only if: (1) it is communicated for the express purpose of securing legal advice for the corporation; (2) it relates to the specific corporate duties of the communicating employee; and (3) it is treated as confidential within the corporation itself.

The *Upjohn* decision evoked a large amount of commentary, much of which has been critical. In addition to the decision's failure to articulate the scope of the privilege of corporations more clearly, another frequent criticism has been *Upjohn's* reliance upon a utilitarian rationale without at the same time limiting the privilege to instances where it is likely to be effective for its stated purpose. Thus, a lower level corporate employee sufficiently sophisticated to factor an evidentiary privilege into his decision to communicate with a corporate attorney is unlikely to be reassured by a privilege which is waivable in the exclusive discretion of the corporation. At a minimum, the privilege should apply only to corporate employees who either have, or are expressly conferred, the power to assert the privilege.

Though the *Upjohn* decision is not rested upon constitutional grounds, and is thus not binding upon the states, it has had considerable influence outside the federal system. At the same time, some states continue to subscribe to the control group test, thus adding the identity of the forum in which the privilege will ultimately be asserted to other sources of uncertainty as to its scope.

An *Upjohn* extension of the corporate attorney-client privilege almost necessitates extension of the privilege in other organizational structures. While under the control group test the scope of the corporate privilege might be roughly likened to that available to a proprietorship, extension to lower level employees without a corresponding extension to employees of various other entities is probably politically as well as theoretically indefensible.

Where the entity in question is governmental, however, significantly different considerations appear, which have led a number of states substantially to limit the privilege for such entities. On the federal level, cases arising from the investigation of President Clinton have held that any privilege applicable to communications between government attorneys and government officials will not apply to prevent disclosure in the face of a grand jury subpoena.

As noted above, there are situations which draw into question the application of the conventional rule that a corporation's privilege may be asserted or waived by the management of the corporation. One such situation is the derivative stockholder's action, in which both parties claim to be acting in the corporate interest. In the leading case of *Garner v. Wolfinbarger*,[6] the court addressed the problem thus raised by recognizing a qualified privilege on the part of the corporate management, but one which may be pierced by a showing of good cause by the shareholders. Several federal Courts of Appeal and some states have explicitly adopted the *Garner* approach and some cases have expanded it beyond derivative shareholder actions. Yet, although probably the

---

[6]   430 F.2d 1093 (5th Cir. 1970).

prevailing doctrine in dealing with disputes between shareholders and corporations, the *Garner* approach has been criticized as injecting too much uncertainty into the application of the privilege.

§ 88 The Professional Relationship

The privilege for communications of a client with her lawyer hinges upon the client's belief that she is consulting a lawyer in that capacity and her manifested intention to seek professional legal advice. It is sufficient if she reasonably believes that the person consulted is a lawyer, though in fact she is not. Communications in the course of preliminary discussion with a view to employing the lawyer are privileged though the employment is in the upshot not accepted. The burden of proof rests on the person asserting the privilege to show that the consultation was a professional one. Payment or agreement to pay a fee, however, is not essential. But where one consults an attorney not as a lawyer but as a friend or as a business adviser or banker, or negotiator, or as an accountant, or where the communication is to the attorney acting as a "mere scrivener" or as an attesting witness to a will or deed, or as an executor or as agent, the consultation is not professional nor the statement privileged. There is some conflict in the decisions as to whether the privilege is available for communications to an administrative practitioner who is not a lawyer. However, the privilege will generally be applicable even where the services performed by a lawyer are not necessarily available only from members of the legal profession.

Ordinarily an attorney can lawfully hold herself out as qualified to practice only in the state in which she is licensed, and consultation elsewhere on a continuing basis would traditionally not be privileged, but exceptionally by custom she might lawfully be consulted elsewhere in respect to isolated transactions, and Uniform Evidence Rule 502(a)(3) requires only that she be authorized or reasonably be believed to be authorized "in any State or country."

Traditionally, the relationship sought to be fostered by the privilege has been that between the lawyer and a private client, but more recently the privilege has been held to extend to communications to an attorney representing the state. However, disclosures to the public prosecuting attorney by an informer are not within the attorney-client privilege, but an analogous policy of protecting the giving of such information has led to the recognition of a privilege against the disclosure of the identity of the informer, unless the trial judge finds that such disclosure is necessary in the interests of justice. Communications to an attorney appointed by the court to serve the interest of a party are of course within the privilege. A communication by a lawyer to a member of the Board of Governors of the state bar association, revealing a fraudulent conspiracy in which he had been engaged and expressing his desire to resign from the practice of law was held not privileged.

Wigmore argued for a privilege analogous to the lawyer-client privilege for "confessions or similar confidences" made privately by persons implicated in a wrong or crime to the judge of a court.[7] As to judges generally there seems little justification for such a privilege if the policy-motive is the furtherance of the administration of justice by encouraging a full disclosure. Unlike the lawyer the judge needs no private disclosures in advance of trial to enable her to perform her functions. In fact, such revelations would ordinarily embarrass rather than aid her in carrying out her duties as a trial judge. The

---

[7] 8 Wigmore, Evidence § 2376 (McNaughton rev. 1961).

famous case of *Lindsey v. People*,[8] however, raised the question whether the judge of a juvenile court does not stand in a special position with regard to confidential disclosures by children who come before her. The majority of the court held that when a boy under promise of secrecy confessed to the judge that he had fired the shot that killed his father the judge was compellable, on the trial of the boy's mother for murder, to divulge the confession. The court pointed out that a parent who had received such a confidence would be compellable to disclose. In the case of this particular court the need for encouraging confidences is clear, but in most cases the most effective encouragement will come from the confidence-inspiring personality of the judge, even without the aid of assurances of secrecy. The court's conclusion that the need for secrecy for this type of disclosure does not outweigh the sacrifice to the administration of justice from the suppression of the evidence seems justifiable.

§ 89 Subject-Matter of the Privilege: (a) Communications

The modern justification of the privilege, namely, that of encouraging full disclosure by the client for the furtherance of the administration of justice,[9] might suggest that the privilege is only a one-way one, operating to protect communications of the client or his agents to the lawyer or his clerk but not vice versa. However, it is generally held that the privilege will protect at least those attorney to client communications that would have a tendency to reveal the confidences of the client. In fact, only rarely will the attorney's words be relevant for any purpose other than to show the client's communications circumstantially, or to establish an admission by the client by his failure to object. Accordingly, the simpler and preferable rule, adopted by a number of statutes and the Uniform Evidence Rules and by the better-reasoned cases, extends the protection of the privilege also to communications by the lawyer to the client.

An even more embracive view, adopted by statute in a few states, would protect against disclosure by the attorney of any knowledge he has gained while acting as such, even information obtained from sources other than the client. Such an extension finds no justification in the modern utilitarian theory of the privilege. In any event, the more widely prevailing rule does not bar divulgence by the attorney of information communicated to him or his agents by third persons. Nor does information so obtained become privileged by being in turn related by the attorney to the client in the form of advice.

The commonly imposed limitation of protection to communications passing between client and attorney, while logically derived from the policy rationale of the privilege, does raise certain problems of construction where the information acquired by the attorney does not come in the conventional form of oral or written assertions by the client. Initially it is fairly easy to conclude, as most authority holds, that observations by the lawyer that might be made by anyone, and which involve no communicative intent by the client, are not protected. Conversely, testimony relating intentionally communicative acts of the client, as where he rolls up his sleeve to reveal a hidden scar or opens the drawer of his desk to display a revolver, would as clearly be precluded as would the recounting of statements conveying the same information. Much more problematic are cases in which the client delivers tangible evidence such as stolen property to the attorney, or confides facts enabling the attorney to come into the possession of such evidence. Here the

---

[8]   181 P. 531 (Colo. 1919).

[9]   See supra § 87.

decisions are somewhat conflicting, reflecting the virtual impossibility of separating the act of confidence which may legitimately be within the privilege from the preexisting evidentiary fact which may not. To resolve the dilemma, one carefully reasoned argument is that the privilege should not operate to bar the attorney's disclosure of the circumstances of acquisition, since to preclude the attorney's testimony would offer the client a uniquely safe opportunity to divest himself of incriminating evidence without leaving an evidentiary trail.

Difficulties also arise in applying the communications-only theory when one assisting the lawyer, e.g., an examining physician, learns and communicates to the lawyer matters not known to the client. The privilege seems to apply with respect to the communication itself. If the physician is considered as aligned with the client, his knowledge would be that of the client and not privileged; but if aligned with the lawyer, the privilege seems to apply, as held in the leading case.

The application of the privilege to writings presents practical problems requiring discriminating analysis. A professional communication in writing, as a letter from client to lawyer for example, will of course be privileged. These written privileged communications are readily to be distinguished from preexisting documents or writings, such as deeds, wills, and warehouse receipts, not in themselves constituting communications between client and lawyer. As to these preexisting documents two notions come into play. First, the client may make communications about the document by words or by acts, such as sending the document to the lawyer for perusal or handing it to him and calling attention to its terms. These communications, and the knowledge of the terms and appearance of the documents that the lawyer gains thereby are privileged from disclosure by testimony in court. Second, on a different footing entirely, stands the question, shall a lawyer who has been entrusted with the possession of a document by his client be subject to an order of court requiring him to produce the document at the trial or in pretrial discovery proceedings whether for inspection or for use in evidence? The policy of encouraging full disclosure does of course apply to encouraging the client to apprise his lawyer of the terms of all relevant documents, and the disclosure itself and the lawyer's knowledge gained thereby as we have seen are privileged. It is true also that placing the documents in the lawyer's hands is the most convenient means of disclosure. But the next step, that of adding to the privilege for communications a privilege against production of the preexisting documents themselves, when they would be subject to production if still in the possession of the client, would be an intolerable obstruction to justice. To prevent the court's gaining access to a relevant document a party would only have to send it to his lawyer. So here this principle is controlling: if a document would be subject to an order for production if it were in the hands of the client it will be equally subject to such an order if it is in the hands of his attorney. An opposite conclusion would serve the policy of encouraging the client to make full disclosure to his lawyer right enough, but reasonable encouragement is given by the privilege for communications about documents, and the price of an additional privilege would be intolerably high. There are other doctrines that may impel a court to recognize a privilege against production of a preexisting document,[10] but not the doctrine of privilege for lawyer-client communications.

---

[10]   See infra § 96.

§ 90 Subject-Matter of the Privilege: (b) Fact of Employment and Identity of the Client

When a client consults an attorney for a legitimate purpose, he will seldom, but may occasionally, desire to keep secret the very fact of consultation or employment of the lawyer. Nevertheless, consultation and employment are something more than a mere private or personal engagement. They are the calling into play of the services of an officer licensed by the state to act in certain ways in furtherance of the administration of justice, and vested with powers of giving advice on the law, of drafting documents, and of filing pleadings and motions and appearing in court for his client, which are limited to this class of officers.

Does the privilege for confidential communications extend to the fact of consulting or employing such an officer, when intended to be confidential? The traditional and still generally applicable rule denies the privilege for the fact of consultation or employment, including the component facts of the identity of the client, such identifying facts about him as his address and occupation, the identity of the lawyer, and the payment and amount of fees. Similarly, factual communications by the lawyer to the client concerning logistical matters such as trial dates are not privileged.

Several reasons have been advanced as a basis for denying protection to the client's identity, most notably that "the mere fact of the engagement of counsel is out of the rule [of privilege] because the privilege and duty of silence do not arise until the fact is ascertained."[11] Additionally, it is said that a party to legal proceedings is entitled to know the identity of the adversary who is putting in motion or staying the machinery of the court. Such propositions, however, shed little light on the real issue, i.e., whether client anonymity is in some cases essential to obtaining the proper objectives of the privilege.

The inadequacy of a purely simplistic rule excluding client identity from the coverage of the privilege was revealed by the facts of the leading case of *Baird v. Koerner*,[12] in which the court upheld a claim of privilege by an attorney who had mailed a check for back taxes to the IRS on behalf of an anonymous client. Any other result on the facts of *Baird* would seem inconceivable, and the decision has served a wholesome purpose by introducing an element of flexibility into the general rule. However, a number of decisions following *Baird* arguably vastly extended the exceptions to the rule. Thus it was variously stated that exception is made "when the disclosure of the client's identity by his attorney would have supplied the last link in a existing chain of incriminating evidence ...,"[13] or "where ... a strong probability exists that disclosure of such information would implicate the client in the very criminal activity for which legal advice was sought."[14] Such decisions may have blazed a false trail in making the exceptions to the rule turn too largely upon the question of the severity of potential harm to the client rather than upon considerations germane to the privilege.

Today there is a marked trend toward refocusing upon the essential purpose of the privilege by extending its protection to client identity and fee arrangements only if the net effect of the disclosure would be to reveal the nature of a client communication.

---

[11] People ex rel. Vogelstein v. Warden of County Jail of New York County, 270 N.Y.S. 362 (Sup. Ct. 1934).

[12] 279 F.2d 623 (9th Cir. 1960).

[13] In re Grand Jury Proceedings, 680 F.2d 1026, 1027 (5th Cir. 1982) (en banc).

[14] United States v. Hodge & Zweig, 548 F.2d 1347, 1353 (9th Cir. 1977).

Protection should certainly be denied where agencies performed by attorneys are no necessary part of the attorney's unique role nor appropriate for immunization from public disclosure and scrutiny. Arguably, general application of a rule of disclosure seems the approach most consonant with the preservation of the repute of the lawyer's high calling. At the same time, much should depend upon the client's objective in seeking preservation of anonymity, and cases will arise in which protection of the client's identity is both proper and in the public interest.

§ 91 The Confidential Character of the Communications: Communications Intended to Be Made Public; Presence of Third Persons and Agents

It is of the essence of the privilege that it is limited to those communications that the client either expressly made confidential or which he could reasonably assume under the circumstances would be understood by the attorney as so intended. This common law requirement seems to be read into those statutes that codify the privilege without mentioning the confidentiality requirement. A mere showing that the communication was from client to attorney does not suffice, but the circumstances indicating the intention of secrecy must appear. Wherever the matters communicated to the attorney are intended by the client to be made public or revealed to third persons, obviously the element of confidentiality is wanting. Similarly, if the same statements have been made by the client to third persons on other occasions this is persuasive that like communications to the lawyer were not intended as confidential.

A split of authority has arisen, especially in federal court cases, about the status of preliminary conversations concerning documents that are to be published to third parties as well as drafts of those documents. Some courts have held that such conversations and drafts are not confidential based upon the intent of the client ultimately to publish the information. Other courts have found them to be within the privilege at least to the extent that the information was not ultimately disclosed. At least one court has held that privilege may attach to preliminary drafts, but only "if they were prepared or circulated for the purpose of giving or obtaining legal advice and contain information or provisions not included in the final version."[15] If the goal of the attorney-client privilege is to encourage a free flow of communications between attorney and client, preliminary conversations and drafts reflecting those conversations ought to be protected. The client and her attorney ought to be able to discuss the precise terms of the disclosure, including drafting wording reflecting the best way to communicate the information, without the risk that matters ultimately determined not to be disclosed would be unprivileged.

Questions as to the effect of the presence of persons other than the client and the lawyer often arise. At the extremes answers would be clear. Presumably the presence of a casual disinterested third person within hearing to the client's knowledge would demonstrate that the communication was not intended to be confidential. On the other hand if the help of an interpreter is necessary to enable the client to consult the lawyer his presence would not deprive the communication of its confidential and privileged character. Moreover, in cases where the client has one of his agents attend the conference, or the lawyer calls in his clerk or confidential secretary, the presence of these intermediaries will be assumed not to militate against the confidential nature of the

---

[15] Andritz Sprout-Bauer, Inc. v. Beazer East, Inc., 174 F.R.D. 609, 633 (M.D. Pa. 1997).

consultation, and presumably this would not be made to depend upon whether the presence of the agent, clerk or secretary was in the particular instance reasonably necessary to the matter in hand. It is the way business is generally done and that is enough. As to relatives and friends of the client, the results of the cases are not consistent, but it seems that here not only might it be asked whether the client reasonably understood the conference to be confidential but also whether the presence of the relative or friend was reasonably necessary for the protection of the client's interests in the particular circumstances.

§ 91.1 The Confidential Character of the Communications: Joint Consultations and Employments; Controversies Between Client and Attorney

When two or more persons, each having an interest in some problem, or situation, jointly consult an attorney, their confidential communications with the attorney, though known to each other, will of course be privileged in a controversy of either or both of the clients with the outside world, that is, with parties claiming adversely to both or either of those within the original charmed circle. But it will often happen that the two original clients will fall out between themselves and become engaged in a controversy in which the communications at their joint consultation with the lawyer may be vitally material. In such a controversy it is clear that the privilege is inapplicable. In the first place the policy of encouraging disclosure by holding out the promise of protection seems inapposite, since as between themselves neither would know whether he would be more helped or handicapped, if in any dispute between them, both could invoke the shield of secrecy. And secondly, it is said that they had obviously no intention of keeping these secrets from each other, and hence as between them it was not intended to be confidential. In any event, it is a qualification of frequent application and of even wider potentiality, not always recognized. Thus, in the situation mentioned in the previous section where a client calls into the conference with the attorney one of the client's agents, and matters are discussed which bear on the agent's rights against the client, it would seem that in a subsequent controversy between client and agent, the limitation on the privilege accepted in the joint consultation cases should furnish a controlling analogy.

A step beyond the joint consultation where communications by two clients are made directly in each other's hearing is the situation where two parties separately interested in some contract or undertaking, as in the case of borrower and lender or insurer and insured, engage the same attorney to represent their respective interests, and each communicates separately with the attorney about some phase of the common transaction. Here again it seems that the communicating client, knowing that the attorney represents the other party also, would not ordinarily intend that the facts communicated should be kept secret from him. Whether the doctrine of limited confidentiality should be applied to communications by an insured to a nonlawyer agent of the insurer bound by contract to provide the defense for both has provoked differing judicial reactions. Where the statement is made directly to the attorney hired by the insurer, there is no question that the privilege applies in an action brought by a third person, nor does it seem disputed that there is no privilege where the controversy is between the insured, or someone claiming under him, and the company itself over the company's liability under the policy.

Another step beyond the joint client situation is the instance where two or more clients, each represented by their own lawyers, meet to discuss matters of common interest—commonly called a joint defense agreement or pooled information situation. Such communications among the clients and their lawyers are within the privilege. Although it originated in the context of criminal cases, the doctrine has been applied in civil cases and to plaintiffs in litigation as well as defendants. It is commonly said that the doctrine applies only where the parties are involved in litigation, but some courts have applied it in other instances.

The burden of showing the common interest is on the party claiming the privilege. Such an agreement may not be found to exist even where two clients jointly consult lawyers with regard to related matters. For example, in a matter involving the Whitewater investigation, the court held that matters discussed between Hilary Rodham Clinton and her lawyers and lawyers representing the Office of the President were not within the common interest doctrine. Mrs. Clinton's interests were in avoiding personal liability, criminal or civil; the White House as a governmental institution did not have a similar interest.

The weight of authority seems to support the view that when client and attorney become embroiled in a controversy between themselves, as in an action by the attorney for compensation or by the client for damages for the attorney's negligence, the seal is removed from the attorney's lips. Though sometimes rested upon other grounds it seems that here again the notion that as between the participants in the conference the intention was to disclose and not to withhold the matters communicated offers a plausible reason. As to what is a controversy between lawyer and client the decisions do not limit their holdings to litigation between them, but have said that whenever the client, even in litigation between third persons, makes an imputation against the good faith of his attorney in respect to his professional services, the curtain of privilege drops so far as necessary to enable the lawyer to defend his conduct. Perhaps the whole doctrine, that in controversies between attorney and client the privilege is relaxed, may best be based upon the ground of practical necessity that if effective legal service is to be encouraged the privilege must not stand in the way of the lawyer's just enforcement of his rights to be paid a fee and to protect his reputation. The only question about such a principle is whether in all cases the privilege ought not to be subject to the same qualification, that it should yield when the evidence sought is necessary to the attainment of justice.

§ 92 The Client as the Holder of the Privilege: Who May Assert, and Who Complain on Appeal of Its Denial?

A rule regulating the competency of evidence or of witnesses—a so-called "exclusionary" rule—is normally founded on the policy of safeguarding the fact-finding process against error, and it is assertible by the party against whom the evidence is offered. The earmarks of a privilege, as we have seen, are first, that it is not designed to protect the fact-finding process but is intended to protect some "outside" interest, other than the ascertainment of truth at the trial, and second, that it cannot be asserted by the adverse party as such, but only by the person whose interest the particular rule of privilege is intended to safeguard.[16] While once it was conceived that the privilege was set up to protect the lawyer's honor, we know that today it is agreed that the basic policy

---

[16] See the discussion in supra § 72 of the distinction between competency and privilege.

of the rule is that of encouraging clients to lay the facts fully before their counsel. They will be encouraged by a privilege that they themselves have the power to invoke. To extend any benefit or advantage to someone as attorney, or as party to a suit, or to people generally, will be to suppress relevant evidence without promoting the purpose of the privilege.

Accordingly it is now generally agreed that the privilege is the client's and his alone, and Uniform Rule 502(b) vests the privilege in the client. It is thought that this would be recognized even in those states that, before modern notions of privilege and policy were adequately worked out, codified the rule in terms of inadmissibility of evidence of communications, or of incompetency of the attorney to testify thereto. These statutes are generally held not to be intended to modify the common law doctrines.

It is not surprising that the courts, often faced with statutes drafted in terms of obsolete theories, and reaching these points rarely and usually incidentally, have not worked out a consistent pattern of consequences of this accepted view that the rule is one of privilege and that the privilege is the client's. It is believed that the applications suggested below are well grounded in reason and are supported by some authority, whether of text or decision.

First, it is clear that the client may assert the privilege even though he is not a party to the cause wherein the privileged testimony is sought to be elicited. Second, if he is present at the hearing whether as party, witness, or bystander he must assert the privilege personally or by attorney, or it will be waived. Third, it is generally held that, if he is not present at the taking of testimony, nor a party to the proceedings, the privilege may be called to the court's attention by anyone present, such as the attorney for the absent client, or a party in the case, or the court of its own motion may protect the privilege. Fourth: While if an asserted privilege is erroneously sustained, the aggrieved party may of course complain on appeal of the exclusion of the testimony, the erroneous denial of the privilege can only be complained of by the client whose privilege has been infringed. This opens the door to appellate review by the client if he is also a party and suffers adverse judgment. If he is not a party, the losing party in the cause, by the better view is without recourse. Relevant, competent testimony has come in, and the privilege was not created for his benefit. But the witness, whether he is the client or his attorney, may refuse to answer and suffer an adjudication of contempt and may, in some jurisdictions at least, secure review on habeas corpus if the privilege was erroneously denied. This remedy, however, is calculated to interrupt and often disrupt progress of the cause on trial. Does a lawyer on the witness stand who is asked to make disclosures that she thinks may constitute an infringement of her client's privilege, owe a duty to refuse to answer and if necessary to test the judge's ruling on habeas corpus or appeal from a judgment of contempt? It seems clear that, unless in a case of flagrant disregard of the law by the judge, the lawyer's duty is merely to present her view that the testimony is privileged, and if the judge rules otherwise, to submit to her decision or pursue the possibility of an appeal.

§ 93 Waiver

Since as we have seen, it is the client who is the holder of the privilege, the power to waive it is his, and he alone, or his attorney or agent acting with his authority, or his representative, may exercise this power. In the case of the corporation, the power to claim or waive the privilege generally rests with corporate management, i.e., ultimately with the board of directors.

Waiver may be found, as Wigmore points out, not merely from words or conduct expressing an intention to relinquish a known right, but also from conduct such as partial disclosure which would make it unfair for the client to invoke the privilege thereafter.[17] Finding waiver in situations in which forfeiture of the privilege was not subjectively intended by the holder is consistent with the view, expressed by some cases and authorities, that the essential function of the privilege is to protect a confidence that, once revealed by any means, leaves the privilege with no legitimate function to perform. Logic notwithstanding, it would appear poor policy to allow the privilege to be overthrown by theft or fraud, and in fact most authority requires that to effect a waiver a disclosure must at least be voluntary.

Given the scope of modern discovery and the realities of contemporary litigation, a question of great practical importance today is whether a voluntary but inadvertent disclosure should result in waiver. In earlier times, the burden of avoiding such a disclosure of privileged matter was relatively slight compared to that encountered today where enormous quantities of documents may be sought by an opponent through discovery. Under current conditions, some privileged material is likely to pass through even the most tightly woven screen. Since the consequences of such an oversight are potentially staggering, the question is raised as to whether traditional waiver doctrine ought to be modified. Not surprisingly, the decisions in the area have been somewhat divergent. However, while some courts apparently still adhere to a rather strict approach to waiver, others have considered factors such as the excusability of the error, whether prompt attempt to remedy the error was made, and whether preservation of the privilege will occasion unfairness to the opponent. The costs of attempting to avoid waiver under a strict rule would argue strongly for modification along these lines, and it is believed that the decisions are tending in this direction.

Closely related to the inadvertent waiver issue is the question of the scope of waiver. The traditional rule has been that waiver as to one document waives the privilege for other documents relating to the same subject matter. However, under modern practice, where the volume of documents may be enormous, a broad subject matter waiver may be inappropriate. Thus, in instances of inadvertent waiver, even some courts applying a strict waiver policy have limited the scope of the waiver to the document itself rather than extending it to all documents dealing with the same subject matter. Others have narrowed the scope of the subject matter significantly. A persuasive argument has been made that the treatment of the inadvertent and scope of waiver issues be analyzed in terms of fairness and that the "principal concern is selective use of privileged material to garble the truth, which mandates giving the opponent access to related privileged material to set the record straight."[18]

In 2008, Congress sought to alleviate some of the more troublesome aspects arising from both inadvertent waiver and the broad scope of waiver in some courts. Federal Rule of Evidence 502 now provides that inadvertent disclosures do not operate as waivers, provided the privilege holder took reasonable steps to prevent disclosure and to rectify the error. The Rule also provides that the scope of waiver is limited to other disclosures

---

[17]   *See* 8 Wigmore, Evidence § 2327 (McNaughton rev. 1961).

[18]   Marcus, The Perils of Privilege: Waiver and the Litigator, 84 Mich. L. Rev. 1605, 1607–08 (1986).

of the same subject matter that "ought in fairness to be considered together." The rule applies in federal courts to disclosures made in either federal or state proceedings. Rule 502 also provides that a federal court order finding that there is no waiver is binding in other federal or state proceedings, even with regard to third parties.

Turning then to the specific contexts in which waiver may be argued to occur, it will be recalled that as noted in an earlier section the commencement of a malpractice action against the attorney by the client will constitute a waiver of the privilege by the latter.[19] There are, in addition, a variety of other types of actions in which the advice of an attorney will sometimes be relied upon in support of a claim or defense. It has accordingly become established that if a party interjects the "advice of counsel" as an essential element of a claim or defense, then that party waives the privilege as to all advice received concerning the same subject matter. While there can be no doubt of the desirability of a rule preventing a party from relying upon the advice of counsel as the basis of a claim or defense while at the same time frustrating a full exploration of the character of that advice, the problem of defining when such an issue has been interjected is an extremely difficult one. The cases are generally agreed that filing or defending a lawsuit does not waive the privilege. By contrast, specific reliance upon the advice either in pleading or testimony will generally be seen as waiving the privilege. Some decisions have gone much further, and have extended the doctrine broadly to cases in which a mental state asserted by the client is sought to be shown inconsistent with the advice of counsel. Such extensions seem dubious lacking full acceptance of the Benthamite principle that the privilege ought to be overthrown to facilitate the search for truth.

Of course, if the holder of the privilege fails to claim his privilege by objecting to disclosure by himself or another witness when he has an opportunity to do so, he waives his privilege as to the communications so disclosed.

By the prevailing view, which seems correct, the mere voluntary taking the stand by the client as a witness in a suit to which he is party and testifying to facts which were the subject of consultation with his counsel is no waiver of the privilege for secrecy of the communications to his lawyer. It is the communication that is privileged, not the facts. If on direct examination, however, he testifies to the privileged communications, in part, this is a waiver as to the remainder of the privileged consultation or consultations about the same subject.

What if the client is asked on cross-examination about the communications with his lawyer, and he responds without asserting his claim of privilege? Is this a waiver? Unless there are some circumstances which show that the client was surprised or misled, it seems that the usual rule that the client's failure to claim the privilege when to his knowledge testimony infringing it is offered, would apply here, and that the decisions treating such testimony on cross-examination as being involuntary and not constituting a waiver are hardly supportable.

How far does the client waive by calling the attorney as a witness? If the client elicits testimony from the lawyer-witness as to privileged communications this obviously would waive as to all consultations relating to the same subject, just as the client's own testimony would. It would seem also that by calling the lawyer as a witness he opens the door for the adversary to impeach him by showing his interest. And it seems reasonable

---

[19] See supra § 91.1.

to contend as Wigmore does[20] that if the client uses the lawyer to prove matter that he would only have learned in the course of his employment this again should be considered a waiver as to related privileged communications. But merely to call the lawyer to testify to facts known by him apart from his employment should not be deemed a waiver of the privilege. That would attach too harsh a condition on the exercise of the privilege. Unless the lawyer-witness is acting as counsel in the case on trial, there is no violation of the Model Rules of Professional Conduct, and if he is, it recognizes that his testifying may be essential to the ends of justice. Moreover, these are matters usually governed not by the client but by the lawyer, to whom the ethical mandate is addressed.

In an earlier section[21] discussing a witness's use of a writing to refresh his recollection for purposes of testifying, it was pointed out that, under both common law and Federal Evidence Rule 612, if a witness consulted a writing to refresh his recollection while testifying, opposing counsel is entitled to inspect it, to cross-examine the witness upon it, and to introduce in evidence portions that relate to the testimony of the witness. It was further pointed out that if the document were privileged, e.g. an attorney-client communication, such act of consultation would effect a waiver of the privilege.[22] And finally, the problem area was said to be when the privileged writing was consulted by the witness prior to testifying. At common law, authority generally was against requiring disclosure of writings consulted prior to testifying, and under that view the problem of waiver of privilege does not arise. However, an increasing number of cases have allowed disclosure, and Federal Evidence Rule 612 gives the trial judge discretion to order disclosure. Should this discretionary power of the judge extend also to deciding whether a waiver of privilege has occurred? Or should it be said that on the one hand waiver never occurs, or on the other that it always occurs? The Report of the House Committee on the Judiciary took a strict no-waiver position,[23] but no language to that effect was incorporated in Rule 612. Nor was there included any specific provision that privilege should always be waived. The discretionary provision was inserted almost as a matter of necessity to limit disclosure of the potentially vast volume and variety of documents that might be consulted before testifying to those truly bearing on the testimony of the witness, and similar considerations are pertinent to the waiver question. While the cases are mixed, the preferred view seems to be that the judge's discretion extends not only to the threshold question whether connection with the testimony is sufficient to warrant disclosure but also to the question whether its importance is sufficient to override the privilege, given all the circumstances.

When at an earlier trial or stage of the case the privilege has been waived and testimony as to the privileged communications elicited without objection, the prevailing view is that this is a waiver also for any subsequent hearing of the same case.

This result has traditionally been justified on the ground that once the confidence protected by the privilege is breached the privilege has no valid continuing office to perform. It should be noted, however, that the same result may here be supported by the distinguishable consideration that to allow a subsequent claim of the privilege would unfairly disadvantage the opponent who has reasonably assumed that the evidence

---

[20]   8 Wigmore, Evidence § 2327 (McNaughton rev. 1961).

[21]   See supra § 9.

[22]   See *id.*

[23]   House Comm. on Judiciary, Federal Rules of Evidence, H.R. Rep. No. 650, 93d Cong., 1st Sess., p. 13 (1973).

would be available. The same reasons seem to apply where the waiver was publicly made upon the trial of one case, and the privilege later sought to be asserted on the hearing of another case.

Should the same rule of once published, permanently waived, apply to out-of-court disclosures made by the client or with his consent? Authority is scanty, but it seems that if the client makes or authorizes public disclosure, this should clearly be a waiver. Even where the privileged matter is privately revealed, or authorized to be revealed, to a third person, waiver has generally resulted and this conclusion may be supported by analogy to the cases which deny privilege when a third person is present at the consultation.[24] The federal courts are split on the issue of whether a disclosure to a government agency necessarily constitutes a complete waiver of the privilege. One Court of Appeals has held that it does not, announcing in effect a rule of selective waiver.[25] A few courts have at least suggested that the waiver may not apply as to others if the client has clearly communicated its intent to retain the privilege, such as by entering into a confidentiality agreement with the federal agency. The majority of courts dealing with the issue have found a complete, rather than selective waiver.

It has been pointed out that considerations of fairness to the opponent rarely enter in where the disclosure is neither public nor made in the context of the litigation.

§ 94 The Effect of the Death of the Client

The accepted theory is that the protection afforded by the privilege will in general survive the death of the client. This settled view was fixed more firmly by the United States Supreme Court in *Swidler & Berlin v. United States*.[26] In *Swidler*, the Court held that the government, which sought information about an interview between the late Deputy White House Counsel Vincent W. Foster and his attorney shortly before Foster's suicide, had failed to make a showing sufficient to justify an overturning of the common law rule. The government had urged that the survival of the privilege be balanced against the government's need for the information in a criminal investigation. The Court rejected the concept of a privilege so qualified, emphasizing that the knowledge that communications will remain confidential even after death "encourages the client to communicate fully and frankly with counsel."[27]

In reaching its decision in *Swidler*, the Court acknowledged the existence of exceptions to the privilege both in instances where the communications are in furtherance of crime or fraud[28] and in cases involving the validity or interpretation of a will or other dispute between parties claiming by succession from the testator at his death. This testamentary exception has been reached by different routes. Sometimes the testator will be found to have waived the privilege in his lifetime, as by directing the attorney to act as an attesting witness. Wigmore argues, as to the will contests, that communications of the client with his lawyer as to the making of a will are intended to be confidential in his lifetime but that this is a "temporary confidentiality" not intended to require secrecy after his death[29] and this view finds approval in some decisions. Other

---

[24]   See supra § 91.

[25]   Diversified Industries, Inc. v. Meredith, 572 F.2d 596 (8th Cir. 1977) (en banc).

[26]   524 U.S. 399 (1998).

[27]   *Id.* at 407.

[28]   See infra § 95.

[29]   8 Wigmore, Evidence § 2314 (McNaughton rev. 1961).

courts say simply that where all the parties claim under the client the privilege does not apply. The distinction is taken that when the contest is between a "stranger" and the heirs or personal representatives of the deceased client, the heirs or representatives can claim privilege, and they can waive it. Even if the privilege were assumed to be applicable in will contests, it could perhaps be argued that since those claiming under the will and those claiming by intestate succession both equally claim under the client, each should have the power to waive.

The doctrine that the privilege is ineffective, on whatever ground, when both litigants claim under the deceased client has been applied to suits by the heirs or representatives to set aside a conveyance by the deceased for mental incapacity and to suits for the enforcement of a contract made by the deceased to make a will in favor of plaintiff. The cases encountered where the party is held to be a "stranger" and hence not entitled to invoke this doctrine are cases where the party asserts against the estate a claim of a promise by the deceased to pay, or make provision in his will for payment, for services rendered.

None of this authority would seem to be eroded by the *Swidler* case. But certainly the survival of the privilege in the ordinary situation is now entrenched. The *Swidler* case is, of course, binding in the federal courts, and likely to be persuasive to the states, especially those that have held that way in the past. The principal question remaining is whether there will be other inroads on the privilege in special situations. For example, in *Swidler*, the dissent raised the specter of a deceased client's confession to a crime with which another is now charged.[30] In apparent response, the majority suggested that constitutional considerations might compel disclosure in such a situation.[31] It is difficult to imagine that the privilege would survive such a set of facts.

The issue of survival of the privilege may also be affected by state statutes. Almost half of the states have statutes giving the personal representative the right to claim the privilege, thus acknowledging its survival. Presumably, the right to claim the privilege would also give the representative the right to waive it. California's statute provides that the privilege survives only so long as the estate is still in administration.[32]

§ 95 Consultation in Furtherance of Crime or Fraud

Since the policy of the privilege is that of promoting the administration of justice, it would be a perversion of the privilege to extend it to the client who seeks advice to aid him in carrying out an illegal or fraudulent scheme. Advice given for those purposes would not be a professional service but participation in a conspiracy. Accordingly, it is settled under modern authority that the privilege does not extend to communications between attorney and client where the client's purpose is the furtherance of a future intended crime or fraud. Advice secured in aid of a legitimate defense by the client against a charge of past crimes or past misconduct, even though he is guilty, stands on a different footing and such consultations are privileged. If the privilege is to be denied on the ground of unlawful purpose, the client's guilty intention is controlling, though the attorney may have acted innocently and in good faith. As to when the client must be shown to have had the guilty purpose, the traditional and apparent majority rule is that the purpose must exist at the time the legal advice is sought. However, some cases have

---

[30]   Swidler & Berlin v. United States, 524 U.S. 399, 413 (1998) (dissent by O'Connor, J.).

[31]   *Id.* at 409 n.3.

[32]   Cal. Evid. Code § 954.

held that the exception applies where the client has used the lawyer's advice to engage in or assist a crime or fraud, irrespective of the client's intention at the time of consultation.

Both the procedure and standard for determining the application of the crime-fraud exception have been troublesome for the courts. The question of whether and when the court can examine documents in camera in aid of its application of the exception was decided for the federal courts in *United States v. Zolin*.[33] The judge may inspect documents in camera when there is a "factual basis adequate to support a good faith belief by a reasonable person" that such an inspection "may reveal evidence to establish the claim that the crime-fraud exception applies."[34] Although the Supreme Court has not addressed the quantum of proof necessary for the second stage of the inquiry—the determination of whether the exception in fact applies—the federal and state courts considering the issue have used a similar standard. Although variously expressed, what is required is a prima facie case that the communication was in furtherance of crime or fraud, or in other words, that the one who seeks to avoid the privilege bring forward evidence from which the existence of an unlawful purpose could reasonably be found. Although the trial judge may consider information offered by the party opposing review, there is no requirement that such consideration be given. On the other hand, the court must determine that the communication was itself in furtherance of the crime or fraud, not merely that it has the potential of being relevant evidence of criminal or fraudulent activity.

Concern has been expressed by the criminal defense bar about the uncertainty and seeming ease with which the crime-fraud exception has been applied. But especially given the courts' concern for secrecy in grand jury proceedings—the most common setting in which the exception is raised—it seems unlikely that it will become more difficult for the prosecution to establish the existence of the exception.

Questions arise fairly frequently under this limitation upon the privilege in the situation where a client has first consulted one attorney about a claim, and then employs other counsel and brings suit. At the trial the defense seeks to have the first attorney testify to disclosures by the client which reveal that the claim was fabricated or fraudulent. This of course may be done, but if the statements to the first attorney would merely reveal variances from the client's later statements or testimony, not sufficient to evidence fraud or perjury, the privilege would stand.

It has been questioned whether the traditional statement of the area of the limitation, that is in cases of communications in aid of crime or fraud, is not itself too limited. Wigmore argued that the privilege should not be accorded to communications in furtherance of any deliberate scheme to deprive another of his rights by tortious or unlawful conduct.[35] A few courts have expanded the exception to include intentional torts; most courts considering the issue have not.

Stricter requirements such as that the intended crime be malum in se or that it involve "moral turpitude," suggested in some of the older decisions, seem out of place here where the only sanction proposed is that of opening the door to evidence concededly

---

[33]   491 U.S. 554 (1989).

[34]   *Id.* at 572.

[35]   8 Wigmore, Evidence § 2298, at 577 (McNaughton rev. 1961).

relevant upon the issue on trial. There further seems no apparent reason why the exception should not be applied equally to the work product privilege.

§ 96 Protective Rules Relating to Materials Collected for Use of Counsel in Preparation for Trial: Reports of Employees, Witness-Statements, Experts' Reports, and the Like

A heavy emphasis on the responsibility of counsel for the management of the client's litigation is a characteristic feature of the adversary or contentious system of procedure of the Anglo-American tradition. The privilege against disclosure in court of confidential communications between lawyer and client, as we have seen, is largely supported in modern times by the policy of encouraging free disclosure by the client in the attorney's office to enable the lawyer to discharge that responsibility.[36] The need for this encouragement is understood by lawyers because the problem of the guarded half-truths of the reticent client is familiar to them in their day-to-day work.

Closely allied to this felt need of promoting a policy of free disclosure by the client to permit the managing of the lawyer's affairs most effectively in the interests of justice, is a feeling by lawyers of a need for privacy in their work and for freedom from interference in the task of preparing the client's case for trial. Certainly if the adversary were free at any time to inspect all of the correspondence, memoranda, reports, exhibits, trial briefs, drafts of proposed pleadings, and plans for presentation of proofs, which constitute the lawyer's file in the case, the attorney's present freedom to collect for study all the data, favorable and unfavorable, and to record his tentative impressions before maturing his conclusions, would be cramped and hindered.

The natural jealousy of the lawyer for the privacy of her file, and the court's desire to protect the effectiveness of the lawyer's work as the manager of litigation, have found expression, not only as we have seen in the evidential privilege for confidential lawyer-client communications, but in rules and practices about the various forms of pretrial discovery. Thus, under the old chancery practice of discovery, the adversary was not required to disclose, apart from her own testimony, the evidence that she would use, or the names of the witnesses she would call in support of her own case. The same restriction has often been embodied in, or read into, the statutory discovery systems.

Counterbalancing this need for privacy in preparation, of course, is the very need from which the discovery devices spring, namely, the need to make available to each party the widest possible sources of proof as early as may be so as to avoid surprise and facilitate preparation. The trend has been in the direction of wider recognition of this latter need, and the taboo against the "fishing expedition" has yielded increasingly to the proposition that the ends of justice require a wider availability of discovery than in the past. Accordingly there has developed an impressive arsenal of instruments of discovery, including interrogatories to the adverse party, demands for admissions, oral and written depositions of parties and witnesses, production of documents or things, entry upon land, and physical and mental examinations. In recent years some disenchantment with discovery has surfaced with claims that it was used as an instrument of harassment, was unduly time-consuming, and was excessively costly. In an effort to reduce the abuse of discovery and to attempt to insure the flow of information from party to party, the Federal Rules of Civil Procedure were amended in 1993 and

---

[36] See supra § 87.

again in 2000, principally to provide for mandatory disclosure of information without the need for invocation of particular discovery devices.[37] These amendments have some impact on the application of the privileges discussed later in this chapter.

Attorney-Client Privilege. In the first place, of course, it is recognized that if the traditional privilege for attorney-client communications applies to a particular writing that may be found in a lawyer's file, the privilege exempts it from pretrial discovery proceedings, such as orders for production or questioning about its contents in the taking of depositions. On the other hand, if the writing has been in the possession of the client or his agents and was there subject to discovery, it seems axiomatic that the client cannot secure any exemption for the document by sending it to an attorney to be placed in his files.[38]

How do these distinctions apply to a report made by an agent to the client of the results of investigation by himself or another agent of facts pertinent to some matter that later becomes the subject of litigation, such as a business dispute or a personal injury. It has usually been held that an agent's report to his principal though made in confidence is not privileged as such, and looked on as a mere preexisting document it would not become privileged when sent by the client-principal to his lawyer for his information when suit is brought or threatened.[39] The problem frequently arises in connection with proceedings for discovery of accident reports by employees, with lists of eyewitnesses, and in connection with signed statements of witnesses attached to such reports or secured separately by investigators employed in the client's claim department or by an insurance company with whom the client carries insurance against liability. Uniform Evidence Rule 502(b) extends the privilege to confidential communications for the purpose of facilitating the rendition of legal services to the client to communications "(4) between representatives of the client or between the client and representatives of the client . . . ." The import of this provision remains largely unexplored.

Whether a communication by the client's agent, on behalf of the client, to the latter's attorney would be privileged, has been discussed elsewhere.[40] Under the Supreme Court decision in *Upjohn Co. v. United States*[41] the attorney-client privilege will protect intra-corporate communications made for the purpose of securing legal advice if, additionally, the communication relates to the communicating employee's[42] assigned duties and is treated as confidential by the corporation. In *Upjohn*, the communications in question were made by the employees directly to General Counsel and other lawyers representing the corporation in the investigation. An analogous rule would seem appropriate for application to agency situations not involving corporations.

By contrast, routine reports of agents made in the regular course of business, before suit is brought or threatened, have usually, though not always, been treated as pre-existing documents which not being privileged in the client's hands do not become so when delivered into the possession of his attorney. It is clear, however, that these classifications are not quite mutually exclusive and that some cases will fall in a doubtful borderland. And the law is in the making on the question whether a report of accident

---

[37] Fed. R. Civ. P. 26(a).

[38] See supra § 89.

[39] See *id.*

[40] See supra §§ 87.1, 91.

[41] 449 U.S. 383 (1981).

[42] See supra § 87.1.

or other casualty, by a policy-holder or his agents to a company insuring the policy-holder against liability, is to be treated as privileged when the insurance company passes it on to the attorney who will represent both the company and the insured. Reasonably, the insurance company may be treated as an intermediary to secure legal representation for the insured, by whom the confidential communications can be transmitted as through a trusted agent. A report to a liability insurer can have no purpose other than use in potential litigation.

Work Product. The discussion thus far has centered upon the extent to which the attorney-client privilege, just as any other privilege, can be invoked as a bar to discovery. Another, and much more frequently encountered limitation upon discovery of materials contained in the files of counsel, is furnished by the so-called "work product" doctrine, exempting trial preparations, in varying degrees, from discovery.

The seminal case on the work product privilege is *Hickman v. Taylor*,[43] decided by the Supreme Court in 1947. The case involved a suit under the Jones Act arising out of the deaths of crew members in a tugboat sinking. After a public hearing on the incident at which the surviving crew members testified, an attorney for the tug owners obtained signed statements from the survivors. The lawyer also interviewed other persons, in some instances making memoranda. Plaintiffs sought the statements, both written and oral. The defendants and their attorney refused and were held in contempt.

The United States Supreme Court affirmed the judgment of the Court of Appeals, which had reversed the contempt citation. The problem, said the Court, was to balance the interest in privacy of a lawyer's work against the interest supporting reasonable and necessary inquiries. Proper preparation of a client's case demands that information be assembled and sifted, legal theories be prepared, and strategy be planned "without undue and needless interference."[44] If the product of this work (interviews, statements, memoranda, etc.) were available merely on demand, the effect on the legal profession would be demoralizing. Discovery may be had where relevant and non-privileged facts, necessary for preparation of the opposing party's case, remain hidden, or the witness unavailable. The burden is on the party seeking to invade the privacy of the lawyer to show justification; this is "implicit in the rules as now [in 1947] constituted."[45] There had been no attempt in *Hickman* to show need for the written statements. And as for the oral statements, to require the attorney to reproduce them would have a highly adverse effect upon the legal profession, making the lawyer more an ordinary witness than an officer of the court. Under the circumstances of this case, no showing could be made that would justify requiring disclosure of the mental impressions of counsel as to what the witnesses told him.

Considerable disagreement in the lower courts as to the meaning of *Hickman v. Taylor* followed that decision, no doubt resulting at least in part from the labored path followed by the Court to the conclusion that the matter of a qualified work product privilege was in fact covered by its own rules as then written. Finally after more than 20 years, the Court in 1970 adopted an amended Federal Rule of Civil Procedure 26(b), with subdivision (3) directed in specific terms to the scope of the qualified work product protection. Nonetheless, *Hickman v. Taylor* remains a "brooding omnipresence," much

---

[43]   329 U.S. 495 (1947).

[44]   *Id.* at 511.

[45]   *Id.* at 512.

cited and quoted by the courts, and in fact still governs an important area of the qualified work product protection.

These salient provisions of Rule 26(b)(3) should be noted:

(1) The document or thing must have been "prepared in anticipation of litigation or for trial." If this scope seems unduly limited, it must be remembered that litigation is the frame of reference for work product. When the lawyer is engaged in rendering other services, e.g., the drafting of a contract, information that she needs will most likely be communicated by the client, falling within the attorney-client privilege. Information from outside sources is viewed as a peculiar characteristic of the litigation situation.

(2) *Hickman v. Taylor* on its facts dealt only with work produced by an attorney, leaving open a troublesome question as to the status of the product of claim adjusters, investigators, and the like. The rule, however, is specific, speaking of documents prepared "by or for another party or by or for that other party's representative (including the other party's attorney, consultant, surety, indemnitor, insurer, or agent)."

(3) The opposing party can obtain work product only if "the party shows that it has substantial need for the materials to prepare its case and cannot, without undue hardship, obtain their substantial equivalent by other means."

(4) The judge in ordering discovery of covered materials is directed to "protect against disclosure of the mental impressions, conclusions, opinions, or legal theories of a party's attorney or other representative concerning the litigation." Literally read, the rule appears to protect mental impressions and the like of the lawyer only against disclosure that would be incidental to disclosure of documents and tangible things, in this regard being absolute in terms. If, however, counsel had not reduced a witness's statement to writing and counsel's deposition were taken in an effort to discover what the witness had said, Rule 26(b)(3) literally would not apply. Under these circumstances, however, it seems inconceivable that courts would not fall back upon *Hickman v. Taylor* and require an extraordinarily strong showing of need, as has indeed been the case.

(5) A person, whether a party or a witness, is entitled to a copy of his or her own statement merely by requesting it; no showing of need is required.

The rule, it should be observed, does not immunize facts, or the identities of persons having knowledge of facts, or the existence of documents as contrasted with the documents themselves. Nor does the rule spell out the breadth of application or the duration of the qualified privilege that it recognizes. Case law is meager on such significant questions as whether the privilege applies at trial or whether it can be invoked in other proceedings.

Amendments to Rule 26 since 1993 affect claims of privilege and work product protection, especially with regard to documents and the preparation of experts to testify. Rule 26(a)(1)(A)(ii) now requires at least a description of all documents, electronically stored information and tangible things in the possession or control of a party that the disclosing party may use to support its claims or defenses, unless solely for impeachment. Although the Advisory Committee's Note to the 1993 amendment stresses that the disclosing party does not, by describing documents, waive its right to object to production on the basis of privilege or work product protection, Rule 26(b)(5)(A) now requires that any claim of privilege or protection must be made expressly and describe the nature of the documents, communications, or things not produced or disclosed in a manner that, without revealing information itself privileged or protected, will enable other parties to assess the applicability of the privilege claim.

Rule 26(a)(2) now requires experts whose testimony may be used at trial to submit a report disclosing the expert's opinions and other related information, including all data or other information considered by the witness in forming opinions. The Advisory Committee's Note emphasizes that the amendment means that litigants should not be able to argue that "materials" furnished to their experts used in forming their opinions are protected from disclosure. Courts considering the issue under the amended rule have differed as to whether "materials" includes mental-impressions communications between the attorney and the expert.

§ 97 Discovery in Criminal Cases: Statements by Witnesses

The development of discovery in criminal cases has, for a variety of reasons, lagged far behind that available in the civil area. The pros and cons of the continuing debate on the subject are outside the scope of the present treatment, though it is pertinent to observe that the trend seems clearly in the direction of more liberal discovery in the criminal area. This expansion of criminal discovery, like its earlier civil analog, has raised the question whether "work product" should be afforded protection, and even the more advanced rules and proposals on the subject do undertake to provide such protection.

A distinguishable question which has drawn considerable attention is whether disclosure should be granted of material at, as opposed to before, trial. At a fairly early date, both federal and state decisions had espoused the view that when the statements of prosecution witnesses contradicting their trial testimony are shown to be in the hands of the government the defendant is entitled to demand their production at the trial. But despite this background, the famous *Jencks*[46] case was widely viewed as a startling incursion into new territory. The Supreme Court held in that case that the trial court had erroneously denied defense requests to inspect reports of two undercover agents who were government witnesses. It was not required, said the Court, that defendant show that the reports were inconsistent with the witnesses' testimony; if they related to the same subject, defendant was entitled to make the decision whether they were useful to the defense. The dissent condemned the holding as affording the criminal "a Roman holiday for rummaging through confidential information [in government files] as well as vital national secrets."[47] This view was echoed in widespread protests by the press, by the Department of Justice, and in the halls of Congress where the so-called Jencks Act of 1959[48] was hastily enacted. Despite this background, the Act was for the most part a codification of the decision that had been so vehemently attacked.

---

[46]   Jencks v. United States, 353 U.S. 657 (1957).

[47]   *Id.* at 681–682.

[48]   18 U.S.C.A. § 3500.

Federal Rule of Criminal Procedure 26.2 was adopted in 1980 and covers much of the same ground as the Jencks Act, but with some significant differences. A highly significant change effected by Rule 26.2 was the expansion of coverage to include statements by defense witnesses and prospective witnesses as well as those for the government. This change was stimulated by the Supreme Court's decision in *United States v. Nobles.*[49] As under the Act, the penalty for refusal is striking of the testimony, with the further provision that if the refusing party is the government a mistrial may be declared if justice requires. A defendant cannot, of course, be allowed to abort a trial by refusing to deliver a statement.

The difference between the Act and Rule 26.2 with regard to a definition of a "statement" may also be significant. Subsection (a) of the Act as amended provides that no statement by a government witness or prospective witness should be the subject of subpoena, discovery, or inspection until the witness has testified on direct examination in the trial. Subsection (b) provides that after a witness called by the government has testified on direct the court should, on motion of defendant, order the government to produce any statement (as later defined) relating to the subject matter of his testimony. Under subsection (c) the court will examine the statement and excise portions not related to the testimony. If, under subsection (d), the government elects not to comply with the order to produce, the testimony is to be stricken or, if justice requires, a mistrial is to be declared. In subsection (e), "statement" as used in subsections (b), (c), and (d) is defined; the definition is very precise and narrow, designed to include only statements that beyond any reasonable question represent with a very high precision the words used by the witness. It will be observed that subsection (a) was designed to bar disclosure of any statement of a witness, regardless of how precise or imprecise a rendition it might be, unless and until the witness had testified for the government. After that testimony had been given, then disclosure was allowed and required but only as to highly precise statements, as defined in (e). If a writing were not a statement at all, in the broad sense of (a), the Act does not affect it. As determined by the Supreme Court in *Palermo v. United States,*[50] writings that were statements in the broad sense of (a), but not within the strict definition of (e), or within (e) but whose maker did not testify, remain locked away, except as they might be obtainable under *Brady v. Maryland,*[51] or possibly under Evidence Rule 612 as discussed below.

Rule 26.2 does not contain the prohibition of subsection (a) of the Act against compelling disclosure of a statement, in the broad sense, unless and until the witness has testified on direct. Thus Rule 26.2 deals only with compelling production of statements within the strict definition of subsection (e) of the Act, which is essentially repeated as subdivision (f) of the Rule. As a companion to Rule 26.2, there was at the same time added to Rule 17 of the Criminal Rules, which deals with subpoenas, a new subdivision (h) Rule 17(h) now reads: "No party may subpoena a statement of a witness or of a prospective witness under this rule. Rule 26.2 governs the production of the statement."

It is unclear whether Rule 17(h) means a statement only as defined in Rule 26.2(f) or a statement within the broader definition of subsection (a) of the Jencks Act.

---

[49]   422 U.S. 225 (1975).

[50]   360 U.S. 343, 351 (1959).

[51]   373 U.S. 83 (1963).

In an earlier section[52] attention was directed to the need to examine the relationship between Criminal Rule 26.2 and Evidence Rule 612. That section pointed out that when a witness while testifying refers to a writing to refresh his or her memory, an opposing party is entitled to inspect it, to cross-examine upon it, and to introduce in evidence portions related to the testimony of the witness; if the reference for refreshing was prior to testifying, access to and use of the writing is subject to the court's discretion. If the writing consulted for refreshment is the statement of a witness or prospective witness, the potential for conflict between Criminal Rule 26.2 and Evidence Rule 612 exists. If the writing is a statement within the strict definition of Rule 26.2(f), the conflict is in reality no more than an overlap, as under either rule disclosure is required once the witness has testified on direct. But when the statement is a statement in the broad sense, as under subsection (a) of the Act, but not within the strict definition of subsection (e) of the Act, the construction in *Palermo* as previously observed, was that no disclosure was available. The confusion is compounded by the fact that Rule 612 opens with the phrase, "Except as otherwise provided in criminal proceedings by section 3500 of title 18, United States Code . . ." and has not been amended. What is the effect of the exception? Does subsection (a) of the Act continue with its former effect? Did *Palermo* survive, pro tanto, the subsequent enactment of Rule 612? A fully satisfactory resolution probably lies only in the legislative sphere. But if one accepts the argument that Rule 26.2 fully supersedes the Jencks Act, the problem goes away. If a statement comes within Rule 26.2 it must be produced after the witness testifies. If it is not within Rule 26.2, it may be produced in the discretion of the court under Rule 612. However, if subsection (a) of the Jencks Act is still alive and the *Palermo* case is still good law, there is no power in the court to order production of a statement that comes within the Jencks Act and does not come within Rule 26.2.

---

[52]   See supra § 9.

Chapter 11

THE PRIVILEGE FOR CONFIDENTIAL INFORMATION SECURED IN THE COURSE OF THE PHYSICIAN-PATIENT RELATIONSHIP

Table of Sections

---

§ 98 The Statement of the Rule and Its Purpose

The common law knew no privilege for confidential information imparted to a physician. When a physician raised the question before Lord Mansfield whether he was required to disclose professional confidences, the great Chief Justice drew the line clear. "If a surgeon was voluntarily to reveal these secrets, to be sure, he would be guilty of a breach of honor and of great indiscretion; but to give that information in a court of justice, which by the law of the land he is bound to do, will never be imputed to him as any indiscretion whatever."[1]

The pioneer departure from the common law rule was the New York statute of 1828 which in its original form was as follows: "No person authorized to practice physic or surgery shall be allowed to disclose any information which he may have acquired in attending any patient, in a professional character, and which information was necessary to enable him to prescribe for such patient as a physician, or to do any act for him as a surgeon."

Another early act which has been widely copied is the provision of the California Code of Civil Procedure of 1872, § 1881, ¶ 4, "A licensed physician or surgeon cannot, without the consent of his patient, be examined in a civil action as to any information acquired in attending the patient which was necessary to enable him to prescribe or act for the patient."

The rationale traditionally asserted to justify suppression in litigation of material facts learned by a physician is the encouragement thereby given to the patient freely to

---

[1]   The Duchess of Kingston's Trial, 20 How. St. Trials 573 (1776).

245

disclose all matter that may aid in the diagnosis and treatment of disease and injury. To obtain this end, so the argument runs, it is necessary to secure the patient from disclosure in court of potentially embarrassing private details concerning health and bodily condition. The validity of this utilitarian justification of the privilege has been questioned by many on the ground that the average patient, in consulting a physician, will have his or her thoughts centered upon his illness or injury and the prospects for betterment or cure, and will spare little thought for the remote possibility of some eventual disclosure of his condition in court. Other, more recent analyses, recognize the weakness of the utilitarian justification for the privilege but find the privilege supportable on the basis of humanitarian concerns that support creation of a private enclave that enables the patient to make informed, independent choices among medical options.

Whatever the rationale for the privilege, the number of states adhering to the common law and refusing any general physician-patient privilege has slowly but steadily dwindled. Only six states and the federal courts now fail to recognize a general physician patient privilege.

Over the same period, there has been a strong trend toward the recognition of a related privilege protecting communications between psychotherapists of various descriptions and their patients. Although psychiatrists, being medically trained, have always come within the ambit of the older physician-patient privilege where that privilege is recognized, it has been argued that accepted practice in the treatment of mental illness involves considerations not encountered in other medical contexts. The following statement is frequently quoted in this regard.

> Among physicians, the psychiatrist has a special need to maintain confidentiality. His capacity to help his patients is completely dependent upon their willingness and ability to talk freely. This makes it difficult if not impossible for him to function without being able to assure his patients of confidentiality and, indeed, privileged communication . . . . A threat to secrecy blocks successful treatment.[2]

The uniqueness of this relationship led to the inclusion in the proposed Federal Rules of Evidence of a psychotherapist-patient privilege even though no general physician-patient privilege was proposed. The Uniform Rules of Evidence have retained this privilege, but make the rule optionally one extending to confidential communication to a physician as well as to a psychotherapist or mental health provider. In the same vein, all of the states that continue to reject a general physician-patient privilege have enacted privileges applicable to the more limited psychotherapeutic context. Most expand the privilege to cover communications to social workers.

The action of the states was bolstered by the recognition of a psychotherapist-patient privilege by the United States Supreme Court in *Jaffee v. Redmond*.[3] Relying on a utilitarian rationale, the Court emphasized that "the mere possibility of disclosure may impede development of the confidential relationship necessary for successful treatment."[4] The Court also noted the appropriateness of the recognition of the privilege in the federal courts in light of the universal recognition of such a privilege in the states.

---

[2]   Report No. 45, Group for the Advancement of Psychiatry 92 (1960).

[3]   518 U.S. 1 (1996).

[4]   *Id.* at 10.

The holding extended the privilege not only to psychiatrists and psychologists but, over the dissent of two justices, to licensed social workers as well. The Court also held that the privilege it recognized was absolute, rejecting the balancing test applied by the Court of Appeals in the *Jaffee* case and by some states.

The Court, confined to the facts before it, could not detail all of the contours of the privilege it announced. It explicitly left open the application of the privilege if a serious threat of harm to the patient or to others can be averted only by means of a disclosure by the therapist. The lower federal courts have just begun to flesh out the dimensions of the privilege. The remaining sections of this chapter will discuss the general physician-patient privilege, but note specifically cases dealing specially with the psychotherapist-patient privilege.

One theory absent from the Court's analysis in *Jaffee* was any suggestion that the recognition of the privilege was constitutionally required. However, there have been arguments made that certain aspects of the physician-patient relationship involve some sort of a federal constitutional guarantee of a right of privacy. In *Whalen v. Roe*,[5] the constitutionality of a New York statute creating a state data bank of the names and addresses of persons obtaining certain drugs by medical prescription was challenged, inter alia, on the ground that patients would be deterred from obtaining appropriate medication by the apprehension that disclosure of their names would stigmatize them as drug addicts. Though garbed in constitutional vestments as an impairment of the right to make personal decisions, this argument bears a striking resemblance to the traditional rationale of privilege. While upholding the statute in *Whalen*, the Supreme Court did so on the basis of reasoning which seemed to suggest the existence of some constitutional right on the part of patients to preserve confidentiality with respect to medical treatment.

Subsequent decisions of lower federal and state courts evidence considerable disagreement concerning the nature and scope, and even the existence, of the constitutionally based right intimated to exist in *Whalen*. A majority of the cases considering the point have involved information conveyed during psychotherapeutic treatment, a context in which the traditional utilitarian justification has been urged to possess particular validity. Nevertheless, even cases of the latter sort have generally been resolved on the particular facts against the claimant of privilege, and it would appear clear that any constitutional right to privacy in medical information is a highly qualified one. In any event, the courts have consistently failed to refer to any protection afforded as a "privilege."

The matter of the protection of patient privacy and its relationship to a physician-patient privilege has been further muddled by the adoption of the Health Insurance Portability and Accountability Act of 1996 (HIPAA) and its implementing regulations. The HIPAA regulatory scheme recognizes a patient's privacy interests but contemplates the disclosure of protected health information in the course of a judicial or administrative proceeding or for law enforcement purposes. Although the issue has been raised, courts asked to consider the question have not been hesitant to find that HIPAA does not codify a general federal physician-patient privilege; nor have they found a limitation on the disclosure of the information in court or grand jury proceedings as provided in the act and regulations.

---

[5]   429 U.S. 589 (1977).

§ 99 Relation of Physician and Patient

The first requisite for the privilege is that the patient must have consulted the physician for treatment or for diagnosis looking toward treatment. If consulted for treatment it is immaterial by whom the doctor is employed. Usually, however, when the doctor is employed by one other than the patient, treatment will not be the purpose and the privilege will not attach. Thus, when a driver at the request of a public officer is subjected to a blood test for intoxication, or when a doctor is appointed by the court or the prosecutor to make a physical or mental examination, or is employed for this purpose by the opposing party, or is selected by a life insurance company to make an examination of an applicant for a policy or even when the doctor is employed by plaintiff's own lawyers in a personal injury case to examine plaintiff solely to aid in preparation for trial, the information secured is not within the present privilege. But when the patient's doctor calls in a consultant physician to aid in diagnosis or treatment, the disclosures are privileged. Moreover, cases decided under the federal psychotherapist privilege have held that therapy session mandated by a patient's employer will be privileged.

If the patient's purpose in the consultation is an unlawful one, as to obtain narcotics in violation of law, or as, by some authority, a fugitive from justice to have his appearance disguised by plastic surgery, the law withholds the shield of privilege.

It has been held that where a doctor has attended a childbirth, the child is a patient and can claim privilege against the doctor's disclosure of facts as to the apparent maturity of the child at birth.

After the death of the patient the relation is ended and the object of the privilege can no longer be furthered. Accordingly, it seems the better view that facts discovered in an autopsy examination are not privileged.

§ 100 Subject Matter of the Privilege: Information Acquired in Attending the Patient and Necessary for Prescribing

Statutes conferring a physician-patient privilege vary extensively, though probably a majority follow the pioneer New York and California statutes in extending the privilege to "any information acquired in attending the patient."[6] Understandably, these provisions have been held to protect not only information explicitly conveyed to the physician by the patient, but also data acquired by examination and testing. Other statutes appear facially to be more restrictive and to limit the privilege to communications by the patient. This appearance, however, may frequently be misleading, for statutes of this sort have been construed to provide a privilege fully as broad as that available elsewhere. The confusion is further compounded by a line of authority that holds that facts observable by anyone without professional knowledge or training are not within the privilege.

While the information secured by the physician may be privileged, the fact that the physician has been consulted by the patient and has treated him or her, and the number and dates of visits, are not within the shelter of the privilege.

The extent to which the privilege attaches to the information embodied in hospital records is discussed in the chapter on Regularly Kept Records.[7]

---

[6]   See supra § 98.

[7]   See infra § 293.

§ 101   The Confidential Character of the Disclosure: Presence of Third Persons and Members of Family; Information Revealed to Nurses and Attendants; Public Records

We have seen that the statutes existing in many states codifying the privileges for marital communications and those between attorney and client usually omitted the requirement that to be privileged such communications must have been made in confidence. Nevertheless, the courts have read this limitation into these statutes, assuming that the legislatures must have intended this common law requirement to continue.[8] The statutes giving the patient's privilege for information gained in professional consultations again omit the adjective "confidential."[9] Should it nonetheless be read in, not as a continuation of a common law requirement, but as an interpretative gloss, spelled out from policy and analogy? Certainly the policy arguments are strong. First is the policy of holding all privileges within reasonable bounds since they cut off access to sources of truth. Second, the argument that the purpose of encouraging those who would otherwise be reluctant, to disclose necessary facts to their doctors, will be adequately served by extending a privilege for only such disclosures as the patient wishes to keep secret.

This principle of confidentiality is supported by those decisions that hold that if a casual third person is present with the acquiescence of the patient at the consultation, the disclosures made in his presence are not privileged, and thus the stranger, the patient and the doctor may be required to divulge them in court. Whether this principle is to be applied when the stranger is a police officer who has escorted the patient to the hospital or doctor's office should, it would seem, turn on whether meaningful acquiescence on the patient's part is to be found on the facts.

If, however, the third person is present as a needed and customary participant in the consultation, the circle of confidence may be reasonably extended to include him and the privilege will be maintained. Thus the presence of one sustaining a close family relationship to the patient should not curtail the privilege. And the nurse present as the doctor's assistant during the consultation or examination, or the technician who makes tests or X-ray photographs under the doctor's direction, will be looked on as the doctor's agent in whose keeping the information will remain privileged. But the application of strict agency principles in this context would seem inconsistent with the realities of modern medical practice, and the preferable view is that of the courts that have based their decisions upon whether the communication was functionally related to diagnosis and treatment.

Many courts on the other hand do not analyze the problems in terms of whether the communications or disclosures were confidential and professional, but rather in terms of what persons are intended to be silenced as witnesses. This seems to be sticking in the bark of the statute, rather than looking at its purpose. Thus these courts, if casual third persons were present at the consultation, will still close the mouth of the doctor but allow the visitor to speak. And if nurses or other attendants or technicians gain information necessary to treatment they will be allowed by these courts to speak (unless the privilege statute specifically names them) but the physician may not.

---

[8]   See supra §§ 80, 91.
[9]   See supra § 98.

When the attending physician is required by law to make a certificate of death to the public authority, giving his opinion as to the cause, the certificate should be provable as a public record, despite the privilege. The duty to make a public report overrides the general duty of secrecy, and in view of the availability of the record to the public, the protection of the information from general knowledge, as contemplated by the privilege, cannot be attained. Accordingly, under the prevailing view, the privilege does not attach.

Today, state and local laws increasingly impose upon physicians requirements to report various types of patient information related to the public health and safety, e.g., the treatment of gunshot wounds, venereal disease, HIV and AIDS, mental illness, and the occurrence of fetal death. Generally, state schemes for the collection and preservation of such data and its use by appropriate authorities have been upheld as against challenges based either upon a constitutional right of privacy or the professional privilege. In some instances, e.g., the reporting of gunshot wounds, the privilege has been held to be qualified to the extent of the reporting requirement, with the result that the physician may testify to any fact included within the report. Conversely, where the physician's report is not required the physician would remain precluded from testifying to the facts in the report, though there is some authority that the privilege, being testimonial, does not bar use of the report to generate other admissible evidence. Many of the reporting systems, however, obviously do not envision general disclosure of the data collected, and maintenance of some degree of confidentiality may in fact be indispensable to constitutionality.

§ 102   Rule of Privilege, Not Incompetency: Privilege Belongs to the Patient, Not to an Objecting Party as Such; Effect of the Patient's Death

As has been pointed out in the discussion of privileges generally,[10] the rule which excludes disclosures to physicians is not a rule of incompetency of evidence serving the end of protecting the adverse party against unreliable or prejudicial testimony. It is a rule of privilege protecting the extrinsic interest of the patient and designed to promote health, not truth. It encourages free disclosure in the sickroom by preventing disclosure in the courtroom. The patient is the person to be encouraged and he is the holder of the privilege.

Consequently, the patient alone during his or her lifetime has the right to claim or to waive the privilege. If the patient is in a position to claim it and does not, it is waived and no one else may assert it. If the patient is not present, is unaware of the situation, or for some other reason is unable to claim the privilege, it is generally held that the privilege may be asserted on his or her behalf by a guardian, personal representative, or the health care provider, the latter being frequently held to have an enforceable duty to invoke the privilege in the absence of waiver by the patient. This necessary rule has unfortunately demonstrated considerable potential for allowing health care providers to advance personal interests under the guise of vindicating the privilege. It is to be hoped that it will not ultimately prove beyond judicial ingenuity in cases of this sort to allow the patient the ultimate decision as to whether the privilege will be invoked.

The adverse party as such has no interest to protect if he or she is not the patient, and thus cannot object as of right.

---

[10]   See supra § 72.

In order to facilitate full disclosure as well as to protect the privacy of the decedent, most courts hold that the privilege continues after death. However, in contests of the survivors in interest with third parties, e.g., actions to recover property claimed to belong to the deceased, actions for the death of the deceased, or actions upon life insurance policies, the personal representative, heir or next of kin, or the beneficiary in the policy may waive the privilege, and, by the same token, the adverse party may not effectively assert the privilege. In contests over the validity of a will, where both sides—the executor on the one hand and the heirs or next of kin on the other—claim under and not adversely to the decedent, the assumption should prevail that the decedent would desire that the validity of his or her will should be determined in the fullest light of the facts. Accordingly in this situation either the executor or the contestants may effectively waive the privilege without the concurrence of the other.

§ 103 What Constitutes a Waiver of the Privilege?

The physician-patient statutes, though commonly phrased in terms of incompetency, are nevertheless held to create merely a privilege for the benefit of the patient, which he or she may waive.

Generally it is agreed that a contractual stipulation waiving the privilege, such as is frequently included in applications for life or health insurance, or in the policies themselves, is valid and effectual.

Another context in which the privilege is waived anticipatorily is that in which a testator procures an attending doctor to subscribe his or her will as an attesting witness. This action constitutes a waiver as to all facts affecting the validity of the will.

The physician-patient privilege, like most other privileges, may also be waived in advance of trial by a disclosure of the privileged information either made or acquiesced in by the privilege holder. Obviously, the law has no reason to conceal in court what has been freely divulged on the public street, and the only question in such cases becomes the voluntariness of the revelation and the scope of the waiver.

Waiver in connection with litigation is an area in which substantial changes have occurred in recent years. A shrinking from the embarrassment which comes from exposure of bodily disease or abnormality is human and natural. It is arguable that legal protection from exposure is justified to encourage frankness in consulting physicians. But it is not human, natural, or understandable to claim protection from exposure by asserting a privilege for communications to doctors at the very same time when the patient is parading before the public the mental or physical condition as to which the patient consulted the doctor by bringing an action for damages arising from that same condition. This, in the oft-repeated phrase, is to make the privilege not a shield only, but a sword.

The conclusion mandated by these considerations clearly is that a patient voluntarily placing his or her physical or mental condition in issue in a judicial proceeding waives the privilege with respect to information relative to that condition. Failure to find a waiver from assertion of a claim or defense predicated upon a physical or mental condition has the awkward consequence of effectively frustrating discovery on a central issue of the case unless one of a variety of temporizing expedients is pressed into service to accommodate the outmoded rule.

Today the once prevalent rule that no waiver results from raising a claim or defense has been widely reversed by statute. Thus, at present, the crucial questions concern the types of issues which sufficiently implicate a party's physical or mental condition, and what actions by a party serve to raise these issues within the meaning of the modern statutes. A claim for damages for personal injuries is of course the paradigm example, and will clearly waive the privilege in all jurisdictions where such waiver by filing is possible at all. Claims for damages for mental suffering have been treated similarly, but here some discernment is called for unless the privilege be seen to evaporate upon the filing of any claim whatsoever. In addition, cases applying the psychotherapist-patient privilege established in *Jaffee v. Redmond*[11] have not agreed as to whether and when a plaintiff who asserts a claim involving distress waives that privilege. With respect to defenses, a distinction is clearly to be seen between the allegation of a physical or mental condition, which will effect the waiver, and the mere denial of such a condition asserted by the adversary, which will not.

A much litigated point since the conversion to more liberal rules of waiver has been whether a waiver effected by filing a claim or defense will permit the waiving party's adversary in litigation to contact physicians on an ex parte basis. Those decisions approving such contacts stress the economies of informal discovery and the anomaly of treating any witness as "belonging" to a party, considerations which suffice to make permissibility of ex parte contact the better rule. A contrary position, however, has been taken by a greater number of courts, and possesses a substantial rationale in the consideration that the waiver following upon the filing of a claim or defense extends only to information relevant to the condition relied upon.

In the criminal area, waiver under the modern statutes has been seen to flow from assertion of the defenses of insanity and diminished responsibility.

Because of the principles discussed above, there will today be fewer occasions in which a cause will come on for trial with the patient's privilege still intact. Since the possibility still exists, however, it should be briefly considered how the privilege may be waived in trial.

How far does the patient's testifying waive the privilege? Doubtless, if the patient on direct examination testifies to, or adduces other evidence of, the communications exchanged or the information furnished to the doctor consulted this would waive in respect to such consultations. When, however, the patient in his or her direct testimony does not reveal any privileged matter respecting the consultation, but testifies only to physical or mental condition, existing at the time of such consultation, then one view is that, "where the patient tenders to the jury the issue as to his physical condition, it must in fairness and justice be held that he has himself waived the obligation of secrecy."[12] This view has the merit of curtailing the scope of a privilege that some view as obstructive, but there are a number of courts that hold that the patient's testimony as to his or her condition without disclosure of privileged matter is not a waiver. If the patient reveals privileged matter on cross-examination, without claiming the privilege, this is usually held not to be a waiver of the privilege enabling the adversary to make further inquiry of the doctors, on the ground that such revelations were not "voluntary."

---

[11]   518 U.S. 1 (1996). See discussion in supra § 98.
[12]   Andrews, J. in Hethier v. Johns, 135 N.E. 603 (N.Y. 1922).

If the patient examines a physician as to matters disclosed in a consultation, or course of treatment, of course this is a waiver and opens the door to the opponent to examine the patient about any other matters then disclosed. And if several doctors participated jointly in the same consultation or course of treatment the calling of one to disclose part of the shared information waives objection to the adversary's calling any other of the joint consultants to testify about the consultation, treatment or the results thereof. Some courts go further and hold that calling by the patient of one doctor and eliciting privileged matter from that doctor opens the door to the opponent's calling other doctors consulted by the patient at other times to bring out any facts relevant to the issue on which the privileged proof was adduced. Arguably, it is not consonant with justice and fairness to permit the patient to reveal his or her secrets to several doctors and then when the condition comes in issue to limit the witnesses to the consultants favorable to the claims. But a substantial number of courts balk at this step.

Though the privilege continues after death of the patient, it may then be waived by the personal representative of the decedent. And where the personal representative is involved in litigation over the decedents estate with other persons claiming through the decedent, or where heirs-at-law are in opposition to one another, any one of the parties may waive the privilege.

§ 104 Kinds of Proceedings Exempted from the Application of the Privilege

The wide variation among state statutes creating and defining the physician-patient privilege renders it difficult to generalize usefully concerning the types of proceedings exempted from the operation of the privilege. Even where the Uniform Rule has been adopted, one or more qualifications have commonly been engrafted upon it. And though the now widely-adopted patient-litigant exception has undoubtedly reduced somewhat the differential application of the privilege, there remain many instances in which the holder of the privilege will not come within that exception. In short, it is indispensable to consult local statutes on the present point.

Probably the most common pattern to be observed in the statutes is that of a broadly defined privilege, applicable to both civil and criminal proceedings, to which a variety of specific exceptions are then attached. But there are states that deny the privilege in criminal cases generally, or in felony cases, or in cases of homicide.

With respect to other exceptions, the privilege has long been viewed as unworkable in worker compensation cases, and in medical malpractice cases and will generally be unavailable in these contexts. In more recent years, proceedings involving child abuse have claimed the attention of the legislatures, and these proceedings are now the most commonly singled out as involving policy considerations more weighty than those underlying the privilege. Other types of proceedings found withdrawn from the operation of the privilege are commitment proceedings, prosecutions for some types of drug offenses, and will contests. The privilege is also sometimes withdrawn in child custody proceedings.

§ 105 The Policy and Future of the Privilege

Some statements of Buller, J., in 1792 in a case involving the application of the attorney-client privilege seem to have furnished the inspiration for the pioneer New York statute of 1828 on the doctor-patient privilege. He said:

The privilege is confined to the cases of counsel, solicitor, and attorney. . . . It is indeed hard in many cases to compel a friend to disclose a confidential conversation; and I should be glad if by law such evidence could be excluded. It is a subject of just indignation where persons are anxious to reveal what has been communicated to them in a confidential manner. . . . There are cases to which it is much to be lamented that the law of privilege is not extended; those in which medical persons are obliged to disclose the information which they acquire by attending in their professional characters.[13]

These comments reveal attitudes that have been influential ever since in the spread of statutes enacting the doctor-patient privilege. One attitude is the shrinking from forcing anyone to tell in court what he or she has learned in confidence. It is well understood today, however, that no such sweeping curtain for disclosure of confidences in the courtroom could be justified. Another is the complete failure to consider the other side of the shield, namely, the loss which comes from depriving the courts of any reliable source of facts necessary for the right decision of cases.

Perhaps the main burden of Justice Buller's remarks, however, is the suggestion that since the client's disclosures to the lawyer are privileged, the patient's disclosures to the doctor should have the same protection. This analogy has probably been more potent than any other argument, particularly with the lawyers in the legislatures. They would be reluctant to deny to the medical profession a recognition which the courts have themselves provided for the legal profession. Manifestly, however, the soundness of the privilege may not be judged as a matter of rivalry of professions, but by the criterion of the public interest.

Some of the analytical weaknesses of the utilitarian rationale of the privilege, except perhaps in the psychotherapeutic context, have been noted earlier.[14] To these must be added the perplexities and confusions arising from judicial and legislative attempts to render tolerable a rule which essentially runs against the grain of truth. The uncertainties of application of a privilege so extensively and variously qualified and restricted certainly undermine any effort to justify it on utilitarian grounds. One familiar with the vagaries of its operation may not be disposed to repose confidence in its protection. Those not so knowledgeable will often find it a snare and a delusion.

A more tenable argument, however, has been increasingly advanced in recent years. This view holds that the privilege should not be viewed as operating to inspire the making of medical confidences but rather as protecting such confidences once made. The legitimate interest in the privacy of the physician-patient relationship should not be subject to casual breach by every litigant in single-minded pursuit of the last scrap of evidence which may marginally contribute to victory in litigation. Arguably the privilege does, at least on occasion, operate to prevent such unwarranted intrusions. The issue is whether the value of such protection is sufficiently great to justify both the suppression of critical evidence in other cases and the costs of administering a highly complex rule.

Regardless of how such a debate might be resolved in one's own mind, complete abolition of the privilege is unlikely given current political realities. One alternative resolution is legislation such as that which exists in North Carolina, which qualifies its statutory privilege with the provision that "the court, either at trial or prior thereto . . .

---

[13]   Wilson v. Rastall, 4 Term. Rep. 753, 759, 100 Eng. Rep. 1287 (K.B. 1792).

[14]   See supra § 98.

may, subject to G.S. 8–53.6, compel such disclosure when, in his opinion disclosure is necessary to a proper administration of justice." Such a balancing was expressly rejected by the Court in *Jaffee v. Redmond*,[15] in connection with the psychotherapist-patient privilege. However, the adoption of such a limitation by statute is certainly possible and may be effective in protecting privacy against trivial intrusion while permitting the use of critical evidence.

---

[15]   518 U.S. 1 (1996); see discussion supra § 98.

Chapter 12

PRIVILEGES FOR GOVERNMENTAL SECRETS

Table of Sections

---

§ 106 Other Principles Distinguished

In discussing the evidentiary privileges and rules of exclusion regarding the production and admission of writings and information in the possession of government officers, other principles should be noted, which may hinder the litigant seeking facts from the government, but which are beyond our present inquiry. Among these are: (a) questions of substantive privilege of government officers from liability for their acts and words, (b) questions as to executive immunity from liability, (c) issues regarding the irremovability of official records, (d) prohibition against suits based on certain types of information, and (e) denial of information on basis of separation of powers.

§ 107 The Common Law Privileges for Military or Diplomatic Secrets and Other Facts the Disclosure of Which Would Be Contrary to the Public Interest

As the activities of modern government have expanded, the need of litigants for the disclosure and proof of documents and other information in the possession of government officials has correspondingly increased. When this need is asserted and opposed, the public interest in the secrecy of "classified" information comes into direct conflict with the public interest in the protection of the claim of the individual to due process of law in the redress of grievances. The proper resolution of this conflict requires careful judicial scrutiny.

A privilege and a rule of exclusion has been recognized for writings and information constituting military or diplomatic secrets of state. The justification for secrecy is obviously extremely strong when the material is vital to national security. In addition to military matters, the privilege has been extended to intelligence-gathering methods or capabilities and sensitive information concerning diplomatic relations with foreign governments. The courts have declined, however, to extend the privilege to matters that are not related to the national defense or international relations.

The Supreme Court has ruled that the government as holder of the privilege must assert it. The government may assert the privilege in actions to which it is not a party. Generally, private parties cannot claim the privilege. When a claim of state secrets privilege would be appropriate but is not made due to oversight or lack of knowledge, the court should assure that notice is given to the appropriate government officer.

The Court has also held that the privilege cannot be waived by a private party. However, when the government is prosecuting a criminal case, it may be forced to forego the privilege for documents essential to the litigation. The fact that similar information has been disclosed earlier does not constitute waiver or prevent the government from claiming the privilege in a later case. However, if the prior disclosure of confidential information revealed the same specific information, then the privilege is waived.

Congress has enacted statutes that interact with and mirror the state secrets privilege: the national security exemption in the Freedom of Information Act (FOIA),[1] the Classified Information Procedures Act (CIPA),[2] and the Foreign Intelligence Surveillance Act (FISA),[3] which applies when state secrets involve electronic surveillance for intelligence purposes.

Although the national security exemption of FOIA is similar to the state secrets privilege, it neither expands nor contracts existing privileges, nor does it create any new privileges. Additionally, important differences exist between the privilege and the FOIA exemptions.

Similarly, CIPA does not create a new evidentiary rule. It recognizes a power in the executive branch to determine that public disclosure of classified information shall not be made in a criminal trial and outlines procedures to protect against the threat of disclosure or the unnecessary disclosure of classified information. CIPA procedures are intended to address situations where a criminal defendant is already in possession of classified information; they do not provide for discovery of classified information. CIPA applies to classified testimony as well as classified documents. It requires a criminal defendant to give particularized notice of an intention to reveal classified information as part of the defense. Upon receiving such notice, the government can seek a ruling that some or all of the information is immaterial, move for substitution of a non-sensitive summary for the information, or admit the facts sought to be proven and thereby eliminate the need for disclosure. Where a determination of privilege prevents the defendant from disclosing classified information, the court may dismiss charges or provide the defendant appropriate lesser relief.

Wigmore seems to regard it as doubtful whether the denial of disclosure should go further than this, but some state statutes occasionally describe the privilege in broader terms, and the English decisions seem to have accepted the wide generalization that official documents and facts will be privileged whenever their disclosure would be

---

[1]   5 U.S.C.A. § 552(b)(1). See generally United States Dep't of Justice, Justice Dep't Guide to the Freedom of Information Act, available at https://www.justice.gov/oip/doj-guide-freedom-information-act-0.

[2]   18 U.S.C.A. App. 3.

[3]   50 U.S.C.A. §§ 1801 et seq.

injurious to the public interest. Whether this wider principle is justified in point of policy is open to serious question.

§ 108   Qualified Privileges for Government Information: The Constitutional Presidential Privilege; Common Law Privileges for Agency Deliberations and Law Enforcement Files

The case of *United States v. Nixon*[4] brought into sharp focus both the limits of the long-standing executive privilege protecting diplomatic and military secrets and the distinguishable question as to whether some broader privilege protects confidential communications between the President and his immediate advisors. In *Nixon*, the Supreme Court recognized a constitutionally based privilege of this nature but held it to be qualified and subject to invasion upon a showing of demonstrable need for evidence relevant to a criminal proceeding. The presidential privilege has occasioned considerable discussion by constitutional scholars, and although of great importance when invoked, it is only occasionally encountered.

Of much greater everyday significance is the enormous quantity of information produced, collected, and compiled by the governmental agencies. Only an extremely small percentage of this governmental information will fall within the previously discussed privilege protecting military and diplomatic secrets. What then of the vast remainder?

Although not within any well-defined evidentiary privilege, securing information from this great store of information was often extremely difficult or impossible. Before amended in 1958, the Federal Housekeeping Act was assumed by administrators to authorize the issuance of regulations requiring governmental personnel in the actual possession of governmental documents and records to decline to produce them even when served with a subpoena issued by a court. These regulations were consistently upheld by the Supreme Court, and although the cases never went so far as to hold that the Act created a statutory privilege, the practical effect was that private litigants were unable to obtain the information. The 1958 amendment to the Act included a provision removing any possible implication that it was intended to create a statutory privilege, and this intent has been followed in subsequent court decisions.

Access to governmental information was even more substantially increased with the enactment by Congress[5] and many state legislatures of freedom of information legislation. While these statutes are directed toward availability of information for the public in general and the news media in particular, they have importance in clearing the way for discovery in litigation. To proceed under the federal Freedom of Information Act, no standing or particularized need for the desired information is required, and any person is eligible to proceed under the provisions of the statute. For present purposes, however, the important question is the extent to which FOIA affects the question of evidentiary privilege for governmental information.

At the time of the enactment of the original federal FOIA in 1966, there was clearly some protection extended by the courts to sensitive government information which did not constitute a military or diplomatic secret. Thus, a qualified common law privilege protected some aspects of government agency policy deliberations, and another, less

---

[4]   418 U.S. 683 (1974).

[5]   5 U.S.C.A. § 552.

clearly defined privilege shielded agency investigative files. In enacting FOIA, Congress recognized the desirability of maintaining some degree of confidentiality in these areas and included them within the exemption provisions of the act.

FOIA itself does not address the question of evidentiary admissibility, and thus cannot be said to be a statutory enactment of the privileges in question. At the same time, it is obvious that the two are critically interrelated and that the exemption provisions mark the outermost limits of the privileges. It would be anomalous in the extreme to deny evidentiary admission on grounds of confidentiality to material available on request to even the casually interested. However, the converse is not necessarily true, and the evidentiary privileges may reasonably protect *less* than the total sum of information denied the general public under the FOIA exceptions. Such a differentiation is justifiable on the ground that the litigant's interest in access to evidence will sometimes be stronger than the ordinary citizen's interest in obtaining information. Accordingly, not all information exempt from disclosure under the FOIA exceptions will necessarily be protected by privilege if sought by discovery processes for purposes of litigation. As the foregoing synopsis suggests, the numerous decisions construing FOIA's exception provisions will be of varying precedential value concerning the scope of the privileges discussed below.

(A)   The Deliberative Process Privilege

This privilege protects communications made between governmental personnel, or between governmental personnel and outside consultants, which consist of advisory opinions and recommendations preliminary to the formulation of agency policy. Like other communications privileges, that protecting governmental agency deliberations seeks to encourage a free flow of communication in the interest of some larger end—here, establishing agency policy only after consideration of the full array of contrasting views on the subject. As with other privileges, the assumption is that total candor will be enhanced, and the quality of governmental decision-making correspondingly improved, by an assurance of at least qualified confidentiality. Also, this privilege is justified by its avoidance of premature and potentially misleading public disclosure of possible agency action and by helping to assure that governmental decision-makers will be judged solely upon the quality of their decisions without regard to the quality of other options considered and discarded.

To come within the rationale of the privilege, the matter sought to be kept confidential must have been communicated prior to finalization of the policy and must have constituted opinion or evaluation as opposed to the mere reporting of objective facts. However, factual information that reflects or reveals the deliberative processes of the agency is protected by the privilege. Whether the communication reflected the view that ultimately became embodied in agency policy, or even whether the communication was considered or totally ignored by the decision-maker is immaterial. Also, the government is not required to identify a particular decision to which the communication contributed as long as the deliberative process involved and the role played by the communication are identified. The privilege, which must be claimed by the agency head, or in most circuits some carefully delegated subordinate, is that of the government, and apparently may be claimed indefinitely. It is not terminated by the adoption of the policy at issue in the communication and likely not by the death of the author of the privileged matter. As further discussed below, the privilege is not absolute and is therefore subject to invasion upon a sufficient showing of necessity. The privilege also does not protect communications which demonstrate government misconduct, which are themselves the subject of the litigation, or which become the formally adopted policy.

The question of privilege for government agency deliberations has arisen with growing frequency in the context of state government. Many of the states enacting FOIA statutes have included exemption provisions protecting policy development materials from mandatory disclosure. Where the question of a true evidentiary privilege has arisen, i.e., where the material is sought for introduction into evidence rather than simply as information, a majority of the cases have upheld the existence of a qualified privilege on the federal model.

(B)   The Privilege for Information and Files Relating to Law Enforcement

Prior to the enactment of the federal FOIA and its state counterparts, a privilege protecting the investigative results of government agencies appears to have been sporadically recognized but ill-defined, frequently being treated as an aspect of a more comprehensive but amorphous privilege for "government information." Clearly, however, disclosure of the files of law enforcement agencies may seriously hamper enforcement efforts by discouraging or compromising confidential informants; disclosing the existence, targets, or methods of investigation; endangering witnesses or law enforcement personnel; or undermining a criminal prosecution or civil enforcement proceeding by revealing the nature of the case in preparation. Congress recognized the legitimacy of these concerns in the enactment of a highly specific exemption to FOIA, which in the most recent iteration of the statute expands its protection to "records or information compiled for law enforcement purposes."[6] Today the exemption and the privilege, at least in federal law, seem inextricably intertwined, leaving no practical reason for distinguishing between them.

To come within the ambit of the privilege, the materials must have been compiled for law enforcement purposes and the agency must demonstrate that disclosure would have one of the six specified results in FOIA Exemption 7. The privilege is qualified and, as with other privileges, may be overcome through a showing of sufficient need. Though it has been said that the privilege, unlike that for agency policy deliberations, expires with the governmental undertaking to which the privileged matter relates, this seems an overly broad generalization. However, the protection will not attach absent an initial government demonstration that production "could reasonably be expected to" bring about one or more of the harms specified by the statute.

With regard to state law in this area, some states expressly confer privilege upon law enforcement records. Others have "classical" official information statutes, which cover at least some of such records under the rubric of communications made by or to a public officer in official confidence when the public interest would suffer from disclosure. Where, however, a state FOIA is in effect, courts appear to accord it primacy in determining the maximum sweep of this privilege.

§ 109 Effect of the Presence of the Government as a Litigant

To the extent that the Freedom of Information Act is available as a means for obtaining government records and information for use in evidence, as discussed in the preceding section, no distinction is made between situations where the litigation is

---

[6]   5 U.S.C.A. § 552(b)(7).

between parties other than the government and those where the government is a party. However, when procedures other than under the Act are used, the difference may be substantial.

When the government is not a party and successfully resists disclosure sought by a party, the result is generally that the evidence is unavailable, as, for example, if a witness died, and the case will proceed accordingly, with no consequences save those resulting from the loss of the evidence. This approach to dealing with the impact of governmental privilege upon litigation between third parties causes no insuperable difficulties where the privilege is a conditional one and a balancing of interests has been made, or where an absolute privilege is involved and the privileged matter does not bear critically on the central issues of the case. The approach may be inappropriate, however, where the invocation of the absolute privilege, such as for military secrets, makes impossible any approximation of a full presentation of the issues. Whether dismissal of the case is warranted where the sovereign has rendered its courts incapable of fairly trying the issues, dismissal has been granted at the behest of the government where continued litigation by adversary means threatens partial or indirect exposure of the protected secret.

The presence of the government in court as a litigant, whether as the moving party in a civil or criminal proceeding or by virtue of consenting to be sued as a defendant, raises the possibility that an exercise of privilege may be handled by ordinary judicial enforcement measures. Accordingly, in a criminal prosecution, the court may give the government the choice of disclosing matters of significance to the defense or having the case dismissed. However, where too many relevant facts remain obscured by the state-secrets privilege to reach a reliable judgment, a government contract as a matter of last resort may be declared unenforceable leaving the parties where they were when the suit was filed.

As the plaintiff in a civil action, the government is subject to the ordinary rules of discovery, and may face dismissal of its action if through the invocation of privilege it deprives the defendant of evidence useful to the defense. There would, however, seem to be no reason why the government, as distinguished from other litigants, should necessarily face dismissal for failure to provide discovery under all circumstances. Only where the governmental claim of privilege shields evidence of such importance as to deny the defendant due process should dismissal automatically result.

Where the government is the defendant, as under the Tort Claims Act, an adverse finding cannot be rendered against it as the price of asserting an evidentiary privilege. This is not one of the terms upon which Congress has consented that the United States be subjected to liability. Accordingly, where the plaintiff's action cannot be proved without disclosure of the privileged matter, the plaintiff will remain remediless, although in light of the extreme nature of this result, some courts seek ways to avoid it.

§ 110 The Scope of the Judge's Function in Determining the Validity of the Claim of Privilege

When the head of department has made a claim of privilege for documents or information under his control as being military or diplomatic secrets is this claim conclusive upon the judge? *United States v. Reynolds*,[7] which remains the Supreme

---

[7]   345 U.S. 1 (1953).

Court's most comprehensive ruling on this privilege, has been extensively mined for the answer to this question. The generally accepted conclusions are that, while the judiciary is not to defer totally to the "caprice" of the executive, the judicial role is a limited one, focused largely upon the process of claiming the privilege rather than upon the merits of its invocation. Thus, the privilege must be asserted through a formal claim by the head of the executive department having charge of the material, and the statement of this official must indicate personal consideration of the claim, the identity (so far as possible) of the privileged material, and the reasons supporting the claim. In some instances, no more will be necessary in order to enable the court to rule in favor of the claim, but it is not unusual for the government to further support its claim with an affidavit, and perhaps other matter, to be reviewed by the court in the absence of opposing counsel.

Whatever material is considered by the court, the standard applied is whether there exists a reasonable danger that disclosure will damage national security. If this danger is found, the privilege is absolute and is not affected by the extent of the litigant's need for the confidential information. That need is considered only when determining how deeply the court will probe to satisfy itself that a privilege claim is justified. Any relevant non-confidential information should be disentangled from other classified information when possible. However, if the information forms a mosaic and disclosure of an apparently innocuous part could lead to the disclosure of classified information, disentangling is not required.

Once outside the restricted area of military and diplomatic secrets, however, a greater role for the judiciary in the determination of governmental claims of privilege becomes not only desirable, but necessary. The head of an executive department or in most circuits a carefully delegated subordinate, who claims the privilege, can appraise the public interest of secrecy as well (or perhaps better) than the judge, but predictably the official's position will tend to minimize the individual's interest. Under the normal routine, the question will come to chief administrators with recommendations from cautious subordinates against disclosure, and in the press of business, they are likely to approve the recommendations about apparently minor matters without much independent consideration. The determination of questions of fact and the applications of legal standards in passing upon the admissibility of evidence and the validity of claims of privilege are traditionally the trial judge's responsibility. As a public official, the judge should have respect for the executive's concern about disclosure, but, at the same time, judicial duties require an appraisal of private interests that must be reconciled with conflicting public policies. A judge may thus be better qualified than the executive to weigh both interests and to strike a proper balance.

The foregoing considerations largely explain why privileges running in favor of government, other than that for military and diplomatic secrets, are uniformly held to be qualified. Thus, where these privileges are claimed, the judge must determine whether the interest in governmental secrecy is outweighed in the particular case by the litigant's interest in obtaining the evidence. Striking a satisfactory balance will, on the one hand, require consideration of the interests giving rise to the privilege and an assessment of the extent to which disclosure will realistically impair those interests. On the other hand, factors which will affect the litigant's need include the significance of the evidence sought for the case, the availability of the desired information from other sources, and the nature of the right being asserted in the litigation. Here, as with other qualified privileges, in camera inspection by the court offers a practical way for testing the claim of privilege without destroying irretrievably the secrecy which the privilege is designed to preserve.

§ 111 The Privilege Against the Disclosure of the Identity of an Informer

For entirely understandable reasons, informers fear disclosure, and if their names were subject to being readily revealed, this important aid to law enforcement would be seriously compromised. On this ground of policy, a privilege is recognized for disclosure of the identity of an informer who has given information about suspected crimes to a prosecuting or investigating officer or to another person to be relayed to such an officer. The privilege runs to the government and may be invoked by its officers who, as witnesses or otherwise, are asked for the information. According to some authority, the privilege also may be asserted by the alleged informer. In some jurisdictions when neither the government nor the informer is represented at the trial, the judge may invoke it for the absent holder, as in other cases of privilege.[8] Whether the privilege is confined to disclosure of identity or extends also to the contents of the communication is in dispute. The policy of the privilege does not appear to require shielding the communication from disclosure, but shielding the contents is required if revealing those contents would likely identify the informer, which is often the case.

The privilege has two important qualifications. The first is that when the identity has already become known to "those who would have cause to resent the communication," the privilege ceases.[9] The second is that, when the privilege is asserted by the state in a criminal prosecution and the evidence of the identity of the informer becomes important to the establishment of the defense, the court will require the disclosure, and if it is still withheld, will dismiss of the prosecution.

While the inherent fairness of this second exception is apparent, its implementation is challenging if the privilege is not to be rendered meaningless by automatic defense allegations of the informer's potential value as a witness. To avoid this result, an in camera hearing is widely used, and sometimes required, to determine the nature of the informer's probable testimony. With or without an in camera hearing, the trial court's task is to assess the balance between the value of that testimony to the defense and the significance of the considerations underlying the privilege in the particular case.

A variant of the second situation occurs when a search or seizure is challenged under the Fourth Amendment and the statement of an informant is essential to probable cause. Although resting less clearly on constitutional grounds, courts frequently employ in camera hearings when they determine that in order to decide probable cause they must resolve questions concerning the informer's existence or nature of the information actually provided by the informer. In recent years, courts have recognized a privilege analogous to the informer's privilege that protects the confidentiality of police surveillance locations so that private citizens permitting the police to use their property will not be subject to retaliation, and to aspects of sensitive surveillance equipment used.

---

[8] See supra § 73.1.

[9] United States v. Roviaro, 353 U.S. 53, 60 (1957).

§ 112 Statutory Privileges for Certain Reports of Individuals to Government Agencies: Accident Reports, Tax Returns, Etc.

A somewhat similar policy to that supporting the privilege for the identity of informers applies to reports that individuals are required by law to make to government agencies for the administration of their public functions. If such statements are admissible against those reporting the information, full and true reporting may be discouraged. On the other hand, these reports often deal with facts highly material in litigation, and an early report to government may be reliable and important to ascertain the facts. The latter interest has generally prevailed with the courts, and in the absence of statutory authority, such reports are not privileged.

Policy arguments that a privilege is needed to encourage frank and full reporting have frequently prevailed with legislatures, and statutory privileges for reports of highway and industrial accidents; tax returns; selective service reports; social security, health, unemployment compensation, and census data; and bank records are common. Whether such privileges are absolute or qualified depends largely on the individual statute, but courts have construed many statutes as granting only a qualified privilege that may be overcome in appropriate circumstances. The privilege is held either by the reporter, the government, or both.

The soundness of a policy extending greater protection to these reports than is required by constitutional guarantees is dubious, and in some instances seems to imply a greater need for accuracy in governmental statistic gathering than in judicial fact-finding. But where the policy has been adopted by statute, any lack of wisdom does not justify judicial incursions against the protection afforded. While federal courts are not obliged to honor privileges created by state statute or court rule, they have occasionally done so, applying a variety of balancing tests to determine whether to honor the privilege.

§ 113 The Secrecy of Grand Jury Proceedings: Votes and Expressions of Grand Jurors; Testimony of Witnesses

The taking of evidence by grand jurors and their deliberations have traditionally been shrouded in secrecy. The ancient oath administered to the grand jurors bound them to keep secret "the King's counsel, your fellows' and your own."

Several objectives are commonly suggested as being promoted by the policy of secrecy: to guard the independence of action and freedom of deliberation of the accusatory body, to protect the reputations of those investigated but not indicted, to prevent the forewarning and flight of those accused before publication of the indictment, and to encourage free disclosure by witnesses. The procedure for attaining them assumes two forms, somewhat loosely described as "privilege." The first is a privilege against disclosure of the grand jurors' communications to each other during their deliberations and of their individual votes. The propriety of such a measure as an assurance of free and independent deliberation can scarcely be doubted, though it may be of slight practical importance in view of the infrequency with which these communications and votes will be relevant to any material inquiry. The second of these privileges involves disclosure of the testimony given by witnesses before the grand jury, and as an area of substantial controversy, deserves thoughtful scrutiny.

While the grand jury in its origins may have been an instrument of, and subservient to, the crown, its position as an important bulwark of the rights of English citizens was established by the end of the 17th century. This latter aspect is evident in the provision of the Fifth Amendment of the Constitution of the United States requiring presentment or indictment as a precondition of prosecution for a capital or infamous crime. During this period, the grand jury's independence from incursion by both prosecution and defense appears to have been well recognized, and prosecutors were admitted only by sufferance. However, the decline in the perceived need for the grand jury as a protector of individual liberties, which caused its abolition in England, seems in this country to have led to predominant emphasis on aiding the prosecution in investigating crime and serving as a powerful instrument of discovery. Thus, we find statutes and rules providing for the presence of prosecuting attorneys and stenographers except when the grand jury is deliberating or voting.

The veil of secrecy surrounding grand jury proceedings does not preclude all subsequent disclosure and use of the testimony and other material presented there. In the federal system, prosecutors have long had the use of grand jury material in criminal prosecutions stemming from the grand jury's investigations. Such use is perfectly consistent both with the practical operation of the grand jury and with the central purpose of that body which justifies its broad investigatory powers. However, government use of grand jury material for purposes other than criminal prosecution, such as in a regulatory proceeding dealing with the same facts, would generally be an abuse of the grand jury system and the federal statutory provisions.

Several decisions of the Supreme Court have examined the statutory provisions and imposed limitations on access to grand jury materials by government agencies. In the first of these decisions, *United States v. Sells Engineering, Inc.*,[10] the Court held that government attorneys, other than those working on the criminal matters before the grand jury, are not automatically entitled to access to grand jury materials without a court order, and further that to obtain such an order, not only must the requirements of the statute be met, but also a "particularized need" for the material must be shown. In *United States v. Baggot*,[11] the Court held that the Internal Revenue Service was not entitled to court ordered access to grand jury materials in connection with a civil tax investigation because such an investigation is not "preliminary to or in connection with a judicial proceeding" as required by the rule.

Finally, in *United States v. John Doe, Inc. I*,[12] the Court qualified somewhat the impact of *Sells Engineering*. First, it allowed the attorney who conducted the grand jury investigation to continue using grand jury materials in civil proceedings related to the investigation. Second, although continuing to recognize that "particularized need" must be shown before disclosure to other government attorneys, the Court noted that the policy concerns supporting grand jury secrecy were "implicated to a much lesser extent" when disclosure involved other government attorneys.

In the federal system, both government agencies and private parties must show a "particularized need" for grand jury material before it is to be released. This requirement, though sometimes criticized by commentators, has consistently been

---

[10]   463 U.S. 418 (1983).

[11]   463 U.S. 476 (1983).

[12]   481 U.S. 102 (1987).

reasserted by the Supreme Court. Clearly, federal grand jury secrecy will enjoy substantial protection for the foreseeable future.

Among others having a potential need for access to transcripts of testimony before a grand jury, perhaps the strongest case may be made for the criminal defendant. The right of an accused to a copy of his or her own recorded grand jury testimony is today recognized by statute or rule in a number of states and in the federal courts. Considerations of basic fairness (and the inapplicability of the justifications for grand jury secrecy in this context) argue strongly for this access. The defense is guaranteed access to the testimony of other grand jury witnesses who testify at trial by the Jencks Act,[13] which requires production of such testimony once they have testified on direct. No infringement of the objectives of secrecy mentioned at the beginning of this section can result from such disclosure, which constitutes the least acceptable minimum. In addition to the specifically recognized grounds for disclosure of grand jury material set out above, several federal courts have recognized the inherent authority of courts to unseal and disclose grand jury material.

Despite the stringent language of the federal rule imposing secrecy on grand jury proceedings, witnesses are pointedly omitted from the list of those bound by its provisions. Whether a federal judge has authority to order grand jury witnesses not to disclose their own testimony in order to protect the integrity of an investigation is unclear. Absent such atypical orders, witnesses are free to divulge their testimony as they see fit after testifying. Indeed, the Supreme Court held that a state statute prohibiting a grand jury witness from ever disclosing testimony before the grand jury violated the First Amendment as applied to a witness who wished to disclose information independently acquired by him to which he had testified.[14] On the other hand, some authorities suggest that witnesses may not be compelled to disclose what their testimony was before the grand jury.

---

[13]　18 U.S.C.A. § 3500.

[14]　*See* Butterworth v. Smith, 494 U.S. 624 (1990).

Title 6

PRIVILEGE: CONSTITUTIONAL

---

§ 114 The History and Development of the Privilege

The legal right of a person to be free of compelled self-incrimination has traditionally been described as a privilege, although it is embodied in federal and state constitutional provisions that do not explicitly use that terminology. The Supreme Court has noted that "[t]he term 'privilege against self-incrimination' is not an entirely accurate description of a person's [Fifth Amendment] constitutional protection against being 'compelled in any criminal case to be a witness against himself.' "[1] Nevertheless, since the most fundamental part of that protection is the right of an accused in a criminal trial not to be compelled to be a witness for the prosecution, it is appropriate to continue to regard the right as a privilege albeit with implications beyond those of other evidentiary privileges.

Because of considerable dispute as to the wisdom of the privilege against self-incrimination, the origin and development of the rule have been of special interest to legal scholars. Unfortunately, important aspects of the matter are still clouded with doubt. What is known suggests that the privilege had its roots in opposition to the use of the ex officio oath by the English ecclesiastical courts and that its development was intimately intertwined with the political and religious disputes of early England. The most significant ambiguity is whether the privilege as finally applied in the common law courts after 1700 represented a logical extension of principle underlying earlier opposition to the procedures of ecclesiastical courts, or rather, whether it reflected condemnation by association of a procedure not inherently inconsistent with prevailing values.

Prior to the early 1200s, trials in the ecclesiastical courts had been by ordeal or compurgation oath, the formal swearing by the party and his oath helpers. Under the "inquisitorial oath," there was active interrogation of the accused by the judge in addition to the accused's uncomfortable consciousness of his oath to reveal the entire truth of the matter under inquiry. There was some formal limitation upon the power of the ecclesiastical courts to use this device.

The oath procedure was subsequently adopted by two controversial courts and used for essentially political purposes. In 1487 the Court of the Star Chamber was authorized to pursue its broad political mandate by means of the oath. The Star Chamber was not even subjected to the requirement of presentation that theoretically provided protection from use of the oath to engage in broad "fishing inquisitions" by the ecclesiastical courts. About one hundred years later the same procedure was authorized for the Court of the

---

[1] U.S. v. Hubbell, 530 U.S. 27, 34 (2000).

High Commission in Causes Ecclesiastical, established to maintain conformity to the recently established church. The freewheeling methods of these politically-minded courts, including the use of torture, undoubtedly stimulated a great deal of additional opposition to the oath procedures.

Required self-incrimination and the use of the oath were not confined to the ecclesiastical courts and the courts of High Commission and Star Chamber. In criminal trials the accused was expected to take an active part in the proceedings, often to his own detriment. He was examined before trial by justices of the peace, and the results of this examination were preserved for use by the judge at trial. Only in limited classes of cases was the examination under oath. This was not out of tenderness for the accused, but rather because it was believed that administering an oath would unwisely permit the accused to eventually place before the jury an influential denial of guilt made under oath.

After 1641, the common law courts began to apply to their own procedure some of the restrictions on use of the oath that had been urged for their ecclesiastical counterparts. By 1700, extraction of an answer in any procedure in matters of criminality or forfeiture was improper. This was the privilege against compelled self-incrimination.

It is difficult to draw many helpful conclusions from the historical origin of the privilege. Wigmore accepts Bentham's suggestion that the privilege as ultimately applied in the common law courts was essentially an overreaction to abusive use of the oath procedure without proper presentment of charges.[2] But perhaps this is too narrow a reading of the historical material. Even if the initial objection was only to the impropriety of putting individuals to their oath without presentation, this policy suggests at least limited objection to the use of information extracted from the mouth of the accused as the basis for a criminal prosecution. This early suspicion of compulsory self-incrimination, even if it extended only to situations where compulsion was exerted before an accusation had been made by some other method, seems to be based upon a perception that compelling an individual to provide the basis for his own penal liability should be limited because the position in which it places the individual, making a choice between violating a solemn oath and incurring penal liability, weighs against important policies of individual freedom and dignity.

There is significant disagreement regarding the early development of the privilege in America. Some evidence of the privilege in early colonial America exists. In any case, it was inserted in the constitutions or bills of rights of seven American states before 1789, and has since spread to all state constitutions except those of Iowa and New Jersey. In both of the latter states, however, it was accepted as a matter of nonconstitutional law.

§ 115 Current Nature and Status of the Privilege

The privilege is, of course, embodied in that portion of the Fifth Amendment to the United States Constitution providing, "No person . . . shall be compelled in any criminal case to be a witness against himself. . . ." The precise nature of the federal constitutional right created by this language divided the justices of the United States Supreme Court in *Chavez v. Martinez*.[3]

---

[2]   8 Wigmore, Evidence § 2250, at 292 (McNaughton rev. 1961).

[3]   538 U.S. 760 (2003).

Justice Thomas, writing for four members of the Court, took the view that the literal terms of the Fifth Amendment mean that no violation of the provision itself occurs until or unless an accused's in-court testimony as a witness is compelled in the course of a criminal trial or a statement made out-of-court or in another proceeding is used in that trial. The Court has authority under the Fifth Amendment to create "prophylactic rules" to safeguard the core constitutional rights, he added. One of these rules is an evidentiary privilege that protects a person who is not on trial for a criminal offense from being compelled to give testimony, because that testimony may later be used in a manner that violates the core of Fifth Amendment protection.

Justice Kennedy, writing for three justices, read the Fifth Amendment provision more broadly:

> [T]he Self-Incrimination Clause is a substantive constraint on the conduct of the government, not merely an evidentiary rule governing the work of the courts . . . . The Clause protects an individual from being forced to give answers demanded by an official in any context where the answers might give rise to criminal liability in the future.[4]

The provision, in other words, "provides both assurance that a person will not be compelled to testify against himself in a criminal proceeding and a continuing right against government conduct intended to bring about self-incrimination."

Justice Souter, joined by Justice Breyer, indicated that evidentiary use of testimony or statements by the accused is "the core of Fifth Amendment protection." He appeared to also believe that this Fifth Amendment core protection could be extended to include protection against other governmental activity if that is shown to be desirable to protect the basic or core guarantee.

Whether this doctrinal division among the justices makes much practical difference is open to question. *Chavez* itself involved an effort to establish civil liability for damages on the basis of coercive out-of-court interrogation. A majority declined to impose such liability on the basis of Fifth Amendment law; four justices reasoned that under Justice Thomas's analysis such expansion was doctrinally prohibited and two reasoned that Chavez had not shown that the conceptually-permissible expansion was appropriate. Justice Thomas commented that even under his approach, the prophylactic nature of the privilege of one not on trial on criminal charges to withhold an answer would not alter the case law addressing penalties for violating that privilege.

For many and perhaps most purposes, it is probably of no significance whether the constitutional right of a witness to refuse to engage in testimonial and incriminating conduct is based on a "prophylactic rule" developed to safeguard the core Fifth Amendment right, as Justice Thomas argued, or is itself an aspect of that core Fifth Amendment right. Courts might, however, be persuaded to less vigorously develop the protections afforded one not at the time an accused in a criminal case if convinced that the right at issue is a judicially-promulgated prophylactic rule rather than a core Fifth Amendment provision.

The Fifth Amendment privilege is, of course, applicable to the states by virtue of the Fourteenth Amendment. So holding in *Malloy v. Hogan*,[5] decided in 1964, the Supreme

---

4   *Id.* at 791.

5   378 U.S. 1 (1964).

Court relied heavily upon the basic proposition that "the American system of criminal prosecution is accusatorial, not inquisitorial." "[T]he Fifth Amendment privilege," the Court continued, "is its essential mainstay . . . . Governments, state and federal, are thus constitutionally compelled to establish guilt by evidence independently and freely secured, and may not by coercion prove a charge against an accused out of his own mouth."

Malloy also rejected as "incongruous" the contention that the availability of the federal privilege to a witness in a state proceeding should be determined according to a less stringent standard than is applicable in a federal proceeding. "[T]he same standards," it concluded, "must determine whether an accused's silence in either a federal or state proceeding is justified."

Much recent self-incrimination discussion has focused upon the Supreme Court's construction of the Fifth Amendment's privilege. In some senses, this is unfortunate. Similar privileges are recognized in all states as a matter of either or both state constitutional provision or case law, and versions of the privilege are sometimes embodied in statutory provisions or court rule. Commentators and courts have increasingly recognized state courts' right and perhaps duty to construe state constitutional and statutory provisions "independently" of the Supreme Court's construction of even identically-phrased federal constitutional provisions. This jurisprudence of "new federalism" emphasizes that there is no single privilege against compelled self-incrimination. Specifically, discussion of legal protection against compelled self-incrimination must recognize the possibility that state law provides citizens with greater protection than does the Fifth Amendment privilege.

State privileges sometimes differ in phraseology from the Fifth Amendment. Seldom, however, do these differences in terminology strongly suggest how current questions of construction should be resolved. The Fifth Amendment provides that no person is to be "compelled in any criminal case to be a witness against himself." State constitutional provisions, in contrast, sometimes specify that no person may be "compelled to give evidence against himself." While this suggests the possibility that the protection afforded by the state provisions is broader, it is difficult to regard the difference in language as necessarily controlling.

§ 116 Policy Foundation of the Privilege Under Federal Constitutional and State Law

Inquiry into the policies that do or might support the privilege often seems a frustrating and perhaps fruitless task. Despite the privilege's rich history, vigorous arguments have been made that the dangers of the Court of Star Chamber no longer exist and that the privilege has outlived its rationale. Even proponents of the privilege acknowledge that its popularity and acceptance was not based upon a careful scrutiny of its rationale and that its incorporation into our legal tradition occurred without thorough examination. Modern discussion has tended to undertake largely de novo development of justifications.

Whether a conceptually adequate justification exists may have little significance to the basic questions under modern law. Stuntz noted that judicial and academic writings tend to be dominated by standard explanations for the privilege that fail to explain adequately even the basic aspects of Fifth Amendment privilege law. This, he added, "lead[s] to a widespread sense that many of [the Fifth Amendment privilege's] rules and limitations are simply inexplicable."[6]

Critics of the privilege, of course, stress that the privilege may lack a satisfactory and principled basis. In addition, they urge that the privilege involves disruptive difficulties of application and excessive costs. First, the privilege deprives the state of access to a valuable source of reliable information, the subject of the investigation himself, and therefore purchases whatever values it attains at too great a cost to the inquiry for truth. The subject may be an especially valuable source of information when the alleged crime is one of the sophisticated "white collar" offenses, and in such situations the privilege may deny the prosecution access to the only available information.

Moreover, the privilege may as a practical matter be impossible to implement effectively. Although the law may extend the theoretical right to remain silent at no or minimal cost, in fact it is inevitable that inferences will be drawn from silence and that the inferences will be acted upon. Since these inferences are drawn from inherently ambiguous silence, they are less reliable than inferences from other sources, including compelled self-incriminatory testimony. The result is that one who chooses to invoke the privilege is not protected, but rather is subjected to potential prejudice in a manner ill designed to promote even the person's own best interest.

Rationales for the privilege can usefully be divided into systemic ones, based on the role of the privilege in maintaining an appropriate criminal justice system, and individual ones, resting on the value of the privilege in implementing the interests or values of those suspected or accused of crime. These rationales may overlap, as is demonstrated by the argument that the privilege serves as a valuable means of preventing the conviction of innocent criminal defendants.

One who is under the strain of actual or potential accusation, although innocent, may be unduly prejudiced by his own testimony for reasons unrelated to its accuracy. For example, he may have physical traits or mannerisms that would cause an adverse reaction from the trier of fact. He might, under the strain of interrogation, become confused and thereby give an erroneous impression of guilt. Or, his act of testifying may permit the prosecution to introduce his prior criminal convictions, ostensibly for impeachment purposes, and the trier of fact may uncritically infer his guilt from these. The privilege affords such an individual the opportunity to avoid these dangers possibly flowing from discussing an incriminating situation and thereby creating an unreliable but prejudicial impression of guilt.

Whether these considerations support the privilege is at best problematic. Few defendants may give misleading impressions of guilt, and juries may be more skilled at evaluating evidence than is sometimes believed. Even when there is a significant risk that testifying will create an erroneous impression of guilt, practical considerations are likely to lead many defendants to testify nevertheless. To the extent that these risks are real ones, other reforms in criminal procedure might better protect against them; the admissibility of prior convictions to impeach, for example, might be limited.

The privilege may also protect the innocent in less direct ways. It constitutes one part, but an important part, of our accusatorial system which requires that no criminal punishment be imposed unless guilt is established by a large quantum of especially

---

[6]   Stuntz, Self-Incrimination and Excuse, 88 Colum. L. Rev. 1227, 1228 (1988).

reliable evidence. By denying the prosecution access to what is regarded as an inherently suspect type of proof, the self-incriminating admissions of the accused, the privilege forces the prosecution to establish its case on the basis of more reliable evidence. This arguably creates an additional assurance that every person convicted is in fact guilty as charged. Some, however, argue that the privilege is an ineffective means of encouraging the making of the guilt-innocence decision on reliable evidence. In many situations, for example, it denies defendants the right to call witnesses whose testimony might well be reliable and exculpatory.

Other systemic arguments run that the privilege serves to deny governments powers that might otherwise be abused, particularly in especially sensitive areas. It may also serve to maintain public confidence in the legal system by preventing the degeneration of trials into spectacles that many would find offensive. Of course, the privilege may in fact do neither. Public confidence in the legal system, to the contrary, may even be reduced when courts are compelled to eschew what appears to be the most reliable sources of information. To the extent that the privilege does accomplish these purposes, it may do so inefficiently, as by failing to identify and restrain those governmental powers most offensive and likely to be abused or those aspects of criminal procedure most offensive to the population in general.

Recent defenses of the privilege have tended to rely less upon systemic rationales than upon individual ones. These arguments, which again somewhat overlap, suggest that the privilege prevents the treatment of suspects and defendants in ways that would be offensive to notions of "privacy" or "individual autonomy." As the privilege applies to out-of-court law enforcement interrogation, for example, it may serve to prohibit interrogation techniques that, given the public's increased sensitivities, may now be as offensive as physical torture was at an earlier time in the privilege's development.

As applied in either the in-court or out-of-court situations, the privilege may prevent the treatment of suspects and accuseds in ways that are unacceptably "cruel." Intolerable cruelty may arise simply from compelling the accused to participate in the process itself. Or, the privilege may prevent the treatment of such persons in ways unacceptable because such treatment is inconsistent with developed notions of human dignity. Even a guilty person, for example, may be regarded as retaining aspects of dignity that are violated when that person is compelled to actively participate in the process of bringing punitive sanctions down upon the person.

Gerstein[7] has developed a somewhat similar argument based on privacy concerns: Most persons apprehended for a crime which they have committed regard themselves as a part of the same moral community as those who are the victims of criminal offenses. They regard the commission of an offense as a moral as well as a legal matter. For such persons, a confession involves not simply submission to legal liability but the acknowledgement of moral wrongdoing and often the revelation of remorse. A person's judgment of his own moral blameworthiness is special and perhaps unique and thus peculiarly private. This sort of "information," self-acknowledgment of moral blameworthiness, is so "private" that the individual ought to have full control over it. Even if the courts are empowered to convict an accused of a crime, they should not be empowered to force the accused to publicly make the judgment by which the accused

---

[7]   Gerstein, Privacy and Self-Incrimination, 80 Ethics 87, 87 (1970).

condemns himself in his own conscience. An accused ought to be able to decide whether to share this only with his God or those to whom he feels bound by trust and affection.

A related argument runs that compelling even a guilty person to choose among incriminating himself, committing perjury, or suffering penalties such as contempt citation requires such a difficult or offensive choice that the privilege is justified by the need to prevent that choice. Exactly why the choice presented by this "cruel trilemma" is so offensive is not entirely clear. Perhaps it is because a person's natural instincts and personal interests so strongly suggest that the person should lie in an effort to avoid criminal liability that it is somehow unfair to punish the person for following those instincts. If no reasonable person could be expected to do other than what the witness did, fairness seems offended by punishing the individual. Perhaps the choice is offensive simply because the state is forcing the person to act. In many cases, Judge Frank argued, "the state would be forcing him to commit a crime and then punishing him for it."[8] Yet the law often puts witnesses and others to choices that seem no less difficult or "unfair." To single out a group of persons for solicitude, most of whom find themselves in their position because of their own criminal acts, may be inappropriate.

Stuntz[9] argues that other efforts to explain the privilege unsatisfactorily assume that the activity protected is in some sense "justified." He suggests that a more satisfactory explanation rests on quite different excuse grounds. Were the privilege not recognized, our legal system would be compelled to make available an excuse defense to those defendants who, when called as prosecution witnesses, perjured themselves rather than admit guilt. But such a defense would invoke quite heavy systemic costs. By removing the deterrents to perjury, for example, the defense would lead to a flood of perjurious testimony impairing juries' ability to accurately resolve cases. Recognizing the privilege avoids the need to pay those costs.

Allen and Mace[10] attempt to explain the Supreme Court's Fifth Amendment privilege law. Keying on the requirement that the compelled activity be testimonial, they conclude that the federal constitutional privilege means "the government may not compel revelation of the incriminating substantive results of compelled cognition." They thus construe the case law as stressing official responsibility for generating an incriminating thought process at least as much as the manner in which the government obtains the results of that thought process. Perhaps this indicates an implicit focus upon a notion of autonomy in thought—the privilege should appropriately limit the government's ability to generate and then exploit thoughts because this impinges upon the most central of peoples' autonomous functioning.

Modern versions of the privilege must be regarded as supported by varying combinations of the considerations discussed above. Particular requirements imposed by them often must rest upon combinations of some but less than all of the considerations. The core situation covered by all versions of the privilege, direct trial examination of the sworn defendant under threat of contempt citations as to whether the defendant committed the crime charged, implicates all of these considerations to a singularly significant degree. Whether or not other situations come within the privilege, however, must depend upon what considerations are implicated, the comparative weight given

---

[8]   U.S. v. Grunewald, 233 F.2d 556, 591 (2d Cir. 1956) (Frank, J., dissenting).

[9]   Stuntz, Self-Incrimination and Excuse, 88 Colum. L. Rev. 1227 (1988).

[10]   Allen & Mace, The Self-Incrimination Clause Explained and Its Future Predicted, 94 J. Crim. L. & Criminology 243 (2004).

those considerations, and the degree to which they are implicated. The variety of purposes and rationales that can be called into play and the absence of historical or other guidelines for applying those purposes and rationales, however, mean that courts have extraordinary flexibility in constructing policy analyses with which to address particular issues presented by the privilege in its various forms.

With regard to the Supreme Court's development of the Fifth Amendment privilege, the Court's expansive discussion in *Murphy v. Waterfront Comm'n of N.Y. Harbor*,[11] suggested that the Court regarded a broad and flexible array of policy considerations as both supporting the federal constitutional privilege and as relevant to its content:

> [The privilege] reflects many of our fundamental values and most noble aspirations: our unwillingness to subject those suspected of crime to the cruel trilemma of self-accusation, perjury or contempt; our preference for an accusatorial rather than an inquisitorial system of criminal justice; our fear that self-incriminating statements will be elicited by inhumane treatment and abuses; our sense of fair play which dictates a fair state-individual balance by requiring the government to leave the individual alone until good cause is shown for disturbing him and by requiring the government in its contest with the individual to shoulder the entire load; our respect for the inviolability of the human personality and of the right of each individual to a private enclave where he may lead a private life, our distrust of self-deprecatory statements; and our realization that the privilege, while sometimes a shelter to the guilty, is often a protection to the innocent.[12]

In *United States v. Balsys*,[13] however, a majority deprecatingly characterized the *Murphy* discussion as at most a "catalog [of] aspirations furthered by the [Fifth Amendment Self-Incrimination] Clause." The values reflected in the decision, it continued, are not "reliable"—or, almost certainly in the Court's view, appropriate—"guides to the actual scope of protection under the Clause."

Most specifically, *Balsys* construed *Murphy's* discussion as asserting that the federal constitutional privilege is designed to protect, and should be construed as protecting, "personal inviolability and the privacy of a testimonial enclave." This "comparatively ambitious conceptualization of personal privacy underlying the Clause," it concluded, rested upon *Murphy's* incorrect conclusion that earlier and narrower views of the Clause as reflecting the Framers' intent to embody the English common-law privilege in the Constitution were mistaken. With regard to the specific issue raised by *Balsys* and addressed by the *Murphy* discussion, *Balsys* concluded—contrary to the *Murphy* discussion—that the common-law rule, embodied in the English common-law privilege, was clear. Considerations of personal testimonial integrity or privacy, as stressed in the *Murphy* discussion, would not support "a significant change in the scope of traditional . . . [Fifth Amendment] protection" as is suggested by the common-law rule.

What, then, is the significance for Fifth Amendment purposes of the policies that support the privilege or, in *Balsys'* terms, the aspirations furthered by the federal constitutional privilege? The Supreme Court has acknowledged that "the privilege has never been given the full scope which the values it helps to protect suggest." Moreover,

---

[11] 378 U.S. 52 (1964).

[12] *Id.* at 55.

[13] 524 U.S. 666 (1998).

"[t]he policies behind the privilege are varied, and not all are implicated in any given application of the privilege." *Balsys* suggests that the Court regards the major consideration in defining the content of the Fifth Amendment as the Framers' apparent intent to embody in the Fifth Amendment the English common-law privilege as then understood. More "ambitious conceptualization[s]" of the policies that might be furthered by the privilege are unlikely to move the Court to particular interpretations of that privilege as broader than its English common-law predecessor. As *Balsys* itself acknowledged, the *Balsys'* discussion rejects a reading of *Murphy* that if accepted would "invest[ ] the Clause with a more expansive promise."

§ 117 Where the Privilege Applies: Distinction Between the Privilege of an Accused in a Criminal Case and the Privilege of a "Witness"

When the English common law courts began to apply the privilege in their own proceedings, it soon became clear that the privilege could be invoked not only by a defendant in a criminal prosecution but also by a witness whose conviction could not procedurally be a consequence of the proceeding. There is no historical indication that this was recognized as an important step in the growth of the privilege, and the written decisions offered no rationale.

The Fifth Amendment prohibits compelling a person "in any criminal case to be a witness against himself." This and the terms of early state constitutional provisions as well can be read as prohibiting only compulsion to cause an individual to give oral testimony in a criminal proceeding in which that person is the defendant. Several authorities have argued that this was their original meaning. Nevertheless, in 1924 the Supreme Court rejected the contention that the Fifth Amendment applied only where the prosecution in a criminal trial sought to compel the testimony of the accused:

> The privilege is not ordinarily dependent upon the nature of the proceeding in which the testimony is sought or is to be used. It applies alike to civil and criminal proceedings, wherever the answer might tend to subject to criminal responsibility him who gives it. The privilege protects a mere witness as fully as it does one who is also a party defendant.[14]

Courts now universally accept that state constitutional provisions as well as the Fifth Amendment applies to and may be invoked by one who is not the defendant in an actual trial of a criminal case. Some discussion refers to what might be two different privileges: that of the accused in a criminal case itself and that of a witness.

Justice Thomas, joined by three other members of the United States Supreme Court, suggested in *Chavez v. Martinez*[15] that this distinction might at least coincide with Fifth Amendment doctrine. No violation of the provision itself occurs, he reasoned until or unless an accused's in-court testimony as a witness is compelled in the course of a criminal trial or a statement made out-of-court or in another proceeding is used in that criminal trial. This is arguably the privilege of an accused in a criminal case. Under its authority to create "prophylactic rules" to safeguard the core constitutional rights, he added, the Court has created an evidentiary privilege that protects a person who is not on trial for a criminal offense from being compelled to give testimony, because that

---

[14]   McCarthy v. Arndstein, 266 U.S. 34, 40 (1924).

[15]   538 U.S. 760 (2003).

testimony may later be used in a manner that violates the core of Fifth Amendment protection. This is arguably the privilege of one not an accused but rather a witness.

Justice Thomas's view was not accepted by the Supreme Court as a whole, and whether it is may have little practical significance. There is a real possibility, however, that the courts may less rigorously develop and apply what the judges perceive is only a "prophylactic" privilege protecting those who are not the accused in an actual criminal case.

Precisely what the right to refuse to engage in compelled self-incriminating conduct means undoubtedly differs in various situations. Perhaps some general distinctions can usefully be drawn depending upon whether the person relying on the right is an accused in a criminal action or in some sense merely a witness. It is unlikely, however, that in any meaningful sense there are two different rights or privileges. Nevertheless, this chapter does address separately for some purposes the privilege as it applies to the accused in a criminal case and as it applies to others.

Insofar as it is important to determine whether a situation implicate the privilege of an accused in a criminal case or that of others, it is necessary to identify when a criminal case commences. The *Chavez* plurality declined to offer a definitive answer as to the precise moment a "criminal case" commences. It did, however, indicate that "a 'criminal case' at the very least requires the initiation of legal proceedings" and therefore police interrogation during an investigation does not occur in a criminal case.

The privilege of the accused, then, is best considered as implicated when a person's compelled testimonial conduct may immediately contribute to a judicial finding that the person is guilty of a criminal offense. In other situations, the person can invoke the privilege but not the status of an accused and thus has the privilege of a witness.

The term "privilege of a witness" suggests that the privilege is limited to proceedings of some formality in which a person can be a witness. This is clearly not the case. In *Miranda v. Arizona*,[16] the Supreme Court made clear that the privilege has application to out-of-court custodial interrogation by law enforcement officers.[17] Concern is sometimes expressed over whether the privilege applies to situations in which, out-of-court, a suspect is not in custody within the meaning of *Miranda*, not interrogated within *Miranda's* meaning of that term, or both.

In fact, the Fifth Amendment privilege probably applies to any situation in which a person might engage in testimonial self-incriminating conduct. As Justice Marshall argued, there is simply no logic in suggesting that the right to remain silent created by the privilege applies only if some governmental official attempts to compel a person to speak.[18] What protection the so-called privilege of a witness provides to someone in the out-of-court presence (but not the custody) of a law enforcement officer may, however, be much different than the protection the privilege provides to one who is a witness before a legislative committee.

---

[16]   384 U.S. 436 (1966).

[17]   See infra § 149.

[18]   Jenkins v. Anderson, 447 U.S. 231, 250 n.4 (1980) (Marshall, J., dissenting).

§ 118 Asserting the Privilege

The privilege against compelled self-incrimination "is not self-executing," and "may not be relied upon unless it is invoked in a timely manner." A taxpayer who makes incriminating admissions on a tax form rather than refusing to provide the information on the basis of the privilege, for example, cannot later successfully claim that those admissions are inadmissible because they constituted compelled self-incrimination. This is not a matter of waiver, but rather a substantive requirement of the right to be free from compelled self-incrimination.

In some situations, the need to so assert the Fifth Amendment privilege is relaxed. Where any response by the person is likely to be testimonially self-incriminating, the person need not affirmatively invoke the privilege. Thus a gambler was not required to invoke the privilege rather than simply fail to file a return required by federal gambling tax statutes, because any response to the statutory demand—including the submission of a claim of privilege—was likely to be incriminating. Nor must a person invoke the privilege if an official penalty is placed on the very action of invoking it.

An actual accused person involved in a criminal action is less likely to be required to affirmatively invoke the privilege than one who is only a witness. The accused's privilege is violated if in a jury trial the jury attention is called to the accused's failure to testify even if the accused has taken no affirmative action to invoke the right to not testify under the privilege.[19] The privilege of one undergoing custodial interrogation by law enforcement officers is violated if the officers do not warn the person of the Fifth Amendment's application and before any interrogation elicit an effective waiver of the right to the presence of counsel.[20] In these contexts, the privilege is truly one to remain silent or completely passive, not simply a right to invoke the privilege and thus avoid compelled self-incrimination.

When the privilege must be invoked, how explicitly must be person invoke it? On the infrequent occasions when this has arisen, the courts have been inconsistent. Where a witness stated he was acting on his "preference" to not testify rather than asserting any privilege, he was held nevertheless to have invoked the privilege, since "[a] witness can invoke his Fifth Amendment rights by the act of refusing to testify." On the other hand, a defendant who had previously declined to reveal the identity of his associate in crime was held not to have invoked the privilege during a sentencing hearing when he again refused to do so. Defense counsel stated, "I have to object to that for a number of reasons . . . I think it's totally inappropriate . . . . There could be many reasons for not disclosing [the information]. . . . [I]t could be that it could incriminate him, it could be other reasons as well." The controlling question should be whether the witness or defendant made sufficiently clear to the trial judge the reliance on the privilege to alert the judge to the need to make whatever inquiries necessary to determine whether reliance on the privilege was appropriate on the facts.

The matter was apparently raised by *Hiibel v. Sixth Judicial Dist. Court of Nev., Humboldt Cty.*,[21] in which the Supreme Court held that the Fifth Amendment did not bar Hiibel's prosecution for refusing to provide his name to a police officer. Although the Court relied primarily upon its conclusion that Hiibel had failed to show that providing

---

[19] See infra § 126.

[20] See infra § 149.

[21] 542 U.S. 177 (2004).

his name posed a sufficient risk of incrimination to trigger the privilege, it also noted that Hiibel had apparently refused to provide his name "only because he thought his name was none of the officer's business." Perhaps, particularly in situations involving a minimal risk of incrimination, a person seeking to bar penalization for out-of-court conduct must at the time of that conduct have articulated reliance on the privilege or at least upon a legal right to act or not act on the basis of a risk of incrimination.

§ 119 Personal Nature of the Privilege

Courts frequently describe the privilege against compelled self-incrimination as being personal in nature. These often offhand comments are, however, somewhat misleading.

The privilege is clearly personal in the sense that only the person who is at risk of incrimination can rely upon it. A witness, therefore, cannot refuse to provide information on the ground that it would incriminate someone else and thus intrude upon their interests. If a lawyer is called as a witness before a grand jury, for example, he cannot rely on the privilege as a basis for refusing to respond to questions on the ground that the answers would incriminate his client. A criminal defendant cannot invoke the privilege of witnesses, codefendants, or even co-conspirators or accomplices. Nor, generally speaking, can a criminal defendant successfully complain that the self-incrimination rights of such persons were violated in the litigation process.

There has been some suggestion that the personal nature of the privilege means that it can only be invoked by the personal act or statement of the holder and thus that a lawyer cannot invoke it on behalf of the holder. This is unnecessary and undesirable. When a lawyer, acting under authorization of the client and on behalf of the client, invokes the client's privilege, there is nothing to be gained by requiring the client to invoke the privilege himself. On the other hand, it is reasonable (and perhaps necessary) to require that the decision as to whether or not to invoke the privilege be made by the client and not the lawyer. If the lawyer's authorization is in reasonable doubt, the trial judges should have authority to require that the client's authorization be established.

§ 120 Incrimination: A "Real and Appreciable" Risk of Contributing to Prosecution and Convictions

The privilege applies only if compelled action is incriminating. As is developed later in this chapter,[22] this means that it protects only against criminal liability. Two other aspects of the requirement of incrimination are also important.

First, and despite the terminology of the Fifth Amendment and many other formulations of the privilege, the privilege is not limited to compelled testimony that is actually introduced into evidence at a criminal trial. Rather, it protects against any conduct meeting the other requirements that would furnish a link in the chain of evidence usable to prosecute the person. This means that it protects against compulsion to engage in conduct that may lead to evidence that could be used in the trial of a criminal offense.

Second, the danger of incrimination in the above sense must be "real and appreciable." Early in the development of the Fifth Amendment privilege, the courts

---

[22] See infra §§ 121–123.

established that a danger only "imaginary and unsubstantial" will not support invocation of the privilege.

In several early decisions, the United States Supreme Court invoked this formulation of the required risk as a basis for holding the privilege inapplicable, and "real and appreciable" risk language is sometimes repeated. As now applied, however, the requirement is probably of little if any significance. Courts, for example, sustain claims of the privilege where criminal liability would rest on prohibitions against sexual activity seldom and perhaps never enforced.

Some courts have expressly embraced what is clearly the functional rule: Whether a sought disclosure is incriminating turns on the possibility rather than the likelihood of its use to prosecute. If a court finds the possibility of future prosecution and that the disclosure would contribute to any such prosecution, that ends the inquiry. The court should not attempt to assess how likely it is there will be a prosecution.

The Supreme Court restated and applied the requirement in *Hiibel v. Sixth Judicial Dist. Court of Nev., Humboldt Cty.*[23] The privilege applies, *Hiibel* stated, only if the person reasonably believed the disclosures sought could be used in a criminal prosecution or could lead to other evidence that might be so used. A reasonable person cannot have a reasonable apprehension that the person's name will be incriminating, at least without any support. Disclosure of one's name, the Court explained, "is so likely to be so insignificant in the scheme of things as to be incriminating only in unusual circumstances." Hiibel himself had not offered even an after-the-fact explanation as to how the disclosure of his name could have been used against him in a criminal case. Had he offered such an explanation, apparently, the trial court would have been required to determine whether a reasonable person could believe that the name could itself be used or could lead to other evidence that might be used in a criminal case.

Application of the general requirement of a real and appreciable risk to some more specific problems in the administration of the privilege does present difficulties. These are considered elsewhere in this chapter in connection with the compulsory production of documents and tangible items[24] and the task of determining whether a witness's response to a question is sufficiently related to criminal liability to support invocation of the privilege.[25]

§ 121 Limitation of the Privilege to Protection Against Criminal Liability: (a) In General

The privilege protects its holders only against the risk of legal criminal liability. It provides no protection against the disgrace and practical excommunication from society which might result from disclosure of matter which, under the circumstances, could not give rise to criminal liability.

If the risk of criminal liability is removed there is no privilege. It is clear, then, that the privilege does not apply when prosecution and conviction is precluded by passage of the period of limitations, pardon, prior acquittal, or a grant of immunity. When prior conviction removes the risk of criminal liability, then the privilege is similarly rendered

---

[23]   542 U.S. 177 (2004).

[24]   See infra § 138.

[25]   See infra § 132.

inapplicable. Whether that risk is actually removed by prior conviction, however, presents some special problems.

If direct appeal from a conviction is pending or remains available, a convicted defendant might, despite his conviction, harbor hope that his conviction will be reversed on appeal and that any disclosures he makes would be used to incriminate him upon any retrial that follows. Because of this possibility, the courts have generally held that a convicted defendant retains the protection of the privilege until appeal is exhausted or until the time for appeal expires. The risk of a reversal and retrial is not so remote as to constitute a negligible risk under the prevailing standard.

Whether the possibility that a conviction might be invalidated in collateral attack should render the privilege available is another matter. Collateral attack is generally available at any time, so regarding the risk of retrial after a successful attack of this sort as preserving protection would dramatically expand the protection of the privilege. The best solution is to treat the possibility of successful collateral attack and retrial as raising the question of whether the facts present a "real and appreciable" danger of incrimination. In the absence of some specific showing that collateral attack is likely to be successful, a conviction should be regarded as removing the risk of incrimination and consequently the protection of the privilege. Most courts, however, treat the finality of a conviction as unqualifiedly removing the risk of incrimination.

The privilege does not protect against all adverse determinations in criminal litigation other than a finding of guilt. The Supreme Court reasonably assumed in *Estelle v. Smith*[26] that a finding of competency to stand trial would not be incrimination. Clearly removal of a procedural barrier to continuation of a prosecution should not be incrimination.

Whether the privilege protects against more severe punishment is less clear. *Minnesota v. Murphy*[27] indicated—albeit in dictum—that revocation of probation is not be incrimination for Fifth Amendment privilege purposes despite the fact that it increases the severity of the punishment inflicted for a crime.

On the other hand, *Estelle v. Smith* appeared to regard a defendant as protected by the privilege from having to reveal information usable only to establish a fact—his "dangerousness"—that could lead to imposition of death rather than life for the crime of which he was convicted.

A defendant's Fifth Amendment privilege applies at sentencing, the Supreme Court held in *Mitchell v. United States*.[28] Further, it applies as the privilege of an accused insofar as the sentencing entity cannot draw an adverse inference from the defendant's failure to testify "in determining the facts of the offense." This reaffirmed that a trial court cannot at sentencing compel the defendant to admit guilt or penalize the defendant's refusal to do so. Despite the conviction, acknowledgement of facts relating to the crime might later prove incriminating regarding that offense.

But *Mitchell's* language left unclear whether the Fifth Amendment privilege provides protection against being compelled to make admissions that would only increase the severity of punishment. Could the sentencing judge in *Mitchell* draw an

---

[26] 451 U.S. 454 (1981).
[27] 465 U.S. 420 (1984).
[28] 526 U.S. 314 (1999).

adverse inference regarding facts that would not indicate liability for additional convictions but would support the assessment of a more severe sentence? Does the incrimination from which the defendant is protected include an increase in the severity of punishment?

In actual fact, at issue in *Mitchell* was whether Mitchell was protected by the privilege from having to disclose facts related to the amount of drugs attributable to Mitchell for federal sentencing purposes. The Government did not contend that these facts were not incriminating, but rather argued that by pleading guilty she had waived her Fifth Amendment protection. A fair reading of *Mitchell* makes clear that the Court assumed that facts that would tend to increase the severity of the punishment imposed by the trial court were incriminating for purposes of Fifth Amendment law.

Mitchell explicitly disclaimed addressing whether a sentencing judge or jury might properly give weight to a defendant's silence at sentencing insofar as it tended to show lack of remorse or failure to accept responsibility for the crime. Lower courts have sometimes attempted to read *Mitchell* as permitting sentencing authorities to consider silence in these ways, but doing so is difficult if not impossible. Some courts bar sentencing authorities from giving any such effect to silence.

§ 122 Limitation of the Privilege to Protection Against Criminal Liability: (b) Distinguishing Criminal and Noncriminal Legal Liability

It is clear that the privilege does protect against the risk of conviction for what are technically criminal offenses and equally clear that it does not protect against the imposition of liability for damages on the basis of traditionally civil causes of action. Whether it protects against types of liability that are between these two poles is less certain.

In 1886, the Supreme Court held that "proceedings instituted for the purpose of declaring the forfeiture of a man's property by reason of offenses committed by him, though they may be civil in form, are in their nature criminal."[29] Thus the Fifth Amendment privilege protects against forfeiture, at least where such action is based on conduct that could also serve as the basis for a criminal prosecution. In *Application of Gault*,[30] the Court held that the federal constitutional privilege protected against compelled disclosures that could lead to a finding that a child was delinquent. This determination apparently rested largely upon the fact that such a finding could result in a loss of liberty which the Court concluded was indistinguishable from the imprisonment that might follow criminal conviction.

But in *Baxter v. Palmigiano*,[31] the Court almost offhandedly held that disciplinary penalties imposed upon convicted prison inmates were not "incrimination" and did not themselves invoke the protection of the Fifth Amendment privilege. Two years later, the Court held that a civil penalty imposed under the Federal Water Pollution Control Act for discharge of harmful substances into navigable waters was not "incrimination" within the Fifth Amendment meaning.

---

[29]   Boyd v. U.S., 116 U.S. 616 (1886).
[30]   387 U.S. 1 (1967).
[31]   425 U.S. 308 (1976).

This line of decisions came to a head in *Allen v. Illinois*,[32] in which the Court considered whether the Fifth Amendment protected against being found a sexually dangerous person under the nominally civil Illinois Sexually Dangerous Persons Act. Under the Act, a person may be found a sexually dangerous person only upon proof that he has engaged in criminal sexual misconduct. If such a finding is made, the person can be committed for an indeterminate period to a maximum-security institution run by correctional authorities. Generally, the Court held, the legislature's designation of liability as civil in nature will be sufficient to take it out of Fifth Amendment coverage. A "civil" label must be disregarded and the Fifth Amendment applied, however, upon " 'the clearest proof' that 'the statutory scheme [is] so punitive either in purpose or effect as to negate [the State's] intention' that the proceeding be civil . . . ." The Illinois courts had determined that the proceedings were essentially civil in nature. Allen failed to make the required showing that the scheme was punitive in purpose or effect. Contrary to indications in *Gault*, the fact that liability may result in involuntary incarceration is insufficient to require application of the privilege.

Under *Allen*, a litigant seeking to establish that the Fifth Amendment protects against a nominally civil form of liability has a difficult task and is unlikely to succeed. In that case, the Court assumed that the Fifth Amendment privilege does not protect against compulsory hospitalization for mental illness. Lower courts have held that the privilege does not protect members of the bar against disciplinary proceedings or judges against judicial discipline. Nor is protection afforded against civil penalties for practicing dentistry without a license, revocation of medical license, termination of parental rights, or liability for civil contempt of court. Criminal contempt, however, is probably incrimination within the meaning of the privilege.

Although the privilege does not protect against a certain type of legal liability, one who is the subject of a proceeding to impose that liability can still invoke the privilege. Most likely, the person does not have the privilege of an accused in a criminal case. A refusal to respond to particular questions must be addressed on the basis of the answers tending to create criminal liability, not simply their tendency to increase the risk of the proceeding itself being successful.

§ 123 Limitation of the Privilege to Protection Against Criminal Liability: (c) Incrimination Under the Laws of Another Jurisdiction

A witness may assert the privilege on the basis of concern regarding criminal liability in the courts of a jurisdiction other than the one in which the witness's testimony is being sought. These situations can be divided as follows: (a) a witness in either state or federal court claims danger of incrimination under the laws of a foreign country; (b) a witness in a state court claims danger of incrimination under the laws of another state; (c) a witness in a state court claims danger of incrimination under federal law; and (d) a witness in a federal court claims a danger of incrimination under state law.

Traditionally, most courts took the position that the privilege protected only against incrimination under the laws of the sovereign which was attempting to compel the incriminating information. In part, the basis for such holdings was the view that the risk of prosecution by another sovereign was so low as not to invoke protection under the

---

[32]   478 U.S. 364 (1986).

privilege. It has also been argued, however, that this result follows from the rationale for the privilege. To the extent that the privilege is based upon concern regarding brutality and other such excesses that a sovereign might commit when attempting to compel a person's assistance in achieving his own conviction, that risk is seldom presented when the only potential criminal liability lies under the laws of another jurisdiction. In such cases, the compelling sovereign is unlikely to have sufficient interest in incriminating the person to perform acts that invoke the rationale for the privilege.

With regard to the Fifth Amendment privilege, this traditional position was rejected by the Supreme Court in *Murphy v. Waterfront Commission*.[33] Murphy and several others had been subpoenaed to testify before the Waterfront Commission of New York Harbor regarding a work stoppage at certain New Jersey piers. They were granted immunity from prosecution under New York and New Jersey law but invoked their Fifth Amendment privilege on the ground that their responses would tend to incriminate them under federal law. The Supreme Court agreed that the Fifth Amendment privilege protects state witnesses from liability under federal as well as state law. Noting the high degree of cooperation among jurisdictions, it reasoned without extended discussion that most and perhaps all of the policies and purposes of the Fifth Amendment privilege are defeated when a witness possessing protection against incrimination under both state and federal law can be "whipsawed" into incriminating himself under both bodies of law by simply being called as a witness in the courts of first one and then the other jurisdiction. The defense of the traditional view noted earlier was dismissed as based upon too narrow a view of those policies supporting the Fifth Amendment privilege.

The court recognized, however, that to expand Murphy's Fifth Amendment protection in state courts to include protection against incrimination under federal law without providing the states with a means of obtaining his testimony would ignore the interests that both levels of Government have in investigating and prosecuting crime. Consequently, it held that when a state compels testimony incriminating under federal law, as for example under a grant of immunity, the Federal Government is prohibited from making any incriminating use of that compelled testimony and its fruits. Since Murphy and his companions were thus adequately protected against the use of their compelled testimony in securing their federal convictions, they could be compelled to testify.

Murphy expressly resolved only situation (c) above. But it removed any conceptual basis for the traditional view that the privilege was inapplicable in situations (b) and (d). In both situations, witnesses have protection. But the jurisdiction seeking their testimony may nevertheless compel it if the witness can be assured that the compelled testimony and evidence derived from it cannot be used to incriminate him under the laws of the other jurisdiction. This assurance is provided by the federal constitutional prohibition against the use of involuntary statements in either federal or state protections.

There is, then, general agreement that a federal witness is protected against incrimination under state law and that a state witness is protected against incrimination under the law of other states. Similarly, it is clear that in either situation the witness can be granted immunity by the forum jurisdiction and compelled to answer. Neither the testimony nor evidence derived from it, however, will be usable in the other jurisdiction.

---

[33] 378 U.S. 52 (1964).

Situation (a) above was addressed by the Supreme Court in *United States v. Balsys*.[34] *Murphy*, as construed in *Balsys*, did not reject either the reading of the common-law privilege as limited to incrimination under the law of the sovereign seeking to compel the testimony or the significance of the common-law rule in defining the content of the Fifth Amendment privilege. Rather, *Murphy* rested on the limited rationale that since the Fifth Amendment privilege is binding on the States as well as the federal government, for purposes of applying this aspect of the Fifth Amendment "the state and federal jurisdictions were as one." There is, however, no reason to similarly regard the federal government and a foreign sovereign "as one," and therefore the common-law derived "same sovereign principle" applies. Since the foreign sovereign is not the same as that seeking the testimony, incrimination under the law of that sovereign does not trigger the privilege.

If the matter turned instead on a comparison of the likely costs and benefits of expanding the Fifth Amendment privilege to cover incrimination under the laws of foreign sovereigns, *Balsys* reasoned alternatively, the result would be the same. Despite the relatively few cases in which claims of incrimination under the laws of a foreign sovereign might be raised, expansion of the privilege would result in loss of some evidence that might cause serious adverse consequences for domestic law enforcement. Since the Court has no role in conducting foreign relations, it could not properly assume expansion of the privilege would stimulate legislation and international agreements that would minimize this cost. Expansion of the privilege might not benefit those who might invoke an expanded privilege. Their silence in reliance on an expanded privilege might be used to deport them to countries where they would face criminal prosecution.

Balsys left open the possibility that the Fifth Amendment privilege could be invoked on the basis of a showing that a potential foreign prosecution that would be in essence brought by the foreign sovereign on behalf of the American jurisdiction seeking the testimony. Merely showing that the American jurisdiction supports foreign prosecution by treaty agreement to provide that foreign jurisdiction with evidence of criminal guilt is not sufficient. Rather, *Balsys* suggests, the issue would be raised only by a showing that the two jurisdictions had enacted substantively similar criminal codes targeting "offenses of international character," and that the American jurisdiction was seeking the testimony "for the purpose of obtaining evidence to be delivered to other nations as prosecutors of a crime common to both nations."

§ 124 Limitation of the Privilege to Compelled "Testimonial" Activity

The Fifth Amendment privilege and those of almost all states protect only against compulsion to engage in testimonial self-incriminating activity. Exploration of what the courts mean by testimonial activity is necessary to consideration of the basis and wisdom of this limitation.

As early as 1910, the United States Supreme Court held that the Fifth Amendment prohibits only the compelled extraction of "communications." This was reaffirmed in *Schmerber v. California*,[35] which explained that the privilege "protects an accused only from being compelled to testify against himself, or otherwise provide the state with evidence of a testimonial or communicative nature." The word "witness" in the Fifth

---

[34]   524 U.S. 666 (1998).

[35]   384 U.S. 757 (1966).

Amendment text, the Court noted in *United States v. Hubbell*,[36] explains the application of protection to communications "that are 'testimonial' in character."

In *Doe v. United States*,[37] the Court approved the approach urged by the Government: an act is "testimonial" within the meaning of the Fifth Amendment privilege if it "explicitly or implicitly, relate[s] a factual assertion or disclose[s] information." It then elaborated that this means that compelled action is "testimonial" only if the action is sought as an indication of the subject's intentional expression of his knowledge or belief concerning factual matters. This approach was reaffirmed in *Pennsylvania v. Muniz*.[38]

Therefore, the privilege is implicated when, but only when, the Government imposes compulsion to cause the subject to act in a manner that the subject intends as a disclosure of his perception of, or belief as to, factual matters. Consequently, the government is not prohibited from compelling actions because it does so to learn the subject's thoughts. The privilege prohibits only compulsion to require the subject to intentionally reveal his thoughts.

Physical as well as verbal activity may be testimonial under this definition. The "vast majority" of verbal statements will be testimonial, however, because "[t]here are very few instances in which a verbal statement, either oral or written, will not convey information or assert facts."[39]

Thus the privilege does not bar compulsion upon a suspect to put on a blouse for purposes of determining whether it fits him, to cause a suspect to cooperate in the extraction of a blood sample which would suggest his guilt, to require a suspect to participate in a lineup, or to obtain a voice sample from a suspect. When compelled production of documents or other items involves compelled testimonial activity is a specialized problem considered elsewhere.

Some of these generalizations may be too broad. *United States v. Mara*,[40] for example, seemed to treat compelled production of a handwriting sample as nontestimonial. Some subsequent lower court decisions, however, have reasonably concluded such compelled activity becomes testimonial under certain circumstances. "Obtaining a handwriting sample by dictation," one court explained, "allows the examiner to pose spelling questions to the subject, which are answered in the written exemplar. It also allows the examiner to assess the degree of the subject's sophistication, the level of his education, the scope of his vocabulary, and his educational level." This most likely makes the production of the exemplar a testimonial act.[41]

Even during trial, a criminal defendant can be compelled to engage in incriminating conduct before the jury if that conduct is not testimonial. The defendant can, of course, be compelled to be in the courtroom. Courts have upheld trial judges' requirements that defendants display a tattoo to a witness on the stand, show the jury the defendant's

---

[36]   530 U.S. 27 (2000).

[37]   487 U.S. 201 (1988).

[38]   496 U.S. 582 (1990).

[39]   *Doe*, 487 U.S. at 213.

[40]   410 U.S. 19 (1973).

[41]   U.S. v. Kallstrom, 446 F. Supp. 2d 772, 776 (E.D. Mich. 2006).

teeth, and put on the jacket, mask and cap worn by the perpetrator of the charged crime and say the words spoken by the perpetrator—"Give me the money" and "Hurry up."

In *Muniz*, the Supreme Court addressed the testimonial nature of several aspects of a stationhouse sobriety test. The officer conducting the test first asked Muniz his name, address, height, weight, eye color, date of birth, and current age. Next, in an apparent effort to test Muniz' ability to calculate, he asked, "Do you know what the date was of your sixth birthday?" Finally, the officer instructed him, as he performed several physical dexterity tests, to count.

The *Muniz* majority assumed that the first questions, as to Muniz' name, address, height, weight, eye color, date of birth, and current age, did call for testimonial responses. It made clear, however, that the Fifth Amendment did not bar the officers from compelling Muniz to speak in order to determine whether he would slur his words. Slurred speech and other evidence of lack of muscular coordination do not involve testimonial components and thus their compelled demonstration does not invoke the Fifth Amendment privilege.

Controversy focused upon the second question—concerning whether Muniz knew the date of his sixth birthday—to which Muniz had responded, "No, I don't." Justice Brennan, speaking for a bare majority of five justices, explained that this question did not require exploration of the "outer boundaries of what is 'testimonial,' " because the "core meaning" of that concept made clear that Muniz' response to the question was testimonial. That the police were seeking to ascertain the physical nature of Muniz' brain processes was not controlling, he continued, if that inquiry was pursued by means that called for testimonial responses from the suspect. The question posed to Muniz called for a testimonial response, because it demanded that he communicate his perception or belief concerning the result of his mental processes. Functionally, he was communicating that he believed or knew that he was unaware of the date of his sixth birthday.

Applying *Muniz*, a California court held impermissible the "Romberg [field sobriety] test." An officer administering the test has the suspect stand, tilt his head back, close his eyes, and tell the officer when he thinks 30 second has passed. "The probative value of the Romberg test," the court explained, "lies firmly in the accuracy of the subject's estimation as communicated to police. Because the test requires the suspect to communicate an implied assertion of fact or belief (i.e., that 30 seconds has elapsed), the test is similar to the sixth birthday question in *Muniz,* which called for a testimonial response."[42]

A response to a police demand that a person state that person's name, it was argued in *Hiibel v. Sixth Judicial District Court of Nevada, Humboldt County,*[43] is no more testimonial than a response to a demand that a person stand to reveal their height. The Supreme Court did not reach the question, but offered that this "may qualify as an assertion of fact related to identity" and thus might be testimonial. Production of demanded identity documents, it added, might also be testimonial.

Whether a suspect's refusal to participate in a breath test for blood alcohol level is testimonial remains uncertain. The Supreme Court commented in *South Dakota v. Neville*[44] that there is "considerable force" in the argument that a suspect's refusal to

---

[42] People v. Bejasa, 140 Cal. Rptr. 3d 80, 93 (Ct. App. 2012).

[43] 542 U.S. 177 (2004).

[44] 459 U.S. 553 (1983).

participate in a breath test for blood alcohol is like flight and thus noncommunicative conduct rather than a testimonial communication. It did not reach the issue because the Court held that in any case the refusal was not compelled. Lower courts have tended to characterize refusals as nontestimonial. The Massachusetts court, perhaps the leading authority to the contrary, has reasoned that a refusal is akin to the refusing person's stating, "I have had so much to drink that I know or at least suspect that I am unable to pass the test."

Best analyzed, such conduct is not testimonial. Although it does reveal the suspect's perception that he is too intoxicated to pass the test, it does not do so by compelling the suspect's intentional communication of his perception that he is so intoxicated. The suspect does not intend the response as an assertion of the fact inferred from it—that the suspect is conscious of his state of intoxication.

Muniz left unresolved whether recitation of letters or numbers in a specified sequence—reciting the alphabet, for example—is testimonial. Arguably these recitations involve implied assertions of the suspects' beliefs. Such a recitation of the alphabet can be viewed as an implied—but testimonial—assertion, "I believe E follows C." Nevertheless, most lower courts have held that such action is not testimonial. This is best based on the proposition that such a recitation does not involve an intentional disclosure of the person's beliefs but are rather a rote recitation of "a set of generic symbols" or—in the words of the Massachusetts court—"the reflexive functioning of the [person's] mental processes."

Muniz suggested that the testimonial requirement should be applied—at least in part—by using a functional analysis based on the rationale for the privilege. At its core, the privilege is designed to protect those suspected of crime from modern-day analogues of the historic trilemma of self-accusation, perjury or contempt. "Whatever else it may include . . .," Justice Brennan explained in *Muniz*, "the definition of 'testimonial' evidence . . . must encompass all responses to questions that, if asked of a sworn suspect during a criminal trial, could place the suspect in the 'cruel trilemma.' " Arguably neither suspects asked to consent to tests nor those commanded to recite numbers or letters are placed in this posture. Offering what the persons perceive as more favorable but false answers to the officers' demands are simply not options.

Precisely why the privilege should be limited to compulsion to engage in "testimonial" activity has seldom been addressed. Certainly the language of most if not all constitutional provisions does not require this result. To the contrary, a broader construction of the privilege is somewhat suggested by the terms of some formulations of it, as for example those providing that no person "shall be compelled to give evidence against himself." Such nuances in terminology have not, however, been regarded as of much significance.

In *Doe*, the Supreme Court noted that so limiting the privilege is consistent with the history of the Fifth Amendment privilege and its predecessors, which were historically intended to prevent the use of legal compulsion to extract sworn communications from accuses of facts, which would incriminate them. The Court acknowledged that the policies supporting the privilege would be served to some extent by applying the privilege more broadly. It did not, however, develop precisely why that does not argue persuasively for a broader formulation of the privilege's protection. "[T]he scope of the privilege," the *Doe* majority simply observed, "does not coincide with the complex of values it helps to protect." But this observation is of little help in explaining why the testimonial requirement is imposed to determine the extent to which the scope will coincide with those values.

Doe conceded that the privilege is based in part upon the need to limit the Government's ability to compel the accused to "assist in his prosecution" in a broader sense, and that this purpose would be served by expanding the privilege to nontestimonial situations. It then simply assumed that the protected interests in "privacy, fairness, and restraint of governmental power" are not impermissibly offended by compelling the accused to cooperate in the prosecution's use of his body to develop "highly incriminating testimony." Apparently this assumption was based in part at least on the conclusions that other federal Constitutional provisions also serve that same purpose, arguably so effectively that the Fifth Amendment need not be developed so as to provide additional limits.

States remain free, of course, to define the protection afforded by their constitutional, statutory, or case law privileges more broadly and as not limited to compelled testimonial conduct. Traditionally, there was considerable authority that some state privileges prohibited any compelled activity, whether testimonial or not, giving rise to incriminating evidence or information implicating the person so compelled. After the Utah Supreme Court's rejection of this position in 1985, however, apparently only Georgia still adheres to this approach.

Under the approach of the Georgia courts, the privilege prohibits only compulsion to engage in certain affirmative actions that are self-incriminating but not necessarily testimonial. It "prohibits compelling a suspect to perform an act that itself generates incriminating evidence; it does not prohibit compelling a suspect to be present so that another person may perform an act generating such evidence." It does, therefore, bar compelling a suspect to produce a handwriting exemplar or to give a breath sample. But it does not bar compelled but passive submission to a surgical procedure required for removal of a bullet from the suspect's body, the taking of blood samples for chemical analysis, or the removal of a suspect's shoes. A person cannot be compelled to engage in an act which will create evidence incriminating the person, although the person can be compelled to act so as to assist authorities in obtaining already existing evidence of this sort.

Perhaps the rationales of the privilege simply cannot support a broad construction of the privilege that would expand its application to nontestimonial compelled activity. To the extent that the privilege is designed to minimize cruelty, arguably that purpose might be best effectuated by prohibiting compulsion to engage in any volitional affirmative act, since such situations provide an incentive to engage in potentially abusive persuasion until the subject complies. As the Utah court noted in the leading rejection of this position, however, other constitutional provisions are available to condemn excessive coercion.[45] Moreover, the incentive for extreme, and thus cruel, persuasive measures is greatest in situations where communicative cooperation is sought, because there the subjects retain the power to control the contents of the sought responses.

Any use of a suspect himself to develop evidence with which to bring about the suspect's own downfall might be regarded as offending privacy concerns underlying the privilege; the more the compelled participation by the suspect intrudes upon the privacy

---

[45]   American Fork City v. Crosgrove, 701 P.2d 1069, 1074 (Utah 1985).

of the person's thoughts, the greater this privacy intrusion might be. It is doubtful, however, whether today privacy considerations are of sufficient significance in supporting the privilege to serve as a foundation for defining its scope.

Difficulties in determining what forms of cooperation are sufficiently affirmative to come within a prohibition against compelled affirmative cooperation argue against defining the scope of a privilege in those terms. Yet, as *Muniz* illustrated, defining the privilege as limited to testimonial activity itself presents serious difficulties.

§ 125   Requirement of Compulsion

The privilege protects against "compelled" self-incriminatory and testimonial activity. What compulsion means varies with the context of the testimonial activity, although the recent history of the privilege has involved significant expansion of the concept of compulsion.

Traditionally, the privilege was limited to situations in which "legal" compulsion, compulsion imposed under authority of law, was exerted upon the witness. Consequently, the privilege was inapplicable to police questioning, since law enforcement officers have no authority to compel answers to their inquiries. In *Miranda v. Arizona*,[46] however, the Supreme Court rejected this approach as a matter of Fifth Amendment law and held the privilege implicated in out-of-court custodial interrogation by police. Reasoning that coverage of such activity was necessary to avoid rendering the privilege at trial a mere empty formality, the Court rejected the requirement that the compulsion be legal. The Fifth Amendment privilege applies to and protects citizens in situations in which their freedom to abstain from self-incrimination "is curtailed in any significant way."

On the other hand, the requirement of compulsion is the conceptual basis for many of the procedural requirements that must be met for successful reliance upon the privilege and consequently serves to limit its effect. Most important, as a general rule, compulsion is present only if a witness has asserted a right to refuse to disclose self-incriminating information and this refusal has been overridden. The need for compulsion also explains the recent holdings that the Fifth Amendment privilege does not protect the contents of self-incriminatory documents from compelled production.

Application of the requirement of compulsion has presented special difficulties when the offered evidence tends to show a suspect's refusal to submit to a procedure such as a blood alcohol or breath test. Much of the difficulty arises from failure to recognize that the leading Supreme Court decision, *South Dakota v. Neville,*[47] holds that—at least in this context—compulsion triggers the privilege only if it is "impermissible,"

At issue in *Neville* was the admissibility of a driver's refusal to submit to a blood alcohol test, offered by the prosecution as evidence of the driver's intoxication. To the extent that the refusal may have been testimonial, the Court held, any compulsion exerted upon the driver to take the test did not render the refusal compelled within the meaning of the Fifth Amendment privilege. The criminal process often requires suspects and defendants to make choices, the Court explained, and the Fifth Amendment does not necessarily preclude this:

---

[46]   384 U.S. 436 (1966).

[47]   459 U.S. 553 (1983).

> [T]he values behind the Fifth Amendment are not hindered when the state
> offers a suspect the choice of submitting to the blood-alcohol test or having his
> refusal used against him. . . . [T]he state could legitimately compel the suspect,
> against his will, to accede to the test. Given, then, that the offer of taking a
> blood-alcohol test is clearly legitimate, the action becomes no *less* legitimate
> when the State offers a second option of refusing to take the test, with the
> attendant penalties for making that choice.[48]

The refusal, therefore, is not an act compelled by the officer and trial use of evidence of
that refusal is not barred by the privilege.

The leading state court analyses concluding that refusals are compelled do not take
issue with *Neville's* function requirement of impermissible compulsion. Rather, they find
that at least as a matter of state law the compulsion involved is impermissible.

The Oregon Supreme Court in *State v. Fish*,[49] for example, addressed evidence of a
refusal to submit to field sobriety tests. The court regarded the tests as calling for
testimonial self-incriminating responses and thus beyond the power of the state to
require. Although South Dakota could compel Neville to submit to the blood draw,
Oregon could not permissibly compel Fish to submit to the field sobriety tests. The
compulsion upon Fish, unlike that on Neville, was not *permissible* compulsion and thus
Fish held it triggered the privilege.

§ 126 Privilege as Applied to an Accused in a Criminal Proceeding: (a) Inferences from and Comment upon the Accused's Reliance upon the Privilege in the Trial

A defendant's refusal to testify in a criminal case itself, the most basic invocation of
the privilege imaginable, cannot be penalized by use of that action as tending to prove
the defendant's guilt in that trial. Implementing this, however, has proven somewhat
troublesome.

In *Griffin v. California*,[50] the Supreme Court held that the Fifth Amendment
privilege was violated by a prosecutor's argument which urged the jury to draw an
inference of guilt from a defendant's failure to testify when his testimony could
reasonably have been expected to deny or explain matters proved by the prosecution and
a jury instruction that authorized the jury to draw that suggested inference. So
encouraging the jury to infer guilt from the defendant's reliance upon the privilege, the
Court concluded, constituted an impermissible penalty for exercising the privilege,
despite the risk that even without argument or instruction the jury might do it anyway.
"What the jury may infer given no help from the court is one thing," noted the Court.
"What they may infer when the court solemnizes the silence of the accused into evidence
against him is quite another."

In 1999, the Court reaffirmed *Griffin*. Rejecting the argument that the rule is
useless because jurors will inevitably draw adverse inferences from defendants' silence,
it explained:

---

[48]   *Id.* at 565 (emphasis in original).
[49]   893 P.2d 1023 (Or. 1995).
[50]   380 U.S. 609 (1965).

> The rule against adverse inferences from a defendant's silence in criminal proceedings . . . is of proven utility . . . . It is far from clear that citizens, and jurors, remain today so skeptical of the principle or are often willing to ignore the prohibition against adverse inferences from silence . . . . [T]he rule prohibiting an inference of guilt from a defendant's rightful silence has become an essential feature of our legal system . . . [and] is a vital instrument for teaching that the question in a criminal case is not whether the defendant committed the act of which he is accused. The question is whether the Government has carried its burden to prove the allegations while respecting the defendant's individual rights.[51]

Under *Griffin*, any explicit—or "direct"—invitation to a jury—by the trial judge, the prosecutor, or even counsel for a codefendant—to consider the defendant's failure to testify as tending to prove guilt is prohibited. Arguments and instructions that have other primary functions are often held permissible, even though they may also serve to call juries' attention to defendants' failure to testify. For example, the Supreme Court upheld an instruction permitting the jury to infer knowledge that property was stolen from evidence of possession of recently-stolen property, if the possession was not satisfactorily explained. Without elaboration, it simply observed that the instruction could not fairly be understood as a comment on the defendant's failure to testify.

A comment or argument is impermissible even if it does not invite reliance on the defendant's failure to testify if it calls that failure to the jury's attention. A prosecutor improperly commented on the accused's reliance on the privilege, for example, by observing to the jury, "Mr. Marshall [the defendant] did not take the stand" and "[w]e don't have Mr. Marshall's thoughts." This is so even if the argument or comment includes a disclaimer that the accused has the right to not testify. Thus a prosecutor acted improperly in commenting, "And let's step back and let's talk about credibility, folks, because that woman sitting there, she has an absolute[ ] right not to testify."

Courts have, however, had some difficulty identifying those arguments by prosecutors that are at most prohibited "indirect" references to the defendant's failure to testify. Lower courts have generally held that arguments possibly referring to the defendant's failure to testify must be considered in context and are impermissible under *Griffin* only if the prosecutor "manifestly intended" to comment on the defendant's silence or if the character of the argument was such that a jury would "naturally and necessarily" construe it as a comment on the defendant's failure to testify. The prosecution violated *Griffin*, for example, when the lead prosecutor stood in front of the defendant in the courtroom, gestured towards her, and demanded in a loud voice, "Just tell us where you were. That's all we are asking, Noura!"

Generally, prosecutors may safely argue that the State's evidence, or particular parts of it, are "uncontradicted." If the state of the evidence is that the only possible contradictory testimony would be from the defendant, however, such argument constitutes an impermissible indirect comment on the defendant's failure to testify. Similarly, an argument stressing the lack of any evidence becomes impermissible if the only evidence that might be presented would be the testimony of the accused.

Otherwise proper comment on the defendant's silence at trial is permissible if it is a fair response to evidence or argument made by the defendant. Thus in United States

---

[51] Mitchell v. U.S., 526 U.S. 314, 329–30 (1999).

v. Robinson[52] when defense counsel argued to the jury that the prosecution had unfairly denied the defendant the opportunity to explain his actions, the prosecutor was permitted to respond in argument that the defendant had "every opportunity," if he chose to use it, "to explain this to the ladies and gentlemen of the jury."

§ 127 Privilege as Applied to an Accused in a Criminal Proceeding: (b) Impeachment and Substantive Use of Prior Invocation of the Privilege or Silence

A criminal defendant may have invoked the privilege prior to the trial on the criminal accusation. This may have occurred out of court during the pretrial events that led to the present trial, it may have occurred in a prior trial of the same case, or it may have happened in a different proceeding. May the prosecution use any of those prior invocations of the privilege against the defendant, perhaps only to impeach the defendant if he testifies or perhaps as affirmative proof of guilt?

Griffin v. California[53]—discussed in the last section—prohibits use of a defendant's invocation of the privilege in the present trial to prove guilt. It does not, however, address the prosecution's ability to use evidence that the accused invoked the privilege in other contexts. A defendant who testifies and thus waives the privilege is generally held to have waived it for—but only for—the trial in which this occurs.[54] Does this approach work against the accused as well as for him, so that an invocation of the privilege in an earlier context can be used by the prosecution in the present—and arguably different— proceeding?

In *Raffel v. United States*,[55] the Supreme Court held that a defendant who testified at trial had no federal constitutional protection against cross-examination concerning his failure to testify at a prior trial on the same charge. This seemed to rest largely on a waiver notion—the Court stressed that a defendant who takes the witness stand subjects himself to such cross-examination as is generally permitted. But other language in the opinion suggested that the basis of decision was rather that such a defendant has no right that warrants protection. Any Fifth Amendment right to be free from penalties for invoking the privilege, the Court suggested, extends only to penalties imposed in the same trial or proceeding in which the defendant invoked the privilege.

Precisely when and how the privilege protects out-of-court silence remains somewhat unclear. Under *Jenkins v. Anderson*,[56] *Raffel* permits a testifying defendant to be cross-examined about prior out-of-court silence even if that silence is, as a general matter, protected. *Jenkins* left open whether it is in fact protected. Impeachment of a testifying defendant with prior in-court reliance on the privilege or out-of-court invocations of it is clearly permissible as a matter of privilege law.

Whether the prosecution can make substantive use of the defendant's prior invocations is less clear. Insofar as *Raffel* suggested that neither the letter nor the reason for the privilege suggests that invoking the privilege has any effect in any trial or tribunal other than that in which it occurs, it was simply wrong. This is clear from the

---

[52]   485 U.S. 25 (1988).

[53]   380 U.S. 609 (1965).

[54]   See infra § 129.

[55]   271 U.S. 494 (1926).

[56]   447 U.S. 231 (1980).

quite complicated case law on the validity of various burdens on the exercise of the privilege.

If the prior invocation was in a formal proceeding, the question should probably be whether permitting its substantive use in a later criminal prosecution is an unacceptable burden on an exercise of the privilege. Given the significant chilling effect this would undoubtedly have, such use of a prior formal invocation of the privilege should be barred.

Whether the prosecution may use out-of-court silence or invocation of the privilege is less certain. Discussion tends to become mired in whether the privilege protects silence in such situations and, if so, whether the situations involved any necessary compulsion to trigger its protection.

In fact, the privilege almost certainly applies in out-of-court situations, whether the person is in custody or not. As applied, however, it does not require affording the person a right to counsel or even a right to warnings. But it does protect the person's right to refuse to make self-incriminating admissions. Invocations of that right should be treated the same as more explicit in-court invocations of the right to refuse to give self-incriminating testimony under oath. Thus the prosecution should be barred from using as substantive evidence of guilt proof that the defendant expressly invoked that right ("I refuse to say anything because I believe there is too great a risk that anything I say will be incriminating.") or that the defendant indicated a desire to consult with counsel.

If the prosecution offers evidence that the accused, before trial and out of court, was silent in the face of circumstances that would cause a reasonable person to protest, the question under the self-incrimination privilege should be whether it is likely enough that the silence reflects reliance on the privilege's right to refuse to respond. This is considered in Section 161. In view of the widespread public perception that such persons do have a right to refuse to respond and the difficulty of determining on a case-by-case basis what motivated silence, such silence should be treated as an invocation of the privilege. The prosecution should be barred by the privilege from using it to prove the guilt of the defendant on trial.

§ 128 Privilege as Applied to an Accused in a Criminal Proceeding: (c) Instructing the Jury Regarding the Privilege

Whether instructions directing jurors to give no weight to a defendant's failure to testify can in fact be effective, of course, is open to dispute. In *Carter v. Kentucky*,[57] the Supreme Court nevertheless held that the Fifth Amendment requires trial judges upon request to instruct juries that no inferences are to be drawn from defendants' failures to testify. "No judge can prevent jurors from speculating about why a defendant stands mute in the face of a criminal accusation," the Court reasoned, "but a judge can, and must if requested to do so, use the unique power of the jury instruction to reduce that speculation to a minimum."

It is widely recognized, however, that reasonable persons differ with regard to when, if ever, such an instruction is likely to do more good than harm. The instruction, of course, reminds jurors of the defendant's failure to testify and emphasizes it albeit by stressing the law's demand that the failure be given no significance. Some lawyers, in at least some situations, believe that the giving of such an instruction increases rather than decreases the likelihood that the jury will actually consider the defendant's failure to

---

[57]   450 U.S. 288 (1981).

testify. In light of this, may or should such an instruction be given if the defendant does not request it or if the defendant actively opposes it?

In *Lakeside v. Oregon*,[58] the Supreme Court found no Fifth Amendment defect in a trial judge's giving of such an instruction over the defendant's objection. *Griffin* was concerned only with adverse comment, the Court reasoned. It then rejected as "speculative" Lakeside's argument that the jury might, in the absence of instructions, take no notice of his failure to testify but if given cautionary instructions might totally disregard those directives and draw an inference from his failure to testify. Sound nonconstitutional policy may direct that a trial judge respect a defendant's desire that cautionary instructions not be given, the Court commented, and states remain free to prohibit cautionary instructions over defendants' objection as a matter of state law.

It is difficult to find any significant interests furthered by the giving of such an instruction over the defendant's objection. Moreover, in light of the uncertainty as to whether and when such an instruction is more favorable to an accused than the absence of any instruction, there is little reason to permit the instruction if the defendant affirmatively objects. As the Pennsylvania Supreme Court noted, permitting the trial judge to decide whether to give the instruction removes the judge from the role of impartial presider and inserts that judge into the role of advocate for the defendant. This is clearly undesirable.

An increasing number of jurisdictions require trial judges to omit the instruction if the defendant objects. This is sometimes by statute, and sometimes by constitutional or nonconstitutional case law.

§ 129 Privilege as Applied to an Accused in a Criminal Proceeding: (d) "Waiver" of the Privilege by Voluntary Testimony

The extensive protection afforded by the privilege to one who is the accused in a criminal case is diminished by the act of the accused in testifying during the trial. Unlike the situation of a witness, who loses the privilege only by testifying to incriminating facts, the accused suffers this reduction in his rights merely by testifying, regardless of the incriminatory content of his testimony. In *Brown v. United States*[59] the Supreme Court explained:

> [The accused] has the choice, after weighing the advantage of the privilege against self-incrimination against the advantage of putting forward his version of the facts and his reliability as a witness, not to testify at all. He cannot reasonably claim that the Fifth Amendment gives him not only this choice but, if he elects to testify, an immunity from cross-examination on the matters he has himself put in dispute. It would make of the Fifth Amendment not only a humane safeguard against judicially coerced self-disclosure but a positive invitation to mutilate the truth a party offers to tell.[60]

The diminution of the accused's rights under the privilege occurs only if the accused testifies in the criminal case itself. Pretrial and out-of-court disclosure of incriminating facts, as to law enforcement officers, does not impair the defendant's protection at the trial itself. Moreover, testimony at a hearing before trial or even during trial on an issue

---

[58]   435 U.S. 333 (1978).

[59]   356 U.S. 148 (1958).

[60]   *Id.* at 155–56.

other than guilt will not affect the accused's protection under the privilege with regard to the trial itself. Participating during trial in a demonstration not involving testimony does not impair the accused's ability to remain off the witness stand and avoid cross-examination or comment on the failure to testify. Of course, having testified in another trial of even the same exact criminal charge does not prevent the accused from relying on the privilege.

The effect of a defendant's participating in entry of a plea of guilty was explored by the Supreme Court in *Mitchell v. United States*.[61] Despite the offer of such a plea, the Court made clear, a criminal defendant has the right to refuse to take the witness stand at a hearing on whether the plea should be accepted. Apparently the defendant may even refuse to participate in an in-court plea colloquy at which the accused is not sworn. If the defendant participates in such a colloquy, even under oath, admissions so made will not be given the same effect as testimony at a contested trial. This is because the defendant's participation in the colloquy does not selectively put matters related to the offense into issue and thus involves no risk of misleading the court as to matters put into issue by the defendant.

The major problem in applying this rule has been defining the extent to which an accused loses the protection of the privilege by testifying. Traditionally, many courts have taken the position that a defendant who testifies becomes subject to cross-examination under the jurisdiction's applicable rules and loses the right to invoke the privilege in response to any question proper under that jurisdiction's rules concerning the permissible scope of cross-examination. Under this approach, a testifying defendant may be questioned concerning all matters permitted by that rule and credibility. Such a defendant may not invoke the privilege on the ground that answers to such questions would incriminate the defendant further regarding the offenses on which the trial is being held. Nor can the defendant invoke it on the ground that the answers would create liability for other offenses.

This last statement is subject to one exception. Courts generally enforce the position adopted by Federal Rule 608(b)[62] that a criminal defendant, like other witnesses, does not by testifying lose the right to invoke the privilege regarding criminal misconduct relevant to the case only because that conduct tends to show the accused's lack of credibility. If such misconduct is relevant to some other issue, however, the privilege cannot be invoked by the defendant to avoid incriminating answers to questions about it.

Under the traditional approach, the extent to which a testifying accused's protection is diminished is determined by the jurisdiction's choice of a rule for cross-examination in general. If the jurisdiction limits cross-examination to the scope of direct examination, a defendant on trial for several offenses could, at least in theory, testify regarding less than all of the charged offenses and avoid cross-examination concerning those not addressed on direct. In practice, the courts in these jurisdictions tend to require only a reasonable relationship to matters covered by direct and thus and to find no right to refuse to respond to questions with relatively attenuated relation to the matters inquired into on direct examination. At least occasionally, however, courts hold cross-examination exceeds the permissible limits and the defendant can thus invoke the privilege.

---

[61]   526 U.S. 314 (1999).

[62]   Fed. R. Evid. 608(b).

A defendant's loss of protection by virtue of testifying in his own defense should not be tied to the jurisdiction's rules concerning permissible cross-examination. There is no reason why the scope of an important constitutional right should vary depending upon the jurisdiction's choice of a cross-examination rule. Determining the scope of cross-examination is essentially a matter of control over the order of production of evidence. The primary policy served by limiting cross-examination is the orderly conduct of the trial; ordinary witnesses usually have no legitimate interest that is affected by the scope of permitted cross-examination. Defining the protection of the privilege, on the other hand, involves the fairness of requiring defendants to forfeit the protection of the privilege in order to place their own versions of the facts before triers of fact. This affects defendants' interests which are, generally speaking, protected by the privilege. The scope of protection retained by a testifying defendant should not be tied to the scope of cross-examination of the ordinary witness.

Testifying defendants are required to submit to cross-examination to provide reasonable assurance that their testimony, like that of other witnesses, is subjected to procedures providing assurance of accuracy. The extent to which a defendant forfeits the privilege by testifying should be related to this rationale for decreased protection because of his testifying. Thus a defendant who testifies should have no right to invoke the privilege regarding questions on cross-examination that the trial court, in the exercise of discretion, determines are necessary to provide the prosecution with a reasonable opportunity to test the defendant's assertions on direct.

If a defendant has testified in his own defense and impermissibly refused to respond to cross-examination in mistaken reliance upon his privilege, what action should or may the trial court take? As in the case where an ordinary witness invokes the privilege on cross-examination,[63] the trial court has substantial discretion as to how to respond. But in view of a defendant's particularly important interest in having his version of the events go to the trier of fact, a trial judge should be especially reluctant to strike the defendant's testimony on direct examination. A judge should strike the testimony only after considering and rejecting alternative measures such as striking only part of the testimony on direct examination or directing that the jury consider in assessing the defendant's credibility his improper reliance upon his privilege.

The loss of protection has traditionally been regarded as effective throughout the trial in which the accused testifies. During that proceeding the privilege does not reattach if the accused physically leaves the witness stand, and the accused can be recalled and required to testify again if this is otherwise procedurally proper. On the other hand, the trial on guilt is regarded by some courts as a different proceeding than the sentencing hearing, so a defendant's waiver of the privilege by testifying at trial does not affect that defendant's ability to decline to testify at the sentencing.

§ 130 Privilege as Applied to a Witness: (a) Invoking the Privilege

The privilege, as applied to persons who are not defendants in a criminal prosecution, provides only a right to decline to respond to certain inquiries. It provides no right to be free from all inquiries designed to elicit self-incriminatory responses. Further, although the Supreme Court has unfortunately referred offhandedly to a

---

[63] See infra § 134.

witness's "privilege of silence," in fact the privilege provides a witness no absolute right to remain silent but only a right to refuse to respond to incriminating questions.

Generally, a witness must submit to questioning and invoke the privilege in response to each specific question. A witness has no right to refuse either to appear or to be sworn as a witness. Ordinarily, then, a witness must submit to a series of questions and assert the privilege in response to each one.

Courts justify the requirement that witnesses so raise their privilege on the basis of the limited protection afforded witnesses by the privilege in this context and the need to accommodate considerations other than the witnesses' interest in avoiding compelled self-incrimination. Parties to litigation have obvious interests in being able to produce relevant testimony, and society as a whole has an important interest in the accurate and efficient resolution of litigation. The trial judge and not the witness himself must determine whether a witness's claim of the privilege is justified. Requiring specific assertion of the privilege when the testimony or information is sought permits efficient resolution of witnesses' claims in a manner that accommodates these other interests. A claim of the privilege by a witness alerts the court and the parties to the need to immediately inquire into the basis for that claim when the facts are fresh and can most accurately be developed. It also guides that inquiry by identifying the nature of the possible incriminatory risks that must be investigated.

In criminal trials, the rights of the accused necessarily affect the matter of witnesses' invocations of the privilege. If such action by a witness interferes with a defendant's ability to present the testimony of that witness, this may infringe upon the defendant's right to produce testimony and thus make a defense to the charges. If the action interferes with a defendant's ability to cross-examine a prosecution witness, this may infringe upon the defendant's right to confront witnesses produced against that defendant.

In some situations, a trial judge may properly permit a witness to make what is often called a "blanket" invocation of the privilege. Such action excuses the witness from invoking the privilege on a question-by-question basis and may even excuse the witness from being required to take the stand and oath. Although a defendant's right to compel the testimony of witnesses argues against permitting a witness called by the defendant to such a blanket invocation generally, a trial judge may in exceptional circumstances permit even a witness called by the defense in a criminal trial to make a blanket invocation of the privilege. Such blanket invocations are clearly disfavored.

In *Carter v. Commonwealth*,[64] for example, the defendant offered a witness to testify that he was not present at the charged shooting. The witness had admitted herself shooting the victim, the witness's attorney advised the judge that she intended to exercise her privilege, and the witness (not under oath) confirmed that intention to the judge. By accepting this as a proper blanket invocation of the privilege, the trial judge erred. The judge was required to consider how the witness would have responded to particular questions, whether some or all of the answers would be incriminating, and whether the defense might have been entitled to answers to some relevant questions despite the witness's right to refuse to answer others.

---

[64] 576 S.E.2d 773 (Va. Ct. App. 2003).

A trial judge properly permits a witness to make a blanket invocation of the privilege only if the judge, after adequate inquiry, determines the witness could legitimately refuse to answer essentially all relevant questions. In making this determination, and in deciding how rigorously to press for support for the claim that the privilege would be available to all questions, the judge may properly consider whether requiring the witness to attempt to explain or justify the claim of a right to avoid all questions would itself "result in injurious disclosure." The judge may also consider whether the witness would be entitled to so invoke the privilege on cross-examination as to require that any relevant direct testimony elicited be struck. It is also relevant—if it is the case—that denial of a blanket invocation would result in putting before a jury only the witness's invocation of the privilege.

Whether to permit blanket invocations of the privilege necessarily involves considerable discretion, and trial judges' decisions to permit this action will be reversed only for abuse of discretion. Nevertheless, a trial judge by failing to inquire into the merits of a witness's blanket assertion of the privilege may abuse that discretion.

Ordinarily, it is desirable that the jury not know that a witness has invoked the privilege, since neither party to litigation is entitled to draw any inference from a witness's invocation. Therefore, if a party anticipates that his witness will invoke the privilege, he should alert the trial court of this. The witness's invocation and the court's inquiry into the justification for the witness's reliance on the privilege should take place out of the presence of the jury. But where it is not clear in advance whether a witness will invoke the privilege, a trial judge has discretion whether to interrupt the presentation of the case to conduct an anticipatory inquiry or, instead, to proceed despite the risk that the jury will therefore observe the witness's reliance on the privilege.

§ 131 Privilege as Applied to a Witness: (b) Rights to Be Warned and to Counsel

A witness at risk of losing the privilege against self-incrimination by testifying to self-incriminating facts generally has no "right" to be warned of the privilege and its potential loss by the testimony the witness is about to give.

A trial judge who becomes aware that the questioning of a witness raises the risk that the witness by responding will incriminate himself, however, has substantial discretion as to whether and how to respond. The judge may, for example, stop the questioning briefly to warn the witness that she may decline to give self-incriminating answers and perhaps assure that the witness has a clear opportunity to assert a desire to withhold answers. In addition, the judge may suggest that the witness may wish to consult with an attorney. The judge may also take more drastic steps as, for example, by temporarily stopping the trial so that the witness may consult with an attorney and even by appointing an attorney to consult with the witness.

Appellate courts sometimes advise trial judges to exercise their discretion sparingly and in light of the loss of relevant and reliable evidence that may result from such action. In any case, warning or other action to protect the privilege of witnesses is best done out of the presence of the trial jury.

Ordinarily, this process protects only the interests of the witness. Noncompliance with any requirements as might apply does not prejudice the legitimate interests of the parties, so they may not complain of the trial judge's failure to take adequate steps to protect the interests of the witnesses. This rule applies in criminal litigation as well as civil, and generally speaking the accused has no standing to object to or seek relief simply from the trial court's disregard of a witness's rights under the privilege. If a defendant can show that the violation of a witness's rights under the privilege affected the reliability of the testimony, however, the defendant may have a due process basis for complaint.

A trial judge's admonitions of a witness in a criminal trial may also infringe the defendant's Sixth Amendment right to present all potentially exculpatory evidence. As the Supreme Court recognized in *Webb v. Texas*,[65] trial judges' efforts to protect defense witnesses' interests may impermissibly intrude upon defendants' right to produce evidence.

Perhaps the most that can be generally said with confidence in such situations is that trial judges have a special duty to seek an accommodation between witnesses' self-incrimination interests and defendants' interests in full production of relevant evidence. The judge is not barred from alerting the witness to her self-incrimination right, but the judge's authority to caution the witness "should be exercised sparingly and with great caution." In deciding whether and how to proceed, the judge should consider, among other factors, the actual risk of the witness being prosecuted, and must take special care to assure that any decision not to testify is that of the witness herself. Of course, the prosecution's interest in being able to challenge the credibility of defense testimony must also be given adequate consideration. The witness must therefore be alerted to the duty after testifying on direct examination to submit to appropriate cross-examination.

A neutral and objective warning, however, is within the court's discretionary authority. For example, no violation of *Webb* or abuse of discretion occurred when, prior to trial, the trial judge contacted a proposed defense witness by telephone, explained to the witness that she was implicated in the offense of which the defendant was accused, that she had a right not to incriminate herself or to waive that right and testify on the defendant's behalf.

§ 132 Privilege as Applied to a Witness: (c) Resolving a Witness's Claim of the Privilege

When a witness claims a right under the privilege to refuse to answer questions, determining whether the witness must be excused from providing the demanded response is sometimes a difficult task. Usually the question is whether the demanded response, if given, would be incriminatory. Sometimes this is clearly the case because the question on its face calls for an incriminating response. The difficulties arise from facially innocent questions, as, for example, "Do you know John Bergoti?"

The witness himself, of course, is not the final arbiter of whether his invocation is proper. Rather, the court itself must determine whether the refusal to answer is in fact justifiable under the privilege. Any other position would subordinate the effective operation of the judicial system to the desires of witnesses.

Traditionally, a witness invoking the privilege was required to produce information from which the court could find a sufficient risk of incrimination and perhaps even to convince the court that such a risk existed. In order to sustain the witness's reliance on the privilege the court was required to "see, from the circumstances of the case, and the

---

[65] 409 U.S. 95 (1972).

nature of the evidence which the witness is called to give, that there is reasonable ground to apprehend danger to the witness from his being compelled to answer."

Traditional analysis, however, was cast into doubt by *Hoffman v. United States*,[66] which must be the point of reference for modern application of witnesses' Fifth Amendment privilege. "To sustain the privilege," the Supreme Court explained in *Hoffman*, "it need only be evident from the implications of the question, in the setting in which it was asked, that a responsive answer to the question or an explanation of why it cannot be answered might be dangerous because injurious disclosure could result." The trial court erred in rejecting Hoffman's claim of a right to refuse to answer the question there at issue, the Court concluded, because "it was not '*perfectly clear*, from a careful consideration of all the circumstances in the case, that the witness is mistaken, and that the answer[s] *cannot possibly* have such tendency' to incriminate."

Despite *Hoffman's* prominence, its precise significance is not entirely clear. The Court's first statement is consistent with traditional doctrine: Unless the court can conclude that further inquiry would create a danger of injurious disclosure it cannot sustain a claim of privilege. If this conclusion cannot be drawn from circumstances already available for scrutiny, the witness has the obligation to bring the necessary circumstances to the attention of the court. But the Court's second statement indicates that a trial judge must permit the witness to refuse to answer in reliance on the privilege unless the judge can conclude that the witness's invocation is improper. This, of course, would reallocate at least the burden of producing information and indicates that in the absence of a sufficient factual basis for the conclusion, the claim of privilege must be allowed.

Lower courts disagree on how *Hoffman* is to be read. Some construe it as requiring that a witness's claim to the privilege be sustained unless it is perfectly clear from all the circumstances that the answer to the question cannot possibly have any tendency to incriminate the witness. This suggests that the party seeking the witness's testimony over the witness's claim of the privilege has both the burden of producing information or evidence on which the witness's claim can be evaluated and—once that information or evidence is produced—of persuading the trial judge that the required risk of incrimination is absent. Other courts read *Hoffman* as sometimes at least imposing upon a witness invoking the privilege some obligation to support that claim.

The difficulty with placing any burden on the witness relying on the privilege, of course, is that sometimes meeting this burden will itself require disclosure of self-incriminating facts. In light of this, *Hoffman* is best read as follows: A witness invoking the privilege need not carry a burden of persuasion requiring the witness to persuade the judge that the answer sought would be incriminating. But where the question, considered in light of the evidence in the case and other information properly taken into account, is one which the trial judge could reasonably regard as presenting no more than an imaginary and unsubstantial risk of incrimination, the witness has the burden of putting into the record—by evidence, logical argument, or persuasion—a basis for regarding that conclusion as insufficiently supported. In the words of the Idaho courts, such a witness "must sketch a plausible scenario" under which the answer would be incriminating. Although a witness might produce evidence in support of a claim of the privilege under this approach, such evidence is not necessary. Argument of counsel

---

[66]   341 U.S. 479 (1951).

presenting logical possibilities may well be sufficient. But a conclusory assertion by or on behalf of the witness that responses "may well include" or "could easily include" incriminating information is not enough.

Although there are some suggestions that a trial court is required to hold a hearing on whether a witness's claim of privilege protection is proper, courts generally find that trial judges have discretion as to how to resolve such claims and whether to hold a specific type of factual hearing is a matter within that discretion. Claims to privilege protection are often resolved on the basis of proffers of counsel and this is apparently appropriate. A trial judge would probably act impermissibly in rejecting a witness's claim to the privilege without granting the witness's request for a factual hearing at which the witness would have an opportunity to establish the basis for his claim. In a criminal trial, a defendant's right to compel testimony undoubtedly entitles the defendant to at least a minimally fair procedure for determining whether a defense witness can avoid testifying by invoking the privilege.

Hoffman itself made clear a judge is not limited to the formal record in the case but may consider news media reports, general information, and perhaps even specific factual information which he has from other sources. In an effort to minimize the risk that a witness will have to make incriminatory disclosures to establish that he is not required to do so, some courts have entertained ex parte submissions and conducted in camera proceedings.

As in other situations, state courts are of course free to construe state formulations of the privilege as more protective of the underlying interests than the Fifth Amendment as applied in *Hoffman*.

§ 133 Privilege as Applied to a Witness: (d) "Waiver" by Disclosure of Incriminating Facts

A witness may lose the protection of the privilege by certain disclosures of the incriminating facts about which the privilege entitles the witness to refuse to testify. In *Mitchell v. United States*,[67] the Supreme Court stated:

> It is well established that a witness, in a single proceeding, may not testify voluntarily about a subject and then invoke the privilege against self-incrimination when questioned about the details. The privilege is waived for the matters to which the witness testifies, and the scope of the waiver is determined by the scope of relevant cross-examination.[68]

Mitchell and other discussions refer to this as a rule of "waiver." That may not be strictly accurate. It does not require that the witness at the time of the testimony actually have understood and intended to give up a known right to invoke the privilege when questioned about details. The rule is perhaps based in part on a somewhat waiver-like rationale that a witness *should know* that by voluntarily testifying the witness loses the protection of the privilege as provided by the rule.

The rule rests primarily on the need to avoid leaving a trier of fact with the limited version of relevant information that would be before it if a witness was permitted to at will pick a point at which to invoke the privilege. In the leading case, *Rogers v. United*

---

[67] 526 U.S. 314 (1999).

[68] *Id.* at 321.

States,[69] the Supreme Court explained that to permit a claim of the privilege on questions asked on proper cross-examination "would open the way to distortion of facts by permitting a witness to select any stopping place in the testimony."

Most discussions agree that loss of the privilege is not based primarily on waiver considerations, and thus the witness's actual knowledge that further disclosure will be required is neither a requirement for finding the witness has lost protection or for determining the scope of a witness's loss of protection. In *Garner v. United States*,[70] the Supreme Court stated explicitly that a person may lose the protection of the Fifth Amendment privilege without making a knowing and intelligent waiver as that term in ordinarily used in constitutional analysis. Nevertheless, courts sometimes refuse to find that disclosure by a witness costs the witness the privilege if the facts show that the witness made the disclosure without awareness of the legal significance of doing so or regard the witness's actual understanding of the result of the original testimony in determining the effect of that testimony.

At least one influential discussion of the rule suggests that a witness loses the protection of the privilege only by testifying to actually incriminating matters. But clearly the question is not whether the voluntary testimony was itself incriminating but rather whether the further questions are necessary to test the accuracy of what was disclosed in the testimony, whether incriminating or not.

The privilege's protection is not lost simply by any disclosure by a witness of incriminating knowledge. It is clear, for example, that a witness cannot be denied the right to refuse to answer a question asked in court because the witness previously answered that question in out-of-court discussion with an investigator. On the other hand, actual in-court testimony is not the only way in which the privilege's protection might be lost. An admission made in an affidavit submitted in a proceeding may result in the affiant's inability to invoke the privilege when asked about the substance of that admission later in the proceeding. Apparently loss of protection can be incurred only by testimony or sworn submissions.

How is the scope of a witness's loss of protection properly determined? Some courts read the Supreme Court's case law as directing a relatively mechanical inquiry whether, in view of the witness's prior disclosures, the answer to the question at issue would increase the risk of incrimination. Only if the answer would not increase the risk of incrimination has the witness lost the right to invoke the privilege in response to the question.

Some courts have applied a more functional approach based upon the Second Circuit's decision in *Klein v. Harris*.[71] *Klein* reasoned that the Supreme Court's rationale for holding that testimony may lead to loss of the privilege's protection should inform the criterion to be applied both to determine when protection is lost and to determine the scope of any loss that occur. Thus:

> A court should only infer a waiver of the fifth amendment's privilege against self-incrimination from a witness' prior statements if (1) the witness' prior statements have created a significant likelihood that the finder of fact will be left with and prone to rely on a distorted view of the truth, and (2) the witness

---

[69]   340 U.S. 367 (1951).

[70]   424 U.S. 648 (1976).

[71]   667 F.2d 274 (2d Cir. 1981).

had reason to know that his prior statements would be interpreted as a waiver of the fifth amendment privilege against self-incrimination.[72]

This approach has been criticized as inconsistent with the Supreme Court's analyses of self-incrimination law. Nevertheless, some courts have used it.

A witness's loss of the privilege by testifying applies throughout but not beyond the "proceeding" in which the witness has given the incriminating testimony. This is apparently because the shift from one proceeding to another sufficiently increases the risk of further incrimination that the witness should be entitled to decide anew whether to disclose incriminating information.

Applying this approach, the courts agree that testimony in one trial does not bar a witness from refusing to testify as to those same matters in another trial. More dispute exists concerning the effect of testifying at an early stage of what might be regarded as a single unit of litigation. Most courts hold that testimony at a grand jury proceeding, or other pretrial event or hearing does not preclude a witness from invoking the privilege at trial.

§ 134   Privilege as Applied to a Witness: (e) Effect in a Criminal Trial of Prosecution Witness's Reliance on the Privilege

Special problems of potentially constitutional dimensions are presented in a criminal case if a prosecution witness invokes the privilege. These situations implicate criminal defendants' right to cross-examine witnesses who testify against them, as protected by the Sixth Amendment and many state constitutional provisions.

In *Namet v. United States*,[73] the Supreme Court suggested that prosecution misconduct sufficient to render a conviction invalid might occur if the prosecution, knowing that a witness will invoke the privilege, calls that witness before the jury and then makes a "conscious and flagrant attempt to build its case out of inferences arising from use of the [self-incrimination] privilege." Alternatively, such action creates significant risk that the jury will rely upon an inference of the defendant's guilt from the questions themselves or from the witness's invocation of the privilege in response to them. This might constitute an impermissible use of "testimony" not subject to cross-examination by the defendant.

In *Douglas v. Alabama*,[74] the Court gave constitutional status to the second possibility identified in *Namet. Douglas* held that a defendant's Sixth Amendment right to effective cross-examination was violated when the prosecution was permitted to extensively question a witness regarding a pretrial statement implicating the defendant and the witness refused on self-incrimination grounds to respond to all questions.

If the prosecution calls a witness who simply invokes the privilege but gives no actual testimony harmful to the defendant, the lower courts have been reluctant to grant defendants relief, at least where little more than the witness's reliance on the privilege is put before the jury. In *People v. Gearns*,[75] for example, the prosecution was permitted to call a witness other testimony made clear was an associate of the defendant. As he

---

[72]   *Id.* at 287.

[73]   373 U.S. 179 (1963).

[74]   380 U.S. 415 (1965).

[75]   577 N.W.2d 422 (Mich. 1998).

had previously indicated he would, the witness refused to answer questions despite being ordered to so. The Michigan Supreme Court found harmless evidentiary error but no confrontation violation because the prosecution had not elicited any testimony from the witness. On federal habeas corpus review,[76] the Sixth Circuit held that the state court had mistakenly assumed that a confrontation violation could occur only if substantive testimony was elicited. In some situations, the Court of Appeals made clear, simply putting a witness's invocation of the privilege before the jury violates confrontation by permitting an inference that the witness and the defendant engaged in criminal conduct together or that the witness has knowledge of the defendant's guilt. This was not shown to have occurred in *Gearns*.

If the prosecution is permitted to ask numerous and perhaps leading questions, the question is whether this shows a sufficient effort by the prosecution to build or shore up its case by inferences from the witness's reliance on the privilege. Among the relevant considerations are the prosecutor's certainty that the witness will invoke the privilege, the number and nature of the questions as to which the privilege is invoked, the importance to the prosecution's case of those matters as to which the jury might have drawn an inference from the witness's invocation of the privilege, whether other evidence has been introduced on those matters, and the giving, and likely effectiveness, of an instruction to the jury to draw no inference from the witness's action.

If a prosecution witness invokes the privilege only after having given considerable testimony, a somewhat different problem—also involving confrontation considerations—is presented. In such situations, the trial court must appraise the impact of the witness's action upon the defendant's ability to test the credibility of the testimony already given. The assessment must include the nature of the precluded inquiry and the directness of its relationship to critical aspects of the witness's direct testimony, whether the area of inquiry was adequately covered by the other questions that were answered, and the overall quality of the cross-examination viewed in relation to the issues actually litigated at trial.

If the witness's invocation of the privilege does preclude effective cross-examination, the witness's testimony on direct examination—or at least that part not subject to challenge by cross-examination—must be struck. On the other hand, if the witness's action does not have this effect, the trial judge can properly take measures short of striking the witness's direct testimony. These might include having the witness invoke the privilege before the jury or instructing the jury to consider the testimony in light of the defendant's reduced ability to cross-examine. Trial courts have considerable discretion both in evaluating the effect of witness's invocation of the privilege and in fashioning an appropriate remedy.

§ 135 Privilege as Applied to a Witness: (f) Effect in a Criminal Trial of Defense Witness's Invocation of the Privilege

If in a criminal trial a potential or actual defense witness invokes the privilege, problems with significant constitutional ramifications are raised. Several situations must be distinguished. All implicate a criminal defendant's right to produce evidence and compel testimony in defense against criminal charges. This right, of course is guaranteed by the Sixth Amendment and many state constitutional provisions.

---

[76] Thomas v. Garraghty, 18 Fed. Appx. 301 (6th Cir. 2001).

The first is where the circumstances make clear a potential defense witness will not testify for the defense unless granted immunity. As a general rule, whether to seek immunity for a witness is the prerogative of the prosecution. Trial courts thus generally lack authority to grant immunity at the request of criminal defendants.

In some situations, a defendant's inability to secure testimony from a defense witness may make the prosecution a violation of the defendant's constitutional rights. Trial courts thus may have inherent power to grant immunity to defense witnesses or to dismiss criminal charges or otherwise penalize the prosecution unless the prosecution seeks immunity for a defense witness. An accused faces a difficult task in establishing that the constitutional right to compel testimony means that the trial court has authority to grant immunity or must put pressure on the prosecution to initiate immunity. Most likely this is permissible only upon a finding that the prosecution's refusal to grant immunity is a bad faith effort to use its discretion to distort the judicial fact-finding process. At least one court, however, has recognized a broader power in the courts to grant use immunity to defense witnesses at the defense request.

A second type of situation occurs where a defense witness improperly and in violation of the trial judge's directions insists on invoking the privilege. As a general rule, a defendant is not entitled to have a witness invoke the privilege before the jury. But the lack of any other appropriate relief for a defendant wronged in this way may mean in this limited situation putting the witness on the stand to improperly refuse to testify may be appropriate. This is especially likely to be the case if the defense presents sufficient evidence to permit the jury to find that the witness rather than the defendant committed the charged offense.

The third type of situation is presented if a defense witness invokes the privilege only in response to the prosecution's efforts to cross-examine. The prosecution, of course, is entitled to a fair opportunity to test the credibility of defense testimony. Consequently, in an appropriate case the trial court can properly strike a defense witness's testimony on direct examination. But such action endangers the defendant's Sixth Amendment right to present testimony.

Trial judges have considerable discretion in dealing with these situations. If the witness's actions frustrate the entire cross-examination process, the trial court may and should strike the testimony or, if this is addressed before the witness testifies, bar the witness from testifying. But they should be reluctant to impose this drastic remedy. Less severe alternatives, such as striking only those portions of the testimony on direct which cannot be adequately tested on cross-examination or barring in advance questioning on those matters which cannot be so tested, should first be considered. Excluding or striking the testimony without careful consideration of these alternatives can be error.

§ 136   Burdens on Exercise of the Privilege

The Fifth Amendment privilege, according to *Malloy v. Hogan,*[77] gives one enjoying it not only the right to remain silent in the face of incriminatory questions but also a right "to suffer no penalty . . . for such silence." This undoubtedly overstates the Fifth

---

[77]   378 U.S. 1 (1964).

Amendment's protection. Nevertheless, it is clear that on some occasions the privilege bars the imposition of penalties for, or burdens on, exercising the privilege.[78]

The Supreme Court has exercised particular care in protecting an accused in a criminal case against one burden—the drawing of adverse inferences from the accused's reliance on the privilege.[79] Even the privilege of an accused in a criminal case itself,[80] however, does not mean that an accused is constitutionally entitled to be completely free of any penalty or burden in that criminal case itself from the accused's reliance on the privilege in that case.

The case law does not attempt to distinguish which privilege is at issue. In *McKune v. Lile*,[81] for example, the imprisoned defendant complained regarding pressure to speak regarding the offense of which he was convicted, possible perjury for testifying at his trial on that offense, and other offenses for which no charges had been brought. Depending on how a "criminal case" is defined, the first might have involved complaints regarding the privilege of an accused, since his punishment for the convicted offense would be increased in harshness. No member of the Court argued that the permissibility of the burdens at issue depended on whether he relied on his privilege as the accused in the criminal case or his privilege as a witness. On the other hand, the Court has clearly treated the drawing of an adverse inference in a criminal proceeding as more dangerous to the privilege than the drawing of such an inference in a civil proceeding.

A line of older cases invalidated a number of penalties for invoking the Fifth Amendment privilege. A teacher cannot be discharged for invoking the privilege before a congressional committee. Similarly, an attorney cannot be disbarred for relying upon the privilege and refusing to produce documents during a judicial investigation into his alleged professional misconduct, a police officer was improperly dismissed for refusing to sign a general waiver of immunity during an investigation of the "fixing" of traffic tickets, architects called before grand juries investigating public contracts could not on the basis of their refusal to waive their privilege be barred from state public contracting for five years, and an officer of a political party cannot be barred from party or public office for five years for refusing to testify or waive immunity when called before a grand jury to testify concerning the conduct of his office.

On the other hand, the Fifth Amendment does not forbid the drawing of adverse inferences against parties to civil actions when they invoke the privilege during that litigation. This appropriately "accommodates the right not to be a witness against oneself while permitting civil litigation to proceed." The accommodation reflects in part that the party against whom the privilege is invoked in civil litigation cannot avoid the impact of this by granting immunity, while that option is available to at least one party in a criminal case. It also reflects that the holder of the privilege has a somewhat less important interest in being able to avoid "be[ing] a witness" in civil litigation, because

---

[78]   Identifying improper penalties or burdens must be distinguished from defining what constitutes "incrimination," as discussed in supra §§ 121–123. The privilege's basic requirements are violated if a person is compelled to testify in a criminal trial in which that person is a defendant or the person's out-of-court testimonial communications are compelled and then used as evidence of guilt in such a trial. Where this does not occur, but the person is placed at a disadvantage because the person demanded the protection of these basic requirements, the issue is a burden or penalty one.

[79]   See supra § 126.

[80]   See supra § 117 (distinction between privilege of accused in a criminal case and privilege of a witness).

[81]   536 U.S. 24 (2002).

less is at stake than in criminal cases and the litigant is not pervasively influenced by the Government's sole interest in convicting the person.

In *Baxter v. Palmigiano*,[82] a 7 to 2 majority held that in a prison disciplinary proceeding, prison authorities could consider an inmate's invocation of the privilege as tending to show the alleged disciplinary infraction. No majority could be reached in *McKune v. Lile*,[83] however, on how to evaluate a convicted and imprisoned defendant's claim that a reduction of the quality of the conditions of his confinement as a result of his reliance on the privilege was an impermissible burden on his exercise of his rights.

The *McKune* plurality found guidance in the case law determining when prison conditions can support a due process challenge. It suggested that reducing the quality of an inmate's prison life in reaction to the inmate's reliance on the privilege does not violate the Fifth Amendment if the reductions are related to legitimate penological objectives and "do not constitute atypical and significant hardships in relations to the ordinary incidents of prison life." Justice O'Connor disagreed with the plurality's reliance on due process case law and was troubled at the plurality's failure to base its approach on a comprehensive theory of the Fifth Amendment privilege. She agreed with the plurality that no violation of the privilege occurred because in her view the alterations in the defendant's prison conditions were not so "great" as to constitute compulsion.

Although *McKune* failed to provide a framework for determining whether a penalty upon an exercise of the Fifth Amendment privilege is constitutionally invalid, it made clear that a majority of the Court was willing to be more flexible than the earlier case law suggested. Specifically, the majority is clearly willing to give considerable weight to the social values served by burdening exercise of the privilege and to balance these against the impact of the burden on the privilege.

Baxter and the earlier case law suggested that when an adverse inference was permissible, it nevertheless could not be the sole basis on which to penalize the party invoking the privilege. *McKune* cast considerable doubt on whether this is the case. The plurality explicitly rejected the argument that a burden on the exercise of the privilege is necessarily improper if that burden is imposed "automatically" as a result of invocation of the privilege. The severity of the burden as well as its automatic nature must be considered. Justice O'Connor appeared to agree.

Penalty issues may arise in civil litigation during trial. Unlike the case in criminal litigation, comment on reliance on the privilege by a party or witness is often permissible. One court explained: "In a civil proceeding [an adverse inferences that may logically be drawn from exercise of the privilege] is permissible, where appropriate, not as a sanction or remedy for any unfairness created by exercise of the privilege but simply because the inference is relevant and outside the scope of the privilege." Some courts reason that the spirit if not the letter of self-incrimination law dictates that some limit be placed—even in the civil context—of adverse inferences drawn from reliance on the privilege. The Tennessee court, for example, concluded:

> [T]he trier of fact may draw a negative inference from a party's invocation of the Fifth Amendment privilege in a civil case only when there is independent evidence of the fact to which a party refuses to answer by invoking his or her

---

[82] 425 U.S. 308 (1976).
[83] 536 U.S. 24 (2002).

Fifth Amendment privilege. In instances when there is no corroborating evidence to support the fact under inquiry, no negative inference is permitted.[84]

Special issues may also arise in the civil context when a party is called upon to plead or participate before trial. They most commonly occur as a result of a party's invocation of the privilege during discovery. When this occurs, courts have the power to respond appropriately even if the response results in a disadvantage being placed upon the party who invoked the privilege. The purpose of such action, and the objective of the court in fashioning an appropriate response for a particular case, should not be to sanction the party who invoked the privilege but rather to provide a remedy for the party disadvantaged by his opponent's reliance upon the privilege.

Trial courts have considerable discretion in fashioning relief in these situations. Dismissal, judgment against the party invoking the privilege or the striking of pleadings is clearly permissible, at least in some situations. But the constitutionally-based need to minimize penalization of the exercise of a fundamental right requires that alternatives be considered. These include delaying the civil litigation pending resolution of criminal matters, excluding evidence on matters about which one party invoked the privilege, and permitting impeachment of a party by pre-trial invocation of the privilege be considered first. The remedy imposed should be no more burdensome on the party invoking the privilege than is necessary to prevent unfair and unnecessary prejudice to the other party.

Arguably courts should be particularly willing to impose vigorous penalties such as dismissal where a civil plaintiff invokes the privilege, and thus uses the privilege's shield as a sword to force an unfair advantage. Fundamental notions of fairness are violated if a party comes into court seeking relief from another and then relies upon his privilege to conceal information that might defeat his claim. A civil litigant's involuntary involvement in a lawsuit, in contrast, suggests that in fashioning a remedy for the litigant's invocation of the privilege more weight be given to that litigant's self-incrimination interests.

Nevertheless, the appellate courts have recently required that trial judges carefully consider whether means short of dismissal can provide sufficient relief even where a civil plaintiff invokes the privilege. A Colorado court, agreeing with this "modern trend," held that a trial judge faced with a civil plaintiff's invocation of the privilege must consider (1) whether the defendant has a substantial need for the withheld information; (2) whether the defendant has alternative means of obtaining the withheld information; and (3) whether the court can fashion a remedy short of dismissal that will prevent unfair and unnecessary prejudice to the defendant.

§ 137 Privilege as Related to Documents and Tangible Items: (a) Protection of Contents and Limits on Use of "Private" Papers

Boyd v. United States[85] indicated that the Fifth Amendment privilege against compelled self-incrimination prohibited the seizure and use in evidence of a person's private papers to prove the person's criminal guilt. This suggested the privilege protected the substantive contents of documents and perhaps other physical items. The conceptual

---

[84]   Akers v. Prime Succession of Tennessee, Inc., 387 S.W.3d 495, 506 (Tenn. 2012).

[85]   116 U.S. 616 (1886).

basis for this position was never entirely clear, but it seemed to rest upon combined Fourth and Fifth Amendment protection.

In *Fisher v. United States*[86] and decisions following it the Supreme Court has rejected the conceptual basis of *Boyd* by making clear that no violation of the Fifth Amendment privilege occurs in the absence of compulsion to put incriminating thought into the contents of documents. "[A] person may be required to produce specific documents even though they contain incriminating assertions of fact or belief because the creation of those documents was not "compelled" within the meaning of the privilege." Thus *Boyd's* notion that the Fifth Amendment privilege protects a privacy interest in the contents of certain private or personal document is no longer viable. The privilege, as generally construed, does not protect any interest in the contents of private papers or documents voluntarily created.

Therefore, where officers learned that a suspect had kept a journal in which he had made entries indicating his guilt of a double murder, the suspect had no protected privacy interest in the content of that private document. He consequently was not entitled to resist a subpoena for its production, or to oppose its offer into evidence at his trial, on the ground that the Fifth Amendment prohibits the seizure or use against him of the contents of his private papers.

States remain free, of course, to construe state privileges more broadly and as protecting the privacy of personal papers. The New Jersey Supreme Court has construed the state's common law privilege as retaining a *Boyd*-like protection for the content of at least some private papers.[87] Other jurisdictions, however, have shown no inclination to follow this approach.

§ 138 Privilege as Related to Documents and Tangible Items: (b) Compulsory Production and Incrimination by the "Act of Production"

One in possession of documents or tangible items may have a right under the privilege to refuse a demand—usually made by subpoena—to produce those items. Under *Fisher v. United States*,[88] *United States v. Doe*,[89] and *United States v. Hubbell*[90] this is the case, however, only if the act of production involves a self-incriminating testimonial communication.

By producing an item in response to a subpoena a person may make one or more of several explicit or implicit representations: (a) the person believes that items described by the subpoena exist; (b) the person believes that such items are within the person's possession or control; and (c) the person believes that the items produced are within the description of the subpoena. Any such representations are unquestionably testimonial communications. Under *Fisher*, *Doe*, and *Hubbell*, whether the Fifth Amendment applies to a demand for production of items depends upon whether any communications of these sorts as might be involved in a particular case involve a real and appreciable risk of incrimination.

---

[86]   425 U.S. 391 (1976).

[87]   Matter of Grand Jury Proceedings of Guarino, 516 A.2d 1063, 1070 (N.J. 1986).

[88]   425 U.S. 391 (1976).

[89]   465 U.S. 605 (1984).

[90]   530 U.S. 27 (2000).

Under *Fisher* and *Doe*, if the information available to the prosecution is such that the item's existence, the person's possession of it, and its authenticity as what the demand calls for are "foregone conclusion[s]," the act of production does not add significantly to the incriminating information available to the government. In this event, testimonial communications involved in production do not create the "real and appreciable risk" of self-incrimination necessary to invoke the privilege. Thus, the privilege provides no basis for refusing the demand for production.

Hubbell made clear that the question is whether the prosecution's derivative use of the testimonial aspects of the act of production would be incriminating. Further, *Hubbell's* willingness to find incriminating derivative use and depreciating reference to the foregone conclusion analysis suggest that at least as applied pre-*Hubbell* that analysis may have been insufficiently sensitive to the risks that demanded productions would be derivatively incriminating.

To overcome an assertion of the privilege made in response to a subpoena calling for production of documents, then, the prosecution must establish two things. First it must show that it already has sufficient information that the documents exist and are in the person's possession. The broader the language of the subpoena, the more difficult this task becomes. The prosecution must establish the existence and possession of the documents with reasonable particularity, although this does not require actual knowledge of each and every responsive document.

Second, it must show that it can establish independent of the act of production that the documents are in fact what they purport to be. This showing may, for example, be that prosecution handwriting experts will be able to establish (if it is the case) that produced documents were written by the witness asserting the privilege. Under *Hubbell*, the prosecution must negate the possibility that by selecting and assembling documents for production, the witness will not be tacitly providing information that will contribute to the prosecution's ability later to authenticate those documents.

An in camera examination of the documents by the court may be an appropriate manner of resolving whether the act of production is sufficiently likely in the specific case to be testimonially incriminating.

Although many of the cases involve demands for documents, the protection of the privilege extends to other demands. The privilege was violated, therefore, by compelled production of recordings and a court's order of protection requiring a subject possibly in illegal possession of a pistol to "[s]urrender any and all firearms owned or possessed."

If one on whom a demand for production is made can decline to comply in reliance on the privilege, this basis for refusal to comply can be eliminated by giving the person immunity from the results of the acknowledgments made by the act of production of the item sought. This is the case even it the item is a document with incriminating contents, since one in possession of a document with self-incriminating contents has no Fifth Amendment protection for the contents of those documents. Immunity must be as broad as the protection of the privilege. Thus under *Hubbell* it must provide protection against even derivative use of the testimonial aspects of the act of production.

§ 139 Privilege as Related to Documents and Tangible Items: (c) "Required Records" and Items Possessed Pursuant to Regulatory Schemes

Compelled production of documents that would otherwise be prohibited by the Fifth Amendment privilege is permitted if those documents are "required records." Further, compelled production of items or even persons may be permitted if the items or persons are in the witness's custody pursuant to a regulatory scheme similar to those making documents required records.

In *Shapiro v. United States*,[91] the Supreme Court held that the Fifth Amendment privilege against compelled self-incrimination was no barrier to the compelled production of documents that were required records, that is, records that the law requires the witness to keep. As later developed, the *Shapiro* doctrine permits compelled production only if all of three additional requirements be met. First, the purposes of the government's activity that imposes the requirement that the records be kept must be "essentially regulatory." Second, the records required and demanded must be of the sort that the regulated persons or businesses would customarily keep. Third, the records must have some "public aspects."

The first requirement focuses upon the nature of the government's purpose in imposing the regulatory scheme. Usually, the judicial inquiry is simply whether the regulatory scheme is a generally permissible one. If so, a demand for records kept pursuant to it meets the first *Shapiro* requirement. Simply because the government relies in part upon criminal sanctions does not mean that the scheme is not essentially regulatory. However, if the scheme focuses upon those selected for attention because they are suspected of criminal activities or upon conduct which is criminal, the scheme is not regulatory, and the exception does not apply.

The second requirement is met if the documents sought are the type of records usually kept in connection with the regulated activity. A subpoena for records and contracts relating to an attorney's representation of a named client called for records within the rule, for example, because these are required and customarily kept by persons engaged in the practice of law.

The third requirement may be the most troublesome to apply, because of uncertainty as to what public aspects must exist and what is required to establish them. Unquestionably, the records need not be "public" in the sense that the general public has access to them or a right of access. Rather, the question is generally posed as whether the records are closely enough related to a sufficiently important "public" interest. In an unusual refusal to apply the required records rule, for example, the Seventh Circuit held that even if the Internal Revenue Code required taxpayers to keep records supporting claims made in tax returns, the limited nature of the taxpayer-Internal Revenue Service relationship was insufficient to give the records the "public aspects" that the *Shapiro* rule requires.

The required records rule is of questionable wisdom. One court summarized the case for the rule:

---

[91]   335 U.S. 1 (1948).

[W]hen the criteria for the required-records exception are met, the exception applies regardless of whether the act of producing the requested records would involve self-incriminating testimony by the record holder.

The courts have cited several reasons for [compelling the production of documents under the required-records regardless of whether the act of producing the requested records would involve self-incriminating testimony by the record holder]: (1) a person engaged in a regulated activity in which record keeping is required by statute or law is deemed to have waived the privilege against self-incrimination with respect to the act of producing the required records; (2) the record holder admits little of significance in the way of existence or authentication by producing records that the law requires to be kept in furtherance of public policy; and (3) the public interest in obtaining records required by a regulatory scheme normally outweighs the private interest in nondisclosure because invocation of the privilege frustrates the regulatory purpose of the scheme.[92]

This is essentially a conclusion that the need for disclosure outweighs the relatively minimal intrusion upon protected interests caused by compelled production.

A balancing analysis of this sort may have been appropriate when *Shapiro* was decided, given the then-current assumption that the Fifth Amendment protected against the self-incriminating contents of documents.[93] Such broad protection is perhaps properly limited by balancing analyses of this sort. Now that the federal constitutional privilege applies only to the act of production, however, the quite limited protection afforded self-incrimination interests may not justify limitation by such a balancing of interests. Nevertheless, the courts have refused to read post-*Shapiro* developments in Fifth Amendment doctrine as superseding the required records rule or so undermining its justification as to demand that it be abandoned.

State courts remain free, of course, to construe their state privileges as embodying no similar exception. They have not, however, done so.

Baltimore City Department of Social Services v. Bouknight[94] suggests that the principle underlying the *Shapiro* required records rule will apply beyond the limited area of production of documents.

Bouknight upheld the compelled production by Bouknight of a child placed by a juvenile court with her, over her Fifth Amendment objections that by producing the child she would be acknowledging control over the child and that this might aid her prosecution. The Court relied heavily upon *Shapiro*. It explained *Shapiro* as resting on the principle that "[w]hen a person assumes control over items that are the legitimate object of the government's non-criminal regulatory powers, the ability to invoke the privilege is reduced." This same principle, the Court continued, applied in *Bouknight*. By finding the child within the jurisdiction of the juvenile court, the state subjected him to a noncriminal regulatory scheme. When Bouknight accepted custody, she assumed certain obligations attending that custody, including that of producing the child for "inspection."

---

92   State v. Gomes, 648 A.2d 396, 401 (Vt. 1996).

93   See generally supra § 137.

94   493 U.S. 549 (1990).

The required records exception, or at least the principle on which it is based, is obviously not limited to documentary records. It may render the privilege unavailable as a bar to compelled production of other items or even persons where custody of the items or persons is pursuant to a noncriminal regulatory scheme of the same sort as renders documentary records subject to compelled production.

As applied, the required records rule or principle operates to deprive a witness of the power to successfully resist a demand that an item or person be produced. *Bouknight* noted the possibility that in these situations, as where an organizational agent is compelled to produce organizational property despite the self-incriminating effects of doing so, the incriminating testimonial admissions made by the production cannot be used against the witness. Whether compelled production under the required records approach in fact generates what is in effect use immunity has not been resolved.

§ 139.1 Privilege and Compelling Assistance in Accessing Data in Electronic Devices

The increased use of electronic devices—such as computers and cell phones—to store information and the protection of such information by encryption has given rise to law enforcement efforts to compel suspects or others to cooperate in authorities' efforts to gain access to such stored information. To what extent does the privilege to be free from compelled self-incrimination enable a person to resist these efforts?

The issues are similar to those raised by compelled production of documents and other physical items as discussed in Sections 137 to 139. In the electronic device context, the law enforcement efforts often take the form of a subpoena, search warrant or court order directing the subject to supply or enter a password, decrypt information in a device, or permit the use of a digit to gain access to the contents of a device.

The better view is that the privilege does not protect the substance of the information in an electronic device,[95] just as in the context of documents it does not protect the substance of the documents' contents.[96] Rather, the important questions are whether the act of complying with the demand amounts to a testimonial communication of incriminating information and, if so, whether a version of the foregone conclusion doctrine defeats what would otherwise be the privilege's protection.

There is general agreement that disclosing a password or other information to be used by law enforcement to gain access to a device or using such information by the subject to provide authorities with access is testimonial because it implicitly conveys that the subject knows the information necessary to access the device and thus has had access to it. This is analogous to the "act of production" protection of the privilege against compelled production of documents or items. In recognition of the different situation, the protection in this context might usefully be called "act of compliance" protection.

On the other hand, passively permitting law enforcement officers to manipulate one's fingers to gain access to a device has no such communicative aspects and is not testimonial.

---

[95] This is reflected in the courts' development of the foregone conclusion doctrine as discussed later in this section. The definition of this exception to the privilege's protection as requiring proof only that the person protected has access to the contents of the device assumes that the substance of the sought information—like the incriminatory contents of a document to be produced—is not protected.

[96] See supra § 137.

There is also agreement that to the extent compelled participation in enabling authorities to access devices is initially prohibited by the privilege, this prohibition is subject to a version of the foregone conclusion exception first recognized regarding the act of production protection the privilege provides against compelled production of documents and items.

Some courts construe the foregone conclusion exception in this context as requiring that authorities establish that they already know of the existence and location of the information sought. This is unsupported by the rationale for the exception, which is to exempt from protection situations in which the compelled "testimony" implicit in the conduct of complying does not provide incriminating information beyond what authorities already have. Compliance does not implicitly convey anything about the substance of the information and thus the exception should not require proof that authorities already know that substance.

The better view is that the foregone conclusion exception in this context requires only proof that authorities already know what compliance would convey—that the subject has the ability to access the device. In *State v. Johnson*,[97] for example, authorities seeking the passcode to Johnson's phone produced evidence that Johnson had, in the presence of law enforcement agents, entered his password in the phone to enable a defense expert to examine the phone. That Johnson had access to the information stored in the phone was therefore a forgone conclusion and he could be compelled to disclose the password.

§ 140 The Privilege as Related to Corporations, Associations, and Their Agents: (a) The Privilege of the Organization

Only natural persons have the Fifth Amendment privilege against compelled self-incrimination. Neither corporations nor unincorporated associations such as labor unions have a privilege.

Many of the rationales for the privilege support its limitation to "natural individuals." Organizations, for example, do not possess the "dignity" which is offended by compelled self-incrimination. An organization cannot be subjected to torture or "equally reprehensible methods that are necessary to compelling self-incrimination or that are invited by the right to do so."

Further, a corporation, unlike a natural person, is "a creature of the State" holding privileges subject to the laws of the State and the terms of its charter. Legislatures reasonably reserve a right to investigate such organizations to assure that they have not exceeded their powers and to conduct such investigations by demanding even self-incriminating information from the organizations. If this is not permitted, many necessary investigations into possible abuses by corporations of their immense power would necessarily fail, because such abuses could can sometimes—and perhaps often—only be ascertained by information obtained from the organizations themselves.

Thus, if a demand for production of documents or items is made upon an organization, the officers or agents of the organization who respond have no right to refuse to respond because doing so will incriminate the organization.

---

[97]   576 S.W.3d 205 (Mo. Ct. App. 2019).

State courts remain free, of course, to construe state privileges as affording protection to such entities. They have not, however, tended to do so.

§ 141 The Privilege as Related to Corporations, Associations, and Their Agents: (b) Agents' Ability to Invoke Their Personal Privilege and the "Collective Entity" Rule

An officer or agent of an association is, of course, protected by that person's own Fifth Amendment privilege against compelled self-incrimination, even though the association itself has no privilege. Such a person's ability to invoke that protection in response to a demand for production of documents or other items, however, is limited by the so-called "collective entity" rule.

Under the collective entity rule, an organization agent who holds items or documents of the organization may not invoke the person's personal privilege in response to demands for production of the items or documents of the organization. When a corporation custodian produces corporation documents, "the custodian's act of production is not regarded as a personal act, but rather an act of the corporation."

The Supreme Court first justified the collective entity rule on the grounds that significant public interests justified limiting the protection afforded organizational agents by the privilege, and that those agents in effect assumed the risk of this reduced protection by becoming agents of the organization. Permitting a claim of privilege by a corporation agent, the Court explained, would be "tantamount to a claim of privilege by the corporation," and thus would circumvent the privilege's inapplicability to such organizations. This, moreover, "would have a detrimental impact on the Government's efforts to prosecute 'white collar crime,' one of the most serious problems confronting law enforcement authorities." Further, by accepting the position as agent of the organization, a person incurs certain obligations, including that of producing organizational documents regardless of the self-incriminating repercussions.

In *Braswell v. United States*,[98] the Supreme Court held that the personal protection afforded the organizational agent who is compelled to produce organizational items requires that the agent's act of production not be used against him individually. Suppose, for example, the Government subpoenas the records of Corporation A from X, president of that corporation. X produces the records. Later, X is prosecuted and the prosecution wishes to show that X possessed the records and was aware of their contents. To prove this, the prosecution may show: (a) X was president of Corporation A; (b) documents of this sort are generally in possession of and familiar to the president of an organization like Corporation A; and (c) these documents were produced by an agent of Corporation A in response to a subpoena for documents of this sort. But the prosecution may not show in support that X himself personally produced the documents on behalf of Corporation A.

Braswell in effect mandates that an organizational agent who in response to compulsion produces organizational documents or items be given automatic use immunity protecting the agent from the use against him of testimonial communications made by the act of production. Under this approach, the collective entity rule can be regarded as based on the lack of any significant risk of incrimination by whatever testimonial communications are made by production.

---

[98]   487 U.S. 99 (1988).

The Supreme Court has indicated that the collective entity rule requires the custodian of organizational property to do no more than produce the document or item or explain under oath the nonproduction of the items. A custodian, the Court said, "may decline to utter upon the witness stand a single self-incriminating word."[99] Subsequently, however, the Court suggested an organizational agent obligated to produce items might also have no right to resist giving testimony merely "auxiliary to the production" of the items because such testimony would not involve an increased risk of incrimination beyond what resulted from the act of production. A witness who has explained nonproduction by testifying the witness does not have the items sought most likely cannot, however, be compelled to testify as to where the items are now located if that information would be personally incriminating.

A witness is deprived of the right to rely on his personal privilege to resist a demand for documents or items only if there is a collective entity sufficient to invoke the collective entity rule. Under *Bellis v. United States*,[100] whether a unit is sufficient to trigger the rule depends upon whether the unit is recognizable as an entity apart from its individual members, probably on the basis of its performance of organized and institutional activity. *Bellis* added:

> The group must be relatively well organized and structured, and not merely a loose, informal association of individuals. It must maintain a distinct set of organizational records, and recognize rights in its members of control and access to them.[101]

A corporation will generally if not always be a sufficient collective entity. Unincorporated associations present greater difficulties. A labor union, of course, is a sufficient unit to invoke the rule. *Bellis* itself makes clear that a partnership will often be sufficient.

The partnership in *Bellis* was a law firm that had been in existence for nearly fifteen years and had three partners and six employees. It maintained a bank account and held itself out as an entity with an independent institutional identity. Size is relevant but not necessarily determinative, the Court commented. "[A]n insubstantial difference in the form of [a] business enterprise," it continued, should not control. Despite their noncorporate nature, partnerships such as law and stock brokerage firms are often large, impersonal, and perpetual in duration. The personal interest of any particular partner in the financial records of the organization is "highly attenuated." A different case might be presented, the Court noted, if the partnership had been a "small family" one or if "there were some other pre-existing relationship of confidentiality among the partners."

Single-member limited liability companies—or LLCs—have been described in this context as "hybrids of both corporations and sole proprietorships." As might be expected, they are sufficient to trigger the collective entity rule.

A person loses the right to invoke the person's own privilege only if the demand is for items belonging to the organization held by the person in his capacity as an agent of the entity. With regard to records, the agency rationale for the collective entity rule indicates that agency law provides an appropriate source for standards. Records are

---

[99]   Wilson v. U.S., 221 U.S. 361, 385 (1911).

[100]   417 U.S. 85 (1974).

[101]   *Id.* at 92–93.

organizational ones possessed as an agent of the organization if the person in developing and possessing them acted within the scope of his agency relationship with the entity.

States, of course, remain free to construe state privileges as affording broader protection to organizational agents than is provided by the Fifth Amendment.

§ 142 Removing the Danger of Incrimination by Granting Immunity: (a) In General

The privilege protects only against formal legal liability. Consequently, if the risk of criminal liability is removed by a grant of effective immunity, the privilege no longer applies.

Generally, the availability of formal immunity to witnesses is closely tied to statutory authority for such immunity and statutorily-provided procedures for conferring and enforcing it. Early statutes sometimes provided for immunity for a witness who simply testified about a matter, permitting witnesses to insulate themselves from prosecution by volunteering information. Modern statutes, in contrast, tend to provide for immunity only if a witness invokes the privilege, the prosecution seeks a grant of immunity, and the trial judge grants it. This is the case, for example, under the federal statute.[102]

Most jurisdictions appear to assume that formal immunity sufficient to permit compelling a witness to testify can be conferred only where and as authorized by statute. Under this approach, courts have no authority to themselves develop systems for granting immunity. The New Mexico Supreme Court in *State v. Belanger*,[103] however, characterized "use" immunity—distinguished in the next section from "transactional" immunity—as essentially a matter of evidence. "New Mexico courts," it noted, "control issues of evidence and testimony . . . ." Further, "[i]n granting use immunity, courts are acting upon their inherent power to control their courtroom and to establish procedural rules." Thus, it concluded, the court itself "controls use immunity rules." Pursuant to this authority, it promulgated an evidence rule authorizing trial courts to grant use immunity on request of criminal defendants.

Many courts recognize prosecutors' power independent of statutory authorization to confer "informal"—or "pocket"—immunity by entering into an agreement with a witness. The immunity provided by these arrangements most likely does not supplant the privilege. A witness can invoke the privilege despite the agreement not to do so.

Immunity does not protect the witness from prosecution for perjury committed in the giving of the immunized testimony. In such a prosecution, the testimony relied upon as being false may, of course, be used against the witness. It is less clear whether immunized testimony may be used to prove that the witness committed perjury other than during the immunized testimony. Almost certainly it must protect the witness against prosecution for perjury committed prior to the immunized testimony.

Immunity creates special difficulties when a person's suspected behavior may constitute crimes subject to prosecution by different prosecutors. Massachusetts requires a prosecutor seeking formal immunity for a witness to notify other prosecutors and the attorney general. This provides them with an opportunity to be heard on whether the

---

[102] 18 U.S.C.A. §§ 6001–6005.
[103] 210 P.3d 783 (N.M. 2009).

court should grant the request.[104] Whether formal procedures of this sort can be circumvented by informal immunity agreements is not settled.

§ 143 Removing the Danger of Incrimination by Granting Immunity: (b) "Transactional" Versus "Use" Immunity

Immunity is of two kinds. "Transactional" immunity confers full immunity from prosecution for all offenses related to matters about which the witness testifies, that is, often all offenses arising out of the "transaction" that was the subject of the compelled testimony. "Use" immunity, on the other hand, provides no bar to prosecution but protects the witness from use against that witness of the compelled testimony and evidence directly or indirectly derived from that testimony.

Some immunity statutes permit only the granting of transactional immunity or only both transactional and use immunity. Others, such as the federal statute, authorize only the granting of use immunity.[105] The Vermont court has construed its statute as authorizing use immunity but also as giving the trial judge discretion to find—on the facts of the particular case—that use immunity would not adequately protect the witness and thus to refuse to compel testimony unless the prosecution seeks transactional immunity.[106]

Counselman v. Hitchcock,[107] decided in 1892, was widely regarded as indicating that the Fifth Amendment privilege permitted compelled testimony over a claim of the privilege only upon a granting of transactional immunity. In *Kastigar v. United States*,[108] however, the Supreme Court held that a grant of transactional immunity is not necessary in order to compel a witness to testify over an assertion of his privilege. The sole concern of the privilege, reasoned the majority, is the prevention of compulsion to give testimony that leads to the infliction of penalties affixed to criminal acts. "Immunity from the use of compelled testimony, as well as evidence derived directly and indirectly therefrom," it concluded, "affords this protection."

Use immunity that does not provide protection against derivative use is not sufficient to supplant the privilege and compel testimony by one with a right to claim it.

The *Kastigar* dissenters and other critics of use immunity argue that even use immunity extending to derivative use is inadequate because, given practical realities, use immunity cannot eliminate or sufficiently minimize the possibility that in actuality compelled testimony will contribute to conviction of the immunized witness. In response, the *Kastigar* majority held that once a defendant establishes that he has previously testified under a grant of immunity concerning matters related to his prosecution, the prosecution, upon defense objection, must affirmatively prove that the evidence it offers against the defendant is derived from a legitimate source wholly independent of the previously compelled testimony. This burden of proof is adequate, the Court concluded, to assure that compelled testimony will not be used to incriminate the witness forced to give it. At such a so-called *Kastigar* hearing, the prosecution must prove its nonuse of the immunized testimony by a preponderance of the evidence.

---

[104] Mass. Gen. L. ch. 233, § 20E(d).

[105] 18 U.S.C.A. § 6002.

[106] State v. Ely, 708 A.2d 1332, 1340 (Vt. 1997).

[107] 142 U.S. 547 (1892).

[108] 406 U.S. 441 (1972).

Lower courts agree that under *Kastigar*, the prosecution must prove that it will make no "evidentiary" use of immunized testimony if it proceeds against a witness who has given immunized testimony. All evidence offered at trial and before any indicting grand jury, then, must be shown to have had a source other than—or independent of—the immunized testimony. A general assertion by the prosecution that its evidence has an independent source is not sufficient. Rather, the prosecution must proceed item-by-item and witness-by-witness and demonstrate its source for the proffered testimony. The same is true regarding evidence elicited by cross-examination; *Kastigar* is violated if a prosecutor's consideration of a defendant's immunized testimony enables the prosecutor to elicit significant testimony on cross-examination of defense witnesses.

When the evidence at issue as potentially derived from immunized testimony is testimony of a witness, the prosecution's task is often quite difficult, especially if the evidence shows that the witness has been exposed to the immunized testimony. At least in those situations, the prosecution may be required to proceed line-by-line through the witness's testimony and demonstrate that the substance of the testimony was not affected by the immunized testimony. As a practical matter, the prosecution may be able to meet its burden only if it has "canned" the testimony—by producing and filing a sworn version of it—before the witness was exposed to the immunized testimony.

Lower courts disagree on whether use immunity does—and constitutionally must—prohibit the prosecution from all "nonevidentiary" use of immunized testimony. One court explained the term:

> Nonevidentiary use . . . is that which does not culminate directly or indirectly in the presentation of evidence against the immunized person. Such use includes "assistance in focusing the investigation, deciding to initiate prosecution, refusing to plea bargain, interpreting evidence, planning cross-examination and otherwise generally planning trial strategy."[109]

Some courts regard use immunity as sufficient to negate the Fifth Amendment right not to testify to self-incriminating matters only if it prohibits nonevidentiary use. Most, however, reject this approach. The prosecution's burden at a *Kastigar* hearing is, of course, greatly increased if it must prove that it is making no nonevidentiary use of immunized testimony.

Probably the leading decision regarding nonevidentiary use as impermissible, *United States v. McDaniel*,[110] has been read as holding that proof that prosecutors were exposed to and aware of immunized testimony of the defendant is sufficient to establish that nonevidentiary use was made of that testimony. This is apparently on the rationale that the prosecution cannot, as a practical matter, produce satisfactory evidence that prosecutors so exposed to immunized testimony did not make use of that testimony. Opponents of the nonevidentiary use approach argue, of course, that at least if that approach is applied as required by this reading of *McDaniel*, use immunity effectively precludes prosecution and thus becomes transactional immunity.

A significant number of state courts have construed state constitutions as requiring transactional immunity. Most often, this is based on conclusions that practical difficulties in applying use immunity mean that in actual fact use immunity does not

---

[109] U.S. v. Slough, 677 F. Supp. 2d 112, 131 (D. D.C. 2009) (quoting U.S. v. North, 910 F.2d 843, 857 (D.C. Cir. 1990)).

[110] 482 F.2d 305 (8th Cir. 1973).

provide adequate assurance that immunized testimony will not be used against the witness in a subsequent prosecution. The Alaska Supreme Court, for example, stressed that faded memories and other difficulties of proof will often make impossible accurate determinations as to whether immunized testimony in fact affected the prosecution's evidence and that no procedural way is available to adequately protect witnesses from nonevidentiary use against them of compelled testimony.

Some courts have found use immunity adequate under state constitutional standards only if it involves safeguards more stringent than those required by *Kastigar* as a matter of Fifth Amendment law. The Pennsylvania Supreme Court, for example, upheld use immunity but only on the condition that the prosecution is required to prove that its evidence "arose *wholly* [from] independent sources" and to prove this by clear and convincing evidence. States may in other ways exceed what is required by Fifth Amendment law. Kansas, for example, requires that at a *Kastigar* hearing the prosecution prove by clear and convincing evidence it made no use of immunized testimony.[111]

---

[111] Kan. Stat. Ann. § 22–3102(b)(2).

Chapter 14

CONFESSIONS

Table of Sections

§ 144 "Confessions" and Admissibility

Among the most frequently raised evidentiary issues in criminal litigation are those relating to the admissibility of self-incriminating admissions by the defendant. These issues are the subject of the present chapter.

Traditional analysis sometimes required inquiry into whether a self-incriminating statement by a defendant was a "confession"—a statement admitting all facts necessary for conviction of the crime at issue—or an "admission"—an acknowledgment of one or more facts tending to prove guilt but not of all the facts necessary to do so. Most major limitations upon the admissibility of confessions now also apply to admissions and even exculpatory statements. This chapter, therefore, will assume unless a particular discussion requires otherwise that no distinction need be drawn among self-incriminating acknowledgements.

Confessions are out-of-court statements quite frequently offered to prove the truth of matters asserted therein and thus are potentially subject to exclusion pursuant to the prohibition against hearsay. Nevertheless, there is general agreement that the prosecution is entitled to introduce confessions, although the conceptual basis for this position is somewhat unclear.

Given the general principle that defendants' confessions are admissible to prove guilt, confession law becomes primarily a collection of rules that prevent the use of particular categories of confessions. To some extent, some confession law rules are examples of the sort of exclusionary sanctions discussed in Chapter 15. Under these, exclusion of confessions is mandated by a perceived need to implement policies other than the accurate ascertainment of the "truth." For example, the requirement that confessions be excluded if they are shown to be sufficiently related to an unlawful arrest is designed to maximize compliance with the rules governing arrest and prompt presentation.

The traditional voluntariness mandate,[1] on the other hand, is more closely related to the objective of accurate ascertainment of guilt or innocence at trial. Whether the modern voluntariness demand and other confession law requirements—such as the well-known *Miranda v. Arizona*[2] rules[3]—still do and should serve that function, perhaps among others, is a major issue in modern confession law.

§ 145 *Corpus Delicti* or Corroboration Requirement: (a) In General

Almost all American jurisdictions have some form of a rule requiring corroboration of at least some out-of-court statements by the accused otherwise admissible against that accused in a criminal prosecution. The rule has sometimes been incorporated into statute or court rule. Constitutional considerations, however, most likely do not demand it.

There are several quite different formulations of the requirement, some of which are variations of what is often called the requirement of independent proof of the *corpus delicti*. Another, applied by the federal courts and some state tribunals, is a more flexible approach. The two basic approaches are described in two sections that follow.

This section addresses some general aspects of the rule, focusing upon the rationale for it, whether it does (and should) address evidence sufficiency, admissibility, or both, and whether it is a matter for the judge, the jury, or perhaps both.

Rationale for Requirement.[4] The requirement has traditionally been based upon concern that convictions might result from false confessions. Widespread agreement remains that the need to assure accuracy of convictions remains at least a major basis for the requirement. There has, however, been no consensus on the nature and sources of inaccuracy that support the rule.

Traditionally and generally, the requirement appears to have a relatively modest objective—protecting against the risk of conviction for a crime that never occurred. Thus the target inaccuracies are very limited. A Maryland court, for example, commented that

---

[1]   See infra § 149.

[2]   384 U.S. 436 (1966).

[3]   See infra §§ 150–153.

[4]   Different formulations of the requirement, see infra §§ 146 & 147, might, of course, be supported by somewhat different rationales.

the requirement serves the limited purpose of preventing a mentally unstable person from confessing to and being convicted of a crime that never occurred.

Sometimes, however, the objectives are stated more broadly although frequently quite generally. The Delaware court, for example, asserted that its rule "serves to protect those defendants who may be pressured to confess to crimes that they either did not commit or crimes that did not occur." The Washington court indicated that the rule is designed to combat, first, risks of inaccuracy arising from misinterpretation or misreporting by witnesses who testify to what defendants admitted and, second, risks of inaccuracy with regard to what defendants said. These latter sources of inaccuracy, the court continued, include not only force or coercion but also the possibilities that a confession was "based upon a mistaken perception of the facts or law." The Michigan Supreme Court indicated that the requirement serves "to minimize the weight of a confession and require collateral evidence to support a conviction," which it regarded as desirable on the apparent assumption that confessions are of dubious reliability and prosecutors should be encouraged to develop and use other evidence of guilt.

Whether considerations beyond accuracy can also support the requirement is doubtful. It has been argued that the corroboration requirement serves to combat improper police practices in securing confessions generally, and thus serves to discourage law enforcement actions offensive for reasons other than inaccuracy. At best, however, the requirement achieves this objective indirectly, and the function is almost certainly more effectively accomplished by other legal requirements relating to confessions.

Admissibility, Evidence Sufficiency, or Both? Many formulations of the corroboration rule put it as a matter of admissibility of a confession, often in addition to its role as a measure of evidence sufficiency. Reported decisions often contain appellate courts' expressions of expectation that trial judges will demand sufficient other evidence before permitting the prosecution to put evidence of an out-of-court confession before the jury. Despite their general statements, appellate courts have been unwilling to enforce any requirement of admissibility by reversing convictions supported by sufficient evidence because the trial court failed to require that evidence before admitting the confession. Trial judges' discretion regarding the order of proof permits them to in effect admit confessions subject to later presentation by the prosecution of the required corroborating evidence. It may be that any formal requirement of admissibility is relatively meaningless as a practical matter because trial judges will know that noncompliance will seldom or never lead to appellate reversal.

Appellate reversals of convictions on the basis of the rule are sometimes put as reversals for the procedural error of admitting a confession in violation of the rule. This, of course, indicates the rule is only a procedural one and appellate reversals for its violation are not findings of evidence sufficiency automatically requiring acquittals.

The Alaska Court of Appeals in *Langevin v. State*[5] addressed the matter at length. It acknowledged that "the majority position in this country is that a defendant is entitled to an acquittal if the government introduces evidence of the defendant's out-of-court confession but fails to satisfy the *corpus delicti* rule." This, it concluded, is based on a perception of the rule that makes adequate corroborating evidence an "implicit element" of the charged offense. Alaska, however, has an "evidentiary foundation" conception of

---

5   258 P.3d 866 (Alaska Ct. App. 2011).

the corroboration rule under which the rule simply addresses whether a trial judge should permit the prosecution to introduce an out-of-court admission or confession as part of its case. When raised on appellate review of a conviction, the rule permits at most a finding that the trial judge procedurally erred and the convicted appellant is entitled to a new trial.

As *Langevin* recognized, most appellate courts treat the corroboration requirement as applied on appellate review as relating to evidence sufficiency, perhaps as well as admissibility. Consequently, a convicted defendant who prevails on appeal is entitled to acquittal.

Nevertheless, the theoretical admissibility requirement of the corroboration rule remains firmly entrenched. When the Utah court jettisoned the *corpus delicti* approach and adopted the trustworthiness standard, for example, it turned explicitly to whether the rule as retained should continue to serve a "gatekeeping" function by imposing an admissibility requirement. Citing only its recognition that no other type of evidence is as potentially prejudicial to defendants as confessions, it held:

> [B]efore a confession may be admitted, the trial court must determine as a matter of law that the confession is trustworthy. When making its determination, the trial court must review the totality of the circumstances. Only after a confession is deemed trustworthy by a preponderance of the evidence may it be admitted into evidence.[6]

The rationale generally given for the corroboration requirement, as discussed above, does not argue for the rule as a limit on admissibility. A rule of admissibility has been defended as encouraging objective jury determinations of whether the prosecution has proved crimes were committed, but unless jury verdicts on that matter are required mid-trial, a rule of admissibility does not well serve this objective.

The only possible basis for an admissibility requirement must rest on a need to encourage the trial judge to scrutinize carefully the non-confession evidence before deciding to let the prosecution prove a confession and, in all probability, go to the jury. A judge may do this more objectively if forced to do it towards the end of the prosecution's case by marshaling the evidence to decide if the prosecution should be permitted to introduce the confession as the finale of its presentation.

Whether this is a needed practice by trial judges, and if so whether it can actually be compelled by a rule of confession admissibility, is at best doubtful. On balance, there is no reason for the corroboration requirement to be framed or discussed as one of admissibility. The courts should stop pretending that it is a rule of this sort.

Judge, Jury, or Both? Is the requirement only for the court or should the jury be instructed to apply it as well? Wigmore assumes that the trial judge applies the rule first, and if the case goes to the jury the "same question" is then posed for the jury. The jury must then address, "without reference to the judge's ruling, whether the corroboration exists to satisfy them."[7] Some courts regard the jury as playing no role in applying the requirement. At least a few appear to conceptualize the jury's evaluation as the major one, with the judge's ruling merely a preliminary screening decision. Insofar

---

[6]   State v. Mauchley, 67 P.3d 477, 490 (Utah 2003).

[7]   7 Wigmore, Evidence § 2073, at 531 (Chadbourn rev. 1978).

as the rule is one of evidence sufficiency, its nature suggests that the jury should at least play a role in its application.

Other courts have taken far different approaches. The Court of Appeals for the District of Columbia Circuit reasoned that as applied in the federal system, the corroboration requirement is "something of a hybrid rule having elements both of admissibility and sufficiency." Juries, of course, are to evaluate the credibility of confession evidence and the sufficiency of the evidence as a whole, but the corroboration rule does not add anything specific to the jury's consideration of these matters. Thus, it concluded, a jury charge is not required[8] or, apparently, even appropriate. Several other federal courts of appeals have agreed.

The District of Columbia Court of Appeals in 2011 joined "[t]he majority of jurisdictions that have considered this issue" and held that the sufficiency of corroboration evidence is not a matter for jury consideration. It relied in large part on the unacceptability of an approach that would empower juries to "overrule" trial judges' decisions that confessions are adequately corroborated.[9] Characterization of the rule as one of substantive law defining evidence sufficiency does not require that the issue be submitted to the jury, a Maryland court concluded. It is best viewed as establishing a requirement of sufficient evidence to go the jury rather than one of sufficiency of evidence to convict for jury application.[10]

An instruction demanding the jury consider whether the prosecution has presented sufficient corroborating evidence may be too ambitious to be of practical value. The Alaska Court of Appeals explained:

> Under this approach, if the trial judge rules that *corpus delicti* is satisfied, the jury would hear the defendant's confession, only to later be asked to set the confession to one side and determine whether the government's remaining evidence is sufficient to establish the *corpus delicti*. One might doubt whether jurors, having heard the defendant's confession to a heinous crime, could dispassionately discharge this duty.[11]

Statements to Which the Requirement Applies. There is widespread agreement that the requirement, whatever the local formulation of it, applies not only to "confessions", defined as complete and conscious admissions of guilt of a crime, but also to "admissions"—acknowledgments of facts relevant to guilt—because these involve the risks which the requirement is designed to reduce. Most courts at least assume it applies to statements intended when made to be exonerating—so-called "exculpatory statements"—but this position has been challenged. The requirement is not limited to statements made to law enforcement officers and consequently applies to statements made to private persons. It does not, however, apply to incriminating statements made prior to or during the offense.

---

8   U.S. v. Dickerson, 163 F.3d 639, 641–43 (D.C. Cir. 1999).

9   Fowler v. U.S., 31 A.3d 88, 91–93 (D.C. 2011).

10   Riggins v. State, 843 A.2d 115, 141 (Md. Ct. Spec. App. 2004).

11   *Langevin,* 258 P.3d at 870.

§ 146 *Corpus Delicti* or Corroboration Requirement: (b) Requirement of Independent Proof of the *Corpus Delicti*

The traditional formulation of the corroboration requirement, still applied by many jurisdictions, demands that there be some evidence other than the confession that tends to establish the *corpus delicti*. Generally, the evidence need not do so beyond a reasonable doubt. If sufficient independent evidence exists, that independent evidence and the confession may both be considered in determining whether guilt has been proved beyond a reasonable doubt. Only "slight" corroborating evidence is often required, and this can be circumstantial as well as direct.

There is some dispute regarding the definition of *corpus delicti*, which literally means the "body of the crime." To establish guilt in a criminal case, the prosecution must ordinarily show that (a) the injury or harm constituting the crime occurred; (b) this injury or harm was done in a criminal manner; and (c) the defendant was the person who inflicted the injury or harm. Wigmore maintains that *corpus delicti* means only the first of these, that is, "the fact of the specific loss or injury sustained," and does not require proof that this was occasioned by anyone's criminal agency.[12] Some courts have agreed.

Most courts, however, define *corpus delicti* as involving both (a) and (b). This means that the corroborating evidence must tend to show the harm or injury and that it was occasioned by criminal activity. It need not, however, in any manner tend to show that the defendant was the guilty party. Thus, in a homicide case, the *corpus delicti* consists of proof that the victim died and that the death was caused by a criminal act, but it need not tend to connect the defendant on trial with that act.

The traditional approach has been to require that the elements of the offense be carefully distinguished and that the corroborating evidence tends to show each of those elements. A growing number of courts, however, are abandoning the strict requirement that the corroborating evidence always tend to prove all elements of the *corpus delicti*. Thus the corroborating evidence need only tend to show the "major" or "essential" harm involved in the offense charged and not all of the elements technically distinguished. This tendency is most pronounced in homicide cases, where defendants are often tried for offenses that involve requirements beyond simply the causing of death in a criminal manner.

This approach is somewhat troublesome as applied to certain modern crimes that—unlike homicide offenses—do not involve a single and tangible injury or loss that can readily be characterized as constituting the "major" or "essential" harm involved in the offense. This is arguably the case, for example, where the crime is an inchoate one, such as conspiracy or attempt. Nevertheless, creative analysis in defining the essential features of even such crimes permits application of the modern *corpus delicti* approach to such offenses.

State v. Angulo,[13] illustrates the trend and its possible implication. Defendant Angulo's confession to penetration and thus rape of a child was used although the corroborating evidence did not tend to establish penetration but only acts constituting molestation or attempted rape. Finding no error, the appellate court relied in part on the

---

[12]   Wigmore, Evidence § 2072, at 524–25 (Chadbourn rev. 1978).

[13]   200 P.3d 752 (Wash. Ct. App. 2009).

fact that the gravamen of the child rape—a sexual act with a minor—was corroborated. Perhaps the *corpus delicti* should be so defined as including only the gravamen of the offense. *Angulo* went on, however, to more questionably add that the corroboration requirement is designed to assure only whether *a* crime was committed, not *which* crime was committed. Thus the corroborating evidence need only indicate that the events or incident on which the prosecution is based involved some crime. This is quite likely an erroneous conclusion regarding the function served by the requirement and an overstatement of implications of general trend toward flexible definitions of the *corpus delicti* needing corroboration.

Felony murder cases have presented special difficulty. Under the traditional application of the *corpus delicti* formulation, the elements of felony murder include the predicate felony as well as the fact of death and the causing of it in a criminal way; thus, corroborating evidence would have to tend to prove that predicate felony. Most courts, however, have balked at this and have held that the corroborating evidence need not tend to prove the predicate felony.

The general rule in felony murder cases is sometimes regarded as reflecting the general principle that elements affecting only the degree or seriousness of the crime are not part of the *corpus delicti* that needs to be corroborated. Thus in a prosecution for burglary that would be first degree burglary because it was committed in the nighttime, the time of the entry could be proved by the confession alone because the time of entry determined only the degree of burglary committed.

Situations involving multiple related crimes have also posed difficulty under the *corpus delicti* rule. Where an accused is being tried for several offenses, must the prosecution support the application of the *corpus delicti* requirement to each offense, one by one? Under such an approach, the statement may be used only to convict of those offenses also shown by the corroborating evidence. Some courts have clearly relaxed the rule's requirements for these situations. The Pennsylvania court, for example, held that if a statement incriminates the defendant regarding multiple offenses and the prosecution complies with the *corpus delicti* rule regarding one offense, the statement can be used to establish guilt of other offenses if two requirements are met. First, the connection between the crimes must be close. Second, permitting such use of the statement must, on the facts, pose no significant risk of convicting the accused for crimes that did not occur.[14]

Some courts assume that *mens rea* is part of the *corpus delicti* and must be shown by at least some independent evidence. This has not been critically considered, however, and at least several courts have disagreed. On principle, corroboration should be required since *mens rea* is generally necessary to show that the injury or harm constituting the crime was done in a criminal manner. Given the ease of meeting the requirement, requiring some independent proof—which may be circumstantial, of course—from which the necessary mental state can be inferred should not be a difficult burden.

---

[14]   Com. v. Taylor, 831 A.2d 587, 596 (Pa. 2003).

§ 147 *Corpus Delicti* or Corroboration Requirement: (c) Requirement of Evidence Tending to Establish Truthfulness of Statement

Some jurisdictions have, to some extent at least, rejected the traditional requirement of independent evidence tending to prove the *corpus delicti* of the charged offense in favor of an alternative standard for determining whether a confession is adequately corroborated. This alternative approach is based on the United States Supreme Court's analysis developed in *Opper v. United States.*[15]

In *Opper,* the Court held as a matter of federal evidence law that a conviction in federal court could not rest upon an uncorroborated confession. The "better rule," *Opper* continued without extensive explanation, would not require that the corroborating evidence establish the *corpus delicti* but rather that it be "substantial independent evidence which would tend to establish the truthfulness of the statement." In *Smith v. United States,*[16] the Court added that *Opper* requires corroboration for those elements of an offense "established by admissions alone." Some state courts and a few legislatures have adopted this position. In 2003, for example, the Utah Supreme Court carefully examined the matter in *State v. Mauchley*[17] and adopted *Opper's* analysis.

Some jurisdictions take more complicated approaches. In 2014, for example, the Tennessee Supreme Court—drawing on decisions from New Mexico and New Jersey— adopted what it called a "modified trustworthiness approach:"

> When a defendant challenges the admission of his extrajudicial confession on lack-of-corroboration grounds, the trial court should begin by asking whether the charged offense is one that involves a tangible injury. If the answer is yes, then the State must provide substantial independent evidence tending to show that the defendant's statement is trustworthy, plus independent prima facie evidence that the injury actually occurred. If the answer is no, then the State must provide substantial independent evidence tending to show that the defendant's statement is trustworthy, and the evidence must link the defendant to the crime.
>
> When the crime involves a tangible injury, the State must present independent prima facie evidence that the loss or injury actually occurred. Unlike the traditional *corpus delicti* rule, the State is not required to demonstrate that the injury resulted from someone's criminal act. Nor must the State link the defendant to the injury.
>
> Whether or not the charged offense involved a tangible injury, the corroboration rule requires the State to introduce substantial independent evidence that the defendant's confession is trustworthy. To establish trustworthiness, the State's independent evidence must corroborate essential facts contained in the defendant's statement.[18]

One advantage of the trustworthiness approach is that its flexibility permits it to provide some—and arguably adequate—protection against conviction on the basis of inaccurate confessions to nonexistent crimes while avoiding serious problems sometimes

---

[15] 348 U.S. 84 (1954).

[16] 348 U.S. 147 (1954).

[17] 67 P.3d 477 (Utah 2003).

[18] State v. Bishop, 431 S.W.3d 22, 58–59 (Tenn. 2014).

involved in the *corpus delicti* formulation. Application of the *corpus delicti* formulation may have been a relatively simple task that accomplished the purpose of the corroboration requirement when crimes were few and were defined in simple and concise terms. But modern statutory criminal law has increased the number and complexity of crimes. Simply identifying the elements of the *corpus delicti* thus provides fertile ground for dispute. Requiring that the corroborating evidence tends to establish each element once the *corpus delicti* is defined may pose an unrealistic burden upon the prosecution without significantly furthering the requirement's objective of providing assurance against conviction on the basis of inaccurate confessions. This is especially the case with regard to crimes that may not have a tangible *corpus delicti*, such as attempt offenses, conspiracy, tax evasion and similar offenses. The modern approach of requiring corroboration of only the "major" or "essential" harm involved in an offense, although conceptually reasonable, may often founder on difficulty in identifying the major or essential harm.

As the Utah court stressed in *Mauchley*, the prosecution may under the trustworthiness approach use independent evidence of the crime to show a statement's trustworthiness. Where such evidence is lacking, it added, the prosecution may rely on the same types of evidence used in other areas to bolster the credibility and reliability of an out-of-court statement:

> [These f]actors . . . include the following: evidence as to the spontaneity of the statement; the absence of deception, trick, threats, or promises to obtain the statement; the defendant's positive physical and mental condition, including age, education, and experience; and the presence of an attorney when the statement is given.[19]

The trustworthiness approach has the further—and perhaps more important— benefit of providing some protection against convictions based on false confessions to actual crimes. As implemented, the trustworthiness standard in at least some cases demands production by the prosecution of evidence confirming not simply the occurrence of the charged crimes but the defendants' identity as the perpetrators.

As applied to modern crimes, in summary, the trustworthiness approach is most likely easier than the *corpus delicti* rule to apply, as effective in accomplishing the modest realistic traditional objectives of the corroboration requirement, provides some protection against false admissions to actual crimes, and is less likely to lead to occasionally unreasonable results.

§ 148 *Corpus Delicti* or Corroboration Requirement: (d) Future of the Requirement

Wigmore maintains that no corroboration rule is needed and that existing corroboration requirements are, in the hands of unscrupulous defense counsel, "a positive obstruction to the course of justice."[20] Commentators have often agreed.

Given the development of other confession law doctrines, especially Fifth Amendment protections as promulgated in *Miranda v. Arizona*[21] and the voluntariness requirement, concerns regarding law enforcement interrogation practices do not provide

---

[19]   *Mauchley*, 67 P.3d at 489.
[20]   7 Wigmore, Evidence § 2070, at 510 (Chadbourn rev. 1978).
[21]   384 U.S. 436 (1966). See generally infra § 150.

significant support for the corroboration requirement. Whether courts can justify retaining the doctrine for the purpose of encouraging investigatory techniques other than interrogation with reasonable expectation of success is at best questionable; the corroboration requirement as applied most likely provides little significant pressure for pursuing such alternatives.

Similarly, the requirement as administered is quite unlikely to provide much protection against inaccuracies resulting from mistakes in reporting, suspects' misunderstandings of the law or facts, or pressures too subtle to invoke *Miranda* or voluntariness protection. Any protection the requirement provides against false confessions by mentally disturbed persons could as well be provided by careful scrutiny of the evidence by conscientious judges. The requirement may, however, serve to trigger such scrutiny in appropriate cases by trial judges otherwise too rushed by the press of business to recognize such evidentiary deficiencies. Generally speaking, there is still some reason to be concerned about convictions for offenses never committed, and a reasonable corroboration requirement serves to provide some protection at minimal cost.

If a requirement of corroboration is to be retained, the complexity of the *corpus delicti* approach—as discussed in Section 146—tends only to detract from the requirement's real function. The "truthfulness" approach—discussed in Section 147—is best designed to pursue the realistic objectives of a corroboration requirement. Those objectives should include the provision of some protection from inaccurate convictions for actual crimes.

There is insufficient justification for treating the rule as one related to admissibility of defendant's admissions. The requirement should be only one of evidence sufficiency. If juries are adequately instructed on the prosecution's burden of proof, there is no need to submit the corroboration requirement to those juries. The rule should be one applied by trial judges and appellate courts, not juries.

Thus, a trial judge should have a duty to assure, if the prosecution's case rests for all practical purposes upon the defendant's out-of-court confession or admission, that the prosecution has produced reasonable evidence other than that confession or admission to establish the trustworthiness of the confession or admission. On appeal from a conviction, the issue should be whether the record contains sufficient evidence to justify a reasonable judge or jury in concluding the confession or admission is trustworthy.

§ 149 Voluntariness, in General

The common law rule requiring voluntariness of an out-of-court confession as a condition for admission into evidence was developed only in the mid-1700s. Early discussions made clear that the rationale for the requirement was the perceived lack of reliability of statements motivated not by guilt but by a desire to avoid discomfort or to secure some favor.

In its first confession case, *Hopt v. Utah*,[22] the Supreme Court of the United States adopted as a matter of federal evidence law what it characterized as the well-developed common law requirement of voluntariness. That requirement, the Court explained, commands that a confession be held inadmissible:

---

[22] 110 U.S. 574 (1884).

when the confession appears to have been made either in consequence of inducements of a temporal nature, held out by one in authority, touching the charge preferred, or because of a threat or promise by or in the presence of such a person, which, operating upon the fears or hopes of the accused, in reference to the charge, deprives him of that freedom of will or self-control essential to make his confession voluntary within the meaning of the law.[23]

Thirteen years later, in *Bram v. United States*,[24] the Court commented that whenever an issue arises in federal criminal trials as to the voluntariness of a confession, "the issue is controlled by that portion of the Fifth Amendment to the Constitution of the United States, commanding that no person 'shall be compelled in any criminal case to be a witness against himself.' " This, the Court continued, embodies the common law rule of voluntariness.

Because the Fifth Amendment was not held binding on the states until 1964, the *Bram* analysis did not impose the voluntariness requirement upon the states as a matter of federal constitutional law. The Court's 1936 holding in *Brown v. Mississippi*,[25] however, made clear that a state court conviction resting upon a confession extorted by brutality and violence violated the accused's general right to due process guaranteed by the Fourteenth Amendment. Subsequent cases established that any use in a state criminal proceeding of a coerced confession violated the federal standard. After the Fifth Amendment was applied to the states, the Court characterized the due process standard developed in *Brown* and its progeny as "the same general standard which [is] applied in federal prosecutions, a standard grounded in the policies of the privilege against self-incrimination."

Despite the traditional emphasis upon the federal constitutional requirement of voluntariness, state constitutional and evidence law in most if not all jurisdictions also imposes similar requirements.

In *Blackburn v. Alabama*,[26] the Supreme Court explained that "a complex of values underlies the stricture against use by the state of confessions which, by way of convenient shorthand, this Court terms involuntary." The traditional criterion for determining the admissibility of a confession challenged under the federal constitutional voluntariness requirement was articulated by Justice Frankfurter in 1961:

> The ultimate test . . . [is] voluntariness. Is the confession the product of an essentially free and unconstrained choice by its maker? If it is, if he has willed to confess, it may be used against him. If it is not, if his will has been overborne and his capacity for self-determination critically impaired, the use of his confession offends due process.[27]

Physical coercion or the threat of it, of course, necessarily shows that the defendant's will was overborne and his confession involuntary. But the Court was increasingly presented with claims of "psychological" rather than physical coercion. Application of the voluntariness standard became more difficult as cases increasingly

---

[23] *Id.* at 585.
[24] 168 U.S. 532 (1897).
[25] 297 U.S. 278 (1936).
[26] 361 U.S. 199 (1960).
[27] Culombe v. Connecticut, 367 U.S. 568, 602 (1961).

relied upon these claims of more subtle influences than were presented by the earlier decisions.

Since 1961 the constitutional question of voluntariness has been carefully distinguished from the question of the accuracy or reliability of particular confessions. In *Rogers v. Richmond,*[28] the Court held that due process did not permit a trial court to resolve the admissibility of a confession challenged on voluntariness grounds by using "a legal standard which took into account the circumstances of probable truth or falsity." Evidence that a challenged confession (or some subpart of it) is accurate, then, is totally irrelevant to the voluntariness inquiry.

In *Colorado v. Connelly,*[29] the Court held that the Fourteenth Amendment's due process requirement of voluntariness imposed no absolute requirement that a confession reflect "an essentially free and unconstrained choice" by the defendant. Official and coercive activity "is a necessary predicate to the finding that a confession is not 'voluntary' within the meaning of the Due Process Clause of the Fourteenth Amendment." In the absence of this predicate, a showing that a confession reflected little or no meaningful choice by the defendant—because of private coercion or undisclosed mental impairment, for example—does not does not even raise an issue as to federal due process voluntariness.

Connelly provided little guidance for determining what constitutes the official coercion necessary to require the Fourteenth Amendment analysis to proceed to the mind of the suspect. *Connelly's* facts illustrate the difficulty. Connelly's statement was made in response to hallucinatory voices, but the officer who took it was unaware of Connelly's impairment. The Court summarily concluded that the taking and later the trial use of Connelly's statement to the officer did not violate the Fourteenth Amendment. It appeared to distinguish *Blackburn v. Alabama*[30] on the basis that in *Blackburn* police learned during interrogation that Blackburn had a history of mental problems. Nevertheless, they continued the interrogation and "exploited this weakness with coercive tactics" such as prolonged questioning in a tiny room. Exploitation of a known impairment in a manner that impairs the suspect's ability to decide whether to confess can constitute the coercion necessary for involuntariness.

Pre-*Connelly* Supreme Court case law reflected consideration of numerous factors in evaluating a voluntariness challenge. The Court gave significant weight to the time of the day or night of the interrogation, the length of interrogation, the quality of the conditions in which the defendant was held before confessing, and similar matters. These have been evaluated in light of various characteristics of the accused that presumably affect the impact of these factors upon the accused. Thus the Court has found suggestion of involuntariness in the accused's youth, physical illness, injury, or infirmity, low educational level, and little or no prior experience with law enforcement practices and techniques. Whether or not officers warned the suspect of his right to silence and explained that right, where there is no specific obligation to do so, is relevant to voluntariness; in any case, the extent of the suspect's actual appreciation of his rights is clearly significant. These factors remain relevant under *Connelly*, but only after official coercive activity has been found.

---

[28]   365 U.S. 534 (1961).

[29]   479 U.S. 157 (1986).

[30]   361 U.S. 199 (1960).

More recently, on the other hand, the Court in *Bobby v. Dixon*[31] disapproved of the lower court's position that involuntariness was at least strongly suggested by proof that officers urged the defendant to "cut a deal" before his accomplice did so. Nothing in the Court's holdings suggests, it explained, that officers may not do this.

The Supreme Court's due process voluntariness law contains no hint that voluntariness necessarily and always requires awareness of the legal right to refuse to make a self-incriminating statement. To the contrary, in a general review of voluntariness law, the Court commented that in none of its decisions had the Court required that the prosecution prove "as part of its initial burden" on voluntariness that the defendant was aware of his right to refuse to answer police queries. Although the defendant's awareness of his right is relevant, like nearly all other considerations it is to be considered in evaluating the totality of the circumstances.

One court effectively summarized the analysis:

> Many factors can bear on the voluntariness of a confession. . . . [W]e look to all elements of the interrogation, including the manner in which it was conducted, the number of officers present, and the age, education, and experience of the defendant. Not all of the multitude of factors that may bear on voluntariness are necessarily of equal weight, however. Some are transcendent and decisive. We have made clear, for example, that a confession that is preceded or accompanied by threats or a promise of advantage will be held involuntary, notwithstanding any other factors that may suggest voluntariness, unless the State can establish that such threats or promises in no way induced the confession. A confession that is preceded or accompanied by any physical mistreatment would obviously be regarded in the same way. Those kinds of factors are coercive as a matter of law. When shown to be present, the State has a very heavy burden, indeed, of proving that they did not induce the confession.

> Other factors, such as the length of interrogation, team or sequential questioning, the age, education, experience, or physical or mental attributes of the defendant, do not have that broad, decisive kind of quality but assume significance, and may become decisive, only in the context of a particular case— based on the actual extent of their coercive effect. Lying between these two kinds of factors is a third—factors that may not be coercive as a matter of law but that need to be given special weight whenever they exist.[32]

As this makes clear, the analysis has considerable flexibility.

State constitutional, statutory or case law requirements of voluntariness need not, of course, be construed as having the same contents as the due process requirement. Of course, state law cannot make admissible statements involuntary under the federal constitutional case law. It can, however, impose additional limits upon admissibility of statements voluntary under due process law. These limits, unlike due process voluntariness, most likely can emphasize reliability as the benchmark for admissibility. A Georgia statute, for example, makes a confession inadmissible if it was "induced by . . . the slightest hope of benefit or remotest fear of injury."[33] The Georgia court has

---

[31]   565 U.S. 23 (2011).

[32]   Williams v. State, 825 A.2d 1078, 1092–93 (Md. 2003).

[33]   Ga. Code Ann. § 24–8–824.

construed this statute when applied to confessions voluntary under due process analysis as requiring state law scrutiny focusing on whether hope of benefit or fear of injury affected the reliability of the confessions.

As lower courts confront the implications of *Connelly's* limitations on federal due process voluntariness, they may be receptive to arguments that statutory or state constitutional voluntariness requirements are not subject to an absolute requirement of official coercion. Such arguments may find support in pre-*Connelly* state cases imposing absolute requirements that confessing defendants have made meaningful decisions to confess.

§ 150 Self-Incrimination (*Miranda*) Requirements: (a) In General

In 1966, the Supreme Court, clearly dissatisfied with the due process voluntariness requirement, decided *Miranda v. Arizona.*[34] This decision revolutionized federal constitutional confession law and has become the focus of subsequent confession law development and analysis.

On the doctrinal level, *Miranda's* significance lies, first, in its holding that custodial law enforcement interrogation implicates the Fifth Amendment's privilege against compelled self-incrimination even though police have no legal authority to compel answers to their questions. "As a practical matter," the Court reasoned, "the compulsion to speak in the isolated setting of the police station may well be greater than in courts or other official investigations [where the legal power to compel answers may be exercised]."

The focus of the Court's concern in *Miranda* was what the Court perceived as the "inherently compelling pressures" of custodial interrogation. Without proper safeguards, the Court reasoned, these will inevitably work "to undermine the individual's will to resist and to compel him to speak where he would not otherwise do so freely." Modern in-custody interrogation, it stressed, is "psychologically rather than physically oriented" and inherently involves "compulsion." In the absence of protective devices, therefore, "no statement obtained from the defendant [in this context] can truly be the product of free choice."

To provide the protective devices necessary to protect the privilege in the custodial interrogation context, the Court developed what have come to be characterized as per se or "prophylactic" rules. These are requirements designed to assure that specific decisions are legally acceptable but which, for protective purposes, apply even to situations where on the facts the suspects' decisions may not have fallen below standards imposed by the law. A confession obtained in violation of these requirements must, as a matter of Fifth Amendment law, be excluded from evidence even if application of voluntariness standards to the particular facts of the case would not lead to a finding that the confession was involuntary.

Although this has been somewhat overshadowed by later developments, it is clear that the *Miranda* Court regarded the major source of protection for those undergoing custodial interrogation to be the right to an attorney. The suspect's Fifth Amendment interests, reasoned the majority, can only be protected by affording the suspect an attendant right to counsel. This means not simply the right to consult with counsel before

---

[34] 384 U.S. 436 (1966). The Court explicitly declined to overrule *Miranda* in 2000. Dickerson v. U.S., 530 U.S. 428, 443–44 (2000).

questioning, "but also to have counsel present during any interrogation . . . ." Counsel must be available regardless of the financial ability of the suspect. Consequently, an attorney must be provided at public expense for those indigent defendants who wish the assistance of counsel.

The most well-known *Miranda* requirement is that of warnings. While "no talismanic incantation" of the language used in the opinion is necessary, officers must give the suspect essentially the following admonitions:

1.   You have the right to remain silent;

2.   Anything you say can [and will] be used against you in court;

3.   You have the right to consult with a lawyer and to have the lawyer with you during interrogation; and

4.   If you cannot afford an attorney, one will be appointed for you prior to any questioning if you so desire.

The first three elements are "absolute prerequisite[s]" to acceptable custodial interrogation. Failure to give even one of them cannot be "cured" by evidence that the suspect was already aware of the substance of the omitted warning[s]. Omission of the fourth element, on the other hand, is not fatal if the suspect was known to already have an attorney or to have ample funds to secure one. If, however, there is any doubt as to the applicability of the fourth element, this will be resolved against the prosecution. The warnings must be given prior to any interrogation.

Neither the right to remain silent nor its attendant right to counsel during interrogation is mandatory. Both are subject to waiver. In all cases where the prosecution offers at trial a self-incriminating statement made during custodial interrogation, it must show a voluntary and intelligent waiver of the privilege against self-incrimination itself, that is, the right to silence. If the statement was made during interrogation at which no lawyer was present on the suspect's behalf, the prosecution must also show an effective waiver of the right to counsel.

Miranda waivers need not be "express," the Court reaffirmed in *North Carolina v. Butler*.[35] Obviously, evidence that the suspect specifically articulated that she was aware of the right and was choosing not to exercise it constitutes strong, but not necessary, evidence of waiver. At the other extreme, *Miranda* itself expressly stated that waivers would not be presumed from a suspect's silence after the warnings or from the fact that the suspect eventually provided a confession. The showing required of the fact of waiver, and the possible need under some circumstances to assert the *Miranda* rights, are addressed more fully in Section 152; the voluntariness and intelligence required is considered in Section 153.

Special problems are presented if officers interrogate a suspect in violation of *Miranda*, they then comply with *Miranda* and again interrogate the suspect, and the prosecution offers only incriminating admissions made after compliance. A split majority of the Court in *Missouri v. Seibert*[36] addressed these situations. Seven years later a unanimous Court applied *Seibert* in *Bobby v. Dixon*.[37]

---

35   441 U.S. 369 (1979).

36   542 U.S. 600 (2004).

37   565 U.S. 23 (2011) (per curiam).

In *Seibert* itself, the first interrogation was productive and Seibert gave a quite complete confession which she repeated after the interrogating officer complied with *Miranda*. Further, the testimony indicated that the officer had been trained to do this for the explicit purpose of obtaining incriminating admissions in disregard of *Miranda*, then complying with *Miranda*, and finally soliciting admissions after this compliance on the assumption that the later admissions could be used in evidence. *Seibert* clearly disapproved of this activity, but the majority split on the rationale.

The *Seibert* plurality reasoned that the key consideration was whether the *Miranda* warnings could be effective in this context involving a single coordinated and continuing interrogation. The warnings could not be effective, the plurality concluded, because a warned suspect led through questions the suspect answered shortly before is unlikely to understand the warning as giving the suspect a meaningful right to remain silent during the latter part of the interrogation. The officer's subjective intention is apparently relevant but it is not the focus of the analysis. Justice Kennedy, the fifth member of the *Seibert* majority, found controlling the officer's deliberate use of a two-step strategy to undermine the *Miranda* requirements. Where an officer acts with such an intention, the postwarning admissions should be inadmissible unless the officer has taken effective curative measures before those admissions were elicited.

Dixon, an unsigned opinion, found *Seibert* inapplicable to the facts before the Court with no discussion of the effect of the split Court in *Seibert*. *Dixon* stressed that the prewarning statement did not admit involvement in the murder at issue and police did not use that statement to elicit the postwarning confession to the murder. Moreover, four hours passed and circumstances dramatically changed between the two interrogation sessions. Thus "Dixon received *Miranda* warnings before confessing to [the] murder [and] the effectiveness of those warnings was not impaired by the sort of 'two-step interrogation technique' condemned in *Seibert* . . . ."

Despite the rigor with which the *Miranda* Court fashioned per se Fifth Amendment requirements out of the very general language of the constitutional provision, post-*Miranda* decisions have shown no inclination to continue this approach by developing more such requirements. This was made obvious in *Moran v. Burbine*,[38] rejecting a per se rule requiring police to inform a suspect of an attorney's efforts to reach him. The Court acknowledged that such a rule "might add marginally to *Miranda's* goal of dispelling the compulsion inherent in custodial interrogation." "[O]verriding practical considerations," however, argued against such a rule. The complexity that would accompany any such rule would decrease *Miranda's* clarity and ease of application. Further, such a requirement would cause some suspects to decline to make voluntary but self-incriminating statements and thus "work a substantial and . . . inappropriate shift in the subtle balance struck in [*Miranda*]."

State courts are, of course, free to read state constitutional self-incrimination provisions as imposing the same requirements which *Miranda* found in the Fifth Amendment privilege. Such action would seem to be a prerequisite to state law holdings that state law imposes more stringent versions of specific *Miranda* requirements than are demanded by Supreme Court case law. A few state courts have explicitly embraced a version of the *Miranda* requirements as independently required by their state constitutions.

---

[38]   475 U.S. 412 (1986).

§ 151　Self-Incrimination (*Miranda*) Requirements: (b) Applicability of *Miranda*; "Custody," "Interrogation," and Exceptions

Miranda v. Arizona[39] applies only if a suspect is in "custody" and is "interrogated." Only if both of these prerequisites exist does a situation present the extreme risks to the suspect's privilege against compelled self-incrimination that justifies the extraordinary protection afforded by the *Miranda* requirements. Each of these terms has become something of a term of art, and their definitions are considered in this section. In addition, the Supreme Court has recognized several exceptional situations in which, despite the existence of both custody and interrogation, either the extreme risks with which *Miranda* is concerned are lacking or those risks are outweighed by countervailing considerations. These exceptions are also addressed here.

Custody. Custody is not limited to "stationhouse custody," but can occur in a suspect's own home. It does not require that the officers' purpose in detaining the suspect relate to the offense which is the subject of the interrogation. On the other hand, not every deprivation of a suspect's liberty constitutes custody.

Custody exists only if the circumstances are such as would cause a reasonable person to perceive that his freedom has been curtailed to a degree associated with a formal arrest. This depends on the objective circumstances of the situation, not on the subjective views of the officer or the suspect.

If an officer makes a formal arrest by explicitly informing the suspect that an arrest has been made, of course, this constitutes custody. In addition, however, a suspect is in custody despite the lack of a formal arrest if the officer detaining the suspect treats the suspect in a manner that a reasonable person would regard as involving an arrest "for practical purposes." Relevant considerations include the length of the detention, any express or implied communication by the officer of the officer's intent to arrest the suspect, and the length, vigor, and subject of questioning and other investigatory efforts by the officer.

Under this approach, a person detained for brief field investigation under what is often called a *Terry* stop is usually not in custody. A motorist subjected to a "traffic stop"—a detention that a reasonable person would perceive as involving issuance of a citation and release—is similarly not in custody.

Interrogation. The meaning of interrogation was addressed in *Rhode Island v. Innis,*[40] refusing to limit *Miranda* to situations involving "express interrogation:"

> [T]he term "interrogation" under *Miranda* refers not only to express questioning, but also to any words or actions on the part of the police (other than those normally attendant to arrest and custody) that the police should know are reasonably likely to elicit an incriminating response from the suspect.[41]

Whether law enforcement conduct is the "functional equivalent" of express questioning focuses primarily upon the perspective of the suspect. Evidence that the words or conduct at issue were intended by the officer to elicit self-incriminating

---

[39]　384 U.S. 436 (1966).

[40]　446 U.S. 291 (1980).

[41]　*Id.* at 301.

admissions from the suspect does not itself establish that interrogation took place. It may, however, tend to show that the officer knew or should have known that the words or conduct were sufficiently likely to elicit the desired response.

Applying the *Innis* standard, the Court has been quite reluctant to characterize situations as involving the functional equivalent of express questioning. *Innis* itself illustrates this approach. A comment by one officer to another—"God forbid one of [the neighborhood's impaired children] might find a weapon . . . and . . . hurt themselves."— in a suspect's presence was held in *Innis* not to constitute interrogation; the facts did not establish that the officers should have been aware that their comments would move the suspect to make a self-incriminating admission as to the location of a gun he had hidden in the area. Permitting a suspect's wife to talk to a suspect arrested for the murder of the couple's young son was similarly held not to constitute interrogation.

Even express questions put to a suspect may not constitute interrogation, if—given the other purposes of the questioning—the risk of those questions eliciting a self-incriminating response is minimal. Police inquiry of a suspect whether he would submit to a blood alcohol test, for example, does not constitute "interrogation." No interrogation took place when an officer explained to a suspect how a breathalyzer examination worked, the legal aspects of the applicable Implied Consent Law and then inquired whether he understood and will be willing to submit to the test. Nor was there interrogation when, during a videotaping, an officer instructed the suspect how he was to perform physical sobriety tests and inquired whether the suspect understood the instructions.

Exceptions to Miranda Requirements. Miranda does not apply to some situations involving both custody and interrogation as those are defined under the Court's case law.

If the questioning is done by an officer functioning in an undercover capacity, the Court held in *Illinois v. Perkins*,[42] *Miranda* has no application. Where a suspect is unaware that he is conversing with his captors, the majority reasoned, the situation does not present the interaction between custody and interrogation creating the risk of coercion that justifies the extraordinary *Miranda* protections. *Miranda* also does not apply, the Court held in *New York v. Quarles*,[43] in certain situations in which police inquiries are supported by particularly pressing concerns for public safety. Where compliance with *Miranda's* mandates would create an immediate and high risk to public safety, the costs are excessive.

A plurality of the Court in *Pennsylvania v. Muniz*[44] recognized another exception for "routine booking questions" asked during the processing of an arrested suspect. This exception, which is almost certain to be accepted by a majority of the Court, covers questions designed to elicit biographical data necessary to complete the booking process and to provide pretrial services. Thus, in *Muniz, Miranda* was regarded by the plurality as inapplicable to questions concerning Muniz's name, address, height, weight, eye color, date of birth, and current age.

---

[42]　496 U.S. 292 (1990).

[43]　467 U.S. 649 (1984).

[44]　96 U.S. 582 (1990).

§ 152 Self-Incrimination (*Miranda*) Requirements: (c) Prohibition Against Interrogation

Under certain—and limited—circumstances, *Miranda v. Arizona*[45] gives a person undergoing custodial interrogation a right not to be interrogated at all. Essentially, the right is one to be free of efforts by officers to persuade the defendant to make a self-incriminating admission or otherwise give up the right to remain silent. In these situations, the risk of any admission being involuntary is sufficient to justify barring all efforts to elicit such an admission.

As an initial matter, interrogation of a suspect in custody is barred until the person has been adequately warned and has waived one or more rights. The case law, however, initially focused on situations in which defendants affirmatively asserted their rights.

Edwards Rule and Reassertion of Waived Right to Counsel. A suspect who has initially waived counsel may, of course, change his mind. If the suspect during permissible interrogation indicates "in any manner" that the suspect now wishes to have the assistance of counsel, interrogation must cease until counsel is present.

In *Edwards v. Arizona*[46] the Supreme Court held that a suspect who had affirmatively invoked his right to counsel could not be further approached by officers until a lawyer was present, even if that approach did not consist of efforts to persuade him to waive his right but only an inquiry regarding his continued unwillingness to do so. Under *Edwards*, police-initiated inquiries regarding possible admissions or questioning are barred until a lawyer is present. *Arizona v. Roberson*[47] made clear that a reapproach is impermissible even if it concerns a different offense than that under actual or possible discussion when the suspect invoked his right to counsel. The unacceptable risk that an officer's eagerness to secure the suspect's waiver will result in an involuntary waiver is not eliminated because the reapproach is for a different offense.

After a suspect has initially waived the right to counsel, *Davis v. United States*[48] held, *Edwards* is triggered only by a clear and unambiguous request for counsel. A suspect's words are sufficiently clear under *Davis* only if a reasonable officer hearing them would, given the circumstances, understand them to be a request for the assistance of counsel. An ambiguous or equivocal reference to counsel that a reasonable officer would at most construe as indicating that the suspect might be invoking the right to counsel—such as Davis' statement, "Maybe I should talk to a lawyer."—is of no legal significance. Stressing the need for bright lines to guide officers, *Davis* rejected the argument that an ambiguous or equivocal reference to counsel, although not triggering *Edwards'* total bar to reapproaching the suspect, should require officers to limit further inquiries of the suspect to ascertaining whether in fact the suspect does desire to invoke his right to assistance of counsel.

A suspect's request for counsel may be sufficiently limited that continued questioning of some sort does not violate *Edwards*. In *Connecticut v. Barrett,*[49] for example, Barrett made clear to officers that he would not give a written statement until

---

45   384 U.S. 436 (1966).
46   451 U.S. 477 (1981).
47   486 U.S. 675 (1988).
48   512 U.S. 452 (1994).
49   479 U.S. 523 (1987).

his lawyer was present, but that he had "no problem" in talking orally with the officers about the incident. This, the Supreme Court held, invoked Barrett's right to counsel only with regard to interrogation designed to produce a written statement. Thus *Edwards* did not bar further interrogation reasonably designed only to elicit an oral statement.

Edwards prohibits only a reapproach by police. If the suspect—without being so reapproached—takes action that demonstrates a desire on the suspect's part for further generalized discussion about the investigation, the *Edwards* bar to further interrogation disappears. In *Oregon v. Bradshaw,*[50] a plurality indicated that the suspect's question— "Well, what is going to happen to me now?"—made while he was being transferred from the stationhouse to jail could have been reasonably interpreted by the officer as evidencing the suspect's desire to open up further discussion concerning the investigation. Although the suspect had previously invoked his right to counsel, police acceptably again warned him of his rights and, when he waived the right to counsel, interrogated him.

A significant change in circumstances may end an *Edwards* prohibition against reapproaching the suspect. This occurs, under *Maryland v. Shatzer*[51] if the suspect is released from custody, remains at liberty for at least fourteen days and is then again taken into custody. This period of liberty eliminates the coercive impact of the initial custody and thus the need for the extraordinary protection afforded by the *Edwards'* bar to reapproach.

Invoking the Right to Silence. Edwards' bar to reapproaching a suspect does not apply to a suspect who invokes the right to remain silent but not the *Miranda* right to counsel. A suspect who—for example, asserts, "I have nothing to say."—is not, under *Michigan v. Mosley,*[52] protected by a per se or total prohibition against reapproach. Interrogation must cease for the moment, but officer may later reapproach the suspect. If after reapproach the suspect waives his rights, however, the situation may require an unusually effective demonstration that the waiver was voluntary.

The *Davis* requirement that an invocation of a *Miranda* right be unambiguous and unequivocal, under *Berghuis v. Thompkins,*[53] applies to invocations of the right to remain silent as well as to the right to counsel.

If counsel is in fact present, *Miranda* itself suggested there "may be some circumstances in which further questioning would be permissible" although the suspect indicated he wished to remain silent. The fact that the interrogation was over objection, of course, would be a circumstance tending to show that any admissions ultimately made were involuntary and hence inadmissible.

Waiver Compared to Invocation of Miranda Rights. Miranda itself suggested that no custodial interrogation could occur unless and until the suspect was warned and both (a) had counsel present or effectively waived the right to counsel; and (b) had effectively waived the right to remain silent. Waiver could be implied rather than express. Do the requirements of unambiguous and unequivocal assertions of rights apply only after the

---

[50]   462 U.S. 1039 (1983) (plurality opinion).

[51]   559 U.S. 98 (2010).

[52]   423 U.S. 96 (1975).

[53]   560 U.S. 370 (2010).

rights have been initially waived and during interrogation the suspect seeks to undo those waivers?

This was considered in *Thompkins*, addressing whether the prosecution showed the required initial waiver of the right to silence. The Court acknowledged that *Miranda* itself suggested even an implied waiver must be in some sense "specifically made," but it added the Court had retreated from that position. Further, "the law can presume that an individual who, with a full understanding of his or her rights, acts in a manner inconsistent with their exercise has made a deliberate choice to relinquish the protection those rights afford . . . ." As a result:

> Where the prosecution shows that a *Miranda* warning was given and that it was understood by the accused, an accused's uncoerced statement establishes an implied waiver of the right to remain silent.[54]

Thompkins involved only the right to silence and not the right to counsel. Much of the Court's language was broad and general and the Court's rationale would seem to apply to the right to counsel as well.

Under *Thompkins*, officers who have warned a suspect and laid the basis for a finding the suspect understood the right to counsel and—to some extent—to avoid interrogation need not also elicit an affirmative answer to questions such as, "And are you willing to talk with us?" Instead, they may simply begin interrogation.

This for all practical purposes requires that a suspect wishing after being warned to rely on the *Miranda* rights must not simply avoid waiving them but must affirmatively invoke them and do so with the clarity demanded by *Davis*.

State courts need not, of course, follow *Thompkins* in developing state law. The Supreme Judicial Court of Massachusetts, for example, rejected the *Thompkins* approach as inappropriately placing on a defendant who has made an uncoerced admission the burden of proving he did not effectively waive his interrogation rights.[55]

Anticipatory Assertions of the Rights. Can a suspect bar officers from approaching the suspect by anticipatorily asserting that the suspect wishes the presence of counsel at any interrogation? In *Montejo v. Louisiana*,[56] the Court strongly suggested this could not be done.

Courts need not struggle with whether defendants' statements at preliminary court appearances constitute invocations of the *Miranda* right to counsel at interrogations, *Montejo* reasoned, because the *Miranda* rights cannot be invoked in this manner. "What matters," the Court explained, "is what happens when the defendant is approached for interrogation, and (if he consents) what happens during the interrogation—not what happened at any preliminary hearing."

If the *Miranda* rights cannot be anticipatorily invoked during a court appearance, they certainly cannot be anticipatorily invoked during law enforcement custody that precedes an approach for interrogation. A number of courts recognize an exception for situations in which interrogation has not yet begun but is imminent.

---

54   *Id.* at 384.
55   Com. v. Clarke, 960 N.E.2d 306, 320 n.12 (Mass. 2012).
56   556 U.S. 778 (2009).

§ 153   Self-Incrimination (*Miranda*) Requirements: (d) Effectiveness of Waivers; Voluntariness and Intelligence

The Fifth Amendment as construed in *Miranda v. Arizona*[57] requires for admission of a self-incriminating statement that the prosecution show that the making of the statement itself was an effective waiver of the right to remain silent and, unless a lawyer were present, that before and during the interrogation the person waived the right to assistance of counsel. To be effective, waivers must be both "voluntary" and "intelligent."

The requirement that waivers of self-incrimination rights during custodial interrogation be "intelligent" is separate and distinct from the demand that such waivers be "voluntary." As best defined, the demand that the waivers be intelligent addresses the information of which a suspect must have actually been aware for the suspect's decision to be effective. The requirement that the waivers be "voluntary," on the other hand, requires that the suspect's decision have been free of unacceptable influences.

The basic question is whether the standards for determining the effectiveness of such waivers are stricter than those imposed by the due process requirements of voluntariness. The fact of custodial interrogation argues for stricter standards than are embodied in due process voluntariness, since suspects' interests are placed at greater risk by custodial interrogation than they are under in those situations to which only the more general due process standard applies. Correspondingly appropriate protection might best be afforded by imposing stricter requirements for determining the acceptability of suspects' decisions to provide the prosecution with evidence or with access to them for questioning without the protection of counsel.

On the other hand, suspects protected by the privilege against self-incrimination as construed in *Miranda* will have been provided warnings, and they are protected against interrogation until they waive their right to counsel. Perhaps these aspects of self-incrimination law provide adequate protection against the increased threat generated by custodial interrogation. Stricter standards for voluntariness, then, may be unnecessary. Moreover, given the difficulty of articulating useful standards in this area, courts may be unable to distinguish meaningfully between two standards, one applicable to custodial interrogation situations and another applicable to other situations.

In fact, the Supreme Court has made clear, voluntariness in *Miranda* waiver law is generally the same as in the due process standard. "There is obviously no reason," the Court commented in *Colorado v. Connelly*,[58] "to require more in the way of a 'voluntariness' inquiry in the *Miranda* waiver context than in the Fourteenth Amendment confession context." No notice was taken of arguments that such reasons exist, no authority was cited, and no discussion was provided.

Voluntariness. Connelly held specifically that a waiver of *Miranda* rights, like a decision to confess under due process voluntariness, need not constitute an exercise of "free will" or "free choice" by the suspect. "Voluntariness" as is required for a *Miranda* waiver is only put into question if the facts show official coercion or overreaching and, as a result, the decision was not voluntary in the more ordinary sense of that term.

The prosecution's burden of showing *Miranda* voluntariness is especially heavy if the suspect was reapproached after earlier invoking his right to remain silent. Under

---

[57]   384 U.S. 436 (1966).

[58]   479 U.S. 157 (1986).

Michigan v. Mosley,[59] the admissibility of any statements so obtained depends upon the effectiveness of that waiver, which in turn depends upon "whether [the suspect's] 'right to cut off questioning' was 'scrupulously honored.' " What constitutes sufficient respect for this right is not entirely clear.

Generally, the prosecution can meet its burden of proving at least a prima facie showing of voluntariness by eliciting from the interrogating officer that the suspect had not been threatened or promised anything, and appeared to freely decide for himself to forego the assistance of counsel and to provide an incriminating statement. If the defense introduces evidence suggesting official overreaching and a significant impact of that overreaching upon the suspect, of course, the prosecution may well have to respond with more detailed and persuasive evidence in order to meet its burden of persuasion.

Intelligence. "Intelligence," as used in *Miranda's* waiver criteria, involves only an understanding of the basic abstract Fifth Amendment rights of which a suspect must be informed: that there is a legal right to remain silent during custodial interrogation; that anything said can be used in evidence to convict her of a crime; that she is entitled to consult with a lawyer and to have a lawyer present during custodial interrogation; and that if she decides to speak to law enforcement officers she is entitled to discontinue such discussion at any time she wishes. It is not necessary that she be aware of factual or legal matters bearing upon the wisdom of exercising any of those options. In fact, ignorance of any or all of those matters is totally irrelevant to the effectiveness of the waiver.

Consequently, a defendant who has previously made an incriminating statement which is in fact inadmissible against her need not understand the inadmissibility of that statement in order to effectively waive her rights and again admit those same facts. The Court has strongly hinted that a defendant who acknowledges participation in a robbery under circumstances that, unknown to her, create felony murder liability for a killing committed by a companion has made intelligent waivers of her rights despite ignorance as to the legal effect of the admissions. A suspect's waiver of the right to counsel is not rendered ineffective by ignorance concerning the subjects about which the officers intended to question her if she waived counsel's help. In *Moran v. Burbine*,[60] the Court held that a suspect's waiver of counsel was not rendered unintelligent by his unawareness that there was a specific attorney ready and willing to represent him during questioning if he wished representation.

In light of *Connelly*, which held that a *Miranda* waiver can be rendered involuntary only by official coercion, is official coercion also a prerequisite to consideration of the possibility that a *Miranda* waiver is insufficiently intelligent or knowing? The issue was not addressed in *Connelly* itself. *Connelly's* general discussion, however, suggests that official misconduct is necessary. If the "voluntariness" of a waiver is put into issue only by a preliminary showing of official coercion, a similar showing would seem necessary to challenge the "intelligence" of that waiver. Thus *Connelly* apparently means that a trial court need not consider a defendant's claim that because of mental illness or retardation, intoxication or emotional distress she failed to actually understanding the warnings, unless the court first finds that official coercion occurred and played a causal role in this failure to develop the required understanding.

---

[59] 423 U.S. 96 (1975).
[60] 475 U.S. 412 (1986).

The Court's position that an intelligent waiver of *Miranda* rights requires at most only an abstract understanding of those legal matters covered in the *Miranda* warnings serves several purposes. First, it avoids the difficult task of determining and articulating what broader information would be required. Second, it eliminates what would sometimes be an impossible task for the prosecution. Officers in some situations would simply be unable to provide a suspect with sufficient information concerning a crime, their investigation of it, or the suspect's legal position to render any waivers effective. They would, then, be barred from productive interrogation of the suspect. A construction of *Miranda* that so limits officers can reasonably be viewed as excessively solicitous of those interests of suspects that the self-incrimination privilege properly protects.

On the other hand, this position arguably renders *Miranda* ineffective in assuring that suspects' confession decisions reflect what in ordinary terms are "meaningful" decisions. In many situations, awareness of the abstract law would for most persons be only a relatively minor consideration in deciding whether to invoke either or both the rights to representation or counsel.

Assuring that suspects' choices are meaningful in such a broad, tactical sense, however, is most likely beyond the purposes of the *Miranda* requirements. The exceptional risks to suspects' privilege caused by custodial interrogation that justify the *Miranda* requirements probably arise exclusively from potential improper influences on suspects' volition. Custodial interrogation may not pose similarly severe risks to suspects' access to factual information or their abilities to intellectually assimilate or use it. Since the *Miranda* requirements are imposed for reasons at most indirectly related to suspects' ability to make intellectually informed and reasoned decisions, waiver criteria are appropriately formulated so as to require relatively minimal intellectual understanding of facts useful in making "wise" decisions.

States, of course, remain free to construe state constitutional requirements differently and some have done so. Several, for example, have held that police failure to permit an attorney to consult with a client undergoing interrogation renders the client's waivers ineffective.

§ 154 General Right to Counsel Requirements

Miranda v. Arizona[61] and analogous state self-incrimination decisions recognize a right to counsel based upon the privilege against self-incrimination as it applies during custodial law enforcement interrogation. General constitutional rights to counsel, such as that in the Sixth Amendment, focus upon representation at trial, but they also apply to certain pretrial situations in which suspects may make self-incriminating admissions. Since an exclusionary sanction attaches to violations of these rights to counsel, failures to comply with them permit challenges to the admissibility of confessions. Two primary issues are presented: first, under what circumstances is a confessing suspect protected by these general rights to counsel; and second, what protections are afforded a suspect by these provisions?

Sixth Amendment Right to Counsel. The Sixth Amendment applies if adversary judicial proceedings against the suspect have begun and police attempt to deliberately elicit self-incriminating admissions from the suspect. "Deliberate elicitation" of

---

[61]   384 U.S. 436 (1966).

admissions probably differs minimally if at all from "interrogation" as defined in case law under *Miranda.*

When adversary judicial proceedings begin is not entirely clear. Detention by the police or even formal arrest is not sufficient. On the other hand, a formal charge, as by the filing of an indictment, is clearly enough. It is not, however, required. In *Michigan v. Jackson,*[62] the Court held that an "arraignment", by which it apparently meant an arrested person's post-arrest appearance before a judicial officer, does trigger the Sixth Amendment right. In most situations, this post-arrest appearance will be the definitive point.

The Sixth Amendment right does not, generally speaking, protect a suspect from being approached in the absence of counsel by officers seeking to persuade him to provide a self-incriminating statement. A suspect entitled to Sixth Amendment protection is apparently entitled to at least the same admonishments required by *Miranda,* although generally not more. The Court has left open the possibility that a waiver of the Sixth Amendment right to counsel may require that the defendant be informed, or perhaps that the suspect know from some source, that the matter has progressed beyond general police investigation to adversary judicial proceedings.

The Sixth Amendment embodies a version of the *Edwards* rule.[63] A suspect who invokes his Sixth Amendment right to counsel as it applies in the law enforcement interrogation context cannot be re-approached by officers. But the Sixth Amendment right to counsel, unlike *Miranda's* right to representation, is "offense-specific." Therefore, a suspect who has by requesting counsel invoked his Sixth Amendment version of the *Edwards* rule may be approached by officers concerning other offenses as to which matters have not progressed sufficiently so as to give him a Sixth Amendment right to counsel as to those other offenses.

The Sixth Amendment right to counsel during questioning, like the Fifth Amendment right, can be waived. A waiver of the Sixth Amendment right must, of course, be both voluntary and intelligent. The Supreme Court has rejected the arguments that "because a Sixth Amendment right may be involved, it is more difficult to waive than the Fifth Amendment counterpart." Generally, then, a waiver of the Sixth Amendment right to counsel requires no more than an effective waiver of *Miranda* rights.

Sixth Amendment protection differs—and exceeds—Fifth Amendment-*Miranda* protection in three primary ways. First, a suspect whose Sixth Amendment right has attached has a Sixth Amendment right to counsel if efforts are made to elicit a self-incriminating admission from the suspect by a police officer functioning in an undercover capacity or a private citizen acting under the direction of law enforcement officers without disclosing that purpose; *Miranda* does not apply where the interrogator's official status is concealed from the suspect.

Second, the Sixth Amendment right to counsel, unlike *Miranda,* does not require that the suspect be in "custody." Thus, a suspect from whom an officer seeks to elicit a self-incriminating admission after the suspect had been released on post-indictment bail is protected by the Sixth Amendment right to counsel.

---

[62]   475 U.S. 625 (1986).

[63]   See supra § 152.

Finally, if a suspect is in fact represented by counsel and the Sixth Amendment has attached, the Sixth Amendment protects the defendant-counsel relationship more rigorously than it is protected by the Fifth Amendment and *Miranda*. In *Moran v. Burbine*[64] the Supreme Court indicated that officers' interference with defense counsel's efforts to contact a client undergoing custodial interrogation, although not discovered by the client until later, would render the client's waiver of his right to counsel ineffective. Officers' simple failure to inform such a client that defense counsel is attempting to contact the client would apparently have the same effect.

Despite *Burbine's* emphasis on existing attorney-client relationships, the Sixth Amendment does not mean that law enforcement officers are barred from approaching suspects simply because those suspects are represented.

State Constitutional Rights to Counsel. State courts seeking to impose greater limits upon law enforcement questioning though their state constitutions have tended to rely upon explicit constitutional rights to counsel rather than rights derived from constitutional self-incrimination privileges. This has been the case even if so applying the state rights requires construing them as applicable earlier in the criminal process than the analogous Sixth Amendment right. Several state courts have held state law rights to counsel bar officers from approaching suspects who have accepted representation or requested counsel regarding charges as to which adversary judicial proceedings have begun.

State courts' willingness to so apply state constitutional rights has been most common where officers have either or both interfered with counsel's access to a suspect undergoing interrogation or have failed to inform such a suspect of counsel's ready availability. The New York court has vigorously developed that state's right to counsel and held that under certain circumstances a suspect's right to counsel during questioning is "indelible," meaning that it can only be effectively waived in the presence of counsel. The New Jersey court has applied the state's right to counsel to the period between the filing of a complaint (or issuance of an arrest warrant) and indictment. During that period, prosecutors or police can initiate conversations with defendants, but they must inform the defendants that a complaint has been filed or a warrant issued.

§ 155   Special Problems: Promises Made to Suspects and Deception of Suspects

Promises and deception, two types of circumstances at least relevant to the effectiveness of defendants' decisions to confess, have presented special difficulty. Courts have tended to draw no distinction between whether the matter at issue is the effectiveness of the defendant's waiver of a constitutional right to remain silent or the right to counsel to protect the right to silence, on the one hand, or the more general voluntariness of the defendant's statement on the other.

Promises. Early voluntariness law placed particular emphasis on "promises" of some benefit in the criminal prosecution as among the influences rendering confessions inadmissible. Modern voluntariness standards, self-incrimination demands, and right to counsel requirements have incorporated at least some of this early "promise law."

During the vigorous application of the voluntariness requirement in the early 1800s, what today would be regarded by most courts as quite innocuous references to possible

---

[64]   475 U.S. 412 (1986).

benefits were regarded as per se tainting subsequent confessions. *Bram v. United States*[65] arguably incorporated such an approach into federal due process voluntariness, on the apparent ground that suspects are particularly sensitive to such inducements and the impact on particular defendants of particular promises is "too difficult to assess."

But in *Arizona v. Fulminante*[66] the Supreme Court indicated that this early language suggesting a rigid rule that promises render a confession involuntary does not state the current standard for determining the federal constitutional voluntariness of a confession. Instead, the Court approved an approach under which the federal constitution requires no more than that courts consider promises as part of the totality of the circumstances when they determine the voluntariness of defendants' confessions.

Some state courts have been reluctant to abandon traditional law's special concern for promises. They are, however, often unclear on whether they are defining requirements of state constitutional or evidence law as demanding more than federal constitutional law, or rather applying federal constitutional law with minimal significance given to *Fulminante*.

Any theoretical remaining emphasis on promises is mitigated by an increasing willingness to define "promise" narrowly and perhaps artificially as limited to what purport on their faces to be guarantees of some benefit to be delivered if the suspect confesses. What is often characterized as an exhortation to tell the truth, a prediction that confessing will result in more lenient treatment, or even an indication that in return for a confession an officer will "do what he can" or that "things will go easier" are held not to constitute promises within the meaning of a rule giving specific effect to promise. One court was probably accurate when it commented that an "express promise" can itself render a confession inadmissible but evidence of an "implied promise" is simply one factor in a totality of the circumstances voluntariness analysis.

Even if a prohibited promise is found, the evidence may not satisfactorily prove that the suspect relied upon it in deciding to confess. If the defendant first raised the possibility of the benefit he authorities later promised, the promise is less likely to render the defendant's decision legally ineffective. This is apparently on the ground that the defendant's initiative shows that the effect of the promise was not such as to impair the defendant's decisionmaking in the manner or degree necessary to render the confession involuntary.

There is general agreement that a promise of complete immunity from prosecution or its equivalent in return for a confession will render a resulting confession involuntary. A promise not to pursue charges for the most serious offenses committed by admitted actions may have the same effect. Furthermore, a promise that a confession would be kept confidential has been held to similarly render a confession inadmissible.

Some approaches emphasize the risk of inaccuracy. Several statutes and some case law provide that confessions are inadmissible if made in response to promises likely to stimulate a false confession by an innocent suspect. Whether this is consistent with federal due process voluntariness law's position that the accuracy of a particular confession is irrelevant to its voluntariness[67] is open to question.

---

[65]   168 U.S. 532 (1897).

[66]   499 U.S. 279 (1991).

[67]   See supra § 149.

Several courts have suggested that although officers may inform a suspect that cooperation may benefit the suspect, they may not tell that suspect that lack of cooperation—and a failure to confess—may result harsher treatment. "The first may contribute to the informed nature of the decision. But the second has no legitimate purpose 'and can only be intended to coerce.'" Thus a confession was inadmissible because interrogators told the defendant that if he did not cooperate they would ask for a "lot of jail time" and would make it "real uncomfortable" for him and that they would file a "recommendation that he was uncooperative."

Despite proof of the making of a disapproved promise, some courts have made clear, a statement may be admissible if the evidence shows the promise did not sufficiently influence the defendant's decision to confess. Precisely what effect the promise must have had is not entirely obvious from the discussions. One jurisdiction apparently gives the prosecution the chance to avoid exclusion by proof that the confession was made independent of the promise. "A statement obtained by threat or promise of advantage is involuntary under Maryland law regardless of the other circumstances," the courts of that state have held, "unless the State can establish that such threats or promises in no way induced the confession."[68]

Despite the apparent relaxation of promise law, some appellate courts sustain convicted defendants' claims that promises of leniency—perhaps in combination with other factors—rendered confessions inadmissible. One court—characterizing the situation as involving "false" promises because the promised leniency did not materialize—explained:

> The reason we treat a false promise differently than other somewhat deceptive police tactics (such as cajoling and duplicity) is that a false promise has the unique potential to make a decision to speak irrational and the resulting confession unreliable. Police conduct that influences a rational person who is innocent to view a false confession as more beneficial than being honest is necessarily coercive, because of the way it realigns a suspect's incentives during interrogation. "An empty prosecutorial promise could prevent a suspect from making a rational choice by distorting the alternatives among which the person under interrogation is being asked to choose." The ultimate result of a coercive interrogation is unreliable.[69]

The task of a court considering a defendant's claim of involuntariness "is to examine whether [the defendant] was not able to make a rational decision due to promises made by the interrogating [officer]."

Deception. If evidence that officers deceived the defendant convincingly demonstrates that the defendant lacked some information necessary to make his confession admissible under the applicable legal standard, of course, the evidence necessarily demonstrates that this legal standard was not met. The legal standards apparently require quite little in terms of a defendant's awareness,[70] however, and this approach therefore gives little significance to proof of deception.

---

[68]   Ford v. State, 175 A.3d 860, 867 (Md. Ct. Spec. App. 2017) (quoting Hill v. State, 12 A.3d 1193, 1201 (Md. 2011)), judgment aff'd, 197 A.3d 1090 (Md. 2018).

[69]   U.S. v. Villalpando, 588 F.3d 1124, 1128–29 (7th Cir. 2009) (quoting U.S. v. Montgomery, 555 F.3d 623, 629 (7th Cir. 2009)).

[70]   See supra §§ 149 (voluntariness), 153 (waiver of *Miranda* rights).

Officers' misrepresentations that the criminal law does not cover what the defendants are being asked to admit are likely to render the confession inadmissible. If confessing defendants need not know the law criminalizes what they are confessing, apparently officers are barred from misrepresenting the criminal law does not cover the conduct. Perhaps such misrepresentations are, or are akin to, promises of nonprosecution.

Courts sometimes seem open to arguments that deception should have some significance beyond disproving that the defendant had the awareness required to make an admissible confession. Some courts put the possible rule as one prohibiting misrepresentations offending notions of fairness or due process. No consensus has developed, however, on how to implement this.

The uncertain state of the law is almost certainly the result of uncertainty as to why law enforcement deception of suspects might be inappropriate and—if it is inappropriate at all—how inappropriate it is. Is it undesirable because—and thus only when—it might or does lead to an inaccurate confession? Or is it simply "wrong"—perhaps immoral in some sense—for public officials to lie and to exploit those lies? Even if such action is wrong, it is inappropriate enough to demand condemnation by excluding confessions to serious criminal conduct?

Common law voluntariness appears, from the minimal case law available, to have regarded proof of deception as largely if not entirely irrelevant to admissibility. The Supreme Court addressed the issue under Fourteenth Amendment due process voluntariness in *Frazier v. Cupp*.[71] Officers falsely told Frazier that a companion (Rawls) had been taken into custody and had confessed. Rejecting the attack on the later confession almost offhandedly, the Supreme Court—offering no authority, discussion, or rationale—simply stated, "[T]he fact that the police misrepresented the statements that Rawls had made is, while relevant, insufficient in our view to make this otherwise voluntary confession inadmissible."

In *Miranda v. Arizona*,[72] the Court, again with no substantive discussion or citation of authority, commented, "[A]ny evidence that the accused was . . . tricked . . . into a waiver [of the *Miranda* rights] will, of course, show that the defendant did not voluntarily waive his privilege." Although *Frazier* was decided after *Miranda*, the Court in *Frazier* amazingly made no mention of the obvious tension between the implications of the *Miranda* dictum and the *Frazier* analysis. In several subsequent cases presenting *Miranda* issues, the Court has failed to respond to or reach defendants' claims that their *Miranda* waivers were rendered ineffective by police deception. In *Colorado v. Spring*,[73] the Court recognized and left open the possibility that affirmative misrepresentations by officers might have significance for the effectiveness of a *Miranda* waiver beyond its logical relevance to the intelligence of that waiver.

Lower courts generally say that deception is not necessarily sufficient by itself to make an otherwise admissible confession inadmissible, but deception is a factor to consider in determining whether necessary voluntariness has been demonstrated. Under what circumstances deception is sufficient to tip the scales in favor of involuntariness is not clear. What is clear is that it will not be easily or frequently found.

---

[71]   394 U.S. 731 (1969).

[72]   384 U.S. 436 (1966).

[73]   479 U.S. 564 (1987).

One court commented that deception will not have this effect simply because it influenced the suspect's decision to confess, "as long as the decision [to confess] results from the suspect's balancing of competing interests." Perhaps the inquiry must be—in part at least—whether the deception and other circumstances so affected the defendant's emotion or reasoning as to prevent the suspect from making a minimally sufficient balance between those considerations militating against the wisdom of confessing and those favoring such action. The inquiry may, however, need to go beyond this.

Some courts have turned to the risk of deception leading to unreliability as the controlling factor—or at least one of the controlling considerations. Thus "a confession induced by deception or trickery . . . is not inadmissible, unless the method used was calculated to produce an untruthful confession or was offensive to due process." The Nebraska court has focused not on the general tendency of the deception used to produce inaccurate confessions, but rather on whether on the facts of the specific case the particular deception used "produced a false or untrustworthy confession."[74] This reference to accuracy poses the same problems here as when it is used to address the significance of promises.

The Seventh Circuit has indicated deception will render a statement involuntary if it "destroy[s] the information that [the suspect] require[s] for a rational choice" in at least part because it renders the confession unreliable.[75] Applying this approach, it held a confession to killing an infant by violent shaking involuntary because officers misrepresented to the defendant (who had acknowledged gently shaking the baby) that medical reports excluded all other possible causes of the child's death. The court explained:

> In this case a false statement did destroy the information required for a rational choice. Not being a medical expert, Aleman could not contradict what was represented to him as settled medical opinion. He had shaken Joshua, albeit gently; but if medical opinion excluded any other possible cause of the child's death, then, gentle as the shaking was, and innocently intended, it must have been the cause of death. Aleman had no rational basis, given his ignorance of medical science, to deny that he had to have been the cause.
>
> . . . .
>
> A trick that is as likely to induce a false as a true confession renders a confession inadmissible because of its unreliability even if its voluntariness is conceded. If a question has only two answers—A and B—and you tell the respondent that the answer is not A, and he has no basis for doubting you, then he is compelled by logic to "confess" that the answer is B. That was the vise the police placed Aleman in. They told him the only possible cause of Joshua's injuries was that he'd been shaken right before he collapsed; not being an expert in shaken-baby syndrome, Aleman could not deny the officers' false representation of medical opinion. And since he was the only person to have shaken Joshua immediately before Joshua's collapse, it was a logical necessity

---

[74]   State v. Nissen, 560 N.W.2d 157, 170 (Neb. 1997) (per curiam).

[75]   Aleman v. Village of Hanover Park, 662 F.3d 897, 906–07 (7th Cir. 2011) (quoting U.S. v. Rutledge, 900 F.2d 1127, 1129–30 (7th Cir. 1990)).

that he had been responsible for the child's death. Q.E.D. A confession so induced is worthless as evidence . . . .[76]

Some courts distinguish between deception regarding "intrinsic" facts—facts relating to the crime to which the suspect confessed and the suspect's guilt of it—and misrepresentation as to "extrinsic" facts—facts concerning other matters. Deceiving a suspect regarding extrinsic facts creates a particularly high risk, first, of overbearing the suspect's will by distorting what would otherwise be a rational choice whether to confess or remain silent, and, second, that the confession will be unreliable. Misrepresentations as to extrinsic facts are generally treated as entitled to more weight as tending to show involuntariness than misrepresentations as to intrinsic facts.

§ 156 Delay in Presenting Arrested Person Before Magistrate

Statutes and court rules in virtually every state as well as Rule 5(a) of the Federal Rules of Criminal Procedure require that arrested persons be brought with some dispatch before judicial officers for what, under the Federal Rules, is called the "initial appearance." Controversy continues as to the appropriate effect of violation of the applicable requirement on the admissibility of a confession obtained during the delay. The Supreme Court's development of the so-called *McNabb-Mallory* Rule and Congress's modification of it have served as a basis for analysis.

These cases present two distinguishable issues that are sometimes not separated by the courts. First is whether particular delay is improper, especially if that delay is for purposes of questioning the suspect prior to the appearance before the magistrate and the resulting judicial warnings, appointment of counsel and perhaps release from custody on bail. Second is the effect of delay determined to be improper on the admissibility of a confession given during that improper delay.

McNabb-Mallory Rule. In *McNabb v. United States,*[77] the Supreme Court held that statements elicited from a defendant during a period in which federal officers had failed to comply with what is now Federal Rule of Criminal Procedure 5(a)'s requirement of presentation before a magistrate without "unnecessary delay" were inadmissible at the defendant's subsequent federal criminal trial. This holding, the Court made clear, was not of constitutional dimensions but rather was an exercise of the Court's supervisory power. The impact of this exclusionary requirement was increased by the Court's construction of the substance of the Rule 5(a) requirement. In *Mallory v. United States,*[78] the Court held that if officers delayed presenting a defendant before a magistrate in order to interrogate him, the delay was "unnecessary" within the meaning of Rule 5(a).

Thus the so-called *McNabb-Mallory* Rule was in part a substantive rule—any delay in presentation for purposes of interrogation was unnecessary under Rule 5(a)—and in part a remedial rule—a confession obtained during delay that had become unnecessary for Rule 5(a) purposes was for that reason automatically inadmissible. Whether the Court in fact possessed a supervisory power sufficient to support its development of an exclusionary sanction of this sort has been questioned. The Supreme Court has never suggested that the *McNabb-Mallory* Rule or any similar prophylactic rule is required by the federal Constitution. Rather, the Court has assumed that delay is merely a factor in

---

[76] *Id.* at 906–07.

[77] 318 U.S. 332 (1943).

[78] 354 U.S. 449 (1957).

constitutional analysis of the voluntariness of a confession and presumably the effectiveness of waivers of Fifth and Sixth Amendment rights. In any case, a violation of a state prompt presentation requirement does not constitute an automatic violation of any federal constitutional requirement and, generally speaking, goes only to the voluntariness of the confession.

Congressional Modification or Rejection of McNabb-Mallory. In 1968, Congress responded to the *McNabb-Mallory* Rule by enacting what was codified as Section 3501 of Title 18 of the United States Code.[79] Section 3501(c) provides that in a federal criminal prosecution, a voluntary confession made by an arrested person within six hours of arrest or detention "shall not be inadmissible solely because of delay in bringing such person before a magistrate . . . ." Under Section 3501(a), a confession "shall be admissible [in a federal prosecution] if it is voluntarily given." Section 3501(b) specifies that among the factors to be considered in determining voluntariness is "the time elapsing between arrest and arraignment of the defendant . . . ."

Under Section 3501, a confession made within six hours of arrest cannot be excluded from a federal prosecution simply because of delay in presenting the defendant and will be inadmissible only upon a determination that it is involuntary. When a confession given during a period of improper delay lasting longer than the six hour "safe haven" in the statute was addressed by the Supreme Court in *Corley v. United States.*[80] Sections 3501(a) and (b), *Corley* held, simply do not address the *McNabb-Mallory* situation. Section 3501(c) means that delay in presentment is not itself a basis for excluding a confession given during the six-hour period after arrest. But if a confession is given after the expiration of that six-hour period and the delay in presentment was unreasonable or unnecessary "under the *McNabb-Mallory* cases," the delay alone still requires exclusion.

In reaching this result, the *Corley* majority stressed that reading the statute otherwise would leave the federal prompt presentation requirement "without any teeth." This, in turn, was particularly significant since that requirement is not "just some administrative nicety." Rather, it is an important safeguard against the risk of governmental overreaching by extended secret questioning. The prompt presentation demand "has always mattered in very practical ways and still does."

State Positions. State courts and legislatures have taken a wide variety of approaches. Agreement that *McNabb-Mallory* is not constitutionally-based and thus binding on the states assures that states are free to reject the Supreme Court's approach.

A few state courts, acting under supervisory authority, have adopted state versions of *McNabb-Mallory*, requiring suppression of confessions obtained during delay that has become improper because of failure to present the accused before a judicial officer. Maximum flexibility is provided by the approach of the Kansas court, which has held that trial courts have broad discretion to fashion and apply remedies for violation of the right of prompt presentation, including exclusion of statements made during impermissible delay.

The requirement of exclusion is sometimes qualified by a requirement that the defendant show that the delay caused or at least contributed to the defendant's decision to confess. Under the Montana court's approach, the prosecution can escape exclusion by making a showing that the evidence at issue was not reasonably related to the delay.

---

[79]   Pub. L. 90–351, Title II, § 701(a), 82 Stat. 210 (1968), codified as 18 U.S.C.A. § 3501.

[80]   556 U.S. 303 (2009).

Given that for other reasons compliance with *Miranda v. Arizona*[81] and other requirements must be shown, defendants under this approach have a difficult and perhaps impossible task in making cases for exclusion.

Several state legislatures have, in varying degrees, followed Congress' lead. In several jurisdictions, state statures follow the federal model. Other states provide unqualifiedly by statute that delay in presenting a defendant does not by itself render inadmissible those confessions obtained during improper delay. The Maryland court, to reconcile such a statutory provision with the right of presentation, concluded that any deliberate and unnecessary delay in presenting a defendant before a magistrate as required by state law "must be given very heavy weight in deciding whether a confession is voluntary."

The majority of state courts treat delay in presentation as merely a factor to consider in determining the voluntariness of decisions made during the delay and thus in deciding the admissibility of challenged confessions. Given the flexibility of the voluntariness analysis, weight may be given to showings that delay was for purposes of using the delay to interrogate. Nevertheless, successful challenges to admissibility under the approach are unusual.

The Massachusetts Supreme Judicial Court effectively articulated in *Commonwealth v. Rosario*[82] that the basic question for state courts having authority to embrace or reject *McNabb-Mallory* as a matter of state law: Is prompt presentation important enough to protecting suspects' self-incrimination rights to justify enforcing the requirement by excluding all statements made after delay becomes improper? Relying heavily upon the federal statute, the Massachusetts court concluded that *Miranda* and voluntariness requirements were sufficient to protect suspects' self-incrimination rights during brief post-arrest questioning, and therefore otherwise admissible statements made within six hours of arrest are not to be excluded on presentation delay grounds. To minimize the need to define what delays are reasonable, the court held that statements obtained after delay has exceeded six hours are to be excluded, unless the delay is caused by "reasons not attributable to the police, such as a natural disaster."

In 2014, the Massachusetts court recognized that the *Rosario* rule of exclusion is a minority position but nevertheless reaffirmed it. It stressed the predictability of the bright-line rule excluding statements made after six hours of improper delay. Further, the court reasoned that its approach avoided the inconsistency in outcomes resulting from treating delay as only a factor in determining involuntariness.

Under exclusionary approaches, should a volunteered admission—one made without police interrogation—be automatically inadmissible? The Massachusetts court, applying *Rosario*, held not. "The [*Rosario*] exclusionary rule," it explained, "was created to give protection to arrestees from the potentially coercive environment resulting from police questioning." When an admission was volunteered, "there was no police misconduct that offended a policy the exclusionary rule was meant to safeguard. Instead, suppression would only hinder legitimate information gathering."

---

[81] 384 U.S. 436 (1966), discussed in supra § 150. The criteria for determining the effectiveness of defendants' decisions in these situations is addressed in supra § 153.

[82] 661 N.E.2d 71 (Mass. 1996).

Waivers of Right to Prompt Presentation. The courts agree that whatever rights defendants have in the jurisdiction to exclusion of a confession based at least in part on delay in presentation is lost if the prosecution shows the defendants effectively waived the right to prompt presentation. Thus they ignore the warnings of Massachusetts Chief Justice Liacos in *Rosario.* He argued that giving effect to waivers, particularly those made after nonpresentation has become improper, will "undoubtedly eviscerate the [general] rule." In any case, he also argued that the need for a meaningful and bright-line requirement of presentation suggests the right to prompt presentation be nonwaivable.

Whether giving effect to waivers is defensible on sound policy grounds depends in part on whether the courts will require proof that offered waivers reflected meaningful choices. There seems, however, no possible defense of the position taken by the District of Columbia Court of Appeals in *Brown v. United States*[83] that a waiver of *Miranda* rights is also necessarily a waiver of prompt presentation rights. Such an approach gives virtually no independent significance to the right of prompt presentation.

§ 157 Reliability or Trustworthiness as Admission Requirement

A major theme of American confession law is the ambiguity of the role that a trial judge's assessment of a confession's accuracy, reliability or trustworthiness plays in determining the admissibility of that confession.

The federal due process requirement is clearly unconcerned with inaccuracy that cannot be attributed to official action. Even when official action is involved, the Supreme Court has mandated a focus on voluntariness that is divorced from the accuracy of the confession.[84] If a defendant's Fifth Amendment rights under *Miranda v. Arizona*[85] or Sixth Amendment right to counsel[86] is implicated, there is no more emphasis on reliability. State courts applying what appear to be state law voluntariness requirements sometimes look to the tendencies of the type of official action to stimulate a false confession.[87] Generally, the legal literature assumes that the trustworthiness of a confession is a matter for the jury.

The real problem in a jury trial system of course is whether juries are unlikely to recognize the untrustworthiness of at least some confessions, so that exclusion is appropriate to avoid jury misuse of them. In 1986, the Supreme Court offhandedly commented that the reliability of a criminal defendant's out-of-court admissions "is a matter to be governed by the evidentiary laws of the forum," thereby suggesting the existence of a body of law addressing this. In fact, little law of this sort exists.

As Richard Leo has pointed out,[88] the most obvious source of such a body of law would be trial courts' authority to exclude evidence on the ground that its probative value is outweighed by its danger of undue prejudice. State courts have occasionally

---

[83] 979 A.2d 630 (D.C. 2009).

[84] See supra § 149.

[85] 384 U.S. 436 (1966), discussed in supra § 150. The criteria for determining the effectiveness of defendants' decisions in these situations is addressed in supra § 153.

[86] See supra § 154.

[87] See supra § 149.

[88] Leo, Miranda and the Problem of False Confessions, in The Miranda Debate 279 (Leo and Thomas eds. 1998).

commented that defendants can challenge confessions on this basis and on rare occasions have reviewed admissibility under this approach.

Defendants seldom argue specifically why particular confessions might create a risk of jury misuse or undue prejudice. The mere fact that a jury is likely to consider an out-of-court statement as devastating to a defendant's case, of course, is not enough to trigger this analysis. Defendants must point out why juries are not likely to recognize indicia of unreliability and thus properly determine probative value.

As a practical matter, and regardless of the doctrine, it seems like that lower courts often apply a requirement of voluntariness as at least implicating trustworthiness. It is also likely that this application occurs with the attitude that generally trustworthiness is a matter for the factfinder, and the implicit trustworthiness aspect of voluntariness is invoked only by a showing of extraordinary factors that strongly suggest unreliability.

Insofar as the requirement of corroboration is an admissibility demand, it may require what amounts to an admissibility inquiry into trustworthiness. This is clearly the result of the Utah court's adoption of the trustworthiness approach to corroboration in *State v. Mauchley*.[89] *Mauchley* also developed how a preliminary inquiry into trustworthiness might proceed:

> In cases . . . where there is no evidence of a crime independent of the confession, the State may nevertheless "establish the trustworthiness of the confession with other evidence typically used to bolster the credibility and reliability of an out-of-court statement."

> Factors used in other areas of the law to bolster the credibility and reliability of an out-of-court statement include the following: evidence as to the spontaneity of the statement; the absence of deception, trick, threats, or promises to obtain the statement; the defendant's positive physical and mental condition, including age, education, and experience; and the presence of an attorney when the statement is given. We conclude that these factors also have applicability in determining the trustworthiness of confessions.

> We emphasize, however, that since a demonstrably wrong statement may indicate that a confession is false, the overall facts and circumstances related in the confession must be consistent with " 'facts otherwise known or established.' " For example, if a man spontaneously confesses that he fondled a child, but the evidence demonstrates he was never in physical proximity with the child, his confession is likely untrustworthy because the facts related in the confession are inconsistent with otherwise known or established facts.[90]

If the facts contain independent evidence of the offense, that of course may also be used to evaluate trustworthiness:

> One of the ways a confession may be bolstered by independent evidence is by showing a person's confession demonstrates the individual has specific personal knowledge about the crime.

> While not exclusive, three factors tending to demonstrate personal knowledge include the following: (1) providing information that "lead[s] to the

---

[89]   67 P.3d 477 (Utah 2003).

[90]   *Id.* at 488–89 (citations omitted).

discovery of evidence unknown to the police," (2) providing information about "highly unusual elements of the crime that have not been made public," and (3) providing "an accurate description of the mundane details of the crime scene which are not easily guessed and have not been reported publicly," because "mundane details [are] less likely to be the result of [suggestion] by the police." Examples of mundane details may include the following: "how the victim was clothed, disarray of certain furniture pieces, presence or absence of particular objects at the crime scene," "or which window was jimmied open."

Here, too, the degree of "fit between the specifics of a confession and the crime facts" is critical because the "fit" determines whether a confession should be deemed trustworthy. If a person merely provides information already known by the police or the public, or if the information provided is inaccurate, a confession may be untrustworthy.[91]

It would be preferable for courts to explicitly recognize that a defendant may reasonably object to the admissibility of an out-of-court statement on the ground that there are significant indications that the statement is untrustworthy, the jury is not likely to properly consider these indications, and thus that the jury will give the evidence regarding the statement more weight than it is entitled to be given. Such an objection calls for an inquiry and this inquiry is distinct from that into voluntariness.

The approach set out in *Mauchley* is an excellent framework for an inquiry of this sort. Reality dictates, however, that application of this approach accommodate the traditional notion that the credibility of evidence that the defendant confessed is ordinarily for the trier of fact. A defendant seeking to exclude a confession as untrustworthy must establish to the satisfaction of the judge that unusual considerations mean that the jury is unlikely to objectively evaluate the trustworthiness and hence the weight properly given to the prosecution's evidence in the case before the court.

§ 158   Mandatory Recording of Interrogations and Confessions

Traditionally, the means by which law enforcement and prosecution authorities preserve and present at trial a criminal defendant's out-of-court incriminating statements goes to the weight of the evidence rather than to its admissibility. Some have long urged, however, that law enforcement be required to record such statements and perhaps also the interrogations that lead to them, and that such requirements be enforced by limits on admissibility of evidence of such statements. Such requirements have proliferated in recent years.

Proponents of a recording requirement argue that criminal defendants' rights to have involuntary admissions excluded and to have law enforcement misconduct during questioning identified and penalized can be enforced only if courts can be provided a specific and accurate record of what occurred during law enforcement interviews of defendants. Only recordings can provide such records. Others contend that such a requirement is often impractical, and generally expensive. Moreover, recording may discourage suspects from making admissions for reasons entirely unrelated to those interests the legal limits on interrogations and the use of admissions are designed to further.

---

[91]   *Id.* at 489 (citations omitted).

What authority courts have to impose requirements that admissions be recorded or to exclude evidence where such requirements have been violated is questionable. There is universal agreement that federal constitutional considerations demand neither recording nor exclusion of evidence of admissions because questioning or statements were not recorded.

In 1980, the Alaska Supreme Court announced that law enforcement officers were required to record interrogation of suspects, when recording was feasible. Five years later in *Stephan v. State*,[92] the court made clear this was an aspect of state constitutional due process, which required that it be enforced by an exclusionary rule barring the use of evidence of admissions related to a violation of that rule.

Several courts have imposed somewhat similar requirements in the exercise of their supervisory authority. In what is probably the leading decision, *State v. Scales*,[93] the Minnesota Supreme Court held that all custodial interrogations including any information about rights, any waiver of those rights, and all questioning were to be electronically recorded where feasible and must be recorded when questioning occurs at a place of detention. Suppression is required of any statements obtained in violation of the recording requirement if—but only if—the violation is found "substantial."

The Massachusetts Supreme Judicial Court, emphasizing the complexities of the undertaking in *Scales*, nevertheless found that lack of responsiveness to its expressed preference for recording justified some supervisory action. It found sufficient action short of that taken in *Scales*:

> [W]hen the prosecution introduces evidence of a defendant's confession or statement that is the product of a custodial interrogation or an interrogation conducted at a place of detention (e.g., a police station), and there is not at least an audiotape recording of the complete interrogation, the defendant is entitled (on request) to a jury instruction advising that the State's highest court has expressed a preference that such interrogations be recorded whenever practicable, and cautioning the jury that, because of the absence of any recording of the interrogation in the case before them, they should weigh evidence of the defendant's alleged statement with great caution and care. Where voluntariness is a live issue . . ., the jury should also be advised that the absence of a recording permits (but does not compel) them to conclude that the Commonwealth has failed to prove voluntariness beyond a reasonable doubt.[94]

The New Jersey Supreme Court in *State v. Cook*,[95] decided in 2004, indicated a willingness to exercise its supervisory authority. It established an advisory committee to study and make recommendations on the use of electronic recordings of custodial interrogations. In 2005, after receiving the report of that committee, it adopted New Jersey Court Rule 3:17 directing recording.[96] Law enforcement's failure to record a statement as required by the rule "shall be a factor for consideration by the trial court in determining the admissibility of a statement, and by the jury in determining whether the statement was made, and if so, what weight, if any, to give to the statement." Where

---

[92]   711 P.2d 1156 (Alaska 1985).

[93]   518 N.W.2d 587 (Minn. 1994).

[94]   Com. v. DiGiambattista, 813 N.E.2d 516, 533–34 (Mass. 2004).

[95]   847 A.2d 530 (N.J. 2004).

[96]   N.J. Ct. Rule 3:17.

a required recording was not made, "the court shall, upon request of the defendant, provide the jury with a cautionary instruction."

Since *Stephan, Scales* and *Cook*, courts have generally been unwilling to adopt recording requirements, either as mandates of state constitutional law or pursuant to judicial supervisory authority. The Connecticut Supreme Court, for example, after an extensive discussion, stressed that its unwillingness to impose recording requirements under either authority was due in large part to the complexity of the matter and its perception that the nature of the relevant considerations made the matter better suited to legislative resolution. It also expressed reservations concerning the use of its supervisory authority to promulgate requirements impacting so dramatically matters outside the judicial process.

A number of legislatures have, however, acted and imposed requirements that at least some custodial interrogations be recorded. Court rules also sometimes incorporate such demands.

These requirements usually apply to custodial interrogations of persons suspected of serious offenses. They are also limited to interrogations that occur in locations under relatively long-term law enforcement dominance, where equipment for recording can be expected to be made available with relative ease. Recording is often not required if the suspect objects.

The evidentiary consequences of these requirements vary. Some statutes appear to make compliance irrelevant to admissibility. Missouri, for example, provides that "[n]othing in [the statute requiring recording] shall be construed as a ground to exclude evidence."[97] Kansas specifies that the "[l]ack of an electronic recording shall not be the sole basis for suppression of the interrogation or confession."[98]

Other provisions make clear that noncompliance requires—at least sometimes—exclusion of a statement made during an unrecorded interrogation. Illinois, for example, provides by statute that in a statement made during custodial interrogation at a place of detention that is not recorded is presumed inadmissible.[99] This presumption "may be overcome by a preponderance of the evidence that the statement was voluntarily given and is reliable, based on the totality of the circumstances." Others, such as the Texas statute, make unexcused noncompliance a basis for exclusion.

Some recording requirement provide for an adverse jury instruction as a consequence of improper nonrecording. The Oregon statute, for example, provides that if the prosecution introduces a confession improperly not recorded:

> upon the request of the defendant, the court shall instruct the jury regarding the legal requirement [of recording] and the superior reliability of electronic recordings when compared with testimony about what was said and done.[100]

If a recording requirement is to be imposed, one important question is how complete a recording should be required. Should it be sufficient that the prosecution has a recording of the statement it wishes to introduce? Or should the record also include all custodial interrogation, the warnings and waivers before custodial interrogation begins,

---

[97]   Mo. Stat. Ann. § 590.700, subd. 3(6).

[98]   Kan. Stat. Ann. § 22–4620(f)(2).

[99]   725 Ill. Comp. Stat. Ann. 5/103–2.1(b).

[100]   Or. Rev. Stat. Ann. § 133.400(3)(a).

or perhaps even all interaction between the defendant and officers in which improper influences on the defendant might be brought to bear? The New Hampshire Supreme Court focused on this and held—pursuant to its supervisory power—that although it would impose no requirement of a recording, the prosecution could use a recording to prove a statement made during custodial interrogation only if the entire interrogation was recorded.

Statutory requirements generally demand that the entire custodial interrogation resulting in the confession be recorded. North Carolina, for example, requires an electronic recording have been made "of the custodial interrogation in its entirety . . . ." "In its entirety" is then defined with unusual specificity as:

> An uninterrupted record that begins with and includes a law enforcement officer's advice to the person in custody of that person's constitutional rights, ends when the interview has completely finished, and clearly shows both the interrogator and the person in custody throughout. If the record is a visual recording, the camera recording the custodial interrogation must be placed so that the camera films both the interrogator and the suspect. Brief periods of recess, upon request by the person in custody or the law enforcement officer, do not constitute an "interruption" of the record. The record will reflect the starting time of the recess and the resumption of the interrogation.[101]

As the discussion of legislation and court rules earlier in this section made clear, a major question is whether any recording requirement imposed should be made enforceable by exclusion of some or all statements made during interrogations unrecorded in violation of the requirement. An exclusionary penalty, of course, might reasonably be regarded as the only way of providing an effective incentive for law enforcement compliance with any recording mandate imposed. On the other hand, some courts or legislatures may find a recording requirement acceptable only if it is not burdened by the complexities and costs of an exclusionary sanction. A recording requirement without an exclusionary penalty may have some value and is certainly preferable to no such requirement.

Insofar as a recording requirement is enforced by a rule excluding evidence, perhaps the major question is what should be required to trigger the right to have evidence excluded? The evidence rule would provide the maximum motivation, of course, if the fact of noncompliance alone is sufficient to require exclusion. But the courts have been reluctant to by judicial decision so mandate the exclusion of evidence of potentially reliable confessions. Under the Minnesota approach as adopted in *Scales*, for example, a defendant's failure to claim that an unrecorded statement was tainted by a violation of the requirements of *Miranda v. Arizona*[102] or was involuntary or otherwise inadmissible means the violation of the recording requirement is not substantial and need not (and perhaps must not) result in exclusion. In *Stephan*, the Alaska Supreme Court indicated that the due process recording requirement did not require exclusion "if no testimony is presented that the [unrecorded] statement is inaccurate or was obtained improperly."

As discussed earlier, legislatures have split on whether to provide an exclusionary penalty for noncompliance with recording requirements. The Illinois provision,

---

[101] N.C. Gen. Stat. Ann. § 15A–211(c)(2).

[102] 384 U.S. 436 (1966).

considered earlier, in effect requires exclusion only of unrecorded statements the prosecution cannot prove are voluntary and reliable.

In the absence of any formal requirement that a statement or interrogation be recorded, the absence of a recording is evidence bearing on whatever issues may be presented. Officers' unexplained failure to record an interrogation where recording was possible might sufficiently impair their credibility that their testimony will not suffice to meet the prosecution's burden of proving compliance with *Miranda v. Arizona* or voluntariness.

§ 159 Evidence Obtained as a Result of Inadmissible Confessions

At early common law, the involuntariness of a confession did not affect the admissibility of other evidence obtained by use of that statement. If, for example, a suspect was coerced into confessing to a murder and also into revealing the location of the murder weapon, the weapon, if located, could be used in evidence. The rationale for this position was that the confession was excluded because of its untrustworthiness. If the "fruits" of that confession were themselves sufficiently probative of the defendant's guilt, the reason for excluding the confession did not extend to that derivative evidence and hence it was admissible. American courts applying the voluntariness requirement adopted this position.

As criminal evidence became permeated with exclusionary flavor after *Mapp v. Ohio*[103] and *Miranda v Arizona*,[104] American courts quite uncritically adopted for confession cases the "fruit of the poisonous tree" doctrine as developed in Fourth Amendment case law. This was apparently on the rationale that voluntariness law had come to serve purposes other than assuring the reliability of evidence, and encouraging law enforcement compliance with rules designed to accomplish these broader objectives required exclusion of "fruits" as well as involuntary confessions themselves.

The Supreme Court made clear that at least the Fifth Amendment issue is not that easily resolved. In *United States v. Patane*,[105] the Court held that federal constitutional law did not require the exclusion of physical evidence obtained by using information in a statement itself inadmissible because it was tainted by a violation of the requirements of *Miranda*. No majority of the justices agreed on a rationale for this, however.

Justice Thomas, writing for three members of the Court, reasoned that the nature of the Fifth Amendment privilege precluded a rule requiring exclusion. The Self-Incrimination Clause is violated only by the use at trial of a defendant's compelled testimony, and thus the clause itself cannot be violated by the evidentiary use of nontestimonial evidence obtained as a result of a voluntary out-of-court statement. Prophylactic rules such as those imposed by *Miranda* are justified only if they are necessary to assure that compelled statements themselves will not be used at trial. Permitting the use of the fruits of a statement creates no danger that the statement itself will be used at trial.

---

[103] 367 U.S. 643 (1961), discussed in infra § 166.
[104] 384 U.S. 436 (1966).
[105] 542 U.S. 630 (2004).

The *Miranda* requirements do not constitute "a direct constraint on the police," Justice Thomas continued. Thus there is no reason to apply a fruit of the poisonous tree as a means of encouraging police compliance with those requirements themselves.

Justice Souter, writing for three and perhaps four justices, reasoned that the *Miranda* requirements are closely enough related to the core protections afforded by the Fifth Amendment that the need to encourage law enforcement compliance with them justifies the exclusion of the fruit of a statement obtained in violation of them. Justice Kennedy, writing for himself and Justice O'Connor, did not reach whether the need to deter *Miranda* violations themselves could justify a constitutional rule excluding the fruit of a statement. Assuming that deterrence of *Miranda* violations was a proper consideration, he concluded that "the important probative value of reliable physical evidence" meant that proponents of a fruit of the poisonous tree rule had failed to make their case.

Patane involved physical evidence obtained as a result of a statement tainted by a *Miranda* violation. But the result confirmed the Court's earlier holdings that no fruit of the poisonous tree analysis applied to the testimony of witnesses found as a result of such a statement or an incriminating out-of-court statement by the accused made after compliance with *Miranda* but made subsequent to the tainted and inadmissible statement.

Patane reaffirmed the indications given nearly twenty years earlier in *Oregon v. Elstad*[106] that the same approach would not be taken to evidence obtained as a factual consequence of an involuntary out-of-court statement.

Elstad and *Patane* make clear that if a confession is involuntary, neither the rule permitting evidentiary use of the fruits of a *Miranda* violation nor its rationale apply. Consequently, at least a subsequent confession given by the defendant is not free from challenge as tainted by the events stimulating the first confession. On the other hand, *Elstad* reaffirmed that a suspect from whom a confession has been coerced is not, as a result, perpetually disabled from thereafter giving an admissible confession, and *Patane* gave no reason to question this.

Precisely what standard determines whether a subsequently given confession is suppressible because of successful voluntariness challenge to the admissibility of the initial confession, however, is not entirely clear. The major question is whether the prosecution establishes admissibility by proving that the second and challenged confession is itself voluntary or whether it must prove more. There are two major possibilities.

First, a defendant may simply need to persuade a court that the prosecution has failed to establish the voluntariness of the challenged subsequent confession. While the Court has left open whether there is a formal presumption that a confession is involuntary if it was given after an initial involuntary statement, the prosecution's burden of proving voluntariness at least imposes a practical need to overcome an inference of involuntariness. As a practical matter, then, the prosecution may need to establish that the influences rendering the first statement involuntary were no longer operative or controlling at the time of the second.

---

[106] 470 U.S. 298 (1985).

Second, a more conventional fruit of the poisonous tree analysis, as used in Fourth Amendment exclusionary sanction analysis, may apply. If the defendant—perhaps aided by a presumption—establishes that "but for" having made the first and involuntary statement the defendant would not have made the second and challenged confession as and when he did, the second confession becomes inadmissible fruit unless the prosecution establishes that the taint of the coercion was attenuated. Whether this approach really differs in substance from the first is by no means clear.

If a defendant challenges nonconfession evidence as the inadmissible result of an involuntary confession, presumably the second approach distinguished above will apply. Such evidence is inadmissible fruit of the involuntary confession if "but for" the confession the evidence would not have been obtained as it was. The prosecution can escape exclusion by showing an exception, such as attenuation of taint or inevitable discovery, applies.

State law, of course, need not track the Supreme Court's federal constitutional law. After *Elstad*, some state courts incorporated the Supreme Court's approach into any *Miranda*-like requirement of state law. Other state tribunals, however, rejected *Elstad*. Massachusetts has also rejected *Patane*, reasoning that "[t]o apply the *Patane* analysis to the broader rights embodied in [our state constitution] would have a corrosive effect on them, undermine the respect we have accorded them, and demean their importance to a system of justice chosen by the citizens of Massachusetts in 1780."[107] The court adopted "a common-law rule" making physical evidence obtained as a result of a statement inadmissible. Several other state courts have also rejected *Patane* as a matter of state law.

The Wisconsin Supreme Court held that state constitutional considerations bar the use of physical evidence obtained as a result of a deliberate *Miranda* violation. It stressed the need for a strong deterrent of the "particularly repugnant" law enforcement conduct involved.[108] In addition, however, it emphasized that the scope of the exclusionary penalty imposed by state constitutional law would be determined in part by what is appropriate to assure the integrity of the state judiciary. That judiciary would be "systemically corrupted" by an exclusionary sanction encouraging law enforcement "to intentionally take unwarranted investigatory shortcuts to obtain convictions."

§ 160 Judicial Confessions, Guilty Pleas, and Admissions Made in Plea Bargaining

Most confession law involves self-incriminating admissions made by suspects to law enforcement officers during the pre-judicial stages of a criminal investigation. But the prosecution sometimes seeks trial use of self-incriminating admissions made by the defendant during what is essentially the judicial processing of a case. These admissions can usefully be broken down into three categories: "judicial" confessions, guilty pleas, and admissions made in connection with plea bargaining.

Judicial Confessions. A so-called "judicial confession" is an incriminating admission made in court or judicial proceedings. It may consist of a defendant's testimony in a different (and perhaps civil) proceeding or in a prior hearing during the criminal prosecution in which it is offered. It may also be a "stipulation" or even the pleadings in

---

[107] Com. v. Martin, 827 N.E.2d 198, 203 (Mass. 2005).
[108] State v. Knapp, 700 N.W.2d 899, 918 (Wis. 2005).

this or other litigation. Under the general rules governing admissions, these judicial confessions are admissible, subject of course to compliance with such requirements as any right to counsel the defendant may have had at the time.

Guilty Pleas. A defendant's guilty plea and statements made in connection with its offer to and acceptance by the trial court are admissible as admissions. Pleas of guilty to minor offenses may sometimes constitute questionable evidence of actual guilt, but this is best handled by considering on a case-by-case basis the probative value of particular pleas weighed against the risk of undue prejudice likely to arise from their admission into evidence.

Federal Rule 410[109] prohibits the use of a withdrawn guilty plea and also bars the use of statements made in the course of proceedings in which such pleas are submitted to and accepted by the trial court. This is apparently on the rationale that permitting use of the plea would frustrate the policy objectives supporting the right to withdraw that plea. State statutes or court rules generally are similar.

Admissions Made in Connection with Plea Bargaining. There is general agreement that admissions made in connection with plea negotiations that do not result in final pleas of guilty must be excluded in order to encourage the desirable or at least necessary process of plea bargaining. This is provided for in federal litigation by Federal Rule 410. State statutes and court rules often address the matter as well, although there is considerable variation among the provisions.

These provisions typically make inadmissible statements made "in the course of plea discussions." Considerable difficulty arises in determining what are "plea discussions," and when particular statements are made "in the course" of such discussions.

Some provisions, such as the federal ones, limit protection to statements made in connection with discussions with a prosecutor, on the rationale that discussions between law enforcement officers and defendants do not involve the sort of negotiations that should be encouraged by exclusion of admissions made during those negotiations. Thus generally no protection is afforded admissions made to law enforcement officers, even under versions of the rule that are not explicitly limited to statements made to prosecutors. Nevertheless, admissions made to a law enforcement officer will be protected if the evidence shows that the officer was apparently acting as the authorized agent of a prosecutor.

Whether statements were sufficiently related to actual or perceived plea discussions—and thus are protected—is frequently disputed. Admissions made by defendants in the hopes of obtaining information from authorities rather than negotiating a plea bargain are, of course, not covered. More significantly, there is no protection for statements made by defendants who are simply seeking to obtain leniency. One court found no protection for admissions made during negotiations for pretrial diversion which would not require a plea of guilty.

These situations are frequently addressed by using a two part analysis often attributed to *United States v. Richardson.*[110] Under this approach, an admission is protected only if both of two requirements are met. First, the defendant must have made

---

[109] Fed. R. Evid. 410. See infra § 266.
[110] 582 F.2d 1356 (5th Cir. 1978) (en banc).

the admission with an actual expectation that he was in the process of negotiating a plea bargain. Second, was that expectation must have been objectively reasonable given the totality of the circumstances.

Perhaps most troublesome are situations in which defendants made admissions in what might be characterized as efforts to begin or simply interest the prosecution in beginning plea negotiations. Some courts seem to require that before the admissions are made, the prosecutors have somewhat explicitly entered into discussions of specific possible quid pro quo exchanges. The Florida Supreme Court, however, has reasonably rejected an absolute requirement that a plea offer have been made.

Under the most reasonable approach, plea negotiations do not require any express or actual formal agreement by the parties that they are negotiating a possible plea bargain. Admissions should be protected if the defendant believes prosecution authorities to whom the admissions are made are receptive to bargaining and prosecution authorities have by words or conduct justified this belief. Thus protection was properly extended to statements made at a meeting "orchestrated" by the defendant because he "wanted to orchestrate a deal" and law enforcement officers and a prosecutor agreed to and did attend without informing the defendant they would be present only to collect incriminating statements to be used against defendant at trial.

Waiver of Protection for Admissions Made in Connection with Plea Bargaining. The Supreme Court held in *United States v. Mezzanatto*[111] that the protection of the federal provisions is subject to waiver. This has encouraged development of "proffer" agreements in which defendants before entering into negotiations waive some or all statutory or rule protection for admissions made in connection with those negotiations.

These agreements may be formal and in writing. They may also, however, be considerably less formal. An agreement to waive the protection may be found on evidence that the prosecutor orally announced that admissions made in the discussion would be admissible and the defendant—understanding this—participated and made admissions.

Mezzanatto held a waiver effective when the prosecution offered an otherwise-protected admission to impeach a testifying defendant. Lower courts have generally held, however, that its rationale also applies when the prosecution offers otherwise-protected admission in its case-in-chief to prove guilt. So enforcing waivers will not frustrate the general purpose of Rule 410 to encourage plea negotiations.

The admissibility of admissions made pursuant to these proffer agreements is determined by the terms of the agreement. If a plea is entered pursuant to the agreement and the defendant exercises his right to withdraw the plea, the agreement is probably breached and otherwise-protected admissions may be used. Agreements often provide that the defendant must be completely truthful and that defendant is not to personally or "through counsel" made representations materially different from statements made or information provided. Violation of these provisions, even by counsel rather than the defendant personally, permits use of admissions.

Proffer agreements sometimes give the prosecution the right to use "derivative evidence"—evidence other than the defendants' statements themselves but obtained by the prosecution's use of those statements. Admissibility of such evidence has been

---

[111] 513 U.S. 196 (1995).

upheld, at least where the proffer agreement "clearly" gives the prosecution the right to use information contained in statements that themselves cannot be used.

Waivers might be subject to a perhaps-implied requirement of good faith on the part of the prosecution. Thus a defendant might be relieved of a waiver in a proffer agreement upon proof that the prosecution never intended to try and reach a plea agreement but instead participated for the purpose of obtaining usable admissions by the defendant.

Permissible Use of Plea Bargain Admissions. The federal provisions permit use in perjury prosecutions of otherwise inadmissible pleas and statements related to pleas and plea negotiations. State provisions often but not always provide similarly. As a result of 1980 amendment, the federal provisions also embody a provision permitting the use of such statements against a defendant when some other statement made in the course of the same plea proceedings or negotiations has been introduced and the statement at issue "ought in fairness be considered contemporaneously with it."

Use of Admissions to Impeach Testifying Defendant. Whether an admission otherwise subject to exclusion may be used to impeach a defendant who testifies is not explicitly addressed under the federal provisions. The original version of Federal Rule 410 contained an explicit but limited exception permitting the use of "voluntary and reliable statements" made in court and on the record, even if they were otherwise inadmissible under Rule 410, but only "where offered for impeachment purposes." Congress eliminated this language in the 1975 amendment of the rule. The Second Circuit has held that this "unusually clear legislative history" demonstrates a Congressional intention "to preclude use of statements made in plea negotiations for impeachment purposes" and other federal courts have agreed. State provisions generally do not address the matter, and the silent provisions are usually read to bar impeachment use of the statements.

§ 161 "Tacit" and "Adoptive" Confessions and Admissions

Under the general rules regarding admissions,[112] the prosecution is generally permitted in a criminal case to prove that an accusatory statement was made in the hearing of the defendant and that the defendant's response was such as to justify the inference that he agreed with or "adopted" the statement. The adopting response may, of course, be an express affirmative agreement with the statement. It may also be conduct from which the defendant's belief in the accuracy of the statement can be inferred; where this is the case, the evidence amounts to what in this text is regarded as an "adoptive" confession. Adoption can be also inferred from the defendant's failure to deny the accusation, so a type of adoptive admission can arise from either silence or an "equivocal response" not a clear denial. Where the accusation is so adopted by the defendant's silence, the evidence thereby rendered admissible, the accusation and the defendant's adopting silence, is a "tacit" confession.

The foundation necessary has been articulated in various ways. Best put, admission requires preliminary proof that (1) someone made an accusatory statement that a person who considered himself innocent would, under the circumstances, deny; (2) the defendant heard and understood the accusatory statement; (3) the defendant had the opportunity and ability to deny the statement; and (4) the defendant manifested his adoption of it or, in the case of a tacit admission, adopted it by his silence.

---

[112] See infra § 262 as to the nature of admissions.

Here, as in civil litigation, admission is based on the assumption that human nature is such that innocent persons will usually deny false accusations. Critical reconsideration of this assumption, especially as it applies in the criminal context, had led to increasing limitations upon adoptive confessions in criminal litigation. Use of this evidence in criminal trials is also affected by federal and state constitutional considerations. These matters, especially as they concern tacit confessions adopted by defendants' silence, implicate the requirements imposed by the privilege against compelled self-incrimination in general, the Fifth Amendment's requirements as specifically developed in *Miranda v. Arizona*,[113] and general considerations of minimal procedural fairness.

Doyle v. Ohio[114] held that federal Due Process barred cross-examination of a testifying defendant by use of pretrial silence after the defendant was taken into custody and warned pursuant to *Miranda* of the right to remain silent. The Supreme Court characterized silence after such warnings as "insolubly ambiguous," and appeared to be influenced by that conclusion. Subsequent decisions by the Court made clear, however, that *Doyle's* holding was based instead on the perceived unfairness of explicitly representing to a suspect that the suspect has the right to silence and then penalizing the suspect for exercising that right. Finding the rationale for the prohibition applicable, the Supreme Court subsequently barred the substantive use of post-warning custodial silence to prove guilt.[115]

Doyle's rationale, so construed, would seem to not apply if the silence relied upon occurred before the defendant was advised of the right to remain silent. Consequently, the Supreme Court's Due Process case law poses no barrier to cross-examination use of silence prior to receipt of the *Miranda* assurance of the right to remain silent. Although the cases explicitly found no barrier to impeachment use, it follows that federal Due Process also permits pre-warning silence to be used substantively—as the basis of a tacit confession—to prove a suspect's guilt.

Even in the absence of warnings, it is quite possible the criminal justice system effectively conveys to people at least some of the essence of the *Miranda* rights, and particularly that one has a right to remain silent in dealings with law enforcement. Much the same unfairness might be found in following this general dissemination of a right of silence with use at trial of pre-warning silence to prove guilt, despite the Supreme Court's failure to find sufficient unfairness to trigger federal Due Process.

A number of lower courts have concluded—despite the apparent limits of the Supreme Court's case law—that the Fifth Amendment bars the use of silence if the defendant was in custody although no explicit warning of the right to silence was given. Some have extended this bar to silence before the defendant was taken into custody. Others, however, have limited the bar to situations covered by *Doyle* and subsequent Supreme Court decisions—those in which the *Miranda* warning of the right to remain silent was given.

Apart from Due Process concerns, silence during interaction with public officials—whether pre or post-warning—might constitute invocation of the right to remain silent. Its use to prove guilt as the basis of a tacit confession might be an impermissible burden

---

[113]   384 U.S. 436 (1966).

[114]   426 U.S. 610 (1976).

[115]   Wainwright v. Greenfield, 474 U.S. 284, 295 (1986).

on the exercise of the self-incrimination privilege that creates the right to remain silent. As is developed in section 127, there is considerable authority for the proposition that the Fifth Amendment and perhaps some state law versions of the privilege bar the use of pre-warning silence on this constitutional ground.

Whether the Fifth Amendment has this effect was cast into considerable doubt by *Salinas v. Texas.*[116]

A split five justice majority in *Salinas* held the prosecution's use in its case-in-chief of a defendant's pre-custody and pre-warning silence after a law enforcement question did not violate the Fifth Amendment. Justice Alito's plurality opinion announcing the judgment—joined by two other members of the Court—reasoned that Salinas could rely on the Fifth Amendment privilege only if he invoked it and he did not. Thus the plurality did not address whether proved reliance on the privilege could be burdened by using that reliance as evidence of guilt. Justice Thomas, writing for himself and Justice Scalia, concurred in the judgment on the ground that using Salinas's silence did not compel him to give self-incriminating testimony and thus no violation of the Fifth Amendment occurred. Four justices contended the Fifth Amendment protects against penalizing reliance on the privilege in the pre-custody and pre-warning context and reliance on the privilege is shown when—as in *Salinas*—the circumstances justify an inference that a suspect's silence reflects reliance on the privilege.

The analysis of the *Salinas* plurality suggests that in non-custodial interrogation situations mere silence cannot invoke the privilege. Use of such silence, then, cannot constitute a penalty imposed upon reliance on the privilege because the defendant has not effectively relied on the privilege. State courts, of course, remain free to construe state privileges as barring use of silence in these situations. The Hawai'i Supreme Court construed that state's constitutional privilege as barring this use of silence, at least where that silence occurs during non-arrest detention.

The factors considered in developing and formulating constitutional limits on the use of silence as the basis for tacit confessions have also been considered by courts addressing possible evidence law limits on this sort of evidence. This is particularly the case with what *Doyle* suggested was the "insolubly ambiguous" nature of silence in this context.

Generally, modern courts have been increasingly critical of the traditional assumption that silence in the face of an accusation is reliable proof that the silent person agrees with the accusation. Less than unequivocal expressed agreement with the accusation—and especially silence—may—given widespread knowledge of *Miranda*—reflect not agreement but instead a decision to invoke what even an innocent suspect believes to be an available and useful right of silence that may reduce the risk of wrongful prosecution or conviction.

The Supreme Court has held that the minimal probative value of a defendant's silence renders evidence of such silence inadmissible to impeach as a matter of federal evidence law.[117] The Connecticut Supreme Court held on state law grounds that an adoptive admission based on silence is admissible only if no explanation other than assent to the accusatory statement is "equally consistent." Some state courts have more

---

[116]   570 U.S. 178 (2013).

[117]   U.S. v. Hale, 422 U.S. 171 (1975); Stewart v. U. S., 366 U.S. 1, 5 (1961); Grunewald v. U.S., 353 U.S. 391, 421 (1957).

severely curtailed prosecution use of tacit admissions. The Alabama Supreme Court, for example, barred all use of either pre- or post-arrest silence, explaining that "neither logic nor common experience any longer support the tacit admission rule, if indeed, either ever supported it."

Other courts have held that admissibility turns on case-specific probative value/risk of undue prejudice balances, and some have encouraged trial judges to engage in more critical appraisals of the competing considerations.

§ 162   Use of Otherwise Inadmissible Confessions for Impeachment

The exclusionary sanctions applicable to confessions are subject to the limitations applicable to exclusionary sanctions generally, including the limitation which often permits the prosecution to use inadmissible evidence to impeach a defendant who testifies in his own defense at trial.[118] Confession law's complexity, and especially the distinction between the voluntariness requirement and other exclusionary rules, results in particular difficulties applying the impeachment exception to confession law.

In a line of cases beginning with *Harris v. New York*,[119] the Supreme Court held that the impeachment exception to federal constitutional exclusionary requirements permits the use of confessions obtained in violation of *Miranda v. Arizona*[120] and at least some Sixth Amendment right to counsel requirements for such impeachment purposes. Those obtained in violation of "core" Sixth Amendment demands, however, seemed possibly to be inadmissible even for this purpose.

Rejecting any distinction among Sixth Amendment violations, the Court in *Kansas v. Ventris*[121] held that apparently all confessions obtained in violation of the Sixth Amendment right to counsel could be used for impeachment. The Sixth Amendment violation occurs when the confession is elicited, not when it is used. The Court found no reason to distinguish these cases from all others in which use at trial of tainted evidence does not itself constitute a violation and thus use for impeachment is constitutionally acceptable.

Harris' impeachment exception to the federal constitutional exclusionary sanctions attaching to confessions does not extend to certain situations in which voluntariness concerns are implicated. In *Mincey v. Arizona*[122] the Court found constitutional error in the use of an involuntary confession to impeach a testifying defendant. "*[A]ny* criminal trial use against a defendant of his involuntary statement," the Court announced, "is a denial of due process . . . ." This is apparently because involuntariness—unlike *Miranda* violations—render confessions at least somewhat untrustworthy, and consequently less valuable as indicators of defendant perjury. The prosecution's interest in using them for impeachment is therefore reduced. Further, law enforcement activity that has sufficient impact to render confessions involuntary is more offensive to constitutional values than activity that merely violates *Miranda's* prophylactic rules. This increases the need for maximum deterrence, which is provided by excluding the confessions for all purposes. In

---

[118]   See generally infra § 183.

[119]   401 U.S. 222 (1971).

[120]   384 U.S. 436 (1966).

[121]   556 U.S. 586 (2009).

[122]   437 U.S. 385 (1978).

these cases, then, the need for full deterrence outweighs the prosecution's reduced interest in using the confessions even for the limited purpose at issue.

As in other exclusionary sanction situations, state courts and legislatures remain free to reject the federal constitutional model and to apply state law exclusionary requirements unqualified by impeachment exceptions. Some have done so.

§ 163 Determining Admissibility and Credibility

The close relationship between some requirements of admissibility and the weight that confession evidence is properly given in determining guilt have generated considerable disagreement on the role of judge and jury in resolving the various issues presented when the prosecution offers evidence of a defendant's confession. Some of the issues, of course, are constitutional ones.

Roles of Judge and Jury. In *Jackson v. Denno*,[123] the Supreme Court held that the due process clause of the Fourteenth Amendment requires that upon proper demand the trial judge determine the voluntariness of a challenged confession. *Jackson* held constitutionally impermissible what had previously been known as the "New York procedure," under which the trial judge conducted a preliminary inquiry and excluded a challenged confession only if its involuntariness was so clear as to present no issue. If the evidence presented a fair question as to voluntariness or any factual matters relevant to voluntariness, the confession was submitted to the jury with directions to determine voluntariness and to consider the confession on the issue of guilt or innocence only if it was found to be voluntary.

Under the New York procedure, the Court reasoned, jurors might first conclude that a defendant committed the crime charged and then be unable or disinclined to determine the voluntariness of a challenged confession without regard to its accuracy. This would, of course, violate the right to have voluntariness determined without regard to reliability. Alternatively, the jurors might first address the confession and conclude that it was involuntary but reliable; they might then be unable or disinclined to ignore that confession in assessing the sufficiency of the prosecution's evidence on guilt. This would endanger the right to have guilt or innocence determined without consideration of an involuntary confession.

Defendants have no federal constitutional right to jury consideration of claims of involuntariness rejected by trial judges. The Court in *Lego v. Twomey*[124] found neither a basis for concluding that juries are somehow "better suited" than trial judges to determine voluntariness, nor convincing grounds for regarding trial judges' resolutions of voluntariness challenges as sufficiently unreliable to entitle defendants to "a second forum for litigating [their] claim[s]."

Defendants do have a federal Due Process right to contest the credibility—as distinguished from the voluntariness—of a confession admitted into evidence. Once the prosecution is permitted to introduce evidence that the defendant made incriminating admissions, the Court held in *Crane v. Kentucky*,[125] the defendant is entitled to introduce

---

[123] 378 U.S. 368 (1964).
[124] 404 U.S. 477 (1972).
[125] 476 U.S. 683 (1986).

evidence concerning the circumstances under which he made them if those circumstances bear upon the credibility of the admissions.

Federal constitutional considerations, then, permit the trial judge to be given sole responsibility for resolving voluntariness issues. Under this "orthodox" approach, the trial judge resolves all factual disputes and determines voluntariness. No issues related to voluntariness are submitted to the jury. Many jurisdictions follow this procedure.

Federal constitutional requirements also permit what is known as the Massachusetts or "humane" procedure under which the trial judge makes a full inquiry into and determines voluntariness. If the trial judge finds the challenged confession voluntary, however, the issue of voluntariness is then submitted to the jury for reconsideration, and the jury is instructed to consider the confession on the defendant's guilt only if it first finds it voluntary. A number of jurisdictions take this approach.

The wisdom of this approach is questionable. Most if not all considerations relating to voluntariness will also be relevant to credibility, so the defendant will have an opportunity to present them to the jury. Whether jurors are ever or often able or inclined to distinguish credibility and voluntariness and to disregard a credible but involuntary confession is at best doubtful, and the task of adequately submitting both matters to the jury without confusing the jurors is a difficult and perhaps impossible one. Careful submission of credibility, then, is preferable to the humane procedure.

What is submitted to a jury depends, of course, on the jurisdiction's approach. Under *Crane*, a defendant challenging before the jury the credibility of the prosecution's evidence that he confessed is certainly entitled to adequate jury instructions on the jury's obligation to evaluate credibility. Under nonconstitutional law, juries are often told that they are to consider, in light of all the circumstances, the weight to give to such evidence, and this is probably sufficient under *Crane*.

Some jurisdictions go further at least in certain types of cases, as for example by instructing juries to view with caution evidence that the defendant made an oral admission of guilt or even to so view evidence that the accused made an out-of-court incriminating statement. Recent developments regarding recording of out-of-court statements by suspect have sometimes included requirements of jury instructions concerning the special risks of evidence of unrecorded statements; this is considered in Section 158 supra.

Jurisdictions following the humane procedure require juries to address the voluntariness of any self-incriminating statements they find the accuseds made. This is a different task than determining the weight to be given such statements in light of their apparent credibility, and a jury is to be told to first determine voluntariness and then, if it finds the confession voluntary, to consider what if any weight to give to it.

Hearing and Burden of Proof. Jackson means that generally a trial judge is required to hold a hearing on the admissibility of a challenged confession—a "*Jackson v. Denno* hearing"—if the party against whom it is offered objects and requests such a hearing. A few courts, regarding some confession requirements as too important to fall to defense counsel's default, require that even in the absence of a demand for a hearing, trial judges conduct a hearing, entertain evidence, and determine voluntariness of a proffered confession.

A defendant's federal constitutional right to a fair determination of voluntariness means that a trial judge's conclusion that a challenged confession is voluntary "must appear from the record with unmistakable clarity." It is not constitutionally necessary, however, that the trial judge make formal findings of fact on contested subissues or write a formal opinion. Nevertheless, sound policy and particularly the practicalities of effective appellate review strongly suggest specific findings concerning disputed subquestions of fact as well as a clear ultimate determination of the major issues.

Lego held that when a defendant challenges the prosecution's proffer of a confession, the federal constitution requires that the prosecution prove the voluntariness of the confession but that the prosecution need only establish this by a preponderance of the evidence. Voluntariness does not have to be established beyond a reasonable doubt or even by clear and convincing evidence.

No basis had been presented for believing that traditional determinations of admissibility based on a preponderance of the evidence were unreliable or otherwise "wanting in quality." Whatever might be accomplished by imposing a higher standard, the Court concluded, would be outweighed by the cost of denying juries evidence probative on defendants' guilt or innocence. Fourteen years later, the Court summarily held that the prosecution's burden of proving compliance with Fifth Amendment *Miranda* requirements is no greater.

States remain free to impose higher standards. Many do require the prosecution to establish voluntariness and sometimes compliance with other requirements, such as those imposed by self-incrimination demands, by clear and convincing evidence or even beyond a reasonable doubt.

Chapter 15

THE PRIVILEGE CONCERNING IMPROPERLY OBTAINED EVIDENCE

Table of Sections

---

§ 164   Introduction

Traditionally, out-of-court impropriety in the manner by which evidence was obtained did not affect its admissibility. This was primarily, of course, because the courts regarded the need for all probative evidence to assure the most accurate resolution of lawsuits as more important than other objectives that might be furthered by excluding relevant but improperly obtained evidence. In addition, however, courts regarded inquiries into possible impropriety in the development of evidence as too costly and time-consuming to justify whatever other objectives might be furthered by excluding evidence because of impropriety in obtaining it.

Probably the most important recent development in the law of evidence as applied in criminal litigation has been the rejection of this approach and the resulting increase in requirements that evidence be excluded because of the manner in which it was obtained—so-called "exclusionary rules."[1]

Discussions sometimes assume the existence of "the exclusionary rule," suggesting that there is only one remedial requirement involved. This is unfortunate and misleading. Litigation and discussion is often dominated by considerations of the Supreme Court's construction of the Fourth Amendment to the United States Constitution as requiring the exclusion in both state and federal criminal prosecutions of evidence tainted by a violation of that provision. But this ignores that exclusion may be required because evidence was obtained by violating other legal requirements, many of them not embodied in the federal constitution. Moreover, the contents of these exclusionary requirements need not necessarily be the same as that of the Fourth Amendment exclusionary demand.

Generally, then, discussion best avoids simplistic reference to "the exclusionary rule" as a single rule covering a range of situations. Instead, this area should be conceptualized as containing numerous possible exclusionary rules or sanctions. An exclusionary sanction may attach to any legal requirement that could be violated in the gathering of evidence. There are potentially as many exclusionary sanctions as there are legal requirements of this sort. The Fourth Amendment exclusionary sanction may provide a benchmark for analysis of issues presented by other exclusionary sanctions. But it is important to recognize that other such sanctions may differ in content from the Fourth Amendment's rule. Whether and how they should differ are hard issues that tend to be obscured by discussion of "the exclusionary rule."

It is, of course, difficult to separate discussion of exclusionary sanctions from consideration of the underlying rules enforced by these sanctions. Nevertheless, the contents of those rules are not matters of evidence law. Consequently, this chapter focuses upon the exclusionary consequences rather than the underlying legal requirements violated.

Many legal requirements relating to the admissibility of confessions, such as the *Miranda* requirements and directives that an arrested person be promptly presented before a magistrate, are probably exclusionary sanctions within the meaning of this chapter. For convenience, however, these are treated in Chapter 14, devoted generally to confessions.

§ 165 Policy Bases for Exclusionary Sanctions[2]

Exclusionary sanctions result in exclusion of what would otherwise be relevant and competent evidence, and therefore involve a considerable cost. Consequently, they bear

---

[1] These requirements are appropriately characterized as rules of privilege rather than rules of competency; see the discussion in supra §§ 72 & 72.1 concerning the distinction between rules of privilege and those of competency. Generally speaking, their purpose is not to facilitate the accurate ascertainment of facts by safeguarding against unreliable or misleading evidence but rather to further other interests embodied in the requirements violated by the manner in which the evidence was obtained.

[2] The purposes which exclusionary rules might serve have been discussed primarily in the context of the federal constitutional requirements, but this discussion can quite easily be generalized. How the Supreme Court has developed the conceptual bases for these federal constitutional requirements is considered later. See infra § 167. While this case law is a model that might be applied in other contexts, the Court's selection of those objectives legitimately served and the comparative significance given them is certainly not beyond reasonable dispute. Some state courts' development of state exclusionary requirements, for example, have rejected at least parts of this model in developing the conceptual bases for these state law rules. See infra § 168.

a significant burden of justification. Such justification might be provided by several quite different functions which these sanctions might serve.

Promotion of Accurate Results. Can exclusionary rules be defended on the ground that they result in rejection of evidence that might otherwise increase the risk that trials would lead to inaccurate results? Some exclusionary sanctions may be supported, at least to some extent, on this basis. If counsel's presence at lineups reduces the risk of suggestiveness, for example, exclusion of eyewitness testimony tainted by the witness's identification of the defendant at a lineup conducted in violation of this right might to some extent result in rejection of unreliable evidence that might otherwise be credited beyond what can be defended on objective grounds.

Most exclusionary sanctions, however, cannot be supported on these grounds. To the contrary, the fact that the evidence excluded by these requirements is not only relevant and competent but also highly reliable increases the difficulty of justifying the requirements.

Prevention of Future Violations. A major function served by exclusionary sanctions, of course, is the prevention of future violations of the underlying legal requirements. Prevention might be effectuated in at least two quite different ways: deterrence and "education" or "assimilation."

Deterrence consists of motivating persons to consciously choose not to violate legal requirements because of a desire to avoid rendering evidence inadmissible. Usually in exclusionary sanction debates this means encouraging law enforcement officers to comply with legal requirements in a conscious effort to assure the admissibility of the products of their investigative efforts. But detractors of the exclusionary sanction approach argue that any expectation that deterrence will work effectively is naive, in part because law enforcement officers will often perceive the threat of exclusion as far less meaningful than other considerations influencing their conduct.

Exclusion will be a possibility only if the case is actively contested. Most criminal cases are not ultimately litigated, so the technical admissibility of evidence will not be a consideration. In the infrequent cases in which exclusion becomes a real possibility, the threat materializes only long after the officers' role in the case is finished. A threat to exclude, made in the context of plea bargaining and protracted processing of criminal cases, may be a threat of such minimal and distant significance that it cannot be expected to overcome, in the officers' minds, other considerations that suggest different courses of action.

In actuality, other considerations may be more immediately pressing and make stronger cases for officers' attention. If an officer believes that compliance with legal requirements endangers his personal safety, he is unlikely to ignore that risk because of the possibility of legal challenges to the admissibility of the products of his actions at some distant time. Similarly, the expectations of the officer's peers and immediate supervisors may well conflict with what the law requires and may compete quite effectively with evidentiary rules for the officer's response.

Moreover, the legal requirements with which the officer is expected to comply may be so unclear as to frustrate efforts to ascertain and follow them. Or they may appear to the officer as unrealistic, meaningless or both, and thus invite circumvention.

There is even a risk that to the extent an exclusionary sanction may convey a meaningful deterrent message to law enforcement officers, the result may be that officers will find it most advantageous to completely forego formal prosecution and instead rely upon "street justice" to encourage what they perceive as desirable behavior. If the result of an evidentiary rule is to encourage law enforcement agencies to engage in informal and largely extra-legal activities rather than to encourage them to comply with legal requirements so that prosecution remains possible, the rules have arguably effectuated the worst of all possibilities.

Perhaps the lesson is that generalization about the likely deterrent effect of exclusionary sanctions is difficult or impossible. Some law enforcement activities may be far more subject to being influenced by evidentiary rules than others. Some legal requirements might far more than others lend themselves to effective implementation by means of exclusionary requirements.

Prevention of undesired law enforcement activity, however, may be accomplished in ways other than deterrence. The Supreme Court has noted the possibility that the long-term effect of excluding evidence may be to demonstrate the seriousness with which society regards the underlying legal requirements. This, in turn, may cause law enforcement officers and policymakers to incorporate the requirements into their value system and, presumably, to accept them unconsciously as demanding compliance regardless of the consciously-perceived effect of noncompliance.

How effective exclusionary sanctions are in enforcing various legal requirements in different contexts remains addressed largely on the basis of intuition. Some empirical research has been undertaken, but in part because of severe methodological problems it is inconclusive.

Judicial Integrity Considerations. Exclusionary sanctions might be justified in whole or in part on the basis of what the Supreme Court in *Elkins v. United States*[3] called "the imperative of judicial integrity." But two very different approaches are sometimes confused in discussions of judicial integrity.

One argument is that because evidence was improperly obtained, courts' use of that evidence is simply and inherently "wrong" and thus to be avoided. Of course, the nature of the argument means that it is incapable of utilitarian analysis or empirical verification. At its base, it rests upon an intuitive notion of "right" or "integrity." Whether any such notion of "right" can provide strong support for a costly evidentiary rule, of course, is at best problematic.

Another argument often regarded as a judicial integrity consideration has, in contrast, a clearly utilitarian end and thus is—in theory at least—susceptible to efforts to verify it. This approach was articulated by Justice Brandeis in *Olmstead v. United States*:[4]

> In a government of laws, existence of the government will be imperiled if it fails to observe the law scrupulously . . . . Crime is contagious. If the Government becomes a lawbreaker, it breeds contempt for law; it invites every man to become a law unto himself; it invites anarchy.[5]

---

[3]   364 U.S. 206 (1960).

[4]   277 U.S. 438 (1928).

[5]   *Olmstead*, 277 U.S. at 485 (Brandeis, J., dissenting).

This means, he continued, that the government, like a private litigant, should be denied access to the courts if it comes with unclean hands. If the government bases its request for aid from the courts on illegally obtained evidence, "aid is denied despite the defendant's wrong. It is denied in order to maintain respect for law; in order to promote confidence in the administration of justice; in order to preserve the judicial process from contamination."

Essentially, this argument is that if illegally seized evidence is used by the government acting through its courts, government in general and its courts in particular will lose the respect of the governed and consequently will be rendered less able to perform their governing functions. In the case of courts, this means that they will be less able to resolve disputes among citizens.

Despite the rhetorical flourish with which Justice Brandeis demonstrated this argument can be made, it may simply be inconsistent with reality. Whether the courts' ability to command respect and compliance is affected by evidentiary rules is, of course, open to doubt. But to the extent that it is, this argument may distort the effect of those rules. General respect for the judiciary may well suffer when the courts are perceived as ignoring reliable evidence because of impropriety in the manner it was obtained, particularly if doing so requires the acquittal of persons clearly guilty of serious antisocial acts.

Remedy for Wrongs Done in the Illegality. Superficially, at least, exclusionary sanctions would seem to perform a unique and perhaps appropriate remedial function, and thus might be justified on that basis. The law's objective, the argument might run, should be to place a wronged person as close to his previous condition as is feasible. Only an exclusionary sanction can replace such a person in a position in which he need not fear the use against him of the fruits of wrong done to him.

On the other hand, the substance of the underlying legal requirements violated may make clear that persons whose rights are violated have no legitimate interest in being free of criminal liability that looms only because of the violations of their rights. If they have no such legitimate interest, the fact that an exclusionary sanction frees them of such liability is of little or no significance.

The right to be free of unreasonable searches, for example, may protect only persons' interest in being free of the privacy invasion occasioned by such searches. That this privacy interest enables them to withhold from the government evidence of their criminal activity would then be at most an undesirable side effect of the privacy right. If the right to be free from unreasonable searches is so conceptualized, no person who is unreasonably searched has a legitimate interest in having the government deprived of the power to use against them evidence found as a result of that search. Their interest in an effective remedy for the violation of their privacy, then, does not include an interest in being returned to a condition in which they need not fear the government's use of the discovered evidence against them in a criminal prosecution.

If the underlying legal requirements are so conceptualized, the tendency of exclusionary sanctions to provide unique protection against criminal liability is of no legitimate remedial significance. Since the victims of the underlying wrongs have no legitimate interest in being free of the use of the evidence against them, the unique ability of exclusionary sanctions to bring about this result does not significantly support the exclusionary sanctions.

Even if exclusion does tend to some extent at least respond in a logical manner to the harm done, it may not be "appropriate" because it provides an excessive remedy. This is especially the case if exclusion of evidence frustrates the prosecution. Acquittal of a demonstrably guilty person may simply be too heavy a cost even to make a victimized person whole.

§ 166   Federal Constitutional Exclusionary Sanctions: (a) Development

Federal constitutional exclusionary sanctions have served as a model for modern exclusionary requirements. The Supreme Court's case law developing the federal sanctions—and the decisions molding the Fourth Amendment exclusionary requirement in particular—have similarly framed much of the discussion of exclusionary requirements in general.

Exclusion as a response to Federal constitutional illegality in obtaining evidence appears to have originated in confusion concerning the substance of Fourth and Fifth Amendment protection. In *Boyd v. United States*,[6] an unsuccessful claimant in a forfeiture action sought relief from a judgment of forfeiture on the ground that the trial court erred in receiving into evidence an invoice which the claimant had been compelled to produce by order of the trial court. Both the Fourth and Fifth Amendments were invoked. The Supreme Court held that the compulsory production of the document was subject to scrutiny under the Fourth Amendment. To determine whether it was reasonable, the Court turned to the Fifth Amendment's prohibition against compelled self-incrimination. Finding an "intimate relationship" between the two provisions, the Court concluded that compelled production or other seizure of a person's private books or papers to be used in evidence against him was violative of the Fifth Amendment. Ultimately, the Court held that the admission into evidence of the invoice, given the manner in which it was obtained, violated both the Fourth Amendment prohibition against unreasonable searches and seizures and the Fifth Amendment prohibition against compelled self-incrimination.

Twenty years later, in *Adams v. New York*,[7] the Court nevertheless refused to require exclusion where only the defendant's Fourth Amendment rights were violated. Such cases were governed by what the Court described as "the weight of authority as well as reason," embodied in the rule that courts will not pause to inquire as to the means by which competent evidence is obtained.

A decade later, however, in *Weeks v. United States*,[8] the Court embraced exclusion as a Fourth Amendment remedy. The Fourth Amendment as it applied in federal criminal litigation, *Weeks* held, imposed an exclusionary sanction. "If letters and private documents can thus be [improperly] seized and held and used in evidence against a citizen accused of an offense," the Court reasoned, "the protection of the Fourth Amendment declaring his right to be secure against such searches and seizures is of no value, and, so far as those thus placed are concerned, might as well be stricken from the Constitution."

---

[6]   116 U.S. 616 (1886).

[7]   192 U.S. 585 (1904).

[8]   232 U.S. 383 (1914).

Weeks, of course, was inapplicable to state litigation, and doubt remained even whether the Fourth Amendment itself was binding on the states. In *Wolf v. Colorado*,[9] the Court for the first time directly addressed these issues. Concluding that the core of the Fourth Amendment, the security of one's privacy against arbitrary intrusion by the police, was basic to a free society and therefore implicit in the concept of ordered liberty, the Court held that under *Palko v. Connecticut*[10] the Fourth Amendment prohibition against unreasonable searches and seizures was enforceable against the States through the Due Process clause of the Fourteenth Amendment.

But *Wolf* then distinguished the prohibition against unreasonable searches and seizures from the exclusionary remedy applied in federal criminal litigation and found the latter not binding on the States. By 1961, however, the Court was prepared to reconsider *Wolf's* second conclusion.

In *Mapp v. Ohio*,[11] this second holding of *Wolf* was reversed. Since *Wolf*, the majority explained, more than half of those states considering whether to adopt an exclusionary sanction as a matter of state law had decided to do so. The weight of the relevant authority, then, could no longer be said to oppose the *Weeks* rule. More important, however, the Court read experience as contradicting *Wolf's* assumption that remedies other than an exclusionary rule could be relied upon to enforce Fourth Amendment rights. The experience and decisions of the state courts as well as the Supreme Court's own decisions recognized the "obvious futility of relegating the Fourth Amendment to the protection of other remedies . . . ." Consequently, the *Weeks* exclusionary rule was held an essential part of both the Fourth and Fourteenth Amendments and therefore binding on the states as well as the federal government.

Mapp was undoubtedly a bold holding made on minimal grounds. Functionally, the Supreme Court read the general terms of the Fourth Amendment as delegating to the federal courts the power to develop remedies appropriate to enforcement of the clear substantive commands of the provision. The framers must have anticipated that the guarantees of the provision be enforceable in federal courts. Since they failed to provide for remedies that enabled this, they must have intended that the courts have authority to develop such remedies as are appropriate given such considerations as the magnitude of the threats posed to the underlying guarantees and the effectiveness of less costly alternatives than exclusion of resulting evidence.

Having determined that an exclusionary sanction was an essential part of the Fourth Amendment right to be free from unreasonable searches and seizures, the Court proceeded to apply it uncritically to other federal constitutional rights. It has made clear, however, that these various federal constitutional exclusionary sanctions are not identical in content.

Until *Hudson v. Michigan*,[12] it was generally assumed that any violation of at least the Fourth Amendment triggered exclusionary rule analysis under *Mapp*. *Hudson*, however, held that at least one category of Fourth Amendment violations will not do so. Fourth Amendment violations consisting of entry of premises to execute a search

---

9   338 U.S. 25 (1949).

10   302 U.S. 319 (1937).

11   367 U.S. 643 (1961).

12   547 U.S. 586 (2006).

warrant in a "no knock" manner violating Fourth Amendment requirements simply cannot support an exclusionary rule challenge to evidence found in the premises.

Hudson's conceptual basis is somewhat unclear. Some of the Court's discussion suggests the holding rests on the lack of proof in these cases of sufficient factual causation between the Fourth Amendment violation and the discovery of the challenged evidence. Other parts suggest that whatever factual causation may exist is usually if not inevitably of a sort that demands a finding that the taint was attenuated and thus the evidence is admissible despite the factual causation.

Overall the *Hudson* discussion indicates that the holding rested on neither causation nor attenuation of taint grounds. Rather, the Court is now willing to identify categories of Fourth Amendment violations that are, as a matter of Fourth Amendment exclusionary sanction law, insufficient to trigger the exclusionary remedy. A defendant's challenge to admissibility of evidence relying on such a violation must fail without inquiry into whether the defendant has proved causation or the prosecution has established attenuation of the taint.

Why were no knock entry violations held insufficient to trigger the exclusionary requirement, and what does this suggest regarding what other violations might be similarly characterized? *Hudson* was not entirely clear. Certainly the result was influenced by the Court's perceptions that the Fourth Amendment announcement requirement is one particularly difficult for officers to understand and meet. It also took into account that these cases often involve at most a minimal causal link between the violation and the discovery of the evidence and present factors militating in favor of a finding of attenuation of taint. It was also undoubtedly influenced by the majority's increasing disenchantment with exclusion of evidence as a constitutional remedy.

In addition, however, *Hudson* indicated that exclusion is appropriate as a response only to Fourth Amendment requirements that protect Fourth Amendment interests in shielding evidence from government observation or physical seizure. The requirement of announcement before entering premises to execute a warrant protects other Fourth Amendment interests—the security of "life and limb" and property and certain aspects of privacy and dignity. Since the challenge to the evidence did not rest on interests related to the protection of evidence from government acquisition, *Hudson* explained, "the exclusionary rule is inapplicable."

Post-*Mapp* applications of the federal constitutional exclusionary requirements generally assumed these requirements are mandatory. If the facts before a trial judge trigger one of the rules but no recognized exception to the exclusionary demand, the judge is required to exclude the evidence. The judge has no general discretion to admit or exclude evidence based on the judge's case specific evaluation of the propriety or wisdom of exclusion.

The continuing validity of this assumption was cast into doubt by *Herring v. United States.*[13] *Herring* held that in at least one context exclusion is not required—or apparently permitted—if a defendant shows only a "negligent" violation of the Fourth Amendment. Specifically, *Herring* held exclusion was not required by a showing that the challenged evidence was tainted by an arrest made in reliance on police records erroneously indicating—as a result of negligent recordkeeping by officers of another

---

[13]   555 U.S. 135 (2009).

county—a warrant was outstanding for the defendant. Whatever deterrence might be provided by excluding evidence tainted by merely negligent police recordkeeping, *Herring* held, is not worth the cost.

Where *Herring* applies, it appears to require a defendant seeking exclusion of evidence under *Mapp* to at least show more as a basis for triggering exclusionary rule analysis than a mere Fourth Amendment violation. This analysis can be triggered by a showing of "deliberate, reckless, or grossly negligent conduct." Alternatively, at least "in some circumstances" a showing of "recurring or systemic negligence" will suffice. Justice Breyer suggested in dissent that trial courts will have to engage a "case-by-case, multifactored inquiry into the degree of police culpability."

If *Herring* applies, it may permit or require more than an inquiry into whether the defendant has shown at least gross negligence or reoccurring or systemic negligence. It may in at least some situations allow trial courts to balance on a case-by-case basis the proven law enforcement culpability against the need for deterrence in the type of situation presented.

Obviously, identifying those situations to which *Herring* applies presents a major issue of Fourth Amendment exclusionary rule law. The Court noted that that the constitutionally-deficient law enforcement conduct before it related to maintaining law enforcement records, and specifically an arrest warrant database. *Herring* may apply only to such situations.

In *Herring*, the merely negligent held insufficient to trigger exclusionary rule analysis was by law enforcements officers of a county other than that employing the arresting officers. This apparently caused the *Herring* majority to characterize the negligence as "attenuated from" the law enforcement action directly causing the acquisition of the evidence. Perhaps, then, *Herring* applies only where the constitutionally-deficient law enforcement conduct is attenuated in this manner from the law enforcement that in a direct sense infringed the objecting defendant's Fourth Amendment protected interests.

Herring might be read as an expansion of the so-called "good faith" exception[14] to the Fourth Amendment exclusionary requirement. But the Court's discussion did not focus on the government's defensive response to *Herring's* challenge to the admissibility of the evidence. Rather, it suggested the defect was one in the attack itself: a defendant— at least in the context involved—must show more than a merely "negligent" law enforcement violation of Fourth Amendment requirements.

Recent developments reflect the Supreme Court's increasing disenchantment with exclusionary remedies for federal constitutional rights; this is developed in the next section. Quite predictably, therefore, in 2009 the Court summarily rejected a suggestion that it should craft a new and broad "exclusionary rule" barring state courts from admitting testimony from "jailhouse snitches."[15]

---

[14] See infra § 182.
[15] Kansas v. Ventris, 556 U.S. 586, 593 n.* (2009).

§ 167 Federal Constitutional Exclusionary Sanctions: (b) Policy Bases and Analytical Approach

As the Supreme Court developed the federal constitutional exclusionary requirements, primarily the Fourth Amendment sanction, it narrowed the policy considerations on which those requirements are based. It also formulated a consistently-applied approach to framing the subissues raised in developing the contents of those requirements. In the course of this process, the Court made several basic choices regarding the potentially-relevant policy considerations.

First, the Court has made clear that the federal constitutional rules do not serve a significant legitimate remedial function. This is because as the Court envisions the constitutionally-cognizable injuries done, exclusion of evidence simply does not tend to make victims whole. "[T]he ruptured privacy of the victims' homes and effects," it explained in the context of search and seizure law, "cannot be restored. Reparation comes too late."

If exclusion of evidence cannot restore the violated privacy, why cannot it at least reduce one effect of the privacy violation by replacing the victim to a position wherein he does not face criminal prosecution based on evidence obtained as a result of the violation of his privacy interests? The Court has not directly addressed this question. But most likely it views the prosecution's possession of and ability to use incriminating evidence as entirely unrelated to the legitimate interests of the defendant. The prosecution has a right to possession of this evidence; the defendant has no ultimate right to withhold it from the prosecution. To the extent that an improper search results in the prosecution being able to implement its interest in obtaining such evidence, the search violates no protected interests, that is, no constitutionally-cognizable "rights," of the defendant. The wrong to the defendant consisted entirely of violating his privacy. To the extent that this violation of privacy factually resulted in the prosecution obtaining access to incriminating evidence, this in no way contributes to the constitutionally-offensive aspects of the search, that is, those aspects as to which the defendant has a legitimate claim to remedy.

Consequently, to deprive the prosecution of the ability to use this evidence would in no way restore the defendant in a manner to which he has any legitimate claim. His only legitimate claim is for restoration of his violated privacy, which is in no way accomplished by depriving the prosecution of evidence.

The second basic decision made by the Court was adoption of the view that considerations of judicial integrity have only a "limited role" in Fourth Amendment theory and, consequently, in determining the content of the provision's exclusionary mandate. This was accomplished by holding that the "primary meaning" of judicial integrity in this context is such that it is violated when, but only when, courts' use of illegally obtained evidence encourages future violations of the sort that provided the prosecution access to the evidence at issue. Consequently, whether particular use of illegally obtained evidence offends judicial integrity considerations involves essentially the same question as whether it serves a preventive purpose: will the admission of the evidence encourage future illegality of the sort committed to obtain the evidence at issue?

A third basic policy decision concerns what almost by default has become the basic justification for the federal constitutional requirements—the need to prevent future violations of the underlying constitutional demands. Traditionally, the Court appeared to assume that this would be accomplished by conscious deterrence—law enforcement officers would be motivated by the exclusionary sanction to consciously comply with the constitutional rules. In *Stone v. Powell*,[16] with regard to the preventive function of the Fourth Amendment exclusionary rule, the Court indicated that the long-term "educative" effect is "[m]ore important[ ]" than the tendency of the threat of exclusion to consciously deter officers from future violations. Nevertheless, it has not followed this pronouncement and in post-*Powell* analyses has assumed that prevention is accomplished primarily if not exclusively by deterrence.

A final policy decision was evidenced more recently in the Court's case law. Beginning with *Herring v. United States*,[17] the Court has stressed the importance of the "culpability" of the law enforcement conduct in determining the exclusionary consequences of that conduct. To some extent, this is closely related to its emphasis on deterrence. "The extent to which the exclusionary rule is justified by . . . deterrence principles," it announced in *Herring*, "varies with the culpability of the law enforcement conduct." But the case law also suggests the Court has come to view exclusion as a punishment imposed on law enforcement that must be justified by a demonstration that the triggering conduct was blameworthy. Later in *Herring* the Court observed:

> To trigger the exclusionary rule, police conduct must be sufficiently deliberate that exclusion can meaningfully deter it, and sufficiently culpable that such deterrence is worth the price paid by the justice system.[18]

This suggests a need for culpability independent of the need for the deliberateness necessary to invoke the deterrence rationale.

Building on these basic decisions regarding the relevant considerations, the Court has developed a consistent formula for framing specific subissues regarding the content of the federal constitutional exclusionary rules. First articulated in *United States v. Calandra*,[19] this approach puts the issue as one of proposed expansion of the exclusionary requirement beyond the core demand that evidence obtained as a direct result of activity violating the constitutional requirements be excluded when offered by the prosecution to prove the defendant's guilt in the prosecution's case-in-chief at a criminal trial. The analysis requires identification of, first, the increased effectiveness of the exclusionary sanction in accomplishing its purpose that would result from the proposed expansion, and, second, the costs of doing so. The critical question is whether the incremental increase in effectiveness is worth the cost that must be paid.

Generally, in inquiring into the potential for increased effectiveness the Court focuses upon deterrence and inquires as to the incremental deterrent effect which would be achieved by the proposed expansion. With regard to the costs, of course, the loss of reliable evidence of offenders' guilt is the major concern. But in addition the Court has taken into account other considerations, such as administrative costs and disruption of the criminal justice system in general and criminal trials in particular. In *Calandra*, for example, the specific issue before the Court was whether the Fourth Amendment exclusionary rule should be applied to grand jury proceedings by permitting witnesses to decline to respond to questions based upon information obtained in violation of the

---

[16]   428 U.S. 465 (1976).

[17]   555 U.S. 135 (2009).

[18]   *Id.* at 144.

[19]   414 U.S. 338 (1974).

witnesses' Fourth Amendment rights. Permitting this, the majority stressed, would require that grand jury investigations be frequently halted for extended inquiries into the manner in which particular information was acquired. The result would be serious interference with the effective and expeditious discharge by grand juries of their historic role and functions.

In recent case law, a majority of the Court has shown increasing willingness to give minimal weight in its analyses to those considerations traditionally favoring reliance on exclusion of evidence. In *Hudson v. Michigan*,[20] for example, the majority suggested legal and social changes since *Mapp* have made reliance on the costly remedy of exclusion less necessary and less appropriate. Law enforcement agencies have become more professional, it added, and have emphasized internal discipline.

Nearly as dramatic has been the willingness of a majority of the Court to characterize exclusion of evidence as a disfavored and last resort remedy under federal constitutional and nonconstitutional law. If the Vienna Convention on Consular Relations authorizes the federal courts to develop a judicial remedy for violations of the Convention, the Court explained in *Sanchez-Llamas v. Oregon*,[21] that remedy must conform with United States domestic law. Domestic United States law, it then made clear, accepts exclusion of evidence only where that approach provides more a more effective and less-costly remedy than alternatives. That is not the case, *Sanchez-Llamas* held, with violations of the Convention.

What *Hudson* and *Herring* portend for the future of federal constitutional exclusionary requirements is far from clear. In *Hudson*, Justice Kennedy concurred in part to express confidence that "the continued operation of the exclusionary rule, as settled and defined by our precedents, is not in doubt." No such confidence was expressed three years later by any of the Justices in *Herring*.

Given the relevant policy considerations, the Court expressly stated in *Hudson*, "[s]uppression of evidence . . . has always been our last resort . . . ." Whether this is accurate as a statement of historical fact is at best questionable. Clearly, however, it accurately states the position of a majority of the current Court.

§ 168 State Constitutional Exclusionary Sanctions

Despite the prominence of *Mapp v. Ohio*.[22] and Fourth Amendment case law in exclusionary sanction discussion, the exclusionary remedy was first developed in state constitutional litigation. State decisions provide bases of increasing importance for modern exclusionary sanctions, independent of *Mapp* and its progeny. Proponents of exclusion as a means of enforcing legal requirements, dissatisfied with the Supreme Court's development of federal rights and exclusionary remedies, have increasingly sought to persuade state courts to develop state constitutional rights—and state constitutional exclusionary requirements—as more rigorously protective of those suspected or accused of crime.

States' power to accept or reject an exclusionary approach was confirmed by the Supreme Court in *California v. Greenwood*.[23] Under California law, the warrantless

---

[20] 547 U.S. 586 (2006).

[21] 548 U.S. 331 (2006).

[22] 367 U.S. 643 (1961).

[23] 486 U.S. 35 (1988).

search of Greenwood's trash constituted an unreasonable search under a state constitutional provision similar to the Fourth Amendment, yet state constitutional law did not require exclusion of the resulting evidence. All agreed that *Mapp* and its rationale did not require, as a matter of Fourth Amendment law, exclusion of evidence obtained in violation of the state constitution but not in violation of any federal provision. Further, the Court held, the Due Process Clause of the Fourteenth Amendment did not bar the state from depriving Greenwood of a remedy for police conduct violating state but not federal constitutional law. California could have defined unreasonable searches as encompassing no more official activity than was covered by the Fourth Amendment. Since the state has the power to permit police activity not barred by the Fourth Amendment, it necessarily also has the lesser included power to prohibit such activity but to enforce that prohibition by means other than excluding evidence from criminal trials.

A few states provide by statute that evidence obtained in violation of state constitutional provisions is inadmissible. In most states, however, the issue is whether state constitutions expressly or by implication embody exclusionary rules.

State constitutional provisions, like their federal counterparts, seldom expressly address the admissibility of evidence obtained in violation of them. When a state court is asked to construe such provisions to require the exclusion of evidence, then, it must choose whether or not to interpret its constitution with the same vigor and flexibility exercised by the Supreme Court in *Mapp*. Thus, state courts are faced with the same basic question as the Supreme Court faced in *Mapp*—does general language prohibiting certain official conduct require or permit exclusion of evidence resulting from prohibited conduct? Seldom have state courts addressed directly and creatively the difficult question of whether such general constitutional provisions provide the courts with authority to mandate as pervasive and controversial requirements as exclusionary sanctions. Language accepting an exclusionary sanction for violations of state constitutions has sometimes simply offhandedly crept into discussion and become accepted law without any focused and careful consideration as to the propriety of this position. In some situations, state judicial attention has been focused upon whether a state exclusionary sanction should be developed as identical in content to federal constitutional exclusionary sanctions, rather than on whether a state exclusionary sanction is even justified. State constitutional exclusionary rules, then, have sometimes developed with little or no careful scrutiny of their propriety or wisdom.

Several state courts have addressed in more depth the propriety of construing their state provisions as the Supreme Court construed the Fourth Amendment in *Mapp*. Each has chosen to follow the *Mapp* approach. The most significant consideration in these analyses has been the courts' perceptions that exclusionary sanctions have become generally accepted and thus are appropriately read into a state provision in the absence of a demonstrated reason to read the state provision otherwise. As the intermediate Connecticut appellate court explained in accurately predicting that the state's highest court would recognize a state constitutional exclusionary rule:

> [T]he [exclusionary] rule has gained overwhelming judicial acceptance as the most effective method of guaranteeing the protection against unreasonable invasion of privacy secured by constitutional search and seizure provisions.[24]

---

[24]   State v. Brown, 543 A.2d 750, 763 (Conn. Ct. App. 1988).

Perhaps most amazing is the lack of diversity in the holdings. No highest state court seems recently to have squarely held that a state provision analogous to the Fourth, Fifth or Sixth Amendment does not require exclusion.

A state court's adoption of a state constitutional exclusionary rule, and even its explicit approval of *Mapp's* interpretive approach, does not mean that it is technically or logically bound to follow the Supreme Court's lead in developing the state remedy or even in framing the issues. Most importantly, the state court remains free to redefine for state law purposes the considerations bearing upon how the state remedy will be developed and the comparative importance of those considerations.

The Supreme Court has emphasized the federal constitutional exclusionary sanctions' function in deterring future violations of the substantive requirements of the amendments and has framed exclusionary rule issues so as to tailor the remedies to serve that function. Some state courts have taken the same approach to state provisions.

A few state courts have rejected this framework in developing their own state constitutional exclusionary sanctions. The Oregon Supreme Court, for example, explained:

> [T]his court . . . explicitly has rejected the view that the Oregon exclusionary rule is predicated upon a deterrence rationale. Instead, this court has held that the Oregon exclusionary rule is a constitutionally mandated rule that serves to vindicate a defendant's personal rights. In other words, the right to be free from unreasonable searches and seizures under Article I, section 9 [of the Oregon Constitution], also encompasses the right to be free from the use of evidence obtained in violation of that state constitutional provision. . . . [T]he aim of the Oregon exclusionary rule is to restore a defendant to the same position as if "the government's officers had stayed within the law."[25]

This emphasis on providing an effective remedy has also been embraced by some other courts. While these courts have not extensively developed the bases or significance of this position, it appears to reject the Supreme Court's assumption that exclusion of evidence resulting from official lawlessness does not provide an appropriate remedy to those who suffer privacy intrusions or other harms from that official lawlessness.

Some state courts view state constitutional exclusionary requirements as serving a broader view of judicial integrity than the Supreme Court has found implicated in the federal constitutional requirements. The Hawaii Supreme Court, for example, has held that the Hawaii constitutional exclusionary requirement is to be construed in part as best furthers the policy that "the courts should not place their imprimatur on evidence that was illegally obtained by allowing it to be admitted into evidence in a criminal prosecution."[26]

State judicial independence in this area has resulted in some restrictive modifications of state constitutions. Florida's state constitutional search and seizure provision has long provided that evidence obtained in violation of it was inadmissible. In 1982, this was supplemented with a specific directive that it be construed "in conformity with" the Supreme Court's construction of the Fourth Amendment, thus limiting

---

[25]   State v. Hall, 115 P.3d 908, 920 (Or. 2005) (citations omitted).

[26]   State v. Torres, 262 P.3d 1006, 1018 (Haw. 2011) (quoting State v. Bridges, 925 P.2d 357, 366 (Haw. 1996)).

exclusion of evidence to those situations in which the evidence "would be inadmissible under decisions of the United States Supreme Court construing the 4th Amendment to the United States Constitution." In the same year, California voters created a state constitutional "Right to Truth-in-Evidence" section providing that except as enacted by a two-thirds vote of both houses of the state legislature, "relevant evidence shall not be excluded in any criminal proceeding." This has effectively deprived the California courts of power to develop state constitutional exclusionary sanctions requiring exclusion of relevant evidence where such exclusion is not mandated by the federal constitution.

§ 169 Exclusion for Nonconstitutional Illegality: (a) In General

Both federal and state constitutional requirements apply only where a defendant establishes that challenged evidence was obtained as a result of a violation of a constitutional rights. But criminal defendants frequently seek exclusion as a remedy for violation of nonconstitutional legal requirements. When, if ever, exclusion is available on such bases presents a more difficult question than is often recognized. Modern law's acceptance of exclusion as an appropriate remedy for the violation of constitutional requirements has tended too often to lead to uncritical acceptance of exclusion as similarly available upon a showing of any illegality. This is simply not the case.

Challenges to relevant evidence on grounds that it was obtained in violation of nonconstitutional legal requirements raises several distinguishable concerns addressed in the next three sections. First is whether courts have legislatively-provided authority to exclude evidence on these bases.[27] Second is whether courts have autonomous authority to exclude evidence on these grounds.[28] Third is the content of any such exclusionary requirements as exist.[29]

Generally, the number and nature of nonconstitutional legal requirements potentially affecting the development of evidence suggests that an exclusionary sanction be more sparingly applied than it is with regard to constitutional requirements. The Michigan Supreme Court explained:

> The exclusionary rule is particularly harsh in that it is neither narrowly tailored nor discerning of the magnitude of the error it is intended to deter. By taking no cognizance of the effect of a police error upon a particular defendant, or of the actual guilt or innocence of a defendant, the exclusionary rule [applied to nonconstitutional illegality] lacks proportionality.[30]

Earlier, the same court had suggested that applying an exclusionary sanction to violations of nonconstitutional law would be to discard highly relevant evidence in response to "a technical deficiency" in official conduct. But this suggestion that all nonconstitutional requirements are mere technical ones oversimplifies the matter as much as uncritical application of exclusion to all illegality in obtaining evidence.

---

[27] See infra § 170.

[28] See infra § 171.

[29] See infra § 172.

[30] People v. Hawkins, 668 N.W.2d 602, 609 n.9 (Mich. 2003).

§ 170 Exclusion for Nonconstitutional Illegality: (b) Legislative Requirements

Legislatures unquestionably have authority to direct that legal requirements be implemented by excluding evidence obtained in violation of those requirements, or to give courts of the jurisdiction discretionary power to develop exclusionary remedies. Exercises of this authority may be explicit or implicit, and the two possibilities are best considered separately.

Explicit Legislative Exclusionary Requirements. A few jurisdictions have relatively broad statutory requirements of exclusion. Since 1925, Texas has statutorily excluded from criminal trials evidence obtained in violation of the laws or constitutions of either the United States or Texas. North Carolina has a somewhat narrower provision, requiring the suppression of certain evidence obtained in violation of its Criminal Procedure Act. These provisions, however, are exceptional. Most states have neither any general explicit legislative directive for exclusion of illegally obtained evidence nor explicit delegation to the courts of authority to develop any such exclusionary requirement.

Somewhat more frequently, legislatures have provided exclusionary remedies for particular statutes. The primary example is the federal electronic surveillance statute,[31] which contains its own statutory exclusionary remedy. Under this statute, states are authorized to provide by state law for state law enforcement officers to engage in certain electronic surveillance, and state statutes enacted pursuant to this contain exclusionary requirements similar or identical to that in the federal statute.

Other statutory provisions also sometimes explicitly require exclusion. Exclusion may be authorized indirectly, as in the Tennessee "implied consent" statute which provides that it is not to affect the admissibility of evidence in prosecutions for aggravated assault or homicide by the use of a motor vehicle. Apparently it may affect admissibility in other prosecutions.

Legislatures occasionally make clear that exclusion is not available. Oregon provides generally that courts may not exclude relevant and otherwise admissible evidence on the ground that it was obtained in violation "of any statutory provision," unless exclusion is required by the United States or Oregon Constitution, the rules of evidence, or the rights of the press. More frequently, legislatures provide that specific statutory provisions are not to serve as the basis of exclusion.

Implied Legislative Exclusionary Requirements. Legislative authority to exclude evidence may sometimes be implied from statutory provisions that lack the sort of explicit requirement discussed above, and many courts have recognized this. When a statute is appropriately construed as authorizing or requiring exclusion, however, has proved to be a difficult question for many courts.

In several early cases, the Supreme Court uncritically held that evidence obtained in violation of certain federal statutory requirements must be excluded. It left unclear, however, whether these holdings rested on readings of legislative intent or were rather exercises of the Court's own power to develop exclusionary requirements.

---

[31] Omnibus Crime Control and Safe Streets Act of 1968, title II, codified as 18 U.S.C.A. §§ 2510 et seq.

Some lower courts have been willing on quite scant bases to find implied legislative exclusionary requirements. In *United States v. Chemaly*,[32] for example, the court held that federal legislation limiting currency searches at the border required exclusion of evidence obtained in violation of its terms. Emphasizing the long acceptance among courts of exclusion as a remedy for even nonconstitutional illegality, the court reasoned that Congress assumed that in the absence of an explicit directive to the contrary courts would enforce the statute by excluding evidence obtained in violation of it; therefore, congressional silence regarding exclusionary sanctions was an implied directive that such a remedy be applied. There is a discernible tendency on the part of some courts to pursue this analysis under statutes imposing requirements similar to, but more stringent than, constitutional mandates. This is apparently on the assumption that when a legislature imposes requirements similar to constitutional ones enforced by exclusionary sanctions, it ordinarily assumes that its statutory directives will also be enforced by such sanctions.

The Iowa Supreme Court reaffirmed—and expanded—its earlier decision to exclude evidence because officers violated a statutory provision giving a person arrested a right to contact an attorney or family member. It acknowledged "the general presumption against implied statutory exclusionary rules," but explained that "an exclusionary rule is warranted for violations of those statutes . . . which involve fundamental rights or have constitutional overtones."

Most courts, however, are more reluctant to find unexpressed legislative intentions that exclusionary sanctions be available. The case discussions emphasize several considerations. If other statutes passed by the legislative body have expressly directed exclusion, legislative failure to similarly provide in the statute at issue suggests to many courts a legislative intention that no such remedy be available for statutes silent on the matter. If the overall purpose of legislation is to increase law enforcement power, courts have also reasoned, the legislature is unlikely to have intended to impede this general objective by imposing an exclusionary sanction, and thus courts should be reluctant to read one into such statutes.

The same approach has been taken where the statutory provision limits law enforcement power. That an Idaho statute limiting arrests for traffic offenses provides no significant remedy for improperly arrested defendants or repercussions for police making improper arrests is "concerning," the Idaho Supreme Court commented, but it nevertheless refused to find an implied suppression remedy.

At least one court requires that an intent to affect the admissibility of evidence be expressly stated in the statute relied upon by the defendant. The Michigan Supreme Court took this position, overruling earlier decisions uncritically excluding evidence for violation of statutes and court rules.

Another announced that exclusion was available only if, first, the statute was designed to protect against improper government conduct, and second, the specific violation must have infringed "the legislative intent or 'spirit' behind the law, such that to effectuate the purpose behind the statue the evidence should be suppressed."

The Wisconsin Supreme Court in *State v. Popenhagen*[33] abandoned its earlier insistence that a statute expressly provide for an exclusionary remedy. It then found

---

³² 741 F.2d 1346 (11th Cir. 1984), opinion reinstated on reh'g, 764 F.2d 747 (11th Cir. 1985).
³³ 749 N.W.2d 611 (Wis. 2008).

sufficient legislative authorization for an exclusionary remedy in a statute authorizing the issuances of subpoenas in language recognizing that motions could be addressed to a court which issued a subpoena. Motions, it reasoned, include motions to suppress evidence obtained as a result of a subpoena issued in violation of the statutory requirements.

Exclusion is more likely to be found available if the statutory provision violated is construed as protecting those targeted by official action. A statutory provision requiring the presence of a veterinarian during execution of certain search warrants, for example, was construed as intended to protect possibly-abused animals that might need emergency care. Evidence obtained by a search conducted without a veterinarian's presence was therefore admissible despite noncompliance with the statute. The underlying assumption is that the legislature is unlikely to have intended exclusion as a remedy for violating statutory provisions not designed to protect those targeted by official action.

On balance, courts should be reluctant to find implied authority in statutes for exclusion of evidence. Exclusion is an exceptionally costly remedy, and its propriety is highly questionable. Legislative silence almost certainly reflects, in most cases, the absence of a consensus that the provisions being enacted are appropriately enforced by such a remedy. Unless there is reasonably clear evidence of such a consensus, generally reflected in the terms of the statute itself, a statute should not be regarded as empowering the courts to exclude evidence obtained in violation of its requirements.

Popenhagen's approach, practically speaking, is not one based on even implied legislative provision for exclusionary remedies. As the dissent noted, under the majority's approach almost any statute could be read as authorizing suppression. The Wisconsin court was in effect asserting judicial authority to develop an exclusionary remedy where the legislature has not barred that approach.

§ 171 Exclusion for Nonconstitutional Illegality: (c) Judicially Developed Requirements

In the absence of legislative or constitutional authorization, courts may nevertheless have independent power to develop and apply exclusionary requirements. Some courts claim such power without identifying its source. If the matter is carefully examined, such judicial power might be based either upon the authority given many courts to promulgate rules relating to procedure and evidence or upon the power claimed by some courts to exercise what is often called "supervisory authority" over litigation and the behavior of some persons whose actions in some way affect that litigation.

Rulemaking Power. Many American courts have power to promulgate rules of evidence and procedure, granted by statute or constitutional provision. This power has been implemented through widespread adoption of evidence rules. Might this power permit a court to promulgate an exclusionary rule applicable to violation of nonconstitutional, as well as perhaps constitutional, legal requirements?

Such action has been taken by the Alaska Supreme Court, which adopted a general exclusionary rule as part of its Criminal Rules and then incorporated this into its Evidence Rules. Under Alaska Rule of Evidence 412, evidence "illegally obtained" may not be used over proper objection by the defendant in a criminal prosecution "for any purpose," with limited exceptions applicable to perjury prosecutions.

Whether this is an appropriate exercise of the rulemaking power is at best problematic. Rulemaking authority is given to courts in large part because of their exceptional ability to address such matters as how to most efficiently and effectively arrive at accurate resolutions in litigated cases. The extent to which exclusionary requirements will interfere with these interests is, of course, an important consideration in deciding whether an exclusionary sanction is appropriate. But far more important are such considerations as the extent to which violations occur and whether other measures hold reasonable promise of discouraging them. The final decision must balance the costs of an exclusionary sanction and the potential benefits of it. This decision is no more than peripherally within courts' area of particular expertise and is clearly the sort of judgment that is ordinarily for legislative decision. Given the nature of exclusionary sanctions, despite their "evidentiary" form, they are best regarded as beyond general judicial evidentiary and procedural rulemaking authority.

Courts' "Supervisory" Power—the Federal Model. Some American courts have held, or indicated in dicta, that they have supervisory authority over judicial proceedings broader than ordinary rule-making power. This authority may give those courts the power to judicially-develop exclusionary requirements invoked by violation of nonconstitutional legal requirements. Whether such authority exists in particular jurisdictions and, if so, whether it authorizes such rigorous judicial lawmaking often poses difficult issues.

The most widely-noted model for such authority is the Supreme Court's reliance upon what it has described as its "supervisory power" authority to develop such exclusionary rules for litigation in the lower federal courts. Whether the Court's perception of its power is soundly based is, at best, questionable.

The seminal Supreme Court decision is *McNabb v. United States*,[34] holding that suppression was required of evidence obtained in violation of what was then the statutory requirement that an arrested person be presented before a magistrate without unnecessary delay. In *Rea v. United States*,[35] the Court held that a federal officer who had obtained evidence in violation of Rule 41 of the Federal Rules of Criminal Procedure should be enjoined from using that evidence in a state prosecution. Implicitly, *Rea* approved the suppression of this evidence in the federal litigation and explicitly held that Rea was entitled to the additional injunctive relief he sought. Both decisions rested upon what the Court described as its "supervisory power." In *McNabb*, the Court equated an exclusionary rule with other rules of evidence, particularly those, apparently rules of privilege, that are based on considerations other than simply "evidentiary relevance." Development of legal requirements of both sorts, the Court concluded, was permissible pursuant to its "duty" to establish and maintain "civilized standards of procedure and evidence" in the federal courts. *Rea's* discussion went further and suggested that the underlying power was not only to provide for the proper processing of litigation but also to "prescribe standards for law enforcement . . . to protect the privacy of the citizen . . . ."

Since *Rea*, the Court has continued to insist that it has such power. It has obviously, however, become more reluctant to exercise it and in fact has not found occasion to do so. In *Lopez v. United States*,[36] for example, the Court reaffirmed its "inherent power" to

---

[34]   318 U.S. 332 (1943).

[35]   350 U.S. 214 (1956).

[36]   373 U.S. 427 (1963).

exclude "material" evidence because of illegality in the manner it was obtained, but commented that this power should be "sparingly exercised." Since Lopez could show no "manifestly improper" conduct by the law enforcement officers, invoking the power in his case would not be justified. In *United States v. Caceres*,[37] the Court suggested that it had the power to exclude evidence on a "limited individualized approach" for the violation of federal administrative regulations. But exclusion under this power would not be appropriate in the case before it, the Court concluded, since the investigators had made a reasonable, good faith attempt to comply with what they understood to be the applicable legal requirements, and the actions they took would clearly have been permitted had they followed the regulations.

Most recently, the Court in *United States v. Payner*[38] considered an argument that it should exercise its supervisory power to exclude evidence obtained by "gross illegality" from a person other than the defendant who moved to suppress it. Again reaffirming its supervisory exclusionary power, the Court offered that "Federal courts may use their supervisory power in some circumstances to exclude evidence taken from the defendant by 'willful disobedience of law.'" But it then made clear that the exercise of this power is to be informed by the same considerations and conclusions reached in developing the federal constitutional exclusionary requirements. The Fourth Amendment case law makes clear that as a general rule, the purposes of exclusion are adequately achieved if the remedy is made available to those whose interests were violated by the underlying illegality. This should also apply where exclusion might be justified under the supervisory power, and thus under that power federal courts should not suppress otherwise admissible evidence on the ground that it was unlawfully obtained from a third party not before the court.

Both the scope and legitimacy of the supervisory power as applied and discussed in this line of cases have been severely criticized. The Supreme Court's refusal, since *McNabb* and *Rea*, actually to exercise what it continues to insist is the federal courts' supervisory power to develop exclusionary rules for nonconstitutional violations suggests that the tribunal is becoming at least ambivalent concerning the legitimacy of this authority.

The lower federal courts continue to assume that some power to develop exclusionary rules exists, perhaps most significantly, implicitly relying on *Rea*, that violations of some of the nonconstitutional requirements for search warrants imposed by Rule 41 of the Federal Rules of Criminal Procedure under some circumstances require or permit exclusion. The courts are, however, increasingly reluctant to exercise this power.

In *Sanchez-Llamas v. Oregon*[39] the Court first explained *McNabb* and other cases as ones in which "the excluded evidence arose directly out of statutory violations that implicated important Fourth and Fifth Amendment interests." In the next paragraph, however, the Court suggested that they rested at least in part on the basis that the statutory right violated was a right "connected to the gathering of evidence."

---

[37]   440 U.S. 741 (1970).

[38]   447 U.S. 727 (1980).

[39]   548 U.S. 331 (2006).

In *Corley v. United States*,[40] the Court held the *McNabb* exclusionary requirement still effective regarding confessions made after delay in presentment that both exceeded six hours and was unreasonable or unnecessary. *Corley* did not revisit or discuss the conceptual basis for the basic exclusionary mandate.

Courts' "Supervisory" Power—State Court Decisions. State courts may also have supervisory powers similar to that invoked in *McNabb-Rea*, and these might be relied upon as a basis for state court developed exclusionary requirements. Generally, however, state courts have engaged in little discussion of this possibility. When state tribunals mention supervisory power, they tend to avoid explicit comment upon whether they possess such power and whether it would support development of exclusionary sanctions. Rather, they simply find that the situations before them are not sufficient to invoke any such sanctions as they might have power to develop. Even state courts embracing such power to exclude evidence generally provide little substantive discussion of the basis for this power and the decision to exercise it in particular situations.

In what is probably the leading state court decision, *State v. Pattioay*,[41] the Hawaii Supreme Court held that its inherent supervisory authority to prevent and correct "errors and abuses" in the lower courts permitted it to develop exclusionary remedies mandating exclusion of evidence obtained in violation of non-constitutional legal requirements. The power, it cautioned, is to be exercised with restraint and discretion and only in exceptional circumstances.

Pattioay appeared to conceptualize the use of illegally obtained evidence by parties to litigation in an effort to obtain favorable action by the courts as sufficient abuse of the courts to justify exercise of the supervisory power. This in turn led it to adopt a rationale for exclusion broader than the deterrent-based federal constitutional rules. Use in a criminal trial of evidence tainted by official illegality, it emphasized, "would be to justify the illegality." Even if exclusion does not sufficiently serve to deter illegality of the sort involved, then, such exclusion is justified as a means of precluding judicial "justification" of the underlying illegality in a manner that would offend notions of what some courts and commentators regard as judicial integrity.

In general, American courts have been insufficiently critical regarding their power, or the lack thereof, to develop exclusionary sanctions for nonconstitutional violations in obtaining evidence. This is no doubt due in large part to the prominence of federal constitutional exclusionary rule case law in any consideration of exclusionary sanction matters. On one hand, this case law encourages an uncritical assumption that courts have power to develop similar exclusionary requirements for nonconstitutional illegality. On the other, resentment at being constitutionally compelled to accept what is regarded by some as an unwise remedy for constitutional violations encourages equally uncritical rejection of exclusion as an authorized remedy where such a remedy is not constitutionally mandated.

Whether the courts of a particular jurisdiction have the power to develop exclusionary sanctions, and whether they should exercise any such power as they may have, must depend in large part upon the nature and breadth of judicial authority in that jurisdiction and the tradition with which it has been developed and applied. Proper resolution of these issues, in any case, requires careful consideration of the argument

---

[40]   556 U.S. 303 (2009); see supra § 156.
[41]   896 P.2d 911 (Haw. 1995).

that the major factors in deciding whether exclusionary sanctions are appropriate are factors that require legislative rather than judicial action.

§ 172 Exclusion for Nonconstitutional Illegality: (d) Substance of Exclusionary Requirements

The exclusionary requirements developed as part of federal constitutional law are, as an initial matter, unqualified. This means that a showing that evidence was obtained as a factual result of a violation of the underlying constitutional requirement demands exclusion of that evidence. Most exclusionary requirements applicable to nonconstitutional violations, on the other hand, are qualified. A right to exclusion, in other words, often demands that a defendant show more than a violation of a nonconstitutional legal requirement and that the challenged evidence was obtained as a factual result of that violation.

The limits or qualifications of these nonconstitutional exclusionary sanctions is developed in this section. Three types of limitations can usefully be distinguished.

First, those nonconstitutional legal requirements whose violation will trigger a possible right to exclusion have sometimes been limited. The case law suggests several approaches towards so limiting exclusionary requirements. Exclusionary requirements could be applied only if the legal requirement applies generally or frequently to official activity designed to collect evidence for use in criminal prosecutions. Given the evidentiary motivation of those affected by the legal requirements, exclusion might be expected to most effectively encourage compliance with the law in these cases.

Exclusion might also be limited to those legal requirements that are related in some sufficient way to constitutional commands. Perhaps the cost of exclusion is justified only if the violated legal requirement protects the same or similar interests as are protected by constitutional rules, although the legal requirement that is violated by infringements is not significant or basic enough to give rise to a constitutional intrusion.

Case law under the federal electronic surveillance regulatory scheme suggests that at least in the context of a set of legislative requirements, exclusion may reasonably be mandated only upon proof of a violation of a statutory requirement directly or importantly related to the underlying legislative objective. Although the federal statutory exclusionary sanction is unqualified, the Supreme Court has held that it is triggered only by those statutory provisions that "directly and substantially implement" the congressional purpose of reasonably limiting use of electronic surveillance techniques. Consequently, failure to secure approval of an application for a surveillance order from the Attorney General or Assistant Attorney General did require exclusion of the resulting evidence, but a failure simply to specify on the documents the official who had in fact authorized the application did not. State exclusionary requirements embodied in similar state electronic surveillance statutes have been similarly construed.

If a legal requirement does not directly and substantially implement a constitutionally-related purpose or the ultimate objective of a legislative scheme, the courts tend to label it "technical" and to treat it as insufficient to trigger an exclusionary sanction.

A second type of limitation upon nonconstitutional exclusionary sanctions makes exclusion available only to those defendants who show more than simply that the evidence at issue was obtained by means of a violation of a sufficient legal requirement.

Often the case law requires a showing of either an "intentional" violation of the underlying legal requirement or prejudice in some sense as a result of that violation. As this approach is applied, prejudice means that the defendant suffered the harm that the legal requirement was designed to prevent. When this approach is invoked in response to proof that officers failed to follow nonconstitutional requirements for search warrants, for example, prejudice apparently requires proof that the search would not have occurred had the requirements been met or at least that the search would have been significantly less intrusive if this had been the case.

Exclusion may be required if but only if the acquisition of the evidence did not involve a "good faith" effort to determine and comply with the law. The Florida courts have taken this position with regard to the statutory procedure for obtaining medical records.

A similar but more flexible analysis would provide for exclusion only upon proof of a legal violation that was in some sense "substantial." Under a North Carolina statute embodying a demand for a substantial violation of law, determining whether an underlying violation was substantial requires consideration of: (a) the importance of the particular interest protected by the legal requirement; (b) the extent of the deviation from lawful conduct; (c) the extent to which the violation was willful; and (d) the extent to which exclusion will tend to deter future violations of the same sort.

A third type of limitation upon the right to exclusion gives a trial court discretionary authority to exclude evidence where on the facts of the case before the court exclusion is determined to sufficiently further the objectives of exclusionary sanctions to warrant the cost involved. This was the thrust of *Commonwealth v. Mason,*[42] in which the Pennsylvania Supreme Court explicitly announced that a showing that evidence had been obtained in violation of the Pennsylvania Rules of Criminal Procedure established only that "exclusion *may* be an appropriate remedy." Exclusion is to be in fact ordered only if the trial judge, after considering the nature of the case and the particular facts, determines that exclusion and its costs would be proportional to the benefits to be gained. Trial judges were cautioned to give particular emphasis to the likelihood that exclusion would prevent future misconduct similar to that which gave rise to the violation before the court.

A similar approach to the Alaska Evidence Rule barring use of "illegally obtained" evidence was adopted by the Alaska Court of Appeals:

> [F]actors to consider in determining whether to apply the exclusionary rule in cases where a government officer violated a statute . . . are: (1) "whether the statutory requirement . . . restriction [was] 'clear and widely known;' " (2) whether the statute was primarily enacted to protect the rights of individual citizens rather than to generally benefit society; (3) whether admission of the evidence would make courts accomplices to the willful disobedience of the law; and (4) whether the police have engaged in "widespread or repeated violations" of the statute.[43]

---

[42]   Com. v. Mason, 490 A.2d 421 (Pa. 1985).

[43]   State v. Avery, 211 P.3d 1154, 1159 (Alaska App. 2009) (quoting Berumen v. State, 182 P.3d 635, 641 (Alaska App. 2008)).

§ 173 Use of Illegally Obtained Evidence in Noncriminal Litigation

Most exclusionary sanction issues arise in criminal litigation. Perhaps because of American courts' increasing acceptance of exclusion as a response to illegality in obtaining evidence, however, litigants sometimes attempt to invoke exclusionary remedies in various types of civil litigation. When, if ever, exclusionary sanctions are appropriate outside of criminal litigation presents a number of difficult questions.

Distinctions here as elsewhere must be drawn among the various exclusionary sanctions that do or might exist. The Supreme Court's case law addressing the application of the federal constitutional exclusionary requirements outside of criminal litigation provides an attractive model that has been widely but not universally followed in other contexts.

Soon after *Mapp v. Ohio*,[44] the Supreme Court held the Fourth Amendment exclusionary rule applicable in a state proceeding for forfeiture of an automobile on the basis that the vehicle had been used in a crime. Forfeiture was clearly a penalty for a criminal act, the Court reasoned, and it would therefore be incongruous to exclude the evidence in a criminal prosecution but admit it in a forfeiture proceeding based on the same criminal activity.

The matter was addressed again in *United States v. Janis*,[45] a civil proceeding for a tax refund in which the Government counterclaimed for the unpaid balance of the assessment. The assessment was based upon information concerning Janis' illegal bookmaking activities; that information had been obtained by state law enforcement officers acting pursuant to a defective search warrant but nevertheless in the "good faith" belief that the search was lawful. Use of the evidence was permissible, the Court reasoned, because "exclusion from federal civil proceedings of evidence unlawfully seized by a state criminal law enforcement officer has not been shown to have a sufficient likelihood of deterring the conduct of the state police so that it outweighs the societal costs imposed by the exclusion."

Janis involved an intersovereign situation—the government that committed the illegality in obtaining the evidence was not the same government that sought to use it. Thus, the Court's result may have rested in part upon a conclusion that excluding evidence in a federal civil proceeding is unlikely to influence state officers. In *I.N.S. v. Lopez-Mendoza*,[46] however, the Court arrived at a similar result in an intrasovereign case. At issue was whether evidence obtained in violation of the Fourth Amendment by federal immigration officers was admissible in a federal civil deportation proceeding. *Janis*, the Court nevertheless observed, provided the framework for analysis: the likely social benefits of excluding the evidence must be balanced against the likely costs. The intrasovereign nature of the situation suggested that the deterrent benefits were likely to be greater than in *Janis*. But other considerations suggested they would still be quite small: the Government itself disciplines officers who violate the Fourth Amendment and excludes evidence arising from intentional violations, and INS officers know that there is only a small likelihood that any arrestee will actually challenge the officers' actions in a formal proceeding. On the cost side, application of the rule would impede the busy deportation system. Since immigration enforcement often involves continuing violations

---

[44]   367 U.S. 643 (1961).

[45]   428 U.S. 433 (1976).

[46]   468 U.S. 1032 (1984).

of the law, application of an exclusionary rule in this context "would require the courts to close their eyes to ongoing violations of the law," a cost of a particularly offensive character. The *Janis* balance, the Court concluded, came out against application of the Fourth Amendment exclusionary rule.

Under *Janis* and *Lopez-Mendoza*, whether the federal constitutional exclusionary rules are applicable in civil litigation turns upon whether the increased prevention of unconstitutional conduct accomplished by application of the exclusionary requirement to civil cases of the sort at issue is worth the costs of so expanding those sanctions. The two decisions suggest that the Court is generally satisfied that sufficient prevention is provided by exclusion of unconstitutionally obtained evidence in criminal litigation. A civil litigant seeking to show that exclusion is justified under *Janis-Lopez-Mendoza* has an extremely difficult task.

Lower courts are understandably hesitant to exclude evidence in civil contexts. Nevertheless, at least some remain reluctant to characterize the federal constitutional sanctions as never applicable to noncriminal litigation.

There is general agreement that whether the federal constitutional exclusionary rule applies in a technically noncriminal proceeding depends at least in part upon the type of proceeding. Many analyses also require consideration of the facts of the specific case, assuming that parties' objections to evidence require case-specific analyses. Several courts have distinguished at least five factors that are relevant to these analyses:

(1)   the nature of the noncriminal proceeding;

(2)   whether the proposed use of unconstitutionally seized material is intersovereign or intrasovereign;

(3)   whether (in intrasovereign situations) the search and the noncriminal proceeding were initiated by the same agency;

(4)   whether there is an explicit and demonstrable understanding between the two governmental agencies; and

(5)   whether the noncriminal proceeding fell within the "zone of primary interest" of the officers that conducted the search.

The *Janis-Lopez-Mendoza* analysis is most likely to lead to exclusion when unconstitutionally obtained evidence is offered in proceedings which, although civil, are brought by governmental authorities for what is essentially a public purpose. Governmental activity may be conducted with the prospect of such litigation in mind, and thus exclusion in such litigation may discourage impropriety in the investigatory activity. There is widespread agreement, for example, that the exclusionary rule applies in proceedings to have a child declared delinquent. Such rules have also been applied in proceedings to collect a tax on illegal drugs and a school disciplinary hearing.

Under the *Janis-Lopez-Mendoza* approach, it is quite unlikely that the federal constitutional rules will ever be applicable in civil actions between private parties. If the evidence was wrongfully obtained by public officers, exclusion would not penalize them and officers would not likely be influenced in their future conduct by such exclusion. If the evidence was wrongfully obtained by private persons, the Supreme Court would almost certainly reason that exclusion would at most deter similar private action in the future, a concern beyond the scope of the underlying federal constitutional rules being enforced.

Most courts, moreover, do not apply the federal constitutional exclusionary rules to administrative proceedings concerning employment or professional disciplinary matters, school disciplinary proceedings, drivers' license suspension or revocation proceedings, civil tax assessment or collection proceedings, civil eviction, forcible-entry and detainer actions, or even child protection proceedings or actions to compel treatment for impaired persons. Some attempt to draw finer lines; several courts have held that the Fourth Amendment exclusionary rule does not apply under federal Occupational Safety and Health Act proceedings to correct a violation but it does apply to proceedings to punish past violations by assessing penalties for them.

In a plurality portion of the lead opinion, *Lopez-Mendoza* left open the possibility that the Fourth Amendment exclusionary rule might apply in noncriminal actions such as deportation proceedings upon proof that the evidence was obtained by "egregious violations of Fourth Amendment or other liberties that might transgress notions of fundamental fairness and undermine the probative value of the evidence obtained." One court has held that proof of "bad faith"—that the officers should have known their conduct was unreasonable and hence unconstitutional—requires exclusion, even if the violation did not affect the probative value of the evidence at issue. Perhaps if the underlying official activity is particularly offensive, the increased need to discourage such activity justifies the costs of adding to the exclusionary disincentive by rejecting its fruits even in civil litigation.

State courts, of course, are technically free to reject the approach taken in *Janis* and *Lopez-Mendoza* and to construe state constitutional provisions as fully applicable to civil litigation. The Oklahoma Supreme Court exercised this power in *Turner v. City of Lawton*,[47] holding evidence unconstitutionally obtained inadmissible in an administrative proceeding to dismiss a firefighter. The court accepted the state search and seizure provision as creating a right to exclusion as a necessary remedy for the preceding violation of privacy, regardless of the necessity for exclusion to discourage future violations of the underlying legal requirements. In order to achieve the remedial objective of the state exclusionary requirement, then, the Oklahoma court extended its rule to civil litigation in order to replace the wronged person as close as possible to his condition before the wrongful search occurred.

Rhode Island has by statute barred the admission of evidence obtained in violation of the state's search and seizure provision when such evidence is offered "[i]n the trial of any action in any court of this state." Clearly this applies a limited exclusionary rule to civil litigation.

One court has more ambiguously indicated that trial judge's discretion in admitting evidence gives them some authority in civil proceedings to exclude evidence illegally obtained.

§ 174 Use of Illegally Obtained Evidence in Criminal Proceedings on Matters Other than Guilt

Evidence may be offered against a criminal defendant in the course of criminal litigation but other than at the trial on guilt or innocence. It may, for example, be used in an effort to have pretrial release denied or revoked, at a preliminary hearing to determine whether a defendant is to be "bound over" for grand jury consideration or trial,

---

[47]   733 P.2d 375 (Okla. 1986).

before a grand jury in support of a proposed indictment charging the defendant with an offense, at sentencing in support of a more severe disposition, in support of an effort to revoke probation once granted, or to substantiate a claim that parole after imprisonment should be denied or revoked. An exclusionary rule's determination that illegally obtained evidence must be inadmissible to prove defendants' guilt does not require the further conclusion that such evidence should be unavailable for any or all of these or similar purposes.

The Fourth Amendment issue was addressed most extensively in *Pennsylvania Board of Probation v. Scott*,[48] in which the Supreme Court made clear that the critical question is whether the deterrence benefits of so expanding the Fourth Amendment exclusionary rule would outweigh the costs incurred. At issue in *Scott* was specifically whether evidence obtained in violation of the Fourth Amendment could be used to establish that a convicted defendant had violated the conditions of his parole. The costs of requiring exclusion in parole revocation proceedings would be exceptionally high, the Court reasoned, indicating that exclusionary rule issues would delay and impede the necessarily flexible and administrative procedures of parole revocation.

Probably more important, the deterrent benefits would most likely be low. Where law enforcement officers do not know that suspects are parolees, the remote possibility that this may be the case—and thus that fruits of misconduct will be unusable for parole violation purposes—is unlikely to influence the officers. Regular law enforcement officers who know a suspect is a parolee are unlikely to be influenced by the admissibility of the fruits of their actions in parole revocation proceedings. Parole officers specifically charged with parole concerns, on the other hand, are less likely than regular officers to perceive themselves engaged in the "adversarial" process of ferreting out crime, and thus are likely to respond adequately to less costly alternatives to exclusion, such as departmental training and discipline and civil damage liability.

Scott's assessment of law enforcement officers' motivations is arguably quite naive. The state court below, like some others, sought a more sophisticated balance by directing that the Fourth Amendment exclusionary rule be applied where—but only where—the defendant challenging the evidence established that the officer who obtained it knew the suspect was a parolee. Thus the state court sought to limit application of the rule to those situations in which deterrent benefits were most certain. Rejecting this approach, the Supreme Court clearly concluded that even in these cases the potential deterrent benefit was minimal. In addition, however, it reasoned that a need to address the officers' awareness in exclusionary rule litigation would unacceptably increase the complexity of applying the rule and consequently the costs of doing so.

Scott thus supplemented the earlier holding in *United States v. Calandra*[49] that the Fourth Amendment does not require that evidence obtained in violation of its terms be kept from influencing grand jury decisions to indict. Together, *Scott* and *Calandra* leave no doubt that the Supreme Court is firmly convinced that exclusion at trial from the guilt-innocence process will generally satisfy federal constitutional requirements. Defendants are unlikely to be able to convince the Court that law enforcement officers unaffected by the admissibility of evidence at trial are likely to be sufficiently influenced by its admissibility for other purposes to justify what the Court regards as the

---

[48]   524 U.S. 357 (1998).

[49]   414 U.S. 338 (1974).

considerable cost of expanding the federal constitutional exclusionary demands to proceedings other than the determination of guilt at trial.

The Supreme Court has not addressed the applicability of the federal constitutional exclusionary rules at pretrial stages except for grand jury proceedings. Most likely, considerations of practicality tip the scales in favor of not apply exclusionary sanctions for granting, limiting, or revoking pretrial release. The Vermont Supreme Court, however, has held the prosecution may sometimes be required to make a prima facie case for admissibility. It stressed that a finding the prosecution has failed to make this showing would not control whether the evidence must be suppressed for purposes of trial.

Applicability of the federal constitutional requirement at preliminary hearings has likewise not been definitely decided. In federal litigation, however, Rule 5.1(e) of the Federal Rules of Criminal Procedure specifically provides that "[a]t the preliminary hearing, the defendant . . . may not object to evidence on the ground that it was unlawfully acquired." A number of state statutes and rules follow this approach.\ At least a few permit challenges at the preliminary hearing. The Hawai'i Supreme Court, over dissent, held that both state and federal constitutional considerations require exclusion of illegally obtained evidence from the preliminary hearing.

Whether the federal constitutional requirements apply post-trial in sentencing has also not been resolved by the Court. Almost certainly, however, the Court would reason, under *Scott* and *Calandra*, that whatever minimal incremental deterrence would be achieved by so applying the requirements would be outweighed by the costs. Particular weight would undoubtedly be given to the cost involved in requiring sentencing courts to exercise their considerable discretion without the benefit of all relevant and reliable evidence. Many lower courts hold—or at least state unqualifiedly—that these exclusionary requirements do not apply at sentencing. Some, however, leave open that they may apply in exceptional circumstances, such as where the defendant shows the officers sought the evidence at issue for the purpose of increasing the severity of the defendant's sentence.

Courts have rejected arguments that the federal constitutional exclusionary requirement applies to revocation of probation or supervised release. Some have left open the possibility exclusion might be required if the unconstitutional conduct was engaged in for the purpose of revoking probation or was in some sense egregious.

State courts again are free to reject the *Scott-Calandra* approach or the Supreme Court's application of it to some or all nontrial stages of criminal proceedings. An Oregon court has done so by holding that the Oregon constitutional exclusionary requirement, intended not simply to deter but also to adequately vindicate the right to privacy, requires that evidence obtained in an unreasonable search or seizure be excluded from sentencing. Adequate vindication requires assurance that those whose rights are violated be free from increased punishment based on the fruits of the violations. The Pennsylvania Supreme Court held that, since "the primary purpose of the exclusionary rule under [our state constitution] is protecting the individual privacy rights of our citizens, as opposed to deterring police misconduct," this purpose is served by applying the state constitutional exclusionary rule to parole and probation revocation proceedings.

§ 175   "Standing" and Personal Nature of Rights

The Fourth Amendment exclusionary rule and most other exclusionary sanctions permit a criminal defendant to seek suppression of evidence only on the basis of a claim that the evidence was obtained in an improper manner that violated the defendant's own rights. Put negatively, this requirement of "standing" precludes a defendant from objecting to evidence on the basis that it was obtained illegally but in a manner that violated only the rights of another person. Courts sometimes suggest that this reflects the "personal" nature of the rights enforced by exclusionary requirements, but in actuality the standing requirement is best conceptualized as an aspect of the exclusionary remedy rather than of the underlying rights.

Fourth Amendment Standing. The Fourth Amendment standing requirement was first developed under pre-*Mapp v. Ohio*[50] law. It was explained in *Jones v. United States*[51] as based upon language in the Federal Rules of Criminal Procedure authorizing a motion to suppress only by "[a] person aggrieved by an unlawful search and seizure." This was read by the Court as applying the "general principle" that constitutional protections can be claimed only by those parties to litigation that belong to the class of persons for whose sake the constitutional protection is given. The Fourth Amendment exclusionary requirement is not designed to exclude evidence on grounds of unreliability or prejudicial effect. Rather, it is a means of making effective the underlying Fourth Amendment protection against official invasion of privacy and the security of property. "[I]t is," the Court concluded, "entirely proper to require of one who seeks to challenge the legality of a search as the basis for suppressing relevant evidence that he allege, and if the allegation be disputed that he establish, that he himself was the victim of an invasion of privacy." After *Mapp*, this approach was incorporated into the Fourth Amendment exclusionary rule as applied to the states.

As first announced and applied, the standing requirement was sometimes read as invoking a distinct body of law distinguishable from that defining the content of the Fourth Amendment's coverage. In *Rakas v. Illinois*,[52] however, the Supreme Court rejected such an approach and made clear that the inquiry necessitated by the Fourth Amendment standing requirement involves application of the case law defining the scope of Fourth Amendment coverage and, in particular, the extent of a particular defendant's rights under that provision. When a defendant objects to the admissibility of the results of a search or seizure, the standing question is whether, under substantive Fourth Amendment law, the search or seizure violated the rights of the objecting defendant.

Rakas also adopted a quite restrictive view of substantive Fourth Amendment law, at least as applied to searches of automobiles. A mere passenger in an automobile, the Court held, has no privacy interest in the automobile. Officers' search of the vehicle, then, does not violate the Fourth Amendment rights of the passenger, and the passenger consequently cannot challenge the reasonableness of such a search.

Careful application of *Rakas* requires consideration of all possible poisonous trees. A passenger in a stopped automobile is seized. The passenger clearly has standing to

---

[50]   367 U.S. 643 (1961).

[51]   362 U.S. 257 (1960).

[52]   439 U.S. 128 (1978).

raise the reasonableness of that seizure and may be able to establish that a search of the vehicle is the fruit of that seizure.

The Supreme Court has justified the Fourth Amendment's standing limitation in terms of the underlying policy concerns:

> The deterrent values of preventing the incrimination of those whose rights the police have violated have been considered sufficient to justify the suppression of probative evidence even though the case against the defendant is weakened or destroyed. But we are not convinced that the additional benefits of extending the exclusionary rule to other defendants would justify further encroachment upon the public interest in prosecuting those accused of crime and having them acquitted or convicted on the basis of all the evidence which exposes the truth.[53]

Nonconstitutional Federal Exclusionary Requirements. The Supreme Court has developed and applied standing as a limit on another, nonconstitutional exclusionary requirement. In *United States v. Payner*,[54] the Court rejected the argument that federal exclusionary requirements based on the courts' supervisory power should not require standing as did the constitutional requirements. The "same social interests" are implicated by both supervisory power exclusionary requirements and the Fourth Amendment exclusionary rule, it reasoned, and the values assigned to those interests do not change when the basis for the exclusionary sanction is the supervisory power rather than the Fourth Amendment. Consequently, even construction of the supervisory power exclusionary sanction is governed by the Court's conclusion that any increased deterrence that would be provided by abandoning standing is outweighed by the inevitable increased loss of reliable evidence.

The Supreme Court has similarly read statutory exclusionary sanction language as incorporating a requirement of standing. Under the federal electronic surveillance statute, suppression of the results of an improper interception of a covered communication is required upon the motion of any person against whom the interception was directed. Without discussing the specific terminology chosen by Congress, the Court has held that the legislative history of the statute indicated a Congressional purpose to permit objections to evidence only by persons with standing under existent standing rules.

"Automatic" Standing. Fourth Amendment law beginning in 1960 relaxed ordinary standing requirements in limited situations covered by what was characterized as the "automatic" standing rule. Under this rule, a defendant charged with possession of an item at the time of a search or seizure was permitted to challenge that search or seizure regardless of general standing requirements. In part, the automatic standing rule was based on concern that in the cases covered defendants would often have to make an admissible judicial confession of guilt, i.e., possession, to establish standing. Such defendants' testimony establishing standing, given at the hearing on the admissibility of the item, might well be admissible against the defendants at trial. The resulting "dilemma," the Court concluded, was unacceptable. As the Court has recognized in *United States v. Salvucci*,[55] this part of the rationale was destroyed by *Simmons v.*

---

[53] Alderman v. U.S., 394 U.S. 165, 174–75 (1969).
[54] 447 U.S. 727 (1980).
[55] 448 U.S. 83 (1980).

United States,[56] holding that testimony given at a motion to suppress evidence is not admissible against the defendant at a subsequent trial. A defendant who, to establish standing, judicially admits possession need not fear that the prosecution will use that admission at trial to establish his guilt.

But the automatic standing rule was also based in part upon perceived offensiveness of contradictory prosecutorial arguments that defendants had close enough relationships to items to be guilty of possession of them but not sufficient relationships to give them standing to challenge the searches by which the prosecution obtained the items. In *Salvucci*, however, the Court concluded that there was no inherent inconsistency between such claims. Since the automatic standing rule had therefore "outlived its usefulness in [the] Court's Fourth Amendment jurisprudence," it was overruled.

The standing requirement is firmly entrenched in the Fourth Amendment and probably in those other exclusionary requirements over which the Supreme Court has substantive development power. But in *Alderman* the Court acknowledged that Congress or states could extend the right of exclusion to persons without standing in the Fourth Amendment sense.

Standing Under State Law Exclusionary Requirements. State courts developing state law exclusionary requirements have generally, but not universally, followed the Supreme Court's Fourth Amendment model. The most dramatic deviation was that of the California Supreme Court, which in 1955 announced that all of the reasons persuading it to adopt exclusionary requirements suggested further that defendants should be able to invoke those requirements regardless of whether they had been the victims of the illegality relied upon.[57]

The California court's rejection of standing rested on several bases. First, the California court sought greater assurance of a deterrent effect than satisfied the Supreme Court, and this was provided by requiring exclusion regardless of the challenging defendant's standing. In addition, however, the California tribunal gave greater weight to judicial integrity considerations than has the Supreme Court. It conceptualized judicial integrity as broader than the Supreme Court's later analysis finding judicial integrity implicated only if judicial use of evidence encourages future violations of the underlying legal requirement. Judicial integrity, as broadly conceptualized, was compromised by use of illegally obtained evidence regardless of whether the victims of the illegality were before the court.

Whatever the controlling rationale, the California approach was nullified by the 1982 amendment to the state constitution barring judicial development of exclusionary sanctions.

The Louisiana courts, in contrast, continue to construe that state's Constitution as dispensing with any standing requirement regarding unreasonable searches and seizures.

Several state courts have retained a standing requirement as a matter of state constitutional law but have held that it is more readily met than the Fourth Amendment requirement as construed by the Supreme Court. The New Jersey Supreme Court concluded that Fourth Amendment law, as construed and applied in *Rakas*, has "the

---

[56]   390 U.S. 377 (1968).

[57]   People v. Martin, 290 P.2d 855 (Cal. 1955).

potential for inconsistent and capricious application," and "will in many instances produce results contrary to commonly held and accepted expectations of privacy." It consequently held that a defendant need only assert a possessory, proprietary or participatory interest in either the area searched or the item seized in order to have standing. The Vermont Supreme Court also took this approach.

The Supreme Judicial Court of Massachusetts has indicated it will be receptive to recognition of "target" standing in certain limited situations. It explained:

> In considering art. 14 [of the Massachusetts Constitution], we have ... suggest[ed] that "[u]nconstitutional [searches of] small fish intentionally undertaken in order to catch big ones may have to be discouraged by allowing the big fish, when caught, to rely on the violation of the rights of the small fish, as to whose prosecution the police are relatively indifferent." We also have suggested that at least where "distinctly egregious police conduct" is involved, the need to create a deterrent effect may require, or at least make appropriate, recognition of target standing.

> We reaffirm ... that in a case where the police engage in "distinctly egregious" conduct that constitutes a significant violation of a third party's art. 14 rights in an effort to obtain evidence against a defendant, it may be appropriate to permit the defendant to rely on the standing of the third party to challenge the police conduct.[58]

The Massachusetts courts, however, appear not to have encountered any cases in which defendants have established a right to target standing under this analysis.

A few state courts retain automatic standing as a matter of state constitutional law. This has been the position of the highest courts in, among other states, Massachusetts, Pennsylvania and New Jersey. Most state courts, however, have followed the Supreme Court's lead and rejected automatic standing.

Disagreement with the Supreme Court's Fourth Amendment case law, such as *Rakas*, may be best addressed as a matter of the substantive law triggering the exclusionary sanction rather than exclusionary rule law. If the result in *Rakas* is inappropriate, the blame may be attributable to the Court's definition of protected privacy rather than the exclusionary rule law that links the ability to challenge evidence to whether the defendant's privacy was violated.

§ 176 Scope of Exclusion: (a) Evidence Acquired as a Result of Illegality ("Fruit of the Poisonous Tree")

Some—but not all—prohibitions against the use of improperly obtained evidence extend beyond evidence obtained as an immediate and direct result of the impropriety. Many, following the "fruit of the poisonous tree" aspect of the Fourth Amendment exclusionary rule, demand the exclusion of all derivative evidence—evidence obtained as a factual result of the impropriety—unless an exception to the exclusionary demand applies. The relationship between this approach and what is often regarded as the separate "independent source" rule presents a continuing problem discussed in the next section.

---

[58] Com. v. Santiago, 24 N.E.3d 560, 564 (Mass. 2015) (citations omitted).

Fourth Amendment "Fruit of the Poisonous Tree" Rule. In *Silverthorne Lumber Co. v. United States,*[59] the Supreme Court construed the Fourth Amendment exclusionary rule as requiring exclusion of evidence obtained even as an indirect result of violation of defendants' Fourth Amendment rights. If a defendant establishes a Fourth Amendment violation—a "poisonous tree"—and that evidence was obtained as a factual result of that violation—that the evidence is "fruit" of the poisonous tree—the defendant is entitled to have the evidence excluded unless the prosecution establishes the applicability of an exception to the general requirement of exclusion. American courts have generally—and arguably uncritically—accepted that other exclusionary sanctions must or at least should be similarly defined.

If a defendant establishes that law enforcement officers, who possessed adequate basis for a search, were motivated to make a second search by information obtained in a first and unreasonable search, the Supreme Court held in *Murray v. United States,*[60] the results of the second search are fruit of the initial illegality. This is so even if the second search was made pursuant to a warrant which was obtained without use of the results of the first and unreasonable search. The challenged evidence nevertheless is a result or fruit of the first and unreasonable search.

Generally, the taint flows only forward and renders inadmissible only that evidence obtained after, and as a factual consequence of, the unreasonable search. Moreover, part of a search may be reasonable and other parts may be unreasonable. Officers searching pursuant to a valid search warrant, for example, may search within the terms of the warrant and discover and seize some evidence. But at various times, they may exceed the scope of search authorized by the warrant and during some of these transgressions they may find and seize other evidence. Usually, only that evidence located and seized while the officers were engaged in the unreasonable aspects of the search, that is, while they were acting beyond the authority of the warrant, is tainted by the officers' improper action and thus rendered inadmissible.

If evidence was acquired by exploiting illegality only in the sense that the illegality prevented illegal removal or destruction of the evidence, exclusion is not required. The Fourth Amendment position, the Supreme Court's discussion in *Segura v. United States*[61] suggests, is based on the policy position that defendants not be permitted to benefit from the loss of opportunities to engage in conduct barred by law.

Amazingly, the Fourth Amendment fruit of the poisonous tree rule developed with little discussion of its rationale or justification. In 1984, however, the Supreme Court retrospectively explained the "core rationale" for the rule in terms of standard Fourth Amendment exclusionary sanction analysis: Although the fruit of the poisonous tree rule increases the cost of the exclusionary sanction, that cost is justified by the need to provide sufficient deterrence assuring adequate disincentive for the prohibited conduct. Only by threatening officers with the inadmissibility of the indirect as well as the direct results of their Fourth Amendment transgressions can adequate incentive for avoiding those transgressions be provided.[62]

---

[59]   251 U.S. 385 (1920).

[60]   487 U.S. 533 (1988).

[61]   468 U.S. 796 (1984).

[62]   Nix v. Williams, 467 U.S. 431, 442–43 (1984).

Initial Requirement of "But For" Causation. As a consequence of the fruit of the poisonous tree rule, under exclusionary rules generally a defendant must show both an illegality sufficient to trigger the exclusionary sanction and a causal relationship between that illegality and the prosecution's possession of the evidence challenged. If but only if that relationship is shown does attention turn to whether the prosecution can show that the evidence is nevertheless admissible because of the nature of that relationship (attenuation of taint)[63] or despite that relationship (inevitable discovery).[64]

Fourth Amendment case law indicates that the defendant must show that "but for" the illegality, prosecution authorities would not have acquired the challenge evidence. The major question is whether this should be applied literally, so that causation is shown if the defendant demonstrates that prosecution authorities would not have gained possession of the evidence precisely when and as they did but for the illegality.

The matter is put quite effectively by the search warrant "no-knock" cases, in which the only Fourth Amendment violation is the officers' failure to announce their authority to enter and to permit the occupants to admit them. Often the evidence suggests that the unreasonable unannounced entry caused the officers to discover and seize the challenged evidence only slightly sooner than would have been the case had they paused to make a proper entry.

In *Hudson v. Michigan*,[65] discussed substantively in Section 166, all nine members of the Court agreed that a violation of the Fourth Amendment requires exclusion of evidence only if the violation was a but-for cause of obtaining the evidence. The Justices split 5 to 4—or perhaps 4 to 5—on whether the necessary but-for causality exists in a "no knock" search warrant entry situation. A clear majority, however, took the view that in these cases either there is no but-for causality or the but-for causality that exists necessarily means the taint of the violation is attenuated.

Hudson, then, confirmed that under the Fourth Amendment exclusionary rule "but for" causation is required. It also made clear the justices disagree on precisely what such causation requires and thus when it does not exist.

Limits on Excludable "Fruit" Under Fourth Amendment Law. Insofar as Fourth Amendment law requires exclusion of fruit of the poisonous tree, there is one indication that at least as applied to some situations the fruits doctrine is qualified by some objective limits on those fruit subject to the exclusionary requirement.

When law enforcement officers violate a defendant's Fourth Amendment rights by unreasonably entering his home to there make an otherwise proper arrest of him, the Supreme Court held in *New York v. Harris*,[66] a defendant simply cannot challenge the admissibility of statements made by him subsequent to that arrest and after he was removed from his home. This is apparently the case regardless of the strength of his claim that such a statement was caused by the illegal entry and without the prosecution needing to establish the applicability of any exception to the exclusionary requirement.

Harris reflects the Court's conclusion that in the specific context there presented, an adequate balance of deterrence expectations and costs requires that defendants be

---

[63] See infra § 179.

[64] See infra § 181.

[65] 547 U.S. 586 (2006).

[66] 495 U.S. 14 (1990).

permitted to challenge the admissibility of some fruits of an unreasonable entry—statements made as a result of that entry and while the defendant is still being detained in the unreasonably entered home. Permitting such defendants' to challenge the admissibility of statements obtained later, however, would trigger loss-of-evidence and increased-litigation costs exceeding whatever marginal deterrence against unreasonable entries of homes might be expected.

Under *Harris*, the fruit of the poisonous tree doctrine is clearly not sacrosanct, even in the Fourth Amendment context. The definition of challengeable fruit may be limited, where that can be done with reasonable clarity and when the characteristics of the type of situation at issue suggest such action as a means of achieving optimum balance between the deterrent benefits and costs of exclusion.

Harris may have been superseded by *Hudson v. Michigan*,[67] discussed in Section 166. *Hudson* held that a Fourth Amendment violation consisting of making an otherwise permissible entry of premises to execute a valid search warrant but in noncompliance with Fourth Amendment "knock and announce" requirements would simply not invoke the constitutional exclusionary remedy. Perhaps *Harris*-type entry without a warrant will now similarly not constitute a poisonous tree triggering the exclusionary rule. Most likely, however, the possibility that seeking a warrant would prevent the entry entirely means that *Harris* remains effective.

Applicability of "Fruits" Rule to Other Exclusionary Requirements. In a series of cases leading up to *United State v. Patane*,[68] the Supreme Court made clear that the fruit of the poisonous tree rule as developed in Fourth Amendment case law is not a necessary concomitant of a federal constitutional exclusionary requirement.

In *Patane*, a split majority of the Court held that the exclusionary remedy for a violation of *Miranda v. Arizona*,[69] although a Fifth Amendment matter, required only the exclusion of the out-of-court statement obtained by interrogation conducted in violation of the requirements of *Miranda*. Physical evidence, testimony of witnesses, and subsequent statements by the suspect are not rendered inadmissible simply because they were obtained as a result of the excluded statement.

The Justices split in *Patane* over whether the nature of the *Miranda* requirements were such that the *Miranda* exclusionary rule conceptually permitted a fruit of the poisonous tree aspect. Justice Thomas's plurality opinion announcing the judgment rested heavily upon his conclusion that the *Miranda* requirements were not direct constitutional constraints on the police and for this reason simply did not conceptually permit an exclusionary penalty extending to derivative evidence. Thus, these justices reasoned, the Court need not—and in fact could not—reach whether excluding derivative evidence would be sound constitutional policy. Justice Kennedy's ground for concurring in the result reached by the plurality relied less on this rationale than on a judgment that the evidence at issue—physical items obtained by using information in an inadmissible statement—was reliable and particularly useful to the accurate resolution of contested criminal cases.

A majority of the *Patane* Court, then, appeared to agree that that the nature of the *Miranda* exclusionary sanction did not preclude developing that sanction as extending

---

[67]   547 U.S. 586 (2006).

[68]   542 U.S. 630 (2004).

[69]   384 U.S. 436 (1966).

to fruit of *Miranda* violations. They agreed that whether the *Miranda* federal constitutional exclusionary requirement should and would extend to fruit of the poisonous tree depended on balancing the value of excluding fruit as a means of deterring conduct violating the constitutional provision against the costs of doing so. That majority disagreed on how the balancing should come out. Justice Kennedy, writing for himself and Justice O'Connor, concluded that "[i]n light of the important probative value of reliable physical evidence, it is doubtful that exclusion can be justified by a deterrence rationale sensitive to both law enforcement interests and a suspect's rights during an in-custody interrogation." Justice Souter, writing for himself and Justices Stevens and Ginsburg, concluded that the need to avoid creating an incentive for police to ignore the *Miranda* requirements by permitting use of derivative evidence is worth the price it involves.

Shortly before deciding *Patane,* the Supreme Court remanded *Fellers v. United States*[70] for a determination whether a showing that officers elicited a statement from Fellers in violation of his Sixth Amendment right to counsel requires suppression of later statements "on the ground that they were fruits of previous questioning conducted in violation of the Sixth Amendment . . . ." The court of appeals held that the rationale for not applying a fruits rule to a violation of the *Miranda* Fifth Amendment requirements also controlled where the offered tree was poisoned by a violation of the Sixth Amendment.

As the Court's case law culminating in *Patane* recognizes, whether an exclusionary requirement properly extends to derivative evidence or fruits should turn on whether so extending it will serve the purposes of the exclusionary requirement well enough to justify the cost paid by the increased loss of reliable evidence. A major consideration, of course, is the importance of legal requirement being enforced. Where an exclusionary sanction applies to violation of a nonconstitutional legal requirement, the nonconstitutional nature of that legal requirement suggests its respect is somewhat less important and thus argues against defining the sanction as extending to derivative evidence.

§ 177 Scope of Exclusion: (b) Evidence with an "Independent Source"

In *Silverthorne Lumber Co. v. United States,*[71] Justice Holmes announced for the Supreme Court that facts acquired in violation of the Fourth Amendment do not, for that reason, "become sacred and inaccessible." "If," he continued, "knowledge of them is gained from an independent source they may be proved like any others . . . ." The "independent source" rule or "concept," based on this comment in *Silverthorne Lumber Co.,* has been a source of some uncertainty in exclusionary rule analysis. Among the problems has been distinguishing independent source from "inevitable discovery" as discussed in Section 181.

In *Murray v. United States,*[72] the Supreme Court emphasized that the independent source "concept" has been used in two distinguishable ways. Justice Holmes' *Silverthorne Lumber Co.* dictum used it to describe situations in which the prosecution has both tainted and untainted evidence of a particular fact and offers only the untainted evidence to prove that fact. For example, police might improperly arrest X, question him, and

---

[70] 540 U.S. 519 (2004).

[71] 251 U.S. 385 (1920).

[72] 487 U.S. 533 (1988).

obtain from him an admission to being in the vicinity of V's home the night it was burglarized. But an alert citizen might report to police seeing X in V's neighborhood on the night of the break-in. The fact that the prosecution obtained inadmissible evidence indicating X's presence near the scene of the offense would not bar it from proving his presence, because it could do so by evidence with an "independence source," that is, evidence obtained in a manner not factually related to the improper arrest. This, *Murray* indicated, was the more specific and most important use of the term independent source.

The other and more general use of the term, *Murray* continued, describes situations in which all of the prosecution's evidence of a particular fact is untainted by its improper activity. For example, police might improperly arrest X and question him, but X may not reveal anything about the location of his victim's body. A citizen, however, may report to police that she observed X hide a body in a particular location; police following up on this information might then discover the body. The prosecution's evidence regarding the body is admissible despite the improper arrest of X because that evidence has an independent source.

Conceptually, the *Murray* discussion makes clear, "independent source" is simply a label reflecting a conclusion that particular challenged evidence was not obtained in a manner causally related to the Fourth Amendment violation. The rule or—"concept"— merely describes several ways in which the prosecution can argue that a defendant seeking to invoke the exclusionary rule has not established the necessary causal link between the triggering illegality and the obtaining of the challenged evidence.

In *United States v. Wade*,[73] however, the Supreme Court addressed the situation in which the prosecution offers a witness to make an in-court identification, the defendant shows the witness identified the defendant at a lineup conducted in violation of the defendant's Sixth Amendment right to counsel, and the prosecution argues the witness's observation of the crime is an independent source for the offered testimony. To prevail, the Court made clear, the prosecution must shoulder the burden of proof and that burden is clear and convincing evidence. *Wade* may reflect the Court's view that independent source analysis in the lineup/eyewitness context presents unique risks of inaccurate application and this justifies—in this context—placement of the burden on the prosecution and increasing that burden to clear and convincing evidence.

Some courts uncritically place the burden of proof regarding independent source generally on the prosecution without considering the tension between that position and a defendant's apparent burden of establishing that challenged evidence is the fruit of the conduct relied upon as the poisonous tree. Others require the defendant to make some sort of preliminary showing of causation, after which the prosecution has the burden of establishing that an independent source in some sense negates this preliminary showing.

Courts have been particularly troubled by the problems presented where officers have acted improperly but the prosecution relies upon evidence obtained in the execution of a later search warrant. When can a subsequently-issued warrant as an independent source of the challenged evidence? If the warrant is obtained without disclosing to the magistrate any information not derived from the illegality but the officers were motivated to seek the warrant because of that illegality, *Murray* made clear, the warrant could not constitute an independent source. Suppose the information derived from the

---

[73]   388 U.S. 218 (1967).

illegality is submitted to the magistrate but it is accompanied by other untainted information itself sufficient to support the issuance of the warrant? *Murray* suggests the warrant can be an independent source only if the tainted information did not nevertheless influence the magistrate's decision to issue the warrant. Some lower courts, however, have stated the standard as involving no inquiry into the issuing magistrate's decisionmaking. Under this approach, a warrant can constitute an independent source of evidence sized under it if there was sufficient untainted information submitted to the magistrate to support issuance of the warrant. The difficulty of inquiring into magistrates' mental processes suggests outcomes may often turn on which party has the burden of persuasion.

§ 178 Effect of Illegality upon "Jurisdiction" over Criminal Defendants and Exclusion of "Identity"

The very presence of many criminal defendants before trial courts could be regarded as the "fruit" of earlier official illegalities and hence in some way tainted by that activity. This is particularly so when the illegality consist of improper arrests, in the absence of which the defendants would almost certainly have never been apprehended. Nevertheless, there is agreement that ordinary illegality in an investigation does not deprive the trial court of "jurisdiction" in any sense or otherwise interfere with the court's power to proceed with the trial. Thus it does not provide a basis for a motion to dismiss the charges or for other relief which automatically ends the proceedings.

As a matter of federal constitutional law, the Supreme Court has held since *Ker v. Illinois*,[74] decided in 1886, that there is no federal constitutional bar to a court exercising jurisdiction over the person of a criminal defendant regardless of manner in which the presence of the person was obtained. After this was reaffirmed in *Frisbie v. Collins*,[75] it became widely-called the *Ker-Frisbie* rule.

In *United States v. Blue*,[76] the Court explained why this was not changed by the Court's commitment in *Mapp v. Ohio*[77] and its progeny to exclusionary sanctions as the primary means of implementing many federal constitutional rights:

> Our numerous precedents ordering the exclusion of . . . illegally obtained evidence assume implicitly that the remedy does not extend to barring the prosecution altogether. So drastic a step might marginally advance some of the ends served by exclusionary rules, but it would also increase to an intolerable degree interference with the public interest in having the guilty brought to book.[78]

That interference, of course, would be caused by depriving the prosecution of all possibility of convicting the defendant. Exclusionary sanctions, where applied, always leave open at least the theoretical possibility that the defendant can be convicted by evidence with an independent source.

Reluctance to read exclusionary sanctions as depriving courts of the power to proceed against defendants may affect analysis of other exclusionary sanction issues. In

---

[74]   119 U.S. 436 (1886).

[75]   342 U.S. 519 (1952).

[76]   384 U.S. 251 (1966).

[77]   367 U.S. 643 (1961).

[78]   *Blue*, 384 U.S. at 255.

United States v. Crews,[79] for example, the victim made an in-court identification of the defendant, who had been illegally arrested. The Court of Appeals held that the defendant's presence at trial had been used by the prosecution in presenting that testimony; the witness testified that she was comparing her memory of the perpetrator with the defendant's appearance, with which she was familiar because she observed him in the courtroom, and on that basis she concluded that he was the perpetrator. This constituted an impermissible evidentiary use of the fruits of the illegal arrest, the Court of Appeals concluded.

Five members of the Supreme Court, however, rejected this approach and characterized Crews' argument as precluded by *Ker* and its progeny. A holding that a defendant's face can be considered suppressible evidence, Justice White explained, "would be tantamount to holding that an illegal arrest effectively insulates one from conviction for any crime where an in-court identification is essential." This, he concluded, was inconsistent with the rationale of *Ker's* successors.

A majority of the Court is strongly committed to the proposition that federal constitutional exclusionary sanctions should not, directly or indirectly, be applied or expanded to completely bar criminal proceedings.

Four years after *Crews,* the Court in *I.N.S. v. Lopez-Mendoza,*[80] and without discussing *Crews,* added:

> The "body" or identity of a defendant or respondent in a criminal or civil
> proceeding is never itself suppressible as a fruit of an unlawful arrest, even if
> it is conceded that an unlawful arrest, search, or interrogation occurred.[81]

State courts have adopted the *Ker-Frisbie* approach that illegality in the investigation and development of evidence does not affect the jurisdiction of the courts over the defendant or the prosecution. It does not require or even permit dismissal of the prosecution. Exclusionary sanctions, in other words, are no more than evidence rules that affect the admissibility of certain evidence.

One isolated judicial defense of the position that an unlawful arrest should fatally taint the jurisdiction of the trial court was predicated largely upon considerations of broadly-defined judicial integrity:

> By basing the court's jurisdiction on an illegal warrantless arrest of the
> defendant in his home, the court legitimizes the illegal conduct which produced
> the arrest. Courts should not be parties to invasions of the constitutional rights
> of citizens.[82]

Lower courts have disagreed on the implications of *Crews* and *Lopez-Mendoza's* comment that the identity of a defendant is never suppressible fruit of an improper arrest. The New York Court of Appeals concluded that under *Crews* and *Lopez-Mendoza* "a defendant may not invoke the fruit-of-the-poisonous-tree doctrine when the only link between improper police activity and the disputed evidence is that the police learned the defendant's name," and the Supreme Court dismissed review as improvidently granted. Other courts—probably most courts—read the language as simply restating the *Ker-*

---

[79]   445 U.S. 463 (1980).

[80]   468 U.S. 1032 (1984).

[81]   *Id.* at 1039–40.

[82]   State v. Smith, 388 N.W.2d 601, 612 (Wis. 1986) (Abrahamson, J., concurring).

Frisbie rule that jurisdiction over a defendant is not affected and thus is not "suppressible." Under this approach, *Crews* and *Lopez-Mendoza* have no application to what one court described as "evidence about identity, such physical evidence establishing a defendant's identity (fingerprints, photographs, etc.), as well as testimonial evidence by an eyewitness about their in- or out-of-court identifications of the defendant as the perpetrator of a crime." This means that despite *Crews* and *Lopez-Mendoza*, "[a]ll evidence about identity is potentially suppressible as fruit of the poisonous tree stemming from unconstitutional police conduct. However, suppression is not automatic—any such evidence may be admitted where the [prosecution] sufficiently proves that it was either untainted by the illegal conduct, or because it was discoverable through an independent source."

§ 179   Exceptions to Exclusion: (a) Attenuation of Taint

The Fourth Amendment exclusionary sanction, and most others modeled upon it, are subject to exception for evidence obtained after the "taint" of the illegality triggering the exclusionary requirement has become "attenuated." Given the nature of this exception, it applies only to "derivative" evidence that is subject to challenge initially only because it is "fruit of the poisonous tree."

This exception, unlike the "independent source" doctrine, does not rest on the lack of an actual causal link between the original illegality and the obtaining of the challenged evidence. Rather, the exception is triggered by a demonstration that the characteristics of that causal link are such that the impact of the original illegality upon the obtaining of the evidence is sufficiently minimal that exclusion is not required despite the causal link.

In *United States v. Leon,*[83] the Supreme Court explained that in the federal constitutional context, the attenuation of taint doctrine is the product of the principles underlying the federal constitutional exclusionary requirements. To some extent, it identifies those cases in which the taint upon evidence is so minimal that admitting the evidence does not compromise the integrity of the court. More importantly, however:

> [T]he "dissipation of taint" concept . . . "attempts to mark the point at which the detrimental consequences of illegal police action become so attenuated that that the deterrent effect of the exclusionary rule no longer justifies its cost."[84]

Generalization as to what is sufficient to establish attenuation of taint is difficult. *Utah v. Strieff*[85] explained that attenuation occurs if the connection between the unconstitutional conduct and official acquisition of the evidence at issue is "remote or has been interrupted by some intervening circumstance." Most of the Supreme Court case law at least until *Strieff* in 2016 applied the doctrine to situations in which a confession made by a defendant in custody begun in violation of the Fourth Amendment is challenged as an inadmissible fruit of the arrest. This gives rise to difficulty in determining when in general terms a causal connection between unconstitutional conduct and acquisition of evidence is fatally "remote" or fatally "interrupted by some intervening circumstance."

---

[83]   468 U.S. 897 (1984).

[84]   *Id.* at 911, quoting Brown v. Illinois, 422 U.S. 590, 609 (1975) (Powell, J., concurring in part).

[85]   136 S. Ct. 2056 (2016).

Strieff confirmed that three considerations or factors bear upon whether attenuation occurred:

1. "the 'temporal proximity' between the unconstitutional conduct [or, in more general terms, the primary illegality] and the discovery of [the] evidence [at issue];"

2. "the presence [and characteristics] of [any] intervening circumstances;" and

3. "the purpose and flagrancy of the official misconduct."

In *United States v. Ceccolini*,[86] the Court observed that "[o]bviously no mathematical weight can be assigned to any of the [relevant] factors . . . ." This is an understatement, but some additional guidance is provided by the Court's case law.

Temporal Proximity. The longer period of time between the primary illegality and obtaining the challenged evidence, the more likely it is that the taint of that illegality has become attenuated. In *Strieff,* an officer lacking the constitutionally-required reasonable suspicion stopped Strieff to inquire about his activity regarding suspected drug premises the officer had seen Strieff leave. Within minutes the officer learned there was an outstanding arrest warrant for Strieff and arrested him; a search incident to that arrest revealed contraband. "[S]uch a short time interval counsels in favor of suppression," the Court announced. In fact, in *Rawlings v. Kentucky*,[87] the Court indicated that the 45 minutes that elapsed between Brown's illegal detention and his making of the statement at issue was a "relatively short period of time" that might under some circumstances preclude attenuation of the taint.

Intervening Circumstances. What number and type of intervening circumstances are sufficient to attenuate a particular taint is an especially difficult question. The more intervening events, clearly, the more likely the taint is to have become attenuated. Some case law suggests that if one of the intervening circumstances involves judicial action, this is entitled to particular significance in finding attenuation. A major thread running through the attenuation cases is the significance of proof that the chain of events involved a voluntary decision by someone to cooperate with investigating authorities. If the decision was that of the defendant, the factor is entitled to particular weight.

In *Strieff,* the Court stressed the officer's discovery and reliance upon the valid arrest warrant as an intervening circumstance strongly favoring attenuation of the taint of the stop. "[T]he warrant was valid, it predated [the officer's] investigation, and it was entirely unconnected with the stop," the Court noted. Further, the warrant mandated an arrest.

Purpose and Flagrancy. Strieff characterized this third factor as " 'particularly' significant." This is apparently because it serves most directly to fashion the exception to cover situations in which deterrence of the type of activity involved makes a relatively weak case for the need for costly deterrence.

Flagrancy, *Strieff* made clear, requires more than a showing that the law enforcement activity violated constitutional requirements. Thus attenuation of taint is less likely to have occurred if the illegality was an extensive deviation from the

---

[86]   435 U.S. 268 (1978).
[87]   448 U.S. 98 (1980).

underlying legal requirement. Impropriety beyond that constituting the poisonous tree argues against attenuation; *Strieff* emphasized that the arrest warrant was valid and supported the arrest and that the search made was a reasonable one incident to the arrest.

Purposes militating against attenuation, *Strieff* suggested, include a completely speculative hope that the law enforcement activity will turn up evidence of wrongdoing—an intent to conduct a fishing expedition. The officer in *Strieff*, in contrast, "sought information from Strieff to find out what was happening inside a house whose occupants were legitimately suspected of dealing drugs."

Strieff also made clear that attenuation is less likely if the facts show the officers were aware that their actions violated constitutional norms. The officer in *Strieff*, in contrast, was merely negligent. Attenuation is also less likely if the constitutional violation was part of systemic or recurrent police misconduct; nothing suggested this in *Strieff*.

The difficulty of applying attenuation analysis is illustrated by the Supreme Court's application of it to the situation in which the challenged evidence consists of the in-court testimony of a witness located by exploitation of information obtained as a result of an improper search or seizure. In *Ceccolini*, the Court refused to adopt a per se rule under which such evidence could never be the excludable fruit of a Fourth Amendment violation. But it did hold that the attenuation analysis should be applied in such cases in a manner appropriately accommodated to the situation. When a criminal defendant seeks suppression of live-witness testimony, "a closer, more direct link between the illegality and that kind of testimony is required," as compared to cases in which exclusion of other kinds of evidence is sought. This apparently means that attenuation is to be more readily found, given that the evidence at issue—eyewitness testimony—is of exceptional importance and therefore exclusion is appropriate only if the facts show a particularly close relationship between the illegality and discovery of the evidence.

In *Ceccolini*-type cases as in other potential attenuation situations, the case for attenuation is dramatically strengthened by a showing of an intervening autonomous decision. The willingness—or eagerness—of the witness in *Ceccolini* to testify was an important consideration favoring attenuation.

The attenuation of taint qualification to the federal exclusionary requirements, of course, does not mean that other exclusionary demands must be similarly limited. Nevertheless, courts have—perhaps uncritically—assumed that other exclusionary requirements extending to fruit of the poisonous tree are also qualified by similar limitations. The Texas Court of Criminal Appeals, for example, adopted the approach of Supreme Court case law for purposes of the state's statutory exclusionary rule, because that case law "appears to be the best available framework" for determining whether the effect of illegality is sufficient to justify exclusion.

The Washington Supreme Court in *State v. Eserjose*,[88] in contrast, left open whether the exclusionary rule of article I, section 7 of the Washington Constitution is subject to an attenuation of taint exception. Four members of the court argued that it should not be:

---

[88]   259 P.3d 172 (Wash. 2011).

> An attenuation exception ... is fundamentally at odds with our article I, section 7 protection. ... [T]his attenuation exception allows illegally obtained evidence to be admitted. Nor does such a doctrine respect our paramount concern of protecting individual privacy, as it would deny a remedy to those whose privacy has been unconstitutionally invaded. Additionally, application of the exception would necessarily be speculative, a departure from our otherwise nearly categorical exclusionary rule.
>
> More importantly, nothing in the attenuation doctrine ... suggests how time, intervening circumstances, or less egregious misconduct can infuse the fruits of an illegal seizure with the authority of law required by article I, section 7. ... Evidence obtained in violation of a person's constitutional rights, even if attenuated, still lacks the authority of law and should be suppressed.[89]

A few state courts, most likely disturbed by *Strieff's* finding of attenuation on the basis of discovery of an arrest warrant minutes into an improper stop, have explored as a matter of state law alternatives to the Supreme Court's attenuation of taint analysis. The Washington Supreme Court in *State v. Mayfield*[90]—decided after *Eserjose*—concluded that the federal attenuation analysis failed to give adequate significance to the state constitutional exclusionary rule's policy of broadly protecting the individual right to privacy. This is in part because the federal analysis admits evidence obtained in ways that violate citizens' privacy and thus fails to adequately protect that privacy by denying the state the benefits of such official action. The court therefore adopted a narrow attenuation analysis based on tort law:

> We now explicitly adopt a state attenuation doctrine that is satisfied if, and only if, an unforeseeable intervening act genuinely severs the causal connection between official misconduct and the discovery of evidence. If such a superseding cause is present, then the evidence is not properly viewed as "fruit of the poisonous tree" but, instead, as "fruit" of the superseding cause. In such a case, the State derives no benefit from its officers' unconstitutional actions. And because a superseding cause must, by definition, be unforeseeable, this narrow attenuation doctrine will not encourage officials to violate article I, section 7 in the hopes of discovering evidence.[91]

The Indiana Supreme Court, in contrast, sought to incorporate into state constitutional attenuation analysis the state constitutional law's emphasis upon totality-of-the-circumstances reasonableness. It did this by embracing the Supreme Court's three-factor approach but adding that other relevant considerations could also be taken into account.

§ 180 Exceptions to Exclusion: (b) Intervening Illegal Conduct

If, in response to officers' illegality sufficient to trigger an exclusionary sanction, suspects engage in further criminal conduct, the courts have regarded that further criminal conduct as bases for law enforcement action somehow independent of the initial illegalities. Thus evidence of those further illegalities, or evidence derived from them, is admissible despite the original improper conduct of the officers.

---

[89] *Id.* at 189 (Johnson, J., dissenting).
[90] 434 P.3d 58 (Wash. 2019).
[91] *Id.* at 74.

Often the further illegality consists of forcible resistance to the officers' conduct. In the leading decision, *United States v. Bailey*,[92] the defendant responded to his arguably improper arrest by struggling with the arresting officer. "But for" the unlawful arrest the officer would not have observed the defendant's resistance—because it would not have occurred. Nevertheless, the constitutional deficiency of the arrest did not require exclusion of evidence regarding the resistance. In a more rigorous application of the analysis, a Texas court applied it to a situation in which a suspect responded to an unlawful search of his car by grabbing the contraband and placing it in his mouth. Although the unlawfulness of the search precluded the prosecution from proving the defendant's possession before his criminal effort to destroy the contraband, the *Bailey* analysis permitted the prosecution to prove his criminal possession of it during and after his grabbing the drug.

The precise nature of the doctrine being applied in these cases is not always clear. Some courts appear to regard the doctrine as simply a specialized application of the attenuation of taint doctrine, under which intervening voluntary criminal conduct usually and perhaps inevitably attenuates the taint of illegality preceding that conduct. This approach, of course, is consistent with the general significance given in attenuation analysis to intervening voluntary conduct.[93]

Other courts appear to regard the doctrine as a separate exception to exclusionary requirements, based on considerations distinguishable from those supporting the attenuation of taint doctrine. An Indiana court, for example, announced:

> Like the many federal and state courts before us, we agree that the purpose of the Fourth Amendment's exclusionary rule—to deter police misconduct—is not advanced by suppressing evidence of a new crime committed by the defendant after an illegal search or seizure. We therefore hold that notwithstanding a strong causal connection in fact between an illegal search or seizure by law enforcement and a defendant's response, if the defendant's response is itself a new and distinct crime, then evidence of the new crime is admissible notwithstanding the prior illegality.[94]

The rule is generally based on the proposition that whatever incremental deterrence of official illegality accomplished by excluding this evidence would be outweighed by the costs involved. Among those costs is the loss of the opportunity to discourage unlawful and perhaps violent responses to questionable law enforcement activity or perhaps actually encouraging such responses. The Colorado court also commented that excluding such evidence would result in only minimal deterrence, apparently on the assumption that officers' responses to attacks on them are unlikely to be affected by later admissibility or inadmissibility of evidence.

The exception is generally assumed to apply only if the defendant engaged in further criminal acts. An unwise response to official illegality that simply reveals a past digression by the defendant will not invoke it. One court reasoned that the rationale for the exception—discouraging violent responses to even improper law enforcement conduct—did not justify the exception's application to evidence that a suspect responded to an unconstitutional detention by giving a false name to the office.

---

92   691 F.2d 1009 (11th Cir. 1982).

93   See supra § 179.

94   C.P. v. State, 39 N.E.3d 1174, 1182 (Ind. Ct. App. 2015).

Several courts have held that the exception only permits use of evidence of the new criminal conduct. Thus, where an officer suspected drug activity and attempted an improper stop, and the suspect struggled, and the officer eventually recovered drugs, the exception permitted use of evidence of the suspect's resisting detention. It did not, however, permit the use of evidence of the drugs. This discourages criminal responds to police conduct, removes a potential incentive for improper law enforcement action, and "preserves the integrity of the rationale underlying much of our constitutional seizure analysis."

Other, and probably most, courts applying the rule permit the admission of evidence of crimes other than the one responsive to the officers' initial improper activity. In *Bailey* itself, the prosecution was permitted to use evidence of Bailey's criminal attack on the officers and drugs found in a search made incident to the arrest for that attack. Conceptually, this approach is consistent with the view that the so-called new crime rule is simply a specialized application of attenuation of taint analysis under which attenuation permits the use of all evidence obtained after the taint of the initial misconduct became attenuated.

§ 181 Exceptions to Exclusion: (c) Inevitable Discovery

Many exclusionary requirements are subject to an exception often called the "inevitable discovery" rule. Evidence otherwise inadmissible becomes usable under this exception upon a showing that if the evidence had not been improperly secured as it was, the prosecution would nevertheless "inevitably" have obtained it in a "legitimate" manner.

Unlike the so-called independent source rule,[95] which is invoked by proof that the challenged evidence was in actual fact not obtained as a factual result of the illegality, this exception rests on proof regarding hypothetical scenarios. This characteristic also distinguishes inevitable discovery from attenuation of taint,[96] which is invoked by a showing regarding the actual causal link between the illegal conduct and obtaining the evidence.

Inevitable discovery was incorporated into federal constitutional exclusionary analysis in *Nix v. Williams*,[97] a Sixth Amendment right to counsel case. The rationale for the exclusionary remedy, the Court reasoned, ordinarily requires only that the prosecution be denied any advantages that might flow from its misconduct. This preventive purpose does not require that the prosecution be put in any worse a position than it would be in had it not committed the primary illegality. Since no reason exists to deny the prosecution any advantage it can establish that it would have enjoyed had its officers eschewed improper action, only an inevitable discovery exception can properly limit the exclusionary requirement as dictated by its rationale.

State courts have tended to construe state exclusionary requirements as qualified by an exception somewhat similar to *Williams's* federal constitutional doctrine. A significant number, however, have been persuaded by the risk that the exception may be misapplied in operation to limit the exception more rigorously than the Supreme

---

[95]   See supra § 177.

[96]   See supra § 179.

[97]   467 U.S. 431 (1984).

Court found appropriate in fashioning the exception to the federal constitutional exclusionary sanctions.

Williams rejected the contention that the nature of the issues posed by the exception requires an unusually high burden of proof on the prosecution. Some state courts, however, have reasoned that the conjecture inherent in application of the exception justifies imposing upon the prosecution the task of proving the exception applies by clear and convincing evidence.

Williams also rejected the holdings below that the exception requires a showing that the evidence was obtained by officers acting in actual "good faith," reiterating that even where officers act in bad faith the purposes of the exclusionary requirement do not justify putting the prosecution in a worse position than it would have occupied had its officers acted properly. Several state courts, however, have required that the officers have acted in good faith. The Alaska Supreme Court, for example, concluded that an unqualified exception poses a sufficient risk of encouraging law enforcement "shortcuts" to demand that as a matter of state constitutional law it be limited to situations in which the officers did not act in bad faith to accelerate the discovery of the challenged evidence.

The exception is generally agreed to require proof that the prosecution would—not might or could—have obtained the challenged evidence in a proper manner. Courts differ somewhat in their statements of the applicable standard. The Montana court colorfully stated that "[i]t must appear that, as certainly as night follows day, the evidence would have been discovered without reference to the violation of the defendant's rights." Others have announced that legitimate discovery must be "truly inevitable" or "certain as a practical matter." Federal circuits differ. Some require only a reasonable probability that the evidence would have been obtained properly. Others direct the exception be limited to situations in which the trial courts find, with a high level of confidence, that each of the contingencies necessary to the legal discovery of the contested evidence would be resolved in the prosecution's favor.

Some courts have sought to minimize the risk that inevitability will be uncritically found by requiring that the prosecution establish that the legitimate discovery of the evidence would have occurred as a result of an alternative line of investigation that was actually being actively pursued at the time of the illegal conduct. Perhaps the leading case, *United States v. Cherry*,[98] reasoned in part that without proof that police had begun active pursuit of the legal line of investigation at the time of their illegal conduct, application of the inevitable discovery exception based on that legal line of investigation would involve the sort of "speculative elements" that *Williams* assumed were not involved in the exception. Others reject this requirement, although proof that such an alternative investigation was actually underway strongly supports the contention that it had the independence necessary to trigger the exception.

Clearly some courts are uncomfortable with the inevitable discovery exception, especially as applied to some types of situations, and this discomfort has given rise to a variety of possible limitations on the doctrine. Some discussions suggest that the exception is not to be applied where the illegality is particularly serious or infringes a central aspect of the governing law. Others suggest that it is not to be applied to situations in which excessive speculation would necessarily be involved.

---

[98]   759 F.2d 1196 (5th Cir. 1985).

The exception might, as some courts have held, be limited to "derivative" as contrasted with "primary" or "direct" evidence. Under this distinction, direct or primary evidence is that which is actually discovered and seized during the illegal conduct. Derivative evidence, on the other hand, is evidence obtained later by means of information derived from illegal conduct. Some courts have limited the exception to evidence of the latter sort. If the exception is limited to derivative evidence, it becomes an exception not to the basic exclusionary requirement but only to the corollary that renders inadmissible all fruit of the poisonous tree. Most courts have refused to limit the exception to derivative evidence. Perhaps, however, they have failed to fully explore the possibility that such a limitation might be the most appropriate way of preventing the exception from effectively nullifying some or most of the legal requirements enforced by exclusionary requirements.

State courts and legislatures are not, of course, bound to include this exception in state exclusionary requirement, and some have rejected it. A split Washington Supreme Court held in *State v. Winterstein*[99] that the state constitutional exclusionary rule had no inevitable discovery exception. The majority relied in part on its conclusion that the doctrine "is necessarily speculative." More importantly, it emphasized that the Washington exclusionary requirement—unlike the Fourth Amendment exclusionary rule—is designed to protect privacy by providing a remedy whenever privacy is impermissibly invaded. This rationale for the state law requirement is inconsistent with the inevitable discovery exception's denial of a remedy where deterrent considerations are viewed as insufficient to support exclusion.

§ 182 Exceptions to Exclusion: (d) "Good Faith"

Whether illegally obtained evidence should be excluded if the officers who gathered it mistakenly believed (or could have believed) that their actions complied with legal requirements is among the most controversial issues posed by existing exclusionary requirements. A limited "good faith" exception to the federal constitutional exclusionary rules for at least some situations of this sort has been recognized by the Supreme Court. State courts and legislatures have sometimes, but not always, followed suit.

Federal Constitutional Exception. In *United States v. Leon*[100] and *Massachusetts v. Sheppard*[101] the Supreme Court held that evidence obtained in searches conducted pursuant to defective search warrants was nevertheless admissible if the prosecution established that reasonable officers would have believed the warrants and therefore the searches complied with constitutional requirements. Three years later, in *Illinois v. Krull*,[102] the Court similarly held admissible evidence obtained in a warrantless search upon proof that given an invalid statute purporting to authorizing the search, a reasonable officer would have believed the statute valid and the search therefore constitutionally permissible.

The "good faith" label attached to the doctrine developed in *Leon, Sheppard* and *Krull* is arguably misleading. The exception does not require proof that the officers actually and subjectively—in "good faith," as that term is generally used—believed their actions within constitutional limits. The inquiry is whether under all the circumstances

---

[99]   220 P.3d 1226 (Wash. 2009).

[100]   468 U.S. 897 (1984).

[101]   468 U.S. 981 (1984).

[102]   480 U.S. 340 (1987).

"a reasonably well trained officer" would have known that the actions at issue were constitutionally impermissible. If not, the exception applies whether the officer actually making the search knew the actions were improper. In fact, and despite the general statement of the rule, the exception does not require proof that the officers actually— subjectively—relied on the warrant or legislation.

Emphasizing the preventive purpose of the Fourth Amendment exclusionary rule, *Leon, Sheppard* and *Krull* reasoned that in at least some situations the rule cannot be expected to deter objectively reasonable law enforcement activity and should not be applied in an effort to do so. This is particularly so, *Leon* continued, where officers have obtained a search warrant. The magistrate has responsibility for determining such matters as whether probable cause exists; officers cannot be expected to question magistrates' resolution of those issues. "Penalizing the officer for the magistrate's errors, rather than his own," the Court concluded, "cannot logically contribute to the deterrence of the Fourth Amendment violations." Similarly, *Krull* reasoned, officers cannot ordinarily be expected to question the judgment of a legislature that passed a statute authorizing a search, so no contribution to deterrence can logically be expected from penalizing the officer for errors of the legislature. Consequently, any benefits derived from excluding evidence in such situations cannot justify the substantial costs of exclusion.

Given that officers' ability to rely on a warrant or legislation must be objectively reasonable, exclusion is required despite a warrant or authorizing statute if the defect in the warrant or statute is so clear that a reasonably well trained officer would recognize that defect. In the case of reliance upon a warrant, *Leon* added, exclusion is required if the officer in applying for the warrant misled the issuing magistrate by including information he knew was false or would have known was false except for his reckless disregard for the truth or if the warrant was issued by a magistrate lacking the impartiality required by the Fourth Amendment.

Eight years after *Krull*, the Court decided *Arizona v. Evans*,[103] which it later characterized as "appl[ying] the good-faith exception in a case where the police reasonably relied on erroneous information concerning an arrest warrant in a database maintained by judicial employees." *Herring v. United States*[104] applied *Evans* to "a case where police employees erred in maintaining records in a [similar] warrant database" and the defendant showed only simple negligence and no systemic error or reckless disregard of constitutional requirements.

Davis v. United States[105] held the Fourth Amendment exception applied to a situation involving no basis for reliance on a warrant or statute. Rather, in *Davis* the Government showed state officers acting within the Eleventh Circuit made the search in a manner permissible under the Eleventh Circuit's interpretation of Supreme Court Fourth Amendment case law rejected—after the search—by the Court. The Fourth Amendment good faith exception, *Davis* held, means "[e]vidence obtained during a search conducted in reasonable reliance on binding precedent is not subject to the exclusionary rule."

---

[103]   514 U.S. 1 (1995).

[104]   555 U.S. 135 (2009).

[105]   564 U.S. 229 (2011).

Davis explained:

> The basic insight of the *Leon* line of cases is that the deterrence benefits of exclusion "var[y] with the culpability of the law enforcement conduct" at issue. When the police exhibit "deliberate," "reckless," or "grossly negligent" disregard for Fourth Amendment rights, the deterrent value of exclusion is strong and tends to outweigh the resulting costs. But when the police act with an objectively "reasonable good-faith belief" that their conduct is lawful, or when their conduct involves only simple, "isolated" negligence, the " 'deterrence rationale loses much of its force,' " and exclusion cannot "pay its way."[106]

Applying this, *Davis* continued:

> Although the search turned out to be unconstitutional . . ., all agree that the officers' conduct was in strict compliance with then-binding Circuit law and was not culpable in any way.
>
> Under our exclusionary-rule precedents, this acknowledged absence of police culpability dooms Davis's claim. Police practices trigger the harsh sanction of exclusion only when they are deliberate enough to yield "meaningfu[l]" deterrence, and culpable enough to be "worth the price paid by the justice system." The conduct of the officers here was neither of these things. The officers who conducted the search did not violate Davis's Fourth Amendment rights deliberately, recklessly, or with gross negligence. Nor does this case involve any "recurring or systemic negligence" on the part of law enforcement. The police acted in strict compliance with binding precedent, and their behavior was not wrongful. Unless the exclusionary rule is to become a strict-liability regime, it can have no application in this case.[107]

The major issue posed by this line of cases is whether the Fourth Amendment exception will be extended to other and perhaps all situations in which reasonable officers would regard their conduct as complying with federal constitutional standards. Until *Herring* and *Davis*, the Court's discussions suggested the exception was limited to situations in which the facts proved a fairly-objective basis for an officer's objectively reasonable good faith belief that the conduct was constitutional—an erroneous decision by some authority a police officer could not ordinarily be expected to question. This could be a decision by a legislature—reflected in a constitutionally-ineffective statute—or a judicial decision—reflected in an invalid warrant or a judicial misrepresentation that a valid warrant was outstanding. On its facts, *Davis* did not deviate from this—the appellate then-binding though erroneous case law was similar to the invalid warrants of *Leon* and *Sheppard* and the ineffective statute of *Krull*.

The stated rationales for *Davis* and *Herring* as discussed in *Davis*, however, placed little or no emphasis on the existence of an erroneous decision by an entity officers could not reasonably be expected to disregard. Rather, *Davis* stressed instead the lack of officer culpability rising above mere negligence. Such culpability, of course, will also be lacking in many situations involving no erroneous decision by an authoritative entity.

Davis strongly suggests some version of the good faith exception will eventually apply where the facts show no more than that a reasonable police officer would have

---

[106]   *Id.* at 238 (citations omitted).
[107]   *Id.* at 239–40.

realized the conduct was unconstitutional. A defendant seeking suppression, in other words, will have to refute the prosecution's prima facie case—or perhaps even a simple claim—of "good faith." This refutation will—consistent with *Davis*—require a showing the officer acted "deliberately, recklessly, or with gross negligence" or of "recurring or systemic [mere] negligence" on the part of law enforcement.

Pre-*Davis*, however, most lower courts assumed the Fourth Amendment exception applied only where the facts showed some authoritative basis for a belief the action was constitutional. It did not, for example, permit admission of evidence obtained in a search made by an officer who mistakenly but perhaps reasonably believed grounds existed for a warrantless exigent circumstances search.

When a reasonable officer could not regard a search warrant as constitutionally valid under *Leon* and *Sheppard* was addressed by the Supreme Court in *Groh v. Ramirez*.[108] The good faith exception would be inapplicable where a warrant contained no description whatsoever of the property or persons to be seized. The Supreme Court stressed that the officer himself had prepared the document, and that even a "simple glance" might have revealed the "glaring deficiency."

Leon's good faith exception—at least as defined prior to *Davis*—raised a number of subquestions. Some courts declined to apply the exception where officers executing a valid search warrant erroneously exceed their authority under a valid warrant. The only error in such situations is that of the officers executing the warrant. Arguably, there thus remains sufficient likelihood that exclusion might encourage greater care in ascertaining the existence or effect of warrants. If *Davis* has the implications suggested earlier in this section, of course, the exception would cover these situations.

Another question is whether the right of officers to rely on a facially valid warrant precludes a defendant from establishing that the warrant itself was tainted by earlier misconduct and thus evidence obtained as a result of the warrant's execution is excludable fruit of that original poisonous tree. Under the better view, a warrant can trigger the exception only if the warrant itself was untainted. If the warrant was issued on the basis of excludable evidence, the warrant and evidence obtained pursuant to it are all fruit of the original poisonous tree. Such laundering of tainted information through a magistrate should not render the fruits doctrine inapplicable. The matter might be viewed not as a good faith exception problem but rather as whether the warrant is or could be an independent source of the challenged evidence; this is addressed in Section 176.

State Constitutional Requirements. State courts have differed in their construction of state constitutional exclusionary requirements. Some, of course, have followed the Supreme Court's approach and read state constitutional requirements as qualified by *Leon*-like exceptions. Others, including the Supreme Courts of New Mexico and Washington, have refused to read such an exception into their constitutions. Wisconsin in 2001 adopted a somewhat narrower exception than was provided for under *Leon-Sheppard-Krull.*

These state tribunals have, to some extent, rejected the Supreme Court's assumption that the effect of the exception on the deterrent value of the exclusionary requirement can be measured and that it is acceptable given the cost incurred by the

---

[108]   540 U.S. 551 (2004).

loss of reliance evidence. More importantly, however, some state courts have rejected the Supreme Court's assumption that the deterrent analysis is appropriate, and have found the exception unacceptable given the broader policy bases of state exclusionary requirements. The New Mexico Supreme Court, for example, reasoned that the exception was incompatible with the purpose of the state constitutional requirement "to effectuate in the pending case the constitutional right of the accused to be free from unreasonable search and seizure." "Denying the government the fruits of unconstitutional conduct at trial," the court concluded, "best effectuates the constitutional proscription of unreasonable searches and seizures by preserving the rights of the accused to the same extent as if the government's officers had stayed within the law."

In addition, the New Mexico court reasoned, the state provision serves important considerations of judicial integrity, defined more broadly than that consideration in Fourth Amendment analysis, and the exception is inconsistent with this state law objective. The Iowa court also stressed the remedial function of the state's constitutional exclusionary rule and the impediment a good faith exception would place to performing that function. Moreover, it rejected the Supreme Court's conclusion that exclusion of evidence is either ineffective in or unnecessary for assuring that judges and legislators perform adequately.

Nonconstitutional Exclusionary Requirements. State statutory exclusionary requirements may be phrased to provide or construed as containing no good faith exception. The Georgia Supreme Court has so construed its provision, and the Texas statutory exclusionary rule has an exception limited to evidence obtained in reasonable reliance on warrants actually issued on probable cause. The North Carolina statutory exclusionary requirement, in contrast, broadly provides that evidence is not subject to suppression if the person committing the illegality "acted under the objectively reasonable, good faith belief that the actions were lawful."

§ 183   Exceptions to Exclusion: (e) Use of Illegally Obtained Evidence to Impeach Testifying Defendant

Most exclusionary sanctions bar only the use of improperly obtained evidence at trial to prove the guilt of the defendant. Thus they are subject to an exception or qualification that permits the use of such evidence to cross-examine and impeach a defendant who testifies at trial.

In *Harris v. New York*[109] the United States Supreme Court reaffirmed its pre-*Mapp v. Ohio*[110] holding in *Walder v. United States*[111] that federal constitutional exclusionary requirements sometimes permit the use of otherwise inadmissible evidence to impeach a testifying defendant. *United States v. Havens*[112] made clear that evidence tainted by violations of the Fourth Amendment could be used for impeachment. Statements elicited in violation of *Miranda v. Arizona*,[113] *Harris* held, could be used to impeach. But a statement that is involuntary, *Mincy v. Arizona*[114] confirmed, cannot be. Statements elicited in violation of the Sixth Amendment right to counsel as it applies to pretrial

---

[109]   401 U.S. 222 (1971).
[110]   367 U.S. 643 (1961).
[111]   347 U.S. 62 (1954).
[112]   446 U.S. 620 (1980).
[113]   384 U.S. 436 (1966).
[114]   437 U.S. 385 (1978).

elicitation of self-incriminating statement were held usable for impeachment in *Michigan v. Harvey*[115] and this was reaffirmed in *Kansas v. Ventris*.[116]

Justice Scalia's opinion for the Court in *Ventris* clarified the rationale for the cases' distinction:

> Whether otherwise excluded evidence can be admitted for purposes of impeachment depends upon the nature of the constitutional guarantee that is violated. Sometimes that explicitly mandates exclusion from trial, and sometimes it does not. The Fifth Amendment guarantees that no person shall be compelled to give evidence against himself, and so is violated whenever a truly coerced confession is introduced at trial, whether by way of impeachment or otherwise. The Fourth Amendment, on the other hand, guarantees that no person shall be subjected to unreasonable searches or seizures, and says nothing about excluding their fruits from evidence; exclusion comes by way of deterrent sanction rather than to avoid violation of the substantive guarantee. Inadmissibility has not been automatic, therefore, but we have instead applied an exclusionary-rule balancing test. The same is true for violations of the Fifth and Sixth Amendment prophylactic rules forbidding certain pretrial police conduct.[117]

Impeachment use of evidence, under *Ventris*, is necessarily impermissible only if the trial use of the evidence is itself at least a part of the violation of the defendant's right on which exclusion for guilt-innocence purposes is based. This explains *Mincy's* holding that involuntary statements cannot be used for impeachment. In the other situations, the violations of the defendants' rights are complete before trial begins. Whether the exclusionary remedy is appropriately applied to bar impeachment use in those situations depends on a balancing of the incremental deterrence that would be accomplished by so expanding exclusion against the costs of doing this.

In all situations in which it has engaged in this balancing analysis, the Court has concluded that given the deterrence accomplished by excluding evidence offered on guilt, little—and thus insufficient—additional deterrence would be provided by excluding unconstitutionally obtained evidence offered only to impeach the testifying defendant. The value of what little deterrence might be achieved, further, would be outweighed by the exceptionally high and offensive cost of permitting potential perjury to go unchallenged. Consequently, impeachment use is permissible.

Walder had suggested that impeachment use of unconstitutionally obtained evidence was permissible only if the testifying defendant went beyond simply denying guilt and testified to collateral matters. Such a position would leave a defendant free to present at least a basic contention of innocence without giving up the right to be free from unconstitutionally obtained evidence. *Harris*, however, rejected this approach. Thus, impeachment is permitted on the basis of testimony by a defendant simply denying guilt of the charged crime.

Further, *Harris* and its progeny sometimes allow impeachment on the basis of testimony given on cross-examination as well as on direct. This is permitted, under

---

[115]   494 U.S. 344 (1990).

[116]   556 U.S. 586 (2009).

[117]   *Id.* at 590.

United States v. Havens,[118] only if the testimony on cross-examination was in response to questions "plainly within the scope of the defendant's direct examination." Whether a defendant's testimony on direct reasonably suggests inquiry by the prosecution on cross-examination into events involving tainted information is "necessarily case specific," and trial judges have considerable discretion in resolving particular cases.

Impeachment is permitted as long as there is some "inconsistency" between the otherwise inadmissible evidence and the defendant's trial testimony. The Supreme Court has suggested that impeachment use must be "otherwise proper," indicating that local rules limiting impeachment might somehow be incorporated into the federal constitutional exception. There is no basis or rationale for constitutionally requiring a state to follow its ordinary cross-examination and impeachment rules when *Harris-Walder* evidence is offered. As a matter of nonconstitutional evidence law, there seems neither basis nor rationale for disregarding limits on impeachment simply because the witness is a criminal defendant and the evidence is inadmissible to prove guilt because of constitutional exclusionary requirements. On the other hand, there is no justification for applying a stricter standard than applies to other evidence offered to impeach.

Only a defendant's personal testimony at trial will trigger the opportunity to use otherwise excluded evidence. In *James v. Illinois*[119]—although only by a close 5 to 4 vote—the Court declined to expand the exception to permit the use of unconstitutionally obtained evidence to "impeach"—or rebut—defense testimony from witnesses other than the defendant. Such an expanded exception would weaken the deterrent value of the basic exclusionary requirement. Further, permitting such rebuttal use of testimony would discourage defendants from presenting potentially meritorious defensive contentions, since defense counsel lack control over non-defendant witnesses.

It follows from *James* that unconstitutionally obtained evidence is not somehow rendered admissible by defense counsel's opening statement. Of course, unconstitutionally obtained evidence does not become admissible to prove guilt because it is offered in the prosecution's rebuttal case rather than its case-in-chief.

Although the Supreme Court has never expressly so held, defendants are undoubtedly entitled to a limiting jury instruction directing the jurors to consider the evidence only on the defendant's credibility and not on guilt.

State courts addressing the contents of state—generally constitutional—exclusionary requirements have seldom been willing to reject any impeachment exception. Nevertheless, they have expressed concern regarding the scope and effect of exceptions based on the Supreme Court's federal constitutional model.

To the extent that state exclusionary requirements rest on broader rationales than the federal constitutional ones, of course, impeachment exceptions may be less appropriate in the state context. Thus, an Oregon court focused on that state exclusionary rule's remedial function. Putting the victim of official misconduct back in the position the victim was in before that misconduct required making the fruits of that misconduct unavailable for any official purpose, the court reasoned, and this is accomplished by excluding those fruits even when they are offered to impeach testifying defendants.

---

[118]   446 U.S. 620 (1980).

[119]   493 U.S. 307 (1990).

Some state tribunals, responding to such concerns, have adopted impeachment exceptions more limited than *Walder-Harris*. The Vermont Supreme Court, for example, emphasized what it viewed as the need to preserve a defendant's right to an unfettered opportunity to testify in his own defense. On this basis it rejected the *Havens* approach and held that evidence obtained in violation of the state provision could only be used to impeach a defendant's testimony on direct examination. Hawaii, rejecting *Harris* but not *Walder*, held that evidence obtained in an unconstitutional search may not be used to impeach a testifying defendant's testimony "as to his actions," but may be used to contradict the defendant's testimony regarding "the corroborative circumstances."

Title 7

RELEVANCE

Chapter 16

RELEVANCE

Table of Sections

§ 184   Relevance as the Presupposition of Admissibility

In the law of evidence, truth matters. To facilitate judgments based on an accurate understanding of the facts, the system of proof presupposes that the parties may present to the court or jury all the evidence that bears on the issues to be decided. Of course, many rules, such as those involving privilege, hearsay, and judicial economy, limit this system of free proof and keep probative evidence from the finder of fact. Nevertheless, unless there is some such distinct ground for refusing to hear the evidence, it should be received. Conversely, if the evidence lacks probative value, it should be excluded. Federal Rule of Evidence 402 and the corresponding Revised Uniform Rule adopt these two axioms of the common law. These rules succinctly provide that "relevant evidence is admissible" unless excluded by other laws or rules and that irrelevant evidence "is not admissible."

§ 185   The Meaning of Relevancy and the Counterweights

To say that relevant evidence is generally admissible while irrelevant evidence is not would be of little value without a suitable definition of relevance. This section clarifies the meaning of relevance. It then outlines the factors that can make even relevant evidence inadmissible.

There are two components to relevant evidence: materiality and probative value. Materiality concerns the fit between the evidence and the case. It looks to the relation between the propositions that the evidence is offered to prove and the issues in the case. If the evidence is offered to help prove a proposition that is not a matter in issue, the evidence is immaterial. What is "in issue," that is, within the range of the litigated controversy, is determined mainly by the pleadings, read in the light of the rules of pleading and controlled by the substantive law. Thus, in a suit for worker's compensation, evidence of contributory negligence would be immaterial, whether pleaded or not, since a worker's negligence does not affect the right to compensation. In an action to enjoin the enforcement of a statute prohibiting "partial-birth abortions" as void for vagueness, expert testimony as to a fetus's capacity to sense pain is immaterial, since it relates only to the state's interest in enacting the law and not to the claim of vagueness. In a prosecution for knowingly entering a military base for an unlawful purpose, defendant could not introduce prior statements showing that he "wished to pound the missile into scrap metal . . . to make an instrument of peace [as a result of] his concern about nuclear war and world starvation."[1] In a prosecution for driving while

---

[1]   U.S. v. Dorrell, 758 F.2d 427 (9th Cir. 1985).

having a breath alcohol concentration above a statutorily established limit, expert testimony that the air that enters the measuring instrument does not come from deep within the lungs is inadmissible, since the statute rationally regards shallower samples as indicating impairment. In such cases, the truth or falsity of the proposition that the evidence is offered to prove has no implications for an element of the claim or offense charged or to a recognized defense.

However, some evidence that is merely ancillary to evidence that bears directly on the issues may be admissible. Leeway is allowed even on direct examination for proof of facts that merely fill in the background of the narrative and give it interest, color, and lifelikeness. Models, maps, diagrams, charts, photographs, videotapes, and computer animations can be material as aids to the understanding of other material evidence. Moreover, the parties may question the credibility of the witnesses and, within limits, produce evidence assailing and supporting their credibility.

The second aspect of relevance is probative value, the tendency of evidence to establish the proposition that it is offered to prove. Federal Rule and the Uniform Rule of Evidence 401 incorporate these twin concepts of materiality and probative value. They state that " '[r]elevant evidence' means evidence having any tendency to make the existence of any fact that is of consequence to the determination of the action more probable or less probable than it would be without the evidence." A fact that is "of consequence" is material, and evidence that affects the probability that a fact is as a party claims it to be has probative force.

There are at least two ways to think about whether an item of evidence has probative value. First, one can simply ask whether learning of this evidence makes it either more or less likely that the disputed fact is true. Take, for example, evidence that a defendant charged with assaulting a neighbor has a reputation for being nonviolent. Knowing that someone has this reputation seems to make it less likely that he would commit an assault, presumably because we accept the underlying generalization that a smaller proportion of people with a reputation for nonviolence assault their neighbors than is the case for people generally. If we denote the reputation evidence as E and the hypothesis that the defendant committed the assault as H, then we can say that the probability of the hypothesis H given the evidence E is less than the probability of H without considering E. In symbols, $P(H \mid E) < P(H)$. (The vertical bar is read as "given" or "conditioned on," and "<" means "is less than.") Because E changes the probability of the assault, it is relevant.

Sometimes, however, this direct mode of reasoning about the probability of an hypothesis will be more difficult to apply because the effect of E on the probability of H will not be so apparent. A second approach considers the probability of the evidence given the hypothesis, $P(E \mid H)$. Evidence that is more likely to arise when H is true than when H is not true supports H; evidence that is less likely to arise under H than not-H supports not-H. Evidence of either type is probative of H. But evidence that is just as likely to arise when H is true as when H is false is of no use in deciding between H and not-H— it is irrelevant. In the example of the assault and the reputation for nonviolence, it seems less probable that a person who committed the assault would have such a reputation than that a person who did not commit the assault would have that reputation. Therefore, $P(E \mid H) < P(E \mid \text{not-}H)$, and the evidence has some probative value—it points toward not-H.

Indeed, the "likelihood ratio" of $P(E \mid H)$ to $P(E \mid \text{not-}H)$ can be used to grade the probative value of the evidence E—the larger the ratio, the more strongly the evidence supports the hypothesis H. Consider a behavioral pattern said to be characteristic of abused children. If research established that the behavior is equally common among abused and non-abused children, then its likelihood ratio would be one, and evidence of that pattern would not be probative of abuse. If the behavior were two times more common among abused children, then it would have rather modest probative value. And if it were a thousand times more common among abused children, its probative value would be greater still.

So far, we have offered the likelihood ratio as a qualitative measure of probative value: the larger the ratio, the stronger the evidence in favor of the hypothesis H. But we have not specified precisely how much stronger a larger likelihood ratio is than a smaller one. A formula known as Bayes' rule enables us to interpret the likelihood ratio for H and not-H as the ratio of (1) the odds in favor of H as opposed to not-H given the evidence E to (2) the odds without E. The ratio of these "posterior" to "prior" odds is called the "Bayes factor." The Bayes factor measures just how much the evidence multiplicatively changes the odds of H. For example, if the prior odds that H is true are 1:3 (corresponding to a prior probability of 1/4) and the Bayes factor is 18, then the odds are increased to 18:3 (or 6:1, corresponding to a posterior probability of 6/7).

Probative evidence often is said to have "logical relevance," while evidence lacking in substantial probative value may be condemned as "speculative" or "remote." Speculativeness usually arises with regard to dubious projections into the future or questionable surmises about what might have happened had the facts been different. For example, a calculation of lost wages in a wrongful death case that arbitrarily assumes that the deceased's salary would have grown at a constant rate year after year can be excluded as speculative. Remoteness relates not to the passage of time alone, but to the undermining of reasonable inferences due to the likelihood of supervening factors. For example, testimony that the defendant in an automobile accident case was speeding just a few minutes before the collision is relevant to whether defendant was speeding at the moment of the collision, but testimony that defendant exceeded the speed limit two years before the accident is likely to be excluded as too remote. The two-year-old incident offers some indication that the driver was speeding, but many factors affect how fast a driver goes at a particular time, and these factors would change over a two-year period.

Under our system, molded by the tradition of jury trial and predominantly oral proof, a party offers his evidence not en masse, but item by item. An item of evidence, being but a single link in the chain of proof, need not prove conclusively the proposition for which it is offered. It need not even make that proposition appear more probable than not or more probable than any single alternative. Whether the entire body of one party's evidence is sufficient to go to the jury is one question. Whether a particular item of evidence is relevant to the case is quite another. It is enough if the item could reasonably show that a fact is slightly more probable than it would appear without that evidence. Even after the probative force of the evidence is spent, the proposition for which it is offered still can seem quite improbable. Thus, the common objection that the inference for which the fact is offered "does not necessarily follow" is untenable. It poses a standard of conclusiveness that very few single items of circumstantial evidence ever could meet. A brick is not a wall.

But if even very weak material items of evidence are relevant, what sort of evidence is irrelevant for want of probative value? The long-standing distinction between "direct" and "circumstantial" evidence offers a starting point in answering this question. Direct evidence is evidence which, if believed, resolves a matter in issue. Circumstantial evidence also may be testimonial, but even if the circumstances depicted are accepted as true, additional reasoning is required to reach the desired conclusion. For example, a witness's testimony that he saw A stab B with a knife is direct evidence of whether A stabbed B. In contrast, testimony that A fled the scene of the stabbing would be circumstantial evidence of the stabbing (but direct evidence of the flight itself). Similarly, testimony of a witness that he saw A at the scene would be direct evidence that A was there, but testimony that he saw someone who was disguised and masked, but had a voice and limp like A's, would be circumstantial evidence that the person seen was A.

Although direct evidence is not necessarily any stronger than circumstantial evidence, direct evidence from a qualified witness offered to help establish a provable fact can never be irrelevant. Circumstantial evidence, however, can be so unrevealing as to be irrelevant. For instance, evidence that the government awarded a firm a lucrative contract is irrelevant on the issue of whether the firm damaged property leased to it because there is no reason to suppose that firms that handle large government contracts are more likely to damage such property than are other lessees.

In short, to say that circumstantial evidence is irrelevant in the sense that it lacks probative value is to say that knowing the evidence does not justify any reasonable inference about the fact in question. Cases involving such evidence are few and far between. That more than one inference could be drawn is not enough to render the evidence irrelevant. Fleeing the scene of a crime, for instance, could mean that the defendant, being conscious of guilt for the crime charged, actually is guilty; or it could mean that defendant is innocent but fled to avoid being apprehended for some other reason entirely. However, the premise that, in general, people who flee are more likely to be guilty than those who do not is at least plausible, and as long as there is some plausible chain of reasoning that leads to the desired conclusion, the evidence is probative of that conclusion. As a result, most evidence seriously offered at trial has *some* probative value. Even when the courts denominate evidence as devoid of probative value, one may often wonder whether the evidence is not more properly excludable on grounds of materiality or insufficient probative value given the countervailing considerations that can bar the use of relevant evidence.

Yet, how can a judge know whether the evidence could reasonably affect an assessment of the probability of the fact to be inferred? In some instances, scientific research may show that the fact in issue is more likely to be true (or false) when such evidence is present than when it is not. Ordinarily, however, the answer must lie in the judge's personal experience, general knowledge, and understanding of human conduct and motivation. If one asks whether an attempted escape by a prisoner charged with two serious but factually unconnected crimes is relevant to show consciousness of guilt of the first crime charged, the answer will not be found in a statistical table of the attempts at escape by those conscious of guilt as opposed to those not conscious of their guilt. The judge can only ask, could a reasonable juror believe that the fact that the accused tried to escape makes it more probable than it would otherwise be that the accused was conscious of guilt of the crime being tried? If the answer is affirmative, then the evidence is relevant. In other situations, the judge may need to consider not only whether the evidence reasonably could support the proposition for which it is offered, but also whether its absence might warrant the opposite inference. That is, where a jury would expect to receive a certain kind of evidence, testimony explaining why that evidence is not available could be helpful and should be considered relevant.

In sum, relevant evidence is evidence that in some degree advances the inquiry. It is material and probative. As such, it is admissible, at least prima facie. But this relevance does not ensure admissibility. There remains the question of whether its value is worth what it costs. A great deal of evidence is excluded on the ground that the costs outweigh the benefits. Rule 403 of the Federal and Uniform Evidence Rules categorize most of these costs. This rule codifies the common law power of the judge to exclude relevant evidence "if its probative value is substantially outweighed by the danger of unfair prejudice, confusion of the issues, or misleading the jury, or by considerations of undue delay, waste of time, or needless presentation of cumulative evidence." Such factors often blend together in practice, but we shall elaborate on them briefly in the rough order of their importance. First, there is the danger of prejudice. In this context, prejudice (or, as the rule puts it, "unfair prejudice") does not simply mean damage to the opponent's cause—for that can be a sign of probative value, not prejudice. Neither does it necessarily mean an appeal to emotion. Prejudice can arise, however, from facts that arouse the jury's hostility or sympathy without regard to the probative value of the evidence. Thus, evidence of convictions for prior, unrelated crimes might lead a juror to think that because the defendant already has a criminal record, an erroneous conviction would not be quite as serious as it would otherwise be. A juror influenced in this fashion may be satisfied with a less compelling demonstration of guilt than should be required. This rationale has been used in innumerable contexts—for example, to preclude inquiry into a medical expert's work in abortion clinics after the expert had testified about the cause of infertility in a woman who used an intrauterine device, to cut salacious scenes from a videotape of a two-million-dollar birthday party given by a corporate CEO accused of looting the company to pay for half of the party and for many other extravagances, to preclude disclosure of the value of stock given to a White House official charged with illegal lobbying, to preclude expert testimony on the extrapolation of a single blood alcohol test to a much earlier time, to limit the number and nature of gruesome photographs of murder victims, to prevent the disclosure of sexually explicit Facebook communications between a murder defendant and other women after he allegedly killed his girlfriend, and to exclude videotapes of an injured plaintiff's rehabilitative therapy or daily activities. Second, whether or not "emotional" reactions are at work, relevant evidence can confuse, or worse, mislead a trier of fact who is not properly equipped to judge the probative worth of the evidence. Third, certain proof and the answering evidence that it provokes might unduly distract the jury from the main issues. Finally, the evidence offered and the counterproof could consume an inordinate amount of time.

Analyzing and weighing the pertinent costs and benefits is no trivial task. Wise judges may come to differing conclusions in similar situations (or the same conclusions in different situations). Even the same item of evidence may fare differently from one case to the next. It may become cumulative of what has gone before. It may be easy for the advocate to make the same point with other, less prejudicial evidence. The issues on which the evidence bears may be more important in one case than another, and the efficacy of cautionary instructions to the jury may be unclear. Accordingly, much leeway is given trial judges who must fairly weigh probative value against probable dangers. On the theory that the trial judge is best situated to make these judgments as the case unfolds, the standard of review on appeal—'abuse of discretion'—is highly deferential.

That a different outcome would have been more appropriate is not sufficient. Only when the trial court "exceeds the bounds of reason," is "clearly wrong," "patently absurd," or "arbitrary, capricious, or whimsical, or . . . manifestly unreasonable" is reversal required. Nevertheless, even broad discretion can be abused, and some appellate courts have urged trial courts to articulate the reasoning behind their relevance rulings. In certain areas, such as proof of character, comparable situations recur so often that relatively particularized rules channel the exercise of discretion. In others, less structured discretion remains prominent. One way or another, however, admissible evidence must satisfy the cost-benefit calculus we have outlined.

Chapter 17

CHARACTER AND HABIT

Table of Sections

§ 186   Character, in General

Evidence of the general character of a party or witness almost always has some probative value, but in many situations, the probative value is slight and the potential for prejudice large. In other circumstances, the balance shifts the other way. Instead of engaging exclusively in the case-by-case balancing outlined in Chapter 16, the courts pass on the admissibility of evidence of character and habit according to a number of rules with some exceptions that reflect the recurring patterns of such proof and its usefulness. These rules categorically exclude most "character evidence"—defined as evidence offered solely to prove a person acted in conformity with a trait of character on a given occasion. This exclusionary rule applies to businesses and other organizations as well as natural persons.

Character evidence that is not categorically excluded is admissible, subject to the other rules of evidence. Thus, in considering evidence of bad character that is offered for a legitimate purpose, many courts emphasize the need for careful case-by-case balancing of probative value against prejudice lest "the minute peg of relevancy will be completely obscured by the dirty linen hung upon it."[1]

Before turning to the details of the rules specific to character evidence, it may be helpful to sketch two general considerations that have shaped them and guide their application. The first is the purpose for which the evidence of character is offered. If a person's character is itself an issue in the case, then character evidence is crucial and skepticism of inferences from very general character traits to highly situation-specific conduct is less apposite because, in principle at least, the evidence is not introduced to support these ancillary inferences. But if the evidence of character merely is introduced as circumstantial evidence of what a person did or thought, it is less critical. Other, and probably better, evidence of the acts or state of mind may be available, and an exclusionary rule creates an incentive to produce it. Furthermore, jurors may regard personality traits as more predictive of individual behavior than they actually are. Exclusion is therefore much more likely when the character evidence is offered solely to help prove that a person acted in one way or another. Federal Rule of Evidence 404(a), which basically codifies common law doctrine, provides that subject to enumerated exceptions, "[e]vidence of a person's character or character trait is not admissible to prove that on a particular occasion the person acted in accordance with the character or trait." Federal Rules 413 to 415 set forth additional, and more controversial, exceptions to this rule of exclusion.

In the manner of the common law, Rule 404 does not exclude evidence just because it reveals a person's character. It excludes such evidence only when it is part of a particular mode of reasoning—a chain of inferences that employs the evidence to establish that the person (1) is more inclined to act or think in a given way than is typical, and (2) is therefore more likely to have acted or thought that way on a particular occasion. Because the character-evidence rule is directed at reasoning based on inferred behavioral dispositions or propensities, it can be described as a "propensity rule" that only curtails the admission of "propensity evidence." Although this description is a helpful heuristic, it should be understood that not all propensities are character traits. An amputee may have a tendency to limp, and a person with a cold may have a tendency to sniffle. These behaviors are not particularly blameworthy or praiseworthy—they are

---

[1]   State v. Goebel, 218 P.2d 300, 306 (Wash. 1950).

not seen as qualities or defects of a person's moral character—and jurors are not likely to misestimate the ability of these conditions to predict behavior on a given occasion. At the other pole, portraying a wife accused of murdering her husband-to-be as "a bad mother, an unloyal fiancée, a self-absorbed manipulator, and even, quite literally, a witch" to show that "despite the lack of any readily apparent motive, she was the kind of person who would shoot her husband-to-be" is quite clearly propensity evidence of character.[2]

The second consideration is the type of evidence offered to establish an individual's character. Character is susceptible of proof by evidence of conduct that reflects some character trait, by a witness's opinion based on personal observations, or by testimony as to reputation generally. As one moves from the specific to the general in this fashion, the pungency and persuasiveness of the evidence declines, but so does its tendency to arouse undue prejudice, to confuse and distract, and to raise time-consuming side issues. Traditionally, when character evidence could come in at all, the relatively neutral and unexciting reputation evidence was the preferred type. Thus, prior to the adoption of the Federal Rules, the other methods of proving character could be employed only in narrowly defined situations. Roughly stated, when character was being used as circumstantial evidence of conduct, it could be proved only by reputation evidence. When character was in issue, it could be proved by specific instances or by reputation.

Federal Rule of Evidence 405(a), however, allows opinion testimony as well as reputation testimony to prove character whenever any form of character evidence is appropriate. Some states go further, allowing proof of specific acts that have been the subject of a criminal conviction. And, as at common law, when character is "in issue," as discussed in the next section, it also may be proved by testimony about specific acts.

§ 187 Character in Issue

A person's characteristic behaviors may be a fact that under the substantive law determines rights and liabilities of the parties. For example, because truth is a defense in an action for defamation, in an action of slander for the statement that the plaintiff "is in the habit of picking up things," the defendant can introduce evidence of plaintiff's thefts to prove that the statement was true. A complaint for negligence may allege that the defendant allowed an unfit person to use a motor vehicle or other dangerous object, or that an employer was negligent in hiring or failing to supervise an employee with certain dangerous character traits. In deciding who should have custody of children, fitness to provide care is of paramount importance. Nuisance claims naturally require proof of the conduct constituting the nuisance. Civil rights and employment discrimination cases challenging allegedly discriminatory business practices require proof of the practices. When character has been put in issue by the pleadings in such cases, evidence of character must be brought forth.

In view of the crucial role of character in this situation, the courts usually hold that it can be proved by evidence of specific acts. The hazards of prejudice, surprise and time-consumption implicit in this manner of proof are more tolerable when character is itself in issue than when this evidence is offered as an indirect indication of how the defendant behaved on a specific occasion. Federal Rule 405(b) reflects this approach. "When a person's character or character trait is an essential element of a charge, claim, or defense," the rule permits evidence of "relevant specific instances of the person's

---

[2]   Dunkle v. State, 139 P.3d 228, 238 (Okla. Crim. App. 2006).

conduct." (This proviso is logically superfluous in that proving character as an essential element does not rely on a propensity inference from the character trait to some other fact. Consequently, the Rule 404 ban does not come into play, and the question of how character can be proved under one of the rule's exceptions does not arise. Nevertheless, pointing to the correct outcome for proof by specific acts in this situation does no harm.)

In deciding whether character is truly in issue, courts must ascertain whether a character trait is an "operative fact"—one that under the substantive law determines rights and liabilities of the parties. "The relevant question should be: would proof, or failure of proof, of the character trait by itself actually satisfy an element of the charge, claim, or defense? If not, then character is not essential, and evidence should be limited to opinion or reputation."[3]

Yet, some older cases do not simply permit evidence of specific acts to prove character when it is in issue. They insist on it. There is no reason to exclude reputation evidence, which ordinarily is the preferred mode of proof of character. Proof by means of opinion testimony is slightly more debatable, but most of the arguments against opinion evidence do not apply when character is in issue. For example, the possibility that specific acts may be inquired into on cross-examination (which may prompt barring specific-act evidence when character is not in issue) is hardly of concern, since the door to such evidence already is open.

The phrase "character in issue" sometimes invites confusion. A defendant in a criminal case generally can bring in evidence of good character to show that he is not the type of person who would have committed the offense charged. Although courts sometimes speak loosely of this strategy as putting the defendant's character in issue, the defendant is using character solely as circumstantial evidence. When the defendant makes his character an issue in this manner, it merely means that the prosecution is allowed to bring forth certain kinds of rebuttal evidence of bad character. It does not justify evidence of specific acts, opinions, and reputation by either party. That free-wheeling approach to character evidence is limited to the unusual situation in which an offense, claim, or defense for which character is an essential element is pled.

§ 188   Character as Circumstantial Evidence: General Rule of Exclusion

Even when a person's character is not itself in issue as defined in the preceding section, litigants may seek to introduce character-type evidence. In ascertaining whether such evidence is admissible, the purpose for which the evidence is offered remains of the utmost importance. In some cases, even though a person's character is not itself in issue, evidence of a character trait is relevant to proving a material fact that is distinct from whether the person acted in conformity with that trait on an occasion that is the subject of the litigation. In other words, the evidence has "special" or "independent" relevance as part of a chain of reasoning that does not include the propensity inference described in Section 186.

Thus, when extortion is charged, the defendant's reputation for violence may be relevant to the victim's state of mind. In these cases, the reputation itself, not the character that it tends to prove, is the significant fact; reputation is not used as evidence

---

[3]   New Mexico ex rel. Balderas v. Real Estate Law Center, P.C., 409 F.Supp.3d 1122, 1167 (D. N.M. 2019) (quoting U.S. v. Keiser, 57 F.3d 847, 856 (9th Cir. 1995)).

of how the person with the character traits behaved on a given occasion. Thus, a plaintiff alleging assault and subsequent emotional distress may introduce evidence of the defendant's past conduct to show the extent of her fear and its emotional impact. Likewise, a defendant charged with assault or homicide who argues self-defense may offer evidence of his knowledge of the victim's violent nature on the theory that it shows his reasonable belief that he needed to resort to force. So too, in a sexual assault case, a man's previous violent acts toward his wife may be admissible on the issue of whether she consented.

In contrast, evidence that an individual is the kind of person who behaves in certain ways almost always has some value as circumstantial evidence of how this individual acted (and perhaps with what state of mind) in the matter in question. For instance, on average, persons reputed to be violent probably commit more assaults than persons known to be peaceable. Yet, evidence of character in any form—reputation, opinion from observation, or specific acts—generally will not be received to prove that a person engaged in certain conduct or did so with a particular intent on a specific occasion, so-called circumstantial use of character. The reason is the familiar one of prejudice outweighing probative value. Used for this purpose, character evidence typically is of relatively slight value, but it still is laden with the dangerous baggage of prejudice, distraction, and time-consumption. As indicated in Section 185, prejudice can arise in two ways—misestimation of probative value and departure from legal norms. Misestimation would occur if jurors were to think that a character trait is more predictive than it actually is, or if they were to create incorrect, broad character portraits from isolated traits. And, jurors would depart from the norms that they are expected to apply if they were to view a conviction of an accused who actually is innocent of the specific charges as less serious because of the bad acts or traits of character that he has displayed.

At the same time, there are important exceptions to this general rule of exclusion, and this rule, it bears repeating, applies only when the theory of relevance is that the person or organization has a trait that it usually follows and therefore probably followed on the occasion in question. In light of the various true exceptions to the rule as well as the limits within which the rule operates, some writers prefer to state the general rule as one of admissibility subject to exceptions for exclusion. The next six sections consider various applications of the rule of exclusion and the most important exceptions to it.

§ 189　Character for Care in Civil Cases

The rule against using character evidence solely to prove conduct on a particular occasion has long been applied in civil cases, notwithstanding suggestions that exclusion is not justified in this context. The rule is invoked most uniformly when specific-act evidence is proffered. Of course, we are speaking of specific acts other than those at bar. No doubt, evidence that someone acted negligently says something about that person's character. But we are concerned here with character as circumstantial evidence, that is, as evidence of a propensity to behave in a certain way, which, in turn, makes it more likely that such behavior occurred on the occasion in question. When this is the theory of admissibility, the character evidence is inadmissible, but a previous accident or negligent act that does something more than show character or predisposition may be admissible.[4]

Negligence cases illustrate the point. Evidence of negligent conduct of the defendant on other occasions may reflect a propensity for negligent acts, thus enhancing the probability of negligence on the occasion in question, but this probative force has been thought too slight to overcome the usual counterweights. In an action for malpractice against a surgeon, for example, a similarly botched surgery on another patient is not admissible to show that a surgeon was negligent in performing the surgery on the plaintiff, but previous post-operative infections in patients may be admissible to show knowledge of a problem requiring precautions. That a locomotive engineer suing his employer for injuries suffered in a derailment had been disciplined for improperly driving trains four times in his career was not admissible to show that he was contributorily negligent in the derailment, but the "history of rule infractions and resulting interruptions of employment" should have been admitted "to support a lower lost earnings projection."[5] The same categorical approach applies to evidence of other negligent acts of the plaintiff, as well as other instances of careful conduct.

Most courts also reject proof of an actor's character for care by means of reputation evidence or opinion testimony. In the past, a minority of courts had admitted these types of evidence, often under the guise of evidence of "habit," when there were no eyewitnesses to the event. A few even did so if there were eyewitnesses with conflicting stories. The Federal and Uniform Rules do not make such fine distinctions. The prevailing pattern is to exclude all forms of character evidence in civil cases when the evidence is employed merely to support an inference that conduct on a particular occasion was consistent with a person's character.

This pattern persists despite psychological studies of "accident proneness." It has been argued that research establishing that drivers with inadequate training, defective vision, and certain attitudes and emotional traits are at risk for automobile accidents should prompt a relaxation of the rule against evidence of character for negligence. The argument was that because a small number of drivers with identifiable characteristics account for the bulk of the accidents, they must drive improperly as a routine matter, and this provides a better-than-usual basis for inferring that the accident in issue resulted from such negligent driving. Presumably, the reform would be to admit evidence of previous accidents combined with proof that the particular driver fits the "accident proneness" profile. In a similar vein, the possibility of a "pyromania exception" has been discussed.

A somewhat different proposal asks that aggregate and individual data concerning the actions of physicians should be admissible in malpractice cases. For example, in deciding whether the removal of a patient's appendix was unnecessary surgery, the jury might be invited to consider whether the defendant physician performs appendectomies on a far larger percentage of patients than is normal. Although evidence of previous accidents or similar happenings should not be freely admitted, a suitable expert testifying about a departure from the customary standard of care should be permitted to rely on such information and to explain this analysis to the jury. Moreover, where the

---

[4]   Dallas Ry. & Terminal Co. v. Farnsworth, 227 S.W.2d 1017, 1020 (Tex. 1950) (in an action for an injury allegedly due to the abrupt starting of a street car, testimony that the driver had started abruptly once before on the same trip admissible to show motorman was nervous and in a hurry).

[5]   National R.R. Passenger Corp. v. McDavitt, 804 A.2d 275, 290–91 (D.C. 2002).

statistically measured departure from the customary pattern is itself so great as to make it plain that the defendant is behaving differently from the norm, this statistic should be provable. Conversely, a defendant might wish to establish statistically that a pattern is within the normal range. The statistical pattern can be proved without going into the prejudicial, distracting, or time-consuming details of other incidents. The value of the evidence is greatest in cases where each surgery or other event, viewed in isolation, could be a matter of reasonable professional judgment. In these situations, the need for such evidence justifies taking the risks associated with defendant's seeking to prove reasonable care in each of the other incidents.

§ 190 Bad Character as Evidence of Criminal Conduct—General Rule of Exclusion for Other Crimes

If anything, the rule against using character evidence to prove conduct on a particular occasion applies even more strongly in criminal cases. Indeed, some courts have intimated that the rule has constitutional underpinnings. In criminal cases, unless and until the accused gives evidence of his good character, the prosecution may not introduce evidence of his bad character. Nor may the prosecution suggest bad character by insinuations, implications, or direct comments. The evidence or statements would not be irrelevant, but particularly in the setting of the jury trial, the dangers of prejudice, confusion and time-consumption outweigh the probative value.

This broad prohibition includes the specific and frequently invoked rule that the prosecution may not introduce evidence of other criminal acts of the accused unless the evidence is introduced for some purpose other than to suggest that because the defendant is a person of criminal character, it is more probable that he committed the crime for which he is on trial. As Federal Rule 404(b) puts it:

> Evidence of a crime, wrong, or other act is not admissible to prove a person's character in order to show that on a particular occasion the person acted in accordance with the character. . . . This evidence may be admissible for another purpose, such as proving motive, opportunity, intent, preparation, plan, knowledge, identity, absence of mistake, or lack of accident.

§ 190.1 Bad Character as Evidence of Criminal Conduct—General Rule of Exclusion for Other Crimes—Permissible Uses That Are Not True Exceptions

As Rule 404(b) indicates, there are numerous uses to which evidence of criminal acts may be put, and those enumerated are neither mutually exclusive nor collectively exhaustive. Nor are the enumerated purposes all of the same type. Some are phrased in terms of the immediate inferences sought to be drawn (such as plan or motive) while others are phrased in terms of ultimate facts (such as knowledge, intent or identity) that the prosecution seeks to establish. With these points in mind, examination is in order of the principal purposes for which the prosecution may introduce evidence of a defendant's bad character. Although it is common for courts to refer to the usual categories of nonpropensity character evidence as "the exceptions" to a rule of exclusion, it would be more accurate to call them "pseudo-exceptions" or "quasi-exceptions." They are not true exceptions because there is no rule against admitting evidence of other crimes per se— "[t]he rule does not prohibit character evidence generally, only that which lacks any purpose but proving character."[6] Thus, rather than carving out exceptions to the categorical rule of exclusion, the quasi-exceptions help demarcate the boundaries of the rule. After listing the quasi-exceptions, some general observations will be offered about the use of other-crimes evidence for these purposes.

§ 190.2 Bad Character as Evidence of Criminal Conduct—General Rule of Exclusion for Other Crimes—Permissible Uses That Are Not True Exceptions—Unified Plan

Evidence of other crimes is outside the rule of categorical exclusion when introduced to prove the existence of a larger plan, scheme, or conspiracy, of which the crime on trial is a part. For example, when a criminal steals a car to use in a robbery, the automobile theft can be proved in a prosecution for the robbery. Although some courts construe "common plan" more broadly (especially in sexual abuse and domestic violence cases), each crime should be an integral part of an over-arching plan explicitly conceived and executed by the defendant or his confederates. This linkage will be relevant as showing motive, and hence the doing of the criminal act, the identity of the actor, or his intention. "This type of plan evidence is admissible because it is based on the permissible inference that, regardless of character, a person who has formulated a plan is more likely to carry out the elements of the plan."[7]

§ 190.3 Bad Character as Evidence of Criminal Conduct—General Rule of Exclusion for Other Crimes—Permissible Uses That Are Not True Exceptions—"Signature" Crimes

Uncharged crimes by the accused may be admissible when they are so nearly identical in method as to earmark them as the handiwork of the accused. The phrase of which authors of detective fiction are fond, modus operandi, may be employed. Much more is demanded than the mere repeated commission of crimes of the same class, such as serial murders, robberies or rapes. The pattern and characteristics of the crimes must be so unusual and distinctive as to be like a signature. For example, in *Rex v. Smith*,[8] the "brides of the bath" case, George Joseph Smith was accused of murdering Bessie Mundy by drowning her in the small bathtub of their quarters in a boarding house. Mundy had left all her property to Smith in a will executed after a bigamous marriage ceremony. The trial court allowed the prosecution to show that Smith "married" several other women whom he drowned in their baths after they left him their property. In all the drownings, Smith took elaborate steps to make it appear that he was not present during the drownings. The Court of Criminal Appeal affirmed the resulting conviction on the ground that the evidence in connection with Mundy's death alone made out a prima facie case, and the other incidents were properly admitted "for the purpose of shewing the design of the appellant."

In *Rex v. Smith*, an elaborate pattern of conduct characterized the different murders, but the "signature" quasi-exception also applies when the state proves that a specific implement, such as a particular gun known to have been used by the defendant in one crime, also was used in the separate crime with which the defendant is now

---

[6]   U.S. v. Bowie, 232 F.3d 923, 930 (D.C. Cir. 2000).

[7]   State v. Verde, 296 P.3d 673, 682 (Utah 2012) (separate acts of "entic[ing] teenage males to be his friends with the motive of exploiting their trust for his sexual gratification" is not a "plan").

[8]   (1915) 11 Cr. App. R. 229, described in Marjoribanks, For the Defence: The Life of Edward Marshall Hall 321 (1929).

charged. As in *Smith*, the crimes could be remarkably similar in many other idiosyncratic details, but even a few sufficiently individuating common aspects could mark the defendant as the likely perpetrator of both crimes.

§ 190.4 Bad Character as Evidence of Criminal Conduct—General Rule of Exclusion for Other Crimes—Permissible Uses That Are Not True Exceptions—Rebutting Claims of Accident or Innocently Performed Acts

Uncharged crimes are not categorically excluded when introduced to show, by similar acts or incidents, that the act in question was not performed inadvertently, accidentally, involuntarily, in self-defense, or without guilty knowledge. *Rex v. Smith* falls in this category. The death of one bride in the bath might be an accident, but three drownings cannot be explained so innocently. Another classic example of the "improbability" logic is the "baby farming" case of *Makin v. Attorney General of New South Wales*.[9] The remains of thirteen infants were discovered in places where the couple, John and Sarah Makin were living or had lived, and the Crown charged the Makins with the murder of two of these children. One was identified by his clothing and hair. His mother testified that the Makins had agreed to adopt her son in exchange for only three pounds. The jury convicted the Makins of murdering the boy whose remains had been identified. On appeal, the couple argued that all the evidence concerning other missing children should not have been admitted. The Privy Council rejected this argument. Although its opinion did little to explain the basis for this conclusion, counsel for the Crown had stressed that "the recurrence of the unusual phenomenon of bodies of babies having been buried in an unexplained manner in a similar part of premises previously occupied" implied that the deaths were "wilful and not accidental."

In these "no-accident" cases, the similarities between the act charged and the extrinsic acts need not be as extensive and striking as is required under purpose (3), and the various acts need not be manifestations of an explicit, unifying plan, as required for purpose (1). In some instances, it is possible to express numerically the probability of the concatenation of events occurring by accident, as when an abnormal number of cardiac arrests in a hospital occurs in the presence of a particular doctor or nurse. In these situations, testimony as to the entire sequence and its improbability has been admitted.

There is some debate as to whether the no-accident logic is just propensity reasoning in disguise, but it clearly differs from the usual propensity chain of inferences. There, the reasoning is that (1) a defendant who committed a similar offense is predisposed to commit the offense charged, and therefore (2) it is more probable that he did so. The no-accident reasoning is that (1) looking at each event in isolation, it would be difficult to say whether the defendant was responsible; but (2) looking at the events as a whole, either the defendant is remarkably unlucky or he is the cause of both events. The different logical structure makes a requirement of strong proof that defendant was responsible for the other incidents inapposite.

---

[9]   69 Eng. Law T. (N.S.) 778, 58 J.P. 148, 1893 WL 9238 (Privy Council 1893).

§ 190.5 Bad Character as Evidence of Criminal Conduct—General Rule of Exclusion for Other Crimes—Permissible Uses That Are Not True Exceptions—Motive

Uncharged crimes introduced to establish motive fall outside the rule of categorical exclusion. The evidence of motive may be probative of the identity of the criminal or of malice or specific intent. Thus, evidence that a store had fired an employee for stealing money from the cash register was admissible "to explain why he would return to that same store to rob it";[10] evidence that a daughter was threatening to end an incestuous relationship was admissible to show the father's motivation to murder her; and evidence of the need to silence a victim of a series of frauds to prevent the revelation of these crimes to her next defrauded paramour were admissible to show her reason for strangling the first man and leaving his body in a footlocker in the woods.

This reasoning commonly is applied in cases in which a husband charged with murdering his wife had previously assaulted or threatened her, evincing not merely a general disposition toward violence, but a virulent hostility toward a specific individual. A few states have adopted by legislation a specific rule allowing evidence of past acts of domestic violence, by the same defendant against the same victim, to be admitted in prosecutions involving domestic violence without worrying about the purpose for the evidence. In other words, these statutes create a true exception to the propensity rule, and a defendant is not entitled to a limiting instruction.

The unusual probative value of a specific motive also can justify admission when the defendant is charged with conduct that interferes with the enforcement of the law. The prosecution then may prove that the defendant committed a crime that motivated the interference. Finally, a variation of the reasoning permits proof of a consciousness of guilt as evidenced by criminal acts of the accused that are designed to obstruct justice or to avoid punishment for a crime.

The motive theory should not apply, however, when the "motive" is so common that the reasoning that establishes relevance verges on ordinary propensity reasoning or when "motive" or "intent" is just another word for propensity. Prior incidents involving guns, for example, are not admissible just to show that defendant was motivated by a desire to derive "a thrill from creating violence,"[11] and prior sexual assaults are not admissible just to show the "motive" of "sexual gratification."[12]

§ 190.6 Bad Character as Evidence of Criminal Conduct—General Rule of Exclusion for Other Crimes—Permissible Uses That Are Not True Exceptions—Opportunity

Uncharged crimes can be admissible to establish opportunity by demonstrating that defendant had access to or was present at the scene of the crime or possessed certain distinctive or unusual skills or abilities employed in the commission of the crime charged. For example, a defendant might be shown to have neutralized sophisticated burglar alarm systems in other burglaries, to be a skilled shoplifter, or to know how to build pipe bombs with "a time delay and . . . an explosive filler, igniter, power source,

---

[10]   State v. Reid, 186 P.3d 713 (Kan. 2008) (as described in State v. Wells, 221 P.3d 561, 569 (Kan. 2009)).

[11]   U.S. v. Brown, 880 F.2d 1012, 1014 (9th Cir. 1989).

[12]   People v. Wilson, 824 N.E.2d 191, 193 (Ill. 2005).

and wiring."[13] Of course, the skill or knowledge must be rare if it is to possess enough probative value to offer a meaningful alternative to propensity reasoning.

§ 190.7 Bad Character as Evidence of Criminal Conduct—General Rule of Exclusion for Other Crimes—Permissible Uses That Are Not True Exceptions—Malice, Deliberation or Specific Intent

Uncharged crimes fall outside the categorical rule of exclusion when offered to show, without considering motive, that defendant acted with malice, deliberation, or the requisite specific intent. Thus, weapons seized in an arrest have been held admissible to show an "intent to promote and protect" a conspiracy to import illicit drugs. Many no-accident cases could be said fall under this quasi-exception. For example, other incidents of a high school coach's physical contact with students might be admitted to shed light on whether his physical contact was "for the purpose of sexual gratification."[14]

§ 190.8 Bad Character as Evidence of Criminal Conduct—General Rule of Exclusion for Other Crimes—Permissible Uses That Are Not True Exceptions—Identity

Although proof of identity is indisputably one of the ultimate purposes for which evidence of other criminal conduct will be received, it is rarely a distinct ground for admission. Almost always, identity is the inference that flows from one or more of the theories just listed. The second (larger plan), third (distinctive device), and sixth (motive) seem to be most often relied upon to show identity. Certainly, the need to prove identity should not be, in itself, a ticket to admission. In addition, the courts tend to apply stricter standards when the desired inference pertains to identity as opposed to state of mind.

§ 190.9 Bad Character as Evidence of Criminal Conduct—General Rule of Exclusion for Other Crimes—Permissible Uses That Are Not True Exceptions—Completing the Story

Other crimes may be admissible to complete the story of the crime on trial by placing it in the context of nearby and nearly contemporaneous happenings. Prosecutors frequently elicit testimony about uncharged crimes to tell a more complete story of events connected with the alleged criminal acts. For example, in a prosecution for the murder of one child, the state was allowed to show that the defendant shot the child along with his other children and his wife while they were asleep.[15] Similarly, when police found drugs in a washing machine in an apartment complex, they were allowed to testify that the defendant, on trial only for possession, resisted arrest with nearly superhuman power when they found him hiding in a nearby dryer.[16]

It may seem axiomatic that uncharged crimes that are part of the "same transaction," that are "intrinsic" to, or "inextricably intertwined" with the crime actually charged do not offend the propensity rule. However, these phases, like the unhappy Latin incantation, "res gestae," often obscure what they purport to describe. Evidence of acts that are truly intrinsic to the crime charged or that are part of that very transaction

---

13   U.S. v. Zajac, 748 F. Supp. 2d 1327, 1335 (D. Utah 2010).

14   State v. McFarland, 721 S.E.2d 62, 72 (W. Va. 2011).

15   People v. Ciucci, 137 N.E.2d 40 (Ill. 1956), judgment aff'd, 356 U.S. 571 (1958).

16   U.S. v. Marrero, 651 F.3d 453 (6th Cir. 2011).

certainly is admissible. Because the subject of the evidence is not *other* crimes, these "integral acts" can be proved as direct evidence of the offense at bar.

The complete-the-story rationale, in contrast, applies to evidence of extrinsic crimes that might seem to be circumstantial evidence of the offense in question—and hence not allowed via propensity reasoning—but nevertheless can be justified on another basis. But what, exactly, is this other basis? What, in other words, is the legitimate function of the prejudicial background information about the defendant's other crimes? Some courts have said that there is none—that a mere desire to "complete the story" has no force, and there must be a separate, nonpropensity rationale for admitting the evidence. Certainly, much of what is said to "complete the story" or to be "intertwined" is admissible to show preparation, intent, or motive. But the question remains—Is there any other background information that shows a defendant's involvement in other crimes and that serves a nonpropensity purpose?

We think that there is. Specifically, other-crime evidence should be admissible to complete the story if it satisfies "the offering party's need for evidentiary richness and narrative integrity in presenting a case."[17] This is a narrow quasi-exception. The word "need" is critical. Not every story needs lurid embellishment, and courts frequently stretch the complete-the-story logic too far. The rationale should be applied only (1) when reference to the other crimes is essential to a coherent and intelligible description of the offense at bar, (2) when the incomplete story that the defendant would prefer leaves a gap that would frustrate "the jurors' expectations about what proper proof should be,"[18] or (3) when the material in question is necessary to a fair understanding of the behavior of individuals involved in the criminal enterprise or the events immediately leading up to them.

As an example of a case in the last category, suppose that a private individual goes to the authorities because an acquaintance threatened to kill an undercover agent and asked for her help obtaining dynamite and cocaine. The police have her arrange for a buy through another undercover agent, but by the time the sale is consummated, the purchaser has lost interest in the dynamite, and he only buys the cocaine. At a trial for this buy, the prosecution has the woman testify to the defendant's original death threat and effort to acquire explosives.[19] This testimony does not run afoul of the propensity rule if used solely to explain the woman's role in the drug buy. If believed, it shows that she had good reason to approach the police, avoiding surmises (or countering suggestions from the defendant) about why she would be involved in this drug buy and whether she might have had a reason to set him up. This is not a propensity use of the evidence, and omitting this part of the story could detract from the jurors' evaluation of the credibility of her testimony.

§ 190.10 Bad Character as Evidence of Criminal Conduct—General Rule of Exclusion for Other Crimes—Sex Crimes

The law has vacillated on proof of similar sex crimes to show a passion or propensity for unusual and abnormal sexual relations. Initially, proof of other sex crimes was

---

[17]   Old Chief v. U.S., 519 U.S. 172, 183 (1997) (referring to the reason for "the familiar, standard rule . . . that a criminal defendant may not stipulate or admit his way out of the full evidentiary force of the case as the Government chooses to present it," *id.* at 186–87).

[18]   *Id.* at 188.

[19]   These facts are a simplified version of U.S. v. Green, 617 F.3d 233 (3d Cir. 2010).

confined to offenses involving the same parties, but many jurisdictions now admit proof of other sex offenses with other persons, at least as to offenses involving sexual aberrations. Furthermore, courts in many of the jurisdictions that still do not overtly admit evidence of sex crimes with other victims as revealing an incriminating propensity achieve a similar result by stretching to find a nonpropensity purpose. Federal Rules of Evidence 413 and 414, added by Congress in 1994, allow the broadest conceivable use of "similar crimes" in sexual assault and child molestation cases, making "evidence of defendant's commission" of other such offenses "admissible . . . for its bearing on any matter to which it is relevant." Both the manner in which Congress adopted these rules and their content have been the subject of widespread criticism.[20] Federal courts have rebuffed due process and other constitutional challenges. These opinions reason that the safeguard of case-by-case balancing of probative value (including the value of propensity inferences, of course) and prejudicial effect are adequate to assure fair trials. Similar legislation has had a mixed reception in the states, with some courts striking down laws departing from the modern common law ban on propensity evidence.

Unlike the quasi-exceptions for which other-crimes evidence is admissible to support reasoning that differs in some meaningful way from the ordinary propensity chain of inferences, the sex-crime exception flouts the general prohibition of evidence whose only purpose is to invite the inference that a defendant who committed a previous crime is disposed toward committing crimes, and therefore is more likely to have committed the one at bar. Although one can argue for such an exception in sex offense cases in which there is some question as to whether the alleged victim consented (or whether the accused might have thought there was consent), a more sweeping exception is difficult to justify. It rests either on an unsubstantiated empirical claim that one rather broad category of criminals are more likely to be repeat offenders than all others or on a policy of giving the prosecution some extra ammunition in its battle against alleged sex criminals.

§ 190.11 Bad Character as Evidence of Criminal Conduct—General Rule of Exclusion for Other Crimes—Balancing and Other Limitations and Procedures

A number of procedural and other substantive considerations affect the admissibility of other crimes evidence pursuant to the quasi-exceptions and the exception for sexual misconduct. To begin with, the fact that the defendant is guilty of another relevant crime need not be proved beyond a reasonable doubt. The measure of proof that the defendant is guilty of the other crime has been variously described, ranging from "sufficient . . . to support a finding by the jury," to "a preponderance," to "substantial," to "clear and convincing." If the applicable standard is satisfied, then the other crimes evidence should be potentially admissible even if the defendant was acquitted of the other charge. This appears to be the majority rule, although there are variations on just when the acts involved in acquittals may be "relitigated."

Second, the specific connection between the evidence and the permissible purpose should be clearly articulated. The "court should not just ask *whether* the proposed other-act evidence is relevant to a non-propensity purpose but *how* exactly the evidence is relevant to that purpose—or more specifically, how the evidence is relevant without

---

[20] The Judicial Conference opposed the amendments and also drafted a more circumscribed alternative version.

relying on a propensity inference. Careful attention to these questions will help identify evidence that serves no permissible purpose."[21]

Third, the issue on which the other crimes evidence is said to bear should be the subject of a genuine controversy. For example, if the prosecution maintains that the other crime reveals defendant's guilty state of mind, then intent should be disputed. Thus, if the defendant does not deny that the acts were deliberate, the prosecution may not introduce the evidence merely to show that the acts were not accidental. Likewise, if the accused does not deny performing the acts charged, the exceptions pertaining to identification are unavailing. Thus, if opportunity or motive is manifest, that rationale cannot justify the evidence of other bad acts.

Fourth, even if one or more of the valid purposes for admitting other-crimes evidence is appropriately invoked, there is still the need to balance its probative value against the usual counterweights described in § 185. When the sole purpose of the other-crimes evidence is to show some propensity to commit the crime at trial, there is no room for ad hoc balancing. The evidence is then unequivocally inadmissible—this is the meaning of the rule against other crimes evidence. But the fact that there is an accepted logical basis for the evidence other than the forbidden one of showing a proclivity for criminality does not ensure that the jury will not also rely on a defendant's apparent propensity toward criminal behavior. Accordingly, modern authority recognizes that the problem is not merely one of pigeonholing, but of classifying and then balancing. Moreover, a number of opinions suggest that the balancing should be less friendly toward admission than is typical for Rule 403 decisions. They emphasize the need for exacting scrutiny of both the probative value of the evidence and the likely prejudicial impact. To implement more rigorous balancing, the Rule 403 balancing standard, which is written so as to lean toward admission, might be replaced with a requirement that probative value for a permissible purpose outweigh prejudicial effect.

In deciding whether the danger of unfair prejudice and the like substantially outweighs the incremental probative value, a variety of matters must be considered, including the strength of the evidence as to the commission of the other crime, the similarities between the crimes, the interval of time that has elapsed between the crimes, the need for the evidence, the efficacy of alternative proof, and the degree to which the evidence probably will rouse the jury to overmastering hostility. A detailed limiting instruction may be required, but such instructions are not panaceas. Finally, "to reduce surprise and promote early resolution on the issue of admissibility," case law or rules may require a party to notify the opponent of the intention to introduce certain types of evidence of other crimes or bad acts.

§ 191 Good Character as Evidence of Lawful Conduct: Proof by the Accused and Rebuttal by the Government

The prosecution, as we saw in the preceding section, generally is forbidden to initiate evidence of the bad character of the defendant merely to imply that, being a bad person, he is more likely to commit a crime. This rule, in turn, is a corollary of the more general proscription on the use of character as circumstantial evidence of conduct. Yet, when the table is turned and the defendant in a criminal case seeks to offer evidence of good character to imply that he is unlikely to have committed a crime, the general rule

---

[21] U.S. v. Gomez, 763 F.3d 845, 856 (7th Cir. 2014) (en banc).

against propensity evidence is not applied. In both situations, the character evidence is relevant circumstantial evidence, but when the accused chooses to rely on an inference from good character, the problem of prejudice is altogether different. Now, knowledge of the accused's character may prejudice the jury in his favor, but the magnitude of the prejudice or its social cost is thought to be less. Thus, the common law and the federal rules provide a "mercy rule" that permits the defendant, but not the government, to open the door to character evidence.

Not all aspects of the accused's good character are open to proof under this exception. The prevailing view is that only pertinent traits—those involved in the offense charged—are provable.[22] One charged with theft might offer evidence of honesty, while someone accused of murder might show that he is peaceable, but not vice versa. A few general traits, like being law-abiding, seem relevant to almost any accusation.

The common law has vacillated as regards the methods of establishing the good character of the accused. A rule of relatively recent origin limits proof to evidence of reputation for the pertinent traits. This constraint prevents a witness from giving a personal opinion and also prohibits testimony concerning specific acts or their absence.

The Federal Rules reinstate the earlier common law approach. Rule 405(a) provides, in part, that: "When evidence of a person's character or character trait is admissible, it may be proved by testimony about the person's reputation or by testimony in the form of an opinion."

This liberalization was not achieved without debate. It allows expert opinion testimony about an accused's character traits, subject to the court's residual power to screen for prejudice, distraction, and time-consumption. Nevertheless, like the common law rules, it does not allow evidence of particular incidents. For example, a federal inspector charged with accepting a bribe from a meat packer can call a character witness to show his reputation for being honest, but he may not call other meat packers to testify that he did not solicit bribes from them.[23]

Where reputation evidence is employed, it may be confined to reputation at approximately the time of the alleged offense. Traditionally, only testimony as to the defendant's reputation in the community where the accused resided was allowed, but urbanization has prompted the acceptance of evidence as to reputation within other substantial groups of which the accused is a constantly interacting member, such as the locale where defendant works.

When defendant does produce evidence of his good character as regards traits pertinent to the offense charged, whether by way of reputation or opinion testimony, he frequently is said to have placed his character "in issue." The phrase is potentially misleading. That a defendant relies on character witnesses to indicate that he is not predisposed to commit the type of crime in question does not transform his character into an operative fact upon which guilt or innocence may turn.[24] Defendant simply opens

---

[22]   A distinct situation, involving different rules, can arise if the accused takes the stand as a witness. If he does not testify that he has character traits that are inconsistent with the charges against him, the prosecution cannot introduce, by way of rebuttal, evidence that he lacks these traits. But the prosecution may impeach credibility by evidence of bad character for veracity. See supra §§ 41–44; infra § 197.

[23]   U.S. v. Benedetto, 571 F.2d 1246 (2d Cir. 1978).

[24]   For further explanation of the proper meaning of character in issue, see supra § 187.

the door to proof of certain character traits as circumstantial evidence of whether he committed the act charged with the requisite state of mind.

Ordinarily, if the defendant chooses to inject his character into the trial in this sense, he does so by producing witnesses who testify to his good character. By relating a personal history supportive of good character, however, the defendant may achieve the same result. Whatever the method, once the defendant gives evidence of pertinent character traits to show that he is not guilty, his claim of possession of these traits—but only these traits—is open to rebuttal by cross-examination or direct testimony of prosecution witnesses. The prosecution may cross-examine a witness who has testified to the accused's reputation to probe the witness's knowledge of the community opinion, not only generally, but specifically as to whether the witness "has heard" that the defendant has committed particular prior criminal acts that conflict with the reputation vouched for on direct examination. Likewise, if a witness gives his opinion of defendant's character, then the prosecution can allude to pertinent bad acts by asking whether the witness knew of these matters in forming the opinion.

This power of the cross-examiner to reopen old wounds is replete with possibilities for prejudice. Accordingly, certain limitations should be observed. First, the general responsibility of trial courts to weigh probative value against prejudice does not vanish because reference to other crimes or wrongs takes the form of insinuation or innuendo rather than concrete evidence. The extent and nature of the cross-examination demands restraint and supervision. Some questions are improper under any circumstances. For instance, questions about the effect of the current charges on reputation or opinion usually are barred on the grounds that they would require a reputation witness to speculate about the community as a whole, and that it is unfairly prejudicial to ask any witness to indulge in a hypothetical assumption of the defendant's guilt; however, some jurisdictions do not apply this per se rule to opinion witnesses. Second, as a precondition to cross-examination about other wrongs, the prosecutor should reveal, outside the hearing of the jury, the basis for believing in the rumors or incidents so that the court can determine whether there is a substantial basis for the cross-examination. Finally, when cross-examination is allowed, a jury instruction explaining the limited purpose of the inquiry may be advisable.

The other prosecutorial counterthrust to the defendant's proof of good character is not so easily abused. The government may produce witnesses to swear to defendant's bad reputation or, in most jurisdictions, their opinion of defendant's character. As with defense character witnesses, the strictures concerning pertinent traits and remoteness apply. The courts had divided over the admissibility as rebuttal evidence of judgments of convictions for recent crimes displaying the same traits, but with the adoption of the federal rules, few jurisdictions allow any proof of specific instances of misconduct as rebuttal evidence.

§ 192   Character in Civil Cases Where Crime Is in Issue

As explained in the preceding section, in criminal cases the law relaxes its ban on evidence of character to show conduct to the extent of permitting a defendant to produce evidence of good character. In civil litigation it is not unusual for one party to accuse another of conduct that amounts to a criminal offense. For instance, much of the conduct that is the subject of civil antitrust, securities, and civil rights cases as well as a substantial proportion of more traditional civil actions, could also provide grist for the public prosecutor's mill.

Where the homologous crimes are largely regulatory or administrative, it may seem inappropriate to accord the civil party the same dispensation given criminal defendants whose lives or liberties are in jeopardy. But what of the party whose adversary's pleading or proof accuses him of what would be an offense involving moral turpitude, as in an action for conversion, a complaint arising from an alleged incident of police brutality, or a suit for a breach of a fire insurance policy in which the insurer refuses to pay because it believes that the insured set the fire? Some courts have thought that the damage that may be done to the party's standing, reputation and relationships warrants according the civil defendant the same special dispensation. These courts therefore permitted the party to introduce evidence of good reputation for the traits involved.

But this has never been the majority view. Since the consequences of civil judgments are less severe than those flowing from a criminal conviction, most courts have declined to pay the price that the concession would demand in terms of possible prejudice, consumption of time, and distraction from the issue. Defendants in civil cases accused of assault and battery, personal cruelty, setting fires, fraud, and more are barred from presenting evidence of their character. Although the balance may be arguable, the Federal and Uniform Rules of Evidence adhere to the majority position. Rule 404 bars evidence of character in civil as well as criminal cases to show how a person probably acted on a particular occasion,[25] and the grace given by Rule 404(a)(1) to an "accused" who wishes to introduce evidence of his or her good character does not extend to civil defendants.

§ 193 Character of Victim in Cases of Assault, Murder, and Rape

A well established exception to the rule forbidding character evidence to prove conduct applies to homicide and assault cases in which there is a dispute as to who was the first aggressor. Under this exception, the accused can introduce evidence of the victim's character for turbulence and violence. The majority rule is that evidence must be directed to the victim's reputation or opinion rather than to specific acts—evidence of past acts of violence generally is not a permissible mode of proof. However, some jurisdictions allow the victim's violent character to be proved by convictions, and a minority position is that even specific acts without convictions can be proved as long as they shed sufficient light on who the first aggressor was. In response, the prosecution may adduce evidence that the victim was a characteristically peaceful person.

This line of proof and counterproof openly relies on the victim's tendency to act in accordance with a general trait of character—a violent or a peaceful disposition.

---

[25] See supra § 189. Some complications arise in assault and battery cases. When the issue is simply whether the defendant committed the act, the majority approach described above excludes defendant's evidence of his character for peacefulness. But when the defendant pleads self-defense, he usually may show plaintiff's reputation for turbulence if he proves it was known to him. The rationale is that the evidence then shows defendant's reasonable apprehension, and therefore is not used to prove that plaintiff acted in conformity with the character trait. Of course, this is also not an instance of the defendant's introducing evidence of his own good character. Likewise, since the exceptions described supra § 190 apply in civil as well as criminal cases, evidence of defendant's bad character may be used to show malice to justify punitive damages. Finally, when there is a dispute as to who committed the first act of aggression, many courts, regardless of their alignment on the general question of defendant's use of good character evidence, seem to admit evidence of the good or bad character of both parties for peacefulness as shedding light on their probable acts.

Consequently, it does not require proof that the defendant was aware of the victim's violent reputation or acts. But such awareness could have additional relevance. It could help to justify defendant's conduct by showing that the defendant reasonably believed that he was in immediate danger and needed to respond with the deadly (or other) force that he actually employed. Used only for this purpose, the evidence does not transgress the policy against employing character evidence to show conduct. This "quasi-exception" for character evidence that shows reasonable fear is universally available, but a minority of jurisdictions still do not embrace the true exception for victim-character evidence. They will not admit evidence of the victim's violent or belligerent propensity to show who was the first aggressor.

In the minority jurisdictions, obviously the defendant must know of the victim's reputation or specific acts if the evidence is to be admissible, and the defendant cannot argue that the victim's aggressive character proves that the victim was the first attacker. In the majority jurisdictions, the defendant can use the victim-character evidence to determine who attacked whom, but he cannot refer to specific acts that he knew nothing about.

Federal Rule 404(a)(2) adopted the majority position by enumerating a true exception. It speaks to "pertinent"[26] character traits of the victims of crimes generally and specifically to the trait of nonviolence in homicide cases. It exempts from the usual rule of exclusion a defendant's "evidence of an alleged victim's pertinent trait" and the prosecution's "evidence to rebut it"; and, "in a homicide case, the prosecutor may offer evidence of the alleged victim's trait of peacefulness to rebut evidence that the victim was the first aggressor."

That the character of the victim is being proved renders inapposite the usual concern over the untoward impact of evidence of the defendant's poor character on the jury's assessment of the case against the defendant. There is, however, a risk of a different form of prejudice. Learning of the victim's bad character could lead the jury to think that the victim merely "got what he deserved" and to acquit for that reason. Nevertheless, at least in murder and perhaps in battery cases as well, when the identity of the first aggressor is really in doubt, the probative value of the evidence ordinarily justifies taking this risk.

In some jurisdictions, a claim of self-defense may not trigger, in itself, the prosecution's power to introduce rebuttal evidence of the victim's nonviolent nature. By one view, such counterproof is allowed only when the accused opens the door specifically by evidence of the victim's character for belligerence. The rule quoted above clearly follows the contrary view in homicide cases. Since a dead victim cannot attest to his peaceable behavior during the fatal encounter, Rule 404(a)(2)(C) provides that whenever the accused claims self-defense and offers any type of evidence that the deceased was the first aggressor, the government may reply with evidence of the peaceable character of the deceased.

A similar exception to the general rule against the use of character to prove conduct pertained to the defense of consent in sexual assault cases. In the past, the courts generally admitted evidence of the victim's character for chastity, although there were

---

[26]   See supra § 191.

diverging lines of authority on whether the proof could be by specific instances and on whether the prosecution could put evidence of chastity in its case in chief.

In the 1970s, however, nearly all jurisdictions enacted criminal "rape shield" laws "to protect rape victims from degrading and embarrassing disclosure of intimate details about their private lives, to encourage reporting of sexual assaults, and to prevent wasting time on distracting collateral and irrelevant matters."[27] The reforms ranged from barring all evidence of the victim's character for chastity to merely requiring a preliminary hearing to screen out inadmissible evidence on the issue.

Federal Rule of Evidence 412 lies between these extremes. As originally promulgated, Rule 412 applied only to prosecutions for sexual assault. Reversing the traditional preference for proof of character by reputation, in criminal cases the rule bars all reputation and opinion evidence of the victim's past sexual conduct, but it permits evidence of specific incidents if certain conditions are met. Procedurally, the proponent of the evidence ordinarily must give written notice before trial, and the court must conduct an in camera hearing before admitting the disfavored evidence. Substantively, in criminal cases Rule 412 distinguishes between evidence of past sexual behavior of the victim with the accused and sexual conduct involving other individuals. If the evidence pertains to past conduct with an accused who claims consent, it may be admitted to prove or disprove consent. But if the evidence pertains to acts of the victim with other individuals, the defendant may use it only to prove that someone else was the "the source of semen, injury, or other physical evidence." Finally, the rule specifies that if the constitution mandates it, the defendant may introduce evidence of the victim's prior sexual conduct.

Resort to an undefined, residual provision to avoid an otherwise unconstitutionally sweeping ban on proof of the victim's character is inferior to an articulation of the full range of allowable uses of sexual history evidence. It places trial courts in the awkward position of having to make constitutional rulings rather than being able to apply a self-contained and structured rule of evidence. Uniform Rule of Evidence 412 and many state laws and provide a more structured approach that seems preferable to the obscurity of the federal rule.

Be that as it may, a number of cases have identified circumstances in which a defendant is constitutionally entitled to introduce evidence of an alleged victim's sexual conduct under the due process or confrontation clauses. For example, in *Olden v. Kentucky*,[28] the Supreme Court held that a rape defendant's right to confront his accusers entitled him to inquire into the alleged victim's cohabitation with another man to show that she had a reason to falsely accuse the defendant.[29]

A 1994 amendment extends the federal rape shield law to all civil cases "involving alleged sexual misconduct."[30] This augmented rule surely reaches civil suits for sexual

---

[27]   U.S. v. Torres, 937 F.2d 1469, 1472 (9th Cir. 1991).

[28]   488 U.S. 227 (1988).

[29]   A state court had prevented this inquiry, not on the basis of a rape shield law, but on the ground that it was unfairly prejudicial because the jury would have learned that the victim, a white woman, was living with a black man. Drawing on *Olden*, one court summarized situations in which the right to confront one's accusers or to present a full and fair defense requires the admission of past sexual behavior as including the following: "to expose a possible motive to lie," "to rebut the presumption of a victim's sexual naiveté," and "to respond when the prosecution has 'opened the door' by offering evidence of the victim's chastity." State v. Robinson, 803 A.2d 452, 457 (Me. 2002).

[30]   Fed. R. Evid. 412(a).

assaults that could be (or were) the subject of criminal actions, and it probably extends to civil rights claims for sexual harassment. However, the shield is weaker in the civil context than in criminal cases, where the rule excludes all evidence of the victim's sexual character—no matter how probative—that is not within the categorical exceptions. In contrast, Rule 412(b)(2) adopts a balancing test with the scales tilted against admission. It forbids admission of any type of evidence for sexual disposition unless the "probative value substantially outweighs the danger of harm to any victim and of unfair prejudice to any party."

Under state laws, evidence of the victim's sexual experience generally is admissible, upon notice, for specified purposes: to demonstrate that the victim, having had previous voluntary sexual relations with defendant, consented to the alleged attack or that defendant reasonably believed there was consent; that the victim has a motive falsely to accuse defendant; that the witness characteristically fantasizes sexual assaults; that the witness knowingly brings false accusations of sexual misconduct; that a young child who gave a detailed account of a sexual assault already possessed the knowledge to do so; or that someone else may have been the source of semen or trauma to the witness. Other exceptions also have been articulated in various states.

A recurring difficulty under all the statutes arises in determining the conduct that is shielded from inquiry. The shield laws certainly apply to evidence of other acts of sexual intercourse or contact, for these laws are intended to protect victims from the embarrassment of having to disclose these acts. Concern for personal privacy and for not discouraging victims from complaining extends as well to private behavior that implies sexual intercourse or contact, such as the use of contraceptives or the presence of venereal disease. As one moves to conduct that is less directly linked to sex acts, however, the applicability of a rape shield law becomes more arguable. Should modes of dress, prior accusations of rape, sexual innuendos, banter, flirting, and statements about sexual desires or knowledge be considered "sexual conduct" or "sexual behavior" that is exempt from inquiry or proof? The statutes and cases are divided.

The rape shield laws have survived constitutional attacks, albeit with occasional surgery. They reflect the judgment that most evidence about chastity has far too little probative value on the issue of consent to justify extensive inquiry into the victim's sexual history. Given the recognition of this notion in the case law emerging during the period preceding their enactment, however, whether special rape shield laws were necessary to alter the law is questionable. Furthermore, there is scant evidence that the reforms have achieved the goals of increasing reports or convictions of rapes. Thus, the true value of the rape shield laws may be symbolic rather than instrumental.

§ 194 Evidence of Character to Impeach a Witness

The familiar practice of impeaching a witness by producing evidence of bad character for veracity amounts to using a character trait to prove that a witness is testifying falsely. As such, it involves a species of propensity reasoning and is subject to the argument that the jury will overvalue it. Unlike propensity evidence to show the conduct alleged in a complaint, indictment, or information, however, the propensity inference from impeachment evidence of a witness's general truthfulness normally goes only to the conduct of the witness while testifying. Its purpose is to suggest that the witness should be believed now—not that the witness probably did or did not act as alleged in the civil complaint or criminal charge. When the witness is not a party, the threat that evidence will induce the jury to penalize or reward parties because of *their* bad or good character is usually absent. Moreover, the need for the evidence of a witness's character is greater. As a result, a distinct set of rules govern witness-character evidence. Chapter 5, on impeachment, discusses these rules.

§ 195 Habit and Custom as Evidence of Conduct on a Particular Occasion

Although the courts frown on evidence of traits of character when introduced to prove how a person or organization acted on a given occasion, they are more receptive to evidence of personal habits or of the customary behavior of organizations. To understand this difference, one must appreciate the distinction between habit and character. The two are easily confused. People sometimes speak of a habit for care, a habit for promptness, or a habit of forgetfulness. They may say that an individual has a bad habit of stealing or lying. Evidence of these "habits" would be identical to the kind of evidence that is the target of the general rule against character evidence. Character is a generalized description of a person's disposition, or of the disposition in respect to a general trait, such as honesty, temperance or peacefulness, that usually is regarded as meriting approval or disapproval. Habit, in the present context, is more specific. It denotes one's regular response to a repeated situation. If we speak of a character for care, we think of the person's tendency to act prudently in all the varying situations of life—in business, at home, in handling automobiles and in walking across the street. A habit, on the other hand, is the person's regular practice of responding to a particular kind of situation with a specific type of conduct. Thus, a person may be in the habit of bounding down a certain stairway two or three steps at a time, of patronizing a particular pub after each day's work, or of driving his automobile without using a seatbelt. The doing of the habitual act may become semi-automatic, as with a driver who invariably signals before changing lanes.

Evidence of habits that come within this definition has greater probative value than does evidence of general traits of character. Furthermore, the potential for prejudice is substantially less. By and large, the detailed patterns of situation-specific behavior that constitute habits are unlikely to provoke such sympathy or antipathy as would distort the process of evaluating the evidence.

As a result, many jurisdictions accept the proposition that evidence of habit is admissible to show an act. These courts only reject the evidence categorically if the putative habit is not sufficiently regular or uniform, or if the circumstances are not sufficiently similar to outweigh the dangers of prejudice, distraction and time-consumption. The Federal, Uniform, and Model Rules all follow this pattern. In the past, however, some jurisdictions excluded evidence of habit altogether, and others admitted it only if there were no eyewitnesses to testify about the events that were said to have triggered the habitual behavior.

Even the jurisdictions that were reluctant to accept evidence of personal habits were willing to allow evidence of the "custom" of a business organization, if reasonably regular and uniform. This may be because there is no confusion between character traits and business practices, as there is between character and habit, or it may reflect the belief that the need for regularity in business and the organizational sanctions that may exist when employees deviate from the established procedures give extra guarantees that the questioned activity followed the usual custom. Thus, evidence that a letter was written and signed in the course of business and put in the regular place for mailing usually will be admitted to prove that it was mailed. Similarly, regular adherence to a standard protocol of informing research subjects of the known risks and benefits of a drug can counter allegations that some subjects were not properly informed. But admissible business practices can include ones that depart from official or acknowledged company policy.

The existence of the personal habit or the business custom may be established by a knowledgeable witness's testimony that there was such a habit or practice. Evidence of specific instances may also be used. Naturally, there must be enough instances to permit the finding of a habit, the circumstances under which the habit or custom is followed must be present, and, as always, there are the limitations for cumulativeness, remoteness, unnecessary inflammatory quality, and so on.[31]

---

[31]   See supra § 185.

Chapter 18

SIMILAR HAPPENINGS AND TRANSACTIONS

Table of Sections

---

§ 196 Other Claims, Suits, or Defenses of a Party

Should a party be permitted to cast doubt on the merits of the claim at bar by demonstrating that an opponent has advanced similar claims or defenses against others in previous litigation? Two conflicting goals shape the rules of evidence in this area. Exposing fraudulent claims is important, but so is protecting innocent litigants from unfair prejudice. The easy cases are those in which one of these considerations clearly predominates. If the evidence reveals that a party has made previous, very similar claims and that these claims were fraudulent, then almost universally the evidence will be admissible despite the dangers of distraction and time-consumption with regard to the quality of these other claims, and despite the general prohibition on using evidence of bad character solely to show conduct on a given occasion.[1] At the other pole, if the evidence is merely that the plaintiff is a chronic litigant with respect to all sorts of claims, the courts consider the slight probative value overborne by the countervailing factors. This evidence they usually exclude.

In between lie the harder cases. Suppose the evidence is that the party suing for an alleged loss, such as fire damage to his property or personal injury in a collision, has made many previous claims of similar losses. The evidence surely is relevant. The probability of so many similar accidents happening to the same person by chance alone can be vanishingly small. Yet, rare events do happen. There will always be some people who suffer the slings and arrows of outrageous fortune. In itself, this fact gives no indication of prejudice. Presumably, a jury can come to a reasonable judgment as to the relative likelihood of the alternatives. Nevertheless, there is a form of prejudice inherent in this situation. The jury may disapprove of a person precisely because that person is litigious. The judge, balancing probative value against prejudice, should admit the evidence only if there is a basis for concluding that the other claims were fabricated.

This foundation could be supplied by distinct evidence of fraud, or it might be inferred when the probability of coincidence seems so negligible as to leave fraud (or being the victim of someone else's repeated malevolent acts) as the only plausible explanations. The likelihood of repeated, substantially identical claims depends on the number of claims and the probability of each incident. In addition, the degree of

---

[1]   See supra Ch. 17.

similarity among the claims is important, inasmuch as a series of disparate but bona fide claims seems more likely than a string of very similar ones.

So far, we have discussed evidence of a party's other claims introduced to raise a question about the instant claim or suit. Evidence of a witness's past accusations or defenses introduced to attack the veracity of that witness presents comparable problems. In these situations, a litigant might seek to prove that the other accusations have been false as circumstantial evidence that the testimony just delivered is also false. Although this is a species of character evidence to show conduct, it usually will be admissible to impeach the witness. Even without proof that the other accusations were false, the very fact that the witness repeatedly accuses many others of the same kind of behavior may seem too extraordinary to be explained as a mere coincidence. The logic and issues here are perfectly analogous to those already addressed with regard to the filing of repeated, similar suits or claims.[2] However, in keeping with the customary relaxation of the standard of admissibility on cross-examination, it is generally easier to elicit admissions about the other claims on cross-examination than it is to introduce the evidence by the testimony of the proponent's witnesses.

§ 197 Other Misrepresentations and Frauds

In cases alleging fraud or misrepresentation, proof that the defendant perpetrated similar deceptions frequently is received in evidence. Admission is not justified on the theory of "once a cheat, always a cheat," for that would contravene the ban on using character traits solely as propensity evidence of conduct on the occasion. Rather, at least one of three well entrenched alternate theories typically is available. To begin with, evidence of other frauds may help establish the element of knowledge—by suggesting that defendant knew that the alleged misrepresentation was false or by indicating that defendant's participation in an alleged fraudulent scheme was not innocent or accidental.

Second, the evidence may be admissible with respect to the closely related element of intent to deceive. In *Butler v. Watkins*,[3] for example, an inventor in New Orleans claimed that the Patent Nut and Bolt Company engaged in negotiations to make use of his patent, in bad faith, to keep him from marketing it while the company sold other such devices. He offered letters showing that this English manufacturing company had similar negotiations with a different inventor to keep a similar invention from entering the market that same year. The trial court excluded the letters as extrinsic because they involved a different patentee, and the company prevailed at trial. The Supreme Court reversed, stating that if "similar negotiations . . . conducted . . . deceitfully in order to keep [the other inventor's device] out of the market that year . . . tends to show . . . the same animus . . . ."[4] When other misrepresentations are used to show intent or knowledge, they need not be identical nor made under precisely the same circumstances as the one in issue.

---

[2] When the witness is a party, the relevance of the other claims is two-fold. Not only do the other claims indicate that the party-witness is the sort of person who institutes false actions or raises false defenses, but they also suggest that the party-witness is generally untruthful. Since both "claim-mindedness" and veracity come into play, courts that reject the "claim-mindedness" proof may allow the cross-examination of the party-witness. The party-witness may also make specific statements on direct examination that open the door to cross-examination about other claims.

[3] 80 U.S. 456 (1871).

[4] *Id.* at 465.

Finally, if the uttering of the misrepresentations or the performance of the fraudulent conduct is contested, then other misrepresentations or fraudulent acts that are evidently part of the same overall plan or scheme may be admissible to prove the conduct of the defendant. For example, evidence that defendants had "salted" ore samples that other intended buyers took from a mine is "competent and cogent evidence tending to establish their complicity in the like fraud now under consideration" since all the fraudulent acts were "in furtherance of same general design."[5]

The requirement of a common plan or scheme is well recognized, but it should not be necessary in civil cases. When there is conflicting testimony as to the making of the misrepresentation at issue, the value of evidence of other, very similar misrepresentations—whether or not part of the same plan or scheme—in resolving the controversy should be sufficient to outweigh the danger of prejudice. As it is, the courts often manage to discern a larger plan when the various acts could well be described as separate transactions or are content to describe the other acts as loosely defined "pattern-or-practice evidence."

§ 198 Other Contracts and Business Transactions

Evidence concerning other contracts or business dealings may be relevant to prove the terms of a contract, the meaning of these terms, a business habit or custom, and occasionally, the authority of an agent. As to many of these uses, there is little controversy. Certainly, evidence of other transactions between the same parties readily is received when relevant to show the meaning they probably attached to the terms of a contract. Likewise, when the existence of the terms is in doubt, evidence of similar contracts between the same parties is accepted as a vehicle for showing of a custom or continuing course of dealing between them, and as such, as evidence of the terms of the present bargain. Also, when the authority of an agent is in question, other similar transactions that the agent has carried out on behalf of the principal are freely admitted. Finally, evidence of misconduct in other business dealings may be relevant to claims of bad faith or knowledge in the transaction at bar, as when an insurer repeatedly refuses to make proper payments of underinsured motorist claims.

In the past, many courts had balked when contracts with others were offered to show the terms or the making of the contract in suit. It is hard to understand why any hard and fast line should be drawn. As an historical matter, these decisions perhaps may be explained as manifestations of the perennial confusion between the sufficiency of an item of evidence to prove the proposition for which it is offered and its relevance to that proposition. In addition, these decisions reflect the beguiling power of the mystical phrase *res inter alios acta*.[6] Yet, it seems clear that contracts of a party with third persons may show the party's customary practice and course of dealing and thus supply insights into the terms of the present agreement. Indeed, even if there are but one or two such contracts, they may be useful evidence. When, in a certain kind of transaction, a business has adopted a particular mode of handling a bargaining topic or standardized feature, such as a warranty, discount or the like, it is often easier for it to cast a new contract in the same mold than it is to work out a new one. Moreover, some practices

---

[5]   Mudsill Min. Co. v. Watrous, 61 F. 163, 179 (6th Cir. 1894).

[6]   The maxim "*Res inter alios acta, aliis neque nocere neque prodesse potest*" means "A thing done between some can neither harm nor profit others." The maxim "*Res inter alios acta alteri nocere non debet*" states a key tenet of the principle of res judicata—that a person is not bound by litigation in which that individual does not participate.

become so accepted in an industry that they may shape the meaning of most contracts in that field. As to these, evidence in the form of contracts or transactions involving neither of the parties may nevertheless be probative of the commercial relationship that exists between the parties.

Inasmuch as there is no general danger of unfair prejudice inherent in evidence of other business transactions, strict rules or limits on admissibility are inappropriate. The courts should admit such evidence in all cases where the testimony as to the terms of the present bargain is conflicting and where the judge finds that the risk of wasted time and confusion of issues does not substantially outweigh the probative value of the evidence of the other transactions. Many jurisdictions therefore leave evidence of other contracts or business dealings to the trial judge to evaluate on a case by case basis.

§ 199 Other Sales of Similar Property as Evidence of Value

When the market value of property needs to be determined, the price actually paid in a competitive market for comparable items is an obvious place to look. Indeed, when presented with the sometimes wildly disparate estimates of professional appraisers, courts have remarked that the sales prices of comparable properties are the best evidence of value. The testimony of witnesses with first-hand knowledge of other sales, or reliable price lists, market reports, or the like may be received to show the market price.

The less homogeneous the product, the more difficulty there is in measuring market value in this way. Thus, cases involving land valuation, especially condemnation cases, frequently discuss the admissibility of evidence of other sales. A dying rule excludes the evidence entirely save in exceptional circumstances. The dominant view gives the judge discretion to admit evidence of other sales. The inquiry focuses on whether these sales have been sufficiently recent, and whether the other land is sufficiently nearby and alike as to character, situation, usability, and improvements, as to make it clear that the two tracts are comparable in value. A weaker standard for similarity applies when the other sales are used as the basis for an expert judgment as to value instead of being introduced as independent evidence of value.

Because the value sought is what, on average, a willing buyer would have paid a willing seller, prices on other sales of a forced character, such as execution sales or condemnation awards for other tracts, generally are inadmissible. Many courts also exclude the condemnor's evidence of prices it paid to other owners on the theory that sales made in contemplation of condemnation do not approximate the relevant market price. Other courts, following what seems the better reasoned view, allow such evidence in the judge's discretion.

Of course, any other sale must be genuine, and the price must be paid or substantially secured. Although actual sale prices rather than asking prices typically *are* required, unaccepted offers made by a party may be admissible as statements of a party-opponent. When the evidence of unaccepted offers comes from the mouth of the seller, however, the traditional rule is that the testimony is too unreliable to warrant admission, because "[o]ral and not binding offers are so easily made and refused in a mere passing conversation, and under circumstances involving no responsibility on either side, as to cast no light upon the question of value"[7] and because "the person

---

[7]   Sharp v. U.S., 191 U.S. 341, 349 (1903).

making such offer . . . may have so slight a knowledge on the subject as to render his opinion of no value."[8] Unaccepted offers are admitted more easily when the offeror is available for examination or when there have been no consummated sales. In addition, some courts allow expert appraisers to refer to such offers as part of the basis for their valuation, although this theory does not make the offers admissible for their truth.

§ 200 Other Accidents and Injuries

The admissibility of evidence of other accidents and injuries is raised frequently in negligence and product liability cases. At one time, a few courts applied a rigid rule of exclusion. The modern cases commit the matter to the trial judge for a weighing of the advantages and disadvantages of admitting or excluding the evidence; many opinions stress the trial judge's discretion. In light of the prejudice that such evidence can carry with it, and because of the rule that evidence of other accidents or their absence is not admissible solely to show a character or propensity for careful or careless behavior,[9] most judges will scrutinize it carefully. Usually, a nonpropensity purpose and a showing of sufficient similarity in the conditions giving rise to the various accidents are required. Of course, exactly identical circumstances cannot be realized, but the burden of showing substantial similarity falls on the proponent of the evidence. As regards the permissible purposes, in practice these tend to blend together in that more than one typically is available. For clarity of analysis, however, we shall try to isolate each valid purpose for admitting evidence of other accidents.

To begin with, evidence of other accidents or close calls may be admissible to prove the existence of a particular physical condition, situation, or defect. For instance, the fact that several persons slipped and fell in the same location in a supermarket can help show that a slippery substance was on the floor. At the same time, this proof is a bit sensational. Unless the defendant strenuously disputes the presence of the condition, the court may reject the evidence of the similar accidents as unduly prejudicial and cumulative.

Second, the evidence of other accidents or injuries may be admissible to help show that the defect or dangerous situation caused the injury. Thus, instances in which other patients placed on the same drug therapy contracted the same previously rare disease is circumstantial evidence that the drug caused the disease in plaintiff's case. As typically developed at trial, such evidence of other accidents is a crude version of a retrospective epidemiologic study. Since many unsuspected factors could contribute or cause the observed effects, the conditions of the other injuries and the present one must be similar. Some courts look to four "factors . . . when admitting evidence of other incidents to support a claim that the present accident was caused by the same defect: (1) the products are similar; (2) the alleged defect is similar; (3) causation related to the defect in the other incidents; and (4) exclusion of all reasonable secondary explanations for the cause of the other incidents."[10]

Although the use of evidence of other accidents to prove the existence of a condition (the first purpose listed above) can overlap the use of the evidence to prove that the condition caused plaintiff's injuries, ordinarily, the need to use the evidence for this second purpose is plainer. Causation is frequently in genuine dispute, and

---

[8] *Id.* at 348.

[9] See supra § 189.

[10] Watson v. Ford Motor Co., 699 S.E.2d 169, 179 (S.C. 2010).

circumstantial evidence may be of great value in pursuing this elusive issue. Thus, receptivity to evidence of similar happenings to show causation is heightened when the defendant contends that the alleged conduct could not possibly have caused the plaintiff's injury.

Third, and perhaps most commonly, evidence of other accidents or injuries may be used to show the risk that defendant's conduct created. If the extent of the danger is material to the case, as it almost always is in personal injury litigation, the fact that the same conditions produced harm on other occasions is a natural and convincing way of showing the hazard. The requirement of substantial similarity is applied strictly here. However, statistical analyses in which the differences are likely to be randomly distributed should be more readily admissible than testimony about particular accidents.

Finally, the evidence of other accidents commonly is received to prove that the defendant knew, or should have known, of the danger. Of course, if defendant's duty is absolute, this theory is inapposite. In negligence cases, however, the duty is merely to use reasonable care to maintain safe conditions. Even in many strict product liability cases, demonstrating that the product is defective or unreasonably dangerous for its intended use requires an analysis of foreseeable risks.

When the evidence of other accidents is introduced to show notice of the danger, subsequent accidents are not admissible under this rationale. The proponent probably will want to show directly that the defendant had knowledge of the prior accidents, but the nature, frequency or notoriety of the incidents may well reveal that defendant knew of them or should have discovered the danger by due inspection. Since all that is required is that the previous injury or injuries be such as to call defendant's attention to the dangerous situation, the similarity in the circumstances of the accidents can be considerably less than that which is demanded when the same evidence is used for one of the other valid purposes. Nonetheless, it remains necessary to show that the other accidents are similar in that they were or should have been recognized as the result of the same defect of conditions that caused the accident in question.

Having surveyed the utility of a history of accidents in establishing liability, we now consider the admissibility of a history of safety for exculpatory purposes. One might think that if proof of similar accidents is admissible in the judge's discretion to show that a particular condition or defect exists, or that the injury sued for was caused in a certain way, or that a situation is dangerous, or that defendant knew or should have known of the danger, then evidence of the absence of accidents during a period of similar exposure and experience likewise would be receivable to show that these facts do not exist. Indeed, it would seem perverse to tell a jury that one or two persons besides the plaintiff tripped on defendant's stairwell while withholding from them the further information that another thousand persons descended the same stairs without incident.

Yet, for many years decisions laid down just such a general rule against proof of absence of other accidents. Admittedly, there are special problems with proving the nonexistence of something. In particular, an absence of complaints does not necessarily mean that accidents have not been occurring. "Stair climbers other than the plaintiff may have tripped but not fallen, or fallen without being hurt, or been hurt without complaining, or complained to someone other than the witness who testifies to the lack of complaints. Moreover, the plaintiff may have been the first to pass after a deteriorating condition became sufficiently dangerous to cause a serious accident."[11] While these factors should be considered in balancing probative value against the usual counterweights, they do not justify a flat rule of exclusion. In some cases, excluding such proof of safety may be justified on the ground that the persons passing in safety were not exposed to the same conditions as those that prevailed when the plaintiff's injury occurred. The evidence of a thousand safe descents down the stairs would be far less convincing if it were revealed that all of these were made in daylight, while the two or three accidents occurred at night in poor lighting. However, the possibility that a very general safety record may obscure the influence of an important factor merely counsels for applying the traditional requirement of substantial similarity. When the experience sought to be proved is so extensive as to be sure to include an adequate number of similar situations, the similarity requirement should be considered satisfied.

Neither can the broad proscription be justified by the other considerations that affect the admissibility of evidence. The problems of prejudice and distraction over "collateral issues" seem much more acute when it comes to proof of other accidents than when evidence of an accident-free history is proffered. Indeed, the defendant will seldom open this door if there is any practical likelihood that the plaintiff will dispute the safety record.

Consequently, few recent decisions can be found applying a general rule of exclusion. A large number of cases recognize that lack of other accidents may be admissible to show (1) absence of the defect or condition alleged, (2) the lack of a causal relationship between the injury and the defect or condition charged, (3) the nonexistence of an unduly dangerous situation, or (4) want of knowledge (or of grounds to realize) the danger.

---

[11]   Lempert et al., A Modern Approach to Evidence 311 (4th ed. 2011).

Chapter 19

INSURANCE AGAINST LIABILITY

Table of Sections

---

§ 201 Insurance Against Liability as Proof of Negligence

A formidable body of cases holds that evidence that a party is or is not insured against liability is not admissible on the issue of negligence. Federal Rule of Evidence 411 codifies this line of cases. It states that "evidence that a person was or was not insured against liability is not admissible to prove whether the person acted negligently or otherwise wrongfully." The rule is limited to insurance for liability and does not include other forms of insurance.

This rule rests on two premises. The first is the belief that insurance coverage reveals little about the likelihood that one will act carelessly. Subject to a few pathological exceptions, financial protection will not diminish the normal incentive to be careful, especially when life and limb are at stake. Similarly, the argument that insured individuals or firms are more prudent and careful, as a group, than those who are self-insurers seems tenuous and also serves to counteract any force that the first argument may have. Thus, the relevance of the evidence of coverage is doubtful. In addition, there is concern that the evidence would be prejudicial—that the mention of insurance invites higher awards than are justified, and conversely, that the sympathy that a jury might feel for an uninsured defendant who must pay out of his own pocket could interfere with its evaluation of the evidence under the appropriate standard of proof. Although empirical research into these possible forms of prejudice yields no clear answers, the "shallow pocket" hypothesis seems better supported.[1]

Despite these concerns and the general rule that evidence of the fact of insurance coverage is inadmissible to show negligence or reasonable care, such evidence frequently is received. As with the exclusionary rules discussed in Chapters 17 (Character and Habit) and 18 (Similar Happenings and Transactions), the evidence may be admitted for some other purpose, providing of course that its probative value on this other issue is not substantially outweighed by its prejudicial impact. Thus, Federal and Uniform Rule 411 states that "the court may admit this evidence for another purpose, such as proving a witness's bias or prejudice or proving agency, ownership, or control."

Caselaw elaborates on these "other purposes." Varied opinions recognize that the fact that persons rarely purchase liability insurance to cover contingencies for which they are not responsible makes evidence that a party is insured relevant to questions of agency, ownership, and control of vehicles and premises. More commonly, the fact of

---

[1] *See* Vidmar, The Performance of the American Civil Jury: An Empirical Perspective, 40 Ariz. L. Rev. 849 (1998).

insurance can be relevant to the bias of a witness. This is most obvious when the witness is an investigator or other employee of the insurance company.

Cross-examination affords the usual means of revealing bias, and the fact that the witness is being compensated (even if the insurer is not identified) is fair game. Moreover, it is well established that the trial court has discretion to allow more candid and complete disclosure that this employer is actually the defendant's insurer. But bias also is an issue with some experts who are not employees of the insurer. These witnesses can face pressures or incentives comparable to those arising from the employment relationship. Consequently, the cross-examiner is usually allowed to exposure a "substantial connection" to the insurance carrier. However, the phrase "substantial connection" is hardly self-defining. In imbuing it with meaning, most courts have concluded, on the one hand, that evidence that an expert witness merely has the same insurance carrier as the defendant is normally not admissible. Likewise, being paid to appear in the single case at bar does not require the insurance carrier to be named as the source of the compensation. On the other hand, when the expert has a clear and substantial financial interest in the insurer's not having to pay its insured for a judgment, the need to disclose this influence dominates. Deriving a significant fraction of income from insurers, working for companies that rely on insurers for a major part of their revenue, or having other close ties to insurance carriers can constitute the substantial connection.

Plainly, the purposes enumerated in Rule 411 do not exhaust the possibilities. Evidence of insurance may be admitted when it is an inseparable part of an admission of a party bearing on negligence or damages. That a defendant is insured can be important to rebut a suggestion that the defendant is too poor to pay a large judgment; conversely, that a defendant in not insured can be relevant to plaintiff's demand for punitive damages. And, there are some less common uses.[2]

Furthermore, there are two other ways in which the fact of insurance can be brought home to the jury. Witnesses have been known to make unexpected and unresponsive references to insurance. In these situations, the court has the power to declare a mistrial, but it is a rare case in which the judge will do more than strike the reference and instruct the jury to ignore it. Finally, in the examination of prospective jurors, most jurisdictions allow questions about employment by or interest in insurance companies.

Despite its nearly universal acceptance, the wisdom of the general prohibition on injecting insurance into the trial, as it currently operates, is questionable. When the rule originated, insurance coverage of individuals was exceptional. In the absence of references to insurance at trial, a juror most probably would not have thought that a defendant was insured. Today, compulsory insurance laws for motorists are ubiquitous, and liability insurance for homeowners and businesses has become the norm. Most jurors probably assume that defendants are insured. Yet, few courts will allow a defendant to show that he is uninsured, unless the plaintiff has opened the door to such evidence. At a minimum, such a defendant, and indeed any party, should be entitled to an instruction that there has been no evidence as to whether any party is insured

---

[2]   *E.g.*, Kubista v. Romaine, 549 P.2d 491, 496 (Wash. 1976) (evidence that defendant's insurer had encouraged plaintiff to go to school to learn a new trade and had promised to take care of him admissible to rebut defense that plaintiff could have mitigated damages by going back to work earlier).

because the law is that the presence or absence of insurance should play no part in the case.

More fundamentally, the underlying soundness of the general rule forbidding disclosure of the fact of insurance has been the object of scathing criticism. Stripped to its essentials, the debate is not really over the application of the doctrines of relevancy and its counterweights. Hardly anyone questions the premise that the evidence is irrelevant to the exercise of reasonable care. Neither does anyone contend that a party has a right to put irrelevant evidence into the record. Rather, the arguments for the abandonment of the policy of secrecy are either pragmatic or idealistic. The pragmatic argument is straightforward. The conspiracy of silence is hard to maintain. Its costs include extensive and unnecessary arguments, reversals, and retrials stemming from elusive questions of prejudice and good faith. This state of affairs might be tolerable if the revelations of insurance were truly fraught with prejudice. But, as we have suggested, most jurors probably presuppose the existence of liability insurance anyway, and the heart of the policy of nondisclosure is surrendered when jurors are examined about their connection with insurance companies. Consequently, the extent to which evidence of coverage or its absence is prejudicial is unclear. Even the direction in which such prejudice might work is obscure. In sum, the rule has become a hollow shell, expensive to maintain and of doubtful utility.

The other principal argument against the rule of secrecy arises from a certain conception of fairness—a conception that holds that the jury should know who the "real" parties in interest are. The insurance company, which under its policy has the exclusive right to employ counsel, defend the suit, and control the decision as to settling or contesting the action, is a party in all but name.

Unfortunately, this argument begs the question. If the substantive law is that the depth of the defendant's pocket has nothing to do with liability or damages, then why should the jury be apprised of this fact? To be sure, in many cases the relative wealth of the parties is manifest. A multinational corporation cannot disguise itself as a struggling member of the proletariat. But where admittedly irrelevant characteristics can be removed from the courtroom without great strain, it is hard to see why they should be retained. In the end, therefore, it is the more pragmatic analysis that should be decisive. The benefits of a half-hearted policy of secrecy are not worth the costs. If disclosure of the fact of insurance really is prejudicial, the corrective is not a futile effort at concealment, but the usual fulfillment by the court of its function of explaining to the jury its duty to decide according to the facts and the substantive law, rather than upon sympathy, ability to pay, or concern about proliferating litigation and rising insurance premiums.

Chapter 20

EXPERIMENTAL AND SCIENTIFIC EVIDENCE

Table of Sections

I. SCIENTIFIC TESTS IN GENERAL

§ 202 Pretrial Experiments

The dominant method of factual inquiry in the courts of law is observational. Witnesses relate what they have seen under naturally occurring conditions, and the judge or jury, observing the witnesses, accepts or rejects their testimony with varying degrees of confidence. In many fields of science, naturalistic observations of people or things are also a principal means of gathering information (though the observations are made in a more structured fashion and are presented and analyzed in a different way). In some scientific disciplines, the major method for collecting data involves manipulating the environment. In its simplest and ideal form, a controlled experiment holds constant all extraneous variables so that the experimenter can measure the impact of the one factor of interest.

The opportunities for applying the experimental method to factual controversies that arise in litigation are immense, but they generally go unrecognized and unused. Some of the more frequently encountered types of experiments are tests of the composition or physical properties of substances or products; tests of the flammability or explosive properties of products; tests of the presence or effects of drugs and other products on human beings or other organisms; tests of firearms to show characteristic, identifying features, or capabilities; tests of the visibility of objects or persons under certain conditions; and tests of the speed of moving vehicles and of the effectiveness of brakes, headlights or other components. Some of these experiments can be simple affairs, such as driving an automobile along a stretch of road to determine where a particular object on the road first becomes visible, or driving from one place to another to estimate how long the trip might take. Others are more complicated, requiring sophisticated machinery, statistical analysis of the results, or other specialized knowledge or procedures. Testimony describing the experiments may be received as substantive evidence, or the experiments may form the basis for an expert opinion. Although scientific or engineering experts conduct most pretrial experiments, the simplest experiments are often the most convincing, and scientific sophistication is not always necessary or cost-effective.

§ 202.1 Pretrial Experiments—the Substantial Similarity Requirement as Applied

Pretrial experiments that do not demand scientific expertise for their interpretation are the main subject of this section. These experiments will be admitted as evidence if their probative value is not substantially outweighed by the usual counterweights of prejudice, confusion of the issues, and time consumption. The only form of prejudice that might operate in this context is that of giving experimental results more weight than they deserve, and that can depend on how they are presented. If the interpretation of the experiment does not entail expert scientific testimony, the danger of misusing the findings is not likely to be excessive. The extent to which the presentation will be distracting or time-consuming will vary from case to case. As for probative value, the courts often speak of the need for similarity between the conditions of the experiment and those that pertained to the litigated happening. The burden of showing substantial similarity is on the proponent.

In practice, however, the similarity requirement is not applied to all pretrial experiments, or if it is nominally applied, the notion of "similarity" becomes almost infinitely flexible. In the words of one state supreme court, "[s]ubstantial similarity does not require identity of conditions, but only that degree of similarity which will insure that the results of the experiment are probative."[1] The requirement is at its strictest when the experiment seeks to replicate the event in question to show that things happened (or did not happen) as alleged. But even in these case-specific experiments, differences between the experimental and actual conditions that only could make it harder for the experiment to be favorable to the proponent should be no obstacle to admission. Furthermore, an event can never be perfectly reenacted or simulated. There are too many details to keep track of, and some defy precise recreation. For example, the human agent in the happening to which the experiment pertains may be deceased, the vehicle may be destroyed, the surrounding circumstances may be known only vaguely, or the process of duplicating what actually happened may be too dangerous. Consequently, although the similarity formula is sometimes overrigidly applied, most courts recognize that the requirement is a relative one. If enough of the obviously important factors are duplicated in the experiment, and if the failure to control other possibly relevant variables is justified, the court may conclude that the experiment is sufficiently enlightening that it should come into evidence. This determination typically is subject to review only for an abuse of discretion.

On the other hand, the similarity requirement either is not applied or is highly diluted when the pretrial experiment does not purport to replicate the essential features of a particular happening. There are many perfectly acceptable experiments of this nature. For example, if one party contends that certain acts or omissions could not produce—under any circumstances—the result in question, then the other party may conduct an experiment to falsify this hypothesis. Of course, the closer the experiment is to the conditions that actually pertained, the more useful the experiment will be, but merely refuting the opposing party's sweeping claim may be sufficiently valuable to make the evidence admissible.

Similarly, the proponent may offer to prove that something was not the cause of the actionable result by means of an experiment showing that some other agent can bring about the same result. For example, when homeowners claimed in *Coon v. Utah Construction Co.*[2] that vibrations from defendant's heavy trucks on an adjacent highway enlarged cracks in the foundation and masonry walls, the construction company

---

[1]   Hermreck v. State, 956 P.2d 335, 339 (Wyo. 1998) (holding admissible an experiment using a ten-year-old girl on a 20-inch bicycle to determine how long it would take a seven-year-old boy on a 16-inch; bicycle to go from a standing start at the side of the road to the place where defendant's truck struck the bicycle).

[2]   228 P.2d 997 (Utah 1951).

commissioned tests of the level of vibrations. The vibrations in the house were no greater when the company's trucks went by than when other traffic did—and a person walking on the floor caused much greater vibration.

Finally, the experiment may be introduced solely to illustrate or demonstrate a scientific principle or empirical finding that a jury, perhaps with the aid of an expert witness, can apply to the specifics of the case. Thus, experiments showing general properties of materials are admitted without confining the experiments to the conditions surrounding the litigated situation. Most of these analyses are referred to as tests rather than experiments. When this label is attached, the question becomes one, not of similarity, but of authentication—making sure that the right material was tested and that it underwent no essential alterations before testing. In addition, tests for composition or properties often are highly scientific, thus triggering an inquiry into their scientific validity and reliability as described in the next section.

§ 202.2 Pretrial Experiments—Substantial Similarity Reconceptualized

At a conceptual level, the "substantial similarity" standard is somewhat frustrating. Its value lies in calling attention to the possible effect of differences on the implications of an experiment for the situation at bar. However, the requisite degree of similarity is not always obvious. One could say that when experiments reveal properties or traits that clearly apply under a wide range of conditions, substantial similarity is present even if the conditions are quite different. After all, there is little point in controlling for irrelevant conditions, and if physical theory indicates that the gross differences are superficial and inconsequential, the circumstances are similar in the relevant respects. More generally, whenever the marginal benefits of a more refined experiment do not exceed the marginal costs and the experiment is probative, the substantial-similarity requirement should be deemed satisfied.

Although some opinions adopt such an approach to finding substantial similarity, others treat the requirement as stating a preference for duplicating conditions to the greatest extent feasible. Yet, many useful experiments fall short of this Procrustean demand, and the courts that speak in these terms usually do not exclude an experiment just because a slightly more fastidious one could have been conducted. One device that they use to achieve a sensible result is to accept experiments elucidating "properties" as falling outside the rule demanding maximum similarity. As we have seen, that rule is applicable to efforts to re-create or simulate an accident or other event that is the subject of the litigation.

To confine the substantial-similarity rule to re-creations and simulations, however, one needs some principle that explains what makes the experimental findings pertain to general properties or traits and why a more detailed simulation is unnecessary. For instance, in *Council v. Duprel*,[3] the Supreme Court of Mississippi held an experiment with herbicides admissible, because it "was not an effort to duplicate the conditions existing on appellant's farm" but merely an attempt "to establish the fact that 2,4-D is far more destructive to cotton than 2,4,5-T."[4] Of course, the question for the jury was whether 2,4-D was more destructive on appellant's farm, and an experiment could have been designed to control for possible differences in soil conditions, humidity, and other

---

[3]   165 So. 2d 134 (Miss. 1964).

[4]   *Id.* at 150.

variables. But if the herbicidal quality of the chemical is largely independent of these variables, it can be considered a general property, and controlling for those variables would have been of little value. Thus, deciding when an experiment is acceptable as an investigation of a "property" as opposed to a re-creation of the conditions of the accident involves the same inquiry as deciding when the experimental conditions are substantially similar to the ones of interest.

In short, whether the experiment is an effort at re-creation or a study of general properties, the core question is whether matching the variables that are different would make the experiment so much more revealing as to be worth the additional effort and expense. Focusing directly on marginal costs and benefits gives some definition to the substantial-similarity test; indeed, it makes that language superfluous.

§ 202.3 Pretrial Experiments—Procedural Improvements

In view of the widespread use of experiments to re-create or simulate accidents, explosions, product failures, and some crimes, it is appropriate to consider procedures to improve the design and implementation of case-specific experiments before they are conducted. Consideration might be given to excluding experiments unless the adversary has had reasonable notice, an opportunity to make suggestions, and to be present during the experiment. Also worthy of consideration is appointment by the court of an impartial person to conduct or supervise an experiment. Such prophylactic procedures could lead to findings that would invite much less in the way of time-consuming or distracting attack and defense at trial.

§ 203 Standards for Admitting Scientific Evidence

To deal effectively with scientific evidence, attorneys must know more than the rules of evidence. They must know something of the scientific principles as well. Although they can rely on suitably chosen experts for advice about the more arcane points, they must have a sufficient grasp of the field to see what is essential and what is unnecessary detail and verbiage if they are to develop or counteract the evidence most effectively. In one product liability case, counsel's complaint that an expert's calculations of energy and pressure—using formulas in existence for centuries—should have been excluded as "scientific 'Sanskrit' " provoked this lecture from the Court of Appeals:

> Law must apply itself to the life of a society driven more and more by technology and technological improvements. Judges and lawyers do not have the luxury of functional illiteracy in either of these two cultures [the sciences and humanities]. Sometimes, as in this case, effective presentation, cross-examination, and evaluation of expert testimony require lawyers and judges to fill in gaps in their scientific, engineering, or mathematics educations or refresh their memories about them.[5]

In this chapter, we cannot explore in any depth the vast body of knowledge that comes into play in the forensic applications of science and medicine. Only a superficial sampling of a few areas will be attempted. We shall focus on some of the problems that can arise in making measurements and in interpreting data. Sections 204 through 207.2 deal with laboratory, clinical, or field tests (organized somewhat arbitrarily by scientific discipline) in which statistical analysis of the data does not play a major role. Sections

---

[5]   Lapsley v. Xtek, Inc., 689 F.3d 802, 811 (7th Cir. 2012).

208 through 211 concern studies in which statistical analyses are prominent. In the remainder of this section, we discuss some general points concerning the admissibility of all such evidence and the weight that it should receive.

Most of the case law centers on the threshold question of admissibility. The principles of relevancy outlined in Chapter 16 are as applicable to scientific evidence as to any other kind, and the doctrines governing all expert testimony discussed in Chapter 3 operate here as well. The screening of scientific evidence under these general principles can be described as a relevancy-helpfulness review. However, many courts apply a more specialized rule for admissibility when expert witnesses are called to testify about scientific tests or findings. Two approaches are dominant—general acceptance and scientific soundness. Under the former, the proponent must show that the scientific community agrees that the principles or techniques on which the expert relies are capable of producing accurate information and conclusions. Under the latter standard, general acceptance remains an important consideration, but the court must consider other factors to decide for itself whether the expert's methodology is scientifically valid. Both the general-acceptance and the scientific-soundness tests require a binary determination. Evidence either possesses the necessary quality and is admissible (subject to the other rules of evidence), or it lacks the essential quality and is inadmissible. A third approach—the relevancy-plus standard—considers the degree of general acceptance, the extent of scientific soundness, and still other factors in evaluating probative value for the case at bar.

§ 203.1   Standards for Admitting Scientific Evidence—the General-Acceptance Requirement

The notion of a special rule for scientific evidence originated in 1923 in *Frye v. United States*.[6] Frye was a murder prosecution in which the trial court rebuffed defendant's effort to introduce results of a "systolic blood pressure test," a forerunner of the polygraph. On appeal, the defendant relied on the traditional rule governing expert testimony, but the Court of Appeals for the District of Columbia, without explanation or precedent, superimposed a new standard:

> Just when a scientific principle or discovery crosses the line between the experimental and demonstrable stages is difficult to define. Somewhere in this twilight zone the evidential force of the principle must be recognized, and while courts will go a long way in admitting expert testimony deduced from a well-recognized scientific principle or discovery, the thing from which the deduction is made must be sufficiently established to have gained general acceptance in the particular field in which it belongs.[7]

The opinion did not state clearly whether "the thing" that needed "to have gained general acceptance" was the link between conscious insincerity and changes in blood pressure or the ability of an expert to measure and interpret the changes, or both. The court concluded, however, that the deception test lacked the requisite "standing and scientific recognition among physiological and psychological authorities."[8]

---

[6]   293 F. 1013 (D.C. Cir. 1923).

[7]   *Id.* at 1014.

[8]   *Id.*

Many courts adopted the *Frye* standard in the ensuing years with scant discussion. The theories or tests that have fallen prey to its influence at one time or another include polygraphy, graphology, hypnotic and drug induced testimony, voice stress analysis, voice spectrograms, various forms of chemical spectroscopy or inferences from the spectra, infrared sensing of aircraft, retesting of breath samples for alcohol content, computer simulations of the movements of bodies in accidents, psychological profiles of battered women and child abusers, post traumatic stress disorder as indicating rape, effect of "weapon focus" on eyewitness identification, penile plethysmography as indicating sexual deviancy, the Personality Assessment Inventory test as indicating hypervigilance, therapy to recover repressed memories, astronomical calculations, ear prints, blood-group typing, and DNA testing. In the jurisdictions that follow *Frye*, the proponent of the evidence must prove general acceptance by surveying scientific publications, judicial decisions, or practical applications, or by presenting testimony from scientists as to the attitudes of their fellow scientists.

§ 203.2 Standards for Admitting Scientific Evidence—the Retreat from General Acceptance

Especially since the early 1970s, the *Frye* standard was subjected to critical analysis, limitation, modification, and finally, outright rejection. Some courts found the *Frye* standard satisfied in the teeth of expert testimony that the technique in question was too new and untried and the test results too inconclusive for court use. While asserting the continuing vitality of the *Frye* standard, other courts held that general acceptance goes to the weight rather than the admissibility of the evidence. Still others reasoned that the standard applies only to tests for truthfulness, to relatively esoteric applications of science, to the "hard sciences" or to very general principles or methodology rather than to the body of studies or results being applied to reach a conclusion in the case at bar. Many opinions simply ignored the standard, and many others blithely equated it with a requirement of showing the accuracy and reliability of the scientific technique. Finally, in the 1970s and 1980s, a strong minority of jurisdictions expressly repudiated *Frye*.

The adoption of the Federal Rules of Evidence intensified the retreat from *Frye*. These rules do not explicitly distinguish between scientific and other forms of expert testimony, and they do not mention general acceptance. As originally adopted, Rule 702 majestically provided that "[i]f scientific, technical, or other specialized knowledge will assist the trier of fact to understand the evidence or to determine a fact in issue, a witness qualified as an expert by knowledge, skill, experience, training, or education, may testify thereto . . . ." Some courts construed the omission of any direct reference to "general acceptance" as evincing a legislative intent to overturn the well-established common law requirement.

§ 203.3 Standards for Admitting Scientific Evidence—the Scientific-Soundness Requirement

Although the more convincing view is that the federal rules left the viability of the general-acceptance standard open to further common law development, in *Daubert v. Merrell Dow Pharmaceuticals*,[9] the Supreme Court determined that the rules

---

9   509 U.S. 579 (1993).

"superseded" *Frye*[10] and "displaced" general acceptance as "the exclusive test for admitting expert scientific testimony."[11] Plaintiffs in *Daubert* were two young children born with missing or malformed limbs. Together with their parents, they sought damages from the maker of Bendectin, a drug approved by the Food and Drug Administration as safe and effective for the relief of nausea and vomiting during pregnancy. Plaintiffs' case foundered when they were unable to point to any published epidemiological studies concluding that Bendectin causes limb reduction defects. The district court granted summary judgment for Merrell Dow, and the Ninth Circuit Court of Appeals affirmed on the theory that under *Frye*, there could be no admissible expert testimony of causation without some peer-reviewed, published studies showing a statistically significant association between exposure to Bendectin and limb reduction defects. Having determined that *Frye* no longer governed, the Supreme Court remanded the case to the court of appeals, which adhered to its original decision on other grounds.

However, the Supreme Court did not simply hold, as had the courts in a significant minority of federal and state jurisdictions, that with *Frye*'s demise, the relevancy-plus standard governs scientific expert testimony. Instead, it read into the phrase "scientific . . . knowledge" in Rule 702 a requirement of a "body of known facts or . . . ideas inferred from such facts or accepted as truths on good grounds" in accordance with "the methods and procedures of science."[12] In addition, the Court emphasized that scientific analysis must "fit" the facts of the case.[13] The Court then offered an abstract discussion of how the requirement of scientifically "good grounds" might be satisfied. It suggested inquiring into such matters as the degree to which a theory has been tested empirically, the extent to which it has been "subjected to peer review and publication," the rate of errors associated with a particular technique, and the extent of acceptance in the scientific community.[14]

Following this 1993 opinion, an untold number of lower court opinions have elaborated on such factors. The Supreme Court soon discussed their application in another toxic tort case, *General Electric Company v. Joiner*,[15] and then again in *Kumho Tire Co. v. Carmichael*,[16] a fatal automobile accident case that turned on an engineer's opinion that a tire failed because of a manufacturing defect. In 2000, an amendment to Rule 702 codified the major themes of these opinions. The current rule, which governs all expert testimony, demands that: "(a) the expert's . . . specialized knowledge will help the trier of fact to understand the evidence or to determine a fact in issue; (b) the testimony is based on sufficient facts or data; (c) the testimony is the product of reliable principles and methods; and (d) the expert has reliably applied the principles and methods to the facts of the case."

---

[10]   *Id.* at 589 n.6.

[11]   *Id.* at 589.

[12]   *Id.* at 590.

[13]   *Id.* at 591.

[14]   *Id.* at 594.

[15]   522 U.S. 136 (1997).

[16]   526 U.S. 137 (1999).

§ 203.4 Standards for Admitting Scientific Evidence—Assessment of the Requirements

Frye's general-acceptance standard and *Daubert*'s scientific-soundness inquiry do not exhaust the range of "tests" for scientific evidence, and neither opinion offers any reasons for choosing among the many possibilities. Proponents of the general-acceptance test argue that it assures uniformity in evidentiary rulings, that it shields juries from any tendency to treat novel scientific evidence as infallible, that it avoids complex, expensive, and time-consuming courtroom dramas, and that it insulates the adversary system from novel evidence until a pool of experts is available to evaluate it in court. Most commentators agree, however, that these objectives can be met with less drastic constraints on the admissibility of scientific evidence. In addition to the *Daubert* approach of looking directly to reliability or validity rather than to the presence or absence of general acceptance, it has been suggested that a panel of scientists rather than judges screen new developments for validity or acceptance, that a substantial acceptance test be substituted for the general acceptance standard, that scientific evidence be admitted freely, coupled with testimony of an expert appointed by the court if it finds that the testimony would be subject to substantial doubt in peer review by the scientific community, and that the traditional standards of relevancy and the need for expertise—or a somewhat more detailed relevancy-plus analysis—should govern.

The last method for evaluating the admissibility of scientific evidence is the most appealing. General scientific acceptance is a proper condition for taking judicial notice of scientific facts, but it is not suitable as a determinant of the admissibility of scientific evidence. Any relevant conclusions supported by a qualified expert witness should be received unless there are distinct reasons for exclusion. These reasons are the familiar ones of prejudicing or misleading the jury or consuming undue amounts of time.

This traditional approach to the evidence does not make scientific testimony admissible on the say-so of a single expert. Neither does it go to the other extreme of insisting on a fully formed scientific consensus. It permits general scientific opinion of both underlying principles and particular applications to be considered in evaluating the worth of the testimony. In so treating the yeas and nays of the members of a scientific discipline as but one indication of the validity, accuracy, and reliability of the technique, the traditional balancing method focuses the court's attention where it belongs—on the actual usefulness of the evidence in light of the full record developed on the power of the scientific test.

Furthermore, unlike the general-acceptance standard and the scientific-soundness "validity assessment" as it is usually performed, the relevancy approach is sensitive to the perceived degree of prejudice and unnecessary expense associated with the scientific technique in issue. Not every scrap of scientific evidence carries with it an aura of infallibility. Some methods, like handwriting identification and ascertaining the trajectories of bullets, are demonstrable in the courtroom. When the methods involve principles and procedures that are comprehensible to a jury, the concerns over the evidence exerting undue influence and inducing a battle of the experts have less force. On the other hand, when the nature of the technique is more esoteric, as with some types of statistical analyses and chemical tests, when subjective judgments are misleadingly presented as hard science, or when the inferences from the scientific evidence sweep broadly or cut deeply into sensitive areas, a stronger showing of scientific validity (and hence probative value) should be required. This could result in the categorical exclusion of certain types of evidence, such as polygraphic lie detection and statements made while under the influence of a "truth" serum. By attending to such considerations, the rigor of the requisite foundation can be adjusted to suit the nature of the evidence and the context and manner in which it is offered.

Using a legal standard that recognizes that scientific validity and acceptance are matters of degree rather than yes-or-no judgments diminishes the severity of many of the problems that have plagued the general acceptance and scientific soundness standards. Courts in *Frye* and *Daubert* jurisdictions have been forced to draw (and tempted to manipulate) an often obscure line between "scientific" evidence and other expert or lay testimony. Focusing at the outset on the costs and benefits of the particular evidence makes it less crucial to decide exactly when evidence is so "scientific" or "novel" that the special test for novel scientific evidence applies. Similarly, predictability is not easily attained in the face of ambiguity and disagreement as to how general the acceptance in the scientific community must be, who can speak for that community, and the "particular field" to which the scientific evidence belongs and in which it must be accepted. Although such issues arise under any effort to assess the probative value of scientific evidence, they are less critical when a court can consider the number of fields in which a technique is used, the rigor required in those fields, and the degree of its acceptance in those fields, without having to label the technique as generally accepted. Finally, attending to the probative value of conclusions as well as methodologies softens the brittle distinction between the two that can be awkward to apply in *Frye* jurisdictions (and in *Daubert* jurisdictions that have not softened the distinction by later decisions or amendments to their rules of evidence).

Of course, it might be argued that the relevancy-plus approach is no less amorphous and manipulable than the general-acceptance and scientific-soundness standards. There is truth in this charge, but courts and commentators have identified the varied considerations that determine the balance of probative value and prejudice of scientific evidence. Applying these to various types of scientific evidence offers a more honest and sensitive basis for making admissibility decisions than the more cramped tests that have characterized this area of the law of evidence.

Whatever the standard for admissibility may be in a particular jurisdiction, arguments as to the weight that the jury should give to the evidence will be important. Indeed, skills in building cases with admissible scientific evidence and demolishing these same structures have become valuable as the forensic applications of science have grown more commonplace. Attention to possible infirmities in the collection and analysis of data can cut superficially impressive scientific evidence down to its proper size. To begin with, one might consider the process by which the forensic scientist makes raw measurements. Does subjective judgment play an important role? If so, are standards to guide the process of reaching conclusions in place? Do different experts tend to find very different measured values, so that the measurement process is unreliable? Are the variations randomly distributed about some true mean, or are they biased in one direction or another? Are enough replicate measurements made in light of the variability of individual measurements? Then there are problems of interpretation. Is the quantity being measured the real item of interest, or at least a suitable proxy for that variable? Are the inferences drawn from the measurements adequately supported? In brief, considering the probable errors introduced at each stage of the scientific analysis, is the final result likely to be reliable, accurate, and meaningful? The remainder of this chapter describes particular scientific (and pseudo-scientific) tests and studies both with regard to these weight-related factors and to the validity of the reasoning of the scientific experts who bring their specialized knowledge and training to the courtroom.

Before turning to particular areas and types of scientific evidence, however, one additional feature of scientific evidence deserves mention. The fundamental problem of scientific expert testimony is that judges and juries are compelled to evaluate scientific claims with little or no prior knowledge of the field. We call on scientists because they have knowledge that legal decision makers lack, then we ask those decision makers to evaluate intelligently that mysterious knowledge. How can they perform this task without becoming "amateur scientists"?[17] Procedures permitting and encouraging professional scientists to contribute their expertise to screening and assessing scientific evidence can help resolve this conundrum. In particular, requiring adequate pretrial disclosure of the witness's scientific reasoning in written form and adequate detail for review by other scientists would be valuable. And, a century of calls for court-appointed, testifying experts or expert advisers or managers may have had some effect.

II. PARTICULAR TESTS

§ 204 Physics and Electronics: Speed Detection and Recording

Forensic applications of physics and electronics include motor vehicle accident reconstruction, analysis of tape recordings, and detecting and recording speed and other aspects of the movements of vehicles. This section surveys the evidentiary features of speed detection and recording devices.

§ 204.1 Physics and Electronics: Speed Detection and Recording— Mechanical Timing Devices

The branch of classical mechanics that deals with the motion of objects is called kinematics. The physicist defines average velocity as the distance travelled along a given direction in a specified time period divided by the length of this time period. Speed is the absolute value of velocity. (The difference between speed and velocity is that the latter includes information as to the direction of travel, while the former merely states how fast the object is moving.) Average acceleration is the change in velocity for a unit of time divided by the time elapsed. It states how quickly an object is speeding up, slowing down, or changing direction. Measuring such quantities without some mechanical aid is difficult to do accurately, although it can be easy enough to ascertain whether one vehicle is moving faster or slower than another. A more elaborate application of these principles of kinematics to the detection and conviction of traffic offenders is recorded in an English case at the turn of the century in which a constable took readings from a watch with a second hand.[18] A progression of more sophisticated timing mechanisms followed, from the stopwatch, as employed by a stationary observer or by observers in aircraft, to the Visual Average Speed Computer and Record (VASCAR). When a suspected violator's vehicle reaches a clearly marked point, such as an intersection, the operator activates the timer. When the police car reaches the same point, the operator activates a mechanism for recording the distance the police car travels as measured by its odometer. When the target vehicle reaches a second clearly marked point down the road, the police officer shuts off the timer, and when the police car arrives at this second point, he turns

---

17   *Daubert*, 509 U.S. at 601 (Rehnquist, C.J., concurring in part and dissenting in part).
18   Gorham v. Brice (1802) 18 T.L.R. 424 (K.B. Div.).

off the distance switch. The computer divides the measured distance by the measured time elapsed and displays this average speed.

Initially, the courts required expert testimony concerning the principles and operation of the VASCAR. However, the kinematic principles, which date back to the time of Galileo and Newton, are so well established that they, like the ability of an electronic computer to divide two numbers, easily can be the subject of a kind of judicial notice. The more serious issue, which goes to the weight and (in an extreme case, the admissibility) of the evidence, is the accuracy of the device under operational conditions. Errors can arise from a poorly calibrated odometer, from turning on and off the switches at the wrong times, and so on. A foundation indicating that the device is properly calibrated and the operator well trained in its use is usually required.

§ 204.2 Physics and Electronics: Speed Detection and Recording— Tachographs and Event Data Recorders

A speed detector and recorder not so closely tied to police work is the tachograph. It consists of a tachometer and a recording mechanism that furnishes, over time, the speed and mileage of the vehicle to which it is attached. It is used on trains, trucks and busses. Its readings have been admitted in civil and criminal cases, on a showing the particular device works accurately and an identification of which portion of the record generated pertains to the events in issue.

A more advanced kinematic recording instrument is the aircraft flight recorder. It records time, airspeed, altitude, attitude (orientation of axes relative to some reference line or plane, such as the horizon), magnetic heading, vertical acceleration, and other instrument readings. These records can be extremely valuable in analyzing aircraft crashes. Admissibility turns on evidence of authenticity and expert testimony to explain how the machine operates and to interpret the marks on the chart.

Similar devices, known as Event Data Recorders, are installed in trains and some commercial and private trucks, buses, and automobiles. Some devices record specific data on sudden deceleration and air bag deployment. Others reveal when a train's bell and horn are activated. To date, no serious doubts have been raised about the general acceptance or validity of Event Data Recorders for recording information immediately before crashes. Naturally, foundational evidence that the instruments are performing as expected and recording the events in question is necessary.

§ 204.3 Physics and Electronics: Speed Detection and Recording— Radar

Radar equipment provides another means of measuring velocity. Military or aircraft pulse-type radar uses the velocity-distance-time relationships previously discussed. The radar antenna transmits microwave radiation in pulses. The equipment measures the time it takes for a pulse to reach the target and for its echo to return. The fact that the radiation travels at a known speed (the speed of light) fixes the distance to the target. The changes in the distances as determined from the travel times of later pulses permit the target's velocity to be computed. Police radar, however, relies on different principles. In its simplest form, the radar speedmeter used by police agencies transmits a continuous beam of microwaves of uniform frequency, detects the reflected signals, and measures the difference in frequency between the transmitted and reflected beams. It converts this frequency difference into the speed of the object that has reflected the radiation. This conversion is based on the Doppler effect. Electromagnetic radiation coming from an object moving relative to the observer is shifted to a higher frequency if the object is approaching, and to a lower frequency if the object is receding. For the range of velocities of interest in traffic court, the extent of this Doppler shift is directly proportional to the relative speed. When the radar set is at rest relative to the ground, it therefore gives the speed of the vehicle being tracked.

A more complicated version of the Doppler shift detector processes signals received at two distinct frequencies. This refinement allows the unit to be used conveniently in a moving vehicle. The shift in frequency of the beam as reflected off the road surface gives the speed of the police vehicle. The shift in frequency as reflected off the target vehicle gives its speed relative to the police car. In effect, circuitry in the radar unit adds the relative speed to the police car's speed to yield the ground speed of the target.

Most of the early cases admitting radar evidence of speeding involved testimony showing not only that the target car had been identified and that a qualified operator had obtained the reading from a properly functioning device, but also explaining the Doppler effect, its application in the radar speedmeter, and the scientific acceptance of this method of measuring speed. Within a few years, the courts began to take a type of judicial notice of the underlying scientific principles and the capability of the device to measure speed with tolerable accuracy. Expert testimony on these subjects is no longer essential.

The question of what must be proved to establish that the specific instrument was operating accurately has provoked more controversy. Decisions range from holdings that the evidence is inadmissible without independent verification of the accuracy of the system at the time and place of the measurement to holdings that lack of evidence of testing goes to the weight but not the admissibility of the results. In many jurisdictions, statutes provide for admissibility and specify the requisite type of showing of accuracy. Revelations that police radar units operating under field conditions may not be as reliable as had once been assumed underscore the importance of demonstrating the accuracy of the equipment.

Regardless of whether the jurisdiction has a particularized rule for the extent and type of testing needed for admissibility, evidence pertaining to the accuracy of the reading is admissible. There are many ways in which errors can creep into the system. Stationary radar readings will be wrong if the transmission frequency changes, if the receiver misevaluates the frequency difference, if the radar is not held motionless, or if radiation from another source is attributed to the suspect's vehicle. Moving radar, being a more complex device, has more room for error. Acceleration of the patrol car, "cosine error," and "shadowing" can lead the instrument to underestimate the patrol car's speed, and hence to overstate the target vehicle's speed.

Some of these sources of error can be minimized or excluded by careful operating procedures and on-site tests. These include the use of tuning forks vibrating at frequencies such that their linear motions will cause the speedmeter to register particular speeds if it is receiving properly, use of an internal, electronically activated tong for the same purpose, and simply checking that, when aimed at another police car, the radar reading corresponds with that car's speedometer reading. Of course, after a few years of use, tongs may not vibrate at the presumed frequency, an internal oscillator may need adjustment, and a car's speedometer may not be accurate. At least on the question of admissibility, however, most courts recognize that independent errors are unlikely to be identical. They tend to hold that some combination of these methods is sufficient to warrant admissibility. Furthermore, a number of decisions, sometimes aided by statute, hold that tested radar readings can amount to proof beyond a reasonable doubt.

§ 204.4 Physics and Electronics: Speed Detection and Recording— Laser Pulses

Yet another device uses a laser to generate many pulses of infrared radiation per second. Like pulse radar, laser-based speed detection uses the reflection times of the pulses to determine the speed of the reflecting object via the distance-time-velocity formulas. The physical principles that the device relies on are eminently sound, and the only possible ground for questioning the scientific basis of such speed measurements is whether the instrument properly implements them. After some hesitation, the courts have agreed that laser devices can measure vehicular speed accurately. Indeed, not only do some courts accept the general principles of laser-based speed detection, but they even dispense with hearings on the general acceptance or validity of specific instruments and admit the evidence when the proponent demonstrates compliance with the manufacturer's recommendations for proper operation and calibration. The better view, however, is that "[a]lthough the underlying principles of laser technology may be the same from one device to another, generally judicial notice as to the reliability of a speed-measuring device is device-specific."[19] That is, the proponent of the evidence should bear the burden of showing that the instrumentation validly implements the recognized scientific principles to produce reliable measurements of speed, either indirectly—by evidence of general acceptance (in *Frye* jurisdictions)—or directly—by evidence of scientific soundness (in *Daubert* jurisdictions). Only after a suitable period of judicial acceptance without significant controversy should a court rely on previous opinions as the sole basis for establishing general scientific acceptance or validity for instrumentation. As with radar and other instruments that measure speed, once the general acceptance and validity of both the theory and the measuring instrument have been established, the case-specific issues of the accuracy and authenticity of particular measurements may be subject to further rules.

§ 205 Biology and Medicine

The forensic applications of the biological sciences and medicine are far too extensive and varied to be discussed fully here, but we shall consider two groups of laboratory tests of biological samples that commonly provide crucial evidence. These are chemical tests for drunkenness and for DNA types. In addition, we describe immunogenetic and other tests for blood and tissue types that were the precursors of the modern DNA tests.

§ 205.1 Biology and Medicine—Drunkenness

Physiologically, the amount of alcohol in the brain determines the degree of intoxication. Except in an autopsy, however, a direct measurement of this quantity is not feasible. Nevertheless, samples of blood, urine, saliva, or breath can be taken, and the alcohol level in these samples can be measured. Using these measurements to determine whether a person is intoxicated raises two technical problems—the accuracy

---

[19]   State v. Starks, 964 N.E.2d 1058 (Ohio Ct. App. 2011).

of the measurement itself and the relationship between the concentration of alcohol in the sample and the degree of intoxication.

Analysis of blood samples gives the most accurate results. Various chemical and other techniques are available to measure the concentration of ethyl alcohol in the sample. When proper procedures are followed and the sample is correctly obtained and preserved, these give reliable estimates. Of course, there is always room for error in measurements. Estimates are not necessarily true values. Good scientific practice requires that the probable range of errors that arise even when chemical or other tests are performed properly be quantified and described along with the more familiar "point estimates" of alcohol concentration long encountered in court.

Even where the measured values are very precise, moving from an estimated value for the blood alcohol concentration (BAC) to the degree of intoxication during the crucial period creates uncertainty. Substantial variability in tolerances for alcohol, absorption rates, and clearance rates, both among individuals and within the same individual from one situation to another, complicates efforts to deduce the true extent of intoxication at the time of an arrest or accident. In particular, one cannot assume that BAC inevitably is higher at the time of an accident than it is afterwards, for the concentration rises after drinking, then drops. Extrapolations based on direct measurements of BAC therefore seem more perilous than is generally recognized, and there have been suggestions that BAC should be measured at several different times to ascertain whether the first reading is from the early period of rising BAC or the later period of declining BAC. However, even with two measurements, the situation may not be clearcut.

Determinations resting exclusively on concentration of alcohol contained in a sample of breath (BrAC) pose additional problems. To be sure, various instruments have been shown to be accurate in measuring BrAC in laboratory studies, and arguments that particular instruments are not generally accepted or sufficiently accurate for the purpose of determining BrAC usually fail. As with tests of blood, however, errors can arise from operating conditions, individual biological variability, and extrapolation to the time in question. Moreover, there is an inherent problem with breath testing. A formula must be used to convert BrAC to BAC. Traditionally, a single number is used as a multiplier in making this conversion, but the true value of this parameter is debatable. Certainly, the conversion ratio varies among individuals and even within the same individual over time. Although most studies suggest that the conventional figure of 2100 tends to understate the blood alcohol level, a small fraction of individuals will have blood alcohol concentrations that are lower than those deduced from this value. Nevertheless, the use of the single proportionality constant for all individuals remains contentious, particularly as more of the variables that affect the conversion ratio are becoming known.

These cautions concerning the scientific proof do not necessarily make the blood and breath test evidence inadmissible. On the contrary, when the tests are properly conducted and analyzed, the evidence can be of great value in deciding questions connected with intoxication. Since the general links from breath-alcohol concentration to blood-alcohol level to intoxication, as well as the accuracy of measurements made under ideal conditions are well established, under the usual principles governing scientific evidence, the test results should be admissible if founded on a showing of authenticity and satisfactory care in the collection of the sample and its analysis. Expert testimony ordinarily would be needed to establish that the party with the measured or inferred BAC was intoxicated during the period in question. Some courts have emphasized the need for care in admitting retrograde extrapolations, but arguments that all extrapolations are so uncertain as to be inadmissible under *Frye* or *Daubert* have not prevailed.

In the context of traffic offenses, specialized statutes and regulations provide shortcuts to the application of the common law principles and evidence codes in determining the admissibility of blood and breath test evidence. In proceedings involving driving or control of a vehicle while under the influence of intoxicating liquor, these laws typically make chemical test evidence of BAC admissible as long as it is obtained by certified persons following procedures that the state department of health or the state police have prescribed. If the procedures are sufficiently rigorous, then, under the first wave of statutes, the results of this testing would trigger two rebuttable presumptions: if BAC at the relevant time was at or above a specified level (such as 0.08%), that the individual was under the influence; and if BAC was at or below a smaller level (such as 0.05%), that he was not. An intermediate reading usually was deemed "competent evidence" for consideration along with the other evidence in the case. In most jurisdictions, a party offering test results pursuant to such a statute had to lay a foundation by producing witnesses to explain how the test was conducted, to identify it as duly approved under the statutory scheme, and to vouch for its correct administration in the particular case.

By the early 1980s, as concern with the carnage due to drunken driving escalated, nearly all states placed still more emphasis on chemical testing by providing for the admissibility of BrAC measurements obtained with approved equipment and procedures, and all states have enacted "per se" laws making it a crime to drive while having a BAC or BrAC (or in several states, a urine alcohol concentration) in excess of a specified amount. Some of these statutes create a presumption that BAC is equal to or greater than BrAC, simplifying the prosecution's case; others seek to circumvent defense challenges to converting BrAC to BAC by redefining the offense in terms of breath rather than blood alcohol. Furthermore, to avoid the need to present testimony extrapolating from later to earlier measurements, some statutes create a presumption as to what the BAC or BrAC was at the time of driving, or leave it to a jury to infer that the concentration exceeded the allowed amount, at least when the test was administered with "a reasonable time." Finally, not content with a permissive inference or presumption, some legislatures even redefined the offense to consist of having a given BAC or BrAC within several hours after operating a motor vehicle. By and large, these laws have weathered constitutional challenges with regard to sampling breath rather than blood and using concentrations a later time without extrapolating backward. The result is a potentially confusing mosaic of laws and rules in which a set of overlapping offenses with various statutory provisions for admitting evidence of BAC or BrAC in traffic cases is superimposed on the more general evidence code or common law rules.

§ 205.2 Biology and Medicine—Blood and Other Tissue Types

Another group of chemical tests—those that identify blood, tissue and DNA types—are often the subject of courtroom testimony. DNA testing has come to dominate the field, but inasmuch as the particularized case law and legislation began in response to blood and tissue typing, we begin with an exposition of the earlier technologies.

Elucidating the biochemical mechanisms by which a multicellular organism distinguishes between self and non-self—between its own cells and foreign substances—is a major research problem in biology. The topic is fundamental to understanding the way in which the body responds to infections from microorganisms, to grafts of foreign tissues or materials, and to blood transfusions, and it is central to the study of allergies, tumors, and autoimmune diseases. Protruding from the surface of cells are various molecules, called in this context, antigens. For instance, individuals with type A blood have the molecule known as an A antigen on their red blood cells. The red blood cells are not the only ones to possess antigens. Human Leucocyte Antigens (HLA) are found on the surface of most human cells, and there is an elaborate nomenclature for these. The full set of antigens that a cell possesses distinguishes it from the cells of other organisms. It is conceivable that each person is uniquely identifiable in this way. In addition to the immunologically crucial antigens, cells and bodily fluids contain chemicals such as enzymes and other proteins that can differ from one person to another.

Most enzymes and serum proteins are identified by a technique called electrophoresis, in which an electric field is applied to separate the molecules according to their electric charge. Although electrophoresis is a standard technique in biochemistry, its application to aged or dried blood stains was marked by controversy. Difficulties arose because thin gel multisystem testing is used only in crime laboratories, because few outside investigations of the effects of aging and environmental contamination were undertaken, and because crime laboratories did not submit to routine proficiency testing. Nevertheless, almost all appellate courts that encountered challenges to electrophoretic identifications concluded that both the multisystem and the more generally used electrophoretic procedures are scientifically accepted and that the findings can be admitted into evidence.

A different type of test is used to detect antigens. The antigens react with other biologically produced molecules, called antibodies. Serologic tests consist of exposing a suspected antigen to its corresponding antibody and observing whether the expected reaction occurs. Errors involving misinterpretation, mislabeling, poor reagents, and the like are always possible, but workers in this field report that with stringent procedures and quality control standards, the risk of error can be made very small.

The forensic use of these tests arose principally in two areas—identifying the perpetrators of violent crimes or sexual offenses from traces of blood or semen, and ascertaining parentage in child support cases, criminal cases, and other litigation. In general, the courts moved from an initial position of mistrust of such evidence to the present stage of taking judicial notice of the scientific acceptance or acceptability of serologic and related tests. From the outset, it was recognized that if the suspect's antigens do not match those in the sample found at the scene of a crime, then the incriminating trace does not consist of his blood. For a considerable time, however, there was a difference of judicial opinion concerning evidence of a match. Since some combinations of antigens are relatively common, a few courts dismissed the positive test results for these antigens as irrelevant. The better view—and the overwhelming majority position—is that positive findings are neither irrelevant nor so inherently prejudicial as to justify a rule against their admission.

Serologic tests have been used in paternity litigation at least since the 1930s. The underlying logic is based on elementary principles of human genetics. Roughly speaking, portions of the DNA contained in the chromosomes of the nucleus of a cell—the genes—

direct the synthesis of proteins. Different versions (or alleles) of these genes oversee the synthesis of the different antigens. Consequently, by ascertaining which antigens are present in an individual (the phenotype), one learns something about that individual's alleles (the genotype). As such, the antigens are genetic markers. Knowing the phenotypes of the child, mother, and putative father and applying the laws of inheritance, a geneticist can say whether it would be possible for a child with the observed phenotype to have been born to the mother and the alleged father. That is, the medical expert can state that the biological father—whoever he may be—must have certain genetic characteristics, which can be compared to those that the alleged father has. In this way, a man falsely accused—one who does not have the necessary characteristics—can be excluded.

With an appropriate foundation, such negative test results are nearly always admissible, although the weight accorded to an exclusion varies. A few cases can be found upholding liability despite serologic proof of nonpaternity. Perhaps the most notorious involved the comedian Charlie Chaplin.[20] In most states, however, a properly conducted blood test that excludes the defendant is conclusive.

Positive immunogenetic findings are another matter. The traditional rule in this country was that serologic tests are inadmissible for this purpose. At one time, when only a few, widely shared antigens were known, this approach made some sense. For example, under the early ABO system, a positive test result merely meant that the accused was, on average, one of the 87% of the male population possessing the requisite genotypes. Such evidence is not very probative, and the fear that the jury would give it more weight than it deserved, cloaked as it was in the garb of medical expertise, prompted many courts to exclude it as unduly prejudicial. With the plethora of genetic markers that became known, however, it was commonplace to determine that the biological father had immunogenetic traits shared by one in several thousand men of the same race. As laboratories came to test reliably for more and more antigens, positive test results became too probative to be ignored.

As a result, evidence that the accused has immunogenetic traits consistent with the claim that he is the biological father was received regularly. In most states, this was a consequence of statutory innovation. In other instances, it was an example of the common law lugubriously digesting a technological advance. The battle over the admissibility of serologic and related tests to prove paternity is over, but disputes over efforts to give an exact statement of the "probability of paternity" linger.[21]

§ 205.3 Biology and Medicine—Principles of DNA Typing

Red blood cell grouping, blood serum protein and enzyme analysis, and HLA typing went a long way toward identifying individuals in suitable cases, but they were overshadowed by forensic adaptations of DNA technology. There is no single method of DNA typing. As with immunogenetic testing, the probative value of the laboratory findings depends on the procedure employed, the quality of the laboratory work, and the genetic characteristics that are discerned. We shall describe some of these procedures and the theory that lies behind them, and then consider the case law.

---

[20] Berry v. Chaplin, 169 P.2d 442, 450–51 (Cal. Ct. App. 1946).
[21] See infra § 211.

DNA is found in all nucleated cells, including those in bodily fluids such as blood and saliva. The DNA molecule has two long strands that spiral around one another, forming a double helix. Within the double helix are units, called nucleotide bases, that link one strand to the other, like the steps of a spiral staircase. There are four of these bases, which can be referred to by their initials, A, T, G and C. The A on one strand pairs with T on the other, and the G bonds to C. The lengthy sequence of AT and GC "stairs" within the DNA includes all the genes and regulatory sequences (for turning certain genes on and off and modulating the output of genes). The genes are mostly a series of base pairs whose order determines the composition of proteins and related products synthesized by various cells. These DNA sequences are called "coding" because the order of the base pairs specifies the order of the subunits that make up the protein that the gene encodes. However, most of the DNA in human beings (and many other organisms) is noncoding. Indeed, much of it has no known function, and even within functional regions, the variants in many sequences from one person to another are of little or no consequence to health or bodily function. But whether functional or not, essentially all the DNA in all of an individual's bodily cells are faithful copies of the genome of the fertilized cell that grew into that individual.

Examining cell surface antigens (such as the ABO and HLA systems) or blood serum enzymes or proteins gives some information about the underlying DNA sequences—if the markers differ, then the DNA must differ. In contrast, DNA typing works with the DNA molecule itself and is not limited to identifying variations in coding sequences. With appropriate technology, one can detect differences in the base pair sequences anywhere in the DNA molecules of human cells. Because 99.9 percent of the DNA sequence in any two people is identical, the technical challenge is to detect the relatively rare stretches of DNA that vary among individuals. Two categories of procedures have been used, and more are under development. In PCR-based testing, small portions of DNA molecules are "amplified" by heating and cooling with an enzyme called DNA polymerase. Even if the sample contains only a small number of DNA molecules to start with, the polymerase induces a chain reaction that generates millions of identical fragments. Various procedures then can be used to characterize these small DNA fragments. Indeed, "massively parallel sequencing" or "next generation sequencing" generates the DNA sequences of many fragments at the same time ("in parallel") and uses computer-intensive computational methods to align the fragment sequences and thus infer the order of the base pairs of practically all of the genome.

§ 205.4　Biology and Medicine—STR Profiling

At present, the most popular PCR-based technology is STR testing. STRs (short tandem repeats) consist of repeated occurrences of a core pattern of a few base pairs. For example, the sequence AATGAATGAATG denotes a small STR consisting of three repeats of AATG on one strand of the DNA molecule. Another individual might have seven repeats at the same location in the genome. The location at which the sequences differ are called "loci," and the variants at each locus are known as "alleles." The STR alleles differ in the number of repeats and hence their lengths—the more repeats, the longer the allele. Electrophoresis separates the fragments according to their size. A graph known as an electropherogram should have peaks that correspond to the pairs of alleles that are present at each locus.

As with serologic tests, individual alleles may be common in the population and hence a given single-locus pair might not be not especially revealing. However, a series of STRs can narrow the percentage of the population that could have been the source of the sample. Testing for ten, twenty, or even more STRs—can be very discriminating.

§ 205.5 Biology and Medicine—Mitochondrial Sequencing

Another form of PCR-based testing uses mitochondrial DNA (mtDNA). Mitochondria are small structures outside of the cell nucleus, in which certain molecules are broken down to supply energy. The mitochondrial genome is minuscule compared to the chromosomal genome in the cell nucleus. However, it has discrete alleles that can be detected with sequencing procedures that determine the order of the base pairs one after the other. The mitochondrial DNA has three features that make it useful for forensic DNA testing. First, the typical cell, which has but one nucleus, contains between 75 to 1,000 identical mitochondria. Hence, for every copy of chromosomal DNA, there usually are hundreds of copies of mitochondrial DNA. This means that it is possible to detect mtDNA in samples containing too little nuclear DNA for conventional typing. Second, the mtDNA contains a region of about a thousand base pairs that varies greatly among most individuals. Finally, mitochondria are inherited mother to child, so that siblings, maternal half-siblings, and others related through maternal lineage possess the same mtDNA sequence. This last feature makes mtDNA particularly useful for associating persons related through their maternal lineage—associating skeletal remains to a family, for example. However, the mt-DNA alleles are not as distinctive as a series of STR alleles; hence, an mtDNA match is much less definitive.

§ 205.6 Biology and Medicine—RFLP-VNTR Profiling

The typing procedure that dominated the first decade or so of forensic DNA cases but was supplanted by the PCR-based methods is known as RFLP (restriction fragment length polymorphism) testing. It involves "digesting" DNA into fragments with enzymes ("restriction enzymes") from bacteria, separating the restriction fragments according to length by gel electrophoresis, blotting the array of fragments onto a nylon membrane, tagging the fragments with a radioactive probe, then placing X-ray film to the membrane to give an image with dark bands at the locations of the tagged fragments. The process can be repeated with other probes, and each probe yields a picture (known as an autoradiogram) with one or two bands. There will be one band if DNA in the sample came from a person who inherited the same allele from each parent; but more commonly, there will be two bands per probe because the individual inherited one allele from one parent and a different allele from the other parent. The locations of the bands from all the probes is the DNA profile seen on an autoradiograph.

With RFLP testing, the region within the long DNA molecules that are profiled depends on the particular combination of probe and restriction enzyme. Within some regions are stretches of DNA known as VNTRs (variable number of tandem repeats). Like STRs, VNTRs result from repetitions of core sequences. However, the repeated units are much longer (about 30 to 60 base pairs), and so are the alleles (which can consist of many thousands of base pairs). A probe that detects the core repetitive sequence will detect these variable length fragments. Because the number of repeating units at a VNTR locus varies greatly within a population, the probes that detect this type of repetitive DNA are exquisitely informative. However, gel electrophoresis is not capable of measuring the lengths of VNTRs down to the level of a single repeat unit. This limitation made for some complications in deciding whether two VNTR bands "match" and how many people in the general population might be found to have similarly matching bands.

A major advantage of the polymerase chain reaction over immunogenetic and RFLP testing is that it requires very little biological material, and it permits smaller (more degraded) DNA fragments to be analyzed. PCR-based procedures also can be automated and take less time to complete. For such reasons, they dominate forensic testing.

§ 205.7 Biology and Medicine—Admissibility of DNA Typing

The judicial reception of DNA evidence can be divided into at least five phases. The first phase was one of rapid acceptance. Initial praise for RFLP testing in homicide, rape, paternity, and other cases was effusive. Indeed, one judge proclaimed "DNA fingerprinting" to be "the single greatest advance in the 'search for truth' . . . since the advent of cross-examination."[22] In this first wave of cases, expert testimony for the prosecution rarely was countered, and courts readily admitted RFLP findings.

In a second wave of cases, however, defendants pointed to problems at two levels—controlling the experimental conditions of the analysis, and interpreting the results. Some scientists questioned certain features of the procedures for extracting and analyzing DNA employed in forensic laboratories, and it became apparent that declaring matches or nonmatches among the RFLPs due to VNTR loci in two samples was not always trivial. Despite these concerns, most cases continued to find forensic RFLP analyses to be generally accepted, and a number of states provided for admissibility of DNA tests by legislation. Concerted attacks by defense experts of impeccable credentials, however, produced a few cases rejecting specific proffers on the ground that the testing was not sufficiently rigorous. Moreover, a minority of courts, perhaps concerned that DNA evidence might well be conclusive in the minds of jurors, added a "third prong" to the general acceptance standard. This augmented *Frye* test requires not only proof of the general acceptance of the ability of science to produce the type of results offered in court, but also of the proper application of an approved method on the particular occasion. Such matters are better handled as aspects of the balancing of probative value and prejudice (that also may be addressed at a pretrial hearing) rather than as an inherent part of the special screening test for scientific evidence.

A different attack on DNA profiling begun in cases during this period proved far more successful and led to a third wave of cases in which many courts held that estimates of the probability of a coincidentally matching VNTR profile were inadmissible. These estimates relied on a simplified population-genetics model for the frequencies of VNTR profiles, and some prominent scientists claimed that the applicability of the mathematical model had not been adequately verified. A heated debate on this point spilled over from courthouses to scientific journals and convinced the supreme courts of several states that general acceptance was lacking. A 1992 report of the National Academy of Sciences proposed a more "conservative" computational method as a compromise, and this seemed to undermine the claim of scientific acceptance of the less conservative procedure that was in general use.

In response to the population-genetics criticism and the 1992 report came an outpouring of critiques of the report and new studies of the distribution of VNTR alleles

---

[22]   People v. Wesley, 533 N.Y.S.2d 643 (County Ct. 1988), aff'd, 589 N.Y.S.2d 197 (App. Div. 1992), order aff'd, 633 N.E.2d 451 (N.Y. 1994).

in many population groups. Relying on the burgeoning literature, a second National Academy panel concluded in 1996 that the usual method of estimating frequencies of VNTR profiles in broad racial groups was sound. In the corresponding fourth phase of judicial scrutiny of DNA evidence, the courts almost invariably returned to the earlier view that the statistics associated with VNTR profiling are generally accepted and scientifically valid.

In a fifth phase of the judicial evaluation of DNA evidence, the courts concluded that the newer PCR-based methods rested on a solid scientific foundation and were generally accepted in the scientific community. Thus, in little more than a decade, DNA typing made the transition from a novel set of methods for identification to a "gold standard" for forensic technology. However, one should not lump all forms of DNA identification together. New techniques and applications continue to emerge. These range from the use of new genetic systems and instrumentation to the typing of DNA from plants and animals. Even with existing systems, efforts to push PCR to its limits in copying DNA fragments from only a few cells ("low template" or "touch" DNA samples) have generated controversy. So have the procedures that analysts follow in interpreting complex mixed stains, including complicated software designed to automate or assist in the interpretive process. Before admitting such evidence, it will be necessary to inquire into the biological and statistical principles and knowledge that would justify inferences from these new technologies or applications.

§ 206   Psychology

The law and its procedures have long attracted the interest of psychologists and psychiatrists. Their preeminent contributions as expert witnesses have come in presenting clinical diagnoses or evaluations in criminal and other cases. Traditionally, such diagnoses were seen as the contributions of skilled witnesses rather than the products of scientific tests and procedures. However, less conventional forensic applications received more searching analyses, and modern courts typically apply the special tests for scientific evidence discussed in Section 203 to evidence derived from psychological and psychiatric theories and tests. In this section, we survey issues arising from expert testimony about physiological indicators of deception, "truth" drugs and hypnosis, eyewitness identifications, and "profiles" of certain types of offenders or victims.

§ 206.1   Psychology—Detection of Deception

Popular belief has it that lying and consciousness of guilt are accompanied by emotion or excitement that expresses itself in bodily changes—the blush, the gasp, the quickened heartbeat, the sweaty palm, the dry mouth. The skilled cross-examiner may face the witness with his lies and involve him in a knot of new ones, so that these characteristic signs of lying become visible to the jury. This is part of the demeanor of the witness that the jury is told it may observe and consider with regard to credibility.

Internal stress also has been thought to accompany the process of lying. It is said that more than 4,000 years ago the Chinese would try the accused in the presence of a physician who, listening or feeling for a change in the heartbeat, would announce whether the accused was testifying truthfully. As explained below, most modern "lie detectors" operate on the same general principle.

§ 206.2 Psychology—Detection of Deception—Theories and Instruments for Lie Detection

While an interrogator puts questions to the suspect, the polygraph monitors and records several autonomic physiological functions, such as blood pressure, pulse rate, respiration rate and depth, and perspiration (by measuring skin conductance). In the most commonly used procedure, the "diagnosis" is made by comparing the responses to "control" questions with the reactions to "relevant" questions. Control questions attempt to force the subject to lie about some common transgression. In an embezzlement case, for instance, a control question might be, "Have you ever stolen anything?" A relevant question is one that relates to the matter under investigation. If the autonomic disturbances associated with the relevant items seem greater or more persistent, then the subject is judged to be dissembling. In making this judgment, most practitioners employ some type of numerical scoring system, and this process may be performed by a computer. Other analysts apply a less structured procedure and insist that polygraphic lie detection is a "clinical judgment" that depends on "intrinsic emotional states," "medical conditions," and "unique" interviews.

The validity and reliability of the control-question test are hotly contested. Polygraph examiners claim that, properly administered, it is a highly effective means of detecting deception, and they cite figures such as 80%, 90%, 95%, 99%, and even 100% for its accuracy. Although some controlled experiments and other studies have been interpreted as showing that such accuracy is possible, most psychologists and other scientists reviewing the literature are not impressed with these bold assertions. They see methodological flaws undermining the conclusions, they suggest figures in a much lower range, and they point out that the percentage figures of "accuracy" are inappropriate measures of validity. Attempts to determine the rate of false positives—of saying that someone is lying when he is actually telling the truth—also have been controversial. Some writers claim that these errors rarely occur but there are also studies and analyses that put the expected rate of false positives in excess of 35%. The skeptics also dispute the underlying theory. At best, the control question technique registers physiological correlates of anxiety, which is not the same thing as consciousness of guilt or lying. Questions can provoke inner turmoil even when they are answered truthfully. As one critic has put it, "the polygraph pens do no special dance when we are lying."[23] In addition, there are numerous countermeasures that a suspect can use to mislead the analyst, some of which are said to be effective and difficult to detect. It is feared that if the polygraph came into widespread use in court cases, these could cause the rate of false negatives—saying that the suspect is telling the truth when he is lying—to become intolerably high.

Another group of devices that measure a physiological response to detect when a person is consciously concealing knowledge are the voice stress analyzers. They analyze the frequency spectrum of a speaker's voice to detect subaudible, involuntary tremors said to result from emotional stress (microtremors). The scientific literature on these lie detection devices indicates that they do not actually measure microtremors and have no validity. Nonetheless, they are used in interrogations. Another technique, known as

---

[23] Lykken, as quoted in Kleinmuntz & Szucko, On the Fallibility of Lie Detection, 17 Law & Soc'y Rev. 85, 88 (1981).

layered voice analysis, which relies on unspecified vocal characteristics, also performs no better than chance in laboratory tests.

Finally, neuroscientists have experimented with instruments that measure blood flow (fMRI) or electrical activity within the brain (EEG). Despite enthusiastic reports from the small number of scientists seeking to use such instruments for detecting deception or memories, robust demonstrations of reliability and validity remain to be seen.

§ 206.3   Psychology—Detection of Deception—Admissibility of Lie-Detector Results

The courts have not greeted the modern methods of lie detection with enthusiasm. Indeed, *Frye v. United States*,[24] the case that announced the general-acceptance standard for the admissibility of scientific evidence, involved a primitive version of the polygraph. In the succeeding decades, many courts treated the early decision as if it established that polygraph results were inadmissible regardless of any improvements in the technology. With the erosion of the general-acceptance requirement and the explosive growth of polygraphy in American government and business, however, a substantial number of courts were willing to take a fresh look at the evidentiary value of the most commonly used polygraph tests. Three principal positions on admissibility have emerged, with considerable back and forth movement into and out of each category. First, there is the traditional rule that the test results are inadmissible when offered by either party, either as substantive evidence or as relating to the credibility of a witness. As a corollary, the willingness or unwillingness of a party or witness to submit to examination is also inadmissible. Second, a substantial minority of jurisdictions have carved out an exception to the rule of unconditional exclusion. In these jurisdictions the trial court has the discretion to receive polygraph testimony if the parties stipulated to the admission of the results prior to the testing and if certain other conditions are met. Third, in a small number of jurisdictions, admission even in the absence of a stipulation is said to be discretionary with the trial judge. Even in most of these jurisdictions, however, admission of unstipulated results is so rare as to be aberrational.

The widespread and strongly rooted reluctance to permit the introduction of polygraph evidence is grounded in a variety of concerns. The most frequently mentioned is that the technique is not generally accepted in the scientific community or is "unreliable" due to inherent failings, a shortage of qualified operators, and the prospect that "coaching" and practicing would become commonplace if the evidence were generally admissible. Because there is intense disagreement in the literature as to the premise that even a truly expert polygrapher is capable of distinguishing truthful statements from intentional falsehoods in realistic situations at rates significantly above chance levels, admissibility under the *Frye* standard is, at best, doubtful. Likewise, whether polygraphy possesses the modicum of demonstrated validity demanded under the federal rules as interpreted in *Daubert v. Merrell Dow Pharmaceuticals*[25] is open to grave question. Estimating a realistic error rate seems to be especially difficult.

Yet, the decisive arguments against admission go beyond the search for the artificial level of "acceptance" or "reliability" compelled by *Frye* and *Daubert*. After all, a great deal of lay testimony routinely admitted is at least as unreliable and inaccurate, and

---

[24]   293 F. 1013 (D.C. Cir. 1923).

[25]   509 U.S. 579 (1993).

other forms of scientific evidence involve risks of instrumental or judgmental error. Rather, the more compelling argument against admissibility adjusts the requisite quantum of acceptance or validity to the type of evidence in question. If the probative value of polygraph readings is slight (or would be if the barriers to admissibility were dropped), then their value easily is outweighed by the countervailing considerations. These counterweights are the danger that jurors would be unduly impressed with the "scientific" testimony on a crucial and typically determinative matter, that judicial and related resources would be squandered in producing and coping with the expert testimony, and that routine admissibility would put undesirable pressure on defendants to forfeit the right against self-incrimination.

Some of these concerns may be overstated, and the miscellaneous other reasons that courts sometimes give for excluding polygraph tests may not withstand analysis. It sometimes is said that polygraph results would not aid the jury because the credibility of a witness is susceptible to resolution without expert testimony. But talk of "prejudice to the jury process," of "usurping the jury's function," and affirmations that "the jury system is not yet outmoded," or that "the jury is the lie detector," may reflect this cramped view of the scope of expert testimony in addition to the previously catalogued concerns. The real issue, of course, is not whether juries can decide which witnesses to believe without polygraph or other such testing, but rather how much this testing would enhance those decisions—and at what cost.

Even from this more balanced perspective, however, opening up the matter to the discretion of the trial courts—without providing more detailed standards than the usual balancing prescription—could lead to untoward results. Nor is the "stipulation-only" approach satisfactory. Whether polygraph testimony should be admitted is doubtful, but if it is to be received, clear standards should be developed as to whether such testimony is admissible solely for impeachment purposes, how important the testimony must be in the context of the other evidence in the case for admissibility to be warranted, what level of training and competence examiners should have, what precautions should be taken against deceptive practices on the part of examinees, and what procedures would be best to give an independent or opposing expert a meaningful opportunity to view or review the examination and analysis. When all is said and done, the game simply does not seem worth the candle. A categorical rule of exclusion for polygraph results is a logical and defensible corollary to the general principles of relevancy.

The case against admitting diagnoses of deception from the newer neuroimaging technologies is even stronger, since such cutting-edge technologies are less well studied yet potentially more impressive to jurors. And voice stress analysis, having less scientific support than polygraphy, is almost universally inadmissible, although some states allow test results to be admitted pursuant to stipulation.

§ 206.4 Psychology—Detection of Deception—Hypnosis and Drugs

Psychologists and psychiatrists have used hypnosis and hypnotic drugs for diagnosis and therapy. Resort to these techniques became prevalent in the treatment of traumatic war neuroses during World War II, and the methods have been applied to the treatment of pain, amnesias, catatonic conditions, and psychosomatic disorders. They have also been employed to test the truthfulness of a witness's testimony as well as to enhance recall.

Although the scientific study of hypnosis began over 200 years ago, a single, satisfactory explanation of the phenomenon has yet to emerge. The scientific studies do make it clear, however, that people who are hypnotized or given "truth serum" do not always tell the truth. Indeed, subjects have been known to feign, quite convincingly, a hypnotized state. Even though some studies suggest that in certain circumstances hypnosis can enhance memory, the effect is not apparent in experimental studies, and it is clear that hypnosis can alter memory. Hypnotized persons are highly suggestible, and some authorities believe that when a hypnotist encourages a subject to relate everything he can possibly remember, the subject produces fragments and approximations of memory in an effort to be cooperative. In addition, the subject may accept as his own recollections distortions inadvertently suggested by the hypnotist. Finally, the hypnotic session may reinforce the witness's confidence in erroneous memories.

Forensic applications of hypnosis can generate a variety of constitutional and evidentiary issues. A party might seek admission of statements a witness made while under hypnosis or narcoanalysis to show directly the existence of certain facts, to impeach or buttress credibility, or to show the basis for a psychiatric or psychological opinion. Similarly, a party might offer the in-court testimony of a previously hypnotized or drugged witness.

The courts have been most reluctant to admit such statements or testimony. In the first case to raise the issue, a California court stated in 1897 that "the law of the United States does not recognize hypnotism."[26] Since then the courts nearly always excluded statements made under hypnosis or narcoanalysis, regardless of whether these statements are offered as substantive evidence or as bearing on credibility.

Posthypnotic testimony as to recollections enhanced or evoked under hypnosis has produced more divergent holdings. A few courts have said that such testimony is generally admissible with objections as to its accuracy bearing on the weight that the finder of fact should give it. But even in these jurisdictions there is a tendency to insist on rigorous safeguards for the hypnotically refreshed memories to be admissible. The far more prevalent view is that testimony about the posthypnotic memories is inadmissible.

There are two exceptions to this per se rule of exclusion. First, the usual rule permits a witness to testify to memories recorded and preserved before the hypnotic session. To that extent at least, the witness remains competent to testify. Under this exception, proof that these memories existed prior to hypnosis must go well beyond a subject's posthypnotic recollections of the timing of his or her memories. Once hypnotized, it may be impossible for the subject to separate untainted, prehypnotic recollections from later, possibly tainted or confabulated memories.

The desirability of this exception is debatable. For a time, California excluded *all* testimony of a hypnotized witness—even testimony consistent with statements made before the hypnotic session. This strict rule responds to the concern that the hypnotic session enhances the witness's confidence in all his recollections, thereby insulating the witness from meaningful cross-examination. The strict rule also obviates the need to determine whether the hypnotic session has tainted the witness's current testimony about the earlier statements or the events. In that regard, courts applying the exception

---

[26]　People v. Ebanks, 49 P. 1049, 1053 (Cal. 1897).

for preserved memories sometimes look for compliance with various safeguards that help establish that the hypnosis does not taint the testimony about prehypnotic statements.

Second, in *Rock v. Arkansas*,[27] the Supreme Court held that the constitution precludes categorical exclusion of the hypnotically refreshed testimony of a criminal defendant who cannot present a meaningful defense without that testimony. Even so, a defendant's testimony may be excluded unless rigorous safeguards are employed during hypnosis.

Most of the courts adopting a per se exclusionary rule for hypnotic and posthypnotic statements relied on the *Frye* test of general scientific acceptance, although the same result can be reached by examining scientific validity under *Daubert* or inquiring directly into the relative costs and benefits of the testimony. Indeed, the more modern cases support their invocation and application of the general acceptance standard by examining scientific testimony or literature on the value of hypnosis for recovering memories and by referring to the usual concerns with scientific evidence—its suspected tendency to over-awe the jury and to consume time and resources—in a matter of particular sensitivity.

When an expert uses narcoanalysis or hypnosis to determine whether a subject is insane, incompetent, or mentally incapacitated, the case for admissibility is much stronger. A few courts have excluded expert opinions based on these techniques, but this position seems difficult to defend even under the restrictive general-acceptance standard. Most courts recognize that the opinions of the experts may be admitted and that the revelation of the details of what the subject said while under hypnosis or drugs is within the trial judge's discretion. Thus, the trial court may permit the expert to give an explanation of the underlying information along with an opinion, but still curb the introduction of the statements made under hypnosis or narcoanalysis.

§ 206.5 Psychology—Eyewitness Testimony

For many years, expert testimony has been received to show that mental disorders may have affected the testimony of eyewitnesses. In the 1970s, criminal defendants also began to call on psychologists to offer expert opinions on the factors that ordinarily influence the reliability of eyewitness identifications. Typically, the expert testifies to generalizations from experiments in which students or other subjects have witnessed a film or other enactment or description of the kind of events that are the subjects of courtroom testimony. In such studies, the accuracy of the recall of faces or facts is then tested under a variety of conditions. The overall findings indicate that such witnesses often make mistakes, that they tend to make more mistakes in cross-racial identifications as well as when the events involve violence or weapons, that errors are easily introduced by misleading questions asked shortly after the witness has viewed the simulated happening, and that the professed confidence of the subjects in their identifications bears no consistent relation to the accuracy of these recognitions.

Testimony about such research findings has been received in some cases and rejected in others. By and large, rejection was the norm, especially in the 1970s and 1980s, when the evidence seemed novel. Given the extreme deference usually accorded trial court decisions on the need for expert testimony, these decisions were almost invariably upheld. By 1990, a handful of appellate courts had held that exclusion of

---

[27]   483 U.S. 44 (1987).

expert testimony on highly pertinent aspects of eyewitness identifications constituted an abuse of discretion or that this testimony is not categorically excluded. But one opinion after another displayed a distinct distaste for such testimony. A few jurisdictions seemed to prohibit it entirely. In 1995, the Court of Appeals for the First Circuit would only say that "[q]uite recently, several circuits have suggested that such evidence warrants a more hospitable reception. . . . It may be that a door once shut is now somewhat ajar."[28] In 1997, the Eleventh Circuit spoke of a continuing "attitude of disfavor"[29] and was unimpressed with "nascent case law more receptive to expert testimony on eyewitness reliability."[30]

The unsympathetic opinions argued that since an appreciation of the limitations on eyewitnesses' perceptions and memory is within the ken of a lay jury, broad-brush psychological testimony about these mechanisms would not appreciably assist the jury and that cross-examination is sufficient to expose unreliable identifications. They pointed also to the standard concerns with scientific evidence—that lay jurors will overstate its importance and that its introduction will entail undue expense and confusion. Some courts were dubious of the scientific validity of the psychological research. The more poorly reasoned opinions spoke of invading the province of the jury.

Nevertheless, the matter could not be disposed of this easily. Concern over the reliability of eyewitness testimony lies at the heart of the Supreme Court's right to counsel and due process decisions in cases involving lineups and other pretrial identification procedures. It may well be that without some counteracting influence, juries give too much weight to the witness's assertions of recognition. Studies consistently expose eyewitness misidentification as the leading cause of false convictions in rape and, to a lesser extent, homicide cases. To contend that juries know how to evaluate the reliability of the identifications without expert assistance, while simultaneously maintaining that the assistance would have too great an impact on the jury's deliberations, smacks of makeshift reasoning. Admittedly, there are dangers— some obvious and some subtle—in translating laboratory and classroom demonstrations of witness fallibility into conclusions about the accuracy of a particular witness's identification in a real-life setting. Nevertheless, it is clear that the researchers have something to offer and that when a case turns on uncorroborated eyewitness recognition, the courts should be receptive to expert testimony about the knowledge, gleaned from methodologically sound experimentation, of the factors that may have produced a faulty identification and that are present in the case at bar. Although the researcher must be circumspect in stating inferences about a particular witness's testimony, the pertinent research findings can assist the jury in evaluating a crucial piece of evidence. While expert testimony on the psychology of eyewitness identifications may not be necessary or appropriate in many cases, in those instances in which the case turns on the eyewitness testimony and the expert's assistance could make a difference, the scientific knowledge generally should be admitted, either through expert testimony or judicial instructions concerning factors affecting eyewitness accuracy that are important to assessing the identification in question and that are not well understood by most jurors.

Indeed, in rejecting the argument that admission of an eyewitness identification made in highly suggestive circumstances—but for which the state was not responsible—

---

[28]   U.S. v. Brien, 59 F.3d 274, 277 (1st Cir. 1995).

[29]   U.S. v. Smith, 122 F.3d 1355, 1357 (11th Cir. 1997).

[30]   *Id.* at 1358.

violates the right to due process of law, the Supreme Court in *Perry v. New Hampshire*,[31] took solace in the fact that in some states "in cases involving eyewitness identification of strangers or near-strangers, trial courts will routinely admit expert testimony [on the dangers of such evidence]."[32] Although it seems doubtful that this practice is truly routine, appellate courts have generally moved from a position of skepticism and hostility to an increasingly open stance toward presenting jurors with the research findings on the psychology of eyewitness testimony. No longer can trial judges summarily reject expert psychological testimony on pertinent factors that influence eyewitness identifications as automatically unhelpful to jurors; a "particularized inquiry" is necessary.

§ 206.6 Psychology—False Confessions

Psychological testimony on the phenomenon of false confessions is functionally and structurally similar to the expert testimony on eyewitness identification discussed in the previous subsection. In both situations, the expert provides background information that might contradict lay impressions and that the jury can apply to the case at hand, if persuaded to do so. The expert normally does not comment directly on the accuracy of identification or the falsity of the confession, but leaves it to the jury to apply the generalizations derived from empirical studies to the particular identification or confession that is presented through other witnesses. This type of testimony has been denominated "social framework" evidence.[33] For false confessions, experts have tried to estimate the prevalence of false confessions (to counteract the assumption that they are rare) and to discover the factors that prompt suspects to confess (which are presented as if they are risk factors for false confessions). Unfortunately, the research on prevalence and risk factors has significant gaps.

As with testimony offered to educate jurors on the fragility of eyewitness identification, the four key issues for admissibility of this false-confession testimony are (1) general acceptance or scientific validity of the relevant research findings; (2) the jurors' pre-existing knowledge; (3) the importance of the confession; and (4) the length and complexity added to the trial. Although prevalence and risk-factor testimony should not be excluded on the basis of the slogan that it usurps the jury's role, whether and when it merits admission in light of these four considerations is an open question.

§ 206.7 Psychology—Profiles and Syndromes

Psychological studies sometimes show a correlation between certain traits or characteristics and certain forms of behavior. When this is the case, one can construct a diagnostic or predictive "profile" for such behavior. For instance, studies of "accident prone" persons indicate that such factors as having poor eyesight, being relatively young or old, and acting impulsively, aggressively or rebelliously are prevalent in this group. Physicians regard certain patterns of physical injuries in children, which they designate the "battered child syndrome," as indicating repeated physical abuse.

Likewise, analysis of individuals apprehended while smuggling drugs through airports shows that these persons tend to arrive from major points of distribution, to

---

[31]   565 U.S. 228 (2012).

[32]   *Id.* at 247 (quoting and adding bracketed material to State v. Clopten, 223 P.3d 1103, 1113 (Utah 2009)).

[33]   Monahan & Walker, Twenty-Five Years of Social Science in Law, 35 Law & Hum. Behav. 72 (2011).

have little or no luggage with them, to look nervously about, to arrive in the early morning, and to have large amounts of cash in small bills. Police often present a flexible version of this profile in describing how a defendant came to their attention, explaining the nature of illegal drug smuggling, or suggesting that the defendant is in fact a courier. Used for the last purpose, this profile evidence usually is inadmissible as evidence of bad character or as an opinion on the defendant's intent.

In civil commitment and criminal proceedings at which a person's dangerousness to others is an issue, unvalidated clinical predictions of violence have long been admitted. In the aftermath of *Daubert*, however, the use of statistical (actuarial) risk assessment instruments has commanded more attention, even in *Frye* jurisdictions.

More generally, we all evaluate information in the light of some set of factors that could be called a "profile." Jurors, for example, can be said to bring to the courtroom their preconceived "profiles" which they then apply to decide who is lying and who is telling the truth, and who is likely to have committed an offense and who is innocent. Although there is no fundamental difference between the psychological and medical profiles and the more common, impressionistic ones, the former may have been derived in a more systematic and structured way and have been tested by verifying that they give correct diagnoses or predictions when applied to new cases. The correlations obtained in such prospective or cross-validated studies measure the validity of the better-defined profiles.

Particularly in criminal cases, litigants have sought to introduce expert testimony as to a long list of profiles said to be scientifically constructed or validated. These include the following:

- The "battered woman syndrome" (BWS) has been invoked to support pleas of self-defense in murder cases, to establish the killing was not premeditated, to buttress defenses of duress in cases in which women aided their abusive partners in criminal activity, to explain inconsistencies in a woman's statements or behavior, and in various other situations. Indeed, prosecutors have found uses for the syndrome, as have civil litigants. Yet, criticism of its scientific underpinnings has been intense.

- Prosecutors in sexual abuse cases have relied on the "rape trauma syndrome" (RTS, a form of post-traumatic stress disorder) or related behaviors that are said to be common among victims of rape to negate a claim of consent, to explain conflicting statements or actions of the complainant, to prove sexual assault. Conversely, defendants have introduced evidence that a complainant did not experience the syndrome's symptoms.

- In sexual abuse cases involving children, prosecutors have relied on a similar "child sexual abuse accommodation syndrome" (CSAAS) to prove the fact of abuse or to explain the child's delay in reporting the abuse, a retraction of the accusation, or other behavior apparently inconsistent with abuse. They also have relied on expert testimony that children who report sexual abuse generally are truthful.

- In child abuse and homicide cases, prosecutors have called witnesses to establish that defendants exhibited the "battering parent syndrome" or "child battering profile" to describe "the type of person who would abuse a child." In the same vein, defendants have pointed to the presence of factors in the profile in other individuals who might have abused the child.

- So too, defendants accused of sexual offenses have offered testimony to the effect that they did not fit the profiles for sexual offenders.

- Prosecutors have offered expert testimony on the characteristics of batterers and the risk factors for lethal domestic violence.

When the plaintiff or the government offers evidence that the defendant fits an incriminating profile, it may be excluded under the rule that prohibits evidence of character to show conduct on a particular occasion. The same reasoning applies when a defendant, seeking to create doubt about his own conduct, produces evidence that another person fits the profile. Yet, arguably the rule should not bar admission in all such cases. After all, the rule against character evidence rests on the premise that the marginal probative value of character traits generally is low while the potential for distraction, time-consumption and prejudice is high. When the profile is not itself likely to arouse sympathy or hostility, the argument for applying the rule against character evidence to prove conduct on a particular occasion is weakened. Conversely, if it were shown that the profile was both valid and revealing—that it distinguishes between offenders and nonoffenders with great accuracy—then the balance might favor admissibility. It is far from clear, however, that any existing profile is this powerful.

When the profile evidence is used defensively (to show good character, to restore credibility, or to prove apprehension in connection with a claim of self-defense), it falls outside of or under an exception to the rule against character evidence. Admissibility then should turn on the extent to which the expert testimony would assist the jury viewed in the light of the usual counterweights. The qualifications of the expert, the degree of acceptance in the appropriate scientific community, the reliability and validity of using the profile for a particular purpose, and the need for the evidence in light of what most jurors know about the behaviors in question thus affect the admissibility and of course the weight of the profile evidence. For example, it is not entirely clear how the "battered woman syndrome" helps show the reasonableness of the use of deadly force within the traditional doctrine of self-defense. The effect of the syndrome evidence in such situations is to redefine the substantive law. This result suggests the need for a stronger scientific base than now exists for the expert testimony.

The form or specificity of the testimony—whether the expert crosses the line between the general and the specific or tries to evaluate the truthfulness of the witness or a class of witnesses—also is important. Even courts that allow generalized or "social framework" testimony to explain what otherwise appear to be abnormal or unusual behavior, often vehemently reject expert opinions on the applicability of the profile or the credibility of a witness in a given case.

In some ways, profile evidence resembles expert testimony describing the results of psychological research into eyewitness identifications and confessions to establish a framework for evaluating the statements of other witnesses-the reports of eyewitnesses or the confessions of defendants. Logically, the variables affecting eyewitnesses and confessions could be presented as defining a profile or syndrome for mistaken identifications or false confessions, but this is not normally done. Perhaps the greater initial receptivity of the appellate courts to psychological profile evidence stems from the fact that this type of testimony seems more like the clinical assessments routinely received from psychologists and physicians. In addition, considering the subject matter of most of the psychological profiles that have come to the attention of the courts, it is likely that a growing sensitivity to women's and children's issues has played a major role.

§ 207 Criminalistics: Identifying Persons and Things

Many of the techniques of scientific criminal investigation, or criminalistics, are aimed at identifying people or things. Fingerprinting, studying the trajectories and characteristics of bullets and firearms, examining questioned documents, detecting and identifying poisons and other drugs, microscopically comparing hairs and fibers, and matching blood stains are among the better known examples. In addition, there is a vast array of less familiar techniques for detecting and analyzing "trace evidence" of criminal or other activity. These include other applications of microanalysis, odontology, anthropology, entomology, and somewhat esoteric chemical and physical tests used in connection with fingerprints, firearms, glass fragments, hair, fibers, adhesive tape, paints, explosions and fires, questioned documents, and recordings.

While most of these methods are unquestionably of great value in many investigations, their use in the courtroom can pose problems. To emphasize the scientific quality of the analysis, or in an effort to be as precise as possible, or in response to demands from the court or counsel, expert witnesses may state the results or implications of their tests in quantitative, probabilistic terms—a practice that causes difficulty for the courts. Furthermore, some analytic procedures or tests are themselves specially adapted or developed for forensic purposes and well known primarily in law enforcement circles. Consequently, the test of general scientific acceptance does not always work well in this context, and this incongruity can result in important opinions on the standards governing the admissibility of scientific evidence. Although newer, technologically sophisticated tests or procedures tend to be validated for forensic use and to receive outside scrutiny, historically much of forensic science has been a practical craft, lacking an academic tradition that prized rigorous validation of methods and assumptions. Two examples—identification of latent fingerprints and spectrographic analysis of human voices—will serve to illustrate these observations.

§ 207.1 Criminalistics: Identifying Persons and Things— Fingerprinting

Fingerprints may have been used as a means of identification in ancient China, but their use in criminal investigations in the Western world only began in the late 19th Century. In the United States, fingerprints were introduced in evidence for the first time in *People v. Jennings*,[34] a 1910 murder trial in Illinois. Four witnesses testified for the prosecution that they had examined thousands of fingerprints in their careers and that the fingerprints in question came from the defendant. The Illinois Supreme Court upheld the resulting conviction, concluding "that there is a scientific basis for the system of finger print identification . . . [and] that this method of identification is in such general and common use that the courts cannot refuse to take judicial cognizance of it."[35] Yet, the ability of examiners to match latent prints—those naturally deposited on paper, metal, glass, or other surface—to rolled, inked prints had never been carefully studied.

---

[34]   96 N.E. 1077 (Ill. 1911).

[35]   *Id.* at 1082.

For nearly a century, neither these studies nor much other fundamental research into the premises and claims of fingerprint examiners was undertaken. This state of affairs created a quandary: if *Frye* requires general acceptance among scientists (as opposed to fingerprint analysts) that the origin of a latent print can be attributed to a single individual with 100% confidence (as fingerprint examiners traditionally reported), or if *Daubert* demands scientific demonstrations of the validity of the assumptions of those working in the field or scientifically plausible estimates of error rates in actual identifications, how can such testimony of infallible individualization continue to be admissible?

No opinion provided a satisfactory answer. Instead, courts that have been willing to apply, nominally at least, the strict scrutiny normally accorded scientific evidence were content with long usage in law enforcement and in the courtroom in lieu of acceptance and extensive research in the scientific community. They accepted litigation-driven, unpublished studies that probably could not withstand scientific peer review as scientific fact. They confused a second examiner's approval of a co-worker's conclusion with scientific peer review. They maintained that the lack of many publicized cases of false identifications means that the false-positive error rate is essentially zero. And, when all else fails, they have observed that "the *Daubert* standard offers a list of flexible factors to be used as appropriate for various types of expert testimony"[36] as if flexibility itself is a ground for admitting the evidence.

The courts go to these extremes because, even without extensive scientific study, it seems obvious that fingerprint comparisons are probative and valuable. The difficulty lies in saying how probative they are and in pretending that a probability is a certainty. Experiments testing the validity and reliability of fingerprint analysts show that trained analysts using their personal judgments and thresholds can achieve low false positive rates (a fraction of a percent) and moderate false negative rates (around 10% or less) in matching latent prints to exemplars. Experiments also reveal that expectation bias can affect the outcomes in some cases. But with blind verification and procedures to reduce the chance of cognitive bias, fingerprint matches can be very strong evidence of identity.

Even though very few opinions have disapproved of the traditional description of a match as *necessarily* excluding everyone else in the world as a possible source of the latent print, this claim of global individualization exceeds the bounds of what is scientifically demonstrable and what is recommended in the field. Fortunately, there is no shortage of alternative ways to explain the meaning of a match. These include statements (when justified) that the matching features are very unusual in the general population, that it would be improbable to find another source that matches so well in a geographic area, and that the match is much more probable when the latent print and the exemplar come from the same individual than when they originate from different people. In addition, automated systems for estimating the probabilities of matches for prints of varying quality and completeness under competing hypotheses about the true source are coming close to fruition.

---

[36]   U.S. v. Havvard, 260 F.3d 597, 600 (7th Cir. 2001).

§ 207.2 Criminalistics: Identifying Persons and Things—Voice Spectrograms

Identification of speakers by means of spectrographic analysis of their voices illustrates the premature adoption for courtroom use of a seemingly impressive identification technique. However, having been developed more recently than fingerprinting and firearms-mark comparisons, and being more clearly scientific in nature, it received experimental study and review from scientists outside of the forensic-science community earlier in its lifecycle than the more entrenched identification methods.

Complex sound waves, such as those involved in speech, can be understood mathematically as sums of simple waveforms of various frequencies. The frequency spectrum of such a sound wave is, in effect, a list of each such constituent frequency and its relative importance in describing the composite sound. Since the 1940s or 1950s, electronic devices that analyze sound waves into these frequency components have been available. A spectrogram is a graphic representation of this information, that is, a picture of the frequency spectrum of a sound wave. In the 1960s, it was proposed that the spectral characteristics of a speaker's voice could identify that speaker. The theory was that individuals have different but largely stable patterns in the way they manipulate their lips, teeth, and so on in speaking. From the outset, this hypothesis has been controversial. If it is false, then comparisons of spectrograms should not produce consistently correct identifications. Despite a few early (and seemingly extravagant) claims of accurate identifications, subsequent studies providing better approximations of realistic forensic conditions reported misidentifications at rates ranging from 18% (12% false negatives and 6% false positives) to 70 and 80% (including 42% false positives). Many scientists therefore doubt the reliability and validity of the current technique.

Most courts applying the general scientific acceptance test to voice spectrographic evidence have held the evidence inadmissible. In fact, this evidence inspired some of the most spirited and thoughtful defenses of the general acceptance standard for scientific evidence. On the other hand, faith in the method and a belief that jurors will not find it overly impressive prompted some courts to bend the *Frye* test to the breaking point to conclude that the evidence should be admissible. Use of the technique has declined, however, and in *Daubert* jurisdictions, courts are increasingly likely to exclude the evidence. Whatever standard may be applied, it seems that unless further research makes the validity of the technique plainer, the courts will remain divided over or opposed to the admissibility of voice spectrographic identification.

III. STATISTICAL STUDIES

§ 208 Surveys and Opinion Polls

Samuel Johnson once remarked that "You don't have to eat the whole ox to know the hide is tough." In the past, courts required litigants to dismember and devour an ox or two to prove a point—either because of skepticism about the value of sampling and opinion polling or because of the hearsay rule. In *Irvin v. State*,[37] for example, the Florida Supreme Court upheld the trial judge's refusal to admit a public opinion survey in a

---

[37] 66 So. 2d 288 (Fla. 1953).

pretrial hearing on the theory that the poll was "hearsay based upon hearsay" and that it was "useless" in revealing public attitudes toward the defendant, a black who had been convicted of rape but alleged that the verdict was the result of racial prejudice.[38] The court regarded as much more informative the opinions given by selected witnesses who testified in court that the defendant could get a fair trial in the county, and it cited as an "illustration of the friendliness of the white people for the colored in the community . . . the recent construction of an elaborate memorial to a colored soldier who had been killed in World War II."[39]

With the development and implementation of scientific survey methods, the courts are much more receptive to proof based on sample data. Rule 703 of the Federal and Uniform Rules largely circumvent hearsay objections by allowing an expert to form an opinion on the basis of a survey produced in a reasonably reliable manner. Specially commissioned surveys or samples have been used to support motions for a change of venue in response to pretrial publicity, to show consumer perceptions in trademark and misleading advertising cases, to unmask community standards in obscenity prosecutions, to select a set of representative cases for adjudication and extrapolation in a class action, and for numerous other purposes. Advocates have also relied on pre-existing research involving sample data in product liability, food and drug, environmental, constitutional, and other cases. The modern opinions have said that case-specific surveys are generally admissible if they are conducted according to the principles accepted by social scientists and statisticians for gathering and analyzing survey data. This section therefore gives an overview of these principles—adherence to which affects the weight as well as the admissibility of survey evidence. In a great many cases, courts have examined whether the conclusions of the survey researchers rest on data collected in such a way as to permit fair inferences about the relevant factual questions.

Although many refinements are possible, the basic ideas behind scientific survey techniques are simple. The researcher tries to collect information from a manageable portion (a sample) of a larger group (a population) in order to learn something about the population. Usually some numbers are used to characterize the population, and these are called parameters. For example, the proportion of all consumers who would mistake one product for another because of a similarity in the brand names is a population parameter. Sample data lead to statistics, such as the proportion of the persons in the sample who are confused by the similarity. These sample statistics are then used to estimate the population parameters. If 50% of the sample studied exhibited confusion between the products with the similar brand names, then one might conclude that 50% of the population would be confused. Under some circumstances, statistical methods enable the researcher not only to make an estimate, but to indicate how much such an estimate could differ from the unknown parameter just because of the luck of the draw— that is, to quantify the sampling error that may be lurking in the estimate.

Sampling underlies almost every pertinent research effort. Descriptive surveys, like those introduced in connection with change of venue motions, are almost always confined to a sample of the entire population. Surveys looking for causal explanations (such as a survey of homicide rates in states that do and states that do not have capital punishment) usually involve samples. Even experiments designed to investigate

---

[38]   *Id.* at 291–92.

[39]   *Id.* at 292.

causation, such as a clinical trial of a new drug, typically produce only sample data. Many such surveys are nonverbal. Since an employer's records can be inspected, no one needs to poll the current employees to obtain data on the distribution of wages paid to men as opposed to women.

What factors are likely to make surveys produce accurate as opposed to misleading estimates? We can identify two major categories of errors: random errors and nonrandom errors. There are many potential sources of nonrandom, or systematic errors. In personal surveys, these include the specification of the population to be sampled, the technique for eliciting responses, the wording of the questions, the method for choosing and finding respondents, and the failure to pose questions that address the proper issues. Unless those sources of nonrandom error cancel each other out, any estimates made on the basis of the sample data will be biased. Making the sample size larger offers no protection against bias. It only produces a larger number of biased observations.

Random errors arise at two levels. The first is with respect to the observations on each unit sampled. In a nonverbal study, a measuring instrument (such as an instrument to determine breath alcohol content) might well give slightly different readings even on identical samples. A person seeking to get rid of an interviewer may say whatever pops into mind. The process for making individual measurements or observations is rarely perfectly reliable. The second kind of random error results from variability from one sample to the next. One sample of air expelled from the lungs may be slightly different from the next in its concentration of alcohol. Even though great care may be taken to assure that the people selected for interviews are representative of the population, there can be no guarantee that another sample selected by the same procedure would give identical responses. As such, even if all the answers or measurements are individually free from error, sampling variability remains a source of statistical, or chance error.

If methods known as probability sampling are employed, however, the magnitude of the sampling error (but not of the nonrandom errors) can be estimated. Probability sampling also has been shown to be very effective in producing representative samples. The reason is that unlike human beings, blind chance is impartial. Probability sampling uses an objective chance process to pick the sample. It leaves no discretion to the interviewers. As a result, the researcher can compute the chance that any particular unit in the population will be selected for the sample. Stated another way, a probability sample is one in which each unit of the sampling frame has a known, nonzero probability of being selected. Other samples, either "convenience" samples or "quota" samples, do not have this property, and they are acceptable only in special circumstances. A common type of probability sampling is simple random sampling, in which every unit has the same probability of being sampled. It amounts to drawing names at random without replacement.

The statistics derived from observations or measurements of random samples permit one to estimate the parameters of the population. In a consumer confusion survey for instance, some proportion of the sample of consumers who are interviewed will indicate confusion between the products. If the sample is a simple random sample, and if there are no nonrandom errors, then this sample proportion is an unbiased estimator of the proportion for all consumers. But it is only an estimate. Another random sample probably would not include precisely the same persons, and it probably would produce a slightly different proportion of responses indicating confusion. There is no single figure that expresses the extent of this statistical error. There are only probabilities. If one were to draw a second random sample, find the proportion of confused consumers in this group, then do the same for a third random sample, a fourth, and so on, one would obtain a distribution of sample proportions fluctuating about some central value. Some would be far away from the mean, but most would be closer. Pursuing this logic in a rigorous way, the statistician computes a "confidence" or "coverage" interval and gives an "interval estimate" for the population proportion. The analyst may report that at a 90% confidence level, the population proportion is 50% plus or minus 10%. This means that if the same method for drawing samples and interviewing the customers were repeated a very large number of times, and if a 90% confidence interval were computed about each sample proportion, close to 90% of the resulting interval estimates would be correct. The intervals obtained from these hypothetically repeated samples would vary, but about 90% of them would include the population proportion, whatever that number happens to be.

Although testimony as to confidence intervals often is received in cases involving survey evidence, its meaning apparently remains obscure in many cases. Note that a confidence of, say 90% does not necessarily mean that the interval estimate has a 90% probability of being correct. Strictly speaking, all that the classical statistical methodology reveals is that the particular interval was obtained by a method that gives intervals that would capture the true proportion in 90% of all possible samples. But each such interval estimate could be different. Thus, the "confidence" pertains to the process rather than to any particular result. Therefore, the common view that "[a] 95% confidence interval means that there is a 95% probability that the 'true' [value] falls within the interval"[40] is mistaken. Despite this difficulty in interpreting a confidence interval, the technique does give the finder of fact an idea of the risk of error in equating the sample proportion to the population figure. If the interval is small, even for a high level of "confidence," then the sample proportion is reasonably accurate, in the sense that taking more, or larger samples probably would give similar results.

The width of the confidence interval depends on three things. For a given sample, there is a trade-off between the level of confidence and the narrowness of the interval. One can be sure that the population proportion lies somewhere between zero and one. The confidence is 100%, but the interval is so broad as to be useless. Lowering the confidence level narrows the range of the estimate, but there is more risk in concluding that the population value lies within the narrower interval. Second, for a given confidence and a fixed sample size, the width of the interval depends on how homogeneous the population is. If nearly every consumer would be confused (or nearly no one would be), then there will be minimal sampling variability, since almost all the possible samples can be expected to look alike. Hence, the confidence interval for any sample will be very narrow. On the other hand, if the population is highly variable, then there are more chances to draw aberrant samples, and the computed confidence interval for any sample will be larger. Third, whatever the makeup of the population, larger samples give more reliable results than smaller ones. However, the point of diminishing returns rapidly is reached in that adding the same amount to the sample size does little to narrow the confidence interval. It is wrong to believe that one always needs to sample

---

[40] DeLuca by DeLuca v. Merrell Dow Pharms., Inc., 791 F. Supp. 1042 (D. N.J. 1992), judgment aff'd, 6 F.3d 778 (3d Cir. 1993).

a substantial proportion of a large population to obtain an accurate estimate of a population parameter.

In assessing the statistical error of a survey, therefore, the courts should look to the interval estimates rather than to untutored intuitions as to how large a sample is needed. Deciding what level of confidence is appropriate in a particular case, however, is a policy question and not a statistical issue. Finally, in making use of surveys, it is important to remember that the statistical analysis does not address the nonrandom sources of error. A small confidence interval with a high confidence coefficient is not worth much if the data collection is badly flawed.

§ 209 Statistical Evidence of Association and Causation

Survey evidence, as we described it in the previous section, involves sampling from some population, deriving statistics from the sample data, and offering some conclusion about the population in light of these sample statistics. In this section, we describe applications and extensions of this approach used to supply and interpret evidence on the issue of causation.

§ 209.1 Statistical Evidence of Association and Causation—Types of Studies

When causation is at issue, advocates have relied on three major types of information—anecdotal evidence, observational studies, and controlled experiments. Anecdotal reports can provide some information, but they are more useful as a stimulus for further inquiry than as a basis for establishing association or causation. Observational studies can establish that one factor is associated with another, but considerable analysis may be necessary to bridge the gap from association to causation. Controlled experiments are ideal for ascertaining causation, but they can be difficult to undertake.

"Anecdotal evidence" means reports of one kind of event following another. Typically, the reports are obtained haphazardly or selectively, and the logic of "post hoc, ergo propter hoc" does not suffice to demonstrate that the first event causes the second. Consequently, although anecdotal evidence can be suggestive, it can also be quite misleading. For instance, some children who live near power lines develop leukemia; but does exposure to electrical and magnetic fields cause this disease? The anecdotal evidence is not compelling because leukemia also occurs among children who have minimal exposure to such fields. It is necessary to compare disease rates among those who are exposed and those who are not. If exposure causes the disease, the rate should be higher among the exposed, lower among the unexposed. Of course, the two groups may differ in crucial ways other than the exposure. For example, children who live near power lines could come from poorer families and be exposed to other environmental hazards. These differences could create the appearance of a cause-and-effect relationship, or they could mask a real relationship. Cause-and-effect relationships often are subtle, and carefully-designed studies are needed to draw valid conclusions. Thus, some courts have deemed attempts to infer causation from anecdotal reports unsound methodology.

Typically, a well-designed study will compare outcomes for subjects who are exposed to some factor—the treatment group—and other subjects who are not so exposed—the control group. A distinction must then be made between controlled experiments and observational studies. In a controlled experiment, the investigators decide which subjects are exposed to the factor of interest and which subjects go into the control group. In most observational studies, the subjects themselves choose their exposures. Because of this self-selection, the treatment and control groups of observational studies are likely to differ with respect to important factors other than the variable whose effects are of primary interest. These other factors are called confounding variables or lurking variables. With observational studies on the health effects of power lines, family background is a possible confounder; so is exposure to other hazards.

Whether the data come from observational or experimental studies, the conclusions that can be drawn will involve further statistical assessments. Parties in environmental and product liability cases typically rely on statistical reasoning to establish that a chemical or other agent is carcinogenic or toxic. In civil rights cases, parties seeking to prove (or disprove) that a class or an individual has been subjected to unlawful discrimination may find statistical evidence useful. In antitrust litigation, a party may use statistical analysis to show illegal conduct and its effects. In business litigation generally, a party may apply statistical techniques to estimate lost profits or other damages resulting from illegal conduct. In these and many other sorts of cases, the statistics, and inferences drawn from them, if in accordance with normal statistical practice, will be admissible via the testimony of a suitably qualified expert.

The weight that may be given such testimony will depend, of course, on the skill of counsel and the ability and preparation of the witness. In addition, the methods that the expert uses to analyze and interpret that data, so as to assist the court or jury in understanding it, will be crucial in determining the admissibility and impact of the evidence. The remainder of this section outlines one of the statistical concepts most frequently encountered in connection with sophisticated statistical proofs. Because most cases addressing the usefulness of this concept arose in discrimination litigation, it draws on a few of the developments in this area to illustrate some general points about the presentation of statistical evidence.

§ 209.2 Statistical Evidence of Association and Causation—Magnitude and Significance of Disparities

The courts have relied heavily on statistical evidence in cases in which a criminal defendant alleges that he was indicted by an unconstitutionally selected grand jury or an unconstitutionally empaneled petit jury. There is no constitutionally permissible basis for systematically excluding, say, members of defendant's race from the population of citizens who are eligible for jury duty. Where direct evidence of discrimination is unavailable, or where additional proof is desired, statistical methods have been pressed into service. The usual procedure is to compare the proportion of the persons eligible for jury service who are in the class allegedly discriminated against with the corresponding proportion appearing on jury venires or pools. Substantial underrepresentation over a significant period of time is taken as evidence of discrimination.

In early cases, the courts made purely intuitive assessments of the disparity in the proportions. In time, formal statistical reasoning to evaluate the quantitative evidence became *de rigueur*. The logic begins from the assumption that selection of potential jurors is a random process, like blindly drawing differently colored marbles from an urn, in which the chance that a person will be selected is the same in each instance. Under the "null" hypothesis that everyone has an equal chance of being selected, the probability of picking a member of the protected class each time is simply the overall proportion of these individuals in the eligible population. The alternative to this hypothesis is not always specified clearly, but it usually amounts to the claim that the chance of picking a protected class member is not equal to the population proportion. The statistical analyst compares the proportion of the protected class actually chosen for jury service to the proportion expected if each selection were made by the random process described above. This probability of a disparity as large or larger than the reported one is called a "p-value." It states the chance that so large a disparity would come about purely as a matter of bad luck or coincidence. The p-value thus expresses how improbable or surprising such extreme outcomes are when null hypothesis is true. If the p-value is very small, it is taken to indicate that the null hypothesis is implausible. If the p-value is large, it is taken to indicate that this hypothesis is consistent with the data. In this way, the p-value serves as an index of the statistical force of the quantitative evidence—the smaller the p-value, the more unlikely it is that the statistical disparity was the result of the chance process. It should be noted, however, that even though small p-values are needed to reject the null hypothesis (coincidence) as implausible, the p-value does not directly measure the probability of coincidence. Confusing the probability that the disparity would arise simply by coincidence with the probability that coincidence is in fact the explanation for the disparity is so common that it goes by its own name—the transposition fallacy.[41]

The p-value is by no means the only quantity that indicates the strength of statistical evidence. For various reasons, some statisticians and scientists do not think that it is the best. One problem with its use in court is the tendency of some expert witnesses or judges to assume that because there is an arbitrary convention of insisting on p-values of .05 or less before labeling scientific findings "statistically significant," this same number should be required before the factfinder may consider or rely on the quantitative results from a single study. It is hard to see why an "almost significant" result (for which $p = .051$, for instance) should be ignored when a "barely significant" one (for which $p = .049$ or the like) should be credited. Another difficulty is the tendency to portray the absence of significance at the .05 level as statistical proof that there is no association. Sometimes a study with a large p-value does support the null hypothesis, but in other instances, the large p-value is just a reflection of the limited power of the study to detect an association. A final caveat is that a p-value is not a statement of how large the observed disparity is—with a large enough sample, even a trivial difference can have a small value and be deemed statistically significant.

In sum, if the p-value is not to be misleading, its meaning must be clearly understood—a goal that can be thwarted by the specialized meanings of everyday terms like "significance" and "confidence." The p-value is not itself evidence of anything. It is merely one measure of the extent to which a statistical disparity indicates that something other than chance is necessary to explain the data, and it is an incomplete measure at that. This is not to deny that the p-value is a useful concept. Properly understood, it may assist the court or jury in assessing the statistical data.

Statistical evidence of disparities also commonly is used in employment discrimination cases. There is more difficulty in defining the relevant population from which employees are drawn, there are more variables to consider, the sample sizes tend to be smaller, and the mechanics of computing p-values may differ, but the meaning of

---

[41] See infra § 210.

the p-value and of "statistical significance" is the same. When complicated statistical models are used to account for the effects of many variables, however, many subtle errors are possible, and an uncritical acceptance of the estimates derived from these models and their calculated p-values can be dangerous. For example, just as one cannot accept a small p-value at face value when it has been obtained by subdividing the data and performing many significance tests, given enough latitude in the number of variables and the form of a statistical model, a statistician eventually can construct a particular model that will fit the data remarkably well and have impressively small p-values for the quantities of interest. This same model easily can be worthless in the sense that it probably would not work well with any other data. In short, for this form of scientific testimony, the battle is not usually over the admissibility of statistical evidence in general or over the use of concepts like the p-value to assess the evidence. Rather, the battlelines are drawn when it comes to the admissibility of flawed applications, to the weight that should be given the evidence, and to transforming methods and conventions of statistical inference into rules of law.

IV.　PROBABILITIES AS EVIDENCE

§ 210　Identification Evidence and Probabilities

The previous two sections discussed the use of probability calculations in connection with statistical studies. When the statistical analyst takes properly collected sample data, computes statistics such as a proportion, a difference between two means, or a regression coefficient, and calculates a p-value or a confidence interval for each such statistic, the courts are willing to rely on the probabilities in assessing the force of the statistical evidence. Especially in criminal cases, however, the courts are more reluctant to admit probability calculations intended to show the identity of a wrongdoer. This section examines the admissibility of probability calculations relating to the myriad forms of identification evidence—eyewitness testimony, DNA tests, fingerprints, bitemarks, questioned document examinations, microanalysis, and so on. The next section focuses on the role of probability calculations in paternity litigation.

At the outset, two preliminary points of clarification may be helpful. First, although the phrase "probability evidence" is a convenient shorthand for testimony or argument involving probability calculations, the term is something of a misnomer. The probabilities are not themselves evidence. They are numbers ranging from zero to one that may be used in drawing conclusions from the statistical or other evidence. The topic of this section is whether or when overtly attaching a probability number to identification evidence is permissible. A somewhat different question is whether statistical evidence alone is sufficient to support a verdict. Psychologists have detected an aversion to decisions based on "naked statistical evidence" under certain conditions, and philosophers, economists, and legal commentators have presented theories to justify or to counter the apparent opposition of some courts to verdicts that seem to rest exclusively on statistical evidence. Positions have ranged from denying that there is any generally accepted rule of law precluding such verdicts, to offering economic (incentive-based) justifications for such a rule, to opposing verdicts based on an explicit probability for fear that they will undermine the expressive function of verdicts, to reconceptualizing the burden of persuasion, to positing unconventional theories of probability.

Second, it should be clear that any global objection to using group statistics to draw inferences on individual instances is untenable. Courts sometimes suggest that evidence about a class of objects cannot be used to support a conclusion about a particular member of the class—especially when the inference concerns personal behavior. When it comes to inanimate objects, however, the courts are much quicker to recognize the usefulness of generalizations derived from the experience of others. For example, government statistical reports showing that Volkswagen vans are more likely to eject occupants in an accident than are other vans are readily admissible. A statistician might try to reconcile these intuitions by reasoning that the group-based judgments about people are weaker because there is more variability among human beings or the circumstances they confront than there is among mere objects like Volkswagen vans. But surely this depends on the characteristics in question. People are very similar in some dimensions and highly variable in others. So are Volkswagen vans. And even as to the highly variable features, it seems hard to deny that the statistical evidence as to people is relevant under Rule 402.

A more convincing explanation for resistance to the introduction of probabilities derived from experience with groups of individuals might be that where the statistical indicators pertain to volitional conduct, the courts are cautious because they place great weight on a conception of human autonomy and dignity that the coldly statistical analysis would undermine. To put it another way, shying away from the statistical predictions reflects a belief that everyone should have the opportunity to depart from the statistical norm.

This normative theory does not deny the truism that all evidence is statistical or probabilistic. Plainly, we rely on generalizations derived from experience with other members of the same group all the time. Law schools admit students with high grades and test scores in part because other students with these credentials have achieved success. Banks issue credit cards based on ratings that reflect the behavior of other individuals. Surgeons perform drastic operations on patients because other patients have experienced beneficial effects. Legislatures enact statutes making it an offense to drive with a blood alcohol concentration exceeding an amount seen to impair the functioning of a sample of persons. The Constitution spares defendants from capital punishment when their IQ scores fall below a specified number taking into consideration the standard error of measurement derived from on the test scores of other people. Juries tend to convict or acquit defendants because of hunches or beliefs about how certain classes of people behave, and they award damages in wrongful death cases with the assistance of mortality tables that reflect the experiences of many other men or women. We are all guilty of such "profiling." We could not survive without it.

So, too, any expert giving any opinion on whether the scientific test identifies the defendant as being the person who left the incriminating trace, such as a fingerprint, bullet, or bloodstain, necessarily bases this conclusion on an understanding or impression of how similar the items being compared are and how common it is to find items with these similarities. If these beliefs have any basis in fact, it is to be found in the general experience of the criminalists or more exacting statistical studies of these matters. In brief, the reluctance to allow testimony or argument about probabilities must be justified, if at all, on the basis of something other than an undifferentiated claim about the logical or epistemological weakness of relying on probabilities derived from statistics about other persons or things. In fact, more conventional concerns about probability evidence surface in the decisions in this area. These relate to the probative value of the explicit quantification and the tendency of the seemingly impressive numbers to mislead or confuse the jury.

To begin with, for more than a hundred years there have been attempts to compute the probability of observing a conjunction of certain incriminating characteristics by assuming that each characteristic is statistically independent and that the probabilities of these presumably independent characteristics could be obtained by introspection. In the most notorious of these cases, *People v. Collins*,[42] police apprehended a man and a woman fitting descriptions supplied by eyewitnesses near the scene of a robbery. The prosecutor proposed figures for the frequencies of such things as an interracial couple in a car, a girl with a ponytail, a partly yellow automobile, a man with a mustache, and so on. A mathematics professor testified to the rule that the joint probability of a series of independent events is the product of the probabilities of each event. Applying this rule to the "conservative estimates" that he had propounded, the prosecutor concluded that there was but one chance in 12 million that any couple possessed the distinctive characteristics of the defendants, and he argued that "the chances of anyone else besides these defendants being there, . . . having every similarity, . . . is something like one in a billion."[43]

In *People v. Collins* and other such cases, the appellate courts hold that it is error to admit such testimony on the ground that the hypothesized values that are multiplied together are sheer speculation. In addition, *Collins* and opinions in similar cases decry the use of the multiplication rule on the ground that the events are obviously far from independent. Because the fallacious computations and are presented in the guise of expert analysis, they are excluded under the principle that their prejudicial impact clearly outweighs their probative value.

In another group of cases, there are some data for calculating the joint probability. While some forensic experts are content to describe the points of similarity between the incriminating traces and material taken from the defendant or his belongings and to leave it to the jury to decide how unlikely it would be to find all these similarities by mere coincidence, from time to time, the experts testify to vanishingly small probabilities. The appellate responses to estimates that have some empirical basis are more divided. When the probabilities of the individual characteristics or events are well founded, there are three possibilities regarding the joint events to consider—the events could be statistically independent, positively correlated (tending to occur together), or negatively correlated. When statistical independence is established, multiplication of the individual probabilities is allowed. When the events seem positively correlated, however, the simple multiplication rule yields an excessively small probability, and admission of the testimony constitutes error. When the underlying events or characteristics are negatively correlated, multiplication of the unconditional probabilities understates how improbable the joint event is. As such, the conservative computation should be admissible to show that the event is improbable. In the exceptional case that finds error even in the admission of computations that the court considers well founded, the rationale seems to be that the jury would misconstrue the meaning of the probability or overemphasize the number, or that it would be too difficult to explain its true meaning.

In evaluating these decisions, it is important to distinguish between explicit calculations of the probability of guilt or coincidence and the presentation of relevant background statistics. If the offender, whoever he or she might have been, left a bloodstain at the scene of the crime that matches the defendant's blood types, the

---

[42]   438 P.2d 33 (Cal. 1968).

[43]   *Id.* at 37.

scientific evidence cannot be interpreted intelligently without some knowledge of how frequently these blood types occur in the relevant population. We have already remarked that if the expert offers any conclusion as to whether the defendant left the incriminating trace, he or she is relying, either explicitly or sub rosa, on estimates of these quantities. Without being informed of such background statistics or the relative likelihoods for different sources, the jury is left to its own speculations (or exposed to inadequately validated claims of uniqueness). When the available data do not permit a reasonable calculation, but it is obvious that the match is probative, this may be tolerable. But where reasonable estimates of the population frequencies are available, they should not be kept from the jury. Thus, courts routinely admit testimony estimating such frequencies, often without objection.

To be sure, there are risks in this policy. A juror who hears that only one out of every five, or for that matter, one out of every 10,000 persons, possesses the traits that characterize the true offender, may be tempted to subtract this statistic from one to arrive at the incorrect conclusion that the remainder is the probability that the defendant is guilty. In the statistical literature, this reasoning is known as the transposition fallacy. Nevertheless, it should not be so difficult for defense counsel to correct any such misapprehension by pointing out that the frequency estimate merely establishes that the defendant is one member of a class of persons who have the incriminating characteristics. The distribution of these characteristics in the population at large simply determines whether this class of persons whom the scientific evidence would identify as a possible offender is large or small.

In principle, a statistician could do more than state the frequency at which the scientific tests would implicate persons. First, in those cases in which the identifying characteristics were not the very basis on which the defendant was picked from the general population, the expert could be explicit about the p-value for the findings.

Second, valiant efforts have been made to calculate conditional probabilities pertaining to the number of people in some populations who have the incriminating characteristics. Indeed, the opinion in *People v. Collins* sported a mathematical appendix purporting to show that the conditional probability of there being more couples with the characteristics of the Collins's given that there was at least one such couple was 0.41. One could imagine admitting testimony about these probabilities.

Third, when it is feasible to compute the likelihood ratio or Bayes factor that indicates the probative value of the evidence, an expert might present this quantity. This approach has been followed in a growing number of DNA cases and is becoming the procedure of choice now that "probabilistic genotyping" software is used in interpreting complex DNA mixtures. It is generally accepted among European and Australian forensic scientists and laboratories. and has been recommended by the American Statistical Association and the Royal Society.

Finally, the expert could apply Bayes' rule to show jurors how the frequency data would increase a previously established probability that the person tested is the one who left the incriminating traces. This last proposal has been attacked on both philosophical and practical grounds. It has been said in reply that the pragmatic objections are the more persuasive. Certainly, having an expert testify to the "probability of guilt" given the evidence would be inadvisable. But whether the benefits of using this method of statistical inference solely to educate the jury by displaying the probative force of the evidentiary findings would be worth the costs in terms of time-consumption and possible confusion is a closer question. Outside of the parentage testing area, fully Bayesian calculations rarely are seen in court.

In general, it appears that the explicit use of the theories of probability and statistical inference, either as a basis for the opinions of the experts themselves or as a course of education for jurors in how to think about scientific identification evidence, remains controversial. As long as counsel and the experts do not try to place a scientific seal of approval on results not shown to be scientifically based, however, there is room for judicious use of these theories to put the identification evidence in reasonable perspective.

§ 211　Paternity Testing

Problems of questioned or disputed parentage have plagued mankind, perhaps ever since the origin of the species. The Talmud tells of a case in which a widow married her brother-in-law before the required three-month waiting period after the death of her husband. She gave birth to a child scarcely six months later. The rabbis reasoned that either the child was a full term baby fathered by the deceased husband or a premature child of the second husband. Since the mother had shown no visible signs of pregnancy three months after her first husband's death, the matter was not easy to settle. As one rabbi said, "it is a doubt."

Many legislators, courts, and commentators have concluded that genetic and statistical methods permit such doubts to be dispelled. Section 205.2 described the methods of detecting genetic markers and the principles of human genetics that allow this information to be applied to cases of disputed parentage. We saw that states now admit the results of DNA, blood, and tissue typing tests not merely to exclude the alleged father as the biological father, but, when he is not excluded, to help prove that he is the father. To assist the trier of fact in interpreting positive results, the expert, under generally applicable evidentiary principles, may give reliable estimates of the frequencies that characterize the distribution of the pertinent genotypes or genetic markers in the male population. That is, the expert may testify to the proportion of men that the test would exclude—a parameter that is sometimes converted into the "probability of exclusion." This probability and its complement, the probability of inclusion, are essentially the same as those sometimes used to indicate the significance of matching features in other forms of scientific identification evidence.

Yet, many experts believe that testimony limited to the test results and the probability of exclusion is incomplete and sometimes misleading. They prefer to testify to "the probability of paternity," and almost all jurisdictions allow such testimony in civil cases. Yet, even though most states have statutes that permit positive test results to be received into evidence, not all of these statutes say whether the probabilities derived from the test results also are admissible. At the other extreme, statutes adopted across the country not only allow such testimony, but rely on the "probability of paternity" to trigger a presumption of paternity. In the absence of a statute explicitly authorizing the expert to give the "probability of paternity," admissibility should turn on whether probability testimony is sufficiently likely to aid the jury in properly assessing the probative value of the positive findings. To answer this question, one must first understand what the "probability of paternity" is. This section indicates how this probability is computed. It then argues that one version of this approach is not suited for courtroom use and suggests some alternative methods of assisting the jury or court to weigh the positive test results along with the other evidence in the case to reach a decision as to paternity. Finally, it discusses special concerns that have been raised about probability computations involving DNA typing. It concludes with the suggestion that in most cases, testimony as to the numerical probability of paternity is no longer necessary.

§ 211.1 Paternity Testing—the Meaning of the "Probability of Paternity" and Its Components

The probability of paternity, as conventionally computed, is a deceptively simple application of an elementary result in probability theory discovered by the Reverend Thomas Bayes in the nineteenth century. Bayes' formula can be interpreted as showing the effect of a new item of evidence on a previously established probability. Suppose we let A stand for the event that the alleged father is the biological father. Its probability (before we learn the outcome of the laboratory tests) is $\Pr(A)$, and the corresponding odds on A as compared to not-A are $\mathrm{Odds}(A) = \Pr(A) / \Pr(\text{not-}A) = \Pr(A) / [1 - \Pr(A)]$. For instance, if $\Pr(A)$ is 1/2, or 50%, its odds prior to learning of the test are 50:50, or $1/2 / 1/2 = 1$. Many testifying experts take the prior odds to be 1 on the theory that doing so shows that they are neutral as between plaintiff and defendant. Although this conception of "neutrality" cannot withstand examination, adopting these odds does amount to assuming that the accusation of paternity is as likely to be true as to be false.

Bayes' rule tells us how to update these odds to account for the test results T. In particular, it says to multiply the prior odds by a quantity called the Bayes factor, or (in simple cases) the likelihood ratio, to produce the new odds that the alleged father is the biological father, which we write as $\mathrm{Odds}(A \mid T)$, for the odds of A given the test results T. In symbols, $\mathrm{Odds}(A \mid T) = \mathrm{LR} \times \mathrm{Odds}(A)$, where LR is an abbreviation for likelihood ratio. For the standard assumption that the prior odds are 1, the posterior odds of paternity are just $\mathrm{Odds}(A \mid T) = \mathrm{LR}$.

This likelihood ratio can be computed as the ratio of two probabilities. The numerator is the probability that the types T would be found if the alleged father really were the biological father. The denominator is the probability that the types T would be found if the alleged father were not the biological father. In other words, the likelihood ratio states how many times more probable it is that the tests would show the types T if the alleged father were the biological father than if he were not. The computation of the numerator is relatively simple. It is just the probability that a man with the phenotypes of the alleged father and a woman with the mother's types would produce an offspring with the child's types.

The computation of the denominator is trickier. The denominator is the probability that a man other than the alleged father would produce an offspring with the child's types. But which man? Some "alternative men" could not produce this type of child. They are the ones whom the tests would exclude. Others would have the same probability of producing this type of child as does the alleged father. These are the ones who have the same types that he does. Still others would produce this type of child with other probabilities. Their types differ from the alleged father's but are still consistent with the genotypes of the biological father. The conventional solution is to invent a "random man"—or, more precisely, to model the paternal contribution as a random draw from the pool of all the alleles in the male population. Suppose, for example, that given the allele frequencies estimated in the male population, it is 5,000 times more likely to obtain a child with the observed types from a man with the alleged father's types than from the imaginary "random man." This figure is known as the "paternity index." Bayes' formula then states that Odds $(A \mid T) = 5000 \times$ Odds (A). For prior odds of 1, this means that the odds that the alleged father is the biological father are 5000 to 1. There are 5,000 chances that he is the father compared to one that he is not. The corresponding probability of paternity is 5000/5001 = .9998, or 99.98%. These are the kind of numbers that the experts testifying to the "probability of paternity" produce.

§ 211.2 Paternity Testing—Admissibility of the "Probability of Paternity" and Its Components

Should the results of these calculations ever be admissible? Resorting to the "random man" to form the likelihood ratio and postulating prior odds of 1 creates two problems for a courtroom presentation. First, the random-draw-from-the-gene-pool assumption for the probability $\Pr(T \mid \text{not-}A)$ in the denominator of the paternity index (PI) takes the event not-A to mean that the biological father is not closely related to the defendant. If that is the only alternative event that needs to be considered, all is well. Letting U represent unrelatedness, the following version of Bayes' rule is mathematically correct:

$$\Pr(A \mid T) / \Pr(U \mid T) = \text{PI} \times [\Pr(A) / \Pr(U)],$$

where PI = $\Pr(T \mid A) / \Pr(T \mid U)$.

But if the alternative to A includes relatedness to the defendant, the paternity index is not the Bayes factor for odds on the event that the alleged father is the biological father as against the event that he is not. The correct Bayes factor is a weighted average of the likelihoods for every possible alternative man, where the weights are proportional to the prior probability for each man. Although the likelihoods are small for unrelated men, they can be orders of magnitude larger for close relatives, who may well form a non-negligible part of the population of conceivable fathers. As such, it could be misleading to describe the conventional paternity index as the factor to use in computing the posterior odds of paternity. A careful expert would have to say that the computed posterior probability assumes that the biological father is unrelated to the defendant and that the paternity index is not necessarily the Bayes factor for the claim that the defendant is the biological father. Rather, it is only useful for considering the degree to which the test data support the defendant's paternity relative to that of an unrelated man. Second, the choice of prior odds also requires care. It is tempting to dismiss the blanket prior odds of one as contrived, speculative, and lacking any scientific basis. This starting point may be "standard," but it is far from "neutral," as laboratories are wont to claim. It assigns fully half the prior probability to a single man and distributes the rest equally among every other man in the population. Multiplying by such prior odds thus sounds like some of the classic cases in which an expert multiplied together probabilities that had no basis in fact.[44] Here, however, there are some hard data suggesting that these prior odds understate the incidence of truthful accusations of paternity in civil cases and therefore favor the alleged father, who would be the objecting party.

Nonetheless, to serve up any single number computed in this fashion as "the" probability of paternity connotes more than the mathematical logic can deliver. Most persons hearing that the probability of paternity is 99.98% would think that the alleged

---

[44] See supra § 210.

father's role in the affair is conclusively confirmed. Indeed, the parentage-testing community has standardized phrases, which they call "verbal predicates," to characterize the numbers. Yet, in view of the way in which the "probability of paternity" is calculated, many men—all those who share the alleged father's types—would have had "probabilities of paternity" of 99.98% had they been tested. Some nonexcluded men (for serological and HLA types) might have even higher "probabilities of paternity." In more than one case, a man later shown to be sterile had a "probability of paternity" exceeding 95% as determined from HLA typing. Unless an expert can somehow explain that the calculated "probability of paternity" is not the chance that the alleged father, as distinguished from all other possible fathers, is the biological father, the expert should not be allowed to put this "probability" before the jury. Furthermore, it would appear that any accurate explanation of why the "probability of paternity" does not mean the probability that the alleged father, rather than any other man, is the biological father, and then of what it does mean, would be hopelessly confusing. Consequently, testimony as to the "probability of paternity," computed with a fixed and undisclosed prior probability of one-half, should not be allowed. Such testimony seems unable to fulfill its only legitimate function—assisting the jury in weighing the positive test results along with the other evidence in the case. The same rule of exclusion should apply to the "verbal predicates."

This rule would not prohibit the introduction of the genetic evidence and an explanation of its significance. The fact that competently performed genetic tests prove the alleged father's phenotypes or genotypes to be consistent with the claim of paternity is always relevant and useful evidence, and several ways to convey the probative value of the test results are available. First, the strength of this evidence, like other forms of identification evidence, can be shown to some extent by testimony about the probability of exclusion or, better, the likelihood ratios for unrelated men and relatives.

Second, there is also a strong argument for using a Bayesian approach to help the jury evaluate the evidence. Instead of viewing the evidence from the position of a laboratory, which, having nothing else to go on, is driven to such artifacts as using prior odds of one, one can adjust the focus to the trial, where other evidence is available to the decisionmaker. As noted in section 210, the expert could show the jury how the test results would affect not merely a prior probability of one-half, but a whole spectrum of prior probabilities. It could be made clear to the jurors that the purpose of this exposition is not to compel them to assign a prior probability to the other evidence in the case, but to permit them to gauge the strength of the positive test findings and to weigh these findings, along with the other evidence, in the manner that they think best. By using variable instead of fixed prior odds, the expert can display the statistical force of the evidence without attempting to quantify—on the basis of incomplete information—the one thing that the jury must decide with the benefit of all the evidence in the case: the probability of paternity.

However, as noted earlier, using the likelihood ratio with respect to unrelated men as the Bayes factor in a single illustrative table does not account for the possibility that a true father is a close relative of the defendant. Moreover, the simplest table assumes that there is no ambiguity or doubt about the determination of phenotypes or genotypes and the frequencies of the related alleles in the relevant population. To cope with these complications, a table could give a range of posterior probabilities for each prior probability used in the table.

Finally, in most civil cases at least, there is a cornucopia of DNA loci to test within the fresh and uncontaminated samples that can be obtained from the mother, child, and putative father. With enough loci, even very close relatives will have small likelihoods compared to the defendant's. For such evidence, detailed calculations of the troublesome "probability of paternity" is largely beside the point. Given the exquisite power of DNA loci to discriminate among individuals, it has been suggested that:

> [W]e are approaching the point where explicit statistical analysis can be relegated to the background. Today, exclusions rarely are interpreted in terms of a paternity index or a probability of paternity, presumably because these numbers are so close to zero as to give no more guidance to a judge or jury than a simple statement that if the test results are correct, then it is practically impossible for the tested man to be the father. Likewise, an inclusion for which the paternity index is clearly astronomical perhaps may be more profitably described as demonstrating that it is practically impossible for the putative father to be anything but the biological father.[45]

---

[45]   Kaye, DNA Paternity Probabilities, 24 J. Fam. L. 279, 303–04 (1990).

Title 8

REAL EVIDENCE, OTHER NONTESTIMONIAL EVIDENCE, AND DEMONSTRATIVE AIDS

Chapter 21

REAL EVIDENCE, OTHER NONTESTIMONIAL EVIDENCE, AND DEMONSTRATIVE AIDS

Table of Sections

§ 212   Introduction

The subject of this Chapter is the admissibility of the types of nontestimonial evidence that are commonly used at trial. Objects, drawings, photographs and sound recordings exemplify the traditional types of such evidence.[1] In the contemporary courtroom, many new types have emerged, with the advent of videotape and computer graphics in particular. As a result, the problem of satisfactorily labeling the larger class that would include all such types has proved difficult. It has been variously referred to as real, autoptic, demonstrative, tangible, and objective. Perhaps "nontestimonial evidence" and "tangible exhibits" are the most content-neutral descriptions.

However, although convenient, the use of any single term to denominate all such evidence can be at best confusing and at worst harmful to a clear analysis of what should be required to achieve its admission into evidence. This is because not all nontestimonial evidence is offered for the same purpose or received on the same theory. Therefore, each section of this Chapter focuses on a specific type: real evidence; demonstrative aids; photographs; video, film and sound recordings; demonstrations and experiments in court; computer-generated simulations and models; and views. Use of this organization should not be taken as a return to categorical formalism, however, since each type will be discussed functionally in terms of its relevance and use at trial.

The following brief discussion of the key legal concepts which concern the admissibility of all types of nontestimonial evidence—relevance, authentication, and judicial discretion to exclude—introduces the important questions that will concern us throughout this Chapter.

---

[1]   The admissibility of writings is treated independently in infra Ch. 22 (authentication of writings) and infra Ch. 23 (the requirement of the originals of writings, recordings and photographs, and the exceptions thereto).

Relevance. Some types of evidence discussed in this Chapter are offered on the theory that the trier of fact obtains information relevant to a fact of consequence just from perceiving them, irrespective of whether any witness testifies to what he or she also perceives. Some common examples are a weapon allegedly used in the crime charged, a day-in-the-life film of a personal injury plaintiff, or a computer-generated simulation of the alleged cause of a collision. Such items are "substantive" evidence, with independent probative value for proving a fact of consequence in the case. By contrast, other types are offered on the relevance theory that they only "illustrate" the facts or opinions testified to by a witness. They are relevant if they aid the trier in understanding the witness's testimony, which itself makes a fact of consequence more or less probable. Examples include duplicates of objects involved in the events underlying the litigation, drawings, diagrams and models. The term "demonstrative aid" will be employed here to identify these and other types of evidence whose relevance is illustrative, rather than substantive. Some courts refer to these aids as "pedagogic aids" or "devices."

The two theories of relevance will be referred to in this Chapter as the "illustrative" use and the "substantive" use of evidentiary items. The distinction between the two theories becomes important in assessing how the rules of evidence should be applied and what is a sufficient foundation for a particular exhibit. A problem arises because this distinction cannot be rigidly maintained; that is, it becomes blurred when an item of evidence that is allegedly offered solely as illustrative of a witness's testimony also inevitably serves as an independent source of substantive information.

Most commonly, this problem occurs with the use of photographs, film and video recordings, and computer-generated exhibits. For example, surveillance videotapes may be offered to illustrate the testimony of a percipient witness, but they might also convey data to the trier that the testifying witness did not or could not perceive. This raises the important question of what foundation is sufficient for the admission of such recordings, a question which is treated in depth in Sections 215 and 216 infra. Computer-generated exhibits also blur the distinction between illustrative and substantive evidence because of their persuasive power and because the computer itself sometimes functions like an expert.

Authentication. In all jurisdictions, the requirement of authentication applies to all of the types of evidence discussed in this Chapter. An item may be admitted into evidence only after the proponent has offered some evidentiary foundation to show that the item really is what the proponent claims it to be. This is the burden of authentication, denominated by Federal Rule 901 as "Authenticating or Identifying Evidence." The requisite standard of proof for authentication is a prima facie case, or "evidence sufficient to support a finding."

First the proponent asserts that a proffered item is relevant to prove (or disprove) a fact of consequence in the case. This assertion of relevance then determines what it is the proponent claims an offered item to be for purposes of authentication, typically that it is connected to a specific person or to one of the litigated events in the case. For example, in a prosecution for possession of an illegal substance, if a plastic bag of white powder is offered into evidence, the government would assert that the bag is relevant both because the defendant possessed the bag and because its contents are illegal. The requirement of authentication would be satisfied by evidence sufficient to support a finding that it is the very bag that was seized from the possession of the defendant. It is this "connection" to a person that is commonly proved to identify or authenticate the exhibit. Other facts beyond the scope of Federal Rule 901, such as the illegal contents of the bag, may also be necessary to make an item relevant.[2]

The proponent's claim as to what an item is, and thus the connection that must be proved for purposes of authentication, will vary with the type of item offered and with its relevance as substantive or illustrative evidence in the instant case. There is no single formula that must be satisfied in every case, as will be evident in the discussion of specific types of tangible exhibits that follows in this Chapter. Over time, courts have distilled the elements of an adequate foundation into criteria that they apply routinely. Federal Rule 901(b) and most state evidence rules contain a set of options with such criteria for satisfying the authentication requirement. These options include some well-established requirements for particular types of exhibits, as well as the more general options of using either the testimony of a witness who has personal knowledge or of relying on circumstantial evidence such as contents and appearance, both of which can apply to many different types.

Functions of Judge and Jury in Authentication. Evidence sufficient to support a finding means evidence upon which a reasonable jury could find by a preponderance of the evidence an item to be what the proponent claims it is. This standard gives the judge a limited screening role on the issue of "sufficiency." If a witness has personal knowledge and gives direct testimony on the matter, this is sufficient. The judge does not weigh credibility but takes the testimony at face value. The opponent is permitted to contest the witness's credibility before the jury, and the jury decides the ultimate question of authenticity.

When the authenticating evidence is circumstantial, the question whether a jury could reasonably find the facts as claimed by the proponent is more difficult and the judge must be accorded some latitude of judgment. And while this exercise of judgment is reviewed under an "abuse of discretion" standard, appellate courts still decide whether the requisite minimum standard of "sufficiency" under Federal Rule 901(a) has been satisfied. Appellate courts conduct their own review of the record to determine whether there was sufficient evidence that could support a reasonable jury finding on the facts that authenticate an item.

Judicial Discretion to Exclude. Nontestimonial evidence appeals to the senses of the trier of fact. The trier derives its own sensory perceptions from such exhibits and does not have to rely on the reported perceptions of witnesses. This distinctive characteristic of the evidence treated in this Chapter raises specific issues of probative danger and probative value.

Probative Dangers. Since "seeing is believing," it is today often felt that this kind of evidence possesses an immediacy and apparent reality which endow it with particularly persuasive effect. In all jurisdictions, the judge has discretionary authority to exclude such evidence if its admission would raise significant dangers for the jury's reasoning, and if those dangers substantially outweigh the exhibit's probative value, as provided, for instance, in Federal Rule 403. Most of the probative dangers listed in this Rule are frequently made the basis of objections to the admission of the types of evidence discussed here.

---

2   See infra § 213 for discussion of authentication of real evidence by a percipient witness or proof of chain of custody.

Exhibits or demonstrations which portray gruesome events such as personal injuries, autopsies of crime victims, or the details of tort or crime sites, are frequently objected to as raising *unfair prejudice*, a term which the drafters of Federal Rule 403 define as suggesting "decision on an improper basis, commonly, though not necessarily, an emotional one."[3] Such types of evidence have the capacity to generate emotional responses such as pity, horror, revulsion, or contempt, and may "arouse the jury's hostility or sympathy for one side," as discussed in Section 185 supra, thus influencing the outcome in an unfair way. Where the danger of such a response substantially outweighs the probative value of the evidence for the issues in the case, exclusion is appropriate.

Again, even if no essentially emotional response is likely to result, video and film recordings, and computer-generated animations and simulations may convey an impression of objective reality to the jury. Thus, courts have recognized the danger that such evidence is *misleading* if its contents do not correspond closely enough to the actual conditions and context of the events that are at issue at trial. In another sense of the term, an exhibit might be misleading if the jury will not be able to estimate its probative worth accurately, typically because it may overestimate the item's value due to the immediacy of the apparent reality it portrays. A related probative danger is *confusing the issues*, which could occur if the jury's attention is distracted by an impermissible use of an exhibit, or by the dramatic power of an exhibit, from a careful evaluation of the issues in dispute.

Further, certain types of exhibits present logistical difficulties for the courts. Since courts are basically structured, architecturally and otherwise, to receive the testimony of witnesses, the presentation of various forms of real evidence or demonstrative aids may require that the court physically move to receive them, or that unwieldy objects or paraphernalia be introduced into the courtroom. These actions may cause *undue delay* and *waste of time*. Finally, while oral testimony is easily incorporated into a paper record for purposes of appellate review, demonstrative evidence will sometimes not be susceptible to similar preservation and transmission.

The judge's evaluation of the probative dangers just mentioned will obviously vary greatly with the characteristics of the particular item offered, and the purpose and need for its introduction in the particular case. Since the wide variety of exhibits, and the facts of consequence they are sought to prove, are virtually unlimited (other than by the imagination and resources of trial counsel), it is appropriate and inevitable to accord the trial judge broad discretion in ruling upon admissibility. As an essential part of the exercise of discretion under Federal Rule 403, the judge must also attempt to estimate the probative value of the proffered evidence.

Probative Value. Certain types of the evidence discussed here are accorded significant probative value. Some objects reveal information that bears directly on issues in the case, such as whether the object does or does not possess a perceptible feature, characteristic, or quality. If the object is produced so that the jury may perceive the quality, or its absence, for themselves, this exhibit will be regarded as highly probative; for example, the exhibition of the person if a party seeks damages for the loss of a limb or for an injury leaving a disfiguring scar. Similarly, the exhibition of clothing or other tangible objects may constitute probative evidence on the issue of a relevant condition.

---

[3]   Fed. R. Evid. 403 advisory committee's note.

Often the probative value of a proffered exhibit and the fact at issue requires an inference that is more difficult. For example, to prove identity, a shirt worn at the time of arrest by the defendant in a robbery prosecution is exhibited to the jury to demonstrate its similarity to (and thus its identity as) the shirt worn by the robber, as described by witnesses. How probative is the actual shirt to the issue of identity? Most courts and commentators agree that the primary measure of probative value is the strength of the inference that establishes the connection between the proffered item and the material fact in the case—here, the inference that the defendant and the robber own the same shirt. There is no precise or accurate way to estimate this strength. It is affected by many facts, such as the amount of detail in the witnesses' description and the presence or absence of matching details on the shirt. Other factors also affect the judicial determination of probative value, for example the need for the shirt for purposes of identification in the context of other available evidence or the importance of the issue of identification in the case.

Balancing. Pursuant to Federal Rule 403, the trial judge possesses broad discretionary power to weigh the probative value of the evidence against whatever unfair prejudice, risk of misleading or confusing the jury, or waste of time are entailed, and to determine admissibility accordingly. The desirability of judicial discretion to deal with highly individual situations is particularly well illustrated by the question of the admissibility of photographs portraying a murder victim or the decedent in a wrongful death case as they were "in life." Both the materiality and the potential prejudicial effect of such photographs will vary markedly with the type of case in which they are offered, a fact which renders the careful use of judicial discretion indispensable.

Federal Rule 403 provides some guidance on the question whether the ultimate balancing of probative value and probative danger justifies exclusion of an exhibit. It provides that exclusion is justified when the danger substantially outweighs probative value. This balancing test favors admissibility and seems to require the judge to accept some risks of an exhibit's negative impact on the jury.[4]

As with other circumstantial evidence, of course, an exhibit offered for a proper relevant purpose may give rise to an improper inference as well. Thus, introduction of a gun taken from a defendant upon arrest and shown to be similar to that used in the commission of the crime charged may imply both that the defendant was the robber and that the defendant is a dangerous person given to carrying firearms. In this circumstance, the judge may give a limiting instruction that directs the jury to consider the exhibit only for its proper use. The traditional judicial assumption that the jury can and will adhere to such limiting instructions, and that the risk of unfair prejudice is therefore reduced, justifies admission in these circumstances.

§ 213 Real Evidence

Objects offered as playing an actual and direct part in the incident or transaction giving rise to a trial, for example the alleged weapon in a murder prosecution, are commonly called "real" evidence. Such objects are treated as independent substantive sources of evidence because the trier of fact may draw inferences from the objects themselves about some fact of consequence.

---

[4]   See supra § 185.

For purposes of authentication, if the proponent asserts that the proffered weapon is relevant because it was found at the scene of the crime, then an adequate foundation to authenticate the exhibit would be testimony that the weapon offered is the weapon which was found there. The offered item may possess characteristics that are fairly unique and readily identifiable. If so, the testimony of a percipient witness such as "I recognize the carved handle on this weapon; it is the same as the handle of the weapon I found at the crime scene; this is the weapon I found" will be sufficient to support a finding that the weapon is what it is claimed to be. On the other hand, if the offered evidence is of such a nature as not to be readily identifiable, the foundation required for authentication will be substantially more elaborate. Typically it will entail testimony that traces the chain of custody of the item from the moment it was found to its appearance in the courtroom, with sufficient completeness to render it reasonably probable that the original item has neither been exchanged nor altered.

If the condition of the item of real evidence is important to its identity, the unchanged condition is part of the authentication requirement. It could be the subject of testimony from a percipient witness, or even inferred from the object being relatively impervious to change. If the item is readily subject to tampering or adulteration, such as illegal drugs or other chemicals, a more rigorous chain of custody may be required. If the item has been subjected to testing, the technician becomes part of the chain. Cases decided under Federal Rule 901, however, make it clear that a complete chain of custody need not always be proved. The standard of proof requires only evidence from which the trier could reasonably believe that an item still is what the proponent claims it to be. If there is some specifically identified risk of misidentification or alteration, the proponent of the exhibit should produce evidence to overcome this risk or suffer exclusion. It should, however, always be borne in mind that foundational requirements are essentially requirements of logic, and not rules of art. Thus, even an altered item of real evidence may still be admissible if the pertinent features which make it probative remain unchanged.

Real evidence consisting of samples drawn from a larger mass are also generally held admissible to authenticate the total mass, subject to the foregoing requirements pertaining to real evidence generally and to the further requirement that the sample be established to be accurately representative of the mass. Further, where a mass of material is offered in toto, it will generally be sufficient for the witness to describe the mass and not each constituent item.

Once an item of real evidence has been authenticated, it is still potentially subject to the judge's discretion to exclude pursuant to Federal Rule 403. However, it is customary for judges to treat real evidence as being highly probative and thus of considerable assistance to the jury, sometimes with little analysis of what the jury would learn for purposes of deciding a fact of consequence in the case. Thus, the admission of even gruesome objects has been upheld if they played a part in the litigated events.

§ 214 Demonstrative Aids

It is today increasingly common to encounter the use of demonstrative aids throughout a trial. These aids are offered to illustrate or explain the testimony of witnesses, including experts, or to present a summary or chronology of complex or voluminous documents. Counsel also rely on such aids during opening and closing statements. Demonstrative aids take many forms; the types discussed in this Section are duplicates, models, hand drawn maps, charts, drawings, diagrams, and computer-generated pedagogic aids. Unlike real evidence, the availability of which will frequently depend upon circumstances beyond counsel's control, opportunities for the use of demonstrative aids are limited only by counsel's ingenuity and ability to generate them. The potential of these aids for giving clarity and adding interest to spoken statements has brought about their widespread use, which will undoubtedly continue in the future.

Relevant for "Illustrative" Use Only. Demonstrative aids are defined here by the relevant purpose for which they are offered at trial, which is to illustrate other admitted evidence and thus to render it more comprehensible to the trier of fact. They have been called "derivative" evidence because, in theory at least, demonstrative aids do not have independent probative value for determining the substantive issues in the case. They are relevant, again in theory, only because of the assistance they give to the trier in understanding other real, testimonial and documentary evidence. Summaries and charts of documentary evidence used for this illustrative purpose must be distinguished from summaries admitted as substantive evidence under Federal Rule 1006, discussed in Section 241 infra.

Authentication as "Fair and Accurate" Representation of Other Evidence. When a demonstrative aid is presented, its foundation differs considerably from the requirements for authenticating real evidence. It is not an object that itself was specifically connected to the parties or played a part in the events underlying the litigation. Its source and how it was created may be of no significance whatever. Instead, the theory justifying its admission is that the item is a fair and accurate representation of relevant testimony or documentary evidence that has otherwise been admitted in the case. Typically, an aid will be identified by a witness, during the witness's testimony, as a substantially correct representation of something the witness once perceived and is now describing. This satisfies the sufficiency standard of Federal Rule 901(b)(1), as discussed in Section 212 supra. Whether the admission of a particular demonstrative aid will in fact be helpful, or will instead tend to confuse or mislead the trier, is a matter within the sound discretion of the trial court, in most jurisdictions decided pursuant to Federal Rule 403 and Federal Rule 611(a).

Status as Exhibit. While all jurisdictions allow the use of demonstrative aids throughout trial, there is some diversity of judicial opinion concerning their precise evidentiary status. Some jurisdictions treat such items as admissible exhibits which may be used by a reviewing court and sometimes viewed by the jury during deliberations. Other courts treat them differently, either admitting them for "demonstrative purposes" only or refusing to admit them at all as exhibits. These courts then differ on whether to allow them into the jury room during deliberations.

A major issue in recent case law is the evidentiary status of summaries and charts that present voluminous documentary evidence and testimony that have been admitted at trial in a mode "more akin to argument than evidence . . . [which] may reflect to some extent, through captions or other organizational devices or descriptions, the inferences and conclusions drawn . . . by the summary's proponent."[5] Such summaries blur the line between demonstrative aids that are simply illustrative and summaries admitted as evidence by Federal Rule 1006, which must be shown to the court to be accurate and nonprejudicial. Courts have resolved the tension between the helpfulness of such

---

[5]   U.S. v. Milkiewicz, 470 F.3d 390, 397–98 (1st Cir. 2006).

conclusion-laden summaries and the risk of undue influence on the jury by giving explicit limiting instructions that such summaries are not themselves evidence and may not be relied on by the jury as substantive proof.

Even if all types of demonstrative aids are not permitted into the jury room, there appears to be no reason to deny admission and formal status as an exhibit to such items. It is, unfortunately, common for many demonstrative aids to be displayed and referred to without ever being formally offered or admitted into evidence. Numerous appellate courts have commented upon the difficulties created on appeal when crucial testimony has been given in the form of indecipherable references to an object not available to the reviewing court. The clearly preferable practice is for the proponent to offer a demonstrative aid into evidence as an exhibit, to authenticate it by the testimony of a witness, and formally to introduce it as part of the witness's testimony, in which it will be incorporated by reference. When the record is not so perfected many courts have presumed that the illustrative items and testimony referring to them support the verdict, making it in the interest of both parties to clarify the record.

As stated above, it has also become customary for counsel to make use of demonstrative aids during opening statements and closing arguments. The status of these aids is unclear, whether created by the attorney's use of chalkboards and large pads of paper or as power point slide shows. It has been suggested that if these aids either will be, or have been, admitted as exhibits for use during trial, their status is unchanged by counsel's usage; but if their use is only to dramatize counsel's own words or to suggest counsel's inferences about the substantive evidence, then they should be viewed as part of the counsel's statement or argument and should not be available to the jury during its deliberations.

Duplicates. A duplicate item may often properly be used in lieu of real evidence. Articles actually involved in a transaction or occurrence may be lost or unavailable, or witnesses may be unable to testify that the article present in court is the identical one they have previously observed. Where only the generic characteristics of the item are significant, no objection would appear to exist to the introduction of a substantially similar duplicate. The relevant purpose of such items is to illustrate the characteristics of an object that a witness is testifying was involved in the events at issue. While admissibility is generally viewed as within the discretion of the trial court, it has been suggested that it would constitute reversible error to exclude a duplicate testified to be identical to the object involved in the occurrence. On the other hand, if there is an absence of testimony that the object to be illustrated ever existed, the introduction of a duplicate may foster a mistaken impression of certainty and thus merit exclusion.

Models, Hand Drawn Maps, Drawings and Diagrams. These demonstrative aids, as distinguished from duplicates, are by their nature less easily confused with real evidence. They are relevant under the theory that they illustrate and explain live testimony, and they are authenticated simply on the basis of testimony from a witness that they are substantially accurate representations of what that witness is trying to describe. Such aids may be created outside of court or by a witness during the trial itself.

Probative dangers may exist because aids of this kind can be more misleading than helpful due to inaccuracies, variations of scale, distortion of perspective, etc. If discretionary control pursuant to Federal Rule 403 is applied, probative value is measured by the degree to which the judge thinks that the item will assist the trier of fact in understanding a witness's testimony. When the trial court has exercised its discretion to admit, it will only rarely be found in error. This is particularly true if the potentially misleading features have been pointed out by witnesses for the proponent, or could have been exposed upon cross-examination.

Computer-Generated Pedagogic Aids. The use of all types of computer-generated evidence has increased dramatically during recent years, and the trend seems certain to continue as courtrooms become even better equipped to present all forms of computer displays. There are certain types of computer-generated exhibits (CGEs) that fit comfortably within the class of demonstrative aids as defined here. Their purpose is to display, and to help the jury understand, evidence that is otherwise admitted. Thus, they are also referred to as "pedagogic" aids. As such, these aids are subject to the general view that they are not themselves evidence and would not be used by the jury during deliberations. However, some courts treat such aids as subject to the process of admission as exhibits because they are important tools for educating juries. Commonly used types of such aids are now described.

Static Images. Static images are non-moving images, or still illustrations, that are created by, or stored in, a computer and are projected at trial onto a large screen or individual monitors by a computer display system. Drawings, objects, scenes or mechanisms can be displayed in this way. When used to illustrate the testimony of a witness, these types of CGEs are treated by courts and commentators no differently from more traditional modes of presentation on chalkboards or easels.

Enhanced Images. Enhanced images are presented in static form for the most part, but are subject to computer-driven manipulation to achieve, for example, highlighting, enlargement, split screen presentation and emphasis through the use of zoom, different colors, arrows and the like. Again, while this type of manipulation is more engaging, efficient and perhaps effective than similar techniques created to emphasize points in testimony without a computer, it remains within the category of demonstrative aid so long as it accurately illustrates what a witness has to say. The authenticating testimony from a witness would establish the substantial accuracy of the CGE as reflecting what the witness is trying to describe, and any potential probative dangers in the enhancement would be considered by the trial judge pursuant to Federal Rule 403.

Animations. Computer-generated animations present a series of static images which the computer can show in rapid succession. This creates the illusion of motion, like a cartoon. Many simple animations are offered to illustrate the factual testimony of a witness. For example, an animated CGE might portray the simple motion of a person walking; or, the images can move in rotation to show an object from different perspectives; gradual enlargement can show an object or scene from different distances. These simple animations are not used for the purpose of recreating or simulating an event. The authenticating testimony from a witness would establish that the animated CGE is a fair and accurate representation of what the witness is trying to describe, and admission of the animation would be within the discretion of the trial judge pursuant to Federal Rule 403.

More complex "re-creation" animations illustrate the events that form the basis of the parties' dispute. They are offered as illustrative of the expert opinion of a testifying expert witness. Thus, as a demonstrative aid, they could be authenticated by the expert's testimony that the animation fairly and accurately represents that opinion. Critics of the use of re-creation animations are concerned that they are not simply illustrative; that they incorporate hearsay from persons who provide information to the animators, the hearsay opinions of the animators themselves, and the technical principles used in the computer software to generate the animation. The re-creation animation may thus serve as a conduit for independent substantive, and potentially inadmissible, evidence. This is a serious objection. If the animation, or any illustrative demonstrative aid, also conveys substantive evidence to the jury beyond the scope of the foundation that it simply "illustrates" a witness's testimony, then this foundation is not adequate. Recent empirical research also questions the adequacy of judicial evaluation of the risk of undue prejudice to jury decision making under Federal Rule 403.

Summaries and Charts as Pedagogic Aids. In addition to illustrating the testimony of a witness, CGEs can also be developed to summarize and display evidence (particularly documentary evidence) that has already been admitted at trial. These pedagogic aids are welcomed as effective trial management aids pursuant to Federal Rule 611(a), so long as they are limited in scope to summarizing admitted exhibits. Even if Federal Rule 901 does not necessarily apply when the summary or chart will not be an exhibit, a foundation for the accuracy of the summary should be presented by the proponent. The trial court's decision to permit the use of summary charts and witnesses is reviewed for abuse of discretion.

§ 215 Photographs

Photographs can be admitted under two theories of relevance: as illustrative of a witness's testimony (also called the "pictorial testimony" use of a photograph) and as independent substantive evidence to prove the existence of what the photo depicts (also called the "silent witness" use of a photograph).

Photographs Relevant as Illustrative Only. Photographs have been most commonly admitted into evidence under the same relevance theory as the demonstrative aids just discussed. As illustrative evidence, a photograph is viewed merely as a graphic portrayal of oral testimony. It is authenticated if the witness testifies that the photograph is a correct and accurate representation of relevant facts personally observed by the witness. Accordingly, under this theory, the witness who lays the authentication foundation need not be the photographer, nor need the witness know anything of the time, conditions, or mechanisms of the taking of the picture. Instead, the witness need only have personal knowledge of the facts represented or the scene or objects photographed. Under the Federal Rules and Uniform Rules, this foundation would fall within Rule 901(b)(1). Once personal knowledge is shown, the witness can say whether the photograph correctly and accurately portrays what the witness saw. The photograph thus verified is admissible as a graphic portrayal of the verifying witness's testimony.[6]

Admission of an authenticated photograph is also subject to Federal Rule 403. If the photograph fails to portray the relevant facts with complete accuracy, such as if changed conditions have occurred, it may be misleading. The photograph may still be admissible in the trial court's discretion if the changes are not substantial, are easily explained, or do not reduce the probative value of the image. Photographs that present gruesome details, such as crime scene or autopsy photos, or photos of persons with personal

---

[6]   *But see* Santee, More Than Words: Rethinking the Role of Modern Demonstrative Evidence, 52 Santa Clara L. Rev.105, 123–124 (2012):

> It is impossible to express in words everything that a photograph depicts because words can never describe an image the same way as a photograph. Thus, even if the verbal testimony were so elaborate that it covered every detail of the photograph, the photograph is still further evidence because it necessarily conveys the information in a different manner.

injuries, may be objected to as unfairly prejudicial but typically are admitted. Color and enlarged photographs have generally been viewed as admissible provided the photo represents the scene depicted with substantial accuracy.

The illustrative theory of relevance pursuant to which photographs are admitted is clearly a viable one and has undoubtedly served to facilitate the introduction of the general run of photographs. But it would press the theory too far to deny to photographs the status of exhibits, or to deny them substantive effect when they are used as independent sources of information for the jury, as some courts have done in treating photographs as if they have only an illustrative function at trial.

Photographs Relevant as Independent Substantive Evidence. It might be posited that every photograph conveys more to the senses of the trier than simply what a testifying witness is trying to remember and describe. The masking of the substantive effect of photographs under the rubric of "illustrative evidence" has been cogently criticized both for its lack of conceptual honesty and because of the consequences seen to flow from it.[7] These consequences include inadequate authentication, an instruction to the jury that a photograph may be used for illustrative purposes only, and not permitting the photograph to be used during jury deliberations. Once the photograph is understood as having the capacity to add relevant information on its own, independent of a witness, then it should be acknowledged that the photographic image is itself a source of substantive information and is not merely illustrative. In appropriate cases, this acknowledgment would lead courts to grant photographs full evidentiary status only after subjecting the accuracy of their contents to closer scrutiny under Federal Rule 901 and Federal Rule 403.

Photographs are subjected to such scrutiny when no witness has viewed what they portray. X-ray photographs are clearly understood to be relevant sources of independent substantive information and are consistently admitted. The authentication foundation typically required is that a reliable scientific process was correctly utilized at a specific time and place to obtain the photographic product offered in evidence.

Under this doctrine, commonly referred to as the "silent witness" theory of admission, photographic evidence is shown to be accurate by proof of the reliability of the photographic process. This foundation, including the time and place the photograph was taken, is now used to authenticate photographic evidence of all types as substantive evidence in virtually all jurisdictions. Such a foundation satisfies Federal Rule 901(b)(9) which requires "evidence describing a process or system and showing that it produces an accurate result." In addition to validating the accuracy of the process of reproduction, a complete foundation could also require evidence of the competence of the operator, the condition of the equipment, and the unchanged condition of the product, perhaps by chain of custody. In most cases, due primarily to the well-established reliability of the photographic process, the requisite foundation simply identifies the subject of the photographic product. However, if a photograph is understood to convey highly significant substantive information to the trier of fact, or when there is significant risk of tampering such as now exists with digital images, the court could require a more complete foundation.

---

[7]   Mnookin, The Image of Truth: Photographic Evidence and the Power of Analogy, 10 Yale J. L. & Human.1,3,11,18, 20 (1998). Mnookin argues that treating the photographer as unnecessary to authenticate the accuracy of an "illustrative" photograph should be "understood as a legal fiction" since in many cases the photograph is treated as substantive proof, speaking "with a certain probative force in itself."

Posed Photographs. Posed photographs are artificially reconstructed scenes in which people, automobiles, and other objects are placed and photographed so as to conform to the descriptions of the original crime or collision given by the witnesses. They are typically admitted under the illustrative theory of relevance. However, it should be noted that such photographs are similar to the re-creation animations discussed in Section 214 supra. That is, their process of production may incorporate hearsay information and opinions about the reconstruction that go beyond the testimony of witnesses at trial. If so, then they too may convey substantive evidence to the trier and their "illustrative" foundation is inadequate.

Under existing case law, when the posed photographs portray the positions of persons and objects as reflected in the undisputed testimony, their admission has been generally approved. Frequently, however, a posed photograph will portray only the version of the facts supported by the testimony of the proponent's witness. The dangers inherent in this situation, i.e., the tendency of the photographs unduly to emphasize certain testimony and the possibility that the jury may confuse one party's reconstruction with objective fact, have led some courts to exclude photographs of this type. The current trend would appear to be to permit photos of disputed reconstructions.

§ 216 Video, Film and Sound Recordings

Video, film and sound recordings of objects, properties and events as they happen outside the courtroom are commonplace in criminal prosecutions and personal injury actions. Also commonplace are filmed re-enactments that portray events as they are alleged to have taken place. As judges, counsel and the lay public have become accustomed to the prevalence of such recordings in court, their persuasive potential is both widely acknowledged and the subject of concern. As with photographs, it is important for courts to acknowledge that films and videos are often not merely illustrative of a witness's testimony, but are potential independent sources of substantive information for the trier of fact. The traditional foundation for such recordings as an illustrative demonstrative aid may therefore not be adequate.

Unscripted Video and Film Recordings. The recordings discussed here are not simulations or re-enactments of disputed events. They purport to present reality to the trier of fact. Unscripted recordings include views of a polluted site, surreptitious filming of an allegedly incapacitated plaintiff shoveling snow or playing baseball, police films taken after the arrest of an allegedly intoxicated driver, after-the-fact videos of a crime scene, and cell phone or automated surveillance camera recordings of events that become the subject of trial.

If the recorded events are relevant to prove a fact of consequence in the case, then the recording has been held to be relevant in one of two ways—as illustrative of the testimony of a percipient witness or as substantive evidence that itself is probative of the disputed facts. As with photographs, these two different theories of relevance demand different standards for the authentication and ultimate admissibility of the recording.

Unscripted Recordings Relevant as Illustrative Evidence. When moving pictures were first offered into evidence, they were frequently objected to and sometimes excluded on the theory that they afforded manifold opportunities for fabrication and distortion. Even those older decisions which upheld their admission appear to have done so on the basis of elaborate foundation testimony detailing the methods of taking, processing, and projecting the film. It has now become the general practice, however, that as with still photographs, unscripted video and film recordings may be authenticated by testimony that the recording fairly and accurately reproduces events perceived by the witness.

Under this theory, the requisite authentication foundation may be laid pursuant to Federal Rule 901(b)(1) by the photographer or by any witness who was present when the film was made and who therefore perceived the events filmed. Objections that a video or film is unduly prejudicial or distorted in some significant way, or has been edited and is therefore misleading, are resolved pursuant to Federal Rule 403.

The problem just identified in Section 215 supra regarding still photographs is even more salient when the court is dealing with moving pictures. That is, when a percipient witness testifies to the accuracy of the video or film, there is a judicial tendency to treat it solely as illustrative of, and therefore cumulative of, that testimony. This misrepresents the nature and capacity of the visual medium as an independent source of substantive evidence. Unscripted recordings are potentially fraught with hidden hearsay dangers.[8] First, they often present more information to the trier of fact than witnesses could possibly see or hear; and, they can also present less information than existed at the scene. The film maker chooses what to record and what to omit. Second, the information that films do present is constructed by the film maker's perspective and choices. A video or film may convey a particular point of view to the observer, intentionally or not. In short, even an unscripted film or video is not a "transparent" version of reality.

If courts overlook this capacity of visual recordings to convey independent substantive evidence that is both chosen and constructed by the film maker, then admission of a film or video solely on the basis of testimony from a percipient witness may be inadequate. Relying on the illustrative theory of relevance discourages courts from requiring the parties to engage in careful scrutiny of the actual filming process and the production of the recording. Such scrutiny could help the jury understand the choices made by the film maker and the limits of the recording as wholly objective evidence. Although a camera cannot be cross-examined, a film maker can be.

Unscripted Recordings as Substantive Evidence. Without a percipient witness to testify as to their accuracy, visual recordings, again as with still photographs, are subjected to more careful scrutiny under the "silent witness" theory of authentication. Recordings such as a tape from an automatic surveillance camera can be authenticated as the accurate product of an automated process, the foundation required by Federal Rule of Evidence 901(b)(9). However, admission of such videotapes has also been upheld upon a more tenuous foundation.

Courts acknowledge that these videotapes are independent sources of substantive evidence; indeed, they seem to treat these tapes as unimpeachable eyewitnesses "testifying" to the true version of what happened. Yet even automated cameras do not record everything and do record only from the perspective of where they are situated. Enhancing and editing add a human element of subjectivity which should also be examined and understood by the jury. An inquiry into the effect of possible limits on the "truth-value" of the tapes could aid the jury in understanding their message.

---

[8]   For the original treatment of these points, see Silbey, Judges as Film Critics: New Approaches to Filmic Evidence, 37 U. Mich. J.L. Reform 493 (2004).

Judicial acknowledgement of the capacity of video and film evidence to distort the substantive information that they appear to present as ultra-realism might not change the outcome of many judicial decisions on admissibility. But it could result in a more vigorous application of the authentication standard under Federal Rule 901, acknowledgement of the underlying hearsay issue, a more thorough discussion of probative value under Federal Rule 403, and a more realistic understanding of the unrealistic aspects of this type of evidence by the jury.

Scripted Recordings. An even more serious issue of departure from reality is posed by scripted moving pictures, such as day-in-the-life films taken of an injured party pursuing ordinary day-to-day activities, offered for the purpose of bringing home to the trier of fact the implications and significance of the injury for which damages are sought. These films are not spontaneous but are designed and produced by representatives of the injured party. Underlying the footage, therefore, there may be intent both on the part of the film maker and the injured person to display the effects of injury in a particular way, presumably to communicate to the trier the gravity of the harm suffered. With this understanding of their purpose, some courts have acknowledged the assertive nature of day-in-the-life films and have attempted to use the rules of evidence to assure accuracy. In general, however, admission of such films is left to the sound discretion of the trial judge.

Recorded Reenactments. A still different set of problems is presented by videotapes which do not record original events in controversy, but rather represent one party's staged reproduction of those events, using real people rather than animated figures. Such reenactments are increasingly used in criminal and tort cases due to advances in crime scene and accident reconstruction.

These recorded reenactments are admitted as illustrative or demonstrative evidence to aid the jury's understanding of an expert's opinion as to what happened. They are authenticated by testimony from the expert that they fairly and accurately represent his opinion, and that they accurately represent the testimony in the record that the expert relies on. On this basis, the reenactment video should not be available to the jury during deliberations. They are also subject to exclusion under Federal Rule 403. Filmed reenactments may in some cases be more properly classified as out-of-court demonstrations or experiments.[9] Courts require that the filmed events be prepared under, and demonstrate, conditions "substantially similar" to the event in question as shown by admitted evidence.

The extreme vividness and verisimilitude of pictorial evidence is truly a two-edged sword. Thus, many of the issues to be identified in Section 218 infra pertaining to simulations and re-creation animations also apply to recorded reenactments. Not only is there danger that the jury may confuse art with reality. The impressions generated by the evidence may prove particularly difficult to limit by judicial instruction or, if the film is subsequently deemed inadmissible, to expunge by instruction. The latter difficulty may be largely eliminated if the court holds a preliminary viewing in chambers and conducts a prior hearing on admissibility.

Sound Recordings. Narration of events perceived will sometimes be offered as an integral part of a film or videotape, raising the possibility that the filmed portrayal is

---

[9]   See infra § 217.

admissible while the sound recording may not be. The common-sense expedient in such cases, suggested by some decisions, is to suppress the sound.

More commonly, modern technology provides many modes of recording communications from persons who are heard but not seen; for example, tape recordings, answering machines and voice messages. As with video or film recordings of real events, if a percipient witness overheard the voices as they were recorded, this witness may provide the required authentication foundation by testifying that the sound recording is an accurate record of what the witness did hear. In such a case, no chain of custody is required either, since the purpose of proving the chain is to show that the recording is in the same condition as when first recorded.

If no witness testifies that he overheard the crucial information being recorded, then the record must be authenticated by the "silent witness" process; that is, testimony concerning the accuracy of the recording system and the absence of tampering, often through its chain of custody.

Under either foundation, sound recordings are treated as independent substantive evidence of messages, conversations or other sounds. It would blink reality to consider them solely as illustrative evidence. The recorded voices, inflections of speech and other sounds defy adequate description by the testifying witness and are inevitably subject to interpretation directly by the trier.

Since messages and conversations are frequently hearsay statements offered for the truth of the matters asserted, authentication is by no means a guarantee of admissibility. Other evidentiary problems include objections under Federal Rule 403 as to the completeness and audibility of the recording, and whether and under what conditions transcripts of the recording should be made available to the jury while listening to the recording. A transcript must itself be authenticated by evidence sufficient to support a finding that it is an accurate rendition of the authenticated tape recording. The transcript is usually treated as a demonstrative aid to the jury's understanding of the recording; thus, it is not admitted as evidence of the recording's contents and is not taken into the jury room during deliberation.

§ 217   Demonstrations and Experiments

Demonstrations and experiments conducted in the courtroom typically involve a testifying witness engaging in action before the trier of fact to illustrate or explain what the witness is trying to describe. Like a demonstrative aid, if it assists the trier's understanding, it is relevant. Typically, this action is not a tangible exhibit and cannot be recorded and retained. Therefore, strict compliance with the requirement of authentication is not necessary. However, it is part of the witness's testimony, and the testimony should include a description of what the witness is doing, and why, which will make a record for appellate review. The conducting of a demonstration or an experiment is always subject to the discretion of the trial court pursuant to Federal Rule 403.

Demonstrations. The exhibition of a wound or physical injury, e.g., the injury sustained by a plaintiff in a personal injury action, will frequently be probative evidence of a material fact. Not surprisingly, therefore, exhibitions of physical injuries to the jury are commonly allowed. In most jurisdictions the matter is viewed as subject to the discretion of the trial court, but has sometimes been said to be a right of the injured party. A trial court is rarely reversed for permitting a bodily exhibition. Thus, when the exhibition is permitted, no abuse of discretion is generally found even though the injury displayed was particularly shocking, or even where the injury's nature or existence need not have been proved because it has been admitted by the opponent.

The physical characteristics of a person may also constitute relevant evidence. For example, the scars or physical condition of a victim may tend to prove the nature of an assault, or a physical trait of a person may be relevant to prove or disprove the identity of the perpetrator or involvement in a crime or tort. Though some awkwardness is encountered in treating persons as exhibits, bodily exhibitions for these purposes are within the trial court's discretion and have frequently been allowed. When the prosecution seeks to exhibit traits of the defendant, the question has long been analyzed under the heading of self-incrimination and the demonstration has been allowed so long as it may be classed as "nontestimonial." Similarly, it has generally been held that it is open to the defendant to display his physical characteristics to the trier of fact without incurring the necessity of taking the stand.

It is also within the discretion of the trial court to permit the injured person to perform actions or submit to manipulation by a physician, although judicial opinion has been somewhat more divided concerning the propriety of going beyond mere exhibition. The probative dangers inherent in such demonstrations include undue emotional response on the part of the jury and the fact that manifestations of pain and impairment of function are easily feigned and difficult to test by cross-examination. Nevertheless, discretion is frequently exercised in favor of permitting the demonstration.

In addition to active demonstrations of physical injuries, in-court reenactment of material events by participating witnesses has been held permissible to illustrate testimony. Some demonstrations are videotaped out of court and the video is introduced during the testimony of the person who participated in the demonstration.

Experiments. There is no formal distinction between an in-court demonstration and an in-court experiment, although it might be said that a demonstration becomes an experiment when the witness, particularly an expert witness, attempts to reenact some aspect of an event in order to show a specific result that is at issue in the trial. The results of such an experiment are generally proved through the testimony of the experimenting witness describing what the experiment is and what is occurring.

Unlike experiments performed out of court, the results of which are generally communicated through expert testimony, in-court experimentation may involve considerable confusion and delay, and the trial judge is viewed as in the best position to judge whether the probative value of the experiment is substantially outweighed by such costs. The probative value of in-court experiments is determined by the similarity of the conditions between the experiment and the alleged out of court event, a requirement which is applicable to experimental evidence generally. This requirement may be particularly difficult to meet under courtroom conditions, and many proposed courtroom experiments have been held properly excluded on this ground. Involving the jury in an experiment is subject to careful scrutiny by the court to insure its substantial similarity to the out-of-court events.

Simple demonstrative experiments by a witness are usually permitted and may be strikingly effective in adding vividness to the spoken word. It should not be overlooked, however, that this vividness may create the risk of undue emotional response by the jury.

Recorded Experiments and Demonstrations. Out-of-court experiments and demonstrations are frequently filmed or videotaped so that the jury may observe the results rather than merely having them described by an expert witness. The fact of filming does not alter the basic requirement of "substantial similarity" that is applicable to experiments and demonstrations. However, the more realistic and life-like the experiment, the greater becomes the judicially-perceived danger that the recording is unduly persuasive because it may cause the jury to confuse the filmed event with the actual one in litigation. Thus, where the film or tape may appear to present a replication of the original event, the required similarity has been rigorously enforced. Experiments intended to demonstrate the nature or capacity of physical objects, or the general principles of science, do not present the visual reproduction of the event itself and there is less chance of jury confusion; the similarity requirement is therefore not so strictly imposed as part of the foundation for the recording. Even if the experiment is aimed at demonstrating general principles of science, the court still has discretion to exclude if it is a veiled attempt at a recreation of the event or is prejudicial.

§ 218 Computer-Generated Simulations and Models

In recent years, technology has added a new weapon to the arsenal of the trial lawyer in the form of the computer-generated exhibit (CGE). As discussed previously in Section 214, to the extent that CGEs such as computer-generated animations represent simply a new type of illustrative evidence, their admissibility is controlled by the basic principles applied to all demonstrative aids. That is, since their relevance is limited to helping the jury understand the testimony of a witness, authentication is often limited to the witness's statement that the exhibit is a fair and accurate representation of what the witness saw, or of what an expert witness has concluded from the admitted evidence. There is no need to apply principles of evidence law that require more information about the creation of the demonstrative aid.

This Section discusses computer-generated simulations and models, which are not just illustrative evidence. These two forms of CGEs create their own version of disputed events, typically in personal injury cases and criminal prosecutions. Their creation requires the use of scientific data, principles and methods to formulate a computer-generated conclusion about the events at issue. This conclusion is sought either to be introduced directly through the CGE or to be used by an expert to form an opinion. Simulations and models are therefore viewed as independent sources of substantive evidence for the trier of fact and are admissible only after satisfying evidentiary requirements beyond those applicable to demonstrative aids.

The adequacy of the typical foundation for these two types of CGE exhibit is addressed in this Section. That some computer animations occupy the borderland between illustrative and substantive evidence is also discussed. A summary of the debate over the impact of animations and simulations on accurate jury decision making concludes the Section.

Computer-Generated Simulations. The purpose of a computer-generated simulation is to determine how an event "must have happened" and then to provide a visual image of that conclusion. A simulation adds information beyond the testimony of percipient witnesses, both in terms of the data inputs into the computer and the programming which analyzes and then graphically portrays the outputs.

For example, empirical or recorded data, such as size and shape of an object, time, altitude, and velocity are entered into a computer program from several different sources. The data is then processed according to formulae programmed into the computer and the relative paths of all objects throughout the pertinent time period are independently plotted. The computer tracks and accurately depicts each object relative to all other objects throughout the time span, taking into account known laws of physics, such as gravity, inertia, friction and drag.

Computer-generated simulations that re-create and graphically depict disputed events are generally considered to be sources of substantive evidence for the trier. Even when simulations are introduced through the testimony of an expert opinion witness, the graphic simulation itself is independently relevant to prove a fact of consequence— how an occurrence would have happened. The computer-generated "opinion" is determined by the scientific principles that an expert has programmed into the computer. Thus the simulation must be authenticated as an accurate result of a system or process, pursuant to Federal Rule 901(b), by a set of factors: (1) sufficiency of the factual basis that serves as input, and its substantial similarity to the real event; (2) reliability of the underlying technical or scientific principles; (3) accuracy of the specific computer operating system; and (4) appropriateness and accuracy of the mathematical formulae creating the model that is programmed into the computer.[10]

Moreover, there are issues akin to hearsay. A simulation is the work product of many out-of-court actors whose knowledge and beliefs affect the reliability of the simulation, including (1) the sources of the factual basis for the simulation; (2) the sources of the underlying scientific and technical formulae and assumptions made by the programmers; and (3) the design, testing, selection and operation of the computer program. Testing these out-of-court hearsay sources could be conducted through examination of the necessary witnesses in court, and/or under the rules governing the admissibility of a testifying expert's opinion, in particular under Federal Rules 702 and 703.

Computer-Generated Models. Computer models can also be used to test hypotheses of experts as to what did or could happen concerning events related to litigation. The inputs contain variables as well as known information; the computer runs these inputs through formulae based on scientific principles. Based on the various results of the model, depending on the variable inputs, the expert may be able to form a conclusion about his hypotheses and will then base his opinion upon these results. Typically, there is no graphic image created by this type of "data model" as that term is used here. The foundation for such models parallels the foundation described above for simulations. Since the model is used to formulate a testifying expert's opinion, the validity of the scientific principles and methods under *Daubert* and other case law is of paramount concern.[11]

What Is the Appropriate Foundation for "Re-Creation" Animations Portraying the Opinions of Testifying Expert Witnesses? A frequently used type of animation is the "re-creation" animation which is developed to portray the pre-existing opinion of an expert as to "what happened." This animation is more complex than the simple animation, as

---

[10]   These factors are drawn from Joseph, Modern Visual Evidence at § 701 [4][c] (2018).

[11]   See supra § 203.

has been discussed in Section 214 supra, although it is also created as a series of individual drawings displayed to portray full motion.

A distinction is drawn by both courts and commentators between the computer-generated simulations just described and re-creation animations. Re-creation animations are described as "illustrative" of an opinion that the testifying expert has already arrived at, whereas simulations have helped to generate that opinion and thus are "substantive" evidence. This distinction is reminiscent of the dichotomy between the "illustrative" evidence theory and the "silent witness" theory for admitting photographs and film and video recordings.[12]

This distinction has justified the admission of re-creation animations on the basis of a simpler foundation than simulations. That is, as previously described in Section 214, re-creation animations must only be shown to be relevant to the issues in the case, authenticated as a fair and accurate depiction of an expert's opinion. In addition, of course, they are subject to trial court discretion under Federal Rule 403, pursuant to which the court evaluates the animation's probative value in terms of how much it will aid the trier in understanding and evaluating that opinion and determines whether the animation's probative dangers substantially outweigh its value. Compare this simple foundation with that prescribed for simulations in the footnotes under *Computer-Generated Simulations* and *Computer-Generated Models*, supra.

Under these standards, exactly how much information courts will require about the creation of the animation is a matter of discretion; and courts are not always consistent in labeling the particular exhibit. In determining the accuracy of re-creation animations, courts have required that the event shown on the animation must conform to the testimony about that event at trial. A few courts have also required testimony from, or about, the specific sources of data that were relied on by the animator. The expert whose opinion is depicted by the animation will have to testify about the basis for that opinion and the scientific or technical principles upon which it is based, as must any testifying expert, but not about the scientific or technical validity of the underlying computer program. Trial courts also give elaborate instructions to the jury concerning the limited purpose of the animation as illustrative evidence, and appellate courts rely on the fact that instructions were given to reduce the probative danger that the animation misled the jury.

It must be recognized that there can be significant similarities in the methods by which both re-creation animations and simulations are created. Because of these similarities, the re-creation animation may also reflect substantive knowledge and information beyond that of the testifying expert. It too may make its own independent evidentiary contribution to the trial. It thus partakes of a dual "illustrative evidence"/"substantive evidence" identity, a duality shared with photographs and video and film recordings.[13] This simply means that the rigid distinction between a simulation and an animation cannot always be maintained and that courts should not rely on these labels alone to resolve the question of what foundation for admissibility they should require. When courts fail to acknowledge this dual identity, they only rely on the foundation for "illustrative" evidence to assure the accuracy of the animation. This foundation may be inadequate.

---

12   See supra §§ 215–216.
13   See supra §§ 215–216.

Are Animations and Simulations Misleading "Razzle Dazzle" or Necessary Explanations of Complexity? Both supporters and critics of the increasing use of computer re-creation animations and simulations in trials have concerns about their effect on jury decision making.[14] Courts have excluded computer simulations pursuant to Federal Rule 403 on the grounds that their probative dangers substantially outweigh their probative value. The principal dangers that have been identified are that animations and simulations will over-persuade the jury, overwhelm traditional testimony about what happened, and can mislead due to inaccuracy and bias in the creation of the exhibit. The fact that an animation or simulation includes factual inputs from only one side's version of the disputed events has also been considered problematic.

Supporters of the use of animations and simulations in the courtroom contend just the opposite. They assert that it is the complexity of the issues tried to juries, and the tedium of the evidence, that will overwhelm the accuracy of jury decision making in contemporary litigation unless the jury receives the substantial help in understanding the evidence that such CGEs provide.[15]

Surely there is some truth in both positions. Thoughtful judges seem convinced that short, simple, clear and concise animations that are "clinical and devoid of drama so as to prevent jury reliance on an improper basis"[16] are not unfair and are helpful to the jury. Empirical research on the impact of CGEs on decision makers may help to identify what issues, concerning both the preparation of the exhibit and the impact of the images it displays, should be carefully scrutinized. In the adversary system, courts must rely on the opposing party to raise these issues. Thus, adequate opportunity for pre-trial examination of simulations and animations and for interrogation of their creators is essential. The evolving standards for admission of simulations and re-creation animations place the decision whether to admit them squarely within the discretion of the trial court judge. As the Tenth Circuit stated in *Robinson v. Missouri Pacific Railroad*, district courts should exercise their discretion "carefully and meticulously"[17] and appellate courts should not shrink from providing helpful and enforceable guidelines.

§ 219 Views

Courts have sensibly recognized that if a thing cannot be brought to the observer, the observer must go to the thing. Venturing forth to observe places or objects that are material to litigation, but which cannot feasibly be brought, or satisfactorily reproduced, within the courtroom, is termed a "view." While statutes or court rules concerning views are in effect in nearly all states, it is frequently said that even without express statutory authorization there is an inherent power in the trial judge to order a view by the jury, or, in a judge-tried case, to take a view personally. This power extends to views of personal property and real property in criminal as well as civil cases.

Since a view is often time-consuming and disruptive of the ordinary course of a trial, the trial judge is in most instances vested with wide discretion to grant or refuse a view.

---

[14] Fiedler, Note, Are Your Eyes Deceiving You?: The Evidentiary Crisis Regarding the Admissibility of Computer Generated Evidence, 48 N.Y. L. Sch. L. Rev. 295 (2003); Goode, The Admissibility of Electronic Evidence, 29 Rev. Litig. 1 (Fall 2009).

[15] Joseph, Modern Visual Evidence § 1.01 (2018).

[16] Com. v. Serge, 837 A.2d 1255, 1263 (Pa. Super. Ct. 2003), aff'd, 896 A.2d 1170 (Pa. 2006).

[17] Robinson v. Missouri Pacific R. Co., 16 F.3d 1083, 1088 (10th Cir. 1994).

It is to be noted, however, that a number of state statutes provide that in certain types of cases, notably eminent domain, either party is entitled to a view upon request as a matter of right. Where the grant of a view is discretionary with the trial court, factors to be considered include the importance of the information to be gained by the view to the issues in the case, changed conditions, practicality, and whether the same information has been secured from maps, photos or diagrams and testimony from witnesses. A district court's rationale that a requested view would be "time consuming, difficult to control, and [un]necessary in order for the jury to fully appreciate the case, especially in light of the numerous photographs and reports, and the relevant testimony . . . allowed into evidence" was upheld as paralleling the standards in other Circuits.[18]

The appropriate procedures to be followed in connection with views are widely regulated by statute. At common law, and generally in civil cases today, the presence of the trial judge at a view is not required, although some circuit courts have held that the judge must attend the view since his or her oversight "is as important during the view as in the course of the trial."[19] Unauthorized views by one or more jury members are of course improper and can constitute reversible error. Attendance at the view by the parties and their counsel is generally permitted though subject to the discretion of the trial judge. The judge in a bench trial may take a view, though to do so without allowing the parties to attend invites a claim of error. In criminal cases, the rights of the defendant to have the judge present at the view, and to be present personally, are frequently provided for by statute. Moreover, when testimony is taken at the view, or the view itself is deemed to constitute evidence, the right of the defendant to be present in all probability possesses a constitutional underpinning.

Statutory and constitutional considerations aside, the advisability of trial court attendance at views is strongly suggested by the numerous cases in which unauthorized comments, obviously hearsay, have been made to the jury, or other improper events have occurred during the course of the view. Presence of the trial judge would seem to afford the best guarantee against the occurrence of events of this nature. On the other hand, where the trial judge is present to rule on admissibility, and provision for preparation of a proper record is made, there would appear no inherent vice in receiving testimony or allowing demonstrations or experiments during a view. These practices, however, have been looked upon with disfavor by appellate courts, and some jurisdictions appear to hold reception of testimony or experiments during a view improper under any circumstances.

The evidentiary status of a view has been a troublesome problem for courts, since what the jury perceives is relevant both as real proof and as a demonstrative aid. A large number of jurisdictions have held that a view is not itself evidence; like a demonstrative aid, its purpose is only to assist the trier of fact in understanding and evaluating the evidence. It is therefore common practice in these jurisdictions to so instruct the jury, and to tell jury members that they may take into account what they have seen only so long as it is supported by evidence they received in the courtroom. One justification for this doctrine is that facts garnered by the jury from a view are difficult or impossible to embody in the written record, and thus review of questions concerning weight or sufficiency of the evidence becomes impracticable. However, many other types of demonstrative aids are to some extent subject to the same difficulty. It is unreasonable

---

[18]   Kelley v. Wegman's Food Markets, Inc., 98 Fed. Appx. 102, 104 (3d Cir. 2004).

[19]   Clemente v. Carnicon-Puerto Rico Management Associates, L.C., 52 F.3d 383, 386 (1st Cir. 1995).

to assume that jurors will apply the metaphysical distinction suggested in the instruction and will ignore the evidence of their own senses if it conflicts with the testimony of the witnesses. Commentators have condemned the downgrading of views to non-evidentiary status. A substantial number of courts now hold that a view has full status as an independent source of evidence for the trier of fact. This is the preferable position, at least when it is acknowledged that a view alone cannot logically be considered to constitute sufficient evidence of a fact the establishment of which ordinarily requires the introduction of expert testimony.

§ 220 Exhibits in the Jury Room

Under modern American practice it is common to allow many types of tangible exhibits to be taken by the jury into the jury room for consideration during the deliberations, provided that the exhibits have been formally admitted into evidence. The question whether a particular exhibit may be taken into the jury room is widely viewed as subject to discretionary control by the trial judge, but in some jurisdictions jury access to at least certain types of exhibits is apparently made mandatory either by judicial holding or legislative enactment.

Current practice with regard to written exhibits differentiates between the relevance of the writings. Legal rights and liabilities are frequently a function of particular words and figures and may be drastically affected by seemingly minor variations in phraseology. Thus crucial documents, such as deeds, contracts, or ledger sheets may frequently be of vital help to the jury and should be carefully scrutinized. However, writings which are testimonial in nature, such as depositions, dying declarations in writing, etc. are typically not taken in with the jury. Courts have frequently commented that such writings, viewed as simply a different form of testimony, should not be unduly emphasized over oral testimony in the case. For this reason, the transcript of an audio recording which may be given to the jury during the playing of the recording is usually treated as a demonstrative aid to the jury's understanding. Thus it is not admitted as evidence of the recording's contents and is not taken into the jury room during deliberation. Written or recorded confessions in criminal cases, however, are in many jurisdictions allowed to be taken by the jury despite their obvious testimonial character. This exception may be justified on the theory that their centrality in the case warrants whatever emphasis may result.

The need for allowing the jury to take tangible exhibits other than writings into the jury room seems somewhat weaker, at least if the jury has made an in-court examination of the exhibit. The persuasive force of real evidence and demonstrative aids arguably does not need additional augmentation. Further, the relevant characteristics of many tangible exhibits are sufficiently gross as not to require the close examination appropriate to writings, while at the other end of the spectrum there may be risk in allowing independent jury inspection of the finer features of tangible exhibits which require exposition and interpretation by an expert. Nevertheless, the sending of tangible exhibits to the jury room is today so well established as to be practically irreversible.

A major problem stemming from relatively free jury access to tangible exhibits other than writings is that of controlling the jury's experimenting with them in the jury room. Judicial limitations upon the introduction of evidence of experiments become largely meaningless if the jury is allowed to conduct experiments of its own devising in the jury room. In attempting to distinguish between proper and improper jury use of tangible exhibits, the most commonly drawn distinction is between experiments which constitute merely a closer scrutiny of the exhibit and experiments which go "beyond the lines of the evidence" introduced in court and thus constitute the introduction of new evidence in the jury room. The decisions reached under this standard are perhaps not totally reconcilable. Most courts, however, emphasize the immunity of jury-conducted experiments from scrutiny by the parties as their most objectionable feature. Thus, it would seem correct to say that jury experimentation is improper if reasonable grounds to attack such an experiment exist and, in addition, if nothing happened during the in-court proceedings to make such an attack inappropriate. Specifically, experiments which are merely reruns of in-court experiments, or which use techniques of examination not markedly different from those employed during trial, are not generally held to fall within the proscribed class. On the other hand, jury experiments utilizing techniques or equipment substantially different from any employed in court tend to be held error, at least where counsel has not specifically acquiesced in the experiment.

Federal Rule 606, however, limits the admissibility of juror testimony about events that occur during deliberations to "whether extraneous prejudicial information was improperly brought to the jury's attention" or "an outside influence was improperly brought to bear on any juror." It has been suggested that experimenting with physical evidence that has been admitted as an exhibit does not fall within these permissible topics of jury testimony. Improper experimenting inside the jury room as grounds for impeaching a verdict may therefore be difficult to prove under the Federal Rules, unless the experimentation is viewed as resulting in "extraneous" prejudicial information.

Title 9

WRITINGS

Chapter 22

AUTHENTICATION

Table of Sections

---

§ 221 General Theory: No Assumption of Authenticity

As discussed in Chapter 21, in all jurisdictions the requirement of authentication applies to all tangible and demonstrative exhibits. The discussion here will be limited to the authentication of writings and voice communications. To summarize what has gone before, the requirement of authentication requires that the proponent, who is offering into evidence a writing or a voice communication, produce evidence sufficient to support a finding that the writing or voice communication is what the proponent claims it is.

The proponent's assertion as to why the writing is relevant determines what the proponent claims the writing is, typically that it has some specific connection to a person or organization, whether through authorship or some other relation. It is this connection that must be proved to authenticate the writing.

In the everyday affairs of business and social life, it is customary simply to look at the writing itself for evidence as to its source. If the writing bears a signature purporting to be that of X, or recites that it was made by X, we assume, nothing to the contrary appearing, that it is exactly what it purports to be, the work of X. At this point, however, the law of evidence has long differed from the common-sense assumption upon which we conduct our own affairs. Instead it adopts the position that the purported signature or recital of authorship on the face of a writing is not sufficient proof of authenticity to secure the admission of the writing into evidence. The same attitude has traditionally extended as well to the authority of agents, with the result that if an instrument recites that it is signed by A as agent for P, not only must additional proof be given that A actually did the signing, but also of the fact that A was P's agent and authorized to sign.

The principal justification urged for this judicial skepticism toward the recital of authorship in documents is that it constitutes a necessary check on the perpetration of fraud. To use an example: In a suit for libel, the alleged libelous writing must be authenticated by evidence to show that defendant authored or published it. This

553

requirement protects the defendant from the risk that the libelous writing is not his work but that of some third person. It is also possible that plaintiff has fabricated the writing to generate a claim for relief. The requirement of authentication also protects the defendant from the possibility of mistake, such as mistaken attribution of a writing to one who fortuitously happens to possess the same name, etc., as the true author.

However, requiring proof of what may be correctly assumed in 99 out of 100 cases is at best time-consuming and expensive. At the worst, the requirement will occasionally be seen to produce results which are virtually indefensible.

Traditional requirements of authentication admittedly furnish some guarantee against fraudulent or mistaken attribution of a writing. Nevertheless, it has frequently been questioned whether this benefit is not outweighed by the time, expense, and occasional untoward results entailed by the traditional skeptical attitude toward authenticity of writings. It is also clear, however, that simply handing a writing to the jury without any contextual information at all would be confusing and perhaps misleading. The requirement of satisfying the authentication standard of Federal Rule 901 is not a heavy one. Typically, it places the burden of locating a witness with some knowledge of the writing on the proponent; the opponent may cross-examine the witness about it; and the trier of fact then gets the added benefit of additional foundational information about the writing. The following sections present the most common modes of satisfying the authentication requirement.

In some instances, testimony or other secondary evidence about the contents of a writing will be offered rather than the writing itself. This is permissible through the operation of the so-called "best evidence" rule or its exceptions.[1] The original writing should still be authenticated, for the connection between the original writing and an individual is still necessary to relevance when the writing is described in testimony.

§ 222 Authentication by a Percipient Witness

Proof of Authorship. The simplest form of testimony authenticating the author of a writing is the production of a witness who swears that he saw a specific person write and/or sign the proffered writing. The testimony of a percipient witness satisfies the requirement that evidence sufficient to support a finding be presented. The witness may be anyone—the author or signer, acknowledging execution; a person who simply observed the event; or, a formal subscribing or attesting witness who must be called before other witnesses may authenticate the writing.

The Federal Rules of Evidence dispensed with the requirement of calling attesting witnesses except when the writing to be offered is one required by the law of the jurisdiction to be attested. When attesting witnesses are so required, it is not required that the attesters give favorable testimony establishing the writing. So even if they profess want of memory or even deny that they attested, the writing may be established by other proof; and conversely, if they support the writing, other proof may establish that it is not authentic.

Proof of Other Connections. A writing may also be authenticated by testimony from a percipient witness that other connections exist between the writing and a particular person, and it is those connections that make that writing relevant. For example, a

---

[1]   See infra Ch. 23.

writing may be relevant because a certain person found it, read it or possessed it, and an observer to that act may properly authenticate the writing.

§ 223   Authentication by Proof of Handwriting

The Federal Rules of Evidence formalized the common law's two principal methods of authenticating a document by the handwriting of its author. These are testimony from lay witnesses as to their nonexpert opinion, and comparison of the proffered document with authenticated specimens by the trier of fact or an expert.

Nonexpert Opinion. A witness giving her lay opinion about another person's handwriting must first testify that she is familiar with that person's handwriting from her own personal knowledge. The nonexpert's qualification as to how familiarity was gained is typically required to be shown but is minimal. Once shown, anyone thus familiar with the handwriting of a given person may supply authenticating testimony in the form of an opinion that a writing or signature is in the handwriting of that person, except that Federal Rule 901(b)(2) requires that this familiarity not have been acquired for purposes of the current litigation. Adequate familiarity obtained from experience prior to trial may be present if the witness has seen the person write or has seen writings purporting to be those of the person in question under circumstances indicating their genuineness. Examples of the latter situation include instances where the witness has had an exchange of correspondence with the person, or has seen writings which the person claims to have authored, or has been present in an office or other place where genuine writings of a particular person in the ordinary course of business would naturally be seen. Finally, it is not required that the authenticating witness's identification be absolutely certain or even categorical in nature. Weaknesses in the foundation for the witness's opinion, or lack of certainty, will usually be said to affect the "weight" of the opinion, not its admissibility. But at some point, a lay witness's opinion may be so conclusory and unsubstantiated that the authentication requirement of evidence sufficient to support a finding is not satisfied.

Comparison by Trier or Expert Witness. Another well-established doctrine permits authentication of proffered handwritten writings by comparison with handwriting specimens or exemplars. The specimen may be admitted at trial solely for the purpose of making this comparison. The general rule is that the specimen must be authenticated pursuant to the "sufficiency" standard of Federal Rule 901. Once the specimen is admitted for purposes of comparison, the genuineness of the proffered writing alleged to be the work of the same author becomes a question for the trier of fact. The proponent may, but need not, offer the testimony of an expert witness to aid the trier. Analogous holdings may be found in the relatively more rare cases of authentication by typing technique or word usage patterns (psycholinguistics), both of which, like handwriting identification, proceed on the basis of comparisons between the document in question and exemplars of known origin.

There is good reason to doubt that lay opinion or the jury's own comparison is meaningful in cases where the authenticity is actually disputed and requires distinguishing a skilled forgery from a genuine writing. Certainly, it is incredible that an unskilled layman who saw the person write once a decade before could make such a differentiation. The prevalent judicial view holds the testimony of bona fide handwriting experts to be evidence of greater reliability and persuasiveness. However, the admissibility of handwriting analysis, and in particular the opinions of handwriting experts as to the identity of the author of a particular handwriting sample, have been subject to recent challenge in criminal cases under the United States Supreme Court opinions in *Daubert* and *Kumho Tire*.[2]

The minimal qualifications required of the ordinary lay witness or juror to authenticate a writing by identification of handwriting are defensible only on the basis that no more than one in a hundred writings is questioned. The current permissive standards allow the admission of the general run of authentic documents with a minimum of time, trouble, and expense. It has been argued that even greater savings in these commodities might safely be achieved by simply presuming the authenticity of writings for purposes of admissibility in the absence of proof raising a question as to genuineness.

§ 224 Authentication by Distinctive Characteristics and Other Circumstances

Many written documents are authenticated by proof of appearance, contents, substance and other distinctive characteristics, taken in conjunction with the circumstances of its source, location, condition etc. It is clear that authentication by such circumstantial evidence is uniformly recognized as permissible. Certain patterns of circumstantial evidence have in fact been so frequently held to authenticate particular types of writings that they have come to be recognized as distinct rules, e.g., the ancient documents rule and the public records rule. These formalized provisions of the Federal Rules are treated in Sections 225–226 infra. Treated here are some of the other familiar patterns which are commonly used to prove the source of a writing, such as that its contents refer to a particular person's knowledge, or that it has been written in reply to prior correspondence. These same concepts are now applied to authenticate newer forms of electronic communication, such as email, text messages etc.[3]

It is important to bear in mind, however, that authentication by circumstantial evidence is not limited to situations which fall within one of these recurrent patterns. Rather, proof of any circumstances which will support a finding that the writing is what it is claimed to be will suffice to authenticate the writing.

Contents Refer to a Person's Knowledge. When a signed letter is received "out of the blue" with no previous correspondence, the traditional "show me" skepticism of the common law prevails, and the purported signature is not sufficient as authentication, unless authenticity is confirmed by additional facts.

One circumstance recognized as sufficient is that the letter discloses knowledge that the purported signer would be likely to have or that otherwise identifies a person as the probable author. The knowledge need not be uniquely held by the purported signer, but the smaller the group of persons with such knowledge, the stronger the desired inference of authorship.

Reply Letter. Moreover, a convenient practice recognizes that if a letter has been written to a specific recipient, and the letter now offered in evidence purports to be written by the recipient in reply to the first letter (that is, its contents either refer to the first letter, or are responsive to its terms) and has been received without unusual delay,

---

[2]   Daubert v. Merrell Dow Pharmaceuticals, Inc., 509 U.S. 579 (1993); Kumho Tire Co., Ltd. v. Carmichael, 526 U.S. 137 (1999). See supra §§ 13 & 207.

[3]   See infra § 227.

these facts authenticate it as a reply letter. This result rests in part upon the generalization that the author would know of the terms of the first letter in view of the presumed regularity and dependability of the mails in delivering the first letter.[4] It is also supported by common experience which tells us that reply letters do come from the person addressed in the first letter. The proponent may also show that the original message was communicated in some manner other than the mail, and that a reply was timely received.

Today, the reply letter concept as a means of authentication may be applied in cases involving many forms of electronic communication, including email. The first step in authentication of the reply letter is to prove that the first letter was dated, was duly mailed at a given time and place, and was properly addressed. Seemingly, oral testimony to these facts should suffice as to proving the existence of the first letter if the reply letter refers to it by date. If, however, the reply letter refers to the first letter only by reciting or responding to its content, then the content of the first letter becomes important. It might then be necessary to satisfy the requirement of producing the original letter. If the party-opponent is the purported author of the reply and has possession of the first letter, it would be necessary to give him notice to produce it at trial before a copy could be used to prove its terms.[5]

Identification of Source. Proving a connection to a particular source, other than by the signature of an individual, is also a common means of authenticating documents. It is generally held that business records may be authenticated as to their source by the testimony of one familiar with the books of the business entity, such as a custodian or supervisor, who has not made the record itself or seen it made. The testimony can be based on knowledge of how a business's records are produced, filed and retrieved, or by comparison of the proffered records with known records of the business. Business records are also now self-authenticating under Federal Rule 902(11) and 902(12).[6] Other foundation proof may be required before the records will be accepted as evidence of the facts recorded under the hearsay exception for business records.[7]

§ 225 Ancient Documents

A writing that has been in existence for a number of years will frequently be difficult to authenticate by a percipient witness. Where the maker of an instrument, those who witnessed the making, and even those familiar with the maker's handwriting, had over the course of years died or become unavailable, the need to resort to authentication by circumstantial evidence was apparent. The circumstances which raised an inference of the genuineness of an aged writing were quite varied, and any combination of circumstances sufficient to support a finding of genuineness were held appropriate authentication. Facts indicative of genuineness include unsuspicious appearance, emergence from natural custody, prompt recording, and, in the case of a deed or will, possession taken under the instrument. Age itself may be viewed as giving rise to some inference of genuineness in that inaccuracies might have been already discovered.

The frequent necessity of authenticating ancient writings by circumstantial evidence, plus the consideration that certain of the above facts probative of authenticity

---

[4]   See infra § 234.

[5]   See infra § 237.

[6]   See infra § 229.1.

[7]   See infra §§ 284–294.

are commonly found associated with genuine older writings, led common law courts to develop a rule of thumb for dealing with the question. Under this rule, a writing was sufficiently authenticated if the party who offered it produced sufficient evidence that the writing was thirty years old, that it was unsuspicious in appearance, and further proved that the writing was produced from a place of custody natural for such a document. The Federal Rules, the Uniform Rules, and most state derivatives, continue the rule but reduce the required documentary age to twenty years. In addition to the foregoing requirements, some jurisdictions, if the writing is a dispositive one such as a deed or a will, impose the additional condition that possession must have been taken under the instrument. The documents which may be authenticated under Federal Rule 901(b)(8) and its state law counterparts, however, are not limited to dispositive instruments, and these terms have been applied to allow authentication of a wide variety of writings.

In the case of a writing which purports to be executed by an agent, executor, or other person acting under power or authority from another, proof of the facts which authenticate the writing as an ancient document gives rise to a presumption that the person signing was duly authorized.

Under Federal Rule 901(b)(8), the third requirement—that the document be in such condition as to create no suspicion concerning its authenticity—has been interpreted narrowly by some courts. The only issue that the proponent must address is whether there is any suspicion that the document is not the type of document it is claimed to be. Whether it is accurate goes to its weight and is a matter for the trier of fact.

Despite the utility of the ancient documents rule, it is merely a rule of authentication, the satisfaction of which does not necessarily guarantee the admission of the authenticated document. The writing may be proved genuine and yet remain inadmissible as hearsay or secondary evidence. Confusion has been generated by a partial overlap between the requirements of the present authentication rule and those of the hearsay exception for certain types of ancient documents. Today, Federal Rule 803(16) provides for the admission of a "statement in a document that is at least 20 years old that was prepared before January 1, 1998, and whose authenticity is established." If secondary evidence is offered, the preferable and majority view is that satisfaction of the ancient document requirements will serve to authenticate an ancient copy of an original writing.

§ 226   Public Records and Reports

If a writing is claimed to be an official report or record of a public governmental agency and is proved to have come from the proper public office where such official papers are kept, it is generally agreed that this authenticates the offered document as genuine. This result is founded on the assumption that the public employees having custody of such records will carry out their public duty to receive and maintain only genuine official papers and reports. Thus it is the official duty of custody, rather than the duty of preparation, which constitutes the document a genuine public record. Similarly, where a public office is the depository for private papers that have been recorded or filed there, such as wills, conveyances, or income tax returns, the proof that such documents have come from the custody of the proper office is usually accepted as sufficient authentication. This again can be sustained on the principle that the official custodian has a public duty to verify the genuineness of the papers offered for recording or filing and to accept only the genuine.

As is discussed in Section 229.1 infra, any need for testimonial proof of production from proper official custody is today frequently avoided by resort to several means of "self-authentication" of public records. However, use of self-authentication procedures are not exclusive or mandatory, and proof of the facts necessary to secure admission of a public record may be made by any witness with competent knowledge. While the necessary testimony will most frequently be provided by the record's custodian, this also is not required.

The question of the authenticity of official records is not determinative of the ultimate admissibility of such records. It is quite possible for a public record to be perfectly genuine and yet remain inadmissible, typically for reasons of hearsay. Today, Federal Rule 803(8) provides a hearsay exception for public records that set out the office's activities, matters observed under a duty to report (except by law enforcement in criminal cases), and factual findings from a legally authorized investigation (except not against a criminal defendant).

Should the rule which accepts, as prima facie genuine, documents which are shown to emerge from official custody be extended to writings found in private custody? Since the circumstances of private custody are infinitely more varied than those of public custody, a new rule in an already rule-ridden area seems inadvisable. No such rule is needed, provided that, in their discretion, courts recognize that proof of private custody, together with other circumstances, is frequently strong circumstantial evidence of authenticity.

§ 227 Electronic and Computer-Generated Documents

Due to the enormous growth in electronic correspondence and commerce in recent years, the recording, communication and preservation of digital information pervade society. Understandably, then, electronic writings (also known as e-evidence) are increasingly used in both civil and criminal litigation. The first generation of e-evidence included computer-generated documents and data files, emails and Internet website postings, including chat rooms. Now courts frequently deal with text messages and social network communications and postings. The authentication of such electronic writings can be hotly contested when authorship is in dispute. There are no subsections of Federal Rule 901(b) that address these new electronic technologies specifically, but Rule 901(b) provides flexibility in applying the requisite standard of sufficiency set forth in Federal Rule 901(a). Courts have emphasized that the threshold set by the sufficiency standard raises a question for the jury and have used the flexibility of Federal Rule 901(b) to develop analogies to traditional writings in admitting all forms of e-evidence.

Again, it must be emphasized that authentication does not secure admissibility of electronic documents into evidence. As with more traditional forms of written evidence, if the electronic or computer-generated writing is used to prove the truth of its contents, the hearsay rule must be satisfied. In addition, the "best evidence" requirement to produce the original document or its authorized substitute may apply.[8]

Emails. Emails can be authenticated by their authorship. However, the electronic signature that they bear may not be sufficient to identify the author because of the risk

---

[8]   See infra Ch. 23.

of manipulation of email headers. Additional data such as the address that an email bears, the use of the "reply" function to generate the address of the original sender, the content of the information included in the email and other circumstances such as "appearance, contents, substance, internal patterns, or other distinctive characteristics . . . taken together with all the circumstances" can suffice.[9] Emails are also deemed authenticated when produced by, and then offered against, a party opponent.

Evidence that the email to be authenticated is a timely response to an earlier message addressed to the purported sender would be analogous to the reply letter doctrine discussed in Section 224 supra, which is based upon the presumed regularity and dependability of the mails. Applying this doctrine, an email response to an original email message that was sent to the responder's email address has been held sufficient to authenticate the source and genuineness of the response. There are also "a variety of technical means by which email transmissions may be traced."[10]

Text Messages. Text messages sent between cell phone users are treated the same as emails for purposes of authentication. Typically, such messages are admitted on the basis of identifying the author who texted the proffered message. Ownership of the phone that originated the message is not sufficient. Like email, authorship can be determined by the circumstances surrounding the exchange of messages; their contents; who had the background knowledge to send the message; and whether the parties conventionally communicated by text message.

Proving text messages in court often presents additional challenge, however, because their contents are regularly purged by the telephone carrier. Thus, transcripts made by law enforcement at the time the cell phone is seized are often proffered as evidence of the messages and must be authenticated as an accurate transcription.

Website Data and Postings. Information appearing on private, corporate and government websites is often proffered as evidence in litigation. Printouts of Web pages must first be authenticated as accurately reflecting the content and image of a specific web page on the computer. Such accuracy can generally be established if the printout has a URL address and date stamp and is accompanied by an affidavit from a percipient witness, such as trial counsel. Often the printout is relevant only if posted by a particular source (such as the website owner) and thus must be authenticated as having been posted by that source. In the recent past, courts have expressed skepticism about attributing documents obtained from a website to the organization or individual who maintains the site. Private website postings are not self-authenticating and therefore require additional proof of the source of the posting or the process by which it was generated. Courts have also recognized that specific authentication issues exist for website printouts obtained from web archive services. Generally, courts require the testimony of someone with knowledge of the reliability of the archive service. Information retrieved from government websites, however, has been treated as self-authenticating, subject only to proof that the webpage does exist at the governmental web location. Issues of completeness of electronic records can be treated as a matter of evidentiary weight, rather than authentication and admissibility, as long as the complete records are available.

---

[9]   Fed. R. Evid. 901(b)(4).

[10]   Joseph, Modern Visual Evidence § 1503[1](f) (2018).

Chat Room Communications. Authentication of chat room communications is not accomplished through identification of the website owner. Rather, the author of the identity-protected posting must be identified. Authorship can be determined by content and circumstances. Courts have noted the need for flexibility in their approach to authenticating this evidence, as several of Federal Rule 901(b)'s provisions are simply not usable. Authentication can be accomplished with evidence linking an individual to a screen name used in chat room conversations; evidence that an individual possessed information sent to the chat room participant; evidence from an individual's computer hard drive showing that a user of the computer used a particular screen name.

Testimony from a chat participant as to the accuracy of a transcript of the online conversation is sufficient. When computer text files of chat postings have been created, their completeness goes to the weight of the evidence, not admissibility, when all of the files are available.

Social Network Postings and Messaging. Many new types of writings, potentially relevant as evidence in civil and criminal trials, are retrieved from internet sites known as "social networks" or "social media." Social networking websites permit their members to share information with others. Members create their own individual web pages (their profiles) on which they post their own personal information, photographs and videos, and from which they can send and receive messages to and from others whom they have approved as their "friends." "Creating a Facebook account is easy . . . anyone at least thirteen years old with a valid email address could create a profile."[11]

Despite the seeming novelty of social network-generated documents, courts have applied the existing concepts of authentication under Federal Rule 901 to them. In the existing case law, the key issue is typically one of authorship—who authored/posted the proffered document in question. Of course, a witness with personal knowledge of authorship could satisfy the Federal Rule 901(b)(1) foundation. But in most of the existing case law, it is the criminal defendant against whom the document is offered, and the defendant does not testify and/or denies authorship. Thus, as with other forms of electronic evidence, courts look to circumstantial evidence to establish authorship such as the name, birth date, or profile picture attached to a social networking account or the content of posts or messages sent from the account. Courts have generally taken one of two approaches to the authentication issue. Some courts have imposed a heavier burden of authentication on this evidence due to the courts' perception of increased dangers of falsehood and fraud in that electronic medium. While these courts purport to apply the relatively lenient standard of Federal Rule 901, they have excluded social networking evidence absent significant corroboration of the identity of the author. For these courts, it appears that the mere possibility that someone other than the purported author could have created the social networking evidence is sufficient to exclude the evidence for lack of authentication.

Other courts have held that concerns about false authorship go to the weight of social networking evidence, as opposed to its admissibility. For these courts, once a proponent has made a prima facie showing that social networking evidence was created by its purported author, concerns about the vulnerability of social networking evidence to false authorship are left to evaluation by the jury.

---

[11]   Smith v. State, 136 So. 2d 424, 432 (Miss. 2014).

In addition, some courts have found that other risks inhere in photographs posted on social networks. Such photos have been excluded in the absence of expert testimony that the photos are not composites or "faked," due to "the untrustworthiness of images downloaded from the internet."[12] And courts have yet to grapple with some of the other tools of social network sites, such as the ability of owners to post "tags" in photos, identifying themselves or other members of the site by name and location. Persons so tagged are informed only if they are the owner of the site. Otherwise, a person's photo may be tagged incorrectly on a third person's site, and the person wrongly tagged may never be informed. New features, such as adding a caption or a comment on photos posted by others, involve additional risks of error.

In sum, courts have not yet reached a consensus on how best to address social networking evidence and a number of issues unique to this type of evidence have yet to be addressed. However, the approach by courts imposing a heavier burden on social networking evidence is reminiscent of the conservative response many courts had to the advent of other technologies such as the telegraph, the computer, and the internet. With time the trend may well shift towards this latter category of cases as courts become more familiar with the social networking medium and the perceived dangers of this evidence dissipate. Given that many of the cases taking a lenient approach to social networking evidence have arisen in only the last two to three years, this shift may already be occurring. In addition, solutions to the problems of identity-security may be developed within the social network technology itself.

Computer-Generated Documents. When a computer is simply used as a typewriter, computer-generated documents may be authenticated by any of the means discussed in Sections 222–224 supra. Documents stored in a computer frequently need to be authenticated by proof of a connection to a particular person, either to show authorship or possession of the document. The mere presence of a document in a personal or business computer file will constitute some indication of a connection with the person or persons having ordinary access to that file. However, much will depend on the surrounding facts and circumstances, and it is reasonable to require that these include some additional evidence of authenticity.

Authenticity may also depend on the accuracy of the process by which computer documents are generated. To lay this foundation, a qualified witness should have general knowledge of who prepares the printouts, how they are prepared, and the way the system records and retrieves information. If the records are pre-existing and are simply stored in a computer, or are identified as belonging to a party-opponent and are thus admissible as party admissions regardless of their accuracy, the information about their retrieval will suffice. Basic computer operations relied on in the ordinary course of business are admitted without an elaborate showing of accuracy. The accuracy of the individual computer will not be scrutinized unless specifically challenged, and even perceived errors in the output are said to go to the weight of the evidence, not its admissibility.

When a computer is used to create a data compilation, how much information will be required about data input and processing to authenticate the output will depend on the nature and completeness of the data, the complexity of the manipulation, the routineness of the operation, and verifiability of the result. A more elaborate foundation may be required to satisfy Federal Rule 901(b)(9) if the computer is performing more

---

[12] People v. Beckley, 110 Cal. Rptr. 3d 363, 366–67 (Ct. App. 2010).

complex manipulations. Testimony about the computer equipment, the hardware and software, the competency of the operators, the procedures for inputting data and retrieving the outputs may be necessary, particularly if these elements are challenged. The hearsay nature of the output will also require the satisfaction of a hearsay exception, typically the business or public records exceptions to the hearsay rule. The use of computers to generate demonstrative aids and simulations is discussed in Sections 214 and 218 supra.

§ 228 Voice Identifications and Telephone Calls

Modern technology makes commonplace the receipt of oral communications from persons who are heard but not seen. The problems of authentication raised by these communications are substantively analogous to the problems of authenticating writings, although no document or other exhibit is necessarily involved. It has long been established that if a communication made to or from a disembodied voice is relevant only if it is connected to a particular person, this connection must be proved prior to the admission of any evidence proving the content of the communication. Federal Rule 901(b)(5) & (6) provide illustrations for proving voice identifications and for authenticating telephone calls that will meet the sufficiency standard of Rule 901(a).

Voice Identifications. Self-identification by a speaker during a telephone conversation is not sufficient to authenticate the speaker's voice and to permit a witness to testify about the call. The requisite additional proof may take the form of lay opinion testimony by the witness that he is familiar with the speaker's voice and can identify him. Or identification may be accomplished by circumstantial evidence pointing to the identity of the speaker, such as if the communication received reveals that the speaker had knowledge of facts that only he (or very few others) would be likely to know. These same modes of identification are also recognized where communications have been made or received on an apparatus other than a telephone.

Voice communications are frequently recorded, whether knowingly or not, on telephone answering machines, 911 calls, and police radio transmissions. In such cases, the recording itself must be authenticated as well as the voice or voices identified. The identification of the voices in taped communications may be made through context and chain of custody, comparisons, and testimony by those familiar with the voice. It is a common strategy in the prosecution of crimes involving illegal drugs for a government agent to testify that the defendant participated in recorded drug-related conversations based solely on the agent's comparison of the recorded voice with defendant's voice heard in live interviews, court appearances, wire taps and other recordings.

Finally, since the recordings treated here are almost invariably statements, it must constantly be borne in mind that authentication is by no means a guarantee of admissibility, and that recordings will often raise evidentiary problems of hearsay and compliance with the requirement to produce the original recording.[13]

Telephone Calls to a Listed Number. Suppose that a witness testifies that she placed a telephone call to a number assigned to or listed for a specific person, and that the person who answered identified himself as that person. Are these two facts sufficient proof of that person's identity? This foundation would satisfy Federal Rule 901(b)(6). Thus, most courts today view proof of proper placing of a call plus self-identification of

---

[13] See infra § 233.

the speaker as sufficient proof of authenticity to admit the substance of the call. For the application of this principle to cell phone text messages and emails, see Section 227 supra. It is likewise held that where it is shown that the witness has called the listed number of a business establishment and has spoken with someone who asserts that he speaks for the concern, or speaks about matters within its ordinary course of business, this is sufficient proof that the speaker was authorized to speak for the employer.

§ 229 Escapes from the Requirement of Producing Evidence of Authenticity: Modern Procedural Practice

As the foregoing sections clearly imply, the authentication of writings and other communications by formal proof may prove troublesome, time consuming, and expensive even in cases where no legitimate doubt concerning genuineness would appear to exist. The ultimate explanation for the continuing insistence upon the furnishing of such proof may not rest on common sense, but rather on arguments of fairness in allocating the burden of presenting proof between the adversaries, and concern about sharp practices should the burden of such proof be lifted. In addition, various procedural devices afford escape from authentication requirements and avert some of the impatience which might otherwise be engendered by formal authentication requirements. Legislatures, too, have frequently nibbled at the problem by enacting statutes relieving the rigors of authentication in what would otherwise be particularly troublesome contexts. Among these "escapes from authentication," the following are particularly noteworthy.

Requests for Admission. Under the practice in the federal courts as provided by Rules 36 and 37(c)(2) of the Federal Rules of Civil Procedure, and under analogous rules or statutes in many states, a party may serve upon an adversary a written request for admission of the genuineness of any relevant document described in the request. If the adversary unreasonably fails within a specified time to serve an answer or objection, genuineness is admitted. If genuineness is denied and the requesting party thereafter proves the genuineness of the document at trial, the latter may apply for an order of court requiring the adversary to pay her the reasonable costs of making the authenticating proof.

Securing Admission at Pretrial Conference. Under Rule 16 of the Federal Rules of Civil Procedure, and under analogous rules and statutes in many states, it is provided that a pretrial conference of the attorneys may be called by the court to consider among other things, "the possibility of obtaining admissions of fact and of documents which will avoid unnecessary proof." Such a conference is now preceded in the federal system not only by pretrial discovery but by mandatory initial disclosures of documents in the possession, custody and control of the disclosing party that the party may use to support its claims or defenses, pursuant to Federal Rule of Civil Procedure 26(a)(1)(A)(ii). Of course, stipulations as to genuineness of documents often are secured in informal negotiation between counsel. But a skillful judge may create at a pretrial conference an atmosphere of mutual concession unusually favorable for such admissions. This function of the pretrial practice has been considered one of its most successful features.

Writings That "Prove Themselves." In addition, there are certain kinds of writings that are said to "prove themselves" or to be "self-authenticating" on the ground that they are so likely to be authentic that the proffering party does not need to offer any extrinsic evidence of authenticity. Such writings are the subject of Section 229.1 which follows.

§ 229.1 Self-Authentication Under Federal Rule of Evidence 902

A self-authenticating writing, once tendered to the court, will be accepted in evidence for what it purports to be, without the shepherding angel of an authenticating witness. Statutes have often provided that certain classes of writings shall be received in evidence "without further proof." These are writings that are often, in some manner, vouched for on their face by an official. This helpful attribute has most commonly been given by statute to (1) deeds, conveyances or other instruments, which have been acknowledged by the signers before a notary public, (2) certified copies of public records, and (3) books of statutes which purport to be printed by public authority.[14]

This relatively limited concept of self-authentication has been greatly expanded by the Federal Rules of Evidence. Federal Rule 902 accords prima facie authenticity, meaning that no extrinsic evidence of authenticity is required, to many kinds of writings beyond acknowledged documents and certified public records.

It must be emphasized that presumptive authenticity, as provided for by Rule 902, does not preclude the opponent from challenging the authenticity of the offered writing, such as with proof that the document is a phony or bears a forged signature. Nor does it resolve questions as to the source or accuracy of information that is reported in self-authenticated documents. Objections can still be made that inadmissible hearsay statements or expert opinions are included in, for example, newspapers or periodicals.

Executed, Acknowledged and Certified Documents and Records. Federal Rules 902 (1) through (4) provide for the presumptive authenticity of classes of writings which can qualify only when the acknowledgment is certified by execution under seal or by attestation or certification, indicating that at least some public officer has paid attention to the genuineness of the document. Federal Rule 902(8) provides the same presumption for documents and instruments which have been acknowledged by the signer(s) before a notary public.

But how is the court to know without proof that the signature or seal appearing on the document or certificate is actually that of the official whose name and title are recited? This presumption is supplied by the traditional doctrines which recognize the seal or signature of certain types of officers, including the keeper of the seal of state, as being of themselves sufficient evidence of the genuineness of the certificate, perhaps based on assumptions about the difficulties of forgery. Moreover, in many state codes, particular provisions supplement or clarify tradition by specifying that the seals or signatures of certain classes of officialdom shall have this self-authenticating effect.

Public and Commercial Writings That Are Difficult to Forge. Newer classes of writings are self-authenticating under Federal Rule 902 based on their appearance and/or self-evident content alone. Included are all books, pamphlets and other publications that purport to be issued by public authority; newspapers and periodicals; and trade inscriptions and labels indicating ownership, control or origin.

If the justification for the presumption of their genuineness is that they are very difficult to forge, it must be acknowledged that recent technologies weaken this justification. If the justification rests on the assumption that most writings offered at trial are genuine, and the burden should be placed on the opponent to prove lack of authenticity as Federal Rule 902 provides, then this approach might well be extended to

---

[14] Proof of statutes of sister states and of foreign countries is discussed in infra § 335.

apply to all writings that on their face have a connection with the party against whom offered.

Self-Authenticating by Operation of Law. Federal Rule 902(9) adheres to those principles of general commercial law that have recognized certain types of commercial paper as self-authenticating; and Federal Rule 902(10) applies any federal statute that endows signatures, documents or anything else with presumptive authenticity.

Records of Regularly Conducted Activities. The concept of self-authentication has recently been extended further by reform measures which confer self-authenticating effect on records of regularly conducted activities. In 2000, these principles were fully integrated into the Federal Rule 902. Subsections (11) and (12) provide for self-authentication based on a written certification that the record conforms to the terms of the hearsay exception for records of activities that are "regularly conducted," typically by businesses. This exception previously required testimony in court from the custodian of records or other qualified person.[15] Now, the certification, notice to the adverse party of a party's intent to use Federal Rules 902(11) or 902(12), together with the records themselves, can suffice if provided to the opponent for verification and potential challenge.

Courts have been strict in requiring that the person making the written declaration specifically state familiarity with the creation and maintenance of the proffered records. One question has been whether the written declaration must contain a factual showing of its conformity to the terms of the business records hearsay exception set forth in Federal Rule 803(6)(A) to (C), or can simply recite conclusions. Most reported cases have referred to the certification as being only a verbatim recitation of the required terms of the business records exception. But recent cases have required proof that those terms have actually been satisfied by the proffered records. Unsubstantiated conclusions often require the opponent to depose the author of the written declaration in order to establish whether there are possible grounds to challenge compliance with Federal Rules 902(11) and 902(12).

---

[15]   *See* infra § 292.

Chapter 23

THE REQUIREMENT OF THE PRODUCTION OF THE ORIGINAL WRITING, RECORDING, OR PHOTOGRAPH AS THE "BEST EVIDENCE"

Table of Sections

---

§ 230 The "Best Evidence" Rule: Not a General Principle of Evidence Law

Thayer tells us[1] that the first appearance of the "best evidence" phrase is a statement in 1700 by Holt, C.J. (in a case in which he admitted evidence questioned as secondary) to the effect that "the best proof that the nature of the thing will afford is only required."[2] This statement given as a reason for receiving evidence, that it is the best which can be had, is a liberalizing principle. Not surprisingly, it gives birth to a converse and narrowing doctrine that a party must produce the best evidence that is available— second-best will not do. And so before 1726 we find Baron Gilbert in one of the earliest treatises on Evidence saying, "the first . . . and most signal rule in relation to evidence is this, that a man must have the utmost evidence the nature of the fact is capable of . . . ."[3] Blackstone continues the same broad generalizing and combines both the positive and negative aspects of the "best evidence" idea when he says, ". . . the best evidence the nature of the case will admit of shall always be required, if possible to be had; but if not

---

[1]   Thayer, Preliminary Treatise on Evidence at the Common Law 489 (1898).

[2]   Ford v. Hopkins (1700) 1 Salk. 283, 91 Eng. Rep. 250.

[3]   Gilbert, Evidence 15–17 (2d ed. 1760) (quoted by Thayer at 490).

possible, then the best evidence that can be had shall be allowed."[4] Greenleaf in this country in 1842 was still repeating these wide abstractions.

Thayer, however, writing in 1898, points out that these broad principles, though they had some influence in shaping specific evidence rules in the 1700s, were never received as adequate or accurate statements of governing rules, and that actually "the chief illustration of the Best Evidence principle, the doctrine that if you would prove the contents of a writing, you must produce the writing itself" is an ancient rule far older than any notion about the "best" evidence.[5] Most modern textwriters agree that there is no general governing principle that the "best evidence" of a disputed fact must be produced.

§ 231   The "Best Evidence" Rule: The Original Document Requirement

The only actual rule that the "best evidence" phrase denotes today is the rule requiring the production of an original writing, recording or photograph. This requirement is enforced against the proponent of any "secondary evidence" of the original; that is, testimony or exhibit that presents a version of the contents of the original. The rule is this: In proving the content of a writing, recording or photograph, where the terms of the content are material to the case, the original document must be produced unless it is shown to be unavailable for some reason other than the serious fault of the proponent, or unless secondary evidence is otherwise permitted by rule or statute.

The sections in this Chapter follow this basic framework, discussing first the reasons for the rule which inform the scope of the basic requirement to produce the original or, in most circumstances, a duplicate. Next presented are the excuses for not producing an original that is unavailable and the policy of no preferences for the types of secondary evidence that may then be used to prove the original's content. Following the excuses are the rules that permit the presentation of secondary evidence without an excuse which demonstrates that the original is unavailable. The Chapter concludes with sections on the allocation of questions of fact between judge and jury and appellate review of judicial rulings admitting secondary evidence.

§ 232   The Reasons for the Rule

Since its inception in the early 18th century, various rationales have been asserted to underlie the "best evidence rule" as applied to writings. Many older writers have claimed that the rule is essentially directed to the prevention of fraud. Wigmore, however, vigorously attacked this thesis on the analytical ground that it does not square with certain recognized applications and non-applications of the rule. Most modern commentators follow his lead in asserting that the basic premise justifying the rule is the central position which the written word occupies in the law. Because of this centrality, presenting to a court the exact words of a writing is of more than average importance, particularly in the case of operative or dispositive instruments such as deeds, wills or contracts, where a slight variation of words may mean a great difference in rights. In addition, it is to be considered (1) that there has been substantial hazard of inaccuracy in some of the commonly utilized methods of making copies of writings, and (2) oral testimony purporting to give the terms of a writing from memory is probably

---

4   Blackstone, Commentaries 368 (1768) (quoted by Thayer at 491).

5   Thayer, supra at 497–506.

subject to a greater risk of error than oral testimony concerning other situations generally. The danger of mistransmission of critical facts through the use of written copies or recollection justifies preference for original documents.

At the same time, it has long been observed that the opportunity to inspect original writings may be of substantial importance in the detection of fraud. Not surprisingly, then, prevention of fraud has long been sporadically cited as at least an ancillary justification for the rule. And some modern authorities go so far as to assert that fraud prevention constitutes the principal current justification for the rule. For unless this additional justification is accepted, applying the rule to copies produced by modern copying techniques, which virtually eliminate any possibility of mistransmission, would make little sense. To accept fraud prevention as the exclusive basis for the rule, however, forces reexamination of the question raised by Wigmore, why is the rule not equally applicable to chattels?

Finally, it is sometimes intimated that the rule should be viewed to protect not only against mistaken or fraudulent mistransmissions but also against intentional or unintentional misleading through introduction of selected portions of a comprehensive set of writings to which the opponent has no access. This seems to engraft upon the best evidence rule an aspect of the rule of completeness that is now the subject of Federal Rule 106 and Uniform Rule 106.[6]

The advent of modern discovery and related procedures, including compelled disclosure of exhibits and pre-trial conferences, which permit examination of original documents or secondary evidence before trial rather than at it, have substantially reduced the need for the evidentiary rule requiring an original. The availability of these alternatives is not uniform in all jurisdictions and is limited in the criminal sphere. Thus, the original documents rule remains a continuing and important requirement, although it is foreseeable that further extensions of discovery and pre-trial disclosures may ultimately render the rule obsolete in civil cases.

§ 233   The Scope of the Rule: Writings, Recordings and Photographs

At common law, the requirement that the original be produced was limited to "writings." Today, the scope of this requirement has been broadened to writings, recordings and photographs. All three types of evidentiary items exhibit a fineness of detail lacking in chattels generally; this detail will often be of critical importance; and prevention of loss of this fine detail through mistransmission is a basic policy objective of the rule requiring production of originals.

Writings and Recordings. The basis for concern about mistransmission of fine detail when proving the contents of writings and recordings that consist of letters, words or numbers, or their equivalent, is obvious. The terms "writing" and "recording" are now broadly defined to include any form of data compilation, including digital evidence. Sound recordings, by tape recorder or other electronic means, clearly involve similar considerations of mistransmission where their content is sought to be proved. Thus, inclusion within the scope of the rule is warranted.

Photographs, Video and Film Recordings. Photographs have also been brought within the rule when their contents are sought to be proved as a source of independent substantive evidence. And, "photograph" is broadly defined to include X-ray films, and

---

[6]   See supra § 56.

film and video recordings. The rationale for bringing all such films within the scope of the rule when their contents are sought to be proved is that secondary evidence, such as a verbal description of contents of the photograph by a witness, bears the risks of error and incompleteness similar to writings. Certainly, the original of a photograph may reveal indices of tampering which secondary evidence of its contents would not betray, and this is likely to be of unusual importance where photographic products are offered "to speak for themselves" as substantive evidence. It has been held, however, that the requirement of an original does not apply when the photograph is being used as a demonstrative aid, to illustrate a witness's testimony about what a witness has seen.

This broad extension of the rule to nonverbal graphic representations rejects the strict limiting principle of the common law rule that applied only to writings. Thus the requirement of an original may now be extended to other such representations which exhibit a wealth of detail.

Inscribed and Uninscribed Objects. Writings can be generally distinguished from objects with respect to the amount and importance of the detail they exhibit. However, chattels bearing more or less detailed inscriptions are far from uncommon. Thus, when an object such as a policeman's badge, a flag, or a tombstone bears a number or words, the terms of which are relevant, it must be considered whether the object shall be treated as a writing. It would seem unnecessary, however, to classify as a writing any object that carries an inscription of any sort whatsoever. In the final analysis, it is perhaps impossible to improve upon Wigmore's suggestion, followed by a number of courts, that the judge shall have discretion to apply the present rule to inscribed objects or not in light of such factors as the need for precise information as to the exact inscription, the ease or difficulty of production, and the simplicity or complexity of the inscription.

§ 234 What Constitutes Proving the Content

When a writing, recording or photograph is offered "in order to prove its content," it is apparent that the danger of mistransmission of that content is significant. Secondary evidence of the content should not be permitted without reason. This principle applies when the contents of a document are facts of independent legal significance, and when the proponent is using the contents of a document that record the happening of an out-of-court event to prove that event in court.

Contents of Writings, Recordings and Photographs Relevant as Facts of Independent Legal Significance Are Within the Best Evidence Rule. There are certain issues in legal disputes whose resolution, under the governing principles of substantive law, require knowledge of the exact contents of a writing, recording, or photograph. In these instances, the contents are relevant as facts of independent legal significance, are not within the definition of hearsay,[7] and are within the best evidence rule. In some of these cases, the Statute of Frauds or parol evidence rule endows a writing with either indispensability or primacy. The underlying transactions are viewed as written transactions, and writings embodying them, such as deeds, contracts, judgments etc., are universally considered to be within the best evidence rule when the legal effect of the writing is actually at issue in the litigation. In other cases, substantive legal rules of tort and criminal law treat the contents of writings, recordings, or photographs as out-of-

---

7   See infra § 249.

court conduct that must be proved; and in still other cases, the contents of a document are at issue because they prove notice.

Out-of-Court Events May Be Proved by Testimony from a Witness with Independent Firsthand Knowledge of the Event When Writings, Recordings or Photographs of Those Events Also Exist. There are writings, recordings and photographs, essentially unlimited in variety, which record the facts of out-of-court actions and events. When the proponent is trying to prove the happening of such past events, the best evidence rule does not demand that such documents be used. The substantive law does not regard the document as the essential or primary repository of these events. Testimony by a witness with independent firsthand knowledge that describes such events is primary, not secondary, evidence. It is not being offered to prove the contents of a document just because a documentary record also exists. In such cases, testimony is permitted under the best evidence rule and there is no need to produce the original documentary record, or to explain its absence. Examples in the case law abound.

Obviously, some permissible uses of testimony to prove the happening of an event may seem counterintuitive when the written record or recording would appear to be more reliable than the witness's description. However, admission of the witness's description does not deprive the record of its probative value, and the writing may also be admitted in the trial court's discretion.

When Writings, Recordings and Photographs Are Offered by the Proponent to Prove an Event, the Best Evidence Rule Applies. When a party offers a writing, recording or photograph as a record that proves the happening of an event, the document is being offered to prove its contents. The best evidence rule applies. Even when an event might be proved by testimony, sometimes the party attempting to prove the event chooses to offer the contents of a writing, recording or photograph for that purpose. For example, a conversation between two people is an event that may be proved either by testimony from the participants (or from anyone else who heard the conversation) as to what was said or by a tape recording made of the conversation. If the proponent chooses to prove what was said during the conversation by use of the tape recording, then the tape is being offered to prove its own contents. The requirement of the original tape would apply. Testimony by a witness as to what that witness had previously heard on the tape recording, or a written transcript of the original recording, would be rejected unless the original is shown to be unavailable. The same is true, of course, when a written record is offered as proof of out-of-court events. The original record must be offered; oral testimony as to what a witness had previously seen in the record will be rejected unless the original is unavailable. In addition, such use of a written record reflects the hearsay statements of its author and a hearsay exception must be found as well.

Witnesses may also testify that an event did not occur because relevant records contain no mention of it. This negative type of testimony is usually held not to constitute proof of contents and thus not to require production of records. But care in the application of this exception is required, since testimony as to what does not appear may easily involve a questionable description by the witness of the details which do appear.

Testimony from a Witness Without Independent Firsthand Knowledge Who Relies on the Contents of a Writing, Recording or Photograph. Sometimes a witness testifies to the existence of a fact or event as to which that witness has no firsthand knowledge. In such circumstances, the witness is usually relying on a writing, recording or photograph that the witness has read or observed outside of court. When the proponent of the witness's testimony does not present that document in court, there is likely to be a violation of the best evidence rule. This is the case when, for example, a recording or photograph is a "silent witness" to events that no person has in fact observed. Courts may also mistakenly treat testimony by a lay witness that is based on documents used by the witness out of court as lay opinion. However, under Federal Rule 701, lay opinions must be based on firsthand knowledge.[8] Only qualified experts may rely for their opinions on information made known to them prior to trial pursuant to Federal Rule 703.[9] Permitting testimony about specific facts that a lay witness has gleaned from specific writings would seem to violate the principle and policies of the best evidence rule.

Proving "a Fact" About a Writing. It is sometimes held that the use of testimony that states "a fact" about a writing, recording, or photograph is permissible. Presumably this does not raise the danger of mistransmission because the testimony is offered to prove an issue other than the exact terms of the document's content. Common examples of such issues are that a certain document is in existence, its type, or the history of events surrounding its creation, execution, assignment and issuance or delivery. In such cases, Rule 1002 does not apply, and testimony may be given without producing the document.

A Functional Approach. It must be acknowledged that courts are often challenged in the application of the question whether it is only "a fact" about the document that the proponent is seeking to prove. Uncertainty is often resolved by judicial treatment of a document's contents as "collateral" and thus excused from the basic requirement.[10] Courts must also make a distinction between contents of a document that are treated as facts of independent legal significance and contents that are treated as records of out-of-court events and transactions. This distinction, formal and doctrinal, can be difficult to apply.

Perhaps an alternative approach to determining when an original writing, recording or photograph must be produced would be to abandon the distinction between transactions that are essentially written (and thus have independent legal significance) and events that are essentially nonwritten. Application of the rule could turn upon the trial judge's determination of such functional factors as the centrality of the writing to the litigation, the importance of bringing the precise terms or content before the trier, and the danger of mistransmission in the absence of the original. These factors already come into play in decisions concerning inscribed objects, and collateral documents. The common-sense flexibility which such an approach would provide must be weighed against loss of whatever predictability for the parties, and opportunity for appellate control, inhere in a more categorical approach.

§ 235   What Is an "Original"?

"Original" Determined by Substantive Law. What should be the application of the basic rule where two documents, X and Y, exist, X having been created first and Y being some variety of reproduction of X? Copies, of course, are frequent and in most cases the document first prepared will be the one whose initial production is required by the rule. But the problem is not always so simple. For example, X may be a memorandum prepared by the sender and given to an assistant to send by e-mail or facsimile and Y is the e-mail or fax actually received by the addressee. Or, X may be a libelous handwritten

---

[8]   See supra § 11.

[9]   See supra § 15.

[10]   See infra § 239.

letter given to a stenographer for copying and sending, and Y the letter actually received by the addressee. Or, X may be an account sheet in the creditor's books and Y the bill made up therefrom and sent to the debtor.

In any of the above cases, if a party in court offers document Y in evidence, what determines whether the document is "the original writing itself" offered to prove its own terms, or merely a "copy" offered to establish the terms of X? The answer here clearly does not depend upon the chronology of creation or the ordinary semantic usage which would denominate Y as a "copy." Instead it will depend upon the substantive law of contracts, defamation, property, and the like. The question to be asked, then, is whether, under the substantive law, the creation, publication, or other use of Y is relevant as affecting the rights of the parties in a way material to the litigation. If the answer to this question is affirmative, proving the contents of Y is the fact of consequence in the case. That Y happens to be a copy of another writing is completely immaterial. There are, then, many instances in which the terms of "copies" are the facts sought to be proved.

Counterparts. It will also frequently occur that a written transaction, such as a contract or deed, will be evidenced by several counterparts or identical copies, each of which is signed by the parties or, at any rate, intended to be equally effective as embodying the transaction. Such multiple counterparts have also been called "duplicate (or triplicate, etc.) originals," a term which has often caused confusion in its application. Each counterpart intended to have equal legal effect is admissible as an "original." The proponent need not produce or account for the other counterparts. However, before secondary evidence may be resorted to, it has been held that all of the counterparts must be shown to be unavailable.

Photographs, Computer Printouts and Electronic Messaging. Federal Rule 1001(d) provides that the "original" of electronically stored information includes "any printout—or other output readable by sight—if it accurately reflects the information," and that the "original" of a photograph "includes the negative or a print from it." Obviously, where data are originally entered and stored in a computer, nothing akin to a conventional documentary original will be created. Thus, all printouts are equally admissible once the proponent has fulfilled the burden of showing that the computer's hardware and software accurately retrieved the stored data. Other admissibility issues such as the hearsay nature of the information recorded, or whether the computer accurately processed the original data and thus satisfies the authentication requirement of Federal Rule 901(b)(9), will also require resolution.

§ 236   When Is a "Duplicate" Admissible in Lieu of the Original?

The primary policy underlying the original documents requirement is to secure accurate information from the contents of material writings, free of the dangers of mistransmission, such as the mistakes of memory and hand-copying. It follows, therefore, that any form of copying which generally produces an accurate duplicate of an original should be viewed as sufficient to fulfill this policy. Requiring the original, or accounting for it, places costs, burdens of planning, and hazards of mistake upon the litigants; these costs are probably not worth imposing when risks of inaccuracy are reduced to a minimum by the offer of an accurate copy. At the same time, if the original document requirement is also supported by the ancillary purpose of fraud prevention, even copies produced by photographic or xerographic printing processes are not totally free of the risk of alteration that might not be discernable. Thus, in some circumstances, a copy is not as desirable as the original writing.

Federal Rules 1001 and 1003 make reasonable accommodation between these purposes of the basic rule and the realities of modern copying by defining "duplicate" broadly, and by providing for the general substitution of duplicates for originals unless there is good reason to require the original.

The Development of Accurate Copies. The treatment of copies under the rule requiring production of the original document can only properly be understood when viewed in light of the technological history of copying itself. In its earliest stages, the rule appears to have developed against a background of copying performed by individuals of the Bob Cratchit sort, transcribing manually not always under the best of conditions. Errors under such circumstances were routinely to be expected. Presumably influenced by the infirmities present in such modes of copying, the courts generally declined to accept subsequently created copies as equivalent to originals.

The advent of carbon paper, however, made possible the creation of copies of substantially greater reliability and legibility. Here, since the copy is made by the same stroke as the original, courts made a factual distinction between these copies and copies produced subsequent to the original by the older methods. It moreover became common, as it is today, to create multiple counterparts of a contract or transaction through the use of carbon paper, with each copy duly signed either through the same medium or individually. The fact that many true counterparts are made by the use of carbons, coupled with the notion that writings generated simultaneously by the same stroke are in some way superior, caused some courts to treat all carbons as if they were duplicate originals, i.e., as admissible without accounting for the original. This line of thinking supported the acceptance, as primary evidence of the contents of a particular book or newspaper, any other book or newspaper printed from the same sets of fixed type, or the same plates or mats. A like result would be reached as to all copies run off in the same mechanical printing process.

Today, copying by various photographic and other electronic processes has become commonplace, replacing the carbon. These processes, of course, produce facsimiles of an extremely high degree of accuracy and thus might have been expected, as have carbons, to win recognition as duplicate originals. In fact, an early judicial step in this direction was taken in a celebrated federal court of appeals decision which held that "recordak" photographs of checks which had been paid and were preserved by a bank as part of its regular records were admissible under the federal Business Records Act. Subsequently, a uniform act was prepared under which photographic copies, regularly kept, of business and public records are admissible without accounting for the original. This act has been widely adopted. In some cases, however, in which photographs of writings were offered to show the terms of the original without the aid of specific statutes, the photographic copies have been treated as secondary evidence, inadmissible unless the original is accounted for. The only explanation for these strange results would be that courts became fixed upon simultaneous creation as the characteristic of accuracy and were for a time unwilling to modify that concept in the face of newer technological methods.

Photographic, Electronic and Digital Copies Are Duplicates. Now, any process or technique which accurately reproduces the original is defined as a duplicate and is generally admissible to the same extent as the original. Copies produced manually, by hand or typewriter, are not included. But a duplicate of a duplicate may be found admissible. Enhanced re-recordings of audio or videotapes may also qualify as duplicates if the process of enhancement accurately reproduces the original, even if editing is required to remove background noise or irrelevant or prejudicial segments. A prepared transcript of the audio portion of a recording is often used at trial when the original is difficult to hear accurately. If viewed as a demonstrative aid that helps the jury understand the contents of the recording, the transcript presents no problem under the best evidence rules. Such use of a transcript is a matter of discretion for the trial court.[11]

Exceptions to the Use of Duplicates as Originals. There are two exceptions in Federal Rule 1003 to the use of a duplicate in lieu of an original document: The opponent may raise a genuine question as to the authenticity of the original, or there are circumstances making it unfair to admit the duplicate instead of the original. In both situations, production of the original may reveal indicia of putative fraud such as watermarks, types of paper and inks, alterations, etc., that may not be discernable on the copy. Decided cases suggest that the requisite challenge to authenticity must be relatively specific. Unfairness usually involves some infirmity with the duplicate itself; for example, an incomplete copy that fails to reproduce some vital part of the original document. Unfair conduct by the proponent which alters the copy or prevents the proponent from examining the original may also justify exclusion of a duplicate.

If a duplicate as defined under Federal Rule 1001(e) is used to challenge the authenticity of an original which is being offered into evidence, on the ground that the original has been altered after copying, it would seem absurd to read Federal Rule 1003 to bar admission of the duplicate.

§ 237 Excuses for Nonproduction of the Original

The requirement of producing the original of a writing, recording or photograph is principally aimed, not at securing an original document at all hazards and in every instance, but at securing the best obtainable evidence of its contents. There are many reasons why, as a practical matter, an original document is not available and cannot be produced, and the requirement to do so ought to be excused. This section examines these excuses.

Originals Lost or Destroyed. If the original has been lost or destroyed, its production is excused, and other evidence of its contents becomes admissible. Failure to recognize this excuse for complying with the basic rule would mean a return to the bygone and unlamented days in which to lose one's paper was to lose one's right. This cost of rigid enforcement of the basic rule is too high. Recognition of the excuse also squares with the rule's ancillary purpose to protect against the perpetration of fraud, since proof that failure to produce the original is due to inability to do so without bad faith tends logically to dispel the otherwise possible inference that the failure stems from design.

Loss or destruction may sometimes be provable by direct evidence, such as testimony from a witness who destroyed the document. But more often the only available evidence will be circumstantial, usually taking the form of testimony that an appropriate search for the document has been made without locating it. In such cases, the adequacy of the showing will be largely dependent upon the thoroughness and appropriateness of the search. It has been held that when a writing is last known to have been in a particular place or in the hands of a particular person, then that place must be searched,

---

[11] See supra § 216.

or the person produced. It is believed, however, that these statements are best considered as general guides or cautions, rather than strict and unvarying rules. Virtually all jurisdictions view the trial judge as possessing some degree of discretion in determining the preliminary question as to whether loss or destruction makes it infeasible to produce the original document.

Such discretion is particularly appropriate since the character of the search required to show probability of loss or destruction will, as a practical matter, depend on the circumstances of each case. Factors such as the relative importance of the document and the lapse of time since it was last seen bear upon the extent of search required before loss or destruction may be inferred. The only general requirement, however, should be that all reasonable avenues of search should be explored to the extent that reasonable diligence under the circumstances would dictate.

If the original document has been destroyed by the person who offers secondary evidence of its contents, that person bears the burden of proving that the destruction was accidental or was done in good faith. Otherwise, the secondary evidence is not admissible. Negligent destruction, or destruction in the ordinary course of business, can rebut the inference of fraud or intention to prevent the original document's use as evidence.

Original Not Obtainable. When the original writing, recording or photograph is in existence and is in the hands of a third person, the proponent must use available judicial process or other procedures to obtain it. If the person in possession is within the geographical limits of the trial court's subpoena power, the safest course is to have a writ of subpoena duces tecum served on the possessor summoning him to bring the document to court at the trial. Some decisions will excuse resort to subpoena if the possessor is privileged not to produce it.

If the writing is in the possession of a third person out of the state or out of the reach of the court's process, a showing of this fact will, in the view of many courts, excuse production of the original writing. This practice has the merit of being an easy rule of thumb to apply, but the basic policy of the original document requirement would tend to support the view that a further showing must be made. Some courts, therefore, require that before secondary evidence is used, the proponent must also show either that he has made reasonable but unavailing efforts to secure the original from its possessor, or circumstances which persuade the court that such efforts, had they been made, would have been fruitless. The burden and practicality of producing an original should be taken into account when secondary evidence is available.

Original in the Possession of the Opponent. A frequently used method of excusing a party's obligation to produce an original writing, recording or photograph is for the party to shift that burden to another party, typically the opponent. This requires a fairly detailed showing by the proponent of secondary evidence: first, that the original was under the other party's control; second, that the proponent notified the other party that the contents would be subject to proof at trial and/or that the opponent should produce it at the trial; and third, that the other party has failed to do so. Observe that the required notice is without compulsive force, but justifies excusing nonproduction of the original by the proponent and the consequent use of secondary evidence of the original's terms. If the proponent actually needs the production of the original itself, he should resort to a request for production of documents or subpoena duces tecum. But when the notice permits resort to secondary evidence, the adversary cannot fairly complain that he was only given the opportunity, not compelled, to preserve the original and make it available if he thinks it important to an accurate resolution of the case.

The safest and almost universal practice is to give written notice beforehand to the opponent or his attorney, describing the particular original documents. The proponent may then call upon the opponent orally at the trial to produce the documents requested. It has been held that the substance of the proponent's complaint or defense may constitute a sufficient implied notice that the proponent is charging the other party with possession of the original and considers its production essential. As to the time of serving notice, it is sufficient if it allows the other party a fair opportunity under the existing circumstances to produce the writing at the trial. Accordingly, if it appears at the trial itself that the other party has the original paper in the courtroom, an immediate notice then and there is timely.

Some exceptions to the requirement of notice before using secondary evidence of an original in the opponent's possession have been recognized. The first is well sustained in reason. It dispenses with the need for notice when the opponent has wrongfully obtained or fraudulently suppressed the writing, presumably because such notice would be futile. Some courts excuse the notice requirement for writings in the hands of the accused in a criminal prosecution so that secondary evidence may be received without notice to the accused to produce.

§ 238 No Preferences Among Types of Secondary Evidence

The basic policy of the requirement that an original writing, recording, or photograph be produced is that of according special protection to the accuracy of the contents presented in court. If the original is unavailable, as just discussed in Section 237, does the same policy require a preference among the secondary methods of proving the content of the original? There are many alternative means of proof, and some means may be more reliable than others, such as (1) a duplicate, as defined and discussed in Section 236 supra; (2) a copy that does not qualify as a duplicate but was made by one who was looking at the original while he copied, or a transcript made while listening to a recording; (3) a copy, however made, which has been compared by a witness with the original and found correct; (4) a secondhand or mediate copy, i.e., a copy of a firsthand copy; (5) a summary or restatement of a writing; (6) testimonial evidence as to the contents of the writing, recording, or photograph, with memory aided by a previously made memorandum or notes; and (7) testimonial evidence from unaided memory. There are many additional variations.

Apart from a special preference that applies only to official and public records, as discussed in Section 240 infra, there are two general approaches to the problem. First there is the view, introduced by some of the English decisions and early espoused by a minority of the American cases, that "there are no degrees of substantive evidence." This position has the virtues of simplicity and easiness of application. In addition, there remains a substantial practical motivation to produce the more satisfactory secondary evidence where it exists. This practical motivation, of course, stems from fear that the opponent will suggest to the trier of fact that an adverse inference may be drawn from failure to produce more satisfactory secondary evidence that has not been shown to be unavailable. These considerations have led the draftsmen of most modern codes of evidence to adopt the so-called "English" view, including the Federal Rules and the

Uniform Rules which contain no provision for "degrees" of secondary evidence, thus no preferences for "types" of secondary proof.

The opposing view, once the majority "American" rule, recognizes a distinction between types of secondary evidence, with a written copy being preferred to oral testimony. This view possesses the common-sense merit that even poor copies are likely to contain more detail than the recollection of the best witness. But whatever its merits, the adherents of this rule have been reduced to distinctly minority status by the widespread state adoption of evidence codes following the pattern of the Federal and Uniform Rules which, as earlier noted, do not recognize degrees of secondary evidence.

Secondary evidence must, of course, be admissible under all other applicable evidence rules. Oral testimony of the contents of detailed documents such as insurance policies may not need to be exact.

§ 239 The Originals of Writings, Recordings and Photographs Involved Only Collaterally Need Not Be Produced

At nearly every turn in human affairs some writing—a letter, a bill of sale, a newspaper, a deed—plays a part. Consequently, any narration by a witness is likely to include many references to events that consist partly of what is contained in written communications or other writings, recordings, or photographs. Witnesses to a tort or crime, for example, may identify the date of the event because they had been reading a particular story in a newspaper dated that day, or might identify the time because they heard a crash at a particular moment in a favorite television program. It is apparent that it is impracticable to forbid such references unless the writing or recording (e.g., the newspaper or the television video) is produced in court. Recognition of an exemption for "collateral" writings, recordings and photographs from the operation of the basic rule has therefore followed.

This exemption is a necessary concession to expedition and efficiency of trials, as well as to clarity of witnesses' narration. In the case of merely incidental references to what is contained in documents, these interests outweigh the need for perfect exactitude in the presentation of these documents' contents and the risk of fraud. The same practical judgment underlies limiting the basic requirement of producing an original to those documents that are offered to prove their contents.[12] In cases where there is uncertainty and confusion as to whether the contents are sought to be proved, the exemption for collateral documents can also be called into play.

While documents are frequently held to be collateral within the meaning of the present exemption, the purposes for which witnesses make references to them are so variegated that the concept of "collateral" defies precise definition. Three principal factors, however, should, and generally do, play a role in making the determination of when a document is collateral to the proceedings. These are: the centrality of the document to the principal issues of the litigation; the complexity of the relevant features of the document; and the existence of genuine dispute as to its contents. Evaluation and weighing of these factors in the particular instance may perhaps best be left to the discretion of the trial judge, and as elsewhere in the application of this essentially administrative rule, exercise of that discretion should be reviewed only for its abuse.

---

[12] See supra § 234.

§ 240 Original Public Records Need Not Be Produced

If the contents of the judgment of a court or of an executive proclamation are to be proved, shall the proponent be required to produce the original writing? The accepted view is that the originals of official records, and of documents that are recorded or filed in public offices, should be retained by their official custodian in the public office designated for their custody. Courts will not require them to be removed, as provided by statutes and rules of evidence. Federal Rule 1005 provides that the original of an official or public record need not be produced and need not be accounted for. Removing the original would be inconvenient for the governmental agency and members of the public who might desire to consult the records, and would entail a risk of loss or damage.

Accordingly, specific types of secondary evidence have been deemed appropriate for admission into evidence in lieu of the original: a copy certified as accurate by a person with authority to make such a certification; or, an examined copy, authenticated by a witness who has personally compared it with the original record. Under Federal Rule 1005, these two types of secondary evidence are given a preference. This helps ensure that the evidence received is the most accurate version of what is probably quite detailed content in the original. If neither of these types can be obtained using reasonable diligence, other evidence of the contents of the original may be admitted.

§ 241 Summaries of Voluminous Writings, Recordings and Photographs

It has long been held that records too voluminous to be conveniently produced and examined in court may be summarized and their import testified to by a witness, usually an expert, who has reviewed the entirety. Federal Rule and Uniform Rule 1006 recognize and clarify this helpful practice by providing that the contents of voluminous documents may also be presented in the form of a chart, summary or calculation. The trial judge has substantial discretion to decide whether the underlying originals are too voluminous to be conveniently examined in court.

Pursuant to Rule 1006, the original documents need not be produced in court. Thus, the rule functions as a form of exemption from the requirement of producing originals. However, the underlying originals must be made available for examination and copying by other parties in time to permit them to check the summary for any errors or inconsistencies and for purposes of cross-examination. These requirements also tacitly assume that reasonable notice be given of the intent to offer a summary. If the originals are no longer available, Rule 1006 would not apply but a summary might be admissible under Federal Rule 1004 as secondary evidence.

Since a summary admitted under this rule is being introduced substantively in place of the matters summarized, the voluminous materials must themselves be shown to be admissible, and courts must be scrupulous in assuring that the summary accurately portrays the contents of the underlying material and that a summary is necessary. So long as they are accurate, however, such summaries may present only one party's side of the case. However, courts guard against summaries that contain inferences and assumptions that are not fully supported by evidence in the record, as well as outright argument.

Federal Rule 1006 is clear that summaries admitted under its terms are evidence themselves, substituting for the voluminous documents that are not admitted into evidence. And because such summaries are substantive evidence, no limiting instruction is given to the jury as to its use and it may be taken into the jury room during deliberations. A distinction can thus be drawn between Rule 1006 summaries and summaries treated as pedagogic aids which illustrate a witness's testimony or summarize or analyze testimony and documents that have themselves already been admitted into evidence at trial. Juries are commonly instructed that such aids are not themselves evidence but should be used only as an aid in understanding the evidence.[13] However, when this distinction is not sharply drawn by trial courts, appellate courts are reluctant to hold any such error to be harmful.

§ 242   Proof of Contents of an Original by Testimony or Written Admission of a Party

Many American courts have followed the lead of Baron Parke's decision in *Slatterie v. Pooley*[14] and have held admissions made by a party opponent orally or in writing to be admissible to prove the content of an original document, without requiring that the original be accounted for. Upon reflection, however, Baron Parke's decision to admit a witness's testimony about a party's oral admission squares rather poorly with the primary policy in favor of obtaining the contents of writings with accuracy. Relying on the witness's perception and memory raises the possibility of erroneous transmission without corresponding justification. Accordingly, some American decisions rejected such testimony.

The possibility of mistransmission is effectively reduced where a witness does not report that a party's oral admission was made. The position adopted by Federal Rule 1007 is that "[t]he proponent may prove the content of a writing, recording, or photograph by the testimony, deposition, or written statement of the party against whom the evidence is offered." In such circumstances, "[t]he proponent need not account for the original." Thus when the party against whom his own writing, recording or photograph is offered and produced in evidence, or when the party himself makes a statement about the contents of a document on the stand in this or some other trial or hearing, or in a deposition, these admissions by the party may be used to prove those contents. Oral testimony by a witness that he heard the party's admission as to the content of a writing, recording or photograph should be excluded.

Of course, the party-opponent's admission must also be relevant, authenticated, and within the hearsay exceptions for admissions. The opponent may contest that the admission was made, although this may be a losing argument since the admission will either be the opponent's own testimony or made by him in writing. And the opponent may contest the reliability of his admission; that is, that it does not accurately represent the contents of the original document.

§ 243   Allocation of Questions of Fact Between Judge and Jury

Application of the rules discussed in this Chapter requires the trial judge to make numerous decisions preliminary to ruling on the admissibility of an original, duplicate, or secondary evidence of a writing, recording or photograph. For example, if a proponent offers a written document as an exhibit, is the writing being offered to prove its contents? If it is, is it the "original"? If it is not the original, is it a "duplicate"? And if it is a

---

[13]   See supra § 214.

[14]   (1840) 6 M. & W. 665, 151 Eng. Rep. 579 (Exch.).

duplicate, is there any serious question of the authenticity of the original, or of unfairness, which would prevent the duplicate's use at trial? If the proffered writing is not a duplicate, is the original unavailable for any of the reasons (e.g., that the original is lost or destroyed) that would provide an excuse for its nonproduction and would permit the use of secondary evidence?

These are only the most basic questions which the judge must answer in the administration of the rules and policies known as "best evidence." Some of these are questions of law, some are questions of fact and some require the exercise of judicial discretion. Clearly, questions of law and questions requiring judicial discretion are for the judge alone to decide and are not presented to the trier of fact. Most preliminary questions of fact are for the judge as well, to be decided under the preponderance of the evidence standard.

However, some fact questions that are dispositive of issues that touch on the merits of the particular case may also be involved in the judge's decisions about the admissibility of a particular document. Federal Rule of Evidence 1008 requires that these fact questions, if raised between the parties, be reserved for the trier of fact.

The following examples illustrate this rule:

(1) When the proponent of a writing offers it as the original or duplicate, the opponent may claim that the original never existed and the proffered writing is a fraud. In a jury trial, if the trial judge decides that the original did not exist, and for this reason excludes the proponent's proffer, the merits of the proponent's claim based on the alleged original document would not get to the jury. Therefore, under Federal Rule 1008(a), the judge would admit the alleged original and let the jury resolve the parties' dispute over its existence.

(2) Similarly, the parties might present competing "originals" of the same writing. In a jury trial, if the judge decides that one is the true original and therefore excludes the other, one of the two parties would not be allowed to present the merits of its claim or defense to the jury. Therefore, under Federal Rule 1008(b), the judge would admit both originals and let the jury resolve the dispute over which is the genuine one.

(3) Finally, the proponent may be offering a writing as secondary evidence to prove the contents of an original which has been lost. In a jury trial, if the judge does not believe that this secondary writing correctly reflects the contents of the original, or decides to admit only the opponent's competing secondary evidence as the correct version of the original, then the merits of the proponent's claim would not go to the jury. Under Federal Rule 1008(c), the judge would admit the proponent's secondary evidence (and the opponent's, if any) and let the jury decide what is the correct version.

However, to reach these questions which Federal Rule 1008 allocates to the trier of fact, the proponent's proffered writing (or testimony) must first be found admissible. Preliminary questions of fact necessary to determine admissibility are still decided by the judge; in example (3), for instance, whether the original was lost, and was lost in bad faith. In addition, the judge will require a showing of sufficient evidence on any issue that is allocated to the jury. In example (1) above, the proponent must still introduce evidence sufficient to support a jury finding that his claimed original is genuine. In example (3), the secondary evidence submitted must be sufficient to support a finding that the contents of the original are what the proponent claims.

§ 243.1 Appellate Review of Rulings Admitting Secondary Evidence

It will be seen from the earlier sections of this chapter that the requirement of the production of original writings, with the several excuses for nonproduction and the exemptions from the requirement itself, make up a fairly complex set of regulations for administration by the trial judge. Mistakes in the application of these rules are, understandably, not infrequent. The purpose of this system of rules, on the other hand, is simple and practical. That purpose is to secure the most reliable information as to the contents of documents, when those terms are disputed. A mystical ideal of seeking "the best evidence" or the "original document" as an end in itself is no longer the goal. Consequently when an attack is made on appeal on the judge's admission of secondary evidence, it seems that the reviewing tribunal should ordinarily make inquiry of the complaining counsel, "Does the party whom you represent actually dispute the accuracy of the evidence received as to the material terms of the writing?" If the counsel cannot assure the court that such a good faith dispute exists, it seems clear that any departure from the regulations in respect to secondary evidence is likely to be harmless error, or not error at all.

Title 10

THE HEARSAY RULE AND ITS EXCEPTIONS

Chapter 24

THE HEARSAY RULE

Table of Sections

§ 244　The History of the Rule Against Hearsay

In an oft-quoted passage, Wigmore calls the rule against hearsay "that most characteristic rule of the Anglo-American Law of Evidence—a rule which may be esteemed, next to jury trial, the greatest contribution of that eminently practical legal system to the world's methods of procedure."[1] How did this rule come about?

The development of the jury was, no doubt, an important factor. In its earlier forms, the jury was in the nature of a committee or special commission of qualified persons in the neighborhood to report on facts or issues in dispute. So far as necessary, its members conducted its investigations informally among those who had special knowledge of the facts. Attesting witnesses to writings were summoned with the jurors and apparently participated in their deliberations, but the practice of calling witnesses to appear in court and testify publicly about the facts to the jury is a late development in jury trial. Though something like the jury existed at least as early as the 1100s, this practice of hearing witnesses in court does not become frequent until the later 1400s. The movement is gradual thereafter to the present conception that the normal source of proof is not the private knowledge or investigation of the jurors but the testimony of witnesses in open court. In the 1500s, it becomes, although not yet the exclusive source of proof, the normal and principal one.

A consciousness of need for exclusionary rules of evidence did not begin to appear until this period of the emergence of witnesses testifying publicly in court. Admittedly, even early witnesses to writings were required to speak only of "what they saw and heard,"[2] and this requirement would naturally be applied to the new class of testifying witnesses. But when the witness has heard the statement of X out of court that X has

---

[1]　5 Wigmore, Evidence § 1364, at 28 (Chadbourn rev. 1974).

[2]　Thayer, Preliminary Treatise on Evidence 101, 519 (1898).

seen an injury inflicted by a blow with a sword, and offered it as evidence of the blow, a new question was presented. Certainly, the earlier requirement of knowledge must have predisposed the judges to skepticism about the value of hearsay.

The value of hearsay and its sufficiency as proof is the subject of discussion in this gestation period. Through the reigns of the Tudors and the Stuarts, a drumfire of criticism and objections by parties and counsel against evidence of oral hearsay declarations gradually increases. While the evidence was constantly admitted, the confidence in its reliability was increasingly questioned. It was derided as "a tale of a tale"[3] or "a story out of another man's mouth."[4] Parallel with this increasingly discredited use of casual oral hearsay was a similar development with respect to transcribed statements made under oath before a judge or judicial officer, not subject to cross-examination by the party against whom it is offered. In criminal cases in the 1500s and until the middle 1600s, the main reliance of the prosecution was the use of such "depositions" to make out its case. As oral hearsay was becoming discredited, uneasiness about the use of "depositions" began to take shape, first in the form of a limitation that they could only be used when the witness could not be produced at the trial. Neither the lack of an oath nor the unreliability of the report of the oral statement can be urged against such evidence, but only the absence of cross-examination and observation of demeanor.

During the first decade after the Restoration, the century or so of criticism of hearsay had its final effect in decisions rejecting such evidence, first as to oral hearsay and then as to depositions. Wigmore finds that the period between 1675 and 1690 is the time of crystallization of the rule against hearsay. For a time, the rule was qualified by the notion that hearsay, while not independently admissible, could be received to confirm other evidence, and this qualification survived until the end of the 1700s in the limited form of admitting witnesses' prior consistent statements to corroborate their testimony.

Whether the rule against hearsay was, with the rest of the English law of evidence, in fact "the child of the jury"[5] or the product of the adversary system may be of no great contemporary significance. The important point is that the rule against hearsay taking form at the end of the seventeenth century was neither a matter of immemorial usage nor an inheritance from Magna Charta but was a relatively late development of the common law.

Holdsworth thinks that the immediate influences leading to the crystallization of the rule against hearsay, at the particular time in the late 1600s when this occurred, were first, a strong dictum by Coke in his Third Institute denouncing "the strange conceit that one may be an accuser by hearsay,"[6] and second, the rejection of the attempt to naturalize in English law the two-witness requirement of the canon and civil law and the consequent urge to provide some compensating safeguard. As noted earlier, a century of increasing protests against the use of hearsay had preceded the establishment of the rule. However, most of the specific weaknesses of hearsay, which were the underlying reasons for the adoption of the rule and which have explained its survival, were not

---

[3]   Colledge's Trial, 8 How. St. Tr. 549, 663 (1681).

[4]   Gascoigne's Trial, 7 How. St. Tr. 959, 1019 (1680).

[5]   Thayer, Preliminary Treatise on Evidence 47, 180 (1898).

[6]   Coke, Third Institute 25 (1641).

clearly acknowledged until after the beginning of the 1700s when the newly established rule came to be rationalized by the judges and the text writers.

§ 245 The Reasons for the Rule Against Hearsay; Exceptions to the Rule

The factors upon which the value of testimony depends are the perception, memory, narration, and sincerity of the witness:

(1) *Perception.* Did the witness perceive what is described and perceive it accurately?

(2) *Memory.* Has the witness retained an accurate impression of that perception?

(3) *Narration.* Does the witness's language convey that impression accurately?

(4) *Sincerity.* Is the witness, with varying degrees of intention, testifying falsely?

In order to encourage witnesses to put forth their best efforts and to expose inaccuracies that might be present with respect to any of the foregoing factors, the Anglo-American tradition evolved three conditions under which witnesses ordinarily are required to testify: oath, personal presence at the trial, and cross-examination. The rule against hearsay is designed to ensure compliance with these ideal conditions, and when one of them is absent, the hearsay objection becomes pertinent.

In the hearsay situation, two "witnesses" are involved. The first complies with all three of the ideal conditions for the giving of testimony but merely reports what the second "witness" said. The second "witness" is the out-of-court declarant whose statement was not given in compliance with the ideal conditions but contains the critical information.

Oath. Among the earliest of the criticisms of hearsay, and one often repeated in judicial opinions down to the present, is the objection that the out-of-court declarant who made the hearsay statement commonly speaks or writes without the solemnity of the oath administered to witnesses in a court of law. The oath may be important in two aspects. As a ceremonial and religious symbol, it may induce a feeling of special obligation to speak the truth, and it may also impress upon the witness the danger of criminal punishment for perjury, to which the judicial oath or an equivalent solemn affirmation would be a prerequisite condition. Wigmore considered the oath requirement incidental and not essential and supported his argument by reference to the practice of excluding hearsay statements made under oath. But the fact that the oath is not the only requirement of the rule against hearsay does not prove it is unimportant. Similarly, the fact that the oath lacks the power that it had in an earlier age does not mean it no longer has significance; although affirmation is now commonly permitted as a substitute, the oath (or affirmation) requirement for witnesses remains firm.

Personal Presence at Trial. Another long-asserted objection is the lack of opportunity for observation of the out-of-court declarant's demeanor, with the light that this may shed on credibility. In addition, the solemnity of the occasion and possibility of public disgrace can scarcely fail to impress the witness and testifying falsely becomes more difficult if the person against whom it is directed is present.

Moreover, personal presence eliminates the danger that the witness reporting the out-of-court statement may do so inaccurately. Also, reporting the spoken word is likely subject to special dangers of inaccuracy beyond the fallibility common to all reproduction from memory of matters of observation, and the risk of such inaccuracy is one of the weaknesses of hearsay. As Wigmore points out, however, not all hearsay is subject to this danger. Written statements can be produced in court and can be tested with reasonable accuracy for genuineness and freedom from alteration. Moreover, as Morgan notes, the reporting in court of spoken words for nonhearsay purposes, as in proving the making of an oral contract or the utterance of a slander, is subject to this same risk of misreporting. Neither argument seems conclusive. Moreover, no general distinction is made between written and spoken hearsay.

Cross-Examination. The lack of any opportunity for the adversary to cross-examine the absent declarant whose out-of-court statement is reported is today accepted as the main justification for the exclusion of hearsay. As early as 1668, hearsay was rejected because "the other party could not cross-examine the party sworn."[7] Judicial expressions stress this as a principal reason for the hearsay rule. Cross-examination, as Bentham pointed out, was a distinctive feature of the English trial system, and the one that most contributed to the prestige of the institution of jury trial. He called it "a security for the correctness and completeness of testimony."[8] The nature of this safeguard which hearsay lacks is indicated by Chancellor Kent:

> Hearsay testimony is from the very nature of it attended with all such doubts and difficulties and it cannot clear them up. A person who relates a hearsay is not obliged to enter into any particulars, to answer any questions, to solve any difficulties, to reconcile any contradictions, to explain any obscurities, to remove any ambiguities; he entrenches himself in the simple assertion that he was told so, and leaves the burden entirely on his dead or absent author.[9]

In perhaps his most famous remark, Wigmore described cross-examination as "beyond any doubt the greatest legal engine ever invented for the discovery of truth."[10]

Hearsay That Is Admitted. Eminent judges have spoken of the "intrinsic weakness"[11] of hearsay, but the unreliability of hearsay can be easily overstated. Hearsay is not by its inherent nature unworthy of any reliance in a judicial proceeding. The contrary is proved by the fact that courts are constantly admitting hearsay evidence under the numerous exceptions to the hearsay rule. If otherwise inadmissible hearsay evidence is received without objection, it typically may be considered and, if apparently reliable, is sufficient to sustain a verdict or finding of fact. Also, hearsay is widely used to establish probable cause, in administrative proceedings, at sentencing, and more generally, much of our learning comes in the form of hearsay.

Hearsay evidence exhibits a wide range of reliability, including mere third hand rumors to sworn affidavits of credible observers and ranging virtually from the highest to the lowest levels of trustworthiness. Although varying levels of reliability are found in most testimonial or circumstantial evidence, which is similarly based upon the

---

7   2 Rolle's Abr. 679, pl. 9 (1668).

8   Rationale of Judicial Evidence, b. II, ch. IX, and b. III, ch. XX (1827).

9   Coleman v. Southwick, 9 Johns. 45, 50 (N.Y. Sup. 1812).

10   5 Wigmore, Evidence § 1367, at 32 (Chadbourn rev. 1974).

11   *See, e.g.,* Marshall, C.J., in Mima Queen v. Hepburn, 11 U.S. 290 (1813).

frailties of human perception, memory, narration, and veracity, such evidence is not subject to a general rule of exclusion. The effort to adjust the rules of admissibility to variations in the reliability of hearsay has been a major motivating factor in the movement to liberalize evidence law.

Nevertheless, broad support exists for a general policy of requiring that testimony be given by witnesses in open court, under oath, and subject to cross-examination, which is the objective of the rule against hearsay. The problem lies in the operation of the rule that excludes evidence as a means of effectuating that policy.

§ 246   A Definition of Hearsay

A definition cannot furnish in a sentence or two ready answers to all the complex problems of an extensive field, such as hearsay. It can, however, provide a helpful general focus, mark a starting point, and serve as a memory aid in arranging some of the solutions.

The definition of hearsay in Rule 801 of the Federal Rules of Evidence, which is in effect in the federal courts and provides the model for all but a handful of states, has two major components. First, a "statement" is defined as "a person's oral assertion, written assertion, or nonverbal conduct, if the person intended it as an assertion." Second, "hearsay" is "a statement that: (1) the declarant does not make while testifying at the current trial or hearing; and (2) a party offers in evidence to prove the truth of the matter asserted in the statement." This definition is affirmative in form; it says that an out-of-court assertion, offered to prove the truth of the matter asserted, is hearsay. For example, witness W reports on the stand that declarant D has stated that X was driving a car at a given time and place. The proponent is trying with this evidence to prove that X did so act. The out-of-court assertion is being offered to prove the truth of the matter asserted, and by definition, it is hearsay.

The definition does not in terms say that everything not included within the definition is not hearsay, but that was the intended effect of the rule, according to the Advisory Committee's Note. The rule's definition means, therefore, that out-of-court conduct is not hearsay if it is not an assertion or, even if it is assertive, it is not offered to prove the truth of the matter asserted.

Despite the importance of forms of the word "assert" in the definition of hearsay, that term is nowhere defined. The contemporary dictionary meaning is to state positively or strongly. However, in the pre-Rule world of evidence, the word "assert" carried no connotation of being positive or strong.[12] A favorite of writers in the field for at least a century and a half, the word simply means *to say that something is so*, e.g., that an event happened or that a condition existed. Unfortunately, this definition is nowhere set out, and as a consequence, contemporary courts sometimes exclude from the hearsay definition questions or imperative statements apparently categorically (or at least ordinarily) because they are not directly assertive. More appropriately nuanced opinions find such statements hearsay despite their form if the circumstances and/or wording demonstrate an intent to assert.

Another formulation of the definition of hearsay that is different from the federal model is sometimes used. It measures the out-of-court statement against the policy underlying the hearsay rule and classifies as hearsay statements whose evidentiary

---

[12]   Webster's Third New International Dictionary (1993).

value depends upon the credibility of the declarant without the assurances of oath, presence, or cross-examination. While the assertion-oriented definition of hearsay used by the Federal Rules and the definition based on the dangers behind the rule (sometimes termed declarant-oriented) often reach the same result, they also sometimes differ. This treatise in its original edition advanced the assertion-oriented approach and has continued to do so throughout its subsequent revisions, although later editions have moderated that approach.

When conduct or statements are not assertive or when they are assertive but are not used to prove the truth of the matter asserted, the statement should generally not be treated as hearsay because it does not fit the literal definition and because under these circumstances the danger of insincerity is usually significantly reduced. Although not perfect, this approach is relatively simple to apply and reaches a reasonable result in most situations even as judged by the rule's underlying policy. However, analysis based on whether the statement is used to prove the specific point asserted is sometimes inadequate. Where a realistic appraisal of the statement and its circumstances reveal that the danger of insincerity has not been meaningfully reduced, hearsay treatment is appropriate. However, the burden should be on the opponent to show that an exception to the normal application of the hearsay definition should be recognized. These general principles will be further applied in the succeeding sections and particularly in the analysis of "implied assertions" in Section 250.

Not in Presence of Party Against Whom Offered. A remarkably persistent bit of courthouse folklore is that statements are inadmissible if not made in the presence of the party against whom they are offered. As the above discussion reveals, this objection is not related to the basic concept of hearsay. Substitute the following for the final sentence in the section: The presence of the party against whom an out-of-court statement is offered can, however, have significance that permits its admission in a few specific circumstances, e.g., when a statement spoken in the party's presence is relied upon to establish notice,[13] when failure to deny a statement is the basis for claiming that the party adopted the statement,[14] or when the statement of the other is admitted as nonhearsay to provide context for the party's admission.

§ 247 Distinction Between Hearsay Rule and Rule Requiring Firsthand Knowledge

The requirement of firsthand knowledge is a rule more ancient than the hearsay rule, and while having some kinship in policy, should be distinguished from it. This rule mandates that witnesses are qualified to testify to facts susceptible of observation only if it appears that they had a reasonable opportunity to observe the facts.[15] Thus, if a witness testifies that on a certain day a flight arrived on time at X airport and from her other testimony it appears she was not in X at that time and could therefore only have spoken from conjecture or report of other persons, the proper objection is not hearsay but want of personal knowledge. Conversely, if the witness testifies that his brother told him that he came in on the flight and it arrived on time, the objection for want of knowledge of when the plane arrived is inappropriate. The witness purports to speak from his own knowledge of what his brother said, and as to this, he presumably had knowledge. If the

---

[13]   See infra § 249.

[14]   See infra § 261.

[15]   See supra § 10.

testimony in this latter case was offered to show the time of the plane's arrival, the appropriate objection is hearsay.

The distinction is one of the form of the testimony, whether the witness purports to give the facts directly upon his or her own credit (though it may appear later that the statement was made on the faith of reports from others) or whether the witness purports to give an account of what another has said and this is offered to establish the truth of the other's report. However, when either from the phrasing of the testimony or from other sources, the witness appears to be testifying on the basis of reports from others, although not to their statements, the distinction loses much of its significance, and courts may simply apply the label "hearsay."

§ 248 Instances of the Application of the Hearsay Rule

A few examples of the rejection of evidence under the general hearsay rule excluding extra-judicial assertions offered to prove the facts asserted will indicate the scope of its operation. Evidence of the following oral statements has been excluded: on the issue whether deceased had transferred his insurance to his new automobile, testimony that he said he had made the transfer; to prove that veniremen had read newspaper articles, testimony of deputy sheriff that attorney said that one venireman said that another had read the articles; to prove that driver was driving with consent of insured owner, testimony that owner said after the accident that the driver had his permission; in rebuttal of defense of entrapment, criminal reputation of defendant to show predisposition; to show defendant's control of premises where marijuana was found, testimony of police officer that neighbors said person of same name occupied the premises; and statements of child to social workers describing sexual abuse.

Instances of exclusion of written statements as hearsay when offered in court as evidence of their truth are likewise frequent. Thus, the following have been determined to be hearsay: written estimates of damages or cost of repairs made by an estimator who did not appear as a witness; written appraisal of stolen trailer by appraiser who did not testify; invoices from third parties as independent evidence of the making of repairs; the written statement of an absent witness to an accident; newspaper accounts as proof of the facts reported; statements in will that testator's second wife had agreed to devise property to his children as proof of that agreement; medical report by a physician who did not testify to prove that plaintiff had sustained injuries in a subsequent accident; and manufacturer's advertising claims as proof of product's reliability.

§ 249 Some Out-of-Court Utterances That Are Not Hearsay

The hearsay rule forbids evidence of out-of-court assertions to prove the facts asserted in them. If the statement is not an assertion or is not offered to prove the facts asserted, it is not hearsay. A few of the more common types of nonhearsay utterances are discussed in the present section.

Verbal Acts. When a suit is brought for breach of a written contract, no one would think to object that a writing offered as evidence of the contract is hearsay. Similarly, proof of oral utterances by the parties in a contract suit constituting the offer and acceptance which brought the contract into being are not evidence of assertions offered testimonially but rather verbal conduct to which the law attaches duties and liabilities. Other obvious instances are evidence of the utterance by the defendant of words relied on as constituting a slander or deceit for which damages are sought. Additional cases illustrating the principle are described in the footnote.

Verbal Parts of Acts. The legal significance of acts taken alone and isolated from surrounding circumstances may be unclear. Thus, the bare physical act of handing over money to another person is susceptible of many interpretations. The possibilities include: loan, payment of a debt, bribe, bet, gift, and no doubt many other kinds of transactions. Explanatory words which accompany and give character to the transaction are not hearsay when under the substantive law the pertinent inquiry is directed only to objective manifestations rather than to the actual intent or other state of mind of the actor. As used by most courts, the "verbal parts of acts" concept has been tightly limited to words that constitute operative legal conduct and renders the doctrine an adjunct to the verbal acts doctrine. A narrow range for this doctrine seems appropriate.

Utterances and Writings Offered to Show Effect on Hearer or Reader. A statement that D made a statement to X is not subject to attack as hearsay when its purpose is to establish the state of mind thereby induced in X, such as receiving notice or having knowledge or motive, or to show the information which X had as bearing on the reasonableness, good faith, or voluntariness of subsequent conduct, or on the anxiety produced. The same rationale applies in self-defense cases to proof by the defendant of communicated threats by the person killed or assaulted. If offered to show the defendant's reasonable apprehension of danger, the statement is not offered for a hearsay purpose because its value does not depend on its truth.

In the situations discussed above, the out-of-court statement will frequently have an impermissible hearsay aspect as well as a permissible nonhearsay aspect. For example, an inspector's statement that a customer's tires are defective admitted to establish notice of the defective condition (with other proof being required to establish the condition) is susceptible of being used improperly by the trier of fact as proof that the tires were in fact defective. Unless the need for the evidence for the proper purpose is substantially outweighed by the danger of improper use, the appropriate result is to admit the evidence with a limiting instruction.[16]

One area where abuse may be a particular problem involves statements by arresting or investigating officers regarding the reason for their presence at the scene of a crime. The officers should not be put in the misleading position of appearing to have happened upon the scene and therefore should be entitled to provide some explanation for their presence and conduct. They should not, however, be allowed to relate historical aspects of the case, such as complaints and reports of others containing inadmissible hearsay. Such statements are sometimes erroneously admitted under the argument that the officers are entitled to give the information upon which they acted. The need for this evidence is slight, and the likelihood of misuse great. Instead, a statement that an officer acted "upon information received," or words to that effect, should be sufficient.

Prior Inconsistent and Consistent Statements Used to Affect Credibility. A common technique to impeach the credibility of a witness is to show that on a prior occasion the person made a statement inconsistent with his or her testimony on the stand. The theory of impeachment does not depend upon the prior statement being true and the present one false. Instead, the mere fact that the witness stated the facts differently on separate occasions is sufficient to impair credibility. By "blowing hot and cold," doubts are raised

---

[16]   See supra §§ 59 & 185.

as to the truthfulness or accuracy of both statements.[17] Thus, the prior statement is not offered for its truth and is not hearsay. It is important to note that as a consequence of the theory of admissibility, statements offered under this theory may not be used for their truth and do not constitute substantive evidence. Similarly, once a witness's testimony has been impeached, prior consistent statements may be offered under some circumstances in rehabilitation,[18] and when offered for this limited purpose, they are also nonhearsay.

Automatic Machine Generated Data and Animal Reactions. As noted in Section 245, the benefits of cross-examination animate hearsay theory, and therefore certain situations where cross-examination is impossible or ineffectual may be categorized as nonhearsay. As long understood with animal responses and more recently with some machine-generated data, particularly automatically generated measurements and objective data, treating the evidence as hearsay is inappropriate. Instead, issues under the rubric of expert testimony and authentication take predominance.

However, as can be most clearly seen when the results are from machine generated evidence, human agency is at some level necessarily involved, although the degree and immediacy of the involvement varies, and often interpretation is laced throughout reading the machine's response. As with many areas that may appropriately be treated as nonhearsay, careful analysis is required regarding the nature of human involvement and extent of human judgment reflected in the results in determining whether the machine response should be treated as nonhearsay. Although not ruled by easy labels, this area of nonhearsay is growing because of the advancing sophistication of automated responses and expansion of computer-generated data in modern life.

Indirect Versions of Hearsay Statements; Group Statements. If the purpose of testimony is to use an out-of-court statement to prove the truth of facts stated, the hearsay objection cannot be eliminated by eliciting the content of the statement in an indirect form. Thus, when offered as proof of the facts asserted, testimony regarding "information received" by the witness and the results of investigations made by other persons are properly classified as hearsay.

Statements of collective or group decisions presented by the testimony of one member of the group should be treated similarly except where expert opinions are involved. For example, when the statement involves a decision reached after consultation by a group of doctors, the opinion reached and the statements of others supporting it should be admissible because the expert opinion rule allows such opinions to be based on reliable although inadmissible evidence.[19] However, the statements of other experts should still not be received for their truth and only to support the opinion,[20] but the theoretical validity of even this accepted limited use is subject to some debate.

Reputation. In the earlier stages of jury trial, when the jurors were expected to seek out the facts by neighborhood inquiries (instead of having the witnesses bring the facts through their testimony in court), community reputation was a frequent source of information for the jurors. When in the late 1600s the general doctrine excluding hearsay

---

[17] See supra § 34.

[18] See supra § 47.

[19] See supra § 15; Fed. R. Evid. 703. Business records also allow admission of opinions and diagnoses. See infra § 287.

[20] See infra § 324.3.

began to take form,[21] the use of reputation either directly by the jurors or through the testimony of the witnesses was so well established in certain areas that exceptions to the hearsay rule for reputation in those areas was soon recognized.

Reputation is a composite description of what the people in a community have said and are saying about a matter. A witness who testifies to reputation testifies to a generalized version of a series of out-of-court statements. Whether reputation is hearsay depends on the same tests applied to evidence of other out-of-court statements[22] and sometimes may not be hearsay at all. Thus, in an action for defamation where an element of damages is injury to the plaintiff's reputation, evidence that the plaintiff's reputation was bad before the slander is not hearsay when presented regarding damages. Proof of reputation in the community offered as evidence that some person there had knowledge of the reputed facts is similarly not hearsay.

On the other hand, evidence of reputation is hearsay when offered to prove the truth of the fact reputed and hence depends for its value on the veracity of the collective asserters. It should be excluded when it fits within no exception. However, several hearsay exceptions have been recognized for reputation as to character and certain other issues.[23]

Prior Statements of Witnesses Offered for the Truth; Admissions of Party-Opponents. Some prior statements of witnesses offered for their truth and admissions by party-opponents are excluded from the hearsay rule by the Federal Rules under theories separate from the definition of hearsay discussed above. These statements are discussed in later sections.[24]

§ 250 Conduct as Hearsay and "Implied Assertions"

Nonverbal Conduct. The examination thus far into what is and is not hearsay has been confined to out-of-court words, either spoken or written. Under the definition in Section 246, if they constitute an assertion and are offered as proof that the matter asserted happened or existed, they are hearsay.

In some situations, non-verbal conduct may be just as assertive as words. If, in response to a question "Who did it?," one of the auditors held up her hand, no one would contend that this gesture could be treated as different from an oral or written statement. Other illustrations are the act of pointing to a particular person in a lineup as the equivalent of saying "That's the person," or the sign language used by persons with impaired speech or hearing. These are clear instances of "non-verbal conduct [that] the person intended . . . as an assertion,"[25] which under our hearsay definition receives the same treatment as oral or written assertions. The only difference is that an oral or written assertion is assumed in the first instance to have been intended as such by virtue of being assertive in form, while in the case of the non-verbal conduct an intent to assert must be found by the judge as a precondition to classification as hearsay. The conduct, however, need not be so extreme as to constitute an assertion in itself if, in context, it is assertive.

---

[21] See supra § 244.

[22] See supra § 246.

[23] See infra § 322.

[24] See infra § 251 (prior statements) & Ch. 25.

[25] Fed. R. Evid. 801(a).

In other situations, the conduct is just as clearly nonassertive. Thus, an uncontrollable action or reaction by its very nature precludes any intent to make an assertion. Two cases illustrate the difference. In the first, an officer testified he went to the murder suspect's home and asked defendant's wife for the shirt he was wearing when he arrived home after the murder was committed. She handed the officer a shirt on which blood stains were later found.[26] In the second case, a murder suspect was described by witnesses as wearing a jacket with a fur-lined collar. The officer who arrested defendant at his home testified that he asked defendant if he had a jacket with a fur-lined collar, and that defendant turned to his wife and said, "I don't have one like that, do I dear?" His wife fainted.[27] In the first case, the suspect's wife was found to have intended to assert that the shirt produced was the one requested, and therefore her conduct was hearsay. In the second, the conduct was considered nonassertive and hence not hearsay. The disputed area lies between these extremes.

Nonassertive Nonverbal Conduct. The celebrated 19th century case of *Wright v. Tatham*[28] is the focal point of this debate. By will, John Marsden, a country gentleman, had left his estate to one Wright, who had risen from a menial station to the position of steward and general man of business for Marsden. The legal heir, Admiral Tatham, brought proceedings to recover the manors of the estate, alleging that Marsden was not competent to make a will. Defendant Wright, supporting the will, offered in evidence several letters that had been written to the deceased by third persons who were no longer alive.

The theory of the offer was that the letters indicated the writers' belief that Marsden was mentally competent from which it might be inferred that he was in fact competent. The letters were admitted, and the will sustained. However, upon retrial after reversal, the letters were excluded, and the verdict was against the will. The House of Lords ended eight years of litigation by upholding the ruling that the letters were inadmissible as equivalent to hearsay evidence of the opinions of the writers. The holding was perhaps most pithily put by Baron Parke in these words:

> The conclusion at which I have arrived is, that proof of a particular fact which is not of itself a matter in issue, but which is relevant only as implying a statement or opinion of a third person on the matter in issue, is inadmissible in all cases where such a statement or opinion not on oath would be of itself inadmissible; and, therefore, in this case the letters which are offered only to prove the competence of the testator, that is the truth of the implied statements therein contained, were properly rejected, as the mere statement or opinion of the writer would certainly have been inadmissible.[29]

To describe the evidence in *Wright v. Tatham* as "implied statements," i.e. implied assertions, as suggested by Baron Parke is to prejudge the issue, for it is to extrajudicial assertions that the hearsay rule applies.

Before turning to the letters actually at issue in the case, let us examine one of the best known examples used by the House of Lords. That is the nonverbal conduct of a deceased captain embarking on a ship with his family after he conducted a full inspection

---

26   Stevenson v. Com., 237 S.E.2d 779 (Va. 1977).

27   People v. Clark, 86 Cal. Rptr. 106 (Ct. App. 1970).

28   7 Adolph. & E. 313, 112 Eng. Rep. 488 (Exch. Ch. 1837), and 5 Cl. & F. 136 (H.L. 1838).

29   7 Adolph. & E. at 388, Eng. Rep. at 516.

of it to establish its seaworthiness. The line of reasoning suggested is that (a) the captain's conduct tends to prove that he believed the ship to be seaworthy and (b) from this belief, the conclusion might be drawn that the ship was in fact seaworthy. This, the judges said, was the equivalent of an out-of-court statement by the captain that the ship was seaworthy and hence inadmissible hearsay. Functional equivalence can, however, be misleading. The vital element of intent to assert does not appear to be present in the example.

After *Wright v. Tatham*, the hearsay issue often went unrecognized, and when noticed, the earlier cases tended to favor the objection. Now, however, Federal Rule 801(a)[30] and numerous decisions treat nonverbal conduct as nonhearsay unless an intent to assert is shown.

Is this result consistent with the policies that underlie the hearsay rule? The question should be answered through an evaluation of the dangers that the hearsay rule is designed to guard against, i.e., imperfections of perception, memory, narration, and particularly sincerity. Such an analysis rejects the view that nonassertive nonverbal conduct, from which may be inferred a belief, from which in turn may be inferred the happening of the event which produced the belief, is the equivalent of an assertion that the event happened and hence hearsay. Prior to raising their umbrellas, people do not say to themselves in soliloquy form, "It is raining," nor does the motorist go forward on the green light only after making an inward assertion, "The light is green." The conduct offered in the one instance to prove it was raining and in the other that the light was green involves no intent to communicate the fact sought to be proved, and purposeful deception is much less likely in the absence of intent to communicate. True, the threshold question whether communication was intended may on occasion present difficulty, yet the probabilities against intent are generally so great as to justify putting the burden of establishing it upon the party urging the hearsay objection.

Even though the risks arising from purposeful deception may be slight or nonexistent in the absence of intent to communicate, the objection remains that the actor's perception and memory are untested by cross-examination for the possibility of honest mistake. However, in contrast to the risks from purposeful deception, those arising from the chance of honest mistake seem more sensibly to be factors useful in evaluating weight and credibility rather than grounds for exclusion. Moreover, the kind of situation involved is ordinarily such as either to minimize the likelihood of flaws of perception and memory or to present circumstances lending themselves to their evaluation. While the suggestion has been advanced that conduct evidence ought to be admitted only when the actor's behavior has an element of significant reliance as an assurance of trustworthiness, a sufficient response here too is that the factor is one of evaluation, not a ground for exclusion. Moreover, undue complication ought to be avoided in the interest of ease of application. The same can be said with respect to the possibility that the conduct may be ambiguous so that the trier of fact will draw a wrong inference. Similar arguments exclude nonassertive verbal conduct including questions and commands from the hearsay rule, although the analysis is generally more difficult and the reduction of hearsay dangers somewhat less clear.

Silence as Hearsay. One aspect of the conduct-as-hearsay problem is presented by cases where a failure to speak or act is offered to support an inference that conditions

---

[30]   See supra § 246.

were such as would evoke silence or inaction in a reasonable person. The cases are likely to fall into two classes: (1) evidence of absence of complaints from other customers as disproof of claimed defects of goods or food or from other persons who would have been affected, as disproof of a claimed injurious event or condition, and (2) evidence from members of a family that a particular member never mentioned an event or claim to or disposition of property, to prove nonoccurrence or nonexistence. Often the presence of an arguable hearsay question is neither noted nor discussed.

Although common law cases were divided as to the hearsay status of this kind of evidence, the evidence is not hearsay under the definition of hearsay in Section 246 because it is not intended as an assertion. Support for admissibility, aside from any question of hearsay, may be stronger in the cases of absence of complaints than in other cases of silence. The other cases present a variety of situations, some of which suggest motivations for silence other than nonoccurrence of the disputed event that call for evaluation of whether the probative value of the evidence is outweighed by its prejudicial effect. Silence as an admission by a party-opponent is treated elsewhere.

So-Called "Implied Assertions"; Out-of-Court Assertions Not Offered to Prove the Truth of the Matter Asserted. The preceding discussion relates to hearsay aspects of nonassertive nonverbal conduct. The actual issue in *Wright v. Tatham*, on which the discussion is largely based, involved verbal conduct that was, in a measure at least, assertive—letters that made some affirmative statements. They raise the hearsay status of certain types of assertive conduct.

If one of the letters had said, "Marsden, you are competent to make a will," it would clearly fall within the definition of hearsay as an out-of-court assertion offered to prove the truth of the matter asserted, but that was not the case. The letters, though assertive in form, were not offered to prove the truth of what was asserted. The letter from the cousin describing conditions found on his voyage to America, for example, was not offered as evidence of conditions in America but as evidence that the writer believed Marsden to be of reasonable intelligence, from which belief competency might be inferred. Under these conditions, should the evidence be treated as hearsay?

Although the application of the principle is sometimes complicated, the basic answer under the Federal Rules and contemporary judicial analysis is that an out-of-court assertion is not hearsay if offered as proof of something other than the matter asserted. The theory is that questions of sincerity are generally reduced when assertive conduct is "offered as a basis for inferring something other than the matter asserted."[31] This argument is somewhat less compelling than for nonassertive conduct since an intent to make some assertion is present, and the danger of insincerity regarding indirect uses of the statement can never be entirely discounted. However, this risk is generally not so great as to mandate treatment as hearsay when the intent does not embrace the inference suggested, and the likelihood of purposeful deception is accordingly substantially reduced.

Clearly, the contemporary definition of hearsay is less inclusive than logical and analytical possibilities would allow, and the elimination of all hearsay dangers, would require. Relatively early in his career, noted evidence scholar Edmund Morgan suggested:

---

[31]   Fed. R. Evid. 801(a) advisory committee's note.

> A comprehensive definition of hearsay . . . would include (1) all conduct of a person, verbal or nonverbal, intended by him to operate as an assertion when offered either to prove the truth of the matter asserted or to prove that the asserter believed the matter asserted to be true, and (2) all conduct of a person, verbal or nonverbal, not intended by him to operate as an assertion, when offered either to prove both his state of mind and the external event or condition which caused him to have that state of mind, or to prove that his state of mind was truly reflected by that conduct.[32]

He subsequently concluded that a definition of hearsay expanded to the outer limits suggested by logic and analysis was undesirable, with needless complication of the hearsay rule that outweighed any supposed advantage. Similarly, the contemporary resolution of the issues involved in "implied assertions" reflects ultimately a compromise between theory and the need for a relatively simple and workable definition in situations where hearsay dangers are generally reduced.

Knowledge. On an issue whether a given person was alive at a particular time, evidence that she said something at the time would be proof that she was alive. Whether she said, "I am alive," or "Hi, Joe," would be immaterial; the inference of life is drawn from the fact that she spoke, not from what was said. No problem of veracity is involved. In terms of the definition of hearsay, even the first statement is not offered to prove what is asserted because its relevance does not depend upon its content.

This analysis may be extended to declarations evincing knowledge, notice, or awareness of some fact. Conversation about a matter demonstrates on its face that the person was aware of it, and veracity does not enter into the situation. Caution is appropriate, however, since the self-proving aspect is limited strictly to what is said. Thus, the statement, "I know geometry," establishes no more than that the speaker is aware of the term "geometry," not that she has command of that subject. On the other hand, if the statement is itself a proposition of geometry, it is self-evident that the speaker knows some geometry; whether the statement is prefaced with "I know" is immaterial.

When the existence of knowledge is sought to be used as the basis for a further inference, the hearsay rule may be violated. That possibility becomes a reality when the purpose of the evidence of knowledge is to prove the existence of the fact known. Statements of memory or belief are not generally allowed as proof of the happening of the event remembered or believed, since allowing the evidence would destroy the hearsay rule.[33] For this purpose, knowledge is indistinguishable from memory and belief. However, drawing from evidence of knowledge an inference other than the existence of the fact known will occasionally be possible.

For example, evidence that a person made statements showing knowledge of matters likely to have been known only to a specific person is receivable as tending to prove the identity of the declarant. A similar nonhearsay use of knowledge is illustrated by *Bridges v. State.*[34] In that case, a child victim gave a description of the house and its surroundings and of the room and its furnishings where the crime occurred. Other evidence showed that the description fit the house and room where the defendant lived.

---

[32]   Morgan, Hearsay and Non-Hearsay, 48 Harv. L. Rev. 1138, 1144 (1945).

[33]   See infra § 276.

[34]   Bridges v. State, 19 N.W.2d 529 (Wis. 1945). See infra § 268.

At a superficial level the evidence, which was used to help identify the defendant as the perpetrator, depends for its value upon the observation, memory, and veracity of the child and thus shares some of the hazards of hearsay. Significantly, the testimony has value independent of these factors. Other witnesses established the physical characteristics of the locale, and the child's testimony was not used for that purpose. Assuming other possible sources of her knowledge have been eliminated—as the court determined—the only remaining inference was that she had acquired that knowledge by being in the defendant's room. Evidence of this sort is thus not hearsay.

§ 251 Prior Statements of Witnesses as Substantive Evidence

The traditional view has been that a prior statement, even one made by the witness, is hearsay if it is offered to prove the matters asserted therein. Of course, this categorization has not precluded using the prior statement for other purposes, e.g., to impeach the witness by showing a self-contradiction if the statement is inconsistent with his testimony[35] or to support credibility when the statement is consistent with the testimony and logically helps to rehabilitate.[36] But the prior statement has traditionally been admissible as substantive evidence to prove the matter asserted therein only when falling within an established exception to the hearsay rule. This position has come under substantial attack on both logical and practical grounds.

The logic of the orthodox view is that the previous statement of the witness is hearsay since its value rests on the credit of the declarant, who, when the statement was made, was not (1) under oath, (2) in the presence of the trier, or (3) subject to cross-examination.

The counterargument goes as follows: (1) The oath is no longer a principal safeguard of the trustworthiness of testimony. Affidavits, although under oath, are not exempted from the hearsay rule. Moreover, of the numerous exceptions where evidence is admitted despite being hearsay, only prior testimony must have been under oath.[37] (2) With respect to allowing the trier of fact to observe the demeanor of the witness while making the statement, Judge Learned Hand cogently stated: "If, from all that the jury see of the witness, they conclude that what he says now is not the truth, but what he said before, they are none the less deciding from what they see and hear of that person and in court."[38] (3) The principal method for achieving credibility is clearly cross-examination, and this condition is largely satisfied. As Wigmore, who originally adhered to the traditional view, observed: "Here, however, by hypothesis the witness is present and subject to cross-examination. There is ample opportunity to test him as to the basis for his former statement. The whole purpose of the hearsay rule has been already satisfied."[39]

The question remains whether cross-examination must take place at the time when the statement is made to be effective. The orthodox view urges:

The chief merit of cross-examination is not that at some future time it gives the party opponent the right to dissect adverse testimony. Its principal virtue is

---

[35] See supra § 34.

[36] See supra § 49.

[37] See infra § 301.

[38] Di Carlo v. United States, 6 F.2d 364, 368 (2d Cir. 1925).

[39] 3A Wigmore, Evidence § 1018, at 996 (Chadbourn rev. 1970).

the immediate application of the testing process. Its strokes fall while the iron is hot. False testimony is apt to harden and become unyielding to the blows of truth in proportion as the witness has opportunity for reconsideration and influence by the suggestions of others . . . .[40]

Yet, with inconsistent statements, the witness by definition has changed his or her story; rather than hardening, the story has yielded to something between the giving of the statement and the time of testifying; and the circumstances most frequently suggest that the "something" which caused the change was an improper influence.

An additional persuasive factor against the orthodox rule is the superior trustworthiness of earlier statements based on the general proposition that recency aids memory. The prior statement is always nearer and usually very much nearer to the event than is the testimony. The fresher the memory, the fuller and more accurate it is. The requirement of the hearsay exception for memoranda of past recollection, that the matter have been recorded while fresh in memory,[41] is based precisely on this principle.

These various considerations led to a substantial movement to abandon the orthodox view completely. The Model Code of Evidence provided: "Evidence of a hearsay declaration is admissible if the judge finds that the declarant . . . is present and subject to cross-examination."[42] Substantial support for this position began to appear in reported decisions.

Under the Model Code/Wigmore position, all prior statements of witnesses, regardless of their nature, would be exempt from the ban of the hearsay rule. This complete rejection of the orthodox rule resulted in uneasiness that a practice might develop among lawyers whereby a carefully prepared statement would be offered in lieu of testimony, merely tendering the witness for cross-examination on the statement. The practice seems not to have materialized in the jurisdictions where the orthodox rule was rejected, but the potential for abuse nevertheless remained.

As a consequence, the Advisory Committee adopted an intermediate position, neither entirely admitting nor rejecting prior statements of witnesses where the "declarant testifies and is subject to cross-examination concerning the statement," but exempting from classification as hearsay certain prior statements thought by circumstances to be generally free of the danger of abuse. Under Federal Rule of Evidence 801(d)(1), the exempt statements are: (A) inconsistent statements "given under penalty of perjury at a trial, hearing, or other proceeding or in a deposition"; (B) consistent statements "offered to rebut an express or implied charge that the declarant recently fabricated it or acted from a recent improper influence or motive in so testifying"; and (C) statements that "identif[y] a person as someone the declarant perceived earlier."

Prior Inconsistent Statements. The witness who has told one story earlier and another at trial has invited a searching examination of credibility through cross-examination and re-examination. The reasons for the change, whether forgetfulness, carelessness, pity, terror, or greed, may be explored by the adversaries in the presence of the trier of fact, under oath, casting light on which is the true story and which the false. Certainly, evidence of a prior inconsistent statement, when declarant is on the

---

[40]   State v. Saporen, 285 N.W. 898, 901 (Minn. 1939).

[41]   See infra § 281 (past recollection recorded); § 286 (business records).

[42]   Model Code of Evidence Rule 503(b).

stand to explain it if he or she can, has the major safeguards of examined testimony. The rule admits the inconsistent statement as substantive evidence, which avoids use of a limiting instruction that the jury may have difficulty fully following.

When is a prior statement inconsistent?[43] Where a witness no longer remembers an event, a prior statement describing that event should not be considered inconsistent. Yet the tendency of unwilling or untruthful witnesses to seek refuge in a claim of forgetfulness is well recognized. Hence the judge may be warranted in concluding under the circumstances the claimed lack of memory of the event is untrue and in effect an implied denial of the prior statement, thus qualifying it as inconsistent. The case law generally applies the concept broadly and gives considerable discretion to the trial court to find inconsistency.

As originally drafted by the Advisory Committee and transmitted to the Congress by the Supreme Court, the Federal Rule contained no requirement as to the conditions under which the prior inconsistent statement must be made. However, Congress imposed limitations, adding the requirements that it must be given under oath subject to the penalty of perjury at a trial, hearing, or other proceeding, or in a deposition. The result of the limitation is to confine substantive use of prior inconsistent statements virtually to those made in the course of judicial proceedings, including grand jury testimony, although allowing use for impeachment without these limitations.

Prior Consistent Statements. While prior consistent statements are hearsay by the traditional view and inadmissible as substantive evidence, they have nevertheless been allowed limited admissibility for the purpose of supporting the credibility of a witness, particularly to show that a witness whose testimony was allegedly influenced told the same story before being influenced. As originally promulgated, Federal Rule of Evidence 801(d)(1)(B) exempted from the hearsay rule and therefore admitted for the truth prior consistent statements "offered to rebut an express or implied charge that the declarant recently fabricated it or acted from a recent improper influence or motive in so testifying." As amended effective December 2014, the rule extended nonhearsay treatment to prior consistent statements admitted "to rehabilitate the declarant's credibility as a witness when attached on another ground." The Supreme Court examined the first category of statements admitted as nonhearsay—those involving a charge of recent fabrication—in *Tome v. United States*.[44] There, the Court concluded that the rule imposes a timing requirement and admits only those statements "made before the charged recent fabrication or improper influence or motive."[45]

One frequently encountered situation that raises questions of interpretation regarding timing involves prior consistent statements by a government witness accused by the defendant with providing testimony to gain favor regarding the witness's own criminal liability. The courts have taken two different approaches. One view, which appears to be more in line with the clarity of *Tome*'s approach, holds that when the witness is obviously under investigation or has been arrested when the statements were made, they are inadmissible because the motive to fabricate has already arisen. The other position is that investigation and arrest do not automatically produce the motive

---

[43]   See supra § 34 (inconsistency required for prior statements used to impeach).
[44]   513 U.S. 150 (1995).
[45]   *Id.* at 156.

to lie. Instead, when the declarant's motive to lie commenced must be determined by the trial court on the specific facts of the case.

While prior consistent statements are not universally received for credibility purposes, remaining admissible only if they rehabilitate a witness whose credibility has been attacked and being subject to exclusion under Federal Rule 403 or because they constitute improper bolstering, they are received under Federal Rule 801(d)(1)(B) beyond cases involving charges of recent fabrications and improper influence or motivation. For example, consistent statements are often admitted to explain what would otherwise appear to be an inconsistency in the witness's testimony, and to rebut a charge of faulty memory. The new provision does not alter the requirements imposed by *Tome* for statements offered to rebut charges of recent fabrication or improper influence or motive. It also does not change "traditional and well-accepted limits" on introducing consistent statements for credibility purposes. However, it does mean that if a statement is admitted to rehabilitate a witness's credibility attacked on grounds other than recent fabrication or improper influence or motive, the statement is admissible, not only to affect credibility, but also for its truth and is considered not hearsay.

Statements of Identification. When A testifies that on a prior occasion B pointed to the accused and said, "That's the man who robbed me," the testimony is clearly hearsay. If, however, B is present in court, testifies to the prior identification, and is available for cross-examination, the case fits within the present section as a statement that "identifies a person as someone the declarant perceived earlier." Admissibility of the prior identifications has long-standing case law support, often in the older cases without recognition of the hearsay problem. Justification is found in the unsatisfactory nature of courtroom identification and by the constitutional safeguards that regulate out-of-court identifications arranged by the police. Evidence of such a pre-trial identification is usually permitted even when the witness cannot make an in-court identification.

The Requirement of Testifying and Being Subject to Cross-Examination. With respect to each of the categories of prior statements discussed above, the Federal Rule requires that declarant testify at the trial or hearing and be "subject to cross-examination about a prior statement."[46] The meaning of the witness being subject to cross-examination has been vigorously debated for both prior inconsistent statements and statements of identification. Bogus and real claims of lack of memory, denials, and acknowledgments of both the underlying event and the prior statement appear in various combinations. Until the United States Supreme Court's decision in *United States v. Owens*,[47] some of the possible scenarios described were seen to create difficult problems for adequate cross-examination under either the rule or the Confrontation Clause.

Owens, which dealt with a prior identification by a witness who could not recall the crime at issue because of head injuries he suffered during it, and cases applying its analysis to prior inconsistent statements, have ended the debate. The Court concluded that the requirements of both the hearsay rule and the Confrontation Clause are satisfied as long as the witness takes the stand and responds willingly to questions. Judicial restrictions on cross-examination and claim of privilege would threaten meaningful cross-examination, but lack of memory does not. Lower courts have extended

---

[46]   Fed. R. Evid. 801(d)(1). Constitutional aspects of cross-examination are discussed in infra § 252.

[47]   484 U.S. 554 (1988).

the analysis of *Owens* to statements involving prior inconsistent statements and to feigned lack of memory. Because *Owens* found cross-examination adequate in one of the most difficult fact patterns, few plausible challenges remain.

§ 252 Constitutional Problems of Hearsay: Confrontation and Due Process

(A) Confrontation

The constitutional issues related to admission of hearsay focus primarily on the Confrontation Clause of the Sixth Amendment, which applies to the states through the Fourteenth Amendment. The Clause requires "that in all criminal prosecutions, the accused shall enjoy the right . . . to be confronted with the witnesses against him." In addition, nearly every state constitution has a similar provision. The Confrontation Clause is applicable only to criminal prosecutions and may be invoked only by the accused. Due process has an impact on hearsay admission and the right to cross-examine, but a far less significant role.

Certain facets of the right of confrontation and the right to due process, while relevant to the values affecting the admission of hearsay, do not bear directly upon it. One is the right of an accused to be present at every stage of the trial. Another is the defendant's right to cross-examine witnesses who appear and testify against the defense.[48] A related right is to disclosure by the prosecution of material exculpatory evidence as an element of due process. The Sixth Amendment right to counsel is a thread running through much of this constitutional fabric.

The Confrontation Clause's impact on the admission of hearsay—the principal subject of this chapter—was fundamentally reconfigured by the Supreme Court's decision in *Crawford v. Washington*.[49] *Crawford* rejected the Confrontation Clause analysis of *Ohio v. Roberts*,[50] which the Court had followed for over two decades.

Obviously, a relationship exists between the hearsay rule and constitutional right of confrontation. The hearsay rule operates to preserve the ability of a party to confront adverse witnesses in open court, and the Confrontation Clause does the same for an accused in a criminal case. The nature of that relationship has been the subject of episodic reexamination, and specifically, the extent to which these two concepts and their exceptions coincide is the subject of debate.

In the late 1700s when confrontation provisions were first included in American bills of rights, the general concept of a rule against hearsay had been part of English law for a hundred years, but under certain circumstances hearsay was also admitted. Some argued, the most influential being Dean Henry Wigmore, that the Clause worked chiefly through the hearsay rule, including its exceptions, to regulate the admission of out-of-court statements. But the Confrontation Clause also rejects inquisitorial practices, such as admitting depositions taken in the absence of the accused, which was subsequently abandoned by the English judges and forbidden by statute. These inquisitorial practices and their modern analogs are the focus of *Crawford*.

---

[48]   See supra § 19.

[49]   541 U.S. 36 (2004).

[50]   448 U.S. 56 (1980).

One of the major issues in the debate about the relationship between the Confrontation Clause and hearsay has been whether confrontation recognizes the validity of the traditional hearsay rule—whether it effectively accords hearsay exceptions constitutional status or stands independent of the hearsay rule and imposes its own limits on what hearsay is covered and excluded by the Clause. In *Roberts*, the Supreme Court created an extremely close linkage between hearsay exceptions and statements that satisfy the Confrontation Clause. *Roberts* established a two-part test, the first dealing with the declarant's availability. The second requirement was that the statement must have been made under circumstances providing sufficient "indicia of reliability," which *Roberts* stated "can be inferred without more in a case where the evidence falls within a firmly rooted hearsay exception."[51] This second requirement strongly linked satisfaction of the Confrontation Clause to admission under established hearsay rules. By contrast, *Crawford* focuses, not on the regulation of hearsay generally, but instead on a limited class of hearsay statements—those that are "testimonial."

While the system of analysis developed in *Roberts* was rejected by *Crawford* and subsequently fully overruled,[52] two strands of long-standing confrontation doctrine outside *Roberts'* general framework were left untouched by *Crawford*. The first admits prior confronted testimony offered when the declarant is unavailable at the current trial. The constitutional requirement of unavailability is reasonably rigorously enforced for such statements. *Crawford* endorsed this method of satisfying the Confrontation Clause. The second allows receipt of prior statements when the declarant appears at the present trial, testifies, and is subject to cross-examination. This method of satisfying the Confrontation Clause was recognized in *California v. Green*,[53] where the Court concluded that the Clause did not limit introduction of prior statements if the declarant is produced at the trial for cross-examination. *United States v. Owens*[54] decided that even an imperfect witness who testified and was available to be questioned satisfied the defendant's confrontation right as to prior statements of that witness. It concluded that, absent limitations by the trial court on cross-examination or the witness's invocation of a privilege, the opportunity to cross-examine was constitutionally adequate. *Crawford* recognized the continuing validity of this way to meet the confrontation challenge.

Testimonial Statement Approach. In *Crawford*, the Supreme Court established a new mode of analyzing how the Confrontation Clause regulates admission of hearsay. The case involved tape recorded statements of the defendant's wife that incriminated the defendant in an assault and attempted murder made while she was in police custody being interrogated as also potentially involved in the crime. The Court designated these statements to be part of a new type of hearsay statements—those that are "testimonial."

As to testimonial statements, the Court rejected admission based on judicial determinations that the statements were reliable or trustworthy and created a firm rule of exclusion in the absence of confrontation. To this rule of exclusion, it recognized only a limited number of rather strictly defined exceptions.

Writing for seven members of the Court, Justice Scalia concluded on the basis of history and the text of the Constitution that the core of the Clause applied to testimonial statements. First, history demonstrated that the "principal evil at which the

---

[51] *Id.* at 66.

[52] *See* Whorton v. Bockting, 549 U.S. 406, 420 (2007).

[53] 399 U.S. 149 (1970).

[54] 484 U.S. 554 (1988).

Confrontation Clause was directed was the civil-law mode of criminal procedure, and particularly its use of *ex parte* examinations as evidence against the accused."[55] This civil law procedure, with its roots on the European continent, of private examination by judicial officers stood in sharp contrast to the preferred English common law tradition of "live testimony in court subject to adversarial testing."[56]

The Court then examined the text of the Confrontation Clause in the Sixth Amendment, which provides that in criminal prosecutions, "the accused shall enjoy the right . . . to be confronted with the *witnesses against him*" (emphasis added). The Court derived from that terminology a focus on "testimonial" statements. " 'Witnesses' against the accused" indicated in the Court's judgment that the Clause was to be applied to "those who 'bear testimony.' "[57] "Testimony," in turn, is typically "[a] solemn declaration or affirmation made for the purpose of establishing or proving some fact."[58]

The Court left "for another day" an effort to define testimonial statements comprehensively. However, "[w]hatever else the term covers, it applies at a minimum to prior testimony at a preliminary hearing, before a grand jury, or at a former trial; and to police interrogations. These are the modern practices with closest kinship to the abuses at which the Confrontation Clause was directed."[59]

Without selecting one, the Court noted three possible definitions that "shared a common nucleus":

> The Petitioner's Definition—"*ex parte* in-court testimony or its functional equivalent—that is, material such as affidavits, custodial examinations, prior testimony that the defendant was unable to cross-examine, or similar pretrial statements that declarant would reasonably expect to be used prosecutorially";
>
> Justice Thomas' Definition—"extrajudicial statements . . . contained in formalized testimonial materials, such as affidavits, depositions, prior testimony, or confessions";
>
> Amicus' Definition—"statements that were made under circumstances which would lead an objective witness reasonably to believe that the statement would be available for use at a later trial."[60]

The Court also provided as an example of a statement that is not testimonial "[a]n off-hand, overheard remark."[61] It contrasted "[a]n accuser who makes a formal statement to government officers," which is clearly testimonial, with "a person who makes a casual remark to an acquaintance," which is not.[62] The categories of statements the Court ruled testimonial are also important guides: "prior testimony at a preliminary hearing, before a grand jury, or at a former trial; . . . police interrogations";[63] and "plea allocution[s] showing existence of a conspiracy."[64] Beyond its value as an interpretative guide, the

---

[55] *Crawford*, 541 U.S. at 50.

[56] *Id.* at 43.

[57] *Id.* at 51.

[58] *Id.* at 51 (quoting 1 N. Webster, An American Dictionary of the English Language (1828)).

[59] *Id.* at 68.

[60] *Id.* at 51–52.

[61] *Id.* at 51.

[62] *Id.*

[63] *Id.* at 68.

[64] *Id.* at 64.

Court's bar under the Confrontation Clause to receiving statements made in police custody by a co-participant in crime that implicates the defendant is an important lasting accomplishment of *Crawford*.

Although hearsay exceptions do not match up with the concept of testimonial statements, the Court indicated that most statements in the business records exception and statements in furtherance of a conspiracy are "by their nature . . . not testimonial."[65] While, as discussed below, it suggested that dying declarations might be excluded for historical reasons, the Court took a different view of excited utterances/spontaneous declarations. It stated that its decision in *White v. Illinois*[66] was arguably incorrect in allowing admission of a child's statement to an investigating police officer as a spontaneous declaration. The Court implied that the child's statement might have been testimonial and doubted it would have been admissible at the time the Sixth Amendment was adopted because "to the extent the hearsay exception for spontaneous declarations existed at all, it required that the statements be made 'immediat[ely] upon the hurt received, and before [the declarant] had time to devise or contrive any thing for her own advantage.'"[67] In *White*, the child's statement was made forty-five minutes after the alleged assault.

Crawford Exceptions. The Court set out a limited number of exceptions where testimonial statements may be received. As noted earlier, two lines of authority developed outside of the *Roberts* analysis remain valid after *Crawford*. First, *Crawford* recognized that the confrontation right may be satisfied through a prior opportunity for cross-examination rather than through cross-examination at the current trial if the witness is shown to be unavailable.[68] Second, the *Crawford* Court reaffirmed "that, when the declarant appears for cross-examination at trial, the Confrontation Clause places no constraints at all on the use of his prior testimonial statements."[69] Third, the Court recognized that its concept of "forfeiture by wrongdoing" is consistent with the new approach.[70] Fourth, *Crawford* does not bar the introduction of out-of-court testimonial statements where they are used for a purpose "other than establishing the truth of the matter asserted"—where they are not used for a hearsay purpose.[71] Fifth, the Court recognized that dying declarations that are testimonial under its definition might be admissible on historical grounds. At the time the Constitution was adopted, such statements were apparently accepted as an exception to the common law confrontation principle, which might mean the Confrontation Clause was understood to permit admission of such statements. However, the Supreme Court was cautionary: "If this exception must be accepted on historical grounds, it is *sui generis*."[72] Finally, although not stated by the Court in *Crawford*, the Confrontation Clause certainly does not exclude personal admissions by the defendant.

---

[65] *Id.* at 56.

[66] 502 U.S. 346 (1992).

[67] *Crawford*, 541 U.S. at 59 n.8 (quoting Thompson v. Trevanion, Skin. 402, 90 Eng. Rep. 179 (K.B. 1694)).

[68] *Id.* at 57–58.

[69] *Id.* at 59 n.9.

[70] *Id.* at 62 (citing Reynolds v. United States, 98 U.S. 145 (1878)).

[71] *Id.* at 59 n.9.

[72] *Id.* at 56 n.6.

Primary Purpose of the Interrogation; Ongoing Emergency. In *Davis v. Washington*,[73] the United States Supreme Court provided further explication of the testimonial concept. The *Davis* decision involved two prosecutions for domestic violence. In contrast to *Crawford*, the statements in both cases were made to government officials outside a police station and the declarants were neither under arrest nor were being formally interrogated. The fact patterns thus provide guidance to the meaning of the testimonial concept in less structured questioning situations than occurred in *Crawford*.

Davis concerned an emergency 911 call. There the Court articulated a different test than used in *Crawford*:

> Statements are not testimonial when made in the course of police interrogation under circumstances objectively indicating that the primary purpose of the interrogation is to enable police assistance to meet an ongoing emergency. They are testimonial when the circumstances objectively indicate that there is no such ongoing emergency, and that the primary purpose is to establish or prove past events potentially relevant to later criminal prosecution.[74]

In this test, the Court stated the testimonial determination rested on the "primary purpose of the interrogation," which appeared to focus on the conduct and intention of the government agent asking the questions rather than the declarant where *Crawford* centered its attention. While some disagreement continues within the Court on this point, the perspectives of both questioner and declarant are relevant ("a combined inquiry that accounts for both the declarant and the interrogator"),[75] with ultimately primary emphasis generally being given to the declarant:[76] "it is the statements, and not the questions, that must be evaluated under the Sixth Amendment."[77]

In the *Davis* case, the Court ruled that the statements by the apparent victim of domestic abuse were not testimonial because they were made virtually in the midst of an assault and were describing events as they were happening. It concluded that the purpose of the questioning by the 911 operator was to enable the police to meet the ongoing emergency. This purpose applied even to a statement giving the name of the attacker, which the Court considered potentially important information for the responding officers to have in approaching the scene. However, the Court suggested that the statements became testimonial once the attacker left the building and thus ended the ongoing emergency caused by his violence and his threatening presence.

The Court ruled in the companion case of *Hammon v. Indiana* that statements made under different circumstances to a police officer by another domestic assault victim were testimonial. Although the damage from the altercation was still visible in the house when the police arrived and the defendant was still present, the Court reasoned that police were also present, the victim stated things were fine, and the officers were focused on what had happened rather than what was then happening. The primary purpose no longer concerned an ongoing emergency. In drawing the distinctions between the situations like those in *Davis* and *Hammon*, much will be left to the interpretation and

---

[73]   547 U.S. 813 (2006).

[74]   *Id.* at 822.

[75]   Michigan v. Bryant, 562 U.S. 344, 367 (2011).

[76]   *Davis*, 547 U.S. at 822–23 n.1.

[77]   *Bryant*, 562 U.S. at 367 n.11.

discretion of the trial judge in finding whether the emergency is ongoing or has concluded.

Formality. Davis provided some important clarification regarding the question of the requirement of formality of a testimonial statement. It did not impose the strict level of formality that one of the initial definitions in *Crawford* had prescribed. First, it ruled that formal interrogation, which had occurred in *Crawford*, was not required. It stated: "The Framers were no more willing to exempt from cross-examination volunteered testimony or answers to open-ended questions than they were to exempt answers to detailed interrogation."[78] Moreover, the *Davis* majority ruled that the declarant's words were testimonial even if not memorialized in a signed witness statement. It asserted: "The product of such interrogation, whether reduced to a writing signed by the declarant or embedded in the memory (and perhaps notes) of the interrogating officer, is testimonial."[79]

Although reducing the rigor of the formality requirement, the *Davis* Court stated that "formality is . . . essential to testimonial utterances."[80] While *Davis* provided some clarification, it did not resolve the nature of the formality requirement for some of the Justices. Generally, formality is found for statements made to known police investigators outside of ongoing emergency situations. On the other hand, both Justices Thomas and Alito adhere to a much more exacting standard of formality, which has proven important given the sharp divisions that developed in the Court in later Confrontation Clause decisions.

Ongoing Emergency Revisited. The ongoing emergency concept was expanded outside of the domestic violence context in *Michigan v. Bryant*[81] to quell an ongoing emergency involving an armed assailant, and in *Ohio v. Clark*[82] was applied to statements by a child to teachers regarding child abuse. In *Bryant*, the police spoke with a severely injured individual found in a gas station parking lot about the circumstances of the shooting that caused his injury, which had occurred sometime earlier and at a different location. The Court ruled that statements made by the victim regarding the identification and description of the shooter and the location of the shooting were not testimonial statements because they had the primary purpose of enabling the police to meet an ongoing emergency.

The *Bryant* opinion explained that the limited range of time involved in *Davis* was a function of the fact that the crime was an act of domestic violence targeted against a particular victim by an unarmed perpetrator. In *Bryant*, it reasoned that the perpetrator's use of a gun, his continued possession of that weapon, and his unknown motivation made more expansive inquiries pertinent to the ongoing emergency. The Court considered questions designed to identify and find the attacker legitimately related to concern for public safety regarding an armed attacker whose location and motivation were unknown and therefore did not consider those inquiries to have the primary purpose of developing evidence for trial but rather concerned the ongoing emergency.

---

[78] *Davis*, 547 U.S. at 822 n.1.

[79] *Id.* at 826.

[80] *Id.* at 830 n.5.

[81] 562 U.S. 344 (2011).

[82] 135 S. Ct. 2173 (2015).

Among the other factors the Court found pertinent in the testimonial determination were the serious medical condition of the victim and the informality of the police interrogation. The exact impact of *Bryant* is not clear, but it will permit a broader reading of the time period of an ongoing emergency in armed perpetrator situations, and its multi-factor analysis will effectively give broader discretion to trial judges in evaluating the primary purpose of the law enforcement inquiry and the declarant's motivation. Predictably, a larger group of statements will be ruled nontestimonial after *Bryant* generally, and particularly in armed, unidentified perpetrator cases.

In *Clark*, a preschool teacher noticed injuries to the eye of a three-year-old boy, L.P., and asked him "[w]hat happened." L.P. initially did not respond and then said he "fell." In better light, the teacher noticed additional injuries to the child's face. This teacher notified a more senior teacher who asked L.P., "who did this? What happened to you?" L.P. said something like "Dee, Dee." When asked whether Dee was "big or little," the boy responded, "Dee is big."[83] The senior teacher took L.P. to her supervisor, who lifted the child's shirt, finding more injuries.

At this point the teacher who first observed the injuries called a child abuse hotline to alert authorities to suspected abuse. As a result of the ensuing investigation, Darius Clark, nicknamed "Dee," was charged with multiple counts of endangering children, domestic violence, and felonious assault, including additional multiple assaults against L.P.'s 18-month-old sister, who investigating authorities found to have suffered serious injuries. At Clark's trial, L.P.'s statements were introduced over Clark's Confrontation Clause objection.

The Supreme Court held L.P.'s statements were not testimonial, concluding they were made "in the context of an ongoing emergency involving suspected child abuse."[84] The Court observed that the teachers were unsure who had abused the child, how best to secure his safety, and whether other children might be at risk. As a result, it concluded that both the teachers' questions and L.P.'s answers "were primarily aimed at identifying and ending the threat" and that the teachers' questions "were meant to identify the abuser in order to protect the victim from future attacks."[85] In addition, the conversation was informal and spontaneous, which distinguished it from statements found testimonial in *Crawford* and *Hammond*.

In the *Clark* decision, the Court addressed the previously unresolved issue of whether the government must play a role in the production of the statement for it to be considered testimonial. It stated: "Because as least some statements to individuals who are not law enforcement officers could conceivably raise confrontation concerns, we decline to adopt a categorical rule excluding them from the Sixth Amendment's reach."[86] However, the Court observed that statements made to individuals other than law enforcement "are significantly less likely to be testimonial" and the fact L.P. was speaking to his teachers rather than someone principally charged with uncovering and prosecuting crime "remains highly relevant."[87]

---

[83]   *Clark*, 135 S. Ct. at 2178.

[84]   *Id.* at 2181.

[85]   *Id.*

[86]   *Id.*

[87]   *Id.* at 2182.

The Court also made a general, although not a categorical, observation about the application of the testimonial concept to statements by children: "Statements by very young children will rarely, if ever, implicate the Confrontation Clause."[88] The Court explained that young children would rarely understand the criminal justice system and would be unlikely to intend their statements to be substitutes for trial testimony. Finally, it concluded that the state's mandatory child abuse reporting law, which was applicable to L.P.'s teachers, could not alone convert the conversation "between a concerned teacher and her student into a law enforcement mission aimed primarily at gathering evidence for a prosecution."[89]

Forfeiture by Wrongdoing. One of the exceptions to *Crawford's* strong insistence that testimonial statements must face confrontation arises when the defendant forfeits his confrontation right by wrongdoing that renders the declarant unavailable. *Davis* endorsed the "forfeiture by wrongdoing" exception but like *Crawford* did not answer whether an intent to silence the witness was required under the Confrontation Clause exception as it is under the hearsay exception defined in Federal Rule 804(b)(6).

In answering the intent question, the Court once again examined statements offered in a domestic violence case, this one ending in homicide. In *Giles v. California*,[90] a divided Court ruled that the forfeiture by wrongdoing exception was limited to those instances in which "the defendant engaged in conduct designed to prevent the witness from testifying."[91] However, the Court recognized that the intent to silence or dissuade a victim from testifying or cooperating with authorities might be found in the "domestic violence context" in prior acts of violence and threats. Although the Supreme Court has not ruled on the standard of proof to be used in establishing forfeiture, the lower courts have consistently applied a preponderance standard, which is appropriate.

Forensic Certificates and Reports. Crawford's application to forensic certificates and expert reports has been examined in three cases that sharply divided the Court. While the first two brought many such documents within the testimonial concept, the third excluded some and left the issue muddled and confused. In *Melendez-Diaz v. Massachusetts*,[92] the Supreme Court ruled that sworn certificates of analysis reporting the results of forensic analysis performed by a state laboratory at police request on seized material were testimonial and their admission without the testimony of the analysts violated the Confrontation Clause. The certificates gave the weight of the seized bags and identified their contents.

The *Melendez-Diaz* opinion, which was written by Justice Scalia for five members of the Court, concluded that these forensic certificates were in the core class of testimonial statements because they were functionally identical to live, in-court testimony. In particular, they stated that the substance found was cocaine, which is the precise testimony the analysts would be expected to provide if called at trial.

The Court rejected a number of arguments made by Massachusetts and by Justice Kennedy in his dissenting opinion for four members of the Court. Among them was the argument that the record should be admitted because it was a business or government

---

[88] *Id.*

[89] *Id.* at 2182–83.

[90] 554 U.S. 353 (2008).

[91] *Id.* at 359–60.

[92] 557 U.S. 305 (2009).

record. The Court rejected this argument, which it characterized as misunderstanding the relationship between the business-and-official-records hearsay exceptions and the Confrontation Clause. It stated:

> Business and public records are generally admissible absent confrontation not because they qualify under an exception to the hearsay rules, but because—having been created for the administration of an entity's affairs and not for the purpose of establishing or proving some fact at trial—they are not testimonial. Whether or not they qualify as business or official records, the analysts' statements here—prepared specifically for use at petitioner's trial—were testimonial against petitioner, and the analysts were subject to confrontation under the Sixth Amendment.[93]

The Court described two types of records created for different purposes than the forensic certificates in *Melendez-Diaz* that either would not be testimonial or likely would not be testimonial. Regarding the former, it stated that "medical reports created for treatment purposes . . . would not be testimonial under our decision today."[94] The Court stated that another type of document "may well qualify as nontestimonial records." These are "documents prepared in the regular course of equipment maintenance."[95] Machine calibration records are presumably in this exempt category.

The Court also rejected statutes that require the defendant to subpoena and call forensic analysts. It characterized them as converting the duty under the Confrontation Clause into the defendant's privilege under the Compulsory Process Clause and declared them invalid as a possible alternative to the prosecution producing the analysts. The Court did, however, endorse the mechanism adopted in some states to lessen the burden of confrontation through notice-and-demand statutes. These require the prosecution to provide notice to the defendant of its intent to use an analyst's report as evidence after which the defendant is given a period of time to demand confrontation or lose the right to challenge admission of the evidence. In their "simplest form," the Court indicated these statutes are constitutional.

In *Melendez-Diaz*, the Court was not presented with the situation where the analyst who appears in court and is subject to cross-examination did not perform the underlying analysis. However, that was the situation in *Bullcoming v. New Mexico*,[96] which involved an unsworn lab report. There, the Court rejected surrogate examiner testimony as adequate. It ruled categorically that, when the prosecution introduces the results of an examination "to prove a fact at a criminal trial,"[97] the Confrontation Clause is not satisfied by making available an uninvolved expert for cross-examination as a surrogate for the preparer of the report. Where the testifying expert did not sign the report or certificate and did not personally perform or observe performance of the test reported, cross-examination of the surrogate expert does not provide the confrontation required by the Constitution.

Bullcoming was a five-to-four decision, with Justice Sotomayor providing the decisive fifth vote. In her concurring opinion, she noted that this was not a case where

---

[93] *Id.* at 324.

[94] *Id.* at 312 n.2.

[95] *Id.* at 311 n.1.

[96] 564 U.S. 647 (2011).

[97] *Id.* at 657.

the testifying expert relied upon a report produced by a non-testifying expert, not for its truth, but to form the basis of the testifying expert's opinion. Indeed, the testifying expert in *Bullcoming* had no independent opinion regarding the fact at issue—the defendant's blood alcohol level—but merely acted as a conduit for the admission of the non-testifying expert's results. The next term, the Court in *Williams v. Illinois*[98] reached the unresolved issue of whether the Confrontation Clause was violated when the testifying expert relied on the forensic report of a non-testifying expert to provide the basis for the expert's opinion.

In *Williams*, four members of the Court concluded that *Crawford*'s exception for a statement not used "for the truth of the matter asserted" rendered nontestimonial the testifying expert's use of a report by a non-testifying expert where the report was neither admitted into evidence nor shown to the factfinder. Justice Alito, writing the plurality opinion, reasoned that while reliance on these documents might result in weaknesses in the proof or the irrelevance of inadequately supported propositions, those possible defects would be either matters of state law or due process, not the Confrontation Clause. He also concluded that, since the DNA report at issue was prepared without the primary purpose of accusing a targeted individual but rather to catch a dangerous unidentified rapist who was still at large, it was not testimonial.

Five Justices concluded that the use of the report to support the testifying expert's opinion did not qualify as a "legitimate" or "plausible" nonhearsay purpose and that the use of the statement to provide the basis of the opinion was effectively to use it for the truth within the meaning of the Confrontation Clause. However, one of those five, Justice Thomas, found the report nontestimonial because, although the report was signed, it contained no certification. In his view, it "lacked the requisite 'formality and solemnity' to be considered 'testimonial.' "[99] Accordingly, Justice Thomas concurred in the judgment reached by Justice Alito's plurality opinion, albeit on quite distinct grounds, that the use of the report did not violate the Confrontation Clause. Thus, *Williams* leaves the testimonial treatment of forensic reports confused and more broadly reveals a fundamentally divided Court on basic definitional issues.

Statements Not for the Truth of the Matter Asserted. Given the divisions in *Williams*, how courts should treat other statements that under evidentiary law may arguably be used for a purpose other than their truth remains uncertain. As noted earlier, the Court in *Crawford* stated that "[t]he Clause also does not bar the use of testimonial statements for purposes other than establishing the truth of the matter asserted."[100] It cited for that proposition *Tennessee v. Street.*[101] *Street*, which all the justices endorsed in *Williams* as a proper use of the concept, involved a defendant who claimed that his confession was coerced and that the sheriff who secured it read his co-defendant's confession to him and told him to "say the same thing."[102] The Court approved the response of reading the co-defendant's confession to the jury along with the sheriff's indications of the differences between the statements. Admission was also accompanied by a limiting instruction telling the jury to consider the co-defendant's confession only for impeachment purposes.

---

[98]   567 U.S. 50 (2012).

[99]   *Id.* at 103 (Thomas, J., concurring in the judgment).

[100]   Crawford v. Washington, 541 U.S. 36, 59 n.9 (2004).

[101]   471 U.S. 409 (1985).

[102]   *Id.* at 411.

In principle, the exception for statements that are not offered for the truth is sound because such statements are supposed to make no claims that the declarant's out-of-court statement was truthful, which cross-examination could test. However, varying evidentiary definitions of this concept should not determine the Confrontation Clause exception. The specific argument in *Williams* regarding an expert use of inadmissible hearsay statements presents one clear problem area but is not unique in the challenge of reconciling allowed not-for-the-truth uses of hearsay with the Confrontation Clause or evaluating whether significant truth claims are made by particular types of statements within this general nonhearsay category.

A particularly problematic area in hearsay law described in Section 249 presents a similar problem for confrontation. It involves statements by arresting or investigating officers regarding the reason for their presence at the scene of a crime. As noted in that earlier section, while the officers should not be put in the misleading position of appearing to have happened upon the scene and therefore should be entitled to provide some explanation for their presence, they should not provide detailed accounts of complaints containing inadmissible hearsay. Such statements are all too often erroneously admitted as nonhearsay to give the information upon which the officers acted.[103] When the statements exceed the limited need to explain the officer's presence and go into extensive discussion of historical fact, they can no longer legitimately be admitted under a "not-for-the-truth-of-the-matter-asserted" rationale. When the statements recited are testimonial, the violation is not only of the nonhearsay concept but should implicate the Confrontation Clause as well.

Dying Declarations. Whether dying declarations are an exception to *Crawford's* testimonial principle has still not be explicitly decided by the Supreme Court, but the likelihood appears high that it constitutes such an exception. In *Crawford*, the Court somewhat equivocally stated: "We need not decide in this case whether the Sixth Amendment incorporates an exception for testimonial dying declarations. If this exception must be accepted on historical grounds, it is *sui generis*."[104]

Giles did not decide the issue. However, the Court in *Giles* used the existence of this common law exception so strongly to defeat the argument that killing a witness was sufficient for admission under the exception for forfeiture by wrongdoing that it would be difficult to imagine the Court now deciding that the dying declaration exception was not clearly recognized as its own exception to confrontation. Justice Scalia's opinion also sets out the dimensions of the historically accepted common law hearsay exception in place at the time of the framing, presumably thereby imposing such limits on any modern-day exception to testimonial statements.

(B) Due Process

In contrast to the right of confrontation, which results in exclusion when ruled to be applicable to a statement, the Due Process Clause may require the admission of otherwise inadmissible hearsay if of sufficient reliability and importance. In *Chambers v. Mississippi*,[105] the Supreme Court ruled that due process was denied where several confessions exculpating the accused given under circumstances that provided considerable assurances of their reliability were excluded and where the accused was

---

[103] See supra § 249.
[104] *Crawford*, 541 U.S. at 56 n.6.
[105] 410 U.S. 284 (1973). See infra § 318.

prohibited from cross-examining the confessing person because of the state's "voucher rule." Although the decision appeared to present intriguing possibilities, it was limited to the facts presented and has not proven to be a significant catalyst of further developments. However, it continues to occasionally provide a basis for appellate relief from denial of admission of reliable hearsay despite generally rather strict interpretation.

§ 253 The Hearsay Exceptions Where Declarant Is Unavailable; Admission of Hearsay as a Consequence of Wrongful Procurement of Unavailability

(A) Unavailability

One of the basic challenges to the hearsay rule is how to effectuate through the procedure of excluding evidence a policy of requiring that testimony be given in open court, under oath, and subject to cross-examination. Some of the difficulty arises from the wide variation in the reliability of evidence that is classified as hearsay. The traditional solution has been to recognize numerous exceptions where "circumstantial guarantees of trustworthiness" justify departure from the general rule excluding hearsay. These exceptions are the subject of several of the chapters that follow.

The pattern that has evolved divides the hearsay exceptions into two groups. In the first, the availability or unavailability of the declarant is not a relevant factor—the exception is applied without regard to it. In the second group, unavailability is a requirement of the exception. The theory of the first group is that the out-of-court statement is as reliable or more reliable than would be testimony in person so that producing the declarant would involve pointless delay and inconvenience. The theory of the second group is that, while live testimony would be preferable, the out-of-court statement will be accepted if the declarant is unavailable. To a large extent, the division is the product of history and experience, and as might be expected of a body of law created by deciding cases as they randomly arose, it is not completely consistent. Nevertheless, the division has stood the test of time and use and offers a substantial measure of predictability. Although the full list of exceptions at first glance may appear enormous, many are encountered only rarely, and the actual working collection numbers approximately a dozen.

The importance accorded unavailability in the scheme of hearsay exceptions requires that it be considered in some detail. Although general practice is to speak loosely of unavailability of the witness, the critical factor is actually the unavailability of the witness's testimony. Witnesses may be physically present in court but their testimony nevertheless unavailable. Of course, if unavailability is procured by the party offering the hearsay statement, the requirement is not satisfied. Depositions are briefly discussed in the latter portions of this section.

Federal Rule of Evidence 804(a) provides a convenient list of the five generally recognized unavailability situations, which are examined below:

(1) *Exercise of privilege.* The successful exercise of a privilege not to testify renders the witness unavailable within the scope of the privilege.

(2) *Refusal to testify.* If a witness simply refuses to testify, despite all appropriate judicial pressures, he or she is practically and legally unavailable.

(3) *Claimed lack of memory.* A claim of lack of memory made by the witness on the stand can satisfy the unavailability requirement. If the claim is genuine, the testimony is simply unavailable by any realistic standard. However, the claimed lack of memory might well not be genuine, particularly in former testimony cases where the witness learns that the adversary has discovered new fuel for cross-examination or for other reasons seeks refuge in forgetfulness. This situation is of no great moment when the parallel to the witness who refuses to testify is recognized. The witness who falsely asserts loss of memory is refusing to testify in a way that attempts to avoid a collision with the judge. Under the language of the Federal Rule, the witness must testify regarding a lack of memory and is subject to cross-examination. If that claim is determined to be false, the witness is subject to contempt proceedings, though perhaps less effectively than in cases of simple refusal. An assertion of loss of memory clearly may constitute unavailability. If the forgetfulness is only partial, the appropriate solution would appear to be resort to present testimony to the extent of recollection, supplemented with the hearsay testimony to the extent required.

(4) *Death; physical or mental illness.* Death was the form which unavailability originally assumed with most of the relevant exceptions. Physical disability to attend the trial or testify is a recognized ground. Mental incapacity, including failure of faculties due to disease, senility, or accident, is also recognized as a basis for unavailability. Where the mental or, more frequently, physical condition is temporary, the issue appears to be handled by granting a continuance. Where the disability is of longer duration but not permanent, unavailability should be determined by considering the prospects for quick recovery, the importance of the testimony, and the interest in prompt administration of justice. Physical disability may provide the basis for finding the witness unavailable so that his or her videotaped deposition may be received as prior testimony, as remote testimony of witness (not covered by the Rules of Evidence), or through two-way closed-circuit television. Under the influence of the Confrontation Clause, a higher standard of disability may be required in criminal cases for witnesses testifying against the accused.

(5) *Absence.* Absence of the declarant from the hearing, standing alone, does not establish unavailability. Under the Federal Rule, the proponent of the hearsay statement must in addition show an inability to procure declarant's attendance (a) by process or (b) by other reasonable means. State requirements vary, especially with respect to the latter. Furthermore, the requirements of the Confrontation Clause must be satisfied.

(a) *Process.* The relevant process is subpoena, or in appropriate situations, writ of habeas corpus ad testificandum. If a witness is beyond the reach of process, obviously process cannot procure attendance. Substantial differences in the reach of process exist between civil and criminal cases. For example, service of a civil subpoena may be relatively limited, while a federal criminal subpoena may be served anywhere in the country and under some circumstances even abroad. Although in state courts process in civil cases will usually not be effective beyond state boundaries, all states have enacted the Uniform Act To Secure the Attendance of Witnesses from Without a State in Criminal Proceedings, which in effect permits extradition of witnesses from another state in criminal cases. If a witness against the accused in a criminal case is within the reach of process, the prosecution must resort to process in both state and federal cases.

If a witness cannot be found, process obviously cannot be effective. The proponent of the hearsay statement must, however, establish that the witness cannot be found. For witnesses testifying against the accused, the prosecution must demonstrate a substantial effort, described as a "good-faith effort." A lesser showing may be adequate as to other witnesses in criminal and in civil cases, where confrontation requirements do not apply.

When absence is relied upon as the basis of unavailability and hearsay is offered under the exceptions in Rules 804(b)(2), (b)(3), and (b)(4), the Federal Rule imposes a further requirement. The proponent must demonstrate an inability to take the deposition of the missing witness.

(b) *Other Reasonable Means.* In addition to inability to procure attendance by process, the Confrontation Clause requires the prosecution, before introducing a hearsay statement of the type where unavailability is required, also to show that declarant's attendance cannot be procured through good-faith efforts by other means. Here the standard is one of diligence. In *Barber v. Page,*[106] the Confrontation Clause was held to require a state prosecutor, before using at trial the preliminary hearing testimony of a witness presently incarcerated in a federal penitentiary in an adjoining state, to take appropriate steps to induce the federal authorities to produce him at the trial. When the witness is beyond the reach of process for reasons other than imprisonment, the least that would seem to satisfy confrontation requirements is a request to appear coupled with reimbursement for travel and subsistence expenses. When the Confrontation Clause does not apply, i.e. civil cases and defense witnesses in criminal cases, the authorities are divided as to whether attempts must be made to induce the witness to attend voluntarily. The Federal Rule requires an effort through reasonable means, while others demand only a showing that the witness is beyond the reach of process.

Depositions. Unavailability may appear as a requirement at two different stages in connection with depositions: (1) the right to take a deposition may be subject to certain conditions of which the most common is unavailability to testify at the trial, or (2) the right to use a deposition at the trial in place of the personal appearance of the deponent is usually conditioned upon unavailability. The matter is largely governed by statute or rule.

The use of depositions in criminal cases requires particular consideration in view of the higher standards of confrontation applicable to evidence presented against an accused. Legislation providing for depositions in criminal cases is in effect in a number of jurisdictions. No constitutional problems arise when the deposition is to be taken and used by the accused. When, however, the deposition is to be used against the accused, the unavailability standards of *Barber v. Page,* previously discussed, are applicable. If these standards are met, a meaningful opportunity to confront and cross-examine must also be provided, with its concomitant right to counsel, when the deposition is taken.

---

[106] 390 U.S. 719 (1968).

Children. Particularly in sexual abuse cases, receiving testimony from children often presents difficult questions of unavailability for purposes of the application of both a hearsay exception and the Confrontation Clause. In some jurisdictions, a finding of incompetence will make a witness unavailable. Other courts have found unavailability based upon the inability of the child to remember the events. Often, a finding of unavailability is justified based upon a determination that testifying will cause emotional trauma to the child and that the child is therefore unavailable. Courts finding the child unavailable within the meaning of the hearsay rule have usually also found any Confrontation Clause requirement of unavailability satisfied.

Many states, and the United States Congress, enacted statutes permitting either the introduction of videotaped statements or use of closed-circuit televised testimony, based on a finding that a child witness would suffer emotional or mental distress if required to testify in open court. *Maryland v. Craig*[107] held an individualized finding of potential serious emotional distress sufficient to permit a child to give testimony via closed circuit television outside the physical presence of the accused but subject to cross-examination. The development of technologies that permit high quality audiovisual links and thus would allow simultaneous examination of witnesses at long distances with considerable advantages in terms of cost savings and convenience to witnesses will challenge traditional conceptions of in person confrontation.

(B) Hearsay Exception for Wrongful Procurement of Unavailability

As noted earlier, the final sentence of Federal Rule 804(a) states that a declarant is not unavailable if "the statements' proponent procured or wrongfully caused the declarant's unavailability as a witness in order to prevent the declarant from attending or testifying." This provision requires a specific purpose to render the witness unavailable, but it does not require wrongful conduct.

Federal Rule of Evidence 804(b)(6), which was added in 1997 and subsequently adopted by a number of states, carries the above concept one significant step further. Rather than preventing admission of hearsay where required unavailability results from the proponent's actions, this rule provides for admission of otherwise inadmissible hearsay against a party who wrongfully secured the declarant's unavailability.

Rule 804(b)(6) admits statements "offered against a party that wrongfully caused— or acquiesced in wrongfully causing—the declarant's unavailability as a witness, and did so intending that result." Under the Rule, the party against whom the statement is offered must have (1) directly or through others engaged or acquiesced in conduct (2) that is wrongful (3) with the intent of producing the declarant's unavailability, (4) which was thereby procured. The requisite preliminary factual findings must be made by a preponderance of the evidence. The rule clearly contemplates that this determination, which may overlap with a jury issue, will nevertheless be decided by the trial judge without jury involvement.

A number of issues have been examined by the courts with relatively consistent responses. These include the following: When the party did not secure unavailability through his or her direct actions, how may the defendant's involvement be proven? Must the intention to secure the declarant's absence as a witness be the sole motivation? How

---

[107] 497 U.S. 836 (1990).

may the intent be proven? Does the exception cover the murder of the witness in the trial of the defendant for that murder, or does it only apply to admission of evidence against the defendant in a separate pre-existing crime where the declarant would have been a witness?

Generous interpretations of these requirements have generally resulted, such as easily finding sufficient involvement and freely using circumstantial evidence to prove intent and responsibility, which expands the scope of the exception. Given the distasteful nature of these cases, courts have generally taken a generous view. However, the requirements of the federal hearsay exception are not met simply by showing the defendant made the declarant unavailable through wrongful acts, such as by killing the witness; this is not an exception that automatically admits murder victim hearsay statements against the accused murderer.

Federal Rule 804(b)(6) is unique among hearsay exceptions in admitting evidence without a guarantee of trustworthiness, based on a theory that the opponent's purposeful wrongful action forfeits any objection. Some courts have ruled that trustworthiness must be guaranteed at some level through another mechanism, requiring that trial courts exclude clearly unreliable hearsay because it lacks sufficient probativity under the balancing process of Rule 403.

After approval of the principle that forfeiture by wrongdoing can eliminate the defendant's confrontation right, courts in some states have admitted the evidence under the same concept without the creation of a formal hearsay rule. Others have required that an established hearsay exception must be satisfied.

Chapter 25

AN OPPOSING PARTY'S STATEMENTS/ADMISSIONS

Table of Sections

---

§ 254 Nature and Effect

"Anything that you say can be used against you." This familiar phrase provides a convenient starting point for the examination of admissions as evidence.

As traditionally used with regard to hearsay, an "admission," which the Federal Rules now terms "an opposing party's statement,"[1] are the words or acts of a party or a party's representative that are offered as evidence by the opposing party. They may be express admissions, which are statements of the opposing party or an agent whose words may fairly be used against the party, or admissions by conduct. The major theories that have historically explained and supported the probativity and admissibility of admissions are discussed below.

Morgan's view was that admissions are received as an exception to the hearsay rule. Exceptions to the hearsay rule usually are justified on the ground that evidence meeting the requirements of the exception possesses special reliability and often special need, such as the unavailability of the declarant. However, no objective guaranty of trustworthiness is furnished by the admissions rule. The party is not required to have firsthand knowledge of the matter declared; the declaration may be self-serving when

---

[1]   Fed. R. Evid. 801(d)(2).

made; and the declarant is probably sitting in the courtroom. As Morgan himself admitted, "The admissibility of an admission made by the party himself rests not upon any notion that the circumstances in which it was made furnish the trier means of evaluating it fairly, but upon the adversary theory of litigation. A party can hardly object that he had no opportunity to cross-examine himself or that he is unworthy of credence save when speaking under sanction of an oath."[2]

Wigmore, after noting that the party's declaration generally has the probative value of any other person's assertion, argued that it had a special value when offered against the party. In that circumstance, the admission discredits the party's statements inconsistent with the present claim asserted in pleadings and testimony, much like a witness impeached by contradictory statements. Moreover, admissions pass the gauntlet of the hearsay rule, which requires that extra-judicial assertions be excluded if there was no opportunity for the opponent to cross-examine because it is the opponent's own declaration, and "he does not need to cross-examine himself." Wigmore added that the hearsay rule is satisfied because the party "now as opponent has the full opportunity to put himself on the stand and explain his former assertion."[3]

Strahorn suggested a further theory that classified all admissions when offered against a party, whether words or acts, as conduct offered as circumstantial evidence rather than for its assertive, testimonial value. This circumstantial value is, as noted by Wigmore, the quality of inconsistency with the party's present claim.[4]

On balance, the most satisfactory justification of the admissibility of admissions is that they are the product of the adversary system, sharing on a lower level the characteristics of admissions in pleadings or stipulations. Under this view, admissions need not satisfy the traditional requirement for hearsay exceptions that they possess circumstantial guarantees of trustworthiness. Rather admissions are outside the framework of hearsay exceptions, classed as nonhearsay, and excluded from the hearsay rule.

Federal Rule 801(d)(2) excludes from the hearsay rule, the "opposing party's statement" when it "is offered against an opposing party" and:

(A) was made by the party in an individual or representative capacity;

(B) is one the party manifested that it adopted or believed to be true;

(C) was made by a person whom the party authorized to make a statement on the subject;

(D) was made by the party's agent or employee on a matter within the scope of that relationship and while it existed; or

(E) was made by the party's co-conspirator during and in furtherance of the conspiracy.

The federal rule no longer refers to this class of statements as "admissions," but rather titles this exclusion from the hearsay rule as "an opposing party's statement."[5] No change in application is intended and because the continued widespread use of the

---

[2] Morgan, Basic Problems of Evidence 265–66 (1963).

[3] 4 Wigmore, Evidence § 1048, at 5 (Chadbourn rev. 1972).

[4] Strahorn, A Reconsideration of the Hearsay Rule and Admissions, 85 U. Pa. L. Rev. 484, 576 (1937).

[5] Fed. R. Evid. 801(d)(2).

admissions terminology in the states and its consistent use in this treatise in past editions, it will be maintained.

Regardless of the precise theory, admissions of a party are received as substantive evidence of the facts admitted and not merely to contradict the party. As a result, no foundation by first examining the party, as required for impeaching a witness with a prior inconsistent statement,[6] is mandated for admissions.

When the term admission is used without any qualifying adjective, the customary meaning is an evidentiary admission, that is, words in oral or written form or conduct of a party or a representative offered in evidence against the party. Evidentiary admissions are to be distinguished from judicial admissions. Judicial admissions are not evidence at all. Rather, they are formal concessions in the pleadings in the case or stipulations by a party or counsel that have the effect of withdrawing a fact from issue and dispensing wholly with the need for proof of the fact.[7] Thus, a judicial admission, unless allowed by the court to be withdrawn, is conclusive in the case, whereas an evidentiary admission is not conclusive but is subject to contradiction or explanation.

Confessions of crime are a particular kind of admission, governed by special rules discussed in the chapter on confessions.[8] An admission does not need to have that dramatic effect, be the all-encompassing acknowledgment of responsibility that the word confession connotes, or give rise to, a reasonable inference of guilt. Admissions are simply words or actions of the opposing party inconsistent with that party's position at trial, relevant to the substantive issues in the case, and offered against that party. Moreover, while generally received in evidence because of their typically significant probative value, admissions may be excluded if their probative value is substantially outweighed by the prejudicial impact.

A type of evidence with which admissions may be confused is evidence of declarations against interest. The latter, treated under a separate exception to the hearsay rule,[9] must have been against the declarant's interest when made. Although most admissions are against interest when made, no such requirement is applied to admissions. For example, if a person states that a note is forged and then later acquires the note and sues upon it, the previous statement may be introduced as an admission although the party had no interest when he or she made the statement. Hence the common phrase "admissions against interest" is an invitation to confuse two separate theories of admitting hearsay and erroneously engraft an against-interest requirement on admissions.

Other distinctions between admissions and declarations against interest are that admissions must be the statements of a party to the lawsuit, and they must be offered against the party opponent. By contrast, declarations against interest need not be made by a party but may be made by some third person, and they may be offered by either party.[10] Also, the declaration against interest exception admits the statement only when

---

[6]   *See* Fed. R. Evid. 613(b); supra § 37.

[7]   See infra § 257.

[8]   See supra Ch. 14.

[9]   See infra § 316.

[10]   See *id.*

the declarant has become unavailable as a witness, while unavailability is not required of admissions.[11]

§ 255 Testimonial Qualifications: Mental Competency; Personal Knowledge

In some instances, the mental capacity of a declarant making an admission must be considered. Statements by badly injured persons, possibly under sedation, are an example. While older decisions examined the capacity of the declarant and excluded the evidence if capacity was seriously in issue, the trend in decisions was to view the question as one of weight rather than admissibility and was carried further by the adoption of rules that eliminated formal competency requirements.[12] The adversary roots of admissions suggest this reasoning should be applied with caution to statements by children, but substantive rules of tort liability may provide acceptable standards of responsibility for such admissions.

The requirement that a witness speak from firsthand knowledge is applicable to hearsay declarations generally.[13] However, the traditional view that firsthand knowledge is not required for admissions is accepted by the vast majority of courts and adopted by the Federal Rules.

Eliminating the firsthand knowledge requirement is supported by several arguments. When people speak against their own interest, they have generally made an adequate investigation. While admissions are competent evidence although not against interest when made, the vast majority of admissions that become relevant in litigation concern some matter of substantial importance to declarants upon which they would likely have informed themselves. As a result, most admissions possess greater reliability than the general run of hearsay, even when not based on firsthand observation. Moreover, the possibility is substantial that the declarant may have significant information that the opponent cannot prove. The validity of dispensing with firsthand knowledge for admissions by agents has been questioned by some commentators, but courts have not drawn that distinction.

§ 256 Opposing Party's Statements in Opinion Form; Conclusions of Law

If the lack of firsthand knowledge of the party does not exclude an admission, then neither should the opinion rule. As discussed earlier,[14] the purpose of the latter rule is to regulate the in-court interrogation of a witness so as to elicit answers in a more concrete form rather than in terms of inference. In its modern form, it is a rule of preference for more concrete answers, if the witness can give them, rather than a rule of exclusion.

Thus, the rule limiting lay opinions, which is designed to promote the concreteness of answers on the stand, is grotesquely misapplied to out-of-court statements such as admissions where the declarant's statements are made without thought of the form of courtroom testimony. While counsel may reframe the question in the preferred form if

---

[11]   *See* Fed. R. Evid. 801(d)(2), 804(b)(3).

[12]   *See* Fed. R. Evid. 601; supra § 62.

[13]   *See* Fed. R. Evid. 803 advisory committee's note; infra §§ 280, 290 & 313.

[14]   See supra § 11.

an objection is sustained to testimony in court, the rule can only be applied by excluding an out-of-court statement. Accordingly, the prevailing view is that admissions in the form of opinions are competent.

Another argument sometimes made to exclude opinions within admissions is that they constitute conclusions of law. Most often this issue arises in connection with statements of a participant in an accident that the mishap was the speaker's fault. While conceivably a party might give an opinion on an abstract question of law, such are not the typical statements actually offered. Instead, the statements normally include an application of a standard to the facts. Thus, they reveal the facts as the declarant thinks them to be, to which the standard of "fault" or other legal or moral standard involved in the statement was applied. In these circumstances, the factual information conveyed should not be ignored merely because the statement may also indicate the party's assumptions about the law. However, the legal principle may conceivably be so technical as to deprive an admission of significance, or the party may indeed give an opinion regarding solely an abstract issue of law. In those situations, exclusion is warranted. Also, it should be remembered that evidentiary admissions are subject to explanation.

§ 257 Opposing Party's Statements in Pleadings; Pleas of Guilty

The final pleadings upon which the case is tried state the contentions of each party as to the facts, and by admitting or denying the opponent's pleading, they define the factual issues that are to be proved. Thus, the court must look to the pleadings as part of the record in passing on the relevancy of evidence and to determine the issues to be submitted to the jury. For these purposes, the pleadings need not be offered in evidence. They are used as judicial and not as evidentiary admissions, and they are conclusive until withdrawn or amended.

A party may also seek to use a portion of an adversary's final pleading as a basis for arguing the existence of some subordinate fact or as the foundation for an adverse inference. Some courts permit the party to do this by quoting or reading the pleading as part of the record, while others require that the party, in order to make this use of the final pleading, to introduce the relevant passage from the opponent's pleading as part of its own evidence during the course of the trial. Such a requirement may be preferable in that it allows the pleader to give explanatory evidence, such as that the allegation was made through inadvertence or mistake, and avoids the possibility of a surprise inference from the pleading in closing argument.

Subject to the qualifications developed later in this section, pleadings are generally usable against the pleader. As noted earlier, if they are the effective pleadings in the case, they have the standing of judicial admissions. Amended, withdrawn, or superseded pleadings are no longer judicial admissions but may be used as evidentiary admissions. A party's pleading in one case may generally be used as an evidentiary admission in other litigation. These same principles apply to the use in a subsequent trial of counsel's oral in-court statements representing the factual contentions of the party, even including assertions made during opening statement.

How closely is it necessary to connect the pleading with the party against whom it is to be introduced as an admission? Certainly, showing it to have been sworn to, or signed by, the party would be sufficient. More often, however, the pleading is prepared and signed by counsel, and the older view was that statements contained in such pleadings were presumed to be merely "suggestions of counsel" unless other evidence was produced that they were actually sanctioned by the client. The dominant position, however, is that pleadings shown to have been prepared or filed by counsel employed by the party are *prima facie* regarded as authorized by the client and are entitled to be received as admissions. The party opposing admission may offer evidence that the pleading was filed upon incorrect information and without his or her actual knowledge, but, except in extraordinary circumstances, such a showing goes only to the weight and not to the admissibility of the pleading.

An important exception to the use of the pleadings as admissions must be noted. A basic problem which attends the use of written pleadings is uncertainty whether the evidence as it actually unfolds at trial will prove the case described in the pleadings. Traditionally a failure in this respect, i.e., a variance between pleading and proof, could bring disaster to the pleader's case. As a safeguard against developments of this kind, the common law permitted the use of counts, each a complete separate statement of a different version of the same basic claim, combined in the same declaration to take care of variance possibilities. The same was done with defenses. Inconsistency between counts or between defenses was not prohibited; in fact, it was essential to the successful use of the system. Also essential to the system was a prohibition against using allegations in one count or defense as admissions to prove or disprove allegations in another.

Under the influence of the Field Code of 1848, the view prevailed for a time that there could exist only one set of facts in a case and that inconsistent statements and defenses were therefore not allowable. Nevertheless, uncertainty as to how a case will in fact develop at trial is now recognized as a reality, with a concomitant need for some procedure for dealing with problems of variance. The modern equivalent of the common law system is the use of alternative and hypothetical forms of statement of claims and defenses, regardless of consistency. It can readily be appreciated that pleadings of this nature are directed primarily to giving notice and lack the essential character of an admission. To allow them to operate as admissions would frustrate their underlying purpose. Hence the decisions with seeming unanimity deny them status as judicial admissions, and generally disallow them as evidentiary admissions.

Some courts have exhibited sensitivity to the potential unfairness involved in admitting pleadings where a more skillful pleader would have avoided the pitfalls of creating an admission, particularly where the pleading at issue concerned the conduct of third parties. Another approach is to recognize the potential of an inconsistent pleading to prejudice unfairly a party or to be overvalued in relation to its true probative worth, excluding the pleading in appropriate cases after balancing the relevant factors. A final possible exception, not widely recognized, is denial of status as an admission to amended, withdrawn, or superseded pleadings on the theory that to admit them into evidence contravenes the policy of liberality in amendment.

A recurring question is whether a plea of guilty to a criminal charge should be allowed in evidence in a related civil action. Generally, the evidence is admitted. While a plea of guilty to a traffic offense is in theory no different from a plea of guilty to other offenses, recognition that people plead guilty to traffic charges for reasons of convenience and with little regard to guilt or collateral consequences has led some commentators to argue against admissibility, but courts have generally rejected these arguments. In jurisdictions where allowed, pleas of *nolo contendere* or *non vult* are generally regarded as inadmissible, and in fact that attribute is a principal reason for use of such pleas.

A related question involves whether a plea of guilty can be introduced as an admission in a criminal case where the accused is allowed to withdraw the guilty plea and is subsequently tried on the charge. The result depends on the resolution of competing considerations of policy. On the one hand, a plea of guilty if freely and understandingly made is so likely to be true that to withhold it from the jurors seems to ask them to do justice without knowledge of very important evidence. On this basis, some courts have received admissions in civil cases, leaving it to the adversary to rebut or explain. The competing concern is that if the withdrawn plea is admitted the effectiveness of the withdrawal itself is substantially impaired. In addition, admitting the guilty plea virtually compels the accused to explain why it was initially entered, with resultant encroachment upon the privilege against self-incrimination and intrusion into sensitive areas of the attorney-client relationship. The drafters of the Federal Rules accepted the policy arguments against receiving evidence of a withdrawn guilty plea, and Rule 410 excludes such evidence in both civil and criminal cases.

§ 258 Testimony by the Party as an Admission

While testifying on pretrial examination or at trial, a party may admit some fact that is adverse, and sometimes fatal, to a cause of action or defense. If the party's admission stands unimpeached and uncontradicted at the end of the trial, like unimpeached and uncontradicted testimony generally, it is conclusive against the party. Frequently this situation is what the courts are referring to when they say somewhat misleadingly that a party is "bound" by his or her own testimony. The controversial question is whether the party is "bound" by such testimony in the sense that the party will not be allowed to contradict it with other testimony, or if contradictory testimony has been received, the judge or jury is nevertheless required to accept as true the party's disserving testimony as a judicial admission.

Three main approaches are reflected in the decisions, which to some extent tend to merge and do not necessarily lead to different results in particular situations. First, some courts take the view that a party's testimony in this respect is like the testimony of any other witness called by the party, and the party is free to elicit contradictory testimony from the same witness or to call other witnesses to contradict the statement. Obviously, however, the problem of persuasion may be a difficult one when the party seeks to explain or contradict his or her own words, and equally obviously, the trial judge would often be justified in ruling on a motion for directed verdict that reasonable minds could only believe the party's disserving statement.

Second, others take the view that the party's testimony is not conclusive against contradiction except when testifying unequivocally to matters in his or her "peculiar knowledge." These matters may consist of subjective facts, such as the party's own knowledge or motivation, or they may consist of objective facts observed by the party.

Third, some courts adopt the doctrine that a party's disserving testimony is to be treated as a judicial admission, conclusive on the issue, so that the party may not bring other witnesses to contradict the admission, and if the party or the adversary does elicit such conflicting testimony, it will be disregarded. This third rule often comes with a number of qualifications and exceptions. For example, the party is free to contradict, and thus correct, his or her own testimony; only when the party's own testimony taken as a whole unequivocally affirms the statement does the rule of conclusiveness apply. Also, the rule is inapplicable when the party's testimony may be attributable to inadvertence or to a misuse of language, is merely negative in effect, is explicitly uncertain or is an estimate or opinion rather than an assertion of concrete fact, or relates to a matter as to which the party could easily have been mistaken, such as the swiftly moving events just preceding a collision in which the party was injured.

Of these three approaches the first seems preferable in policy and most in accord with the tradition of jury trial. It rejects any restrictive rule and leaves the evaluation of the party's testimony and the conflicting evidence to the judgment of the jury, the judge, and the appellate court, with only the standard of reason to guide them.

The second theory, binding as to facts within the party's "peculiar knowledge," is based on the assumption that as to such facts the possibility that the party may be mistaken largely disappears. If the facts are subjective ones (e.g., knowledge, motivation), the likelihood of successful contradiction is slight, but even then, the assumption may be questionable. "Often we little note nor long remember our 'motives, purposes, or knowledge.' There are few if any subjects on which plaintiffs are infallible."[15]

The third theory is also of doubtful validity. The party's testimony, uttered by a layman in the stress of examination, cannot with justice be given the conclusiveness of the traditional judicial admission in a pleading or stipulation,[16] deliberately drafted by counsel for the express purpose of limiting and defining the facts in issue. Again, a general rule of conclusiveness necessitates an elaboration of qualifications and exceptions, which represents an unfortunate transfer to the appellate court of some of the traditional control of the jury by the trial judge, or in a nonjury case of the judge's factfinding function. Also, the moral emphasis is wrong. In the early cases where the rule of conclusiveness first appeared, judges were outraged by apparent attempts by parties to play fast and loose with the court. However, this is far from being the typical situation of the party testifying to disserving facts. Instead of the unscrupulous party, it is either the one who can be pushed into an admission by the ingenuity or persistence of adverse counsel or the unusually candid or conscientious party willing to speak the truth regardless of its consequences who is penalized by the rule of conclusiveness.

§ 259   Representative Admissions; Coconspirator Statements

When a party to the suit has expressly authorized another person to speak, it is an obvious and accepted extension of the admission rule to admit against the party the statements of such persons. In the absence of express authority, how far will the statements of an agent be received as the principal's admission by virtue of the employment relationship? The early texts and cases used as analogies the doctrine of the master's substantive responsibility for the acts of the agent and the notion then prevalent in evidence law that words accompanying a relevant act were admissible as part of the *res gestae*. Together, these concepts produced the inadequate theory that the agent's statements could be received against the principal only when made at the time of, and in relation to, some act then being performed in the scope of the agent's duty.

A later theory that gained currency was that the admissibility of the agent's statements as admissions of the principal was measured by precisely the same tests as the principal's substantive responsibility for the conduct of the agent, that is, the words

---

¹⁵   Alamo v. Del Rosario, 98 F.2d 328, 332 (D.C. Cir. 1938).

¹⁶   See supra § 257 (judicial admissions).

of the agent would be received as the admissions of the principal if they were spoken within the scope of the authority of the agent to speak for the employer. This formula made plain that the statements of an agent employed to give information (a so-called "speaking agent") could be received as the employer's admissions, and the authority to act, e.g., the authority of a chauffeur to drive a car, would not carry with it automatically the authority to make statements to others describing the duties performed.

These tests were most frequently used to exclude statements made by employees involved in an accident to someone at the scene regarding the accident when the statement was not made in furtherance of the employer's interest but rather as the employee's description of what occurred. Exclusion represents the logical application of these tests, but the assumption that the determinant of the master's responsibility for the agent's acts should be the test for using the agent's statements as evidence against the master is a shaky one.

The rejection of such post-accident statements coupled with the admission of the employee's testimony on the stand resulted in preferring the weaker to the stronger evidence. Typically, the agent is well informed about acts in the course of the business, the statements are offered against the employer's interest, and while the employment continues, the employee is not likely to make the statements unless they are true. Moreover, if admissions are viewed as arising from the adversary system, responsibility for statements of one's employee is consistent with that theory. Accordingly, even before adoption of the Federal Rules, the predominant view was to admit a statement by an agent if it concerned a matter within the scope of the declarant's employment and was made before that relationship was terminated. Of course, admissibility of the traditional authorized statement was continued.

Federal Rule 801(d)(2)(C) & (D), following the expansive view described in the preceding paragraph, admits statements offered against a party "a person whom the party authorized to make a statement on the subject," and "by the party's agent or employee on a matter within the scope of that relationship" made "while it existed."

The party offering evidence of the alleged agent's admission must first prove that the declarant is an agent of the adverse party and the scope of that agency. This may be done directly by the testimony of the asserted agent, by anyone who knows, or by circumstantial evidence. Traditionally, courts held that evidence of the purported agent's past declarations asserting the agency could not be considered in deciding whether an agency relationship existed. By contrast, the Federal Rule permits such statements to be used by the trial judge in deciding the agency issue but states explicitly that standing alone they are insufficient to establish it. If the preliminary fact of the declarant's agency is disputed, the question is one to be decided by the court under Rule 104(a).

The question also arises whether to be an admission a statement by an agent must be made to an outsider rather than to the principal or to another agent. Typical instances are the railway employee's report of an accident or a letter to the home office from a manager of a branch office of a bank. Historically, though plainly made in the scope of authority, some courts refused to admit such statements unless they were adopted by the principal. Others admitted them even if made in-house. The courts that excluded such statements relied chiefly on the fact that the doctrine of *respondeat superior* does not apply to transactions between the agent and the principal, determining the hearsay question by the rules of substantive liability of principals. However, other analogies could just as reasonably control, such as the fact that statements made by a party not intended for the outside world—entries in a secret diary, for example—are receivable as admissions.

Reliability also favored admissibility of such in-house statements. While slightly less reliable as a class than the agent's authorized statements to outsiders, intra-organization reports are generally made as a basis for some action, and when this is so, they share the reliability of business records. They will only be offered against the principal when they admit some fact damaging to the principal, and this kind of statement by an agent is likely to be trustworthy. No special danger of surprise, confusion, or prejudice from the use of the evidence is apparent.

The drafters of the Federal Rules found the arguments in favor of receiving such in-house admissions persuasive. The expansion has been held to apply both to statements by agents authorized to speak and by those authorized only to act for the principal.

While the Federal Rule greatly expands the scope of statements within a corporation that will qualify as admissions, it leaves a number of difficult issues to be resolved by analysis of the individual facts of the situation. For example, statements made by corporate employees that are admissions of the corporation are not automatically vicarious admissions of other employees of the corporation, and a specific showing of agency between the employees is required. Also, while firsthand knowledge is not required for vicarious admissions of corporate employees, uncertainty about the identity of the person who was the source of a statement may result in exclusion because of a failure to establish that the statement concerned a matter within the scope of the declarant's employment as opposed to "mere gossip."

The general principles developed above are applied in the remainder of this section to special categories of agents and to types of vicarious admissions that are frequently encountered:

Attorneys. If an attorney is employed to manage a party's conduct of a lawsuit, the attorney has *prima facie* authority to make relevant judicial admissions by pleadings, by oral or written stipulations, or by formal opening statement, which unless allowed to be withdrawn are conclusive in the case.[17] Such formal and conclusive admissions, which are usually framed with care and circumspection, are sometimes contrasted with an attorney's oral out-of-court statements, which have been characterized as "merely a loose conversation." Some courts take the view that the client is not "bound" as to such "casual" statements of counsel made outside of court. The use of the word "bound" is obviously misleading. The issue is not whether the client is "bound," as he or she is by a judicial admission, but whether the attorney's extrajudicial statement is admissible against the client as a mere evidentiary admission made by an agent.

A desire to protect the client and the attorney against the hazard of counsel's ill-advised statements produced a tendency in the older cases to restrict introduction of such statements more than those by other types of agents. More recent cases generally measure the authority of the attorney to make out-of-court admissions by the same tests of express or implied authority as would be applied to other agents, and when they meet these tests, admit them as evidentiary admissions. These admissions occur, for example, in letters or oral conversations made in the course of efforts for the collection or

---

[17]   See supra § 257 (judicial admissions).

resistance of claims, or settlement negotiations, or the management of any other business on behalf of the client.

Partners. A partner is an agent of the partnership for the conduct of the firm's business. Accordingly, when the existence and scope of the partnership have been proved, the statement of a partner made in the conduct of the business of the firm is receivable as the admission of the partnership. What of statements of a former partner made after dissolution? The cases are divided, but since a continuing power is recognized in each former partner to do such acts as are reasonably necessary to wind up and settle the affairs of the firm, one former partner should be regarded as having authority to speak for the others in making statements of fact as are reasonably incident to collecting the claims and paying the debts of the firm. Beyond this, it seems that one partner's admissions should be competent only against that partner.

Coconspirators. Conspiracies to commit a crime or an unlawful or tortious act are analogous to partnerships. If A and B are engaged in a conspiracy, the acts and declarations of B occurring while the conspiracy is actually in progress and in furtherance of the design are provable against A, because they are acts for which A is criminally or civilly responsible as a matter of substantive law. But B's declarations may also be introduced against A as representative admissions to prove the truth of the matter asserted. Only statements of the latter sort are at issue within this section on representative admissions. However, courts have seldom discriminated between declarations offered as conduct constituting part of the conspiracy and declarations offered as vicarious admissions of the facts declared. Instead, even when offered as admissions, courts have generally imposed the same test applicable to statements that form part of the conduct of the crime, namely that the declaration must have been made while the conspiracy was continuing and must have constituted a step in furtherance of the venture. Federal Rule 801(d)(2)(E) is consistent with the foregoing analysis, treating as an admission, a statement "made by the party's coconspirator during and in furtherance of the conspiracy." The statement need not be made to a member of the conspiracy but may be made to someone outside the conspiracy and even unwittingly to a government informer as long as a conspiracy exists and the person making the statement is making it during and in furtherance of the conspiracy.

Literally applied, the "in furtherance" requirement calls for exclusion of statements possessing evidentiary value solely as admissions. Under this requirement, statements that merely recount prior events in the conspiracy are not admissible, but the line of admissibility is not always clear since historical statements that advance the goals of the conspiracy are admissible. Courts have generally interpreted generously the requirement that the statement further the conspiracy. Some parallel can be seen between the liberal admissibility of coconspirator statements and admission against the principal of statements relating to the subject of the agency even though the agent was not specifically authorized to make a statement.

The requirement that the statement be made "during . . . the conspiracy" calls for exclusion of admissions and confessions made after the termination of the conspiracy, which generally is held to occur with the achievement or failure of its primary objectives. The "in furtherance" requirement often has a similar limiting effect. Questions arise, of course, as to when termination occurs. Under some circumstances, the duration of the conspiracy is held to extend beyond the commission of the principal crime to include closely connected disposition of its fruits or concealment of its traces, as in the case of police officers engaged in preparing a false report to conceal police participation in a burglary, disposal of the body after a murder, or continuation of a racketeering enterprise that involved on-going concealment to effectuate the scheme. In *Krulewitch v. United States*,[18] the Supreme Court held inadmissible a coconspirator's statement regarding concealment efforts after arrest of the participants and established the position of the federal courts. *Krulewitch* was cited with approval in the Advisory Committee's Note to Federal Rule 801(d)(2)(E), and attempts to expand the "concealment phase" to include all efforts to avoid detection have generally not been accepted. While statements made after the termination of the conspiracy are inadmissible, subsequent acts which shed light upon the nature of the conspiratorial agreement have been held admissible.

Preliminary questions of fact with regard to declarations of coconspirators are governed by Federal Rule 104(a) and must be established by a preponderance of the evidence. The Supreme Court changed longstanding practice in *Bourjaily v. United States*[19] by holding that the putative coconspirator statement itself can be considered by the trial court in determining whether a conspiracy exists and its scope. However, under the federal rules, as amended after the *Bourjaily* opinion, some additional evidence beyond the coconspiracy statement is required to establish these facts.

A conspiracy need not be formally charged for coconspirator statements to be admissible if a conspiracy in fact exists. Likewise, the declarant need not be charged, and acquittal of conspiracy charges does not preclude use of his or her statement. The evidence is similarly admissible in civil cases, where the conspiracy rule applies to tortfeasors acting in concert.

Statements of Government Agents in Criminal Cases. In a criminal prosecution, statements by the agent of an accused may generally be admitted against the accused, but statements by agents of the government are often held inadmissible against the government. "This apparent discrimination is explained by the peculiar posture of the parties in a criminal prosecution—the only party on the government side being the government itself whose many agents and actors are supposedly uninterested personally in the outcome of the trial and are historically unable to bind the sovereign."[20] A more plausible explanation is the desirability of affording the government a measure of protection against errors and indiscretions on the part of at least some of its many agents.

The cases ruling against admissibility involve statements by agents at the investigative level, with statements by government attorneys after the initiation of proceedings being held admissible. An admissibility dividing line based on the agent's position in the government may properly balance the conflicting interests involved. While Federal Rule 801(d)(2) does not specifically address the question, it is very hard to find any support in its language or structure for a blanket exclusion of statements by government agents. However, a balancing approach of the type suggested above appears consistent with its basic approach and the various policy concerns involved.

---

[18]   336 U.S. 440 (1949).

[19]   483 U.S. 151 (1987).

[20]   U.S. v. Santos, 372 F.2d 177, 180 (2d Cir. 1967).

§ 260 Declarations by "Privies in Estate," Joint Tenants, Predecessors in Interest, Joint Obligors, and Principals Against Surety

Historically, courts accepted the notion that "privity," or identity of interest between the declarant and a party justified introduction of the statement of the declarant as an admission of the party. Thus, the declaration of one joint tenant or joint owner against another could be received, but the distinction derived from the law of property was applied so strictly in this context that statements of a tenant in common, a co-legatee or co-devisee, or a co-trustee were excluded.

The more frequent and important application of this property analogy was the use of declarations of a predecessor in title to land, personalty, or choses in action against a successor. The successor was viewed as acquiring an interest burdened with the same liability of having declarations used against him or her as could have been used against the predecessor. The declarations had to relate to the declarant's transactions, intent, or interest in the property, and they must have been made while the declarant was the owner of the interest now claimed by the successor. Under this theory, courts received the declarations of grantors, transferors, donors, and mortgagors of land and personalty against the transferees and mortgagees; of decedents against their representatives, heirs, and next of kin; of a prior possessor against one who claims prescriptive title relying on such prior possession; and of former holders of notes and other choses in action against their assignees. Of course, concepts such as bona fide purchaser and holder in due course may make the evidence irrelevant and therefore inadmissible.

Similarly, when two parties are jointly liable as obligors, the declarations of one were sometimes receivable as an admission against the other. However, the element of authorization to speak in furtherance of the common enterprise, as in the case of agency, partnership, or conspiracy, can hardly be spelled out from the mere relationship of joint obligors, and admissibility of declarations on this basis has been criticized. In fact, most of the cases found in support involve the special situation of declarations of a principal offered as admissions against a surety, guarantor, indemnitor, or other person secondarily liable. These declarations were usually held admissible.

Morgan criticized importing into the law of evidence the property doctrines of identity of interest and privity of estate: "The dogma of vicarious admissions, as soon as it passes beyond recognized principles of representation, baffles the understanding. Joint ownership, joint obligation, privity of title, each and all furnish no criterion of credibility, no aid in the evaluation of testimony."[21]

Following Morgan's view, the Model Code omitted any provision for admitting these declarations, and the Federal Rules followed the same pattern. Most meritorious statements will qualify as declarations against interest, vicarious admissions of agents, or some other hearsay exception more soundly grounded than on the privity concept.

§ 261 Admissions by Conduct: (a) Adoptive Admissions

One may expressly adopt another's statement. That is an explicit admission like any other and calls for no further discussion. In this treatise, the term adoptive admission is used somewhat restrictively to apply to evidence of other conduct of a party

---

[21]   Morgan, Admissions, 12 Wash. L. Rev. 181, 202 (1937).

manifesting circumstantially the party's assent to the truth of a statement made by another.[22]

Adoptive admissions under the Federal Rules are governed by Rule 801(d)(2)(B). In conformity with traditional practice, it provides that a statement is not hearsay if offered against a party and "is one the party manifested that it adopted or believed to be true."

The fact that the party declares that he or she has heard that another person has made a given statement is not alone sufficient to justify finding that the party has adopted the third person's statement. The circumstances surrounding the party's declaration must be examined to determine whether they indicated an approval of the statement.

Actions manifesting adoption or belief can occur in a number of situations involving written documents or electronically transmitted material. One such situation is the republication of material authored by another. Another is the use of documents created by others. Whether the republication or use of the material constitutes and adoption, qualifying as an admission under this provision will depend on a careful examination of the facts.

The question of adoption arises in life and accident insurance cases when the defendant insurance company offers a statement, such as the certificate of the attending physician, which the plaintiff beneficiary attached to the proof of death or disability. The fact that the beneficiary tendered it as an exhibit accompanying a formal statement of "proof" presented for the purpose of having the company pay the claim would appear to be enough to secure its admission. The picture is more complicated, and admission should not follow where the beneficiary expressly disavows the accompanying statement or the document is contrary to those presented in exhibits. The argument for exclusion is particularly strong if accompanying statements, such as the certificate of the attending physician, are required under the terms of the policy.

Does the introduction of evidence by a party constitute an adoption of the statements of witnesses so that they may be used against the party as an admission in a subsequent lawsuit? The answer ought to depend upon whether the particular circumstances warrant the conclusion that in fact an adoption occurred and not upon the discredited notion that a party vouches for its own witnesses. When a party offers in evidence a deposition or an affidavit to prove the matters stated therein, the party knows or should know the contents of the writing so offered and presumably desires that all of the contents be considered on its behalf since only the portion desired could be offered. Accordingly, it is reasonable to conclude that the writing so introduced may be used against the party as an adoptive admission in another suit.

With respect to oral testimony, however, the inference of sponsorship of the statements is not always so clear. Nevertheless, here too circumstances may justify the conclusion that, when the proponent placed the witness on the stand to prove a particular fact and the witness so testified, the party has created an adoptive admission of the fact that may be admitted in a later suit. But how is the party offering the testimony in the later suit to show that a given statement of the witness at the former trial was intended to be elicited by the party who called the witness or was contrary to or outside that intention? The form and context of the question would usually, but not

---

[22]   See § 262 infra (adoptive admissions by silence treated separately).

always, give the clue. In view of the prevailing practice of interviewing one's witnesses before putting them on the stand, it would seem that a practical working rule would admit against the proponent the direct testimony of its own witness as presumptively elicited to prove the facts stated, in the absence of counter proof that the testimony came as a surprise to the interrogator or was repudiated in the course of argument. By contrast, testimony elicited on cross-examination may be drawn out to reveal the witness' errors and dishonesty and should not be assumed to have been relied on by the examiner as evidence of the facts stated. To constitute an adoptive admission, reliance must be affirmatively established.

In the main, preliminary factual issues arising with regard to whether a statement was adopted are to be decided as questions of conditional relevancy under Rule 104(b).[23]

Similar to adoptive admissions are the instances where the party has referred an inquirer to another person whose anticipated statements the party accepts in advance. However, these admissions by reference to a third person are probably more properly classifiable as representative or vicarious admissions, rather than adoptive.[24]

§ 262 Admissions by Conduct: (b) Silence

When a statement is made in the presence of a party containing assertions of facts which, if untrue, the party would under all the circumstances naturally be expected to deny, failure to speak has traditionally been received as an admission. Whether the justification for receiving the evidence is the assumption that the party has intended to express its assent and thus has adopted the statement or that the probable state of belief can be inferred from the conduct is probably unimportant. Since it is the failure to deny that is significant, an equivocal or evasive response may similarly be used against the party on either theory, but if the total response adds up to a clear-cut denial, this theory of implied admission is inapplicable.

Despite the offhand appeal of this kind of evidence, courts have often suggested that it be received with caution, an admonition that is especially appropriate in criminal cases. Several characteristics of the evidence should be noted. First, its nature and the circumstances under which it arises often amount to an open invitation to manufacture evidence. Second, ambiguity of inference is often present. Silence may be motivated by many factors other than a sense of guilt or lack of an exculpatory story. For example, silence may be valued. As indicated at the beginning of this chapter, everyone knows that anything you say can be used against you. Third, the constitutional limitations of *Miranda v. Arizona*[25] apply to the use of this type of evidence in criminal cases, but only if the suspect is interrogated by the police while in custody.[26] Fourth, while in theory the statement is not offered as proof of its contents but rather to show what the party accepted, the distinction is indeed a subtle one; the statement is ordinarily highly damaging and of a nature likely to draw attention away from the basic inquiry whether acquiescence did in fact occur.

Even with the array of circumstances raising doubts regarding the reliability of this kind of evidence, the Supreme Court has not found any absolute federal constitutional

---

[23] See infra § 262 (related issues).

[24] See generally supra § 259.

[25] 384 U.S. 436 (1966).

[26] See supra § 161.

barriers against its use other than those imposed in some circumstances by *Miranda*.[27] Nevertheless, courts have evolved a variety of safeguards against misuse: (1) The statement must have been heard by the party claimed to have acquiesced. (2) It must have been understood by the party. (3) The subject matter must have been within the party's knowledge. At first glance, this requirement may appear inconsistent with elimination of the firsthand knowledge requirement for admissions. However, a person cannot reasonably be expected to deny a matter on which he or she has no knowledge, lacking the incentive or the ability to dispute the accusations. (4) Physical or emotional impediments to responding must not be present. (5) The personal makeup of the speaker, e.g., young child, or the person's relationship to the party or the event, e.g., bystander, may be such as to make it unreasonable to expect a denial. (6) Probably most important of all, the statement itself must be such as would, if untrue, call for a denial under the circumstances. Beyond the constitutional issues that can be raised, the fact that the police are present when an accusatory statement is made may constitute a critical circumstance that eliminates the naturalness of a response.

The above list is not an exclusive one, and other factors will suggest themselves. The essential inquiry in each case is whether a reasonable person under the circumstances would have denied the statement, with answers not lending themselves readily to mechanical formulations.

Most preliminary questions of admissibility in connection with admissions by acquiescence fall within the category of conditional relevancy. While some preliminary issues involved with admissions by silence are entrusted to final determination by the court, questions such as whether the statement was made in the person's hearing and whether there was an opportunity to reply should be submitted for jury determination if the court concludes sufficient evidence has been introduced so that a reasonable jury could find that those facts have been established.

Failure to Reply to Letter, Email, or Other Written Communication. If a written statement is given to a party and read in the presence of others, the party's failure to deny its assertions may be received as an admission, when under the circumstances it would be natural for the person to deny them if he or she did not acquiesce. The principle in operation here is similar to the failure to deny an oral statement. Moreover, if a party receives an email or letter containing several statements, which he or she would naturally deny if untrue, and states a position as to some of the statements but fails to comment on the others, this failure will usually be received as evidence of an admission to those omitted.

More debatable is the question whether the failure to reply at all to a letter or other written communication should be received as an admission by silence. Certainly, such a failure to reply will often be less convincing than silence in the face of an oral charge. Indeed, a "general rule" is sometimes announced that failure to answer a letter generally does not constitute an admission. The negative form of the rule unfortunately tends toward over-strict rulings excluding evidence of material value. The preferable view is that the failure to reply to a letter containing statements which it would be natural under all the circumstances for the addressee to deny if he or she believed them untrue is receivable as evidence of an admission by silence. Two factors particularly tend to show that a denial would be naturally forthcoming: first, where the letter was written as part

---

[27] See *id.*

of a mutual correspondence between the parties, and second, where the proof shows that the parties were engaged in some business, transaction, or relationship which would make it improbable that an untrue communication about the transaction or relationship would be ignored.

The most common instance of this latter situation is the transmission by one party to a business relationship to the other of a statement of account or a bill. Failure to question such a bill or statement is uniformly received as evidence of an admission of its correctness. On the other hand, if the negotiations have been broken off by one party's taking a final stand, thus indicating a view that further communication would be fruitless, or if the letter was written after litigation was instituted, these circumstances tend to show that failure to answer should not be received as an admission.

§ 263 Admissions by Conduct: (c) Flight and Similar Acts

"The wicked flee when no one pursues."[28] Many acts of a defendant after the crime seeking escape are received as admissions by conduct, constituting circumstantial evidence of consciousness of guilt and hence of the fact of guilt itself. In this class are flight from the scene, from one's usual haunts, or from the jurisdiction after the crime; assuming a false name; changing appearance; resisting arrest; attempting to bribe arresting officers; forfeiture of bond by failure to appear or departure from the trial while it is proceeding; escapes or attempted escapes from confinement; and suicide attempts by the accused.

If the flight is from the scene of the crime, evidence of it seems to be wholly acceptable as a means of locating the accused at the critical time and place. However, in many situations, the inference of consciousness of guilt of the particular crime is so uncertain and ambiguous and the evidence so prejudicial that one is forced to wonder whether the evidence is not directed to punishing the "wicked" generally rather than resolving the issue of guilt of the offense charged. Particularly troublesome are the cases where defendant flees when sought to be arrested for another crime, is wanted for another crime, or is not shown to know that he or she is suspected of the particular crime. Some courts appear to accept a general sense of guilt as sufficient.

Many cases currently adopt the rubric that the probative value of flight:

> as circumstantial evidence of guilt depends upon the degree of confidence with which four inferences can be drawn: (1) from the defendant's behavior to flight; (2) from flight to consciousness of guilt; (3) from consciousness of guilt to consciousness of guilt concerning the crime charged; and (4) from consciousness of guilt concerning the crime charged to actual guilt of the crime charged.[29]

Important factors in the analysis are the timing of flight relative to the offense or to other significant events in the case, and the strength of the inference that the defendant was aware of, and motivated by, fear of apprehension for a particular offense. The potential for prejudice of flight evidence should also be weighed against its probative value. Critical scrutiny of the balance between the often weak probative value of this type of evidence and its prejudicial impact is appropriate in each case.

---

28   Proverbs 28:1 (New Rev. Standard).
29   U.S. v. Myers, 550 F.2d 1036, 1049 (5th Cir. 1977).

While the great bulk of the decisions involve criminal prosecutions, flight also finds recognition in civil actions.

§ 264 Admissions by Conduct: (d) Failure to Call Witnesses or Produce Evidence; Refusal to Submit to a Physical Examination

When it would be natural under the circumstances for a party to call a particular witness, or to take the stand as a witness in a civil case, or to produce documents or other objects in his or her possession as evidence and the party fails to do so, tradition has allowed the adversary to use this failure as the basis for invoking an adverse inference. An analogous inference may be drawn if a party unreasonably declines to submit, upon request, to a physical examination or refuses to furnish handwriting exemplars.

Most of the controversy arises with respect to failure to call a witness. The classic statement is: "[I]f a party has it peculiarly within his power to produce witnesses whose testimony would elucidate the transaction, the fact that he does not do it creates the presumption that the testimony, if produced, would be unfavorable."[30]

The cases fall into two groups. In the first, an adverse inference may be drawn against a party for failure to produce a witness reasonably assumed to be favorably disposed to the party. In the second, the inference may be drawn against a party who has exclusive control over a material witness but fails to produce him or her, without regard to any possible favorable disposition of the witness toward the party. Cases in the second group are increasingly less frequent due to the growth of discovery and other disclosure requirements. In either group, if the testimony of the witness would be merely cumulative, the inference is unavailable.

Despite an abundance of cases recognizing the inference, refusal to allow comment or to instruct rarely results in a reversal, while erroneously instructing the jury on the inference or even an erroneous argument by counsel much more frequently requires retrial. The appellate courts often counsel caution. A number of factors support a conservative approach. Conjecture or ambiguity of inference is often present. The possibility that the inference may be drawn invites waste of time in calling unnecessary witnesses or in presenting evidence to explain why they were not called. Failure to anticipate that the inference may be invoked entails substantial possibilities of surprise. The availability of modern discovery and other disclosure procedures serves to diminish both its justification and the need for the inference. Finally, some courts have expressed particular concern in using the instruction in criminal cases against the defendant often citing concerns regarding its implicitly impact on the burden of proof and presumption of innocence. In recognition of these factors, courts often require early notice from a party expecting to make a missing witness argument or intending to request such an instruction.

If a witness is "equally available" to both parties, courts often state that no inference springs from the failure of either to call the witness. This statement can hardly be accurate, as the inference may be allowed when the witness could easily be called or subpoenaed by either party. What is meant instead is that when the witness would be as likely to be favorable to one party as the other, no inference is proper. However, equality of favor is nearly always debatable, and although the judge thinks the witness

---

[30] Graves v. U.S., 150 U.S. 118, 121 (1893).

would be equally likely to favor either party, perhaps both should be permitted to argue the inference.

A party may be at liberty to call a witness but may have a privilege against the witness being called by the adversary, as when in a criminal case the accused may call his or her spouse, but the state may not. Similarly, it may be clear that all the information that a witness has is subject to a privilege which the party may exert, such as the doctor-patient privilege. In these situations, probably the majority of courts would forbid an adverse inference from a failure to call.[31] Of course, an inference from the failure of the criminal defendant to take the stand is constitutionally forbidden.[32] The policy considerations with respect to comment upon the exercise of evidentiary privileges are discussed elsewhere.[33]

The specific procedural effect of the inference from failure to call a witness is seldom discussed. Some courts have said that the party's failure to call the witness or produce the evidence creates a "presumption" that the testimony would have been unfavorable. It is usually phrased in terms, however, of "may" rather than "must" and seemingly could at most be only a "permissive," not a mandatory, presumption.[34] Moreover, unlike the usual presumption, it is not directed to any specific presumed fact or facts which are required or permitted to be found. The burden of producing evidence of a fact cannot be met by relying on this "presumption." Rather, its effect is to impair the value of the opponent's evidence and to give greater credence to the positive evidence of the adversary upon any issue upon which it is shown that the missing witness might have knowledge.

Instead, most courts speak of the party's failure to call the witness as creating an "inference." Some of these courts consider that the party has a right to have such inference explained in the instructions on proper request, while others consider that the instruction is proper but not required. Still others condemn an instruction as a comment on the evidence. Of course, all courts permit counsel to argue the inference where it is an allowable one.

In jurisdictions where the judge retains the common law power to comment on the evidence, a fair comment on failure to produce witnesses or evidence is traditionally allowable. Permitting judicial discretion to instruct on the inference is appropriate. However, a practice that gives a party a right to such instruction is undesirable because it tends to lead to the development of elaborate rules defining the circumstances when the right exists. Making instruction a matter of right does have the advantage of focusing past experience on the problem presented at the trial, but the cost of complex rules far outweighs the gain.

A web of rules also can develop by tightly controlling counsel's argument on the inference. It is wiser to hold that if an argument on failure to produce proof is fallacious, the remedy is the answering argument and the jury's good sense. Thus, the judge should be required to intervene only when the argument, under the general standard, can be said to be not merely weak or unfounded, but unfair and prejudicial.

---

[31]   See supra § 74.1.

[32]   See supra § 132.

[33]   See supra § 74.1.

[34]   See infra Ch. 36 (discussing these terms).

§ 265   Admissions by Conduct: (e) Misconduct Constituting Obstruction of Justice

We have seen in the preceding section that a party's failure to produce evidence that he or she is free to produce or withhold may be treated as an admission. As might be expected, wrongdoing by the party in connection with its case amounting to an obstruction of justice is also commonly regarded as an admission by conduct. By resorting to wrongful devices, the party is said to provide a basis for believing that he or she thinks the case is weak and not to be won by fair means, or in criminal cases that the accused is conscious of guilt. Accordingly, the following are considered under this general category of admissions by conduct: a party's false statement about the matter in litigation, whether before suit or on the stand; subornation of perjury; fabrication of documents; undue pressure by bribery, intimidation, or other means to influence a witness to testify favorably or to avoid testifying; destruction or concealment of relevant documents or objects; attempt to corrupt the jury; and hiding or transferring property in anticipation of judgment.

Of course, it is not enough to show that someone did the acts charged as obstructive. The actor must be connected to the party, or, in the case of a corporation, to one of its superior officers. If the circumstances demonstrate bad faith, courts uniformly recognize the propriety of a sanction. Although many innocent and ordinary explanations will result in no sanction, a number of jurisdictions authorize a remedy in appropriate circumstances where destruction is done with awareness of the need to preserve the evidence and even ordinary negligence. Although sanctions are imposed by courts on the basis of negligence and knowledge of the consequences of evidence destruction, a showing of bad faith or willful destruction will usually be required for more extreme remedies.

A question may well be raised whether the relatively modest probative value of such evidence is not often outweighed by its prejudicial effect. The litigant who would not like to have a stronger case must indeed be a rarity. The real underpinning of the rule of admissibility may be a desire to impose swift punishment, with a certain poetic justice, rather than concern over niceties of proof. In any event, the evidence is generally admitted, despite incidental disclosure of another crime.

What is the probative reach of these various kinds of "spoliation" admissions beyond their great tactical value in darkening the atmosphere of the party's case? They should entitle the proponent at least to an instruction that the adversary's conduct may be considered generally as tending to corroborate the proponent's case and to discredit that of the adversary. This result is worthwhile in itself, and it carries with it the corresponding right of the proponent's counsel to argue these inferences.

However, a crucial and perplexing question remains whether the adverse inference from the party's obstructive conduct substitutes for evidence of a fact essential to the adversary's case. Certainly, the primitive impulse to answer "yes" is strong, and an analogy has been suggested to the practice under statutes and rules permitting the court to enter a default against a party who refuses to provide discovery. When the conduct points toward an inference about a particular specific fact, as in the case of bribing an attesting witness to be absent or destroying a particular document, there is likely to be a greater willingness to allow an inference of that fact although the only available information regarding it is the proponent's claim in the pleadings. Where the conduct is not directed toward suppression of any particular fact, as in attempts to "buy off" the prosecution, to tamper with the jury, or to defeat recovery by conveyance of property, an inference as to the existence of a particular fact not proved is more strained. Without adverting to this distinction, many decisions have supported the general doctrine that the inference from obstructive conduct will not satisfy the need for proof of a particular fact essential to the proponent's case.

Some recent cases have indicated a willingness to rethink these traditionally established principles. Several cases have found intentional actions that result in the destruction of evidence either to shift the burden of proof or to provide affirmative evidence on a critical issue. A few cases have proposed a separate tort for spoliation of evidence. This area of the law appears to be in flux and the patterns of the new order are not yet clear.

§ 266 Admissions by Conduct: (f) Offers to Compromise Disputed Claim in Civil Suits and Plea Negotiations in Criminal Cases

In General. Arguably an offer to accept a sum in compromise of a disputed claim might be used against the party as an admission of the weakness of the claim. Conversely, an offer by the adversary to pay a sum in compromise might be used against that party as an admission of the weakness of his or her position. In either situation, general agreement exists that the offer of compromise is not admissible on the issue of liability, although the reason for exclusion is not always clear.

Two grounds for the rule of inadmissibility are advanced: lack of relevancy and policy considerations. First, the relevancy of the offer will vary according to circumstances, with a very small offer of payment to settle a very large claim being much more readily construed as a desire for peace rather than an admission of weakness of position. Relevancy would increase, however, as the amount of the offer approaches the amount claimed. Second, the policy argument is the promotion of settlement of disputes, which would be discouraged if offers of compromise were admitted. Resting the rule on this latter basis has the advantage of avoiding difficult questions of relevancy. On this ground, the principle should protect one who made the offer and is a party to the suit in which the evidence is offered.

To invoke the exclusionary rule, an actual dispute must exist, preferably some negotiations, and at least an apparent difference of view between the parties as to the validity or amount of the claim. An offer to pay an admitted claim is not privileged since there is no policy of encouraging compromises of undisputed claims, which should be paid in full. If the validity of the claim and the amount due are undisputed, an offer to pay a lesser sum in settlement or to pay in installments would accordingly be admissible.

What is excluded? The offer is excluded, as well as any suggestions or overtures of settlement. How far do any accompanying statements of fact made by either party during oral negotiations or correspondence looking to settlement share the privilege? The historically accepted doctrine held that an admission of fact in the course of negotiations was not privileged unless it was stated hypothetically ("we admit for the sake of the discussion only"), expressly made "without prejudice," or inseparably connected with the offer so that it could not be correctly understood without considering the two together.

The traditional doctrine of denying the protection of the exclusionary rule to statements of fact had serious drawbacks. It discouraged freedom of communication in attempting compromise and involved difficulties of application. As a result, the trend has been to extend the protection to all statements made in compromise negotiations, and this approach is generally followed by Federal Rule 408, reproduced in the footnote.[35]

The rule is designed to exclude the offer of compromise only when it is tendered as an admission of the weakness of the offering party's claim or defense, not when offered for another purpose. Thus, for example, the rule does not call for exclusion when the compromise negotiations are offered to explain delay in taking action or failure to seek employment to mitigate damages, to show the extent of legal services rendered in conducting them, to establish bias, or to show the terms of compromise in another dispute that are part of the current case. Similarly, using the evidence of an effort to settle a civil case is not barred to prove an effort to obstruct a criminal prosecution. As in other situations where evidence is admissible for one purpose but not for another, the probative value for the proper purpose must be weighed against likelihood of improper use, with due regard to the probable efficacy of a limiting instruction.[36]

The use of inconsistent statements made in compromise negotiations for general impeachment of the testimony of a party is fraught with danger of misuse of the statements to prove liability, threatens frank interchange of information during negotiations, and generally should not be permitted. The Federal Rule explicitly prohibits use of statements made during settlement negotiations to impeach by inconsistent statement and contradiction.

A completed compromise agreement, discussed below, may also be admissible for another purpose. For example, a defendant in a personal injury case may call a witness who was injured in the same collision. If the witness has made a claim against the defendant inconsistent with the witness' present favorable testimony, the claim may be proved to impeach the witness. Furthermore, if the witness has been paid or promised money in compromise of his or her claim, this may be shown as evidence of bias or used more generally to impeach.

Evidence of Present Party's Compromise with Third Persons. In an action between plaintiff (P) and defendant (D), a compromise offer or a completed compromise by D with a third person having a claim similar to P's arising from the same transaction may be relevant as showing D's belief in the weakness of the defense in the present action. Nevertheless, the same consideration of policy which prompts exclusion of a compromise offer made by D to P, namely the danger of discouraging such compromises, applies here.

---

[35] Rule 408, Compromise Offers and Negotiations, states:

(a) Prohibited Uses. Evidence of the following is not admissible—on behalf of any party— either to prove or disprove the validity or amount of a disputed claim or to impeach by a prior inconsistent statement or a contradiction:

(1) furnishing, promising, or offering—or accepting, promising to accept, or offering to accept—a valuable consideration in compromising or attempting to compromise the claim; and

(2) conduct or a statement made during compromise negotiations about the claim— except when offered in a criminal case and when the negotiations related to a claim by a public office in the exercise of its regulatory, investigative, or enforcement authority.

(b) Exceptions. The court may admit this evidence for another purpose, such as proving a witness's bias or prejudice, negating a contention of undue delay, or proving an effort to obstruct a criminal investigation or prosecution.

[36] See supra § 59.

Accordingly, the prevailing view is that the compromise offer or payment made by the present defendant is privileged when offered as an implied admission of liability.

Effect of Acceptance of Offer of Compromise. If an offer of compromise is accepted and a contract is thus created, the party aggrieved may sue on the contract and obviously may prove the offer and acceptance. Moreover, if after such a contract is made and the offering party repudiates it, the other may elect to sue on the original cause of action and here again the repudiating party may not claim privilege against proof of the compromise. The shield of the privilege does not extend to the protection of those who repudiate the agreements, which the privilege is designed to encourage.

Compromise Evidence in Criminal Cases. As noted earlier, the policy of protecting offers of compromise in civil cases under Rule 408 does not extend to efforts to stifle criminal prosecution by "buying off" the prosecuting witness or victim. However, the Federal Rule excludes statements made during legitimate civil settlement negotiations from criminal prosecutions when offered to prove liability for, invalidity of, or the amount of the claims, except when the defendant negotiated in the civil case with a public office or agency exercising regulatory, investigative, or enforcement authority. Moreover, the legitimacy of settling criminal cases by negotiations between prosecuting attorney and accused, whereby the latter pleads guilty in return for some leniency, has been generally recognized. Effective criminal law administration would be difficult if a large proportion of the charges were not disposed of by guilty pleas. Public policy accordingly encourages compromise, and as in civil cases, that policy is furthered by protecting from disclosure at trial not only the offer but also statements made during negotiations.

Federal Rule 410 excludes from civil and criminal cases as evidence against a defendant who made a plea or participated in the plea discussions (1) guilty pleas which were later withdrawn, (2) *nolo contendere* pleas, (3) statements made in the course of entering the plea under Rule 11 of the Federal Rules of Criminal Procedure or comparable state procedures for a later withdrawn and *nolo contendere* pleas, and (4) statements made in the course of plea discussions with a prosecuting attorney which did not result in a plea of guilty or which resulted in a plea that was later withdrawn. The rule allows such statements to be admitted for completeness in some instances and in prosecutions for perjury regarding such statements.

The original version of the rule did not explicitly state that its protection extended only to negotiations between the accused and the prosecutor. As a result, some decisions held that efforts to make deals with a considerable variety of federal law enforcement officers were within the rule. The rule accordingly was amended to make clear that only negotiations "with an attorney for the prosecuting authority"[37] fall within its protection. Despite this amendment, issues still arise in non-standard discussions with prosecuting attorneys and in some discussions with law enforcement agents that the defendant contends were plea discussions properly covered by Rule 410. To resolve these issues, a number of courts have used the two-tiered approach developed by the Fifth Circuit's decision in *United States v. Robertson:*[38] "first, whether the accused exhibited an actual subjective expectation to negotiate a plea at the time of the discussion, and, second, whether the accused's expectation was reasonable given the totality of the objective circumstances."

---

[37]   Fed. R. Evid. 410(a)(4).
[38]   U.S. v. Robertson, 582 F.2d 1356, 1366 (5th Cir. 1978).

While the rule permits use of statements made as part of plea negotiations for other purposes, impeachment of the defendant's subsequent testimony is not one of those permissible purposes. However, in *United States v. Mezzanatto*,[39] the Supreme Court held that impeachment was permissible if the plea agreement was drafted to waive the defendant's objection. Indeed, courts have broadly interpreted *Mezzanatto* agreements, which can apply not only to withdrawn agreements but also to initial discussions with the prosecution. If the transaction on which the prosecution is based also gives rise to a civil cause of action, a compromise or offer of compromise in the civil case is protected by Rule 408, which is also effective in the criminal case unless it falls within that Rule's long-standing exception for efforts to obstruct justice in the criminal case or its narrow carve-out for statements made in parallel civil claims by public civil regulatory, investigative, or enforcement authorities.

§ 267   Admissions by Conduct: (g) Safety Measures After an Accident; Payment of Medical Expenses

Subsequent Remedial Measures. After an accident causing injury, the owner of the premises or the enterprise will often take remedial measures, such as repairing a defect or changing safety rules. Are these new safety measures, which might have prevented the injury, admissible to prove negligence as an implied acknowledgment by conduct that due care required that these measures should have been taken before the injury? Particularly when the remedial measures follow the injury immediately, they may be very persuasive of the owner's belief as to the precautions required by due care before the accident. Nevertheless, courts at one time occasionally asserted that the evidence was irrelevant for this purpose. While such remedial changes permit varying explanations, some of which are consistent with due care, the evidence would often meet the usual standards of relevancy if treated only as raising issues of the admissibility of circumstantial evidence and admission by conduct.[40]

The predominant reason for excluding such evidence, however, is not lack of probative significance, but rather a policy not to discourage safety measures. Courts exclude evidence of various types of remedial measures taken after an injury when offered as admissions of negligence or fault, and in some jurisdictions, defects in a product or its design or a need for warning or instruction. These include: repairs and alterations in construction; installation of new safety devices, such as signs, lights, gates, or guards; changes in policies, rules, and regulations or the practice of the business; and the dismissal of an employee charged with causing the injury, but generally not post-accident investigative reports. However, when the remedial measures are taken by a third person, the policy ground for exclusion is absent, and the evidence, if otherwise admissible, is not excluded.

The ingenuity of counsel in suggesting other purposes has made substantial inroads upon the general rule of exclusion. Thus evidence of subsequent repairs or changes has been admitted as evidence of the defendant's ownership or control of the premises or duty to repair; as evidence of the possibility or feasibility of preventive measures; as evidence to explain that the situation at the time of accident was different from when the jury has observed the scene at a later time; as evidence of what was done later to show that the earlier condition as of the time of the accident was as plaintiff claim; and

---

[39]   513 U.S. 196 (1995).

[40]   See supra § 185.

to impeach. The older cases allowed such evidence to prove that the faulty condition later remedied was the cause of the injury by showing that after the change the injurious effect disappeared, but recent cases are more skeptical that this is an appropriate use of such evidence. The modern embodiment of these common law concepts, Federal Rule of Evidence 407, is set out in the footnote.[41]

As noted earlier, not discouraging remedial measures is the principal reason for the rule excluding evidence that such measures were taken. Liberal admission of remedial measure evidence for purposes other than as an admission of negligence seriously undercuts the basic policy of the rule. Hence Rule 407 specifically requires that, when the evidence is offered for another purpose, that purpose must be controverted. Ownership, control, and feasibility of precautionary measures are mentioned as illustrations of other purposes. If the other purpose is not controverted, the evidence is inadmissible. The fact that the other purpose is controverted should not be taken as a guarantee of admissibility; the possibility of misuse of the evidence as an admission of fault still requires a balancing of probative value and need against potential prejudice under Rule 403. The availability of other means of proof is an important factor in this balancing process.[42]

The provision of the rule that permits evidence of remedial measures to be admitted for impeachment is of particular concern in that, if applied expansively, it could "swallow up" the rule. At the same time, impeachment should be permitted in some situations, such as when the witness' testimony constitutes, not simply a general denial of negligence, but a claim that is directly contradicted by the remedial conduct.

Whether subsequent remedial measures should be excluded in product liability cases has been debated in the courts. *Ault v. International Harvester Company*[43] led the movement against application in such cases. The departure is based primarily on a rejection of the assumption that admitting the evidence discourages remedial steps when the enterprise involved is a large manufacturer and a general desire to spread the cost of injuries. A number of state courts, although apparently a dwindling number, have followed *Ault*. The federal courts, by contrast, generally disagreed, and a 1997 amendment to Federal Rule 407 made explicit that the rule applies to product liability cases tried in the federal courts.

The admissibility of recall letters has been approached in a somewhat similar vein, as the first step in the taking of remedial steps. The courts have divided on the question. Those admitting the letters often take the view that the action should not be protected since it is not likely to be deterred because undertaken under regulatory command and not voluntarily.

---

[41] Rule 407, Subsequent Remedial Measures, states:

When measures are taken that would have made an earlier injury or harm less likely to occur, evidence of the subsequent measures is not admissible to prove:

§ 72.1   negligence;

§ 72.2   culpable conduct;

§ 72.3   a defect in a product or its design; or

§ 72.4   a need for a warning or instruction.

But the court may admit this evidence for another purpose, such as impeachment or—if disputed—proving ownership, control, or the feasibility of precautionary measures.

[42] See supra § 185.

[43] 528 P.2d 1148 (Cal. 1974).

Payment of Medical Expenses. Similar considerations of doubtful relevancy and of public policy underlie the general exclusion of evidence of payment or offers to pay medical and similar expenses of an injured person to prove liability. Federal Rule 409, which is set out in the footnote,[44] is in general conformity with the prior case law.

Unlike compromise negotiations, where the discussion of issues is an essential part of the process and requires protection against disclosure, communications are unnecessary to the providing of care. Accordingly, they are unprotected. Also, if the offer to pay is relevant to an issue other than liability for the injury, exclusion is not required by this doctrine.

---

[44] Federal Rule 409 states: "Evidence of furnishing, promising to pay, or offering to pay medical, hospital, or similar expenses resulting from an injury is not admissible to prove liability for the injury."

Chapter 26

SPONTANEOUS STATEMENTS

Table of Sections

§ 268 *Res Gestae* and the Hearsay Rule

The term *res gestae* seems to have come into common usage in discussions of admissibility of statements accompanying material acts or situations in the early 1800s. At this time, the theory of hearsay was not well developed, and the various exceptions to the hearsay rule were not clearly defined. In this context, the phrase *res gestae* served as a convenient vehicle for escape from the hearsay rule in two primary situations. First, it was used to explain the admissibility of statements that were not hearsay at all.[1] Second, it was used to justify the admissibility of statements that today come within the three exceptions discussed in this chapter: (1) statements of present sense impressions, (2) excited utterances, and (3) statements of present bodily condition, mental states, and emotions.

Initially the term *res gestae* was employed to denote words that accompanied the principal litigated fact, such as the murder, collision, or trespass. However, usage developed to the point where the phrase seemed to embody the notion that evidence of any relevant act or condition might also bring in the words that accompanied it. Two main policies or motives are discernible in this recognition of *res gestae* as a password for the admission of otherwise inadmissible evidence. One is a desire to permit each witness to tell his or her story in a natural way by reciting all that happened at the time of the narrated incident, including those details that give it life and color. Events occur as a seamless web, and the naturalness with which the details fit together gives confirmation to the witness's entire account. The other policy, emphasized by Wigmore and those following his leadership, is the recognition of spontaneity as the source of

---

[1]   See infra § 269.

special trustworthiness. This quality of spontaneity characterizes to some degree nearly all the types of statements which have been labeled *res gestae*.

Commentators and courts have criticized use of the phrase *res gestae*. Its vagueness and imprecision are apparent. Moreover, traditional limitations on the doctrine, such as the requirement that it be used only in regard to the principal litigated fact and the frequent insistence of concurrence (or at least a close relationship in time) between the words and the act or situation, have restricted its usefulness as a tool for avoiding unjustified application of the hearsay rule. However, the vagueness of the phrase also made it easier for courts to broaden its coverage and thus permitted the admissibility of certain statements in new situations. The ancient phrase thus played a role in the evolution of evidence law and the expansion of the admission of contemporaneously made hearsay statements.

Although *res gestae* it appears to be a historical relic to be jettisoned from modern hearsay analysis, the United State Supreme Court's decision in *Crawford v. Washington*,[2] revived a bit of interest in some of the restrictions associated with the term. *Crawford* observed that to the extent that a hearsay exception existed at all at the time of the framing of the Constitution and Bill of Rights, "it required that the statements be made 'immediat[ely] upon the hurt received, and before [the declarant] had time to devise or contrive any thing for her own advantage.' "[3]

§ 269 Spontaneous Statements as Nonhearsay: Circumstantial Proof of a Fact in Issue

The types of spontaneous statements discussed in this chapter are often treated by courts as hearsay, and thus to be admissible, they must come within an exception to the general rule excluding hearsay. In many cases, however, this maneuver is unnecessary because the statements are not hearsay in the first place. As developed in an earlier section, hearsay is generally defined as assertive statements or conduct offered to prove what is asserted. But many so-called spontaneous statements are in fact not assertive statements or, if assertive, are not offered to prove the truth of the assertion. For example, it is clear that the statements, "I plan to spend the rest of my life here in New York" and "I have lost my affection for my husband" are hearsay when offered to prove the plan to remain in New York or the loss of affection. On the other hand, statements such as "I have been happier in New York than in any other place," when offered to show the speaker's intent to remain in New York, and "My husband is a detestable wretch," offered to show lack of affection for the husband, will or will not be classed as hearsay, depending upon the position taken with respect to the long debated question whether "implied assertions" are to be treated as hearsay.[4]

If the statement offered in evidence is not classed as hearsay, then no further consideration of the exceptions developed in this chapter is required. If, however, it is considered hearsay, then these exceptions may become pertinent to admissibility. Indeed, often the hearsay definition question is almost entirely academic for statements offered to prove the declarant's state of mind since admissible, even if considered hearsay, under a rather broad exception.

---

[2]   541 U.S. 36 (2004).

[3]   *Id.* at 58 n.8 (quoting Thompson v. Trevanion, Skin. 402, 90 Eng. Rep. 179 (K.B. 1693)).

[4]   See supra § 250.

§ 270 "Self-Serving" Aspects of Spontaneous Statements

The notion that parties' out-of-court statements could not be evidence in their favor because of the "self-serving" nature of the statements seems to have originated with the now universally discarded rule forbidding parties to testify. When this rule of disqualification for interest was abrogated by statute, any sweeping rule of inadmissibility regarding self-serving statements should have been regarded as abolished by implication.

The hearsay rule excludes all hearsay statements unless they fall within some exception to the rule. Thus, no specific rule is necessary to exclude self-serving out-of-court statements if not within a hearsay exception. If a statement with a self-serving aspect falls within an exception to the hearsay rule, the judgment underlying the exception that the assurances of trustworthiness outweigh the dangers inherent in hearsay should be taken as controlling, and the declaration should be admitted despite its self-serving aspects.

Historically, most courts agreed that this was the proper approach when the self-serving statement fell within one of the well-established exceptions, such as the exclusion of business records, excited utterances, and spontaneous statements of present bodily sensations or symptoms. However, with regard to the somewhat more recently developed exceptions, such as statements of present state of mind or emotion, less agreement existed. Some courts applied a purported general rule of exclusion of self-serving statements in this area. Others rejected any blanket rule of exclusion, although the self-serving aspects of the declaration were taken into account in applying a requirement that the statements must have been made under circumstances of apparent sincerity.

The Federal Rules covering hearsay exceptions for spontaneous statements, discussed in the remaining sections of this chapter, make no special provision for self-serving statements. What is clear, however, is that since spontaneity is the principal, and often the only, guarantee of trustworthiness for the exceptions in this chapter, its absence should result in exclusion of the statement. Circumstances indicating a lack of spontaneity, which may be related to the self-serving character of the statement, are accordingly extremely important to the determination of admissibility.

Although reference to spontaneity is helpful, the difficult issue remains: may courts properly exclude statements because of doubts about the sincerity of the declarant as evidenced by the self-serving nature of the statement? Judicial consideration of credibility is not theoretically prohibited in determining an issue of preliminary-fact-finding of the type involved in admitting or excluding hearsay. The chief problem with this approach under hearsay rules modeled on the Federal Rules is legislative intent. The rules give no authorization to such considerations, and indeed the omission of a requirement found in the original Uniform Rule that the statement must not be made in "bad faith" at least suggests a contrary legislative intent. Moreover, in some other exceptions, the self-serving character of a statement, appearing in the form of motive to falsify, is specified as a ground for exclusion.[5]

A somewhat more comfortable place for the general exercise of such judicial judgment is under the balancing of probativity and prejudice authorized by Federal Rule

---

[5]   See, e.g., infra § 288 (accident reports) & § 296 (police reports).

403, although this home is hardly secure since neither the rule itself nor its history gives explicit authorization. Nevertheless, in exercising discretion to exclude evidence where the danger of prejudice, confusing the issues, misleading the jury, or wasting time outweighs its probative value, circumstantial or direct evidence revealing a self-serving motive should logically have a place.[6] Rarely, however, should statements of substantial importance to the case be excluded even under this rule based upon judicial doubts about the declarant's motivation. Under the structure of the Federal Rules, judgments about credibility should generally be left to the jury rather than preempted by a judicial determination of inadmissibility. Leaving the issue to the jury is particularly appropriate when the credibility issue can be readily appreciated by it, as is generally the case when the reason to question credibility rests upon the declarant's self-serving motivation.

§ 271   Unexcited Statements of Present Sense Impressions

Although Wigmore's creative work did much to clarify the murky concept of *res gestae*, his analysis of spontaneous declarations may have led to one unfortunate restricting development of this exception. Professor Thayer, reviewing the *res gestae* cases in 1881, concluded that this was an exception based on the contemporaneousness of statements. He read the law as creating an exception for statements "made by those present when a thing took place, made about it, and importing what is present at the very time . . . ."[7] Wigmore, however, saw as the basis for the spontaneous exclamation exception, not the contemporaneousness of the exclamation, but rather the nervous excitement produced by the exposure of the declarant to an exciting event.[8] As a result, the American law of spontaneous statements shifted in its emphasis from what Thayer had observed to an exception based on the requirement of an exciting event and the resulting stifling of the declarant's reflective faculties. As Professor Morgan noted, this shift was unfortunate.[9] Given the danger of unreliability caused by the very emotional impact required for excited utterances, it makes little sense to admit them while excluding other out-of-court statements that may have equal assurances of reliability and lack the inherent defects of excited utterances.[10]

Under Morgan's leadership, arguments were made for restoring Thayer's view of the law by recognizing another exception to the hearsay rule for statements concerning nonexciting events that the declarant was observing while making the declaration. Although these statements lack whatever assurance of reliability is produced by the effect of an exciting event, other factors offer safeguards. First, since the report concerns observations being made at the time of the statement, possible errors caused by a defect of the declarant's memory are absent. Second, a requirement that the statement be made contemporaneously with the observation means that little or no time is available for calculated misstatement. Third, the statement will usually have been made to a third person (the witness who subsequently testifies to it), who was also present at the time and scene of the observation. Thus, in most cases, the witness will have observed the situation and thus can provide a check on the accuracy of the declarant's statement and

---

6   See generally supra § 185.

7   Thayer, Bedingfield's Case—Declarations as a Part of the Res Gesta, 15 Am. L. Rev. 1, 83 (1881).

8   6 Wigmore, Evidence § 1747 (Chadbourn rev. 1976).

9   Morgan, Res Gestae, 12 Wash. L. Rev. 91, 96 (1937).

10   Morgan, A Suggested Classification of Utterances Admissible as Res Gestae, 31 Yale L.J. 229, 236 (1922).

furnish corroboration. Moreover, since the declarant will often be available for cross-examination, his or her credibility will be subject to substantial verification before the trier of fact.

The courts generally did not rush to the support of the proposed exception for unexcited statements of present sense impressions. A considerable number continued to admit contemporaneous statements under *res gestae* language without emphasis on the presence or absence of an exciting event. In a large proportion of these decisions, an arguably exciting event was present. However, cases recognizing the exception for unexcited statements of present sense impressions began to emerge. The case most commonly cited to illustrate judicial recognition of the exception is *Houston Oxygen Co. v. Davis.*[11] Although an apparently exciting event transpired, the opinion disclaimed reliance upon it and instead expressly based its decision upon the exception for unexcited declarations of present sense impressions. A more compelling case on its facts, decided in the same year, is *Tampa Electric Co. v. Getrost.*[12]

Although judicial acceptance gradually gained momentum, the rulemaking process provided the principal impetus for recognition of the hearsay exception for unexcited statements of present sense impressions. The Model Code of Evidence and the original Uniform Rules included such an exception. Federal Rule 803(1) provides a hearsay exception, without regard to the availability of the declarant, for "[a] statement describing or explaining an event or condition, made while or immediately after the declarant perceived it."

Even though recognized as a hearsay exception, relatively few statements of present sense impression are found in reported cases in comparison with excited utterances. The relative infrequence of such cases likely results from the fact that unexciting events do not often give rise to statements that later becomes relevant in litigation. However, as growing use of electronic communication devices, such as cell phones and text messaging expands the number of occasions when contemporaneous statements of observations are narrated to others, the exception may see more frequent application.

Like all hearsay exceptions and exclusions other than admissions,[13] present sense impressions and excited utterances require that the declarant have firsthand knowledge, which can sometimes be proved entirely by the statement. These two exceptions otherwise differ in a number of important respects. First, no exciting event or condition is required for present sense impressions. Second, while excited utterances "relating to"[14] the startling event or condition are admissible, present sense impressions are limited to "describing or explaining" the event or condition perceived.[15] Tighter correspondence between observation and statement is appropriate given the theory underlying the present sense impression exception. Although fabrication and forgetfulness are reduced by the absence of time lapse between perception and utterance, the lack of a startling event makes the assumption of spontaneity difficult to maintain unless the statements directly pertain to perception. Third, although the time within which an excited utterance may be made is measured by the duration of the stress caused by the exciting

---

[11]   161 S.W.2d 474 (Tex. Comm'n App. 1942).

[12]   10 So. 2d 83 (Fla. 1942).

[13]   See supra § 255.

[14]   See infra § 272.

[15]   See *id.*

event,[16] statements of present sense impression may be made only while or "immediately after" the declarant "perceived" the event or condition. This shortened period is also consistent with the weaker guarantee of trustworthiness of the present sense impression. While principle might seem to call for a limitation to exact contemporaneity, some allowance must be made for the time needed for translating observation into speech. Thus, the appropriate inquiry is whether sufficient time elapsed to have permitted reflective thought.

Some commentators have suggested that corroboration by an "equally percipient" witness should be a further requirement for admitting statements of present sense impression into evidence. The proposal represents a significant departure from the general pattern of exceptions to the hearsay rule. The only instance in which a requirement of corroboration is found is where a statement against penal interest by a third person—a third-party confession—is offered to inculpate or exculpate another person. There, the common law had a firmly established position against admission. In order to increase the acceptability of a change of that position, the Advisory Committee incorporated into Federal Rule 804(b)(3) a requirement that the hearsay statement must be corroborated when the exception was expanded to admit statements that exculpate another person.[17] The present sense impression exception presents no such general need. Its underlying rationale offers sufficient assurances of reliability without the additional requirement of corroboration, and the Federal Rule and most courts have not required it.

Historically, the limitation of the exception in terms of time and subject matter has usually meant that the witness who reports the making of the statement will have perceived the event or at least observed circumstances strongly suggesting it. This aspect is certainly an added assurance of accuracy, but a general justification for admission is not the same as a requirement.

As noted earlier, the explosive expansion of electronic communication devices in modern life, such as cell phones and text and instant messaging, which both facilitate a flow of almost instantaneous communication and frequently create a record of it, is likely to result in the availability of many more statements that qualify under this exception in terms of their spontaneity as potential evidence in litigated cases. Statements through such devices generally mean that the reporting witness or recording will not be in a position to have perceived the event or the circumstances of the observation. This treatise has long taken the position that the presence or absence of a witness who can corroborate the circumstances of the statement is a matter is better left for consideration by the finder of fact as going to weight and sufficiency rather than becoming a complicating admissibility requirement. Whether the requirements of the exception should be modified in response to changes in the availability and quality of the statements through modern electronic communication should be carefully considered if experience with such statements indicates a challenge to the general trustworthiness of these statements.

---

[16]   See *id.*

[17]   See infra § 318.

§ 272 Excited Utterances

While historically often lumped together with the amalgam of concepts under the term *res gestae*,[18] an exception to the hearsay rule for statements made under the influence of a startling event is now universally recognized. Formulations of the exception differ, but all agree on two basic requirements. First, there must be an occurrence or event sufficiently startling to render inoperative the normal reflective thought processes of the observer. Second, the statement of the declarant must have been a spontaneous reaction to the occurrence or event and not the result of reflective thought. These two elements, which define the essence of the exception, together with a third requirement that the statement be one "relating to" the event, determine admissibility.

The rationale for the exception lies in the special reliability that is furnished when excitement suspends the declarant's powers of reflection and fabrication. This factor also serves to justify dispensing with any requirement that the declarant be unavailable because it suggests that testimony on the stand, given at a time when the powers of reflection and fabrication are operative, is no more (and perhaps less) reliable than the out-of-court statement.

The entire basis for the exception may, nevertheless, be questioned. While psychologists would probably concede that excitement minimizes the possibility of reflective self-interest influencing the declarant's statements, they have questioned whether this might be outweighed by the distorting effect of shock and excitement upon the declarant's observation and judgment. Despite these questions concerning its justification, the exception is well established.

The sufficiency of the event or occurrence as an exciting event is usually easily resolved. Physical violence, though often present, is not required. An automobile accident, pain or an injury, an attack by a dog, a fight, seeing a photograph in a newspaper or unexpectedly encountering a feared individual, and a wide range of other events may qualify. The courts look primarily to the effect upon the declarant, and if satisfied that the event was such as to cause adequate excitement, the inquiry is ended.

A somewhat more serious issue is raised by the occasional requirement of proving the exciting event by some proof in addition to the statement itself, which certainly can be considered.[19] Under generally prevailing practice, the statement itself is considered sufficient proof of the exciting event, and therefore the statement is admissible despite absence of other proof that an exciting event occurred. Some courts, however, have taken the position that an excited utterance is admissible only if other proof is presented which supports a finding of fact that the exciting event did occur. The issue has not yet been resolved under the Federal Rules. Fortunately, only a very few cases need actually confront this knotty theoretical problem if the courts view what constitutes independent evidence broadly, as they should where the circumstances and content of the statement indicate trustworthiness.

The second requirement is substantively the most significant: whether the statement was the result of reflective thought or a spontaneous reaction to the exciting event. The most important of the many factors entering into this determination is the

---

[18]   See supra § 268.

[19]   See supra § 53.

temporal element. If the statement occurs while the exciting event is still in progress, courts have little difficulty finding that the excitement prompted the statement, but as the time between the event and the statement increases, courts become more reluctant to find the statement an excited utterance. According to the historical analysis of the excited utterance exception in *Crawford v. Washington*,[20] strict contemporaneousness was required between the event and the statement. That historical limitation, however, did little to encourage courts to construe the modern exception more narrowly.

Passage of time viewed in isolation is not an entirely accurate indicator of admissibility. For example, while courts have held statements made more than twelve hours after a physical beating to be the product of the excitement caused by the beating, other courts have found statements made within minutes of the event not admissible.

A useful rule of thumb is that where the time interval between the event and the statement is long enough to permit reflective thought, the statement will be excluded in the absence of some proof that the declarant did not in fact engage in a reflective thought process. Testimony that the declarant still appeared "nervous" or "distraught" and that there was a reasonable basis for continuing emotional upset will often suffice. The nature of the exciting event and the declarant's concern with it are obviously relevant. Thus, a statement made by the victim's wife one hour after a traffic accident was held admissible where the husband was still in the emergency room and his wife was still concerned about his condition.

Other factors may indicate the opposite conclusion. Although not grounds for automatic exclusion, evidence that the statement was made in response to an inquiry or was self-serving is an indication that the statement was the result of reflective thought. Where the time interval permitted such thought, those factors might swing the balance in favor of exclusion. Proof that the declarant performed tasks requiring relatively careful thought between the event and the statement provides strong evidence that the effect of the exciting event had subsided. Because of the wide variety of factual situations, appellate courts have recognized substantial discretion in trial courts to determine whether a declarant was still under the influence of an exciting event at the time of an offered statement.

Although the exception requires that the declarant be affected by the exciting event, he or she need not be involved in the event. An excited utterance by a bystander is clearly admissible. However, if the identity of the bystander-declarant is undisclosed, the courts have been reluctant to admit such statements, principally because of uncertainty that foundational requirements, including firsthand knowledge and the impact of the event on the declarant, have been satisfied.

The third requirement is that there be a connection between the content of the statement and the event giving rise to it. Whether the excited utterance had to concern the exciting event and the strictness of relationship between the exciting event and the content of the statement was the subject of historical disagreement. Federal Rule 803(2) and other modern formulations of the exception require a connection between the event and the content of the statement but define that connection broadly as "relating to" the event. This terminology is intended to extend beyond merely a description or an explanation of the event. The courts have been quite liberal in applying this requirement. The formulation used by Rule 803(2) has the advantage of simplicity while at the same

---

[20]   541 U.S. 36, 58 n.8 (2004).

time preserving the trustworthiness gained by requiring a relationship between the exciting event or condition and the resulting statement. It also permits clarification of the difference in theory between excited utterances and statements of present sense impressions, discussed in the preceding section.

Another major issue frequently encountered with excited utterances is whether the declarant meets the tests of competency for a witness. In a modified manner, the witness is required to have firsthand knowledge.[21] Direct proof of observation is not necessary; if the circumstances appear consistent with opportunity by the declarant, the requirement is met. If there is doubt, the question should be for the jury.[22] Especially in cases where the declaration is of low probative value, however, the statement is usually held inadmissible if there is no reasonable suggestion that the declarant had an opportunity to observe.

On the theory that there is a countervailing assurance of reliability in the excitement of the event, the other aspects of competency are not applied. Thus, an excited utterance is admissible despite the fact that the declarant was a child and would have been incompetent as a witness for that reason, or the declarant was incompetent by virtue of mental illness.

Courts have occasionally argued that an excited utterance must not be an opinion. Such a blanket limitation is unjustified in view of the nature and present standing of the opinion rule.[23] Where the declarant is an in-court witness, requiring testimony in concrete terms rather than conclusory generalizations is appropriate. But in everyday life, people often talk in conclusory terms, and when these statements are later offered in evidence, the declarant's words obviously cannot be changed to more specific language. Here, as elsewhere, the opinion rule should be applied sparingly, if at all, to out-of-court speech. Nevertheless, courts have sometimes excluded excited utterances on the grounds that they violate the opinion rule, especially in situations in which the declarants' statements place blame on themselves or others. Despite possible danger that these opinions may be given exaggerated weight by a jury, the need for knowledge of the facts usually outweighs this danger, and the better view admits excited statements of opinion.

§ 272.1 Excited Utterances and Other Hearsay Exceptions in Sexual Abuse Cases

Rape cases and other sexual offenses, particularly those involving minors, raise a number of difficult hearsay issues. Several different exceptions may be involved, including statements for the purpose of medical diagnosis and the catchall exception, which are treated elsewhere.[24] The application of the excited utterance exception and several new specific exceptions developed to deal with issues involved with the prosecution of offenses against children are examined here.

Before moving into modern developments, one historical artifact should be noted. Historically, out-of-court statements that a rape victim made a complaint were admissible to corroborate the assault. In terms of a time requirement, the complaint must have been made without a delay that was either unexplained or inconsistent with

---

[21] See supra § 10.

[22] See supra §§ 53 & 58.

[23] See supra § 11.

[24] See infra §§ 277–278 & 324.

the occurrence of the offense, which is generally less demanding than would be imposed under a typical excited utterance analysis. The theory of admissibility was that the statement rebutted an inference that might otherwise undercut the victim's credibility that, because no immediate complaint was made, no crime in fact occurred. Accordingly, if the victim did not testify, evidence of the complaint was not admissible, and only the fact that a complaint was made could be admitted, not its details. Some jurisdictions continue to recognize a role for this exception.

Moving to modern practice, particularly where children are the victims of sexual offenses, many courts have liberally interpreted the allowable period of time between the exciting event and the child's description of it. The theory of these courts is that the general psychological characteristics of children typically extend the period that is free of the dangers of conscious fabrication. In addition, a growing number of states have enacted specific hearsay exceptions to cover the situations where children are involved as witnesses or victims. One of the advantages of this latter approach is that it reduces the pressure to distort the traditional time limitations of the excited utterance exception to deal with this difficult set of cases.

The special exception for the testimony of children is illustrated by the Washington statute, which became a model for many other states. It admits a child's extrajudicial statement if (1) the court finds after a hearing that the time, content, and circumstances of the statement provide sufficient indicia of reliability, and (2) the child either testifies at the proceeding or is unavailable as a witness and, if unavailable, corroborative evidence is produced to support trustworthiness. However, that exception was tailored to satisfy the Confrontation Clause under the analysis of *Ohio v. Roberts*,[25] which rested on a determination of trustworthiness when the child did not testify. The decision of the United States Supreme Court in *Crawford v. Washington*[26] renders the exception unconstitutional in criminal cases as to any statement by a non-testifying child that is found to be testimonial. However, if the statement is nontestimonial, the federal Confrontation Clause does not apply, and when the child testifies and is subject to cross-examination, the Clause is satisfied.

Major efforts have also been undertaken to ameliorate the trauma associated with testifying in court. The most common reform involves the shielding of the child by the taking of testimony by contemporaneous examination communicated to the courtroom by closed-circuit television. This protection has been ruled not to violate the Confrontation Clause if based upon an individualized finding that the child will suffer trauma if required to testify in the presence of the defendant.[27]

§ 273 Statements of Physical or Mental Condition: (a) Statements of Bodily Feelings, Symptoms, and Condition

Statements of the declarant's present bodily condition and symptoms, including pain and other feelings, offered to prove the truth of the statements, have been generally recognized as an exception to the hearsay rule. Special reliability is provided by the spontaneous quality of the declarations, assured by the requirement that the declaration purport to describe a condition presently existing at the time of the statement. This assurance of reliability is not always effective in that some of these statements

---

[25]   448 U.S. 56, 66 (1980).

[26]   541 U.S. 36 (2004).

[27]   Maryland v. Craig, 497 U.S. 836 (1990).

describing present symptoms are almost certainly calculated misstatements. Nevertheless, a sufficiently large percentage are spontaneous to justify the exception.

"Necessity" plays a large role in admission. The alternative of insisting upon the in-court testimony of the declarant, when available, promises little improvement since cross-examination and other methods of exposing deliberate misrepresentation are relatively ineffective. Together, these factors of trustworthiness and necessity not only provide a basis for admitting statements of this type, but also justify dispensing with any requirement of unavailability of the declarant. Being spontaneous, the hearsay statements are considered of greater probative value than the present testimony of the declarant.

Despite suggestions to the contrary in some early cases, declarations of present bodily condition need not be made to a physician to satisfy the present exception. Any person hearing the statement may testify to it. The exception is, however, limited to descriptions of present condition, and therefore it excludes description of past pain or symptoms, as well as accounts of the events furnishing the cause of the condition.

Federal Rule 803(3) defines a hearsay exception, without regard to the unavailability of the declarant, for "[a] statement of the declarant's then-existing . . . physical condition (such as mental feeling, pain, or bodily health) . . . ." Not only does the rule mandate that the statement must be spontaneous by its requirement that the statement describe a "then existing" physical condition, but the Advisory Committee's Note indicates that the rule is a specialized application of the broader rule recognizing a hearsay exception for statements describing a present sense impression, the cornerstone of which is spontaneity. If circumstances demonstrate a lack of spontaneity, exclusion should follow.

§ 274 Statements of Physical or Mental Condition: (b) Statements of Present Mental or Emotional State to Show a State of Mind or Emotion in Issue

The substantive law often makes legal rights and liabilities hinge upon the existence of a particular state of mind or feeling. Thus, such matters as the intent to steal or kill, or the intent to have a certain paper take effect as a deed or will, or the maintenance or transfer of the affections of a spouse may come into issue in litigation. When this is so, the mental or emotional state of the person becomes an ultimate object of inquiry. It is not introduced as evidence from which the person's earlier or later conduct may be inferred but as an operative fact upon which a cause of action or defense depends. While a state of mind may be proved by the person's actions, the statements of the person are often a primary source of evidence.

In many instances, statements used for this purpose are not assertive of the declarant's present state of mind and are therefore not hearsay.[28] Courts, however, have tended to lump together arguably hearsay statements asserting the declarant's state of mind with those arguably nonhearsay that tend to prove state of mind circumstantially, applying a general exception to the hearsay rule and ignoring the possibility that many of these statements could be treated as nonhearsay.

As with statements of bodily condition, the special assurance of reliability for statements of present state of mind rests upon their spontaneity and resulting probable

---

[28] See supra § 246.

sincerity.[29] The guarantee of reliability is assured principally by the requirement that the statements must relate to a condition of mind or emotion existing at the time of the statement. In addition, some formulations of the exception require that the statement must have been made under circumstances indicating apparent sincerity, although Federal Rule 803(3) imposes no such explicit condition.[30]

Such statements are also admitted under a version of the same necessity argument that supports most hearsay exceptions. Often no better way exists to prove a relevant mental or physical condition than through the statements of the individual whose condition is at issue. Even with cross-examination, the alternative of using the declarant's testimony is not likely to be a better, and perhaps an inferior, manner of proof. If the declarant were called to testify, "his own memory of his state of mind at a former time is no more likely to be clear and true than a bystander's recollection of what he then said."[31] As a result, unavailability of declarant is not required.

Common examples of statements used to prove mental state at the time of the statement include: statements of intent to make a certain place the declarant's home offered to establish domicile, statements expressive of mental suffering to prove that element of damages, statements by customers regarding anger to prove loss of good will, statements showing consumer confusion, including consumer survey results, statements of patients regarding lack of knowledge of risk of taking medication in malpractice suit, statements of willingness to allow one to use the declarant's automobile offered to prove that the car was used with the owner's consent, statement of employee that she expected to be discharged to show constructive discharge, statements accompanying a transfer of property regarding intent to defraud creditors, statements of ill will to show malice or the required state of mind in criminal cases, and statements showing fear.

Although the statement must describe a state of mind or feeling existing at the time of the statement, the evidentiary effect of the statement is broadened by the notion of the continuity in time of states of mind. For example, if a declarant asserts on Tuesday a then-existing intention to go on a business trip the next day, this will be evidence not only of the intention at the time of the statement, but also of the same purpose the next day when the declarant is on the road. Continuity may also look backwards. Thus, when there is evidence that a will has been mutilated by the maker, the declarant's subsequent statements of a purpose inconsistent with the will are received to show his or her intent to revoke it at the time it was mutilated. Similarly, whether payment of money or a conveyance was intended by the donor as a gift may be shown by statements of intent existing at the time of the statement whether made before, at the time of, or after the act of transfer. The duration of states of mind or emotion varies with the particular attitudes or feelings at issue and with the cause, and the court may require some reasonable indication that in light of all the circumstances, including the proximity in time, the state of mind was the same at the material time. Whether a state of mind continues is a decision for the trial judge.[32]

Declarations such as those involved here frequently include assertions other than state of mind. For example, the victim may assert that the defendant's acts caused the

---

[29] See supra § 273.

[30] See generally supra § 270.

[31] Mutual Life Ins. Co. v. Hillmon, 145 U.S. 285, 295 (1892).

[32] This is a matter of logical relevancy rather than conditional relevancy. *See* Fed. R. Evid. 104(a) & (b). See generally supra § 53.

state of mind. The truth of those assertions beyond the mental or emotional condition may coincide with other issues in the case, as where the defendant is charged with acts similar to those described. In such circumstances, the normal practice is to admit the statement and direct the jury to consider it only as proof of the state of mind and to disregard it as evidence of the other issues.[33] Compliance with this instruction is probably beyond the jury's ability and almost certainly beyond their willingness. Where substantial evidence has been admitted on the other act, probably little harm results. However, where the mental state is provable by other available evidence and the danger of harm from improper use by the jury of the offered declarations is substantial, the trial judge should exclude the statements entirely, or prohibit the witness from giving the reasons for the state of mind.

Federal Rule 803(3) covers statements of "the declarant's then-existing state of mind (such as motive, intent, or plan) or emotional [or] sensory . . . condition." The rule is generally consistent with the hearsay exception as developed by the courts at common law.

Insanity. A main source of proof of mental competency or incompetency is the conduct of the person in question, showing normal and abnormal response to the circumstances of his or her environment. By this test, every act of the subject's life, within reasonable limits of time, would be relevant to the inquiry. Whether the conduct is verbal or nonverbal, assertive or nonassertive, is inconsequential. It is offered as a response to environment, not to prove anything that may be asserted, and is accordingly not hearsay.[34] Thus, whether declarant says "I am King Henry the Eighth" or "I believe that I am King Henry the Eighth" is insignificant. Both are offered as evidence of irrationality, and niceties of form should not determine admissibility. If, nevertheless, it is argued that abnormal conduct can be simulated, thereby becoming assertive and therefore hearsay, a short answer is that in that event the evidence would be admissible under the present hearsay exception. Such inquiries are largely superfluous, and courts should spend little effort determining whether the statement is nonhearsay or is hearsay evidence showing an abnormal state of mind.

§ 275　Statements of Physical or Mental Condition: (c) Statements of Intention Offered to Show Subsequent Acts of Declarant

As the previous sections made clear, statements of mental state are generally admissible to prove the declarant's state of mind when that state of mind is at issue. But the probative value of a state of mind obviously may go beyond the state of mind itself. Where a state of mind would tend to prove subsequent conduct, can the two inferential processes be linked together, with the declarations of state of mind being admitted as proof of the conduct? For example, can the declarant's statements indicating an intent to kill be admitted to prove not only intent, but also that the declarant did in fact subsequently commit the murder? The answer involves concerns of both hearsay and relevancy.

These issues are somewhat more difficult than the matter of admissibility of statements to show only the state of mind. The special reliability of the statements is less in the present situation since it is significantly less likely that a declared intention

---

[33]　See infra § 276 (discussing the legitimacy of inferring from state of mind the happening of the act claimed to have caused the state of mind).

[34]　See supra §§ 246 & 250.

will be carried out than it is that a declared state of mind is actually held. A statement of intention to kill another is much stronger proof of malice toward the victim at the time of the statement (or subsequently) than it is proof that the declarant committed the murder. Nevertheless, a person who expresses an intent to kill is undeniably more likely to have done so than a person not shown to have had that intent. The accepted standard of relevancy, i.e., more probable than without the evidence,[35] is easily met.

Statements of state of mind are now recognized as admissible to prove subsequent conduct. Thus, out-of-court statements that tend to prove a plan, design, or intention of the declarant may be received, subject to the usual limitations as to remoteness in time and perhaps apparent sincerity[36] common to all statements of mental state, to prove that the plan, design, or intention of the declarant was carried out by the declarant.

The leading case is *Mutual Life Insurance Co. v. Hillmon*,[37] which concerned a suit on life insurance policies by the wife of the insured, Hillmon. The principal issue was whether Hillmon had in fact died. A body had been found at Crooked Creek, Kansas, and the parties disputed whether the body was that of Hillmon. Plaintiff's theory was that Hillmon left Wichita, Kansas, about March 5, 1879 with a man named Brown and that on the night of March 18, 1879, while Hillmon and Brown were camped at Crooked Creek, Hillmon was killed by the accidental discharge of a gun. The defendants, on the other hand, maintained that another individual named Walters had accompanied Hillmon and that the body found at Crooked Creek was Walters'.

Defendants offered testimony that on or about March 5, 1879, Walters wrote to his sister that "I expect to leave Wichita on or about March 5, with a certain Mr. Hillmon."[38] An objection to this and similar evidence was sustained. The United States Supreme Court reversed on the ground that the evidence of the letters should have been admitted:

> The letters . . . were competent, not as narratives of facts communicated to the writer by others, nor yet as proof that he actually went away from Wichita, but as evidence that, shortly before the time when other evidence tended to show that he went away, he had the intention of going, and of going with Hillmon, which made it more probable both that he did go and that he went with Hillmon, than if there had been no proof of such intention.[39]

Although the text of Federal Rule 803(3) does not explicitly address the question of admitting intent for the purpose of proving the doing of the intended act, the Advisory Committee stated that it was to continue. Statements for this purpose are currently routinely admitted. However, a number of subsidiary problems remain to be considered under the rule and the common law decisions.

The suggestion has been made that unavailability of the declarant should be a requirement. In fact, in virtually all the cases admitting the statements of intent as proof of the doing of the intended act, the declarant has been unavailable, and it may well be that the resulting need for the evidence influenced the courts in the direction of

---

[35]   See supra § 185.

[36]   See supra § 274.

[37]   145 U.S. 285 (1892).

[38]   *Id.* at 288.

[39]   *Id.* at 295–96.

admissibility. However, neither the decisions nor the Federal Rule require unavailability.

In a somewhat similar vein, in virtually all the cases admitting the evidence the intent stated was quite concrete, e.g., to do a specific act at a specific time. Again, this quality of specificity is not generally stated as a requirement, but probative value is undeniably enhanced by its presence. Its absence not only detracts from probative value, but if a statement of vague generality, may tend to stray into areas of character evidence that is inadmissible against a criminal defendant.

The danger of unreliability is greatly increased when the action sought to be proved is not one that the declarant could have performed alone, but rather is one that required the cooperation of another person. If completion of a plan or design requires not only the continued inclination and ability of the declarant to complete it, but also the inclination and ability of someone else, arguably the likelihood that the design or plan was completed is substantially less. In *Hillmon* itself, Walters' successful completion of his plan to leave Wichita depended upon the continued willingness of Hillmon to have Walters as a companion and upon Hillmon's willingness and ability to leave at the time planned. However, all parties agreed that Hillmon did in fact go to Crooked Creek, and the Supreme Court had no occasion to consider this aspect of the case.

The issue is made more difficult when the cooperative actions between the declarant and another are themselves at issue. For example, in the homicide prosecution of Frank, a witness testifies that on the morning of the killing the victim said, "I am going out with Frank tonight." While this tends to prove the victim's acts, it also tends to prove that the defendant "went out" with the victim, a fact very much in issue. Despite some rulings to the contrary, courts have generally admitted these statements. The result is that the statement is used as proof of the other person's intent and as proof that this intent was achieved. The additional dangers present here have, however, prompted some courts to impose additional restrictions or requirements. These include: instructing the jury to consider the evidence only to prove the conduct of the declarant, requiring independent evidence to establish the defendant's conduct, permitting the declaration to be used only to explain the declarant's intent, and limiting use of such statements to cases where the declarant is dead or unavailable and to situations where both the statement of intent is shown to be serious and the event is realistically likely to be achieved.

Acceptance of the use of statements of state of mind to prove subsequent conduct and recognition of occasions for its application by the courts have differed among types of situations. In will cases, for example, previous declarations of intention are received as evidence of the decedent's later conduct when those acts are at issue. Such statements are admissible on issues of forgery, alteration, contents of a will, and whether acts of revocation were done by the testator. Despite early decisions to the contrary, or decisions greatly restricting their use, statements of intent to commit suicide have been admitted when offered by the accused in homicide cases to prove that the victim took his or her own life and similarly in insurance cases to show suicide. Historically, there has been some greater resistance, however, to admitting threats of a third person to commit the act with which the accused is charged as evidence that the act was committed by the third person and therefore not by the accused. Greater liberality should follow under the Federal Rules since Rule 803(3) provides no basis to restrict admission of threats by others, and the Federal Rules' flexible approach to relevancy should provide fewer reasons to treat this as a special class of evidence.

Homicide and assault cases present other special problems. If the accused asserts self-defense and knows of threats of the victim against the accused, these threats are admissible to prove the accused's apprehension of danger and its reasonableness. When used for this purpose, the statements of the victim are not hearsay. But uncommunicated threats pose a more serious problem. They are admissible only to show the victim's intention to attack the accused and further that the victim carried out this intention, thus committing the first act of aggression in the fatal altercation. Fear that juries will abuse the evidence has led some courts to admit proof of uncommunicated threats only under qualification. No qualification appears in the Federal Rule 803(3), and under its influence, changes in the qualifications imposed can be anticipated. However, even under the Federal Rule, courts can certainly impose reasonable restrictions on admissibility of such statements to reduce dangers of confusion and misleading under relevancy concerns, which provide the principal focus for determining admissibility of these statements rather than the hearsay doctrine.

The matter of the admissibility of declarations of state of mind to prove subsequent conduct is a far different question from that of the sufficiency of these statements, standing alone, to support a finding that the conduct occurred. In the typical case, it is reasonable to hold that the declarations are themselves insufficient to support the finding and therefore that statements of intention must be admitted in corroboration of other evidence to show the acts.

§ 276   Statements of Physical or Mental Condition: (d) Statements of State of Mind to Show Memory or Belief as Proof of Previous Happenings

As was seen in the preceding section, under the *Hillmon* doctrine, statements of intent to perform an act are admissible as proof that the act was in fact done. By contrast, a statement by the declarant that he or she had in fact done that act would be excluded under this exception to the hearsay rule. Thus, Walters' statement that he intended to go to Crooked Creek is admissible, but a later statement by him that he had been to Crooked Creek would be excluded. As a matter of common experience, this result seems wrong. The first statement, which is admissible, appears inferior as evidence to the second, which would be excluded. While both statements involve the truthfulness of the declarant, the first statement involves the further risk that supervening events may prevent the stated intent from being accomplished. Minds are changed; tickets are lost; popular sayings, literature, and experience are filled with plans that went awry. Accordingly, the argument goes, if the inferior evidence of intent to do an act in the future is admitted as proof that the act was subsequently done, the superior statement that the act has been completed should certainly be admitted to prove it had been done. In other words, hearsay statements of memory or belief should be admitted as proof that the matter remembered or believed did happen.

Forty years after *Hillmon*, in *Shepard v. United States*,[40] the Supreme Court dealt with an aspect of this argument. In *Shepard*, the trial court had admitted in a murder prosecution testimony that the victim, the wife of the physician-defendant, had stated to

---

[40]   290 U.S. 96 (1933).

a nurse, "Dr. Shepard has poisoned me."[41] Reversing, the Supreme Court rejected the argument that the statement was admissible as a declaration of state of mind:

> [*Hillmon*] marks the high water line beyond which courts have been unwilling to go. It has developed a substantial body of criticism and commentary. Declarations of intention, casting light upon the future, have been sharply distinguished from declarations of memory, pointing backwards to the past. There would be an end, or nearly that, to the rule against hearsay if the distinction were ignored.

> The testimony now questioned faced backward and not forward in its most obvious implications. What is even more important, it spoke to a past act by someone not the speaker.[42]

In more formal hearsay terms, forward-looking statements of intention are admitted while backward-looking statements of memory or belief are excluded because the former do not present the classic hearsay dangers of memory and narration. The weakness inherent in forward-looking statements—the uncertainty that the intention will be carried out—may lead to exclusion, but this is under the relevancy doctrine rather than hearsay analysis.

Nevertheless, after the decision in *Shepard*, the blanket exclusion of statements of memory or belief to prove past events was the subject of some re-examination. From the blanket exclusion of statements of memory or belief to prove past events, the courts carved out an area of admissibility for statements by a testator made after the execution of an alleged will. Thus, the testator's statements that he or she has or has not made or revoked a will or made a will of a particular purport were excepted from the ban of the hearsay rule by a preponderance of the decisions. Impetus to recognize such an exception is furnished by the unavailability of the testator who best knew the facts and often was the only person with that knowledge. Special reliability is suggested by the undeniable firsthand knowledge and general lack of motive to deceive, although the possibility exists that a particular testator may wish to deceive his or her relatives. Federal Rule 803(3) explicitly allows the introduction of a statement of memory or belief to prove the fact remembered or believed if it "relates to the validity or terms of the declarant's will," but otherwise does "not include[e] a statement of memory or belief to prove the fact remembered or believed."

Various types of efforts have been made to permit broader admissibility of hearsay in this general area. A few statutes have allowed receipt of statements by deceased persons made in good faith and upon personal knowledge before the commencement of the action. The Model Code of Evidence went much further by allowing any hearsay statement by an unavailable declarant. The original Uniform Rules proposed a narrower exception. Although statements of "memory or belief to prove the fact remembered or believed" were generally excluded, statements were admissible if made by an unavailable declarant describing an event or condition recently perceived while the declarant's recollection was clear and made in good faith prior to the commencement of the action.

As proposed by the Supreme Court, the Federal Rules included an exception for recent perception with the added limitation that the statement must not have been made

---

[41] *Id.* at 98.
[42] *Id.* at 105–06.

in response to the instigation of a person engaged in investigating, litigating, or settling a claim. The entire provision was eliminated by Congress, but limited to civil cases, it was included for a period of time in the Uniform Rules of Evidence. Either the Uniform Rule or the proposed federal rule has been adopted in a handful of states. In addition, California has created a new hearsay exception that admits statements regarding past threats made by unavailable declarants where the threat is recorded in writing or electronically or was made to medical personnel or a police officer.

A recurring problem arises in connection with the admissibility of accusatory statements made before the act by the victims of homicide. If the statement is merely an expression of fear, such as, "I am afraid of D," no hearsay problem is involved, since the statement falls within the hearsay exception for statements of mental or emotional condition. This does not, however, resolve the question of admissibility. The victim's emotional state must relate to some legitimate issue in the case. For example, the victim's emotional state may permit the inference of some fact of consequence, such as lack of consent where the prosecution charges that the killing occurred during the commission of either a kidnapping or rape.

However, the most likely inference that jurors may draw from the existence of fear, and often the only logical inference that could be drawn, is that some conduct of the defendant, probably mistreatment or threats, occurred and caused the fear. The possibility of over-persuasion, the prejudicial character of the evidence, and the relative weakness and speculative nature of the inference, all argue against admissibility as a matter of relevance.[43] Moreover, even if the judgment is made that evidence of fear standing alone should be admitted, statements of fear are rarely stated pristinely. Instead, that state of mind usually assumes the form either of a statement by the victim that the accused has made threats, from which fear may be inferred, or perhaps more likely a statement of fear because of the defendant's threats. Not only does the evidence possess the weaknesses suggested above for expressions of fear standing alone, but in addition it seems unlikely that juries can resist using the evidence for forbidden purposes in the presence of specific disclosure of misconduct of the defendant.

In either event, the cases have generally excluded the evidence. While the same pressing need for the evidence may be present as that which led to the development of the hearsay exception for dying declarations, the case for trustworthiness is often much weaker, and need alone is not a sufficient basis for a hearsay exception. Exclusion is not universal, however, for in some circumstances, statements may be admissible under other hearsay exceptions, such as that for excited utterances or dying declarations.[44] Moreover, the decedent's fear may be relevant for other legitimate purposes beyond proof of the defendant's act or state of mind. Specifically, such statements are admissible where the defense claims self-defense, suicide, or accidental death because in each of those situations the statements look to the future in that decedent's fear makes unlikely and thus helps to rebut defense claims about the declarant's subsequent conduct, which the *Hillmon* concept permits.

---

[43]   See supra § 185.

[44]   See supra § 272 & infra Ch. 32.

Chapter 27

STATEMENTS FOR THE PURPOSE OF MEDICAL DIAGNOSIS OR TREATMENT

Table of Sections

---

§ 277   Statements of Bodily Feelings, Symptoms, and Condition: (a) Statements Made to Physicians Consulted for Treatment

Statements of a presently existing bodily condition made by a patient to a doctor consulted for treatment[1] have almost universally been admitted as evidence of the facts stated, and even courts that otherwise limited the admissibility of declarations of bodily condition have admitted statements made under these circumstances. Since statements made to physicians are usually made in response to questions, many are not spontaneous. Instead, their reliability is assured by the likelihood that the patient believes that the effectiveness of the treatment depends on the accuracy of the information provided to the doctor, which may be termed a "selfish treatment motivation."

As this exception developed, many courts extended it to include statements made by a patient to a physician concerning past symptoms because of the strong assurance of reliability. This expansion is generally sound, as patients are likely to recognize the importance to their treatment of accurate statements of past, as well as present, symptoms. Some courts continued, however, to admit the testimony only for the limited purpose of explaining the basis for the physician's conclusion rather than to prove the fact of the prior symptoms.[2]

A major issue involving the scope of the exception is the treatment of statements made to a physician concerning the cause or the external source of the condition to be treated. In some cases, the special assurance of reliability—the patient's belief that accuracy is essential to effective treatment—also applies to statements concerning the cause. Moreover, a physician who views cause as related to diagnosis and treatment might reasonably be expected to communicate this to the patient and perhaps take other steps to assure a reliable response. However, the result is different when statements as to causation enter the realm of establishing fault. Generally, neither the patient nor the physician is likely to regard them as related to diagnosis or treatment. In such cases, the statements lack any assurance of reliability based on the declarant's interest in proper treatment and should properly be excluded. "Thus a patient's statement that he was

---

[1]   Statements made to nontreating physicians are discussed in infra § 278.

[2]   See supra § 14 (bases for expert's opinion).

struck by an automobile would qualify, but not his statement that the car was driven through a red light."[3]

Federal Rule 803, Statements Made for Medical Diagnosis or Treatment, provides a hearsay exception, regardless of availability of declarant, for

A statement that:

(A) is made for—and is reasonably pertinent to—medical diagnosis or treatment; and

(B) describes medical history; past or present symptoms or sensations; their inception; or their general cause.

The statement need not have been made to a physician; one made to a hospital attendant, ambulance driver, or member of the family may qualify if intended by the patient to secure treatment. Psychologists and social workers have been included within the exception. Nor does the rule require that the statement concern the declarant's condition, and statements by others, most often close family members, may be received if the relationship or the circumstances give appropriate assurances. The rule is broadly drawn as to subject matter, including medical history and descriptions of past and present symptoms, pain, and sensations. The test for admissibility is whether the subject matter of the statements is reasonably pertinent to diagnosis or treatment—an apparently objective standard. Descriptions of cause are similarly allowed if they are medically pertinent, but statements of fault are unlikely to qualify. A related use of the exception to establish the identity of the perpetrator in sexual assault cases is examined in the next section.

§ 278 Statements of Bodily Feelings, Symptoms, and Condition: (b) Statements Made to Physicians Consulted Only to Testify

Historically, many courts drew a sharp line between statements made to physicians consulted for treatment and those made to physicians consulted solely with the anticipation that the physician would testify for the declarant. Courts were hesitant to admit statements made to doctors consulted only for diagnosis because when the declarant does not anticipate that the effectiveness of treatment depends upon the accuracy of his or her statement, the traditional underlying rationale for the exception— a selfish treatment interest—does not exist. Indeed, if the declarant anticipates that enhancement of symptoms will aid in the subsequent litigation, an affirmative motive may exist to falsify or at least to exaggerate.

The precise nature of the restrictions upon statements made to doctors not consulted for treatment differed among the jurisdictions, although a very common pattern permitted the doctor to recite the statements of the declarant for the limited purpose of providing a basis for the doctor's medical opinion. The dubious propriety of these restrictions was probably responsible for the restrictive view taken by the courts as to what constituted consultation solely for purposes of obtaining testimony. An inquiry was made to determine whether there was any significant treatment motive; if this existed, an additional motive to obtain testimony was ignored.

The Federal Rule abandons these restrictions. The Advisory Committee concluded that permitting statements to be admitted as a basis for a medical expert's opinion but

---

[3]   Fed. R. Evid. 803(4) advisory committee's note.

not for their truth was likely to be a distinction lost on juries and rejected the limitation. The general reliance upon "subjective" facts by the medical profession and the ability of its members to evaluate the accuracy of statements made to them is considered sufficient protection against contrived symptoms. Within the medical profession, the analysis of the rule appears to be that facts reliable enough to be relied on in reaching a diagnosis have sufficient trustworthiness to satisfy hearsay concerns.

The result also has its practical dimension. Under prior practice, contrived evidence was avoided at too great a cost and in substantial departure from the realities of medical practice. Rule 803(4) eliminates any differences in the admissibility of statements made to testifying, as contrasted with treating, physicians. Here, as with statements made for treatment, the test for admissibility is whether the statement is medically pertinent to the diagnosis.

The changes in the hearsay exception for statements made for medical diagnosis or treatment have had their biggest impact in cases of child sexual abuse. In this area, a number of courts have admitted a broad range of statements by children, including statements identifying a particular individual as the perpetrator of the offense. Although some cases exclude statements that identify the perpetrator because they merely assign fault, such statements are more frequently admitted if offered under the theory that the perpetrator's identity is pertinent to treatment of the abused child. Statements have been received when made in a number of different situations and to a rather broad array of professionals, although some courts have developed limitations where non-physicians are involved. These uses of the expanded hearsay exception challenge the wisdom of its extension to cover statements made without any treatment purpose, and a number of states have modified their rule or have restricted its application through judicial interpretation so as to require treatment motivation or other evidence of reliability. Federal circuits have also developed somewhat different limiting interpretations of the rule as well. Admission of statements made exclusively for the purpose of diagnosis also raises constitutional issues regarding the right of confrontation in criminal cases when that diagnosis is done for forensic purposes.[4]

---

[4] See supra § 252.

Chapter 28

RECORDS OF PAST RECOLLECTION

Table of Sections

---

§ 279 History and Theory of the Exception

By the middle 1600s, it had become customary to permit a witness to refresh a failed memory by looking at a written memorandum and to testify from a then-revived memory.[1] Frequently, while examination of the writing did not revive memory, the witness recognized the writing as one that he or she had prepared and was willing to testify on the basis of the writing that the facts recited in it were true. By the 1700s, this later procedure was also accepted as proper, although the theoretical difficulty of justifying the new practice was often avoided by labeling it with the somewhat ambiguous term of "refreshing recollection," which clearly was not strictly accurate. In the early 1800s, courts began to distinguish between the two situations and to recognize that the use of past recollection recorded was a far different matter from permitting the witness to testify from a memory refreshed by examining a writing.

As the rule permitting the introduction of past recollection recorded developed, it had four requirements: (1) the witness must have had firsthand knowledge of the event, (2) the written statement must be an original memorandum made at or near the time of the event while the witness had a clear and accurate memory of it, (3) the witness must lack a present recollection of the event, and (4) the witness must vouch for the accuracy of the written memorandum.

With some refinements, this exception appears as Federal Rule 803(5), Recorded Recollection, with no requirement for the unavailability of the declarant. It reads as follows:

A record that:

(A) is on a matter the witness once knew about but now cannot recall well enough to testify fully and accurately;

(B) was made or adopted by the witness when the matter was fresh in the witness's memory; and

(C) accurately reflects the witness's knowledge.

---

[1]   See supra § 9.

If admitted, the record may be read into evidence but may be received as an exhibit only if offered by an adverse party.

The usefulness of the hearsay exception is apparent from the huge variety of items the courts have admitted into evidence under its sponsorship.

Whether recorded recollection should be classed as a hearsay exception or as not hearsay is debatable since the reliability of the assertions rests upon the veracity of a witness who is present and testifying.[2] Which way the argument is decided seems not to have affected the requirements for admissibility, however, and it is convenient to treat recorded recollection as a hearsay exception since at least some failure of memory is required.

Should the writing be admitted into evidence and be allowed to be taken to the jury room? Federal Rule 803(5) resolves the issue by resort to the ancient practice of reading the writing into evidence but not admitting it as an exhibit unless offered by the adverse party.

§ 280 Firsthand Knowledge

The usual requirement of firsthand knowledge[3] that applies to witnesses and hearsay declarants is also enforced in regard to past recollection recorded. Thus, where an inventory was offered and the witness produced to lay the necessary foundation testified that it had been made only partly from his own inspection and partly from information provided by an assistant, the inventory was inadmissible.

§ 281 Record Made While the Witness's Memory Was Clear

Despite some cases suggesting the contrary, the exception as generally stated requires that there be a written formulation of the memory. Federal Rule 803(5) uses the broad term "record," which, for example, a videotape or audio recording would satisfy. Moreover, the original must be produced or accounted for as is generally required when the contents of documents are sought to be proved.[4] However, the record need not have been prepared by the witness personally if the witness read and adopted it. Multiple-participant situations are considered further in § 283.

The record must have been prepared or recognized as correct at a time close enough to the event to ensure accuracy. Some opinions use the older strict formulation that requires the writing to have been either made or recognized as correct "at or near the time" of the events recorded. This requirement finds some support in psychological research suggesting that a rapid rate of memory loss occurs within the first two or three days following the observation of an event. However, the trend is toward accepting the formulation favored by Wigmore, which would require only that the writing be made or recognized at a time when the events were fairly fresh in the mind of the witness.[5] The formula of Federal Rule 803(5) is "when the matter was fresh in the witness's memory." The cases vary as to the length of time lapse allowable, and while the period of time between the event and the making of the memorandum or record is a critically important

---

2   Compare with the treatment of prior statements of a witness in supra § 251.

3   See supra § 10.

4   See generally supra Ch. 23.

5   *See* 3 Wigmore, Evidence § 744 (Chadbourn rev. 1970).

factor, a mechanical approach, looking only to the length of time that has passed rather than focusing on indications that the memory remained fresh, should not be employed.

§ 282 Impairment of Recollection

The traditional formulation of the rule required that the witness who made or recognized the record as correct must testify that he or she lacks any present memory of the event and therefore is unable to testify concerning it. A few courts took a more relaxed position, suggesting that, although the witness retains more present recollection than allowed under the traditional requirement, the prior recorded statement was more complete and more reliable than testimony based upon the witness's memory. An occasional case has supported complete abandonment of the requirement, arguing that failure of memory adds nothing to the credibility of the statement.

Clouded by the passage of time, present recollection is often less accurate than a statement made at a time when recollection was fresh and clear. However, completely eliminating the requirement that the witness must have some memory impairment would likely encourage the use of statements carefully prepared for litigation under the supervision of claims adjusters or attorneys or under other circumstances casting significant doubt upon the reliability of the statement.

These competing concerns are accommodated by phrasing the requirement not in absolute terms but as a lack of sufficient present recollection to enable the witness to testify fully and accurately. This standard of the Federal Rule has assumed the dominating position in preference to eliminating any requirement of impaired memory.

Is the requirement of the Federal Rule that the witness "now cannot recall well enough to testify fully and accurately" satisfied when an apparently reluctant witness seeks to avoid testifying to a particular fact by claiming no memory? A number of courts have answered this question affirmatively. Perhaps that result does no great violence to the underlying hearsay concerns since the witness is still required to establish the accuracy of the statement and is available for at least some limited cross-examination. However, whether this pattern meets the literal requirement of the rule that the witness "now cannot recall" or is consistent with either the historical function of this exception or the intention of the rulemakers is far from clear.

§ 283 Proving the Accuracy of the Record; Multi-Party Situations

As a final assurance of reliability, either the person who prepared the writing or one who read it at a time close to the event must testify to its accuracy. This may be accomplished by a statement that the person presently remembers recording the fact correctly or remembers recognizing the writing as accurate at an earlier time. Also, if present memory is inadequate, the requirement may be met by testimony that the declarant knows it is correct because of a habit or practice to record such matters accurately or to check them for accuracy. At the extreme, some courts find sufficient testimony that the individual recognizes his or her signature and believes the statement correct because the witness would not have signed it if he or she had not believed it true at the time.

No particular method of proving the accuracy of the memorandum is prescribed by Federal Rule 803(5), which merely requires that it be "accurately reflects the witness's knowledge." However, the witness must acknowledge at trial the accuracy of the statement. An assertion of its accuracy in the acknowledgment line of a written statement or such an acknowledgment made previously under oath is not sufficient.

Courts have been relatively liberal in finding that the witness has acknowledged the accuracy of a prior statement, particularly where the witness is apparently hostile or reluctant to testify but does not repudiate the statement. A special danger of misuse of the exception occurs when this weak proof of the statement's accuracy operates in combination with the argument, discussed in the preceding section, that reluctance to testify satisfies the exception's requirement that a witness have insufficient memory of the event. The statement as recorded by the second party may not have accurately reflected the declarant's knowledge, particularly as to details, and the limited examination of a reluctant declarant may not produce its correction.

Typically, past recollection recorded involves one person, with a single witness making the original observation, recording it, and verifying its accuracy. When the verifying witness did not prepare the report but merely examined it and found it accurate, the matter involves a cooperative report, but the substantive requirements of the exception can still be met by the testimony of a single individual—the person who read and verified the report.

A somewhat different type of cooperative report is involved when one person orally reports facts to another person, who writes them down. A store clerk or timekeeper, for example, may report information to a bookkeeper. In this situation, courts have held the written statement admissible if both individuals testify. First, the person reporting the facts testifies to the correctness of the oral report (although at the time of the testimony, the detailed facts cannot be remembered), and second, the recorder of that statement testifies to faithfully transcribing the oral report. Although inartfully drafted by Congress, the Federal Rule continues to permit admission of such multi-party statements.

Chapter 29

REGULARLY KEPT RECORDS

Table of Sections

---

§ 284 Admissibility of Regularly Kept Records

Regularly kept records may be offered in evidence in many different situations, although in most the record is offered as evidence of the truth of its terms. In such cases the evidence is hearsay, and some exception to the hearsay rule must be used if the record is to be admitted. Often no special exception is needed, however, as the record comes within the terms of another exception. For example, if the record was made by a party to the suit, it is admissible against that party as an admission.[1] If the entrant is produced as a witness, the record may be used to refresh memory,[2] or it may be admissible as a record of past recollection.[3] Sometimes the record may be admissible as a declaration against interest.[4] The present chapter is concerned with those situations in which a specific exception to the hearsay rule for regularly kept records is employed.

§ 285 The Origin of the Regularly Kept Records Exception and the Shopbook Vestige

By the 1600s in England, a custom emerged in the common law courts of receiving the "shop books" of tradesmen and craftsmen as evidence of debts for goods sold or services rendered on open accounts. Since most tradesmen were their own bookkeepers, the rule permitted a reasonable means of avoiding the harsh common law rule preventing a party from appearing as its own witness. Nevertheless, theoretical objections to the self-serving nature of this evidence, apparently coupled with abuse of it in practice, led to a statutory curb in 1609 that limited the use of a party's shopbooks to

---

[1]   See generally supra § 254.

[2]   See generally supra § 9.

[3]   See generally supra Ch. 28.

[4]   See generally infra Ch. 33.

a period of one year after the debt was created unless a bill of debt was given or the transaction was between merchants and tradesmen. The higher courts refused to recognize the books at all after the year had elapsed, although in practice such evidence was received in the lower courts with small claims jurisdiction.

During the 1700s, a broader doctrine began to develop in the English common law courts. At first, this doctrine permitted only the use of regular entries in the books of a party by a deceased clerk, but it was expanded to cover books regularly kept by third persons who had since died. By 1832, the doctrine was firmly grounded, and its scope was held to include all entries made by a person, since deceased, in the ordinary course of the maker's business.

The development of the doctrine in America was less satisfactory, however. In the colonies, limited exceptions for the books of a party based on the English statute of 1609 and Dutch practice were in force. In addition to requiring that the entries be regularly made at or about the time of the transaction and as a part of the routine of the business, other common restrictions were that (1) the party using the book not have had a clerk, (2) the party file a supplemental oath to the justness of the account, (3) the books bear an honest appearance, (4) each transaction not exceed a certain limited value, (5) witnesses testify from their experience in dealing with the party that the books are honest, (6) the books be used only to prove open accounts for goods and services furnished the defendant (thus making them unavailable for proof of loans and goods and services furnished under special contract or furnished to third persons on defendant's credit), and (7) other proof be made of the delivery of some of the goods.

Not until the early 1800s did the American equivalent of the English general exception for regular business entries by deceased persons emerge. As the doctrine gained acceptance, however, often no provision was made for the "shop books" of a party, whose admissibility continued to be controlled by the restrictive statutes. This failure made little sense, especially in view of the fact that abolition of the party's disqualification as a witness[5] removed the justification for treating the books of a party as a special problem. Most courts today take the reasonable position that the remaining shop book statutes are alternative grounds for admissibility.

§ 286 The Regularly Kept Records Exception in General

The hearsay exception for regularly kept records is justified on grounds of trustworthiness and necessity that underlie other hearsay exceptions. Reliability is furnished by the fact that regularly kept records typically have a high degree of accuracy. The regularity and continuity of the records are calculated to train the recordkeeper in habits of precision; if of a financial nature, the records are periodically checked by balance-striking and audits; and in actual experience, the entire business of the nation and many other activities function in reliance upon records of this kind. The impetus for receiving these hearsay statements at common law arose when the person or persons who made the entry, and upon whose knowledge it was based, were unavailable because of death, disappearance, or other reason.

The common law exception had four elements: (1) the entries must be original entries made in the routine of a business, (2) the entries must have been made upon the personal knowledge of the recorder or of someone reporting the information, (3) the

---

[5]   See supra § 65.

entries must have been made at or near the time of the transaction recorded, and (4) the recorder and the informant must be shown to be unavailable. If these conditions were met, the business entry was admissible to prove the facts recited in it.

The regularly kept records exception had evolved within the context of simple business organizations, using the typical records of a double-entry system of journal and ledger. In this setting, the common law requirements were not unduly burdensome. Control and management of complex organizations require correspondingly complicated records, however, and business, government, and other institutions were becoming increasingly intricate.

While the theory of the exception was sound, some of the common law requirements were incompatible with modern conditions. The limitation to records of a business was unduly restrictive. The requirement of an original record was inconsistent with modern developments in record keeping. The need to account for nonproduction of all participants in the process of assembling and recording information was a needless and disruptive burden in view of the unlikelihood that any of those involved would remember a particular transaction or its details. Also, what witnesses were required to lay the necessary foundation for the records was sometime uncertain. Since the courts seemed unable to resolve these difficulties, relief was sought in legislation, and even before the enactment of the Federal Rules, the exception was governed by statute or rule virtually everywhere.

The Commonwealth Fund Act and the Uniform Business Records as Evidence Act provided the principal models for the early legislative reforms. Their essential features are now incorporated in Federal Rule 803(6), which provides a hearsay exception, without regard to unavailability of declarant, as follows:

Records of a Regularly Conducted Activity. A record of an act, event, condition, opinion, or diagnosis if:

(A) the record was made at or near the time by—or from information transmitted by—someone with knowledge;

(B) the record was kept in the course of a regularly conducted activity of a business, organization, occupation, or calling, whether or not for profit;

(C) making the record was a regular practice of that activity;

(D) all these conditions are shown by the testimony of the custodian or another qualified witness, or by a certification that complies with Rule 902(11) or (12) or with a statute permitting certification; and

(E) the opponent does not show that the source of information or the method or circumstances of preparation indicate a lack of trustworthiness.

§ 287 Types of Records; Opinions; Absence of Entry

The usual statement of the business records exception to the hearsay rule suggests that oral reports are not within it, even if the other requirements for admissibility are met. The common law cases tended to speak in terms of entries in account books.[6] The Commonwealth Fund Act used the terms "writing or record" and the Uniform Act spoke of "record" as does Federal Rule 803(6). Given that the federal rule both uses the term

---

6   See supra § 285.

report and requires that it be "kept," there is no basis to find oral reports within the rule. The English position, however, is that oral reports may qualify under the exception.

Under the common law exception, the entries were required to be original entries and not mere transcribed records or copies. This restriction was based on the assumption that the original entries were more likely to be accurate than subsequent copies or transcriptions. In business practice, however, daily transactions, such as sales or services rendered, are customarily noted upon slips, memorandum books, or the like by the person most directly concerned. Someone then collects these memoranda and from them makes entries in a permanent book, such as a journal or ledger. In these cases, the entries in the permanent record sufficiently comply with the requirement of originality. They would certainly be admissible if the slips or memoranda disappeared and should be admissible as the original permanent entry without proof as to the unavailability of the tentative memoranda. This practice also serves the interest of convenience, since it is much easier to use a ledger or similar source than slips or temporary memoranda when the inquiry concerns the state of an entire account. Of course, the slips or memoranda would also be admissible if they should be offered.

With regard to opinions in business records, two types of issues arise. The first concerns lay opinions or conclusions, which are largely conclusory forms of expression. The opinion rule should be restricted to governing the manner of presenting live testimony where a more specific and concrete answer can be secured if desired and should have little application to the admissibility of out-of-court statements, including business records.[7] The second and more difficult issue regards expert opinions within business records. Federal Rule 803(6) specifically provides that an admissible regularly kept record may include an "opinion," which will ordinarily be that of an expert. Such opinions should be governed by the ordinary restrictions on expert qualifications and proper subjects for expert opinions. In § 293, these issues are examined for hospital records.

Sometimes the absence of an entry relating to a particular transaction is offered as proof that no such transaction took place. For example, a car rental agency's records showing no lease or rental activity for a certain vehicle may be offered to prove that the defendant, found in possession of the car, stole it. Courts have generally admitted the evidence for this purpose, and Federal Rule 803(7) specifically so provides.

§ 288 Made in the Routine of a "Business"; Accident Reports; Reports Made for Litigation; Indications of Lack of Trustworthiness

The early cases construed the requirement of a "business" literally and excluded, for example, records kept in connection with loans made by an individual not in the business of loaning money to others on the basis that they were not concerned with "business." The Commonwealth Fund Act defined "business" much more expansively to "include business, profession, occupation and calling of every kind." The Uniform Act added "operation of institutions, whether carried on for profit or not."

In Federal Rule 803(6), the term includes "business, organization, occupation, or calling, whether or not for profit." Applying to a "record," of a "business" broadly defined, this rule has broad scope. It has been held to encompass such diverse items as a diary of tips kept by a blackjack dealer, notations on calendar of daily illegal drug sales,

---

[7]   See supra § 11.

performance evaluations of hospital employees, resignation letters, a hospitals scrapbook of newspaper articles showing visiting hours, a restaurant "guest check" with defendant's name written on it, a videotape made by prison of removal of prisoner from his cell, a bill of lading, an automobile lease by dealer, a logbook of malfunctions of a machine, loan counselor's notes of telephone conversations with defendant, e-mail reports of potential security breaches of clients' confidential data, and an appraisal of a painting for purposes of insurance. These examples are all in addition to account books and their counterparts, which might more readily fall within the usual concept of business records. Hospital records are specially treated below in § 293 and computer-stored records are the subject of § 294.

Records, such as diaries, if of a purely personal nature not involved in declarant's business activities, do not fall within the rule, but if kept for business purposes are within the rule. Memoranda of telephone conversations are treated similarly. The breadth of the exception is also demonstrated by cases holding that the activity need not be legal for the record to qualify. Some church records are covered by the business records exception, while those related to the family history of members are the subject of Federal Rule 803(11).

Until recently, under the English rules, both the matter or event recorded and the recording of it must have been performed pursuant to a duty to a third person. Under American law, conduct in the regular course of the business is required instead.

How far Rule 803(6) goes in requiring not only that the record must be made in the regular course of a business, but that "making the record was a regular practice of that activity" is disputed. What might be termed non-routine records, which are nevertheless made in the course of regularly conducted activities, are the focus of concern here. Unusual records, often outside the expertise assured by a business routine, are properly excluded for that reason. Other records of this type will be properly excluded because of motivational concerns arising from the fact they were generated for litigation purposes, discussed immediately below. While an occasional court has focused on the apparent intention of Congress as reflected in the wording of the rule that the making of the memorandum be the "regular practice," the general focus is much more on whether the basic concern of trustworthiness is met for non-routine records.

An important set of concerns revolves around the purpose of the report and the circumstances of its preparation, particularly reports of accidents. The seminal case is *Palmer v. Hoffman*,[8] a suit against railroad trustees arising out of an accident at a railroad crossing. The engineer of the train involved was interviewed two days after the accident by a representative of the railroad and a representative of the state public utilities commission and signed a statement giving his version of the incident. He died before trial, and the statement was offered by the defendants, who contended that the railroad obtained such statements in the regular course of its business.

Affirming the trial court's exclusion of the report, the Supreme Court stated:

[The report] is not a record made for the systematic conduct of the business as a business. An accident report may affect that business in the sense that it affords information on which the management may act. It is not, however, typical of entries made systematically or as a matter of routine to record events

---

[8]　318 U.S. 109 (1943).

or occurrences, to reflect transactions with others, or to provide internal controls . . . . Unlike payrolls, accounts receivable, accounts payable, bills of lading and the like, these reports are calculated for use essentially in the court, not in the business. Their primary use is in litigating, not in railroading.[9]

Consequently, the report was held not to have been made "in the regular course" of the business within the meaning of the federal statute then providing for the admissibility of business records.

While *Palmer* has been subject to various interpretations, the most reasonable reading is that it did not create a blanket rule of exclusion for accident reports or similar records kept by businesses. Rather, it recognized a discretionary power in the trial court to exclude evidence which meets the letter of the exception, but which under the circumstances appears to lack the reliability business records are assumed ordinarily to have. The existence of a motive and opportunity to falsify the record, especially in the absence of any countervailing factors, is of principal concern.

The Federal Rule incorporates this reading of *Palmer* by admitting of reports that otherwise comply with the requirements of the rule if "neither the source of information nor the method or circumstances of preparation indicate a lack of trustworthiness." Logic places the initial burden on the proponent of the documents admission to show that it meets the basic requirements of the rule with the opponent having the burden to show lack of trustworthiness based on the source of information or the method or circumstances of preparation. When records are prepared in anticipation of litigation, they will often, but not always, demonstrate that lack of trustworthiness.

Police reports and records can, of course, meet the requirements for the regularly kept records exception to the hearsay rule, but they also qualify under the hearsay exception for public records and reports.[10] Federal Rule 803(8) contains certain restrictions upon the use of police reports in criminal cases, and the question has arisen whether those restrictions can be avoided by offering police reports under the regularly kept records exception, which imposes no such limitations. The answer, while complicated, is generally "no." This subject is discussed in greater detail in Section 296 infra.

§ 289 Made at or near the Time of the Transaction Recorded

A substantial factor in the reliability of any system of records is the promptness with which transactions are recorded. The formula of Federal Rule 803(6) is "at or near the time." Whether an entry made subsequent to the transaction has been made within a sufficient time to render it within the exception depends upon whether the time span between the transaction and the entry was so great as to suggest a danger of inaccuracy by lapse of memory. In addition, the failure to make a timely record may suggest non-regularity in the making of the statement and may indicate motivational problems related to records prepared for litigation purposes.

---

[9] *Id.* at 113–14.

[10] See generally infra Ch. 30.

§ 290 Personal Knowledge; All Participants in Regular Course of Business

The common law exception for regularly kept records required that the entries have been made by one with personal knowledge of the matter entered or upon reports to the maker by one with personal knowledge. The entrant was required to be acting in the regular course of business, and if the information was supplied by another, that person also was required to be acting in the regular course of business. If the information was transmitted through intermediaries, they were subject to the same requirement. The application of the regular course requirement to all participants in the process of acquiring, transmitting, and recording information was consistent with, indeed mandated by, the theory of the hearsay exception.

Early legislation did not deal clearly with whether the information must initially be acquired by a person with firsthand knowledge and whether that person and all others involved in the process must be acting in the regular course of the business. The Commonwealth Fund Act required that the record be "made in the regular course of . . . business" and provided that "other circumstances . . ., including lack of personal knowledge by the entrant or maker, may be shown to affect its weight, but they shall not affect its admissibility." The Uniform Act also required that the record be "made in the regular course of business," and in addition required that "in the opinion of the court, the sources of information, method and time of preparation were such as to justify its admission." Federal Rule 803(6) requires that the record be "made . . . by—or from information transmitted by—someone with knowledge."

Assuming, as is reasonable, that "knowledge" means firsthand knowledge, then Rule 803(6) answers the first part of the above question affirmatively, to the effect that the person who originally feeds the information into the process must have firsthand knowledge. Also, the person making the record must be in the regular course of business, Rule 803(6) using the term "kept" to describe records produced in the regular course of business.

Any doubts about drafting should be resolved by referring to the underlying theory of the exception, namely, a practice and environment encouraging the making of accurate records. If any person in the process is not acting in the regular course of the business, then an essential link in the trustworthiness chain fails, just as it does when the person feeding the information does not have firsthand knowledge. *Johnson v. Lutz,*[11] the leading case on this point, was decided under the New York version of the Commonwealth Fund Act, which held inadmissible a police officer's report insofar as it was not based upon his personal knowledge but on information supplied by a bystander. Courts generally followed its analysis for various formulations of the exception, including Federal Rule 803(6). Thus, if information going from observation to final recording is to be received under this exception, all parts of the process must be in the regular course of business. One alternative is for someone within the organization to verify the accuracy of the information provided by the "outsider."

Also, when the matter recorded itself satisfies the conditions of some other hearsay exception, the requirement that the person initially acquiring the information must be acting in the regular course of the business does not apply. For example, a police officer

---

[11]   170 N.E. 517 (N.Y. 1930).

may include in a report of an automobile accident a damaging statement by one of the drivers, who later becomes a party to litigation. The statement qualifies as an admission, and the report may be used to prove it was made. That the officer has no firsthand knowledge of the correctness of the statement is immaterial if it was the officer's responsibility to record this type of information. These issues are discussed further in connection with multiple hearsay.[12]

Direct proof that the maker of the statement had actual knowledge may be difficult, and proving specifically the identity of the informant with actual knowledge may be impossible. Evidence that it was someone's business duty in the organization's routine to observe the matter will be prima facie sufficient to establish actual knowledge. This principle does not dispense with the need for personal knowledge but permits it to be proved by evidence of a routine practice and a reasonable assumption that such practice was followed with regard to a particular matter, or by other appropriate circumstances.

§ 291 Unavailability

Historically, if the person who made a business record was present as a witness, the record could be used to refresh recollection, or if that person could not recall the facts, the record might be admissible as past recollection recorded. If, however, the witness could not be produced in court, then these alternative avenues to admissibility for the business record could not be used. A need for a special hearsay exception for business records in such cases was apparent. Unfortunately, as sometimes happens, the reason why the rule came into existence became a requirement, in this instance a requirement of unavailability.

The process of calling a series of participants, only to have them testify that referring to the business record did not refresh their recollection, or at best to give rote testimony that it was their practice to be accurate, was a waste of the court's time and disruptive to the business involved with no corresponding benefit. Yet no other response could reasonably be expected from participants in the keeping of business records under modern conditions. The reliability of the record could be shown by evidence other than the testimony of participants, as had been done when a participant was unavailable. Accordingly, unavailability virtually disappeared as a requirement under common law decisions. Federal Rule 803(6) does not require unavailability, and the unavailability requirement has now almost entirely disappeared from American jurisdictions.

§ 292 Proof; Who Must Be Called to Establish Admissibility

The demise of the requirement of unavailability had its intended impact upon the method of proving business records. No longer was it necessary to call each available participant and exhaust the possibility of refreshing memory or establishing the record as past recollection recorded. Any witness with the necessary knowledge about the particular recordkeeping process could testify that the regular practice of the business was to make such records, that the record was made in the regular course of business upon the personal knowledge of the recorder or of someone reporting in the regular course of business, and that the entries were made at or near the time of the transaction. The Uniform Act provided that the foundation might be laid by "custodian or another qualified witness," and this language was incorporated in Federal Rule 803(6).

---

[12]   See infra § 324.1.

Perhaps the most commonly used foundation witness is a person in authority in the recordkeeping department of the business. Whether or not such a person falls within the term "custodian" may be questioned, but certainly he or she is "a qualified witness." In fact, anyone with the necessary knowledge is qualified; this witness need not have firsthand knowledge of the matter reported or actually have prepared the report or observed its preparation.

Problems may arise when one business organization seeks to introduce records in its possession but actually prepared by another. As discussed later in this section, Federal Rule 803(6) now provides for a certification process that may make it easier to have the organization that prepared the record establish the foundation. Absent such certification, the foundation can often be laid by the organization possessing the records. One related problem is the apparent requirement of the Federal Rule that the organization laying the foundation have made the record. Courts have ignored this problem or have held it satisfied if the second organization incorporates the records into their own. Obviously, mere possession or "custody" of records under these circumstances does not qualify employees of the possessing party to lay the requisite foundation, and reliance by the organization on records created by others, although an important part of establishing trustworthiness, without more is not sufficient. However, when the business offering the records of another has made an independent check of the records, has integrated them into their own business operation in a way that establishes trustworthiness or contains other assurances of trustworthiness, or can establish accuracy by other means, the necessary foundation may be established.

In order to facilitate the introduction of regularly kept records, Congress enacted a statute providing a certification procedure for foreign records in criminal cases. Federal Rule 803(6) was amended in 2000 to permit the foundation for business to be established without the appearance of the custodian or other qualified witness at trial if the requisite information is shown by a certification that complies with Rule 902(11), Rule 902(12), or a statute permitting certification. The provisions of Rules 902(11) and 902(12) require both certification that the requirements of Rule 803(6) have been met and advanced written notice of the intention to rely on this provision to permit the opportunity for challenge.

§ 293 Special Situations: (a) Hospital Records

In the past, specific statutory authority governed the admission of hospital records. Although some courts hesitated to expand the business record exception to hospital records, they are now admissible upon the same basis as other regularly kept records. This result is appropriate, for the safeguards of trustworthiness of records of the modern hospital are at least as substantial as the guarantees of reliability of records of business establishments generally.

History. Under standard practice, a trained attendant at a hospital enters upon the record a "personal history," including an identification of the patient, an account of the present injury or illness, and the events and symptoms leading up to it. This information, which may be obtained from the patient directly or from a companion, is elicited to aid in the diagnosis and treatment of the patient's injury or disease. Is this history admissible to prove assertions of facts it may contain? Two layers of hearsay are involved here, with the first being the use of the hospital record to prove that the statement was made. The primary issue is whether the specific entry involved was an entry made in the regular course of the hospital's business. If the subject matter falls within matters that under hospital practice are regarded as relevant to diagnosis or treatment or other hospital business, it is within the regular course of business.[13] If, on the other hand, the subject matter does not relate to those concerns, the making of the entry is not within the regular course of the hospital's business, and thus it is not admissible even for the limited purpose of proving that the statement was made.

Assuming that the hospital record is admissible to prove that the statement contained in the history was made, is this statement admissible to prove the truth of assertions made in it? In accordance with the general rule, the business record exception cannot support admission of the history because the declarant's action in relating the history was not part of a business routine of which he or she was a regular participant. However, if as is generally the case the history comes within one of the other exceptions to the hearsay rule, it is admissible.[14] The statements may, for example, constitute statements for the purpose of diagnosis or treatment,[15] admissions of a party opponent,[16] dying declarations,[17] declarations against interest,[18] or excited utterances.[19]

Diagnostic Statements. Professional standards for hospital records contemplate that entries will be made of diagnostic findings at various stages. These entries are clearly in the regular course of the operations of the hospital. The problem which they pose is one of the admissibility of an "opinion."[20] In the hospital records area, the opinion is usually one of an expert who would unquestionably be permitted to give it if personally testifying. While the requirement of qualification does not disappear, if the record is shown to be from a reputable institution, it may be inferred that regular entries were made by qualified personnel in the absence of any indication to the contrary.

When an expert opinion is offered by a witness personally testifying, the expert is available for cross-examination on that opinion. If the opinion is offered by means of a hospital record, no cross-examination is possible. Consequently, courts historically tended to limit the scope of opinions that could be introduced by this method. Ordinary diagnostic findings customarily based on objective data and not presenting more than average difficulty of interpretation were usually admitted, but diagnostic opinions that on their face were conjectural were often excluded.

Given that Federal Rule 803(6) specifically includes opinions or diagnoses, this historical distinction based on whether the opinion is objective or conjectural does not appear to survive, at least directly. However, admissibility of all such entries is not assured. First, where indications of lack of trustworthiness are shown, which may result from a lack of expert qualifications or from a lack of factual support, exclusion is warranted. Moreover, inclusion of opinions or diagnoses within the rule only removes the bar of hearsay. In the absence of the availability of the expert for explanation and cross-examination, the court may conclude that the probative value of this evidence is

---

[13] See supra §§ 277–278.

[14] See infra § 324.1.

[15] See supra Ch. 27.

[16] See supra Ch. 25.

[17] See infra Ch. 32.

[18] See infra Ch. 33.

[19] See supra § 272.

[20] See supra § 287.

outweighed by the danger that the jury will be misled or confused.[21] This concern is particularly significant if the opinion involves difficult matters of interpretation and a central dispute in the case, such as causation. Under these circumstances, a court operating under the Federal Rules, like earlier courts, is likely to be reluctant to permit a verdict to be reached on the basis of an un-cross-examined opinion and may require that the witness be produced.

Privilege. In most states, patients have been afforded a privilege against disclosure by physicians of information acquired in attending the patient and necessary for diagnosis and treatment.[22] While hospital records are generally privileged to the extent that they incorporate statements made by the patient to the physician and the physician's diagnostic findings, application of the privilege to information obtained by nurses or attendants is more complicated. On one hand, privilege statutes should arguably be strictly construed, and most do not mention nurses or attendants. On the other hand, information is usually gathered and recorded by them as agents of the physician and for the purpose of aiding the physician in treatment and diagnosis. The answer lies in interpreting the underlying privilege. If it would bar the direct testimony of a nurse or attendant, it should bar use of their hearsay statement under this exception; if it would not, such statements in hospital records should not be privileged.

§ 294 Special Situations: (b) Computer Records

Even though the scrivener's quill pens in original entry books have now been replaced by computer records, the theory behind the reliability of regularly kept business records remains the same. Provided a proper foundation is laid, computer-generated evidence should be admitted under the exception.

Most business records are now processed by computers. Although some commentators initially argued that evidence rules should be amended to add a rule specifically governing computer-generated evidence, this suggestion was not followed. Instead, Federal Rule 803(6) originally applied to a "data compilation, in any form," terminology intended to include records stored in computers, and courts and legislatures have judged the admissibility of such records by the hearsay exception for regularly kept records. The rule now simply uses the term "record," and courts have dealt competently with the admissibility of such evidence by applying Rule 803(6) or its common law or statutory counterparts fluidly to computer records as they became the norm.

The usual conditions for the exception are applicable.[23] The differences between traditional record-keeping methods and sophisticated electronic equipment, however, require some further exploration of foundation requirements. While paper records can be inspected and the process of keeping the record can often be tracked in a step-by-step manner, electronically processed data is not a visual counterpart of the machine record and is not subject to inspection until it takes the form of a printout.

The theory of trustworthiness supporting the regularly kept records exception assumes a reliable method for entering, processing, storing, and retrieving data. Moreover, the rule requires that "neither the source of information nor the method or circumstances of preparation indicate lack of trustworthiness." Issues may arise at any

---

[21]   See generally supra § 185.

[22]   See supra Ch. 11.

[23]   See supra §§ 286–290.

of the stages of the handling of the data regarding (1) computer hardware, (2) software or programming, and (3) accuracy or security.

Serious problems are rarely presented regarding computer hardware because most computer equipment used to produce records otherwise meeting the requirements of the exception is both standard and highly reliable, with few data errors resulting from defects in equipment. Testimony regarding equipment ordinarily need only describe the function that each unit performs in the process and that each is adequate for the purpose. Excursions into theory are not required or ordinarily appropriate.

Human factors involved in the programming of the computer and the development of software afford more frequent potential for errors. However, the trend here is not to require the proponent of the statement to call the programmer to lay the foundation for admission. With regard to questions of inaccuracy and data security, courts have not imposed rigid requirements. Thus, in the typical case, the proponent is not initially required to show periodic testing for programming errors or the elimination of all possibilities of data alteration or errors in data entry or programming.

While a well-laid foundation will touch upon each of the general areas noted above, the trend among courts has been to treat computer records like other business records and not to require the proponent of the evidence initially to show trustworthiness beyond the general requirements of the rule. The fact that the organization relies upon the record in the regular course of its business may itself provide sufficient indication of reliability, absent realistic challenge, to warrant admission.

As noted in an earlier section, in order to qualify under the hearsay exception for regularly kept records, a record must have been made in the regular course of business, and documents made for use in litigation frequently do not meet that requirement. Because of the motivation factor, such records typically lack the trustworthiness contemplated by the exception.[24] Also, the regularly kept records exception requires that entries must be made at or near the time of the event recorded.[25] The application of these general principles to the creation of a computer printout raise several specific problems. These issues are presented by a computer printout that is made (1) long after the data were entered into the system and (2) after litigation has commenced.

The question as to the timeliness of the creation of the record is answered by observing that the time requirement refers to when the entry into the data bank was originally made, not the time the printout was produced. With regard to documents prepared for use in litigation, the arrangement of the data in a form designed to aid litigation should not result in exclusion if the data and the retrieval processes are themselves reliable. For example, when information is recorded in the computer in the sequence in which it was received rather than organized by customers or transactions, reordering the data by computer should not present a barrier to its admission greater than a manual collation of related business records would. The evidence should not be rejected merely because it is not a visual counterpart of the electronic record. However, the court must consider whether the process producing the printout is reliable and whether the record may have been compromised by that process.

Another specific issue encountered with regard to computer records is whether records that are self-generated by the computer are hearsay at all. A frequently

---

[24]   See supra § 288.

[25]   See supra § 289.

encountered example of a record of this type is the trace report produced by telephone company computers when tracking a call made to a specific number. Because such records are not the counterpart of a statement by a human declarant, which should ideally be tested by cross-examination of that declarant, they should not be treated as hearsay, but rather their admissibility should be determined on the basis of the reliability and accuracy of the process involved.

Chapter 30

PUBLIC RECORDS, REPORTS, AND CERTIFICATES

Table of Sections

§ 295 The Exception for Public Records and Reports: (a) In General

The common law developed an exception to the hearsay rule for written records and reports of public officials under a duty to make them, made upon firsthand knowledge of the facts. These statements are admissible as evidence of the facts recited in them. The common law formulation of this hearsay exception has been broadened by decisions, statutes, and rules, discussed in the sections that follow. The most important of these modern formulations of the exception is the Federal Rule.

Federal Rule 803(8) provides, without regard to the declarant's availability, a hearsay exception for the following:

Public Records. A record or statement of a public office if:

(A) it sets out:

    (i)   the office's activities;

    (ii) a matter observed while under a legal duty to report, but not including, in a criminal case, a matter observed by law-enforcement personnel; or

    (iii) in a civil case or against the government in a criminal case, factual findings from a legally authorized investigation; and

(B) the opponent does not show that the source of information or other circumstances indicate a lack of trustworthiness.

The special trustworthiness of official written statements is found in the declarant's official duty and the high probability that the duty to make an accurate report has been performed.[1] The possibility that public inspection of some official records will reveal any inaccuracies and cause them to be corrected (or will deter the official from making them

---

[1]   See supra § 286 (related rationale for business records).

685

in the first place) has been emphasized by the English courts, which have imposed a corresponding requirement that the official statement be one kept for the use and information of the public. This limitation has been criticized, and the American courts have not adopted it. Although public inspection might provide a modest additional assurance of reliability, strictly limiting admissibility to records that are open to public inspection would be unwise because many documents with sufficient reliability to justify admission would be excluded.

The impetus for the development of this hearsay exception is the inconvenience of requiring public officials to appear and testify concerning the subject matter of their records and reports. Not only would this disrupt the administration of public affairs, but it almost certainly would create a class of official witnesses. Moreover, given the volume of business in public offices, the official written statement will usually be more reliable than the official's memory. For these same reasons, the declarant's unavailability is not required. The convenience of proof by certified copy,[2] the simplicity of foundation requirements,[3] and the lack of need for the testimony of a custodian make the official records exception an attractive method of proof when available.

§ 296 The Exception for Public Records and Reports: (b) Activities of the Office; Matters Observed; Investigative Reports; Restrictions on Prosecutorial Use

Under Federal Rule 803(8) matters falling within the hearsay exception for public records and reports are divided into three groups, which track the common law and statutory background:

(A)(i): Activities of the office. The first group includes the oldest and most straightforward type of public records, records of the activities of the office itself. An example is the record of receipts and disbursements of the Treasury Department. In addition to the assurances of reliability common to public records and reports generally, this group has the assurances of accuracy that characterize business records and are routinely admitted.

(A)(ii): Matters while under a legal duty to report. The second group consists of matters observed and reported, both pursuant to duty imposed by law. Rainfall records of the National Weather Service are illustrative. This general category of records is relatively uncontroversial except when the matter is observed by a police officer or other law enforcement personnel.

(A)(iii): Legally authorized investigation. In *Beech Aircraft Corporation v. Rainey*,[4] the Supreme Court resolved an issue that had previously divided lower federal courts. It rejected a narrow interpretation of "factual findings" and held that "factually based opinions and conclusions" could be included within the exception.[5] Under the exception, a wide range of agency findings are admissible.

The Court noted that the primary protection against admission of unreliable evidence was the Rule's provision directing exclusion of all elements of the report—both factual and evaluative—if the court determines that they lack trustworthiness. In

---

[2]   See supra § 240.

[3]   See supra § 224.

[4]   488 U.S. 153 (1988).

[5]   *Id.* at 163.

making the determination of trustworthiness, the four factors to be examined include: the timeliness of the investigation, the skill or experience of the investigator, whether a formal hearing was held, and the bias of the investigator. To be admissible, the record is not required to satisfy all four requirements, and if the record facially satisfies the requirements of the rule, the opponent has the burden to demonstrate lack of trustworthiness.

As the name indicates, these reports embody the results of investigation and accordingly are often not the product of the declarant's firsthand knowledge, required under most hearsay exceptions. Nevertheless, the nature and trustworthiness of the information relied upon, including its hearsay nature, is important in determining the admissibility of the report. Also, the statement must constitute the conclusion of a governmental agency as opposed to a mere accumulation of information, and it must not be an interim or preliminary document.

Restrictions on Use by Prosecution in Criminal Cases. As submitted by the Supreme Court and enacted by the Congress, what is now clause (A)(iii) of the Federal Rule prohibits the use of investigative reports as evidence against the accused in a criminal case. The limitation was included because of "the almost certain collision with confrontation rights which would result" from using investigative reports against the accused.[6]

As transmitted by the Supreme Court to the Congress, what is now clause (A)(ii) simply provided for including in the public records and reports exception "matters observed pursuant to duty imposed by law." In the course of debate on the floor of the House, concern was expressed that the provision might allow the introduction against the accused of a police officer's report without producing the officer as a witness subject to cross-examination. Accordingly, the provision was amended by adding the italicized words to read "matters observed pursuant to duty imposed by law as to which matters there was a duty to report, *excluding, however, in criminal cases matters observed by police officers and other law enforcement personnel.*" It was enacted as so amended.

The amendment raises a number of questions of varying importance:

(1) Can the accused in a criminal case use a report falling under (A)(ii)? Clearly the criminal defendant can use an investigative report which falls under (A)(iii). However, the language of (A)(ii) appears to prohibit the admission of all records of matters observed in criminal cases, which, if read literally, would exclude use by the defense as well as the prosecution. This meaning is not what Congress had in mind, and the cases have construed the provision to permit the defendant to introduce police reports under (A)(ii).

(2) What types of public officials are part of a "legally authorized investigation"? In its broadest form, this term has been construed to include "any officer or employee of a governmental agency which has law enforcement responsibilities."[7] In specific, "law-enforcement personnel" has been held to include a Customs Service chemist analyzing the seized substance in a narcotics case, border inspectors, and I.R.S. agents, but not a city building inspector, medical examiner, or judge. This second inquiry has, however, become somewhat less important as the courts have developed the exceptions examined

---

6   Fed. R. Evid. 803(8)(C) advisory committee's note.

7   United States v. Oates, 560 F.2d 45, 68 (2d Cir. 1977).

below for routine or nonadversarial governmental records and for circumstances where the declarant testifies at trial.

(3) Does the limitation of (A)(ii) apply to routine records? The courts have consistently answered that Congress did not intend to exclude observations characterized as "objective" and "nonadversarial" even though contained in law enforcement reports.

(4) Can the limitation of (A)(ii) and also that of (A)(iii) be avoided by resorting to some other hearsay exception? This question arises when the statement satisfies the requirements of some other hearsay exception that does not prohibit the use of police records and reports or investigative reports against the accused. For example, police reports can often meet the exception for recorded past recollection, and laboratory tests of materials have often been admitted as business records. Neither of these hearsay exceptions contains limitations like those of Rule 803(8)(A)(ii) & 803(8)(A)(iii).

The case first considering this issue answered with an unequivocal and uncompromising "no." It concluded that Congress meant to exclude law enforcement and investigative reports against defendants in criminal cases whatever route around the hearsay rule was chosen.[8] However, subsequent consideration by other courts has led to direct disagreement by some and to a number of exceptions. First, the limitations of (A)(ii) and (A)(iii) will not be extended to other hearsay exceptions if the maker is produced as a witness and subject to cross-examination since the essential purpose of Congress was to avoid admission of evidence not subject to cross-examination. Second, this limitation is inapplicable to proof of the absence of an entry in a governmental record.

§ 297 The Exception for Public Records and Reports: (c) Vital Statistics

If the requirement that the out-of-court declarant must have an official duty to make the report were strictly enforced, such matters as a minister's return upon a marriage license indicating that the ceremony had been conducted and the report of an attending physician as to the fact and date of birth or death would not be admissible. Consequently, this requirement has been relaxed with regard to matters involving various general statistics. Where the report was made to a public agency by one with a professional, although not necessarily an "official," duty to make the report, such as a minister or a physician, the courts have generally admitted the record to prove the truth of the reporter's statement. An alternative approach is to regard the maker of the report as acting as an official for purposes of making the report. However, the mere fact that a report is required by law is not sufficient to convert it into a public report. The person making the report—a motorist, for example, completing a required accident report—can scarcely be regarded as acting in a temporary official capacity or under a professional duty.

The law concerning records of vital statistics is largely statutory, and states generally have enacted legislation on the subject. Federal Rule 803(9) covers records in any form of births, deaths, and marriages, if the report is made to a public office pursuant to requirements of law. While the rule looks largely to local law to determine the duty to

---

⁸ *Id.* at 78.

make the report and for its content, it should not be regarded as borrowing and incorporating the local law as to trustworthiness, and the federal rule governs that issue.

As to routine matters, such as place and date of birth or death and "immediate" cause of death, such as drowning or gunshot wound, admissibility is seldom questioned. However, entries in death certificates as to the "remote" cause of death, such as suicide, accident, or homicide, usually are made on the basis of information obtained from other persons and predictably involve the questions that have been raised with regard to investigative reports generally, and courts have divided on admissibility. When conclusions of this type are involved, the provisions of Rule 803(8), which is equally applicable and involves a much more careful treatment of the issues, should be applied. Thus, the restrictions on using police and investigative reports against accused persons contained in Federal Rule 803(8)(A)(ii) & 803(8)(A)(iii) should be applied to this aspect of records of vital statistics. Similar tests for the admissibility of investigative reports under Federal Rule 803(8)(A)(iii), such as the expertise and motivation of the preparer and the sources of information used, should prevail.

§ 298 The Exception for Public Records and Reports: (d) Judgments in Previous Cases, Especially Criminal Convictions Offered in Subsequent Civil Cases

Since reports of official investigations are admissible under the official written statement exception, the judgment of a court, made after the full investigation of a trial, might logically also be admissible in subsequent litigation to prove the truth of those facts necessarily determined in the first action, and it certainly should prove the fact of the conviction where relevant. Guilty pleas and statements made in the course of litigation may constitute declarations against interest[9] or statements of a party-opponent[10] and under those exceptions avoid the bar of the hearsay rule. Where the doctrines of res judicata, collateral estoppel, or claim or issue preclusion make the determinations in the first case binding in the second, a judgment in the first case is not only admissible in the second, but it is conclusive against the party as a matter of substantive law. Historically, the courts were often unwilling to admit judgments in previous cases if neither res judicata nor collateral estoppel applied under the theory they were hearsay.

A variety of reasons have been advanced for this rule, particularly in civil cases. Civil cases often involve numerous issues and determining what issues were decided by a judgment may be difficult. This argument, however, should only require that one offering a judgment establish first that the judgment in fact determined an issue relevant to the instant litigation. Another argument advanced is that the party against whom the judgment is offered may not have had an opportunity to be present and participate in the first action. In many cases, the party will in fact have been present and have had, not only an opportunity, but also a strong motive to defend. However, the appropriate question is not the party's opportunity to have been present at the official investigation but whether that investigation provided adequate assurance of reliability.

The argument against admissibility has particular merit for judgments offered against a criminal defendant. When that judgment was rendered against another,

---

9   See infra Ch. 33.
10   See supra Ch. 25 (admissions generally) & § 257 (guilty pleas).

admitting it would violate the defendant's constitutional right of confrontation. Admitting civil judgments rendered against the defendant directly raises constitutional issues as well.

Other arguments against admissibility of prior judgments relate to the danger of undue prejudice and the need for orderly administration of trials. Also, juries may have difficulty grasping the distinction between a prior judgment offered as evidence and one that is conclusive, giving the judgment binding effect even if this is contrary to substantive law. A final argument is that if prior judgments are admissible parties offering them will rely heavily on them and not introduce significant other evidence with the result that the evidence available in the second case does not support a reliable decision. These arguments and the absence of authorization under a specific rule, such as 803(8)(A)(iii) or 803(22), have caused many courts to exclude a prior civil judgment offered in a subsequent civil case when offered under a public records and reports exception.

By contrast, most courts admitted a prior conviction for a serious criminal offense in a subsequent civil action even before codification of a rule of evidence. With serious offenses, the party against whom the judgment is offered was generally the defendant in the criminal case and therefore had, not only the opportunity, but also the motive to defend fully. In addition, because of a heavier burden of proof, a criminal judgment requires significantly more reliable evidence than a judgment in a civil case. The trend was most obvious when the judgment was offered in a subsequent civil case in which the convicted defendant sought to benefit from his criminal offense—for example, a convicted arsonist sues to recover upon his fire insurance policy. The strong desire to prevent this result undoubtedly influenced courts to admit the judgment of conviction, and some courts also held it was conclusive in the civil case. Courts soon moved to a general admissibility of a prior criminal conviction in a civil action against the party who was previously the criminal defendant.

Often the exception is limited to convictions for serious offenses under the theory that convictions for misdemeanors do not represent sufficiently reliable determinations to justify dispensing with the hearsay objections. Judgments of acquittal, however, are still inadmissible in large part because they may not present a determination of innocence, but rather only a decision that the prosecution has not met its burden of proof beyond a reasonable doubt.

Federal Rule 803(22), quoted in the footnote,[11] is generally consistent with these trends and has a number of significant features. First, only criminal judgments of conviction are included. Judgments in civil cases are not included, their effect being left to the law of res judicata or preclusion. Second, it covers only serious crimes, i.e., punishable by death or imprisonment for more than one year, thus eliminating problems

---

[11]   Rule 803(22), Judgment of a Previous Conviction, provides:

Evidence of a final judgment of conviction if:

(A) the judgment was entered after a trial or guilty plea, but not a nolo contendere plea;

(B) the conviction was for a crime punishable by death or by imprisonment for more than a year;

(C) the evidence is admitted to prove any fact essential to the judgment; and

(D) when offered by the prosecutor in a criminal case for a purpose other than impeachment, the judgment was against the defendant. The pendency of an appeal may be shown but does not affect admissibility.

associated with convictions of lesser crimes. Third, the rule does not apply to judgments of acquittal. Fourth, when offered by the government in criminal prosecutions, judgments of conviction of persons other than the accused are admissible only for purposes of impeachment. When the judgment of conviction is offered in a civil case, however, it is treated as are investigative reports generally, and there is no restriction as to the parties against whom the evidence is admissible. Fifth, judgments entered on pleas of *nolo contendere* are not included within the exception.[12] Finally, the provision merely removes the hearsay bar from a qualifying judgment and does not purport to dictate the use to be made of the judgment once admitted. Applicable rules of res judicata or preclusion will be given effect. Otherwise the evidence may be used "substantively" or for impeachment, as may be appropriate.

§ 299 The Exception for Official Certificates: (a) In General

For purposes of the law of evidence, a certificate is a written statement issued to an applicant by an official that recites certain matters of fact. It is not a part of the public records of the issuing office, although a common form of certificate is a statement that a document to which it is attached is a correct copy of such a record. The common law was strict about admitting certificates as hearsay exceptions, for the most part requiring statutory authority.

The relation between certification and a public record may be illustrated by proof of marriage. If the celebrant of a marriage issues a certificate that the marriage was performed and gives it to the parties, this document is not a public record, and admission in evidence must be under some other hearsay exception. If, however, the celebrant makes a "return" of the license, i.e., a redelivery to the issuing official with an endorsement of the manner in which the authority was exercised, then the return becomes a part of the public record and is admissible under that hearsay exception.

Federal Rule 803(12) provides a hearsay exception for certificates of marriage and similar ceremonies performed by the clergy, public officials, or others authorized to perform the ceremony where the certificate is issued at the time of the act or within a reasonable time thereafter. Certification is also provided for a large variety of matters by statutes, with corresponding provisions for admissibility in evidence. Federal Rule 802 continues the effectiveness of such statutes.

§ 300 The Exception for Official Certificates: (b) Certified Copies or Summaries of Official Records; Absence of Record

When a purported copy of a public record is presented in court accompanied by a certificate that the purported copy is correct, a two-layered hearsay problem is presented. First, is the public record within the hearsay exception for that kind of record? Second, is the certificate within the hearsay exception for official certificates? The first question has been considered in the earlier sections of this chapter. The second question involves a specialized application of the certification procedure discussed generally in the immediately preceding section.

The early common law generally required a statutory duty to certify. However, the Supreme Court long ago rejected this position with respect to certification of copies of public records, and the American common law rule remains that a custodian has, by

---

[12]   See supra § 257.

virtue of the office, the implied duty and authority to certify the accuracy of a copy of a public record in the custodian's official possession. The usual practice is to prove public records by copy certified as correct by the custodian, and many statutes so provide. Federal Rule 1005 allows proof of public records by copy, without producing or accounting for the original,[13] and Rule 902(4) provides for authentication by certificate.

In the absence of a statute to the contrary, the usual view has been that the authority to certify copies of public records is construed literally as requiring a copy and does not include paraphrases or summaries. Thus, a certificate saying "our records show X" is not admissible to prove X.

By analogy to the rule that nonoccurrence of an event may be proved by a business record containing no entry of the event where the practice was to record such events, proof of nonoccurrence may be made by absence of an entry in a public record where such matters are recorded. However, absence of the entry or record could at common law be proved only by testimony of the custodian. This limitation has been modified by many statutes, and Federal Rule 803(10) defines a hearsay exception for a certification in accordance with Rule 902 or for testimony that a diligent search failed to disclose a record, report, or entry used to prove the absence of the record, report, or statement or the nonoccurrence or nonexistence of a matter which should otherwise have been recorded. The rule is phrased to include not only proving nonoccurrence of an event of which a record would have been made, but also the non-filing of a document allowed or required by law to be filed. Courts have insisted that the requirement of a "diligent search" must be satisfied but have not required that a specific form of words be used to meet that requirement.

---

[13]   See supra § 240.

Chapter 31

TESTIMONY TAKEN AT A FORMER HEARING OR IN ANOTHER ACTION

Table of Sections

---

§ 301 Introduction

Upon compliance with requirements designed to guarantee an adequate opportunity for cross-examination and after showing that the witness is unavailable, testimony given previously may be received in the pending case. The prior testimony may have been given during a deposition or at a trial. It may have been received in a separate case or in an earlier hearing of the present case.

Depending upon the precise hearsay definition used, this evidence, which is usually called "former testimony," could be classified as an exception to the hearsay rule or considered as nonhearsay under the theory that the requirements of the hearsay concept have been met. The former view is accepted generally today; the latter was espoused by Wigmore.[1] In this treatise, former testimony is classified as a hearsay exception under the general definition of hearsay developed earlier that treats as hearsay all prior statements offered for their truth.[2]

Cross-examination, oath, the solemnity of the occasion, and the accuracy of modern methods of recording testimony all combine to give former testimony a high degree of reliability. Accordingly, to allow its use only upon a showing of unavailability may seem to relegate former testimony to an undeserved second-class status. The result is, however, explained by the strong preference to have available witnesses testify in open court.

This exception was one widely regulated by statute. The predecessor statutes have generally been replaced by rules like Federal Rule 804(b)(1), Former Testimony, which upon a showing of unavailability, excepts from the hearsay rule:

---

[1]   5 Wigmore, Evidence § 1370 (Chadbourn rev. 1974).

[2]   See supra § 246.

Testimony that:

(A) was given as a witness at a trial, hearing, or lawful deposition, whether given during the current proceeding or a different one; and

(B) is now offered against a party who had—or, in a civil case, whose predecessor in interest had—an opportunity and similar motive to develop it by direct, cross-, or redirect examination.

Former testimony may often be admitted without meeting the requirements discussed in this chapter, which are applicable only when the evidence is offered under this exception. When the former testimony is offered for some nonhearsay purpose—to show the commission of the act of perjury, to show that testimony against the accused furnished the motive for retaliation against the witness, to refresh recollection, or to impeach a witness at the present trial by proving that earlier testimony was inconsistent—the restrictions of the hearsay exception do not apply. Likewise, if offered for a hearsay purpose but under some other exception, e.g., as the admission of a party-opponent or past recollection recorded, only the requirements of the other exception must be satisfied.

§ 302 The Requirement of Oath and Opportunity for Cross-Examination; Unavailability

To be admitted under this hearsay exception, former testimony must have been given under the sanction of an oath or affirmation. More frequently at issue is the requirement that the party against whom the former testimony is now offered, or perhaps a party in like interest,[3] must have had a reasonable opportunity to cross-examine.

Actual cross-examination is not required if the opportunity was afforded and waived. Whether cross-examination was conducted or waived, admissibility under this exception is not judged by the use made of the opportunity to cross-examine but rather the availability of the opportunity. This point is amply demonstrated in cases holding that the opportunity to cross-examine at a preliminary hearing in a criminal case provides sufficient opportunity even though few criminal defendants, for a number of reasons, fully exercise that opportunity. However, circumstances may differ sufficiently between the prior hearing and the present trial to bar admission under this requirement, as where questions on a particular subject would have been largely irrelevant at the earlier proceeding. Moreover, as discussed in later sections, the opportunity to cross-examine must have been such as to render the cross-examination actually conducted or the decision not to cross-examine meaningful in the light of the circumstances prevailing when the former testimony was given.[4]

If a right to counsel exists when the former testimony is offered, a denial of counsel when the testimony was taken renders it inadmissible. However, a general finding of ineffective representation at the prior hearing does not automatically require rejection of the testimony; the adequacy of the cross-examination under the facts must be determined. Improper judicial interference may render the opportunity to cross-examine inadequate. However, restrictions upon cross-examination do not have this consequence unless very substantial, some courts holding that they must render the testimony

---

[3]   See infra § 303 (discussing when parties are "in like interest").
[4]   See infra § 304.

inherently unreliable. Similarly, the fact that a party was less able to impeach the witness at the prior hearing will ordinarily not bar its later use under this exception.

The opportunity to cross-examine is not construed literally; rather the party must have the opportunity to develop the testimony through questioning. Thus, if a party calls and examines a witness and this testimony is offered against that same party in a subsequent trial, the witness' testimony may be admitted.

If evidence is offered under the former testimony exception to the hearsay rule, it is offered as a substitute for testimony given in person in open court, and the strong policy favoring personal presence requires that unavailability of the witness be shown before the substitute is acceptable. If the witness is present in court and is available for cross-examination, his or her former testimony may be admitted under some circumstances as a prior statement of a witness.[5] Exclusion of prior testimony for reasons relating to availability will generally occur only when the witness is absent from court but is not unavailable as defined by evidence rules or the Confrontation Clause. Unavailability under the hearsay rule and problems of confrontation, which are issues common to a number of hearsay exceptions, are discussed elsewhere.[6]

§ 303 Identity of Parties; "Predecessor in Interest"

The haste and pressure of trials cause lawyers and judges to speak in catchwords or shorthand phrases to describe evidence rules. Thus "identity of parties" was often spoken of as a requirement for the admission of former testimony. It is a convenient phrase to indicate a situation where the underlying requirement of adequacy of the present opponent's opportunity for cross-examination would usually be satisfied. But as a *requirement*, identity of parties (or, for that matter, identity of issues)[7] is hardly a useful generalization. It both obscures the true purpose of the requirement and must be hedged with too many qualifications to be helpful.

Historically, courts recognized a number of situations where identity of parties has not been required. An important inroad upon strict identity of parties results from the recognition, developed under Wigmore's guidance, that it is only the party against whom the former testimony is now offered whose presence as a party in the previous suit is significant. Second, if both the proponent and opponent of the evidence were parties in the former proceedings where the testimony was taken, the presence of additional parties in either or both proceedings is immaterial. Third, identity of parties is not required as to a party against whom prior testimony is offered when that party is a successor in interest to the corresponding party in the former suit. This notion, to which the label "privity" is attached, is considered to offer adequate protection to the party opposing admission. Finally, if the party against whom the former testimony is now offered, though not a party to the former suit, actually cross-examined the witness (personally or by counsel) about the relevant matters or was accorded a fair opportunity for such cross-examination and had a like motive for such examination, then the former testimony may be received.

The next step in this progression away from the formalistic requirement of identity of parties would be to treat neither identity of parties nor privity as requirements, but

---

[5]   See supra § 251.

[6]   See supra §§ 252–253.

[7]   See infra § 304.

merely as means to an end. Under this view, if a party in the former suit had a motive similar to the present party to cross-examine about the subject of the testimony and was accorded an adequate opportunity for such examination, the testimony could be received against the present party. Identity of interest in the sense of motive, rather than technical identity of cause of action or title, would satisfy the test. Under this perspective, the argument that it is unfair to force upon a party another's cross-examination or decision not to cross-examine loses its validity with the realization that other hearsay exceptions involve no cross-examination whatsoever and that the choice is not between perfect and imperfect conditions for the giving of testimony but between imperfect conditions and no testimony at all.

Exactly how Federal Rule 804(b)(1) should be interpreted regarding these issues remains unclear. As sent to Congress by the Supreme Court, the prior testimony exception would have taken the next step described above and admitted prior testimony if the party against whom that testimony was offered, or a party who had a "similar motive," had an opportunity to examine the witness. The House Judiciary Committee, however, objected to this formulation on the ground that "it is generally unfair to impose upon the party against whom the hearsay evidence is being offered responsibility for the manner in which the witness was previously handled by another party."[8] Accordingly, it substituted a requirement that "the party against whom the testimony is now offered, or in a civil action or proceeding *a predecessor in interest*, had an opportunity and similar motive" to examine the witness,[9] and this version of the rule was enacted.

While the impact in civil litigation of this congressional modification is cloudy, one point is clear: when the testimony is offered against a criminal defendant, the defendant must have been a party to the former proceeding. The rule as enacted eliminates doubts under the Confrontation Clause raised by the Court's version, which would have allowed examination by a substitute. However, by its literal terms the rule insists on identity of prosecution also, which would appear to bar a defendant in a federal prosecution from introducing exculpatory testimony from a related state case given by an unavailable witness. Exclusion of such evidence implicates due process considerations, and quite likely was not intended by Congress.

For civil cases this unfortunately oblique legislative history is more troubling, providing no definitive meaning for the term "predecessor in interest." As enacted, the rule requires that there has been an opportunity to examine the witness by the party against whom now offered or by a "predecessor in interest" with similar motive. The explanation offered by the report of the House Committee is only modestly helpful. After asserting the general unfairness of requiring a party to accept another's examination of a witness, quoted above, the report stated: "The sole exception to this, in the Committee's view, is when a party's predecessor in interest in a civil action or proceeding had an opportunity and similar motive to examine the witness. The Committee amended the Rule to reflect these policy determinations."[10] In adding the language regarding a predecessor in interest, the House Committee presumably meant to make some change. The Senate Committee, however, characterized the difference between the version

---

[8]   House Comm. on Judiciary, H.R. Rep. No. 650, 93d Cong., 1st Sess. 15 (1973), 1974 U.S. Code Cong. & Admin. News 7075, 7088.

[9]   *Id.* (emphasis added).

[10]   *Id.*

transmitted by the Supreme Court and that developed by the House Committee as "not great,"[11] and the Conference Committee remained silent on this point.

This state of legislative history has left little concrete guidance in determining congressional intent. Apparently, the House Subcommittee that drafted this modification intended it to require a "formal relationship" between the parties. How much weight to give such obscure indications of legislative intent is unclear, particularly since even the Senate Judiciary Committee appeared not to understand the significance of the modification, which suggests no Congressional "meeting of the minds." However, to ignore entirely the addition of the "predecessor in interest" language and construe the provision precisely as it was before that change would not be sensible. Thus, those courts that have read the language to mean no more than the general requirement that the prior party have a similar interest appear to have misconstrued the provision. On the other hand, interpreting the actions of Congress to require a strict privity approach, while not unreasonable, appears too rigid.

Courts construing the "predecessor in interest" language have taken several discrete approaches that appear consistent with the murky intent of Congress. One interesting approach is the so-called community of interest analysis. This approach requires some connection—some shared interest, albeit far less than a formal relationship—that helps to insure adequacy of cross-examination. A second approach appears consistent with congressional concerns about fairness and is even more broadly applicable than the community of interest analysis. It requires courts to ensure fairness directly by seriously considering whether the prior cross-examination can be fairly held against the later party. The testimony can be excluded if the objecting party shows that the cross-examination was inadequate by, for example, setting out the additional questions or lines of inquiry that he or she would have pursued. The opportunity to challenge the adequacy of the prior cross-examination directly, while ostensibly available in all situations, is not applied with rigor where there is no change in the identity of the party between the different proceedings.[12] The suggested interpretation accomplishes all that we know for certain was intended by the published legislative history—an interpretation of the term "predecessor in interest" that makes it fair to hold the present party responsible for the actions of another.

§ 304 Identity of Issues; Motive to Cross-Examine

Questions of identity of the issues involved in the former and present proceedings often arise in association with questions about identity of parties. This is to be expected because any supposed requirement of identity of issues is, like the rule about parties,[13] merely a means of fulfilling the policy of securing an adequate opportunity and sufficient motive for cross-examination.

While occasionally stated as a requirement that the issue in the two suits must be the same, the policy underlying this exception does not require that all the issues (any more than all the parties) in the two proceedings must be the same. At most, the issue on which the testimony was offered in the first suit must be the same as the issue upon

---

[11]   Senate Comm. on Judiciary, S. Rep. No. 1277, 93d Cong., 2d Sess. 28 (1974), 1974 U.S. Code Cong. & Admin. News 7051, 7074.

[12]   See supra § 302 & infra § 304 (discussing the ready admission in criminal trials of testimony from preliminary hearings).

[13]   See supra § 303.

which it is offered in the second. Additional issues or differences with regard to issues upon which the former testimony is not offered are of no consequence. Moreover, insistence upon precise identity of issues, which might have some appropriateness if the question were one of res judicata or estoppel by judgment, is out of place with respect to former testimony where the question is not of binding anyone but merely of salvaging the testimony of an unavailable witness. Accordingly, even before the enactment of the Federal Rules, the trend was to demand only "substantial" identity of issues.

Thus, neither the form of the proceeding, the theory of the case, nor the nature of the relief sought need be the same between the proceedings. Such formalism is not warranted by a policy of insuring adequacy of opportunity and motive for cross-examination. For example, in criminal cases where the first indictment charges one offense (robbery) and the second alleges another distinct offense (murder of the person robbed), that the two indictments arise from the same transaction is usually considered sufficient. The requirement has become, not a mechanical one of identity or even of substantial identity of issues, but rather that the issues in the first proceeding, and hence the purpose for which the testimony was offered, must have been such as to produce an adequate motive for testing on cross-examination the credibility of the testimony. How this requirement has been applied gives definition to the general rule.

In criminal cases, one important pattern involves introducing testimony from the preliminary hearing at trial; analogously, in a civil case, testimony from a discovery deposition is admitted. In another frequently encountered situation, testimony given against the accused in an earlier criminal trial is offered against the same accused in a civil case to which the criminal defendant is a party. Although an occasional exception will be found, prior testimony is generally admitted in these situations.

Somewhat in contrast, cases examining the admissibility of prior grand jury testimony of a witness against the government have reach mixed results. The typical fact pattern involves a witness who testified before the grand jury giving testimony that in some aspect exculpates the defendant and is unavailable at trial, usually because the witness asserted the Fifth Amendment privilege against self-incrimination. In *United States v. Salerno*,[14] the Supreme Court rejected the view that "adversarial fairness" requires admission of such testimony obtained by the government under a grant of immunity regardless of whether the "similar motive" test of Rule 804(b)(1) is satisfied.

Militating against admission, the government may be still investigating the crime and not yet be the opponent of the witness. It faces a relatively low burden of proof and has little incentive to contest an exculpatory statement if the case is strong and challenging the statement would reveal still secret information. On the other hand, the commitment to prosecute may be clear and the challenge of the exculpatory testimony obvious, yielding strong motivation to challenge it. Generally resting their results on specific facts that went to the existence of a "similar motive," the lower court decisions are somewhat divided on whether exculpatory grand jury testimony was admissible.

Courts do not require that the party at the earlier proceeding actually have conducted a full cross-examination of the witness. The cases emphatically hold that judgments to limit or waive cross-examination at that earlier proceeding based on tactics or strategy, even though these judgments were apparently appropriate when made, do not undermine admissibility. Instead, the courts look to the operative issue in the prior

---

[14]   505 U.S. 317 (1992).

proceeding, and if basically similar and if the opportunity to cross-examine was available, the prior testimony is admitted. However, at some extreme point, differences in the nature of the proceeding, the stakes involved, and even factual details with regard to the same core issue will result in exclusion of the prior testimony.

§ 305 The Character of the Tribunal and of the Proceedings in Which the Former Testimony Was Taken

If the accepted requirements of an oath, adequate opportunity to cross-examine on substantially the same issue, and present unavailability of the witness are satisfied, then the character of the tribunal and the form of the proceedings are immaterial, and the former testimony should be received. Accordingly, when these conditions are met, testimony has been received when taken before an arbitrator or a committing magistrate at a preliminary hearing,[15] in a sworn examination before the comptroller by the corporation counsel of a person asserting a claim against a city, at a driver's license revocation hearing or a broker's license revocation hearing, at a Coast Guard hearing or a hearing on motion to suppress, in a bankruptcy proceeding, or at a deposition in a foreign country. Because some of the above requisites were missing, testimony given in a coroner's inquest and a legislative committee hearing and narrative affidavits given during investigations government agents have been excluded. Also, exclusion in particular situations may be mandated by statute.

Some courts have held that, if the court in the former proceeding lacked jurisdiction of the subject matter, the former testimony is inadmissible, but others have concluded that the fact that the court may ultimately be held to lack power to grant the relief sought does not deprive it of power to compel attendance of witnesses and to administer oaths, and accordingly the former testimony was held admissible. A glaring usurpation of judicial power would call for a different ruling, but where the first court has substantial grounds for believing that it has authority to entertain the proceeding, and the party called upon to cross-examine should consider that the existence of jurisdiction is reasonably arguable, the guarantees of reliability are present. The question should be viewed, not as one of limits of jurisdiction, but whether the sworn statement of a presently unavailable witness was made under such circumstances of opportunity and motive for cross-examination as to make it sufficiently trustworthy to be received in evidence.

§ 306 Objections and Their Determination

May objections to the former testimony, or parts thereof, which could have been asserted when it was given, be made for the first time when offered at the present trial? There are sweeping statements in some opinions that this may always be done and in others that it is never allowable. The more widely approved view, however, is that objections which go merely to the form of the testimony—as on the ground of leading questions, unresponsiveness, or opinion—must be made at the original hearing when errors can be corrected. On the other hand, objections that go to the relevancy or the competency of the evidence may be asserted for the first time when the former testimony is offered at trial.

Whether the former testimony meets the requirements of the hearsay exception rule may depend on a question of fact. For example, is the witness unavailable? This and

---

[15] See supra §§ 302 & 304.

other preliminary questions of fact are to be decided by the court.[16] The declarant, whose former testimony is introduced, may be impeached as if he or she were a witness.[17]

§ 307 Methods and Scope of Proof

When only a portion of the former testimony of a witness is introduced by the proponent, the result may be a distorted and inaccurate impression. Under the rule of completeness, the adversary is entitled to introduce such other parts as fairness requires and to have them introduced at that time rather than waiting until the presentation of his or her own case.

Four methods of proof can be used to admit prior testimony:

1. Any firsthand observer of the giving of the former testimony may testify to what was said from unaided memory. This and the next method were frequently used before court stenographers became commonplace. The reporting witness need not profess to be able to give the exact words of the former witness but must satisfy the court that he or she is able to give the substance of all that the former witness has said, both on direct and cross-examination, about the subject matter relevant to the present suit.

2. A firsthand observer may testify regarding the former testimony by using a memorandum, such as counsel's or the stenographer's notes or transcript, to refresh the present memory of the witness.[18]

3. A witness who has made written notes or memoranda of the testimony at the time of the former trial, or while the facts were fresh in his or her recollection, and who will testify that he or she knows that they are correct, may use the notes as memoranda of past recollection recorded.[19]

4. In most states, the official stenographer's transcribed notes of the testimony are admitted when properly authenticated as evidence of the fact and purport of the former testimony, either by statute or under the hearsay exception for official written statements.[20] Although sound advocacy would make proof by any other form almost unthinkable where transcript or an official mechanical recording of the testimony exists, no rule of preference exists in most states to require an official transcript or recording over the unaided memory of a witness to the testimony, for example.

§ 308 Possibilities of Improving Existing Practice

In earlier editions, this treatise argued that hearsay admitted under the former testimony exception should be admitted regardless of the availability or unavailability of the declarant because few exceptions measure up in terms of the reliability of statements under former testimony.[21] For a time, the Supreme Court's analysis of the Confrontation Clause treated former testimony as perhaps uniquely inferior hearsay and

---

[16] See generally supra § 53.

[17] See infra § 324.2.

[18] See supra § 9 (discussing refreshing recollection).

[19] See generally supra §§ 279–283.

[20] See supra Ch. 30.

[21] See McCormick on Evidence § 261 (3d ed. 1984).

required for that reason a showing of unavailability when it was not required for much hearsay, including coconspirator statements and excited utterances.[22] Under such analysis, admitting prior testimony without unavailability was fanciful in criminal cases. The same conclusion is still accurate under the new "testimonial" approach of *Crawford v. Washington*,[23] which treats prior testimony as a firmly prohibited testimonial statement that is admissible only upon a showing that the witness/declarant is unavailable.[24]

The Supreme Court's characterization of prior testimony as uniquely weak hearsay as part of its earlier Confrontation Clause jurisprudence that had the effect of according it second-class status is incongruous as a matter of hearsay law. When compared with some other hearsay, such as declarations of present mental state and spontaneous utterances, where no showing of unavailability is required, prior testimony possesses arguably more substantial guarantees of trustworthiness. The fears that the proponent of prior testimony would routinely resort to the use of such testimony when witnesses are available appears overblown, and when the witness is available, the opponent is able to conduct meaningful cross-examination under Rule 806 even if the declarant is not called on direct examination.[25] However, when the Confrontation Clause is applicable, concerns other than hearsay analysis prevail to make prior testimony dependent on unavailability.

In civil cases, those concerns are not present and the law could be improved by a procedure that admitted prior testimony without requiring unavailability but upon notice to the opponent of intent to offer the testimony, thus affording that party an opportunity to produce available declarants when desired.

A second area where reform regarding the admissibility of prior testimony that should be considered concerns the application of the predecessor in interest concept. Under Federal Rule 804(b)(1), prior testimony is admissible if it "is now offered against a party . . . in a civil cases . . . whose predecessor in interest had . . . had an opportunity and similar motive to develop" the testimony. A very substantial issue is raised by the meaning of "predecessor in interest" and in particular whether the concept applies to situations where no economic or legal relationship exists between the parties.[26]

This problem in defining a predecessor in interest might be avoided if the courts recognized explicitly that the dimensions of the opportunity and motive to cross-examine may differ between the situation where the party itself was involved in the previous litigation and one where an unrelated party conducted the cross-examination. In the former situation, as exemplified by the use of preliminary hearing testimony against criminal defendants at trial,[27] parties have been, and should be, held responsible for previous strategic or tactical judgments and just plain poor lawyering. By contrast, in the situation where the parties are unconnected, the quality of the cross-examination should be scrutinized more carefully. Even if opportunity and motive for cross-examination are adequate, the costs of poor lawyering should not be imposed on a separate party. If courts become willing to examine directly and meaningfully the

---

[22]   White v. Illinois, 502 U.S. 346, 353–57 (1992).

[23]   541 U.S. 36 (2004).

[24]   *Id.* at 57–59.

[25]   See infra § 324.2.

[26]   See supra § 303.

[27]   See supra §§ 302 & 304.

adequacy of the testing of the prior testimony, issues about what constitutes a predecessor in interest will become much less important.

Chapter 32

DYING DECLARATIONS

Table of Sections

§ 309 Introduction

Of the doctrines that authorize the admission of special classes of hearsay, the doctrine relating to dying declarations is the most mystical in its theory and traditionally among the most arbitrary in its limitations. The notion of the special likelihood of truthfulness of deathbed statements was widespread long before the recognition of a general rule against hearsay in the early 1700s. Not surprisingly, nearly as soon as we find a hearsay rule, we also find an exception for dying declarations. The fact that dying declarations were received at the time the Constitution and the Bill of Rights were formed when the hearsay rule was not yet settled led the Supreme Court in *Crawford v. Washington*[1] to suggest that even if such a statement is testimonial it would be admissible as an exception to the Confrontation Clause objection.

§ 310 Requirements That Declarant Must Have Been Conscious of Impending Death and That Declarant Must Be Unavailable

The popular reverence for deathbed statements flows from two important limitations upon the dying declaration exception as developed at common law. Unlike several other limitations, which will be discussed in the next section, these two were arguably rational even though they restricted the exception too tightly.

The first was that the declarant must have been conscious that death was near and certain when making the statement. The declarant must have lost all hope of recovery. A belief in a probability of impending death would arguably make most people strongly disposed to tell the truth and hence guarantee the needed special reliability, but belief in the certainty of impending death, not its likelihood or probability, is the formula that was rigorously required. Perhaps this limitation reflected some lack of confidence in the reliability of "deathbed" statements generally.

---

[1]   541 U.S. 36 (2004).

The description of the declarant's mental state in Federal Rule 804(b)(2), which is set out in full in the footnote, is less emphatic than in the common law cases, merely saying "while believing that declarant's death to be imminent." Evidence that would satisfy the common law would clearly satisfy the rule, and a growing number of courts have recognized that a lesser showing will suffice.

Often this belief in the imminence of death is proved by the declarant's own statements of belief at the time—an expression of a "settled hopeless expectation"[2]—but the declarant need not have made such a statement. The belief may be shown circumstantially by the statements made to the declarant by doctors or others of the hopelessness of the condition, the apparent fatal quality of the wound, or other circumstances, but it must be shown. These preliminary questions of fact are to be determined by the court.[3]

The second historical limitation was that the declarant must be dead when the evidence is offered. However, the Federal Rules do not require that the declarant must be dead, only unavailable, which of course includes death.[4] Since the declarant need not die from the wounds or injuries, the length of time between a statement and death could not be dispositive of the statement's admissibility under the modern exception. Even under the earlier formulations, death was not required to have followed at any very short interval after the declaration. The critical issue throughout is the declarant's belief in the nearness of death at the time of the statement, not the actual swiftness with which death ensues after the statement or the immediacy of the statement after the injury.

§ 311   Limitation to the Use in Criminal Homicide Cases and Subject Matter Restrictions

If the courts in their creation of rules about dying declarations had stopped with the limitations discussed above, the result would have been a narrow, but rational and understandable, exception. The requirement of consciousness of impending death arguably tends to guarantee a sufficient degree of special reliability, and the requirement that the declarant must have died and thus be unavailable as a witness provides an ample showing of the necessity for the use of hearsay. This simple rationale of dying declarations sufficed until the beginning of the 1800s, and these declarations were admitted in civil and criminal cases without distinction and seemingly without untoward results. The subsequent history of the rule is an object lesson in the use of precedents to preserve and fossilize earlier judicial mistakes.

The first error occurred in limiting admissibility to homicide prosecutions. Sergeant East, in his widely used treatise, Pleas of the Crown, wrote that dying declarations are "admissible in this case on the fullest necessity; for it often happens that there is no third person present to be an eye-witness to the fact; and the usual witness on occasion of other felonies, namely, the party injured himself, is gotten rid of."[5] East's statement was seized upon for a purpose not intended, namely, an announcement that the sole justification for the admission of dying declarations is the necessity of punishing murderers who might otherwise escape for lack of the testimony of the victim. This need may exist, but the proposition that the use of dying declarations should be limited to

---

[2]   Shepard v. U.S., 290 U.S. 96, 100 (1933) (quoting Willes, J. in Reg. v. Peel, 2 F. & F. 21, 22).

[3]   See generally supra § 53.

[4]   See supra § 253 (discussing unavailability).

[5]   East, 1 Pleas of the Crown 353 (1803).

instances where it exists surely does not follow. Nevertheless, this proposition was further developed into a series of largely arbitrary limiting rules.

The first of these was the rule that the use of dying declarations was limited to cases of criminal homicide. Although the English courts in the 1700s had not done so, subsequent decisions refused to admit dying declarations in civil cases, whether death actions or other civil cases, or in criminal cases other than those charging homicide as an essential part of the offense. For example, in a rape prosecution, the declarations were held inadmissible even though the victim died before trial. Probably this restriction proceeded from a sense that dying declarations both rest on a somewhat questionable guarantee of trustworthiness and constitute a dangerous kind of testimony, which a jury is likely to handle too emotionally. However, these dangers are not likely to be less serious in a murder prosecution, where the statements are admitted, than they are in a civil action for wrongful death or in a prosecution for rape, where they were excluded.

As proposed by the Supreme Court, the exception for dying declarations was not restricted to any particular type of case. However, led by the House Judiciary Committee, Congress amended the exception and limited it to prosecutions for homicide and civil actions or proceedings. Thus, under the Federal Rule, dying declarations are inadmissible in criminal cases other than homicides.

The concept of necessity, limited to protection of the state against the slayer who might go free because of the death of his victim, produced another consequence. This was the further limitation that not only must the charge be homicide, but the defendant in the present trial must have been charged with the death of the declarant. When a marauder shot a man and his wife at the same time but the defendant was tried separately for the husband's murder, the dying declaration of the wife identifying the defendant as the assailant was excluded under this doctrine. Wigmore could not imagine "a more senseless rule of exclusion."[6] No such limitation appears in the Federal Rule.

A third limitation regarding the subject matter was conceptually sound, but its early formulations were sometimes arbitrary, i.e., declarations were admissible only insofar as they related to the circumstances of the killing and to the events more or less nearly preceding it in time and leading up to it. Under this version, declarations about previous quarrels between the accused and the victim would be excluded, while transactions between them leading up to and shortly before the present attack would be received. Some limitation as to time and circumstances is appropriate to enhance trustworthiness, but proper phrasing is difficult. Federal Rule 804(b)(2) requires only that the statement be one about the "cause or circumstances" of what he believed to an imminent death. Statements identifying an attacker are clearly admissible under this terminology, and those describing prior threats by, or fights and argument with, such person also meet its requirements. Within this more liberal framework, decisions to exclude may be made in terms of remoteness and prejudice under Rule 403.[7]

Finally, occasionally dying declarations have been limited with regard to statements elicited by leading questions. However, no blanket limitation against statements in response to questions is generally recognized or appropriate.

---

[6]   5 Wigmore, Evidence § 1433, at 281 n.1 (Chadbourn rev. 1974).

[7]   See supra § 185.

§ 312   Admissible on Behalf of Accused as Well as for Prosecution

The historical limitation of dying declarations to homicide cases, based on the extreme need for the decedent's statements and the sense of rough justice that admitting such statements against the murderer was only fair, might have led some courts to restrict dying declarations only to use by the prosecution. However, the unfairness of such a result was too apparent, and they have long been received on behalf of the defendant as well.

§ 313   Application of Other Evidentiary Rules: Personal Knowledge; Opinion; Rules About Writings

Other principles of evidence law present recurrent problems in their application to dying declarations. If the declarant did not have adequate opportunity to observe the facts recounted, the declaration will be rejected for lack of firsthand knowledge. When there is room for doubt as to whether the statement is based on knowledge, the question is for the jury. Expressions of suspicion or conjecture are to be excluded, however.

The knowledge requirement has sometimes been confused with the opinion rule, and this confusion may have led courts to make the statement that opinions in dying declarations will be excluded. The traditional opinion rule, designed as a regulation of the manner of questioning of witnesses in court, is generally inappropriate as a restriction upon out-of-court declarations.[8] Accordingly, most courts, including some that have professed to apply the opinion rule here, have admitted statements in which the declarant attributes purpose or lack of justification to the other party, which at one time would have been excluded as opinions if spoken by a witness on the stand.

Another problem is the application of the so-called best evidence rule.[9] Often the dying victim will make one or more oral statements about the facts of the crime and, in addition, may make a written statement, or the person hearing the statement may write it down and have the declarant sign it. When must the writing be produced, or its absence be explained? Any separate oral statement is clearly provable without producing a later writing, but the terms of a written dying statement cannot be proved as such without producing or accounting for the writing.[10] What if the witness who heard the oral statement, which was taken down and signed, offers to testify to what he or she heard? Wigmore argued that the execution of the writing does not call into play the parol evidence rule since that rule is limited to contracts and other "legal acts."[11] To a limited degree, some courts ruled otherwise. They did not exclude evidence of other oral statements made on the same occasion which were not embraced in the writing, but oral declarations embodied in a writing signed or adopted by the deceased were provable only by producing the written statement, if available. The result might be justified by the need for accuracy in transmitting to the tribunal the exact terms of this very important statement. However, these restrictions do not have a justification in modern evidence rules, and whether such limitations continue in any jurisdiction is unclear.

---

[8]   See supra § 11.

[9]   See supra Ch. 23.

[10]   See supra § 233.

[11]   5 Wigmore, Evidence § 1450(b), at 314 (Chadbourn rev. 1974).

§ 314 Instructions Regarding the Weight to Be Given to Dying Declarations

Historically, commentators and courts frequently theorized as to the weight properly to be given to dying declarations. As a result, the practice has grown up in some states of requiring or permitting the judge to instruct the jury that these declarations are to be received with caution or that they are not to be regarded as having the same value and weight as sworn testimony. In other jurisdictions, such instructions have been held to be improper. Others have considered it proper to direct the jury that they should give the dying declaration the same weight as the testimony of a witness.

While there may be merit in a standardized practice of giving cautionary instructions, the direction to give the declaration a predetermined fixed weight seems of questionable wisdom. The weight of particular dying declarations depends upon so many factors varying from case to case that no standardized instruction will fit all situations. Certainly, in jurisdictions where the judge retains common law power to comment on the weight of the evidence, the dying declaration is an appropriate subject for individualized comment. But where the judge lacks this power, as in most states, the wiser practice is to leave the weight of the declaration to the arguments of counsel, the judgment of the jury, and the consideration of the judge on motion for new trial.

§ 315 Suggestions for Changes in the Exception

In a remarkably forward-looking decision involving an action by the executor of the seller to recover on a land sale contract, the Kansas Supreme Court was confronted with a dying statement of the seller of "the truth about the sale."[12] Admission required departure from traditional common law limitations in that the case was civil, not a criminal homicide prosecution, and the statement did not relate to the cause or circumstances of death. In admitting the evidence, the court stated: "We are confronted with a restrictive rule of evidence commendable only for its age, its respectability resting solely upon a habit of judicial recognition, formed without reason, and continued without justification."[13]

As observed in earlier sections of this chapter, there has been some willingness to expand admissibility with respect to the type of case, as witnessed by Uniform Rule 804(b)(2), which would admit dying declarations in all cases. The exclusion of such hearsay under the Federal Rules from criminal cases other than prosecutions for homicide because of Congressional concern about the reliability of this form of hearsay seems to strike the wrong balance. Only a sense of very rough justice will admit statements in the most serious type of cases because the murder of the witness threatens to rob the court of valuable testimony but exclude them because of questionable trustworthiness in less serious criminal prosecutions. Under the terms of the Federal Rule, the need for the testimony is frequently just as great in non-homicide cases because the declarant, while not a murder victim, must be unavailable to testify. As a result, extension of the exception to other criminal cases would appear appropriate.

While the limitation on statements admissible under the exception to the circumstances of the declarant's death was not in the original Uniform Rules, it is a requirement of the Federal Rule, and departure from this limitation is found only in

---

[12]   Thurston v. Fritz, 138 P. 625 (Kan. 1914).

[13]   *Id.* at 627.

occasional rules and statutes. The restriction is generally sound because the connection between these circumstances and the statement helps to enhance its trustworthiness by reducing the dangers of poor memory and insincerity.

Chapter 33

DECLARATIONS AGAINST INTEREST

Table of Sections

---

§ 316 General Requirements; Distinction Between Declarations Against Interest and Admissions

Traditionally, two main requirements have been imposed on the statement against interest exception: first, either the declaration must state facts that are against the pecuniary or proprietary interest of the declarant or the making of the declaration itself must create evidence that would harm such interests;[1] second, the declarant must be unavailable at the time of trial.[2] Under the theory that people generally do not lightly make statements that are damaging to their interests, the first requirement provides the safeguard of special trustworthiness justifying most of the exceptions to the hearsay rule. The second is largely an historical development but operates usefully as a limiting factor. As with hearsay exceptions generally,[3] the declarant must have had firsthand knowledge. Minor qualifications may be added, such as the interest involved must not be too indirect or remote.

While sometimes erroneously called an admission against interest, this exception and the admission exclusion[4] are distinct. The traditional distinctions developed by Wigmore are generally followed. Thus, the admissions of a party-opponent may be introduced without satisfying any of the requirements for declarations against interest. First, while frequently admissions are against interest when made, they need not be and may, in fact, have been self-serving at that time.[5] Second, the party making the admission need not be, and seldom is, unavailable.[6] Third, the party making the admission need not have had personal knowledge of the fact admitted.[7] Accordingly, when the opponent offers a statement of a party, it should be submitted as, and tested by, the requirements for parties' admissions and not those for declarations against interest. On the other hand, statements of nonparties, which may not be introduced as

---

¹   See infra §§ 317–319.

²   See infra § 320.

³   See, for example, supra §§ 280, 290 & 313.

⁴   See supra Ch. 25.

⁵   See supra § 254 & infra § 319.

⁶   See supra § 254.

⁷   See supra § 255.

admissions, may be admitted if they are against interest and if the declarant is unavailable. Moreover, since the Federal Rules do not recognize admissions by persons in "privity" with parties,[8] the instant exception provides one of the principal alternative methods for introducing damaging statements made by a party's predecessor.

The Federal Rules preserve the hearsay exception as broadly developed at common law with respect to statements against pecuniary or proprietary interest and expand the definition to include statements against penal interest. Rule 804(b)(3), Statement Against Interest, admits statements of unavailable declarants as follows:

A statement that:

(A) a reasonable person in the declarant's position would have made only if the person believed it to be true because, when made, it was so contrary to the declarant's proprietary or pecuniary interest or had so great a tendency to invalidate the declarant's claim against someone else or to expose the declarant to civil or criminal liability; and

(B) is supported by corroborating circumstances that clearly indicate its trustworthiness, if it is offered in a criminal case as one that tends to expose the declarant to criminal liability.

§ 317 Declarations Against Pecuniary or Proprietary Interest; Declarations Affecting Claim or Liability for Damages

The traditional field for this exception has been that of declarations against proprietary or pecuniary interest. Common instances of the former are acknowledgments that the declarant does not own certain land or personal property or has conveyed or transferred it. Moreover, a statement by one in possession that he or she holds an interest less than complete ownership has traditionally been regarded as a declaration against interest, though it is obviously ambiguous in that it claims some rights.

The clearest example of a declaration against pecuniary interest is an acknowledgment that the declarant is indebted. Here the declaration, standing alone, is against interest on the theory that to owe a debt is against one's financial interest. This theory is routinely followed even though it may not be applicable in particular circumstances. Less obviously an acknowledgment of receipt of money in payment of a debt owing to the declarant is also traditionally classed as against interest. Here the fact of payment itself is advantageous to the receiver, but the acknowledgment of it is regarded as against interest because it is evidence of the reduction or extinguishment of the debt. Of course, a receipt for money which the receiver is to hold for another is an acknowledgment of a debt. Similarly, a statement that one holds money in trust is against interest.

The exception as developed by English courts narrowly focused it in the areas of debt and property, but the American cases extended the field of declarations against interest to include acknowledgment of facts which would give rise to a liability for unliquidated damages for tort or seemingly for breach of contract. The exception was also extended to statements of facts impairing a defense to a claim of damages otherwise available to the declarant.

---

[8] See supra § 260.

Federal Rule 804(b)(3)(A) is broadly drawn to include statements against pecuniary or proprietary interest in general, and more specifically those tending to subject declarant to civil liability, without being limited to tort or contract, and those tending to invalidate a claim by the declarant against another. This aspect of the rule thus occupies the entire area developed by the common law except for some of the more fanciful English decisions in tenancy cases.

§ 318 Penal Interest; Interest of Prestige or Self-Esteem

In 1844 in the *Sussex Peerage Case*,[9] the House of Lords determined that a declaration confessing a crime committed by declarant was not receivable as a declaration against interest. This decision was influential in confining the development of this exception to the hearsay rule within narrow materialistic limits. It was generally followed in this country in criminal cases for many years. Courts, while not repudiating the limitation, have sometimes justified admission of a third person's confession of crime in the civil context on the basis that the particular crime was also a tort and thus the statement was against material interest by exposing the declarant to liability for damages.

The practice of excluding third-person confessions in criminal cases certainly cannot be justified on the ground that an acknowledgment of facts rendering one liable to criminal punishment is less trustworthy than an acknowledgment of a debt. The motivation for the exclusion was no doubt a different one, namely, the fear of opening the door to a flood of witnesses testifying falsely to confessions that were never made or testifying truthfully to confessions that were false. This fear was based on the likely criminal character of the declarant and the witness who would recount the alleged statement, reinforced by the requirement that declarant must be unavailable, which would make perjury easier to accomplish and more difficult to punish.

Wigmore rejected the argument of the danger of perjury, since that danger is one that attends all human testimony, and concluded that "any rule which hampers an honest man in exonerating himself is a bad rule, even it if also hampers a villain in falsely passing for an innocent."[10] Under this argument, accepted by Justice Holmes in a famous dissent,[11] courts began to relax the rule of exclusion of declarations against penal interest in particular situations or generally. The inclusion of declarations against penal interest in Federal Rule 804(b)(3) has given great impetus to the use of this exception, and most of the recent case law and literature dealing with declarations against interest have centered on this aspect and its concomitant problems.

During the course of the expansion of the hearsay exception to include declarations against penal interest, the situation principally examined was whether a confession or other statement by a third person offered by the defense to exculpate the accused should be admissible. The traditional distrust of declarations against penal interest had evolved in that setting, and as a result, the Federal Rule included a requirement that the statement must be "supported by corroborating circumstances that clear indicate its trustworthiness."[12] While the possibility was recognized that statements against penal interest by third parties inculpating both the declarant and the defendant might also be

---

9   11 Cl. & F. 85, 8 Eng. Rep. 1034 (1844).

10   5 Wigmore, Evidence § 1477, at 359 (Chadbourn rev. 1974).

11   Donnelly v. United States, 228 U.S. 243, 277–78 (1913) (Holmes, J., dissenting).

12   See infra § 319(F) (discussing corroboration requirement).

offered by the prosecution to inculpate the accused, prior to the adoption of the Federal Rules the possibility of their admissibility was raised infrequently in cases or the literature. Under Rule 804(b)(3), admission of such statements has been relatively common. The issues involved in statements against penal interest made by third parties have raised a number of difficult issues, which arise because statements against interest, unlike personal admissions, can be offered against others. These issues will be examined in the next section.

Whether the hearsay exception for declarations against interest should be enlarged to include declarations against "social" interests has been debated. Traditionally, interests of this nature were not regarded as sufficiently substantial to ensure reliability. However, following the pattern of the original Uniform Rule, the Federal Rule, as proposed by the Supreme Court, included statements tending to make the declarant "an object of hatred, ridicule, or disgrace," but it was deleted from the rule by Congress. The provision was reinstated in Uniform Rule 804(b)(3) and has been adopted in a handful of states.

§ 319 Determining What Is Against Interest; Confrontation Problems

The determination of whether a statement is against interest involves three major concerns.

(A) The Time Aspect. As observed at the beginning of this chapter, the theory underlying the hearsay exception for declarations against interest is that people do not make statements that are harmful to their interests without substantial reason to believe that the statements are true. Reason indicates that the harm must exist at the time the statement is made; otherwise it can exert no influence on declarant to speak accurately and truthfully. That the statement later proves to be damaging—or, for that matter, beneficial—is without significance. Rather, the motivation and the statement must be contemporaneous.

(B) The Nature of the Statement. Under Rule 804(b)(3)(A), the statement must be such "a reasonable person in the declarant's position would have made only if the person believed it to be true" in view of the statement's adversity to declarant's interest. The interests involved are the declarant's pecuniary, proprietary, or penal interest. With regard to the latter, the statement need not be a confession, but it must involve substantial exposure to criminal liability.

(C) "Collateral" Statements and Williamson. In the archetypal case of *Higham v. Ridgway*,[13] an entry in the record book of a midwife was introduced showing a charge for attendance upon the mother for birth of a child together with an entry six months later showing payment of the charge offered to prove the date of birth of an individual. The court said the entry payment "was in prejudice of the party making it." However, although the entry of payment may have been against interest, the issue in the case was not payment, but the birth six months earlier. To this the court replied, "By the reference to the ledger, the entry there [of the birth] is virtually incorporated in the other entry [of payment], of which it is explanatory." In civil cases such as *Higham v. Ridgway*, admission of an associated statement may have been acceptable, even though not itself against interest, if it was closely connected to the statement against interest.

---

[13]   10 East 109, 103 Eng. Rep. 717 (K.B. 1808).

However, the generally sound decision to recognize statements against penal interest as qualifying under the exception put substantial new pressures on this element of the exception. When the contextual statement is not about a birth noted in the doctor's bill but rather is an incriminating statement offered by the prosecution against the accused found in a statement against the interest of a third party, both trustworthiness issues and the Confrontation Clause move unavoidably to the forefront.

In *Williamson v. United States*,[14] the United States Supreme Court resolved the most difficult issues presented by contextual statements by focusing on the definition of "statement" as used in this rule. It concluded that the principle behind the rule pointed to a narrow reading to the term—"a single declaration or remark" rather than "a report or narrative"—because only as to the more narrow meaning does the rationale hold that not particularly honest people make self-incriminatory statements only if they believe them to be true.[15] Indeed, one of the most effective ways to lie is to mix falsehood with truth; to mix within a larger report the exculpatory with the self-incriminating. The text of the Rule, the Court concluded, supports that result and overcame ambiguous Advisory Committee comments. The result is that only the specific parts of the narrative that inculpate qualify. The determination of whether a statement in this narrow sense is self-incriminatory requires examination of context. The reasoning of *Williamson* as to the narrow meaning of "statement" under Rule 804(b)(3) should apply as well to statements that are against interest in addition to penal interest, such as pecuniary interest, which would alter the result in cases such as *Higham v. Ridgeway*.

Williamson noted that under the new test statements against interest by third parties can continue to be admitted against the defendant where the statement does not mention the defendant directly but either logical inferences or the operation of law makes it incriminating to the defendant. Also, statements mentioning a defendant may also be admissible if a reasonable person in the declarant's position would realize that being linked to others implicated the declarant in another crime. Applying *Williamson*, federal courts have most frequently admitted third party statements that inculpate a defendant where two general conditions are satisfied: (1) the statement does not seek to curry the favor of law enforcement authorities, and (2) it does not shift blame.

(D) The Factual Setting. Whether a statement was against interest "can only be determined by viewing it in context"[16] and will often require a delicate examination of the circumstances under which it was made. That determination may depend on outside facts that existed at the time the statement was made that were reasonably known by the declarant but may not be disclosed in the statement. For example, whether a statement that declarant is a member of a certain partnership is against his or her pecuniary interest depends upon whether the firm is clearly solvent or is on an uncertain economic footing. Likewise, a statement that one has a contract to purchase a commodity, such as wheat, at a certain price is against or for interest depending upon the price in the market at the time of the statement.

The setting in which the statement is made is of particular importance where statements against penal interest are offered to inculpate the accused. If the declarant was in police custody when he or she made the statement, the statement or the part

---

[14] 512 U.S. 594 (1994).

[15] *Id.* at 599–600.

[16] *Id.* at 603.

implicating others very likely was made to curry favor even if it also inculpates the declarant, and if made to law enforcement agents, it is likely to be considered testimonial under the Confrontation Clause. However, courts have not treated being in custody as conclusively establishing that the statement is self-serving if it is voluntarily given, strongly incriminating of the declarant, and shows no indication of currying favor.

Relationships of friendship, family, and confidence bear on admissibility in a number of different ways. A relation of trust and confidence between speaker and listener could militate against awareness that making the statement might be against declarant's interest, but the possibility of disclosure appears to be enough. Instead, in the context of statements against penal interest, greater significance is attached to the fact a statement made to private individuals, rather than to law enforcement authorities, was not likely made for the purpose of currying favor. Moreover, making these statements to private individuals, particularly in informal settings, generally avoids a violation of the Confrontation Clause under *Crawford v. Washington*,[17] as discussed below in subsection (E). That the statement was made in a *relationship of trust* is also frequently utilized in of determining whether the statement has been corroborated, as discussed below in subsection (F).

(E) "Testimonial" Statements Inculpating Another. Although not impacting the hearsay definition, the Supreme Court's decision in *Crawford*, eliminates the practical importance of whether many of the most problematic statements against interest are admissible. *Crawford* does so through its treatment of the Sixth Amendment's Confrontation Clause. Statements made during police interrogation or the grand jury testimony of another participant in the crime without the right to cross-examine the declarant are now clearly inadmissible under the Confrontation Clause because they are testimonial. Thus, *Crawford* effectively eliminates some of the most problematic applications of the statement against interest exception that appeared to have particularly angered the Court and likely motivated the determination to revamp this constitutional protection.[18] By contrast, statements made to private individuals, particularly if made in an informal setting, generally are not considered testimonial and therefore outside the concern of the Confrontation Clause.

(F) Corroboration. As amended in 2010, Rule 804(b)(3)(B) requires corroboration to all statements against penal interest that inculpate the speaker and are offered into evidence in criminal litigation whether the statement exculpates or inculpates the defendant. The final sentence of Rule 804(b)(3)(B) states: "A statement tending to expose the declarant to criminal liability and offered in a criminal case is not admissible unless corroborating circumstances clearly indicate the trustworthiness of the statement." The Advisory Committee's Note to the 2010 amendment explains: "A unitary approach to declarations against penal interest assures both the prosecution and the accused that the Rule will not be abused and that only reliable hearsay statements will be admitted under the exception."

The federal courts have disagreed on whether the corroboration requirement applies to the veracity of the in-court witness testifying that the statement was made in addition to the clearly required showing that the statement itself is trustworthy. As a matter of standard hearsay analysis, the credibility of the in-court witness regarding the

---

[17]   541 U.S. 36 (2004).

[18]   *Id.* at 63–64 (describing the admission of accomplice confessions as the "unpardonable vice of the *Roberts* test").

fact that the statement was made is not an appropriate inquiry. Indeed, the Advisory Committee's Note stated that "the credibility of the witness who relates the statement is not a proper factor for the court to consider in assessing corroborating circumstances." However, given the strong historical concern over the possibility of perjured testimony that the exculpatory statement was made, some state courts may continue this theoretically unsound practice.

Corroboration of the trustworthiness of the out-of-court declaration focuses on two sets of factors. One set involves the circumstances of the making of the statement and the motivation of the declarant beyond the against-penal-interest character of the statement. Often an important factor in this first set is the nature of the relationship between the declarant and the person to whom the statement was made. A relationship of confidence and trust is generally viewed as providing a corroborating circumstance when the statement is inculpatory or exculpatory of someone who is not a friend or family member. On the other hand, when the statement is exculpatory of a friend or family member, the motivation of the declarant is suspect because of the concern that the statement was made to aid the relative or friend. The other set of factors involves information supporting or negating the content or truth of the statement. Cases rely on various concerns, including the nature and strength of the independent evidence of the conduct described in the statement.

(G) State of Mind of the Declarant. In strictest logic, attention in cases of declarations against interest, as with other hearsay exceptions, should focus on the actual state of mind produced in the declarant by the supposed truth-inducing circumstances, and a reasonable-person standard should not be the focus of attention. That, of course, is not the case. The usual standard is that found in Federal Evidence Rule 804(b)(3)(A): "a reasonable person in the declarant's position would have made only if the person believed it to be true." Difficulties of proof, probabilities, and the unavailability of the declarant all favor the accepted standard. However, statements of a declarant disclosing his or her ostensible actual mental state should certainly be received and should control in an appropriate case.

The exception has often been stated as requiring that there have been no motive to falsify. This is too sweeping, and the limitation can probably best be understood merely as a qualification that even though a statement must be against interest in one respect, if it appears that declarant had some motive, whether of self-interest or otherwise, which was likely to lead to misrepresentation of the facts, the statement should be excluded.

§ 320 Unavailability of the Declarant

The Federal Rule and the vast majority of the states require unavailability. While the requirement of unavailability followed its own course of development at common law with respect to declarations against interest, as was the case with other hearsay exceptions requiring unavailability of the declarant, the pattern is now largely standardized. Unavailability requirements are discussed in detail in Section 253 supra.

<h1 align="center">Chapter 34</h1>

VARIOUS OTHER EXCEPTIONS AND THE FUTURE OF THE RULES ABOUT HEARSAY

Table of Sections

§ 321   Learned Treatises, Industry Standards, and Commercial Publications

When offered to prove the truth of matters asserted in them, learned writings, such as treatises, books, and articles regarding specialized areas of knowledge, are clearly hearsay. Nevertheless, Wigmore argued strongly for an exception for such material.[1] According to his view, permitting such sources to be proved directly would not be as great a change as might at first be supposed because much of the testimony of experts consists of information they have obtained from such sources. Also, admitting the sources would greatly improve the quality of information presented. Wigmore concluded that learned treatises had sufficient assurances of trustworthiness to justify equating them with the live testimony of an expert. First, authors of treatises have no bias in any particular case. Second, they are acutely aware that their material will be read and evaluated by others in their field, and accordingly feel a strong pressure to be accurate.

Virtually all courts permit some use of learned materials in the cross-examination of an expert witness. Historically, several patterns developed. Most courts permitted use where the expert relied upon the specific material in forming the opinion given during direct examination. Some of these courts extended the rule to situations in which the witness admitted to having relied upon some general authorities although not the particular impeaching material, and other courts required only that the witness acknowledge that the material offered for impeachment was a recognized authority in the field and permitted use of the material on that basis despite the fact that the witness may not have personally relied upon it. Finally, some courts permitted use of such material to impeach without regard to whether the witness relied upon or acknowledged

---

[1]   6 Wigmore, Evidence §§ 1690–1692 (Chadbourn rev. 1976).

the authority of the source if either the cross-examiner established, or the court judicially noticed, the general authority of the material.

The material used to impeach was traditionally not admissible as substantive evidence received for its truth. Instead, its only impact was upon the witness' competency or the accuracy of the opinions rendered. Under the common law development of the practice, most courts were unwilling to adopt a broad exception to the hearsay rule for treatises and other professional literature. Although not finding them compelling, Wigmore recognized a number of arguments that could be made against recognizing an exception: (a) professional skill and knowledge shift rapidly, so printed material is likely to be out of date; (b) a trier of fact is likely to be confused by being exposed to material designed for the professionally-trained reader; (c) the opportunity to take sections of material out of context creates a danger of unfair use; and (d) most matters of expertise are really matters of skill rather than academic knowledge of the sort put in writing and therefore personally-appearing witnesses are likely to be better sources of evidence than written material. In Wigmore's view, the only arguably meritorious objection was the basic hearsay objection that the author is not available for cross-examination, but he concluded this concern was outweighed by the need for the evidence and the other assurances of accuracy.

The Federal Rules addressed these various issues by creating a hearsay exception for "learned treatises." Federal Rule 803(18), Statements in Learned Treatises, Periodicals, or Pamphlets, provides:

A statement contained in a treatise, periodical, or pamphlet if:

(A) the statement is called to the attention of an expert witness on cross-examination or relied on by the expert on direct examination; and

(B) the publication is established as a reliable authority by the expert's admission or testimony, by another expert's testimony, or by judicial notice.

The rule historically has been broadly applied including standards and manuals published by government agencies and industry or professional organizations. The rule requires that the reliability of the publication must be established, which demonstrates that it is viewed as trustworthy by professionals in the field. Authoritativeness can be established by the expert of either party or by judicial notice.

The rule also requires that the publication must be called to the attention of an expert on cross-examination or relied upon by the expert in direct examination. This provision is designed to ensure that the materials are used only under the sponsorship of an expert, who can assist the fact finder and explain how to apply the materials. This policy is furthered by the prohibition against admission as exhibits, which prevents sending the materials to the jury room.

While Rule 803(18) defines a hearsay exception, its requirements have an impact beyond hearsay concepts, in effect setting the general standards for the use of such documents to impeach. On the other hand, satisfying its requirements does not automatically guarantee admissibility. Documents that meet the terms of the rule are still excluded if their probative value is outweighed by their prejudicial impact or potential to confuse or mislead.

Courts have developed a somewhat related hearsay exception that includes publications such as reports of market prices, professional directories, city and telephone directories, and mortality and annuity tables used by life insurance companies. The justification for this exception is that the motivation for accuracy is high, and public acceptance depends upon reliability.

Federal Rule 803(17) defines a hearsay exception for such publications, covering "[m]arket quotations, lists, directories, or other compilations that are generally relied on by the public or by persons in particular occupations." While the precise definition of this exception is somewhat difficult, other than by example, some of its basic characteristics are clear. The list must be published in written form and circulated for use by others; it must be relied upon by the general public or by persons in a particular occupation; and it must pertain to relatively straightforward objective facts.

§ 322 Reputation as to Character; Statements, Reputation, and Judgments as to Pedigree and Family History; Reputation Concerning Land Boundaries and General History

(A) Reputation as to Character

Evidence regarding pertinent traits of character are admitted both to prove conduct in conformity with those traits and to impeach the credibility of witnesses, and in modern evidence law, these traits may be proved by evidence of reputation or opinion.[2] Proof of the trait by reputation raises a hearsay issue, which has traditionally been resolved by a hearsay exception that readily admitted such evidence. Federal Rule 803(21), which deals only with the hearsay aspect of the issue, recognizes an exception that admits reputation among associates or in the community when used to establish character.

(B) Statements, Reputation, and Judgments as to Pedigree and Family History

One of the oldest exceptions to the hearsay rule encompasses statements concerning family history, such as the date and place of birth and death of members of the family and facts about marriage, descent, and relationship. Under the traditional rule, declarations are admissible when made by the person whose family situation is at issue and by other members of the family. Under a liberal view adopted by some courts, declarations by nonfamily members with a close relationship to the family are also admitted. These statements were admissible, however, only upon a showing that the declarant is unavailable, that the statement was made before the origin of the controversy giving rise to the litigation in which the statement is offered (i.e., *ante litem motam*), and that there was no apparent motive for the declarant to misrepresent the facts.

Under the strict traditional view, the relationship of declarant to the family had to be proved by independent evidence, but this requirement did not apply where declarant's own family relationships were the subject of the hearsay statement. Firsthand knowledge by declarant of the facts of birth, death, kinship, or the like was not required. The general difficulty of obtaining other evidence of family matters, reflected in the unavailability requirement, furnished impetus for the hearsay exception. Reliability was assured by the probability that absent a motive to fabricate, discussions with relatives (and others intimately associated) regarding family members would be accurate.

---

[2]   See Fed. R. Evid. 404, 405 & 608; supra § 43.

Federal Rule of Evidence 804(b)(4), Statement of Personal or Family History, continues the requirement of unavailability of the declarant[3] and provides a hearsay exception for:

[a] statement about:

(A) the declarant's own birth, adoption, legitimacy, ancestry, marriage, divorce, relationship by blood, adoption, or marriage, or similar facts of personal or family history, even though the declarant had no way of acquiring personal knowledge about that fact; or

(B) another person concerning any of these facts, as well as death, if the declarant was related to the person by blood, adoption, or marriage or was so intimately associated with the person's family that the declarant's information is likely to be accurate.

The rule follows the liberal view in allowing statements by intimate associates of the family. It eliminates the traditional requirements that the statement have been made *ante litem motam* and without motive to misrepresent, leaving these aspects to be treated as questions of weight, or excluded under Rule 403 in extreme cases.[4] The narrow view of what is included in family history is continued.

The traditional hearsay exception went beyond the statements described above and allowed the use of contemporary records of family history, such as entries in a family Bible or on a tombstone, even though the author may not be identifiable. Federal Rule 803(13) follows this pattern in providing a hearsay exception irrespective of the declarant's availability for statements "of fact about personal or family history contained in a family record, such as a Bible, genealogy, chart, engraving on a ring, inscription on a portrait, or engraving on an urn or burial marker."

Matters of family history traditionally have also been provable by reputation in the family and sometimes in the community. Federal Rule 803(19), Reputation Concerning Personal or Family History, continues this pattern. It covers:

[a] reputation among a person's family by blood, adoption, or marriage—or among a person's associates or in the community—concerning the person's birth, adoption, legitimacy, ancestry, marriage, divorce, death, relationship by blood, adoption, or marriage, or similar facts of personal or family history.

The exception requires reputation among family members or members of the community to establish such facts and not simply assertions by individuals. In addition, Rule 803(23) permits admission of judgments "to prove a matter of personal, family, or general history, or boundaries, if the matter: (A) was essential to the judgment; and (B) could be proved by evidence of reputation."

(C) Reputation Regarding Land Boundaries and General History

When the location of boundaries of land is at issue, reputation is admitted to prove that location. Traditionally, the reputation not only had to antedate the beginning of the present controversy, but also it had to be "ancient," i.e., to extend beyond a generation.

---

[3]   See generally supra § 253 (discussing unavailability requirement).

[4]   See supra § 185.

Some recent cases suggest that the requirement is only that the monuments or markers of the original survey must have disappeared. Federal Rule 803(20) dispenses completely with a requirement that the reputation be ancient or that the passage of time have rendered other evidence of the boundaries unavailable.

Reputation is also admissible to prove a variety of facts which can best be described as matters of general history. Wigmore suggested that the matter must be "one as to which it would be unlikely that living witnesses could be obtained."[5] Rule 803(20) does not impose that requirement, although by use of the term "history" some requirement of substantial age is imposed. In addition, the matter must be one of general interest, so that it can accurately be said that there is a high probability that the matter underwent general scrutiny as the community reputation was formed. Thus, when the navigable nature of a certain river was at issue, newspaper accounts and histories describing its use during the nineteenth century were admissible to prove reputation for navigability at that time.

In addition to these well-developed exceptions, reputation evidence is sometimes admitted under statute or local law to prove a variety of other miscellaneous matters. These include ownership of property, financial standing, and maintenance of a house as an establishment for liquor-selling or prostitution.

§ 323 Recitals in Ancient Writings and Documents Affecting an Interest in Property

One method of authenticating a writing is to show that it is at least twenty years old, is unsuspicious in appearance, and came from a place of custody natural for such a writing.[6] Indeed, historically the "ancient documents" rule related only to authentication, but American courts began recognizing a hearsay exception for written statements that met these requirements. Thus, what originated as an aspect of authentication also became an exception to the hearsay rule in some jurisdictions.

Necessity, which produced the special authentication rule, was the primary stimulus for this hearsay exception. After passage of a long period of time, witnesses are unlikely to be available or, if available, are unlikely to recall reliably the events at issue.

As to a guarantee of trustworthiness, the mere age of the writing offers little assurance of truth since the prevalence of lying is unlikely to have changed much in twenty years. Advocates of the exception argued, however, that sufficient assurances of reliability existed. First, the dangers of mistransmission are minimized since the rule applied only to written statements. Second, the age requirement generally assured that the assertion was made before the beginning of the present controversy. Consequently, it was less likely that the declarant had a motive to falsify, and the statements are were less likely to have been influenced by partisanship. Finally, some additional assurance of reliability was provided by insistence, insofar as practicable, that the usual qualifications for witnesses and out-of-court declarants have been met. As a result, the writing was found inadmissible if the declarant lacked the opportunity for firsthand observation of the facts asserted.[7] Finally, the writing must not have appeared suspicious on its face.

---

[5] 5 Wigmore, Evidence § 1597, at 561 (Chadbourn rev. 1974).

[6] See supra § 225.

[7] See generally supra §§ 10 & 247.

Well before the drafting of the Federal Rules, a number of courts accepted a hearsay exception for recitals in an ancient deed. Thus, recitals of the contents and execution of an earlier instrument, of heirship, and of consideration were commonly received to prove those facts. Arguably these cases involve unusual assurances of reliability, especially where possession has been taken under the deed, and the exception could be limited to them. However, a number of courts applied the exception to other types of documents, and Federal Rule 803(16) followed suit, creating an exception for statements in authenticated documents that were at least 20 years old.

While the rule itself contained no limitation as to the kind of document that qualified, as long as it is at least twenty years old and properly authenticated,[8] several limitations were seen as providing some assurance of trustworthiness. The declarant was subject to the general requirement of firsthand knowledge, and by virtue of the authentication requirements, the document must not be suspicious in appearance, which in many situations supported its reliability. In addition, if the document contained or referred to a hearsay statement, the normal requirement of Rule 805 was generally applied,[9] mandating that other hearsay must be itself independently admissible under hearsay analysis.

However, in an amendment that became effective in 2017, the rule was substantially limited because of concerns about the exception's lack of direct guarantees of trustworthiness in the modern context of electronically stored information. Rule 803(16) now provides a hearsay exception only to "[a] statement in a document that was *prepared before January 1, 1998*, and whose authenticity is established."[10]

The Committee's Note on the amended rule succinctly sets out its justification for the change as follows:

> The ancient documents exception to the rule against hearsay has been limited to statements in documents prepared before January 1, 1998. The Committee has determined that the ancient documents exception should be limited due to the risk that it will be used as a vehicle to admit vast amounts of unreliable electronically stored information (ESI). Given the exponential development and growth of electronic information since 1998, the hearsay exception for ancient documents has now become a possible open door for large amounts of unreliable ESI, as no showing of reliability needs to be made to qualify under the exception.[11]

A somewhat related hearsay exception is recognized by Federal Rule 803(15), which covers statements contained in a document "that purports to establish or affect an interest in property if the matter stated was relevant to the document's purpose—unless later dealings with the property are inconsistent with the truth of the statement or the purport of the document." This exception imposes no requirement of age of the document, but it is limited to title documents, such as deeds, and to statements relevant to the purpose of the document.

The circumstances under which documents of a dispositive nature are executed, the character of the statements that will qualify, and the inapplicability of this exception if

---

[8]   See supra § 225.

[9]   See infra § 324.1.

[10]   Fed. R. Evid. 803(16) (emphasis added).

[11]   Fed. R. Evid. 803(16) advisory committee's note to 2017 amendment.

subsequent dealings have been inconsistent with the truth of the statement or the purport of the document, are considered sufficient guarantees of trustworthiness. A companion rule deals with the evidentiary status of such documents that have been recorded.

§ 324 The Residual Hearsay Exception

When proposing the federal rules, despite the extensive array of specific hearsay exceptions in the Federal Rules, the Advisory Committee felt it "presumptuous to assume that all possible desirable exceptions to the hearsay rule have been catalogued and to pass the hearsay rule to oncoming generations as a closed system."[12] Therefore, it proposed, for both available and unavailable declarants, a residual or catchall exception for statements "having comparable circumstantial guarantees of trustworthiness." Cautioning against wholesale modification of the established system of hearsay exceptions by unrestricted admission under the residual exceptions, the Committee observed that the residual exceptions "do not contemplate an unfettered exercise of judicial discretion, but they do provide for treating new and presently unanticipated situations which demonstrate a trustworthiness within the spirit of the specifically stated exceptions."[13]

The House Judiciary Committee deleted the provisions entirely, believing they injected too much uncertainty into the law and arguing that additional hearsay exceptions should be created by amending the rules. The Senate Committee responded by suggesting further restrictions on the proposed exceptions, and they were enacted as modified.

In arguing to restore these exceptions after the House deleted them, the Senate Judiciary Committee stated that it intended that the residual exceptions should be used "very rarely, and only in exceptional circumstances."[14] Although occasionally this language is quoted by a court in supporting its decision to exclude hearsay offered under a residual exception, resort to the exception has been very substantial. Perhaps most surprising is that the predominant use of the exceptions in federal courts, at least as reflected in the reported cases, has been by the prosecution in criminal cases.

In 1997, the two residual exceptions were combined into a single rule, Rule 807, a change that the Advisory Committee stated was not intended to change the meaning of the rules. Rule 807 was substantially amended, effective December 1, 2019. Amended Rule 807 is set out in the text, and for purposes of comparison, the prior version of the Rule is provided in the footnote.[15]

---

[12]   Fed. R. Evid. 803(24) advisory committee's note.

[13]   *Id.*

[14]   Senate Comm. on Judiciary, S. Rep. No. 1277, 93d Cong., 2d Sess. 18 to 20 (1974), reprinted in 1974 U.S. Code Cong. & Admin. News 7051, 7065 to 7066.

[15]   Prior to the 2019 amendment, Rule 807 appeared as follows:

(a)   In General. Under the following circumstances, a hearsay statement is not excluded by the rule against hearsay even if the statement is not specifically covered by a hearsay exception in Rule 803 or 804:

(1)   the statement has equivalent circumstantial guarantees of trustworthiness;

(2)   it is offered as evidence of a material fact;

(3)   it is more probative on the point for which it is offered than any other evidence that the proponent can obtain through reasonable efforts; and

(4)   admitting it will best serve the purposes of these rules and the interests of justice.

Amended Rule 807 provides:

(a) In General. Under the following conditions, a hearsay statement is not excluded by the rule against hearsay even if the statement is not admissible under a hearsay exception in Rule 803 or 804:

> (1) the statement is supported by sufficient guarantees of trustworthiness after considering the totality of circumstances under which it was made and evidence, if any, corroborating the statement; and

> (2) it is more probative on the point for which it is offered than any other evidence that the proponent can obtain through reasonable efforts.

(b) Notice. The statement is admissible only if the proponent gives an adverse party reasonable notice of the intent to offer the statement including its substance and the declarant's name so that the party has a fair opportunity to meet it. The notice must be provided in writing before the trial or hearing—or in any form during the trial or hearing if the court, for good cause, excuses a lack of earlier notice.

The 1997 version of Rule 807 contained five requirements, but as earlier editions of this treatise explained, only three of the five imposed substantial requirements. The amended rule retains those three, two with modifications, and deletes the other two. The two deleted provisions were 807(a)(2), which stated that the hearsay must be "offered as evidence of a material fact" and 807(a)(4), which stated that "admitting it will best serve the purposes of these rules and the interest of justice." The Advisory Committee's Note to the 2019 amendment explains that these provisions were deleted because they "proved to be superfluous in that they are already found in other rules," citing Rules 401 and 102. The three retained provisions deal with the requirements of trustworthiness, "necessity," and notice. These concepts, along with corroboration and "near miss," are examined below.

Sufficient Guarantees of Trustworthiness. Whereas the earlier version had required that the statement have "equivalent circumstantial guarantees of trustworthiness," amended Rule 807(a)(1) requires the statement to be "supported by sufficient guarantees of trustworthiness" and then provides by way of explanation "after considering the totality of the circumstances under which it was made and evidence, if any, corroborating the statement."

The change in language regarding the required showing of trustworthiness from "equivalent circumstantial guarantees" to "sufficient guarantees" should have little impact on admissions decisions, although as the Advisory Committee argues, the change may eliminate some difficulty of application of the previous standard. "Equivalent circumstantial guarantees" meant equivalent to hearsay exceptions found in Rules 803 and 804. However, the guarantees of reliability in the various exceptions vary in strength and nature or do not exist at all as in the exception for forfeiture by wrongdoing under Rule 804(b)(6). As a result, faithful adherence to the requirement of comparison in some instances posed at least theoretical problems. Moreover, for some hearsay that is

---

(b)   Notice. The statement is admissible only if, before the trial or hearing, the proponent gives an adverse party reasonable notice of the intent to offer the statement and its particulars, including the declarant's name and address, so that the party has a fair opportunity to meet it.

arguably trustworthy, no useful comparison can be found in the existing rules.[16] Under the amended trustworthiness standard, courts are to go directly to an assessment of the guarantees of trustworthiness supporting the hearsay statement at issue.

The amendment likely has a somewhat bigger impact in its requirement that courts consider corroborating evidence, where it exists, in determining trustworthiness. Earlier editions of this treatise noted that corroboration has occupied an "uncertain status" but that it has been considered by some courts in determining trustworthiness of the residual exception. Indeed, most, but not all, court have embraced the use of corroborating evidence in the trustworthiness analysis. Uncertainty is now eliminated in the federal courts as a result of this amendment, and such evidence is to be considered in the trustworthiness determination.

Although the factors supporting and undermining trustworthiness are extremely varied and occur in numerous combinations, certain recurring factors are particularly significant to the determination of admissibility. Among these factors are: whether the declarant had a motivation to speak truthfully or otherwise; the spontaneity of the statement, including whether it was elicited by leading questions, and generally the time lapse between event and statement; whether the statement was under oath; whether the declarant was subject to cross-examination at the time the statement was made; the relationship between the declarant and the person to whom the statement was made; whether the declarant has recanted or reaffirmed the statement or the consistency of multiple statements; whether the statement was recorded; and whether the declarant's firsthand knowledge is clearly demonstrated. One factor that should not be considered in evaluating the trustworthiness of the statement is the credibility of the person testifying to having heard it.[17]

The availability of the declarant to be cross-examined also may support the admissibility of statements that otherwise would be found insufficiently trustworthy to be received. On the other hand, the availability of the declarant to testify as a superior alternative to the hearsay and a basis for exclusion is discussed below under the "necessity" heading.

Corroboration. As noted above, amended Rule 807 includes in the required sufficient guarantees of trustworthiness, not only the totality of the circumstances under which the statement was made, but also any evidence corroborating the statement. Corroboration does not bear upon declarant at the time the statement was made but in retrospect offers support to its accuracy and therefore its truthfulness. However, given that both the circumstances of making the statement and corroboration are to be considered, whether the supporting factor falls into one of these categories or the other should not be significant. Corroboration can obviously come in many different forms, such as the statements of other eyewitnesses, independent documentary evidence, and unusual conduct consistent with the statement.

"Necessity." A second factor given varying significance by the opinions is the requirement of Rule 807(a)(2) that the statement must be "more probative on the point for which it is offered than any other evidence that the proponent can obtain through reasonable efforts." Many courts interpret this as a general necessity requirement. However, it does not mean that the hearsay evidence must be essential. Indeed, some

---

[16] *See* Fed. R. Evid. 807 advisory committee's note to 2019 amendment.

[17] *See id.*

courts view the requirement as providing a basis for a trial court to evaluate the need for the statement in the case as compared to the costs of obtaining alternative evidence. Others view it as imposing a requirement of diligence. The requirement also has the effect of imposing a rough "best evidence" requirement on the exception in the sense that where live testimony of the declarant is available and the out-of-court statement is not superior, the exception cannot be used. Also, as the Advisory Committee explained in retaining this requirement unchanged, it helps prevent the residual exception from being used to erode the specific exceptions.

Notice. The third requirement of amended Rule 807(b) is notice by the proponent to the adverse party of the intent to offer hearsay under the residual exception. The amendment changes the notice requirement in a number of ways, which constitute minor substantive changes and/or are clarifying and consistent with the consensus interpretation of courts of the pre-amended Rule. These are examined here in the order they appear in the language of the amended Rule.

First, instead of providing the "particulars" of the statement, the amendment requires the proponent to provide its "substance," which is the terminology used for offers of proof under Rule 103(a)(2). Second, under the pre-amended Rule, the "particulars" included both the declarant's name and address. As a minor substantive change, the address requirement has been deleted as nonsensical for unavailable declarants and unnecessary in cases where the address is known or easily obtainable. Where critical and unavailable to the adversary, the Advisory Committee expects relief should be available from the court through an individual request for address information rather than a generally applicable requirement. Third, in another substantive change intended to reduce disputes regarding whether notice was given, the amended rule requires that notice be made in writing, which under Rule 101(b)(6) includes electronic form. Fourth, the timing of notice has been modified and recognition of exceptions has been formalized. While courts occasionally required strict compliance with this requirement under the pre-amendment Rule 807(b), courts generally were willing to dispense with notice if the need for the hearsay arose shortly before or during the trial and possible injustice could be avoided by the offer of a continuance or other remedies. The amended Rule explicitly recognizes that notice may in some circumstances not be given before trial. The Advisory Committee gives as examples situations where the need to use the residual exception results from events, such as first learning of the existence of a hearsay statement after the trial began or where a witness unexpectedly becomes unavailable. Where notice is not given in the normal course before trial, "for good cause," the court can excuse the failure. In that situation, the court is expected to consider protective measures, such as a continuance to avoid prejudice to the party opposing admission.

"Near Miss." Before being amended in 2019, Rule 807 stated that the exception applied if "the statement is not specifically covered by" any of the specific exceptions. What this language meant with respect to a statement that narrowly, but clearly, failed to qualify under one of the enumerated exceptions was often characterized by the term "near miss." Did such a failure result in automatic disqualification because it was "specifically covered" or prove helpful in supporting admissibility because little else was needed to satisfy the earlier standard of "equivalent circumstantial guarantees" of trustworthiness? The almost unanimous opinion of courts was that failing to qualify under an enumerated exception did not disqualify admission under the residual exception.

As amended in 2019, the language "not specifically covered by a hearsay exception" was changed to "not admissible under a hearsay exception." That change was intended to eliminate the "near miss" confusion and make it clear that "a statement that nearly misses a specific exception can be admissible under Rule 807 so long as the court finds sufficient guarantees of trustworthiness."[18] In addition to assessing the all relevant guarantees of trustworthiness, the court should "take into account the reasons that the hearsay misses the admissibility requirement of the standard exception."[19]

Frequent Applications of the Exception. Courts have employed the exception most extensively in admitting statements made by child witnesses, particularly in sexual abuse cases. They emphasize factors such as the spontaneity and consistency of the statement, the general proposition that young children do not invent allegations of the type involved, the unusualness of explicit sexual knowledge by a young child, or the use of childish terminology to describe sex. Statements tend to be excluded in cases where the court found that they were made in response to leading questions by poorly trained interrogators.

Beyond child sexual abuse cases, the residual exception has been used to admit hearsay in an extraordinarily varied array of cases associated with all the frequently used hearsay exceptions. For example, prior testimony cross-examined by unrelated parties, statements made with death approaching but not imminent, and statements made by private citizens to public agencies or businesses. After *Crawford v. Washington*[20] imposed substantial restrictions on admission of testimonial hearsay,[21] some other uses of the residual exception in criminal cases against the defendant that were popular for a time, such as admitting grand jury testimony and at least formal statements to police officers by victims and witnesses, were eliminated as violations of the Confrontation Clause.

§ 324.1 Hearsay Within Hearsay; Multiple Hearsay

"On principle it scarcely seems open to doubt that the hearsay rule should not call for exclusion of a hearsay statement which includes a further hearsay statement when both conform to the requirements of a hearsay exception."[22] The common law followed this reasoning, and under Federal Rule 805, multiple levels of hearsay are admissible "if each part of the combined statements conforms with an exception to the rule."

In the usual situation, two stages of inquiry are involved. First, does the primary statement qualify under a hearsay exception? If so, the hearsay rule allows its use to prove that the included statement was made, which may end the inquiry. Ordinarily, however, the included statement will be offered to prove the truth of the facts that it asserts. In that event, the second stage of inquiry is required: Does the included statement also qualify under a hearsay exception? If the answer again is in the affirmative, the requirements of Rule 805 are met. However, if the included statement is inadmissible, the rule is not satisfied, and the statements are excluded.

---

[18]   Advisory Committee on Evidence Rules, Report to the Standing Committee at 3, May 14, 2018.

[19]   Fed. R. Evid. 807 advisory committee's note to 2019 amendment.

[20]   541 U.S. 36 (2004).

[21]   See supra § 252.

[22]   Fed. R. Evid. 805 advisory committee's note.

Police reports of accident investigations frequently provide examples of multiple hearsay, with admissibility depending upon the nature of the secondary statement. The primary statement—the written report of the officer—is admissible generally as a public record. Statements of individuals made to the officer either qualify under various exceptions, such as excited utterances or dying declarations, or they fail to meet any additional exception and must be excluded as violating the principle. It is violated, for example, when a police officer testifies that A stated that B confessed to the crime. Although B's confession to A—the included statement likely qualifies as an admission or a statement against interest, A's statement to the police officer—the primary statement—appears to meet no hearsay exception.

Another frequently encountered version of the multiple hearsay problem involves a regularly kept business record that includes a further hearsay statement. If both the primary and the included statements are by persons acting in the routine of the business, then both are admitted under the regularly kept records exception, and no further exception need be invoked. However, if the person whose statement is included is not acting in the routine of the business, it is inadmissible unless another exception is available.

An argument could be made that even if the included statement met some other hearsay exception, the primary statement could not qualify under a hearsay exception because the regularly kept records exception requires that the informant must be produced in the routine of the business. This position has not been accepted, but instead the recorder must have a business interest in recording the information provided by the outsider.

The requirement of a duty to record will lead to a different result depending upon the nature of the business involved. For instance, a hospital intake worker has an interest in a narrower and different type of information when talking to an assault victim about the circumstances surrounding the injury than a police officer. The statement that the victim was shot by a person of a particular race would not be material to the hospital's business and not admissible through the business records exception when made to a hospital employee even if the included statement met another hearsay exception. By contrast, the same statement would be highly relevant to a police officer's duties in locating the assailant, and accordingly the primary statement should be admissible as a public record when offered by the accused.

One of the statements might constitute an admission, which at common law was considered a hearsay exception. Since admissions are not classed as hearsay under the Federal Rules, the question arises whether an admission may qualify as a hearsay exception for purposes of the multiple hearsay rule. One answer has been that admissions are within the spirit and purpose of the rule. An easier answer may be that only one level of hearsay exists since an admission is not hearsay under the Federal Rules, and if the other statement satisfies an exception, no further hearsay difficulty remains.

§ 324.2 Impeachment and Rehabilitation of the Hearsay Declarant

When a hearsay statement is introduced, often the declarant does not testify. It is, however, ultimately the declarant's credibility that determines the value that should be accorded to the statement. How should that credibility be attacked or, where appropriate, supported?

Federal Rule 806, Attacking and Supporting the Declarant's Credibility, provides:

When a hearsay statement—or a statement described in Rule 801(d)(2)(C), (D), or (E)—has been admitted in evidence, the declarant's credibility may be attacked, and then supported, by any evidence that would be admissible for those purposes if the declarant had testified as a witness. The court may admit evidence of the declarant's inconsistent statement or conduct, regardless of when it occurred or whether the declarant had an opportunity to explain or deny it. If the party against whom the statement was admitted calls the declarant as a witness, the party may examine the declarant on the statement as if on cross-examination.

The rule effectively treats the hearsay declarant as a witness for impeachment and rehabilitation purposes. It covers both statements admitted under hearsay exceptions and admissions, but it does not apply to statements that are nonhearsay and not admitted for their truth.

The declarant may be impeached by any of the standard methods of attacking credibility, including prior convictions, inconsistent statements, bias or interest, character for untruthfulness, and defects in testimonial capacity. If impeached, the credibility of the declarant can also be rehabilitated. This principle applies to all witnesses, including a non-testifying defendant who may be impeached with prior convictions when his or her hearsay statement is introduced. With regard to impeachment by prior inconsistent statements, the rule eliminates the requirement, otherwise applicable to statements made by witnesses who testify in person,[23] that an opportunity be afforded for them to explain or deny the inconsistency. When the declarant does not take the stand, the procedure for conducting the impeachment should be relaxed, but separate restrictions in other rules are not eliminated.

If the declarant takes the stand, the Rule permits an adverse party to examine on the statement "as if on cross-examination," which permits use of leading questions.[24] When the statement is admitted against a criminal defendant, the accused can invoke the compulsory process clause to require assistance in securing the declarant's presence.

§ 324.3 Basis for Expert Opinion as a Quasi-Hearsay Exception

Under Federal Rule 703, an expert may base an opinion on facts or data that are not "admissible" if of a type reasonably relied upon by experts in the field. An expert often should be allowed to disclose to the jury the basis for an opinion because otherwise the opinion is left unsupported with little way for evaluation of its correctness. In those situations, the expert may testify to evidence even though it is inadmissible under the hearsay rule, but allowing the evidence to be received for this purpose does not mean it is admitted for its truth. It is received only for the limited purpose of informing the jury of the basis of the expert's opinion and therefore does not constitute a true hearsay exception. As a result, where it constitutes the only evidence on a critical issue—such as the identity of the assailant in a child sexual abuse case—this distinction will prove decisive. In some situations, the fact that the basis is inadmissible hearsay may effectively leave the opinion unsupported.

---

[23] Fed. R. Evid. 613(b). See generally supra § 37.

[24] See Fed. R. Evid. 611(c). See generally supra § 20.

Probably more often the difference between limited admissibility and admission for the truth of the statement is of little significance and threatens no harm. For instance, if the underlying data has no direct relevance to the dispute in the case or if the facts it concerns, although relevant, have already been proved through other admissible evidence, allowing the jury to hear the inadmissible data from the expert will have no significant consequences.

Unfortunately, although limiting instructions are appropriate and required when requested, jurors may be unable or unwilling to follow them. Thus, in those instances where the inadmissible facts or data would have an important impact if used for the truth and would therefore be subject to abuse, a danger exists of Rule 703 improperly becoming a "backdoor" hearsay exception. Two steps must be satisfied. First, the facts "need not be admissible" if "experts in the particular field would reasonably rely on those kinds of facts or data in forming an opinion on the subject." Second, "if the facts or data would otherwise be inadmissible, the proponent of the opinion may disclose them to the jury only if their probative value in helping the jury evaluate the opinion substantially outweighs their prejudicial effect." This second requirement was strengthened by a 2000 amendment to the federal rule. Previously, the inadmissible data was subject to exclusion for prejudice or irrelevancy under Rule 403,[25] but the proponent now has a much more onerous burden in showing how receiving the inadmissible evidence will substantially aid the jury in evaluating the expert's opinion in comparison to being misused by the jury for substantive purposes.

Even to claim a nonhearsay purpose has been challenged in some situations. In *Williams v. Illinois*,[26] five Justices concluded that under the Confrontation Clause the use of the report of other experts to support the testifying expert's opinion did not qualify as a "legitimate" or "plausible" nonhearsay purpose.[27] Moreover, these Justices asserted that the use of the statement to provide the basis of the opinion was effectively to use it for the truth within the meaning of Clause. Whether this critical constitutional analysis will have an effect on the use of materials relied upon by experts for this relatively broadly accepted limited evidentiary purpose beyond the restricts discussed earlier remains to be seen.

§ 325 Evaluation of the Present Rules

In his evidence treatise published in 1842, Professor Greenleaf wrote:

> The student will not fail to observe the symmetry and beauty of this branch of the law . . . and will rise from the study of its principles convinced, with Lord Erskine, that "they are founded in the charities of religion,—in the philosophy of nature,—in the truths of history,—and in the experience of common life."[28]

No one today would apply this evaluation to the rule against hearsay developed in the common law tradition, and far more would agree with the description of Professors Morgan and Maguire approximately a century later that the exceptions appear like "an old-fashioned crazy quilt made of patches cut from a group of paintings by cubists,

---

[25] See generally supra § 185.

[26] 567 U.S. 50 (2012).

[27] *Id.* at 105–06 (Thomas, J., concurring in the judgment). See generally supra § 252.

[28] Greenleaf, Evidence § 584 (1st ed. 1842).

futurists and surrealists."[29] Indeed, a number of contemporary scholars seek the replacement of the pattern of rules with a radically different system.

The common law's insistence upon a high quality of evidence for judicial fact-finding that helped to produce the hearsay rule was sound. However, the rules as they developed appear not to have yielded a quality commensurate with the high price they have exacted. The chief criticisms are that the rules are too complex and that they fail to achieve their purpose of screening good evidence from bad.

First, with respect to the complexity of the rule against hearsay and its exceptions, the number of exceptions naturally depends upon the minuteness of the classification. The Federal Rules contain thirty exceptions and exclusions. Wigmore requires over a thousand pages to cover hearsay, and its treatment occupies one quarter of the original edition of the present work.

Most of the complication, of course, arises in connection with the exceptions, leading readily to the conclusion that a general rule so riddled with exceptions is "farcical."[30] The conclusion may be somewhat exaggerated. While admittedly complicated, probably less than a dozen of the exceptions are encountered with any frequency in the trial of cases. Gaining mastery of these, plus an awareness of the others and a working knowledge of what is and is not hearsay, should not unduly tax the intellectual resources of the legal profession.

The second complaint that the rule against hearsay and its exceptions fail to screen reliable from unreliable hearsay on a realistic basis is more substantial. The trustworthiness of hearsay statements ranges from the highest reliability to quite questionable value. Whether these almost infinitely varying, plastic situations can ever be completely and satisfactorily treated by a set of rules may well be doubted.

If the heart of the problem is that the exceptions are unacceptable in detail, the problem persists. The preceding chapters dealing with hearsay indicate that while some progress has been made in rationalizing the rules and improving their practical workability, they remain quite complex. If the basic difficulty is simply that no hearsay system based on classes of exceptions can truly succeed, a totally different approach would be required. As discussed in Section 327, such proposals, which have been advanced in civil cases in the past but have run into the Confrontation Clause barrier in criminal cases, may have more favorable long-term prospects. Perhaps the most notable recent development has not been a broad revamping of the system of exceptions but rather the substantial flexibility introduced by the frequent admission of hearsay through ad hoc judicial action under the residual exception.

§ 326 The Path of Modern Hearsay Development

Wholesale efforts to reformulate the traditional common law hearsay pattern have been for the most part legislative in nature rather than judicial, and some of the more notable legislative efforts are discussed below.

Pursuant to a suggestion from Thayer, the Massachusetts Hearsay Statute of 1898 was enacted as follows: "A declaration of a deceased person shall not be inadmissible in evidence as hearsay if the Court finds that it was made in good faith before the

---

[29]   Morgan & Maguire, Looking Backward and Forward at Evidence, 50 Harv. L. Rev. 909, 921 (1937).

[30]   Nokes, The English Jury and the Law of Evidence, 31 Tulane L. Rev. 153, 167 (1956).

commencement of the action and upon the personal knowledge of the declarant."[31] After a quarter century of experience under the act, a questionnaire was addressed to the lawyers and judges of the state regarding its merits. The vast majority of those responding thought that its effects were positive. The American Bar Association in 1938 recommended a liberalized version of the act for adoption by the states.

The English Evidence Act of 1938 allowed the introduction of written statements, made on the personal knowledge of the maker or in the regular course of business, if the maker was called as a witness or was unavailable. Even though the maker was neither called nor unavailable, the judge might admit the statement if satisfied that undue delay or expense would otherwise be involved. Statements made by interested persons when proceedings were pending or instituted were excluded from the act. It applied only in civil cases.

These limitations were relaxed, and new ones added in 1968. Under the act, hearsay statements, whether written or oral, were admissible to the extent that testimony of the declarant would have been admissible, regardless of whether he or she was called as a witness, though prior statements were not ordinarily admissible at the request of the proponent if the declarant was called. Notice was required of intent to offer a hearsay statement under the act, and the opposite party had the right to require production of declarant as a witness, if available. The picture was conceptually simplified by the Civil Evidence Act of 1995, which abolishes the hearsay rule as a basis for excluding evidence while retaining the notice requirement, some restrictions on prior statements, and the right of the opponent to call and cross-examine declarants. Like its predecessors, the new act applies only to civil cases. Reforms to English hearsay law in criminal cases have been more modest but still substantial.

The drafters of the Model Code of Evidence of the American Law Institute took a bold course about hearsay. They drafted a sweeping new exception to the hearsay rule that allowed admissibility "if the judge finds that the declarant (a) is unavailable as a witness, or (b) is present and subject to cross-examination."[32] This rule, however, was qualified by other rules which limited its application to declarations by persons with personal knowledge, excluded hearsay upon hearsay, and empowered the trial judge to exclude such hearsay whenever its probative value was outweighed by the likelihood of waste of time, prejudice, confusion, or unfair surprise. In addition to this new rule, the traditional exceptions were generally retained. The liberalizing of the use of hearsay was a chief ground of opposition to the Model Code and no doubt substantially accounted for the failure of the code to be adopted in any jurisdiction.

Nevertheless, the controversy over the Model Code awakened a new interest in the improvement of evidence law. Accordingly, the Commissioners on Uniform State Laws, in cooperation with the American Law Institute and building on the foundation of the Model Code, drafted and adopted a more modestly reformative code, the Uniform Rules of Evidence. The American Bar Association approved this action.

Instead of admitting virtually all firsthand hearsay of an unavailable declarant, the original Uniform Rules, like the Model Code rule quoted above, substituted a hearsay exception for statements by unavailable declarants describing a matter recently perceived and made in good faith prior to the commencement of the action. A similar

---

[31]   Mass. Acts 1898, c. 535.

[32]   Model Code of Evidence Rule 503 (1942).

provision was found for a time in Rule 804(b)(5). However, Congress removed its counterpart from the Federal Rules, and it is no longer part of the Uniform Rules. As to prior statements by witnesses present at the hearing, the original Uniform Rules adopted substantially the broad provisions of the Model Code rule quoted above, but the Uniform Rules follow the much narrower congressional version of Federal Rule of Evidence 801(d)(1).[33] The original Uniform Rules, like the Model Code, retained and liberalized the other traditional exceptions.

The Advisory Committee on the Federal Rules of Evidence approached its task with awareness of the criticisms that had been leveled against the common law system of class exceptions to the hearsay rule. It also was aware that the Model Code's lack of acceptance was largely the result of having exceeded the profession's willingness to accept a fundamentally altered approach to hearsay that permitted broad admissibility of prior statements of unavailable declarants.

In its first draft circulated for comment, the Committee endeavored to rationalize the hearsay exceptions in general terms, while at the same time maintaining continuity with the past. For these ends, two rules were included, one covering situations where it made no difference whether the declarant was available and the other applying only when the declarant was unavailable. The first of these rules opened with the following general provision: "A statement is not excluded by the hearsay rule if its nature and the special circumstances under which it was made offer assurances of accuracy not likely to be enhanced by calling the declarant as a witness, even though he is available."

This general provision was followed by twenty-three illustrative applications derived from common law exceptions, which were not to be considered an exclusive listing. The second of the rules again opened with a general provision: "A statement is not excluded by the hearsay rule if its nature and the special circumstances under which it was made offer strong assurances of accuracy and the declarant is unavailable as a witness." It was also followed by a list, albeit a shorter one, of illustrative applications derived from the common law with again a caution that the enumeration not be considered exclusive.

While the response indicated a willingness to accept a substantial revision in the area of hearsay, the legal community opted for a larger measure of predictability than the proposal was thought to offer. As a result, the two general provisions quoted above were withdrawn, and the two rules were revised by converting the illustrations into exceptions in the common law tradition, with the addition of two residual exceptions to accommodate unforeseen situations that might arise. In this form, the rules, with some alterations, were enacted into law by the Congress as Rules 803 and 804. In addition, rules modeled on the Federal Rules are now in effect in forty-four states, with local changes of varying significance. The pattern of a general rule excluding hearsay, subject to numerous exceptions, has shown substantial resilience.

§ 327 The Future of Hearsay

Regardless of whether the hearsay rule was as a matter of history the child of the jury system,[34] clearly the concern for controlling the use of hearsay is more pronounced in jury cases than in nonjury cases. In part, this attitude may be a product of the close

---

[33] See supra § 251.
[34] See supra § 244.

association between the right to a jury and the right of confrontation in criminal cases. The English developments in the direction of relaxing limitations on hearsay in civil cases[35] were apparently inspired by the virtual disappearance there of jury trials in such cases. Corresponding changes have not transpired with respect to criminal cases where the jury remains.

In America, the constitutional rights of criminal defendants to confrontation and a jury trial and the unwillingness to develop separate rules for criminal and civil cases have to date combined to inhibit wholesale changes in the traditional hearsay exceptions. However, the Supreme Court's decision in *Crawford v. Washington*[36] decoupled Confrontation Clause analysis from hearsay exceptions as to testimonial statements. If the Court were to eliminate that linkage entirely, a major limitation on hearsay reformulation would be removed.

In any case, one may reasonably assume that the civil jury will continue to decline in importance. As noted in an earlier section,[37] courts often exhibit a more relaxed attitude in administering the exclusionary rules of evidence in nonjury cases, including the rule against hearsay. An even more relaxed attitude prevails in administrative proceedings. These trends are likely to continue.

Scholars have suggested that admissibility of hearsay, particularly in civil cases should be made more flexible. Judge Weinstein argued that admissibility should be based upon the judge's ad hoc evaluation of its probative force accompanied by several procedural safeguards. They included: notice to the opponent of the intention to use hearsay, expanding the judge's ability to comment on the weight of such evidence, greater control by judges over juries, and greater control by appellate courts over trial courts.[38] Almost two decades later, Professor Park argued that in civil cases a residual exception should be added that would permit admission without any reliability screening. The exception would require notice to the adversary and would allow the adversary to exercise a rule of preference, which if exercised would require a showing that the declarant was unavailable or, if available, must be called to testify.[39] Despite some attractive features, neither proposal has approached acceptance.

More recently, Judge Richard Posner added his voice to this movement to make the admission of hearsay simpler and more flexible:

> The "hearsay rule" is too complex, as well as being archaic. Trials would go better with a simpler rule, the core of which would be the proposition (essentially a simplification of Rule 807) that hearsay evidence should be admissible when it is reliable, when the jury can understand its strengths and limitations, and when it will materially enhance the likelihood of a correct outcome.[40]

More than fifty years ago, Professor McCormick wrote, much in the Benthamic tradition:

---

[35]   See supra § 326.

[36]   541 U.S. 36 (2004).

[37]   See supra § 60.

[38]   *See* Weinstein, Probative Force of Hearsay, 46 Iowa L. Rev. 331, 338–42 (1961).

[39]   *See* Park, A Subject Matter Approach to Hearsay Reform, 86 Mich. L. Rev. 51, 118–22 (1987).

[40]   U.S. v. Boyce, 742 F.3d 792, 802 (7th Cir. 2014) (Posner, J., concurring).

> Eventually, perhaps, Anglo-American court procedure may find itself gradually but increasingly freed from emphasis on jury trial with its contentious theory of proof. With responsibility for the ascertainment of facts vested in professional judges, the stress will be shifted from the crude technique of admitting or rejecting evidence to the more realistic problem of appraising its credibility. Psychologists meantime will have built upon their knowledge of the statistical reliability of witnesses in groups a technique of testing the veracity of individual witnesses and assessing the reliability of particular items of testimony. Judges and advocates will then become students and practitioners of an applied science of judicial proof.[41]

It becomes increasingly evident that this optimistic statement represents at best a very long-term view and is unlikely ever to be achieved.

Several scholars have argued that although complicated and fraught with substantial problems, the existing system and even its complexity have some benefits that suggest caution in making radical change. These reasons include: the likelihood that oral statements may be misreported, the potential effect of relaxing hearsay rules on the advantage that the prosecution and wealthy organizations enjoy in litigation due to superior facilities for generating evidence, a distrust of the ability and impartiality of trial judges, and certain other process concerns.[42]

Two general propositions appear almost unavoidably true. First, for the considerable future, a hearsay rule and set of specific exceptions strongly resembling the present system will continue. Second, changes will move in the direction of liberalizing admission of hearsay.

---

[41] McCormick, Evidence, 3 Encyclopedia of the Social Sciences 637, 645 (1931, reissue of 1937).

[42] *See* Lempert & Saltzburg, A Modern Approach to Evidence 519 (2d ed. 1982); Mueller, Post-Modern Hearsay Reform: The Importance of Complexity, 76 Minn. L. Rev. 367 (1992).

Title 11

JUDICIAL NOTICE

Chapter 35

JUDICIAL NOTICE

Table of Sections

§ 328 The Need for and the Effect of Judicial Notice

The traditional notion that trials are bifurcated proceedings involving both a judge and a panel of twelve jurors has obviously had a profound impact on the overall development of common law doctrine pertaining to evidence. The very existence of the jury, after all, helped create the demand for the rigorous guarantees of accuracy which typify the law of evidence, witness the insistence upon proof by witnesses having first-hand knowledge, the mistrust of hearsay, and the insistence upon original documents and their authentication by witnesses. Thus, it is that the facts in dispute are commonly established by the jury after the carefully controlled introduction of formal evidence, which ordinarily consists of the testimony of witnesses. In light of the role of the jury, therefore, it is easy enough to conclude that, whereas questions concerning the tenor of the law to be applied to a case fall within the province of the judge, the determination of questions pertaining to propositions of fact is uniquely the function of the jury. The life of the law has never been quite so elementary, however, because judges on numerous occasions take charge of questions of fact and excuse the party having the burden of establishing a fact from the necessity of producing formal proof. These hybrid questions of fact, dealt with by judges as if they were questions pertaining to law, are the raw materials out of which the doctrine of judicial notice has been constructed.

A moment's reflection on the law-fact distinction is in order. The statement that it is necessary in a certain jurisdiction to have a testator's subscription attested by three witnesses if the document is going to be admitted to probate is an assertion that a certain state of affairs obtains. A speaker might actually preface the assertion with the words, "as a matter of fact." Whether the statement is true or false presents, in the everyday vernacular, a question of fact. Persons engaged in social conversation might not agree on the accuracy of the statement but agree to settle their difference by a straw poll of the other persons present. All of which would be of no moment, provided always no one present actually planned his or her estate on the basis of the result of the poll.

If this same conversation took the form of an argument between lawyers in a courtroom during an official proceeding wherein the answer was germane to the disposition of the matter at hand, very different considerations would come into play. The answer could not be seen to vary between cases in the same courtroom or between courtrooms across the jurisdiction. There must exist a standardized answer if the law qua system of dispute resolution is to maintain the necessary appearance of fairness and rationality. It is the apparatus of appellate review and one ultimately highest court in the jurisdiction which guarantees uniformity. Thus, it is the case that, within the vernacular of the law, a question which can have only one right answer must be answered in a courtroom by a judge and is, therefore, a question of law.

The question who did what to whom when, where and in what state of mind implicates another set of considerations. The concrete human actions or inactions which precipitate lawsuits are water over the dam, history as it were. Reflection may suggest that history is actually a current event, because history is our present best judgment as to what happened in the past. Past events cannot be reconstituted; only a facsimile of them can be constructed in the mind's eye on the basis of the evidence presently available. In a courtroom the evidence available is a factor of the rules of evidence and the cleverness as well as industry of the opposing counsel.

If there is produced at trial enough evidence upon which seriously to deliberate about what actually happened in the past, and provided that in a civil case the evidence is not so overwhelming as to make deliberation unnecessary, there is no scientific litmus by which to assay the accuracy of the opposing versions of the affair. A verdict either way is possible. In the law's vernacular, we are met with a question of fact, which in Anglo-American tradition is meet for a jury to decide. But this compels the conclusion that a question of fact is one to which there are two right answers.

This model finds its roots in Lord Coke.[1] *Ad questionem facti non respondent judices: ad questionem juris non respondent juratores.* To questions of fact judges do not answer: to questions of law the jury do not answer. Implicit in this model, however, is the notion inherent in the adversarial system that a judge presides over a trial after the fashion of an umpire who governs the play according to known rules but who does not participate in it. Implied, too, are the notions that trials involve straightforward contract or tort disputes, that complaints are abruptly dismissed if they do not state a familiar cause of action and that the concise elements of a well pleaded common law cause of action make the issues of fact at trial, if it comes to that, few and simple. Finally, the model presupposes that the law itself is composed primarily of private law rules which by and large remain immutable over the life of any one generation.

If during a trial a proposition of fact were to be implicated, the truth of which brooked no dispute among reasonable persons, this proposition would not fit comfortably within the principle that either of two answers is appropriate to a question of fact. The application of common sense to the principles thus far rehearsed leads inexorably to the conclusion that the existence of one right answer signals a question of law. Thus, at least if requested to do so, a judge would have to treat this question of fact as one of law and instruct the jury that the proposition could simply be taken as established in its own right. Indeed, modern thinking is that, given the fact noticed must be true, judicial notice works not merely to excuse producing evidence of its truth to the jury, but the court must instruct to jury that they must accept the fact as true. Second thoughts suggest that in criminal cases such an instruction might run afoul Sixth Amendment wisdom forbidding

---

[1]   Coke's Commentary Upon Littleton 155b (1832 ed.).

a judge to direct a judgment against a defendant. Thus, Congress modified the Federal Rule to require the court in those cases to instruct the jury that it may or may not accept the noticed fact as conclusive.[2] One must be careful to keep in mind that many states adopted the Uniform Rules which made no effort to soften the rule.[3]

With what manner of questions pertaining to facts do judges concern themselves? Whether a well known street was in fact within a local business district as alleged by a litigant, in which case a certain speed limit obtained, may be dealt with by the judge during the trial of a negligence case. That is to say, the judge may instruct the jury that the street in question was within a business district, dispensing thereby with the need to introduce evidence to this effect. Then again, questions of fact arise about which reasonably intelligent people might not have in mind the information in question, but where they would agree that the facts are verifiable with certainty by consulting authoritative reference sources. At a time when Sunday contracts were taboo, for example, the question arose during the trial of a warranty action whether the relevant sales instrument, dated June 3, 1906, had been executed on a Sunday. In this instance the trial judge was reversed for leaving the question to the jury to deliberate upon as a question of fact. Experience reveals, therefore, that two categories of facts clearly fall within the perimeters of judicial notice, these being facts generally known with certainty by all the reasonably intelligent people in the community and facts capable of accurate and ready determination by resort to sources of indisputable accuracy.

In both of the examples enumerated thus far it should be carefully noted that the facts of which judicial notice was taken were "adjudicative" facts. They were facts about the particular event which gave rise to the lawsuit and, like all adjudicative facts, they helped explain who did what, when, where, how, and with what motive and intent. Further, either because they were facts so commonly known in the jurisdiction or so manifestly capable of accurate verification, they were facts reasonably informed people in the community would regard as propositions not reasonably subject to dispute.

Another species of facts figures prominently in discussions of judicial notice which, to employ the terminology coined by Professor K.C. Davis,[4] are denominated "legislative" facts. Judicial notice of these facts occurs when a judge is faced with the task of creating law, by deciding upon the constitutional validity of a statute, or the interpretation of a statute, or the extension or restriction of a common law rule, upon grounds of policy, and the policy is thought to hinge upon social, economic, political or scientific facts. Illustrative of this phenomenon was *Clinton v. Jones*[5] in which the Court refused even on prudential grounds to grant to a sitting president automatic immunity from a civil suit arising from acts occurring before he took office, rejecting the argument that private litigation might interfere with the President's performance of his official duties. All but one of the justices agreed that it was highly unlikely that a civil suit could take up any substantial amount of presidential time. This premise rested upon a certain view of the facts of political life, but these facts were hardly indisputable. Indeed, the presidential deposition taken in the case brought on a maelstrom of legal and political controversy that came close to monopolizing the president's attention. Carefully note, however, that

---

[2] Fed. R. Evid. 201(f).

[3] *Compare* Fed. R. Evid. 201(f) *with* Uniform Rule (g) (2005).

[4] Davis, An Approach to Problems of Evidence in the Administrative Process, 55 Harv. L. Rev. 364 (1942).

[5] 520 U.S. 681 (1997).

these facts were not part and parcel of the disputed event being litigated but bore instead upon the court's own thinking about the tenor of the law to be applied in deciding the dispute.

The generic caption "legislative facts" fails to highlight any distinction between the use of extra-record data by judges when they craft a rule of law, whether of the constitutional or private law variety, and when they resort to extra-record data to assay whether there exist circumstances which constitutionally either legitimate the exercise of legislative power or substantiate the rationality of the legislative product. Resort to a new subdivision like "law-making facts" might not, in its turn, bring home the reality that judges regularly resort to extra-record data not only when enunciating new substantive doctrine, but also employ them in deciding questions which pertain to everything from the alpha of civil jurisdiction to the omega of criminal sentencing.

Concern for legislative facts does signal the recognition both that judges do not "find" the law but rather make it, and that questions of public law have become a staple of the case law menu. A judge may no longer be quite the disinterested umpire in the steady state system suggested by the common law model, but more an active participant making work what has come to be seen as process of adapting law to a volatile socio-political environment. In a very real sense, it may be that a judge used to a steady diet of private law cases and a judge dealing with disputes arising out of a multiplicity of administrative agency actions may actually live in different worlds. At the same time modern procedure and trial practice have served to create a complexity that would confound the serjeants of yesteryear.

The picture is further complicated by a tendency of any bright-line distinction between adjudicative and legislative facts to dissolve in practice. Assume, for example, a statute making it a crime to possess coca leaves or any salt, compound or derivative thereof. If believed, the testimony of witnesses, lay and expert, establishes that defendant possessed a quantity of cocaine hydrochloride and that the item is indeed a salt, compound or derivative of coca leaves. The last proposition is indisputable and subject to judicial notice. If this is an adjudicative fact, a federal judge would not feel free to instruct the jury that, if they were to find the defendant possessed this item, they must find the item was a proscribed one.[6] No such compunction would obtain if it were a legislative fact. Yet one judge might visualize the question in terms of, "What is it that defendant possessed?", which is part of the who, what, when and where litany signaling an adjudicative fact, while another judge might inquire, "What was it that the legislature intended to criminalize?", which access door to the realm of legislative facts. All of which may warn the reader that the judicial notice of fact phenomenon has many of the characteristics of a universal solvent: it cannot be totally contained in any known vessel.

It is axiomatic, of course, that the judge decides whether a given set of facts constitutes an actionable wrong or a certain line of cross-examination is relevant. A judge, unless she is to be reversed on appeal, is bound to know the common and statutory law of her own jurisdiction. Commonly enough even this truism has been incorporated into the law of evidence by saying that judges must judicially notice the law of their own forum. This manner of speaking has served to interpolate into the field of judicial notice the procedural mechanisms by which the applicable law is fed into the judicial process. Foreign law, of course, was once more germane to the topic of judicial notice because that

---

6   *See* Fed. R. Evid. 201(f).

body of law was (for convenience) treated as fact, so much so that the law of a jurisdiction other than the forum had to be pleaded and proved just like any other question of fact, but a peculiar one which only the judge came to decide, which justified its inclusion within the topic of judicial notice. Indeed, lumped along with foreign law as a proper subject for treatment under the caption of judicial notice has been the forum's own administrative law and local municipal ordinances, together with a hotchpot of internal judicial administrative details concerning the courts themselves, such as their own personnel, records, organization and jurisdictional boundaries. The recognition appears to be growing, however, that the manner in which the law is insinuated into the judicial process is not so much a problem of evidence as it is a concern better handled within the context of the rules pertaining to procedure.[7]

One must be careful, however, to note that foreign law can be judicially noticed not as law to be applied to the decision of a case but as a fact to be used in the law-making process. The Supreme Court, for example, ruled that the Eighth Amendment provision prohibiting the imposition of cruel and unusual punishment forbade the imposition of the death penalty on offenders under the age of eighteen when the crime was committed.[8] In so doing the court took judicial notice of the fact that only seven countries in the entire world had since 1990 executed juveniles and that these nations had since abolished or disavowed the practice. "The opinion of the world community, while not controlling our outcome, does provide respected and significant confirmation for our own conclusions."[9]

In a world connected by an electronic web what was once foreign and far away has acquired next door immediacy. At the same time the sheer volume of domestic materials on the web poses a problem when trying to assay the authoritativeness of the source behind the materials being put forward as legislative facts, much less actual adjudicative facts.[10]

§ 329 Matters of Common Knowledge

The oldest and plainest ground for judicial notice is that the fact is so commonly known in the community as to make it unprofitable to require proof, and so certainly known as to make it indisputable among reasonable people. Though this basis for notice is sometimes loosely described as universal knowledge, manifestly this could not be taken literally, and the more reflective opinions speak in terms of "what well-informed persons generally know" or "the knowledge that every intelligent person has." Observe that the progression over time has somewhat widened the circle of facts within "common knowledge." Moreover, though usually facts of "common knowledge" will be generally known throughout the country, it is sufficient as a basis for judicial notice that they be known in the local community where the trial court sits.

What a judge knows and what facts a judge may judicially notice are not identical data banks. A famous colloquy in the Year Books shows that a clear difference has long been taken between what judges may notice judicially and the facts that the particular judge happens personally to know.[11] It is not a distinction easy for a judge to follow in

---

[7]   *Compare* Fed. Rule Evid. 201 *with* Fed. R. Civ. P. 44.1 (determination of foreign law). *But see* a good model of a bad idea in Proposed Rule 203, 171 F.R.D. 330, 386–89.

[8]   *See* Roper v. Simmons, 543 U.S. 551 (2005).

[9]   *Id.* at 578.

[10]   See infra §§ 330–331.

[11]   Anon., Y.B. 7 Hen. IV, f. 41, pl. 5 (1406), from which the following is an excerpt: "Sir, let us put the case that a man kills another in your presence and sight, and another who is not guilty is indicted before you

application, but the doctrine is accepted that actual private knowledge by the judge is no sufficient ground for taking judicial notice of a fact as a basis for a finding or a final judgment, though it may still be a ground, it is believed, for exercising certain discretionary powers, such as granting a motion for new trial to avoid an injustice, or in sentencing.

Similarly, what a jury member knows in common with every other human being and what facts are appropriately circumscribed by the doctrine of judicial notice are not the same thing. Traditionally those facts so generally known within the community as not to be reasonably subject to dispute have been included within the perimeters of judicial notice under the caption of common knowledge. At the same time, however, it is often loosely said that the jury may consider, as if proven, facts within the common knowledge of the community.

When considering the award to make in a condemnation case, a jury were properly concerned whether the value of the remaining fee was diminished by the installation of a natural gas pipeline in the easement which was the discrete subject of the taking. The jurors factored in an amount to compensate for the contingency that, the fee being a farm, deep chisel-style plowing might rupture the pipe and cause an explosion, the very notoriety of which would put off future purchasers of the farm. This possibility was taken seriously by the jurors, themselves residents of a farming community and familiar with local practices. Even though there had not been introduced into evidence any matter pertaining to deep chisel plowing, a court was willing to sustain the award precisely because, given the fund of common knowledge shared by this rural jury, there was no need for formal evidence to establish the point.

Had the same case been transferred for trial to an urban venue, deep chisel plowing would not likely have ever been considered by a jury absent the introduction of evidence alerting them to the practice. It would be manifestly improper were a juror to investigate farming practices and to introduce the subject for the first time in the privacy of the jury room. Information of this kind should be supplied to the jury through the testimony of a witness, and of course a juror is generally viewed as incompetent to perform this role. This leaves open the possibility that a former rural resident might introduce the subject into an urban jury room, pooling with his compatriots his distinct share of the fund of common knowledge. If the fund the jurors can draw upon is knowledge common to the community as a whole, this datum would appear to be illicit specie in an urban venue.

A similar problem would arise were evidence introduced for and against the existence of a real threat posed by deep chisel plowing and one or more of the jurors shared their unique experience with the practice with the rest of the panel. Jurors do not think evidence; jurors think about the evidence, and to think at all requires a person to draw upon his or her experience. The cases are difficult to reconcile. It was held improper to invite jurors with personal experience on farms to share it with their fellows in a case which turned on the question whether an insured horse had indeed been killed by a lightning bolt, while another court held it appropriate to invite jurors with personal experience in and about saw mills to share their insights in a personal injury case arising out of an accident at a saw mill.

---

and is found guilty of the same death, you ought to respite the judgment against him, for you know the contrary, and report the matter to the King to pardon him. No more ought you to give judgment in this case . . . Gascoigne, C.J. One time the King himself asked me about this very case which you have put, and asked me what was the law, and I told him just as you say, and he was well pleased that the law was so."

The parameters of the jury fund of common data may be vague but so are the limits on trial lawyers when they use summations to expose jurors to non-evidence facts masquerading as rhetorical hypotheses. These problems are at least moderated by the availability of voir dire examinations and challenges to exclude from juries those with particularized knowledge about key aspects of the case. Even so, all of this assumes that by and large each venue's jurors share relatively homogenous cultural roots so that, in fact, there does exist a rough-hewn common fund of knowledge in which they all share.

In an increasingly heterogeneous and highly mobile society, further fractured by class divisions, there may no longer exist a common fund of knowledge shared by the jurors resident in a particular venue. Out of academe there has come the suggestion that a common fund can be guaranteed by imposing a definition of that fund's parameters community to community. This judge-imposed construct would not only be the basis for an instruction confining deliberating jurors to this fund but would serve as a benchmark during voir dire examinations and in determining relevancy. The efficacy of any instruction purporting to limit the data jurors use in their thinking about the outcome of a case may be questionable at best. In fact, the very notion of imposing rigorous limitations upon the materials which a jury may use is likely, if taken seriously, to provoke intense debate.

Thus, it is very easy to confound into one common denominator facts to which the evidentiary discipline of judicial notice applies and the residual data the jury members bring along with them as rational human beings. Whereas in the typical vehicular accident case the well-known character of a street can be dealt with informally as background information which helps everyone visualize the scene, the question becomes a formal one to be dealt with as part of the doctrine of judicial notice if the precise character of the street becomes an adjudicative fact in the case being tried. Again, while the meaning of words is normally left to the informal common sense of the jury, the precise meaning of a word in a contract case which may be outcome determinative should be dealt with formally as a problem of judicial notice.

The cases in which judicial notice is taken of indisputable facts commonly known in the community where the facts noticed are actually adjudicative ones appear to be relatively rare. In most instances, not-withstanding the invocation of the language of judicial notice, the facts either involve background information helpful in assaying the evidence relevant to the adjudicative facts or involve facts relevant to the process of formulating the tenor of the law to be applied to the resolution of the controversy. Indeed, there is a growing recognition that the common knowledge variety of fact plays only a very minor role on the judicial notice scene.

§ 330 Facts Capable of Certain Verification

The earlier and probably still the most familiar basis for judicial notice is "common knowledge," but a second and distinct principle has come to be recognized as an even more significant ground for the invocation of the doctrine. This extension of judicial notice was first disguised by a polite fiction so that when asked to notice a fact not generally known, but which obviously could easily be ascertained by consulting materials in common use, such as the day of the week on which January 1 fell ten years ago, the judges resorted to calendars but purported to be "refreshing memory" as to a matter of common knowledge. Eventually it was recognized that involved here was an important extension of judicial notice to the new field of facts "capable of accurate and ready demonstration," "capable of such instant and unquestionable demonstration, if desired, that no party would think of imposing a falsity on the tribunal in the face of an intelligent adversary," or "can be accurately and readily determined from sources whose accuracy cannot reasonably be questioned."

Information obtained from online sources is becoming a frequently used basis for judicial notice. To this point, government and corporate websites and well-recognized mapping services are among the most commonly relied upon sources. While ordinary principles easily reject some proposed uses of judicial notice, such as with unsubstantiated facts and analyses or where inadequate specificity has been provided, standards for determining the indisputable accuracy of varying types of online sites and data are still evolving. The simplest use of judicial notice involving a website is to establish what information is located there as opposed to establishing the accuracy of that content. No doubt additional uses and interesting issues regarding judicial notice of websites will continue to arise.

It is also under this category that courts have taken judicial notice of established scientific principles that have been verified. These principles justify the evidentiary use of radar, blood tests for intoxication and nonpaternity, handwriting identification, and ballistics. Whether the person employing any of these devices was qualified to do so, whether the equipment was properly maintained and whether it was used correctly remain questions of fact.

Attempts to formulate inventories of verifiable facts of which courts will take judicial notice have begun to fall into disrepute because the principle involved can better be illustrated by way of example. Thus, in *State v. Damm*,[12] the defendant was on trial for rape after one of his stepdaughters gave birth to a child. The defense sought a court order authorizing blood tests with the hope of proving the defendant's innocence through a negative result. Even if the tests produced a negative result, however, the testimony recounting the tests would be relevant to the question of guilt or innocence only if it was true that properly administered blood tests evidencing a negative result excluded the possibility of paternity. To leave this preliminary question pertaining to the then present state of scientific knowledge to the jury to decide as best they could on the basis of possibly conflicting testimony would appear absurd. There being only one right answer to the question whether the principle was accepted in the appropriate scientific circles, the question fell within the province of judicial notice. Even so, the trial judge in this particular case was held not to have erred in refusing the request because the defense was not able to produce the data necessary to illustrate to him that the principle was generally accepted within the scientific community or established as valid under the jurisdiction's test for introduction of scientific expert testimony. The result, now likely through DNA, would be the opposite today.

Thus, while the various propositions of science are a suitable topic of judicial notice, the content of what will actually be noticed is subject to change as the tenets of science evolve. It is manifest, moreover, that the principle involved need not be commonly known in order to be judicially noticed; it suffices if the principle is established as valid in the appropriate scientific community. In determining the intellectual viability of the proposition, of course, the judge is free to consult any sources that he or she thinks are reliable, but the extent to which judges are willing to take the initiative in looking up

---

[12]   266 N.W. 667 (S.D. 1936).

the authoritative sources will usually be limited. By and large, therefore, it is the task of counsel to find and to present in argument and briefs such references, excerpts and explanations as will convince the judge that the fact is certain and demonstrable. Puzzling enough in this regard, it has been noted that "nowhere can there be found a definition of what constitutes competent or authoritative sources for purposes of verifying judicially noticed facts."[13] And, it should be noted that after a number of courts take judicial notice of a principle, subsequent courts begin to dispense with the production of these materials and to take judicial notice of the principle as a matter of law established by precedent.

In Federal Courts and many state courts, the test for receiving scientific evidence has undergone a paradigm shift from one based on the general acceptance standard of *Frye*[14] to *Daubert's*[15] multi-factored test of the validity of scientific or technical expert testimony.[16] But while the paradigm has shifted in terms of initial validation of the basis for expert testimony, the practice of courts taking judicial notice of firmly established principles and methodologies of scientific and technical evidence is only modestly affected. Where the theory or basic methodology is so firmly established as to have attained the status of scientific law, the court can take judicial notice directly.[17] Otherwise the initial acceptance of the principle or methodology must be reached by the courts under a *Daubert* analysis. Thereafter, its judicially established acceptance can be recognized through judicial notice as a matter of law as noted above.

In addition to scientific principles, courts take judicial notice under the theory of verifiable facts of a myriad of other matters. Historical facts fall within the doctrine, such as the dates upon which wars began and terminated. Geographical facts are involved, particularly with reference to the boundaries of the district or state in which the court is sitting and of the counties, districts and townships thereof, as well as the location of the capital of the state and the location and identity of the county seats. Whether common knowledge or not, courts notice the identity of the principal officers of the national government and the incumbents of principal state offices. Similarly, while obviously not necessarily a matter of common knowledge, judges take notice of the identity of the officers of their courts, such as the other judges, the sheriffs, clerks, and attorneys, of the duration of terms and sessions, and of the rules of court.

It would seem obvious that the judge of a court would take notice of all of the records of the institution over which he or she presides, but the courts have been slow to give the principle of judicial notice its full reach of logic and expediency. It is settled, of course, that the courts, trial and appellate, take notice of their own respective records in the present litigation, both as to matters occurring in the immediate trial, and in previous trials or hearings. The principle seemingly is equally applicable to matters of record in the proceedings in other cases in the same court, and some decisions have recognized this, but many courts still adhere to the needless requirement of formal proof, rather than informal presentation, of recorded proceedings in other suits in the same court. However, while the claims made by the parties in the other case and action taken by the court in the other proceeding may be noticed, many courts hold that judicial notice may

---

13   Comment, The Presently Expanding Concept of Judicial Notice, 13 Vill. L. Rev. 528, 545 (1968).

14   Frye v. U.S., 293 F. 1013, 1014 (D.C. Cir. 1923).

15   Daubert v. Merrell Dow Pharms., Inc., 509 U.S. 579 (1993).

16   See generally supra § 203.

17   *Daubert*, 509 U.S. at 593 n.11.

not be taken of factual determinations or contested facts in other cases. Matters of record in other courts are usually denied notice even though it would appear manifest that these public documents are logically subject to judicial notice as to the indisputable information in them.

§ 331   Social and Economic Data Used in Judicial Law-Making: "Legislative" Facts

It is conventional wisdom today to observe that judges not only are charged to find what the law is, but must regularly make new law when deciding upon the constitutional validity of a statute, interpreting a statute, or extending or restricting a common law rule. The very nature of the judicial process necessitates that judges be guided, as legislators are, by considerations of expediency and public policy. They must, in the nature of things, act either upon knowledge already possessed or upon assumptions, or upon investigation of the pertinent general facts, social, economic, political, or scientific. An older tradition once prescribed that judges should rationalize their result solely in terms of analogy to old doctrines, leaving the considerations of expediency unstated. Contemporary practice indicates that judges in their opinions should render explicit their policy judgments and the factual grounds therefor. These latter have been helpfully classed as "legislative facts," as contrasted with the "adjudicative facts" which are historical facts pertaining to the incidents which give rise to lawsuits.

Constitutional cases argued in terms of due process typically involve reliance upon legislative facts for their proper resolution. Whether a statute enacted pursuant to the police power is valid, after all, involves a twofold analysis. First, it must be determined that the enactment is designed to achieve an appropriate objective of the police power; that is, it must be designed to protect the public health, morals, safety, or general welfare. The second question is whether, in light of the data on hand, a legislature could reasonably have adopted the means they did to achieve the aim of their exercise of the police power. In *Jay Burns Baking Co. v. Bryan*,[18] for example, the question was whether, concerned about consumers being misled by confusing sizes of bread, the Nebraska legislature could decree not only that the bakers bake bread according to distinctively different weights but that they wrap their product in wax paper lest any post-oven expansion of some loaves undo these distinctions. A majority of the court held the enactment unconstitutional because, in their opinion, the wrapping requirement was unreasonable. Mr. Justice Brandeis, correctly anticipating the decline of substantive due process, dissented, pointing out that the only question was whether the measure was a reasonable legislative response in light of the facts available to the legislators themselves. Then, in a marvelous illustration of the Brandeis brief technique, he recited page after page of data illustrating how widespread was the problem of shortweight and how, in light of nationwide experience, the statute appeared to be a reasonable response to the environmental situation.

Given the bent to test due process according to the information available to the legislature, the truth-content of these data are not directly relevant. The question is whether sufficient data exist which could influence a reasonable legislature to act, not whether ultimately these data are true. This is not the same case as when a court proceeds to interpret a constitutional norm and, while they still rely upon data, the judges qua legislators themselves proceed to act as if the data were true. In *Brown v.*

---

[18]   264 U.S. 504 (1924).

Board of Education,[19] for example, the Court faced the issue whether segregated schools, equal in facilities and faculty, could any longer be tolerated under the equal protection clause. The question was no longer whether a reasonable legislator could believe these schools could never be equal, but whether the judges believed that the very act of segregating branded certain children with a feeling of inferiority so deleterious that it would be impossible for them to obtain an equal education no matter how equal the facilities and teachers. Thus, the intellectual legitimacy of this kind of decision turns upon the actual truth-content of the legislative facts taken into account by the judges who propound the decision. While not necessarily indisputably true, it would appear that these legislative facts must at least appear to be more likely than not true if the opinion is going to have the requisite intellectual legitimacy upon which the authority of judge-made rules is ultimately founded.

When it comes to the utilization of these lawmaking facts, three problems can beset constitutional law decisions. The first is that the forest can sometimes be lost sight of for the trees. That is to say, so much historical and sociological data are rehearsed that an opinion appears to be bottomed upon purely pragmatic considerations and not upon any compelling constitutional norm.[20] The second is that an outpouring of learning appears inordinate to the requirements of the problem at hand.[21] The third is that data can appear to be included as an exercise in fustian excess, often in a losing cause.[22] The first would appear to be a problem of draftsmanship, hard cases perhaps making bad law, but the latter two appear less defensible.

When making new common law, judges must, like legislators, do the best they can in assaying the data available to them and make the best decision they can concerning which course wisdom dictates they follow. Should they, for example, continue to invoke the common law rule of *caveat emptor* in the field of real property, or should they invoke a notion of implied warranty in the instance of the sale of new houses? Should they require landlords of residential units to warrant their habitability and fitness for the use intended? While sociological, economic, political and moral doctrine may abound about questions like this, none of these data are likely indisputable.

Thus, it is that, in practice, the legislative facts upon which judges rely when performing their lawmaking function are not indisputable. At the same time, cognizant of the fact that her decision as lawmaker can affect the public at large, in contradistinction to most rulings at trials which affect only the parties themselves, a judge is not likely to rely for data only upon what opposing counsel tendered her. Obviously enough, therefore, legislative facts tend to be the most elusive facts when it comes to propounding a codified system of judicial notice. This seems to be confirmed by the fact that the Federal Rules of Evidence make no effort to regulate this type of judicial notice.

§ 332 The Uses of Judicial Notice

Judges have been prone to emphasize the need for caution in applying the doctrine of judicial notice. The great writers of evidence, on the other hand, having perhaps a wider view of the needs of judicial administration, advocate a more extensive use of the

---

[19]   347 U.S. 483 (1954).

[20]   Chief Justice Burger's concurring opinion in Doe v. Bolton, 410 U.S. 179, 208 (1972).

[21]   Justice Blackmun's opinion in Flood v. Kuhn, 407 U.S. 258, 260–64 (1972).

[22]   Chief Justice Rehnquist's dissent in Texas v. Johnson, 491 U.S. 397, 421–35 (1989).

doctrine. Thus, Thayer suggests: "Courts may judicially notice much that they cannot be required to notice. That is well worth emphasizing; for it points to a great possible usefulness in this doctrine, in helping to shorten and simplify trials . . . . The failure to exercise it tends daily to smother trials with technicality and monstrously lengthens them out."[23] And Wigmore says, "The principle is an instrument of usefulness hitherto unimagined by judges."[24]

The simple litany that judicial notice encapsulates facts commonly known and facts readily verifiable is useful as a rule-of-thumb but not as a precise litmus test. The courts' willingness to resort to judicial notice is apparently influenced by a number of less specifically definable circumstances. A court is more willing to notice a general than a specific fact, as for example, the approximate time of the normal period of human gestation, but not the precise maximum and minimum limits. A court may be more willing to notice a fact if it is not an ultimate fact, that is, a fact which would be determinative of a case. Suppose, for example, that a plaintiff in a vehicular negligence action specifically alleged that the defendant was driving too fast in a business district and the testimony, if believed, would indicate that the automobile in question caused a long skid mark on the highway surface. The trial judge might be less willing to notice that the street in question was within the business district than to notice that any properly equipped automobile travelling at the maximum speed appropriate in such a district could be stopped within x feet of the braking point. In the first example, the trial judge would appear to be invading the province of the jury to determine the facts pertinent to what had happened, whereas in the second she would be merely establishing rather quickly a piece of data which would aid the jury during their deliberations on the ultimate issue of negligence.

Agreement is not to be had whether the perimeters of the doctrine of judicial notice enclose only facts which are indisputably true or encompass also facts more than likely true. If, on the one hand, the function of the jury is to resolve disputed questions of fact, an argument can be made that judges should not purport to make decisions about facts unless they are indisputable facts. If this argument is accepted, it follows that once a fact has been judicially noticed, evidence contradicting the truth of the fact is inadmissible because by its very nature, a fact capable of being judicially noticed is an indisputable fact which the jury must be instructed to accept as true.[25] If, on the other hand, the function of judicial notice is to expedite the trial of cases, an argument can be made that judges should dispense with the need for time-consuming formal evidence when the fact in question is likely true. If this argument is accepted, it follows that evidence contradicting the judicially noticed fact is admissible and that the jury are ultimately free to accept or reject the truth of the fact posited by judicial notice.

A facile resolution of this conflict suggests itself readily enough. That is, the controversy might be exposed as a misunderstanding caused by a failure to take into account the distinction between "adjudicative" and "legislative" facts. This would be true if the instances where judicial notice was restricted to indisputable facts involved only adjudicative facts whereas potentially disputable facts were only noticed within a legislative context. Whether the decided cases sustain this symmetry is itself a matter of dispute because authority exists which illustrates that some courts are not loathe

---

[23]   Thayer, A Preliminary Treatise on Evidence 309 (1898).

[24]   Wigmore, 9 Evidence § 2583, at 819 (Chadbourn rev. 1981).

[25]   *See* Morgan, Judicial Notice, 57 Harv. L. Rev. 269 (1940).

judicially to notice a potentially disputable fact within what is at least arguably an adjudicative context.

The most recent efforts to deal with judicial notice have exhibited a trend away from extrapolating an all-inclusive definition of a doctrine in favor of promulgating modest guidelines which would regularize what are perceived to be the essential applications of judicial notice. One approach would restrict formalized judicial notice regulation to those situations in which only adjudicative facts are involved.[26] Limiting judicial notice to adjudicative facts and then only to indisputable ones leaves unresolved the question whether a jury in a criminal case should be instructed that they must accept the inexorable truth of the noticed fact. In terms of logic and pure reason it would appear that a jury as a rational deliberative body must accept proper judicially noticed facts. But, viewed through the lens of democratic tradition as a protection against an overbearing sovereign, a criminal trial jury may be a body which ought to be free to return a result which as an exercise in logic flies in the face of reason.

Another approach would narrow the range of judicial notice by reducing the significance of the conflict between questions peculiarly the province of juries and questions of fact handled by judges. Judges have, for example, always dealt with preliminary questions of fact even in jury trials. Thus, while the admissibility of the results of blood tests raises a question of fact pertaining to the reliability of such tests, the judges deal with this question as a preliminary step in ruling on relevancy, a function that is itself peculiarly a judicial one. Indeed, if trials are examined functionally, it can be demonstrated that judges have always had to decide questions pertaining to facts without any apparent infringement of the jury's domain, whether this be in ruling on demurrers, during pretrial hearings, on motions for nonsuit or to set aside verdicts, or at sentencing. This may indicate, after all, that the scope of judicial notice varies according to the function the judge is performing when judicial notice is taken.

It may be the case that there is no easy rule-of-thumb technique adequate unto the day to serve as an easy capsulation of the judicial notice phenomenon. Protagonists of the indisputable-only definition of judicial notice concede that in criminal cases the jury must be left free in the ultimate analysis to determine the truth or falsity of any adjudicative fact. Protagonists of the disputability thesis might be expected to resolve the controversy by suggesting that, whereas in jury cases there is some merit in the notion that judicial notice should be restricted to indisputable facts in order not to infringe on the role of the jury, the disputable theory works quite efficiently within the context of the jury-waived cases, which probably means that it applies in most cases which come to trial. The fact of the matter is that this solution has not received as much notoriety as might be expected.[27]

The very fact that the trend of these recent investigations has been calculated to resolve the problems associated with judicial notice by narrowing the dimensions of that concept has, however, raised a new problem which must be dealt with in the future. If judicial notice is restricted to instances where judges deal with facts in an adjudicative context, the instances where judges deal with legislative facts is left unregulated insofar

---

[26]   See Fed. R. Evid. 201(a) advisory committee's note.

[27]   A possible explanation may be found in the close, if not complete, coincidence between a disputable judicially noticed fact and rebuttable presumption. This relationship has largely passed undetected and without comment. *See* Fringer v. Venema, 132 N.W.2d 565 (Wis. 1965).

as procedural guidelines are concerned. The significance of this problem can be best illustrated within the context of the next section.

§ 333 Procedural Incidents

An elementary sense of fairness might indicate that a judge before making a final ruling that judicial notice will be taken should notify the parties of his or her intention to do so and afford them an opportunity to present information which might bear upon the propriety of noticing the fact, or upon the truth of the matter to be noticed. Although the original version of the Uniform Rules of Evidence required it, only a rare pre-Federal Rules case insisted that a judge must notify the parties before taking judicial notice of a fact on his or her own motion, and Federal Rule 201(e) permits judicial notice before notification of the parties. It may very well be the case that a trial judge need only consider notifying the parties if on her own motion she intends to take judicial notice of a less than obviously true fact. In every other instance, after all, the request by one party asking the judge to take judicial notice will serve to apprise the opposing party of the question at hand. While there may, nevertheless, exist in practice a rough consensus with regard to procedural niceties when trial judges take judicial notice of adjudicative facts, this is not the end of the matter. The cases universally assume the nonexistence of any need for a structured adversary-style ancillary hearing with regard to legislative facts. Indeed, even with regard to adjudicative facts, the practices of appellate courts tend to support the argument that there exists no real felt need to formalize the practice of taking judicial notice.

Legislative facts, of course, have not fitted easily into any effort to propound a formalized set of rules applicable to judicial notice. These facts, after all, tend to be less than indisputable ones and hence beyond the pale of judicial notice. What then of the requirement that, before judicial notice is taken, the parties be afforded a reasonable opportunity to present information relative to the propriety of taking judicial notice and the tenor of the matter to be noticed? By and large the parties have this opportunity during arguments over motions as to the appropriate law to be applied to the controversy, by exchanging briefs, and by employing the technique exemplified by the Brandeis brief. It appears, therefore, that there exists no felt need to formalize the procedures pertaining to the opportunity to be heard with reference to legislative facts. Even so, there are cases where the legislative facts which form the basis of an appellate opinion first appear in the decision itself and counsel never have the opportunity to respond to them. Presumably current practice relies upon the sound discretion of judges to maintain discipline in this regard by presupposing a general insistence among the judges on a fundamental notion of elementary fairness. However ill-defined because rooted in a sense of due process rather than bottomed on a precise calculus of rules, this notion of fairness may prove to be the common denominator which will continue to link together judicial notice of legislative and adjudicative facts.

With regard to the treatment of adjudicative facts by appellate courts, the common starting point is the axiom that in civil cases these tribunals can take judicial notice to the same extent as can trial courts. At the very least, this rule suggests the obvious fact that appellate courts can review the propriety of the judicial notice taken by the court below, and when not reviewing a criminal case tried to a jury can even take judicial notice on their own initiative of facts not noticed below. Despite the fact that Federal Rule 201(d) allows judicial notice to be taken at any stage of the proceeding and provides no limitation on criminal cases, it is doubtful that judicial notice can be taken on appeal in a criminal case tried before a jury given the restricting under Federal Rule 201(f). That provision states that in criminal cases the court may not, unlike in civil cases, instruct the jury that it is to accept the noticed fact as conclusive but instead must instruct that the jury "may or may not" accept that fact.

Nonetheless the recitation of these principles fails to portray the full flavor of the actual practice of appellate courts in taking judicial notice on their own initiative of what would appear to be adjudicative facts.

In this regard the case of *Mills v. Denver Tramway Corp.*,[28] may be instructive. Plaintiff had alighted from a trolley car, walked behind it and crossed the parallel set of tracks, where he was struck by a car going in the opposite direction. Plaintiff appeared to be manifestly guilty of contributory negligence, a sound enough conclusion plaintiff next attempted to overcome by invoking the doctrine of the last-clear-chance. That is, at the penultimate moment of the trial, plaintiff requested a jury instruction to the effect that, if the motorman had had a chance to sound the trolley bell, the harm might still have been avoided, in which case plaintiff was entitled to prevail. The trial judge refused the instruction because no evidence was ever introduced to indicate that the trolley had a bell. The appellate tribunal reversed, giving plaintiff a new trial, reciting the fact that "streetcars have bells." If all trolley cars had bells, a fact the trial court could have taken judicial notice of had it ever been requested to do so, it would be quite appropriate for the appellate court to take notice of the very same fact. But was it an indisputable fact that all streetcars had bells? Arguably most did, in which case the appellate court was taking judicial notice, not of an indisputable fact, but only of a more-than-likely-true fact. More plausibly, the court reasoned that, in all likelihood, the trolley had a bell, in which instance plaintiff should have, as part of his case, proceeded to introduce evidence to substantiate a plausible claim on the last-clear-chance theory. Alternatively, had no bell existed, plaintiff should have made that omission the basis of his claim. In either event, a sense of justice cried out for a trial of the case with all the facts fully developed. If, however, this was the sense of justice which moved the appellate tribunal, their invocation of the statement that "all streetcars have bells," a disputable proposition, sheds no real light either on the question whether judicial notice extends to disputable adjudicative facts or whether the parties must be afforded a hearing before judicial notice is taken. Given the need for appellate courts on occasion to reverse results below on a factual basis, judicial notice serves as a convenient device by which to give the practice the appearance of legal propriety. This being true, it would appear that the chances of adequately formalizing judicial notice even of adjudicative facts at the appellate level may be a slim one indeed.

§ 334 Trends in the Development of Judicial Notice of Facts

It appears that, by and large, agreement has been reached on a rough outline of the perimeters of judicial notice as applied to adjudicative facts at the trial level.[29] A workable procedural format which would appear to guarantee fairness already exists in the event that judicial notice is restricted to indisputable facts. The only question remaining is whether, in order to expedite the trial of cases, judges should be allowed to excuse the proponent of a fact likely true of the necessity of producing formal evidence thereof, leaving it to the jury to accept or reject the judicially noticed fact, and of course,

---

[28]   155 F.2d 808 (10th Cir. 1946).

[29]   See Fed. R. Evid. 201 & Unif. R. Evid. 201 (2005).

allowing the opponent to introduce evidence contradicting it. Indeed, the present controversy might be put in a new light by limiting judicial notice to indisputable facts and then raising the question, whether, as part of the law associated with the burden of proof and presumptions, a judge can properly expedite trials by himself ruling that very likely true facts are presumptively true unless the jury care to find otherwise.

Whatever the ultimate doctrinal synthesis of judicial notice of adjudicative facts comes to be, a viable formulation of rules laying down a similarly rigid procedural etiquette with regard to legislative facts has not proved feasible. Given the current recognition that nonadjudicative facts are inextricably part and parcel of the law formulation process in a policy-oriented jurisprudence, there may be no need to formulate a distinctly judicial notice-captioned procedure with regard to nonadjudicative facts. These data are fed into the judicial process now whenever rules of law are brought to the attention of judges in motions, memoranda and briefs. Thus, whatever rules govern the submission of law in the litigation process have already preempted the nonadjudicative field and made unnecessary separate treatment thereof within the context of judicial notice.

There has been an increasing awareness, moreover, that quite apart from judicial notice, the trial process assumes that the participants bring with them a vast amount of everyday knowledge of facts in general. To think, after all, presupposes some data about which to think. In an automobile accident case, for example, both the judge and the jury constantly draw on their own experiences as drivers, as observers of traffic, and as live human beings, and these experiences are reduced in their minds to propositions of fact which, since they have survived themselves, are probably fairly accurate. This substratum of data the participants bring into the courthouse has, however, tended to confuse the judicial notice scene. On the one hand, this subliminal-like data is sometimes confused with the "common knowledge"-style of adjudicative facts with which formal judicial notice is concerned. On the other hand, judges constantly invoke references to these same everyday facts when they write opinions because, when formally articulated, it is impossible "to think" without reference to them. It may very well be the case that judges have tended, when extrapolating the obvious, to invoke the words, "I take judicial notice of" to explain the presence of these facts in their minds, thereby unnecessarily glutting the encyclopedias with trivia which are, when formally collected, highly misleading indices of the true scope of judicial notice as such.

Federal Rule of Evidence 201 only applies to adjudicative facts, which might suggest that legislative facts simply cannot be fitted into the concept of judicial notice. If they cannot, legislative facts would have to come into the judicial process in the form of "evidence." A problem would then arise if a trial court had to decide the question of law whether it was constitutional totally to exclude from a bifurcated jury in a capital case individuals opposed to the death penalty. After hearing testimony and accepting documentary material, the court might conclude on the basis of available social science materials that either death disqualification produced conviction prone juries or it did not. The court might bottom its decision of the constitutional issue on this "finding of fact." If the social science materials were not clearly inclined to sustain only one conclusion, and the ruling were treated as a factual ruling, the ruling, whichever way it came out, could not be reversed because it would not be clearly erroneous. Law would come to turn on fact and be susceptible to two right answers. This is not going to happen. Legislative facts are not "evidence" in the normal sense of the word, and judicial notice doctrine still obtains as to them. The problem is one of refining that doctrine, and not confusing it with evidentiary proof of adjudicatory facts.

Arguably legislative facts might better be handled by treating them as one would a search for law amidst a canon of conflicting cases, ruling on the tenor of the applicable economic or social rule as if it were a question of law. But as we have seen, judges are constantly asserting facts to be true in many contexts and at many stages of the judicial process, "facts" which while they appeal to common sense and prudence as work-a-day truths, lack the dignity and permanence of something that could be called "law." Law requires more than cracker-barrel folk wisdom behind it to command respect and obedience. What is needed is a new concept, perhaps oriented around the study of thinking-about-facts techniques involved throughout the judicial process. Judge Robert E. Keeton has spearheaded just such an endeavor in the most appropriate context of a William B. Lockhart Lecture, taking as his cue the notion that facts are the premise of innumerable rulings.[30] Oddly enough, this trend if continued would represent a return to Thayer.[31]

To add further spice to this subject mention must be made of the Internet. In *Atkins v. Virginia*,[32] Justice Stevens wrote for the majority that contemporary standards of decency compelled the conclusion that the execution of a mentally retarded individual had become cruel and unusual punishment not permitted by the 8th Amendment. This standard was derived from recent state legislation exempting these persons from execution. Although a majority of states had not yet so amended their laws, the amendments relied upon illustrated a consistency in the direction of change. Appended in a note were the results of opinion polls and the views of religious and professional organizations, together with a note referencing world opinion. The Chief Justice Rehnquist took exception to the use of any standard other than a head count of state practice. Not only did he add an appendix designed to show that polls were not dependable sources upon which to formulate any judgment, he signed off on his opinion with an abrupt "I dissent." Although respectfully dissenting, Justice Scalia made mock of the legislative facts and asserted that the case had not really been decided upon the "fabricated" national consensus but in cavalier fashion upon the feelings about the issue held by the majority. This case presaged an increasingly acrimonious debate about the use of foreign law. And it also raised the potential for real differences in the future when it came to use of the vast data made available on the web.

It was Justice Stevens again who authored a concise summary of this last phenomenon.[33] The information available through the internet to anyone who had access to computers is infinite by human standards, and includes not only books, journals and newspapers, but the law of many jurisdictions. "Publishers include government agencies, educational institutions, commercial entities, advocacy groups, and individuals. Publishers may either make their material available to the entire pool of internet users, or confine access to a restricted group such as those willing to pay for the privilege."[34] The reception of the internet has varied among judges. Early on a Texas district judge

---

[30]   *See* Keeton, Legislative Facts and Similar Things: Deciding Disputed Premise Facts, 73 Minn. L. Rev.1 (1998).

[31]   *See* Thayer, A Preliminary Treatise on Evidence at the Common Law 278–79 (1898).

[32]   536 U.S. 304 (2002).

[33]   Reno v. American Civil Liberties Union, 521 U.S. 844, 849–52 (1997).

[34]   *Id.* at 843.

conditionally denied a motion to dismiss a personal injury action on the ground that the plaintiff's proof that the defendant owned the vessel at the time was based on "electronic" evidence, citing the Coast Guard's on-line data base.[35] The judge was convinced that information gleaned from the web was inherently untrustworthy because anyone could put something of the web and hackers could adulterate what was already there. "Instead of relying on voodoo information taken from the Internet, Plaintiff must hunt for hard copy back-up documentation in admissible form from the United States Coast Guard or discover alternative information verifying what Plaintiff alleges."[36] Then again, Judge Posner cited Wikipedia for an aside noting that a defendant was "a former trainer of the Polish boxer Andrew Golata—the world's most colorful boxer."[37] A matter of little moment unless one adds that the judge is reported to have called Wikipedia "a terrific resource" though "it wouldn't be right to use it in a critical issue."[38]

One might put a perfectly reasonable gloss on this by suggesting that data extracted from the Internet must be authenticated in such a way as to pass the test of verifiable accuracy were its use to establish an adjudicative fact. When it comes to legislative facts one must presume the judge has the requisite common sense and critical sensitivity to use data on a sliding scale of dependability keyed to the weight it bears holding up the decision being made.

§ 335 The Judge's Task as Law-Finder: Judicial Notice of Law

It would appear to be self-evident that it is peculiarly the function of the judge to find and interpret the law applicable to the issues in a trial and, in a jury case, to announce her findings of law to the jury for their guidance. The heavy-footed common law system of proof by witnesses and authenticated documents is too slow and cumbrous for the judge's task of finding what the applicable law is. Usually this law is familiar lore, and if not, the judge relies on the respective counsel to present the statutes, reports, and source books, and these resources are read from informally in discussion or cited and quoted in trial and appellate briefs. Occasionally the judge will go beyond the cited authorities to make her own investigation. In the ordinary process of finding the applicable law, the normal method then is by informal investigation of any sources satisfactory to the judge. Thus, this process has been traditionally described in terms of the judge taking judicial notice of the law applicable to the case at hand. Indeed, when the source-material was not easily accessible to the judge, as in the case of "foreign law" or city ordinances, law has been treated as a peculiar species of fact, requiring formal proof. We shall see, however, that as these materials become more accessible, the tendency is toward permitting the judges to do what perhaps they should have done in the beginning, that is, to rely on the diligence of counsel to provide the necessary materials, and accordingly to take judicial notice of all law. This seems to be the goal toward which the practice is marching.

Domestic Law. As to domestic law generally, the judge is not merely permitted to take judicial notice but required to do so, at least if requested, although in a particular case a party may be precluded on appeal from complaining of the judge's failure to notice a statute where the party's counsel has failed to call it to the judge's attention. This

---

[35]   St. Clair v. Johnny's Oyster & Shrimp, Inc., 76 F. Supp. 2d 773 (S.D. Tex. 1999).

[36]   *Id.* at 775.

[37]   United States v. Radomsky, 473 F.3d 728, 731 (7th Cir. 2007).

[38]   Cohen, Courts Turn to Wikipedia, But Selectively, N.Y. Times, Jan. 20, 2007.

general rule that judicial notice will be taken of domestic law means that state trial courts will notice Federal law, which is controlling in every state, and has been held to mean that in a Federal trial court the laws of the states, not merely of the state where it is sitting, are domestic and will be noticed. Similarly, all statewide or nationwide executive orders and proclamations, which are legally effective, will be noticed. Under this same principle, even the laws of antecedent governments will be noticed.

State and national administrative regulations having the force of law will also be noticed, at least if they are published so as to be readily available. When such documents are published in the Federal Register, it is provided that their contents shall be judicially noticed.[39] Private laws and municipal ordinances, however, were historically not commonly included within the doctrine of judicial notice and these must be pleaded and proved. Municipal ordinances are now in many, but not all, jurisdictions subject to judicial notices, and that trend is likely to continue to grow as such ordinances become readily available in compilations. In the meantime, it would appear appropriate for judges to take judicial notice of both private laws and municipal ordinances if counsel furnish a certified copy thereof.

The Law of Sister States. It is easy to see how the difference of languages and inaccessibility of source books should have led the English courts to develop the common law rule that the laws of foreign nations would not be noticed but must be pleaded and proved as facts. The assumption in the earlier cases in this country that the courts of one state must treat the laws of another state as foreign for this purpose is less understandable and in retrospect seems a deplorable instance of mechanical jurisprudence. Yet it remains today, in nearly every one of the increasingly few states which have not yet adopted a remedial statute, the common law rule that notice will not be given to the laws of sister states. This is probably the most inconvenient of all the limitations upon the practice of judicial notice. Notice here could certainly be justified on the principle of certainty and verifiability, and the burden on the judge could be minimized by casting the responsibility upon counsel either to agree upon a stipulation as to the law or to produce on each side for the benefit of the court all materials necessary for ascertaining the law in question.

Under this hoary practice when a required pleading and proof of the foreign law has been overlooked, or has been unsuccessfully attempted, the resulting danger of injustice is somewhat mitigated by the presumption that the law of the sister state is the same as that of the forum, or more simply the practice of applying local law if the law of the other state is not invoked and proven. But this presumption-tool is too rough for the job in hand, particularly when the materials for ascertaining the laws of sister states are today almost as readily accessible as those for local law, and in any event counsel as officers of the court are available to find and present those materials to the judge in just the same informal and convenient fashion as if they were arguing a question of local law.

In 1936 the Conference of Commissioners on Uniform Laws drafted the Uniform Judicial Notice of Foreign Law Act This legislation provided that every court within the adopting state shall take judicial notice of the common law and statutes of every other state. The 1936 Act pertained to the law of sister states and did not address the issue of the law of other nations. It was supplanted in 1962 when the National Conference of Commissioners on Uniform Laws approved Article IV of the Uniform Interstate and

---

[39]   See 44 U.S.C.A. § 1507.

International Procedure Act. Calculated to address judicial notice of true foreign law, the new Act implicates the law of sister states as well because it imposes the same discipline when the law of any extra-forum jurisdiction was invoked. This act was in turn withdrawn "due to it being obsolete."[40]

The Law of Foreign Countries. At common law, foreign law was treated as a matter of fact: pleading and proof were required, and the jury decided what the foreign law was. As early as 1936 the Uniform Judicial Notice of Foreign Law Act reflected the idea that the tenor of the law of a foreign country was a question for the court and not for the jury. What is significant is the fact that this selfsame 1936 Act, adverted to in the preceding section, contained no provision for the judicial notice of the law of other nations. The parties were left not only to pleading but proving, albeit to a judge and not a jury, the law of other nations.

The longevity of the ancient notion that a party had "to prove" the law of another nation was likely rooted in the fact that the sources of extranational law were not easily accessible even in urban centers. A healthy pragmatism seems to have ameliorated the harshness of any rule demanding strict proof. Sworn to or certified copies of extranational statutes or decisions gave way to the use of copies thereof in a book printed by the authority of the foreign state or proved to be commonly recognized in its courts.

Even so, the very idea that a party was engaged in "proving" a point of extranational law fairly invited complications. The written text of any law suggests that its "black letter" be interpreted in light of any germane decisions, treatises or commentaries. This under common law proof must be accomplished by taking the testimony in person or by deposition of an expert in the foreign law. The adversary of course is free to take the testimony of other experts if he can find them on his side, and the cross-examination of conflicting experts is likely to accentuate the disagreements. This method of proof seems to maximize expense and delay and hardly seems best calculated to ensure a correct decision by our judges on questions of foreign law. It could be vastly improved by pre-trial conferences in which agreements as to undisputed aspects of the foreign law could be secured, and by the appointment by the court of one or more experts on foreign law as referees or as court-chosen experts to report their findings to the court.

Following the lead of several states which by statute have provided that the court must take judicial notice or permit the court to do so in its discretion, the practice obtaining in the federal courts has been codified to make the tenor of foreign law a question of law for the court.[41] Thus, it is that a party who intends to raise an issue of foreign nation law must give notice of his intention to do so, either in his pleadings or by any other reasonable method of written notice. Once the issue of foreign law is raised, the court need not, in its effort to determine the tenor of that law, rely upon the testimony and other materials proffered by the litigant, but may engage in its own research and consider any relevant material thus found.

The unwillingness of the courts to notice the laws of other countries creates difficulties where the party whose case or defense depends, under conflicts rules, upon foreign law and that party fails to prove that law as a fact. There are several solutions. First, the court may decide the issue against that party for failure of proof. This is often a harsh and arbitrary result. Second, the court may simply apply the law of the forum

---

[40]   13 ULA Part II 127 (2002); 2011 Handbook, Nat'l Conference of Commissioners of State Laws 625.

[41]   Fed. R. Civ. P. 44.1; Fed. R. Crim. P. 26.1.

on the ground that no other law is before it, especially if the parties have tried the case as if local law were applicable. Third, the court may presume that the law of the other country is the same as that of the forum, thus reaching the same result as under the second theory but raising intellectual difficulties because the presumption is so frequently contrary to fact. When the doctrine involved is one of common law, but the other nation is not a common law country, some courts will decline to apply the presumption. On the other hand, when the common law rule invoked is a part of the common fund of all civilized systems, such as the binding force of ordinary commercial agreements, the presumption is applied though the foreign country is not a common law country. Moreover, by what is probably the prevailing and more convenient view, if the question would be governed locally by a statute, a like statute in the foreign country may be presumed.

International and Maritime Law. The rules, principles and traditions of "international law," or "the law of nations," will be noticed in Federal and state courts. Maritime law is similarly subject to judicial notice but only insofar as these rules have become part of the general maritime law. Less widely recognized maritime rules of foreign countries are treated like foreign law generally and are required to be proved, unless they have been published here by government authority as the authentic foreign law, or they have been embodied in a widely adopted international convention. Peculiarly enough, the presumption of identity of foreign law with the local law, which would seem to be unusually convenient and realistic in the maritime field, has been narrowly restricted.

The Future of Judicial Notice of Law. When a judge presiding in the presence of a jury decides a question of fact, a sufficiently unique event occurs to merit special treatment because the jury is thought to perform the fact-finding role in common law countries. This appears to explain why judicial notice of facts has been a topic of evidence law ever since Thayer authored his pioneering treatise. There is nothing very remarkable about a judge ruling on the tenor of the law to be applied to the resolution of the controversy, however, because by definition this is the very function judges are supposed to perform. When the sources of law were dubious at best, the job of sorting out the applicable law was shifted to the jury, witness how foreign law and municipal ordinances were treated as questions of fact. When next judges began to rule on the tenor of this law, even though it was still "fact" to be developed by the parties, there may have been some justification for describing this process as judicial notice. As all law has become increasingly accessible and judges have tended to assume the duty to rule on the tenor of all law, the notion that this process is part of judicial notice has become increasingly an anachronism. Evidence, after all, involves the proof of facts. How the law is fed into the judicial machine is more appropriately an aspect of the law pertaining to procedure. Thus, it is that the electronic bleeps sounded by today's data processing equipment may be actually tolling the intellectual death knell of this discrete subject-matter hitherto dealt with as a subdivision of the law of evidence.

Old habits, however, are hard to break. A short time researching the scene at state level will quickly turn up a number of states wherein the Uniform Judicial Notice of Foreign Law Act still obtains, together with a hotchpot of discrete statutes detailing judicial notice of local statutes, some administrative regulations and some if not all municipal ordinances. These materials cry out for rationalization and it is little wonder than that several states, in the process of adopting the Federal Rules of Evidence have added a Rule 202 governing the judicial notice of law. Coming full circle there existed a proposed revision of the Federal model that would add rules creating a coordinated regimen for inputting law into the judicial process through the judicial notice of law mechanism.[42]

Using foreign law as legislative fact can be a controversial practice. A convenient starting point is the opinion by Justice Stevens citing an amicus brief filed by the European Union in support of the proposition that "within the world community the imposition of the death penalty for a crime committed by mentally retarded offenders is overwhelmingly disapproved."[43] This provoked Justice Scalia to object that "irrelevant are practices of the world community, whose notions of justice are (thankfully) not always those of our people."[44] Then, quoting himself, he warned that "We must never forget that it is a Constitution of the United States of America that we are expounding . . . . [W]here there is not first a settled consensus among our own people, the views of other nations, however enlightened the Justices of this Court may think them, cannot be imposed upon Americans through the Constitution."[45]

Using foreign or international law as legislative fact in formulating standards of civilized opinion or behavior is one thing but applying it as law controlling the decision is quite another. The use of Sharia law in domestic relations case, notwithstanding its reversal,[46] catalyzed a frenzy of proposals for legislation at state level designed to prevent this,[47] much of it painting with a broad brush that would ban the use of all foreign and international law.

---

[42]   Proposed Revisions to the Federal Rules of Evidence, 171 F.R.D. 330 (a good model of a bad idea).

[43]   Atkins v. Virginia, 536 U.S. 304, 316 n.21 (2002).

[44]   *Id.* at 347–48 (Scalia, J., dissenting).

[45]   *Id.* at 348 (Scalia, J., dissenting).

[46]   S.D. v. M.J.R., 2 A.3d 412 (N.J. Super. Ct. App. Div. 2010) (reversing opinion below).

[47]   *See, e.g.*, Ariz. Rev. Stat. Ann. §§ 12–3101, 12–3103.

Title 12

BURDEN OF PROOF AND PRESUMPTIONS

Chapter 36

THE BURDENS OF PROOF
AND PRESUMPTIONS

Table of Sections

§ 336 The Burdens of Proof: The Burden of Producing Evidence and the Burden of Persuasion

"Proof" is an ambiguous word. We sometimes use it to mean evidence, such as testimony or documents. Sometimes, when we say a thing is "proved" we mean that we are convinced by the data submitted that the alleged fact is true. Thus, "proof" is the end result of conviction or persuasion produced by the evidence. Naturally, the term "burden of proof" shares this ambivalence. The term encompasses two separate burdens of proof. One burden is that of producing evidence, satisfactory to the judge, of a particular fact in issue. The second is the burden of persuading the trier of fact that the alleged fact is true.

The burden of producing evidence on an issue means the liability to an adverse ruling (generally a finding or directed verdict) if evidence on the issue has not been produced. It is usually cast first upon the party who has pleaded the existence of the fact, but as we shall see, the burden may shift to the adversary when the pleader has discharged its initial duty.[1] The burden of producing evidence is a critical mechanism in a jury trial, as it empowers the judge to decide the case without jury consideration when a party fails to sustain the burden.

---

[1] See infra § 338.

The burden of persuasion becomes a crucial factor only if the parties have sustained their burdens of producing evidence and only when all of the evidence has been introduced. It does not shift from party to party during the course of the trial simply because it need not be allocated until it is time for a decision. When the time for a decision comes, the jury, if there is one, must be instructed how to decide the issue if their minds are left in doubt. The jury must be told that if the party having the burden of persuasion has failed to satisfy that burden, the issue is to be decided against that party. If there is no jury and the judge is in doubt, the issue must be decided against the party having the burden of persuasion.

What is the significance of the burden of persuasion? Clearly, the principal significance of the burden of persuasion is limited to those cases in which the trier of fact is actually in doubt. Possibly, even in those cases, juries disregard their instructions on this question and judges, trying cases without juries, pay only lip service to it, trusting that the appellate courts will not disturb their findings of fact. Yet, even if an empirical study were conclusively to demonstrate both a regular disregard for jury instructions and a propensity on the part of judges to decide issues of fact without regard to their express statements concerning the allocation of the burden of persuasion, rules allocating and describing that burden could not be discarded by a rational legal system. A risk of nonpersuasion naturally exists any time one person attempts to persuade another to act or not to act. If the other does not change her course of action or nonaction, the person desiring change has, of course, failed. If no burden of persuasion were acknowledged by the law, one possible result would be that the trier of fact would purport to reach no decision at all. The impact of nondecision would then fall by its own weight upon the party, usually the plaintiff, who sought a change in the status quo. Although this is generally where the law would place the burden anyhow, important policy considerations may dictate that the risk should fall on the opposing party.[2]

Another possibility would be that the trier of fact would itself assign a burden of persuasion, describing that burden as it saw fit by substituting its own notions of policy for those now made available to it as a matter of law. Such a result would be most undesirable. Considerations of policy that are sufficient to suggest that in some instances the burden of persuasion be assigned to the party desiring a maintenance of the status quo are strong enough to dictate the need for a consistent rather than a case by case determination of the question. Other policy considerations, such as those that have led the law to require that the prosecution in a criminal case prove the defendant guilty beyond a reasonable doubt,[3] are sufficient to require that the jury be explicitly and clearly instructed as to the measure of the burden as well as its allocation. Although judges and juries may act contrary to the law despite the best attempts to persuade them to do otherwise, we can at least give them the benefit of thoughtful guidance on the questions of who should bear the burden of persuasion and what the nature of that burden should be. In jury trials, perhaps the problem has not been in the concept of a burden of persuasion, but rather in the confusing jury instructions that abound on this point of law. In nonjury trials, if judges are not in fact following rules of law allocating the burden, the fault may lie not in the concept but with thoughtless judicial and legislative allocations and descriptions of the burden.

---

[2]   See infra § 337.

[3]   See infra § 341.

§ 337　Allocating the Burdens of Proof

In most cases, the party who has the burden of pleading a fact will have the burdens of producing evidence and of persuading the jury of its existence as well. The pleadings therefore provide the common guide for apportioning the burdens of proof. For example, in a typical negligence case the plaintiff will have the burdens of (1) pleading the defendant's negligence (2) producing evidence of that negligence and (3) persuading the trier of fact of its existence. The defendant will usually have the same three burdens with regard to the contributory negligence of the plaintiff.

However, looking for the burden of pleading is not a foolproof guide to the allocation of the burdens of proof. The latter burdens do not invariably follow the pleadings. In a federal court, for example, a defendant may be required to plead contributory negligence as an affirmative defense and yet, where jurisdiction is based upon diversity of citizenship, the applicable substantive law may place the burdens of producing evidence and persuasion with regard to that issue on the plaintiff. More significantly, reference to which party has pleaded a fact is no help at all when the rationale behind the allocation is questioned or in a case of first impression where there are no established pleading rules.

The burdens of pleading and proof with regard to most facts have been and should be assigned to the plaintiff who generally seeks to change the present state of affairs and who therefore naturally should be expected to bear the risk of failure of proof or persuasion. The rules which assign certain facts material to the enforceability of a claim to the defendant owe their development partly to traditional happen-so and partly to considerations of policy.

The determination of appropriate guidelines for the allocation of the burdens has been somewhat hindered by the judicial repetition of two doctrines, one erroneous and the other meaningless. Statements are found primarily in older cases to the effect that even though a party is required to plead a fact, it is not required to prove that fact if its averment is negative rather than affirmative in form. Such a rule would place an entirely undue emphasis on what is ordinarily purely a matter of choice of forms. Moreover, these statements were probably to be understood as properly applying only to the denial by a party of an opponent's previous pleading, and now one who has the burden of pleading a negative fact as part of its cause of action generally has the accompanying burdens of producing evidence and persuasion. The second misleading doctrine is that the party to whose case the element is essential has the burdens of proof. Such a rule simply restates the question.

The actual reasons for the allocation of the burdens may be no more complex than the misleading statements just discussed. The policy of handicapping a disfavored contention probably accounts for the requirement that the defendant generally has all three burdens with regard to such matters as contributory negligence, statute of limitations, and truth in defamation. Convenience in following the natural order of storytelling may account for calling on the defendant to plead and prove those matters which arise after a cause of action has matured, such as payment, release, and accord and satisfaction.

A doctrine often repeated by the courts is that where the facts with regard to an issue lie peculiarly in the knowledge of a party, that party has the burden of proving the issue. Examples are the burdens commonly placed upon the defendant to prove payment, discharge in bankruptcy, and license. This consideration should not be overemphasized. Very often one must plead and prove matters as to which his adversary has superior access to the proof. Nearly all required allegations of the plaintiff in actions for tort or breach of contract relating to the defendant's acts or omissions describe matters peculiarly in the defendant's knowledge. Correspondingly, when the defendant is required to plead contributory negligence, it pleads facts specially known to the plaintiff.

Perhaps a more frequently significant consideration in the fixing of the burdens of proof is the judicial estimate of the probabilities of the situation. The risk of failure of proof may be placed upon the party who contends that the more unusual event has occurred. For example, where a business relationship exists, it is unlikely that services will be performed gratuitously. The burden of proving a gift is therefore placed upon the one who claims it. Where services are performed for a member of the family, a gift is much more likely and the burden of proof is placed on the party claiming the right to be paid.

In allocating the burdens, courts consistently attempt to distinguish between the constituent elements of a promise or of a statutory command, which must be proved by the party who relies on the contract or statute, and matters of exception, which must be proved by its adversary. Often the result of this approach is an arbitrary allocation of the burdens, as the statutory language may be due to a mere casual choice of form by the draftsman. However, the distinction may be a valid one in some instances, particularly when the exceptions to a statute or promise are numerous. If that is the case, fairness usually requires that the adversary give notice of the particular exception upon which it relies and therefore that it bear the burden of pleading. The burdens of proof will not always follow the burden of pleading in these cases. However, exceptions generally point to exceptional situations. If proof of the facts is inaccessible or not persuasive, it is usually fairer to act as if the exceptional situation did not exist and therefore to place the burden of proof and persuasion on the party claiming its existence.

As has been stated, the burdens of producing evidence and of persuasion with regard to any given issue are both generally allocated to the same party. Usually each is assigned but once in the course of the litigation and a safe prediction of that assignment can be made at the pleading stage. However, the initial allocation of the burden of producing evidence may not always be final. The shifting nature of that burden may cause both parties to have the burden with regard to the same issue at different points in the trial.[4] Similarly, although the burden of persuasion is assigned only once—when it is time for a decision—a prediction of the allocation of that burden, based upon the pleadings, may have to be revised when evidence is introduced at trial.[5] Policy considerations similar to those that govern the initial allocation of the burden of producing evidence and tentatively fix the burden of persuasion govern the ultimate assignment of those burdens as well.[6]

In summary, there is no key principle governing the apportionment of the burdens of proof. Their allocation, either initially or ultimately, will depend upon the weight that is given to any one or more of several factors, including: (1) the natural tendency to place the burdens on the party desiring change, (2) special policy considerations such as those

---

[4]   See infra § 338.

[5]   See infra § 344.

[6]   See infra § 343.

disfavoring certain defenses, (3) convenience, (4) fairness, and (5) the judicial estimate of the probabilities.

§ 338 Satisfying the Burden of Producing Evidence

Let us suppose that the plaintiff, claiming an estate in land for John Smith's life, had the burden of pleading, and has pleaded, that John Smith was alive at the time the action was brought. She seeks to fulfill the burden of producing evidence of this fact.

To do this she may offer direct evidence, e.g., of witness Jones, who saw Smith alive in the clerk's office when the complaint in the action was filed. From this the inference of the truth of the fact to be proved depends only upon the truthfulness of Jones. Or, she may offer circumstantial evidence, which requires a weighing of probabilities as to matters other than merely the truthfulness of the witness. For example, she may secure the testimony of Jones that Jones received a letter in the mail which was signed "John Smith" one month before the action was brought and that she recognized the signature as Smith's. Patently in this latter case, the tribunal may be satisfied that Jones is speaking the truth, and yet the tribunal may decline to infer the fact of Smith's being alive when the action began.

How strongly persuasive must the offered evidence be to satisfy the burden? A "scintilla" of evidence will not suffice. The evidence must be such that a reasonable person could draw from it the inference of the existence of the particular fact to be proved or, as put conversely by one federal court, "if there is substantial evidence opposed to the [motion for directed verdict], that is evidence of such quality and weight that reasonable and fair-minded men in the exercise of impartial judgment might reach different conclusions, the [motion] should be denied."[7]

One problem that has troubled the courts is whether the test for the granting of a directed verdict should vary, depending upon the required measure of persuasion should the case go to the jury. For example in a criminal case where the prosecution must persuade the jury beyond a reasonable doubt,[8] should the test for a directed verdict be whether the evidence could satisfy reasonable people beyond a reasonable doubt? Some courts have said no, perhaps believing with Judge Learned Hand that, although the gravity of the consequences often makes judges more exacting in criminal cases, the line between proof that should satisfy reasonable men and the evidence that should satisfy reasonable men beyond a reasonable doubt is, in the long run, "too thin for day to day use."[9]

However, most courts have applied the stricter test. A clear trend toward universal adoption of the stricter test was effectively solidified into a constitutional dictate in *Jackson v. Virginia*,[10] where the Court held that a federal court reviewing a state court conviction on a habeas corpus petition must determine whether a rational factfinder could have found the petitioners guilty beyond a reasonable doubt. Arguably no trial judge should apply a lesser standard on a motion for a directed verdict.

Generally no difficulty occurs where the evidence is direct. Except in rare cases, it is sufficient, though given by one witness only, however negligible a human being she

---

[7]   Boeing Co. v. Shipman, 411 F.2d 365, 374 (5th Cir. 1969).

[8]   See infra § 341.

[9]   United States v. Feinberg, 140 F.2d 592, 594 (2d Cir. 1944).

[10]   443 U.S. 307 (1979).

may be. But if the evidence is circumstantial, forensic disputes often arise as to its sufficiency to warrant a jury to draw the desired inference. In fact, in few areas of the law have so many words been spoken by the courts with so little conviction. One test frequently expounded in criminal cases is that where the prosecution relies upon circumstantial evidence, the evidence must be so conclusive as to exclude any other reasonable inference inconsistent therewith. The test is accurate enough in criminal cases, but adds little at least to the stricter test for criminal cases discussed above. A similar formula is sometimes expounded in civil cases but seems misplaced in civil litigation. It leaves little for the jury and far exceeds what is needed to prevent verdicts based upon speculation and conjecture. Courts rejecting the formula in civil cases have stated that the burden of producing evidence is satisfied, even by circumstantial evidence, if "there be sufficient facts for the jury to say reasonably that the preponderance favors liability."[11]

Other tests and other phrasings of the tests discussed here are myriad, but irrespective of the test articulated, in the last analysis the judge's ruling must necessarily rest on her individual opinion, formed in the light of her own common sense and experience, as to the limits of reasonable inference from the facts proven. However, certain situations recur and give rise repeatedly to litigation, and a given judge, in a desire for consistency and the consequent saving of time and mental travail, will rule alike whenever the same situation is proved and its sufficiency to warrant a certain inference is questioned. Other judges follow suit and a standardized practice ripening into a rule of law results. Most of these rules are positive rather than negative. They announce that certain types of fact-groups are sufficient to enable the person who has the first duty to go forward with evidence to fulfill that burden, i.e., they enable the party to rest after proving them without being subject to the penalty of an adverse ruling.

Suppose the one who had the initial burden of offering evidence in support of the alleged fact, on pain of an adverse ruling, does produce evidence barely sufficient to satisfy that burden, so that the judge can just say, "A reasonable jury could infer that the fact is as alleged, from the circumstances proved." If the proponent then rests, what is the situation? Has the duty of going forward shifted to the adversary? Not if we define that duty as the liability to a peremptory adverse ruling on failing to give evidence, for if at this juncture the original proponent rests and the adversary offers no proof, the proponent will not be entitled to the direction of a verdict in her favor on the issue, but rather the court will leave the issue to the decision of the jury. But it is frequently said that in this situation the duty of going forward has shifted to the adversary, and this is unobjectionable if we bear in mind that the penalty for silence is very different here from that which was applied to the original proponent. If she had remained silent at the outset she would irrevocably have lost the case on this issue, but the only penalty now applied to her adversary is the risk, if she remains silent, of the jury's finding against her, though it may find for her. Theoretically she may have this risk still, even after she has offered evidence in rebuttal. It is simpler to limit "duty of going forward" to the liability, on resting, to an adverse ruling, and to regard the stage just discussed (where the situation is that if both parties rest, the issue will be left to the jury) as one in which neither party has any duty of going forward.

In the situation just discussed, the party who first had the duty, i.e., the necessity, of giving proof, has produced evidence which requires the judge to permit the jury to

---

[11]   Smith v. Bell Tel. Co. of Pa., 153 A.2d 477 (Pa. 1959).

infer, as it chooses, that the fact alleged is or is not true. It is a permitted, but not a compulsory, inference. Is it possible for the original proponent of evidence to carry her proof to the stage where if she rests, she will be entitled to a directed verdict, or its equivalent, on the issue? Undoubtedly, with a qualification to be noted, this is possible, and when it occurs there is a shifting to the adversary of the duty of going forward with the evidence, in the strictest sense. Such a ruling means that in the judge's view the proponent has not merely offered evidence from which reasonable people could draw the inference of the truth of the fact alleged, but evidence from which (in the absence of evidence from the adversary) reasonable people could not help but draw this inference. Thus, as long ago as 1770, Lord Mansfield told the jury that upon the issue of whether defendant had published a libel, proof of a sale of the book in defendant's shop was, being unrebutted, "conclusive."[12]

In the case first supposed at the beginning of this section, if the plaintiff brought forward the direct evidence of Jones that Smith was alive when the complaint was filed, and there is no contrary evidence at all, or if she brings forward circumstantial evidence (that is, evidence that Smith was seen alive in perfect health 10 minutes before the complaint was filed) which is, in the absence of contrary circumstances, irresistibly convincing, the jury should not be left to refuse to draw the only rational inference.

If we do not permit the jury to draw an inference from insufficient data, as where the proponent has failed to sustain her initial duty of producing evidence, we should not permit the jury to act irrationally by rejecting compelling evidence. Here again the ruling, from repeated occurrence of similar facts, may become a standardized one. However, the statement that one who has the duty of going forward can go forward far enough not merely to escape an adverse peremptory ruling herself, but to subject her opponent to one if the latter declines to take up the gage by producing evidence, has the following qualification. Obviously if the testimony were conflicting as to the truth of the facts from which the inference of the fact in issue is desired to be drawn, and the judge believes the inference (conceding the truth of the premise) is irresistible to rational minds, the court can only make a conditional peremptory ruling. The judge directs the jury, if you believe the evidence that fact A is so then you must find fact B, the fact in issue. In some jurisdictions, if the party seeking the ruling has the burden of persuasion on the issue, as assigned on the basis of the pleadings, she can only get a conditional ruling, though her witnesses are undisputed and unimpeached. But, in either event, if the inference is overwhelming, the jury is instructed not to cogitate over that, but only over the truthfulness of those who testify to the basic data.

We have seen something of the mechanics of the process of "proceeding" or "going forward" with evidence, viewed from the point of view of the first party who is stimulated to produce proof under threat of a ruling foreclosing a finding in her favor. She may in respect to a particular issue pass through three states of judicial hospitality: (a) where if she stops she will be thrown out of court; (b) where if she stops and her adversary does nothing, her reception will be left to the jury; and (c) where if she stops and her adversary does nothing, her victory (so far as it depends on having the inference she desires drawn) is at once proclaimed. Whenever the first producer has presented evidence sufficient to get her to the third stage and the burden of producing evidence can truly be said to have shifted, her adversary may in turn pass through the same three stages. Her evidence

---

[12]　Rex v. Almon, 5 Burr. 2686, 98 Eng. Rep. 411 (K.B. 1770).

again may be (a) insufficient to warrant a finding in her favor, (b) sufficient to warrant a finding, or (c) irresistible, if unrebutted.

§ 339 Satisfying the Burden of Persuasion: (a) The Measure of Persuasion in Civil Cases Generally

According to the customary formulas a party who has the burden of persuasion of a fact must prove it in criminal prosecutions "beyond a reasonable doubt,"[13] in certain exceptional controversies in civil cases, "by clear, strong and convincing evidence,"[14] but on the general run of issues in civil cases "by a preponderance of evidence." The "reasonable doubt" formula points to what we are really concerned with, the state of the jury's mind, whereas the other two divert attention to the evidence, which is a step removed, being the instrument by which the jury's mind is influenced. These latter phrases, consequently, are awkward vehicles for expressing the degree of the jury's belief.

What is the most acceptable meaning of the phrase, proof by a preponderance, or greater weight, of the evidence? Certainly the phrase does not mean simple volume of evidence or number of witnesses. One definition is that evidence preponderates when it is more convincing to the trier than the opposing evidence. This is a simple commonsense explanation which will be understood by jurors and could hardly be misleading in the ordinary case. It may be objected, however, that it is misleading in a situation where, though one side's evidence is more convincing than the other's, the jury is still left in doubt as to the truth of the matter. Compelling a decision in favor of a party who has introduced evidence that is simply better than that of his adversary would not be objectionable if we hypothesize jurors who bring none of their own experience to the trial and who thus view the evidence in a vacuum. Of course, no such case could exist. We expect and encourage jurors to use their own experience to help them reach a decision, particularly in judging the credibility of witnesses. That experience may tell them, for example, that although the plaintiff has introduced evidence and the defendant has offered nothing in opposition, it is still unlikely that the events occurred as contended by the plaintiff. Thus, it is entirely consistent for a court to hold that a party's evidence is sufficient to withstand a motion for directed verdict and yet to uphold a verdict for its adversary.

The most acceptable meaning to be given to the expression, proof by a preponderance, seems to be proof which leads the jury to find that the existence of the contested fact is more probable than its nonexistence. Thus the preponderance of evidence becomes the trier's belief in the preponderance of probability. Some courts have boldly accepted this view.

Other courts have been shocked at the suggestion that a verdict, a truth-finding, should be based on nothing stronger than an estimate of probabilities. They require that the trier must have an "actual belief" in, or be "convinced of" the truth of the fact by this "preponderance of evidence." Does this mean that they must believe that it is certainly true? Hardly, since it is apparent that an investigation by fallible people based upon the testimony of other people, with all their defects of veracity, memory, and communication, cannot yield certainty. Does it mean a kind of mystical "hunch" that the fact must be true? This would hardly be a rational requirement. What it would most naturally be

---

[13] See infra § 341.

[14] See infra § 340.

understood to mean by the jury (in the unlikely event that it should carry analysis so far) is that it must be persuaded that the truth of the fact is not merely more probable than not, but highly probable. This is more stringent than our tradition or the needs of justice warrant, and seems equivalent to the standard of "clear, strong and convincing proof," hitherto thought to be appropriate only in exceptional cases.[15]

Much of the time spent in the appellate courts over the metaphysics of "preponderance" has been wasted because of the courts' insistence upon the cabalistic word. This bemusement with word-magic is particularly apparent in the decisions dealing with the use of the word "satisfaction" or its derivatives in referring to the effect of the evidence on the jury's mind. Some courts, with more logic than realism, have condemned its use as equivalent to proof beyond a reasonable doubt unless qualified by the word "reasonable." Other courts have pragmatically, although perhaps reluctantly permitted its use, even without the qualification. Although certainly juries should be clearly and accurately instructed with regard to the question of the measure of persuasion in civil cases, it is hard to believe that variations in language such as those involved in the courts' difficulties with the use of the word "satisfaction" lead to any differences in jurors' attitudes. Thoughtfully drafted pattern jury instructions should prove helpful in reducing unnecessarily spent appellate court time on these questions. Where no pattern instruction is available, however, trial judges would be wise to search for the locally accepted phraseology and to adhere to it religiously.

§ 340 Satisfying the Burden of Persuasion: (b) Requirement of Clear and Convincing Proof

While we have seen that the traditional measure of persuasion in civil cases is by a preponderance of evidence,[16] there is a limited range of claims and contentions that the party is required to establish by a more exacting measure of persuasion. The formula varies from state to state, but among the phrases used are the following: "by clear and convincing evidence," "clear, convincing and satisfactory," "clear, cogent and convincing," and "clear, unequivocal, satisfactory and convincing." Some courts have used all of these phrases and then some to describe the applicable standard. The phrasing within most jurisdictions has not become as standardized as is the "preponderance" formula, but even here the courts sometimes are surprisingly intolerant of slight variations from the approved expression. No high degree of precision can be attained by these groups of adjectives. It has been persuasively suggested that they could be more simply and intelligibly translated to the jury if they were instructed that they must be persuaded that the truth of the contention is "highly probable." But as former Chief Justice Burger stated:

We probably can assume no more than that the difference between a preponderance of the evidence and proof beyond a reasonable doubt probably is better understood than either of them in relation to the intermediate standard of clear and convincing evidence. Nonetheless, even if the particular standard-of-proof catchwords do not always make a great difference in a particular case, adopting a "standard of proof is more than an empty semantic exercise." . . . In cases involving individual rights, whether criminal or civil,

---

[15]   See *id.*

[16]   See supra § 339.

"[t]he standard of proof [at a minimum] reflects the value society places on individual liberty."[17]

To this end, the United States Supreme Court has held that proof by a clear and convincing or similar standard is required, either by the United States Constitution or by the applicable federal statute, in a variety of cases involving deprivations of individual rights not rising to the level of criminal prosecution, including commitment to a mental hospital, termination of parental rights, denaturalization and deportation.

Not all instances of requirements of proof more than usually convincing concern cases involving individual liberty. Indeed, the requirement of proof of this magnitude for certain types of contentions seems to have had its origins in the standards prescribed for themselves by the chancellors in determining questions of fact in equity cases. However, it has now been extended to certain types of actions tried before juries, and the chancellors' cautionary maxims are now conveyed to the jury in the form of instructions on the burden of persuasion.

Among the classes of cases to which this special standard of persuasion commonly has been applied are: (1) charges of fraud and undue influence, (2) suits on oral contracts to make a will, and suits to establish the terms of a lost will, (3) suits for the specific performance of an oral contract, (4) proceedings to set aside, reform or modify written transactions, or official acts on grounds of fraud, mistake or incompleteness, and (5) miscellaneous types of claims and defenses, varying from state to state, where there is thought to be special danger of deception, or where the court considers that the particular type of claim should be disfavored on policy grounds.

The appellate court, under the classical equity practice, tried the facts de novo, upon the deposition testimony in the record, and thus it was called on to apply anew the standard of clear and convincing proof in its study of the evidence. But in the modern system there are usually restrictions upon appellate review of a judge's findings of fact, even in equity issues. Thus, in the federal courts under Rule 52(a) the trial court's findings will be reversed only when "clearly erroneous." And in jury-tried cases the verdict will be reviewed only to the extent of determining whether there was evidence from which reasonable people could have found the verdict. Will the appellate court, then, today, if there was substantial evidence from which the judge or jury could have made the findings it did, consider the questions whether the evidence met the "clear and convincing" standard, in a case where it applies? The United States Supreme Court, in reviewing a summary judgment in a libel case where the plaintiff's burden was to prove actual malice by clear and convincing evidence, stated that the test on appeal should be "whether the evidence in the record could support a reasonable jury finding either that the plaintiff has shown actual malice by clear and convincing evidence or that the plaintiff has not."[18] However, in some jurisdictions it is for the trial court, not the appellate court, to draw a distinction between evidence which is clear and convincing and evidence which merely preponderates.

---

[17]   Addington v. Texas, 441 U.S. 418, 425 (1979).

[18]   Anderson v. Liberty Lobby, Inc., 477 U.S. 242, 255–56 (1986).

§ 341 Satisfying the Burden of Persuasion: (c) Proof Beyond a Reasonable Doubt

As we have seen with reference to civil cases, a lawsuit is essentially a search for probabilities. A margin of error must be anticipated in any such search. Mistakes will be made and in a civil case a mistaken judgment for the plaintiff is no worse than a mistaken judgment for the defendant. However, this is not the case in a criminal action. Society has judged that it is significantly worse for an innocent person to be found guilty of a crime than for a guilty person to go free. The consequences to the life, liberty, and good name of the accused from an erroneous conviction of a crime are usually more serious than the effects of an erroneous judgment in a civil case. Therefore, as stated by the Supreme Court in recognizing the inevitability of error even in criminal cases, "[w]here one party has at stake an interest of transcending value—as a criminal defendant his liberty—this margin of error is reduced as to him by the process of placing on the other party the burden . . . of persuading the factfinder at the conclusion of the trial of his guilt beyond a reasonable doubt."[19] In so doing, the courts may have increased the total number of mistaken decisions in criminal cases, but with the worthy goal of decreasing the number of one kind of mistake—conviction of the innocent.

The demand for a higher degree of persuasion in criminal cases was recurrently expressed from ancient times, but its crystallization into the formula "beyond a reasonable doubt" seems to have occurred as late as 1798. It is now accepted in common law jurisdictions as the measure of persuasion by which the prosecution must convince the trier of all the essential elements of guilt. In 1970, the Supreme Court explicitly held that the due process clause "protects the accused against conviction except upon proof beyond a reasonable doubt of every fact necessary to constitute the crime with which he is charged."[20]

A simple instruction that the jury will acquit if they have a reasonable doubt of the defendant's guilt of the crime charged in the indictment is ordinarily sufficient. Courts, however, frequently paint the lily by giving the jury a definition of "reasonable doubt." A famous early instance was the oft-echoed statement of Chief Justice Shaw in the trial of Prof. Webster for the murder of Dr. Parkman: "It is that state of the case, which, after the entire comparison and consideration of all the evidence, leaves the minds of jurors in that condition that they cannot say they feel an abiding conviction, to a moral certainty, of the truth of the charge."[21] It is an ancient maxim that all definitions are dangerous and this one has been caustically criticized as raising more questions than it answers. Other definitions, often more carefully balanced to warn against the overstressing of merely possible or imaginary doubts, have become customary in some jurisdictions. Reasonable doubt is a term in common use almost as familiar to jurors as to lawyers. As one judge has said it needs a skillful definer to make it plainer by multiplication of words,[22] and as another has expressed it, the explanations themselves often need more explanation than the term explained.[23] If a definition of the term is not requested by the accused, it is not required. Whether if so requested it is the judge's duty to define the term, is a matter of dispute, but the wiser view seems to be that it lies in

---

19 Speiser v. Randall, 357 U.S. 513, 525–26 (1958).

20 In re Winship, 397 U.S. 358, 364 (1970).

21 Commonwealth v. Webster, 59 Mass. (5 Cush.) 295, 320 (1850).

22 Newman, J. in Hoffman v. State, 73 N.W. 51, 52 (Wis. 1897).

23 Mitchell, J. in State v. Sauer, 38 N.W. 355 (Minn.1888).

the court's discretion, which should ordinarily be exercised by declining to define, unless the jury itself asks for a fuller explanation.

There are certain excuses or justifications allowed to the defendant, which although provable for the most part under the plea of not guilty, are spoken of for some purposes as "affirmative defenses." Among these are self-defense, duress, insanity, intoxication and claims that the accused is within an exception or proviso in the statute defining the crime. Sometimes only the burden of producing evidence will be assigned to the defendant. Under certain circumstances the burden of persuasion with regard to some of these defenses may be allocated to the defendant and correspondingly, the prosecution may be relieved of proving the absence of the defense. The allocation and operation of the burdens of proof with regard to these defenses present difficult policy, as well as constitutional, problems. These problems will be discussed together with the special problems related to presumptions in criminal cases.[24]

Despite occasional statements to the contrary, the reasonable doubt standard generally has been held inapplicable in civil cases, regardless of the nature of the issue involved. For example, when a charge of crime is at issue in a civil action, the threatened consequences of sustaining the accusation, though often uncommonly harmful to purse or prestige, are not generally as serious as in a prosecution for the crime. Accordingly the modern American cases have come around to the view that in the interest of justice and simplicity a reasonable doubt measure of persuasion will not be imposed. Most courts have said that a preponderance of the evidence is sufficient, although some have increased the standard to "clear and convincing."

§ 342 Presumptions, in General

One ventures the assertion that "presumption" is the slipperiest member of the family of legal terms, except its first cousin, "burden of proof." One author has listed no less than eight senses in which the term has been used by the courts.[25] Agreement can probably be secured to this extent, however: a presumption is a standardized practice, under which certain facts are held to call for uniform treatment with respect to their effect as proof of other facts.

Returning for a moment to the discussion of satisfying the burden of producing evidence,[26] assume that a party having the burden of producing evidence of fact A, introduces proof of fact B. The judge, using ordinary reasoning, may determine that fact A might reasonably be inferred from fact B, and therefore that the party has satisfied its burden, or as sometimes put by the courts, has made out a "prima facie" case. The judge has not used a presumption in the sense of a standardized practice, but rather has simply relied upon a rational inference. However, in ruling on a motion for directed verdict the judge may go beyond her own mental processes and experience and find that prior decisions or existing statutes have established that proof of fact B is sufficient to permit the jury to infer the existence of fact A. The judge has thus used a standardized practice but has the court necessarily used a presumption? Although some courts have described such a standardized inference as a presumption, most legal scholars have disagreed. They have saved the term to describe a significantly different sort of a rule, one that dictates not only that the establishment of fact B is sufficient to satisfy a party's burden

---

[24]   See infra §§ 346–348.

[25]   Laughlin, In Support of the Thayer Theory of Presumptions, 52 Mich. L. Rev. 195, 196–207 (1953).

[26]   See supra § 338.

of producing evidence with regard to fact A, but also at least compels the shifting of the burden of producing evidence on the question to the party's adversary. Under this view, if proof of fact B is introduced and a presumption exists to the effect that fact A can be inferred from fact B, the party denying the existence of fact A must then introduce proof of its nonexistence or risk having a verdict directed or a finding made against it. Further some authorities state that a true presumption should not only shift the burden of producing evidence, but also require that the party denying the existence of the presumed fact assume the burden of persuasion on the issue as well.[27]

Certainly the description of a presumption as a rule that, at a minimum, shifts the burden of producing evidence is to be preferred, at least in civil cases. Inferences that a trial judge decides may reasonably be drawn from the evidence need no other description, even though the judge relies upon precedent or a statute rather than personal experience in reaching a decision. In most instances, the application of any other label to an inference will only cause confusion. In criminal cases, however, there are rules that traditionally have been labeled presumptions, even though they do not operate to shift even the burden of producing evidence. The jury is permitted but not required to accept the existence of the presumed fact even in the absence of contrary evidence.[28] In 1979, the Supreme Court has resurrected the term "permissive presumption" to describe these rules.[29] The term presumption will be used in this text in the preferred sense discussed above in referring to civil cases, but with the qualification suggested in referring to criminal cases.

There are rules of law that are often incorrectly called presumptions that should be specifically distinguished from presumptions at this point:

Conclusive Presumptions. The term presumption as used above always denotes a rebuttable presumption, i.e., the party against whom the presumption operates can always introduce proof in contradiction. In the case of what is commonly called a conclusive or irrebuttable presumption, when fact B is proven, fact A must be taken as true, and the adversary is not allowed to dispute this at all. For example, if it is proven that a child is under seven years of age, the courts have stated that it is conclusively presumed that she could not have committed a felony. In so doing, the courts are not stating a presumption at all, but simply expressing the rule of law that someone under seven years old cannot legally be convicted of a felony.

Res Ipsa Loquitur. Briefly and perhaps over simply stated, res ipsa loquitur is a rule that provides that a plaintiff may satisfy his burden of producing evidence of a defendant's negligence by proving that the plaintiff has been injured by a casualty of a sort that normally would not have occurred in the absence of the defendant's negligence. Although a few jurisdictions have given the doctrine the effect of a true presumption even to the extent of using it to assign the burden of persuasion, most courts agree that it simply describes an inference of negligence. Prosser called it a "simple matter of circumstantial evidence."[30] Most frequently, the inference called for by the doctrine is one that a court would properly have held to be reasonable even in the absence of a special rule. Where this is so, res ipsa loquitur certainly need be viewed no differently from any other inference. Moreover, even where the doctrine is artificial—where it is

---

[27]   See infra § 344.

[28]   See infra § 346.

[29]   County Court of Ulster County, N. Y. v. Allen, 442 U.S. 140 (1979).

[30]   Prosser, Torts, § 40 at 231 (4th ed. 1971).

imposed for reasons of policy rather than logic—it nevertheless remains only an inference, permitting but not requiring, the jury to find negligence. The only difference is that where res ipsa loquitur is artificially imposed, there is better reason for informing the jury of the permissibility of the inference than there is in the case where the doctrine simply describes a rational inference. Although theoretically a jury instruction of this kind might be viewed as violating a state rule prohibiting comment on the evidence, the courts have had little difficulty with the problem and have consistently approved and required, where requested, instructions that tell the jury that a finding of negligence is permissible. Obviously these instructions can and should be given without the use of the misnomer "presumption."

The Presumption of Innocence. Assignments of the burdens of proof prior to trial are not based on presumptions. Before trial no evidence has been introduced from which other facts are to be inferred. The assignment is made on the basis of a rule of substantive law providing that one party or the other ought to have one or both of the burdens with regard to an issue. In some instances, however, these substantive rules are incorrectly referred to as presumptions. The most glaring example of this mislabeling is the "presumption of innocence" as the phrase is used in criminal cases. The phrase is probably better called the "assumption of innocence" in that it describes our assumption that, in the absence of contrary facts, it is to be assumed that any person's conduct upon a given occasion was lawful. In criminal cases, the "presumption of innocence" has been adopted by judges as a convenient introduction to the statement of the burdens upon the prosecution, first of producing evidence of the guilt of the accused and, second, of finally persuading the jury or judge of his guilt beyond a reasonable doubt. Most courts insist on the inclusion of the phrase in the charge to the jury, despite the fact that at that point it consists of nothing more than an amplification of the prosecution's burden of persuasion. Although the phrase is technically inaccurate and perhaps even misleading in the sense that it suggests that there is some inherent probability that the defendant is innocent, it is a basic component of a fair trial. Like the requirement of proof beyond a reasonable doubt, it at least indicates to the jury that if a mistake is to be made it should be made in favor of the accused, or as Wigmore stated, "the term does convey a special and perhaps useful hint . . . in that it cautions the jury to put away from their minds all the suspicion that arises from the arrest, the indictment, and the arraignment, and to reach their conclusion solely from the legal evidence adduced."[31]

§ 343 Reasons for the Creation of Presumptions: Illustrative Presumptions

A presumption shifts the burden of producing evidence, and may assign the burden of persuasion as well. Therefore naturally the reasons for creating particular presumptions are similar to the considerations that have already been discussed,[32] that bear upon the initial or tentative assignment of those burdens. Thus, just as the burdens of proof are sometimes allocated for reasons of fairness, some presumptions are created to correct an imbalance resulting from one party's superior access to the proof. An example of such a presumption is the rule that as between connecting carriers, the damage occurred on the line of the last carrier. Similarly, notions, usually implicit rather than expressed, of social and economic policy incline the courts to favor one contention

---

[31]   9 Wigmore, Evidence § 2511 at 407 (Chadbourn rev. 1981).
[32]   See supra § 337.

by giving it the benefit of a presumption, and correspondingly to handicap the disfavored adversary. A classic instance is the presumption of ownership from possession, which tends to favor the prior possessor and to make for the stability of estates. A presumption may also be created to avoid an impasse, and reach some result, even though it is an arbitrary one. For example, presumptions dealing with the survivorship of persons who died in a common disaster are necessary in order that other rules of law may operate, even though there is actually no factual basis upon which to believe that one party or the other was likely to have died first. Generally, however, the most important consideration in the creation of presumptions is probability. Most presumptions have come into existence primarily because the judges have believed that proof of fact B renders the inference of the existence of fact A so probable that it is sensible and timesaving to assume the truth of fact A until the adversary disproves it.

Obviously, most presumptions are based not on any one of these grounds alone, but have been created for a combination of reasons. Usually, for example, a presumption is based not only upon the judicial estimate of the probabilities but also upon the difficulties inherent in proving that the more probable event in fact occurred.[33] Moreover, as is the case with initial allocations of the burdens, the reasons for creation of presumptions are often tied closely to the pertinent substantive law. This is particularly true with regard to those presumptions that are created, at least in part, to further some social policy.

Although it would be inappropriate to attempt to list the hundreds of recognized presumptions, following is a brief discussion of a few illustrative presumptions and the reasons for their creation:

Official actions by public officers, including judicial proceedings, are presumed to have been regularly and legally performed. Reason: probability and the difficulty of proving that the officer conducted himself in a manner that was in all ways regular and legal.

A letter properly addressed, stamped and mailed is presumed to have been duly delivered to the addressee. Reason: probability and the difficulty of proving delivery in any other way.

When the plaintiff has been injured by the negligent operation of a vehicle, then upon proof of further facts he may have the benefit of presumptions in moving against the nondriving defendant. The plaintiff seeking to prove agency may secure the advantage of the presumption that the person driving the vehicle was doing so in the scope of his employment and in the course of the business of the defendant, merely by proving that the defendant was the owner. In a number of states the plaintiff must not only prove ownership to gain the benefit of the presumption of agency, but also that the driver is regularly employed by the defendant. If the plaintiff seeks to prove liability in a state having a statute making the owner liable for acts of one driving with the owner's consent, the plaintiff may secure the advantage of the presumption that the person driving was doing so with the owner's consent merely by showing ownership. In some states the plaintiff must not only prove ownership to gain the benefit of the presumption but also that a special relationship existed between the driver and the defendant. Reasons behind these presumptions: probability, fairness in the light of defendant's

---

[33] See *id.*

superior access to the evidence, and the social policy of promoting safety by widening the responsibility in borderline cases of owners for injuries caused by their vehicles.

When a bailor proves delivery of property to a bailee in good condition and return in a damaged state, or a failure to return after due demand, a presumption arises that the damage or loss was due to the negligence or fault of the bailee. Reason: fairness in the light of the superior access of the bailee to the evidence of the facts surrounding the loss; probability.

Proof that a person has disappeared from home and has been absent for at least seven years and that during this time those who would be expected to hear from the person have received no tidings and after diligent inquiry have been unable to find the person's whereabouts, raises a presumption that the person died at some time during the seven year period. The rule, though not very ancient, is already antiquated in that the seven year period is undoubtedly too long considering modern communications and transportation. Reasons: probability and the social policy of enforcing family security provisions such as life insurance, and of settling estates.

In the tracing of titles to land there is a useful presumption of identity of person from identity of name. Thus, when the same name appears in the chain of title first as grantee or heir and then as grantor, it will be presumed that it was the same person in each case. Reasons: the convenience of enabling the court and the parties to rely upon the regularity of the apparent chain of title, until this is challenged by evidence contesting identity; the social policy of quieting claims based on the face of the record; and probability.

Proof that a child was born to a woman during the time when she was married creates the presumption that the offspring is the legitimate child of the husband. Despite the controversy over whether presumptions generally shift the burden of persuasion upon the opponent,[34] it is universally agreed that in the case of this presumption, the adversary contending for illegitimacy does have the burden. This burden, moreover, is usually measured not by the normal standard for civil cases of preponderance of the evidence, but rather by the requirement of clear, convincing, and satisfactory proof, as most courts say, or even by the criminal formula, beyond a reasonable doubt. In addition, as pointed out elsewhere in this work, the contender for illegitimacy is further handicapped by a rule rendering incompetent the testimony or declarations of the spouses offered to show nonaccess, when the purpose is to bastardize the child.[35] Reasons: social policy, to avoid the visitation upon the child of the sins of the parents caused by the social stigma of bastardy and the common law rules (now generally alleviated by statutes) as to the incapacities of the *filius nullius*, the child of no one; probability.

When violent death is shown to have occurred and the evidence is not controlling as to whether it was due to suicide or accident, there is a presumption against suicide. Reasons: the general probability in case of a death unexplained, which flows from the human revulsion against suicide, and, probably, a social policy that inclines in case of doubt toward the fruition rather than the frustration of plans for family protection through insurance.

---

[34]   See infra § 344.

[35]   See supra § 67.

§ 344 The Effect of Presumptions in Civil Cases

The trial judge must consider the effect of a presumption in a civil jury trial at two stages: (1) when one party or the other moves for a directed verdict and (2) when the time comes to instruct the jury.

Sometimes the effect of a presumption, at either stage, is easy to discern; it follows naturally from the definition of the term. Thus, where a party proves the basic facts giving rise to a presumption, it will have satisfied its burden of producing evidence with regard to the presumed fact and therefore its adversary's motion for directed verdict will be denied. If its adversary fails to offer any evidence or offers evidence going only to the existence of the basic facts giving rise to the presumption and not to the presumed fact, the jury will be instructed that if they find the existence of the basic facts, they must also find the presumed fact. To illustrate, suppose plaintiff proves that a letter was mailed, that it was properly addressed, that it bore a return address, and that it was never returned. Such evidence is generally held to raise a presumption that the addressee received the letter.[36] Defendant's motion for a directed verdict, based upon nonreceipt of the letter, will be denied. Furthermore, if the defendant offers no proof on this question (or if she attempts only to show that the letter was not mailed and offers no proof that the letter was not in fact received) the jury will be instructed that if they find the existence of the facts as contended by plaintiff, they must find that the letter was received.

But the problem is far more difficult where the defendant does not rest and does not confine her proof to contradiction of the basic facts, but instead introduces proof tending to show the nonexistence of the presumed fact itself. For example, what is the effect of the presumption in the illustration given above, if the defendant takes the stand and testifies that she did not in fact receive the letter? If the plaintiff offers no additional proof, is the defendant now entitled to the directed verdict she was denied at the close of the plaintiff's case? If not, what effect, if any should the presumption have upon the judge's charge to the jury? The problem of the effect of a presumption when met by proof rebutting the presumed fact has literally plagued the courts and legal scholars. The balance of this section is devoted to that problem.

(A) The "Bursting Bubble" Theory and Deviations from It

The Theory. The most widely followed theory of presumptions in American law has been that they are "like bats of the law flitting in the twilight, but disappearing in the sunshine of actual facts."[37] Put less poetically, under what has become known as the Thayer or "bursting bubble" theory, the only effect of a presumption is to shift the burden of producing evidence with regard to the presumed fact. If that evidence is produced by the adversary, the presumption is spent and disappears. In practical terms, the theory means that, although a presumption is available to permit the party relying upon it to survive a motion for directed verdict at the close of its own case, it has no other value in the trial. The view is derived from Thayer,[38] sanctioned by Wigmore,[39] adopted in the

---

[36] See supra § 343.

[37] Lamm J. in Mackowik v. Kansas City, St. J. & C.B.R. Co., 94 S.W. 256, 262 (Mo. 1906), quoted in 9 Wigmore, Evidence § 2491 (Chadbourn rev. 1981).

[38] Thayer, Preliminary Treatise on Evidence, ch. 8, passim, and especially at 314, 336 (1898).

[39] 9 Wigmore, Evidence § 2491(2) (Chadbourn rev. 1981).

Model Code of Evidence,[40] and seemingly been made a part of the Federal Rules of Evidence.[41] It has been adopted, at least verbally, in countless modern decisions.

The theory is simple to state, and if religiously followed, not at all difficult to apply. The trial judge need only determine that the evidence introduced in rebuttal is sufficient to support a finding contrary to the presumed fact. If that determination is made, certainly there is no need to instruct the jury with regard to the presumption. The opponent of the presumption may still not be entitled to a directed verdict, but if its motion is denied, the ruling will have nothing to do with the existence of a presumption. As has been discussed, presumptions are frequently created in instances in which the basic facts raise a natural inference of the presumed fact. This natural inference may be sufficient to take the case to the jury, despite the existence of contrary evidence and despite the resultant destruction of the presumption. For example, in the case of the presumption of receipt of a letter, referred to above, the defendant may destroy the presumption by denying receipt. Nevertheless, a jury question is presented, not because of the presumption, but because of the natural inference flowing from the plaintiff's showing that she had mailed a properly addressed letter that was not returned. On the other hand, the basic facts may not present a natural inference of sufficient strength or breadth to take the case to the jury. In such an instance, the court may grant a directed verdict against the party who originally had the benefit of the presumption.

Deviations from the Theory—in General. The "bursting bubble" theory has been criticized as giving to presumptions an effect that is too "slight and evanescent" when viewed in the light of the reasons for the creation of the rules.[42] Presumptions, as we have seen, have been created for policy reasons that are similar to and may be just as strong as those that govern the allocation of the burdens of proof prior to the introduction of evidence.[43] These policy considerations may persist despite the existence of proof rebutting the presumed fact. They may be completely frustrated by the Thayer rule when the basic facts of the presumption do not give rise to an inference that is naturally sufficient to take the case to the jury. Similarly, even if the natural inference is sufficient to present a jury question, it may be so weak that the jury is unlikely to consider it in its decision unless specifically told to do so. If the policy behind certain presumptions is not to be thwarted, some instruction to the jury may be needed despite any theoretical prohibition against a charge of this kind.

These considerations have not gone unrecognized by the courts. Thus, courts, even though unwilling to reject the dogma entirely, often find ways to deviate from it in their treatment of at least some presumptions, generally those which are based upon particularly strong and visible policies. Perhaps the best example is the presumption of legitimacy arising from proof that a child was born during the course of a marriage. The strong policies behind the presumption are so apparent that the courts have universally

---

[40]   Model Code of Evidence Rule 704(2) (1942):

[W]hen the basic fact . . . has been established . . . and evidence has been introduced which would support a finding of the nonexistence of the presumed fact . . . the existence or nonexistence of the presumed fact is to be determined exactly as if no presumption had ever been applicable . . . .", and Comment, "[a] presumption, to be an efficient legal tool must . . . (2) be so administered that the jury never hear the word presumption used since it carries unpredictable connotations to different minds . . . .

[41]   Fed. R. Evid. 301.

[42]   Morgan & Maguire, Looking Backward and Forward at Evidence, 50 Harv. L. Rev. 909, 913 (1937).

[43]   See supra § 343.

agreed that the party contending that the child is illegitimate not only has the burden of producing evidence in support of the contention, but also has a heavy burden of persuasion on the issue as well.[44]

Another example of special treatment for certain presumptions is the effect given by some courts to the presumption of agency or of consent arising from ownership of an automobile.[45] The classic theory would dictate that the presumption is destroyed once the defendant or the driver testifies to facts sufficient to support a finding of nonagency or an absence of consent. Some courts have so held. However, other courts have recognized that the policies behind the presumption, i.e., the defendant's superior access to the evidence and the social policy of widening the responsibility for owners of motor vehicles, may persist despite the introduction of evidence on the question from the defendant, particularly when the evidence comes in the form of the party's own or her servant's testimony. These courts have been unwilling to rely solely upon the natural inferences that might arise from plaintiff's proof, and instead require more from the defendant, such as, that the rebuttal evidence be "uncontradicted, clear, convincing and unimpeached." Moreover, many courts also hold that the special policies behind the presumption require that the jury be informed of its existence.

Deviations from the Theory—Conflicting Presumptions. Frequent deviations from the rigid dictates of the "bursting bubble" theory occur in the treatment of conflicting presumptions. A conflict between presumptions may arise as follows: W, asserting that she is the widow of H, claims her share of his property, and proves that on a certain day she and H were married. The adversary then proves that three or four years before W's marriage to H, W married another man. W's proof gives her the benefit of the presumption of the validity of a marriage. The adversary's proof gives rise to the general presumption of the continuance of a status or condition once proved to exist, and a specific presumption of the continuance of a marriage relationship. The presumed facts of the claimant's presumption and those of the adversary's are contradictory. How resolve the conflict? Thayer's solution would be to consider that the presumptions in this situation have disappeared and the facts upon which the respective presumptions were based shall simply be weighed as circumstances with all the other facts that may be relevant, giving no effect to the presumptions.[46] Perhaps when the conflicting presumptions involved are based upon probability or upon procedural convenience, the solution is a fairly practical one.

The particular presumptions involved in the case given as an example, however, were not of that description. On the one hand, the presumption of the validity of a marriage is founded not only in probability, but in the strongest social policy favoring legitimacy and the stability of family inheritances and expectations. On the other hand, the presumptions of continuance of lives and marriage relationships are based chiefly on probability and trial convenience, and the probability, of course, varies in accordance with the length of time for which the continuance is to be presumed in the particular case. This special situation of the questioned validity of a second marriage has been the principal area in which the problem of conflicting presumptions has arisen. Here, courts have not been willing to follow Thayer's suggestion of disregarding both rival

---

[44]   See supra § 343.

[45]   See *id.*

[46]   *See* Thayer, Preliminary Treatise on Evidence 346 (1898) followed in 9 Wigmore, Evidence § 2493 (Chadbourn rev. 1981).

presumptions and leaving the issue to weighing of circumstantial inferences. They have often preferred to formulate the issue in terms of a conflict of presumptions and to hold that the presumption of the validity of marriage is "stronger" and should prevail. The doctrine that the weightier presumption prevails should probably be available in any situation which involves conflicting presumptions, and where one of the presumptions is grounded in a predominant social policy.

Another and perhaps even better approach to the problem is to sidestep the conflict entirely and create a new presumption. Such a presumption has evolved in cases involving conflicting marriages. Under this rule, where a person has been shown to have been married successively to different spouses, there is a presumption that the earlier marriage was dissolved by death or divorce before the later one was contracted. While of course the presumption is rebuttable, as in the case of the presumption of legitimacy, many courts place a special burden of persuasion upon the party attacking the validity of the second marriage by declaring that the presumption can only be overcome by clear, cogent, and convincing evidence.

Deviations from the Theory—Instructions to the Jury. Because of the strength of the natural inferences that generally arise from the basic facts of a presumption, judges are seldom faced with the prospect of directing a verdict against the party relying upon a presumption. Similarly, conflicting presumptions are relatively rare. However, far more frequently courts have justifiably held that the policies behind presumptions necessitate an instruction that in some way calls the existence of the rule to the attention of the jury despite the Thayerian proscription against the practice. The digests give abundant evidence of the wide-spread and unquestioning acceptance of the practice of informing the jury of the rule despite the fact that countervailing evidence has been adduced upon the disputed inference.

Given the frequency of the deviation, however, the manner in which the jury is to be informed has been a matter of considerable dispute and confusion. The baffling nature of the presumption as a tool for the art of thinking bewilders one who searches for a form of phrasing with which to present the notion to a jury. Most of the forms have been predictably bewildering. For example, judges have occasionally contented themselves with a statement in the instructions of the terms of the presumption, without more. This leaves the jury in the air, or implies too much. The jury, unless a further explanation is made, may suppose that the presumption is a conclusive one, especially if the judge uses the expression, "the law presumes."

Another solution, formerly more popular than now, is to instruct the jury that the presumption is "evidence," to be weighed and considered with the testimony in the case. This avoids the danger that the jury may infer that the presumption is conclusive, but it probably means little to the jury, and certainly runs counter to accepted theories of the nature of evidence.

More attractive theoretically is the suggestion that the judge instruct the jury that the presumption is to stand accepted, unless they find that the facts upon which the presumed inference rests are met by evidence of equal weight, or in other words, unless the contrary evidence leaves their minds in equipoise, in which event they should decide against the party having the burden of persuasion upon the issue. It is hard to phrase such an instruction without conveying the impression that the presumption itself is "evidence" which must be "met" or "balanced." The overriding objection, however, is the impression of futility that it conveys. It prescribes a difficult metaphysical task for the jury, and, in actual use, may mystify rather than help the average juror.

One possible solution, perhaps better than those already mentioned, would be for the trial judge simply to mention the basic facts of the presumption and to point out the general probability of the circumstantial inference as one of the factors to be considered by the jury. By this technique, however, a true presumption would be converted into nothing more than a permissible inference. Moreover, the solution is simply not a feasible one in many jurisdictions without at least a new interpretation of another aspect of the law. The trial judge in most states must tread warily to avoid an expression of opinion on the facts. Although instructions on certain standardized inferences such as res ipsa loquitur are permitted,[47] the practice, wisely or not, may frown on any explanation of the allowable circumstantial inferences from particular facts as "invading the province of the jury."

Where the "bursting bubble" rule is discarded in favor of a rule that operates to fix the burden of persuasion, the problem of alerting the jury to the presumption should not exist. Under this theory, a presumption may ordinarily be given a significant effect without the necessity of mentioning the word "presumption" to the jury at all. There is no more need to tell the jury why one party or the other has the burden of persuasion where that burden is fixed by a presumption than there is where the burden is fixed on the basis of policies apparent from the pleadings. The jury may be told simply that, if it finds the existence of the basic facts, the opponent must prove the non-existence of the presumed fact by a preponderance of evidence, or, in some instances, by a greater standard. Even in those instances in which the presumption places the burden of persuasion on the same party who initially had the burden, there would seem to be no reason to mention the term. If the courts feel that the operation of the presumption warrants a higher standard of proof, the measure of persuasion can be increased as is now done in the case of the presumption of legitimacy. However, unless we are willing to increase the measure of persuasion, nothing can be gained by informing the jury of the coincidence. The word "presumption" would only tend to confuse the issue.

(B)   Attempts to Provide a Single Rule Governing the Effect of Presumptions

Perhaps, the greatest difficulty with the "bursting bubble" approach is that, in spite of its apparent simplicity, the conflicting desires of the courts to adopt it in theory and yet to avoid its overly-rigid dictates have turned it into a judicial nightmare of confusion and inconsistency. This state of affairs has caused legal scholars not only to search for a better rule, but for a single rule that would cover all presumptions.

Many writers came to the view that the better rule for all presumptions would provide that anything worthy of the name "presumption" has the effect of fixing the burden of persuasion on the party contesting the existence of the presumed fact. A principal technical objection to such a rule has been that it requires a "shift" in the burden of persuasion something that is, by definition of the burden, impossible. The argument seems misplaced, in that it assumes that the burden of persuasion is fixed at the commencement of the action. However, as we have seen,[48] the burden of persuasion need not finally be assigned until the case is ready to go to the jury. Thus, using a

---

[47]   See supra § 342.

[48]   See supra § 336.

presumption to fix that burden would not cause it to shift, but merely cause it to be assigned on the basis of policy considerations arising from the evidence introduced at the trial rather than those thought to exist on the basis of the pleadings.[49] Certainly there is no reason why policy factors thought to be controlling at the pleading stage should outweigh factors bearing upon the same policies that arise from the evidence. Just the reverse should be true.

Certainly, some presumptions have been interpreted consistently as affecting the burden of persuasion without a great deal of discussion of a "shifting" burden of proof.[50] The real question is more fundamental: should this rule which is applicable to some presumptions be applicable universally? The answer to that query depends, not on theoretical distinctions between shifting as opposed to reassigning the burden of persuasion, but upon whether the policy behind the creation of all presumptions is always strong enough to affect the allocation of the burden of persuasion as well as the burden of producing evidence.

One of the leading proponents of the rule allocating the burden of persuasion as a universal rule was Professor Morgan. Although Professor Morgan served as a reporter for the Model Code of Evidence, he was unable to persuade the draftsmen of that code to incorporate into it a provision embracing this view of the effect of presumptions. The Model Code instead takes a rigid Thayerian position.[51] However, Morgan also was active in the drafting of the original Uniform Rules of Evidence where he had considerably more success in inducing an adoption of his theory. The original Uniform Rules provided that where the facts upon which the presumption is based have "probative value" the burden of persuasion is assigned to the adversary; where there is no such probative value, the presumption has only a Thayerian effect and dies when met by contrary proof.[52]

The original Uniform Rules, although having much to commend them, presented problems. Obviously, they did not provide for a single rule. Different courts could give different answers to the question whether a particular presumption has probative value. The possibilities of inconsistency and confusion, although reduced by the rules, were still present. Further, the distinction made was a thin one that disregarded the existence of strong social policies behind some presumptions that lack probative value. Certainly if a presumption is not based on probability but rather is based solely upon social policy, there may be more, and not less, reason to preserve it in the face of contrary proof. A presumption based on a natural inference can stand on its own weight either when met by a motion for a directed verdict or in the jury's deliberations. A presumption based on social policy may need an extra boost in order to insure that the policy is not overlooked. Morgan apparently recognized the weakness of the distinction made by the rule and seemed to have agreed to it only to allay fears that a provision giving to all presumptions the effect of fixing the burden of persuasion might be unconstitutional.[53]

An approach almost directly opposite to the one taken in the original Uniform Rules is taken in California's Code of Evidence, adopted in 1965. Under the California Code,

---

[49]   The policies behind the allocation of the burden of persuasion are discussed generally in supra § 337. The policies behind the creation of presumptions are discussed in supra § 343.

[50]   See supra § 343 concerning the presumption of legitimacy.

[51]   Model Code of Evidence Rule 704.

[52]   Original Unif. R. Evid. 14 (1953).

[53]   Morgan, Presumptions, 10 Rutgers L. Rev. 512, 513 (1956).

presumptions based upon "public policy" operate to fix the burden of persuasion;[54] presumptions that are established "to implement no public policy other than to facilitate the determination of a particular action" are given a Thayerian effect.[55] The California approach is an improvement over the Uniform Rules but is still not completely satisfactory. The line between presumptions based on public policy and those that are not may not be easy to draw. Furthermore, although the California distinction is sounder than that made in the Uniform Rules, it is not completely convincing. The fact that the policy giving rise to a presumption is one that is concerned with the resolution of a particular dispute rather than the implementation of broader social goals, does not necessarily mean that the policy is satisfied by the shifting of the burden of producing evidence and that it should disappear when contrary proof is introduced. California asks the wrong question about the policies behind presumptions. The inquiry should not be directed to the breadth of the policy but rather to the question whether the policy considerations behind a certain presumption are sufficient to override the policies that tentatively fix the burdens of proof at the pleading stage.

The Federal Rules of Evidence, as adopted by the Supreme Court and submitted to the Congress, took the approach advocated by Morgan. The proposed Rule 301 provided that "a presumption imposes on the party against whom it is directed, the burden of proving that the nonexistence of the presumed fact is more probable than its existence." However, the draft did not survive congressional scrutiny and Rule 301, as enacted, has a distinct Thayerian flavor:

> In all civil actions and proceedings not otherwise provided for by Act of Congress or by these rules, a presumption imposes on the party against whom it is directed, the burden of going forward with evidence to rebut or meet the presumption but does not shift to such party the burden of proof in the sense of the risk of non-persuasion, which remains throughout the trial upon the party of whom it was originally cast.[56]

Some legal scholars have argued that Federal Rule 301 does not preclude instructions that at least alert the jury to the strength of logic and policy underlying a presumption, even though evidence contrary to the existence of the presumed fact has been introduced. Furthermore, there has been willingness on the part of the federal courts to find that certain acts of Congress create presumptions of greater vitality than that provided by Rule 301 or even that certain presumptions in existence at the time of the adoption of Rule 301 are not subject to the procedure set forth in that rule. On the other hand, the rule has also served as a guideline for courts wishing to give a "bursting bubble" effect to a presumption, even where the court may not necessarily believe itself bound by the dictates of Rule 301.

The matter is further complicated by the fact that many of the states thus far adopting new evidence rules based upon the federal rules, have taken the approach of original Rule 301 and allocate the burden of persuasion based upon the presumption. Likewise, the Uniform Rules of Evidence adopted in 1974 rejected the "bursting bubble"

---

[54] Cal. Evid. Code §§ 605–606.

[55] *Id.* §§ 603–604.

[56] Fed. R. Evid. 301. Rule 301 was restyled in 2011 to read: "In a civil case, unless a federal statute or these rules provide otherwise, the party against whom a presumption is directed has the burden of producing evidence to rebut the presumption. But this rule does not shift the burden of persuasion, which remains on the party who had it originally."

and contained a Rule 301 almost identical to the rule submitted by the Supreme Court to the Congress. The current Uniform Rule maintains this difference from the federal rule.

(C) The Search for the Grail

Despite the best efforts of legal scholars, instead of having one rule to govern all presumptions in all proceedings, we are left in some ways in a more confusing state than that which existed prior to the adoption of the Federal Rules. Neither Morgan's view that all presumptions operate to assign the burden of persuasion nor the Thayerian concept of a disappearing presumption has yet to win the day.

The problem may be inherent in the nature of the concept of a "presumption." At least one author has argued that the concept is an artificial one, an attempt to do through a legal fiction what courts should be doing directly;[57] that the term "presumption" should be eliminated from legal usage and the functions which it serves replaced by direct allocations of the burdens of proof and by judicial comment accurately describing the logical implication of certain facts. In one sense, the suggestion is attractive. The courts should indeed be discussing the propriety of allocating the burdens of proof, rather than the conceptual technical application of a presumption. Yet, both the term and concept of a presumption, however misunderstood, are so engrained in the law that it is difficult to imagine their early demise. Furthermore, as the author recognizes, there are instances in which the evidence introduced at the trial may be such as to give rise to a rule of law which shifts or reassigns the burdens of proof. He calls this a "conditional imperative" and recognizes that in such a case the allocation of the burdens of proof cannot be made prior to trial. While the term "conditional imperative" may be just as good as "presumption," it is no better and the same set of problems which exist with regard to presumptions are just as likely to occur regardless of the label employed.

The answer may be that there is no single solution to the problem. The resistance of the courts and legislatures to a universal rule of presumptions is reflective of the fact that there are policies of varying strength behind different presumptions and therefore a hierarchy of desired results. In one instance, the policy may be such as only to give rise to a standardized inference, a rule of law which gets the plaintiff to the jury but does not compel a directed verdict in its favor. In another instance, the policy may be strong enough to compel a directed verdict in its favor, thus shifting the burden of producing evidence to the opposing party, but not strong enough to reassign the burden of persuasion. In still another instance, the policy may be strong enough to reassign the burden of persuasion.

Attempts to categorize presumptions according to policy considerations have been thoughtful and well-meaning. Unfortunately, they have fallen short of the mark, largely because of the inherent difficulty of the task. Each presumption is created for its own reasons—reasons which are inextricably intertwined with the pertinent substantive law. These substantive considerations have a considerable impact on the procedural effect desirable for a particular presumption. The diversity of the considerations simply defies usable categorization. The law and lawyers are accustomed to considering the dictates of the substantive law in determining the initial allocation of the burdens of proof. The

---

[57] Allen, Presumptions, Inferences and Burden of Proof in Federal Civil Actions—An Anatomy of Unnecessary Ambiguities and a Proposal for Reform, 76 Nw. U. L. Rev. 892 (1982); Allen, Presumptions in Civil Actions Reconsidered, 66 Iowa L. Rev. 843 (1981).

task should not be thought too onerous in connection with the operation of presumptions which, after all, simply operate to reallocate those burdens during the course of the trial.

Rather than attempting to provide a single rule for all presumptions, a task which has thus far proved futile, the drafters of evidence codes might instead provide guidelines for the appropriate but various effects which a presumption may have on the burdens of proof. The courts and legislatures would then have the opportunity to select the appropriate effect to be given to a particular presumption. The term presumption seems likely to be with us forever; it also seems likely that different presumptions will continue to be viewed as having different procedural effects; we can only hope to insure that the concept which the term "presumption" represents is applied constructively and rationally.

§ 345   Constitutional Questions in Civil Cases

Serious questions under the United States Constitution are raised by the creation and use of presumptions in criminal cases. Those questions are discussed in subsequent sections.[58] Although there are constitutional considerations involved in the use of presumptions in civil cases, the problems are simply not of the same magnitude. In a criminal case, the scales are deliberately overbalanced in favor of the defendant through the requirement that the prosecution prove each element of the offense beyond a reasonable doubt.[59] Any rule that has even the appearance of lightening that burden is viewed with the most extreme caution. However, there is no need for this special protection for any one party to a civil action. The burdens of proof are fixed at the pleading stage, not for constitutional reasons, but for reasons of probability, social policy, and convenience.[60] There is no reason why the same policy considerations, as reflected in the operation of a presumption, should not be permitted further to effect an allocation of the burdens of proof during the course of the trial.

Nevertheless, the courts articulate a "rational connection" test in civil cases, which requires that such a connection exist between the basic facts and the presumed facts in order for the presumption to pass constitutional muster. Relatively recent cases have applied the test, but upheld the presumption. Perhaps under certain circumstances a presumption could operate in such an arbitrary manner as to violate fundamental due process considerations, even in a civil case. But to impose a strictly applied "rational connection" limitation upon the creation of presumptions in civil cases would mean that only presumptions based on probability would be permissible. Such a limitation would ignore other, equally valid, reasons for the creation of the rules. Considerations that have been either explicitly rejected or severely limited in criminal cases, such as the comparative knowledge of the parties with regard to the facts and the power of the legislature to do away with a claim or a defense entirely, should remain significant in determining the validity of a civil presumption.

Perhaps the most difficult question with regard to civil presumptions is whether a presumption may operate to assign the burden of persuasion. The question arises from the contrast between two Supreme Court cases considering the validity of presumptions of negligence operating against railroads. In the first, *Mobile, J. & K.C.R.R. v.*

---

[58]   See infra §§ 347–348.

[59]   See supra § 341 with regard to the nature of the prosecution's burden; see infra § 347 with regard to the constitutional limits on the effect that a presumption may have upon that burden.

[60]   See supra § 337.

Turnipseed,[61] decided in 1910, the Court considered a Mississippi statutory presumption of negligence operating against a railroad in an action for death of an employee in a derailment. The statute provided that proof of injury inflicted by the running of railroad cars would be "prima facie evidence of the want of reasonable skill and care" on the part of the railroad. Noting that the only effect of the statute was to impose on the railroad the duty of producing some evidence to the contrary, the court held that the rational connection between the fact proved and the fact presumed was sufficient to sustain the presumption.

However, in 1929, in *Western & Atlantic R.R. v. Henderson,*[62] the Court struck down a Georgia statute making railroads liable for damage done by trains, unless the railroad made it appear that reasonable care had been used, "the presumption in all cases being against the company." In *Henderson* the plaintiff alleged that her husband had been killed in a grade crossing collision. The jury was instructed that negligence was presumed from the fact of injury and that the burden was therefore on the railroad to show that it exercised ordinary care. The Court held that the mere fact of a collision between a train and a vehicle at a crossing furnished no basis for any inference as to negligence and that therefore the presumption was invalid. *Turnipseed* was distinguished on the ground that the Mississippi presumption raised "merely a temporary inference of fact" while the Georgia statute created "an inference that is given effect of evidence to be weighed against opposing testimony and is to prevail unless such testimony is found by the jury to preponderate."[63]

Although perhaps a grade crossing collision differs from a derailment and therefore *Turnipseed* and *Henderson* can be distinguished on their facts, it is nevertheless fair to read *Henderson* as imposing constitutional limitations on the effect of at least some presumptions. However, as has been cogently pointed out, *Henderson* may simply no longer be valid law. The case assumed the necessity of a showing of negligence. But the concept of negligence as a necessary basis for liability has lost most of its sanctity since 1929. Although there is considerable doubt as to what the Court would have done in that year, there is little doubt today that a legislature would be permitted at least to relegate lack of negligence to the status of an affirmative defense. If negligence could be so reduced, a presumption that assigned the burden of persuasion could logically be treated no differently.

Since *Henderson*, the Court has, on at least one occasion, approved a state presumption that operated to fix the burden of persuasion on the party controverting the presumed fact. In that case, *Dick v. New York Life Insurance Co.*[64] the Court approved a North Dakota common law rule that imposed on the defendant insurance company, defending against the operation of an accidental death clause, the burden of persuading the jury that the death of the insured was due to suicide.

The questionable status of *Henderson* in light of recent developments in tort law, the holding of the Court in *Dick*, and the illogic of treating presumptions differently from other rules of law allocating the burden of persuasion, make it relatively unlikely that

---

[61]   219 U.S. 35 (1910).

[62]   279 U.S. 639 (1929).

[63]   *Id.* at 643–644.

[64]   359 U.S. 437 (1959).

there are now serious constitutional limits on the effect that may be given to presumptions in civil cases.

§ 346 Affirmative Defenses and Presumptions in Criminal Cases: (a) Terminology

As has been earlier pointed out, the courts and legislatures do not always use the term presumption in the sense either that the term is used in this text or by the same courts and legislatures on other occasions.[65] The use of loose terminology is perhaps even more prevalent in dealing with presumptions operating in criminal cases than in civil cases. The best example is one that has already been given. The "presumption of innocence" is not a presumption at all, but simply another way of stating the rule that the prosecution has the burden of proving the guilt of the accused beyond a reasonable doubt.[66]

Similarly, the courts and writers have struggled to define and distinguish presumptions and affirmative defenses. Certainly, these procedural devices have factors in common. Yet, as the devices are traditionally defined, there are some significant variations between them that have caused the courts to treat them differently.

1. Affirmative Defenses. The term affirmative defense is traditionally used to describe the allocation of a burden, either of production or of persuasion, or both, to the defendant in a criminal case. The burden is fixed by statute or case law at the beginning of the case and does not depend upon the introduction of any evidence by the prosecution. For example, a crime may be statutorily defined as consisting of elements A and B. However, the accused may be exonerated or the offense reduced in degree upon proof of C. C is an affirmative defense. In some instances, the defendant may simply have the burden of production of evidence with regard to C; in the event that burden is satisfied, the prosecution will then have the burden of persuading the jury of elements A, B, and C beyond a reasonable doubt. In other instances, the defendant will have both the burden of production and the burden of persuasion. Thus, the prosecution will have no burden with regard to C; the defendant must both introduce proof of C and persuade the jury of its existence. Usually, the measure of persuasion imposed on the defendant with regard to an affirmative defense is a preponderance of the evidence.

2. Presumptions. Presumptions have already been defined as a standardized practice under which certain facts are held to call for uniform treatment with respect to their effect as proof of other facts.[67] In civil cases, the term presumption is properly reserved for a rule that provides that upon proof of certain basic facts, at least the burden of producing evidence with regard to certain presumed facts shifts. As has been discussed, a presumption may in some instances operate to allocate the burden of persuasion as well.[68]

A somewhat different terminology has been used more or less consistently in criminal cases. The tendency in criminal cases has been to describe any standardized rule which permits the inference of one fact from another as a presumption, regardless of whether the rule operates to shift the burden of production. Thus, assume a crime

---

[65]   See supra § 342.

[66]   See *id.*

[67]   See *id.*

[68]   See supra § 344.

with three elements, A, B and C. A rule of law provides that fact C may be inferred from proof of A and B. Such a rule is usually described as a presumption, whether or not any burden is actually shifted to the defendant. In most instances, no burden shifts; the presumption operates only to permit the prosecution to make out a prima facie case by proof of A and B alone. The jury will be instructed that it may, but is not required to, infer the existence of fact C from proof of facts A and B.

The United States Supreme Court has resurrected terminology used in the first edition of this text to describe the different effects of presumptions in criminal cases. In *County Court of Ulster County v. Allen*,[69] the court distinguished between mandatory and permissive presumptions. A mandatory presumption is one that operates to shift at least the burden of production. It tells the trier of fact that it must find the presumed fact upon proof of the basic fact, "at least unless the defendant has come forward with some evidence to rebut the presumed connection between the two facts."[70] The Court further sub-divided mandatory presumptions into two parts: presumptions that merely shift the burden of production to the defendant and presumptions that shift the burden of persuasion. A permissive presumption is one that allows, but does not require, the trier of fact to infer the presumed fact from proof of the basic facts. Under the *Allen* decision, these various kinds of presumptions differ not only procedurally, but also with regard to the tests for their constitutional permissibility as well.

§ 347 Affirmative Defenses and Presumptions in Criminal Cases: (b) Constitutionality

Recent years have brought some notable developments with regard to the constitutionality of both affirmative defenses and presumptions.

1. Affirmative Defenses. Historically, many states placed both the burden of production and the burden of persuasion on the accused with regard to several classical affirmative defenses, including insanity and self-defense. The allocation to the defendant of the burdens of proof with regard to insanity survived constitutional challenge in 1952. In *Leland v. Oregon*,[71] the Supreme Court held that the defendant could be required to prove his insanity at the time of the alleged crime beyond a reasonable doubt. On the other hand, some limitations were imposed on the creation or effect of affirmative defenses. For example, one United States Court of Appeals held unconstitutional a state's allocation of the burden of persuasion to the accused with regard to alibi.[72] The court reasoned that an alibi was a mere form of denial of participation in the criminal act, not a true affirmative defense.

Although perhaps foreshadowed by the treatment given the defense of alibi, the real revolution in thought with regard to affirmative defenses occurred in the mid-1970's with two pivotal Supreme Court decisions.

In *Mullaney v. Wilbur*,[73] the Court reversed a Maine murder conviction where the jury had been instructed, in accordance with longstanding state practice, that if the prosecution proved "that the homicide was both intentional and unlawful, malice

---

[69]   442 U.S. 140 (1979).

[70]   *Id.* at 157.

[71]   343 U.S. 790 (1952).

[72]   Stump v. Bennett, 398 F.2d 111 (8th Cir. 1968).

[73]   421 U.S. 684, 686 (1975).

aforethought was to be conclusively implied unless the defendant proved by a fair preponderance of the evidence that he acted in the heat of passion on sudden provocation," in which event the defendant would be guilty only of manslaughter. The placing of this burden on the defendant was said to violate the dictates of *In re Winship*[74] that the due process clause requires the prosecution to prove beyond a reasonable doubt every fact necessary to constitute the crime charged. Although recognizing that under Maine law murder and manslaughter were but degrees of the same crime, the Court noted that *Winship* applied to instances in which the issue is degree of criminal culpability as well as to cases of guilt or innocence.

The *Mullaney* case was surprising in view of the long history in some jurisdictions of placing the burden of reducing the degree of a homicide on the defendant. However, given the holding and rationale of *Winship*, it was not totally unexpected. It was certainly possible, and perhaps fair, to read the *Mullaney* case broadly so as to require the imposition of the burden of persuasion on the prosecution with regard to many, if not all, of the traditional affirmative defenses. Indeed, the opinion was read by several state courts as constitutionally compelling the prosecution to bear the burden of persuasion with regard to various affirmative defenses. Only the existence of the *Leland* opinion, not expressly overruled in *Mullaney*, prevented one federal court from applying *Mullaney* to impose upon a state the burden of persuasion with regard to an insanity defense.[75]

The first real indication that the holding in *Mullaney* had far more narrow limits came when the Court, in *Rivera v. Delaware*,[76] dismissed, as not presenting a substantial federal question, an appeal from a conviction in which the defendant had borne the burden of proving his insanity. The indication became a certainty when the Court decided *Patterson v. New York*.[77] In *Patterson*, the Court upheld a New York procedure under which an accused is guilty of murder in the second degree if he is found, beyond a reasonable doubt, to have intentionally killed another person. The crime may be reduced to manslaughter if the defendant proves by a preponderance of the evidence that he had acted under the influence of "extreme emotional disturbance." The Court held that the New York procedure did not violate due process noting, in the language of *Winship*, " 'every fact necessary to constitute the crime with which [Patterson was] charged had to be proved beyond a reasonable doubt.' "[78] *Mullaney* was distinguished as dealing with a situation in which the defendant was asked to disprove an essential element of the prosecution's case—malice aforethought. New York, unlike Maine, did not include malice aforethought in its definition of murder. By this omission, New York had avoided the defect found fatal in *Mullaney*, even though the defense involved in the Patterson case was but an expanded version of the "heat of passion on sudden provocation" involved in *Mullaney*.

The Court in *Patterson* decided the constitutionality of the allocation of the burden of proof by a formalistic analysis of state law: due process was not violated because the defendant did not have the burden of proof on any fact that state law had identified as an element of the offense. Despite significant and persistent criticism, the durability of

---

[74]   397 U.S. 358 (1970). See discussion in supra § 341.

[75]   Buzynski v. Oliver, 538 F.2d 6 (1st Cir. 1976).

[76]   429 U.S. 877 (1976).

[77]   432 U.S. 197 (1977).

[78]   *Id.* at 206.

this approach was confirmed ten years later in *Martin v. Ohio*.[79] In *Martin*, Ohio had defined the crime of murder as purposely causing the death of another with prior calculation or design and placed the burden of proving self-defense on the defendant. The Court upheld the conviction because the defendant did not have the burden of proving any of the elements included by the state in its definition of the crime. The dictates of *Winship* were not violated so long as the instructions to the jury made it clear that State had the burden of proving all of the elements—including prior calculation and design—beyond a reasonable doubt, and that the self-defense evidence could also be considered in determining whether there was reasonable doubt about any element of the State's case.

The lower courts have, of course, followed the pattern of *Patterson* and *Martin*, holding invalid allocations of the burden of persuasion thought to involve nothing more than the rebuttal of an element of the offense and sanctioning allocations where the jury has been instructed that the affirmative defense is held to come into play only after the state has proven the elements of the crime beyond a reasonable doubt.

The analysis in *Patterson* and *Martin* deals only with the allocation of the burden of persuasion. As suggested by dicta in *Patterson*, the courts have had no trouble with an affirmative defense that simply requires the defendant to bear a burden of production. For example, even though a state includes absence of self-defense as an element of a crime so as to prohibit the allocation of the burden of persuasion to the accused, the accused may be required to introduce at least some evidence of self-defense in order for the issue to go the jury.

2. *Presumptions.* Like affirmative defenses, the Supreme Court's analysis of the constitutionality of presumptions has evolved significantly in recent years. The 1979 decisions in *County Court of Ulster County v. Allen*[80] and *Sandstrom v. Montana*,[81] constitute the watershed in the Court's analysis of the issue.

Prior to *Allen* and *Sandstrom*, the Court had set limitations on the creation and application of presumptions in criminal cases in a series of cases beginning with *Tot v. United States*.[82] In *Tot*, the Court invalidated a presumption contained in a federal firearms statute stating that possession of a firearm was presumptive evidence that the weapon was received in interstate commerce. The Court stated that "a statutory presumption cannot be sustained if there be no rational connection between the fact proved and the ultimate fact presumed, if the inference of the one from proof of the other is arbitrary because of lack of connection between the two in common experience."[83]

Tot was followed by two 1965 cases dealing with presumptions enacted to aid the government in prosecuting liquor cases. In *United States v. Gainey*,[84] the Court applied the rational connection test of *Tot* to uphold the validity of a statute which provided that presence at the site is sufficient to convict a defendant of the offense of carrying on the business of distilling without giving bond, "unless the defendant explains such presence

---

[79] 480 U.S. 228 (1987).

[80] 442 U.S. 140 (1979).

[81] 442 U.S. 510 (1979).

[82] 319 U.S. 463 (1943).

[83] *Id.* at 467.

[84] 380 U.S. 63 (1965).

to the satisfaction of the jury." However, in *United States v. Romano*,[85] the Court struck down as violative of *Tot* an identical presumption with regard to the companion offense of possession of an illegal still. The Court distinguished *Gainey*, noting that the crime of carrying on an illegal distilling business, involved in *Gainey*, was an extremely broad one. A person's unexplained presence at the still made it highly likely that he had something to do with its operation. However, no such natural inference existed with regard to the presumption of possession from unexplained presence involved in *Romano*.

Tot, Gainey and *Romano* left several questions unanswered. Most significantly, the "rational connection" test was vague. Was it a test of relevancy or a test of probative sufficiency? If it was a test of sufficiency, the existence of the presumed fact would have to be shown to be more likely than not to exist or perhaps even have to be shown to exist beyond a reasonable doubt.

The question was partially answered in 1969 and 1970 by two cases involving presumptions in narcotics prosecutions. In *Leary v. United States*,[86] the Court considered a presumption providing that possession of marihuana was sufficient evidence to authorize conviction of transporting and concealing the drug with knowledge of its illegal importation unless the defendant explained his possession to the satisfaction of the jury. The Court held that the presumption of knowledge was unconstitutional, stating:

> The upshot of *Tot, Gainey* and *Romano* is, we think, that a criminal statutory presumption must be regarded as 'irrational' or 'arbitrary,' and hence unconstitutional, unless it can be said with substantial assurance that the presumed fact is more likely than not to flow from the proved fact on which it is made to depend . . . .[87]

In a footnote to this statement, the Court added that because of its finding that the presumption was unconstitutional under this standard, it would not reach the question "whether a criminal presumption which passes muster when so judged must also satisfy the criminal 'reasonable doubt' standard if proof of the crime charged or an essential element thereof depends upon its use."[88]

The next year, the Court dealt with two presumptions in *Turner v. United States*.[89] One was identical with the presumption struck down in Leary, except that the drugs involved in *Turner* were heroin and cocaine rather than marihuana. The other provided that the absence of appropriate tax paid stamps from narcotic drugs found in the defendant's possession would be "prima facie evidence" that he purchased or distributed the drugs from other than the original stamped package. The Court extensively reviewed the legislative records with regard to the statutes and surveyed the records of other narcotics cases for evidence to support or rebut the inferences called for by the statutes. It concluded that the "overwhelming evidence" was that the heroin consumed in the United States is illegally imported and that Turner therefore must have known this fact. Based upon this conclusion, the Court upheld the presumptions of illegal importation and "stamped package" as to heroin. In contrast, the Court struck down the same presumptions with regard to cocaine, finding that it could not be "sufficiently sure either

---

[85]   382 U.S. 136 (1965).

[86]   395 U.S. 6 (1969).

[87]   *Id.* at 36.

[88]   *Id.* at 36 n.64.

[89]   396 U.S. 398 (1970).

that the cocaine that Turner possessed came from abroad or that Turner must have known that it did," and that there was "a reasonable possibility" that Turner had in fact obtained the cocaine from a legally stamped package.

In *Turner*, the Court again found it unnecessary specifically to adopt a test that would require that the presumed fact be shown to exist beyond a reasonable doubt. However, the Court's frequent reference to that standard in *Turner*, coupled with its decision in *In re Winship*[90] recognizing that such a measure of pro of is constitutionally required in criminal cases, seemed to make it likely that the reasonable doubt standard would be applied to test the validity of presumptions.

Not long after *Turner*, the Court applied the rationale of the cases involving statutory presumptions to a common law presumption. In *Barnes v. United States*,[91] the Court upheld a conviction for possession of stolen treasury checks in which the jury had been instructed in accordance with the traditional common law inference that the knowledge necessary for conviction may be drawn from the unexplained possession of recently stolen goods. The Court still refrained from adopting either a more-likely-than-not or a reasonable doubt standard in its review of the presumption, but held rather that the presumption in question satisfied both. The only question that seem to remain after *Barnes* whether the Court ultimately would require that all presumptions be tested by a reasonable doubt standard. Surprisingly, a whole new set of considerations arrived in 1979.

The New York prosecution in *County Court of Ulster County v. Allen*[92] was for illegal possession of, inter alia, handguns. Four persons, three adult males and a 16-year-old girl, were tried jointly. The evidence showed that two large-caliber handguns were seen in the front of the car in an open handbag belonging to the 16-year-old. A New York statute provided that, with certain exceptions, the presence of a firearm in an automobile was presumptive evidence of its illegal possession by all persons then occupying the vehicle. The jury was instructed with regard to the presumption but told that the presumption "need not be rebutted by affirmative proof or affirmative evidence but may be rebutted by any evidence or lack of evidence in the case."

The federal Court of Appeals affirmed the District Court's grant of habeas corpus, holding that the New York statute was unconstitutional on its face because it swept within its compass many individuals who would in fact have no connection with a weapon even though they were present in a vehicle in which the weapon was found.[93]

The Supreme Court reversed, stating that the Court of Appeals had improperly viewed the statute on its face. The Court stated that the ultimate test of any device's constitutional validity is that it not undermine the factfinder's responsibility at trial, based on evidence adduced by the state, to find the ultimate facts beyond a reasonable doubt. Therefore, mandatory and permissive presumptions must be analyzed differently. It is appropriate to analyze mandatory presumptions on their face. Where a mandatory presumption is used, the defendant may be convicted based upon the presumption alone as the result of the failure of the accused to introduce proof to the contrary. The Court reasoned that in such an instance the presumption would be unconstitutional unless the

---

[90]   397 U.S. 358 (1970). See supra § 341.

[91]   412 U.S. 837 (1973).

[92]   442 U.S. 140 (1979).

[93]   Allen v. County Court, Ulster County, 568 F.2d 998 (2d Cir.1977).

basic facts, standing alone, are sufficient to support the inference of guilt beyond a reasonable doubt. In the case of a permissive presumption the jury is told only that it may, but need not, find the defendant guilty based upon the basic facts. Thus, the validity of the presumption must be tested, not in the abstract, but rather in connection with all of the evidence in the case. The Court stated:

> Because this permissive presumption leaves the trier of fact free to credit or reject the inference and does not shift the burden of proof, it affects the application of the 'beyond a reasonable doubt' standard only if, under the facts of the case, there is no rational way the trier could make the connection permitted by the inference. For only in that situation is there any risk that an explanation of the permissible inference to a jury, or its use by a jury, has caused the presumptively rational factfinder to make an erroneous factual determination.[94]

The Court found that the instruction in *Allen* created a permissive, not a mandatory, presumption. The Court considered all of the evidence in the case and found a rational basis for a finding of guilty beyond a reasonable doubt, noting that the jury could have reasonably rejected the suggestion advanced on appeal by the adult defendants that the handguns were solely in the possession of the 16-year-old.

In *Sandstrom v. Montana*,[95] the defendant was charged with deliberate homicide, which under Montana law would consist of purposely and knowingly causing the death of another. Defendant claimed that the degree of the offense should be reduced in that he suffered from a personality disorder aggravated by alcohol consumption. The jury was instructed in accordance with Montana law that the "law presumes that a person intends the ordinary consequences of his voluntary acts." Defendant was convicted, and his conviction was upheld by the Montana Supreme Court. The United States Supreme Court reversed, holding that the jury could have interpreted the instruction with regard to the presumption of intention of the ordinary consequences of voluntary acts as creating either a conclusive presumption or shifting the burden of persuasion with regard to the question of intent to the defendant. Citing *Mullaney* and *Patterson* as well as *Allen*, the Court found that such a shift of the burden would be constitutionally impermissible. The fact that the jury could have interpreted the instruction either as permissive or as shifting only the burden of production did not matter so long as the instruction could also have been interpreted as imposing heavier burdens on the defendant.

Several years later, in *Francis v. Franklin*,[96] the Court held that an instruction in a Georgia homicide prosecution, stating that the "acts of a person of sound mind and discretion are presumed to be the product of a person's will, but the presumption may be rebutted," violated *Sandstrom*. The Court held that the instructions had created the kind of mandatory presumption prohibited by *Sandstrom,* even though Georgia had interpreted such language as amounting to no more than a permissive inference. The fact that the presumption was expressly made rebuttable was not controlling so long as the jury could have interpreted the instruction as shifting the burden of persuasion to the accused.

---

[94]   *County Court of Ulster County,* 442 U.S. at 157.

[95]   442 U.S. 510 (1979).

[96]   471 U.S. 307 (1985).

The upshot of all of these cases seems to be as follows: Presumptions in criminal cases will be divided into mandatory and permissive presumptions. A permissive presumption is one that will permit the jury to find the presumed facts, but neither compels the acceptance of such facts nor allocates a burden of persuasion to the defendant with regard to those facts. Regardless of how the state characterizes the presumption, the courts will analyze the jury instructions to determine their possible effect on the jury. A permissive presumption will be constitutionally acceptable if, considering all of the evidence in the case, there is a rational connection between the basic facts proved by the prosecution and the ultimate fact presumed, and the latter is more likely than not to flow from the former. A mandatory presumption is one that shifts the burden of production or persuasion to the defendant. Although the Supreme Court has not specifically so held, dictum in *Allen* and the holdings of lower court decisions seem to make it clear that a presumption that clearly shifts nothing other than the burden of production will be scrutinized in the same way as a permissive presumption and pass constitutional muster if it meets a rational connection test. Could a presumption that shifts the burden of persuasion be created? The Court in *Allen* suggests the possibility that such a presumption could be constitutional if a rational juror could find the presumed fact beyond a reasonable doubt from the basic facts. Some authors have suggested that such a presumption may not constitutionally exist after *Allen* and *Sandstrom*. The courts have not had occasion to rule on the question. Certainly, the test suggested in *Allen* is a stiff one.

§ 348 Affirmative Defenses and Presumptions in Criminal Cases: (c) Special Problems

Not surprisingly, several questions remain from the active constitutional development in this area of the law.

1. The Creation of Affirmative Defenses. The *Patterson* case tied the question of the constitutionality of affirmative defenses directly to the formalistic notion that a true affirmative defense is one that does not simply go to negative an element of the offense. The question remains as to when something is an element of an offense. Many cases have looked only to the language of the statute although some have considered how the statute has been interpreted by the state courts.

Can the state create an affirmative defense simply by carefully excluding it from the elements of the offense? The answer to this question seems to be a qualified yes. In *Patterson*, the Court suggested that there were constitutional limitations on the creation of affirmative defenses.[97] Those limits may depend upon whether the state may, under the U.S. Constitution, punish the activity without reference to the affirmative defense. For example, assume an offense that has consisted of the elements A, B, C, all of which had to be proved by the prosecution beyond a reasonable doubt. The legislature carefully amends the statute covering the offense so as to make the elements of the offense A and B only, but provides that the accused may be exonerated if the defense proves C by a preponderance of the evidence. Such a new statute would be constitutional if the state may, consistent with the Eighth Amendment and substantive due process, punish the individual to the extent provided by the statute based upon proof of A and B only.

---

[97]   Patterson v. New York, 432 U.S. 197, 210 (1977).

Such an analysis has suggested another, less formalistic, approach to the treatment of affirmative defenses to some legal scholars. Under this approach, if the state can constitutionally exclude an element from an offense, it can require the defendant to bear the burden of persuasion with regard to that element. In other words, in the above example, if the state could exclude C from the definition of the crime, it could make the accused prove C, whether or not C is formally removed as an element of the offense. Other scholars have rejected an Eighth Amendment approach entirely and have proposed tests that would more severely limit the state's options in the creation of affirmative defenses.

As yet, no court has struck down an affirmative defense because the Eighth Amendment prohibited punishment based only upon the elements assigned to the definition of the offense. Indeed, the Eighth Amendment and related concepts of substantive due process have not proved to be an effective check on legislative decisions with regard to punishment. Moreover, no court has used an alternative approach suggested in the law journals to limit the creation of affirmative defenses. Instead, the courts have relied upon the safer, formalistic notions of Patterson.

One possible approach to assessing the validity of affirmative defenses that is neither inconsistent with case law nor directly tied to the Eighth Amendment was suggested by Justice Powell in his dissent in *Patterson*. Powell suggested that the prosecution be required to prove beyond a reasonable doubt at least those factors which "in the Anglo-American legal tradition" had made a difference in punishment or stigma.[98] Although troublesome if taken to its logical extent, the notion that we should consider historical factors has merit. At the very least, it would be appropriate for a court in assessing the validity of the creation of an affirmative defense to take into account not only the statutory language and judicial statements of the elements of the offense, but also the nature of the burden traditionally borne by the state with regard to the same or analogous factors.

2. *Affirmative Defenses or Presumptions?* Despite the differences between affirmative defenses and presumptions as the terms are used by the courts and legal scholars, the impact of these procedural devices on the accused can be identical. Thus, in one state, the accused may have the burden of producing evidence that she acted in self-defense—an affirmative defense. In another jurisdiction, the law may provide that, once the state has proved that the defendant intentionally killed the deceased, there is a presumption of unlawfulness that requires the defendant to introduce evidence with regard to self-defense, although the ultimate burden of persuasion remains with the state. The defendant must introduce some evidence of self-defense in order for the jury to be instructed on the issue. The effect of this presumption is identical to that of the affirmative defense. Both devices used in this way have been held to be constitutional.

An affirmative defense that places the burden of persuasion on the defendant with regard to a factor that is not an element of the offense may be constitutional. Could the state accomplish the same allocation of the burden of persuasion in the form of a presumption, i.e., a rule that states that once the state has proven the elements of the offense, the defendant is presumed guilty unless he proves some other factor? Such a rule simply delays the allocation of the burden of persuasion until after the state has proved its case. It places no different burden on the accused than would an affirmative

---

[98] *Id.* at 226–227.

defense. However, as framed, the presumption would seem to run directly afoul of *Sandstrom*. The matter may simply be one of legislative drafting. The prudent legislature will choose the affirmative defense route rather than the presumption language. It is yet to be seen whether the courts will look to the designation of a procedural device as a presumption or as an affirmative defense or whether they will more realistically decide the constitutionality of the procedural device based upon its actual effect on the defendant.

3.   When Is It Proper to Submit an Issue Involving a Presumed Fact to the Jury? In deciding the question whether a case involving a presumed fact should be submitted to the jury, the trial judge must necessarily be guided by the dictates of *Jackson v. Virginia:*[99] a jury verdict will be upheld, even against collateral attack, only if the evidence was sufficient for a reasonable person to find the defendant guilty beyond a reasonable doubt. In the rare instance in which a mandatory presumption is involved, the problem is not difficult. *Allen* suggests that the presumption will be tested by the constitutional test of whether the presumed fact flows beyond a reasonable doubt from the basic facts. If the presumption meets that test, it is by definition sufficient to get to the jury, provided the other elements of the crime are supported by sufficient evidence. However, because of the rigid requirements for the validity of mandatory presumptions, virtually all presumptions will be permissive. Therefore, under the *Allen* case, the trial judge must look to the rational effect of the presumption in connection with all of the other evidence in the case. Perhaps the best statement of a test for the sufficiency of the evidence under these circumstances is contained in Uniform Rule 303(b):

> (b) Submission to the jury. The court may not direct the jury to find a presumed fact against an accused. If a presumed fact establishes guilt. is an element of the offense, or negates a defense, the court may submit the question of guilt or of the existence of the presumed fact to the jury, but only if a reasonable juror on the evidence as a whole, including the evidence of the basic fact, could find guilt or the presumed fact beyond a reasonable doubt. If the presumed fact has a lesser effect, the question of its existence may be submitted to the jury if the basic fact is supported by substantial evidence or is otherwise established, unless the court determines that a reasonable juror could not find on the evidence as a whole the existence of the presumed fact.

Given the dictates of *Jackson v. Virginia* and *County Court of Ulster County v. Allen,* no other proposed formulation of the rule seems acceptable.

4.   Instructing the Jury on Presumptions. The distinction made in the *Allen* case between permissive and mandatory presumptions, makes the exact language of instructions on presumptions critical. Unless a presumption is strong enough to meet the stringent test for mandatory presumptions, the trial judge must use caution in charging the jury so as to place no burden whatsoever on the defendant.

Again, the Uniform Rules provide a suggested pattern for such an instruction. Uniform Rule 303(c) provides:

> Instructing the Jury. At the time the existence of a presumed fact is submitted to the jury, the court shall instruct the jury that it may regard the basic fact as sufficient evidence of the presumed fact but is not required to do so. In addition,

---

[99]   443 U.S. 307 (1979). See supra § 338.

if a presumed fact establishes guilt, is an element of the offense, or negates a defense, the court shall instruct the jury that its existence, on all the evidence, must be proved beyond a reasonable doubt.

This instruction seems to meet most of the problems raised in the *Allen* case, as well as those suggested by *Sandstrom v. Montana*. One additional problem has been suggested. In *Allen*, the court stated that the prosecution could not rest its case entirely on a presumption unless the facts proved were sufficient to support the inference of guilt beyond a reasonable doubt.[100] Therefore, where the prosecution relies solely upon a presumption and not any other evidence, as in *Allen*, not only must the presumed fact flow beyond a reasonable doubt from the basic facts, but the jury must be able to find the basic facts beyond a reasonable doubt. At least two states have adopted the essence of the Revised Uniform Rule, but, in order to cover this situation, have added language that requires that the basic facts be proved beyond a reasonable doubt.

§ 349　Choice of Law

The significance of the burdens of proof and of the effect of presumptions upon those burdens has already been discussed. Certainly the outcome of litigation may be altered depending upon which party has the burden of persuasion.[101] Where there is little evidence available on an issue, the burden of producing evidence may also control the outcome.[102] Recognizing the impact of these rules upon outcome, the federal courts, applying the doctrine of *Erie Railroad Co. v. Tompkins*,[103] have consistently held that where an issue is to be decided under state law, that law controls both the burdens of proof and presumptions with regard to that issue. Federal Rule of Evidence 302 limits the operation of this rule with respect to presumptions to cases in which the presumption operates "respecting a fact which is an element of a claim or defense as to which state law supplies the rule of decision." "Tactical presumptions," those that operate as to a lesser aspect of the case, will be governed by the federal rule. While no reported case has specifically made the distinction contemplated in the rule, the reasoning is sound. Although tactical presumptions may in some instances influence the outcome of a case, their effect is no greater than that of a rule governing the admission or exclusion of a single item of evidence. As in the case of those rules, the desirability of providing a uniform procedure for federal trials through a fixed rule governing tactical presumptions outweighs any preference for increased certainty of identity of result in state and federal courts.

Of course *Erie* problems are not the only choice of law problems. The question remains, even for federal courts having resolved to apply state rather than federal law: what state's law is applicable? Unlike the federal courts applying the *Erie* rule, the state courts generally have not considered the impact of the burdens of proof and presumptions on the outcome of the lawsuit to be controlling. The general rule expressed is that both the burdens of proof and presumptions are "procedural" in the sense that the law of the forum governs rather than the law of the state whose substantive rules are otherwise applicable. However, as in the case of most general rules with regard to

---

[100]　County Court of Ulster County v. Allen, 442 U.S. 140, 167 (1979).

[101]　See supra § 336.

[102]　See supra § 338. See also supra §§ 342 & 344 as to the operation of presumptions with regard to both the burden of producing evidence and the burden of persuasion.

[103]　304 U.S. 64 (1938).

the subject matter of this chapter, instances in which an exception to this general rule has been held applicable are perhaps as numerous as instances in which the rule has been applied. The principal exception to the basic dogma has been variously phrased but its gist is that the forum will apply the rule of a foreign jurisdiction with respect to the burdens of proof or presumptions where that rule is inseparably connected to the substantive right created by the foreign state.

The general rule and its principal exception have proved difficult to apply. The plethora of conflicting decisions under the test amply illustrates the problems inherent in attempting to distinguish between rules that are inseparably connected with substantive law and those that are not. The distinction is indeed a hollow one. Regardless of the nature of the claim or defense, rules with respect to the burdens of proof always have the same potential effect upon the decision in the case. If insufficient evidence is available, the party having the burden of producing evidence will lose the decision. If the jury is in doubt, the party having the burden of persuasion will lose. As has been observed, cases in which the burden of proof is so closely interwoven with the substantive right as to make a separation of the two impossible constitute either all or none of the litigated cases.

A somewhat better approach to the problem is taken by the Second Restatement of Conflict of Laws which states that the forum will apply its own local law in determining which party has the burdens of proof "unless the primary purpose of the relevant rule of the otherwise applicable law is to affect decision of the issue rather than to regulate the conduct of the trial." The rule sounds very much like the test applied in *Erie* cases. However, the comments and illustrations to the applicable sections of the Restatement indicate that the Restatement is to be interpreted in much the same way as the more traditional statements just discussed; the assumption is that the rule is one concerned with "trial administration," not the decision of the issue. The assumption seems wrong. The burdens of proof are almost always allocated for the primary purpose of affecting the decision in the case where there is no evidence or where the jury is in doubt. To say that these rules merely govern the conduct of the trial, as in the case of rules concerning the admission and exclusion of evidence, gives far too much emphasis to form over substance.

A better approach to the choice of law problem would be to adopt the federal rule used in *Erie* cases as a rule of general application. Such a rule would provide that the law of the state or states supplying the substantive rules of law should govern questions concerning the burdens of proof as well as presumptions operating with regard to a fact constituting an element of a claim or defense.

Table of Statutes

Index

References are to Pages

HAND, LEARNED
Burden of proof, views on, 767
Hearsay, views on, 599

HANDWRITING
Samples, as self-incrimination, 293

HEALTH DATA
Government secrets privilege, 265

**HEALTH INSURANCE PORTABILITY AND
    ACCOUNTABILITY ACT OF 1996
    (HIPAA)**
Physician-patient privilege, as affecting, 247

HEARSAY
       See also Residual Hearsay Exception;
         Spontaneous Statements.
     Generally, 585–618
Absence, unavailability of witness, 615–616
Admissions of party-opponent, 594
    Exceptions distinguished, 620
    Multiple hearsay in, 727–728
Ancient documents
    As authentication, 557
    Exception, generally, 721
Backdoor exception, 730
Character, exception, 719
Children, right to confront, 617
Commercial publications, exception, 717–719
Complexity of present rules, 730
Computer records, status of, 682
Computer-generated simulations, as, 543–544
Confrontation
    Compared, 603–613
    Hearsay exceptions, 101–102
Constitutional problems of, 603–613
Cross-examination
    Hearsay declarant, of, 600, 603, 729
    Lack of, 587–588
    Relation to, 55–56, 77
Death, unavailability of witness, 615
Declarant, impeachment of, 728–729
Definition of, 589–590, 646
Depositions, 7–9
    Unavailability of witnesses, 616
Directories, exception, 719
Due process as requiring admission of, 603–613
Dying declarations, 606
Effect on hearer or reader, 592
Evaluation of present rules, 730
Examples of, 590–591
    Nonhearsay utterances, 591–594
Exceptions. See also specific exceptions.
    Number of, 730
    Reasons for, generally, 587–589
Expert opinion, basis as quasi-hearsay, 729–730
Expert witnesses, impeachment by, 68
Family history, exception, 720
Firsthand knowledge distinguished, 32, 590
Former testimony, 693–694, 701
Future of, 733–734
    Civil cases, 734
    Constitutional limits on change, 733–734
Group statements, 593
Habeas corpus, 616
History of rule, 585–586

Identification, statements of, exclusion, 602
Impeachment of declarant, 728–729
Implied assertions, 597
Inadmissible, instructions to jury, 729–730
Knowledge, assertions offered to prove, 598
Learned treatises, exception, 717–719
Legislative modifications of rule, 731–733
Liberalization of rule, need for, 587–588
Life insurance annuity tables, exception, 719
Market reports, exception, 718
Memory, lack of as unavailability, 615
Mental illness, unavailability of witness, 615
Modern development of rule, 731–733
Multiple hearsay, 727–728
Nonassertive nonverbal conduct as, 595
Nonverbal conduct as, 594–595
Oath, value of, 587
Opinion polls, as, 509
Paternity, exception, 719–720
Pedigree, exception, 719–720
Physical illness, unavailability of witness, 615
Presence of party, 589
Presence of witness at trial, value of, 587–588
Present sense impressions, exemption for, 648–
    650
Prior statements of witnesses as, 599–603
Privilege as constituting unavailability, 614
Public records, exception, 685–686, 688–690
Quasi-hearsay, 729–730
Reasons for rule, 587–589
Records of past recollection, clarification as, 667–
    668
Re-creation animations, as, 544–545
Reform efforts, 731–732
Refusal to testify as constituting unavailability,
    614
Reputation, 593–594, 719–720
Silence as, 596–597
Sound recordings, as, 541
Surveys, status of, 509
Testimonial statements, 604–605
Third party reports, 56–61
Title documents, exception, 722
Truth of matter asserted
    Assertions not offered for, 593
    Assertions offered for, 593
Unavailability
      Generally, 614–617
    Definition of, 615–616
    Good faith in establishing, 616
Unscripted video and film recordings, 538
Variation in reliability of, 731
Verbal acts, 591–592
Verbal parts of acts, 591–592
Views on present rules, 730
Vital statistics, exception, 688–689
Witnesses, hearsay declarants as, 728–729
Wrongful procurement of unavailability, 617–618

HIV/AIDS
Reporting
    Physician-patient privilege, 250

HOSPITAL RECORDS
Multiple hearsay in, 727–728